DICTIONARY OF AMERICAN BIOGRAPHY

AMERICAN
COUNCIL
★ OF ★
LEARNED
SOCIETIES
★

BABSON INSTITUTE,

WELLESLEY HILLS, MASS.

DICTIONARY OF
AMERICAN BIOGRAPHY

DICTIONARY OF AMERICAN BIOGRAPHY

UNDER THE AUSPICES OF THE
AMERICAN COUNCIL OF LEARNED SOCIETIES

EDITED BY

ALLEN JOHNSON

Brearly — Chandler

VOLUME III

CHARLES SCRIBNER'S SONS

NEW YORK

1929

Prompted solely by a desire for public service the New York Times Company and its President, Mr. Adolph S. Ochs, have made possible the preparation of the manuscript of the Dictionary of American Biography through a subvention of more than $500,000 and with the understanding that the entire responsibility for the contents of the volumes rests with the American Council of Learned Societies.

COPYRIGHT, 1929, BY
AMERICAN COUNCIL OF LEARNED SOCIETIES

Printed in the United States of America

CONTRIBUTORS TO VOLUME III

Adeline Adams	A. A—s.	Charles F. Carey	C. F. C.
James Truslow Adams	J. T. A.	W. Ellison Chalmers	W. E. C.
Robert G. Albion	R. G. A.	Wayland J. Chase	W. J. C—e.
Edmund Kimball Alden	E. K. A.	Russell Henry Chittenden	R. H. C.
Albert Allemann	A. A—n.	Allen L. Churchill	A. L. C.
Edward Ellis Allen	E. E. A.	Katherine W. Clendinning	K. W. C—g.
William Henry Allison	W. H. A.	Frederick W. Coburn	F. W. C.
James Parkhill Andrews	J. P. A.	Samuel Gwynn Coe	S. G. C.
John Clark Archer	J. C. A.	Esther Cole	E. C.
Frederick William Ashley	F. W. A.	Rossetter Gleason Cole	R. G. C.
Benjamin Wisner Bacon	B. W. B—n.	Kenneth Wallace Colgrove	K. W. C—e.
Theodore D. Bacon	T. D. B.	Edna Mary Colman	E. M. C—n.
Hayes Baker-Crothers	H. B–C.	John Corbett	J. C.
Ray Palmer Baker	R. P. B—r.	R. S. Cotterill	R. S. C.
James Curtis Ballagh	J. C. B.	Ellis Merton Coulter	E. M. C—r.
Claribel Ruth Barnett	C. R. B.	W. H. B. Court	W. H. B. C.
John Spencer Bassett	J. S. B—t.	Isaac Joslin Cox	I. J. C.
Ernest Sutherland Bates	E. S. B.	Avery O. Craven	A. O. C.
William Agur Beardsley	W. A. B.	Nelson Antrim Crawford	N. A. C.
Charles Francis Dorr Belden	C. F. D. B.	Walter Hill Crockett	W. H. C.
Elbert Jay Benton	E. J. B.	William James Cunningham	W. J. C—m.
Percy W. Bidwell	P. W. B.	Merle E. Curti	M. E. C.
George Blumer	G. B.	Robert E. Cushman	R. E. C.
Roger S. Boardman	R. S. B.	Harrison Clifford Dale	H. C. D.
Herbert Eugene Bolton	H. E. B.	Tyler Dennett	T. D.
Beverley W. Bond, Jr.	B. W. B—d.	Herman J. Deutsch	H. J. D.
Milledge Louis Bonham	M. L. B.	Charles Allen Dinsmore	C. A. D.
Stephen Bonsal	S. B.	Frank Haigh Dixon	F. H. D.
Archibald Lewis Bouton	A. L. B.	Eleanor Robinette Dobson	E. R. D.
Witt Bowden	W. B.	Dorothy Anne Dondore	D. A. D.
Sarah G. Bowerman	S. G. B.	Elizabeth Donnan	E. D.
Charles N. Boyd	C. N. B.	William Howe Downes	W. H. D.
William Kenneth Boyd	W. K. B.	Stella Drumm	S. D.
Benjamin Brawley	B. B.	Raymond Smith Dugan	R. S. D.
Edward Breck	E. B.	William B. Dunning	W. B. D.
Robert Bridges	R. B.	Lionel C. Durel	L. C. D.
George W. Briggs	G. W. B.	J. H. Easterby	J. H. E—y.
Walter Cochrane Bronson	W. C. B.	Linda Anne Eastman	L. A. E.
Robert Preston Brooks	R. P. B—s.	Walter Prichard Eaton	W. P. E.
L. Parmly Brown	L. P. B.	Edwin Francis Edgett	E. F. E.
John S. Brubacher	J. S. B—r.	John H. Edmonds	J. H. E—s.
Kathleen Bruce	K. B.	Arthur Elson	A. E.
George Sands Bryan	G. S. B.	Logan Esarey	L. E.
Oscar MacMillan Buck	O. M. B.	Lawrence Boyd Evans	L. B. E.
Duncan Burnet	D. B.	Paul D. Evans	P. D. E.
Guy H. Burnham	G. H. B.	Harold Underwood Faulkner	H. U. F.
Pierce Butler	P. B.	Albert Bernhardt Faust	A. B. F.
Francis Gordon Caffey	F. G. C.	George Emory Fellows	G. E. F.
Charles T. Cahill	C. T. C.	Gustave Joseph Fiebeger	G. J. F.
William B. Cairns	W. B. C.	Carl Russell Fish	C. R. F.
James Morton Callahan	J. M. C.	Walter Lynwood Fleming	W. L. F.

Contributors to Volume III

Norman Foerster	N. F.	Stephen Leacock	S. L.
Blanton Fortson	B. F.	James Melvin Lee	J. M. L.
Harold North Fowler	H. N. F.	Alexander Leitch	A. L.
L. Webster Fox	L. W. F.	Charles Lee Lewis	C. L. L.
John H. Frederick	J. H. F.	Thomas Ollive Mabbott	T. O. M.
William Little Frierson	W. L. F.	Samuel Black McCormick	S. B. M.
Claude Moore Fuess	C. M. F.	Thomas Denton McCormick	T. D. M.
John F. Fulton	J. F. F.	Philip B. McDonald	P. B. M.
Charles Burleigh Galbreath	C. B. G—h.	William MacDonald	W. M.
Francis Pendleton Gaines	F. P. G.	Walter Martin McFarland	W. M. M.
Curtis W. Garrison	C. W. G.	Arthur Cushman McGiffert	A. C. M.
Karl Frederick Geiser	K. F. G.	Seth Shepard McKay	S. S. M.
George Harvey Genzmer	G. H. G.	Donald L. McMurry	D. L. M.
W. J. Ghent	W. J. G.	Bruce E. Mahan	B. E. M.
Cardinal Goodwin	C. G.	Dumas Malone	D. M.
Colin B. Goodykoontz	C. B. G—z.	James Trimble Marshall, Jr.	J. T. M. Jr.
Armistead Churchill Gordon,		David M. Matteson	D. M. M.
Jr.	A. C. G. Jr.	Brander Matthews	B. M—s.
Harris Perley Gould	H. P. G.	Leila Mechlin	L. M.
Louis Herbert Gray	L. H. G.	A. Howard Meneely	A. H. M.
Jerome Davis Greene	J. D. G.	Newton D. Mereness	N. D. M.
LeRoy R. Hafen	L. R. H.	Robert Lee Meriwether	R. L. M—r.
William J. Hail	W. J. H.	John Campbell Merriam	J. C. M.
Philip May Hamer	P. M. H.	George Perkins Merrill	G. P. M.
Talbot Faulkner Hamlin	T. F. H.	Jane Louise Mesick	J. L. M.
John Louis Haney	J. L. H.	Truman Michelson	T. M.
Thomas LeGrand Harris	T. L. H.	Broadus Mitchell	B. M—l.
Frances B. Hawley	F. B. H.	Mary Hewitt Mitchell	M. H. M.
Marshall DeLancey Haywood	M. DeL. H.	Carl W. Mitman	C. W. M.
Grace Raymond Hebard	G. R. H.	Frank Monaghan	F. M—n.
Burton Jesse Hendrick	B. J. H.	Fulmer Mood	F. M—d.
Ellwood Hendrick	E. H.	Robert E. Moody	R. E. M.
Vivian Allen Charles Henmon	V. A. C. H.	Charles Moore	C. M.
Frederick Charles Hicks	F. C. H.	Mary Atwell Moore	M. A. M.
Homer Carey Hockett	H. C. H.	Samuel Eliot Morison	S. E. M.
Jean MacKinnon Holt	J. M. H.	Richard B. Morris	R. B. M.
Walter Hough	W. H.	Richard L. Morton	R. L. M—n.
Harold Howland	H. H.	Kenneth Ballard Murdock	K. B. M.
Edgar Erskine Hume	E. E. H.	David Saville Muzzey	D. S. M.
Edward Frank Humphrey	E. F. H.	Edwin G. Nash	E. G. N.
Albert Hyma	A. H—a.	Frank Nash	F. N.
Theodore Henley Jack	T. H. J.	Allan Nevins	A. N.
Joseph Jackson	J. J.	Roy F. Nichols	R. F. N.
Edward Hopkins Jenkins	E. H. J.	E. J. M. Nutter	E. J. M. N.
Allen Johnson	A. J.	John W. Oliver	J. W. O.
Edgar Hutchinson Johnson	E. H. J—n.	Henry Fairfield Osborn	H. F. O.
Marie A. Kasten	M. A. K.	Norris Galpin Osborn	N. G. O.
Louise Phelps Kellogg	L. P. K.	Marie Bankhead Owen	M. B. O.
Vernon Lyman Kellogg	V. L. K.	Frank L. Owsley	F. L. O.
Rayner W. Kelsey	R. W. K.	Francis Randolph Packard	F. R. P.
William Webb Kemp	W. W. K.	Leigh Page	L. P.
Frank Richardson Kent	F. R. K.	Edwin William Pahlow	E. W. P.
Pierre van Rensselaer Key	P. V. R. K.	Theodore Sherman Palmer	T. S. P.
Fiske Kimball	F. K.	Fred Lewis Pattee	F. L. P—e.
Edgar Wallace Knight	E. W. K.	Charles Oscar Paullin	C. O. P.
Grant C. Knight	G. C. K.	Frederic Logan Paxson	F. L. P—n.
H. W. Howard Knott	H. W. H. K.	C. C. Pearson	C. C. P.
Conrad H. Lanza	C. H. L.	Theodore Calvin Pease	T. C. P.

Contributors to Volume III

Donald Culross Peattie	D. C. P.	Frederick C. Swanson	F. C. S—n.
Frederick Torrel Persons	F. T. P.	Eben Swift	E. S.
A. Everett Peterson	A. E. P.	Jennette R. Tandy	J. R. T.
James M. Phalen	J. M. P.	Edwin Platt Tanner	E. P. T.
Francis Samuel Philbrick	F. S. P.	Frank A. Taylor	F. A. T.
Paul Chrisler Phillips	P. C. P.	Milton Halsey Thomas	M. H. T.
Ulrich Bonnell Phillips	U. B. P.	Harrison John Thornton	H. J. T.
William Whatley Pierson, Jr.	W. W. P.	Charles Franklin Thwing	C. F. T.
Lewis Frederick Pilcher	L. F. P.	Ezra Squire Tipple	E. S. T.
Henry Augustus Pilsbry	H. A. P.	R. P. Tolman	R. P. T.
John E. Pomfret	J. E. P.	F. E. Tourscher	F. E. T.
Richard Lyle Power	R. L. P.	Francis J. Tschan	F. J. T.
Edward Preble	E. P.	Frederick Tuckerman	F. T.
Richard J. Purcell	R. J. P.	William Treat Upton	W. T. U—n.
Milo Milton Quaife	M. M. Q.	Roland Greene Usher	R. G. U.
Arthur Hobson Quinn	A. H. Q.	William T. Utter	W. T. U—r.
Charles William Ramsdell	C. W. R.	Carl Van Doren	C. V-D.
James Garfield Randall	J. G. R.	George Van Santvoord	G. V-S.
P. Orman Ray	P. O. R.	Henry R. Viets	H. R. V.
Charles Dudley Rhodes	C. D. R.	John Martin Vincent	J. M. V.
Thomas Cole Richards	T. C. R.	Eugene M. Violette	E. M. V.
Franklin Lafayette Riley	F. L. R.	Frank Horace Vizetelly	F. H. V.
Frank H. Ristine	F. H. R.	John Donald Wade	J. D. W.
James Alexander Robertson	J. A. R.	James Elliott Walmsley	J. E. W—y.
David Moore Robinson	D. M. R.	Marjorie F. Warner	M. F. W.
William Alexander Robinson	W. A. R.	W. Randall Waterman	W. R. W.
Frank Edward Ross	F. E. R.	Frank Weitenkampf	F. W.
Henry Kalloch Rowe	H. K. R.	Thomas Jefferson Wertenbaker	T. J. W.
Robert R. Rowe	R. R. R.	Allan Westcott	A. W.
George H. Ryden	G. H. R.	Arthur P. Whitaker	A. P. W.
Joseph Schafer	J. S.	Melvin Johnson White	M. J. W.
Franklin William Scott	F. W. S.	W. L. Whittlesey	W. L. W.
Louis Martin Sears	L. M. S.	Robert J. Wickenden	R. J. W.
Thorsten Sellin	T. S.	James Field Willard	J. F. W.
Muriel Shaver	M. S.	Mary Wilhelmine Williams	M. W. W.
William Bristol Shaw	W. B. S.	H. Parker Willis	H. P. W.
Clifton Lucien Sherman	C. L. S.	James E. Winston	J. E. W—n.
Henry Noble Sherwood	H. N. S.	Clark Wissler	C. W.
Floyd Calvin Shoemaker	F. C. S—r.	Carter Godwin Woodson	C. G. W.
William Adams Slade	W. A. S.	Thomas Woody	T. W.
William E. Smith	W. E. S.	Ernest Hunter Wright	E. H. W.
A. I. Spanton	A. I. S.	Helen Wright	H. W.
Thomas Marshall Spaulding	T. M. S.	Walter L. Wright, Jr.	W. L. W. Jr.
Mary Newton Stanard	M. N. S.	Lawrence Counselman Wroth	L. C. W.
Harris Elwood Starr	H. E. S.	Julien C. Yonge	J. C. Y.
Henry P. Stearns	H. P. S.	Edna Yost	E. Y.
Walter Ralph Steiner	W. R. S.	Frederic George Young	F. G. Y.
Witmer Stone	W. S.		

DICTIONARY OF

AMERICAN BIOGRAPHY

Brearly — Chandler

BREARLY, DAVID (June 11, 1745–Aug. 16, 1790), jurist and statesman, was descended from a family of Yorkshire, England. His American ancestor, John B. Brearly, emigrated in 1680 and settled near Trenton, N. J. David Brearly was born at Spring Grove, the son of David and Mary (Clark) Brearly. He became a lawyer at Allentown, near Trenton. At the opening of the Revolution he was so outspoken in his Whig sentiments that he was arrested for high treason, but was freed by a mob of citizens. In the war he was appointed lieutenant-colonel of the 4th New Jersey, Nov. 28, 1776; and of the 1st New Jersey, Jan. 1, 1777. He resigned Aug. 4, 1779, but served after the war as colonel of militia. His career in civil affairs was more conspicuous. He was a member of the New Jersey constitutional convention, and on June 10, 1779 he was elected chief justice of the supreme court of the state. In this position there came before him for decision a case of considerable importance. A certain Elisha Walton had received a favorable verdict, May 24, 1779, given by a jury of six men, in accordance with a law recently passed by the legislature of the state, the case being tried before a justice of the peace in Monmouth County. The chief justice issued a writ of *certiorari*, returnable at the next session, and the case—*Holmes* vs. *Walton*—was argued at Trenton before Chief Justice Brearly, Nov. 11, 1779. Judge Brearly's opinion was given, probably orally, Sept. 7, 1780, in a significant statement regarding the law which had allowed a jury of six men. In the development of the right to overturn a legislative enactment by judicial decision, this opinion by Judge Brearly has been regarded as especially noteworthy. "No doubt remains that Brearly met the question of constitutionality squarely and on Sept. 7, 1780, announced the principle of judicial guardianship of the organic law against attempted or inadvertent encroachment by the ordinary law" (Austin Scott). The same commentator remarks: "From the 7th of September, 1780, this function of the judiciary, this principle of judicial power over unconstitutional legislation, has held sway in New Jersey." It was approved by the legislature; and reference to it was made by Gouverneur Morris in an address to the Pennsylvania Assembly in 1785.

Brearly was a delegate to the Federal Convention of 1787, and is thus described by Pierce: "As an Orator he has little to boast of, but as a Man he has every virtue to recommend him." He opposed proportional representation, and joint ballot in the election of president. As an adherent of the rights of the small states he seconded the motion for one vote for each state. He was a member of the "grand committee," and he seems to have been regular in attendance at the convention, for he wrote to his colleagues Dayton and Paterson, urging their presence at the sessions. He was closely associated with Paterson. "He (Paterson) here discussed the idea of erasing state boundaries, a scheme which he and his colleague Brearley, seem actually to have had in serious contemplation" (A. C. McLaughlin, *The Confederation and the Constitution*, 1905, p. 216). A further evidence of their connection is the fact that in Paterson's notes of the convention, two of the documents are in Brearly's handwriting (*American Historical Review*, IX, 312–40).

Brearly presided over the state convention which ratified the Federal Constitution. He was a presidential elector, and United States district judge from 1789 until his death. He stood high in Masonic circles, and was vice-president of the New Jersey Society of the Cincinnati. He was a delegate to the Episcopal General Convention of 1786, and was one of the compilers of the prayer-book. About 1767 he married Elizabeth Mullen of Trenton, and on Apr. 17, 1783, he married Elizabeth Higbee.

[W. H. Brearley, *Geneal. of the Brearley Family* (1886). Austin Scott in the *Am. Hist. Rev.*, IV, 457–69, describes the *Holmes* vs. *Walton* case. He summarizes his statement at the end by saying that Brearly was associated with Paterson and Livingston in supporting the New Jersey Plan, and that this plan proposed the "principle of judicial control in our legal system." A. C. McLaughlin, *Courts, Constitution, and Parties* (1912), p. 42, note, observes: "It will not do to stress the connection between *Holmes* vs. *Walton* and this section of the Constitution (the one referring to the 'law of the land') ; it is possible, but we cannot say more, that the case was of influence on the minds of men like Paterson."]

E.K.A.

BREAUX, JOSEPH ARSENNE (Feb. 18, 1838–July 23, 1926), jurist, educator, was descended from an Acadian family which settled in Louisiana. He was the son of John B. Breaux and Margaret (Walsh) Breaux, was born on the family plantation in Iberville Parish, and was educated there until he prepared for college. Completing his college work at Georgetown (Ky.), young Breaux studied law in the University of Louisiana (now Tulane) and was graduated in 1859. He married Eugenia Mille, daughter of a planter, in 1861, and had established himself near the home of his boyhood when the Civil War began. He entered the service first as captain of the 13th Louisiana Infantry, but when this organization was merged with other units upon being mustered into the Confederate army, Breaux transferred to the 8th Louisiana Cavalry as a private. He continued in service, promoted to lieutenant, throughout the war. Resuming the practise of his profession at Lafayette, and a little later at New Iberia (1866), he became an important factor in rehabilitating the Parishes during the hard period of Reconstruction. Of wide acquaintance, very shrewd and conservative in business affairs, he won the confidence of the Creole population. He was chosen president of the First National Bank of New Iberia; but more important than this, he became president of the local school board, and demonstrated his ability to better the deplorable condition of the schools. At that time the only tongue known to large numbers of the country folk in Southwest Louisiana was a very imperfect French which had practically no written form. There were serious difficulties (due to mutual suspicion on the part of Creole and English, to sheer ignorance, to political jealousy) in the path of an effective

system of schools. Fortunately for the state, Breaux was elected state superintendent of public schools (1888). He compiled the school laws then on the statute books, drafted a new school law, and by his influence with the Parishes where he was so well known won its enactment by the legislature; it became the basis of a sound system of public instruction.

Appointed by Gov. Nicholls as associate justice of the supreme court in 1890, Breaux served longer than any justice except Martin, becoming chief justice in 1904 and retiring in 1914. As a judge, he displayed that sense of fair dealing, that kindliness which had won him friends. His knowledge of the law was extensive and exact; but his decisions are rarely well written; indeed, Breaux never acquired ease in writing English; but he arrived at substantial justice and gave shrewd judgments. In 1901, he published a *Digest* of the decisions of the supreme court that was invaluable to the lawyer. He was fond of reading, and was a man of gentle, almost retiring disposition, although physically tall and powerful. His interest in many quiet philanthropies was shown by his gifts to the Charity Hospital of New Orleans for tubercular patients. He was chairman of the board for the State Museum, and for the Confederate Memorial Hall, and was actively interested in the history of the state. Having no direct heirs, he left the bulk of his estate in trust for the benefit of students of law in Tulane University and in Loyola University, with both of which he had long been connected.

[*Who's Who in La. and Miss.* (1918) ; J. S. Kendall, *Hist. of New Orleans* (1922), II, 822 ; obituaries, July 24, 1926, in *Times-Picayune, States,* etc.; memorial in *Phi Beta Kappa Key,* Mar. 1927 ; memorial address by Hon. W. Catesby Jones before the Supreme Court, Nov. 1926.]

P.B.

BRECK, GEORGE WILLIAM (Sept. 1, 1863–Nov. 22, 1920), mural painter, was born in Washington, D. C., son of John and Annie (Auer) Breck. When quite young he went to New York to take up mechanical drafting. Instruction at the Art Students' League marked the beginning of his technical studies and following this, he taught drawing and did some illustrating. Through his realization of the need for special study, he became greatly interested in the possibilities in the development of mural painting and entered the first competition for the Jacob H. Lazarus Scholarship for the Study of Mural Decoration, held under the auspices of the Metropolitan Museum of Art, New York, in 1896. Being the fortunate winner of this scholarship, he had the opportunity of attending the American Academy of Fine Arts in Rome for several years (1897–1902). Probably because of his long absence abroad, very little has been written concerning some of the most active years of the artist's life, but we may safely conclude that the ideal environment of Rome and the many opportunities for helpful and congenial personal contacts laid the foundation for his later successes. At the suggestion of Edwin A. Abbey, while in Rome he was commissioned by the University of Virginia to make a replica of Raphael's "School of Athens" for the Auditorium in Charlottesville. An important event in his life at this time was his marriage, June 10, 1903, to Katharine, daughter of Franklin H. Head of Chicago. He became a member of the New York Architectural League; New York Municipal Art Society; National Society of Mural Painters; the Century Club; the New York City Art Commission (1912–15); the American Fine Arts Society, and for three terms served the Art Students' League as president. At the St. Louis Exposition in 1904, he was awarded a silver medal. During 1904–09 he was director of the Academy of Fine Arts in Rome, but in 1910 established a studio in New York and made his home at Flushing, L. I., where his death occurred in 1920.

During his period of study as an associate member of the American Academy of Fine Arts, at Rome, Breck had an exhibition of his work in the Pratt Institute Department of Fine Arts, Brooklyn, N. Y., Oct. 10–25, 1902. This exhibit included the following: copies—"Jurisprudence," "Group from the Disputa," "Group from Messa di Bolsena," "Mt. Parnassus," "Poetry" and "The Temptation," from Raphael; "Prophet Esaias," from Michelangelo; "Sixtus IV" and two copies entitled "Angel" from Melozzo da Forli; "Fame" from Guercino; four works entitled "Muse," from Lo Spagna; original sketches—"America" and "Sketch for Mural Decoration" made in competition for the Lazarus Scholarship. Other important examples of Breck's work are: two mural paintings in the Watertown, N. Y., Flower Memorial Library, entitled "First Public Commemoration of the Declaration of Independence in Jefferson County, N. Y.," and "Conference between M. de la Barre, Governor of Canada, and the Representatives of the Five Nations" (1904); mosaics in the façade and interior of St. Paul's P. E. Church at Rome, Italy; three medallions for the library of the Hon. Whitelaw Reid, one, "Reflection," a beautiful ceiling panel, symbolic in treatment, the pose of the principal figure, a female, being of interest for its suggestion of grace, poise, and intellectual strength.

[E. H. Blashfield, *Mural Painting in America* (1913), p. 68; *Who's Who in America*, 1920–21; *Am. Art Annual*, XVII, 265, XIX, 436 ("Mural Paintings in Public Buildings in the United States"); Thieme-Becker, *Künstler-Lexikon*, IV, 561; Pratt Institute, Brooklyn, N. Y., Dept. of Fine Arts, *Exhibition of Sculpture, Sketches and Photographs of Work by Hermon A. MacNeil and Copies, Drawings and Sketches by Geo. W. Breck*, Oct. 10–25, 1902.]   J.M.H.

BRECK, JAMES LLOYD (June 27, 1818– Mar. 30, 1876), Episcopalian clergyman, born near Philadelphia, the fourth son among the fourteen children of George Breck and Catherine D. Israell. He was educated at the Rev. Dr. Muhlenberg's academy at Flushing, L. I., and at the University of Pennsylvania. From his boyhood, he showed himself to be of strong character, and was distinguished at school by his industry and perseverance if not by brilliance. At the age of sixteen he had already decided to offer himself to a life of hardship in the mission field. After graduation from the University of Pennsylvania in 1838, he entered the General Theological Seminary in New York. These were the early days of the Catholic Revival in the Episcopal Church, and in the seminary Breck came under the influence of the Rev. Dr. Whittingham, later Bishop of Maryland, who strengthened in him the High Church principles he had acquired from Dr. Muhlenberg. During Breck's stay in New York, Bishop Jackson Kemper returned there from his first missionary journey through the new territories of the Northwest, and appealed for volunteers. Breck saw here the opportunity for a life of service for which he had been waiting. For some time he had had in his mind the formation of a brotherhood of celibate clergy, thus reviving in the Episcopal Church a type of religious devotion in which little or nothing had been attempted since the dissolution of the monasteries by Henry VIII. In this desire he had the support of two other young clergymen, and in 1841 the three set off for Wisconsin. The next fall found the little society established at Nashotah, where the brethren bought land and built their first house. From this centre, Breck worked tirelessly at the three tasks he had set himself: missionary work among the settlers who were swarming into the new territories, the foundation of a theological seminary for the West, and the revival of a disciplined religious community life in the Church. Of the three, the last was probably the dearest to him at this time. It was his inflexible determination to insist on his brotherhood idea, in spite of the growing lukewarmness of his companions, which led him to leave Nashotah after eight years of successful struggle. Breck was nothing if not masterful, and realizing that the work could not develop on lines which he preferred, he resigned the presidency and went to Minnesota. He had not failed, for Nashotah Seminary still exists to propagate his uncompromising Church principles. After a brief and not too encouraging attempt to found a permanent religious order after his own heart at St. Paul, Breck turned with equal enthusiasm to convert the Indians. A man of great stature and commanding personality, capable of doing his forty miles a day on foot over the forest trails, dressed invariably in the full clerical attire of the period, never lacking clean linen in spite of the frequent squalor of his surroundings, Breck made a tremendous impression on the red men. From the outset of his career he had been convinced of the necessity of Church schools and religious education in connection with Christian missions; and during the five years he spent among the Chippewas he opened at Crow Wing and Leech Lake educational, agricultural, and missionary centers which were beginning to exercise a potent influence among the savages. He had already received the earnest commendation of the governor of the territory, when his dreams of a Christianized and civilized Indian population were destroyed by the withdrawal of all United States troops from Minnesota. The Civil War was imminent, and the white missionaries and their converts, now without protection, were in constant danger. With great reluctance, Breck sought a more settled neighborhood, and made new headquarters at Faribault. During his years with the Indians, the force of circumstances seems to have led him to abandon his cherished ideal of an order of celibate clergy living in community under a religious rule, for in 1855 he married Jane Maria Mills, one of his assistants. She died in 1862; and after two years as a widower Breck married his second wife, Sarah Styles, who survived him. In its outcome, the work at Faribault was the largest of all Breck's labors. In the nine years he spent there, he either founded or prepared the way for the cathedral, the Seabury Divinity School, which is the principal Episcopal seminary west of the Mississippi, and the splendid schools for boys and girls now existing there. After nine years, Faribault became too solidly established to tempt this "apostle of the wilderness" to remain longer. He was by nature a pioneer, and his last search for the frontier led him to California. In 1867 he settled at Benicia, not far from San Francisco. There he followed his usual plan of founding a theological seminary and schools for boys and girls; but before he had had sufficient time to establish his latest work on a substantially enduring basis, he died in 1876, prematurely worn out by his incessant toil.

[Chas. Breck, *Life and Letters of the Rev. Jas. Lloyd Breck* (1883); T. I. Holcombe, *An Apostle of the Wilderness* (1903); private papers in possession of Nashotah House; documents in possession of the Wis. Hist. Soc.]   E.J.M.N.

BRECK, SAMUEL (July 17, 1771–Aug. 31, 1862), prominent citizen of Philadelphia, came of a Massachusetts Bay family prominent from the earliest settlement, and was born in Boston as the eldest son of Samuel Breck, a wealthy overseas merchant, and his wife Hannah, only daughter of Benjamin Andrews. The stately family mansion facing the Common was the resort of foreign visitors to Boston, many of whom had social or business connections with the elder Breck. In 1779 the father was appointed by the King of France to be fiscal agent of the French forces and young Samuel, who attended the Latin School, became a favorite with the French naval officers who frequented his home, one of whom, Admiral the Marquis de Vaudreuil, sent the lad, with his father's consent, to be further educated at the famous semi-religious and aristocratic military school at Sorèze, where he spent over four years, and whence he returned to Boston, in July 1787, with a foreign accent and a strong leaning toward the Roman Catholic religion. The latter he soon exchanged for the Episcopalian faith of his father. After a second visit to Europe in 1790, where he was the guest of the painter Copley and Sir William Pepperell in England, and of Noailles, Lafayette, and Vaudreuil in Paris, he was given the sum of $10,000 by his father, with which to "commence merchant." Young Samuel thereupon established a shipping business on Long Wharf, Boston. In 1792 however, partly on account of what was considered by the father to be "an iniquitous system of taxes," and partly because of an affection of his throat, the entire family moved to Philadelphia, where the elder Breck at once assumed a leading position in the social and public life of that city, at the time the national capital, among the honors falling to him being the federal appointment as one of the commissioners to pass on the claims connected with Article XXI of the Treaty of San Lorenzo (Spanish Spoliations) in 1797–99. The younger Samuel married on Christmas Eve, 1795, Jean Ross, daughter of a prominent merchant, and thereafter served his adopted city and state with distinction in many fields. His many historical addresses and dissertations, though of minor importance, are notable for their erudition and polish, the most important being his essay on "Continental Paper Money." He was the founder of the Society of the Sons of New England, and president or a high official of many other societies. He served four years in the Pennsylvania Senate, from 1817 to 1821, introducing, in February 1821, a bill for the emancipation of the slaves still remaining in the state. He was elected (1823) to the Eighteenth Congress, but failed of reëlection because, from a feeling of loyalty toward his old friend, John Quincy Adams, he alone of all the Pennsylvania delegation voted for that statesman for president. From the year 1800 he kept a singularly full diary which is still extant in many manuscript volumes, forming an agreeable and valuable social and political record of Philadelphia for nearly sixty years. His *Recollections,* which are of uncommon interest, together with extracts from the diaries, were published in 1877. While always a bitter opponent of slavery and an ardent churchman, Breck was fanatical on neither subject. His patriotism was proverbial. In his ninetieth year, at a patriotic meeting soon after the fall of Fort Sumter, Breck, at the close of the singing of the national anthem, sprang to his feet and called for three cheers for the United States, adding, "I was a man when they were formed, and God forbid that I should live to witness their downfall!" A year later, as he lay paralyzed on his death-bed, upon hearing cheering news from the front, his voiceless lips moved and with difficulty he raised his only sound hand and waved it feebly three times as if in triumph.

[The numerous MSS. of Breck's diaries and other, mostly unpublished, writings, are the best sources of information in regard to his career. Most of these are in possession of his collateral descendant, Miss Anna Shaw, Morristown, N. J. Among printed sources see *Recollections of Samuel Breck* (1877), ed. by H. E. Scudder; J. Francis Fisher, *Memoir of Samuel Breck* (1863); Jos. Reed Ingersoll, *Memoir of the Late Samuel Breck* (1863).]

E.B.

BRECKENRIDGE, JAMES (Mar. 7, 1763–May 13, 1833), soldier, lawyer, congressman, brother of John Breckinridge, 1760–1806 [*q.v.*], was the grandson of Alexander Breckenridge who emigrated from the north of Ireland to Virginia about 1738. His son Robert Breckenridge, a captain in the French and Indian War, married Letitia Preston and through her their children had influential political connections (M. S. Kennedy, *Seldens of Virginia and Allied Families,* 1911, I, 452–55). During the Revolution, James, the eighteen-year-old son of Robert and Letitia (Preston) Breckenridge, enlisted as a private in a corps of Botetourt riflemen commanded by his relative Col. Preston and in 1781 he was an officer under Gen. Greene in North Carolina. Later he was a major-general of Virginia militia and served in the War of 1812 (Obituary, *Richmond Whig,* May 24, 1833). In the meantime he had taken the academic and law courses in the College of William and Mary, graduating in 1785 (*History of William and Mary College,* 1874, p. 98). The young patriot commenced to practise law in 1787 and soon entered public life. He was a member of the House of Delegates from Botetourt County for thirteen sessions between 1780 and 1824 (E. G. Swem and J. W. Williams, *A Register of the General Assembly of Virginia 1776–1918,* 1918, p. 351). He was a candidate for governor of Virginia against James Monroe, but was defeated. He represented his district in Congress, Mar. 22, 1809 to Mar. 3, 1817 (*A Biographical Congressional Directory,* 1903, p. 410). Breckenridge was a leader of the Federalist party in Virginia. Later, he supported, in the legislature, Jefferson's plans for the University of Virginia, was one of the commission to select a site for that institution and a member of its first Board of Visitors (W. C. Bruce, *History of the University of Virginia,* 1922, I, 210, 212, 220, 221, 236, 290, II, 44). On his ancestral estate near Fincastle, in Botetourt County, Breckenridge built a beautiful home, "Grove Hill," noted for its atmosphere of cordiality, patriotism, and culture, which made a fitting background for its master and was the joy of his descendants for more than a hundred years. There he kept in close touch with ruling spirits in state and national affairs through correspondence with such men as Jefferson, Monroe, Madison, and many other notables whose letters made "Grove Hill" a treasure house of historical data. The mistress of "Grove Hill" was Anne, daughter of Cary Selden, of Elizabeth City County, to whom Breckenridge was married at Old St. John's Church, Richmond, on New Year's Day 1791, by Rev. James Buchanan. He died at the home he had created, leaving many descendants. Portraits represent Breckenridge as a stately, reserved, soldierly-looking man, of thoughtful countenance and rather blond coloring. An editorial in the *Richmond Times-Despatch* declared that "The destruction of 'Grove Hill' by fire, on Oct. 24, [1909] was a genuine sentimental calamity. It was . . . a splendid specimen of late colonial architecture—rich in memories of bygone Virginia."

[In addition to references given above, see *Richmond Enquirer,* May 24, 1833.]

M.N.S.

BRECKINRIDGE, JOHN (Dec. 2, 1760–Dec. 14, 1806), lawyer, statesman, of Scotch-Irish ancestry, was a son of Robert Breckenridge (the spelling of the family name was for the most part, changed in the next generation) whose father came to Virginia about 1738. His mother was Letitia, a daughter of John Preston. Soon after his birth near the present site of Staunton, Va., his family moved on westward into Botetourt County where his father died in 1772, leaving a widow and seven children in exposed frontier surroundings. Though living in as refined a home as could be found in that part of the world, Breckinridge found conditions rough and uncouth. Harboring a strong desire for learning, he managed when nineteen years of age to enter William and Mary College where he remained two years. While a student here, without his previous knowledge he was elected by the voters of Botetourt County to represent them in the legislature. This was more than an attempt of his fellow citizens to save money by designating some one as representative who happened to be residing at the seat of government. On account of his youth he was not allowed to take his seat. Twice more was he elected before he was admitted. He now decided to study law, married in 1785 Mary Hopkins Cabell, a daughter of Col. Joseph Cabell of Buckingham County, and immediately settled in Albemarle County.

The spell of Kentucky, which had seized so many other Virginians, soon gripped him. Letters from two of his brothers and from many friends who were there implored him to move to that land of hope. He abandoned a position in Congress to which he had just been elected and crossed the mountains in 1792, settling near Lexington in Fayette County and developing an estate which he called Cabell's Dale. Here he built an office and began the practise of law. He was soon on the road to a comfortable fortune, being greatly busied with land suits. His ablity as a lawyer recommended him to Gov. Isaac Shelby who appointed him attorney-general for the state in 1795 following his defeat for the United States Senate by Humphrey Marshall. It was while he was in this position that the disputed gubernatorial election took place in 1796. Called upon for an opinion by Benjamin Logan, who had received a plurality of the electoral vote, he refused officially to give a decision, but privately upheld Logan's position. The next year Breckinridge was elected to represent Fayette County in the lower house of the legislature and he was successively reëlected until 1801, being speaker the last two years. In 1801 he was elected to the United States Senate,

but resigned in 1805 to become attorney-general of the United States, an appointment which greatly pleased the West and strengthened President Jefferson there.

Breckinridge impressed himself upon the country as no other representative of the West had done up to that time. He believed that the national government was making little effort to open the Mississippi River, and he emphasized this belief by accepting the presidency of the Democratic Society of Kentucky, organized in Lexington the year he arrived. He also looked with favor on George Rogers Clark's plottings with Genet in their efforts to open the navigation of the Mississippi and he promised a money subscription in the undertaking. In 1794 he wrote, "We have sat down with patience to watch the Event of his [Pinckney's] negotiations & God send, thay may not show us that we may fight or negotiate for ourselves" (Breckinridge Manuscripts, Sept. 15, 1794). His insistence on the rights of the West and his friendship for Jefferson had their weight in the Louisiana Purchase of 1803. Breckinridge's fighting instincts led him to work readily with Jefferson in promoting the Kentucky Resolutions of 1798. Jefferson wrote these celebrated resolutions; Breckinridge changed two of them slightly, introduced them in the Kentucky legislature, and forced their passage. The next year he introduced a new set which he himself wrote. He was not alone a destructive critic; he was a constructive reformer as well. He remade the penal code for Kentucky and eliminated all capital crimes except murder. His constructive ability again was shown in his work in the second constitutional convention of Kentucky. The document it produced was largely due to his efforts. He died when only forty-six years of age, but his widow lived many years thereafter. There were born to them nine children.

[Various letters to and from Breckinridge are in the Breckinridge MSS. in the Lib. of Cong. Other sources of information relating to him are: *Ky. Gazette,* Dec. 15, 22, 1806; E. D. Warfield, *The Ky. Resolutions of 1798* (1887); Richard H. and Lewis Collins, *Hist. of Ky.* (1874); *Biog. Encyc. of Ky.* (1877); H. Levin, ed., *Lawyers and Lawmakers of Ky.* (1897).]

E. M. C—r.

BRECKINRIDGE, JOHN (July 4, 1797–Aug. 4, 1841), Presbyterian clergyman, controversialist, was a descendant of Scotch-Irish settlers in Virginia, a Kentuckian by birth, who feared God but not the face of man. His father, John [*q.v.*], attorney-general in Jefferson's cabinet at the time, died when his namesake was but nine years old, and he was brought up at his birthplace, Cabell's Dale, Ky., by a most capable mother, Mary Hopkins Cabell, daughter of Col. Joseph Cabell of Buckingham County, Va., and by an older brother, his legal guardian. Before entering the College of New Jersey, where he enrolled in 1815 and from which he graduated with honors three years later, he had no thought of becoming a minister, for no one of his family was then a church member, and he had been destined for the law. It was in the face of considerable opposition from home, therefore, that having been converted from his "gay and wild career," he persisted in his determination to preach the gospel. In 1820–21 he was a tutor at Princeton and a student in the theological seminary there. On Aug. 1, 1822, he was licensed to preach by the Presbytery of New Brunswick, and during 1822–23 was chaplain of Congress. He was ordained, Sept. 10, 1823, by the Presbytery of West Lexington, Ky., and installed pastor of the McChord Church, Lexington.

His intellectual strength, eloquence, and ability as a debater quickly lifted him into prominence, but the intensity of his zeal soon wore out a none too robust body. His original intention had been to labor in a foreign field, but conditions outside his control, he states, forbade. He was afire with missionary ardor, however, an aggressive champion of the Protestant faith, and a crusader against heresy and wrong. In Presbyterian circles he stood forth as an uncompromising opponent of the New School theology, and while at Lexington he waged war against the liberalism of President Horace Holley [q.v.] of Transylvania University. Outside the pulpit, his principal medium of attack was the *Western Luminary,* which he edited, and is commonly said to have established. This latter honor, however, probably belongs to the publisher, Thomas T. Skillman (L. and R. H. Collins, *History of Kentucky,* 1874, I, 466; G. W. Ranck, *History of Lexington, Ky.,* 1872, p. 300). In 1826 Breckinridge became associated with Dr. John Glendy at the Second Presbyterian Church, Baltimore, and in 1831, secretary and general agent of the Board of Education of the Presbyterian Church. The General Assembly appointed him professor of pastoral theology in Princeton Seminary in 1836, which chair he relinquished in 1838 to become secretary and general agent of the Board of Foreign Missions. His health was failing, however, and he held the office but two years. At the time of his death, which occurred at his birthplace, he was pastor-elect of the Presbyterian church in New Orleans, and had been chosen president of Oglethorpe University, Ga.

As a controversialist Breckinridge became widely known through two series of debates with Rev. John Hughes [q.v.], later archbishop of New York. The first of these, on the question "Is the Protestant Religion the Religion of Christ?" was conducted in the columns of the *Presbyterian* and the *Catholic Herald* in 1833, and was published under the title *Controversy between Rev. Messrs. Hughes and Breckinridge, on the Subject, etc.* (1834?). The second was carried on in the Union Literary and Debating Institute, Philadelphia, in 1835–36, and was on the question: "Is the Roman Catholic Religion in Any or in All its Principles or Doctrines Inimical to Civil or Religious Liberty?" followed by the question, "Is the Presbyterian Religion . . . Inimical, etc.," published in 1836 under the title, *A Discussion of the Question, Is the Roman Catholic Religion, etc.* Both sides of these controversies were discussed frankly, ably, and at length, the discussions being enlivened with rather acrimonious personalities. The widespread report that on his death-bed he repented his opposition to the Roman Catholic Church and asked for the ministry of a priest seems to have been thoroughly disproved (see R. Davidson, *History of the Presbyterian Church,* 1847, p. 363).

Besides the above, his published works include *Ministerial Responsibility* (1828); *An Address Delivered July 15, 1835, before the Eucleian and Philomathian Societies of the University of the City of New York* (1836); and the tenth lecture in *Spruce Street Lectures on Missions* (1833). After the death of his first wife, Margaret Miller, daughter of Prof. Samuel Miller, of Princeton Theological Seminary, whom he married in January 1823, he published *A Memorial of Mrs. Margaret Breckinridge* (1839). He was married a second time in 1840 to Mary Ann Babcock of Stonington, Conn.

[Besides above-mentioned works, see W. B. Sprague, *Annals Am. Pulpit,* vol. IV (1858); *Baltimore Relig. and Lit. Mag.,* VIII, 475–80.]   H.E.S.

BRECKINRIDGE, JOHN CABELL (Jan. 15, 1821–May 17, 1875), soldier, statesman, was of Scotch-Irish descent. His grandfather John Breckinridge [q.v.] came to Kentucky in 1792 and subsequently became a United States senator and attorney-general under Jefferson. His father, Joseph Cabell Breckinridge, who had married Mary Clay Smith, became a distinguished lawyer and politician but died when only thirty-four years of age. John C. Breckinridge was his only son and was born near Lexington, Ky. He attended Centre College, a Presbyterian school in Danville, and was graduated in 1839. Shortly afterward he spent some time at the College of New Jersey. With his family background it was only natural that he should study law and this he did under the direction of Gov. Owsley. He also pursued further his work in law at Transylvania College during the year 1840–41. The Lexington bar was so well supplied with men of outstanding ability and success that Breckinridge decided that his opportunities there would be rather meager. He first went to Frankfort but soon concluded to settle in a less crowded region further west and chose Burlington, Iowa. Here he remained two years, but the spell of Kentucky was always upon him. Returning to his native state, he at first located for a short time at Georgetown, near Lexington, but becoming bolder and more self-confident, in 1845 he moved back to Lexington and began practise there, later forming a partnership with James B. Beck. He was soon in comfortable circumstances but was on the road to no great fortune. The call for troops in 1846 to invade Mexico failed to enlist either his enthusiasm or his services, he being in this respect unlike most of his fellow Kentuckians. But his ability as an orator had been noted and when in July 1847 a score of dead Kentuckians, officers and privates, killed at Buena Vista and at other battles, were brought to Frankfort for a great military funeral, where 20,000 people gathered, Breckinridge was selected to deliver the commemorative oration. Aided by the solemn splendor of the occasion, Breckinridge talked himself into the army. He was commissioned a major of the 3rd Kentucky Volunteers, whom he led into Mexico. But he was too late to reap any military glory, his chief accomplishment here being his defense of Gen. Pillow in a dispute which arose with Gen. Scott.

In 1849 Breckinridge made his first entry into politics when he ran for the legislature to represent Fayette County. He was elected. It was at this time that the campaign was on for the constitutional convention and that the slavery question was being hotly agitated. Being a Democrat he favored the convention and opposed the emancipationists. In this campaign he came into conflict with his imperious uncle, Robert Jefferson Breckinridge [q.v.], with whom he was hereafter to differ on almost every subject. In 1851 the Democrats chose him as their candidate for Congress representing the Ashland District, which had become under Clay's leadership one of the strongest Whig districts in the state. The Whigs with Gen. Leslie Combs, who stood next to Clay in popularity in the state, expected to win easily. But Breckinridge overturned the

normal 1,500 Whig majority and won by 500 votes. Now there had arisen a successor to Clay, who was to play almost as remarkable a part in Kentucky sentiment. The next year, when he delivered a funeral oration over the dead Clay, his position in the affections of the people was fixed. The next year the Whigs attempted without success to defeat Breckinridge, using this time the ex-governor, Robert P. Letcher. Although Breckinridge was characterized by a dignified bearing and serene nature, in 1854 on the floor of Congress he got himself involved in a heated altercation with Frank B. Cutting, a representative from New York, which came near resulting in a duel. Breckinridge had now definitely established his leadership both in Kentucky and in Congress, but at the end of his second term he decided to resume his law practise in order to repair his private fortune. At this time President Pierce offered him the diplomatic post at Madrid, which he refused.

His record in Congress had so favorably introduced him to the national Democracy that at the party convention in Cincinnati in 1856, when a Southern running-mate for Buchanan was needed, Breckinridge received the nomination. He took an active part in the campaign, making speeches in Indiana, Michigan, and Pennsylvania. His influence in Kentucky gave the state to the Democrats by 6,000 majority. When Buchanan became president in 1857, Breckinridge as vice-president became the presiding officer in the Senate. His four years of service were characterized by poise and justice in his decisions. When on Jan. 4, 1859, the Senate moved from its old chamber to its new quarters Breckinridge was chosen to deliver the parting address. He traced the development of the Union and made a strong plea for its preservation. The Kentucky Democrats now having found their leader decided to keep him before the country. Almost a year and a half before his term as vice-president would expire (December 1859), they elected him to the United States Senate for the term beginning Mar. 4, 1861.

When the Democratic National Convention met in Charleston Breckinridge's name was presented by Arkansas, but not being a candidate and not desiring to interfere with James Guthrie's aspirations, Breckinridge had his name withdrawn. No nomination having been made in Charleston, when the Southern faction of the disrupted convention later met in Baltimore, Breckinridge was selected for president despite the fact that he was still averse to having his name considered. He, however, accepted the nomination. He saw with many misgivings the

8

break-up of the Democratic party and he readily agreed to step aside when Jefferson Davis attempted unsuccessfully to reunite the party. After all efforts toward peace had failed he took an active part in the campaign and stoutly defended himself against the charges of being inconsistent and of holding disunion sentiments. He maintained that he had always stood for the non-intervention of Congress on the subject of slavery in the territories and that slavery could be excluded only when the territory should become a state. A determined effort was made to prove that he was a disunionist but he showed that neither by word nor act had he ever promoted such an idea. In 1859 after he had been elected to the Senate he said, "She [Kentucky] will cling to the Constitution while a shred of it remains . . ." (*Modern Eloquence,* edited by Thomas B. Reed, 1905, VII, 105), and in 1860 at Frankfort he said, "I am an American citizen, a Kentuckian, who never did an act nor cherished a thought that was not full of devotion to the Constitution and the Union" (*Kentucky Statesman,* July 20, 1860). He received 72 electoral votes in November, though he failed to carry his own state.

As the presiding officer of the Senate he appointed the committee on compromise in December 1860, and he used his influence to have the Crittenden Compromise, which came before that committee, adopted. He believed in the abstract right of secession but he was opposed to the adoption of such a course at that time. Yet he was just as thoroughly opposed to the coercion of a state, holding that the Constitution gave the national government no such power. After the inauguration of Lincoln, he returned to Kentucky and took an active part in the political maneuvers there. He stood out for any compromise that would save the Union, but after the firing on Fort Sumter, which set up the second wave of secession, he held that the Union no longer existed, and that Kentucky now had the right to take any course she should please. The logical action would be to call a sovereign convention, and from this time on as long as there was a chance of using this procedure, he worked for it. On Apr. 2 he addressed the legislature and on May 10 he was appointed a member of a small conference which it was hoped would unite the state on a single course of action. The movement failed and two weeks later Kentucky declared her neutrality, a solution which did not meet with Breckinridge's approval. Yet he acquiesced in it when it was established.

Being a member of the United States Senate he attended the special session beginning on July 4, 1861, and assuming that he was to represent his state and uphold her position which she had recently adopted, he opposed Lincoln's whole war policy, refusing to vote men or money. He defended this position by later declaring to the Kentuckians, "I would have blushed to meet you with the confession that I had purchased for you exemption from the perils of the battlefields and the shame of waging war against your Southern brethren by hiring others to do the work you shrank from performing" (*Rebellion Record,* edited by Frank Moore, III, 254). In early September Kentucky abandoned her neutrality when the armies of both sides invaded the state, embraced the Union troops and ordered the Confederates out. The military régime immediately took charge of the state, arresting hundreds of citizens on suspicion and sending them away without trial. Breckinridge fled to escape arrest, and on Oct. 2 the legislature requested him to resign from the Senate, and on Nov. 6, he was indicted for treason in the federal district court at Frankfort. On Dec. 2, 1861, the United States Senate declared him a traitor and went through the formality of expelling him although he had long been in the Confederate army.

In September he had returned to Kentucky and on the 8th of the following month from Bowling Green he issued a burning address to the people of his native state defending his position and castigating those who had sold out the state to the Federal army. In his address he resigned his position in the Senate, saying, "I exchange with proud satisfaction a term of six years in the Senate of the United States for the musket of a soldier" (*Rebellion Record,* III, 258). He helped to organize the provisional government of Kentucky (Confederate) and in November was appointed a brigadier-general under the command of Gen. A. S. Johnston at Bowling Green. In early 1862 he retreated out of Kentucky with the Confederates, taking part in the battle of Shiloh where he commanded the Reserve Corps. He was soon promoted to be a major-general and in the summer of 1862 he defended Vicksburg. He was then ordered to attack Baton Rouge which he did unsuccessfully; in August he fortified Port Hudson to block the Federal advance up the Mississippi River. He was ordered to join Bragg's invasion of Kentucky in the fall of 1862 but the order came too late for him to take part. On Bragg's return to Tennessee Breckinridge joined him and was in the thickest of the fight at Murfreesboro, commanding the 2nd Division of Hardee's corps. After the battle he covered Bragg's retreat with considerable skill. In May 1863 he was attached to Gen. Joseph E. Johnston in Mississippi and was present at the battle of Jackson. He then returned to the Army of Tennessee under Bragg and commanded a division of D. H. Hill's corps at Chickamauga and Missionary Ridge. In 1864 on the death of John H. Morgan he was ordered to southwest Virginia to assume command of the department, where he remained until Gen. Lee called him to the Shenandoah Valley. After some maneuvers in the Valley he was attached to Lee's army and at the battle of Cold Harbor commanded a division. He was with Gen. Jubal Early in the raid on the outskirts of Washington in July 1864, winning victories at Martinsburg and Monocacy. He was afterward ordered back to the department of southwest Virginia where he was located when President Davis made him secretary of war on Feb. 4, 1865. Although Breckinridge had had no military training beyond his Mexican War experiences, his innate ability as a leader of men, his ready adaptability to new circumstances, and his commanding personality made of him an able commander in the Civil War.

After Appomattox he fled southward with the Confederate cabinet, was present as an adviser to Gen. J. E. Johnston on his surrender to Gen. Sherman, and after the cabinet broke up at Washington, Ga., he made his way on horseback to the coast of Florida where he escaped to Cuba. He now embarked for Europe where he remained until 1868 when he went to Toronto, Canada. In March of the following year he was given permission by the federal government to return to Lexington, Ky. Here he was received with the greatest acclaim, and had his disabilities been removed he might have had any office within the gift of the people. He was now undoubtedly the most popular man in the state, and Grant thought it would have been well for the federal government to allow him to hold office. But he disclaimed all political ambitions and in a very retiring manner resumed his law practise. He was made vice-president of the Elizabethtown, Lexington, & Big Sandy Railroad and took a prominent part in the railroad development coming to the state at this time. He strongly favored the building of the Cincinnati Southern Railroad from Cincinnati to Chattanooga and he took a prominent part in the fight incident to the movement.

Breckinridge married Mary C. Burch of Scott County in December 1843. He died in Lexington in 1875 from the effects of a serious operation. In 1886 the state erected a statue of him in Lexington at an expense of $10,000.

[The Breckinridge MSS. in the Lib. of Cong.; *Biog.*

Sketches of Hon. John C. Breckinridge, Democratic Nominee for President, and Gen. Jos. Lane, Democratic Nominee for Vice-President (1860); *Buchanan and Breckinridge: Lives of Jas. Buchanan and John C. Breckinridge, Democratic Candidates for the Presidency and Vice-presidency of the U. S., with the Platforms of the Political Parties in the Presidential Canvass of 1856* (1856); *Famous Adventures and Prison Escapes of the Civil War* (1893); *Battles and Leaders of the Civil War* (1888); *Official Records,* see Index; *Lexington Weekly Press,* May 23, 1875; *Lexington Observer and Reporter,* Mar. 13, 1869; *Ky. Gazette,* May 19, 1875; *McClure's Mag.,* Jan. 1901; Ed. Porter Thompson, *Hist. of the Orphan Brigade* (1898); Richard H. and Lewis Collins, *Hist. of Ky.* (1874); Alexander Brown, *The Cabells and Their Kin* (1895).]

E. M. C—r.

BRECKINRIDGE, ROBERT JEFFERSON (Mar. 8, 1800–Nov. 27, 1871), lawyer, Presbyterian clergyman, college president, born at Cabell's Dale near Lexington, in Fayette County, Ky., was the son of John [*q.v.*] and Mary Hopkins (Cabell) Breckinridge. The father was one of the leaders in the state and nation, being a United States senator and an attorney-general under President Jefferson. Robert was given excellent preparation for college by the leading educators of the state and when sixteen years of age was sent to Jefferson College, where he remained for two years. He spent part of a year at Yale College and then changed to Union College at Schenectady, N. Y., where he was graduated in 1819. He then returned to Lexington to manage his mother's estate, and there studied law. In 1824 he began the practise of his profession, at a time when the Old Court and New Court struggle was hottest. He supported the former, ran for the legislature in 1825, and was victorious. He continued to represent Fayette County at Frankfort until 1828. The death of two of his children had a profound effect upon him, and a severe illness at this time left his health ever afterward impaired. He now turned to religion, joining the Presbyterian Church, and entered upon a new career. In 1831 he was sent to Cincinnati as a delegate from the West Lexington Presbytery to the General Assembly, and the next year he was licensed to preach. In 1832 he removed with his family to Princeton to better prepare himself for the ministry, but before the end of the year he accepted a call to the Second Presbyterian Church in Baltimore, succeeding his brother John, where he continued until 1845. Here he speedily developed into one of the greatest controversialists and crusaders of his times. He was chiefly responsible for the celebrated "Act and Testimony" of June 1834, which led to the division of the Presbyterian Church in 1837 into the Old School and New School. He allied himself with the former group. In 1836 he visited Europe in the interest of his health, acting at the same time as a representative of the General Assembly, and he engaged in Glasgow, Scotland, in a heated controversy over slavery. In 1845 he accepted the presidency of Jefferson College, in Pennsylvania, but after two troublous years there he resigned on account of the rigors of the climate and accepted a call to the First Presbyterian Church in Lexington, Ky. In 1847 Gov. William Owsley appointed him superintendent of public instruction, which position he held until 1851, first through reappointment by Gov. John J. Crittenden in 1848 and then by election in 1851. His labors for the public school system were monumental, increasing the school attendance in his six years of service from 20,000 to 201,000. He left the public schools to accept a professorship in the new Danville Theological Seminary, which the Presbyterians had just established, and he remained in this capacity until 1869 when old age, disease, and disputes brought about his resignation. He died two years later in Danville.

His career was characterized by fierce controversies. In Baltimore he began a bitter attack against the Catholics, so vigorously carried on as to cause his friends to fear for his life. He also strongly opposed the Universalists. In 1831 he unsuccessfully ran for the state legislature in Kentucky on the issue of opposition to slavery and to Sunday mails. He was also a tireless worker in the temperance movement. In 1849 he headed the attempt of the gradual emancipationists to control the constitutional convention of that year, but failed in his election as a delegate. While in Baltimore he opposed the attempt of Maryland to exclude free negroes. During the Civil War he put forth all of his fiery zeal in support of the Union and during the four years of the struggle he was Lincoln's chief counsellor and adviser in Kentucky. He was also the chief supporter of the military régime in the state. He organized the Lincoln support in Kentucky in 1864, headed the delegation to the Baltimore convention, and was made temporary chairman. He was uncompromising in his opposition to Southern sympathizers, even refusing to save members of his own family from Northern prisons and firing squads. He so hopelessly involved the Presbyterian Church in the political rancors of the times that the organization split in 1866. He was an untiring writer and speaker, writing many open letters, pamphlets, and books. His best known works are, *The Knowledge of God, Objectively Considered* (1858) and *The Knowledge of God, Subjectively Considered* (1859). He edited in Baltimore the *Literary and Religious Magazine* and the *Spirit of the Nineteenth Century,* and from 1861 to 1865 in Danville the *Danville Quarterly Review.* He was married three times: first on Mar. 11, 1823, to his cousin Ann Sophronisba Preston, a daughter of Col. Francis Preston of Virginia, who died in 1844; secondly, in 1847 to Mrs. Virginia Shelby, a daughter of Col. Nathaniel Hart, who died in 1859; and thirdly, in 1868 to Margaret White, who survived him.

[Richard H. and Lewis Collins, *Hist. of Ky.* (1874); *Biog. Encyc. of Ky.* (1878); H. Levin, ed., *Lawyers and Lawmakers of Ky.* (1897); J. W. Townsend, *Kentuckians in Am. Letters* (1913), vol. I; *Lexington Dollar Weekly Press,* Jan. 6, 8, 1872.]   E.M.C—r.

BRECKINRIDGE, WILLIAM CAMPBELL PRESTON (Aug. 28, 1837–Nov. 19, 1904), lawyer, editor, congressman, was a son of Robert J. Breckinridge [*q.v.*], and Ann Sophronisba, a daughter of Gen. Francis Preston and a grand-daughter of Gen. William Campbell. He was a grandson of John Breckinridge, attorney-general under President Jefferson. He was born in Baltimore, Md., where his father was pastor of the Second Presbyterian Church. Later when his father became president of Jefferson College in Pennsylvania he attended school there, finishing his college course at Centre College, Danville, Ky., in 1855. He now studied medicine for a year, but deciding that he had a greater liking for law, pursued that subject at the Louisville Law College, was graduated in 1857, and began the practise of his profession in Lexington. When the Civil War broke out his sympathies were strongly with the Confederacy, but because his father was the outstanding leader of the Union cause in the state, he remained inactive until Gen. John H. Morgan invaded the state in July 1862. He then joined Morgan's 2nd Kentucky Cavalry in Georgetown as captain and immediately took a prominent part in the engagement at Cynthiana. In 1863 he was attached to the 9th Kentucky Cavalry as a colonel and continued with Morgan until this unit was detached when the latter made his raid north of the Ohio. He was present at the battle of Saltville, Va., and in various capacities was actively engaged throughout the war. He was a member of the body-guard that accompanied Jefferson Davis on his retreat southward, and when the band broke up he was released from further Confederate service by his distinguished kinsman, John Cabell Breckinridge. He returned to Lexington where he began again the practise of law and where in 1866 he assumed the editorship of the *Lexington Observer and Reporter.* In 1868 he gave up his newspaper work in order to enter more actively into his law practise. He was connected for a time with the Law School of Kentucky University (formerly Transylvania University). In 1869 he ran for county attorney but was defeated on account of his support of the admission of negro testimony in the courts. He was elected to the lower house of Congress in 1884 and was reëlected for four successive terms. In 1894 after a very bitter campaign he was defeated and in 1896 he again suffered defeat. At the latter time he ran on a fusion ticket in support of sound money. In January of the following year he became chief editorial writer on the *Lexington Morning Herald*, a paper managed by his son Desha, and in this capacity he developed journalistic ability of a high order. His writings were smooth and direct. As an orator, by common consent, he was unexcelled by any Kentuckian of his day, and as a lawyer his manner and argument were compelling before a jury. In physique he was manly, robust, and handsome. He was married three times: first, to Lucretia Clay, a grand-daughter of Henry Clay, who died in 1860; secondly, to Issa Desha, a granddaughter of Gov. Joseph Desha, who died in Washington in 1892, and lastly, to Louise Wing. In his later days his fame was clouded by rumors and a court proceeding involving his family relations (Fayette Lexington, pseudonym, *The Celebrated Case of Col. W. C. P. Breckinridge and Madeline Pollard*, 1894). He died in Lexington in 1904.

[Letters and papers in the Breckinridge MSS. in the Lib. of Cong. Sketches and appreciations of his life may be found in *Lexington Leader*, Nov. 20–23, 1904; *Lexington Morning Herald*, Nov. 20–22, 1904; *Biog. Encyc. of Ky.* (1878); Richard H. and Lewis Collins, *Hist. of Ky.* (2 vols., 1874); John W. Townsend, *Kentuckians in Am. Letters* (1913), vol. I; Basil W. Duke, *Hist. of Morgan's Cavalry* (1867); R. U. Johnson and C. C. Buel, eds., *Battles and Leaders of the Civil War* (4 vols., 1887–88).]

E.M.C—r.

BREED, EBENEZER (May 12, 1766–Dec. 23, 1839), early advocate of protection of the shoe industry, was born in Lynn, Mass. He was the youngest of the eight children of Benjamin Breed and Ruth Allen and was of the fifth generation in line from Allen Bread (afterward Breed) who came to Salem, Mass., in 1629 and settled at Saugus, Mass., his portion of the plantation being known as "Breed's End," afterward a part of Lynn. Benjamin Breed is recorded as being a cordwainer and husbandman, combining, as was the custom, two vocations in order that no part of the year might be wasted. Ebenezer Breed's younger days were probably spent in connection with his father's business but letters written later in life indicate that he received more than an ordinary education. He

early moved to Philadelphia and being reared in the Society of Friends was warmly received by several of the more prosperous Quakers, previously residents of Lynn. Foremost among them was Stephen Collins, a successful merchant of the period. Influenced by his early association Breed established himself as a wholesale shoe merchant. In his business he quickly encountered the oppressive economic conditions which beset the not-too-well established industries in the period of adjustment which followed the Revolutionary War. Being of a sanguine temperament, with a Quaker sense of the injustice of poverty from avoidable causes, he early seems to have formed definite ideas regarding the policy to be pursued in building the way to economic independence.

Three years of agitation culminated in a brilliant dinner-party given by Breed to the members of Congress at the Collins Mansion loaned for the purpose. The register of the Lynn Historical Society preserves this fragment of Breed's impassioned plea for the shoemaker: "Will you stand tamely by and see this infant industry swallowed up by the raging lions of Britain and Gaul? Will you see the homes of these operatives destroyed or abandoned and not hold out your strong arms to shield them as they shielded you when war bent his horrid front over our fair land? No, I trust and New England expects that by your suffrages we shall obtain the desired relief when the matter comes before your honorable body." This dinner took place between the meeting of the First Congress, Mar. 4, 1789, and the following July 4, when the first tariff act was passed, providing a duty of fifty cents per pair on boots, seven cents per pair on leather shoes, slippers, galoshes, and ten cents per pair on all shoes or slippers made of silk or stuff. Breed now visited England, where his correspondence shows that he was well received, and he is even said to have had his august moment in the presence of royalty, through his friend Sir Benjamin West. He made many business contacts of great advantage and became an importer of much of the shoe material that came from England and France. He also arranged for the coming of several workmen of unusual skill to the city of Lynn for the purpose of teaching the most advanced methods in the shoemaking art. He visited France for a brief period and is said to have had a few very miserable hours in endeavoring to escape the ravages of the Revolution then in progress.

Among the estimable ladies of Breed's circle in Philadelphia was one to whom he paid fervent court, Polly Atmore, daughter of a prominent Quaker, and before he went abroad in 1792 he had won the promise of her hand in marriage. But, on his return, Polly's father accused him of departing from the precepts of his youthful training in his contact with the wealthy classes abroad and directed that the nuptials be postponed for a year. When the year of probation expired, however, Polly was married to a Mr. Robinson and from that day Breed began to give color to the old Quaker's charge by being constantly in his cups. He gradually lost his health and finally his eyesight and the year 1800 found him back in his native town, an inmate of the poorhouse. A kindly disposed cobbler taught him the art of making shoes and he at various times worked whimsically at his trade, resentfully refusing the aid that well-meaning friends proffered. He died in Lynn and was buried at the public expense.

[F. J. Allen, *The Shoe Industry* (1922); *Vital Records of Lynn, Mass.* (1905–06); *Reg. of the Lynn Hist. Soc.*, 1911; Alonzo Lewis and J. R. Newhall, *Hist. of Lynn* (1865); *Essex Antiquarian*, Salem, Mass., Oct. 1907.]   C. T. C.

BREEN, PATRICK (d. Dec. 21, 1868), diarist of the Donner party, was born in Ireland and came to the United States in 1828. Of his early life nothing appears to be recorded. From Keokuk, Iowa, Apr. 5, 1846, with his wife Margaret and seven children, he set out for the emigrants' rendezvous at Independence, Mo., bound for California. Here he joined the party of George and Jacob Donner, which had come from Springfield, Ill., and which with several other parties left for the West early in May. On July 20, at the Little Sandy, in Wyoming, where more emigrants were found, the Donner party was separately organized and George Donner was elected captain. At Fort Bridger, which was reached five days later, decision was made to try the new Hastings cut-off around the south shore of Salt Lake. Instead, however, of reaching the lake by the known route through Weber Canyon, a roundabout course was taken through the mountains, which caused great delay. Other delays with great loss of live-stock followed, in traversing the Nevada desert, and when the party reached Truckee Lake (since called Donner Lake), snow was falling. Several attempts to proceed were frustrated by the increasing snowfall, and by the middle of November the leaders of the party realized that they were hemmed in, with small chance of rescue. Of the tragedy that followed, in which thirty-six out of a company of eighty-one perished, many of the survivors have left accounts. The narrative that furnishes the most vivid realization of the scene, however, is the diary kept from Nov. 20 to Mar. 1 by Breen. Its bare, scant sentences record divided counsels, quarrels, the sending out of the relief-seekers in mid-December, the exhaustion of the food supply until nothing but hides were left, the increasing weakness and illness of the people, the succession of deaths, the arrival of the first rescue party and the departure of the first contingent of survivors; and it closes with the statement that in two or three days the remainder will start. All of the Breens lived throught the terrible ordeal, though the youngest was a nursing baby. After some shifting about, the family settled, in February 1848, at San Juan Bautista, in San Benito County. The children all lived to maturity, and five of them outlived their parents. The father died at the San Juan home, and six years later his wife followed him.

Breen's title to fame rests on his sole literary production, the diary—"one of the most highly prized treasures," says Bancroft, "of my Library." It is brief—so brief that it omits much the reader would wish to know. Its quality is that of stark literalness unrelieved by any note other than one of patient endurance based on a serene faith in ultimate rescue. Breen was a devout Catholic who had prayers read regularly every day, and his piety converted one of the other members of the party to his creed. He was in no way distinguished among his companions. Indeed, though the women of the party—particularly Tamsen Donner, Margaret Breen and Olvina Murphy—revealed outstanding qualities of greatness, all the men except Stanton seem to have been weak and uncertain, without foresight or any other of the capacities that should have enabled them to prevent an appalling disaster.

[C. F. McGlashan, *History of the Donner Party; A Tragedy of the Sierra* (2nd ed. 1880); Eliza P. Donner Houghton, *The Expedition of the Donner Party and Its Tragic Fate* (1911); H. H. Bancroft, *Hist. of Cal.*, vols. II, V (1885–86); *California and Californians*, ed. by Rockwell D. Hunt (1926), vol. II. The diary is given, with a brief introduction by Frederick J. Teggert, in *Acad. Pacific Coast Hist. Pubs.*, vol. I (July 1910).]   W. J. G.

BREESE, KIDDER RANDOLPH (Apr. 14, 1831–Sept. 13, 1881), naval officer, was born in Philadelphia and appointed a midshipman, from Rhode Island, Nov. 6, 1846. In February 1847 he was ordered to the *Saratoga,* commanded by Commander (afterward Admiral) Farragut and served in her on the Gulf Coast during the war with Mexico. In the spring of 1848 he joined the *St. Mary's* and then served in the *Brandywine* until December 1850. In February 1851 he joined the frigate *St. Lawrence*, and participated in that vessel's voyage to London, laden with articles for the World's Fair. From October 1851 to June 1852 he studied for examination at the Naval Academy, being promoted passed midshipman during the latter month and ordered to the *Mississippi*, flagship of Commodore M. C. Perry [*q.v.*], participating in the famous cruise to Japan. During this cruise he was temporarily attached to the *Macedonian*, which visited the northern end of Formosa to search for coal and to inquire into the captivity of Americans by savages of that island. Returning to the United States in the *Mississippi* in June 1855, in 1858 he was ordered to the *Preble*, and took part in the expedition to Paraguay, and afterward spent some time on the Mosquito Coast, being invalided home with "Isthmus fever" in September 1859. In 1860 he joined the *Portsmouth* on the African Coast, and then the *San Jacinto*, in which he remained until December 1861, the end of her extended cruise, in which 1,500 slaves were captured. During the same month he was ordered to command the third division of Admiral Porter's mortar flotilla, taking part in the opening of the Mississippi River in 1862. Promoted lieutenant commander, the promotion dating from July 16, 1862, he joined Porter's river squadron, commanding the flagship *Black Hawk*, and was present at nearly all the important operations on the Mississippi River and its tributaries. On the conclusion of the Red River expedition he was recommended for promotion. When Porter was ordered to command the North Atlantic blockading squadron in September 1864, he chose Breese as his fleet-captain. This command Breese held until the end of the Civil War. In the storming of Fort Fisher on Jan. 15, 1865, he commanded the storming party of sailors and marines. Admiral Porter in his report, after enumerating and highly praising the devices of Lieutenant Commander Breese, added, "He is a clever, gallant officer, and I strongly recommend his immediate promotion to a commander." Breese's commission followed on July 25, 1866. His duties after the Civil War included those of the assistant superintendency of the Naval Academy under Admiral Porter; those of the inspectorship of ordnance at the Washington Navy Yard; and others connected with the testing of breech-loading arms. He took command of the *Plymouth* of the European squadron on June 29, 1870; was on duty in the Bureau of Ordnance at the Navy Department in December 1872; and became commandant of midshipmen at the Naval Academy in June 1873. He was commissioned captain Aug. 9, 1874. In

1878 he commanded the *Pensacola*, flagship of the Pacific squadron, and was ordered home on sick-leave in 1880, his death occurring the following year.

[Admiral D. D. Porter, *Naval Hist. of the Civil War* (1886); *Report of the Sec. of the Navy, 1861–65*, inclusive; obituary in the *Army and Navy Journal*, XIX, 145; *Navy Register, 1847–80*.]   E. B.

BREESE, SIDNEY (July 15, 1800–June 27, 1878), jurist and politician, was endowed by birth with the prestige of an aristocratic family of New York. On the side of his mother, Catharine Livingston, he was a descendant of John Livingstone, the Scotch divine who negotiated with Charles II in 1650 at Breda, and on his father's side, a descendant of the picturesque soldier-merchant who was master of the port of New York on the eve of the American Revolution (E. E. Salisbury, *Family Memorials*, 1885, II, pp. 477, 503). His father, Arthur Breese, who received an honorary bachelor's degree from Yale College in 1789, followed in the wake of the westward migration, settled at Whitestown in 1793, later removed to Utica, and for seventeen years was clerk of the supreme court of Western New York. He built a spacious house where he entertained Lafayette and other notables who visited that part of the country.

Sidney Breese, the second son in a family of nine, prepared for college under a Presbyterian minister, Rev. Jesse Townsend. Entering Hamilton College, he transferred to Union College and graduated at the age of eighteen, third in his class. Shortly after leaving college, Sidney Breese, like his father, sought his fortune in the West and accepted the invitation of a friend of the family, Elias Kent Kane, to read law at Kaskaskia. It was in the office of the brilliant Kane that the first constitution of the State of Illinois was drafted. Breese was thus early identified with the group of leaders who played a conspicuous part in the development of this frontier state. Admitted to the bar in 1820, he lost his first case through stage-fright and came near to abandoning the profession. In 1821, he was postmaster of Kaskaskia; a year later Kane secured him the appointment of state's attorney; and four years later he received an appointment from President Adams as federal district attorney for Illinois, from which office as a victim of the spoils system, he was removed by President Jackson. This involved him in the bitter struggle in local politics between the Adams faction and the Jackson faction; and for years after he had become a Jacksonian Democrat he was hounded with the charge that once he had distributed "coffin hand-bills" depicting the tyranny of Jackson's martial law in New Orleans (Linder, *Reminiscences*, 144). To advance his political career he edited behind the name of R. K. Fleming the "scurrilous and libelous thumbpaper," the *Western Democrat*, published at Kaskaskia. In 1831 he was an unsuccessful candidate for representative to Congress with a platform in favor of complete state ownership of the public lands. Like Lincoln, Breese played a part in that grim prairie tragedy, the Black Hawk War. Enlisting as a private he was elected to a lieutenant-colonelcy of volunteers, thus furnishing the curious spectacle, in the camp of Gen. J. D. Henry, of a retiring scholar outranking such young warriors as Albert Sidney Johnston, Zachary Taylor, and Robert Anderson who later was the gallant defender of Fort Sumter. At the bar, Breese soon won recognition by his able defense of Judge Smith against impeachment charges in the state legislature (*Senate Journal, 1831–3*, App. 22). This led to his election as judge of the second circuit court in 1835; and, while sitting on this bench, he wrote the opinion in the case of *People* vs. *Field* holding that the governor had power to remove a subordinate from office (*Illinois State Register*, May 24, 1839, pp. 2–3). The reversal of this partisan decision by the supreme court led to the reprehensible action of the Democratic legislature in swamping this court by the addition of five new judgeships, to which were elected, among others, Breese and Stephen A. Douglas.

In 1838, Breese was an unsuccessful candidate for the Democratic nomination as governor. Four years later he again offered himself as a candidate, but withdrew in favor of Thomas Ford, as a result of an alleged bargain which won him the election as United States senator by the legislature in the winter of that year (T. C. Pease, *The Frontier State*, 1918, p. 283). His nomination, however, was contested in an all-night caucus of the Democratic party at Springfield by the supporters of Douglas—an incident which led to years of animosity between the two men.

Breese served one term in the Senate, 1843–49. Although handicapped by a persistent timidity, and impatient with details, he made a minor reputation for learning and scholarship and for five years held the position of chairman of the committee on public lands. With the Democrats of Illinois he took an extreme attitude on the Oregon question, demanding in several speeches a policy of "54° 40′ or fight." He supported Polk's policy of annexation of Texas and the war with Mexico, and made an elaborate reply

to Calhoun's celebrated demand that the American army fall back to a defensive line (*Congressional Globe*, 30 Cong., 1 Sess., App. p. 344). Like many Democrats he opposed grants of public lands for the Cumberland Road and for other internal improvements, but he reluctantly approved of national aid for canals and railways, urging in particular Asa Whitney's project for a railway to the Pacific and the Illinois scheme for a railway parallel with the Mississippi (*Senate Document No. 466*, 29 Cong., 1 Sess.). He was also interested in getting the lead mines of northern Illinois out of the hands of the government and into private ownership.

His congressional record was not sufficiently strong to save him from being replaced in 1849 by a military hero—Gen. Shields. Breese's retirement from the Senate was followed by an episode of considerable personal humiliation. He had prided himself on being the original proposer of the Illinois Central Railway; while a senator, he had introduced a bill to aid in the construction of the road in Illinois, but he lacked the ability to win votes, and he blocked the efforts of his colleague, Douglas, to carry the business through Congress. Thus, when Douglas secured the passage of the Illinois Central Bill in the first session after Breese's retirement, the latter's chagrin led him unwisely to engage in a bitter newspaper controversy with his old rival, in the course of which Douglas was able to show that the project had not originated with Breese, and furthermore, that Breese's bill in the Senate had envisaged a line simply from Cairo to Galena without touching Lake Michigan or reaching to the Gulf (*Illinois State Register*, Jan. 5 and Mar. 13, 1851).

Breese spiritedly plunged once more into local politics. In the autumn of 1850 he was elected without opposition to a seat in the Illinois House of Representatives and in the same year became speaker. For the next few years he camped on the trail of Douglas hoping to win the Democratic nomination for senator; but, with Lincoln and Trumbull as competitors in baiting the author of "squatter sovereignty," Breese did not cut a conspicuous figure.

In 1857 came the turning point in his career. He was elected to the Illinois supreme court to fill a vacancy, being reëlected in 1861 for the full term of nine years and again in 1870. On the bench, the talents of this remarkable man, long warped by his incongruous political aspirations, blossomed into real genius. He became one of the leading jurists of America during a period when the rapid expansion of litigation witnessed the increase of the Illinois reports from the eighteenth to the eighty-ninth volume. Breese brought to the bench an independent method of thinking that sometimes shocked the conservative members of the bar but had a refreshing effect upon the lay mind. His wholesome impatience with the technicalities encumbering the law is illustrated by the case of *Maus* vs. *Worthing* (4 *Ill.* 26), a case in which Lincoln appeared as counsel and in which Breese dissented in vigorous language, holding that judicial proceedings should not be hidebound by arbitrary rules handed down from the past when the result was obviously to obstruct justice, and that judges should not surrender their own judgment to follow blindly the doctrine of *stare decisis* and become slaves to precedent. At the same time he vehemently opposed any tendency to exalt unduly the judiciary and was alert to prevent the courts as guardians of the people's rights from encroaching in their turn upon the liberties of the citizen. During his twenty-three years' service, he gave the opinion of the court in several famous cases, but in particular he attracted national attention by his ruling in one of the well-known "Granger cases," *Munn* vs. *Illinois* (69 *Ill.* 80). In this case, he upheld the validity of an act of the state legislature regulating grain elevators, and the United States Supreme Court, on appeal, sustained the Illinois decision upon every point (94 *U. S.* 113). This decision, rendered in 1876, was the beginning of a series of cases propounding the doctrine of the regulative power of the state over public service companies and all corporations in whose business public interests are involved. Coming at the beginning of the struggle for governmental regulation of big business —three decades before Roosevelt's war on the "trusts"—the case became one of the landmarks in the economic history of America.

The opinion in the case of *Munn* vs. *Ill.* was written in the seventy-sixth year of Breese's life —a tribute to the elasticity and alertness of his mental processes even in his old age. Early in his career, while a member of the circuit court, Breese told a Democratic rally in Montgomery County that it was compatible with judicial dignity for a judge to take an active part in politics, and even late in his career he saw nothing unbecoming in acting as a director of the Baltimore & Ohio Railroad while holding judicial office. His views in regard to the ethics of participating in politics were modified in time, but throughout his service on the bench, Breese maintained a broad sympathy with human affairs which was beneficial in the highest degree to his judicial duties. He was also conspicu-

ous for witty repartee on the bench. His opinions were couched in lucid language. His logic did not equal that of Marshall and his literary ability was inferior to Story's but his opinions were conspicuous for both argument and literary flavor. While still a young man, Breese undertook the task of reporting the decisions of the supreme court of Illinois down to date, with the result that *Breese's Reports,* published at Kaskaskia in 1831, cover the decisions of that court for the first eleven years. It was modestly announced by its editor as prompted by a "desire to discharge in some degree that duty which one of the sages of the law has said every man owes to his profession."

According to a colleague he was short in stature, deep-chested, careful in dress, nearsighted, and always wore spectacles. As a young man he was close-shaven with his black hair cut short; but in later years he suffered his beard to grow long and his hair to hang down over his shoulders, which gave him a venerable appearance. He had a weak voice. In social intercourse he was a combination of amiability and taciturnity, often delighting in learned conversation, frequently lapsing into superciliousness; he was vain, and at times obsessed with a desire to impress his associates with a sense of their inferiority. His vanity on more than one occasion proved his undoing. It led him to break with his benefactor, Kane, and it involved him in several unseemly controversies with the coarser-grained but more agile Douglas, in which he came off second best.

[W. D. Lewis, *Great Am. Lawyers* (1908), IV, 453–95; U. F. Linder, *Reminiscences of the Early Bench and Bar of Ill.* (1879), pp. 141–47; J. D. Caton, *Bench and Bar of Ill.* (1893), pp. 64, 201; *Proc. of the Chicago Bar in Memory of the Hon Sidney Breese* (1878); F. B. Crossley, *Courts and Lawyers of Ill.* (1916), I, 181–83. Breese's *Early Hist. of Ill. . . . until 1763,* ed. by T. Hoyne, was published in 1884, and contains an excellent memoir of Breese by Melville W. Fuller. The Breese-Douglas correspondence concerning the Illinois Central Ry. is reprinted in *Fergus Hist. Series,* no. XXIII, 63–98. His correspondence with Gov. Ninian Edwards is included in the *Edwards Papers* (1884), ed. by E. B. Washburne. Unpublished letters and papers of Breese are preserved in the Ill. State Hist. Lib. at Springfield and the Chicago Hist. Soc.]

K. W. C—e.

BRENNAN, ALFRED LAURENS (Feb. 14, 1853–June 14, 1921), illustrator, was born at Louisville, Ky., the son of John Fletcher and Evangeline (Williamson) Brennan. The father, a Canadian writer and publisher, served in the Northern army in the Civil War; the mother came of Pennsylvania Quaker stock. After the war the family removed to Cincinnati. The son was educated at private schools and Saint Dunstan's College, Prince Edward

Island, 1861–65, and by private tutors 1865–71. The father wanted him to take up printing; the son preferred art. Alfred's art studies began at the School of Design (McMicken bequest, University of Cincinnati), where he won a gold medal and an assistant-professorship in the school for one year. Later he worked with Frank Duveneck and H. F. Farny. After two years in Philadelphia he settled in New York City, about 1879. There he remained with an interval (1903–08) in Brookline, Mass., on an advertising contract, until his death. In pen-and-ink illustrations he attained an unsurpassed skill. Pennell pronounced him "the finest technician in America," and added that "there is probably no one living who has a greater knowledge of the requirements and limitations and possibilities of process." He was brilliant, with a vein of extravagant fancy, "an assiduous cultivator of whimsicality as a fine art." The flavor of his individuality pervaded all he did, even when he re-drew a photograph,—and there was much of that by artists in those days before the developed half-tone. He had a leaning toward classical subjects, illustrating, for example, a Greek play at Harvard. In the eighties and nineties, when this country possessed a remarkable school of pen-and-ink artists: Abbey, Blum, Pennell, Reinhart, Lungren, and others, Brennan was a commanding figure. There is in the work of some in this group the influence of Fortuny, and also of Rico, Vierge, and the Japanese. Harry Wilson Watrous explained this in part by the fact that Blum, Brennan, and others spent much time in the studio of Humphrey Moore, friend of Fortuny.

Brennan's assiduous courtship of the medium resulted in a large number of drawings,—7,000 or more. His illustrations, including delightful head and tail pieces, appeared in the *Century* (in the April 1903 number of which were published his pictures of the restored White House), *St. Nicholas, Life,* and other periodicals, as also in books, among which were F. Marion Crawford's *Katharine Lauderdale* (1894), Anthony Hope's *Phroso* and Charles Erskine Scott Wood's *Maia* (1918). Beside this, he designed book and magazine covers for Harpers', Scribner's, etc., painted in water-colors (exhibition, Keppel Galleries, New York, in 1891), painted portraits in oil (including one of T. L. DeVinne), and etched ("Divination in Tea Leaves" being published in the *American Art Review*). At the time of his death he was doing a series of water-colors reminiscent of his boyhood days. He also wrote magazine criticisms of pictures and books, both over his own name and over the pseudo-

nym "Dirk Laurens." But it is by his pen-and-ink drawings that his position in American art is made secure. He had a picturesque personality, was fastidious, an eccentric dresser, a keen wit, and an expert pistol shot. On Feb. 14, 1883, he married Lucy Lee, a New Yorker, who survived him, with five children, when, after he had been ill in St. Luke's Hospital for two months, death came to him in Flatbush, Brooklyn, N. Y.

[For this sketch the printed accounts of Brennan's life have been verified or corrected by his daughter, Alfreda L. Brennan; *Am. Art Student,* Jan. 1922; *Who's Who in America,* 1906–07; obituaries in *N. Y. Times* and *Evening Post,* June 16, 1921, and the *Am. Art Annual,* vol. XVIII; critical estimates in *Am. Art Rev.,* I, 51 (article on Brennan's etchings by S. R. Koehler); Jos. Pennell, *Pen Drawing and Pen Draughtsmen* (1920), *Adventures of an Illustrator* (1925), and "A Forgotten Master," *Internat. Studio,* vol. LXXIV, pp. clxxxviii–ccii; F. Weitenkampf, *Am. Graphic Art* (1924).]
F. W.

BRENNER, VICTOR DAVID (June 12, 1871–Apr. 5, 1924), sculptor, medalist, was the son of George and Sarah (Margolis) Brenner. He was born in Shavli, Russia, a town of 5,000 inhabitants, not far from the Baltic. The officials were Russian, the cultural influences German. His grandfather was a blacksmith. His father set up the trade of metal-working at home. He also cut gravestones, snipped out silhouettes, carved in soapstone, engraved rings and brooches; in short, turned his hand to various forms of necessary and neighborly plastic art. In this environment of spontaneous artistic endeavor, Victor began to learn his craft at the age of thirteen, or earlier, his father meanwhile instructing him in history, languages, and the Talmud. Seals being then in vogue in Russia, the youth practised seal-making also. After three years, he became an itinerant journeyman in the simple arts he had followed, and later, he spent nine months working at line-engraving. In his eighteenth year he went to Riga, and there learned jewelry engraving. Indeed his whole life, until his final years, was an amazing interplay of earning and learning. On his arrival in America, he found employment as a die-cutter; and just as in a previous generation the young Saint-Gaudens had labored at his cameo-cutter's lathe by day, and studied at Cooper Union in the evening, so Brenner at about the same age was working at his craft by day, and following the Cooper Union courses at night. Later, he studied at the Art Students' League and at the National Academy of Design. In 1894 he was able to set up for himself as die-cutter for jewelry and silver, his early training in Russia serving him in good stead. He prospered, and sent for his family. Prof. Ettinger of the City College chanced to see a Beethoven badge he had made, and brought him to the attention of the American Numismatic Society. That body at once recognized Brenner's artistic ability, and aided him materially in establishing his fame as a medalist. Brenner was indefatigable, ambitious, filled with high ideals. By 1898, through strenuous endeavor, he had earned enough to go to Paris, there to spend three years in study under Roty and Charpentier, the world-famous medalists whose genius was then enhancing the possibilities of bas-relief. Brenner also studied sculpture at the Académie Julien, under Puech, Verlet, and Dubois. In 1900 he gained honorable mention at the Paris Salon, and a bronze medal at the Paris Exposition. Returning to New York with a mind enriched and broadened by study and travel, Brenner was again the practising die-cutter, badge-maker, medalist. He thereby earned yet another period of earnest work in Paris. The year 1906 found him once more in New York, resolved to become known as a sculptor and medalist in the purely artistic field. A Lincoln coin had been proposed in 1886. A few five-cent pieces were struck in nickel, but the project was dropped. About twenty years later, when Brenner, as one of our foremost medalists, was modeling the Panama Canal medal, to be awarded to Canal workers of two years' standing, and was receiving a sitting from Roosevelt, whose portrait is on the obverse, he showed the President a Lincoln plaque of his design. This was largely instrumental in the choice of Brenner as designer of the Lincoln cent, our first portrait coin (issued August 1909). The result was well liked, except for the too prominent initials, V. D. B. Over 22,000,000 of the coins were in circulation before the initials were removed from the final design; even the single letter B, when tried, seemed unduly conspicuous. Aside from his Schenley Memorial Fountain in Pittsburgh (1916), and a number of busts, his work in the round is little known, but how well he realized his ambition to be a medalist of the first rank is shown by the fact that many distinctively artistic societies, such as the National Academy of Design, the Fine Arts Federation of New York, the Art Institute of Chicago, and in particular the American Numismatic Society, sought his services. His designs for medals, plaquettes, and plaques mount into the hundreds, if both obverse and reverse are counted, as they should be. Most of these are struck in bronze or silver, a few are cast. In 1920, at the American Numismatic Society's international exhibition of work by contemporary medalists, sixty-nine pieces by Brenner were

on view, some of them doubling themselves by being shown both in obverse and in reverse. Many of these works were designed for clubs, societies, anniversaries, centennials, conferences. Others, either by portraiture or allegory or both, honored famous persons, quick or dead. The likenesses are excellent. Brenner's studies had given him command of the nude figure, used to advantage in his Sorolla medal, his University of Wisconsin plaquette, and other examples. He was happy in the draped figure also, as in his Fine Arts Federation plaque. Like most medalists, he often over-elaborated the anecdotal details demanded, and so missed sculptural simplicity. His Whistler medal escapes this snare of pictorial insistence. Its reverse, dominated by a peacock crying "Messieurs les Ennemis," is a triumph of imaginative suggestion, with a tang of satire. Indeed every work by Brenner was thoughtfully done. He gave his best, seeking always to make that best still better. He was of sensitive nervous organization, and his close application to his art no doubt shortened his life. His gentle, dark-bearded features often showed a trace of Slavic melancholy. His last years were clouded by long illness. But he was happy in his marriage, in 1913, to Ann Reed, and happy also in his membership in three artistic associations, the National Sculpture Society, the Architectural League of New York, the American Numismatic Society. His work is represented in the Paris Mint, and in the Luxembourg Museum; the Munich Glyptothek; the Vienna Numismatic Society; the Metropolitan Museum, New York; the Museum of Fine Arts, Boston; the American Numismatic Society, New York. He died at the New York Hospital.

[Archives of the Am. Numismatic Soc.; special illustrated article by Paul U. Kellogg, *Survey*, Oct. 2, 1915; obituaries in the *Numismatist*, May 1924, and *N. Y. Times*, Apr. 6, 1924. Illustrations of Brenner's work appear in the *Catalogue of the Exhibition of the Am. Numismatic Soc.*, 1920.] A. A—s.

BRENT, MARGARET (1600–1670/71), America's first feminist, was one of the thirteen children of Richard Brent, lord of Admington and Stoke, and his wife, Elizabeth Reed, daughter of Edward Reed, lord of Tusburie and Witten, all of Gloucester, England. The Brents of Stoke traced their ancestry to Ode Brent, knight (1066), while Elizabeth Reed's family claimed descent from William the Conqueror. The abundant resources of the new world lured Margaret and her sister Mary to accompany their brothers Giles and Fulke Brent to St. Mary's, Md., in November 1638. Blood relationships or political affiliations secured to the Brent pioneers unusual favors in large land grants and high offices.

Margaret, bent upon individual independence, came to Gov. Leonard Calvert [*q.v.*], who later married her sister Anne, armed with letters from Lord Baltimore claiming for the Brent sisters portions of land as large and privileges as great as had been given the first arrivals. Having brought over five men and four maid servants, the sisters were entitled to 800 acres of land under the colonization inducements offered to women. Through their letters they received much larger grants. On Oct. 4, 1639, Margaret obtained from the Assembly a patent for 70½ acres in St. Mary's, which she called "Sister's Freehold." This was the first grant recorded at St. Mary's and Margaret was the first woman of Maryland to hold land in her own right. Later she obtained a tract of 1,000 acres and from time to time accumulated more land as she transported little groups of men and women. Forceful and fearless, she aided Gov. Calvert in suppressing the Claiborne Rebellion by assembling an armed group of volunteers to join his forces on his return from Virginia in August 1646. He proved his confidence in her ability by appointing her his executrix (Letters of Administration granted June 19, 1647). The Provincial court appointed her attorney for Lord Baltimore, that she might collect rents and take care of both estates. In this capacity she entered more law suits than any one in the colony. Because of her heavy responsibilities, she appealed to the Assembly, Jan. 21, 1648 (*Archives of Maryland*, I, 215), for voice in their counsels and two votes in their proceedings, one for herself as a landowner and the other as attorney for Lord Baltimore. Gov. Greene refused her plea. Resenting this action she followed her brother Giles Brent's example and established a new home called "Peace" in Westmoreland County, Va., in 1650. With vast property in both states, as lady of the manor she held court leets annually with feasts and frolics for her people. On Dec. 26, 1663, she made her will. The exact date of her death like that of her birth is not definitely known. Her will was admitted to probate May 19, 1671. Of queenly dignity, keen intelligence, ready sympathy, and great womanly charm, this Portia of Maryland possessed a broad vision far beyond her day.

[W. B. Chilton, "The Brent Family," runs through several volumes of the *Va. Mag. of Hist. and Biog.*, Apr. 1905–Jan. 1913. Hester Dorsey Richardson, *Sidelights on Md. Hist.* (2 vols., 1913), presents documentary proofs of Margaret Brent's business acumen. See also Mary E. W. Ramey, *Chronicles of Mistress Margaret Brent* (1915); Jas. Walter Thomas, *Chronicles of Colonial Md.* (1913) and John L. Bozman, *Hist. of Md.* (1837), vol. II.] E. M. C—n.

BRENTANO, LORENZ (Nov. 4, 1813–Sept. 17, 1891), statesman, journalist, was the son of Peter Paul Bartholomaeus Brentano and his wife Helene Haeger. He was born in Mannheim, Baden, received a classical education, and studied jurisprudence at the universities of Heidelberg and Freiburg. He had degrees from Heidelberg and Giessen. After beginning his career in Rastatt and Bruchsal, he practised law in Mannheim. Several times he was elected to the position of burgomaster of his native city, but was never confirmed by the government. Sent to the Chamber of Deputies in 1845, he joined the radical party of Hecker, Itzstein, and Sander, but he did not take part in the insurrection started by Hecker in 1848, nor in the uprising attempted by Struve and Blind in the following September. However, he courageously and eloquently defended the revolutionists at their trial in Freiburg. Elected to a seat in the Frankfurt Parliament, he attached himself to the liberal side and distinguished himself by his speeches against the then Prince of Prussia, and by his sarcastic refusal of the resulting challenge to a duel by Baron von Fincke. When the Revolution spread over Baden in 1849 and the Grand Duke had fled, Brentano was against his own protests placed at the head of the provisional revolutionary government. In the capacity of "Dictator of Baden" he labored for the maintenance of order, and stood for the confining of the Revolution to the territory of Baden. This was a tactical blunder, for which he was unjustly accused of treachery by Struve and the extremists of the party, who instituted legislation that compelled Brentano to take to flight. From Switzerland he addressed a justification of his acts to the people of Baden. The fugitive emigrated to the United States in 1850, where he heard that the restored reactionary government of Baden had sentenced him to imprisonment for life. He settled at first at Pottsville, Pa., editing a German weekly antislavery paper called *Der Leuchtturm*. In 1851 he bought a farm near Kalamazoo, Mich., which he cultivated zealously for about eight years, but hardly with distinguished success. In 1859 he removed to Chicago, engaged in the practise of law, but in the following year joined the staff of the *Illinois Staatszeitung*. From the proceeds of the sale of his farm in 1862 he bought a half-interest in the paper from George Schneider, who was sent by President Lincoln on an important mission to Helsingfors and northern Europe. Through skill and hard work with the aid of his partner A. C. Hesing, Brentano succeeded in making the *Illinois Staatszeitung* not only one of the most influential dailies of Chicago, but also the leading German Republican paper of the entire Northwest. In 1862 he was elected to the

Illinois state legislature and in 1868 was a presidential elector on the Grant-Colfax ticket. For five years he was president of the Chicago Board of Education.

After a general amnesty had been declared in Germany, Brentano revisited his native land in 1869, and served as United States consul at Dresden, 1872–76. After his return he was elected, in 1876, to the Forty-fifth Congress of the United States, continuing until Mar. 3, 1879. Upon his retirement he spent much time in historical and legal investigations, aiming to compare and contrast the American and European codes and methods of criminal procedure. Illustrative of this type of work was his report of the trial of Guiteau, the assassin of President Garfield. He also wrote a history of the case of *Kring* vs. *Missouri* (107 *U.S.* 221), which was republished in Leipzig. His last political activity was his support of Grover Cleveland for the presidency, which meant a separation from his long allegiance to the Republican party, and his first appearance as an independent voter. The last years of his life he was compelled to spend in retirement owing to a partial stroke of paralysis. He died in Chicago, Sept. 17, 1891. He was married to Caroline Aberle.

When compared with his associates of the revolutionary period of 1848–49, Brentano was described as lacking the magnetic personality and inspiring eloquence of Hecker and certain others of the revolutionary heroes. In speech incisive and intellectual, in action deliberate and calculating, in disposition conservative and cautious, he was the lawyer, not the inspirer of the Revolution in Baden. His greater adaptability enabled him to rise to higher positions in this country than Hecker and Struve and most others of his fellow revolutionists who came to the United States, with the exception of the younger, more brilliant Carl Schurz.

[*Deutsch-amerikanisches Conversations-Lexikon,* by Prof. Alex. J. Schem (1869–74), vol. II; *Chicago und sein Deutschtum, 1901–02* (German-American Biog. Publ. Co., Cleveland, Ohio); *In Memoriam: Lorenz Brentano* (a volume of memorial addresses and obituary articles in leading American and German American newspapers, 1891).]   A.B.F.

BRERETON, JOHN. [See BRIERTON, JOHN, fl. 1572–1619.]

BRETT, WILLIAM HOWARD (July 1, 1846–Aug. 24, 1918), librarian, was born in Braceville, Ohio, the son of Morgan Lewis Brett, a descendant of John Alden, and of Jane (Brokaw) Brett, of Virginian ancestry. His parents were members of the Trumbull Phalanx, a short-lived Fourierist community experiment. Soon after his birth the family moved to the larger town of Warren, where William spent his boyhood. Among his early formative influences were W. N. Porter and his little bookshop, around the corner from the Brett home, to which the small boy made a short back-door cut, and where his intimate and broad acquaintance with books began. At fourteen he became librarian of the high school library, contributing this service until he left school at sixteen to earn his living. He was soon a clerk in Mr. Porter's store, to which he returned at intervals between other ventures during the next dozen years. During the Civil War he made repeated vigorous but unsuccessful attempts to enlist, finally learning to play the fife and drum in order to be enrolled as a musician in the 196th Ohio Volunteer Infantry, with which he managed to get into the actual fighting at once. Following the war he spent a year at the University of Michigan and another at Western Reserve, then located at Hudson, Ohio, but lack of funds prevented completion of his college course. In 1874 he entered the Cobb & Andrews Book Store in Cleveland as a clerk, and in the next ten years he became known as the best-informed bookman in the city. It was therefore natural and fortunate that when, in 1884, the trustees of the Cleveland Public Library were looking for a new librarian, Brett was chosen for the position he was to occupy for the next thirty-four years. He introduced modern methods, reclassified and catalogued the books, and opened up the shelves to give free access to readers. Under his direction this library developed from a small, badly organized institution into a great city-wide system, adding to the main library a net-work of branches, stations, and school libraries, and becoming notable among the libraries of the country for its splendid service. Largely instrumental in organizing the Library School of Western Reserve University in 1894, he was its dean until his death. Among his contributions to library progress was the *Cumulative Index,* which later became the *Reader's Guide to Periodical Literature,* an indispensable tool of all libraries. He was president of the American Library Association for the year 1896–97. He organized and was first president of the Ohio Library Association. In the American Library Association War Service in the World War his work was conspicuous, particularly at Newport News, where he spent some months organizing and directing an efficient dispatch office for books shipped overseas. Of medium height, compactly built, with well-formed blond head alertly held, keen eyes of vivid blue, and a ready smile, he kept always his eager, boyish enthusiasm and a winning friendliness, for his interest in people, like his interest in books, continued to grow with the years.

Struck by an automobile on Aug. 24, 1918, he died after a few unconscious hours. His wife, Alice (Allen) Brett, whom he married in 1879, five children, and six grandchildren survived him.

[The facts about William Howard Brett were gathered chiefly from himself, his family, and lifelong friends, with verification of dates from *Who's Who in America,* and other biographical dictionaries. The *Library Jour.,* Nov. 1918, devoted pages 793–807 to a sketch of his life and appreciations by fellow workers; the *Open Shelf* for Sept.–Oct. 1918, published by the Cleveland Pub. Lib., is entirely a memorial number; and all Cleveland newspapers published obituary notices following his death. His own writings were chiefly professional articles published in the Library periodicals.]
                                L.A.E.

BREVOORT, JAMES RENWICK (July 20, 1832–Dec. 15, 1918), painter, was born in Yonkers township, Westchester County, N. Y., son of Elias and Mary (Brown) Brevoort and notable member of a distinguished old family of this state whose ancestor, Jan Heinrich van Brevoort, emigrated from Holland and settled in New Amsterdam about 1643. His early years were spent in Williamsbridge and Fordham. He attended the local schools and later received most of his art education in the New York studio of the late Thomas S. Cummings, then vice-president of the National Academy of Design. For four years he worked in the office of his cousin James Renwick, architect of Grace Church, New York, assisting him in making drawings for St. Patrick's Cathedral. Brevoort took the full course given in the School of Design of New York University, and on June 28, 1854, received a testimonial from the University certifying that he had devoted several years to the study of architecture. In 1861 he was elected an associate of the National Academy of Design, and a National Academician in 1863. He was a member of the Academy for more than fifty-seven years. In 1872 he began landscape painting and at that time also became a professor of perspective at the school of the National Academy.

He married, first, Augusta Cuthill, who died early. On Apr. 14, 1873, he married, second, in Burlington, Ia., Marie Louise Bascom, recipient of the first medal awarded by the school of the National Academy. Brevoort enjoyed the opportunities for painting in interesting localities and visited nearly all the schools and art centers of Europe, studying the ancient and modern works of art in the galleries of the Old World. Most of his time was spent in England, Holland, and Italy. He was made a member of the Royal Academy at Urbino, the birthplace of Raphael.

His paintings of Italian scenery were very successful, especially those of the Italian lakes. Returning from abroad in 1880, he made his home in Yonkers, N. Y., building a private residence there in 1890. He became a member of the Century Association in 1882 and maintained interest in the organization until his death at his home in Yonkers in 1918. Brevoort was sympathetic and truthful in his portrayal of landscapes and achieved original treatment in his atmospheric effects. All of his work clearly indicated his idealism and fine feeling. His "Harvest Scene with a Storm Coming Up" shows considerable power and the effect of light is done with skill. Representative of Brevoort's style are: "A New England Scene"; "Morning in Early Winter"; "A Gray Day"; "Sunset on a Moor"; "Dawn"; "Spring"; "A Scene in Holland"; "Lake Como"; "The Night Wind Swept the Moorland Lea"; "Storm on an English Moor"; "May Morning at Lake Como"; "Wild November Comes at Last"; "Windy Evening on the Moor."

[H. T. Tuckerman, *Book of the Artists* (1867), p. 566; *Catalog of Collection of Paintings and Sketches and Studies of J. R. Brevoort, Sold 1873;* J. D. Champlin & C. C. Perkins, *Cyc. of Painters and Paintings* (1886), I, 204; C. E. Allison, *Hist. of Yonkers* (1896), p. 406; M. A. Hamm, *Famous Families of N. Y.* (1902), p. 42; *Who's Who in America,* 1916–17; family data.]
                             J.M.H.

BREWER, CHARLES (Mar. 27, 1804–Oct. 11, 1885), sea captain and merchant, was born in Boston, son of Moses, a dry-goods dealer, and Abigail (May) Brewer, both of old New England families. An ancestor, Daniel Brewer, had come from London to Roxbury, Mass., in 1632. His father died in 1813 and the widow carried on the business while Charles, the only boy in a family of five, attended various near-by private schools. Apprenticed to a merchant at the age of fourteen he acquired a knowledge of business but a loathing for the counting room. His mother, who knew his longing for adventure and hoped that the hardships of seafaring life would prove an antidote, allowed him when seventeen to go on a sixteen-months voyage to Calcutta. Undismayed, he next went on voyages to England and the East Indies. In 1823 he sailed on the ship *Paragon* for the Hawaiian Islands. There the loading of sandalwood was interrupted when the vessel was chartered by King Kamehameha II for a state funeral. Returning to Boston, Brewer was promoted to second officer for a trip to England, and during a storm fell from the main yard, bruising one leg so badly that he was permanently crippled. From 1825 to 1829 he was first officer on the brig *Chinchilla,* which used Honolulu as her base for trading cruises between Alaska, Kamchatka, and China. Early in 1829 he returned to Boston, but in October sailed as mate of the brig *Ivanhoe,* which traded between Canton, Honolulu, and Mazatlan in Mexico until 1831. He finally quit the vessel in Honolulu because of a quarrel arising out of a hint to the captain that the attempt to fill water casks on Sunday was an infraction of the laws which American missionaries had induced the Hawaiian king to make so strict that smoking and cooking on the Sabbath were crimes. He then became captain of a small schooner trading between Hawaii and the American coast from Mexico to Alaska. In 1833 he commanded the schooner *Unity,* the second American vessel to enter the Sea of Okhotsk, and later claimed credit for discovering the whale fishery there. In 1834 and 1835 he again visited Okhotsk and Petropavlovsk, and in February 1836 was taken as a partner in a prosperous Honolulu trading establishment by Henry A. Peirce [*q.v.*], who departed for Boston leaving him to manage the local business of bartering cotton goods, rum, and "yankee notions" for sandalwood, furs, and hides. When Peirce returned in 1839, Brewer in turn went to Boston, where he married Martha Turner and set sail with her for Hawaii in March 1841. He again took charge of the business in Honolulu, and when Peirce withdrew in 1843 the firm became C. Brewer & Company. Under this name it still flourishes. In Honolulu, then the Pacific emporium for whalers, fur traders, and China merchants, Brewer prospered greatly and established an enviable reputation for integrity and public spirit. In 1839, when France took umbrage at the refusal of the native king to allow Roman Catholic missionaries to land and threatened hostilities, his was the largest contribution to the fund of $20,000 raised to satisfy the demands of Commander La Place. He gave liberally to local charities, and in 1843 enabled King Kamehameha III, his intimate friend, to finance a mission to England which secured recognition of Hawaiian independence. Another benefaction was the introduction to the islands of the beautiful night-blooming cereus. In 1845 he disposed of most of his Hawaiian interests and took his family to Boston. A business trip to Honolulu in 1847–49 completed his seafaring life, but he continued in the Hawaiian and Far Eastern trade, establishing after the Civil War a company which owned a fine fleet of barks sailing to Hawaii, Manila, and Hong-Kong in the eighties. He retired in 1884 and in the following year died at his home in Jamaica Plain. A man of strong character and sharp tongue, he was at heart kindly in disposition and liberal in giving of the large fortune which he had accumulated.

[Charles Brewer, *Reminiscences* (1884); Josephine Sullivan, *Hist. of C. Brewer and Company, Ltd.* (1926).]

W. L. W. Jr.

BREWER, DAVID JOSIAH (June 20, 1837– Mar. 28, 1910), jurist, was born in Smyrna, Asia Minor. His father, Josiah Brewer, from Berkshire, Mass., was a Yale graduate who had gone to Turkey as a missionary in 1830. His mother, Emilia Field, was the daughter of a distinguished New England clergyman and the sister of Justice Stephen J. Field, David Dudley Field, and Cyrus W. Field. The Brewers returned in 1838 and settled in Wethersfield, Conn. After attending Wesleyan University for two years, young Brewer went to Yale where he graduated with honors in 1856. He then studied law for a year in the office of his uncle, David Dudley Field, spent a year at the Albany Law School where he graduated in 1858, and was promptly admitted to the New York bar. He decided to cast in his lot with the new West and in September settled in Leavenworth, Kan., his home until 1890. He embarked almost at once upon his long judicial career. In 1861 he was appointed commissioner of the federal circuit court for the district of Kansas; in 1862 he was elected judge of the probate and criminal courts of Leavenworth County; from 1865 to 1869 he was judge of the first judicial district of Kansas; from 1869 to 1870 he served as city attorney of Leavenworth. In 1870, at the age of thirty-three, he was elected to the supreme court of Kansas where he sat for fourteen years, being reëlected in 1876 and 1882. In 1884 President Arthur appointed him to the federal circuit court for the eighth circuit. He was appointed by President Harrison in 1889 as associate justice of the United States Supreme Court to succeed Justice Stanley Matthews. He remained on the court until his death. He and his uncle, Justice Field, were colleagues until 1898.

In his constitutional principles Brewer was a moderate conservative. He was a stern defender of personal liberty and property rights. As circuit judge he had refused to follow the dictum in the Granger Cases (*Munn* vs. *Illinois,* 94 *U. S.* 113) that legislative power to fix public utility rates is unlimited (*C. & N. W. Ry. Co.* vs. *Dey,* 35 *Fed.* 866), and spoke for the court in *Reagan* vs. *Farmers' Loan & Trust Co.* (154 *U. S.* 362), holding that due process of law entitles a carrier to a fair return on its investment. His strict regard for what he deemed reasonable freedom of contract led him to agree with the court in invalidating the ten hour law for bakers (*Lochner* vs. *New York*, 198 *U. S.* 45), and to dissent in cases sustaining an eight hour law for miners (*Holden* vs. *Hardy*, 169 *U. S.* 366), and an eight hour law on public work (*Atkin* vs. *Kansas*, 191 *U.S.* 207). He wrote the court's opinion, however, in *Muller* vs. *Oregon* (208 *U. S.* 412), upholding a ten hour law for women in industry. He dissented vigorously in the Chinese Exclusion cases (*Fong Yue Ting* vs. *United States*, 149 *U.S.* 698, *United States* vs. *Sing Tuck*, 194 *U. S.* 161, *United States* vs. *Ju Toy*, 198 *U. S.* 253), because of what he deemed arbitrary denial of personal rights. On the circuit bench he had held that brewers driven out of business by a prohibition act were entitled to compensation (*State* vs. *Walruff*, 26 *Fed.* 178). This doctrine was overruled in *Kidd* vs. *Pearson* (128 *U. S.* 1). He viewed with concern the drift toward federal centralization of power, and one of his ablest opinions is that in *Kansas* vs. *Colorado* (206 *U. S.* 46), in which he vigorously rejected the theory that Congress could deal with national problems by using powers not delegated by the Constitution. Of similar import is his opinion in *Keller* vs. *United States* (213 *U. S.* 138), and his dissent in the Lottery Case (188 *U. S.* 321). That he was not a strict constructionist, however, is shown by his notable opinions in *South Carolina* vs. *United States* (199 *U. S.* 437), sustaining a federal tax on the proceeds of the South Carolina liquor dispensary, in *Wilson* vs. *Shaw* (204 *U. S.* 24), upholding the right of Congress to build the Panama Canal, and particularly in the case of *In re Debs* (158 *U. S.* 564), in which the power of a federal court to issue an injunction in a labor dispute for the protection of federal interests was sustained. Justice Brewer was, in fact, an ardent defender of the use of the injunction (see his address, "Government by Injunction," *National Corporation Reporter*, XV, 848).

A life-long advocate of international peace, Brewer was able to render signal service to that cause as president of the commission created by Congress in 1895 to investigate the boundary between Venezuela and British Guiana after President Cleveland's startling message on that controversy (see *Report of the Commission, etc.*, 3 vols., 1897). With Chief Justice Fuller he served as American representative on the arbitral tribunal which in 1898 made the award which ended the dispute (see Latané, *A History of American Foreign Policy*, ch. XX. The official documents are found in Moore's *Digest of International Law*, VI, 533–83. See also a note by Charles Henry Butler, "The Services of Justices Fuller and Brewer in Questions of Inter-

national Law," *American Journal of International Law*, IV, 909). His continued interest in the cause of peace was evidenced by many speeches and papers. He attended nearly all of the Mohonk conferences (see *Mohonk Addresses*, 1910), and in 1909 addressed the New Jersey State Bar Association on "The Mission of the United States in the Cause of Peace" (*Yearbook*, 1909–10). With Charles Henry Butler he wrote the treatise on international law in the *Cyclopedia of Law and Procedure* (1906). He was a vice-president and supporter of the American Society of International Law from its foundation.

Brewer was unique among his judicial colleagues in the freedom and frequency with which he discussed problems of current interest before popular audiences. He was an orator of distinction, with a smack of the pulpit in his utterances. He was a vigorous anti-imperialist and believed the Philippines should be given independence with guaranteed neutrality (see his address, "The Spanish War, a Prophecy or an Exception," before the Liberal Club of Buffalo in 1899). He favored woman suffrage, and advocated the restriction of immigration. He spoke and wrote widely on legal topics, and on the high duties of lawyers and judges. He believed that fair criticism of the courts was wholesome. He addressed university and popular audiences on the obligations of citizenship (*American Citizenship*, the Dodge Lectures at Yale, 1902). In 1890 he accepted a lectureship on corporations in the law school of the Columbian University (now George Washington University).

Broad sympathies, keen civil interest, and splendid executive ability drew Brewer into many forms of public and social service. For five years before his death he was president of the Associated Charities in Washington (see "Justice Brewer and Organized Charity," *Survey*, XXIV, 119). Always interested in missions he served for years as vice-president of the American Missionary Association. He was a loyal member of the Congregational Church. In 1861 he married Louisa Landon of Burlington, Vt., who died in 1898, and in 1901 he married Emma Minor Mott of Washington, D. C. He was physically large and vigorous, genial in disposition, democratic in his social relations, and a famous story teller.

[There is no adequate biography or memoir. Brief sketches of a general sort are found in Henry Wilson Scott, *Distinguished Am. Lawyers*, p. 75 (sketch by Warren Watson) ; and in H. L. Carson, *The Supreme Court of the U. S.* (1902), II, 538. Obituaries appeared at the time of Brewer's death in numerous popular and legal periodicals. Besides the publications and addresses mentioned in the text he wrote many articles for law journals and popular magazines. These may be readily found in the standard periodical indices. In 1899 he edited with A. E. Allen and Wm. Schuyler *The World's Best Essays,* in ten volumes. His opinions as justice of the Supreme Court are found in 133–216 *U. S.* He wrote the opinion of the court in 526 cases, 70 of which involved constitutional problems. He dissented in 215 cases, in 53 of which he wrote separate opinions and of these 18 related to constitutional problems. He concurred in 38 cases, writing 8 separate concurring opinions.]   R. E. C.

BREWER, MARK SPENCER (Oct. 22, 1837–Mar. 18, 1901), congressman, was born in Addison Township, Oakland County, Mich., and died in Washington, D. C. His ancestor Peter Brewer, a native of Holland, had served in the Revolution and subsequently settled in Dutchess County, N. Y. Peter 2nd removed to Michigan Territory in 1832, and built a log cabin in the wilderness of Oakland County. His fifth son, Mark, spent nineteen years of his life on his father's farm. He studied law in the office of Gov. Wisner and began practise in Pontiac in 1864. As a member of the state Senate from 1872 to 1874, he established a reputation for hard work and good judgment that made him an available candidate for office in times of political emergency. He was elected to Congress in 1876 and in 1878. Appointed by his friend, President Garfield, as consul-general at Berlin in 1881, during four years of service Brewer made studies of the bimetallic standard, the credit and trade system, and wages and labor, in Germany, which enabled him to do effective work on the stump in the critical McKinley-Bryan campaign in 1896. In 1887 he was returned to the House of Representatives, where he served until the Democratic landslide of 1891. On the return of the Republicans to power, President McKinley appointed him a member of the Civil Service Commission, in which capacity he served from January 1898 until his death. He was drawn into the controversy over political contributions from federal office-holders that raged between Senators Chandler and Gallinger of New Hampshire, and made an elaborate report on the subject. Brewer was a man of large influence in Michigan affairs because he stood for sound policies rather than political expediency.

[*Dept. of State: Consular Reports* (1882–84), VI, 20, 184, XII, 40, 304, XIII, 43, 250; *Sixteenth Report* (1900) of the Civil Service Commission; *Mich. Biogs.* (1924); obituary in the *Washington Post*, Mar. 19, 1901.]   C. M.

BREWER, THOMAS MAYO (Nov. 21, 1814–Jan. 23, 1880), ornithologist and oölogist, son of Col. James Brewer, a Revolutionary patriot who took part in the "Boston Tea Party," was born in Boston, Mass., where he spent his entire life with the exception of some winters in Washington and a trip to Europe. He was edu-

cated at Harvard, graduating from the College in 1835 and from the Medical School in 1838. He practised his profession for a few years but realizing that writing was much more to his taste than medicine, and being always an ardent politician, he abandoned his practise and became a regular contributor to the *Boston Atlas,* a noted Whig journal, and later its editor. Subsequently he became associated with the publishing firm of Swan & Tileston (afterward Brewer & Tileston), a business in which he continued until his retirement in 1875. He was always interested in the cause of public education and was an active member of the Boston School Committee from 1844 until his death. In 1849 he married Sally R. Coffin, daughter of Stephen Coffin of Damariscotta, Me. In spite of his devotion to business for practically his entire life, he managed to maintain and develop an early interest in birds and to become one of the leading ornithologists of America, with a well established reputation abroad. He was a close personal friend of Audubon during the latter years of the great painter-naturalist's life and in the second edition of the *Birds of America* are to be found a number of acknowledgments for information furnished by young Brewer. He likewise made the acquaintance of Spencer F. Baird while the latter was still at his home in Carlisle, Pa., and a steady correspondence was kept up between them. Brewer joined the Boston Society of Natural History in 1835 at the age of twenty-one and for over forty years contributed ornithological papers and notes to the Society's *Proceedings.*

His first notable paper was a Supplement (1837) to Prof. Hitchcock's *Catalogue of the Birds of Massachusetts* to which he added forty-five species. Next in 1840 he published a small octavo edition of Wilson's *Ornithology* which for the first time brought this classic within the reach of every one who desired to possess it, and in an appendix Brewer added a synopsis of all the birds then known in North America. In 1857 appeared the first (and only) volume of his *North American Oölogy,* a quarto issued by the Smithsonian Institution as one of its Contributions to Knowledge, in which the eggs of each species were figured in colors, with a full description of the life history and distribution of the birds. Unfortunately the cost of the plates proved so great that the publication had to be discontinued, though it apparently gave Brewer more prestige than any other of his works. In 1875 he was fortunately enabled to publish the remainder of his bird biographies in connection with that now famous classic, the *History of*

North American Birds by Baird, Brewer and Ridgway. The entire biographical portion, amounting to about two-thirds of the letterpress, is by Brewer and demonstrates the breadth of his knowledge of American ornithological literature and his intimate acquaintance with the nests and eggs of our birds. His ornithological work was continued up to a short time before his death, which occurred after an illness of only a few weeks. He was stricken at the height of his ornithological career, just as he had retired from business with the idea of being free to prosecute his studies.

By contemporary biographers Brewer is said to have been greatly esteemed socially, while his warm sympathy, loyalty to his friends, and his convictions of truth and duty, were marked traits in his character. His political experiences, perhaps, seem to have made him fond of argument and he replied quickly to criticism and engaged in wordy controversies, that with Elliot Coues on the merits of the English sparrow being carried on for a long time in the pages of the *American Naturalist*. Being essentially a closet ornithologist he was rather impatient at the younger bird students who ventured to discover new facts regarding bird life not contained in the published accounts and was hence not one to encourage the development of new ornithologists; among the rising generation at Cambridge William Brewster was said to have been the only one who could get along with him.

Brewer may be regarded as America's first oölogist, but in the widest sense of that term, as he considered the breeding habits and life history of the birds, not merely the character and value of the egg-shells,—matters which are the chief concern of many oölogists of to-day.

[Editorial sketch of his life, *Bull. Nuttall Ornith. Club,* Apr. 1880, pp. 102–104; manuscript letters to Baird in Smithsonian Institution; personal recollections furnished by Ruthven Deane.]   W. S.

BREWER, WILLIAM HENRY (Sept. 14, 1828–Nov. 2, 1910), scientist, was of Dutch and French Huguenot ancestry. His father, Henry, was a descendant of Adam Brouwer Berkhoven who came to New Amsterdam in 1642. The name Berkhoven was dropped about 1700, and Brouwer used as the family name, but later changed to Brower and after the Revolution to Brewer. William's mother, Rebecca DuBois, was a descendant of Louis DuBois who in 1660 settled in the Huguenot colony in Ulster County, N. Y. William was born in Poughkeepsie, N. Y., but his boyhoood was spent on a farm near Ithaca. At Ithaca Academy where he had his early schooling, he developed a keen interest in plants and minerals which led to the reading of such books as he could obtain dealing with geology, botany, and chemistry, and especially their applications to agriculture. Encouraged by his parents, he entered in 1848 the new school of science at Yale, now the Sheffield Scientific School, where he graduated in 1852 with the first class to obtain a degree. Under Silliman, Dana, and J. P. Norton his interest in science was greatly stimulated, and in 1855 he went abroad for further study, spending a year at Heidelberg under Bunsen in chemistry, and a year in Munich with Liebig. Botany and geology also occupied his attention, and he made many excursions through Germany, Switzerland, and France botanizing and geologizing. In 1858 he married Angelina Jameson, who died in 1860, and in 1868 he married Georgiana Robinson.

Brewer was a man of great versatility, an explorer in all the sciences underlying agriculture, never a specialist in the modern sense, but contributing much in many fields. For four years, 1860–64, he was in the wilds of California as first assistant to Josiah D. Whitney in the geological survey of the state, gaining intimate knowledge of its geography, geology, and botany. As he wrote in his diary, during the first two years he traveled 2,067 miles on foot, 3,900 miles on mule-back, and 3,210 by other conveyance. Nothing escaped his eyes, mountains were measured and named, valleys mapped, minerals and plants collected. Of plants he collected about 2,000 species, the basis of his work on the flora of California, published by Brewer and Sereno Watson, under the title of "Polypetalæ," in Volume I of the *Geological Survey of California*. From 1864 to 1903 he held the chair of agriculture in the Sheffield Scientific School at Yale. With his broad outlook, his wide knowledge and extended experience, combined with a personality that radiated power and strength of purpose, he was able to bring to fruition many movements for the public good. Betterment of agriculture was his chief thought and to that end he was active, with his colleague S. W. Johnson, in the establishment of the first agricultural experiment station in this country, and for thrty-three years he was on the board of control of the Connecticut station. He made for the tenth census a careful study of the cereal production of the United States with special reference to distribution of production in accordance with geographical and climatic features; the relation of cereal production to the growing of live stock; distribution of woodland and forest systems in the country; also a brief history of American agriculture. As a member of the National Academy of Sciences he was active in the study of many questions submitted by the national government, such as the manufacture of glucose sugar from starch (1882); the sorghum sugar industry; preservation of the forest resources of the country (1896); desirability of scientific explorations of the Philippine Islands (1903). To the annual reports of the Connecticut Board of Agriculture he was a constant contributor for twenty-five years on a great variety of topics of interest to the farmer, such as the origin and constitution of soils; woods and woodlands; tree planting with reference to sanitary effects; pollution of streams; the art of stock breeding. He was a pioneer in public health work, active in the organization of a state board of health for Connecticut (president for sixteen years); of a city board of health for New Haven, and active in the early work of the American Public Health Association. He was influential in the establishment of the Yale Forest School (1900) and lectured there on forest physiography. One of his most important pieces of scientific work was an elaborate study of the development of the American trotting horse as a contribution to knowledge of the evolution of breeds, in which he plotted curves showing how fast horses will ultimately trot and when the maximum will be reached. He also carried on many experiments upon the conditions influencing the suspension of clays in river water with reference to the bearing of river deposits on delta formation.

[The above data are derived largely from diaries, letters, and family records, reinforced by knowledge gained through association extending over many years. In the *Biog. Memoirs Nat. Acad. Sci.*, vol. XII, is a detailed account of Brewer's life and work, written by Prof. R. H. Chittenden.]   R. H. C.

BREWSTER, BENJAMIN HARRIS (Oct. 13, 1816–Apr. 4, 1888), attorney-general of the United States, is best known because of his prosecution of the Star Route frauds in the Post Office Department, 1881–84. He was born in Salem County, N. J., and thought of himself as descended from William Brewster of Massachusetts Bay. His friendly biographer thought the same (Savidge, p. 15), but his name does not appear among the descendants recorded in the history of that family (Emma C. Brewster Jones, *The Brewster Genealogy, 1566–1907,* 1908). However this may be, his parents, Francis Enoch and Maria Hampton Brewster, were of old colonial stock with a tradition of education and standing that they transmitted to their son. Benjamin was a graduate of Princeton College (1834), and soon thereafter he became a leading member of the Philadelphia bar. He was ever a marked man. In infancy he was cruelly

burned about his face, so that the scars gave him a wizened and drawn appearance; he called attention to this by assuming the costume of a fop of the later thirties and continuing the same dress throughout his life. Meticulous in costume, antique in appearance, with high stock and ruffles, he was a tradition from his early life; and his great abilities were advertised by his peculiarities. In 1846 he held a minor federal post, settling certain affairs of the Cherokee Indians. Originally a Democrat, he joined the Republicans and was thereafter associated in Pennsylvania politics with Simon Cameron. Through this connection he served as attorney-general of Pennsylvania in 1867 and 1868, and was repeatedly discussed in connection with political opportunities that did not arrive. He came first into national prominence when Attorney-General Wayne MacVeagh invited him in September 1881 to assume with George Bliss of New York the position of special counsel for the government in the Star Route prosecutions. When MacVeagh retired from the cabinet after the death of Garfield, President Arthur advanced Brewster to the seat thus vacated; and for the remainder of the Arthur administration the Star Route prosecutions formed the largest single duty of the attorney-general's office.

The Star Route frauds, after three years of partial concealment, burst upon the country when, in April 1881, President Garfield removed from office T. J. Brady, the second assistant postmaster-general, after receiving the reports of special investigators upon the management of western mail contracts. Involved with Brady were ex-Senator S. W. Dorsey and others who had for many years carried on an extensive traffic in these contracts. The case was of high political importance because Dorsey, as secretary of the Republican National Committee in the canvass of 1880, was widely credited with having carried the State of Indiana by the use of money. Efforts were made to frighten Garfield from the prosecutions, but in vain. After Garfield was shot, action in the matter halted until his death; immediately after which MacVeagh pressed the cases, with the approval of President Arthur, and brought Brewster into them. There was a long and futile struggle for convictions. Robert G. Ingersoll, chief counsel for the various defendants, was at the top of his power as a lawyer, and convictions could not be secured. There was no doubt however that scandalous mismanagement had crept into the Post Office Department; and that the profits of successful crime had been widely distributed among party workers. The failure to procure convictions was a burden upon Arthur's candidacy to secure renomination in 1884, and upon Brewster.

Brewster retired into private life with President Arthur in 1885, and died in Philadelphia three years later. He was twice married; in 1857 to Elizabeth von Myerbach de Reinfeldts who died in 1868, and in 1870 to Mary Walker, daughter of Robert J. Walker, who survived him. By the second marriage he had a son, born in 1872. Brewster had an oratorical gift, and was much in demand for ceremonial addresses. He cultivated in private a taste for ecclesiastical history. His fastidious social habits and his private means helped to give to the Arthur administration its reputation for social activity, in sharp contrast to that of the administrations immediately preceding 1881.

[The only formal work of value upon Brewster is Eugene C. Savidge, *Life of Benjamin Brewster, with Discourses and Addresses* (1891); but his peculiarities and abilities inspired a large amount of paragraph material in the newspapers of his day.]   F. L. P—n.

BREWSTER, FREDERICK CARROLL (May 15, 1825–Dec. 30, 1898), lawyer, jurist, was the son of Francis Enoch and Maria (Hampton) Brewster and the brother of Benjamin Harris Brewster [*q.v.*]. He was born in Philadelphia, and educated at the Old Friends Select School, and University of Pennsylvania, graduating from the latter in 1841. He then studied law in his father's office and was admitted to the Philadelphia bar in September 1844. His early prominence was due mainly to his association with three sensational criminal cases, in which he appeared for the defense, obtaining acquittals in each. In *Commonwealth* vs. *Cunningham,* very fine legal points were involved. The accused, a policeman, shot a man who was resisting arrest, and it was decided that a well-founded apprehension of bodily harm is sufficient to justify the taking of life. *Commonwealth* vs. *Lenairs,* another murder case with a plea of self-defense, was distinguished more by the local animosities sought to be imported into the trial than by its legal features, and Brewster's successful defense was at the time considered extremely brilliant. In the third case, one Kirkpatrick was accused of conspiracy to poison his brother. It excited great interest in society circles, the trial lasted four weeks and Brewster secured an acquittal in the face of strong public opinion and apparently convincing evidence. From that time forward he was recognized as a leader of the bar. In 1856 he achieved his greatest forensic triumph, appearing for W. B. Mann, in the celebrated political contest between the latter and L. Cassidy for the office of district attorney. Closely following came the fail-

ure of the Bank of Pennsylvania, and the indictment of its president, Thomas Allibone, for conspiracy to defraud the bank of $250,000. Brewster was retained for the defense and after a trial extending over three weeks obtained a verdict of "not guilty." An adherent of the Democratic party, but not prominent in political circles, he was in 1862 elected city solicitor after one of the most bitter contests in the history of Philadelphia. In this capacity he conducted some extremely important litigation. He was counsel in the Schollenberger-Brinton case, which established the constitutionality of the Legal Tender Act of 1862, and the Chestnut Street Bridge case, which established the right of the city to bridge the Schuylkill. On the expiration of his term in 1865 he was reëlected, but resigned in October 1866 in order to accept the position of judge of common pleas of the city and county of Philadelphia, which he occupied for three years. He became attorney-general of the state at the request of Gov. Geary, Oct. 23, 1869, and held this office till the latter part of 1872. On his retirement he resumed active practise in Philadelphia. His association with one *cause célèbre* occasioned a remarkable tribute. In the Mintzer case he had induced the jury to upset a will under unusual circumstances, and one reason adduced for a reversal on appeal was that so irresistible had been his eloquence that no twelve sane men in the world could have failed to be controlled by it! In December 1898 he started for Florida in search of health, but died on the train near Salisbury, N. C. In 1850 he had married Emma, daughter of W. P. C. Barton [*q.v.*].

He was the author of *Reports of Equity, Election and Other Important Cases—Principally in the Courts of the County of Philadelphia 1856–73* (4 vols., 1869–73), *A Treatise on Practice in the Courts of Pennsylvania* (2 vols., 1891), *A Treatise on Practice in the Orphans' Court* (1894) and *A Treatise on Equity Practice in Pennsylvania* (1895). He also made contributions to general literature including *Disraeli in Outline* (1890) and *From Independence Hall around the World* (1895).

[*Green Bag,* XII, 381; F. M. Eastman, *Courts and Lawyers of Pa.* (1922), II, 561; J. T. Scharf and T. Westcott, *Hist. of Phila.* (1884), I, 721; R. D. Coxe, *Legal Phila.* (1908), p. 110; obituaries in the *Phila. Inquirer, Press,* and *Public Ledger,* Dec. 31, 1898.]
                                                        H. W. H. K.

BREWSTER, JAMES (Aug. 6, 1788–Nov. 22, 1866), carriage-builder, railway-promoter, and philanthropist, was born in Preston, New London County, Conn., the son of Joseph and Hannah (Tucker) Brewster. A farm lad, he had some slight schooling in his native town, and in

1804 was apprenticed to learn the wagon-maker's trade with Charles Chapman of Northampton, Mass. In 1809, on reaching his majority, he set out for New York by way of New Haven, where he took a job in a wagon-shop he had chanced to visit, and where in 1810 he opened a little shop of his own. In the same year he was married to Mary Hequembourg. From colonial days, heavy coaches had been built in this country for the town or traveling use of the well-to-do, but in 1810 the American carriage-building industry had yet to be developed. Chaises, sulkies, and one-horse wagons were the common forms of private conveyance. "Brewster wagons" soon became favorably known; and after this beginning, Brewster started in to build vehicles that in finish and general workmanship should equal those of English make. He turned out not only buggies but phaëtons, victorias, coaches, and other forms of equipage, and before long was specializing in fine construction. He is said to have sent to Charleston the first paneled carriage delivered by an American builder for Southern use. His output set the styles in a field in which he had been the pioneer. The spread of turnpikes naturally tended to increase the demand for lighter four-wheeled vehicles. In addition to his New Haven manufactory, Brewster established in New York (1827) a warehouse and a repair-shop.

He was one of a group of New Haven citizens that projected a railway between New Haven and Hartford and obtained a charter for it (May 1833). The charter empowered the company to use "the power and force of steam, of animals, or of any mechanical or other power or any combination of them." The rails originally laid for this road—the first opened in the state—were imported from England at a cost of $250,000, which sum, considerable in that stage of American railroading, Brewster personally guaranteed. For four years he was president of the new company, in whose financing he greatly aided and whose interests were his chief concern during that period. He then resigned and again (1838) became active in the carriage business. This enjoyed a steady growth; and Brewster, in the language of one biographer, "accumulated a handsome competency."

For more than fifty years he was an important factor in the welfare and progress of New Haven. He gave an orphan asylum to the town and provided for much-needed improvements in the local almshouse. At his own expense he extended the street system and widened streets already existing. He presented to Yale a mineralogical cabinet and equipped a company of Civil War volunteers. Probably his chief service was in connection with his efforts toward bettering the condition of the workmen employed in his own and other manufactories. He prohibited the use of liquor in his shop—a decided innovation at that time—and was a constant advocate of temperance. He built Franklin Hall, with an auditorium for evening addresses, and defrayed the cost of annual lecture courses there given on scientific subjects. In these and other ways he helped to attract employees of the better class to New Haven and to raise the standard of living in the community. At his death he was characterized as "one of the best citizens New Haven or any other city ever had" (*Palladium* [New Haven], Nov. 26, 1866).

[J. F. Babcock, *Address upon the Life and Character of the Late Jas. Brewster* (1867); E. C. B. Jones, *The Brewster Genealogy* (1908); E. E. Atwater (ed.), *Hist. of the City of New Haven to the Present Time* (1887). Brewster wrote an autobiography, never put into print.]

G. S. B.

BREWSTER, OSMYN (Aug. 2, 1797–July 15, 1889), printer, publisher, son of Dr. Moses Brewster and Lucy (Watts) Brewster, was born in Worthington, Mass. His formal schooling ended at fourteen when, as "a chubby fair-complexioned boy, dressed in a blue corduroy suit" (*Memorial of Uriel Crocker*, p. 30), he began his apprenticeship at the printer's trade in the shop of Samuel Armstrong on Cornhill, Boston. Seven years of apprenticeship in the "mystery" of this trade were so many years of real education for Brewster; each day's education began at six; there was an hour from seven to eight for breakfast and an hour for dinner; in summer the day ended at dark, but after Sept. 20 it continued after eight by candle-light until ten. At twenty-one, he and a fellow-apprentice, Uriel Crocker, were taken by their employer into partnership. The first stereotyped edition (1824) of Scott's *Family Bible* bears the imprint of S. T. Armstrong, and Crocker and Brewster. Brewster's work was in the bookshop with Armstrong and he carried on that part of the business after the latter's retirement from the firm in 1825 and the consequent change in the firm name to Crocker & Brewster. Books of a religious nature were the chief output so that the bookshop got the reputation of being "the great mart of religious literature for the Orthodox churches" (*New England Historical and Genealogical Register*, XLIV, 138). Worcester's edition of *Watts' Psalms and Hymns* is listed in the firm's catalogue of 1830; so great was the demand for this hymnal that at least four editions followed. Among the school texts published by the firm was Ethan Allen Andrews' *First Lessons in Latin*, and a very complete set of Latin texts by the same author. A very different kind of publication was the series of juvenile books by J. S. C. Abbott, one of the earliest titles being *The Child at Home; or, The Principles of Filial Duty*. The firm's imprint will be found on no book of doubtful character or of questionable morality.

Brewster was one of the old school of booksellers that believed the only way to make money was by hard work, careful publishing and buying, strict attention to business, and close economy. His was the only Boston publishing house which survived the financial panic of 1837. In 1848 he was elected to represent Boston in the Massachusetts House of Representatives, and on four other occasions his fellow citizens honored him thus. For one term (1853) he was a state senator, and he was a delegate from Boston to the state constitutional convention of 1853. He also served for three years (1856-58) on the Boston board of aldermen. He became the first president of the Franklin Savings Bank in 1881 and continued to serve in that capacity until 1887. Another organization which had his ardent support was the Massachusetts Charitable Mechanic Association, of which he was the treasurer for over twenty-five years. The *Annals* of that organization in 1853 was "from the press of Messrs. Crocker and Brewster" and "altogether a beautiful specimen of a book" (*New England Historical and Genealogical Register*, VIII, 92). Brewster enjoyed Crocker as a partner and as a friend (see portrait of the two arm-in-arm in *Memorial of Uriel Crocker*, p. 42) and both were blessed with good health and long lives; it was not until 1876 that they sold out to Houghton & Company. Brewster's home in the latter years of his life was at 32 Hancock St., Boston. He married Mary Jones at Boston, Jan. 15, 1824; she died, Jan. 27, 1872. They had two sons and seven daughters.

[*Memorial of Uriel Crocker* (1891), comp. by Uriel Haskell Crocker; obituary in *Publishers Weekly,* July 27, 1889; sketch of Samuel Armstrong in *Memorial Biogs. of the New Eng. Hist. and Geneal. Soc.* (1880), I, 232–36; *The Brewster Genealogy* (1908), by E. C. B. Jones.]　　　　　　　　　　　　　　　A. E. P.

BREWSTER, WILLIAM (1567–Apr. 10, 1644), Pilgrim father, was an Elder of the Pilgrim Church, first in importance during the Scrooby period, second in importance during the Leyden and Plymouth periods. A deposition of his at Leyden finally settles the dispute about the date of his birth and fixes it in the winter of 1566/67, probably in January. He came to Scrooby in 1571 with his father and mother; his father in 1575 became bailiff of the Manor of Scrooby, one of the exempt estates of the Arch-

bishop of York, and in 1588 was appointed postmaster by Elizabeth when Scrooby was made a post-house on the road between London and York. These positions made the father a man of great importance in the district and provided him with a considerable income. The boy was somehow prepared for the university and entered Peterhouse, Cambridge, in December 1580, where he himself later declared that he acquired his first Separatist ideas. He did not take a degree and perhaps remained at Cambridge only a few months. In the autumn of 1583 he became a member of the household of William Davison, then important in administrative and diplomatic life at the court of Elizabeth, and, becoming one of his trusted retainers, accompanied him on missions to the Netherlands in 1584 and in 1585–86. Despite the disgrace of Davison in 1587 as a result of his part in the execution of Mary Stuart and his consequent retirement from public life, Brewster remained in his service until news of his father's serious illness caused his return to Scrooby in 1589. He served as his father's deputy until the latter's death in 1590 and then was himself appointed to the positions of bailiff and postmaster, retaining both until the exodus to Holland in 1608. He married in 1591 Mary ——, by whom he had before 1620 six children. Gradually he became the protector and then the principal member of a little congregation of Puritans, gathered from Scrooby and the near-by villages. But they did not "separate" from the Established Church until the autumn of 1606 and it was not until a year later that John Robinson joined them. After some investigation of their proceedings by the High Commission at York, which certainly did not amount to persecution, they decided to leave so ungodly a land and finally succeeded in emigrating to Holland in 1608. Finding Amsterdam also uncongenial, they settled at Leyden in 1609. Here, if not earlier, Brewster became elder and teacher of the new church. To earn a living for his family, he became a printer of Puritan books, written by the leaders in England, and shipped back to them for sale and distribution at home. In 1617 the initiation of the plan for emigration to America took him and others to England where he interviewed officers of the Virginia Company and various royal officials to secure permission to colonize and a grant of land. Beyond much doubt he was the principal envoy. Returning to Leyden, he printed in 1618 or 1619 a book which gave great offense to James I. Of this the English government complained to the Dutch authorities in 1619 with such effect that Brewster felt it wiser to discontinue the press altogether and to return with his family to England where he seems to have lived unmolested until the *Mayflower* sailed in 1620. He played therefore no part in the final steps at Leyden for the emigration to America and was not present when the decision was reached, in April 1620, that the majority should remain at Leyden with Robinson their minister, while the minority should attempt the venture with Brewster himself as their leader. It also seems probable that he played no important part in organizing the company which sailed for America direct from England, being fearful of royal interference with his own emigration. He embarked on the *Mayflower* at London with his wife, two sons, and two boys "bound out" to him. At Plymouth, Brewster was the only church officer until 1629, but held services of prayer and praise only; he expounded the Scripture at length, but was forbidden by the rules to preach, baptize, or celebrate the communion. Though he was therefore never a minister in the Pilgrim sense of the word and though they "called" Smith, Roger Williams, Chauncey, and Reynor as their ministers later, he remained throughout his life the real leader of the church at Plymouth and the man chiefly responsible for its doctrines, observances, and worship. Administrative position was foreclosed to him by his position in the church but he was active in counsel and played a part second only to Bradford in all decisions, great and small. He became one of the Undertakers in 1627 who assumed the Pilgrim indebtedness. His library (*Proceedings of the Massachusetts Historical Society,* 2nd ser., III, 261–74; V, 37–85) proves him to have been well read in history, philosophy, and religious poetry and shows that he continued to buy books throughout his life. We have no idea of his personal appearance but we do know from the inventory of his property (*Mayflower Descendant,* III, 15–27) that he wore a violet colored cloth coat, black silk stockings, a ruff, and other clothing, of impeccable modesty, but less severe than the popular tradition attributes to the Pilgrims. Social life at Plymouth was undoubtedly quiet in the extreme but in it Brewster played a very important part, being, says Bradford, "of a very cherful Spirite, very sociable and pleasante amongst his friends." He died Apr. 10, 1644, at Plymouth, possessed of a house, lands, cattle, and personalty worth £107.

[The chief authority for Brewster's life to 1620 is H. M. and M. Dexter, *The England and Holland of the Pilgrims* (1905) and for the period after 1620, Wm. Bradford's *Hist. of Plymouth Plantation* (1856). See also: R. G. Usher, *The Pilgrims and Their History* (1918); J. A. Goodwin, *The Pilgrim Republic* (1888); W. H. Burgess, *The Pastor of the Pilgrims: John Robinson* (1920). In *Mayflower Notes and Queries,* IV, 56 ff., is a complete list of his children and grandchildren. In the *Mayflower Descendant,* vols. I, II, III, etc., has been printed the "Brewster Book" kept by his descendants. The best list of his books printed at Leyden is now that in the *Mayflower Descendant,* XXIII, 97–105, with two not before identified. The known autographs are given in the same series in facsimile: XXII, 1; XXIII, 98; XXIV, 97.]   R.G.U.

BREWSTER, WILLIAM (July 5, 1851–July 11, 1919), ornithologist, was born at Wakefield, Mass., the son of John Brewster, a successful Boston banker, and of Rebecca Parker (Noyes) Brewster. Descended on both sides from old Massachusetts families he inherited all of the characteristics of a New England gentleman, and reared in the atmosphere of Cambridge, with Longfellow and other notable men of letters as family neighbors, he absorbed all of the spirit and tradition of the community. He was educated in the public schools of Cambridge and prepared for Harvard, but being never of robust health and suffering in youth from impaired sight he decided to forego a college course. With no leaning toward a business career he nevertheless in accordance with his father's wish entered his banking office at the age of nineteen but retired within a year convinced that he did not possess business talent and henceforth devoted himself entirely to ornithology, his father sympathizing fully with his decision. He was married on Feb. 9, 1878, to Caroline F. Kettell of Boston. Brewster's attention seems to have been first drawn to birds at the age of ten by a neighbor, Daniel C. French, who was interested in hunting and was something of an amateur taxidermist. He willingly gave the boy and others of his associates instructions in preparing specimens with the result that at the age of fourteen Brewster had several cases of mounted birds and had begun what was eventually to become the finest collection of North American birds in existence, which is now preserved in the Museum of Comparative Zoölogy. Brewster became a skilful taxidermist and always took the greatest pains in preparing his specimens, for a bird skin to him was not only a scientific specimen but an object of beauty to be cherished and admired. Later in life he built a little museum on his home grounds in Cambridge where his collection and library were housed and where ornithologists were welcomed and meetings held. Wrapped up in New England traditions, Brewster's main interests were naturally in the local bird life and he kept detailed daily records of bird observations at Cambridge, Concord, Lake Umbagog, and other New England localities which he visited. He also collected specimens, however, in other parts of the country, visiting Illinois, West Virginia, Colorado, the Gulf of St. Lawrence, North Carolina, and Florida as well as the island of Trinidad, and employed skilful collectors to procure specimens from elsewhere. While he possessed a profound taxonomic knowledge of North American birds and published important papers in this field and while he served for years on the Committee on Classification and Nomenclature of the American Ornithologists' Union, his outstanding publications have dealt with the live bird rather than the dead one. He was one of the founders of the Nuttall Ornithological Club (1876) and of the American Ornithologists' Union (1883), becoming president of both organizations. He was active in behalf of bird and game preservation but in a broad-minded not sentimental way, was president of the Massachusetts Audubon Society, and was a member of the state Game Commission. He was in charge of the bird and mammal collections of the Boston Society of Natural History (1879–87) and of the ornithological collection of the Museum of Comparative Zoölogy from 1885 on. His most notable publications were: *Descriptions of the First Plumage in Various North American Birds* (1878–79), *Bird Migration* (1886), *Birds of the Cambridge Region of Massachusetts* (1906), *Birds of the Cape Region of Lower California* (1902), and the posthumous *Birds of the Lake Umbagog Region, Maine* (1924–25, still unfinished). His short papers and notes were numerous and covered a wide range of ornithological topics, those appearing in the *Bulletin of the Nuttall Club* and its successor the *Auk* numbering no less than 267. He also edited an edition of H. D. Minot's *Land Birds and Game Birds of New England* (1894), which contained many additional notes. Besides his Cambridge home Brewster possessed a large tract of farm land at Concord which he maintained primarily as a wild life preserve where for twenty years no gun was fired and where he studied the balance of nature and delighted in the association with birds and small mammals. Indeed to those who knew him well the name of William Brewster was as closely associated with Concord as was that of Thoreau, for whom he had a great reverence. He likewise had a camp at Lake Umbagog, Me., where he spent a number of seasons collecting data on the life histories of the birds of the region. His deep love of nature was contagious and association with him in the field was a privilege not soon to be forgotten. Probably he never realized the part he played in stimulating the ornithological activities of many others, especially young men. His influence upon the development of American Ornithology, extending, as it did, far beyond his printed papers, cannot well be measured.

[Henry W. Henshaw, sketch in the *Auk,* Jan. 1920; F. M. Chapman, sketch in *Bird Lore,* Sept.–Oct. 1919; obituary in *Boston Transcript,* July 12, 1919; *Who's Who in America,* 1918–19; personal acquaintance.]

W.S.

BRICE, CALVIN STEWART (Sept. 17, 1845–Dec. 15, 1898), railroad builder, senator, was descended on his father's side from the Bruces of Kinnaird, Scotland, and on the maternal side from the fifth Lord Livingston, who died about 1553. His father, William K. Brice, was a Presbyterian minister, a graduate of Hanover College and Princeton Theological Seminary, who came from Maryland to Ohio in 1840 and settled in the village of Denmark, Morrow County, where Calvin Stewart Brice was born. The latter's mother, whose maiden name was Elizabeth Stewart, was a native of Carroll County, Ohio, and is described as "a woman of fine education and exemplary traits of character." While his early education was obtained in the common schools, it is clear that the instruction of his parents had a decided effect upon his mental development, for at the age of thirteen he entered the preparatory department of Miami University, at Oxford, Ohio, and after only a year he was admitted to the freshman class. But his studies were interrupted by the war. On Apr. 1, 1861, though only fifteen years of age, he enlisted in the cause of the Union but was rejected on account of his youth; the following year he enlisted again and served for three months, when he returned to Oxford to complete his college course. He graduated in June 1863 and after teaching three months he recruited Company E of the 180th Ohio Volunteer Infantry, became its captain, and served until July 1865. A few days before the close of the war he was promoted to the rank of lieutenant-colonel for meritorious service. He was then just of age and took up the study of law in the University of Michigan. In the spring of 1866 he was admitted to the bar at Cincinnati. He soon gained distinction as a corporation lawyer, a training that fitted him for the part he was to play in the business and financial world, for in 1870 he gave up the active practise of law and embarked upon railroad enterprise, both as projector and manager. He first attracted notice in the business world when Gen. Ewing and other capitalists planned a railroad from Toledo to the Ohio coal fields. This brought him in contact with Allen G. Thurman, Judge Ranney, and Gov. Foster of Ohio. The plan as Brice outlined it was finally followed and he was given a free hand to carry the project to completion. In the winter of 1870–71 he went to Europe to procure a loan for the purpose of completing the line of the Lake Erie & Louisville Railroad as far as

Lima, Ohio. This road afterward became the Lake Erie & Western of which he became president in 1887. Besides his connection with this road he helped in the construction of the division of the Erie Railroad, known as the Chicago & Atlantic, and was responsible for the location in his home town of Lima of the machine shops of the Lake Erie & Western and the Dayton & Michigan railroads. His ability was now generally recognized and he entered upon many new ventures, all of which were successful. The conception, building, and profitable sale of the New York, Chicago & St. Louis Railway, commonly known as the "Nickel Plate," was in great measure due to him. He was connected with ten other railroads, between Duluth, the Atlantic, and the South, as an investor and an official; but perhaps his greatest project was a railroad in China under concessions from the imperial government to the China-American Development Company, known as "The Brice Chinese Syndicate," which had the exclusive right of way between Canton and Hankow with adjacent mining rights; but his death prevented him from completing the undertaking. The *Way Bill,* commenting upon his services, says: "In all Mr. Brice's official relations with various railroads and other corporate properties, he never accepted a dollar of salary for his services. We do not know of another man in a similar position of whom the same can be said" (*Magazine of Western History,* 1889, X, 719). In addition to his extensive railroad activities, he was a promoter and stockholder in many of the local interests of his home city of Lima; he was identified with the Chase National Bank of New York and one of the leading spirits and directors of the Southern Trust Company. Yet he had time for politics. As a Democrat he was on the electoral ticket of Tilden in 1876 and of Cleveland in 1884. In 1888 he was delegate at large from Ohio to the national Democratic convention at St. Louis where he was elected a member of the national Democratic committee and chairman of the national campaign committee for the ensuing campaign. On the death of William H. Barnum in 1889, he was unanimously elected chairman of the Democratic national committee, and in 1890 he was elected to the United States Senate, to succeed Henry B. Payne, for the term commencing Mar. 4, 1891. He soon became one of the leaders on the Democratic side, being a member of the steering committee and also a member of the Committee on Appropriations. While he took little part in public discussions in the Senate, he followed the proceedings closely, was a skilful questioner, and always commanded respect from the leaders of both parties. On retiring from the Senate he took up his residence in New York City and became prominent in financial circles; but after the advent of Bryan and free silver, he took little interest in politics. He was married in 1870 to Catherine Olivia Meily of Lima, Ohio, by whom he had four sons and two daughters.

[The files of *The Times-Democrat* of Lima, Ohio, especially the issues of Dec. 16, 19, and 20, 1898; *Cong. Record,* 52 Cong. 2 Sess.; obituaries in the *N. Y. Times, N. Y. Tribune,* and *Sun* (N. Y.), Dec. 16, 1898.]

K.F.G.

BRICKELL, ROBERT COMAN (Apr. 4, 1824–Nov. 20, 1900), jurist, of Welsh ancestry, was the eldest son of Richard Benjamin and Margaret Williamson (Coman) Brickell. He was born in Tuscumbia, Ala., at the home of his maternal great-grandfather, Dr. Prout, although his parents were making their home in Huntsville, Ala. From Huntsville they moved to Athens, Ala., where the father published and edited the *Athenian,* a weekly newspaper. Gifted as a writer and speaker he was elected to the state legislature in 1831 and again in 1833 from Limestone County where he died in 1835, leaving his widow and six children in straitened circumstances. Robert Brickell's mother was a woman of strong character, well educated, and devoted to her children in whom she inspired the greatest love and respect. After her husband's death she taught school. Her eldest son, Robert, was a delicate child and was always handicapped by a slight physique. With the exception of six weeks in school in Nashville, Tenn., he was taught only by his parents. When nineteen years of age, he was admitted to the bar after having read law in the private office of Judge Daniel Coleman in Athens. Although retiring in disposition he was such a deep student that his learning at a tender age was regarded as remarkable. In 1851 he located in Huntsville and became the junior partner in the law firm of Cabaniss & Brickell. Three years later Leroy Pope Walker became the head of the firm from which Mr. Cabaniss finally retired. There was hardly a case of any importance in north Alabama in which the powerful firm of Walker & Brickell did not take part on one side or the other in legal battles. Both were advocates of state rights and strong believers in the constitutional right of secession.

In 1873 Brickell was appointed associate justice of the supreme court of Alabama by the Republican governor, David P. Lewis, who knew him to be a profound lawyer, peculiarly fitted for that high judicial office. Brickell entered at once upon the discharge of his duties with a determination to lend every possible assistance in rectifying the chaotic condition of the courts in which partisan decisions had been made in total disregard of time-honored precedents. His decisions from the bench were numerous and able. He became chief justice of the supreme court in 1874 by the selection of his associates and in 1880 was nominated by the Democratic party and elected chief justice of the supreme court by the popular vote. Four years later he resigned his office to resume the practise of law with offices in Montgomery, New Decatur, and Huntsville. In 1894, however, he was persuaded by Gov. Thomas G. Jones, who recognized the state's great need of his service on the bench, to accept an appointment once more as a supreme court judge. Upon the expiration of his term of office he returned to Huntsville and resumed the practise of law, in partnership with his son, Robert C. Brickell, Jr. On Nov. 29, 1876, in Montgomery, Ala., he had married Mary Blassingame Glenn, a niece of the wife of Gov. Benjamin Fitzpatrick. On Nov. 20, 1900, he died following a stroke of paralysis.

He was possessed of a nervous temperament and his gestures were rapid and unstudied. He was especially impressive before a court or jury and on account of his masterly arguments and effective oratorical powers the court room was always filled when it was known that he would speak. His abilities were of especial use to the people of Alabama during the period of Reconstruction when the courts were administered by alien judges.

[P. J. Hamilton, "Robt. Coman Brickell," in *Great Am. Lawyers*, vol. VII (1909), ed. by W. D. Lewis; 127 *Ala. Reports; Report of the Twenty-fourth Annual Meeting, Ala. State Bar Ass.*, 1901, pp. 183–89; Thos. M. Owen, *Hist. of Ala. and Dict. of Ala. Biog.* (1921), vol. III; *Daily Picayune*, June 13, 1873; MSS. in the Ala. State Dept. of Archives and Hist.]   M.B.O.

BRIDGER, JAMES (Mar. 17, 1804–July 17, 1881), fur trader, frontiersman, scout, was the son of James Bridger, inn-keeper of Richmond, Va., and of his wife Chloe. Young Bridger removed with his parents to the vicinity of St. Louis about 1812. Orphaned at the age of thirteen, he was apprenticed to a blacksmith, but true to his pioneer inheritance, was attracted by Ashley's "want ad" in the *Missouri Republican* of Mar. 20, 1822, offering employment to a hundred "enterprising young men" to engage on a fur-trapping venture near the sources of the Missouri River. Joining the expedition, Bridger entered that portion of the West with which he was to become more intimately familiar than any of his contemporaries. During the next twenty years, either as an employee of, or a partner in,

various fur companies, he repeatedly traversed the area between the Canadian boundary and the southern line of Colorado and from the Missouri River westward to Idaho and Utah. He was the first white man, so far as is known, to visit (fall of 1824) Great Salt Lake. Noting the decline of the fur business and the growth of western emigration he established a way-station, Fort Bridger, on the Oregon trail in southwestern Wyoming, in 1843. All the notable figures in the western movement—Wyeth, Bonneville, Whitman, Parker, DeSmet, Frémont, the Donner party, Brigham Young and many others—recorded their indebtedness to him either for reliable information about the country or for hospitality at the "fort." To obtain a monopoly of the emigrant business the Mormons drove him from his holdings in 1853. Retiring for a time to a farm which he had purchased near Kansas City, he soon entered government service as a scout. He had already guided Stansbury on his Utah expedition in 1849 and on his return had led him east through the short-cut of Bridger's pass. In 1857–58 he guided Johnston's army in the Utah invasion, probably a not uncongenial assignment. In 1859–60 he accompanied the Raynolds Yellowstone expedition and in 1861 guided the Berthoud engineering party in their attempt to discover a direct route from Denver to Great Salt Lake. In 1865 and 1866 he acted as guide for the Powder River expeditions and in the latter year measured the distances on the Bozeman trail from Fort Kearny, Nebr., to Virginia City, Mont., a distance of 967 miles. In 1868 he retired from the plains and the mountains. He died at his home near Kansas City.

Bridger took three wives. The first was a Flathead woman who died, 1846, leaving three children. His second wife, a Ute, died, 1849, leaving a daughter. His third wife, a Snake woman, died in 1858. With the sole exception of a few Mormon contemporaries, every one of the scores of pioneers, army men, explorers, and sportsmen with whom he came in contact mentions his services, his intelligence, and his character in the highest terms. Tall, keen-eyed and of commanding personality, this completely illiterate frontiersman placed at the disposal of a multitude of varied western travelers his unrivaled knowledge of the country and of the Indians.

[J. C. Alter, *Jas. Bridger* (1925), which includes the whole of G. M. Dodge's *Biog. Sketch of Jas. Bridger* (1905); Grace R. Hebard and E. A. Briminstool, *The Bozeman Trail* (1922).]   H.C.D.

BRIDGERS, ROBERT RUFUS (Nov. 28, 1819–Dec. 10, 1888), Confederate congressman, manufacturer, railroad president, belonged to a family, long resident in southside Virginia, which came to Edgecombe County, N. C., about 1761 and took up land on Town Creek. There Robert Rufus was born, son of John Bridgers and Elizabeth Kettlewells Routh. Having graduated first in the state university's class of 1841, he was immediately licensed to practise law and three years later was sent to the state House of Representatives. Then he settled down at Tarboro. In 1849 he married Margaret Elizabeth Johnston. He worked at the law very hard and in later life is said to have been offered the attorney-generalship. With "decided gifts" for politics, in the 1850's he helped Henry T. Clark make Edgecombe a "stronghold of Democracy" (J. K. Turner and J. L. Bridgers, *Edgecombe County*, 1920, p. 152) and received three terms (1856–61) and the chairmanship of the judiciary committee in the state House of Representatives. Though not "fervent for secession," he advocated a state convention in frank anticipation that secession would be necessary. In the Confederate Congress (1862–65) he was regular in attendance, always a member of the committee on military affairs, and apparently disposed to support President Davis as far as his people's views would permit (*Congress of Confederate States, Journal*, V, 151, 154; VI, 71, 741). His chief interest, however, had already begun to be business. At Tarboro he had organized and developed a bank, of which he had become president in 1851. Next year he was purchasing large land-holdings out of which, with subsequent purchases, he made "Strabane," a plantation noted for high productivity. Simultaneously he was promoting a Tarboro branch of the Wilmington & Weldon Railroad with such success that the line was finished in 1860 and he became a director of the Wilmington & Weldon. During the war he revamped plants for the mining and manufacture of iron in Lincoln and adjacent counties (the "High Shoals property") which supplied the Carolinas with nails and plows and is said to have been the second largest of its kind in the Confederacy. He urged alike upon his railroad and the Confederate government a policy of large production of cotton and its exportation to meet coming financial obligations abroad. Later the Confederate government is said to have wanted him as secretary of the treasury; in the fall of 1865 the Wilmington & Weldon company—which had resumed business in August with four locomotives and nine cars—elected him president. For the next twenty-three years he labored unremittingly on what was to be the Atlantic Coast Line Railroad. Each year he was unanimously reëlected president of

the Wilmington & Weldon. For thirteen years he was also its general superintendent. For it he built four branch lines, totaling nearly two hundred miles in length. He became president also of the Columbia & Augusta, which continued his road from Wilmington. All of these lines were financed by a Baltimore firm to whom he had appealed in 1867 and for whom, as a condition of assistance, he had bought a controlling interest in Wilmington & Weldon, including the state's stock, during the Holden administration. That he escaped the odium and suspicion which attended the transactions of this firm (see complaint of Wilmington and New Hanover County through their attorneys, 1893) was perhaps due to his personal character as well as to the wisdom of his policies. Men noted that he had not taken advantage of the bankruptcy law when the failure of others overwhelmed him with debt at the time of the war. He knew intimately the lands which his roads served and their people individually. He picked territory for branch roads with remarkable shrewdness and aided businesses all along his lines. He fostered enthusiasm among his men through his policy of promotion to vacancies; in turn he rigidly insisted that they treat his patrons courteously. These were not always characteristics of railroad leaders in that day. And since he declined better positions elsewhere, men deemed him "public spirited." He died in harness, in Columbia, S. C., and was buried amid expressions of general esteem in St. James's churchyard, Wilmington.

[S. A. Ashe, *Biog. Hist. of N. C.* (1905), I, 171; Jerome Dowd, *Sketches of Prominent Living North Carolinians* (1888); *News and Observer* (Raleigh), Dec. 12, 1888; *Wilmington Weekly Star*, Dec. 14, 1888.]   C.C.P.

BRIDGES, ROBERT (d. 1656), Lynn iron manufacturer and magistrate, was a significant figure in the industrial history of America. He reached Massachusetts probably in 1641, for in that year (June 2) he took the oath and became a freeman. He was evidently a man of considerable ability, for from the date of his arrival until his death he took a prominent part in the affairs of the community. He was a member of the Ancient and Honorable Artillery Company in 1641 and became a captain in the militia. In 1644 he was chosen representative to the General Court and appointed a member of the Quarterly Court at Salem. In October 1646 he was elected speaker of the House of Representatives, and in the next year became an Assistant, in which office he continued until his death. For a long time he was the only magistrate in Lynn. An interesting episode in his career was his service as commissioner in 1646 to investigate the troubles between two French governors—the Huguenot, La Tour, and the Catholic, D'Aulnay—who were contending for the possession of Acadia and causing trouble to certain Plymouth traders in Maine. Edward Johnson bears witness to his prominence when he speaks of "the Band of Lyn led by the honored and much respected Capt. Robert Bridges, who is also a magistrate, being endued with able parts, and forward to improve them for the glory of God and his people's good" (*Wonder Working Providence*, ed. by J. Franklin Jameson, 1910, p. 231).

Although Bridges was an important figure for a few years in the administration of the Massachusetts colony, his chief interest to subsequent generations lies in his connection with the first iron works established in America. Bog iron was discovered at an early date in Massachusetts but it was not until 1642 that a serious effort was made to take advantage of the discovery. In that year Bridges took some specimens of the ore from the region of the Saugus River and went to London for the purpose of interesting capital. A company known as "The Company of Undertakers for the Iron Works" was formed and the eleven incorporators contributed £1,000 for the enterprise. Skilled workmen were brought over and the industry established, 1643, at Hammersmith (near Lynn) on the Saugus, so named after the English town from which some of the workmen came. The colonial authorities considered the establishment of these iron works a matter of great importance and aided them liberally with civil and religious immunities equal to any in the colony (Lewis and Newhall, *History of Lynn*, 1865, pp. 212 ff.). Although they continued to be operated to some extent until 1683, the iron works met with indifferent success, and apparently did not long occupy the major attention of their founder.

Bridges seems to have been a stern and unyielding Puritan. He was a member of the court which in 1651 regulated the dress of all persons whose estate did not exceed £200 and forbade dancing at weddings or other events in ordinaries. He also participated prominently in the Quaker persecution by ordering the arrest of Clarke, Crandall, and Holmes at Swampscott ("Ill News from New England," *Massachusetts Historical Society Collections*, 4 ser., II, 27 ff., 1854). Personally he was a man of tact, and his rapid rise and continued public service bear witness to his acceptability to the authorities of Massachusetts. His wife was Mary Woodcock of London (Charles H. Pope, *Pioneers of Massachusetts*, 1900, p. 68).

[Alonzo Lewis, *Hist. of Lynn Including Nahant* (1844); Chas. E. Mann, *The Three Lynn Captains, Robt. Bridges, Thos. Marshall, and Richard Walker* (1911), reprinted from vol. XIV of the *Lynn Hist. Soc. Reg.*; Nathan M. Hawkes, *Hearths and Homes of Old Lynn* (1907), pp. 149–58; J. L. Bishop, *Hist. of Am. Manufactures, from 1608 to 1860* (1864), I, 470 ff.]

H.U.F.

BRIDGES, ROBERT (Mar. 5, 1806–Feb. 20, 1882), physician and botanist, was the son of Culpepper Bridges and his wife Sarah Clifton. He was born in Philadelphia and was educated in that city until he went to Dickinson College, from which he graduated in 1824. He then became a pupil of Thomas T. Hewson in his private medical classes while studying medicine at the University of Pennsylvania, from which he received the degree of M.D. in 1828. Although Bridges did not practise medicine many years he became a fellow of the College of Physicians of Philadelphia in 1842. He served as its librarian from 1867 to 1879, and catalogued the Urinary Calculi in its Mutter Museum. He was one of the vaccine physicians of Philadelphia for some years, and during the cholera epidemic of 1832 he was appointed a district physician. The great interests of his life were botany and chemistry. In 1835 he became a member of the Academy of Natural Sciences, which he subsequently served at various times as librarian, corresponding secretary, vice-president, and finally president in 1864. In 1835 with Dr. Paul B. Goddard he presented to the Academy an Index of the genera in its Herbarium, and in 1843 he presented a new Index along with one of Menke's Herbarium, which had come into the Academy's possession. While yet a student with Hewson, Bridges had assisted Franklin Bache in teaching chemistry to Hewson's pupils and had shown much ability. In 1831 he assisted Bache in his chemical teaching in the Philadelphia College of Pharmacy, of which institution he became a trustee in 1839. In 1842 he was appointed professor of general and pharmaceutical chemistry in the College, becoming emeritus professor in 1879. From 1839 to 1846 he was assistant editor of the *American Journal of Pharmacy*. He was a member of the Committee for the Revision of the Pharmacopœia in 1840 and again in 1870. From 1846 to 1848 he was professor of chemistry in Franklin Medical College. He was a member of the Franklin Institute of Philadelphia (1836) and of the American Philosophical Society (1844). Besides many contributions to transactions and periodicals he edited the American edition of George Fownes's *Elementary Chemistry* and Thomas Graham's *Elements of Chemistry* and assisted George B. Wood in the preparation of several editions of the *United States*

Dispensary, as well as in his teaching of Materia Medica at the University of Pennsylvania. He was never married.

[J. W. Harshberger, *The Botanists of Phila.* (1899); W. S. W. Ruschenberber, in *Proc. Am. Philosophical Soc.,* XXI, 427, 1884.]   F. R. P.

BRIDGMAN, ELIJAH COLEMAN (Apr. 22, 1801–Nov. 2, 1861), missionary to the Chinese, sent out by the American Board of Commissioners for Foreign Missions in 1829, was born in Belchertown, Mass., a descendant of James Bridgman who settled in Hartford, Conn., in 1640; and son of Theodore and Lucretia (Warner) Bridgman. From boyhood, when he was attracted to missionary work through his reading of missionary periodicals, his one unwavering interest was in that field of activity. To prepare himself for it, he went to Amherst College, graduating in 1826, and then to Andover Theological Seminary. On the day he finished his studies there, Sept. 23, 1829, representatives of the American Board asked him to accept an appointment to China, a New York merchant, D. W. C. Olyphant, engaged in trade with Canton, having offered to support a missionary there for a year. It took him but three days to come to a decision. On Oct. 3, he was commissioned; on Oct. 6, at Belchertown, he was ordained; and the next week he was on his way, arriving in Canton the latter part of February 1830. Except for a brief visit to America, because of ill health in 1852, he spent the remainder of his life in China, never seeming to have any desire to leave his work. Here he died at the age of sixty, and his body lies buried in the Shanghai cemetery.

When he arrived in Canton the only Protestant worker in China was the celebrated English missionary and translator, Dr. Robert Morrison, under whose tutelage he soon acquired a good knowledge of the language. The open preaching of Christianity at that time was forbidden, and while he performed all the duties of a clergyman, his chief work was that of a pioneer organizer, educator, and translator. On the formation of the Society for the Diffusion of Useful Knowledge, in November 1834, he was chosen joint secretary with Dr. Charles Gützlaff. He was active in founding the Morrison Education Society, and with Drs. T. R. Colledge and Peter Parker [*q.v.*] called the public meeting in Canton, Feb. 21, 1838, which resulted in the organization of the Medical Missionary Society in China. He was also a member of the North China branch of the Royal Asiatic Society, and the editor of its journal. In 1832 a mission press was started, and in May of that year he began the publication of the *Chinese Repository,* for the spread of information about China among English-speaking people. This periodical, widely read and valued, he edited until 1847, when S. Wells Williams [*q.v.*], who had long assisted him, took sole charge. In 1841 he published his *Chinese Chrestomathy,* to which Williams also contributed, a quarto of 734 pages, and the first practical manual of the Cantonese dialect prepared in China. After Hong-Kong was ceded to Great Britain, he removed to that city where he married, June 28, 1845, Eliza Jane Gillett. Later in the year he returned to Canton but in 1847 removed to Shanghai, and spent much of the remainder of his life working on translations of the Bible. His own version, in preparing which Rev. M. S. Culbertson collaborated, appeared in 1862. On various occasions he was of much assistance to the United States government. Caleb Cushing, in a letter published in the *Presbyterian,* Mar. 8, 1845, speaks of Bridgman's "indispensable service" as translator and adviser during the former's negotiations with China.

[B. N. and J. C. Bridgman, *Genealogy of the Bridgman Family* (1894); Eliza J. G. Bridgman, *Life and Labors of Elijah Coleman Bridgman* (1864); F. Wells Williams, *Life and Letters of Samuel Wells Williams* (1889); D. MacGillivray, *A Century of Protestant Missions in China* (1907); Wm. E. Strong, *The Story of the Am. Board* (1910); *Memorials of Protestant Missionaries to the Chinese* (1867).]   H. E. S.

BRIDGMAN, FREDERIC ARTHUR (Nov. 10, 1847–Jan. 13, 1927), painter, was born at Tuskegee, Ala., the son of Frederick and Lovina (Jennings) Bridgman. On the death of his father, his mother moved to the North with her children, and in view of the boy's earnest desire to become an artist, she took advantage of an opportunity to apprentice him to the American Bank-Note Company in New York, 1863, where he remained at work nearly four years. Meanwhile he studied drawing and painting in an art school in Brooklyn and experimented in painting at home out of business hours. In 1866 he went to France for the purpose of continuing his training and became a pupil of J. L. Gérôme in the École des Beaux-Arts, Paris, where he passed five years. During the early days in Paris he met with but scanty encouragement, but in 1870 two of his pictures, "Cirque en Province" and "De Quoi Parlent les Jeunes Filles," were hung in the Salon, several of his works were engraved in *Le Monde Illustré,* and he sold some of his productions to the Goupil Galleries. His summers were usually spent at Pont-Aven, Brittany, then the favorite resort of a colony of painters. It was there that he painted the spirited picture of a circus above mentioned, which was later exhibited in several American cities under the title of "An American Circus in France." In the summer of 1871 he visited England for a short time; then he traveled to the Pyrenees, where he met Fortuny and other painters, and stayed about two years. Thence he proceeded to Algeria, Egypt, and Nubia, in the winter of 1873-74, and, in company with other painters, made a voyage up the Nile as far as the second cataract. So well did he employ his time that when he returned to Paris in the spring of 1874 he brought with him three hundred sketches and studies, for the most part of landscapes and the ruins of temples, also a quantity of costumes and curiosities which were destined to be utilized in the oriental compositions to which he now devoted most of his attention. One of the most important of these was the "Interior of a Harem," which was shown in the Salon of 1875. The work by which he is best known is largely archeological, as for instance the "Funeral of a Mummy," which appeared in the Salon of 1877. Other scholarly and well-painted reconstructions of the life of antiquity are the "Procession of the Bull Apis" and the picture of an Assyrian king killing lions in the amphitheatre (Salon of 1879), works somewhat reminiscent of Gérôme, and, in the opinion of the critics of the time, exhibiting some of the master's best qualities. Continuing to reside and work in Paris, Bridgman became one of the best-known and most esteemed artists of the large American colony there. Medals came to him from the Salon and elsewhere; he prospered; and his paintings commanded a ready market in the United States, for he sent many of his best things to the American exhibitions, notably to the National Academy and the Society of American Artists. On the occasion of one of his periodical visits to his native land, in 1878, a loan exhibition of twenty-four of his pictures was held in Brooklyn, the collection being known as the Bridgman Gallery. This group contained, among other things, his "American Circus in France," "The Prayer in the Mosque," "The Fête in the Palace of Rameses," "The Pride of the Harem," "Woman of Kabzla," "View on the Upper Nile," and a self-portrait. His painting of "The Diligence" is in the Walker Gallery, Liverpool; "The Destruction of Pharaoh's Host" and two other works are in the Academy of Arts in Leningrad; and several of his pictures have been acquired by American museums. In addition to his accomplishments as a painter, he was the author of several books, a composer of music, and a proficient violinist. He published *Winters in Algeria* (1890), *L'Anarchie dans l'Art* (1898)—originally written in English but translated and published in French, an emphatic protest against what he regarded as the demoralizing tendencies of the radical modernists in painting, sculpture, architecture, music, literature, and criticism; and *L'Idole et l'Idéal* (1901). His musical compositions consist of orchestral pieces and several symphonies. On July 17, 1877 he was married in Paris to Florence Mott Baker of Boston. He died in Rouen, and was buried at Lyon-la-Forêt, a village in Normandy, about twenty miles from Rouen.

[B. N. and J. C. Bridgman, *Geneal. of the Bridgman Family* (1894); G. W. Sheldon, *Am. Painters* (1879); Samuel Isham, *Hist. of Am. Painting* (1905); *Art Jour.*, Feb. 1876; *Am. Art Rev.*, June 1881; *Artist*, XXIX, 138; *Art Amateur*, XL, 76; *Harper's*, Oct. 1881.]

W. H. D.

BRIDGMAN, HERBERT LAWRENCE (May 30, 1844–Sept. 24, 1924), newspaper publisher, explorer, was born in Amherst, Mass., the son of Richard Baxter and Mary (Nutting) Bridgman. After finishing the common schools he entered Amherst College, from which he graduated in 1866. He had done some apprentice work at journalism during his last two years in college, and he now made it his vocation. He began on the *Springfield Republican,* of which he became city editor, and he later worked for the Associated Press and on *Frank Leslie's,* the *Press,* and the *Tribune* of New York. In 1887 he became business manager of the *Brooklyn Standard Union,* a place he retained until his death. He was one of the founders of the American Newspaper Publishers Association, of which he was president for three terms, and was for one term chairman of the New York Publishers Association. He remained a journalist as well as a publisher; usually he had an unsigned editorial in the Sunday issue of his newspapers, and always he was a keen and an assiduous gatherer of news. An associate testifies that "he was a specialist on finding the elusive item in the least likely place," and that his contributions, jotted down in an atrocious hand, "probably worse than Greeley's," on any scrap of paper that chanced to be near, were a feature of the daily grist of copy. To the end he never forgot to be a reporter; and on the sea voyage from which he was not to return alive he sent to his newspaper a round dozen of long descriptive letters.

He is most widely known as an explorer and a patron of exploration, particularly of the Arctic. He became closely associated with Robert E. Peary in 1892 and thereafter was his staunch supporter. In 1894, following the discoverer's return to the Arctic the previous year, he accompanied the *Falcon* relief expedition, which provisioned Peary and brought back Mrs. Peary and their infant daughter, born in the Far North. Three years later, for a brief diversion from the Arctic field, he scaled, with Prof. Libby, the Mesa Encantada, in New Mexico. In 1899 he led the *Diana* relief expedition to the North, and on his return organized the Peary Arctic Club, which gave financial aid to the discoverer in all his subsequent work. Two years later, in the *Erik*, he again brought relief to Peary. In 1904 he turned to Africa, going to the headwaters of the Nile, penetrating to the Congo and returning by the same route—a journey narrated in his book, *The Sudan: Africa from Sea to Center*, published the following year. In 1906 and 1908 he was a delegate from various American societies to international gatherings of explorers in Europe. To the great cape at the northeast extremity of Greenland Peary gave the name of his friend, and it was to him that the discoverer sent his code message, received in Brooklyn, Sept. 6, 1909, announcing the discovery of the Pole. Immediately on receiving further information from Peary, Bridgman took a leading part in exposing the pretensions of Dr. Cook. In 1913 he was again a delegate to an international gathering of explorers in Europe and during the year made an extended tour through the Balkans. In 1915 he was made president of the department of geography of the Brooklyn Institute of Arts and Sciences, and two years later a regent of the state university. In 1923 he journeyed through the Panama Canal to California and Hawaii. A youthful octogenarian, he set out on July 2, 1924, for a vacation on the cruise of the New York State School-ship *Newport*, commanded by Capt. Felix Riesenberg. The journey carried him to England, the Belgian battlefields, Spain, and Madeira. On an early morning of the homeward voyage he was suddenly stricken with cerebral hemorrhage, from which he died. The body was brought to Brooklyn and buried, Oct. 1, with appropriate ceremonies, in Greenwood Cemetery.

Bridgman was twice married: in 1868 to Melia Newhall, who died in 1884, and in 1887, to Helen Bartlett, of New York, a writer, who survived him. He was a man of sturdy physique, with the chest and shoulders of an athlete. His familiar photograph shows a large head with a bald and somewhat peaked crown, a high forehead, keen eyes in which may well have "always lurked," as one writes, "a whimsical smile," and a flowing mustache. He was an indefatigable worker and is said never to have wasted a moment. He had amazingly wide interests and managed somehow to apportion his time so as to serve them all. "Had he lived in a period when there were greater undiscovered spaces," said the *New York Times,* "he would have been a Magellan or a Frobisher. . . . His last voyage, in company with youth, is a fit symbol of the whole life of this man who, with uncommon modesty, great geniality and an adventurous courage, illustrated to youth the best that one generation has to give to the next."

[*Who's Who in America*, 1924–25; *His Last Voage: Herbert Lawrence Bridgman, 1844–1924* (a pamphlet compilation of tributes and of Bridgman's last letters, 1924); Helen Bartlett Bridgman, *Within My Horizon* (1920); Earl D. Babst, *In Memory of Herbert L. Bridgman* (1924); *N. Y. Times*, Sept. 27, Oct. 2 and 5, 1924. See also B. N. and J. C. Bridgman, *Genealogy of the Bridgman Family* (1894) and *Amherst Coll. Biog. Record* (1927).]   W. J. G.

BRIDGMAN, LAURA DEWEY (Dec. 21, 1829–May 24, 1889), blind, deaf, mute, was born in Hanover, N. H., the daughter of Daniel and Harmony Bridgman. A delicate child for a year and a half, at the age of two she had an attack of scarlet fever which left her with sight and hearing lost. For two years she was ill and feeble. As soon as she could walk, she began to explore the room and the house, to follow her mother and to imitate her in every way she could. She thus learned to sew and to knit. In 1837 Samuel Gridley Howe [*q.v.*] heard of Laura's case and visited her home. He found her an attractive child with a nervous organization which made for sensibility and activity, and persuaded her parents to let him undertake her education. In October of that year she became his pupil at the Perkins Institution in Boston. For a year or two Howe himself patiently taught her. The particular significance of her case lay in the fact that she was the first blind, deaf, mute in whose case systematic education had been at all successful. Because of her, others in her situation have had life made more worth while. In the fall of 1839, Laura was sent home with a teacher for the annual three weeks' vacation. The change in her was remarkable. Dr. Howe's success in teaching her the use of language so that she spoke by signs and wrote intelligently was considered such an achievement that his reports of it were translated into several languages. Dickens saw her on one of his American trips and was greatly impressed. At the age of fourteen she had completed *Colburn's Mental Arithmetic* in a little over a year. She finished the study of the continent of Africa in four lessons. At fifteen she visited a woolen factory and a grist-mill and understood and remembered much about both. Three years later she taught a deaf and practically blind child arithmetic for an hour a day. She returned to her father's home in Hanover when she was twenty-three with the understanding that it was to be her permanent home. Intense homesickness, however, for the varied life of the Institution made it advisable for her to return there to live. Here she spent the rest of her life. She had a light share in the household work and helped for an hour in the afternoon, teaching sewing in the workroom. She did perfect work and was a more severe task-mistress than the teacher who had sight. By a provision of Dr. Howe's will an income was secured to her which made her independent. Two years before her death a jubilee celebration of the fiftieth anniversary of her arrival at the Institution was held. Phillips Brooks was among the speakers. Howe had intentionally kept from her all formal religious teaching but in 1862, during a visit at home, she had been baptized in the Baptist church. In his last long report of her, Dr. Howe spoke of her unfailing good spirits, her affections and her enjoyment of life.

[Laura E. Richards, *Laura Bridgman* (1928); M. Howe and F. H. Hall, *Laura Bridgman* (1903); M. S. Lamson, *Life and Education of Laura D. Bridgman* (1878); *Letters and Journals of Samuel Gridley Howe* (1909), ed. by L. E. Richards; Helen Keller, *The Story of My Life* (1905).]   M. A. K.

BRIERTON, JOHN (fl. 1572–1619), was the author of the earliest English work dealing with New England. William Brierton of Hoxne, Suffolk, a grandson of Sir Randle Brereton of Malpas, Cheshire, was a farmer of small estate (J. B. Burke, *Genealogical and Heraldic Dictionary of the Landed Gentry of Great Britain and Ireland,* 1852; *Suffolk Green Book,* X, 200). His fourth son, Cuthbert, settled at Norwich where he prospered as a mercer, attaining in 1576 the civic honor of the shrievalty (H. Le Strange, *Norfolk Official Lists,* 1890). By his marriage to Joan Howse of the same city he had several children ("The Visitation of Norfolk," edited by Walter Rye, *Harleian Society Publications,* XXXII, 1891). John Brierton, the third son, was born in 1572. He attended Norwich Grammar School and at seventeen was admitted to Gonville and Caius College, Cambridge, as a pensioner. He took a bachelor's degree in 1592–93 and proceeded M.A. in 1596. Having taken deacon's orders a few months before, he entered the priesthood at Norwich June 24, 1598. His first charge was the curacy of Lawshall, Suffolk, a parish not far from Hessett (J. Venn, *Biographical History of Gonville and Caius College,* I, 135). Here resided the family of Bacon, cousins of Bartholomew Gosnold [*q.v.*]. With this navigator Brierton and thirty others embarked in a small vessel, the *Concord,* sailing from Fal-

mouth Mar. 26, 1602 (Brierton, *Relation,* 1602). That Brierton sailed with Gosnold has been denied (J. and J. A. Venn, *Alumni Cantabrigienses,* I, 210) but new evidence destroys the objection. Setting a western course Gosnold crossed the Atlantic and made a landfall on the southern coast of Maine. He touched at Cape Cod where with Brierton and three others he spent an afternoon on shore. The leaders of the expedition selected Elizabeth's Isle, now Cuttyhunk, as a base, and remained there about three weeks, busying themselves with trade and undertaking a hasty reconnaissance of the country. Brierton afterward wrote of the New England coast with enthusiasm. The party sailed from Cuttyhunk on June 17 and dropped anchor before Exmouth, Devon, July 23, 1602. On his return to England Brierton was requested by a friend, perhaps Gosnold or Hakluyt, to draw up an account of the voyage. This he did. On Oct. 29, 1602, a stationer of London, George Bishop, who had already brought out Hakluyt's *Principal Navigations,* and who was in 1605 to stand sponsor for Rosier's narrative of the Waymouth voyage, entered at Stationers' Hall the pamphlet published under the title of *A Briefe and True Relation of the Discouerie of the North Part of Virginia* (E. Arber, *Transcript of the Register of the Company of Stationers of London, 1554–1640,* 1875–77, III, 88; L. S. Livingstone, Facsimile Reprint of *Relation,* 1903). Brierton's pamphlet furnishes an optimistic account of the natural advantages of the region which was to become New England, and tells the story of Gosnold's voyage. Some trace of the influence of Verrazano's *Letter,* lately published by Hakluyt, can be detected in it (B. F. De Costa, *New England Historical and Genealogical Register,* XXXII, 77–78). The pamphlet was well received and a second, augmented impression was called for within the year. It is to-day a work of extreme rarity; a copy of the later issue sold in 1926 for £2,200. The writing of this short discourse is Brierton's only significant connection with American affairs. In 1604 he was again at Lawshall (J. Venn, *op. cit.,* I, 135). In 1619 he was rector of Brightwell, Suffolk, a parish but a few miles from Grundisburgh, the home of Bartholomew Gosnold. The date of his death has not been ascertained.

[References cited above. H. S. Burrage, *Early English and French Voyages* (1906) reprints the *Relation.* British Museum Add. MS.. 19,120 f. 112. Walter Rye, *Calendars of the Freemen of Norwich 1317–1603* (1888); *Index to Norfolk Pedigrees* (1896); *Norfolk Families* (1913); W. Hudson and J. C. Tingey, *Records of the City of Norwich* (1910); a sketch of Brierton by J. Westby-Gibson in the *Dict. Nat. Biog.* (1886) is out of date.]   F. M—d.

BRIGGS, CHARLES AUGUSTUS (Jan. 15, 1841–June 8, 1913), clergyman and theological professor, was born in New York City, the son of Alanson and Sarah Mead (Berrian) Briggs. His father was a business man and the son grew up in easy circumstances. He took his college course at the University of Virginia. At the outbreak of the Civil War he served for a few months with the 7th Regiment of New York. He then entered Union Theological Seminary where he remained for two years. After a brief period in business he married, in 1865, Julia Valentine Dobbs of New York and went abroad for four years of theological study in Berlin. Returning to America in 1870 he became pastor of the Presbyterian Church of Roselle, N. J., and in 1874 professor of Hebrew and the cognate languages in Union Theological Seminary. Here he at once made himself felt and under his influence the Seminary became a notable center of Old Testament study. In 1890 a professorship of Biblical theology was founded in memory of Edward Robinson and Briggs became the first incumbent of the new chair. From its foundation Union Seminary, though Presbyterian in its affiliations, had been independent of all ecclesiastical control, but in 1870 at the time of the reunion of the old and new school wings of the Presbyterian Church the General Assembly of the reunited church in an access of good feeling had been given by the Seminary the right to veto appointments to its faculty. At his induction into the new professorship Dr. Briggs, already widely suspect on account of his work in Old Testament criticism, gave an address on the authority of Holy Scripture which deeply offended many conservatives. The result was the veto of his appointment by the General Assembly and his trial for heresy by the Presbytery of New York in 1892. The presbytery acquitted him but the prosecution appealed to the General Assembly which condemned him and suspended him from the ministry. After waiting for some years he took orders in the Episcopal Church and remained a clergyman of that church until his death. In the meantime the Seminary's board of directors declining to recognize the right of the General Assembly to veto the transfer of a professor from one chair to another within the faculty, retained Briggs in his professorship and severed relations with the Assembly. The Seminary thus became again wholly independent and a few years later completely undenominational. His trial for heresy was the most dramatic event of Briggs's career. It seemed to many a futile affair, having to do only with the question whether he was sound in the faith according to the Westminster standards, but the issue was really much broader, and though the decision went against him the trial proved a liberating influence for multitudes and marked an epoch in the history of American Presbyterianism.

In spite of his reputation for radicalism Briggs was thoroughly conservative except in the field of Biblical criticism. His faith in the historic doctrines of the church was profound and unwavering. In his later years, as often happens, he even became suspicious of his younger colleagues who departed further from the traditional faith than he had done. He was particularly sensitive in these years concerning the person of Christ and the Virgin Birth. In matters of Biblical criticism however he maintained his early attitude. The eagerness and energy of his mind were shown when in 1904 at the age of sixty-three he resigned the chair of Biblical theology and turned to the teaching of symbolics and irenics. He had long been deeply interested in church unity, writing frequently upon the subject and discussing it with dignitaries of the Roman Catholic Church as well as of other churches, for he envisaged the reunion of all Christendom, not merely of Protestantism. During his later life his studies were carried on largely with this end in view and his teaching followed similar lines.

To the end of his life he was an untiring worker. A bibliography of his books and articles published two years before his death contains nearly two hundred titles. Most important of the former is probably his *Critical and Exegetical Commentary on the Book of Psalms* published in 1906–07 in two volumes. He was one of the founders and for ten years an editor of the *Presbyterian Review*. For some time he added the duties of librarian to those of professor. The great growth of the McAlpin Collection of British history and theology in the library of Union Theological Seminary was mainly due to his untiring efforts through many years. He was an associate editor of the *Hebrew Lexicon,* of which Francis Brown was editor-in-chief, and the theological articles in that lexicon are mostly from his pen. In recognition of his share in this work he was given the degree of Litt.D. by the University of Oxford. Among the greatest of his services to the cause of Biblical and theological learning are two series—the International Critical Commentary and the International Theological Library—which he planned and edited and in which he had the coöperation of leading scholars.

Briggs had an extraordinarily fertile mind, teeming with ideas on all sorts of subjects. He was a rapid worker, of highly nervous temperament, often impatient of the slower mental processes of others. He held positive opinions and his emphatic enunciation of them made him many enemies, but he had a deeply affectionate nature and was loved as well as admired by a large circle of devoted friends. He died of pneumonia at his home on the Seminary quadrangle at the age of seventy-two, after nearly forty years of service as a professor.

Among the more important of Briggs's writings in addition to his commentary on the Psalms already mentioned, are *American Presbyterianism: Its Origin and Early History* (1885), *Messianic Prophecy* (1886), *The Messiah of the Gospels* (1894), *The Messiah of the Apostles* (1895), *General Introduction to the Study of Holy Scripture* (1899), *Church Unity* (1909), *Theological Symbolics* (1914), and a *History of the Study of Theology* (2 vols., 1916), prepared for publication by Emilie Grace Briggs, his daughter.

[A bibliography of Briggs's writings by Chas. R. Gillett was printed in the volume entitled *Essays in Modern Theology and Related Subjects* (1911) issued by pupils and friends of Dr. Briggs to commemorate his seventieth birthday. For biographical material see Henry Preserved Smith, "Chas. Augustus Briggs," in the *Am. Jour. of Theol.*, Oct. 1913; S. Briggs, *The Archives of the Briggs Family* (1880); obituary in the *N. Y. Times*, June 9, 1913. Publications relating to the Briggs controversy include: C. A. Briggs, *Response to the Charges and Specifications Submitted to the Presbytery of N. Y.* (c. 1891); *The Case against Prof. Briggs* 2 vols. (1892–93); *The Defence of Prof. Briggs before the Presbytery of N. Y.*, Dec. 13, 14, 15, 19, and 22, 1892 (1893). The Lib. of Union Sem. has an extensive file of material on the controversy.]   A.C.M.

BRIGGS, CHARLES FREDERICK (Dec. 30, 1804–June 20, 1877), journalist, author, was born on the island of Nantucket, Mass., the son of Jonathan C. and Sally (Coffin) Barrett Briggs. He early went to sea, sailing to Europe and South America on several voyages, but soon gave up the idea of being a sailor, and engaged in mercantile pursuits in New York. In 1839 he published a novel called *The Adventures of Harry Franco: A Tale of the Great Panic*, in which he made use of his experiences gained on the sea. In several subsequent works of fiction he used as a pseudonym the name of the hero of this first work. In 1843 he wrote *The Haunted Merchant* and the next year founded the *Broadway Journal*. Edgar Allan Poe was a contributor from the first number and soon was made associate editor along with Henry G. Watson, a musical critic. Briggs, with characteristic friendliness, began by admiring Poe and defending him against criticism, but could not long remain blind to his talented associate's temperamental peculiarities and weaknesses. He retired

from the *Journal* in 1845 and in the next two years published *Working a Passage*, another reminiscence of his sailor days, and *The Trippings of Tom Pepper*. Some of his friends were annoyed to recognize themselves in the latter book and the author thereupon determined to write no more fiction. In 1853 he became one of the editors of *Putnam's Magazine*, in association with Parke Godwin and George William Curtis. After three years the magazine suspended and when it resumed ten years later Briggs was again one of its editors. In the interim he was an editor of the *New York Times* under Henry J. Raymond, and during the latter's absence in Europe was given editorial charge of the paper. He held a position also in the New York Custom House during this period. In 1870 he was made financial editor of the *Brooklyn Union* by Henry C. Bowen and acted in that capacity for three years. Benjamin F. Tracy, who then bought the paper, made Briggs editor, but the latter soon left to join the editorial staff of the *Independent*, which Bowen also owned. Briggs served there until a few hours before his death, which came suddenly at his home in Brooklyn. He left a widow and one daughter. Among other activities he was one of the three men who composed the first Board of Commissioners for Central Park, and for twenty-four years he wrote the annual preface for Trow's *New York City Directory*. His association with Poe caused the publishers of the *Encyclopedia Britannica* to have him write the sketch of the poet for that work. He was a friend of James Russell Lowell, with whom he had considerable correspondence at a time when Poe was attacking Longfellow, and, less vigorously, Lowell himself on fancied grounds of plagiarism. Lowell in his *Fable for Critics*, which he presented to Briggs with the privilege of copyrighting it and enjoying the proceeds, gave a deservedly appreciative portrait of him under his pseudonym.

[Obituaries in the *Independent*, June 28, 1877, and in the *N. Y. Times*, *N. Y. Tribune*, *N. Y. Herald*, June 22, 1877.]   H.H.

BRIGGS, GEORGE NIXON (Apr. 12, 1796–Sept. 12, 1861), lawyer and statesman, was the eleventh child of Allen Briggs, a blacksmith notable in his community for his forceful character, and of Nancy Brown, who was of Huguenot descent. He was born at Adams, Mass., a town largely settled by Baptists from Rhode Island, but in 1803–05 resided at Manchester, Vt., and in 1805–13 at White Creek, N. Y. At the age of fourteen he was converted at a Baptist revival and at once began making religious appeals which were highly effective. Throughout his life much of his time was given to religious activity. He spent three years learning the hatter's trade. When asked, late in life, from what college he was graduated, he replied, "At a hatter's shop, madam." A year in a grammar school constituted the whole of his formal education. Assisted by one of his brothers he began the study of law in 1813 with Ambrose Kasson of Adams, Mass., but transferred his studies in 1814 to the office of Luther Washburn of Lanesboro, Mass. In May 1818 he married Harriet Hall, and in the following October was admitted to the bar. He first attracted attention by his defense of an Indian who was charged with murder. In 1824 he was elected town clerk of Lanesboro, and in 1826 he was appointed chairman of the commissioners of highways of Berkshire County. In 1830 he was elected to Congress, where he served from 1831 to 1843. In his youth he had been a Democrat, but in the break-up and reorganization of parties he followed Henry Clay on the protective tariff and became a Whig. In Congress he spoke infrequently, but was consistent in his opposition to the extension of slavery. His strongest speech in the House was delivered against the admission of Arkansas with a provision in its constitution forbidding the abolition of slavery without the consent of the slave-owners.

In 1843 he was the Whig candidate for governor of Massachusetts. No choice having been made by the people, he was elected by the legislature in January 1844. He was reëlected each year until 1851, when he received a plurality of the popular vote but was defeated before the legislature by George S. Boutwell. While he was governor, the Mexican War was fought. He strongly condemned it as unnecessary and unjust and believed it to have been entered upon for the purpose of extending slavery, but in spite of his disapproval, he coöperated loyally in supplying the troops which the federal government asked Massachusetts to furnish (*Address to the Legislature*, Jan. 12, 1847). He opposed the annexation of Texas, not only because it extended slavery but also because he questioned the power of Congress either to acquire foreign territory or to admit such territory to the Union. He also deprecated the mode of the annexation of Texas, and argued that annexation by a resolution of Congress was an invasion of the treaty-making power. He opposed the introduction of slavery into the territory acquired from Mexico and urged that the Massachusetts representatives in Congress should not consent to the admission of another slave-holding state. In state affairs his strongest interest was in education. He appreciated his own lack of academic training and

was a warm friend of the colleges. He supported the policies of Horace Mann and repeatedly called the attention of the legislature to the large number of children who never attended school and constantly urged it to provide greater educational facilities. In his first inaugural address, he used language which, in a slightly modified form, was given currency by Grover Cleveland. Briggs said: "Public offices are public trusts, created for the benefit of the whole people, and not for the benefit of those who may fill them." While he was governor the conviction of Professor Webster of the murder of Dr. Parkman occurred. Public sentiment strongly favored a pardon, but Gov. Briggs refused to interfere.

In 1851 he returned to the practise of law with his youngest son as a partner. In 1853 he was a member of the constitutional convention but his part was not conspicuous. In the same year he was appointed judge of the court of common pleas, the abolition of which in 1858 brought his official career to a close. On Sept. 4, 1861, he was appointed umpire in a dispute between the United States and New Granada. On the same day he received an accidental gunshot wound from which he died eight days later.

Briggs was active in the cause of temperance or total abstinence, and from 1856 to his death he was president of the American Temperance Union. He was the most prominent Baptist layman in the United States and from 1847 to his death he was president of the Baptist Missionary Union. He was a man of high character, and exceptional dignity and urbanity of manner.

[Wm. C. Richards, *Great in Goodness: A Memoir of Geo. N. Briggs, Governor of the Commonwealth of Mass. from 1844 to 1851* (1866), is written in a tone of unctuous piety and omits some of the most important phases of its subject's life. A sketch, not always accurate, by Jos. E. A. Smith, appears in *Memorial Biogs. New Eng. Hist. and Geneal. Soc.,* IV (1885), 297–328, and another by Rev. A. B. Whipple in the *Colls. Berkshire Hist. and Sci. Soc.,* II (1895), 151–81. See also Calvin Durfee, *Williams Coll. Biog. Annals* (1871) and S. Briggs, *Archives of The Briggs Family* (1880). Briggs's most important state papers are his seven inaugural addresses which are printed with the *Acts and Resolves* for the year in which they were delivered.]

L.B.E.

BRIGHAM, AMARIAH (Dec. 26, 1798–Sept. 8, 1849), physician, author, was the son of John Brigham of New Marlboro, Mass. On the death of his father when the boy was only eleven years of age, he was taken to live with an uncle, a physician, who promised to educate him as a doctor. Unfortunately his uncle died a year later so he was obliged to shift for himself and finally found a place in Albany as a clerk in a book-store, where he spent the next three years. Then he equipped himself as a doctor by study in the offices of Dr. E. C. Peet of New Marlboro and Dr. Plumb of Canaan, Conn., besides private study and a year spent in attending lectures in New York. At the end of this time, when almost twenty-one, he commenced practise in Enfield, but moved after two years to Greenfield, Mass., where he practised for seven years. At the end of this period he took a trip abroad but after some months of foreign travel returned to his practise in Greenfield. A little later inducements offered in Hartford caused him to remove thither. In 1837, growing tired of his strenuous practise, he went to New York to accept the professorship of anatomy and surgery in the College of Physicians and Surgeons, but remained only a year and a half, preferring his active life as a physician in Hartford. In 1840 he became a candidate for the office of physician and superintendent of the Retreat for the Insane in Hartford and received the position, only to relinquish it in the fall of 1842 for a similar appointment at the New York State Lunatic Asylum, where he founded the *American Journal of Insanity* in July 1844. There he remained until his death. His writings show him to have had a graceful diction. The first book he published, entitled *Remarks on the Influence of Mental Cultivation on Health* (1832), was designed to show the evil effects of beginning to cultivate children's minds too early. It was well received, reaching a third edition in this country, while Scotch editions issued in Glasgow and Edinburgh by Dr. Robert Macnish and James Simpson, Esq., had previously appeared abroad. In the same year, he also published *A Treatise on Epidemic Cholera* which contained little original matter but was published as a compendium of the existing knowledge of this disease, while in 1840 he wrote *An Inquiry Concerning the Diseases and Functions of the Brain, the Spinal Cord, and Nerves,* which soon found a ready sale and was favorably received by the profession. Some years previously he had written *Observations on the Influence of Religion on the Health of Mankind* (1835) which he hoped would have some influence in discouraging fanatical conduct inimical to the religion of Christ and injurious to the health and physical advancement of mankind. His last writing was published as a small duodecimo volume which was entitled the *Asylum Souvenir.* It consisted of aphorisms and maxims to aid in the restoration and preservation of health. He was married Jan. 23, 1833, to Susan C. Root of Greenfield.

[A good sketch of Brigham by E. K. Hunt is in *Lives of Eminent Am. Physicians and Surgeons* (1861), ed. by Sam. D. Gross, pp. 521–544. It was apparently separately printed in Utica in 1858, together with a sermon on the death of Dr. Brigham by Rev. Chauncey E. Goodrich, and a sketch of him by Chas. B. Coventry. See also *Am. Jour. Insanity,* VI, 185–192.]

W.R.S.

BRIGHAM, JOSEPH HENRY (Dec. 12, 1838–June 29, 1904), agriculturist, was born at Lodi, Ohio, the son of Winfield Scott and Mary Elizabeth (White) Brigham. When he was fourteen years old the family moved to a farm in Fulton County and there he grew to manhood and began a public career rather typical of the more successful who reached maturity in Ohio on the eve of the Civil War. When that struggle began he enlisted as a private in the 12th Ohio Volunteer Infantry, later becoming a captain in the 15th Ohio and still later a colonel in the 69th Ohio. He was married in 1863 to Edna Allman. Military prestige gave him civil leadership in the years following the war and although he returned to his farm he was seldom without some public office. Three times sheriff in his own county, he was, in 1880, elected to the state Senate and from that time to his death, through loyal service to the Republican party, he constantly held elective or appointive positions. In 1882 he was chosen a member of the state board of agriculture; in 1887 he was made a member of the board of control of the state experiment station and also of the board of trustees of the state university; in 1894 he was appointed a member of the board of managers of the Ohio penitentiary and in 1897 President McKinley called him to Washington as assistant secretary of agriculture. Consistently interested in agriculture, he always supervised his own farms and his greatest efforts in public life were for the improvement of the farmer. As state senator he was largely responsible for the establishment of the Ohio Agricultural Experiment Station; for three years he was president of the Wool Growers' and Sheep Breeders' Association; he was early active in the Patrons of Husbandry, rendering efficient service as an Institute lecturer; he served as the Worthy Master of the Ohio State Grange, and in 1889 became Worthy Master of the National Grange, an office to which he was reëlected four times. His services to the National Grange were particularly notable. His annual addresses were practical and his administration efficient. He urged the farmers to gain and keep control of the boards of the state experiment stations; he advocated rural free delivery of mails; he insisted that the state and national departments of agriculture should be kept close to the "dirt farmer" both in personnel and program. In the early 1890's when western farmers were inclined to seek relief from economic ills through union with the

Populist party, Brigham insisted on the "absolute political and religious freedom of the individual" within the order and denied the right of the group to bind the individual,—a move which probably saved the organization from dissension and ruin.

[T. C. Atkeson, *Semi-Centennial Hist. of the Patrons of Husbandry* (1916); *Semi-Centennial Hist. of the Ohio State Grange*; *Jours. of Proc. of the National Grange*; L. H. Bailey, *Cyc. Am. Agriculture* (1907–09); *Evening Star* (Washington), June 30, 1904. See also W. I. T. Brigham, *Hist. of the Brigham Family* (1907).]   A.O.C.

BRIGHAM, MARY ANN (Dec. 6, 1829–June 29, 1889), educator, was born at Westboro, Mass., the daughter of Dexter and Mary Ann (Gould) Brigham. The first of her ancestors in this country is thought to have been Thomas Brigham who came from London to New England in 1635. She was educated at Mount Holyoke Seminary. For some years she taught a private school in her father's house in Westboro, and from 1855 to 1858 instructed at Mount Holyoke. For the next five years she was principal of Ingham University at Leroy, N. Y., and from 1863 until her death in 1889 she was associate principal with Dr. Charles E. West at Brooklyn Heights Seminary. She was chosen to be the first president of Mount Holyoke College after the change from a seminary to an institution of the standing of the other women's colleges in the East, Smith, Vassar, and Wellesley, but she was killed in a railroad wreck near New Haven two months before she was to have taken office. She was a woman of fine personality, both as a teacher and as a friend, with unusual executive ability and scholarship. She had done much to make Brooklyn Heights Seminary, where she had charge of the senior department, a notable school, and it was in recognition of these qualities that she was called to Mount Holyoke. She had been offered the presidency of Wellesley as well as professorships at Smith, Wellesley, and other colleges. Mary Brigham Cottage, one of the dormitories at Mount Holyoke, was named in her honor.

[Catalogues and files of Brooklyn Heights Sem.; letters from Frank W. Forbes of Westboro, Mass., containing information in the Westboro Lib., and from Sidney V. Lowell of Brooklyn, whose daughter was a student of Miss Brigham's; *N. Y. Tribune*, June 30, 1889; *Morning Jour. and Courier* (New Haven), July 1, 1889. See also W. I. T. Brigham, *Hist. of the Brigham Family* (1907).]   M.A.K.

BRIGHT, EDWARD (Oct. 6, 1808–May 17, 1894), Baptist editor, was born in Kington, a market town of Herefordshire on the Welsh border of England. In his childhood his parents emigrated to America, settling in Utica, N. Y., where the senior Edward Bright carried on for a time the business of brewer and maltster, and later opened a tannery. The younger Edward was set to learn a trade, became an expert printer, and as his first business venture he joined the partnership of Bennet & Bright in a publishing enterprise. This was successful, but Bright's religious convictions led him to believe that he ought to enter the ministry of the church, and in 1839 he was licensed to preach. The following year he was ordained, and became pastor of the Bleecker Street Baptist Church, in Utica. As a Baptist he was a loyal denominationalist. He had grown to manhood during a time when the polemical disposition was indulged by champions of different phases of religious opinions, and the rapid growth of the Baptists and their distinctive practises occasioned general criticism. Bright never flinched in defense of his faith. After a brief pastorate his well-known interest in missions made him considered for an official position in the missionary society, and he was elected foreign secretary of the American Baptist Missionary Union with headquarters in Boston. Here his editorial ability had a chance to appear in the production of the serial numbers of the *Baptist Missionary Magazine*.

In 1855 he went to New York and purchased a Baptist newspaper called the *Register*. He changed its name to the *Examiner*. The paper became under his editorial supervision the organ of the Baptist churches in a section of the country which had a commanding influence, and he gave the paper a standing second to none in his own denomination. He conceived it to be his mission to help bear the responsibilities of the denomination through its various organizations. He took a special interest in the activities of the New York State Convention. He was a trustee of the University of Rochester and of Vassar College; he sat on various boards and committees; he was devoted to the missionary and educational affairs of the denomination; he made all its interests the weekly concern of his journal. Sometimes he was criticized; he did not hesitate to criticize others sharply. His forceful manner at times created antagonisms, but his heart was friendly and sympathetic. The paper for which he was responsible never hedged on public questions. The editor had his convictions, expressed them freely, and was ready to back them up if assailed. The *Examiner* won general recognition throughout the East as a thoroughly representative paper, and it absorbed several other sheets whose circulation was limited by their local character. Bright was married twice: first, to Adeline Osborn of Homer, N. Y., and second, to Anna Leslie Reid, of Rochester.

[*Proc. N. Y. Bapt. State Convention,* 1859, pp. 40–42; M. M. Bragg, *The Pioneers of Utica* (1877); Pomroy Jones, *Annals and Recollections of Oneida County* (1851); obituaries in the *N. Y. Times, N. Y. Herald, N. Y. Tribune,* May 18, 1894.]   H. K. R.

BRIGHT, JAMES WILSON (Oct. 2, 1852–Nov. 29, 1926), philologist, was born at Aaronsburg, Pa., the son of Samuel and Eve Margaret Bright. Samuel Bright died when James was very young, leaving his widow and children in rather straitened circumstances. Nevertheless, James went to college, graduating in 1877 from Lafayette, where he had studied under Prof. Francis A. March who was then, next to Child, the best Anglicist in America. His interest in philology aroused, he did graduate work at the Johns Hopkins University, where he was a Fellow in 1880–82. There he studied English, Old Saxon, and Icelandic under Cook and Wood, German and Gothic under Brandt, and Sanskrit under Lanman; and was granted the degree of Ph.D. in 1882. Immediately he was appointed assistant in German and during the year 1882–83 the English and German departments, which logically belong together, were combined, Bright giving courses in Old High German and in the German classical authors. In 1883–84 Bright went to Germany and studied three semesters under Sievers, Paul, and Ten Brink. He returned to America in the latter year, eager to establish a seminary with training such as he had himself secured in Germany. He was made Fellow by courtesy (1884–85) and substituted for Prof. Corson at Cornell during January and February 1885. From March to May he lectured at Johns Hopkins on historical English grammar, and won for himself an instructorship in English. The English department now established its independence and quickly became a center of research in English philology. Bright was one of the pioneers of graduate work in America. He gave his students a sound philological training and was a master of scientific method. He became professor in 1893 and was Caroline Donovan Professor of English Literature from 1905 to 1925, when he retired as professor emeritus. In these years in addition to his own contributions and his editorial work he trained fifty-five doctors of philosophy in English, most of whom hold important professorships to-day in all parts of America.

Bright was one of the original board of editors of *Modern Language Notes* (1886–1915), and was editor-in-chief 1916–25. He gave much of his time to shaping its ideals and to bringing the contributions to a high standard of scholarship. He was also an editor of *Hesperia,* a member of the advisory board of *Modern Philology,* a member of the editorial committee of the Modern Language Association (1904–14), and editor-in-chief of the Albion Series of Anglo-Saxon and Middle English Poetry. He was author and editor of an *Anglo-Saxon Reader,* and *Outlines of Anglo-Saxon Grammar* (1891); *Gospel of St. Luke in Anglo-Saxon* (1893); *St. Matthew in West-Saxon* (1904); *St. John in West-Saxon* (1904); *St. Mark in West-Saxon* (1905); *St. Luke in West-Saxon* (1906). He was joint author of *West-Saxon Psalms* (1907), and *Elements of English Versification* (1910). He was also a contributor of scholarly articles and reviews in the field of English to many philological journals. A member of many learned societies, he was secretary for America of the Early English Text Society and of the Chaucer Society, secretary (1893–1901) and president (1902–03) of the Modern Language Association, and a vice-president of the Simplified Spelling Society of London.

Bright will always be remembered as the founder of a new scientific era in English philology, one who established a new standard in the study of English. His publications in the field of Anglo-Saxon and of the West-Saxon Gospels are models of exact research and of severe scholarship. He was himself a hard taskmaster and a tireless worker. He lived all his life as a graduate student. He never married, though he had an attractive personality,—a man of average height and build with bright gray eyes and light brown hair and mustache. He belonged to the University Club of Baltimore but was a member of few social clubs, though he was in demand in social circles. Coming of Pennsylvania German stock he was always thrifty, serious, and studious, and managed to amass a fortune of more than $160,000 which he left to his relatives, selling most of his books to Goucher College.

[Records of Johns Hopkins Univ.; *Who's Who in America,* 1926–27; *Modern Language Notes,* XLI (1926), pp. v–vi; *Modern Philology,* XXIV (1927), pp. 351–52; *Johns Hopkins Alumni Mag.,* XV (1927), pp. 121–28. A portrait of Bright hangs in Gilman Hall, Johns Hopkins University.]   D. M. R.

BRIGHT, JESSE DAVID (Dec. 18, 1812–May 20, 1875), politician, was the son of David Graham and Rachel (Graham) Bright (A. G. Green, *Historical Sketch of the Bright Family,* 1900). He was born at the village of Norwich, Chenango County, N. Y., a New England settlement on the upper waters of the Susquehanna. With his father, two brothers, Michael G. and George M., and a sister he moved to Madison, Ind., in 1820. His rather limited education was obtained in the public schools. At the age of twenty-two he became probate judge, succeeding Joseph G. Marshall and serving from Aug. 9, 1834 to Mar. 26, 1839 (L. J. Monks, *Courts and Lawyers of Indiana*, 1916). In 1841 he succeeded Gamaliel Taylor as United States marshal of the Indiana district court but almost immediately had to give way to a Whig, Robert Hanna. When in the same year the Internal Improvement trouble disrupted the Whig party, Bright appeared as a state senator from Jefferson County, serving two sessions. From 1843 to 1845 he was lieutenant-governor; he represented the pro-slavery and Gov. Whitcomb the anti-slavery wing of the Democratic party. By careful manipulation of the state Senate he was elected United States senator Mar. 6, 1845; re-elected Jan. 11, 1851, and Feb. 4, 1857. On Mar. 1, 1861, he addressed a letter of introduction "To His Excellency Jefferson Davis, President of the Confederation of States." The bearer of the letter was arrested, and Bright was expelled from the Senate, Feb. 5, 1862, after a debate of twenty days participated in by thirty-three senators. The vote was 32 to 14 and was based perhaps as much on personal and political opposition as on the charge of treason. Bright returned home and stood for reëlection or vindication. The Assembly was Democratic but refused to support him. He therefore retired to a farm which he owned in Kentucky. Later he represented Trimble and Carroll counties in the Kentucky legislature. He owned coal mines on the Kanawha River and in 1874 moved to Baltimore where he died May 20, 1875. He was survived by his wife, Mary E. Turpin, whom he had married about 1840.

Bright was of robust figure, inclined to corpulency, clean-shaven, with large head, black hair and eyes, and wide mouth. He was a man of quick decisions and swift actions. He was a courteous, obliging friend and an implacable enemy; a companion and friend of Clay, Webster, and Breckinridge; an out-spoken enemy of Douglas, Sumner, and Seward. He was a reliable, voting senator, took care of his constituents, but rarely if ever rose to the level of statesmanship.

[W. W. Woollen, *Biog. and Hist. Sketches of Early Ind.* (1883); O. H. Smith, *Early Ind. Trials and Sketches* (1858); *Ind. House and Senate Journals*; *Cong. Globe*; *Indiana State Jour.*, esp. May 21, 1875; *Indianapolis Jour.*, May 21, 1875.]   L. E.

BRIGHT EYES (1854–May 26, 1903), an advocate of Indian rights, was an Omaha, born on the Nebraska reservation, and bore the name of Susette La Flesche. Her father, Joseph La Flesche (Iron Eye, or Inshtamaza, *c.* 1818–88), head chief of the tribe, was the son of a French trader, Joseph La Flesche, who had married an Omaha woman about 1817. Iron Eye, who had some schooling in St. Louis, was a steadfast counselor of "the white man's way" among his people, and he warmly seconded his daughter's efforts toward an education. Susette attended the Presbyterian mission school on the reservation and through the interest of one of her instructors was sent to a private school in Elizabeth, N. J., where she qualified as a teacher. On her return she taught in a government day school on the reservation, where she is said to have exercised a stimulating influence on her pupils. In 1879, through a dramatic episode in Indian history, she came into prominence. The Poncas, a kindred tribe to the Omahas, living on a reservation in South Dakota claimed by the Sioux, had been forcibly removed by the government in 1877 and taken to the Indian Territory. In their new home they suffered greatly from privation and illness, many of them dying. Susette and her father visited them in the following year, giving them such aid as they could afford, and on returning made public an account of their sufferings which awakened much sympathy. Early in 1879 the chief of the Poncas, Machunazha, or Standing Bear, and thirty-four followers, including women and children, left the Territory and started north. After a six-hundred-mile journey, in which they underwent great suffering, they arrived among the Omahas late in March. They were at once arrested by the military, taken to Fort Omaha and ordered to be sent back. Two men on the editorial staff of the *Omaha Herald*—Thomas H. Tibbles [*q.v.*], later to become prominent as a Populist editor and a candidate for vice-president (1904), and W. L. Carpenter—immediately interested themselves in the case and enlisted the services of two leading attorneys of the state, who brought a *habeas corpus* proceeding before Judge Elmer S. Dundy, in the federal district court. The case was tried Apr. 30 and resulted in a decision giving the Poncas their freedom. Encouraged by the victory and at the same time apprehensive of reprisals on the part of the so-called "Indian ring," friends of the Indians thereupon proposed a movement to awaken the public interest. Under the management of Mr. Tibbles, Susette (who now, apparently at the suggestion of others, adopted the distinctively Indian name Inshtatheamba, or Bright Eyes), her brother Francis (later to win distinction as an ethnologist), and Standing Bear made a speaking tour of the East. They attracted great attention and doubtless contributed in no small measure to the abandonment of the policy of arbitrary removals of Indian tribes.

In 1881 Bright Eyes was married to Mr. Tibbles. Later she traveled with him to Scotland, where she made several addresses. She coöperated with her husband in his editorial and political work and was especially active as a writer. She edited, with an introduction, an anonymous narrative, *Ploughed Under, The Story of an Indian Chief,* which was published in 1881 and was widely reviewed. As a writer she was clear and cogent, and as a speaker she was forceful and eloquent, with a manner and bearing of native grace and dignity. Her later years were lived mainly at Lincoln. She died on the reservation, near Bancroft.

[Article by Alice Cunningham Fletcher in *Handbook of Am. Indians* (1907), ed. by F. W. Hodge; Zylyff (Thos. H. Tibbles), *The Ponca Chiefs: An Indian Attempt to Appeal from the Tomahawk to the Courts* (1879); incidental material in Alice Cunningham Fletcher and Francis La Flesche, *The Omaha Tribe* (27th Ann. Report of the Bureau of Ethnology, 1905–06); *Omaha World Herald,* May 28, 1903.] W. J. G.

BRIGHTLY, FREDERICK CHARLES (Aug. 26, 1812–Jan. 24, 1888), lawyer, author, was a native of Bungay, in the county of Suffolk, England, where his father, Henry A. Brightly, was a stereotyper and publisher. He was educated privately, with a view to adopting a naval career, and when quite young served as a midshipman in the East Indian trade, studying navigation in 1829 with J. W. Norie of London. In 1831 he emigrated to the United States, settled in Philadelphia, took up the study of law, and was admitted to the bar in 1839. Devoting much attention to the early history of Pennsylvania, he soon was recognized as an authority on legal questions arising from incidents of the old régime. At the same time he established a reputation for reliability, mainly through an infinite capacity for taking pains, and gradually acquired an extensive practise, chiefly of a consultative nature. In 1847 he published a practical treatise on *The Law of Costs in Pennsylvania,* which was followed by *Reports of Cases decided by the Judges of the Supreme Court of Pennsylvania in the Court of Nisi Prius at Philadelphia and in the Supreme Court, 1809–1851* (1851). His practise was now demanding the greater portion of his time, despite which he prepared a work of intrinsic merit, *The Equitable Jurisdiction of the Courts of Pennsylvania* (1855). The first volume of his *Analytical Digest of the Laws of the United States* appeared in 1858, the second volume, delayed till 1869, bringing the digest up to the latter date. The cordial reception accorded to his books now induced him to retire from practise and confine himself to the literary side of the law. From 1868 onward he compiled a

series of works, which, because of their accuracy, completeness, and lucidity of statement, commanded the confidence of the Pennsylvania bar and obtained a vogue beyond the confines of that state. First came a *Digest of the Decisions of the Federal Courts from the Organization of the Government* (1868), a second volume of which appeared in 1873, followed by *The Bankrupt Law of the United States* (1869); *Leading Cases on the Law of Elections in the United States* (1871); *The Constitution of Pennsylvania as Amended in 1874* (1874); *Digest of the Decisions of the Courts of the State of Pennsylvania, 1754–1877* (2 vols., 1877), and two later volumes bringing the work down to 1891; and *Digest of Decisions of the Courts of the State of New York from the Earliest Period to 1875* (1877), which later was brought down to the year 1884 in a subsequent volume. He also edited the eighth edition of Binn's *Justice or Magistrates Daily Companion* (1870). Another valuable contribution was his work on a well-known text, *Digest of the Laws of Pennsylvania from the Year 1700,* by John Purdon, Jr. He edited the eighth edition in 1853, the ninth edition in 1861, and the tenth edition in 1873, the digest being brought up to date in the intermediate years by annual supplements. He had maintained his interest in the early history of Pennsylvania, and assembled a very valuable library bearing upon this subject. His collection of Pennsylvania laws, colonial and republican, was the most complete in existence. They included The Second Bradford (1728) Laws of Pennsylvania, all the Franklin and Dunlap Laws, complete sets of the Pamphlet Laws, the Ordinances of Philadelphia, and a unique collection of rare legal periodicals.

In 1835 Brightly was married to Sarah Corfield, sister of William Corfield, with whom he had studied law. Shortly after his marriage he became a Catholic and was a prominent figure during the anti-Catholic riots of 1844. The latter years of his life he spent principally at Germantown, where he died.

[In 1885 Brightly published *Bibliotheca Brightliensis,* a descriptive catalogue of his library, some of the notes to which are autobiographic in character. A short obituary notice appeared in the *Am. Ann. Cyc. and Reg.,* 1888, p. 625. See also obituaries in Phila. papers, especially the *Public Ledger,* Jan. 25, 1888.] H. W. H. K.

BRILL, NATHAN EDWIN (Jan. 13, 1859–Dec. 13, 1925), physician, was born in the city of New York where he spent his entire life. He was the son of Simon Brill, a native of Lichtenfeld, Germany, and Adelheid Frankenthal, who was born in Fuerth, Germany. His early education was received in the public schools of New

York City and at the College of the City of New York where he received his A.B. degree in 1877, at the age of seventeen, and his M.A. in 1883. He graduated in medicine in 1880 from the medical department of New York University. During his last year as a medical student, and the first year after his graduation he served as an interne in Bellevue Hospital. About this time he came under the influence of the well-known neuro-anatomist, Edward A. Spitzka, under whom he accomplished at least one good piece of original work. In 1893 he was appointed attending physician to Mt. Sinai Hospital, and for the succeeding thirty years he served that institution faithfully and assiduously, taking a great personal interest in his patients and building up his professional experience, which eventually led to his recognition as one of the leading diagnosticians of his day. He was primarily a clinician, though he by no means disparaged the value of laboratory work. As Dr. Sachs remarks in his brief biography, he was of the opinion that the actual study of the patient at the bedside was of greater importance than any other procedure in practical medicine.

Throughout his life Brill was interested not only in clinical medicine but in public health as well. He also played his part in the administrative aspects of hospital work and in the work of medical institutions, notably the New York Academy of Medicine. Beginning in 1910, he published a series of articles concerning a febrile disease of infectious origin, which was of fairly frequent occurrence in New York City. His description of this condition was so clear-cut that others readily recognized it, and it very quickly became known as Brill's Disease. Subsequently, largely through the efforts of the late Dr. Gedide A. Friedman, it was shown that it was a modified form of typhus fever and that cases were not confined to New York City but had appeared in other cities along the Atlantic seaboard. Brill did valuable work in other fields, notably in connection with diseases of the blood-forming organs. He was one of the first to introduce into this country the operation of splenectomy for thrombocytopenic purpura. He was the first, with his colleague, Dr. Mandelbaum, to put on a firm footing the pathological anatomy and clinical features of the curious and rare disease first described by the French physician, Gaucher.

Brill was a large man, who gave the impression of strength and vitality. One of his biographers describes his nature as diffident, almost repellent. To the writer he always appeared as a genial, charming gentleman, who held his opinions with decided tenacity and was always ready to fight for them. Even after he developed the first signs of the disease which ultimately destroyed him, and had had half his larynx removed, he had the courage to continue to attend medical meetings and to take part in discussions in spite of the fact that he was only able to talk in a whisper. When the growth in his larynx recurred and ultimately rendered him entirely voiceless he accepted his lot with fortitude. He was married, on June 8, 1899, to Elsa M. Josephthal, of New York.

[*Bull. of the N. Y. Acad. of Medicine,* ser. II, vol. II (1926), p. 42; Bernard Sachs, *Seventy-Fourth Annual Report of the Mt. Sinai Hospital,* 1926, p. 50; A. A. Berg, *City College Alumnus,* vol. XXII, 1926, p. 391; *Who's Who in America,* 1924–25; personal acquaintance; dates of birth and marriage from a brother, Henry S. Brill.]
G. B.

BRINCKLÉ, WILLIAM DRAPER (Feb. 9, 1798–Dec. 16, 1862), physician, pomologist, was born at St. Jones' Neck, Kent County, Del. The family of Brincklé or Brinckloe were early settlers in that region, and the first John Brinckloe was lieutenant-colonel of the Kent County militia in 1756. His descendant, John Brincklé, a country doctor, married Elizabeth Gordon, the niece and adopted daughter of Cæsar Rodney, one of the signers of the Declaration of Independence, and William Draper Brincklé was their fifth child. He attended Wilmington Academy, graduated from Princeton in 1816, and in 1819 received his M.D. from the University of Pennsylvania. He began the practise of medicine in Wilmington, but in 1825 settled in Philadelphia, where he was active in the profession over thirty years. From 1827 to 1839 he was physician to the City Hospital, devoted to contagious diseases, and in 1832 was distinguished for his efficiency in an epidemic of Asiatic cholera. In 1859, failing health compelled him to resign his practise, and he died at Groveville, N. J., in 1862. Brincklé was twice married: in 1821, to Sarah T. Physick, niece of Dr. Philip Syng Physick of the University of Pennsylvania, who died in 1830; and in 1832, to Elizabeth Bispham Reeves, daughter of Benjamin Reeves of Philadelphia, who died at Groveville in 1858. Though his success in medicine, as measured by his practise, was considerable, Brincklé's claim to distinction rests chiefly on his work as a pomologist. He originated many varieties of fruits, besides introducing to public notice many others discovered in a state of nature, or valuable old varieties in danger of extinction. Owing to limitations of time and space he worked particularly on small fruits and pears, his experiments with the latter winning for him the name of the "American Van Mons." In one year he raised

254 strawberry seedlings, forty-three of which fruited and were described by him, with their parentage and characteristics, in the *Farmers' Cabinet* (XI, 53–57, 1846). He was a frequent contributor to the *Horticulturist,* founded by A. J. Downing, and he prepared the descriptions for *Hoffy's North American Pomologist,* a collection of colored plates of fruits published by Alfred Hoffy, a Philadelphia engraver, of which only Book I (1860) was ever issued. Most of the fruits originated by Brincklé have been superseded by newer varieties, but his work itself is valuable for the accuracy with which he performed his experiments and recorded his observations. In this scientific attitude toward fruit breeding, as also in adoption of the systematic nomenclature which was just beginning to replace the former haphazard methods of description, he was one of the foremost horticulturists of his day. He was one of the founders of the American Pomological Society, an active member of the Pennsylvania Horticultural Society, and honorary member of other leading pomological societies.

[Emile B. Gardette, *Biog. Memoir of Wm. Draper Brincklé* (1863); biographical notices, mostly signed by initials only, in *Gardener's Monthly,* ed. by Thos. Meehan, vol. V; Brincklé's own articles in *Farmers' Cabinet* and *Horticulturist* (1846–60); *Cyc. Am. Horticulture* (1900), ed. by L. H. Bailey, I, 180, and *Standard Cyc. Horticulture* (1915), III, 1566, give sketches by Wilhelm Miller, evidently based in part on information in *Gardener's Monthly,* 1863, but giving date of Brincklé's death incorrectly as 1863. Another briefer note, in Bailey, *Cyc. Am. Ag.* (1909), IV, 557, refers to the *Cyc. Am. Horticulture* and contains same error in date of death.] M. F. W.

BRINKERHOFF, JACOB (Aug. 31, 1810– July 19, 1880), jurist and legislator, was the eldest son of Henry I. Brinkerhoff and Rachel Bevier, the father a member of an old Dutch family of New York, the mother of Huguenot ancestry (Roeliff and T. Van Wyck Brinkerhoff, *Family of Joris D. Brinckerhoff,* 1887, pp. 11–13, 67). Brinkerhoff was born at Niles, N. Y., and attended the public schools of his native town and the academy of Prattsburg, N. Y. He studied law for two years in a law office in Bath, N. Y. In 1836 he moved to Mansfield, Ohio, where he began the practise of law. He was twice married: to Caroline Campbell of Lodi, N. Y., and after her death, to Marion Titus of Detroit. His public life consisted of two terms as prosecutor of Richland County, two terms as a Democratic member of the House of Representatives (1843–47), and three terms in the supreme court of Ohio (1856–71). In Congress he was identified with a small group of northwestern Democrats, advocates of a low tariff, expansionists, and Free-Soilers. He proposed an amendment to the joint resolution for the annexation of Texas, providing that, "as a fundamental condition, . . . the existence of slavery shall be forever prohibited in one-half of all the annexed territory" (*Congressional Globe,* 28 Cong., 2 Sess., p. 192). This amendment failing, Brinkerhoff voted against the resolution. On the Oregon question he defended the claim of the United States to the whole territory. "We do not want war," he exclaimed, "but if we must have it, we would a great deal rather fight Great Britain than some other Powers, for we do not love her" (*Ibid.,* 29 Cong., 1 Sess., pp. 203 ff.). When President Polk asked for $2,000,000 to negotiate peace with Mexico, Brinkerhoff supported an amendment to prohibit slavery in the acquired territory. The facts in his contention of twenty years later that he was the author of the Wilmot Proviso are shrouded in some doubt. It is quite possible that he may have suggested to Wilmot in part or in entirety the particular verbal form of the proposed amendment (see Brinkerhoff's statement in Congress, Feb. 10, 1847, *Ibid.,* 29 Cong., 2 Sess., p. 377). The Proviso attached to the Two Million Bill in Wilmot's handwriting is in the Manuscript Division of the Library of Congress. Brinkerhoff's alleged original draft, the evidence for his part, has unfortunately been lost (C. B. Going, *David Wilmot,* 1924, ch. ix). Brinkerhoff again became a conspicuous opponent of slavery when the Oberlin rescue cases came before the supreme court of Ohio, 1859. The court sustained the Fugitive Slave Law, the vote of the judges being three to two. Brinkerhoff wrote a dissenting opinion, falling back upon the strict construction theory, and so denying to Congress the power to legislate upon the subject of fugitives from labor (*Ex parte Bushnell, ex parte Langston,* IX *Critchfield's Ohio State Reports,* 221– 29). Through the period of the slavery controversy Brinkerhoff passed from the ranks of the anti-slavery Democrats to the Free-Soil party and then to the Republican party. In 1872 he strongly indorsed the Liberal Republican movement (see *Chicago Tribune,* Feb. 12, 1872). Little is known of his personal traits or his private life. He had a local reputation as a public speaker of more than average ability, quick at repartee, having read much and possessing a remarkable memory (A. A. Graham, *History of Richland County,* 1880, pp. 381–82).

[In addition to references given above, see obituary in *Ohio Liberal* (Mansfield), vol. VIII, No. 14; and *The Recollections of a Life Time* (1900), by Gen. Roeliff Brinkerhoff.] E. J. B.

BRINKERHOFF, ROELIFF (June 28, 1828– June 4, 1911), lawyer, banker, penologist, was descended through his father, George Brinkerhoff, from Joris Brinckerhoff who came to this country from Holland in 1638; and through his mother, Jacomyntie Bevier, from a Huguenot refugee who came in 1650. Roeliff, the youngest of nine children, was born on a farm by the side of Owasco Lake, Cayuga County, N. Y. Outdoor life in central New York, a region of remarkable beauty, taught him many lessons and made of a weakly child a strong healthy man and a lover of nature as well. Eight years in the district school, a year in an academy in Auburn, another at a more famous academy in Homer, N. Y., completed his formal school work. For two years he taught in district schools near his father's farm. A cousin living in Tennessee attracted him to the South. In 1846–47, Roeliff, then eighteen years of age, taught in a planter's private school near Nashville. Then for two years he was a tutor in the family of Andrew Jackson, Jr., at the Hermitage. His work left him ample time for reading in the library of Gen. Jackson. More than three years in the South were a happy experience and a liberalizing education for this particular northern boy. In the summer of 1849 he entered the office of an uncle in Mansfield, Ohio, for the study of law, and three years later he was admitted to the bar. He was soon drawn from the practise of law into journalism as editor and then owner of the *Mansfield Herald* (1855), and from that into the army (1861). Senator Sherman returned to Mansfield in the summer of 1861 to recruit two new regiments and persuaded Brinkerhoff to accept a place in one of them, as quartermaster with the rank of captain. He was in the quartermaster service five years, becoming brigadier-general toward the end. During this service he published a military manual, *The Volunteer Quartermaster* (1865). As a newspaper editor he had become actively interested in politics. Though formerly a Democrat, he was drawn into the Republican party on the slave issue. During the war he spoke often at Union meetings. After the war he returned to civil life, law, and politics. A traditional dislike for protective tariffs made him a restless Republican. In the campaign in Ohio in 1869 he raised the issue of tariff reform. One result was a series of speeches throughout the Middle West in 1869–70 under the auspices of the Free Trade League of New York. He took a conspicuous part in the Liberal Republican movement of 1872, attending the Cincinnati convention and later the New York Conference of tariff reformers. In the following campaign Brinkerhoff was chairman of the executive committee for the Liberal Republicans of Ohio. He was at heart a Jeffersonian and after the defeat of Republican liberalism he returned to the Democratic party.

In 1873, with a neighbor, Mr. Harter, he established the Mansfield Savings Bank. His life as a banker left him leisure to devote to philanthropy and penology. In 1873, he was appointed to the Ohio Board of State Charities. He was a regular attendant upon the meetings of the National Conference of Charities and Corrections and frequently participated in its programs. In 1883, he became a member of the National Prison Association, and after the death of Ex-President Hayes (1893), Brinkerhoff succeeded him in the presidency. He was vice-president of the International Prison Congress which met in Paris in 1895. An interest in archæology and pioneer history led him to take the initiative in founding the Ohio Archæological and Historical Society, of which he was president for fifteen years.

Brinkerhoff was married on Feb. 3, 1852, to Mary Lake Bently, by whom he had two sons and two daughters.

[The chief source is Brinkerhoff's autobiography, *Recollections of a Lifetime* (1900). This is more than personal reminiscences; it is a valuable commentary on men and events by a keen observer of wide acquaintance. Articles on Brinkerhoff appear in the *Ohio Archæol. and Hist. Quart.*, IX (1900), and XX (1911). For genealogy see *The Family of Joris Dircksen Brinckerhoff* (1887), comp. by Roeliff Brinkerhoff. There is a good obituary in the *Mansfield Shield*, June 5, 1911.]

E. J. B.

BRINTON, DANIEL GARRISON (May 13, 1837–July 31, 1899), anthropologist, was born at Thornbury, Pa., of English Quaker descent, the son of Lewis and Ann (Garrison) Brinton. Prepared for college by the Rev. William E. Moore, he entered Yale College in 1854. As an undergraduate he soon made a mark in literary activities, taking two prizes in English composition. The winter of 1856–57 he spent in Florida, doubtless laying the foundation for his future work. In 1857 he again distinguished himself in literature at Yale, and in 1858 received the degree of A.B. He then entered the Jefferson Medical College and graduated with the degree of M.D. in 1861. He spent a year studying at Heidelberg and Paris, and returned to West Chester, Pa., where he practised medicine. He entered the Federal army in the summer of 1862 as acting assistant surgeon. His services soon won recognition and he was rapidly promoted. He was present in many of the great battles of the Civil War, including Chancellorsville and Gettysburg. In the fall of 1863 he suffered a sunstroke, was compelled to relinquish active field-duty, and took up hospital work. He remained in the army till Aug. 5, 1865, when he was discharged with the brevet rank of lieutenant-colonel of volunteers, and on Sept. 28, of the same year, he married Sarah Tillson of Quincy, Ill. He returned to West Chester and resumed his medical practise, till he moved to Philadelphia, becoming assistant editor of the *Medical and Surgical Reporter* in 1867, and editor in 1874. He retired in 1887 to pursue the subjects dearest to him. His first work, *Notes on the Floridian Peninsula* (1859), foreshadowed where his true interests lay. In 1867 he resumed his publication of papers on Americana. In 1884 he became professor of ethnology and archeology in the Academy of Natural Sciences of Philadelphia, and in 1886 professor of American linguistics and archeology in the University of Pennsylvania. He never was a field worker and remained a closet anthropologist, apparently never feeling the necessity of coming into close contact with primitive peoples. On the other hand he delved into the libraries of Europe as well as of this country. It is also to be remarked that he utilized the results of field workers in his writings and spoke appreciatively of them. Possibly his lack of field work was due to his view that he had never fully recovered from the sunstroke which he suffered in the Civil War. It is true that his methods are not the methods of to-day. It is also true that some of his theses have been discarded, such as the denial of Asiatic (Mongolian) origin of American Indians and the affirmation of their derivation from Europe, the conviction that polysynthesis and nominal-incorporation were characteristic of all American Indian languages, that elaborate grammatical categories were the late fruit of the human intellect, and that the Lettic peoples in both appearance and language are a connecting link between the Slavonic and Teutonic peoples. It is also true that his translations from Aztec are inaccurate. His dismissal of the Toltecs as being largely purely legendary has not withstood the test of time. Undeniably no one to-day would defend his position that the likeness of Iroquoian and Algonquian mythology (and similarly in other cases) was due to the sameness of the human mind, and not the diffusion. On the other hand his first work, *Notes on the Floridian Peninsula* (1859) remains to this day of the highest value. His exposure of the fraudulent character of the famous (or rather infamous) Taensa grammar alone would win a place for him among scientists. His *The American Race* (1891) was the first systematic classification of the aboriginal languages of both North and South America. Though based on materials which are hardly ade-

quate, this work shows a keen insight regarding the genetic relationships of American Indian languages and in some cases anticipated what has since been established. In this connection it may be said that he was the first to point out the relationship of Natchezan to Muskogean, though afterward he apparently was doubtful of it. His contention that Serian and Yuman are genetically related is gaining acceptance even if rigorous proof has not yet been furnished. His *Library of Aboriginal American Literature* is especially worth noting, for at that time unfortunately American aboriginal literature was presented in literary English, not in text and translation. The publication of his "Maya Chronicles" (Volume I of his *Library*) in 1882, by itself would establish his reputation. All of these (save one) were published in text and translated into a European language for the first time. These chronicles were the foundation upon which Mayan and Christian chronology have been coördinated, and must be considered a landmark in American archeology. His paper on the mound-builders (*Historical Magazine*, February 1866)—showing that they were plain American Indians, and not (as is unfortunately still fondly believed by the laity) a highly civilized mysterious race who were exterminated by the American Indians—is fundamental. The influence of his scattered writings has been very great. Summing up, we may say Brinton was one of the pioneers, and an able one, of anthropology in this country.

[*The Brinton Memorial Meeting* (1900), containing fully annotated list of Brinton's writings; obituaries by McGee and Chamberlain, in *Science*, n.s., X, 193–96, and *Jour. of Am. Folk-Lore*, XII, 215–25, respectively; brief review and appraisement of Brinton's activities in physical anthropology by A. Hrdlička in the *Am. Anthropologist*, n.s., XVI, 537–40; summary of Brinton's work by Boas in *Globus*, LXXVI, 165, 166; short notices in the *Public Ledger* (Phila.) and *Phila. Press*, Aug. 1, 1899; *Who's Who in America*, 1899; eulogy by Mrs. Helen C. DeS. A. Michael in the *Conservator*, Sept. 1899; sketch, largely autobiographical, in *Fourth Biog. Record of Class of Fifty-Eight, Yale Univ.* (1897); Anson Phelps Stokes, *Memorials of Eminent Yale Men* (1914), I, 351 ff.]   T.M.

BRINTON, JOHN HILL (May 21, 1832–Mar. 18, 1907), surgeon, was born in Philadelphia, the son of George and Margaret (Smith) Brinton. He was graduated with the degree of B.A. at the University of Pennsylvania in 1850, and received his degree of M.D. two years later at the Jefferson Medical College. After a year's post-graduate study in Paris and Vienna, in company with the late Prof. J. M. DaCosta, he returned to Philadelphia, entered upon general practise, and was made demonstrator in operative surgery in the Jefferson Medical College. A year later he was advanced to the position of lecturer on operative surgery which he held until the outbreak of the Civil War. In his *Personal Memoirs* he tells us that he was commissioned brigade surgeon on Aug. 3, 1861, his name being fourth on the list of volunteer surgeons. He served with Grant in the Tennessee and Cumberland River campaign in 1862, and was then ordered for duty in the office of the Surgeon-General in Washington. While there he helped to prepare *The Medical and Surgical History of the War of the Rebellion* (1870–88), writing the article on Gunshot Wounds, and was designated to establish an Army Medical Museum. Later he was relieved from duty in Washington and ordered to active service under Gen. Rosecrans, serving as medical director in the field in the Missouri campaign. He was later made superintendent of the hospitals in Nashville, Tenn., and medical director of the Army of the Cumberland. He resigned from the army on Feb. 11, 1865, returned to Philadelphia, and was again made lecturer on operative surgery at the Jefferson Medical College. Subsequently in 1882 he succeeded Dr. Samuel D. Gross as professor of the practise of surgery and clinical surgery at the same college and continued in this position until May 1906 when he was made an emeritus professor. He was visiting surgeon at St. Joseph Hospital from 1895 until his death, and filled the same position at the Philadelphia Hospital, 1867–82 and at the Jefferson Medical College Hospital from 1877 on. He wrote little, but his writings make us wish he had accomplished more with his pen. His *Personal Memoirs* were written for his children. He also edited John E. Erichsen's *Science and Art of Surgery* (1854) and delivered the valedictory address to the graduating class of the Army Medical School in 1896. Some years previously, in 1869, he had delivered in Philadelphia the Mütter lectures on surgical pathology, with "Gun Shot Injuries" as his subject. On Sept. 13, 1866, he married Sarah Ward, daughter of the Rev. Ferdinand DeWilton Ward of Geneseo, N. Y. "He was a broadly educated, cultivated, courteous, kindly gentleman."

[*Personal Memoirs of John H. Brinton* (1914); notice in the *Jeffersonian*, VIII, 65, 112–13, prepared by a committee of his friends and colleagues at the Jefferson Medical College; *Who's Who in America*, 1906–07; *N. Y. Medic. Jour.*, Mar. 23, 1907; *Public Ledger* (Phila.) and *Press* (Phila.), Mar. 19, 1907; names of parents from a son Dr. Ward Brinton of Phila.]

W. R. S.

BRISBANE, ALBERT (Aug. 22, 1809–May 1, 1890), social reformer, was born in Batavia, N. Y., where his father, James Brisbane, of Scotch descent, was one of the more prominent landowners. His mother, Mary (Stevens) Brisbane, was of English stock, and a student of no little ability. From both of his parents Albert Brisbane inherited a sturdy and vigorous constitution, being, according to his father, "as withy as a rattlesnake." From his mother he got much of his early education, particularly in history and the sciences. When about fifteen years of age he was placed in a Long Island boarding-school, but soon removed to New York City where he studied under several tutors, the most important being John Monesca, whose teaching and social philosophy made a great impression. Before leaving Batavia, Brisbane tells us, he had begun to consider seriously the social destiny of man, and his contact with Monesca furthered his interest in the subject and inclined him to study the problem under the great thinkers of contemporary Europe. At the age of eighteen, therefore, he left New York for Paris where he studied for a time under Cousin, Guizot, and others. Disappointed in the French thinkers he next went to Berlin where he studied social philosophy under Hegel. Socially he found Berlin very pleasant, being welcomed into intellectual circles of a liberal character, but Hegel disappointed him for, he says, "I found in Hegel and among his disciples no idea of a higher social order than the European civilization" (Redelia Brisbane, *Albert Brisbane*, p. 96). Leaving Berlin, he next journeyed to Constantinople to study at first hand the civilization of the Turkish Empire and southeastern Europe. Returning to western Europe, he reached Paris shortly after the Revolution of 1830, convinced that the human misery he had witnessed could be alleviated only by a fundamental reconstruction of society. For a time he dallied with the reform ideas of Saint-Simon, but these he eventually rejected. A few months later, however, he read Charles Fourier's *Traité de l'Association Domestique-Agricole* (1821–22), and was much impressed. "Now for the first time," he says, "I had come across an idea which I had never met before—the idea of *dignifying* and *rendering attractive* the manual labors of mankind" (*Ibid.*, 172). Further investigation convinced him that in Fourier's theory he had "found a hypothesis which explained what I had been seeking to discover—a just and wise organization of human society" (*Ibid.*, 187). Two years of study under the personal direction of Fourier followed, during which Brisbane satisfied himself of the wisdom and validity of Fourier's theories. In 1834 he returned to the United States, but for several years poor health prevented the propagation of Fourierism, the general acceptance of which he firmly believed would result in "the social redemption of the *collective* man." In 1839, however, he organized a society and began lecturing in Philadelphia and New York, and the following year widened his appeal by publishing his *Social Destiny of Man; or, Association and Reorganization of Industry,* an exposition of Fourierism. This was followed in 1843 by *Association; or, A Concise Exposition of the Practical Part of Fourier's Social Science.* The earlier work so much interested Horace Greeley that he not only offered Brisbane the use of the *New York Tribune* but even got out with him a paper devoted wholly to Associationism, the *Future,* which ran for two months, when it was dropped for a column in the *Tribune.* In order to forward his educational campaign still more vigorously Brisbane also took over the editorship of the *Chronicle,* wrote twice a week for a radical democratic paper, the *Plebeian,* edited (1843–45) with Osborne Macdaniel, the *Phalanx,* the "organ of the doctrine of Association," and wrote occasionally for the *Dial.* Under the excitement of the new ideas some forty small and poorly financed experiments in practical associationism were started, a development for which Brisbane was quite unprepared and in which he took no part. The results were disastrous, convincing Brisbane of the unwisdom of "too hasty propaganda" (*Ibid.,* 218). Following the failure of these practical experiments in Fourierism, public interest in the subject waned, and Brisbane dropped his educational propaganda, although many years later, in 1876, he published a *General Introduction to Social Sciences,* the first part of which was devoted to an introduction to Fourier's theory of social organization, and the second part to a translation of the master's Theory of Universal Unity.

Brisbane, wrote one of his contemporaries, was "a well and highly educated man, of active and vigorous mind, with a keen and analytical vision, and a large power of generalization. With a great deal of candor, good temper, and kindliness, he exhibits a certain innocent simplicity of character, and a fervor of faith in abstract convictions, which can rarely fail to awaken in a high degree the confidence, interest and esteem of those who are brought into any intimacy of contact with him" (*Democratic Review,* XI, p. 302). As a practical reformer, however, he was not a success. Not only was the scheme he advocated Utopian in character, but Brisbane himself, modest and somewhat self-distrustful, was quite lacking in any real capacity for leadership. Intellectually, as well as historically, Albert Brisbane belongs among those Utopian socialists of his generation who sought in some new order of society a universal panacea for the evils they saw in the society about them. The later years of

Brisbane's life were devoted to study and travel, and to his inventions, of which his system of transportation by means of hollow spheres in pneumatic tubes and a new system of burial became best known. He married twice, his first wife being Sarah White by whom he had three children, and his second wife Redelia Bates. He died in Richmond, Va.

[The chief source is Redelia Brisbane, *Albert Brisbane: A Mental Biography with a Character Study* (1893). With the exception of the first chapter, a character study by Mrs. Brisbane, this work is autobiographical. For a view of Brisbane at the height of his activity as a social reformer, see the *Democratic Review,* XI, 302.]

W.R.W.

BRISTED, CHARLES ASTOR (Oct. 6, 1820–Jan. 14, 1874), author, was the son of Rev. John Bristed [*q.v.*], and Magdalen, daughter of John Jacob Astor II. He was born in New York City, was prepared for college by tutors, and entered Yale College at the age of fifteen. When he was graduated, in 1839, after having gained three of the four classical prizes, he was influenced by relatives to remain at Yale for a year of graduate work; but he later expressed the opinion that the time was almost wasted, as a New England college town was a good place "to unmake a partially formed scholar." In 1840 he matriculated at Trinity College, Cambridge, England, where he was graduated in 1845 as a foundation scholar. He writes of himself in this period as being dressed "in the last Gothamite fashion" and proud of introducing sherry cobbler at Trinity College dinner parties, though shunning all student excesses. He won the University Latin Essay Prize and on receiving his B.A. degree evaded taking the oaths of allegiance to Church and State then required. After some European travel, he returned to the United States and began writing for his own pleasure, sometimes under the name of Carl Benson. Under this pseudonym he was for some years a regular contributor to the sporting journals, *Porter's Spirit of the Times* and *Wilkes's Spirit of the Times.* His chief works are: *Selections from Catullus, for School Use* (1849); *A Letter to the Hon. Horace Mann* (1850), a reply to some criticisms of Astor and Girard; *The Upper Ten Thousand: Sketches of American Society* (1852), sketches of New York society; *Five Years in an English University* (1852); "The English Language in America" (in *Cambridge Essays,* 1855); *Pieces of a Broken-Down Critic* (1858); *Now Is the Time to Settle It* (1862); *No Surrender* (1863); *The Cowards' Convention* (1864); *The Interference Theory of Government* (1867), against tariff and liquor prohibition; *Anacreontics* (1872); and *On Some Exaggerations in Com-*

parative Philology (1873). As a writer he showed a trained mind and fastidious taste, but considerable self-consciousness. His desire for accuracy caused too great detail and timidity in drawing conclusions from facts. Devotion to classical scholarship is evident in his literary criticisms and translations. He was a member of the American Philological Association and a contributor at its meetings, and was a trustee of the Astor Library from its foundation until his death. On Jan. 14, 1847, he married Laura Brevoort of New York, who died in 1860. In 1867 he married Grace Sedgwick of Lenox, Mass. He had homes in New York City, Washington, Lenox, and South Carolina, but spent most of his later years in Washington, where he was known in literary circles as a scholar and to his friends as a hospitable but not indiscriminate host.

[*The Todd Genealogy* (1867), by Richard Henry Greene; an article by Richard Grant White, Bristed's friend, in the *Galaxy*, Apr. 1874; Bristed's own book, *Five Years in an English University* (1852); long sketch, mainly autobiographical, in *A Quarter-Century Record of the Class of 1839, Yale Coll.* (1865); obituaries in the *Washington Chronicle*, Jan. 16, 1874, and the *N. Y. Tribune*, Jan. 17, 1874, and an obituary editorial in the Washington *Evening Star*, Jan. 15, 1874.]

S. G. B.

BRISTED, JOHN (Oct. 17, 1778–Feb. 23, 1855), author, Episcopal clergyman, was born at Sherborne in Dorsetshire, England, the son of a clergyman in the Anglican church. His general education was received at Winchester College. During his life he followed three different professions. He first studied medicine at Edinburgh and practised it for a short time; next he studied law under Joseph Chitty, editor of Blackstone's *Commentaries,* and was admitted to the Inner Temple; later in life he was to be a clergyman. Before leaving England he began writing and seems to have held ideas considered radical at the time, for Arthur Aikin, editor of the *Annual Review and History of Literature* (vol. II, 1804, p. 408), in commenting on Bristed's book *A Pedestrian Tour through Part of the Highlands of Scotland in 1801* (2 vols., 1804), denounced the young author, not only for borrowing parts of his book without giving credit, but also because he and his companion, traveling as American sailors, had gone about haranguing over the hardships of the poor and the excessive luxury of the rich until they had aroused the hostility of the Scots. Other early books of his were *The Adviser; or the Moral and Literary Tribunal* (4 vols., 1802); *Critical and Philosophical Essays* (1804); *The Society of Friends Examined* (1805); and *Edward and Anna* (1806), a novel. In 1806 Bristed came to New York City and there practised law, lectured, and wrote books

and magazine articles. In 1807 he was an editor of the *Monthly Register, Magazine and Review of the United States,* founded in 1805 by Stephen Cullen Carpenter at Charleston, S. C. Bristed's books of this period include *Hints on the National Bankruptcy of Britain, and on Her Resources to Maintain the Present Contest with France* (1809); *The Resources of the British Empire* (1811); *Oration on the Utility of Literary Establishments* (1814), at the opening of Eastburn's Literary Rooms, New York City; *The Resources of the United States of America* (1818); *Thoughts on the Anglican and Anglo-American Churches* (1823). On Mar. 8, 1820, he married Magdalen, widowed daughter of John Jacob Astor, who died in 1832. Their son, Charles Astor Bristed [*q.v.*] became a writer. Growing interested in theology, Bristed studied under Bishop Griswold of the Episcopal Church, at Bristol, R. I., and later under Bishop Smith of Vermont. In 1828 he returned to Bristol as Bishop Griswold's assistant at St. Michael's, and in 1829 succeeded the Bishop there as rector. He held this office until 1843, when he resigned on account of poor health, continuing to reside in Bristol until his death twelve years afterward. During his later years Bristed was a devoted churchman, giving liberally of his wealth both in private charities and in church extension in Rhode Island. He was especially interested in helping young men preparing for the ministry to carry on their studies. As a preacher, he was sincere, somewhat emotional, and oratorical. His writings show diligent and exhaustive study; interest in history, economic questions, and religion; a strong personal point of view, frequently amounting to prejudice; and a rather ornate style.

[Thos. F. Kirby, *Winchester Scholars* (1888), p. 280; E. A. and G. L. Duyckinck, *Cyc. of Am. Lit.* (1855); Richard H. Greene, *The Todd Genealogy* (1867); W. W. Spooner, ed., *Historic Families of America* (n.d.); obituaries in the *Providence (R. I.) Daily Post,* Feb. 27, 1855, and the *Newport (R. I.) Advertiser,* Feb. 28, 1855.]

S. G. B.

BRISTOL, JOHN BUNYAN (Mar. 14, 1826–Aug. 31, 1909), painter, was born in Hillsdale, N. Y., the son of Abner and Lydia Bristol. He was chiefly self-taught, although he had a few lessons at one time from Henry Ary, portrait painter of Hudson, N. Y. His early life is said to have been a struggle, but he seems to have been one who held tenaciously to a chosen profession and through courage, determination, and inherent talent eventually won success. He was elected associate of the National Academy of Design and a member of the Artists Fund Society in 1861. In 1875 he was made a full Academician. In 1862 he married a daughter of Alanson Church of Great Barrington, Mass., and after this made his home in New York. His summers were for the most part spent in New England with occasional trips to Lake George and Lake Champlain. In 1859 he visited Florida and made many sketches in the vicinity of St. Augustine. A painting entitled "Afternoon on the St. John's River" was the result of this sojourn. He was represented in the Centennial Exposition, Philadelphia, in 1876, and received a medal of honor. He also received honorable mention in the Paris Exposition, 1889, and a bronze medal, Pan-American Exposition, Buffalo, 1901. Among his best-known works are: "An Autumn Afternoon near Bolton, Lake George"; "Mansfield Mountain at Sunrise"; "The Adirondacks from Lake Champlain"; "An Afternoon in Haying Time—Berkshire County." H. T. Tuckerman speaks of him as a "modest and assiduous artist with somewhat of Kensett's repose in his best landscapes, some of which, besides accuracy in detail and true effect in generalization, exhibit a genuine sentiment which elevates their imitative truth" (*Book of the Artists,* 1867, p. 558). In 1905 he was reported by his colleague, Samuel Isham, as "still working with undimmed eye and unwearied hand." He died in New York, Aug. 31, 1909.

[Samuel Isham, *Hist. of Am. Painting* (1905); C. E. Clement and L. Hutton, *Artists of the 19th Century* (1879); *Art Jour.* XXXI, 110–11; *Columbia County at the End of the Century* (1900).]　　　　L. M.

BRISTOW, BENJAMIN HELM (June 20, 1832–June 22, 1896), lawyer, statesman, was born in Elkton, Ky., the son of Francis M. and Emily E. (Helm) Bristow. His father, a leading lawyer and politician of the district, sat in Congress in 1854–55 and 1859–61, and was first a Whig and later an anti-slavery Unionist. These facts shaped Bristow's early life. After graduating from Jefferson College in Pennsylvania in 1851, he studied law in his father's office, was admitted to the bar in 1853, and for a time was his father's partner. On Nov. 21, 1854, he married Abbie S. Briscoe. In 1858 he removed to Hopkinsville, Ky., to practise law, and was there when the Civil War began. Being an ardent Unionist, Bristow aided in recruiting the 25th Kentucky Infantry, and on Sept. 20, 1861, was mustered into service as its lieutenant-colonel. After fighting at Fort Donelson and elsewhere, he was seriously wounded by the explosion of a shell at Shiloh, where his regiment was so badly cut up that it was merged with another. Upon recovering, he helped raise the 8th Kentucky Cavalry, became its lieutenant-colonel, and on

Apr. 1, 1863, was commissioned its colonel. He fought in many skirmishes, and was present when Morgan's raiders were captured at Wellsville, Ohio, in the summer of 1863. Offered a brevet as a major-general, he modestly refused it.

Bristow's war service was cut short by the need for strong Union men in Kentucky politics, where ex-Gov. John A. Wickliffe was leading an organized opposition to Lincoln's emancipation proclamation and other measures. In August 1863, without his knowledge, he was elected to the state Senate from Christian County. Realizing the emergency, Bristow somewhat reluctantly accepted and took his seat in December. He supported all Union enactments, labored for ratification of the Thirteenth Amendment, and was an active worker for Lincoln's reëlection. Resigning from the Senate in 1865, he removed to Louisville, and there was immediately appointed assistant United States attorney; the next spring (May 4, 1866) he was made United States attorney for the Kentucky district. This time he had to play a greater rôle in a more pressing emergency. Kentucky was in a state of lamentable disorder. Ku Klux Klan violence, spontaneous racial clashes, and conflicts between Unionists and former secessionists were everyday occurrences; while gross frauds were practised upon the internal revenue service. Bristow acted with characteristic energy and determination. He obtained twenty-nine convictions for various crimes under the first Federal Enforcement Act, one capital sentence for murder being especially effective in shaking the nerve of the Klan. The lives and property of colored people were rapidly made safe. Attacking the distillers of illicit whiskey, he obtained more than a hundred forfeitures of stocks of liquor (*Some Facts about . . . Bristow,* pp. 12 ff.).

The skill and courage which Bristow displayed attracted national attention, and led at once to higher federal office. Having resigned his United States attorneyship on Jan. 1, 1870, he was practising law in Louisville with John M. Harlan as partner when Congress created the post of solicitor-general. President Grant promptly appointed Bristow the first incumbent. He wrote many opinions, made arguments in several important constitutional cases before the Supreme Court, and won a reputation for mastery of federal jurisprudence. He quit office on Nov. 12, 1872, to accept a highly paid place as counsel of the Texas & Pacific Railroad, but found this step a mistake, for the labor required was administrative while his tastes were for legal work. Returning to Kentucky, he was practising law again when on July 3, 1874, President Grant appointed him secretary of the treasury. This appointment, his predecessor W. A. Richardson having been seriously compromised by contract scandals, was hailed by the press as promising a much-needed reform of the department.

With gratifying rapidity this promise was fulfilled. A drastic reorganization was carried through. The office of supervising architect, made notorious by Mullett, was abolished; the second comptroller and his leading subordinates were dismissed for inefficiency; the detective force was shaken up; and the new Secretary consolidated a number of collection districts in both the customs and internal revenue services. At the same time he argued vigorously for a resumption of specie payments. But his greatest service was in breaking up the notorious Whiskey Ring. This was a powerful and corrupt machine which had been devised by western distillers and their allies in the internal revenue service for the evasion of the whiskey tax, and despite general knowledge of its activities, it seemed impregnable. George W. Fishback, owner of the *St. Louis Democrat,* advised Bristow upon the best means of attacking the Ring in that city. The work of detection was assigned to men wholly outside the Treasury department; instructions were given them in a cipher different from the department code; and by maintaining complete secrecy, a mass of evidence upon the frauds was accumulated. Similar work was done in Chicago and Milwaukee. On May 10, 1875, all the suspected distilleries and rectifying houses in these three cities were seized, and the Ring was shattered at one blow. Books and papers were found proving individual guilt. Nearly 250 civil and criminal suits were instituted forthwith. Within a year Bristow had taken action to recover $3,150,000, had indicted 176 men, and had obtained sentences for 110.

The Ring, fighting back desperately, sought with some success to poison the mind of President Grant against Bristow. Through the attorney-general's office they were able to impede the Secretary's efforts to complete the destruction of the Ring; and by adroit manipulation they induced Grant to believe that Bristow was using his office to scheme for the Republican nomination. His resignation was virtually forced by the President, and was handed in on June 17, 1876 (*North American Review,* October 1876, p. 321). Since the beginning of the year he had been prominently mentioned for the presidency. The conference of moderate Republicans held at the Fifth Avenue Hotel in May regarded him as the best Republican candidate but refrained from an open indorsement (P. L. Haworth, *Hayes-Tilden Election,* pp. 15 ff.). Nominated at the Cincinnati convention in June by John M. Harlan, he received 113 votes on the first ballot, and on the fourth ballot, with 126 votes, stood second only to Blaine.

Bristow's resignation from the Treasury closed his official career, which had covered but fifteen years, two of them spent in military commands. In 1895 Cleveland offered him membership on the Venezuela Boundary Commission, but for personal reasons he declined. Removing from Louisville to New York in 1878, and on October 16 of that year forming the partnership of Bristow, Peet, Burnett, & Opdyke, he remained for the rest of his life one of the leaders of the Eastern bar. He argued many cases before the Supreme Court, and was noted among lawyers for his personal charm, the thoroughness and closeness of his argument, and the skill with which he confined himself to vital points. In 1879 he was elected the second president of the American Bar Association, and for many years was a vice-president of the Civil Service Reform Association. He was a member of the Metropolitan, Union, and Union League clubs. In 1896, while in apparently robust health, he was stricken with appendicitis, and died at his home, 27 West Fiftieth St., within four days.

[The best sketch is David Willcox, "Memorial of Benj. H. Bristow" in *Ann. Report, Ass. of the Bar of the City of N. Y.,* 1897. It is supplemented at some points by the anonymous pamphlet, *Some Facts about the Life and Public Services of Benj. H. Bristow* (New York, 1876). The best treatment of the Whiskey Ring is H. V. Boynton's long paper, "The Whiskey Ring," *North Am. Rev.,* CXXIII, 280–327. Paul L. Haworth's *The Hayes-Tilden Disputed Presidential Election* (1906) treats briefly the Bristow "boom" in 1876.]　　A. N.

BRISTOW, GEORGE FREDERICK (Dec. 19, 1825–Dec. 13, 1898), composer, violinist, teacher, was born in Brooklyn, and spent his entire life in or near New York City. His father was an English organist, William Richard Bristow, who started the son's musical education so early that at the age of eleven he became a violinist in the orchestra of the Olympic Theatre in New York. Piano and organ lessons were given him by his father and by Henry C. Timm, and composition was later studied with G. A. MacFarren. In 1842 he became a violinist in the New York Philharmonic Society, a membership which continued for more than forty years. Bristow was married to Louise Westervelt Holden. His "Concert Overture," *Opus 3,* was played by the Philharmonic Society Nov. 14, 1847; his first symphony, in E flat, appeared in 1845 and a cantata "Eleutheria" in 1849, but the first work to attract general attention was the three-act opera "Rip Van Winkle," which was produced at Niblo's Garden in New York on Sept. 27, 1855 by the Pyne-Harrison English Opera Company, the composer conducting. It had seventeen performances in two months. The libretto, based on Washington Irving's story, was the work of Jonathan Howard Wainwright. Critics complained of the extreme length of the opera, the excessive prominence of solo as compared with concerted numbers, and an apparent monotony of style. The orchestration was praised, as was the staging.

On Mar. 1, 1856, the New York Philharmonic Society played Bristow's second symphony, in D minor, and on Mar. 26, 1859, his third symphony, in F sharp minor. The oratorio "Praise to God" was given first performance on Mar. 2, 1861, by the New York Harmonic Society, of which the composer was conductor. A second opera, "Columbus," was never completed, but the overture was played by the New York Philharmonic Society at the first concert in Steinway Hall, Fourteenth St., Nov. 17, 1866. Bristow's second oratorio, "Daniel," was first performed by the Mendelssohn Union, Dec. 30, 1867. The fourth or "Arcadian" Symphony, in E minor, was played by the New York Philharmonic on Feb. 14, 1874. Five years later Theodore Thomas conducted for the first time Bristow's music to an ode by William Oland Bourne entitled "The Great Republic." Bristow's "Jibbenainosay" overture was produced in 1889, and his symphony "Niagara" during the last year of his life.

Bristow conducted the Harmonic Society 1851–62, was a church organist, and from 1854 till his death was connected with musical work in the New York public schools. He was pianist at the concert in Tripler Hall, New York, on Feb. 20, 1852, at which Theodore Thomas made his first appearance in the United States as a boy violinist, and two Bristow songs were on that program. Bristow was a member of the orchestra which accompanied Jenny Lind at her first concerts in this country, and also played in the Jullien concerts in 1853–54. In addition to the music mentioned above he composed two string quartets, a set of six organ pieces, and a number of smaller pieces. He was one of the first outspoken champions of music by Americans, and as early as 1854 protested, with a group of fellow members of the Philharmonic, against the policy of favoring composers of other countries, particularly those of Germany. He was regarded as an able conductor, and was highly esteemed as a teacher. The record left by Bristow is that

of a serious, industrious and unassuming man who exerted a strong influence for good music during many years, and who deserves an honored place as one of the first Americans to compose music in the larger forms.

[G. H. Curtis, "Geo. Frederick Bristow," *Music,* III, 547–64; Waldemar Rieck, "When Bristow's 'Rip' was Sung at Niblo's Garden," *Musical America,* Dec. 5, 1925; G. L. Ritter, *Music in America* (1883); César Saerchinger in *Musical Quart.,* Apr. 1920; *Musical Record,* Jan. 1899.]   C.N.B.

BROADHEAD, GARLAND CARR (Oct. 30, 1827–Dec. 12, 1912), geologist and engineer, was born near Charlottesville, Va., son of Achilles and Mary Winston (Carr) Broadhead and brother of James Overton Broadhead [*q.v.*]. The father was a farmer, teacher, and surveyor, and a son of John Broadhead who had come to America as a soldier in Burgoyne's army and after the war settled in Albemarle County, Va. When the boy was nine years of age the family moved to Flint Hill, St. Charles County, Mo., twenty-five miles north of St. Louis, where he received his early education mainly in private schools or under tutors. He studied at the University of Missouri, 1850–51, showing most proficiency in mathematics, Latin, and history. He then entered the Western Military Institute at Drenum Springs, Ky., where he came under the tutelage of the geologist Richard Owen and the mathematician and engineer Bushrod R. Johnson. His first position after leaving these schools was that of surveyor on the Missouri Pacific Railroad then under construction. The year following he became assistant engineer in charge of location lines and in 1857 was made resident engineer of construction. Later he became engineer of railway construction in Kansas. During the Civil War, in 1862, Broadhead was commissioned assistant adjutant-general on the staff of Gen. J. B. Henderson, and in the same year he was appointed deputy collector of internal revenue for the 1st district of Missouri, a position which he occupied until the close of the war. Two years later he was appointed by President Johnson an assessor of internal revenue for the 5th district of Missouri and held the office until 1868 when he resigned to accept a position on the Geological Survey of Illinois. He took part in the preparation of the Missouri Mineral Exposition of Philadelphia under the direction of the Smithsonian Institution and became one of the jurors on awards in the division of mining and general geology. For several years subsequent to 1884 he served on the Missouri River Commission and on the board of managers of the Bureau of Geology and Mines of the state.

The survey work along the railway lines of

Missouri offered ample facilities for geological observation of which Broadhead was not slow to avail himself. These brought him into the favorable notice of State Geologist Swallow, who in 1857 employed him in making a geological reconnaissance along the line of the southwestern branch of the Pacific Railroad. Later in the capacity of assistant geologist Broadhead investigated the mineral resources of several counties and made six reports, which, owing to the troubled condition of the times, were not published until thirteen years later during the survey of R. Pumpelly. In 1868 Broadhead became an assistant geologist under Worthen on the staff of the Geological Survey of Illinois where he did good service. In 1871 he was called back to Missouri to become assistant on the survey under Pumpelly as already mentioned, and in turn to become its director on Pumpelly's resignation in 1873, continuing to act during the following year, after which the survey was discontinued. In 1881 he contributed a chapter on the building-stone resources of Missouri to the 10th Census Report on this subject, and later, important articles to the surveys of 1889 and 1900 under Winslow, Keyes, and others. In 1887 he was called to succeed J. G. Norwood in the chair of geology in the University of Missouri, retiring as professor emeritus ten years later, at the age of seventy. "The refrain running through all of his courses of instruction at the Missouri State University during the course of his long professorship there, and through his many public lectures, was the adjustment of man's life and efforts to his geological environment" (Keyes, p. 13). As a man he is described as "genial, courteous and considerate, with wide interests and a truly remarkable detailed knowledge of men and events" (*Ibid.*, p. 17). His best work, as judged by one of his colleagues, consisted first, in his differentiation of the coal measures of Missouri and Kansas, and second, in his establishment of the Ozarkian Series, "the great succession of Late Cambrian rocks found typically developed in Missouri and extending far and wide to the northward in the upper Mississippi valley" (*Ibid.*, p. 17). Broadhead's bibliography comprises nearly two hundred titles, many of which, however, are only brief notes. He was married twice, in 1864 to Marion Wallace Wright, and in 1890 to Victoria Regina Royall.

[C. R. Keyes, *Bull. Geol. Soc. of America*, vol. XXX (1919), containing bibliography of Broadhead's publications, pp. 20–27.]   G. P. M.

BROADHEAD, JAMES OVERTON (May 29, 1819–Aug. 7, 1898), congressman, diplomat, was born at Charlottesville, Albemarle County, Va. His mother, Mary Winston (Carr) Broadhead was of Scottish origin, her ancestors occupying large estates in Virginia. His father, Achilles Broadhead, was a native of Albemarle County. A brother, Garland Carr Broadhead [*q.v.*] later attained eminence as a geologist. Achilles Broadhead was a man of great force of character, intensely patriotic, and a soldier of the War of 1812. James Broadhead received a good classical education, acquiring his preparatory training under his uncle, Dr. Frank Carr, who kept a select school at Red Hills, Va. In 1835, at the age of sixteen years, he entered the University of Virginia, where he spent a year in diligent study, supporting himself wholly by his own effort. In 1837, his father having moved to Missouri, he found employment there as tutor in the family of Edward Bates, at the same time pursuing the study of law under that eminent jurist. In 1842 he was licensed and immediately began the practise of law in Bowling Green, Mo. He soon became interested in politics and in 1845 was sent to the state constitutional convention as a delegate from the second senatorial district. In 1847 he was the Whig candidate of Pike County for the legislature, running against Nicholas P. Minor. Although the county was normally Democratic, Broadhead reversed this condition and was elected. In 1850 he was a candidate for the state Senate and again he was triumphant. He removed to St. Louis in 1859 and formed a partnership with Fidelio C. Sharp. In the agitation preceding the Civil War he took a leading part. Although a Virginian, he held the Union above all else, and in conjunction with Frank P. Blair, Jr., and others, helped to organize the committee of safety in St. Louis for the purpose of resisting the tide of disunion. He also aided in effecting a military organization under the leadership of Gen. Lyon. He was a prominent member of the state convention in 1861 which declared a provincial government to be established favorable to the Union. On the report of the committee of which he was chairman, the offices of governor, lieutenant-governor, secretary of state, and treasurer were declared vacant. A provisional government was organized. While a member of this body Broadhead was appointed provost-marshal-general of the district, embracing Missouri, Southern Iowa, Kansas, Indian Territory, and Arkansas. The skill and power with which he discharged this duty gave additional proof of his ability.

In 1875, he was a member of the state constitutional convention and at once took his place as a leader in that able body of men. He labored incessantly for the formation of the constitution adopted that year. He was retained as special counsel for the government in the famous "Whiskey Ring" cases in St. Louis in 1876. In 1878, he was made president of the American Bar Association. He was a member of the commission which framed the "scheme and charter" of St. Louis under the constitution of 1875. In 1882 he was elected to the Forty-eighth Congress on the Democratic ticket and served with distinction on the judiciary committee of the House. President Cleveland, in 1885, appointed him special commissioner to visit France and examine the archives of the government in relation to the French Spoliation Claims which had long been pressing for an adjustment. Upon his report Congress took the first action toward making provision for payment. Soon after the completion of this duty Broadhead was appointed minister to Switzerland but he resigned in about two years. His success as legislator, counsel in shaping the course of military affairs, and as provost-marshal of a great department demonstrates his ability and versatility. Of all the lawyers in Missouri, he probably enjoyed the widest national reputation, as he was concerned not only in litigation within the state, but in many important controversies in the federal Supreme Court. He was forcible in speech, severely logical, candid, and truthful. His fine personal appearance, his open manly face, his genial and gentle manners, expressed his character. He was married on May 13, 1847 to Mary S. Dorsey, daughter of Edward W. Dorsey of Pike County, Mo.

[H. A. Conard, ed., *Encyc. of Hist. of Mo.*, I, 387–91; L. U. Reavis, *St. Louis: the Future Great City of the World* (biog. ed., 1875), pp. 721–25; *The Bench and Bar of St. Louis* (1884), pp. 8–10; *The Hist. of Pike County, Mo.* (1883), pp. 382–83; *Clinton Democrat*, Aug. 8, 1898; *St. Louis Republic*, Aug. 7, 8, 1898.]

F.C.S—r.

BROADUS, JOHN ALBERT (Jan. 24, 1827–Mar. 16, 1895), Baptist clergyman, was born in the Blue Ridge country of western Virginia, of Welsh ancestry. His father, Edmund Broadus, came from a family of preachers, and though not himself a minister was prominent in religious circles as well as in the Virginia legislature. The mother was Nancy Sims, the daughter of a farmer. Broadus had good schooling, and entered the University of Virginia after a period of teaching. During his college course he was converted in a revival and began to preach. Lack of a theological seminary of his own denomination in the South deterred him from further study, and after another period of teaching he became minister to the Baptist church at Charlottesville, Va., at the same time teaching ancient languages in the University of Virginia as assistant instructor. A new period opened in his life when, after long hesitation, he accepted the chair of New Testament and homiletics in the theological seminary established by the Educational Convention of the Southern Baptists in 1858 at Greenville, N. C. He had had a commanding influence in shaping the curriculum for the new school, and he was one of four prominent ministers chosen to constitute the first faculty. Here he worked with James P. Boyce [*q.v.*], the president, in the closest intimacy. Almost at once the school was threatened with extinction by the entrance of the South into the Civil War. Broadus was sympathetic with the Confederacy, preached in the camps, and, when classes were suspended, made a living by preaching to country churches and acting as corresponding secretary of the Sunday-school Board for three years. During the last year of the war he was aide-de-camp to the governor. The seminary shared in the prostration of the South at the close of the war, and in 1870 Broadus went abroad for a year, partly for his health which was never robust. Upon his return he threw himself into the difficult task of resuscitating the seminary. Removal of the school to Louisville, Ky., proved an advantage, the student enrolment increased, and funds began to be available. At Louisville Broadus heightened his reputation as a scholar and teacher, and wrote much. In 1889 he succeeded Boyce as president of the institution. He published *Lectures on the History of Preaching* (1876); *Commentary on the Gospel of Matthew* (1886); *Sermons and Addresses* (1887); and a *Memoir of James Pettigru Boyce* (1893). In 1889 he delivered at Yale the Lyman Beecher lectures on preaching, which were never published. He was in his earlier life an editorial contributor to the *Religious Herald,* and later wrote frequently for the press of his denomination, and for Sunday-school publications. He was a member of the International Lesson Committee from 1878 until his death. He was trustee of the Slater fund. In his own city he spoke in churches and on the public platform, and was admired and loved as a man. He was twice married: on Nov. 13, 1850, to Maria Harrison, who died seven years later; and on Jan. 4, 1859, to Charlotte Eleanor Sinclair.

[Archbald T. Robertson, *Life and Letters of John Albert Broadus* (1901); A. Broadus, *Hist. of the Broadus Family* (1888); Geo. B. Taylor, *Va. Baptist Ministers* (4th ser. 1913); *Religious Herald*, Mar. 21, 1895; *News and Courier* (Charleston, S. C.), May 6, 8, 1875; *Louisville Commercial*, Mar. 16, 1895; *Courier-Jour.* (Louisville), Mar. 15, 16, 1895.]

H.K.R.

BROCKETT, LINUS PIERPONT (Oct. 16, 1820–Jan. 13, 1893), author, physician, descended from John Brockett, one of the founders of the New Haven Colony, was born in Canton, Conn., the son of a Baptist minister, Rev. Pierpont Brockett, and of Sarah (Sage) Brockett. He had the advantages of three educational institutions, the Connecticut Literary Institute at Suffield, Brown University, and Yale Medical School, from which he was graduated in 1843. After a brief attempt at practise, he left medicine in favor of literature. During 1844 and 1845 he was professor of physiology and anatomy in Georgetown College, Ky. He joined a publishing firm in Hartford in 1847 and continued the connection for ten years. During this time and afterward he contributed to various encyclopedias, among them *Appleton's Annual Cyclopaedia, Johnson's Universal Cyclopedia,* and two foreign encyclopedias. Because of his interest in medico-sociological subjects, in 1854 he was appointed a commissioner to investigate idiocy in Connecticut and published a report in 1856. Always a devoted Baptist, he wrote a volume of church history, *The Bogomils of Bulgaria and Bosnia* (1880), and an appreciative account of the Karen Mission in Bassein. As early as 1847 he began writing on historical subjects, a type of work which finally absorbed his whole time and interest. He published about fifty books, the majority on Civil War subjects. Some of the more important are: *A Geographical History of the State of New York* (with Joseph H. Mather, 1851), *The History and Progress of Education* (1860), *Woman: Her Rights, Wrongs, Privileges, and Responsibilities* (1862), *The Philanthropic Results of the War in America* (1863), *The Life and Times of Abraham Lincoln* (1865), *Our Great Captains* (1865), *A Complete History of the Great American Rebellion* (with E. G. Storke, 1863–65), *The Camp, the Battlefield, and the Hospital* (1866), *Woman's Work in the Civil War* (with Mary C. Vaughan, 1867), *Men of Our Day* (1868), *Grant and Colfax* (1868), *Epidemic and Contagious Diseases* (1873), *Our Western Empire* (1881). He edited *Our Country's Wealth and Influence* (1882), and was editor and chief writer of *Descriptive America* (1884–85). Brockett sometimes used the pseudonym "Capt. Powers Hazelton." In 1846 he married Lucy Maria Thacher of Jordan, N. Y. In 1860 he and his wife and their one child removed to Brooklyn. Here he became editor at different times of the *Brooklyn Monthly* and the *Brooklyn Advance.* He was considered, in editorial offices, in his church, and in social relations, a pleasant, kindly, rather serious man.

From his appearance he might have passed for a clergyman or a college professor. He had a roundish face, with an expression of great serenity, a high, bald forehead, a straight, classical nose, bright eyes which needed spectacles much of his life, a thin-lipped mouth uncovered by a mustache, a tuft chin-beard, and long hair curling about his ears. Intensely patriotic, a strong supporter of the Union, and an enthusiastic admirer of the great men of the Civil War period, he made his histories very eulogistic. He had respect for adequate and reliable sources but in the interpretation of events he placed more emphasis on individuals than on social forces. He esteemed integrity of character, religious principle, loyalty to country, above everything else, but, after these, placed a high value on material success. His style of writing is clear, straightforward, substantial. There is little humor, but much use is made of anecdote, especially to illustrate character. He died at his home on Steuben St., Brooklyn, and his funeral was held at Emanuel Baptist Church.

[Biographical sketch in *The Descendants of John Brockett, one of the Original Founders of the New Haven Colony* (1905), comp. by Edward J. Brockett; obituaries in the *Brooklyn Eagle, N. Y. Tribune, Evening Post* (N.Y.), Jan. 14, 1893.]   S.G.B.

BROCKMEYER, HENRY C. [See BROKMEYER, HENRY C., 1828–1906.]

BROCKWAY, ZEBULON REED (Apr. 28, 1827–Oct. 21, 1920), penologist, was born at Lyme, Conn., the son of Zebulon and Caroline Brockway, both descendants of an old New England family. At twenty-one, equipped with an elementary education and a few years of business experience, he took what proved a decisive step in his life; he became a clerk in the Wethersfield prison. Promotion followed promotion. In 1851 he went to the Albany (N. Y.) County Penitentiary as Amos Pilsbury's deputy; in 1853 he was made superintendent of the Albany Municipal and County Almshouse and in 1854 head of the new Monroe County Penitentiary at Rochester. In 1861 he went to Detroit as superintendent of the new House of Correction, a position he held until 1872, when circumstances forced his resignation. Three years in business life lent credence to the judgment pronounced on him as a boy, "That lad will never become forehanded for he has not the money-getting instinct." He again came into his own when in 1876 he accepted the superintendency of the Elmira State Reformatory for men, which he directed for twenty-five years.

In 1894 his management of the reformatory was investigated by the State Board of Charities which recommended that he be dismissed. The investigation was apparently partisan in character, however, and Gov. Flower, acting upon the report of a special commission appointed by him refused to deprive Brockway of his post (*Documents of the Assembly of the State of New York, 1894, No. 89; Nineteenth Yearbook of the Elmira State Reformatory, 1893–94*). In 1900 he retired from public service to devote himself to charitable and educational work, but in 1905 he was induced to run for mayor of Elmira. He served in that capacity for two years with the same deep sense of duty and uncompromising honesty which characterized his whole life. At the conferences of the National (later the American) Prison Association his fine, white-bearded countenance and patriarchal figure were frequently seen, and his opinions were eagerly sought on all important questions. In 1897–98 he served as president of the Association and in 1910 he was honorary president of the International Prison Congress, meeting in Washington. Married on Apr. 13, 1853, to Jane Woodhouse of Wethersfield, he survived his wife by nine years.

While not the innovator of the "indeterminate sentence" he was the first to put it into our statutes. All punishment had for him but one aim, the protection of society against crime. This he thought could best be secured by reforming the criminal, if possible, or by confining the incorrigible indefinitely. If reformation alone was to be the key to liberty, the fixed sentence had to give way to an absolutely indeterminate sentence and the execution of this sentence had to be entrusted to the administrative authorities of all institutions within a given jurisdiction. He presented his ideas to the National Congress on Penitentiary and Reformatory Discipline (Cincinnati, 1870) in a remarkable paper entitled "The Ideal of a True Prison System for a State" (*Transactions*, pp. 33–65). In the "three years law," drafted by him and passed by Michigan in 1869, he had incorporated some of his ideas (*Acts of the Legislature of the State of Michigan, 1869, no. 145*); they received a more complete expression in the organic law of the Elmira Reformatory, which he drafted and saw accepted by the New York legislature, in 1877 (*Laws of the State of N. Y., 1877, ch. 173*). His original demand for a sentence without minimum and maximum was modified by the legislature, which adopted an indeterminate sentence without a minimum but with the maximum as already defined by the penal laws of the state.

Brockway early experimented with evangelistic forms and methods of reformation, but, with wider experience he lost faith in them. Greatly influenced by continental criminological thought, he gradually embraced a deterministic philosophy of conduct which became the basis for his work at Elmira. There, physical, manual, and military training, together with ethical and esthetic instruction, were the instruments he used in his task of "socializing the anti-social." Reformatory prison treatment—and to him there was no other kind—meant "education of the whole man, his capacity, his habits and tastes, by a rational procedure, whose central motive and law of development are found" in what he elsewhere calls "the ennobling influences of established industrial efficiency" ("The American Reformatory Prison System," in C. R. Henderson, *post*, I, 88–107).

[Brockway's autobiography, *Fifty Years of Prison Service*, was published in 1912 by the Russell Sage Foundation, New York City. For an evaluation of his work see F. H. Wines, "Historical Introduction," pp. 3–38 of "Prison Reform," in vol. I of *Correction and Prevention* (1910), ed. by C. R. Henderson; the minute spread upon the records of the Nat. Prison Ass. (*Proc.*, 1900, pp. 333–34) on the occasion of Brockway's retirement from Elmira; Frank L. Christian's necrology, *Proc. Am. Prison Ass.*, 1921, pp. 121–23; and Crystal Eastman's "A Non-Partisan Mayor" in *Charities and The Commons*, XIX, 953–54, Nov. 2, 1907. There was a brief obituary in the *N. Y. Times*, Oct. 22, 1920. Genealogical data may be found in F. E. Brockway, *The Brockway Family* (1890).]   T. S.

BRODERICK, DAVID COLBRETH (Feb. 4, 1820–Sept. 16, 1859), forty-niner, politician, was born in Washington, D. C. He was of Irish stock, and his father, a stone-mason for a time employed on the national Capitol, was doubtless an immigrant. Of the mother, whose maiden name was Copway, little is recorded except that she was idolized by her son. The boy had little schooling. Before he was fourteen the family moved to New York. About 1837 the father died, and the boy began his struggle for a living for himself, his mother, and his younger brother. Industrious, ambitious, belligerent, of strong physique and able to give a good account of himself in a street brawl, he literally fought his way to the front. By the time he was twenty he was a member of an engine company (of which later he became foreman) and was active in ward politics as an adherent of Tammany Hall. His mother dying and his brother being accidentally killed, he was left without kin. His struggles had molded his character; he was "stubborn, positive, unrelenting and unforgiving," self-centered also, and determined upon his advancement to the utmost of his powers. He owned a saloon, which seems to have netted a good profit, and he became politically prominent. He was a member of the city charter convention of 1846, over which he several times presided, and in the same year he was the unsuccessful Tammany nominee for Congress in the 5th district.

In the spring of 1849 he determined to go to California. Closing his saloon, emptying his casks in the street, and vowing that he would never again "sell or drink liquor, smoke a cigar or play a card," he took passage by way of Panama, and in June arrived in San Francisco. Here he found old friends ready to back him alike in business and politics. He formed a partnership with an assayer for the coining of gold "slugs" of four-dollar and eight-dollar values in metal, which passed readily, because of the scarcity of coin, for five dollars and ten dollars. The business, though highly profitable, was sold some months later, and Broderick turned his attention to the still more profitable enterprise of trading in shore-front lots. From the time he landed he was in politics. In August he was chosen a delegate to the constitutional convention, and in January of the following year was elected to fill a vacancy in the Senate. On the succession of Lieutenant-Governor McDougal to the governorship, in January 1851, Broderick was elected president of the Senate. Though his private life was exemplary, in politics he was unscrupulous. An adept in Tammany methods, he soon became a political boss; and it is said of him that from 1851 (when he was reëlected to the Senate) to 1854 he was "the Democratic party of California." He now determined upon a seat in the United States Senate, and set about to compass the defeat of William M. Gwin, whose term would expire on Mar. 4, 1855. The attempt served for the time only to divide the party and to deadlock the legislature, but on Jan. 10, 1857, he won the election by 79 votes out of 111. At the same time, through a bargain made with his rival, Gwin, he brought about the latter's reëlection and obtained the promise of a monopoly of the Federal patronage for the state.

President Buchanan refused to recognize the bargain, and Gwin, in spite of his promise, continued to distribute the patronage. Broderick turned on both men with bitter resentment. At what time he first developed sentiments hostile to the slave power and to political corruption cannot be said. But he now vehemently attacked the administration, both for its policy in Kansas and for its alleged venality, and he carried the war into his own state, where pro-slavery feeling was for the time dominant and aggressive. His attitude brought him into national prominence, but made him a marked man at home. Both he and his friends felt that he was now regarded as a menace and that means would be taken to get rid of him. A remark made by him

on June 27, 1859, concerning Chief Justice David S. Terry, one of the leaders of the pro-slavery element, brought a challenge from Terry, who resigned his judgeship, and Broderick accepted. They met on the early morning of Sept. 13. The pistol furnished Broderick was so "light on the trigger" that it was prematurely discharged by the act of raising his arm. Terry's bullet struck Broderick in the breast, and he fell mortally wounded. Conveyed to a near-by farmhouse, he lingered for three days. On his deathbed he said: "They have killed me because I was opposed to the extension of slavery and a corrupt administration." The dead body was conveyed to the city, where on Sept. 18 funeral services were held at which Col. Edward D. Baker [q.v.] delivered an eloquent and impressive eulogy. On Feb. 13, 1860, memorial services were held by both houses of Congress. Broderick was buried at the foot of Lone Mountain.

He is pictured by Lynch as a large man, robust, and of great strength, with steel-blue eyes, a large mouth filled with strong white teeth, a ruddy brown beard, and a plentiful shock of "slightly dark" hair. His face, says Lynch, was not attractive. His character has been variously portrayed; Bancroft says that it has been "distorted into something abnormal by both his enemies and his friends." The identification of the man shot down by Terry with the ward-heeler of 1850 is no easy task. He had become a student and a man of thought, an advocate of many measures of broad social significance. He read not only the historians and the statesmen, but the poets, and his favorite bard was Shelley. By whatever circumstances he had been led to a hatred of the slave power and a heightened devotion to the Union, the change was one which in a measure transformed him. Though martyrdom invested him with a glamour beyond his meed, he had given substantial promise of a great and useful career.

[Jeremiah Lynch, *A Senator of the Fifties* (1911); John W. Dwinelle, *A Funeral Oration upon David C. Broderick*, including memorial addresses delivered in Congress, Feb. 13, 1860 (pamphlet, 1860); Jas. O'Meara, *Broderick and Gwin* (1881); H. H. Bancroft, *Hist. of Cal.* (1888); Theodore H. Hittell, *Hist. of Cal.* (1897); Hermann Schussler, *The Locality of the Broderick-Terry Duel* (pamphlet, 1916).]   W.J.G.

BRODHEAD, DANIEL (Sept. 17, 1736– Nov. 15, 1809), Revolutionary soldier, son of Daniel Brodhead II and Hester (Wyngart) Brodhead, was probably born in Albany, N. Y., where his father was a merchant. In 1737 the family removed to Brodhead Manor in Bucks County (now Monroe County), Pa. Here Daniel III grew up in the wild surroundings of the frontier. His father was an extensive landowner and justice of the peace for Bucks County, who died on July 22, 1755. Some months later, on Dec. 11, the Indians made a fierce but unsuccessful attack upon the family home. In 1773 Daniel III moved to Reading, where he became deputy surveyor-general. At the beginning of the Revolution he was chosen delegate to the Pennsylvania Convention, and raised a company of riflemen to join Washington. After the battle of Long Island, he was commissioned lieutenant-colonel of the 4th Pennsylvania and was made colonel of the 8th Pennsylvania in March 1777. After passing the winter at Valley Forge, the regiment was sent, in March 1778, to Pittsburgh, where Gen. Lachlan McIntosh was in command. McIntosh was recalled in April 1779 and Col. Brodhead was appointed commandant in his place. It was at first designed that he should coöperate with Gen. Sullivan in invading the Iroquois country, but the commander-in-chief thought the distances too great for effective action; Brodhead, however, with 600 men made a swift march up the Allegheny, and in thirty-three days terrorized and subdued the Indians of that region (see his report in the *Olden Time*, edited by Neville B. Craig, II, 308–11).

Brodhead was successful in his negotiations with the Delawares, who gave him the name Machingwe Keesuch, "Great Moon." He made a treaty of alliance with them, which, for a time, kept the frontier from invasion. The Delawares finally went on the war-path, however, and Brodhead in the spring of 1781 raided their territory. This expedition is thought to have been undertaken to avoid coöperation with Gen. George Rogers Clark, who was planning an expedition against Detroit. Brodhead also had a serious dispute with Col. John Gibson, and a number of army officers and inhabitants of Pittsburgh asked for his removal. He was tried by court martial and acquitted, but Washington felt obliged to remove him from command. After the close of the war he was brevetted brigadier-general and retired to his home at Milford, Pike County, Pa. He had military ability, but was a martinet in discipline; he was inordinately ambitious and jealous of other officers; and he did not neglect to further his private interests even while commandant. He was not, however, discredited in Pennsylvania, served as its surveyor general, and died respected by his community, which in 1872 raised a monument to him. He was twice married: first, to Elizabeth Dupui; second, to Rebecca, widow of Gen. Mifflin.

[Brodhead papers in Wis. Hist. Lib. are largely published in Louise Phelps Kellogg, *Frontier Advance on the Upper Ohio* (1916) and *Frontier Retreat on the Upper Ohio* (1917). His services are noted in several frontier histories, especially Jos. Doddridge, *Notes on the Settlement and Indian Wars* (Williams ed. 1876); A. S. Withers, *Chronicles of Border Warfare* (Thwaites ed. 1895); C. W. Butterfield, *Hist. of the Girtys* (Cincinnati, 1890); Wills De Hass, *Hist. of the Early Settlements and Indian Wars of Western Va.* (1851); E. W. Hassler, *Old Westmoreland* (1900).]   L.P.K.

BRODHEAD, JOHN ROMEYN (Jan. 2, 1814–May 6, 1873), historian, was a descendant of Jan Jansen Bleecker who came in 1658 to New Netherland to help build up the Dutch power in America, and of Capt. Daniel Brodhead who came six years later, with the English expedition to help destroy it. The son of the Rev. Dr. Jacob and Elizabeth (Bleecker) Brodhead, he was born in Philadelphia and lived there until 1826, when his father was called to a pastorate in his old home, New York. He was educated at Albany Academy and Rutgers College, graduating with honors from the latter institution at seventeen. He then read law in the office of Hugh Maxwell and was admitted to the bar in 1835, only to abandon it after two years to accompany his invalid father to a country home at Saugerties, N. Y. Two years later he went to serve under his relative, Harmanus Bleecker, as attaché to the legation at The Hague. Here he developed a strong interest in the Dutch contribution to the early history of New York, if indeed he did not have this interest when he accepted the position, for he might well have known of the action of the New York legislature (May 2, 1839), authorizing the appointment of an agent to procure from the archives of Europe materials to fill the gaps in the state archives. In any case, after a year at the legation, he resigned and sought the new post, to which Gov. Seward appointed him in 1841. Brodhead spent the next four years in the archives of Holland, France, and England, and in spite of meager appropriations, which necessitated the most rigorous economies, he returned with eighty volumes of manuscript copies of documents. "The ship in which he came back," wrote Bancroft, "was more richly freighted with new materials for American history than any that ever crossed the Atlantic" (*Scribner's Monthly*, XIII, 461). This precious cargo was edited by E. B. O'Callaghan and B. Fernow and published by the State, as *Documents Relating to the Colonial History of the State of New York*, Albany, 1856–86. Brodhead's report was published in 1845 (*Senate Document No. 47, 1845*). After three more enjoyable and stimulating years in the diplomatic service (1846–49), as secretary of legation in London under Bancroft, Brodhead settled down to write his *History of the State of New York*. The first volume (1609–64) was published in 1853. In the same year, he was appointed naval officer of the port of New York, which was one reason why his second volume (1664–91) did not appear until 1871. A third volume (1691–1789) was begun but never completed. In 1856 Brodhead married Eugenia Bloodgood and bought a home in New York. He was an active member of the New York Historical Society and the St. Nicolas Society, a trustee of the Astor Library (1867–71), and a loyal alumnus of Rutgers College, where, with his father, he founded the Brodhead Prize for proficiency in the classics. In politics, he was a Democrat. He died on May 6, 1873, and was buried in Trinity Cemetery. "He was somewhat above average height, graceful in form and attractive in manner. His countenance was mobile and expressive. His general disposition, combined with his position and character, won for him troops of friends, and his stores of incident and anecdote, as well as his general culture, made him welcome wherever he was known" (*Scribner's Monthly*, XIII, 462). His reputation as an historian rests chiefly on his *History of the State of New York,* which remains the standard work for the period covered. He was a thorough, accurate, and conscientious scholar, trained in the classics, in law and diplomacy, and broadened by wide and intimate contact with men and things in two of the courts of Europe. If his descent from both conqueror and conquered did not assure an unpartisan spirit as completely as he thought it would do (see Preface, vol. II), his too favorable treatment of the Dutch burghers may have been caused by a reaction, more intense than he realized, against the ludicrous impression given of them in Irving's *Knickerbocker's History of New York.*

[The fullest account of Brodhead (with portrait) appeared in *Scribner's Mo.,* XIII, 459–63. There was a lengthy obituary in the *N. Y. Tribune,* May 7, 1873. Brief mention of him is made in Justin Winsor, *Narr. and Crit. Hist.* (1884–89), III, IV. Several of his letters (1840–42) are printed in H. L. P. Rice, *Harmanus Bleecker, an Albany Dutchman* (1924). His addresses before the New York Historical Society on its fortieth anniversary (1844) and on the two hundredth anniversary of the conquest of New Netherland (1864), as well as others of his papers appear in the publications of the society. He contributed to *Papers Concerning the Boundary between N. Y. and N. J.* (H. B. Dawson, ed., Yonkers, 1866).]   E.W.P.

BROKMEYER, HENRY C. (Aug. 12, 1828– July 26, 1906), philosopher, was born near Minden, Prussia, the son of Frederick William Brockmeyer (for spelling see below), a Jewish business man of moderate wealth. On his mother's side he was related to Prince Bismarck. He was educated in the common schools of the neighborhood until the age of sixteen, when, rebellious against Prussian militarism, he took passage for New York in an emigrant ship, arriving with twenty-five cents in his pocket and three words of English in his vocabulary. He worked first as a bootblack, then as a currier, and later added tanning and shoemaking to his accomplishments. Living with great frugality, he saved enough on his wages of one dollar a day to start west, traveling, mainly on foot, through Ohio and Indiana, and finally bringing up at Memphis, Tenn. There for two years he conducted a combined tanning, currying, and shoemaking establishment; through employing the cheap labor of broken-down negroes he is said to have been able to manufacture a pair of shoes for six and a quarter cents. Giving up this profitable business for the sake of further education, in 1850 he entered the preparatory department of Georgetown College, Ky. Threatened with dismissal after two years, owing to theological controversy with the president, he returned to the more liberal East and at Brown University, for another two years, engaged in joyous disputation with President Wayland. In 1854 he went west for the second time and located in an abandoned cabin in the woods of Warren County, Mo. For two years he lived the life of a recluse, devoting himself to the study of philosophy. When at last partially reconciled to the ways of civilization, chiefly through the influence of Hegel, he moved in to St. Louis and worked as an iron-molder, while still consecrating his evenings to study (see *A Mechanic's Diary,* by Brokmeyer, 1910). Having accidentally made the acquaintance of William Torrey Harris [*q.v.*], he undertook to instruct him and a group of friends in German philosophy but soon purchased a tract of eighty acres in Warren County, built himself a small cabin, and resumed his solitary life. This was effectively broken in 1858 when he was prostrated by an attack of bilious fever, and, being utterly helpless, would probably have died had he not been discovered by Harris, who brought him to St. Louis and had him properly cared for. As soon as his health was recovered, Brokmeyer resumed his philosophy class whose members pensioned him to the extent of food and lodging while he made a literal translation of Hegel's monumental *Larger Logic* which he completed within a year.

In the summer of 1861 he signalized his acceptance of society by marriage to Elizabeth Robertson, "an estimable lady" of St. Louis. During the Civil War he served in the militia and organized a regiment, for which effort he was rewarded by being arrested and thrown into prison on a charge of disloyalty fomented by personal enemies. Speedily released, he was six weeks later elected as a "War Democrat" to the legislature (1862–64) where he was prominent in opposing all measures looking toward the disfranchisement of Southern sympathizers. In 1866 he was elected to the Board of Aldermen of St. Louis. His first wife having died in 1864, he was married in January 1867 to Julia Kienlen of St. Louis. He had several children whom he ruled with a rod of iron. In 1870 he was elected to the state Senate, his followers buying him a new suit of clothes for the occasion, and in 1875 as a member of the constitutional convention he took a leading part in shaping the state's constitution. In the latter year he was also lieutenant-governor and in 1876–77 was acting governor during the illness of Gov. Phelps. Meanwhile he was far from neglecting his major interest, philosophy. In January 1866 he and his protégé Harris had organized the St. Louis Philosophical Society, of which Brokmeyer was elected president. With his intense, fiery, poetic personality, Brokmeyer became the oracle of a remarkable group composed of Harris, Denton J. Snider, Thomas Davidson, George H. Howison, Adolph Kroeger, J. Gabriel Woerner, and others who for more than a decade spread the glad tidings of German idealism throughout the Middle West and influenced to no inconsiderable degree the development of its culture. The "St. Louis Movement," initiated by Brokmeyer, differed from its predecessor at Concord in being based upon Hegel rather than Kant and in emphasizing society rather than the individual. Its weakness lay in its Hegelian idealization of the actual and in its alliance with the material prosperity of its center. Brokmeyer shared to the full in the current illusions as to the future greatness of St. Louis, "the Athens of America," and rejoiced with the others in the Chicago fire of 1871, pointing out that this rival city, an incarnation of the negative principle, had now negated itself. After 1880 the movement declined, and Brokmeyer declined with it, becoming an attorney for the Gould railroads. His last public appearance was as elector-at-large on the Cleveland ticket in 1884 when he received the largest popular vote ever cast in Missouri up to that time.

With his philosophical followers scattered, unable to get his highly Teutonized translation of the *Larger Logic* published (which he completely revised in 1892), he spent his later years in half-melancholy sorties into the farther West on long hunting and fishing expeditions or in search of health. On these trips, he was accustomed to cut down numerous mahogany and rosewood saplings which he shipped back to St. Louis, where at his leisure he whittled out beautifully polished walking-sticks for his friends; the chips

he frugally utilized for equally æsthetic toothpicks, carefully cut in three different sizes and bottled with elaborately carved corks. He also always made his own shells and fishing tackle. The Creek Indians, in admiration of his hunting ability, officially bestowed upon him the title of "Great White Father," and offered him his choice of the fairest maidens of the tribe—an offer which his Hegelianism compelled him regretfully to decline.

The personality of Brokmeyer was never adequately expressed in his own incoherent writings, which included, among others: *A Foggy Night at Newport* (a poetic drama privately printed in 1860), "The Errand Boy," and "Letters on Faust" (*Journal of Speculative Philosophy*, I, 178–87), the latter characterized by Woodbridge Riley as "neither philosophy nor literature." The manuscript of his *magnum opus*, the first English translation of Hegel's *Larger Logic*, now rests, still unpublished, in the Missouri Historical Society. His published writings mostly appeared under the name "Brockmeyer," as he had a philosophic scorn for the minutiæ of spelling, and spelled his name with or without the "c" and with "i" or "y," according as the mood took him, although the shorter form tended on the whole to predominate. Snider gives the following description of his physical appearance: "He had the quick, almost wild, eye of the hunter; his body was very compactly and stoutly knit without a flabby spot of flesh in it—tall, arrowy and lithe. His face was unshaven, though sparse of beard, which seemed rather furzy on the cheeks but somewhat denser on chin and upper lip. But the most prominent feature was an enormous nose, somewhat hooked, which had the power of flattening and bulging, of curling and curveting and crooking in a variety of ways expressive of what was going on within him. . . . The whole physical man rayed forth at every point two main qualities: agility and strength" (*A Writer of Books*, 1910, p. 303).

[Sketch in L. U. Reavis, *Saint Louis, the Future Great City of the World* (1875), pp. 336–42; *The Early St. Louis Movement* (1921); Denton J. Snider, *The St. Louis Movement* (1920); Woodbridge Riley, *Am. Thought* (1915); *Mo. Hist. Rev.*, I, 149; *St. Louis Republic*, July 27, 1906; J. H. Muirhead, "How Hegel Came to America," *Philosophical Rev.*, May 1928; information as to specific facts from Brokmeyer's son, Mr. Eugene C. Brokmeyer of Washington, D. C.]

E. S. B.

BROMFIELD, JOHN (Apr. 11, 1779–Dec. 9, 1849), philanthropist and merchant, born in Newburyport, Mass., was the son of John and Ann (Roberts) Bromfield. His father was a descendant of a family of merchants, of whom the first came to Boston from England in 1675. His mother had enjoyed all the advantages of an English university which her father had attended, and she in turn instructed her children. Her daughter relates that before the age of eight John could recite long passages from Pope's poetry and a great quantity of other verse and prose. The boy showed such studious habits and such an aptitude for languages and various subjects at Dummer Academy in Byfield and at other schools that, in 1792, his father, then living in Charlestown, wished to send him to Harvard. This could be possible, however, only through financial help from two aunts, and as the boy had an extraordinarily independent nature he refused to go under these conditions. He insisted on becoming an apprentice in some mercantile house and until he was almost twenty-one years old was in the service successively of two Charlestown firms. The failure of the second firm brought him long months of unemployment. In despair he had decided to learn the trade of a carpenter, but suddenly found an opening in Boston which made this unnecessary. As he had shown unusual industry and judgment as well as an agreeable manner during his years of apprenticeship, he was employed from 1800 to 1813 as a trusted agent for Boston firms and individuals in various parts of the world. Under the unfavorable conditions of the Napoleonic wars, his trips were on the whole financial failures, as letters to his family from Liverpool, London, and Rotterdam show.

In 1809 he was sent to China with a large sum of money, and the successful year spent there gave him a small capital as well as a knowledge of the East which made possible later enterprises of his own. In 1813, after another ruinous trip to Europe, he decided it would be prudent to remain in Boston. The China trade and careful investments of his profits gave him sufficient wealth to provide his mother and sister with many comforts and luxuries and to give quietly to individuals whom he knew to be in need. At his death he left an estate of $200,000. He never married. In more or less wretched health, he saw very little of people and lived with books, making frequent trips to see his family, which, after his mother's death in 1828, consisted of his sister and her husband. An extreme reserve, which increased as he grew older, was a further cause of his rather solitary life. The literary interests which were his main recreation had made him familiar with the needs of the Boston Athenæum, and toward the end of his life he made it a gift of $25,000, at first with the condition that his name should not be made known. He finally allowed himself to be overruled on

this point, however, by his friends, among whom was Josiah Quincy. His will showed that he had left to the Massachusetts General Hospital and the McLean Asylum in equal shares $40,000, and to the Massachusetts Eye and Ear Infirmary, the Boston Female Asylum, the Asylum for Indigent Boys, the Farm School at Thompson's Island, the Asylum for the Blind, the Seaman's Aid Society and his native town of Newburyport, each $10,000.

[Ann Bromfield Tracy, *Reminiscences of John Bromfield* (1852); Josiah Quincy, *Memoir of John Bromfield* (1850).]

M. A. K.

BROMLEY, ISAAC HILL (Mar. 6, 1833–Aug. 11, 1898), journalist, familiarly known to the intimates of his day and generation as "Brom" and to newspaper men as "I. H. B.," was one of nine children who crowded the house of their parents—Isaac and Mary (Hill)—at Norwich, Conn. As their names suggest, these parents were God-fearing people who lived ardently in the flaming light of the gospel, in awe and reverence, after the manner and spirit of the times. What might otherwise have imparted to their house an atmosphere of severity in social relations was softened by the innate whimsicality of the mother and the amiability and practical sense of the father. The literature of the family, though gradually increasing, and more or less reluctantly becoming liberal, assigned the place of honor to the Scriptures and *Fox's Book of Martyrs*. From both parents Bromley inherited a profound but undemonstrative religious faith. It was from his mother that he received the keen sense of humor which made him a writer and lecturer of fascinating quality—a picturesque figure in print, on the platform, at the banquet table, and in social intercourse. He inherited but little of the practical temperament of his father. Life was too joyous for that, the battle too strong an appeal to his sense of humor, the material reward too elusive. On Dec. 25, 1855, he married Adelaide Emma Roath whose parents were respectively Jabez and Clarissa, names also strongly suggestive of early nineteenth century social and hereditary influences. Isaac and Adelaide had only one child, another Isaac.

Bromley entered Yale College in August 1849, becoming a member of the notable class of 1853. His college course was interrupted in the sophomore year but, in 1868, the degree of B.A. was conferred upon him and he was enrolled with his class. Thereafter he was numbered among its most distinguished members. He studied law in the office of the Hon. L. F. B. Foster of Norwich, a leader at the bar from whom he imbibed a keen relish for human problems, later to convert it into a newspaper asset. He was admitted to the bar in 1854 but study of Blackstone only whetted his appetite for the wider fields of exploration and adventure which newspaper work seemed to promise him. He sought further preparation for what became his life-work in the post of assistant clerk of the Connecticut House of Representatives, to which he was called in 1856. The year following he became clerk of the House and, in 1858, clerk of the Senate. His first serious newspaper work was undertaken in November 1858 when he began the publication of the Norwich *Bulletin,* a daily whose columns he enlivened with his wit and satire. In August 1862 he enlisted in the 18th Connecticut Volunteers and was commissioned captain. After a varied and useful, but not spectacular service, he resigned, in 1864. A year later he resumed the editorship of the *Bulletin.* In 1866 he served a term in the Connecticut General Assembly and, in 1868, removed to Hartford and became the editor of the *Evening Post,* with which he remained until 1872. Between these periods of change, he visited the Far West and, as he expressed it, "subsequently fooled twenty or thirty small Connecticut towns with a lecture on the subject." Other trips, promoted by a restless desire to see the world and "get the hang of it," preceded his connection with the *New York Tribune,* which began in 1873 and continued ten years. In June 1882, he was appointed by President Arthur as a government director of the Union Pacific Railroad. There followed a series of brief editorial engagements with the *Commercial Advertiser* and the *Evening Telegram* of New York and the *Post-Express* of Rochester. Then, in 1884, he became assistant to the president of the Union Pacific Railroad. He held that office until 1889. In October 1891 he resumed his editorial connection with the *New York Tribune.* He remained in its service until a few months before his death, which occurred at Norwich.

Bromley's fame rested upon his skill and charm as a newspaper correspondent and editorial writer. Through the force of his originality and genius for estimating men and events at their true value, he brought to the editorial page of the *Tribune* a sparkle and thrust which earned him a reputation for influence and power equal to any attributed to the editor-proprietors of his day. His was the proverbial Yankee wit of New England. He was a handsome man, with clear-cut features, and black eyes which blazed with fire under provocation and melted in tenderness when the gentler emotions were touched. He was at ease with all men, in high or in humble walks of life, for he was essentially a man's man. He drew his friends from whatever environment he found himself in and left them quivering with a sense of warm refreshment. "I like the human family" was a familiar confession of his. He was at home with actors and artists; with big and little political chiefs of all tribes; with editors and cub reporters. Bromley was a partisan in his outlook on life but his work was performed during a period in the history of the country when impressions were real and convictions were passions; when partisanship was a masculine virtue.

[The chief sources are Norris G. Osborn, *Isaac H. Bromley* (1920); Jos. Bucklin Bishop, *Notes and Anecdotes of Many Years* (1925); autobiog. sketch in *Yale Coll., Class of 1853* (1883); obituary in *N. Y. Tribune,* Aug. 12, 1898. Five scrap-books of articles from Bromley's pen are in the Yale Univ. Lib. In E. C. Stedman's *Am. Anthology* (1900), there is an exquisite portrayal of "I. H. B." by Wm. Winter.]   N.G.O.

BRONDEL, JOHN BAPTIST (Feb. 23, 1842–Nov. 3, 1903), Catholic missionary and first bishop of Helena, Mont., was the son of Charles Joseph Brondel, a successful chair manufacturer of Bruges in Belgium. Finishing the elementary school conducted by the Xaverian Brothers, he attended the local College of St. Louis (1851–61). On graduation he dedicated his life to the American missions and enrolled in the American College at Louvain as a protégé of Bishop Blanchet of Nesqually, Washington Territory. Ordained (1864) at Mechlin by Cardinal Sterckx, he set forth via Panama for Puget Sound. For ten years he served the scattered white colonists and fur-men, half-breed traders, and Indians from missions at Walla Walla and at Steilacoom on the Sound. At Olympia and Tacoma he erected the first churches. Among the Indians, he was especially successful, even among the distant Chinooks of Alaska. His selection as third bishop of Vancouver (1879) was a merited honor, but one which did not transform the humble missionary.

Four years later, he was further burdened with the administration of the vicariate of Montana, and in 1884 he was transferred to the diocese of Helena as its first bishop. The Jesuits, who had been in the field since the arrival of De Smet, assigned their church in Helena to the Bishop who was welcomed in the name of the Catholics by Hon. Thomas Carter, later a powerful Republican senator. Thereafter, the life of Brondel became the history of his diocese. Regarded as a father by the Crows, Nez Percés, Flatheads, and Blackfeet tribesmen of whom there were 10,000 in Montana, he served the government faithfully on peace missions. Before the end of his life most of the Indians were Catholics and provided with chapels and ten schools. On visitations by stage coach and horse, the Bishop averaged 9,000 miles per year, which quite astounded his French correspondents. His diocese grew during his régime from thirteen to fifty-three priests serving sixty-five churches and a hundred chapels. An orphan asylum, nine parochial schools, an industrial school, a home for the aged, eight hospitals, St. Vincent's Academy in Helena, an Ursuline academy in Miles City, and a Good Shepherd home in Helena gave further evidences of Brondel's administrative activities. As the mines were commercially developed and as railroads replaced trails, the Catholic population of his diocese grew to 50,000.

[L. B. Palladino, *Indian and White in the Northwest* (1893) with introduction by Bishop Brondel whose manuscript diary and letters were used by the author; P. Ronan, *Hist. Sketch of the Flathead Indian Nation* (1890); K. Hughes, *Father Lacombe, the Black-Robed Voyageur* (1911); J. Van Der Heyden, *The Louvain American College* (1909); *Cath. Encyc.*; Kennedy's *Cath. Dir.* (1904); *Cath. News* (N. Y.), Nov. 1903; *Helena Independent,* Nov. 3, 1903.]   R. J. P.

BRONSON, HENRY (Jan. 30, 1804–Nov. 26, 1893), physician, historian, was fifth in descent from John Brownson or Bronson, who was supposed to have settled in Hartford with Thomas Hooker in 1632. He was born in Waterbury, Conn., and was the second son of Judge Bennet Bronson and Anna (Smith) Bronson. His two brothers had graduated from Yale but had died early in their careers, so his father, denying him a college training, had destined him to become a farmer. This plan did not coincide with Henry's wishes, however, and at seventeen or eighteen years of age he was allowed to follow his inclinations and prepare for the medical profession. In 1827 he was graduated with the degree of M.D. at Yale, and shortly thereafter settled in West Springfield, Mass., where he married in 1831 Sarah Miles Lathrop, daughter of the Hon. Samuel Lathrop, a former congressman. A few years later greater opportunities came to him on moving to Albany where he practised in association with Dr. Alden March, his former preceptor. Here he soon was much occupied with a constantly increasing and demanding practise, developing at the same time considerable ability in writing newspaper articles on medical topics. When a cholera epidemic came to Montreal and threatened Albany, he was sent by the mayor and several prominent men to Montreal to study this disease. His letters home upon this malady show him to have been a close observer and form interesting reading even to-day. Not long after his return home he removed to Waterbury, where he practised with success until broken health

necessitated a trip abroad. Upon his return he was elected in 1842 to fill the chair of materia medica and therapeutics at the Yale Medical School, and in 1845 removed his residence to New Haven. This chair he filled, with the exception of a single year, until 1860 when he retired to devote himself largely to historical research and economic study. In 1860 he was chosen president of the New Haven County Bank, and served on the city board of education during 1865–66. He also acted as president of the State Medical Society in 1869 and read, besides his presidential address, several papers which included sketches of the society's history, and short lives of its prominent members. In these papers he gained a reputation as an impartial historian. He also prepared three extended and important studies for the New Haven Colony Historical Society on the history of paper currency in Connecticut, early government in Connecticut, and the early history of medicine in New Haven County. In 1858 he published his valuable *History of Waterbury,* a model of accurate and painstaking research. The inheritance which he had received from his father he increased by wise investments so that he was not dependent upon his profession and on moving to New Haven, relinquished his general practise. Of his fortune he gave liberally, Yale receiving between 1873 and 1890 about $80,000 to establish a professorship of comparative anatomy; the New Haven Hospital $10,000, and the Waterbury Hospital $5,000. After 1870, when he was operated upon for a stone in the bladder, he never enjoyed good health. In 1891 he was severely injured in a runaway accident and died two years later, of cystitis and renal disease, in his ninetieth year.

[Jos. Anderson, *The Town and City of Waterbury, Conn.* (1896), III, 855–57; *Obit. Record Grads. Yale Univ.,* 1894, pp. 253–54; *Trans. Conn. Medic. Soc.,* 1894, pp. 229–30; Memoir by Dr. Stephen G. Hubbard in *Papers of the New Haven Colony Hist. Soc.,* VI (1900), 3–99; and *Representative Citizens of Conn.* (1916), pp. 499–501.]   W. R. S.

BRONSON, WALTER COCHRANE (Aug. 17, 1862–June 2, 1928), educator, anthologist, and editor, for thirty-five years professor of English literature in Brown University, was born in Roxbury, Mass., the son of Benjamin Franklin and Anne Hasseltine (Chaplin) Bronson. Both his father and grandfather, Asa C. Bronson, were Baptist ministers. He prepared for college at the Putnam, Conn., high school, but poor health prevented him from entering college until he was twenty-one years old. He graduated from Brown with high honors in 1887, and spent the following year in the Harvard Divinity School. Interest in literature caused him to abandon his youthful intention of entering the ministry, however, and from 1888 to 1890 he did graduate work at Cornell University. After a brief period as professor at De Pauw University (1890–92) he returned to Brown as associate professor of English literature, becoming full professor in 1905, and later head of the department. On Aug. 17, 1905, he married Elsie Marion Straffin. At the age of sixty-five he voluntarily retired that he might have freedom for study and writing, but the following year death came to him while he was engaged in research work at Oxford, England.

He was a shy, modest man, happy among his books, but not lacking in practical wisdom, and endowed with a shrewd knowledge of human nature, a keen sense of humor, and a kindly, optimistic spirit, which made him a valued counselor, and an attractive personality in the lecture room. He never fell into academic ruts, was as appreciative of the new as of the ancient, and as he grew older his power increased rather than abated. His latest students were the most emphatic in praise of his stimulating force. By nature he was a poet, and his Class Day poem, "Modern Monks," a plea for a broad intellectual life, had an excellence unusual in such productions. His creative tendencies were restrained, however, by an acute critical sense, a liking for research, and his genius for teaching. He held it finer to teach great literature than to produce a middling sort. As a result his contributions to the field of literature were chiefly confined to the stimulation which he gave his pupils, and to admirable historical and editorial work. His *Poems of William Collins* (1898), prepared with meticulous care, is a definitive edition of that author's writings, and his *A Short History of American Literature* (1900) has both accurate and discriminating information, and literary atmosphere. The worth of his *English Essays* (1905), *English Poems* (1907–10), *American Poems* (1912), and *American Prose* (1916) is attested by their wide use. He was also the author of a *History of Brown University* (1914), and was a valued adviser and contributor to the *Dictionary of American Biography*.

[*Providence Jour.*, June 3, 1928; H. R. Palmer, "Walter Cochrane Bronson—In Memoriam," *Brown Alumni Mo.*, July 1928; *Who's Who in America*, 1926–27.]

H. E. S.

BROOKE, FRANCIS TALIAFERRO (Aug. 27, 1763–Mar. 3, 1851), soldier and jurist, son of Richard and Elizabeth (Taliaferro) Brooke, was a native of Smithfield, near Fredericksburg,

Va. His grandfather accompanied Gov. Spotswood in the famous pioneer journey to the Blue Ridge. His father had other sons more or less prominent, one of them, Robert, a governor of Virginia. Francis Brooke was well educated, and at the unusually early age of sixteen he enlisted in the Revolutionary army. As a lieutenant he served under Lafayette and more directly under Harrison, and in his *Narrative* he describes conditions in his state at the time of Cornwallis's campaign in 1781 and Tarleton's raid into the interior. He was sent with his company under the general command of Col. Febiger to the south, and he passed the last months of the war with Gen. Greene, and at Savannah. After the peace he studied law with his brother Robert, and became a district attorney. He also entered political life, and was in the House of Delegates 1794–95, and later in the state Senate. While serving as speaker of the Senate in 1804 he was elected judge of the general court, and henceforth his career was on the bench. In 1811 he was elected judge of the supreme court of appeals, and served with that body for the rest of his life, during six years (1824–30) being its president (*Virginia Reports 2, Randolph's Reports* to *2 Leigh's Reports*). In military affairs he was a vice-president of the Cincinnati, and in the state militia he was appointed major in 1796, lieutenant-colonel in 1800, and brigadier-general in 1802. He was married twice: first, in October 1791 to Mary Randolph Spotswood (a niece of George Washington) who died in 1803; second, in 1804 to Mary Champe Carter, who died in 1846. Near the close of his life Brooke wrote for members of his family his *Narrative*. It is a full and rather naive account, especially detailed for the earlier years. Besides domestic and personal matters, the memoir has some historical value. Brooke records his acquaintance with Greene, Gates, Jefferson, Monroe, and others, and particularly with Washington. The two were neighbors, were quite intimate from Brooke's boyhood, and the *Narrative* gives a fairly close view of the President when off—as well as when on—"dress parade."

[F. T. Brooke, *Narrative of My Life for My Family* (privately printed, 1849), an excessively rare work, reprinted as "Family Narrative" in *Mag. of Hist.*, Extra No. 74, 1921; St. George T. Brooke, "The Brooke Family of Va." in *Va. Mag. of Hist. and Biog.*, Jan. 1902 to Oct. 1912; *Works of Henry Clay* (1855–57), containing many letters from Clay to Brooke.]

E. K. A.

BROOKE, JOHN MERCER (Dec. 18, 1826–Dec. 14, 1906), naval officer and scientist, was born in the Brooke Cantonment near Tampa, Fla., the son of Brevet Major-General George

Mercer Brooke, U. S. A., of Virginia, and Lucy (Thomas) Brooke of Duxbury, Mass., who died when her son was only nine years old. Becoming a midshipman in the United States Navy, Mar. 3, 1841, young Brooke saw service first on the *Delaware,* under Commander David Glasgow Farragut, in Brazilian waters. After a cruise to the Pacific round the Horn in the sloop of war *Cyane,* he entered the Naval Academy, recently established at Annapolis, in 1845, where he was graduated two years later. His next important duty was with the hydrographic party of the Coast Survey under Lieut. Samuel P. Lee, 1849–50; and with Maury at the Naval Observatory in Washington, 1851–53, where he invented a deep-sea sounding apparatus by which specimens from the ocean were first brought to light and the topography of its bottom accurately mapped. For this contribution to science, he received in 1860 from the King of Prussia the gold medal of science from the Academy of Berlin. In 1854, Brooke was attached to the *Vincennes* of the North Pacific and Bering Straits Surveying and Exploring Expedition, commanded by Commodore Cadwalader Ringgold (succeeded by Commodore John Rodgers), and given the duty of determining astronomically the geographical position of primary points and of measuring with the chronometer differences of longitude. Returning to Washington, he was there engaged with Commodore Rodgers, until May 24, 1858, in preparing the charts and records of the expedition for publication. Meanwhile having been promoted to lieutenant Sept. 15, 1855, he was assigned to the duty of surveying a route from California to China, in 1858, and accordingly, in the schooner *Fenimore Cooper,* he made deep-sea soundings and important surveys of several islands in the Pacific and of a considerable part of the east coast of Japan. A cyclone, which wrecked his ship at Giddo, Japan, while he was in conference with the American minister at Yedo, interrupted this work, and forced him to wait at Yokohama, until Feb. 10, 1860, for passage home for himself and his crew on the *Powhatan,* flagship of the Asiatic Squadron. Meanwhile he established cordial relations with the Japanese authorities, and at their request took passage on the Japanese corvette *Candinmarroo* to assist her captain in navigating his ship. This vessel, conveying the first Japanese minister to the United States, sailed in company with the *Powhatan,* but after a stormy passage arrived in San Francisco thirteen days in advance of the American ship. For this service the Japanese offered Brooke a large purse, which he declined. At the outbreak of the

Civil War, he resigned Apr. 20, 1861, and going to Richmond, joined the Virginia state navy and soon afterward entered the navy of the Confederate States, becoming a commander Sept. 13, 1862. Early in June 1861, his plan for reconstructing the U. S. S. *Merrimac* into an ironclad by making use of the "submerged ends principle" was approved by Secretary of the Navy Mallory, for which patent number 100 was granted Brooke by the Confederate government, July 29, 1862, to counteract an attempt to deprive him of this honor. He also prepared, in the Tredegar Iron Works in Richmond, the armor and guns for this ship, renamed the C. S. S. *Virginia.* From March 1863 to the close of the war he was chief of the Bureau of Ordnance and Hydrography. The "Brooke" gun, which he invented, was the most powerful one produced by the Confederates. It was a rifle, made of cast-iron but strengthened by wrought-iron hoops or jackets; it was also unique in the utilization for the first time of what is called the "air space" to diminish the initial tension of the gases. At the close of the war, Brooke became professor of physics and astronomy in the Virginia Military Institute, where a few years later Maury also became a professor. In 1899 he retired from active duty, and seven years later died at his home in Lexington very near the age of eighty. Maury-Brooke Hall at Virginia Military Institute is a memorial to the two distinguished naval officers and scientists. Brooke was twice married, his first wife being Elizabeth Selden Garnett of Norfolk, and the second, Kate Corbin of Mossneck, Va. In appearance, Brooke was slender and active, and had the fair complexion of his New England mother; in later life he wore a full beard. As a member of the Episcopal Church, he had sincere religious convictions but was simple and unpretending in his piety. He was characterized particularly by having high ideals, great determination of purpose, inflexible loyalty to his friends, an intolerance of sham and pretense, and a peculiar fitness for research work of a scientific nature.

[The principal sources of information about Brooke are his letters and papers in the hands of his daughter, Mrs. H. P. Willis, New Brighton, N. Y.; *In Memoriam,* from the minutes of the Academic Board of the Virginia Military Institute, Dec. 31, 1906; John M. Brooke, "The Plan and Construction of the Merrimac," in *Battles and Leaders of the Civil War* (1887–88), I, 715; John M. Brooke, "The Virginia, or Merrimac: her Real Projector" in *Southern Hist. Soc. Papers,* XIX, 3–34; *Official Records (Navy)* ; and the *Navy Register,* 1842–61.]   C. L. L.

BROOKE, JOHN RUTTER (July 21, 1838– Sept. 5, 1926), Union soldier, was born in Montgomery County, Pa., the son of William and Martha (Rutter) Brooke. His first American ancestor came from Yorkshire in 1698. He was educated at Freeland Seminary (in whose buildings Ursinus College was afterward organized) and in West Chester, Pa. Responding to the call for three months' service, at the outbreak of the Civil War, he was mustered in, Apr. 20, 1861, as captain in the 4th Pennsylvania Infantry. This was the regiment which won notoriety by claiming its discharge just before the battle of Bull Run. In spite of the personal appeals of the Secretary of War (Cameron), it marched back from Centreville on the morning of the battle, while the rest of the army moved forward into action. Brooke was mustered out on July 26, 1861, but not sharing the regiment's antipathy to fighting he still sought service, and was again mustered in, Nov. 7, 1861, as colonel of the new 53rd Pennsylvania Infantry, and with it joined the Army of the Potomac. He commanded his regiment in the Peninsular campaign, a brigade at Antietam, and his regiment once more at Fredericksburg. He was finally assigned to the command of a brigade of the 2nd Corps in December 1862, though without promotion. This he commanded at Chancellorsville and Gettysburg. In the latter battle, the 2nd Corps arrived on the field early in the morning of the second day, and was posted near the center of the Union line. When the Confederate attack was made upon the salient held by the 3rd Corps (Sickles), Caldwell's division, to which Brooke's brigade belonged, was sent to its assistance, and took part in the desperate fighting around the wheat-field. Brooke was wounded,—"severely bruised" was his own expression for it,—but continued in command. "Of the merit of Col. Brooke, commanding 4th Brigade, too much can scarcely be said," wrote Gen. Caldwell in his report. "His services on this as well as many other fields have fairly earned him promotion" (*Official Records,* ser. I, vol. XXVII, pt. 1, pp. 380–81). Through the winter of 1863–64 Brooke was in command of the veteran camp at Harrisburg, returning to the army before it took the field for the spring campaign. He sustained and enhanced his reputation for hard fighting, at last receiving appointment as brigadier-general of volunteers, May 12, 1864, the commission itself reciting that it was conferred "for distinguished services during the recent battles of the Old Wilderness and Spottsylvania Court House, Va." In the great assault at Cold Harbor, June 3, he was severely wounded, and was carried from the field insensible. He could not return to duty until September, and being still unfit for field service, was then employed on boards and courts until March 1865, when he took command of a division of the Army of the Shenandoah. He resigned from the army on Feb. 1, 1866, but returned to service on being appointed, July 28, 1866, lieutenant-colonel of the 37th Infantry, in the regular army. He was promoted to colonel, Mar. 20, 1879, to brigadier-general, Apr. 6, 1888, and to major-general, May 22, 1897. At the beginning of the war with Spain he was assigned to the command of the 1st Corps, and put in charge of the camp at Chickamauga Park, Ga., where his own corps, and also the 3rd (Wade's) were stationed. As the responsible commander, he incurred some of the blame for the deplorable sanitary conditions in that camp. Late in July he was sent with part of his troops to participate in the campaign in Porto Rico. Landing at Arroyo, July 31, he advanced to Guayama where he had a slight skirmish, Aug. 5, and then to Cayey. He was preparing to attack the Spaniards at this place,—the guns were laid and awaiting the order to fire,—when notice reached him that the armistice had been concluded. After the Spanish evacuation he was military governor of Porto Rico for a few months, and of Cuba for a year, returning to the United States to take command of the Department of the East. He was twice married: first, Dec. 24, 1863, to Louisa Roberts, who died in 1867, and second, Sept. 19, 1877, to Mary L. Stearns, of Concord, N. H. He died in Philadelphia.

[F. B. Heitman, *Hist. Reg.* (1903), I, 248; *Official Records* (*Army*), 1 ser. XI (pt. 1), XIX (pt. 1), XXI, XXV, XXVII (pt. 1), XXIX (pt. 1), XXXVI (pts. 1, 2, 3); "Report of the Commission to Investigate the Conduct of the War Dept. in the War with Spain," *Sen. Doc. No. 221,* 56 Cong., 2 Sess., VI, 3064–3106, giving Brooke's testimony on conditions at Chickamauga Park; *Harper's Pictorial Hist. of the War with Spain* (1899), II, 393–406; obituary in *Phila. Inquirer,* Sept. 6, 1926.]
T. M. S.

BROOKER, CHARLES FREDERICK (Mar. 4, 1847–Dec. 20, 1926), manufacturer and financier, was descended in the sixth generation from John Brooker, shipwright, who settled in Guilford, Conn., about 1695. He was born in Litchfield, Conn., the son of Martin Cook and Sarah Maria (Seymour) Brooker. One of six children, and the only living son, his early years were divided between work on his father's farm and attendance at the Litchfield and Torrington district schools. His business career commenced at the early age of twelve as clerk in the general store at Torrington and was followed by similar work in Waterbury. His manufacturing career started in 1864 when at the age of seventeen he was employed by Lyman

W. Coe, who the year before had acquired the Wolcottville Brass Company of Wolcottville (later Torrington). Under the guiding hand of Coe, a mid-century leader in the Connecticut brass industry, Brooker's capacity as a salesman and executive developed rapidly; he eventually became secretary of the Coe Brass Manufacturing Company and upon the death of Lyman W. Coe in 1893 succeeded the latter as president.

Brooker was identified with the development of the brass industry of Connecticut for sixty-two years and during most of that period in a prominent capacity. As business organizer, his most important work was the formation of the American Brass Company in 1899, a holding company into which were originally amalgamated four of the leading brass manufacturing units of the Naugatuck Valley. Thirteen years later under his supervision the subsidiary companies were dissolved and the American Brass Company became an operating company. In 1921 the Anaconda Copper Mining Company, the largest producer of copper and zinc in the world, desiring to ally itself more closely with what was then the greatest fabricating interest in the business, approached Brooker with a plan for consolidation. His approval and the ratification by the stockholders resulted in the purchase of the stock of the American Brass Company by the Anaconda Copper Mining Company. Brooker as president of the American Brass Company (1900–20) and later as chairman of the board of directors was the chief figure in these reorganizations. After the consolidation Brooker became a director of the Anaconda Company and of its most important subsidiaries. His business interests, however, extended beyond the metal industries. He was at one time president of the Ansonia National Bank and a director of banks in Torrington, New Haven, Boston, Chicago, and New York. He was also for many years a director of the New York, New Haven & Hartford Railroad Company and of several of its subsidiaries. It was at that time that Brooker's influence was exerted to secure the double-tracking and other transportation improvements necessary for the industrial future of the Naugatuck Valley.

Brooker's interest in politics was life-long, and his influence in Connecticut politics was important. He was elected to the Connecticut House of Representatives in 1875 and to the Senate in 1893 on the Republican ticket, but he preferred to act in an advisory capacity rather than through elective office. He was for many years a member of the Republican state central commit-

tee, a member of the Republican national committee (1900–16) and of the executive committee of the latter organization (1904–08). He represented Connecticut as a delegate at large at the Republican National Conventions of 1900, 1904, 1908, 1912, and 1920. Although a personal friend of Roosevelt he maintained in 1912 his allegiance to the conservative wing of the party.

Tactful in his dealings, and of an approachable disposition, Brooker was a man with a wide circle of friends and numerous club memberships. Comparatively late in life (1894) he married Julia E. Clarke Farrel of Ansonia, who died in 1917. Interested in philanthropy, he founded the Maria Seymour Brooker Memorial at Torrington and the "Julia" day nursery at Ansonia, the former in memory of his mother and the latter of his wife. He was especially interested in the Gaylord Farm Sanitorium, maintained by the New Haven County Anti-Tuberculosis Association, of which he was president. His will contained bequests of over $500,000 to various educational and philanthropic enterprises. Active in business until within a few months of the end, he died at Daytona, Fla., where he had spent his last winter in search of health.

[The records of the Am. Brass Co. supply the chief sources for Brooker's career. A scrap-book of newspaper and other clippings relating to him are preserved in the office of the president at Waterbury. The *Ansonia Sentinel, Torrington Register, Waterbury Democrat,* of Dec. 20, 1926, contain obituary notices. See also *Metal Industry,* Jan. 1927, p. 23. The *Waterbury Republican* for Jan. 12, and the *Torrington Register* for Jan. 25, 1927, contain long reports of a memorial address delivered by John A. Coe, his successor as president of the Am. Brass Co. There are brief references to his work in Wm. G. Lathrop, *The Brass Industry in the U. S.* (1926), pp. 118–21, 156.]   H.U.F.

BROOKS, ALFRED HULSE (July 18, 1871– Nov. 22, 1924), geologist and geographer, was born in Ann Arbor, Mich. His father was Thomas Benton Brooks [*q.v.*], who in company with Raphael Pumpelly made the first systematic investigations of the copper regions of Lake Superior and northern Michigan. His mother's maiden name was Hannah Hulse. When a child of but six months he was taken with his parents to Germany where they remained until he was five years of age. Returning to America, they settled at Newburgh, N. Y., where he received his elementary education in the public schools and from private tutors. After several years of residence in Decatur County, Ga., late in 1889 the Brooks family again went to Germany, remaining until 1891 when Alfred returned and entered Harvard University. He was a hard student, and it is stated by his biographer that throughout his college course he "knew definitely what he wanted and went after it with unremitting enthusiasm." Owing to ill health he was obliged to abandon his studies in 1893 and went to Roseland, Ga., where the family had settled on their return from their second trip abroad. His health soon permitting, he began in connection with A. F. Foerste a geological study of the local Tertiary deposits and in the fall of the same year returned to Harvard and graduated with his class in 1894, with the degree of B.S.

In June 1894 he became a member of a corps of United States geologists working under the immediate direction of C. W. Hayes in the Southern Appalachian regions. In company with numerous Americans, he attended the Geological Congress of 1897 in Russia, but instead of returning directly home, passed a few months of study at the Sorbonne in Paris, devoting his attention principally to petrography and geology under La Croix, Fouqué, Bertrand, and De Launay. While here he was offered once more a position on the United States Geological Survey which he promptly accepted and was assigned in 1898 to field work in Alaska. In 1902, after serving the intervening seasons under various parties, he was placed in entire charge of the geologic work of the territory, and to this he devoted his energies until his death, interrupted only by his army service during the World War.

Brooks was a man of unusual breadth, clearness of vision, and of prompt action. He was not merely a geologist. Far-seeing, he early realized the possibilities of engineering information as applied to modern methods of warfare and in May 1915 submitted to the director of the United States Geological Survey a memorandum suggesting the establishment by the War Department of a roster of the engineers and others in the government service whose special qualifications might be of value were they known to be available. Not content with mere suggestion, Brooks with his customary habit of following up his convictions with action promptly enlisted, in May 1916, in a citizens' training camp at Fort Oglethorpe, Ga., and in December 1916 made application for a commission in the Engineer Officers' Reserve Corps which resulted in his appointment as a captain and his sailing with the American Expeditionary Forces for France on Aug. 15, 1917. He was subsequently appointed Chief Geologist, A. E. F. Little can be said here of his accomplishments, other than to quote from a personal letter from Gen. Pershing accompanying his promotion to the rank of lieutenant-colonel when he left the service. "Your work," wrote Pershing, "was of a constructive character in a field new to military service, and the results of your efforts were becoming manifest to all."

As another has expressed it: he "for the first time 'sold' geology to the military establishment through the sheer force of having delivered useful service." Returning from France, he resumed his position at the head of the Alaskan division and died in the harness Nov. 22, 1924.

Brooks's interests were broad. At first his inclinations were toward topographic work and while this naturally threw him into companionship with geologists it is probable that the real turning-point in his life was due to the influence at Harvard of the magnetic N. S. Shaler [q.v.] and the students with whom he associated. That he should have also become a geographer, under like influences and training, followed almost as a matter of course. Brooks was a likeable, companionable man and thoroughly loyal to his calling and to his friends. His merits were recognized both by the Survey and by other organizations. In 1912 on the retirement of C. W. Hayes from the position of chief geologist of the Survey, the position was offered Brooks, who however, wisely as it proved, refused it, preferring the Alaskan field. He served on the Alaskan Railroad Commission in 1912–13 and his work here in connection with his monograph on Mt. McKinley in 1911 brought him in 1913 the Daly medal from the American Geographical Society and the same year the Malte-Brun medal from the Société de Géographie de Paris. This same year he was designated one of the delegates to the twelfth International Geologic Congress at Toronto. He was made a member of the Department of Commerce party on its trip to Alaska and Japan and was a delegate to the second Pan-Pacific Scientific Congress to Australia.

His publications though numerous and voluminous were necessarily not monographic, though his compilation in 1906 of over 300 pages on the *Geography and Geology of Alaska* is to this day the most complete treatise on the subject extant. In 1914–16 and in 1919–23 he prepared annually for publication detailed statements of the Alaskan mineral industry. Other important publications were his *Geologic Features of Alaskan Metalliferous Lodes* (1911); *The Future of Gold Placer Mining in Alaska* (1915); *Antimony Deposits in Alaska* (1916); *The Future of Alaska's Mining* (1920). As an interesting characteristic of the man it is told of him that in the preparation of his reports he dictated very little but wrote voluminously in a large and not very legible hand. His thoughts often outran his ability to transcribe them and words and sentences were left incomplete. The most singular feature was, however, that he never went over these first drafts, correcting and completing them, but practically disregarded them as having seemingly served merely to formulate his ideas, and wrote an entirely new article, sometimes re-writing several times but leaving all minor cor-rections, such as spelling and punctuation, to his secretary.

Personally Brooks was of medium height, rather stoutly built with an unusually large head, and with sandy hair and beard. He was mar-ried Feb. 23, 1903, to Mabel Baker of Washing-ton, D. C., by whom he had two children.

[Philip S. Smith, *Bull. Geol. Soc. of America*, XXXVII (1926), containing full bibliography.]

G. P. M.

BROOKS, BYRON ALDEN (Dec. 12, 1845–Sept. 28, 1911), teacher, inventor, was born at Theresa, Jefferson County, N. Y., the son of Thompson and Hannah (Parrish) Brooks. Thompson Brooks was the miller of Theresa, and his grist-mill was the environment in which Byron developed his interest in mechanics. As a boy he devised and applied several successful improvements in the mill machinery and further indicated his interest in his eager study of math-ematics, in which science he was far enough ad-vanced to teach at the Antwerp (N.Y.) Acad-emy, when at his father's death in 1861 he had to contribute to the support of the family. In 1866 he entered Wesleyan University at Middle-town, Conn., where he supported himself by tu-toring. Though he lost a year through illness, he completed his work in time to graduate with his class in 1871. From 1871 to 1872 he taught at Dobbs Ferry, N. Y., where he was principal of the Union Free School. From there he went to New York City where he was assistant editor of the *National Quarterly Review* (1873) and a teacher and principal in the public schools. As a writer and educator he became interested in the possibilities of the typewriter and as one having some mechanical skill, he studied the machine and attempted improvements. For his first success-ful improvement he received Patent No. 202,923, Apr. 30, 1878, the feature of which is the loca-tion of both a capital and a small letter on the same striking lever and the shifting of the paper roller by a key to bring either the large or small letter into printing position. He sold this patent for $7,000 to the Remingtons who immediately incorporated the improvement in their next model, the Remington No. 2, the first machine to write other than capital letters and the one from which the universal use of the typewriter dates. Following this success, Brooks devoted consid-erable time to typewriter inventions and obtained more than thirty patents, none of which ap-proached the first in importance. In fact, only

one equally important improvement remained to be made, namely, the provision for visible writ-ing, and though Brooks sought to incorporate this feature in a machine which he manufactured and sold as the Brooks Typewriter, he succeeded in making visible only two lines of printing at a time and for lack of any other outstanding fea-tures the machine was discontinued. In 1900 the Brooks Typewriter Company was sold to the Union Typewriter Company, which Brooks served as patent expert to the time of his death. He also attempted improvements in type-casting and composing machines and was president of the Bandotype Company, formed to promote his inventions in this field. At the time of his death in Brooklyn, N. Y., he was also working on a printing telegraph. Brooks married Sarah Davis of Middletown, Conn., in 1872, and after her death married, in 1906, Ella J. Ball of Brooklyn, N. Y. Brooks wrote *King Saul: A Tragedy* (1876); *Those Children and Their Teachers* (1882); *Phil Vernon and His Schoolmasters* (1885); and *Earth Revisited* (1893).

[C. V. Oden, *Evolution of the Typewriter* (1917); E. W. Byrn, *The Progress of Invention in the Nine-teenth Century* (1900); Records of the Wesleyan Univ. Alumni Council; Patent Office Records; correspon-dence with members of family; obituary in *N. Y. Her-ald*, Sept. 30, and *N. Y. Times*, Sept. 29, 1911, and *Typewriter Topics*, Nov. 1911.]

F. A. T.

BROOKS, CHARLES (Oct. 30, 1795–July 7, 1872), Unitarian educationist, clergyman, was born in Medford, Mass., the son of Jonathan and Elizabeth (Albree) Brooks. He fitted for col-lege under Dr. Luther Stearns who was both teacher and physician. In 1812 he entered Har-vard and graduated in 1816. Remaining for graduate work in theology he took his M.A. de-gree in 1819, delivering the valedictory address in Latin. The next year he became pastor of the Third Congregational Church (Unitarian) at Hingham, Mass., and remained there till 1839. In 1821 he published a *Family Prayer Book* of which eighteen editions appeared. In 1833–34 he visited Europe where he became impressed with the superior excellence of the Prussian schools and resolved to bring about improvement in the schools of Massachusetts. Soon after his return he began, in 1835, through printed arti-cles and addresses to carry his message to the people of his state. Starting with a Thanksgiv-ing Day address in Hingham, he spoke to large audiences in many of the chief towns, describing the needs of the schools of the state, dwelling much upon the theme "As is the teacher, so is the school," and urging that the state establish schools for the training of teachers. At the next session of the legislature he made two addresses to the members. It was at this session, subsequently, that the act was passed establishing the first real state board of education in the United States. At the request of its secretary, Horace Mann, Brooks began what proved to be a carriage journey of more than 2,000 miles back and forth through the state as he addressed the people of town after town. In this way he won to his cause the constituents of the members of the legislature who in 1838 voted the sum needed for the first state normal schools. To still further promote the normal-school movement he addressed the legislatures of New Hampshire, Vermont, Maine, and New Jersey, and bodies of citizens in Rhode Island and Pennsylvania. In 1839 having accepted the professorship of natural history in the University of the City of New York and resigned from his pastorate at Hingham, he went again to Europe where he spent four years in scientific study. On his return to this country because of failing sight he relinquished his professorship and retired to private life. Besides the *Family Prayer Book,* the most important of his published works were *Remarks on Europe, Relating to Education, Peace and Labor, and Their Reference to the United States* (1846), *Elements of Ornithology* (1847), and *History of the Town of Medford, Middlesex County, Mass.* (1855). He was married in 1827 to Cecilia Williams who died in 1837 leaving a son and daughter. In 1839 he was married to Mrs. Charlotte Ann (Haven) Lord. Slender in stature, Brooks was of attractive presence and winning personality. The closing years of his life were spent in Medford where he died.

[Memoir by Solomon Lincoln in *Proc. Mass. Hist. Soc.,* XVIII, 174; John Albree, *Chas. Brooks and His Work for Normal Schools* (1907); Henry Barnard's *Am. Jour. Educ.,* I, 587.]   W.J.C—e.

BROOKS, CHARLES TIMOTHY (June 20, 1813–June 14, 1883), Unitarian clergyman, poet, translator, was born in Salem, Mass., a descendant in the eighth generation of Henry Brooks, who came to Woburn, Mass., some time before 1649, and the son of Timothy Brooks. His mother was Mary King (Mason) Brooks. He prepared for college at the Salem Latin Grammar School, and entered Harvard at the age of fifteen, graduating in 1832. The next three years he spent in the Harvard Divinity School from which he graduated with honors. After supplying several churches for brief periods he was called to the Unitarian Congregational Church, Newport, R. I., beginning work there Jan. 1, 1837, although he was not ordained until June 14. Here he served as pastor until November 1871, and at Newport he made his home till his

death twelve years later. On Oct. 18, 1837, he married Harriet Lyman Hazard, daughter of Benjamin Hazard of Newport. His health was never robust and he suffered long from a throat affection, because of which he spent the winters of 1842 and 1851 in Mobile, Ala., where he took charge of the Unitarian Church. On account of his health he also spent almost a year (1853–54) in India. From October 1865 to September 1866 he was in Europe where he made the acquaintance of many eminent literary people.

Brooks was modest, peace-loving, somewhat disinclined to engage in practical affairs, fond of nature, a delightful companion, with a keen sense of humor, and power of lively repartee. His main interest was always in literature, and he gave as much time as possible to writing. Even in preparatory school he became noted for his proficiency in languages, and at Harvard he studied with avidity, especially German. Accordingly, while he wrote on literary and theological subjects for periodicals, and produced some excellent verse, drolleries, and children's books, he became best known through his translations from the German. His first considerable work of this kind was his translation of Schiller's *William Tell* (1837). The following year he published *German Lyrics,* which constituted vol. XIV of Ripley's Specimens of Foreign Literature. In 1842 appeared his *German Lyric Poetry,* to which Longfellow and others contributed; in 1846, Schiller's *Homage of the Arts;* in 1853 another edition of *German Lyrics;* in 1856, the first part of *Faust* in the original meters and in rhyme, with notes; in 1862, Jean Paul Richter's *Titan,* and in 1864, his *Hesperus.* He also published translations of Leopold Schefer's *Layman's Breviary* (1867) and *World's Priest* (1873), and several of Auerbach's novels. The most notable work of his later days was his English version of Friedrich Rückert's great poem *The Wisdom of the Brahmin,* the first six books of which appeared in 1882, the other two being in manuscript at the time of his death. His original writings include *Aquidneck . . . with Other Commemorative Pieces* (1848), *Songs of Field and Flood* (1853), and *The Old Stone Mill Controversy* (1851).

[W. P. Andrews, *Poems, Original and Translated by Chas. T. Brooks with a Memoir by Chas. W. Wendte* (1885). This contains a full bibliography of Brooks's works. See also *Essex Inst. Hist. Colls.,* vol. XX (1883), vol. XXI (1884).]   H.E.S.

BROOKS, ELBRIDGE STREETER (Apr. 14, 1846–Jan. 7, 1902), author, was born at Lowell, Mass., the son of Elbridge Gerry Brooks, a Universalist minister and anti-slavery man, and

Martha (Monroe) Brooks. During the boyhood of his son, the elder Brooks served churches in Bath, Me., Lynn, Mass., and New York City, and at the public schools of Lynn and New York the boy received his preliminary education. In 1861 he entered the Free Academy, afterward the College of the City of New York, where he remained only until the middle of his junior year. His lifelong connection with publishing houses began at this time with a clerkship with D. Appleton & Company. In 1873 he was with Ford & Company and Sheldon & Company; in 1876 he became head of the English educational and subscription department of E. Steiger & Company; and in 1879 he joined the staff of the *Publishers' Weekly*. He was from 1883 to 1885 literary editor and dramatic critic on the *Brooklyn Daily Times*. In 1884 he became associate editor of *St. Nicholas Magazine* and in 1887 removed to Somerville, Mass., to become an editor for D. Lothrop & Company. His relations with this firm were suspended for a short time between 1892 and 1895, during financial troubles and reorganization, but thereafter continued until his death. In 1891-93 he was editor of *Wide Awake*. In 1870 he married Hannah-Melissa Debaun of New York. One of his two daughters, Geraldine, became a writer.

Brooks began writing works for young people in 1880 and altogether published over forty books of this kind, some of the most popular of which are: *Story of the American Indian* (1887), *Story of the American Sailor* (1888), *Story of the American Soldier* (1889), *True Story of Christopher Columbus* (1892), *Century Book for Young Americans* (1894), issued under the auspices of the Sons of the American Revolution, *True Story of George Washington* (1895), *Boy Life of Napoleon* (1895), *True Story of Abraham Lincoln* (1896), *Century Book of Famous Americans* (1896), issued under the auspices of the Daughters of the American Revolution, *True Story of U. S. Grant* (1897), *True Story of the United States* (1897), *True Story of Benjamin Franklin* (1898), *True Story of Lafayette* (1899). The popularity of his books among young people has continued almost unabated and, although experts in juvenile literature criticize them as "machine-made," they still find them so decidedly interesting that they grudgingly approve them. Until a short time before his death at Somerville, Brooks was to be seen regularly at his office, a man of intellectual appearance, with large head, aquiline nose, deep, keen, spectacled eyes, white hair, and full white beard.

[*Who's Who in America*, 1901-02; *The Origin and Hist. of the Name of Brooks, with Biographies of All the Most Noted Persons of that Name—the Crescent Family Record* (1905); obituaries in the *Boston Transcript*, Jan. 7, 1902, and *Boston Herald*, Jan. 8, 1902.]

S. G. B.

BROOKS, ERASTUS (Jan. 31, 1815–Nov. 25, 1886), journalist, politician, was the son of James and Elizabeth (Folsom) Brooks. His father, while of English birth, had spent most of his life in the United States and had become so thoroughly an American that he commanded the cruiser *Yankee* against his native country in the War of 1812. Erastus was a posthumous son, born in Portland, Me. At the age of eight he was working in a grocery store in Boston for his board and clothes and studying in an evening school. He was later apprenticed to a compositor. While still very young he entered Brown University and supported himself entirely by working at the case in a printing office. He did not graduate but left college to start a paper called the *Yankee* in Wiscasset, Me. He soon went to Haverhill, Mass., and taught school under a school board of which the poet Whittier was a member. But the smell of printer's ink was in his nostrils and before long he was editor and proprietor of the *Haverhill Gazette*. An experience as reporter on the *Portland Advertiser* followed, and in his twentieth year he went to Washington where he wrote correspondence for a group of papers composed of the *New York Daily Advertiser*, the *Boston Transcript*, the *Portland Advertiser*, the *Baltimore American*, the *St. Louis Republican*, and the *New York Express*. Five years later we find him back in Portland, editing the *Advertiser* during the Harrison presidential campaign. At its close he was selected to carry Maine's electoral vote to Washington and remained there a year or two. In 1843 he made a tour from Queenstown to Moscow, writing for his group of papers vivid articles which were widely appreciated. On the return voyage the steamer was wrecked off Sandy Hook and Brooks was one of the few survivors. He then joined his brother James [*q.v.*] in the editorial management of the *New York Express*, subsequently assuming the entire control. His editorial career of thirty-four years was marked by exceptional enterprise and originality. During an epidemic of cholera in the city he got out the paper almost single-handed, acting as reporter and compositor as well as editor, and setting news stories and editorials at the case without first committing them to paper. His enterprise and inventiveness were exemplified in two journalistic "beats." In those days the state election news went first to Thurlow Weed's newspaper in Albany. Brooks took compositors with him to the capital, secured the election results from

Weed, turned a stateroom on the Albany boat into a composing-room, and reached New York with the type all set and ready for the press. The other "beat" was made by telegraph. The inaugural message of Gov. Silas Wright was telegraphed to the *Express* and when the famous pony express established by James Gordon Bennett, who scorned to use the telegraph in preference to it, reached Westchester County with a copy of the message on the way to the *Herald* office, it was met by Brooks's messengers with copies of the *Express* containing the document in print. Brooks took an active part in the controversy over the exemption of Catholic church property from taxation, debating vigorously with Archbishop Hughes the point that, since the property was held in the name of the bishops, it should be taxed like other personal holdings of realty. He was consequently elected, in 1853, to the state Senate on the American or Know-Nothing ticket, and continued to discuss the subject there. In 1856 he was nominated for governor by the same party but was defeated. The same year he was a member of the convention of the party which nominated Fillmore for president and in 1860 of the convention of the Constitutional Union party which named Bell and Everett. He served in the New York state constitutional convention of 1866–67, being made chairman of the committee on charities, and on the constitutional commission of 1872–73. In 1877 the *Express* passed into new ownership and Brooks retired to devote himself to politics and public affairs. He was elected five times from Richmond County to the New York Assembly where he served as a member of the important committees on ways and means, cities, and rules. He was active in many public and philanthropic bodies, was one of the founders of the Associated Press, and was for a time its manager. He was married to Margaret Dawes, daughter of Chief Justice Cranch of the circuit court of the District of Columbia. He died at his home on Staten Island.

[*Biography of the Hon. Erastus Brooks* (privately printed, Boston, 1882); *Am. Ann. Cyc.*, 1886; obituaries in the *N. Y. Mail and Express* and the *N. Y. Times*, Nov. 26, 1886.]   H.H.

BROOKS, GEORGE WASHINGTON (Mar. 16, 1821–Jan. 6, 1882), judge, was born at Elizabeth City, N. C., the son of William C. and Catherine (Davis) Brooks, widow of Capt. Hugh Knox. His ancestors, English in origin, migrated from Virginia to North Carolina (Albemarle), late in the seventeenth century. His schooling was obtained at Belvidere Academy in Perquimans County, a Quaker school of some reputation. Later, under difficulties, he studied law, and was licensed to practise in the county courts in 1844 and in the superior courts in 1846. His industry in his chosen profession soon providing him with an adequate income, he married Margaret Costin, June 20, 1850, and by her had three sons and two daughters. A Whig in politics, he represented his county in the House of Commons in 1852, and by voting with the insurgent element in the Democratic party had a share in preventing the election of a United States senator at that session. By 1861 he had become a considerable owner of lands and slaves, but he believed that slavery was doomed, and throughout the Civil War he was confident that the Federal cause would prevail. In the convention of 1865–66 he again represented his county and spoke bitterly of the trials and tribulations endured by a Southern Union man during the war. His open allegiance to the Union caused President Johnson to appoint him United States judge of the district of North Carolina, in August 1865; the nomination was duly confirmed by the Senate, Jan. 22, 1866. His conduct of this office until his death was marked by industry and sound judgment. One incident in his judicial career must be noticed. In the summer of 1870 North Carolina was, and had been for two years, in the throes of reconstruction:—on the one side corruption so brazen as to amount to rapine; on the other, midnight rovers, ministers of "wild justice," intimidating by their weird symbols and disguises, and flogging here or, if need be, hanging there. The governor, Holden, declared two counties in a state of insurrection, suspended the writ of *habeas corpus,* sent troops and had many prominent citizens arrested, and proposed to try them in a military court constituted by himself. The supreme court of the state was appealed to, but its writ was treated with contempt (64 *N. C.*, 820). The recently adopted Fourteenth Amendment (July 28, 1868) and the Habeas Corpus Act of Feb. 5, 1867 (14 *Statutes at Large, U. S.*, 385) were invoked before Judge Brooks with success, for he issued the writ and as, after notice, no evidence was produced against them, the prisoners were discharged in August 1870, the first instance in which the Amendment was invoked in defense of the personal liberty of a while man. A sound lawyer, Brooks was, as a judge, noted for patience, benevolence, and moral courage.

[John H. Wheeler, *Reminiscences and Memoirs of N. C.* (1884), pp. 365–68; J. G. de R. Hamilton, *Reconstruction in N. C.* (1914), pp. 131, 525 ff.; Samuel Ashe, *Hist. of N. C.*, II (1925), 1108.]   F.N.

BROOKS, JAMES (Nov. 10, 1810–Apr. 30, 1873), journalist, was born in Portland, Me., the son of James and Elizabeth (Folsom) Brooks and the brother of Erastus Brooks [*q.v.*]. His father, of English nativity but a loyal American citizen, was lost while commanding a privateer during the War of 1812. The family was left in poverty. James, after attending a public school in Portland, was bound out to a store-keeper of Lewiston. Fortunately his employer was impressed by the lad's ability, released him from the apprenticeship, and assisted him in gaining an education. He first entered an academy at Monmouth, Me., and was graduated from Waterville College (now Colby University) in 1831 (Waterville College Records). Supporting himself by school-teaching in Portland, he began to study law in the office of John Neal, and was inspired by Neal to write for the *Portland Advertiser*. By the time he was admitted to the Maine bar the *Advertiser* offered him $500 a year, and he took up journalism.

In a period when new enterprise was rapidly being infused into the newspaper world Brooks made a brilliant reputation as a correspondent. His political letters from Washington were copied all over the Union, and James Gordon Bennett was one of the journalists who gained useful lessons from them. Equally good were his letters from the South, and especially those from the Creek, Cherokee, and Choctaw districts at the time the two latter tribes were being forced to remove. Maine seemed too small for his talents, and entrance to the legislature in 1835, followed by an unsuccessful candidacy on the Whig ticket for Congress, failed to hold him there. Returning from a European tour late in 1835, he settled in New York, obtained Whig backing, and on June 20, 1836, began publication of the *New York Express,* first as a morning newspaper only, and later with an evening edition as well. Its fortunes were precarious. Brooks later declared that for many years he had labored sixteen hours daily to supply it with letters, editorials, shipping news, and other matter. But as a commercial rather than a political organ, though it called itself "decidedly Whig," it became firmly established by 1840 (*New York Express,* Apr. 29, 1873: historical review on occasion of removal to a new building).

Until his death Brooks combined editorial labors with political activity, and twice changed his party. He volunteered as a campaign speaker in 1840 for William Henry Harrison, one result being his marriage in that year to a relative of Harrison's, Mrs. Mary L. (Cunningham) Randolph of Virginia. After service in the New York legislature, he was carried to Congress in Zachary Taylor's sweep of 1848, serving two terms as a Whig. He supported Clay's compromise mea-

sures of 1850, and a temporary identification with the Native American party in 1854 bridged over his conversion to Democracy as the slavery struggle grew warmer. He wished at all costs to avoid civil war, his newspaper representing the conservatism of the New York commercial community in this regard. For this reason he supported Buchanan in 1856 and Douglas in 1860; and in the spring of 1861 he argued so vigorously for letting the Southern states "depart in peace" that the office of the *Express* was threatened with mob violence. During the Civil War he was a Democrat of the copperhead type, and was identified with Tilden, August Belmont, and other wealthy men in supporting the Society for the Diffusion of Political Knowledge. The *Express* was characterized by the *Evening Post* in 1863 as a journal "which has called repeatedly upon the mob to oust the regular government at Washington, and upon the army to proclaim McClellan its chief at all hazards."

Brooks was elected from New York City to the Thirty-ninth Congress in 1864; he claimed election again in 1866, but was unseated in favor of William E. Dodge; and thereafter biennially until his death he was reëlected. His position on the Democratic side was one of influence, for he was an aggressive and able debater. Twice his party supported him for speaker, and he served on the Ways and Means and other important committees. His opponents correctly characterized him as "pugnacious" and untiring (T. C. Smith, *James Abram Garfield,* 1925, I, 362). In the stormy years after the war he opposed the impeachment of President Johnson, argued for a conciliatory and rapid process of Southern reconstruction, and hotly denounced the carpet-bag governments. He was prominent also in the demand for tariff reduction and revenue reform. His downfall as a result of the Crédit Mobilier scandal, therefore, attracted wide attention. President Johnson had appointed him a government director of the Union Pacific Railroad on Oct. 1, 1867. In the following December he demanded of the Crédit Mobilier officials a large amount of stock, and after much negotiation was assigned 100 shares at par, $10,000, though the market value was then about $20,000. Further demands from him led to a highly irregular issue of 50 more shares in his name. The House investigating committee in 1873 found him guilty of accepting a bribe for the use of his official influence, and recommended his expulsion; he was, however, let off with a vote of censure. His defense, which rested chiefly on the assertion that the shares in question had really been bought by his son-in-law, C. H. Neilson, has not convinced historical students (cf. James Ford Rhodes, *History of the United States,* vol. VII, 1906, p. 11).

Distress over this affair shortened Brooks's life; he had made a tour of the world in 1872, had contracted a fever in India, and now succumbed, maintaining to the end that he had been made a scapegoat because he was a Democrat. He had been given the satisfaction of an unprecedented majority in his district in 1872, while he retained to the last a host of personal friends. He was of fine presence, well-read, a cultivated linguist, suave and courteous, and held a high place in both Washington and New York society.

[See *Am. Annual Cyc.* (1873), p. 81, for a succinct sketch. The pamphlet *Crédit Mobilier: Speeches of Hon. Daniel W. Voorhees, etc.* (Washington, 1873) contains Brooks's own defense. The pamphlet *Biography of the Hon. Erastus Brooks* (Boston, 1882) contains incidental material. Brooks presents his travel impressions in *Seven Months Run, Up, and Down, and Around the World* (1872). Articles in the *N. Y. Express,* Apr. 29–30, and May 1, 1873, throw light on his career. Many of his speeches were reprinted in pamphlet form; *e.g., Not Reconstruction but Destruction* (1867). Cf. J. B. Crawford, *The Crédit Mobilier of America* (Boston, 1880) and the Poland Committee Report (*House Reports,* 42 Cong., 3 Sess., nos. 77, 78).]
A.N.

BROOKS, JAMES GORDON (Sept. 3, 1801–Feb. 20, 1841), editor, poet, often confused with James Brooks [*q.v.*], was probably born at Red Hook, N. Y., though some authorities give Claverack as his birthplace. His father was David Brooks, an officer of the Revolution, afterward a member of Congress. J. G. Brooks was graduated from Union College in 1818. He studied law at Poughkeepsie but his interest was soon turned in other directions and he never applied for admission to the bar. As early as 1817 he had begun to publish verse and prose in periodicals and in 1819 he adopted the pen name "Florio," by which he long succeeded in concealing his identity as an author from even his friends. In 1823 he went to New York, where for two years he was literary editor of the *Minerva,* which called itself a "literary, entertaining, and scientific journal." The *Minerva* was combined with the *Literary Gazette,* which had a brief existence and was then absorbed by the *American Athenæum.* Brooks continued with these journals until 1827, when he became an editor of the *Morning Courier,* an influential Democratic paper, strong in its support of Andrew Jackson. In 1829 it was merged with the *Enquirer* and later became the *Courier and Enquirer.* Brooks remained with the paper until 1830. At one time previous to 1830 he was also an editor of the *New York Daily Sentinel.* His verse was published in the journals with which he was connected and in the *Commercial Advertiser.* In 1828 he married Mary Elizabeth Aiken of Poughkeepsie, who, under the name of "Norma," was a contributor of verse to periodicals. In 1829 they collected their poems in a volume, *The Rivals of Este, and Other Poems.* The title poem, by Mary Brooks, is a melodramatic narrative of medieval Italian intrigue, in stilted verse. Of her other poems, "Hebrew Melodies," verse renderings of selections from the Psalms and the Prophets, are the best. The longest poem by James Gordon Brooks is "Genius," the Phi Beta Kappa anniversary poem delivered at Yale, Sept. 12, 1826. It is a eulogy of intellect, in stately but uninspired verse. His minor poems are of better quality, especially "Greece," an ode full of feeling for liberty, and "The Last Song," his farewell verse. His poems, better than his wife's, are reflective in tone, conventional in rhyme and meter. After the publication of this volume he wrote little verse. Though his poems were fairly popular in his time, his chief distinction is as a journalist. In 1830 Mr. and Mrs. Brooks removed to Winchester, Va., where he was editor of the *Republican.* In 1838 they returned to New York State and settled in Albany. There he was for about a year editor of the *Albany Advertiser* but got into trouble with the Van Rensselaers, who owned the paper, and resigned, after a fight, in 1839. He was then for a short time an editor of the *New Era* in New York. He died at the old Franklin House in Albany.

[Frederic Hudson, *Journalism in the U. S., from 1690 to 1872* (1873), pp. 280, 346, 425, 517; Rufus Wilmot Griswold, *The Poets and Poetry of America* (1874), p. 278; *Centennial Cat. of Union Coll.* (1895); *Record of the Officers and Alumni of Union Coll. 1797–1884* (1884); *Phi Beta Kappa Cat.* (1923); *Albany Daily Argus,* Feb. 22, 1841; *Troy Daily Whig,* Feb. 22, 1841.]
S.G.B.

BROOKS, JOHN (1752–Mar. 1, 1825), Revolutionary soldier, the son of Caleb Brooks, farmer, and Ruth (Albree), was born in a part of Medford, Mass., now within the boundaries of Winchester, and baptized May 4, 1752 (*Vital Records of Medford,* 1907, p. 31). Dr. Simon Tufts, the local physician, took a liking to the boy, and received him as a medical apprentice in his family in 1766. Graduating, as it were, from Dr. Tufts' college in 1773, John Brooks began to practise medicine in the near-by town of Reading, and (1774) there married Lucy Smith. Interested from boyhood in drilling, he joined the Minute Men, and as captain of the Reading company hastened to Concord on Apr. 19, 1775, joined the fight at Meriam's Corner, and pursued the British in their retreat (W. H. Sumner, *History of East Boston,* 1858, pp. 355–56). Shortly after, he received a majority from the State, and played an important part in the battle of Bunker Hill. He was appointed, on Jan. 1, 1776, to the same rank in the Continental Army and served with constant zeal and energy throughout the war. After taking part in the battles of Long Island and White Plains, he was promoted lieutenant-colonel in the 8th Massachusetts line regiment, which he commanded and gallantly led in the taking of Breyman's fort on Bemis's Heights, Oct. 7, 1777 (*Proceedings of the Massachusetts Historical Society,* III, 273-75). On Mar. 24, 1778, Washington offered him a position on the inspector-general's staff, which he filled with great satisfaction to Baron Steuben, although at times detached for active service with the army in the field. When stationed at Newburgh, in the winter of 1782-83, he was appointed by the discontented officers one of a committee of three to present their claims to Congress. He had already gone on a similar mission to the Massachusetts legislature, for the officers of the state. He brought back to camp the committee's account of their discouraging reception; but his exact relation to the "Newburgh Addresses" remains obscure, on account of the later efforts of every one involved to clear himself and blame others. Brooks was accused of being a member of a conspiracy, and of afterward informing upon it to Washington (L. C. Hatch, *Administration of the American Revolutionary Army,* 1904, pp. 167-70); on the other hand he is represented as having stood by Washington from the first (Charles Brooks, *History of Medford,* p. 138; F. Kapp, *Life of Frederick William von Steuben,* 1859, p. 534). One may infer from his long letter of 1823 in the Pickering Manuscripts that he was not in the secret, and thought the enterprise both reprehensible and desperate. After receiving his honorable discharge (June 12, 1783), Brooks took over the medical practise of Dr. Tufts at Medford, and became a highly successful physician, "the grace and ornament of the profession." Dignified though democratic, interested in people and helpful in their troubles, a useful townsman and faithful member of the First Church (changing with it from Calvinism to Unitarianism), Brooks appeared the ideal republican soldier and citizen, the sort of man every one loved, and delighted to honor. He was president of numerous organizations such as the Cincinnati, the Massachusetts Medical Society and Bible Society, and the Bunker Hill Monument Association. Gov. Bowdoin in 1786 appointed him major-general over the militia of Middlesex, with which he marched to Worcester during the Shays rebellion (*Massachusetts Historical Society Collections,* 7 ser. VI, 133-34). President Washington made him

federal marshal for the Massachusetts district in 1791, and brigadier-general, U. S. A., in 1792 (resigned 1796). President Adams nominated him to a major-generalcy in the provisional army during the difficulties with France. Harvard College adopted him as a Master of Arts in 1787, made him honorary M.D. in 1810, Overseer in 1815, and LL.D. in 1817. From 1788, when he became a silent but active member of the Massachusetts Ratifying Convention, Brooks was a staunch Federalist, but never belonged to the inner circle of leaders. He had already twice (1785-86) been elected to the House, and in 1791 was chosen a state senator for Middlesex County whose Jeffersonian Republicanism lost him further opportunities of the same sort. Like the rest of his party, he strongly disapproved the War of 1812; and said so publicly, when declining a nomination to Congress (Washburn Manuscripts, 55). As adjutant-general of the Commonwealth and of the Council (1812-16) he greatly improved the efficiency of the state militia, the right to control which he considered "one of the most essential attributes of state sovereignty." This quotation, and other matters in his correspondence with Timothy Pickering [*q.v.*], with whom he served on a special commission for the defense of the seacoast in 1814, show that he approved the Hartford Convention, and other measures of his state in 1814, taking the same view of the situation as H. G. Otis [*q.v.*]. Both his sons, however, served in the war. In 1816, when Gov. Strong declined to stand again for governor, Brooks was nominated by the Federalists, and elected, although opposed by Gen. Henry Dearborn [*q.v.*], who had served at the front. He was six times reëlected, 1817-22, by substantial majorities over Republican candidates. Brooks's administrations were known as the "Indian Summer of Federalism" in Massachusetts, and his cordial reception to President Monroe in 1817 inaugurated the "Era of Good Feeling" (*Columbian Centinel,* July 12, 1817). He was a competent governor in a period which his popularity and good manners helped to make a placid one. He sympathized with the maritime rather than the manufacturing interests of Massachusetts, and regretted, while he did not attempt to oppose, the separation of Maine. In 1823, when he refused to stand again, the Republican candidate was elected; and the Federalist party, after dominating Massachusetts for a generation, ceased to exist. Brooks died at his home in Medford, Mar. 1, 1825.

[Memoirs by Chas. Brooks in *Hist. of Medford* (1855) and *New Eng. Hist. and Geneal. Reg.,* XIX, 193-200;

by W. H. Sumner, *Ibid.*, XIII, 102–07 and *Proc. Mass. Hist. Soc.*, III, 271–77; by Rev. A. Bigelow, in *Christian Examiner*, II, 103–17 (1825). See also Knox, Keith, Pickering, and Washburn MSS. in Mass. Hist. Soc.]

S. E. M.

BROOKS, MARIA GOWEN (c. 1794–Nov. 11, 1845), poet, called "Maria del Occidente," was born at Medford, Mass., of Welsh extraction. Her paternal grandfather lost money during the Revolution and moved from Cambridge to Medford. Her father, William Gowen, a goldsmith and a man of cultivation, and the friend of Harvard professors, who perhaps encouraged the child in her reading by the age of nine of Shakespeare, Milton's *Comus,* and Southey's *Madoc,* was further reduced in wealth before his death in 1809. Her mother was Eleanor (Cutter) Gowen. Maria was cared for by John Brooks, a merchant of Boston, who had previously married her older sister Lucretia. He was a widower of nearly fifty, with two sons, but he married Maria Aug. 26, 1810, when she was fourteen or fifteen. She bore him two sons, Horace and Edgar, but although he was not unkind, the marriage was not a happy one. Since there was no understanding of the girl on Mr. Brooks's part, he won her respect, not her love. Mr. Brooks lost money invested in privateers during the War of 1812, and retired to Portland. There Maria, who is described as "a very handsome lady, winning manners, purest blonde complexion, blue eyes, abundant pale gold hair, who sang very sweetly," devoted herself to her sons and step-sons. She also composed a poem which was never published, and fell violently in love with a young Canadian officer, whom she had met but once. Of this passion she gave for the time no sign, but she handled with great delicacy another ardent gentleman's unwelcome attentions, rebuking the lover but retaining the friend. In 1819 the General Court allowed her to change her baptismal name of Abigail, and on July 31 she was baptized Mary Abigail Brooks in King's Chapel. Later she always called herself Maria Gowen Brooks. Her life in the narrow and provincial town was unhappy, but her books were her solace, and in 1820 she published at Boston a small volume, *Judith, Esther, and Other Poems, by a Lover of the Fine Arts.*

In 1823 Mr. Brooks died, and on Oct. 20, Maria sailed for Cuba, to live on the coffee plantation of a brother, William Cutter Gowen. There she was urged to marry a neighboring planter, but declined, and soon visited other relatives in Canada. During her visit she again met the British officer, whose initials were E. W. R. A., and who figures as "Ethelwald" in her novel *Idomen.* She became engaged to him, but in some way they were estranged, and Maria twice attempted suicide by drinking laudanum, at the same time praying that she might be spared if it was God's will. She was restored to health through the ministrations of a friend, and returned to Cuba where she inherited considerable property. At Boston in 1825 she published the first canto of *Zóphiël,* a poem on the love of a fallen angel for a mortal, based on a story in the apocryphal Book of Tobit. About 1826 she began a correspondence with Southey. In Cuba, on the Cafétal San Patricio, near Matanzas, in a little Grecian temple erected for her, dressed all in white, and with a passion flower in her hair, she continued work on *Zóphiël,* which was completed in 1829. She proceeded with her son Horace to Hanover, N. H., where he studied with one of the Dartmouth professors, preparatory to entering West Point. His appointment was delayed. Mrs. Brooks visited Europe with a brother. In Paris she met Washington Irving, and through him Lafayette, who finally procured the appointment of Horace Brooks. In 1831 she stayed for a few weeks at Keswick, where she saw much of Southey who undertook to supervise the publication in London of *Zóphiël* which she signed with the pen name "Maria del Occidente." She became in a sense the American member of the group of Lake poets. *Zóphiël* appeared in 1833 after her return to America; the first American edition consisted of the English sheets with a cancel title; a second American edition appeared at Boston in 1834. The poem had little sale but won, especially by the "Song" beginning "Day in melting purple dying," and the allegory of Marriage, the admiration of John Quincy Adams, Southey, and Lamb. Four letters to Southey, 1833–40, tell much of Maria's life during this period. Her son graduated from West Point in 1835. She completed her prose tale *Idomen,* a curiously involved but beautifully frank account of her unhappy love affair, and published it serially, beginning Feb. 17, 1838, in the Boston *Saturday Evening Gazette,* to which she contributed some minor poems, 1838–40. Her son Edgar and a stepson fell ill and died in Cuba before she could reach them, and to their memory she wrote several odes, and the (touchingly simple) song beginning "My fair haired boy." Meanwhile Mrs. Brooks resided with her son Horace on Governor's Island; and corresponded with Halleck (1842) and E. P. Whipple (1843) about *Idomen,* which the Harpers rejected as "too elevated to sell," but which she published privately in New York in 1843. R. W. Griswold, who praised Maria in the *Southern Literary Messenger,* in

1839, spoke of her as the foremost American poetess in his *Poets and Poetry of America* (1842), endeavored vainly to bring out an edition of her *Works,* and inserted some of her poems in *Graham's Magazine.* In May 1843 she wrote Ticknor about Southey's letters to her; in December she returned to Cuba. On Sept. 3, 1844, she sent a poem to W. B. Force, editor of the Washington *Army and Navy Chronicle.* In 1845 she and her stepson fell ill of a tropical fever. Both died—Mrs. Brooks on November 11, 1845—and were buried beneath a white marble cross at Limonal, near Matanzas. Her poetry had the faults of its time but its three or four best passages have imagination, and exalted passion.

[The chief published sources are Southey's *The Doctor* (1834 f.), chapter LIV; Griswold's articles mentioned above, and those by him in *Graham's Mag.,* Aug. 1848, and in the *Female Poets of America,* 1849—the two latter accompanied by engraved portraits; the introduction to Zadel Barnes Gustafson's edition of *Zóphiël* (1879); Caroline E. Swift's "Maria del Occidente" in *Medford Hist. Reg.* (Oct. 1899), pp. 1-11, 150-66; Ruth S. Granniss's *An American Friend of Southey* (N. Y., privately printed 1913); Thos. Ollive Mabbott, "Maria del Occidente," *Am. Collector,* Aug. 1926. There are manuscripts of Mrs. Brooks's letters and poems in the Boston Pub. Lib., Yale, and the Lib. of Cong., and there is a collection of her books and manuscripts formed by Beverly Chew and and now in the possession of T. O. Mabbott.]   T.O.M.

BROOKS, MARY ELIZABETH AIKEN. [See BROOKS, JAMES GORDON, 1801–1841.]

BROOKS, NOAH (Oct. 24, 1830–Aug. 16, 1903), journalist, author, was born in Castine, Me., the son of Barker Brooks, a master shipbuilder, and Margaret (Perkins) Brooks. His earliest American ancestor on his father's side, William Brooks, of the County of Kent in England, was a passenger on the ship *Blessing,* landing at Scituate, Mass., in 1635. The Perkinses were also an old Massachusetts family. He attended the public schools of Castine until he was eighteen, when he went to Boston to study landscape painting. He soon discovered, however, that the pen fitted his hand better than the brush and began to write. By the time he was twenty-one he was contributing short sketches, essays, and humorous stories to magazines and weekly newspapers and was serving on the staff of a Boston daily, the *Atlas.* When he was twenty-five his writing career was interrupted for a few years. He went to Illinois and entered into a business partnership with an intimate friend, John G. Brooks. The business failed and Noah Brooks moved to Kansas, for a brief stay during which he took an active part in the free state movement, and then on to California with a company of emigrants who crossed the plains with ox teams. Coming to rest in Marysville, Cal., he joined with Benjamin P. Avery [*q.v.*], afterward United States minister to China, in publishing the *Daily Appeal.* In addition to his editorial work Brooks steadily contributed to the *Overland Monthly,* then edited by Bret Harte. A friendship developed between the two men which persisted after Brooks left California. This removal took place in 1862, when he sold out his interest in the newspaper and went East to become Washington correspondent of the *Sacramento Union.* In Washington an acquaintance with Abraham Lincoln, begun in Illinois and continued during the period of the Lincoln-Douglas debates, was renewed at the instance of the President. Brooks became a frequent visitor at the White House and an intimate friend of the Lincoln family. He accompanied the President on trips to the front and after the Baltimore convention which nominated Lincoln and Johnson went to the White House at Lincoln's request to give him an eye-witness's picture of the convention's progress. If it had not been for a severe cold which kept him at home Brooks would have been a guest in the presidential box on the fatal night in Ford's Theatre. Shortly before this the President had invited Brooks to become his private secretary in place of John G. Nicolay, who was to go as consul to Paris, but Lincoln's death came before the change could be effected. Brooks was appointed by President Johnson naval officer in the custom house at San Francisco but was removed at the end of a year and a half for refusal to comply with certain of the administration's political requirements. In 1866 he became managing editor of the *Alta California* in San Francisco. A red-headed youngster setting type for the paper timidly submitted an article to the managing editor which greatly astonished Brooks by the brilliancy of its style. He encouraged the youth's impulse to write and must have felt his efforts to that end repaid some years later when *Progress and Poverty* appeared with the name of the red-haired compositor, Henry George, on the title-page. In 1871 Brooks went to New York and joined the staff of the *New York Tribune.* After five years there he became an editor of the *New York Times* and eight years later was made the editor of the *Newark Daily Advertiser.* In 1892 he retired from journalism. The remaining years of his life were uneventful, except for a tour of Egypt, Turkey, and the Holy Land in 1894 and 1895, and were largely spent at his country home in Castine, which he named "The Ark." He was a jovial companion and a good story-teller, one of the founders of the

Authors Club of New York, and a member of the Century Club, the Lotus Club, and the New England Society. Belonging to the Congregational Church, he took an active part in church affairs and charitable undertakings. He was married in 1856 to Caroline, daughter of Oliver Fellows, of Salem, Mass. His wife and an infant child died just as the Civil War was beginning. Brooks himself died in Pasadena, Cal., where he had gone in the hope of restoring his health.

His published works include *The Boy Emigrants* (1876, 1903), based on the experiences of his first journey to California; *The Fairport Nine* (1880, 1903); *Our Baseball Club* (1884); *The Boy Settlers* (1891, 1906); *American Statesmen* (1893, 1904); *Tales of the Maine Coast* (1894); *Abraham Lincoln and the Downfall of American Slavery* (1894); *How the Republic is Governed* (1895); *Washington in Lincoln's Time* (1896); *Short Studies in American Party Politics* (1896); *The Story of Marco Polo* (1896); *The Mediterranean Trip* (1896); *History of the United States* (1896); *Henry Knox, a Soldier of the Revolution* (1900); *Abraham Lincoln; His Youth and Early Manhood* (1901).

[Biog. sketch by Frederick F. Evans in the *Lamp*, Sept. 1903; obituaries in the *N. Y. Herald, N. Y. Tribune, N. Y. Times*, Aug. 18, 1903.]   H. H.

BROOKS, PETER CHARDON (Jan. 11, 1767–Jan. 1, 1849), merchant, was born at North Yarmouth, Me., where his father, Rev. Edward Brooks (Harvard College, 1757), was minister of the First Parish. Peter's mother was Abigail Brown, daughter of the minister of Haverhill, Mass. His ancestors were among the earliest settlers of Watertown, Mass. His own branch of the family belonged in Medford, whither the Rev. Edward Brooks returned in 1769, when his theology proved too liberal for his down-East parish. The father's death in 1781 left the family almost destitute; and Peter was apprenticed to a merchant in Boston, but on attaining his majority, in 1789 set up as an insurance broker at the Bunch of Grapes tavern. In underwriting vessels, and in his adventures of money in the East Indian trade, Brooks was so uniformly successful that he was able to retire in 1803 with a considerable fortune. He married in 1792 Nancy, daughter of Nathaniel Gorham [*q.v.*]; she bore to him thirteen children. In 1805 he built a mansion house at Medford on the ancestral farm, which he made a model farm. Finding time rather heavy on his hands, he returned to business in 1806 as president of the New England Marine Insurance Company, but retired again after a few years. The Federalists

in 1806 insisted on sending Brooks to the state Senate, an honor which both pleased and worried him, for, as he wrote his brother, "I have not learning enough to make any figure in this way." He was annually reëlected to the state Senate until 1814; to the Council, 1817–19, when his second cousin, John Brooks [*q.v.*], was governor; to the constitutional convention of 1820; and alternately to the House and Senate, 1819–23. He is not associated with any measure excepting a committee report of 1821 denouncing lotteries, which is said to have procured legislation against them. Peter C. Brooks did not speculate, or invest largely in manufactures or railroads or western land, but kept turning his money over in loans and mortgages for which, if we may believe his biographers, he never took over six per cent interest; yet at the time of his death (in Boston, January 1, 1849), he was reputed the wealthiest man in New England. His property was put to good use in various philanthropic enterprises, and in promoting the political ambition of his sons-in-law, Edward Everett and Charles Francis Adams [*qq.v.*].

[Edward Everett, "Peter C. Brooks," in Freeman Hunt, *Lives of Am. Merchants* (1858), I, 133–83; Brooks MSS. in Mass. Hist. Soc., containing his letters to his brother Cotton, a merchant at Haverhill, Mass., and Portland, Me.; Jos. T. Buckingham, *Personal Memoirs* (1852), II, 181–85.]   S. E. M.

BROOKS, PHILLIPS (Dec. 13, 1835–Jan. 23, 1893), Episcopal bishop, was fortunate in his name, which, balanced and virile, clearly indicated the two streams of hereditary influence that shaped his life. The Phillips family had been conspicuous in the religious and educational interests of Massachusetts from 1630, when Rev. George Phillips came from England with Winthrop and settled in Watertown, Mass. His son, Samuel, was pastor in Rowley, Mass., for forty-five years. The next in line, also named Samuel, broke the clerical succession and became a goldsmith, but had a minister's daughter, Mary Emerson, for his wife; and their son, Samuel [*q.v.*], was minister of the South Church, Andover, Mass., for sixty-two years. The latter's three sons, Samuel, John [*q.v.*], and William [*q.v.*], turned to secular pursuits, acquired wealth, and used it for philanthropic and educational purposes. John founded Phillips Exeter Academy, and Samuel's son, Judge Samuel Phillips [*q.v.*], having enlisted the coöperation of his father and two uncles, founded the Phillips Andover Academy. The Judge's wife, Phœbe Foxcroft, brought into the family wealth, social grace, and intellectual life of a high order, her great stature and large dark eyes reappearing in Phillips Brooks. Carrying out her husband's wishes, she, with her son John, established the Andover Theological Seminary. This John was the father of Mary A. Phillips, the mother of Phillips Brooks.

In the Brooks family there was less conspicuous idealism and other-worldliness. The founder of the line in this country was Thomas Brooke, who was a freeman of Watertown in 1636 and must have sat under the ministrations of the Rev. George Phillips. The only minister in this descent was the Rev. Edward Brooks whose liberal tendencies led him to give up his parish, and whose wife was a direct descendant of the Rev. John Cotton [q.v.]. Their two sons were Cotton Brown Brooks and Peter Chardon Brooks [q.v.]. The elder became a merchant in Portland, Me., the younger, a prominent Unitarian layman in Boston, at his death considered to be the richest man in the city. When William Gray Brooks, son of Cotton Brown Brooks, came, at the age of nineteen, to Boston to establish himself in business, he met, at the house of his uncle Peter, his aunt's niece, Mary Ann Phillips, whom he married in 1833. Of this union Phillips Brooks was born, the second of six sons, four of whom entered the ministry.

From each parent he inherited superior virtues in balanced proportion. His mother had all the staunch spiritual passion of the Phillips blood. She was richly endowed with an intense and powerful emotional nature, which revealed itself in a glowing idealism, and the reformer's zeal for the establishment of righteousness. Yet her ethical earnestness and unquestioning faith were blended with an ardent mother love which lavished itself without stint upon her children. This fervor of spirituality was tempered and directed in her son by the more humanitarian qualities of the Brooks lineage. From his father, a substantial business man, accurate and methodical, and keenly observant of the ways of men, he inherited executive ability, fondness for art and literature, a sense of present values, and a disinclination to interfere with the personal rights of others. The son was like his father also in his fortunate habit of writing down, constantly and at length, the thoughts which grew out of his reading and observations.

He was baptized in the First Church of Boston, but when he was four years of age the family identified itself with St. Paul's Episcopal Church. After studying in the Latin School, he was admitted to Harvard in 1851, when not quite sixteen, yet even then he stood six feet, three and one-half inches and weighed 161 pounds. In college he excelled in the languages, and ranked high in logic and philosophy. Much of his time was given to general reading. He showed no sign of being an orator but wrote excellent papers for the societies of which he was a member, and graduated the thirteenth in a class of sixty-six. Intending to give his life to teaching, he secured a position in the Boston Latin School. Over the thirty-five young barbarians of nearly his own age assigned to his charge, he could not maintain discipline and in six months he resigned, deeply chagrined to have failed in his home town, and in his first work. His notebooks of this time are remarkable for their lack of introspection or spiritual struggle. They reveal a mind serene, chiefly concerned with discerning the richness of life and its significance for faith, and naturally inclined to generate and proclaim moral ideas. Almost invariably he wrote as if addressing an audience. One reading these random thoughts sees how impossible it was that he should be anything but a preacher. Yet he hesitated, then suddenly, after the term commenced, went to study in the seminary at Alexandria, Va.

It is indicative of the creative vigor of his mind that he took with him a number of notebooks, which he divided into two equal parts, one for facts and thoughts which he found in his reading, the other for his own reflections. So imperative was the need of self-expression that he filled the latter first, and then overflowed into the former. These meditations reveal the uncommon maturity of his mind and the ripened perfection of his style. For him the seminary years were not a period of distressing intellectual and spiritual unsettlement. There is no record of a prolonged struggle with religious doubts, or of a battle with self to renounce the world, its values, and its ambitions. Neither theological systems nor the findings of the critics interested him overmuch. Life, its varied experiences, its amazing possibilities, alone concerned him. From the first he seems to have had three convictions, unclouded and abiding: God, personal, living, in all and over all; man by nature the child of God and capable of a life abounding in blessedness; Christ the revelation of what God is and man may be. These were to him luminous certainties, the sure intuitions of spiritual genius. His problem was not the attainment of a rational faith, but how to convey to men an understanding of the liberty, the joy, the abounding life one may find in the spirit and by the power of Christ. That this was to be his message Phillips Brooks discovered in his second year in the Seminary and the succeeding years only deepened its glory and significance to his own mind and increased his marvelous power of enforcing it.

An observation written in his note-book when he had just turned twenty-one reveals that unlike most young men he was not inclined to disregard the ways of his fathers and to break new paths. "We shall pretty generally find," he remarks, "that it is with theories as with country roads, they may take us a little out of our way, but if they reach our point at last, it will be the easier and altogether the shortest way to keep by them, gaining in the smoothness and pleasantness which the road builders have made ready for us, much more than we lose by not taking a straight line across rough new fields." All his life Brooks not only kept in the middle of the road, he walked in the old roads. His eye was not for the horizon, but for values, for the unfamiliar beauty of familiar things. He was an interpreter, not a pioneer.

Ordained a deacon at Alexandria, Va., July 1, 1859, he began his ministry in the Church of the Advent, Philadelphia, the following month. Immediately his impressive personality and uncommon eloquence attracted attention. Crowds came to hear him. In January 1862 he became rector of Holy Trinity in the same city. Distinguished success attended his ministry. He was a leader not only in spiritual things, but in the stress of Civil War attained local prominence by his unwavering loyalty to Lincoln and the Union cause. When the body of the martyred President was lying in state in Independence Hall, Brooks preached a sermon of such insight and power on the "Character, Life and Death of Mr. Lincoln" that it attracted wide attention. In July of that same year, 1865, he came again into prominence in a most unique manner. Harvard College appointed a commemoration day in honor of her sons who had died in the war, and Phillips Brooks was invited to make the prayer. What is usually a function became an event. "It was the most impressive utterance," said President Eliot, "of a proud and happy day. Even Lowell's Commemoration Ode did not, at the moment, so touch the heart of his hearers. This one spontaneous and intimate expression of Brooks' noble spirit convinced all Harvard men that a young prophet had risen up in Israel." Another who was present said: "One would rather have been able to pray that prayer than to lead an army or conduct a State." It was no formal prayer written in majestic liturgical sentences; the flowing piety of nine generations of praying men broke forth that day in marvelous utterance.

In the summer of 1865 Brooks went abroad for a year of travel. On his return he was called to become the head of the new Episcopal Theological School in Cambridge. The invitation tempted him but was finally declined. In the meantime his influence was extending its range and deepening its impression, yet the permanent contribution to the spiritual wealth of America which belongs to the Philadelphia pastorate is the carol, "O Little Town of Bethlehem," written for his Sunday-school and sung for the first time at Christmas 1868 to music composed by Mr. Redner. Of a rich poetic nature Brooks easily wrote verse, as his note-books testify, but in this sweet carol he expressed the Christmas feeling with a simple beauty that will be held by his Church in perpetual possession.

Being a son of Boston, his increasing fame attracted the attention of his native city and Trinity Church, the stronghold of Episcopalianism, called him in August 1868 to become its rector. At first he declined, but Trinity, after waiting nearly a year, renewed the call so urgently that Brooks accepted and began his memorable ministry in Boston, Oct. 31, 1869. Trinity Church edifice then stood on Summer St. near Washington, a dignified and impressive structure built of granite in Gothic style. In 1872 the great Boston fire destroyed this church, and the noble building in Copley Square was erected and consecrated on Feb. 9, 1877. The architect, H. H. Richardson, and the decorator, John La Farge, combined their signal artistic abilities to make it an outstanding architectural achievement and a fit tabernacle for the ministry of its great preacher.

Immediately upon coming to Boston Phillips Brooks aroused public interest in his person and message. While Trinity Church was building he preached in Huntington Hall to audiences which packed at both services that large auditorium. Now from the pulpit of his centrally located and magnificent church he commanded the attention of Boston and attracted the notice of religious minds everywhere. The conditions of the spiritual life of his city and of his generation were especially favorable to his peculiar genius. Boston was the capital of Puritanism, and Puritanism was always prone to emphasize the intellectual aspects of Christianity to the exclusion of the æsthetic and emotional elements. Its excessive dogmatism had resulted in the cold intellectualism of Unitarianism. The Episcopalians occupied a mediating position though their ecclesiastical exclusiveness was a limitation. They had not been involved in ancient theological conflicts. Their forms of worship were not uncongenial to an increasing number of people of social aspirations in a city of growing prosperity; they had tradition, they had wealth, but no preacher of preëminent abilities. Accordingly, when this radiant spiritual athlete, having the fervent piety and profound convictions of the most religious, combined with all the intellectual freedom and breadth of tolerance which was the boast of the liberals, stepped into the very center of the arena and preached the eternal verities of religion in undogmatic form and with contagious enthusiasm people flocked to hear him.

Neither in thought nor method was he a pioneer. He was sensitive to the finest spiritual currents of the times. Coleridge, Tennyson, Maurice, Robertson, Bushnell, all had ministered to his thought and enkindled his spirit. In face of the questionings aroused by an awakened scientific spirit, he did not try to reconcile religion and science, or combat a materialistic philosophy with argument. His method of meeting mental doubts he suggests in an essay on the "Pulpit and Modern Scepticism" (*Essays and Addresses*): "It seems to me as if, were I a layman in the days when some doctrine had got loose as it were into the wind and was being blown across the Common and up and down the streets, I should go to church on Sunday, not wanting my minister to give me an oracular answer to all the questions that had been started about it which I should not believe if he did give it, but hoping that out of his sermon I might refresh my knowledge of Christ, get Him, His nature, His work, His desire for me once more clear before me, and go out more ready to see this disputed truth of the moment in His light and as an utterance of Him. . . ."

During January and February of 1877 he delivered his valuable *Lectures on Preaching* before the Yale Divinity School. These addresses unveil as do no other writings of the great preacher his own personal experiences, and his noble conception of the joy and purpose of the Christian minister. Their predominant idea is that "Preaching is the communication of truth by man to men. It has two essential elements, truth and personality. . . . Preaching is the bringing of truth through personality." Therefore the preacher must apprehend and live the truth he enunciates; he must love and reverence men. His description of religion as "the life of man in gratitude and obedience and gradually developing likeness to God" is classic in completeness and suggestiveness. In this year Harvard College conferred on him the degree of S.T.D. and in 1878 was published his first volume of sermons. In February of 1879 he delivered in Philadelphia the Bohlen Lectures on "The Influence of Jesus." His fame having spread to England

he was invited by Dean Stanley to preach in Westminster Abbey on July 4, 1880, and the following Sunday at the expressed wish of the Queen he preached before Her Majesty in the Royal Chapel at Windsor, this being the first instance of this distinction coming to an American. The next year he was invited to be the preacher to Harvard University and professor of Christian ethics. To this call he gave long and earnest consideration, as he was strongly inclined to accept the opportunity there offered to influence the students. Reluctantly he declined it. Harvard then abolished the office of preacher and adopted the plan of having a group of ministers selected from different denominations officiate successively for short periods. Oxford gave Brooks the degree of D.D. in 1885, and Columbia in 1887. He declined election as assistant bishop of Pennsylvania in 1886. In October of the same year the General Convention entertained a resolution to change the name of the church from Protestant Episcopal to "The American Church," or "The Church of the United States." Against this he protested vigorously on the ground that the denomination was not large enough to make such a pretentious claim, and that the assumption of such a name doomed the Episcopal Church to become the church of those who accepted the theory of an apostolical succession conferring certain exclusive privileges. The resolution was lost in the convention, but Brooks was apprehensive that the attempt might be renewed and preached a sermon in his own pulpit against the proposition in which he declared that if the change was made he "did not see how he or any, who did not believe in apostolical succession could remain in the Episcopal Church." This sermon had an important influence in this country and in England.

In the Lenten season of 1890 he conducted a memorable series of services at the noon hour in Trinity Church, New York, addressing crowded audiences of the business men of Wall St., who recognized in him a great man, having full knowledge of the world in which he lived, speaking to them in no conventional way of the deepest satisfactions of life.

In the earlier part of his ministry Phillips Brooks was little interested in the machinery of denominational administration. Conventions he disliked and their discussions seemed to him for the most part trivial; bishops he held in good-humored toleration. But his friend, Bishop Potter of New York, affirms that in his later years Brooks experienced a fundamental change of mind regarding the episcopate. "He came to see that what he had reckoned a calling of dry routine might be transformed . . . into a ministry of noblest opportunities and most potential service." Therefore, when at the death of Bishop Paddock there was a spontaneous movement on the part of the churches of the diocese for his election to the vacant bishopric, he was not only willing, but anxious to accept it. The election occurred Apr. 29, 1891, and he was chosen on the first ballot by a large majority of the clergy and a larger majority of the laity of the diocesan convention. Immediately strong opposition was aroused among the narrower elements of the church throughout the nation. He was accused of doctrinal unsoundness and of ecclesiastical latitudinarianism. For some ten weeks the issue was in doubt, and it was not until July 10 that the presiding bishop announced that the election was confirmed by a majority of the bishops. These misrepresentations of his teachings and of his churchmanship he endured in dignified silence. The consecration took place in Trinity Church, Oct. 14, 1891. Many had feared, and some had hoped, that one who was so conspicuously of the prophetic spirit would hold the canons of his church in slight regard, and would treat the red tape of administrative office with disdain. Quite the contrary. During the fifteen months of his incumbency he scrupulously obeyed the laws of the church and faithfully enforced them, yet his chief service was the unusual spiritual inspiration which his presence brought to the churches committed to his charge. Then on Jan. 23, 1893, after a short illness, when he had just passed his fifty-seventh birthday, he died, and the news fell upon the city and multitudes beyond as a crushing public calamity. A great tower of spiritual light had been extinguished. More impressive than the funeral services in Trinity Church were the thousands of reverent men and women gathered in Copley Square whose sense of personal bereavement was expressed in prayer and hymns. The city of Boston held a memorial service in his honor, sermons of commemoration were preached everywhere in this country and in England. Ninety-five thousand dollars came spontaneously from the people for a bronze statue. This was afterward executed by Saint-Gaudens and stands near Trinity Church. The Phillips Brooks House was established at Harvard, dedicated to Piety, Charity, and Hospitality, and a memorial window has been placed in St. Margaret's, Westminster.

Phillips Brooks's supreme contribution to this country was himself. A great bishop, a greater preacher, he was greatest as a superbly molded and an harmoniously developed man, glowing with human sympathy and spiritual light. He is

the "only one I ever knew," writes his intimate friend, Dr. Weir Mitchell, "who seemed to me entirely great." Physically he was majestic, standing six feet four inches, weighing in his prime three hundred pounds, broad shouldered, well proportioned, with a perfectly smooth, open face lighted by luminous brown eyes. "He was the most beautiful man I ever saw," said Justice Harlan of the United States Supreme Court. "I sat opposite to him once at dinner, and could not take my eyes off him." His dress was unconventional, his manner simple without the slightest suggestion of ecclesiastical *hauteur*; little children instinctively loved him, and to all he gave the impression of sincere and radiant goodness. He enjoyed his religion; he had abundant humor and "the deep wisdom of fine fooling," yet wrong awoke in him the blazing wrath of a strong man. Success made him humble, and his steady prosperity increased his eagerness to give of himself unsparingly.

Extreme rapidity of utterance characterized his public speech. Stenographers reckoned that he spoke 213 words a minute. This was due to the excessive energy of his emotions. He kindled in the presence of an audience, his tremendous vitality energized his whole being so that when he attempted to retard his speech all his mental processes slowed down and self-consciousness confused him. "He spoke to his audience as a man might speak to a friend, pouring forth with swift, yet quiet and seldom impassioned earnestness the thoughts and feelings of a singularly pure and lofty spirit. The listeners never thought of style or manner, but only of the substance of the thoughts. . . . In this blending of perfect simplicity of treatment with singular fertility and elevation of thought, no other among the famous preachers of the generation that is now vanishing approached him. . . ." (James Bryce, *The Westminster Gazette*, Feb. 6, 1893).

Because he kept voluminous journals, and had a wide correspondence, Brooks left a wealth of material for his literary executor. This was put at the disposal of Prof. A. V. G. Allen who published in two large volumes what must always be the standard biography of the great preacher (*Life and Letters of Phillips Brooks*, 1900). Its chief defects are the mass of unimportant letters embodied, the tone of excessive laudation, and a lack of humor on the part of the author which led him to treat as of solemn moment experiences common to all.

Brooks's principal writings were his *Yale Lectures on Preaching* (1877), *The Influence of Jesus* (1879), *Essays and Addresses* (1892), and volumes of sermons entitled: *Sermons* (1878), *The Candle of the Lord* (1881), *Sermons Preached in English Churches* (1883), *Twenty Sermons* (1886), *The Light of the World* (1890), *New Starts in Life* (1896), *The Law of Growth* (1902).

[There is a *Memorial Sermon* (1893) by his brother, Rev. Arthur Brooks; *Phillips Brooks* (1903), a study by Bishop Wm. Lawrence; an analysis of Brooks as a preacher in *Representative Modern Preachers* (1904), by Prof. L. O. Brastow, and a singularly interesting contrast in *Huxley and Phillips Brooks* (1903), by W. Newton Clarke. There are sections devoted to Brooks in the memoirs of contemporaries such as *My Education and Religion* (1925) by G. A. Gordon, *Memories of a Happy Life* (1926) by Bishop Wm. Lawrence, *Men I Have Known* (1897) by Dean F. W. Farrar, *Reminiscences of Bishops and Archbishops* (1906) by Bishop Henry C. Potter.]   C. A. D.

BROOKS, PRESTON SMITH (Aug. 6, 1819–Jan. 27, 1857), South Carolina congressman, was the eldest son of Whitfield Brooks and Mary P. Carroll, and was born on the Brooks plantation at Edgefield, S. C. He was educated at the South Carolina College, graduating in 1839, and practised law for a short time after his graduation. During the Mexican War he served as the captain of the Ninety-six Company of the Palmetto Regiment, and was known as an admirable drill officer and an inflexible disciplinarian. He was married twice, in 1841 to Caroline H. Means, and after her death, in 1843, to her cousin, Martha C. Means.

Brooks had served two years in the South Carolina legislature, previous to his war service, but after the disbanding of his regiment he engaged in his chosen work of agriculture, until 1852 when he was elected to the Thirty-third Congress. He served through this and the succeeding Congress, speaking rarely but remembered for two or three speeches of unusual oratorical ability. On May 20, 1856, Senator Charles Sumner of Massachusetts, during the discussion of the Kansas-Nebraska bill, delivered a coarse and violent speech in the Senate, denouncing by name Brooks's uncle, Senator A. P. Butler of South Carolina, who was at the time absent from the Senate. Two days later Brooks, who claimed to have waited for an apology from Senator Sumner and to have searched for him on the streets, found him seated at his desk in the Senate room, after the adjournment of the Senate, struck him over the head repeatedly with a gutta percha cane, which was broken by the blows, and left him apparently insensible on the floor. Senator Sumner is said never to have recovered fully from his injuries. A special investigating committee of the House reported in favor of the expulsion of Brooks, but the report (*House Report No. 182,* 34 Cong., 1 Sess.) on a strictly party vote failed of the necessary two-thirds majority. Brooks, however, resigned after a speech in his own justification, and was unanimously reëlected by his constituents.

The Brooks-Sumner episode created intense excitement, most of which was partisan, the North fiercely denouncing Brooks, while Southern states and communities passed resolutions approving his conduct, and presented him with a number of gold-headed canes and at least one gold-handled cowhide. A month after the assault Brooks was charged in a speech by Anson Burlingame [*q.v.*], representative from Massachusetts, with cowardice and lack of fair play. Brooks challenged Burlingame to a duel; the latter accepted but named as the place the Canadian side of Niagara Falls, which it was difficult, if not impossible, for Brooks to reach with safety. Brooks said Burlingame might as well have named Boston Common and refused to go. His refusal was of course capitalized in the North as revealing lack of courage. He lived less than a year after this event, dying at Brown's Hotel, Washington, Jan. 27, 1857. He was striking in appearance, six feet in height, said to be the handsomest man in the House, of a winning presence, and, except when under the influence of a hasty temper, gentle and gracious in manner. He is said to have suffered in the last months of his life from the fear that his attack on Sumner had hurt the section he was trying to defend.

[There is a large scrap-book of articles, mostly laudatory, concerning Brooks, in the possession of his granddaughter, Mrs. Lucile A. Rion of Greenville, S. C. This includes newspaper sketches of his life. Of easily accessible references, see speeches in House and Senate, Jan. 29, 1857, *Cong. Globe,* 34 Cong., 3 Sess.; Edward L. Pierce, *Memoir and Letters of Chas. Sumner,* vol. III (1893); John Bigelow, *Retrospection of an Active Life* (1909–13); Jas. E. Campbell, "Sumner, Brooks, Burlingame, or the Last of the Great Challenges," in *Ohio Arch. and Hist. Soc. Pubs.,* XXXIV (1925), 435–73.]   J. E. W—y.

BROOKS, RICHARD EDWIN (Oct. 28, 1865–May 2, 1919), sculptor, was born at Braintree, Mass. His father, John Brooks, a spinner by trade, was a native of England; his mother, Julia (Arnold) Brooks, was born in Scotland. The fact that Richard Brooks grew up in the vicinity of the granite quarries of Quincy doubtless had to do with his choice of profession. He is said to have begun to model and carve when a mere boy. He early obtained employment in the workshop of a terra-cotta company, and later established a business of his own, doing many kinds of commercial sculpture, but always endeavoring to improve himself. He studied for a time in Boston under T. H. Bartlett. His first important order was for a bust of Gov. Russell, and the result was so satisfactory that the young sculptor was encouraged to go to Paris and devote himself to study. There his masters were Aubé and Injalbert. His first Salon subject was "Chant de la Vague,"—a graceful nude female figure presumably seated on the shore of the sea —for which he received honorable mention in 1895. His next important exhibit was the statue of Col. Thomas Cass which now stands in the public gardens in Boston, as fine a statue of a quiet, soldierly figure as any which an American sculptor has yet produced. For this figure Brooks was honored with a gold medal at the Paris Exposition in 1900, and in 1901 at Buffalo he received a gold medal for an exhibit comprising the statue of Col. Cass, two portrait busts, a number of medals and two interesting examples of applied art,—a curious candlestick and a necklace. Among his later awards was a silver medal for medals, Panama-Pacific Exposition, San Francisco, 1915.

Brooks lived a great part of his professional life in Paris. In 1911, shortly after the Metropolitan Museum acquired two of his bronzes, "The Bather" and "The Song of the Wave," he came to this country to superintend the erection of his statue of Gen. Hood in Baltimore. At that time he planned to establish a studio in Washington, partly no doubt because his colleagues, Paul Bartlett, the son of his old master, and Frank D. Millet, the well-known mural painter, had studios there. He returned to Paris in the winter of 1911–12 to complete certain commissions. These occupied him so long that it was January 1914 before he opened his studio in Washington. He had some years earlier executed statues of John Hanson and Charles Carroll for Statuary Hall in the United States Capitol, had lately completed statues of William H. Seward and Ex-Gov. John H. McGraw for Seattle, and had received a commission for a statue of Col. Wadsworth of colonial fame for Hartford, Conn. The Wadsworth statue was executed in the studio of Robert Hinckley, portrait painter, on Massachusetts Ave. Among Brooks's other well-known works are statues of John Haynes and Roger Ludlow of Connecticut for the façade of the Connecticut State Capitol at Hartford. In 1915 he executed for the Corcoran School of Art in Washington a bronze portrait tablet of the late E. F. Andrews, first principal of the school. This work was interrupted by the sculptor's illness and his temporary absence in Bermuda. It was unveiled on May 27, 1917, in the vestibule of the school. In an exhibition held by the Society of Washington Artists in the Corcoran Gallery of Art he showed a spirited figure of a boxer and two reclining figures purposed as architectural ornament. In a previous exhibition held under the same auspices he exhibited two frames of portrait medals. As a portrait medalist, Brooks excelled, having caught from the French the lightness of touch and subtlety of expression which mark their work in this field. Brooks was a member of the National Sculpture Society and National Institute of Arts and Letters. He was a man of medium height, rather slight build, great refinement of feature, and alertness of expression. He was found ill in his studio by one of his models and died suddenly after being taken to the hospital.

[Lorado Taft, *Hist. of Am. Sculpture* (rev. ed. 1924) ; *Am. Art Annual*, vol. XVI (1919) ; obituary in *Boston Transcript*, May 3, 1919 ; files of the Washington *Star* ; Vital Records of Braintree, Mass.]   L. M.

BROOKS, THOMAS BENTON (June 19, 1836–Nov. 22, 1900), geologist and mining engineer, was born at Monroe, N. Y., the son of John Brooks and Sarah Ketchum Brooks, his wife. His early training was limited to instruction at home, the district public schools, two years (1856–58) at the Union College School of Engineering, and in 1858–59 a single course of lectures under J. P. Lesley at the University of Pennsylvania. He had, however, the happy faculty of learning from observation, and sufficiently mastered the use of the newly introduced plane table, while serving as an axman with the topographic branch of the Geological Survey of New Jersey, to supersede his immediate superior. This was when he was but seventeen years of age, and prior to his Union College training. While in college he made surveys in the mountain regions west of the Hudson and later worked with a Coast Survey party in the region of the Gulf of Mexico. With the outbreak of the Civil War, Brooks enlisted as a private, being then twenty-five years of age, and was mustered into service as first lieutenant, Company A, New York Volunteer Engineers, in September 1861, serving until the fall of 1864 and resigning only at the earnest request of his parents after the death of his brother in the trenches before Petersburg. He won recognition for conspicuous bravery during the sieges of Forts Pulaski and Wagner and at the time of his resignation had risen to the rank of colonel by brevet.

After his retirement from the army he served a year on the Geological Survey of New Jersey under Dr. G. H. Cook and in 1865 became vice-president and general manager of the Iron Cliff mine, near Negaunee in the Marquette District of Michigan. Here he began the geological work upon which his reputation is mainly based. In 1869 he was employed, in recognition of his authority on the iron bearing formations, to take charge of the economic division of the state geological survey of the Upper Peninsula under Alexander Winchell. The difficulties encountered in this work are to-day little comprehended, except by those who have likewise worked in the region. The country was—at that time—heavily wooded and swampy. Outcrops were poor and often entirely lacking; prospect holes were few, and fewer yet were mines. There were no maps other than the very defective and often misleading ones furnished by the Land Office. The geological structure was exceedingly complicated owing to repeated folding of the rocks. Nevertheless, by his pertinacity and originality Brooks succeeded in producing a work of value from a scientific standpoint as well as of the greatest use to the prospector and to those who came after him—a work indeed concerning which it has been said that it was only superseded after twenty years of study by an able corps of geologists with a hundredfold better facilities.

For use in his work Brooks designed the dial compass and adapted the dip needle to the purposes of the prospector. Determined to carry through his undertaking to a successful conclusion, notwithstanding the meagerness of the appropriation, he worked without salary and exhausted his vitality to an extent from which he never fully recovered. Broken in health he went abroad and finished writing his report in 1873 while residing in London and Dresden. This report was written with the intention of making it a manual of information as complete as possible, relating to the finding, extracting, transporting, and smelting of the iron ores of the Lake Superior region. With this in view he presented first, an historical sketch of the discovery and development of the iron mines; second, the geology of the Upper Peninsula, including the lithology; third, the geology of the Marquette iron region; fourth, the geology of the Menominee iron region; fifth, the Lake Gogebic and Montreal River iron ridge; sixth, a chapter on exploration and prospecting for ore; and seventh, the magnetism of rocks and the use of the magnetic needle in exploring, concluding with chapters on the methods and cost of mining specular and magnetic ores and their chemical composition.

In 1876 he returned to the United States to reside for a winter at Monroe, thence moving to a suburb of Newburgh, N. Y., where he lived the life of a country gentleman. In 1883, in company with a friend and business associate, Raphael Pumpelly [q.v.], he purchased some eight and one-half square miles of land in Decatur County, Ga., where the two families for several years

lived a truly ideal communistic life. In 1889 the Brooks family went once more abroad to obtain for his children the advantage of German educational facilities of which Brooks had a very high opinion. He was twice married, first to Hannah Hulse, who died in 1883 and by whom he had five children, one of whom, Alfred Hulse Brooks [q.v.], won distinction as a geologist, and second, in 1887, to Martha Giesler, a Prussian by birth.

[Full bibliography of Brooks's publications in *Bull. 746, U. S. Geol. Survey*; biographical sketch in D. N. Freeland, *Chronicles of Monroe in the Olden Time* (1898); memorial by Bailey Willis, *Science*, n.s., XIII (1901); G. P. Merrill, *Contributions to a Hist. of State Geol. and Natural Hist. Surveys* (1920), being Bull. 109 of the U. S. Nat. Museum.] G.P.M.

BROOKS, WILLIAM KEITH (Mar. 25, 1848–Nov. 12, 1908), zoölogist, was the second of four brothers, sons of Oliver Allen and Ellenora (Kingsley) Brooks. His ancestry goes back to Thomas Brooke, who was a freeman of Watertown, Mass., in 1636 and later settled in Concord. On the maternal side Brooks was descended from John Kingsley, who came to Dorchester, Mass., about 1638, from England. He was born in Cleveland, Ohio, to which place his father had removed from Burlington, Vt., in 1835, and became one of the early merchants of that city. He grew up in a large, comfortable, old-time home on Euclid Ave., attending the public schools, where he was a quick pupil, and living the normal boy life of that time in the Middle West. A congenital defect of the heart prevented his joining in athletic sports. The assiduous study of several books on natural history—*Thompson's History of Vermont, Wood's Natural History*—and association with the sons of the geologist, Prof. J. S. Newberry, then a neighbor, showed the bent of his mind at this time. His country walks were collecting trips. He learned to stuff birds, became interested in aquaria, and established a sort of museum in the barn. His first microscope was made for him by Charles F. Brush, afterward well known for inventions in electric lighting. While in public school Brooks had private tuition in Greek; ever after, that language had a charm for him second only to the natural sciences. In 1866 he entered Hobart College where, as he wrote years after, "I learned to study, and I hope, to profit by, but not blindly follow, the writings of that great thinker on the principles of science, George Berkeley." Two years later he transferred to the junior class of Williams College, where he was graduated in 1870.

Having no taste for business life, Brooks decided to teach, and for the following two years was a master at DeVeaux College, Niagara

Falls. In 1873 he entered the Harvard graduate school, where he came for a brief time under the influence of Louis Agassiz. At Harvard it is said that his life was studious and generally solitary save for the companionship of a great St. Bernard dog, "Tige," who always walked with him when he went abroad, and who occupied most of his bed at night.

He spent the summer of 1873 at Agassiz's seaside laboratory at Penekese, and after that a part, at least, of every summer at the shore. In 1875 he was at A. Agassiz's laboratory at Newport. In 1878 he founded the Chesapeake Zoölogical Laboratory, which he directed for many years. Subsequently he worked at the United States Fish Commission laboratories at Woods Hole, Mass., and at Beaufort, N. C., and in 1905 and 1906 at the marine laboratory of the Carnegie Institution at Tortugas, Fla.

During 1875 and 1876 Brooks was an assistant in the museum of the Boston Society of Natural History; but museum work did not attract him, and on the founding of Johns Hopkins University in 1876 he applied for one of their fellowships, and was appointed associate in biology. In 1883 he was made associate professor of morphology, in 1889 professor of morphology, and in 1894 head of the biological department. As a teacher he was noted for the vividness and picturesqueness of his lectures and for his ability to stimulate his students to individual investigation.

Brooks was the author of about a hundred papers, fourteen relating to oysters, their embryology and conservation, seventeen to tunicates, twenty-six dealing with molluscan structure and embryology. Other important papers relate to the Crustacea; the significance of their larval stages in phylogeny being lucidly discussed. The life history of the Hydromedusæ was dealt with in one of his most beautiful and satisfactory papers. His principal books are *The Law of Heredity* (1883), and *The Foundations of Zoölogy* (1899). Of the latter David Starr Jordan wrote: "It belongs to literature as well as to science; it belongs to philosophy as much as to either, for it is full of fundamental wisdom about realities which alone is worthy of the name of science." His essay on "The Origin of the Oldest Fossils and the Discovery of the Bottom of the Ocean" (*Journal of Geology,* July–August 1894) offered a highly original solution of one of the great problems of zoölogy and paleontology. His only text-book was an excellent *Handbook of Invertebrate Zoölogy* (1882).

In personal appearance Brooks was short and stout, with straight brown hair and heavy dark-brown mustache. He was rather thoughtless about dress, deliberate in movement and speech, undemonstrative in manner. "If he had no answer ready when a question was asked he usually gave no answer until he was ready—it might be several days later—when he would answer as naturally as if the question had been asked only a moment before." He enjoyed a good joke. "In spite of quiet reserve, he was usually a very companionable man, and his company was sought and prized by his friends." In 1878 he married Amelia Katharine Schultz, a woman of charming personality. They lived at the beautiful estate "Brightside," on the shore of Lake Roland, seven miles from Baltimore.

[Edwin G. Conklin, "Biog. Memoir of Wm. Keith Brooks," *Nat. Acad. Sci. Biog. Memoirs,* vol. VII (1910); Edward G. Spaulding, "Prof. Brooks's Philosophy," *Pop. Sci. Mo.,* Feb. 1911.]　　H.A.P.

BROOKS, WILLIAM ROBERT (June 11, 1844–May 3, 1921), astronomer, was born at Maidstone, England, the son of Rev. William and Caroline (Wickings) Brooks. The family came to America in 1857 and settled in Darien, N. Y. William was educated in the English and American public and private schools. A prolonged trip to Australia and back at the age of seven and eight, and his voyage to America at thirteen, probably started his interest in astronomy. He made his first telescope when he was fourteen years old, just in time to get a view of Donati's great comet of 1858. His first astronomical lecture was delivered in his father's church at the age of seventeen. He became much interested in the development of photography and was one of the pioneers in its application to celestial observation. He was for a time employed at the Shepherd Iron Works in Buffalo and there gained practical experience as a mechanician and draftsman which was of great value to him in constructing his astronomical instruments. In 1868 he married Mary E. Smith and in 1870 moved to Phelps, N. Y., and established himself as the village photographer. During his leisure hours Brooks applied himself to the construction of his telescopes. With the third one he discovered his first comet in 1881; the fourth, a reflector of nine inches aperture, was the chief instrument of the "Red House Observatory," a primitive structure in the apple orchard. With this instrument he discovered ten more comets. Encouraged by his success he now, regardless of his small income, devoted all his time to astronomy. A studious and thorough worker, he was calm of temperament and a well-liked citizen. His interesting presentation and his generous wit brought him much in demand as a lecturer. In 1888 he moved to Geneva, N. Y., where he was given charge of the William Smith Observatory. At Geneva he discovered sixteen more comets, bringing his total up to twenty-seven, only one less than the record number by Pons. He became professor of astronomy at Hobart College in 1900. His cometary discoveries brought him many prizes and medals.

["A Comet Finder," *Century Mag.*, XLVII, 838; "Photographing by Venus Light," *ibid.*, LXII, 529; obituaries in the *Monthly Notices of the Royal Astronomical Soc.*, LXXXII, 246, Geneva (N.Y.) *Daily Times*, May 4, 1921; letter from Anna C. Brooks, daughter of William Robert Brooks.]   R. S. D.

BROOKS, WILLIAM THOMAS HARBAUGH (Jan. 28, 1821–July 19, 1870), Union soldier, was born at New Lisbon, Ohio. In an environment and at a period when attainment of a higher education was difficult, young Brooks eagerly accepted appointment, July 1, 1837, as a cadet at the United States Military Academy. Not a brilliant student, but with work marked by industry and thoroughness, he was graduated in the year 1841, Number 41 in a class which had been reduced by elimination from 113 original cadets to 52 successful graduates. His first assignment was to the 3rd Infantry, and his first field service after joining his regiment was against hostile Seminole Indians in Florida, 1842–43. This was followed, up to the beginning of the war with Mexico, by arduous duty at various isolated frontier posts. In 1846 he joined Gen. Taylor's army, and took part in the battles of Palo Alto (May 8), and of Resaca de la Palma (May 9), receiving his first lieutenancy Sept. 21 of the same year. Thereafter, he participated in nearly all the important battles and engagements of the war—Monterey, Vera Cruz, Cerro Gordo, Ocalaca, Contreras, Churubusco, and the final capture of the City of Mexico. He was brevetted a captain, Sept. 23, 1846, for gallant and meritorious services at Monterey; and on the same date brevetted a major for similar distinguished services at Contreras and Churubusco. At Contreras, working under the direct supervision of that distinguished soldier, Capt. Robert E. Lee, Brooks had made a particularly hazardous and difficult night reconnaissance of a ravine which served as the approach to the enemy's position, when the successful assault was made by Scott's army the following day. For a time thereafter, he served as acting adjutant-general for Gen. Twigg's division, a duty of marked responsibility for so young an officer; and later, from Aug. 19, 1848, until Nov. 10, 1851, when he received his captaincy in the regular army, Brooks served as Gen. Twigg's aide-de-camp. There followed a long period of difficult field service in New Mexico and Texas, which included almost continuous scouting against hostile Indians, and one skirmish with the warlike Navajos in New Mexico, Oct. 10, 1858. During this prolonged period of exposure to danger and to the rigors of climatic extremes, Brooks's ill health required several sick-leaves.

With the outbreak of the Civil War, Brooks was well prepared, except as to impaired physical condition, for promotion to high command, so that his advancement, Sept. 28, 1861, from captain in the regular army to brigadier-general of volunteers, followed naturally and logically. He took part with distinction, in McClellan's Peninsular campaign, being engaged in the siege of Yorktown (Apr. 5–May 4, 1862), the skirmish of Lee's Mills (Apr. 16), the action at Golden's Farm (June 28), and in the battles of Savage Station (June 29) and of Glendale (June 30, 1862). Meanwhile, Mar. 12, 1862, he had become a major in the regular service. In the Maryland campaign of the Army of the Potomac, which followed, Brooks was engaged in the action at Crampton Pass (Sept. 14), the battle of Antietam (Sept. 17), and in the march to Falmouth, Va., during which he commanded his division, from Oct. 22, 1862. In the subsequent Rappahannock campaign, he commanded his division from December 1862 to May 1863; commanded the Department of Monongahela, June 1863 to April 1864; commanded a division of the 18th Corps, Army of the James, April to June, and a division of the 10th Corps, June to July 1864. As division commander, Brooks participated in the battles around Richmond, including Cold Harbor and the siege of Petersburg. But he had been wounded in the battle of Savage Station, and again at Antietam, so that just as victory was about to crown with success the final campaigns of the Union Army, his health broke down completely, and he was forced to resign from the service, June 14, 1864. After a period of rest and recuperation, he moved to Huntsville, Ala., where he engaged in farming until his death, July 19, 1870. His premature end at the age of forty-nine years was mourned not alone by a large circle of army friends and acquaintances, but by his more recent Southern neighbors, who, at a time when the status of former Union officers was strained, loved Brooks for his amiable disposition, simplicity of character, and sound common sense.

[G. W. Cullum, *Biog. Reg.* (3rd ed., 1891); sketch by Gen. Z. B. Tower in *Annual Reunion, Ass. Grads. U. S. Mil. Acad.*, 1871; Justin Smith, *The War with Mexico* (1919); C. M. Wilcox, *Hist. of the Mexican War* (1892); *Battles and Leaders of the Civil War* (1887–88).]   C. D. R.

BROPHY, TRUMAN WILLIAM (Apr. 12, 1848–Feb. 4, 1928), oral surgeon, was born at Goodings Grove, Ill., the son of William Brophy and Amelia (Cleveland) Brophy. He received his academic education at Elgin Academy, Elgin, Ill., 1863–65 and at Dyrenforth's College, 1867–69; and his professional training from the Pennsylvania College of Dental Surgery, where he graduated with the degree of D.D.S., in 1872. In 1880 he graduated from Rush Medical College with the degree of M.D. Early in his career he became interested in the surgery of the mouth. This determination of his life's work was made through an interesting incident. While visiting surgical clinics in the leading cities of the eastern states, he attended in New York a clinical demonstration to medical students given by Dr. Lewis Sayre, the distinguished orthopedic surgeon. Dr. Sayre presented a case of extreme cleft palate and double harelip in an infant two weeks old, a condition which, should the child survive, meant a repulsive and life-long deformity. The mother, in obvious poverty, had brought her baby to the great surgeon, hoping that it might be cured. Dr. Sayre took the child in his hands and explained the details and extent of the deformity—calling attention to the wide cleft between the maxillary bones. By grasping the child's face he could press the flexible bones nearly to contact, saying that if only it were possible to carry the bones to actual contact, with freshened edges, and to immobilize them, and so to effect a union, "we could go far toward correcting the most conspicuous deformity known to mankind." He then stated to his audience the fact that such an operation had never been performed—"we have no way of doing it." The child was returned to the pale-faced and disappointed mother with the conclusive though kindly word that surgery could do nothing in that sad case.

Brophy was deeply stirred by the pathos of the incident and at the same time fired with enthusiasm to devise a way to overcome a surgical difficulty so intricate and so important. As it turned out, his long professional career was devoted to this problem of reconstruction whereby from the vestiges of natural parts were produced, in so far as possible, a hard palate of normal breadth, a flexible soft palate, and a well-shaped lip and nose. After much study and experimentation, he hit upon a plan to immobilize the maxillæ, when brought into contact, by means of lead plates secured by silver wire, and this kind of splint was first used by him on a human subject in 1886. When the union of the bones was established, the cleft lip was united, and later the edges of the soft palate were brought together. This procedure, with minor improvements, has become the accepted method the world over for the treatment of a deformity which had been considered hopeless of correction except by mechanical appliances. During a period of over forty years Brophy performed this operation throughout the United States and in foreign countries, and the relief of human suffering due to him is beyond calculation.

He was distinguished not only as an oral surgeon but also as an educator and writer. He was dean of the Chicago College of Dental Surgery for forty years. He took an active and prominent part in the work of local and national and international dental and medical associations, during the same period, and was a constant writer in the field of oral and facial surgery. An exhaustive book of reference, *Oral Surgery*, was brought out by him in 1915; also *Cleft Lip and Palate*, in 1923. He was married twice: on May 8, 1873, to Emma Jean Mason, who died in 1899; and on Mar. 31, 1908, to Mrs. E. W. Strawbridge.

[Sketch in the *Dental Cosmos*, Apr. 1928; bibliography in *Index to Dental Periodical Lit.*, 1886–1927.]

W. B. D.

BROSS, WILLIAM (Nov. 4, 1813–Jan. 27, 1890), journalist, was the eldest son of Deacon Moses Bross of Sussex County, N. J. When he was a child of nine his family moved to Milford, Pa., where they lived until he was grown. Deacon Bross went into the lumber business when work was started on the Delaware & Hudson Canal, and William was his father's assistant. In 1832 he began his studies at Milford Academy and in 1834 he entered Williams College. He was an earnest student and in 1838 was graduated with honors. Shortly after, in 1839, he married the only daughter of Dr. John T. Jansen of Goshen, N. Y. He secured a position as principal of Ridgebury Academy where he taught 1838–43. He then taught in Chester Academy for five years. In 1848 he moved to Chicago as a partner in the bookselling firm of Griggs, Bross & Company, remaining in this business a year and a half, after which the firm was dissolved. After this, in connection with the Rev. J. A. Wight, he started (1849) the *Prairie Herald,* a religious newspaper which continued for about two years with only moderate success. In 1852 Bross joined with John L. Scripps in starting a paper called the *Democratic Press.* The paper was rather conservative and especially marked for its commercial and financial features. When the Republican party was formed in 1854, the political course of the paper was changed, Bross became an ardent Republican, and his strong advocacy of the doctrines of the new party led him to speak in their behalf. He soon became known as a strong and effective speaker as well as a comprehensive writer. Into this paper Bross introduced the feature of publishing a review of Chicago's business at the beginning of each year. The paper also served as an outlet for his deep enthusiasm for the future prospects of Chicago and the Northwest. Most of his predictions for the former became statistical facts. During the panic of 1857 the *Democratic Press* united with the *Tribune* under the name of the *Press Tribune*. Two years later the first half of the name was dropped and the paper remained the *Tribune*. Bross was a personal friend of Abraham Lincoln, and the *Tribune* very early advocated Lincoln's nomination for president of the United States. In 1864 Bross was elected lieutenant-governor of Illinois. During his term of office he was influential in repealing the so-called Black Laws of Illinois. Immediately after the Chicago fire in 1871, he began working for the rebuilding of the city. He brought considerable aid from other cities through personal contacts which he had made. Bross seemed deeply concerned with religious and moral welfare and often spoke before various religious groups. He was an energetic, resolute man of medium height, robust frame, and square features, and was known as a toiler. Both his speaking and writing were effective because of the frank determination behind each effort that he made. In 1876 he wrote a brief *History of Chicago* dealing chiefly with the commercial progress of the city and its physical advantages. During a vacation near his old home in 1887, he wrote a biographical sketch, *Tom Quick*, which contained an old legend of the Deleware. His death occurred in Chicago.

[*Biog. Sketches of the Leading Men of Chicago* (1868); *Biog. Encyc. Ill.* (1875); *Hist. Encyc. Ill.* (1897); obituaries in *Chicago-Herald*, and *Inter-Ocean*, Jan. 28, 1890, and esp. *Chicago Tribune*, Jan. 28–31, 1890. A paper read before the Chicago Hist. Soc., Jan. 20, 1880, entitled *Chicago and the Sources of Her Past and Future Growth*, and his *Hist. of Chicago* show Bross's interest and knowledge of social and economic tendencies. His religious views are evident from the address before Williams College Alumni, entitled *America as a Field for the Exertions of the Christian Scholar* (1866).]   M. S.

BROUGH, JOHN (Sept. 17, 1811–Aug. 29, 1865), governor of Ohio, was the son of John Brough, a Londoner who came to Ohio in 1806, and in December 1810, by license of the court, opened a tavern "under the court house" in Marietta. In this two-story log building, the first "temple of Justice" in the Northwest Territory, John Brough, eldest of five, was born. The mother, Jane Garnet, died in October 1821, the father a year later. A pioneer editor gave the boy a home and taught him to set type. Printing offices were to be his college, for even in his few terms in Ohio University at Athens (of which he was later a trustee, 1840–43) he supported himself by typesetting. Before he was twenty, he started in Marietta a Democratic paper, the *Western Republican,* sold it in 1833, bought the *Ohio Eagle* in Lancaster, Ohio, and made it a pathway into politics. The Ohio Senate chose him as its clerk for two terms, 1835–37. At twenty-six he was a member of the House and as chairman of the committee on banking and currency, he aided materially in the state's recovery from the panic of 1837. The legislature electing him auditor of state for six years, 1839–45, he reorganized the state system of accounts, corrected many abuses, added to the tax list a million acres of untaxed lands, raised the state's credit from 67 to par,—and made many enemies. Upon the Whig victory of 1844 Brough returned to journalism. He bought the *Cincinnati Advertiser,* changed its name to *Cincinnati Enquirer,* and became its editor. At the same time he practised law. He also entered actively into state politics. Well-informed in public affairs, clear-thinking, self-possessed, clever in argument, favored with a massive frame and a powerful voice, he was deemed the best Democratic speaker in Ohio. From 1848 to 1863 his energies were wholly given to railroads, as president, successively, of the Madison & Indianapolis Railroad, the Bellefontaine Line, and the Indianapolis, Pittsburgh & Cleveland Railroad. He made Madison, Ind., his home, then Indianapolis, and finally Cleveland.

At the outbreak of the Civil War, refusing to follow his party into opposition, he greatly aided the government in the transport of troops and supplies. As the war progressed Ohio was rent with discord. Secret organizations to resist the draft spread fear among the loyal. There was grave peril that the election would be carried by the disaffected, sore over conscription and angered by the arrest of their magnetic leader Vallandigham. In June 1863 before a great meeting at Marietta, his boyhood home, Brough spoke so movingly in support of the Union that within a week he was nominated by the Republicans for governor. The fierce campaign brought out a record poll; Vallandigham's vote surpassed that of all his Democratic predecessors, but Brough's unprecedented majority of 100,099 remained unequaled for forty years.

Inaugurated Jan. 11, 1864, the new governor's great energies were first directed to securing increased taxes for the support of the soldiers' families. The number of welfare agencies near the armies was next increased. The hospitals were brought under inspection. A seniority system of promotions in the army displaced advancement based on favoritism, popular sentiment, and political influence. Acrimonious disputes with officers whose powers were diminished by the new policy arose at once. The governor remained firm in the face of disrespect and open hostility. Large numbers of veteran soldiers whose services were needed in the field were engaged in duties that recruits could well perform—manning fortifications, guarding supply depots, military prisons, and long lines of communications. At a conference of the governors in Washington, Brough led a movement to raise fresh troops to serve for one hundred days, without bounty, in fortifications or wherever needed. The President accepted the offer and Brough telegraphed home a call for 30,000 men. Within sixteen days 34,000 were organized, equipped, and sent forward, releasing an equal number of veterans for Grant's army. He continued to have the confidence of Lincoln and Stanton, grateful for his instant response to calls for support; but powerful enemies within and without the army finally combined to defeat him for a renomination. His last days were embittered but he was not to be moved from any chosen course. He wrote to a friend (February 1865): "I have no fear of any assaults that may be made upon my public acts. . . . They may be marked by errors but not by weakness or dishonesty. And so time and truth will prove them." He still had hosts of friends who overlooked offensive manners and incorrect personal habits in their admiration for his great executive ability, his incorruptible honesty, his zeal, energy, and devotion to the public service. But although he believed he could be renominated and elected, he issued an address "to the people of Ohio" on June 15, 1865, withdrawing as a candidate, "owing the people of the state too much to embarrass their future action for the gratification of [his] own ambition" and doubting whether his health would sustain him through a vigorous campaign. That fear was too soon realized. He did not live to complete his term of office. A sprained ankle compelled the use of a cane and his great weight injured the hand on which he leaned. Gangrene in both foot and hand ended his life after two months of intense suffering. His ashes rest in Woodland Cemetery in Cleveland.

Brough married: first, Achsa Pruden in 1832. She died in 1838, leaving a son and a daughter.

He married second, Caroline A. Nelson in 1843, who bore him two sons and two daughters. She survived him by twenty-five years.

[*Ohio Archæol. and Hist. Quart.*, XIII, 40–70; corrected in some details by vol. XVII, 105–11. Much valuable material about his administration as governor appears in Whitelaw Reid, *Ohio in the War* (1867), I, 166–71, 182–237, 1022–26; and in E. O. Randall and D. F. Ryan, *Hist. of Ohio* (5 vols. 1912). A sympathetic appraisal of him appeared in the *Cincinnati Commercial*, Aug. 30, 1865.]

F. W. A.

BROUGHAM, JOHN (May 9, 1810–June 7, 1880), actor, playwright, was born in Dublin, of Irish and French ancestry. He studied at Trinity College and the Peter Street Hospital, but, when he was twenty, family adversity cut short his medical career, and he went to London and drifted into the theatre, in July 1830. In 1831 he was a member of Mme. Vestris's company at the Olympic, following her to Covent Garden, where, so he always affirmed, he supplied Dion Boucicault [*q.v.*] with the idea of *London Assurance*. In 1840 he managed the London Lyceum, and wrote several plays for its repertoire. He began his American career as Felix O'Callaghan in *His Last Legs* at the Park Theatre, New York, Oct. 4, 1842 (*New York Daily Express*, Oct. 4, 1842), and thereafter was chiefly identified with the United States. He joined Burton's company as an actor and playwright at the famous Chambers Street Theatre, New York, and while there wrote many plays and burlesques, including a dramatization of *Dombey and Son* in which Burton played Captain Cuttle. For this he received, he later declared, only $250. In 1850 he opened Brougham's Lyceum, on the corner of Broadway and Broome St., New York, but lost on the venture because the public thought the theatre walls unsafe after an adjoining building was torn down. He then revived *King John* at the Bowery, and later joined Wallack's company, meanwhile continuing prolific as a playwright. For Wallack, he made, among other works, a dramatization of *Bleak House*, and wrote perhaps his most famous burlesque, *Pocahontas*. That Indian maiden had already served as the heroine of more than one romantic play, and Brougham had lively fun with them all, though his burlesque is marred for us to-day by its incessant stream of puns. He presently rejoined Burton, and wrote another famous burlesque, *Columbus*, one of his most interesting plays, not without a touch of dignity and pathos amid its fun. In 1860 he went to England and acted there for five years, and also made for Charles Fechter an English version of *The Duke's Motto*, for which he declared he was rewarded with a box of cigars.

He returned to America in 1865 and never went abroad again. On Jan. 25, 1869 he opened Brougham's Theatre on West Twenty-fourth St., New York, with *Better Late Than Never* and *The Dramatic Review for 1868,* a forerunner of the reviews of the twentieth century (See *New York Herald,* Jan. 25, 26, 1869). But the owner of the theatre, the notorious Jim Fisk, Jr., was dissatisfied with the box office returns, or pretended to be, and took the house away from him. This was his last effort at management. On Jan. 17, 1878, after he had become distressingly poor, a testimonial benefit was held for him at the Academy of Music, and yielded the sum of $10,000 which was settled on him as an annuity. He died on June 7, 1880. Brougham was first married to Emma Williams, an English actress and beauty, from whom he soon separated. His second wife was Annette Nelson (Mrs. Hodges), daughter of an English naval officer, but herself an actress. She died in 1870. He wrote, during his fifty years on the stage, about seventy-five dramatic pieces and played a great variety of parts. His best work as author was probably his broadly comic and burlesque writing, and his best work as actor was his impersonation of comic characters (especially Irish) who were also gentlemen. His burlesques had a contemporary freshness, and his acting a genial ease, which foreshadowed more modern methods. He himself was gay, full of contagious animal spirits, kindly, generous to a fault, unfailingly courteous, and something of a scholar. His witty curtain speeches were famous, and socially he was extremely popular, being a handsome man of medium height and sturdy stature, with a sparkling discourse, a ready wit, and charming manners. In all business matters he was a trusting child, however, and his later life was clouded by his financial distresses resulting from this temperamental carelessness.

[*Life, Stories, and Poems of John Brougham* (1881), ed. by Wm. Winter; *Appleton's Annual Cyc.,* 1880; Wm. Winter, *Other Days* (1908), and *The Wallet of Time* (1913); *N. Y. Times, N. Y. Tribune,* June 8, 1880.]   W. P. E.

BROWARD, NAPOLEON BONAPARTE (Apr. 19, 1857–Oct. 1, 1910), governor of Florida, is notable for his filibustering expeditions in aid of the Cuban revolutionists, and for his promotion of the drainage of the Everglades. Some of his ancestors were residents of Spanish Florida; his father, also Napoleon Bonaparte Broward, who married Mary Parsons, was a farmer of Duval County. There the son was born and lived until the fighting of the Civil War forced a removal to Hamilton County. An or-

phan at twelve, the future governor worked on the old farm near Jacksonville and attended a country school for several winters. While still a boy he was employed as deck-hand on a steamboat, and on reaching manhood went to Cape Cod and followed the sea for two years. Returning to the St. John's River he was owner and captain of a steamboat until his appointment as sheriff of Duval County in 1889, to which office he was elected in 1892 and again in 1896. But the water never ceased to call him and meanwhile he had built and operated the steamer *Three Friends,* in 1896 commanding her on several filibustering expeditions, successfully landing men and munitions on the coast of Cuba. In 1900 he served in the Florida House of Representatives, and was appointed a member of the state board of health.

A growing interest in the state's welfare and her future led him to the question of the drainage of the Everglades, and with this as a platform and aided by the fame of his Cuban expeditions he was elected governor of Florida in 1904. The project of drainage had been discussed for fifty years and a foundation for the work had been laid by the former administration, but Broward from the stump developed for it a wide popular support of which it was in need. During his term of office (1905–09) dredging was begun (October 1906) and 13.22 miles of canal were completed (see message [on drainage] to the legislature, May 3, 1905). On his recommendation, the legislature created a Board of Control for all state institutions of higher education; these schools were consolidated, and the University of Florida and the Florida Female College (later Florida State College for Women) were established. Other recommendations, at least partly carried out, were greater state aid for common schools, taxation of franchises, primary election legislation, and a resolution proposing an amendment to the constitution to create a board of drainage commissioners. Broward also proposed and strongly advocated state life insurance, and a resolution memorializing Congress to segregate the entire negro race in the United States under a government of its own (see biennial messages to the legislature, Apr. 4, 1905; and Apr. 2, 1907). In the primary election of 1910 Broward was nominated as Democratic candidate for United States senator (virtually equivalent to election), but died before the vote was taken. He was survived by his wife, Annie Douglas, and nine children.

[In addition to his messages to the Fla. legislature (to be found in the *Journals* of both houses) see Caroline M. Brevard, *A Hist. of Fla.,* vol. II (1925); *Fla. Ed. Makers of America* (1911), IV, 17–23; *Certain*

*Live Public Questions, An Open Letter of Gov. Bro-
ward* (Tallahassee, 1907); and an obituary in the
Times-Union, Jacksonville, Fla., Oct. 2, 1910, as well
as obituaries in other Fla. newspapers.]   J.C.Y.

BROWER, JACOB VRADENBERG (Jan.
21, 1844–June 1, 1905), explorer, archeologist,
was born at York, Mich., and at thirteen years
of age moved with his parents, Abraham Duryea
and Mary R. Brower, to Minnesota. Here he
continued his common school education. The
young man saw service in the volunteer army
and navy, and at a later period held various state
and federal appointments. Much remaining to
be done to complete the knowledge of the region of the sources of the Mississippi, in 1889
Brower undertook exploration about Lake Itasca. During this work he discovered traces of
ancient habitations, which impelled him to devote his energies to archeology, especially of the
rich fields of Minnesota and Kansas. As Itasca
State Park Commissioner (1891–95) for which
office he was particularly fitted on account of
his explorations of the region, he continued to
note sites of archeological interest. Continuing
his geographic studies, in 1896 he traced the
sources of the Missouri River. In this period
he rediscovered Quivira, the legendary locality
in central and eastern Kansas reached by the
Coronado expedition in 1541. Always exploring with an indefatigable energy, he located the
surprising number of 1,125 ancient aboriginal
mounds at Mille Lac, Minn., evidently a populous ancient Indian center. In the prolific field
of Minnesota archeology no one has done more
than Brower. In one decade he contributed
100,000 specimens to the State Historical Society at St. Paul. Not only did he collect, but he
made it a rule to publish promptly. That he
found means to publish, and most voluminously,
indicates an enviable situation rarely accorded
to scientific men. As an example of his perseverance, after a fire which destroyed the notes
of years of research, he calmly began the work
anew. Necessarily most of his contributions
were confined to the essential preliminary investigations which science demands as a groundwork. Other more original contributions resulted from excavations in graves, mounds, and
village sites. While not having the training required by present day archeologists, Brower accomplished much by self-education and in following the lead of Henry R. Schoolcraft. Of his
published writings the most important are, *Pre-
historic Man at the Headwater Basin of the
Mississippi* (1895); *Quivira* (1898); *Harahey*
(1899); *Mille Lac* (1900); *Kathio* (1901); and
Kakabikansing (1902). His historical and geographical works include *The Mississippi River*

and Its Source (1893); *The Missouri River and
Its Utmost Source* (1896); *Minnesota: Discovery of Its Area, 1540–1665* (1903); *Kansas:
Monumental Perpetuation of Its Earliest History 1541–1896* (1903); *Itasca State Park, an
Illustrated History* (1904); and many shorter
articles. These works were published mainly at
his own expense, and at the height of his productive period he issued usually one volume a
year. In appearance Brower was like the ideal
pathfinder, over six feet, quite erect and slender,
but muscular, and capable of feats of endurance.
He was unmarried.

[*Who's Who in America*, 1903–05, Am. Anthropologist, n.s. VII, 362; obituary in the *Daily Pioneer
Press* (St. Paul), June 2, 1905.]   W.H.

BROWERE, JOHN HENRI ISAAC (Nov.
18, 1792–Sept. 10, 1834), sculptor, made a unique
and valuable contribution to American culture
in a series of life masks of great Americans.
The son of Jacob Browere and Ann Catherine
Gendon, he was born in 1792, at 55 Warren St.,
New York. He was of Dutch descent, and was
one of the many claimants to heirship from An-
neke Jans, through Adam Brouwer, who came
from Holland to settle in Long Island in 1642.
The man's name was really Berkhoven, but the
name of his business of brewer clung to him
and to his descendants. Young Browere entered Columbia, but was not graduated. At
nineteen, he married Eliza Derrick of London,
England. He studied art with Archibald Robertson, who had come to America from Scotland in 1791 with a commission from the Earl
of Buchan to paint for his gallery at Aberdeen
a portrait of Washington, and who later with
his brother Alexander opened the Columbian
Academy in Liberty St., New York, where for
thirty years they taught drawing and painting.
Browere's brother, captain of a trading vessel
to Italy, took Browere abroad, and for nearly
two years the young man traveled afoot in
Italy, Austria, Greece, Switzerland, France, and
England, "studying art, especially sculpture."
On his return to New York, he made a bust of
Alexander Hamilton, from a miniature by Robertson. Experimenting to produce life masks
by means of a molding material superior to that
in general use, he at length perfected a composition and a process now unknown, and in
1825, his bust of Lafayette brought him fame.
His ambition was to create a portrait gallery
of great characters, to be interpreted, he hoped,
in bronze. That hope was not realized. "Pecuniary emolument," he wrote to Madison, "has
never been my aim." And later, "I have expended $12,087 in the procuration of the specimens

I now have." Included among "specimens" bequeathed to his family were busts of John Adams, John Quincy Adams, Charles Francis Adams, Jefferson, Madison, and Van Buren; Charles Carroll of Carrollton, De Witt Clinton; Generals Philip Van Cortlandt, Alexander Macomb, Jacob Brown; Commodore David Porter, who declared the mask to be "a perfect facsimile of my person, owing to the peculiar neatness and dexterity which guide his scientific operation"; Secretary of the Navy Samuel Southard, Secretary of the Treasury Richard Rush, Justice Barbour, Henry Clay; Drs. Mitchill, Mott, and Hosack; Edwin Forrest and Tom Hilson, actors; Thomas Emmet, Col. Stone, Maj. Noah; that historic trio, Paulding, Williams, and Van Wart; Gilbert Stuart, and other famous men. Dolly Madison at fifty-three was the only woman whose face was handed down by Browere.

The times were not ripe for his plan of permanency in bronze. Abandoning his scheme because of lack of support, and because of what he called "the jealous enmity" of his fellow artists, Browere at one time considered giving some of his works to the South American republics, to incite them to a wider freedom. A versatile individualist, of active mind, he not only wrote verses, but painted pictures, and profitably exhibited them; yet to his wrath he was kept out of the National Academy of Design. A feud with Trumbull was later patched up. Browere made both friends and foes. When the press attacked him for rumored ill treatment of the aged Jefferson under the "process," he retorted that his method was infinitely milder than the usual course, and obtained from Jefferson a satisfactory indorsement.

He died in 1834, after a few hours' illness of cholera, "at his house opposite the old milestone in the Bowery," and was buried in the Carmine Street churchyard. On his deathbed, he directed that the heads of some of his most important works should be sawed off, and packed away for forty years. This was not done. Some of the busts were shown at the Centennial of 1876, but it is doubtful whether their value as records was then appreciated. He left a wife and eight children. His second child, Alburtis (1814–87) became a painter of considerable note. A small water-color made by him of his father shows an energetic manly profile, with upstanding hair, stock, and coat collar. Alburtis knew Browere's process but, like his father, did not divulge the secret. He is said to have added to many of the life masks the draperies which perhaps enhanced them as busts, but which in no way contributed to their paramount virtue, historic authenticity.

[The chief authority on Browere is Chas. Henry Hart, who published in 1898 a well-illustrated book, *Browere's Life Masks of Great Americans*. Hart had previously written an article on these life masks, published in *McClure's Mag.*, IX, 1053–61. Further information is given in letters of famous Americans, notably Jefferson, Madison, John Adams, and others whose masks were made by Browere.]   A.A—s.

BROWN, AARON VENABLE (Aug. 15, 1795–Mar. 8, 1859), congressman, governor of Tennessee, was the sixth child of Rev. Aaron Brown, a Methodist minister, and his second wife, Elizabeth Melton. He was born in Brunswick County, Va., where his father was one of the seven justices from 1800 to 1813. With the exception of his very early training, the younger Brown received all of his education in the state of North Carolina. He was sent when very young to Westrayville Academy in Nash County where he received instruction from John Bobbitt, one of the best teachers and scholars of that time. After spending two years at this place he entered the University of North Carolina in 1812. He was graduated in 1814, valedictorian of his class, showing ability as an orator, even at this early date. While he was still in school his family moved to Giles County, Tenn., nine miles south of Pulaski. After graduation, young Brown also moved to Tennessee, began the study of law with Judge Trimble in Nashville and after two years was admitted to the bar. He practised for a time in Nashville, then took over the law business of Alfred M. Harris in Pulaski, and later formed a partnership with James K. Polk of Maury County which lasted until Polk's public life called him out of the state. Together, they built up a very large practise and also became close personal friends.

In 1821, Brown was elected to the Senate of Tennessee from Lincoln and Giles counties and served until 1827 with the exception of 1825. Again in 1831 he was elected to represent Giles County in the lower house of the state legislature. He exerted all his efforts to have the number of capital crimes reduced, and presented to the legislature a scholarly and philosophical dissertation in defense of his position (*Speeches*, pp. 376, 557 ff.). In 1839 he was elected to Congress over E. J. Shields, a prominent Whig who had served in the two preceding Congresses, and in 1841 and 1843 he was reëlected. He served on the committee which formulated the tariff bill of 1842 and spoke against the bill on the ground that it violated the spirit of the compromise tariff law of 1833 (*Congressional Globe*, 27 Cong., 2 Sess. App., 482). He championed in his speeches the whole Democratic program of the "reoccupation of Oregon" and the "reannexation of Texas," and made a speech against receiving, referring or reporting abolition petitions (*Ibid.*, 28 Cong., 1 Sess., 128).

In 1845, Brown decided to retire from public life and was on his way home from Washington when he received word that he had been nominated for governor of Tennessee by the Democrats. He accepted with reluctance. His opponent was Ephraim H. Foster, a popular Whig. During the campaign Brown made some of his most famous speeches and showed marked ability as an orator. He was elected by a majority of 1,600. An important school program was inaugurated during his administration: a number of male and female academies, including a medical college at Memphis, were established and the Tennessee Deaf and Dumb School at Knoxville was incorporated. The East Tennessee & Virginia Railroad (now the Southern) was granted a charter in 1847. (*Acts of Tennessee 1845–46.*) Brown was governor during the time of the Mexican War and the call for 2,800 soldiers was answered by no less than 30,000 volunteers though only four regiments were accepted. In 1847 he was defeated for reëlection by Neill S. Brown. Aaron Brown was a member of the Nashville convention of 1850 and was author of the Tennessee Platform. He opposed the compromise pending in Congress at this time though he finally acquiesced—but on the other hand, he opposed disunion as a remedy, offering in its stead sectional retaliation by refusing to trade with the North. He was a member of the Democratic convention in 1852 and was chairman of the committee which reported the Baltimore platform on which Pierce was elected. In the Cincinnati convention of 1856, he received 29 votes for the vice-presidency. His last official office was that of postmaster-general in Buchanan's cabinet, in which position he showed a great deal of administrative ability, establishing a much shorter mail route to California by way of the isthmus of Tehuantepec, another route overland from Memphis to St. Louis and San Francisco, and a third across the continent by way of Salt Lake (*Congressional Globe,* 35 Cong., 1 Sess., App., 19–28, 2 Sess., App., 21–26). He was for many years a leader in the Democratic party and his approbation and support were sought in all important measures.

He was first married to Sarah Burruss of Giles County who died leaving four children. In 1845, he was married to Mrs. Cynthia (Pillow) Saunders and had one child, a son.

[*Nashville Republican Banner,* Mar. 9, 1859; Public Papers of Aaron V. Brown in Tenn. State Archives; A. V. Brown, *Speeches, Congressional and Political, and Other Writings* (1854); *Jour. of the Senate of Tenn.,* 1821, '22, '23, '26; *Jour. of the House of Tenn.,* 1831; *Acts of Tenn.,* 1845–46; *Cong. Globe,* 26, 27, 28, 35 Congresses; John Livingston, *Portraits of Eminent Americans Now Living,* vol. I (1853); Family Records furnished by Old Glory Chapter of D. A. R. in Tenn. State Lib. Many encyclopedias give Brown's middle name as Vail, but he himself made the statement that his name was Venable and not Vail, *Speeches,* p. 507.]
F.L.O.

BROWN, ADDISON (Feb. 21, 1830–Apr. 9, 1913), jurist, author, came of Puritan stock, his father, Addison Brown, tracing his descent from the earliest settlers in Massachusetts, and his mother, Catharine Babson (Griffin) Brown, having among her ancestors Rev. John Rogers, president of Harvard in 1682, and Thomas Dudley, second governor of Massachusetts. He was born at West Newbury, Mass. His early education having been obtained privately at Bradford, Mass., he entered Amherst College in 1848, but proceeded to Harvard in 1849, where he graduated in 1852, being placed second in his class, which included Joseph H. Choate. The following year he entered the Harvard Law School, graduated LL.B. in 1854, and was admitted to the New York bar in 1855. He practised law in New York City for twenty-six years, acquiring a good connection, though he was never identified with any outstanding litigation. He was appointed United States district judge for the southern district of New York by President Garfield June 2, 1881, during a recess of the Senate, and the appointment was repeated by President Arthur the same year. Remaining on the bench for over twenty years, he acquired a high reputation as a judge in the particular class of cases which chiefly came before him, *i.e.,* those involving bankruptcy and admiralty law, and in professional circles was considered as perhaps the finest admiralty lawyer who ever occupied the position. Most of his opinions are reported in 8–115 *Federal Reporter.* The outstanding incident of his judicial career was his refusal in 1895 to issue an extradition order in the case of Charles A. Dana, whom it was sought to have removed from New York to Washington for trial on a charge of libeling the United States government. Prompted by failing health he retired from the bench Sept. 3, 1901. In 1902 he prepared and published *Index Digest of Decisions of Hon. Addison Brown, U. S. District Judge for the Southern District of N. Y., 1881–1901.* Thenceforward he lived a somewhat retired life till his death, which occurred in New York City.

Throughout his life he was deeply interested in scientific investigation, and an address delivered by him in 1891 before the New York Scientific Alliance on "The Need of Endowments for Scientific Research and Publication" was published by the Smithsonian Institution. He was an enthusiastic student of botany, on which subject he was widely recognized as an authority. One of the founders of the New York Botanical Garden, he drafted the act of the New York legislature passed in 1891, under which it was established, became one of its scientific directors, and was its president for two years. He also was an extensive contributor to the botanical collections of Harvard University. In collaboration with Nathaniel L. Britton he wrote *Illustrated Flora of the Northern United States, Canada and the British Possessions* (3 vols., 1896–98), a work of a very elaborate character, containing over 4,000 illustrations embracing every recognized species, a revision of which he had just completed at the time of his death. He also wrote *The Elgin Botanical Garden, Its Later History and Relation to Columbia College, the New Hampshire Grants and the Treaty with Vermont in 1790* (1908), which appeared as a Bulletin of the New York Botanical Garden. Another subject to which he devoted much study was astronomy, and his observations on the corona of the solar eclipse of 1878 were published through the Smithsonian Institution. He was married twice: in 1856 to Mary C. Barrett, who died in 1887, and in 1893 to Helen Carpenter Gaskin.

[G. W. Edes, *Annals of the Harvard Class of 1852* (1922); *Proc. of the Bar in Memory of Hon. Addison Brown . . . June 3, 1913* (1913). An appreciation of his judicial career appeared in *Case and Comment*, n.s., IV, 125, and the obituary notice in the *N. Y. Times*, Apr. 10, 1913, is comprehensive and sympathetic.]

H. W. H. K.

BROWN, ALBERT GALLATIN (May 31, 1813–June 12, 1880), congressman, governor of Mississippi, was born in Chester District, S. C. In 1823 his father, Joseph Brown, a poor but ambitious farmer, braved the dangers and hardships of a long, overland journey through a savage-infested wilderness to establish a new home for his wife and two sons in southern Mississippi. They settled a few miles south of Jackson, the new capital of the state, in what is now Copiah County. Albert Gallatin Brown, the second son, was given such meager school advantages as a frontier settlement afforded, though much of his early life was devoted to farm work. These experiences gave him a life-long sympathy for the farming class and a genuine interest in the welfare of all other laborers. At the age of sixteen he entered Mississippi College, at Clinton, which was a few miles from his home. His college career was limited to three years in that institu-

tion and six months in Jefferson College, at Washington, the old territorial capital of Mississippi. Because of financial limitations he was unable to complete his education at Yale or Princeton, as he desired. His six months of military training at Jefferson College resulted in his election to the office of colonel of the militia of Copiah County, at the age of nineteen, and in his promotion a year later to the rank of brigadier-general. Meantime, he was studying law in the office of E. G. Peyton, at Gallatin, the county seat of Copiah County. Within a year he passed a creditable examination before the supreme court of the state and was admitted to the bar before he reached his majority, the court having failed to ask his age. In the autumn of 1833 he entered upon the practise of law in partnership with his law preceptor. Two years later he gave up a lucrative practise to enter politics, and was elected to the state legislature. Although his father had been a Federalist of the old school, the son was a most ardent Jacksonian Democrat. As chairman of a committee to consider the recommendation of Gov. Lynch in favor of the National Bank, Brown made an adverse report (*Speeches*, pp. 19–26), which with his speeches on the subject put him in the forefront of his party in the state. In his absence, 750 of the 900 voters of his county in 1838 signed a paper demanding that he should either support a candidate for the United States Senate who was favorable to the Bank, or resign. He promptly resigned and announced his candidacy for reëlection to fill the vacancy. After a spirited campaign he was triumphantly returned to his vacant seat. Shortly thereafter he was unanimously nominated for Congress on the Democratic ticket. At that time the Bank issue absorbed the attention of the voters of Mississippi, the Whigs having swept the state in the preceding election. As congressmen were then elected on a general state ticket, Brown and his colleague, Jacob Thompson, canvassed the entire state; they were elected by a large majority. Young Brown took his seat in Congress in December 1839, and entered into active participation in the debates, as a champion of the Independent Treasury and other Democratic measures. The most important of his early speeches in Congress was delivered Apr. 17, 1840, in defense of Van Buren's administration (*Ibid.*, pp. 27–47). After the adjournment of Congress in 1840 he made a vigorous but unsuccessful canvass of Mississippi in behalf of Van Buren, who had been renominated for president on the Democratic ticket. Brown's first wife, Elizabeth Frances Taliaferro of Virginia, having died in October 1835, about five months after their marriage, he was married a second time, Jan. 12, 1841, to Roberta E. Young of Alexandria, Va. At the end of his term in Congress (1841) he declined a renomination; but he was induced to run for circuit judge, and defeated the former incumbent by a vote of almost three to one. Two years later he resigned this office to accept the Democratic nomination for governor. His platform declared that the "Union Bank Bonds" had been issued in violation of the state constitution and should be repudiated. The opposing candidates were the nominee of the Whig party and a distinguished ex-senator, who had been nominated by "the independent bond-paying Democrats" of the state. After a heated campaign Brown was elected by a large majority over the combined votes of his two opponents. This election settled the fate of the Union Bank Bonds. In his inaugural address Brown made a strong plea for the establishment of a free school system and for a liberal support of higher education in the state (*Ibid.*, pp. 55–66). His plan for the common schools was not followed by the legislature, and the system which was created proved ineffective, but better results followed his efforts to establish a state university. At the end of his second term as governor he returned to the lower house of Congress, taking his seat in the latter part of January 1848, two months after the beginning of the session. In his last legislative message (Jan. 3, 1848) he recommended the establishment of a state normal school, a school for the blind, and a lunatic asylum, and he urged again, as he had repeatedly urged before, the payment in full of the "Planters Bank Bonds" (*Ibid.*, pp. 92–105). Feb. 10, 1848, he made a bold defense in Congress of the policies of President Polk, and especially of the Mexican War (*Ibid.*, pp. 105–19). From this time until 1854, Brown was an active participant in the sectional debates in the House of Representatives, and from 1854 until the secession of his state he was in the forefront of the more serious controversies in the Senate. He opposed the Wilmot Proviso, the compromise measures of 1850, Know-Nothingism, and the Topeka constitution. He was a man of striking personality, with a handsome and animated face, an open and pleasing countenance, dark curly hair and beard, an expressive mouth, kindly eyes, and a well-proportioned forehead. His manner was courteous and void of ostentation or vanity. His early speeches, though somewhat ornate, were convincing and persuasive; later his speeches were more direct and bold, even to the point of audacity. Reuben Davis, who knew Brown well, says: "He was the best-balanced man I ever

knew. . . . In politics, he had strategy without corruption, and handled all his opponents with skill, but never descended to intrigue" (*Recollections,* pp. 164–5). In 1860 many Democratic papers advocated Brown's nomination for the presidency. In a conference of senators and congressmen from Mississippi, held at Jackson Nov. 22, 1860, at the request of Gov. Pettus to advise with him in reference to secession, Jefferson Davis, Brown, and L. Q. C. Lamar voted against a resolution to call a convention for the purpose of seceding "by separate State action"; the other three congressmen and the Governor voted in favor of the resolution, and the vote was then made unanimous (Mayes, *Lucius Q. C. Lamar,* pp. 86–7).

After secession Brown organized the "Brown Rebels" of which he became captain. He served with this company in the 18th Mississippi Regiment in Virginia, until his election to the Confederate Senate from Mississippi. He served in that body from Feb. 18, 1862, to Mar. 18, 1865. In the Reconstruction period he advised the people of his state "to meet Congress on its own platform and shake hands." As this policy was very unpopular, he never ran for public office after the war, but spent his last days quietly at his home near Terry, Hinds County, Miss., in his old age declaring his disgust with politics. He died June 12, 1880, and was buried in Greenwood Cemetery, Jackson. His two sons, Robert Y. Brown and Joseph Albert Brown, became lawyers, but following their father's advice, neither of them ever entered politics.

[Principal sources of information are the newspapers of Miss., 1835–80, and the *Cong. Globe,* 26, and 30–36 Cong., inclusive. M. W. Cluskey, *Speeches, Messages and Other Writings of the Hon. Albert G. Brown* (1859), contains a biographical sketch, from the *Democratic Rev.* of 1849, with additions by the editor of the volume to cover the period from 1849 to 1859. This book contains seventy-two documents, which are invaluable to students of the political history of the ante bellum period. See also *Biog. and Hist. Memoirs of Miss.* (1891); Jas. D. Lynch, *Bench and Bar of Miss.* (1881); Dunbar Rowland, *Official and Statistical Reg. of Miss.* (1908) and *Mississippi* (1907); *Miss. Hist. Soc. Pubs.,* vols. I–XIV (1898–1914); Edward Mayes, *Lucius Q. C. Lamar* (1896); Reuben Davis, *Recollections of Miss. and Mississippians* (1889).]   F.L.R.

BROWN, ALEXANDER (Nov. 17, 1764–Apr. 3, 1834), banker, one of America's first millionaires, landed in Baltimore, Md., in 1800, seeking his fortune. The son of William and Margaretta (Davison) Brown, born at Ballymena, County Antrim, Ireland, he had been keeper of a small but successful linen store in Belfast. While no precise reason is known for his coming to America, it is altogether likely that the rampant lawlessness in Ireland and the precariousness of all existence there in the late eighteenth century dictated his decision. He brought with him his wife, Grace Davison, and his oldest son, William, then sixteen years old, leaving his other three sons, George, John, and James, in England. He also brought with him a stock of Irish linens and the date of his business start in America is fixed by the appearance Dec. 20, 1800, of an advertisement in the *Federal Gazette and Baltimore Daily Advertiser,* announcing that these linens, three dozen "very nice mahogany hair bottom chairs" and four eight day clocks would be "sold very low." From this modest start as an importer of Irish linen, the swiftness with which the Alexander Brown house expanded, the way in which it developed into one of the greatest business and banking firms in the country, the scope of its affairs and the extent of its influence, constitute one of the commercial romances of American history. During all his life Brown made Baltimore his home and business headquarters and from there directed the banking, the trading and importing operations, the movement of his ships, and the world-wide commercial activities he had begun in the new republic and which his sons were helping him to carry on. One by one he took his sons into partnership and sent them out to establish branches. William, the eldest, went to Liverpool in 1809 and started the firm later known as Brown, Shipley & Company. John A. Brown [*q.v.*] went to Philadelphia and organized what later became the firm of Brown Brothers & Company, while James [1791–1877, *q.v.*] entered the field in New York, establishing Brown Brothers & Company there. The modest linen import business Alexander Brown had begun in 1800 grew into an export business as well. First he had undertaken the exporting of cotton to Great Britain, then tobacco. From this as a natural and indispensable adjunct, an international banking business developed. Family and business connections and acquaintanceships in England put the Baltimore firm in an exceptionally advantageous position to handle matters of this sort—a better position, in fact, than almost any other firm of American merchants then occupied. The change in Alexander Brown's business from that of mercantile house to that of a merchant banking house, was inevitable and rapid. Continuing to expand, he became a ship-owner, for his extensive importations and exportations made it profitable for him to buy and build ships.

It was through his foresight, intuition, and courage in the handling of these ships and their cargoes at a time in the world's history when ocean travel was slow and hazardous, not only

from wind and weather but from privateers and war-vessels, that Alexander Brown achieved his greatest business triumphs and most of his international reputation as a trader and banker. His alertness and carefulness kept his firm and its branches on an even keel during the War of 1812, and in the years following the war. Many of the oldest and strongest banking and mercantile houses in the country failed during those years. Brown suffered losses but not great ones, and about 1824 his firm began a period of swift growth. From then until the founder died its record of prosperity in America and England was virtually unbroken. The scope of its trading extended far beyond the early fields of linen, tobacco and cotton, and included everything merchantable from champagne to indigo. Yet Alexander Brown was cautious about scattering his strength and frequently had to curb the ambitions of his sons to go into other lines of business such as insurance. His reputation, and that of his firm everywhere, for soundness and integrity seems to have been based on a principle he often repeated in his correspondence with his son William, "It is essential for us in all our dealings not only to be fair but never to have the appearance of unfairness."

Brown was identified with every progressive development and civic movement in Baltimore in its early days, helping to incorporate the Maryland Institute of Art, to establish a municipal water-works, to erect the nation's first monument to George Washington, and so on. He and his son, George Brown [1787–1859, *q.v.*], were among the founders of the Baltimore & Ohio Railroad, were, in fact, more responsible than any others for the idea of building the road. When in the last year of his life the Bank of Maryland failed suddenly, and disaster threatened the entire community, a group of merchants and bankers called upon Brown for his advice. He assured them calmly but emphatically, "No firm inherently solvent will be allowed to fail," thus pledging himself to save the business men of Baltimore.

His death on Apr. 3, 1834, at the age of seventy was called by newspapers, in Liverpool and London as well as in this country, the passing of one of the foremost mercantile figures in America. His wealth was estimated at about $2,000,-000,—a great sum in those days. The firm he established, Alexander Brown & Sons, now the oldest banking house in the United States, still exists in Baltimore as one of the most highly respected institutions of its kind in the country. The branches established by the sons, severed now from the parent bank, are to-day directed by their descendants and known throughout the world.

[Old letter books and ledgers dating back to 1800 and now in the vaults of the firm of Alexander Brown & Sons, in Baltimore, form the chief sources of information; many of these were written by Alexander Brown himself. Much of the story is told in the privately printed volume, *A Hundred Years of Merchant Banking* (1909), issued by the late John Crosby Brown of N. Y.; *Experiences of a Century* (1919), issued by Brown Bros. & Co. of Phila., and *The Story of Alexander Brown & Sons* (1925), by F. R. Kent. See also Mary E. Brown, *Alexander Brown and His Descendants* (privately printed, 1917) and a sketch of Sir Wm. Brown in *Dict. Nat. Biog.*, III, 37.]   F.R.K.

BROWN, ALEXANDER (Sept. 5, 1843–Aug. 25, 1906), historian, was born at Glenmore, Nelson County, Va. He was the son of Robert Lawrence Brown and Sarah Cabell (Callaway) Brown. He studied under Horace W. Jones, noted as a molder of the minds and characters of boys, and in his library acquired his taste for history. In 1860 he matriculated at Lynchburg College. The outbreak of the Civil War interrupted his education, and at the age of seventeen he enlisted in the Confederate army. In December 1864 the explosion of a powder-boat, near Fort Fisher, N. C., rendered him almost totally deaf. For several years after the war he was a salesman in Washington, D. C., but his deafness unfitted him for business, and he returned to Nelson County, where he engaged in farming. He led a retired life, devoting every spare moment to historical research. His interest centered in the first two decades of Virginia history, and he spared no effort in searching out original evidence on that period. Year after year he labored patiently, writing to librarians and historians, securing experts to search the archives and copy manuscripts, and practising rigid economy to meet the costs. He married Caroline Augusta Cabell on Dec. 27, 1873. His wife died in 1876, and on Apr. 28, 1886, he married Sarah Randolph Cabell.

His first work, *New Views of Early Virginia History,* appeared in 1886. There followed, in 1890, *The Genesis of the United States,* a collection of documents, many never before published, relating to the founding of the British Empire in America. *The Cabells and Their Kin* appeared in 1895, *The First Republic in America* and *The History of Our Earliest History* in 1898, and *English Politics in Early Virginia History* in 1901.

Brown contended that the history of early Virginia had been falsified by the Court party in England, to discredit the liberal group in the London Company. This was done by suppressing the Company's records, and licensing Captain John Smith's "incorrect, unjust, and ungen-

erous" works. Brown devoted himself to correcting this age-old injustice and to vindicating the true heroes of the founding of Virginia--Sir Edwin Sandys and those who labored with him to set up liberal institutions. He forced historians to reconstruct their views on the early history of Virginia. Although some of his conclusions have not been fully accepted, his place as the leading authority in his field is established.

[*Encyc. Va. Biog.*, ed. by L. G. Tyler, III (1915), 256–57; *Who's Who in America,* 1906–07. Many facts relating to Brown's life and work appear in the prefaces of *The Genesis of the United States* and *The First Republic in America.*]   T.J.W.

BROWN, ALEXANDER EPHRAIM (May 14, 1852–Apr. 26, 1911), inventor and manufacturer, was the son of Fayette Brown [*q.v.*] and his wife Cornelia Curtis. The father had a noteworthy part in Cleveland's industrial development as a banker, iron manufacturer, and owner of a fleet of ore boats. Alexander E. Brown was one of five children. He received his early education in the Cleveland public schools, completing the course at the old Central High School. In the autumn of 1869 he entered the Brooklyn Polytechnic Institute, Brooklyn, N. Y., graduating in an engineering course in June 1872. Immediately after graduation he joined the United States Geological Survey, and for six months was engaged in the exploration of the Yellowstone region. During the ensuing two years he was employed as chief engineer for the Massillon Iron Bridge Company of Massillon, Ohio, and from 1875 to 1878 was employed as an engineer in construction work and in superintending iron mines in the Lake Superior iron region. During part of 1878 and 1879 he was in Cleveland, connected as a mechanical engineer with the Brush Electric Company, then known as the Telegraph Supply Company, a corporation developing the inventions of the founder, Charles F. Brush.

During the year 1879 Alexander Brown made his most important invention, that of the Brown hoisting and conveying machine for handling coal and iron ore at the lake ports. In the following year patents were obtained, and the first Brown hoisting and conveying machine was set up on the ore docks in Cleveland. The Brown Hoisting Machinery Company was organized to manufacture such machinery, with Brown's father as president and himself as vice-president and general manager. In 1910, upon the death of his father he became president, a position which he held until his own death. As a result of Brown's achievement, the construction of lake boats for transportation of bulky materials was revolutionized. Before his time the largest lake boats did not exceed 1,200 tons capacity. He made the operation of such small craft unprofitable; lake boats of 8,000, 10,000, and even 12,000 tons came into use. It became possible to unload a 12,000-ton ore vessel in as many hours as it formerly took days to unload a 500-ton boat.

Brown was identified with many professional and social organizations. He was an engineer and inventor of great ability and versatility. Nearly fourscore patents in various fields are on record in Washington. On Nov. 14, 1877, he was married to Carrie M. Barnett, the daughter of Gen. James Barnett. Their son, Alexander C. Brown, succeeded his father as president of the Brown Hoisting Machinery Company.

[Elroy M. Avery, *Hist. of Cleveland* (1918), III, 533–34; *Who's Who in America,* 1910–11; the Reports of the Cleveland Board of Trade; an article by Alexander C. Brown in *Trade Winds,* a Cleveland publication, Apr. 1925; obituaries in the *Cleveland Plain Dealer* and *Cleveland Leader,* Apr. 27, 1911.]   E. J. B.

BROWN, ANTOINETTE. [See BLACKWELL, ANTOINETTE LOUISA BROWN, 1825–1921.]

BROWN, BEDFORD (1792–Dec. 6, 1870), senator, was the son of Jethro B. and Lucy (Williamson) Brown of Caswell County, N. C. Both parents were of good English stock, the Williamsons being socially prominent. As the representative of the large and politically-minded planters who dominated Caswell, young Brown, after two years at the state university, was sent to the lower house for four years (1815–18, 1823) and then to the Senate (1828–29). Having fought successfully for Jackson electors in 1824 and 1828, in 1829 he was chosen speaker by the Senate; and when President Jackson transferred United States Senator Branch to his cabinet, Brown essayed to back Thomas Ruffin for the unexpired term. "In the scrambling," however, Brown was elected—by mistake, apparently, in the casting of one vote. In the federal Senate his importance consisted chiefly in his support, whole-hearted and vigorous, of the Jackson and Van Buren administrations, particularly as to nullification and fiscal policy. Though never of the Jacksonian inner circle, he was trusted by its members; and it was as an administration candidate that he participated in the legislative elections of 1834 and secured a full term. His retirement from the Senate was melodramatic. A Whig legislature having sent him resolutions condemning Jacksonian policies and referring to "party servility," he announced in the Senate that he "desired his public course should be tested by the popular will of his State," and so would resign after the coming legislative elections (Jan. 14, 1839; *Congressional Globe,* 25 Cong., 3 Sess., p. 117). The legislature, how-

ever, being won by the Whigs, accepted his resignation (1840); and when two years later he sought reëlection from a Democratic legislature, the Calhoun wing of his party blocked him despite his own presence in the Senate and the efforts of his powerful friends outside the state. Disgusted, he moved to Missouri about 1844, but by 1852 had returned and begun anew the game of national politics. State rights within the Union was now his leading principle. In the Democratic national convention of 1856 he favored Buchanan and in that of 1860, Dickenson, on a platform guaranteeing the rights of the Southern States through constitutional amendment (Brown, *Remarks . . . in the Senate of North Carolina, on Dec. 19, 1860*). Back again in the state Senate (1858–63), he led the fight against secession in 1860. His speech of Dec. 19, which was reprinted and circulated, berated alike abolitionists and advocates of a "Southern 'higher law,'" and urged a policy of terms within the Union. Failing in this, in the secession convention and at first in the Senate he advocated a "most vigorous prosecution of the war"; but by the summer of 1863 this mood had passed. The war over, his old Unionist attitude caused Governors Vance and Worth to enlist him—unsuccessfully—as a mediator in Washington. He served in the constitutional convention of 1865. He was elected to Congress in 1865 and to the constitutional convention of 1867, but was denied a seat in each. Though he supported Holden for governor, his county was ravaged by the Reconstructionists and he himself when he sought amelioration from President Grant met curt rebuff.

Brown owned a large plantation in Caswell and lived there, on the aristocratic "Locust Hill." Tall, spare, smooth-shaven, firm of carriage, he cultivated the arts of dress and deportment. His intellectual equipment was mediocre. A deep, husky voice and a slow, labored style made him an unusually poor speaker; but a protruding lower jaw and a habit of clinching his teeth gave him an appearance of resoluteness and, when he was angry, of dangerous fierceness. Some laughed at his pompousness, but none questioned his individual courage. President Jackson was his personal friend and, perhaps, his model. The great Jackson leaders, though they flattered him, really liked him; and he treasured their letters. He was married to Mary L. Glenn, and their son, Bedford Brown (1825–1897), became a noted physician (see Kelly and Burrage, *American Medical Biographies,* 1920, p. 148).

[There is no biography of Bedford Brown. See David Schenck, *Personal Sketches* (1885); *Biog. Hist. of N.*

C., vol. I (1905), ed. by S. A. Ashe; J. G. de Roulhac Hamilton, *Party Politics in N. C. 1835–1860* (1916); *The Correspondence of Jonathan Worth* (1909), and *The Papers of Thos. Ruffin* (1918–20), ed. by J. G. de R. Hamilton; *The Papers of Archibald D. Murphy* (1914), ed. by Wm. H. Hoyt. Brown's correspondence was published in the *Trinity Coll. Hist. Soc. Papers* (1906–07).]   C. C. P.

BROWN, BENJAMIN GRATZ (May 28, 1826–Dec. 13, 1885), senator, governor of Missouri, was born at Lexington, Ky., the son of Mason and Judith (Bledsoe) Brown. His father, Mason Brown, was a jurist of some note who served as judge of a Kentucky circuit court and, from 1856 to 1859, as secretary of state. His grandfather, John Brown, was the first United States senator from Kentucky. The Browns were related to the Prestons, Breckenridges, Blairs, Bentons, and other well-known Kentucky families.

Brown entered Transylvania University but withdrew in 1845 and entered Yale University, where he was graduated in 1847. He then studied law in Louisville, was admitted to the Kentucky bar, and, in 1849, moved to St. Louis. The same year he took the stump in support of Thomas H. Benton's attack upon the "Jackson Resolutions" adopted by the Missouri legislature that year. He again came actively to the support of Benton in the Atchison-Benton senatorial contest of 1852–53. Appreciating the importance of the large German vote in St. Louis, he early cultivated its support; and, largely as a result, he was elected, and reëlected, to the lower branch of the state legislature between 1852 and 1859. For upward of two decades the St. Louis Germans constituted the principal element in his political following. In the Missouri legislature of 1857, Brown took an especially prominent part. A joint resolution was introduced declaring emancipation of the slaves to be impracticable, and that any movement in that direction was "inexpedient, impolitic, unwise, and unjust." In reply to this, Brown, at some personal risk, it is said, made an able and forceful anti-slavery speech in which he advocated and prophesied the abolition of slavery in Missouri on economic grounds—more out of regard to the interest of poor white laborers than as an act of humanity to the slaves. This incident has been regarded by some as the beginning of the Free-Soil movement in Missouri (*Speech of Hon. B. Gratz Brown of St. Louis on the Subject of Gradual Emancipation in Missouri, Feb. 12, 1857*, Pamphlet, 1857). Brown's speech apparently made him the Free-Soil Democratic candidate for governor the same year. He failed of election by the narrow margin of about 500 votes.

Between 1854 and 1859, most of Brown's energies were absorbed in newspaper editorial work for the *Missouri Democrat*—a paper of strong Free-Soil, and, later, Republican, principles. In its columns, Brown persistently assailed the institution of slavery in Missouri and advocated emancipation. In 1856 he fought a duel with Thomas C. Reynolds over differences growing out of editorials relating to the Know-Nothing movement in St. Louis. Brown was shot near the knee, and limped during the rest of his life.

In the formation of the Republican party in Missouri in 1860 Brown took an active part and was a delegate-at-large to the Chicago convention which nominated Lincoln. At the opening of the Civil War, he became colonel of the 4th Regiment of Missouri (three months) Volunteers, and energetically coöperated with Gen. Lyon and Frank P. Blair, Jr., in circumventing the Missouri secessionists.

In the state election of 1862 the abolition of slavery was the outstanding issue, especially in the eastern part of the state. Brown led the radicals, who insisted upon immediate emancipation, in opposition to the gradual emancipationists led by his cousin, Frank P. Blair, Jr. Although the policy of the latter was indorsed two years later by the state convention which adopted an ordinance for the gradual extinction of slavery, Brown's faction won a majority of the seats in both branches of the next legislature, and nominated him for the United States Senate. After a prolonged contest, Brown was elected on the thirty-second ballot (1863) for the unexpired term of W. P. Johnson, who had been expelled as a secessionist. He took the oath of office Dec. 14, 1863, and served until Mar. 4, 1867. In 1864, he was one of the signers of the call for the Cleveland convention of radicals who opposed the renomination of Lincoln and nominated Frémont and Cochrane.

While in the Senate, Brown served upon the committees on military affairs, Indian affairs, Pacific railroad, printing, public buildings and grounds, and also as chairman of the committee on contingent expenses. Although frequently taking part in Senate debates, he made only one extended speech. This was in support of an amendment to a bill to promote enlistments in the army, confirming and making of full effect as law the President's emancipation proclamation, and adding a section declaring the immediate abolition of slavery in all states and territories of the United States, as a war measure (Mar. 8, 1864. *Congressional Globe*, 38 Cong., 1 Sess., pt. II, pp. 984–90). His next longest speech was in opposition to the proposed reading and writing tests for voting in the District of Columbia and in advocacy of woman suffrage for the District. "I stand," he declared, "for universal suffrage, and as a matter of fundamental principle do not recognize the right of society to limit it on any ground of race, color, or sex . . . I recognize the right of franchise as being intrinsically a natural right . . ." (Dec. 12, 1866. *Congressional Globe,* 39 Cong., 2 Sess., pt. I, p. 76). He also spoke, or introduced resolutions, in favor of the eight-hour day for government employees, approving retaliation for rebel mistreatment of Northern prisoners of war, advocating government construction, ownership, and operation of telegraph lines, and urging the establishment of the merit system in the civil service. His speeches are noteworthy for their obvious sincerity and absence of buncombe, their dignified simplicity of diction, and unusual directness and incisiveness.

Before the end of his senatorial career, Brown became prominently identified with the so-called Liberal movement in Missouri for the repeal of the drastic test-oaths prescribed in the Missouri constitution of 1865 and aimed at sympathizers with the Confederate cause. Later, this Liberal movement, which came to embody a reaction against the radical Republican reconstruction policy and in favor of amnesty for former rebels and reconciliation between the sections, culminated in the nomination of Brown for governor, in 1870, and his triumphant election by a majority of more than 40,000. At the same election, constitutional amendments were approved repealing the obnoxious test-oaths.

In his messages as governor (1871–73), Brown recommended constitutional amendments reorganizing the courts, including the grand jury system, and the better regulation of railroads through the creation of a board of railroad commissioners. The bankruptcy of a number of railroads whose bonds had been guaranteed by the state embarrassed his administration, and resulted in a loss to the state of approximately $25,000,000.

The success of the Liberal movement in Missouri encouraged liberals and reformers in other states and led directly to the launching of the Liberal Republican party in 1872 in opposition to the renomination of President Grant and in favor of tariff and civil service reform and abandonment of radical Republican reconstruction policies. Brown's prominence naturally led to serious consideration of his availability as the presidential candidate of this independent movement; and at the Cincinnati convention of the Liberal Republicans, in May 1872, he stood

fourth on the first ballot for the presidential nomination, receiving ninety-five votes. Suspecting that his delegates were being enticed away by the friends of Charles Francis Adams, Brown unexpectedly appeared in Cincinnati, obtained permission to address the convention, and in his speech astonished the delegates by warmly urging the nomination of Horace Greeley. On the sixth ballot Greeley was nominated, and, later, Brown himself received the vice-presidential nomination. Afterward, Carl Schurz and others charged that the ticket was the result of a deliberate bargain between the friends of Greeley and Brown (F. Bancroft, *Speeches, Correspondence, and Political Papers of Carl Schurz,* 1907–08, II, 362–63). Brown's nomination, however, seems to have been of little or no help to the Liberal Republican campaign, although he participated actively in the canvass. In August he attended a class banquet at Yale, became intoxicated, and made a speech in bad taste, criticizing things eastern (E. D. Ross, *The Liberal Republican Movement,* 1919, p. 156). Following this campaign, Brown gave up active participation in politics and devoted himself to the practise of law, making a specialty of railway cases. By 1876 he had virtually gone over to the Democratic party. He attended that party's national convention, where "loud calls for Gratz Brown brought that gentleman to the rostrum, accompanied by a round of applause" (*Official Report of the Proceedings,* p. 91). In his brief response, he expressed sympathy with Democratic demands for reform and the belief that former Liberals would warmly support those demands. Brown's death in 1885 was the direct result of overwork, following close upon a serious illness, in completing a report as referee in an important railroad case pending in the federal court at St. Louis. In person, Brown is described as of medium height, of very slender figure, and "immediately noticeable for his wealth of red hair and beard."

[A disparaging sketch by a political opponent in 1872, pointing out Brown's weaknesses, appears in E. Chamberlin, *The Struggle of '72* (1872), pp. 540–47. A more favorable, and generally more satisfactory sketch is printed in W. B. Davis and D. S. Durrie, *An Illus. Hist. of Mo.* (1876), pp. 482–83. Other Missouri histories contain scattered references to Brown's opposition to secession, advocacy of emancipation in Missouri, and administration as governor, especially, W. F. Switzler, *Illus. Hist. of Mo.* (1879); and *The Province and States* (1904), ed. by W. A. Goodspeed, vol. IV. The Brown-Reynolds duel is described in some detail in W. B. Stevens, *St. Louis—the Fourth City, 1764–1911* (1911), I, 377–85; *Mo. Hist. Rev.,* XIX, 423–26. Brown's senatorial speeches appear in the *Cong. Globe* for the 38th and 39th Congresses. For his political campaign speeches one must consult contemporary newspaper files. Interesting light on Brown's appearance at the Cincinnati convention is shed by H. Watterson, "The Humor and Tragedy of the Greeley

Campaign," *Century*, LXXXV, 27–45. His connection with the earlier stages of the Liberal Movement may best be traced in T. S. Barclay, "The Liberal Republican Movement in Mo.," *Mo. Hist. Rev.*, vol. XX.]

P. O. R.

BROWN, CHARLES BROCKDEN (Jan. 17, 1771–Feb. 22, 1810), novelist, journalist, the first person in the United States to make authorship his principal profession, was descended from James Brown, a Quaker who came to America before William Penn. Charles Brockden Brown was the son of Elijah Brown, a merchant of Philadelphia, and his wife, Mary Armitt. Born into a family in good standing and in fair circumstances, he had at the outset such advantages as the time and place could offer him, except the advantage of robust health. Whether because his being frail made him studious or his being studious made him frail, at least he was both frail and studious. At home and in the school of Robert Proud [*q.v.*] which Brown attended between the ages of eleven and sixteen, the boy gave himself up to violent reading in miscellaneous directions, and thereby got, in an ambitious, uncritical society, an early reputation for scholarship which then or later was never quite justified by the facts. Nor was he eager merely to read. While still at school he produced versions of parts of the Bible and of Ossian, and planned three epics on the grandiose themes of Columbus, Pizarro, and Cortez—thus showing himself to be a contemporary of Joel Barlow [*q.v.*] and a forerunner of Irving and Prescott. Brown's earliest published work was a series of papers called "The Rhapsodist," contributed to the *Columbian Magazine* (Philadelphia, August–November, 1789), and devoted to glorifying the romantic revolutionary soul.

Romance and revolution, however, did not constitute a career in the Philadelphia of the early republic. Brown was accordingly in 1787 apprenticed to Alexander Wilcocks, a Philadelphia lawyer. The law, in the words of Brown's first biographer, "to a mind so ardent in the pursuit of information, opened a wide and inexhaustible field for indulgence. It is withal, in this country, one of the roads to opulence, and the most certain path to political importance and fame" (William Dunlap, *The Life of Charles Brockden Brown*, 1815, I, 15). What was perhaps more attractive, the law was generally thought of as a calling so close to literature that both might naturally be followed by the same man. Brown, along with his legal studies, still found time to speculate and debate, particularly at the meetings of the Belles Lettres Club which he and eight of his friends established for the improvement of their minds during the hours

not claimed by the law. Had he been, as his family hoped and expected, only an amateur in literature, Brown might have ridden his two horses at once. But he had in him too many of the instincts of a professional writer, and in 1793 gave up the law altogether, against the advice of his parents and his elder brothers who presumably saw themselves obliged to support him in his adventure.

Authorship had hitherto occupied the major attention of few Americans and had provided a livelihood for none. Brown, taking so precarious a step, must have seemed to sentence himself to be either a dilettante or a vagabond. He did not become a vagabond. Instead, he only drifted back and forth between Philadelphia and New York, possibly for a time a teacher in his native town, but primarily reading and forming designs for masterpieces. What drew him to New York was less the chances which that town gave him for a literary career than the presence there of Elihu Hubbard Smith [*q.v.*] whom Brown had encountered as a medical student in Philadelphia and who in New York was somehow contriving to write verse and prose as well as heal the sick. At Smith's house in Pine Street Brown met, along with others, Samuel Latham Mitchill [*q.v.*], James Kent [*q.v.*] and William Dunlap [*q.v.*], men of promise who belonged to the Friendly Society, a club which for Brown filled the place of the Belles Lettres Club in Philadelphia. His first visit to New York he apparently made in 1793, another certainly in 1795. From 1798 to 1801 he lived there almost continuously. Without much question the Friendly Society furnished the most stimulating companionship of Brown's life. New York did for him what Philadelphia could not do.

Politically inclined to the party of Jefferson, Brown had by 1795 already come to accept most of the radical doctrines current in the United States, but he owed his special impetus to William Godwin, in whose *Caleb Williams* (1794) he saw "transcendant merits." Before undertaking a novel, however, the young philosopher wrote a treatise in dialogue on the rights of women. A part of the work was published in New York early in 1798, with the title *Alcuin: A Dialogue,* and with a note by Elihu Hubbard Smith; the remainder first appeared in the Dunlap *Life* five years after Brown had died. Because the original *Alcuin* is extremely rare, and has never been reprinted, most comments upon the treatise have gone on the assumption that the portion available in the *Life* is the same as that in the separate book. This accident of bibliography has had few serious results, for *Alcuin* had no appreciable influence at the time and is not now important, though the curious will find in it various enlightened, if unexciting and undramatic, arguments for the equality of the sexes and the freedom of divorce (David Lee Clark, *Brockden Brown and the Rights of Women,* University of Texas Bulletin, No. 2212, Mar. 22, 1922).

The admirer of *Caleb Williams,* not content with argument, next proceeded to fiction. Toward the end of 1797 Brown wrote a romance presumably to be identified as the "Sky-Walk" which he announced in a letter to the *Weekly Magazine* (Philadelphia) of Mar. 17, 1798, but of which the manuscript was lost before it could be published. Whatever his practise may have been, Brown's theory of fiction was impressive. "The value of such works," he told the readers of the *Weekly Magazine,* "lies without doubt in their moral tendency. . . . The world is governed, not by the simpleton, but by the men of soaring passions and intellectual energy. By the display of such only can we hope to enchain the attention and ravish the souls of those who study and reflect." At the same time, Brown did not mean to write for geniuses alone. He held that the same novel which could stir thinkers by its ideas might capture ordinary people with its plot—or, in his own less simple words, that "a contexture of facts capable of suspending the faculties of every soul in curiosity, may be joined with depth of views into human nature and all the subtleties of reasoning."

With the principles of his art thus thought out and with his model chosen, Brown now plunged into the two fecund, nervous years which saw the composition of all his noteworthy books. *Arthur Mervyn,* begun in Philadelphia before the summer of 1798, was completed in New York, and was published in two parts in 1799 and 1800. *Wieland* appeared in 1798, and *Ormond* and *Edgar Huntly* in 1799; only the less interesting *Clara Howard* and *Jane Talbot* have so late a date as 1801. Writing at such speed, Brown had little opportunity to grow in experience or to vary his materials. His novels all bear the marks of haste, immaturity, and Godwin.

Brown's indebtedness to Godwin is to be found chiefly in a fondness for the central situation of *Caleb Williams:* an innocent and more or less helpless youth in the grasp of a patron turned enemy. *Arthur Mervyn,* to take the clearest example, brings a young man from the country to Philadelphia, makes him blunder into the secret of a murder, and subjects him to crafty persecutions from the murderer. In *Ormond* by a variation of the formula the victim is a wo-

man, Constantia Dudley, pursued by the philosophical villain Ormond until she is obliged to kill him in self-defense. Constantia was a favorite heroine of Shelley, to whom she seemed a perfect type of virtue harassed by evil men. But Brown's victims do not suffer the gradual, increasing agony of Godwin's, for the reason that Brown could not construct a plot as Godwin could. The disciple had neither the steady art nor the weighty conviction of the master. Furthermore, American life, loose-knit and easygoing, afforded in Brown's decade an inadequate setting for a story of social persecution.

The method which Brown derived from Godwin is less notable than the material which he took, at first hand, from native conditions. In 1793 he had fled with his family to the country to escape the epidemic of yellow fever which then visited Philadelphia; five years later, just after his arrival in New York, he had gone through a similar invasion of the plague which caused the death of his friend Smith. His letters show how deeply he was moved by the only personal contact he ever had with such affairs of danger and terror as he ordinarily wrote about. Composing *Ormond* almost before the later epidemic had passed, Brown transferred his impressions from the New York of 1798 to the Philadelphia of 1793, as he did in *Arthur Mervyn,* perhaps for some gain in perspective; but in both he wrote with his eye on the fact as nowhere else in his books. With unsparing, not to say sickening, veracity, he represented the physical horrors of the plague, and he was even more veracious in his account of the mental and spiritual horrors which accompanied it. Less successful than his handling of the plague was his handling of the frontier in *Edgar Huntly.* American novelists, he said in his preface, ought no longer to make use of "puerile superstition and exploded manners, Gothic castles and chimeras. . . . The incidents of Indian hostility, and the perils of the Western wilderness, are far more suitable." So far as his knowledge and his prepossessions went, Brown succeeded in this experiment. But he knew little of the frontier and little of the Indians. He merely used a new setting for actions not strikingly unlike those in his Godwinian plots. Huntly is not a frontiersman; he is a sleep-walker, whose adventures might almost be his dreams. Of the Indians, the visible ones are none of them so memorable as the old woman called Queen Mab, who, never appearing in person, stands as a symbol of the vanquished race. Always what interested Brown was the tormented states of mind which he studied in his characters.

This clearly appears in his most compact, most reflective, and most powerful novel, *Wieland*. Its plot was founded upon the deeds of an actual religious fanatic of Tomhannock, New York, who in a mad vision had heard himself commanded to destroy all his idols, and had murdered his wife and children with ferocious brutality (Carl Van Doren, "Early American Realism," *Nation*, Nov. 12, 1914). With this theme Brown involved the story of a trouble-breeding ventriloquist, in order to make the mysterious voices credible. As ventriloquism itself was mysterious in 1798, the solution of the plot probably did not then seem so trivial as it now seems. And Brown did not rely too much upon his trivial solution. He saw, perhaps better than he understood, that the essential mystery in Carwin was not his ventriloquism, but the driving spirit of malice which forced him to meddle in other people's lives without really intending to do harm. Moreover, the murderer, though stung into activity by the voices which he hears, would of course not have acted but for the depths of frenzy already sleeping in his nature. For Brown, who after all was only twenty-seven when he wrote *Wieland*, such cases of speculative pathology were more real, or at least more arousing, than any of the customary aspects of behavior which he might have chosen to represent.

Maturity did not turn the novelist to another reality in fiction, for after this short burst Brown wrote no more novels. (For a detailed account of his other imaginative writings produced in the same period see Carl Van Doren, "Minor Tales of Brockden Brown 1798–1800," *Nation*, Jan. 14, 1915.) Possibly he had exhausted his creative vein. At any rate, he had modified his schemes for freedom. His novels earned him little money. *The Monthly Magazine and American Review* (New York), founded by the Friendly Society and edited chiefly by Brown from its hopeful beginnings in April 1799, came to a gloomy end in December 1800. The next year he went back to Philadelphia, as if to signalize the return of a prodigal, and became a partner with two of his brothers in a mercantile house. At first it prospered, but losses at sea, due both to storms and to the French and British navies, brought this firm near bankruptcy in 1804 and forced it to dissolve in 1806. From 1807 till his death Brown traded independently on a small scale. Though a busy journalist, he could not by his pen alone support the wife, Elizabeth Linn of New York, whom he had married in November 1804, and the four children born to them.

His writings during this latter period were almost wholly hack work. He edited and wrote for the *Literary Magazine and American Register* (1803–07), which a Philadelphia publisher had asked him to undertake, and the *American Register or General Repository of History, Politics, and Science* (1807–11). In addition he translated Volney's *Tableau* under the title *A View of the Soil and Climate of the United States* (1804), wrote three pamphlets on political matters, and planned *A System of General Geography* which never got beyond the prospectus (1809?). Writing, for Brown, was more than a career; it was an itch. "This employment," he told a friend, "was just as necessary to my mind as sustenance to my frame. It was synonymous with a vital function. . . . Had I been exiled to Kamschatka, I must have written as a mental necessity, and in it I have still found my highest enjoyment" (John Bernard, *Retrospections of America 1797–1811*, 1887, p. 254). The sole evidence that his imagination still worked in him is the story that he wrote two acts of a tragedy for John Bernard, and, told that the play would not act, burned the manuscript and kept the ashes in a snuff-box (*Ibid.*, pp. 254–55). Romance had been only a chapter in Brown's life, and it belonged primarily to New York. The later Philadelphia chapter was plain prose.

Brown's place in literary history is not altogether due to the fact that he was the first American who tried to live by his pen or even that he was the first American novelist who won an international hearing. He continues to be occasionally read for his intrinsic merits—for the somber intensity which, given a chance with any but superficial readers, outweighs his shambling structure and his verbose, stilted language. Like Poe and Hawthorne, whom he in several respects anticipates, Brown had a personal acquaintance with the dark moods which he enlarged and projected in his novels. He had an eager intellectual curiosity which gives his work, even at its most naïve, a certain air of range and significance. It is now useless to debate whether, in more favorable circumstances, he might have done more and better work. Writers must be judged by the books they write, not by the books they might have written. Nevertheless, it is difficult not to feel that a community both more critical and more responsive than the United States was at the end of the eighteenth century might have enabled Brown to husband and direct his powers to greater advantage. As it was, he first squandered his strength and then failed to regain it. Authorship was a profession which, as matters stood, he had to pay an extravagant price to enter.

[The original source of information concerning Brown is *The Life of Chas. Brockden Brown* (2 vols., 1815), which was begun by Paul Allen and completed by Brown's friend, Wm. Dunlap, whose name alone appears on the title-page. An abridged version of the work was issued in London in one volume as *Memoirs of Chas. Brockden Brown* (1822). Dunlap was extremely inaccurate, but he has been followed by most later writers on the subject. A critical biography, however, has been prepared by David Lee Clark and is now awaiting publication. A printed abstract of this work, made in 1923, may be consulted in the Lib. of Columbia Univ. See also *The Cambridge Hist. of Am. Lit.* (vol. I, 1917, pp. 287–92 and pp. 527–29) for the most precise recent account of Brown's life and an extended bibliography of the writings by and about him.]

C.V–D.

BROWN, CHARLES RUFUS (Feb. 22, 1849–Feb. 1, 1914), Baptist clergyman, educator, was the son of Rev. Samuel Emmons and Elvira (Small) Brown. Born in East Kingston, N. H., in a Baptist manse, he was reared conscientiously in an evangelical home. In his teens he was a student at Phillips Exeter Academy. Attracted to the sea, near which he lived for a time, he was admitted to the Naval Academy at Annapolis. His training gave him qualities of precision and discipline that served him well as an instructor in later years, but in 1874 he abandoned a naval career for a professional life in the ministry. In order to prepare himself for this he attended Newton Theological Institution (1874–75) and Harvard College, graduating from the latter in 1877, and he then pursued theological studies at Newton and Union seminaries, and at Berlin and Leipzig universities in Europe. In 1881 he entered upon the active ministry as pastor of the Baptist church at Franklin Falls, N. H.

His training had fitted him for service as an educator, and after two years he was elected associate professor of Biblical interpretation of the Old Testament at Newton Theological Institution. Three years later he became full professor. For thirty years he directed his department and inspired his pupils with a sense of the values of the Old Testament. The study of Hebrew was never a drudgery in his classes. He was painstaking and accurate himself, and demanded a mastery of the lesson from others, but he had such an appreciation of shades of thought and fineness of expression and worked with such enthusiasm as to kindle interest even in a dull subject. In addition to his work at Newton, he lectured at the University of Chicago in a summer quarter, and was acting professor in Boston University for a term of seven months. He edited the Bible Union Sunday-school Lessons at various times. In 1910–11 he served as director of the American School of Oriental Research at Jerusalem. He never lost his interest in preaching, and during part of one year he was acting pastor of the Main Street Baptist Church in Worcester.

As a scholar he was happiest in his exegetical studies of the Old Testament, and the fruit of his learning appeared in his *Commentary on Jeremiah*, published in 1907, but he was familiar with the languages cognate to Hebrew and prepared *An Aramaic Method*, which was published in 1884. As a man he was outspoken in his assertion of his opinions, honest and courageous by nature, and demanding no more from another than he would give himself. He was conscientiously industrious, setting high standards of workmanship and careful of the smallest details. In 1884 he had married Clarissa L. Dodge. He died at Stoneham, Mass., after months of failing health.

[*Watchman-Examiner*, Feb. 5, 1914; *Who's Who in America*, 1912–13; *Harvard College Class of 1877, 7th Report* (1917); *Boston Transcript*, Feb. 2, 1914.]

H.K.R.

BROWN, CHARLOTTE EMERSON (Apr. 21, 1838–Feb. 5, 1895), club-woman, organizer, was born at Andover, Mass. Her father, Ralph Emerson, clergyman and professor of ecclesiastical history and pastoral theology in Andover Theological Seminary, came of a long ancestry of New England clergymen and educators and was a relative of Ralph Waldo Emerson. Her mother was Eliza Rockwell of Colebrook, Conn. Charlotte was graduated from Abbot Academy at Andover. She early showed an aptitude for languages and could read, write, and speak French before she was twelve. After her school days she mastered several other languages by private study and learned Greek from her brother Joseph Emerson, professor at Beloit College. She spent a year in Montreal, teaching Latin, French, and mathematics, with Hannah Lyman, later first woman principal of Vassar College. Her education was continued by several years of travel and study of music and languages abroad. The Emerson family, having left Andover and having lived for five years in Newburyport, Mass., removed to Rockford, Ill. Charlotte Emerson, eager for further knowledge, took a commercial course of six weeks in Chicago and then became private secretary to her brother Ralph, a Rockford manufacturer. At Rockford she began her work as a club organizer, founding a musical club, the Euterpe, and a French club, as well as the Rockford Conservatory of Music. She also taught modern languages in Rockford Seminary. She married, July 27, 1880, the Rev. William B. Brown, pastor of the First Congregational Church of Newark, N. J. They went abroad for three years, where Mrs. Brown continued the studies which were her absorbing interest in life. On their return they settled in

East Orange, N. J., where she was very soon elected president of the Woman's Club. At about this time the club Sorosis took the lead in a movement for club federation, and Mrs. Brown was one of the committee of seven which formed the General Federation of Women's Clubs and in 1890 she became its first president. Under her leadership the federation membership increased in two years from fifty to 120 clubs, representing twenty-nine states and numbering 20,000 women. The organization of the Fortnightly Club of East Orange was also her work. After her marriage she became much interested in the foreign missions of the Congregational Church and traveled, spoke, wrote, and planned work for the Woman's Board of Missions. She wrote much on different club activities for newspapers and magazines and at the time of her death had gathered material for a projected history of the woman's club movement. She was a person of unusual memory, unlimited enthusiasm, great energy and power of concentration—both as a student and as a business woman. Her efficiency never made her dictatorial, but her tact, consideration for the opinions of others, and coöperativeness caused her to be generally liked. In appearance she was large and impressive, with a full round face, large serious eyes, and an expression indicating poise and placidity. Her death occurred at East Orange and delegations from women's clubs all over the East attended her funeral.

[Benj. K. Emerson, *The Ipswich Emersons* (1900); *American Women*, vol. I (1897), ed. by Frances E. Willard and Mary A. Livermore; obituaries in the *N. Y. Tribune* and *N. Y. Times*, Feb. 6, 1895.]

S.G.B.

BROWN, DAVID PAUL (Sept. 28, 1795–July 11, 1872), lawyer, orator, and dramatist, was the only child of well-born, well-educated, and wealthy parents. His father, Paul Brown, was descended from Quaker ancestors who came from England with Lord Berkeley and settled in New Jersey. In 1790 Paul Brown removed from Berkeley, N. J., to Philadelphia, where he married Rhoda Thackara of Salem, N. J., and where in 1795 their son David Paul was born. David was taught by his mother till he was eight and he owed to her his unusual discrimination in speech. Later he was trained by tutors and attended the best local schools. His parents brought him up in an atmosphere of wealth, and encouraged him to spend money freely and intelligently. After the death of his mother in 1810 he was sent to the home of the Rev. Dr. Daggett, a Massachusetts clergyman, who directed the youth's education until 1812. Although David favored the profession of law, he then took up medicine to please his father and became a pupil of the famous Philadelphian, Dr. Benjamin Rush. Six months later (1813) Dr. Rush died; David was then permitted to transfer his studies to law, with an equally famous lawyer, William Rawle, as his preceptor. He read zealously, attended the courts, and enjoyed the society of such leaders at the bar as Lewis, Tilghman, Ingersoll, Dallas, and Binney. His father died in 1815, leaving him a comfortable fortune. In September 1816, just as he attained his majority, Brown was admitted to the Philadelphia bar and soon afterward to the bar of the supreme court of Pennsylvania, the district and circuit courts, and the Supreme Court of the United States.

His reputation as a public speaker quickly vied with his professional fame. At twenty-four he addressed a notable audience at the celebration of Washington's birthday. Five years later (1824) he delivered the address of welcome to Lafayette. During the same year he won distinction for his brilliant and successful defense of Judge Robert Porter, who had been impeached before the Senate of Pennsylvania. On Dec. 24, 1826, he married Emmeline Catharine Handy. Meanwhile he continued to be honored with invitations to deliver his florid eulogiums whenever a notable occasion suggested a speaker of unusual oratorical repute.

In spite of his growing practise and the numerous demands on his time, he found opportunity to write reviews of current books and likewise to try his hand at poems and plays. His casual poetry, which appeared in the Philadelphia *Sunday Despatch* and elsewhere, is largely negligible. His efforts as a dramatist, however, are more significant. Within two weeks, and principally while riding on horseback to a fashionable suburban spa, he composed a tragedy in verse entitled *Sertorius; or, The Roman Patriot,* which was produced Dec. 14, 1830, at the Chestnut Street Theatre, Philadelphia, with Junius Brutus Booth in the title rôle. *Sertorius* is a somewhat vapid imitation of Shakespeare's *Julius Cæsar* and Addison's *Cato,* but its sonorous lines were so well delivered by the famous actor that it was presented nine times. It was revived at the Arch Street Theatre, Philadelphia, on Feb. 6, 1832, and figured thereafter in the repertoire of the elder Booth. A romantic comedy, *The Prophet of St. Paul's,* also written in 1830, received a wretched belated performance at the Walnut Street Theatre, Philadelphia, on Mar. 20, 1837, and succumbed after the third performance. It dealt with the popular love-story of Princess Mary and Charles Brandon, Duke of Suffolk. Less significant plays were

The Trial, a tragedy, and a farce called *Love and Honor, or, The Generous Soldier.*

Brown was not concerned over the failure of his dramatic efforts, as they represented mere diversions in the life of a busy lawyer. His skill in cross-examination resulted in his being retained in almost every important criminal case in the Philadelphia courts. Though his practise was lucrative, it did not result in the accumulation of a fortune. He lived on a most lavish scale in accord with his father's theory that a prosperous man should spend his income freely to avoid the evils of indolence. He thought sufficiently well of himself to publish his reminiscences in two large volumes (1856) under the title *The Forum; or, Forty Years Full Practice at the Philadelphia Bar.*

Brown was a man of medium height, compactly built, with a high broad forehead, flashing dark eyes, a large mouth, and a voice of great compass. Friends testified to his amiable disposition, his urbanity of manner, and his other social graces. In court he was preëminently histrionic and perhaps too fond of the orotund phraseology that characterized the old-school lawyer. In 1873 his son, Robert Eden Brown, edited *The Forensic Speeches of David Paul Brown, Selected from Important Trials and Embracing a Period of Forty Years.* Brown regularly declined to consider public office and rarely practised in any courts outside of Pennsylvania.

[In addition to *The Forum* and *The Forensic Speeches* above mentioned, see *Phila. North American and U. S. Gazette,* July 12, 1872, and *Phila. Public Ledger,* July 15, 1872. For an account of the performances of *Sertorius* and *The Prophet of St. Pauls,* see Charles Durang, "The Phila. Stage" (in *Phila. Sunday Dispatch*), ser. III (beginning July 8, 1860), chs. IV, XLVIII, respectively. These plays were printed in Phila., the first in 1830, the second in 1836. See also the reprint of *Sertorius* in M. J. Moses, *Representative Plays by Am. Dramatists,* II (1925), 185–252, which is preceded by a critical note on Brown. A. H. Quinn, *A Hist. of the Am. Drama from the Beginning to the Civil War* (1923), 249–50, cites passing references to Brown in Rees, Wemyss, Wood, and other commentators. For portraits of Brown, see J. T. Scharf and T. Westcott, *Hist. of Phila.* (1884), II, 1549, and *Am. Hist. Reg.* (1896), III, 622.] J.L.H.

BROWN, EBENEZER (1795–Jan. 3, 1889), Methodist clergyman, first manufacturer of detachable collars, was born in Massachusetts, probably at Chesterfield. He entered the Methodist ministry in 1818, being received on trial in that year by the New York Conference and appointed to Stowe (Vt.), in the Champlain District, and in the next year sent to Suffolk, in the New York District. In the same year upon the advice of Bishop McKendree, Brown was selected by Bishop George "to preach to the French inhabitants of the South" (J. M. Reid, *Missions*

and Missionary Society of the Methodist Episcopal Church,* 1879, I, 80). Brown, who for some time had devoted himself to a study of French in preparation for this work, found upon his arrival in New Orleans that the French people had "no ready ear for the Gospel" and he devoted himself to the ministry of a small group of English-speaking Methodists in that city. Brown's mission to the French, although a failure, marked the first missionary enterprise of American Methodism, and Brown, himself, was the first missionary sent out by the Methodist Board. Returning North in 1821 he served pastorates in Middlebury, Vt. (1821), in Hartford, Conn. (1822), and in New York City 1823 and 1824 (*Minutes of the Annual Conferences of the Methodist Episcopal Church for the Years 1773–1828,* 1840). Although a gifted and successful minister, he retired from the active work at the early age of thirty, because of continued ill health.

Shortly after his retirement Brown engaged, about 1827, in the business of a dry-goods merchant at 285 River St., Troy. Just about this time Hannah Lord Montague (1794–1878), daughter of William Lord, a Revolutionary officer, and wife of Orlando Montague, conceived the idea of saving laundry work by cutting off the collars from her husband's shirts. The commercial possibilities of a detachable collar appealed to Brown and in 1829 he "bargained with a number of women to make, wash and iron them, and to accept such goods as were sold by him in payment for their labor. The collars in assorted sizes were placed in paper-boxes, sixteen or more inches in length, and sold to customers and dealers patronizing him" (Weise, p. 174). These first "string collars," as they were known, were worn with the old-fashioned stock tie, and tied around the neck with a string attached to each end of the collar. Brown continued the manufacture until his removal to New York in 1834, when the production was taken up on a larger scale by the firm of Orlando Montague & Austin Granger. Upon his removal to New York, Brown organized the firm of E. Brown & Company which carried on a commission business for many years. His last residence after his retirement was the home of his daughter in Baltimore, where he died in his ninety-fourth year. He was buried at Woodlawn Cemetery, Philadelphia.

[In addition to works cited above consult obituary in the *Christian Advocate* (N. Y.), Jan. 24, 1889; *Seventieth Ann. Report of the Missionary Soc. of the M. E. Ch.* (1888), p. 15; Arthur J. Weise, *Troy's One Hundred Years 1789–1889* (1891), pp. 174 ff.; Geo. B. Anderson, *Landmarks of Rensselaer County, N.Y.* (1897), pp. 275–76 and article by Theodore Sweedy in *N. Y. Times Mag.,* Oct. 31, 1926, p. 2.] H.U.F.

BROWN, ETHAN ALLEN (July 4, 1766–
Feb. 24, 1852), politician, was born at Darien,
Conn., the son of Roger Brown, a considerable
land-owner. He received private instruction in
the classics, but his subsequent education for the
law was delayed by financial embarrassments
due to the Revolution. Business ventures proving profitable, however, in 1797 he entered the
law office of Alexander Hamilton, and was finally
admitted to practise in 1802 (*A Portrait and Biographical Record of Portage and of Summit
Counties, Ohio,* 1898, pp. 136–37). A trip
through western Pennsylvania, then down the
Ohio and the Mississippi to New Orleans, with
a subsequent voyage to Europe to dispose of
flour for which the local market was not advantageous, proved to be the turning-point of
Brown's career. Returning to the West, he purchased a tract of land at what is now Rising Sun,
Ind., and in 1804 established a law practise at
Cincinnati. Professional progress was rapid,
and in 1810 he was appointed by the legislature
to a judgeship of the supreme court of Ohio.
This he resigned in December 1818, having previously been elected governor by a vote of 30,194
as against 8,075 for James Dunlap, also a Democrat (William A. Taylor, *Ohio in Congress,*
1900, pp. 50–51).

Two problems confronted Brown as governor.
The first was the active opposition in the state to
the rechartered Bank of the United States. This
struggle, in which the Governor was actively interested, culminated in virtual nullification when,
in total defiance of the decision of the United
States Supreme Court in *McCulloch* vs. *Maryland,* the State of Ohio forcibly taxed the branch
banks at Cincinnati and Chillicothe (Daniel J.
Ryan, "Nullification in Ohio" in the *Ohio Archæological and Historical Quarterly,* II, 413–
22. See also *Senate Document No. 72,* 16 Cong.,
2 Sess.). The second problem was indicated
in the message to the legislature, Jan. 8, 1819,
wherein the Governor asserted that "Roads and
canals are veins and arteries to the body politic
that diffuse supplies, health, vigor and animation
to the whole system, nor is this idea of their extensive use and beneficial influence new" (Emi-
lius O. Randall and Daniel J. Ryan, *History of
Ohio,* 1912, III, 341). The canals were dug, and
Brown became to Ohio what De Witt Clinton
was to New York.

Reëlected governor in 1820 by a vote of 34,836,
as against 9,426 for Jeremiah Morrow, and 4,348
for William Henry Harrison, Brown resigned in
1822, in order to fill the unexpired senatorial
term of William A. Trimble, deceased. His previous activity in canals now obtained for Brown

the chairmanship of the Committee on Roads and
Canals. He favored particularly the Cumberland Road as helpful alike to Ohio and the nation.
He was friendly, also, to a "grand connection of
the whole coast of the Atlantic by internal navigation," and cited Gallatin's report on a chain
of canals as "sufficient to immortalize his memory" (*Register of the Debates in Congress,* 18
Cong., 2 Sess., Feb. 24, 1825).

Succeeded in the Senate by William Henry
Harrison, Brown held from 1825 to 1830 the congenial post of canal commissioner in Ohio (*The
Democratic Party of the State of Ohio,* 1913, ed.
by Thomas E. Powell and others, I, 54). In
1830 he was named by President Jackson United
States minister to Brazil, remaining there four
years, a conscientious representative of his government during a troubled time in Brazilian
history. The slave trade and American claims
against Brazil were the mission's chief concern.
On Brown's return he was for one year commissioner of the General Land Office at Washington,
a position for which he was well fitted by integrity and experience. Retiring from public life in
1836 at the age of seventy, Brown resided among
his kindred at Rising Sun. Sixteen years later
his sudden death at Indianapolis, where he was
acting as vice-president at a political convention,
called forth the eulogy that his many virtues "reflected honor on offices which are supposed to
confer honor on their incumbents" (John S. C.
Abbott, *The History of the State of Ohio from
the Discovery of the Great Valley to the Present
Time,* 1875, p. 737).

[In addition to authorities cited above, see State Dept.
Despatches, vols. VIII, IX, Brazil, nos. 1–68, with
seven unnumbered, in the Archives of the State Dept.,
Washington, D. C.]   L.M.S.

BROWN, FAYETTE (Dec. 17, 1823–Jan. 20,
1910), banker, inventor, manufacturer, was the
son of Ephraim and Mary (Huntington) Brown.
In 1814 Ephraim Brown, originally of Westmoreland, N. H., joined with a friend and purchased a township in the Connecticut Western
Reserve, now known as North Bloomfield, Trumbull County, Ohio, and the following year he
moved west and settled there with his wife and
several children and became a leader in that
transplanted New England community. There
Fayette was born, the youngest of nine children,
and was brought up in that characteristic atmosphere of thrift and honesty. His elementary education was that afforded by the public schools of
Gambier, Ohio, after which he attended Jefferson College in Pennsylvania. When eighteen
years old, however, he left home and entered the
dry-goods store of an elder brother in Pittsburgh
where he remained until 1851, becoming a mem-

ber of the firm in 1845. Just prior to the termination of the store partnership Brown had formed a partnership with a friend, George Mygatt, to engage in the banking business, and in 1851 he went to Cleveland, Ohio, to join Mygatt, remaining there for the succeeding ten years. At the outbreak of the Civil War in 1861 he accepted an appointment as paymaster in the Union army. After serving for over a year he resigned with the rank of major. Upon his return to Cleveland he became general agent and manager of the Jackson Iron Company, manufacturers of iron and steel. He continued here for the next twenty-five years, building up a reputation as one of the most competent iron manufacturers of his time. During this period he secured four patents, two for hoisting apparatus in connection with the charging of blast furnaces, and two for improvements in blast furnace design. These were issued in 1884 and 1885. It was during this time, too, that Brown became interested in Great Lakes shipping and built up a large fleet of lake steamers, particularly for the transportation of iron ore. In fact, he was the first to bring iron ore by boat from the Lake Superior district to Cleveland. When the Brown Hoisting Machinery Company was organized in 1880 to develop the inventions of his son, Alexander Ephraim [q.v.], Brown assumed the presidency and continued in this capacity until his death. For the first seven years he also continued as general manager of the Jackson Iron Company but relinquished this office in 1887. In later years Brown served also as president of the Union Steel Screw Company, the National Chemical Company, and the G. C. Kuhlman Car Company, respectively, and was also a member of his younger son's firm, H. H. Brown & Company, dealers in iron ore, as well as chairman of the board of directors of the Stewart Iron Company of Sharon, Pa. On July 15, 1847, Brown married Cornelia C. Curtis of Pittsburgh, who died several years before he did. They were survived, however, by their four children, two sons and two daughters.

[*Who's Who in America*, 1910–11; letters from Harvey H. Brown & Co., Cleveland; Patent Office Records; *Cleveland Plain Dealer*, Jan. 21, 1910.]   C. W. M.

BROWN, FRANCIS (Jan. 11, 1784–July 27, 1820), college president, son of Benjamin and Prudence (Kelly) Brown, was born at Chester, N. H. His father was a country merchant of limited means, but thanks to his stepmother, who seems to have had a better appreciation of the boy's possibilities, he secured a good education, attending Atkinson Academy and graduating from Dartmouth College in 1805. After a

year's experience as a private tutor he received an appointment as tutor at Dartmouth. He remained at the college for three years, studying theology in addition to carrying on his teaching duties. On Jan. 11, 1810, he began his pastorate at North Yarmouth, Me., where he remained for the next five years. Here, on Feb. 4, 1811, he married Elizabeth, daughter of Rev. Tristram Gilman of the same town. Soon after ordination he declined the offer of a professorship in languages at Dartmouth, but his continued interest in educational matters is apparent in his service as overseer (1810–14) and trustee (1814–15) of Bowdoin College and in his close friendship with President Appleton of that institution. His pastorate at North Yarmouth was successful but without special incident. By training and association Brown naturally belonged among the conservative and orthodox Congregationalist clergy. Like most members of that body he combined devout Calvinism in theology with fervent Federalism in politics. His faith in the former is set forth in two bulky and controversial pamphlets in defense of Calvin and Calvinism which he published at Portland in 1815 (*Calvin and Calvinism* and *Reply to Rev. Martin Ruter's Letter relating to Calvin and Calvinism*). His political views are to be found in a published sermon (July 23, 1812) on the occasion of the declaration of war against Great Britain, in which he denounced the Madison administration for its subservience to France, "Babylon the great, the mother of harlots and abominations of the earth."

In the meantime there was developing in New Hampshire, its genesis in an obscure parochial quarrel, the controversy which resulted in the "Dartmouth College case." On Aug. 26, 1815, the trustees removed President Wheelock and offered the position to Francis Brown who assumed the duties of president a month later. The local quarrel, because of the religious and political affiliations of the participants, rapidly assumed state-wide importance with legislative intervention as a natural result. Until Chief Justice Marshall handed down the final decision in February 1819 (*The Trustees of Dartmouth College* vs. *Woodward, 4 Wheaton, 518*), the life of the college hung in the balance. With its charter virtually annulled by the Act of June 27, 1816, with a new institution, "Dartmouth University," functioning under the sanction of the state, with funds unavailable because of litigation, with student body depleted, and confronted with public hostility and internal dissension, there was need of the highest qualities of leadership. President Brown proved equal to the occasion. The college work went on in spite of severe handicaps. He conducted classes, raised money, defended the cause before the public, advised with counsel, and by the dignity and tact displayed toward opponents, kept the controversy from degenerating into either a brawl or a comedy as might easily have happened under less competent guidance. His correspondence shows that he had a clear perception of the constitutional and political issues involved, and their bearing on the future of chartered institutions throughout the country. That his services were appreciated elsewhere is seen by the fact that Hamilton and Williams honored him with the degree of D.D.

His health broke under the strain of constant work and anxiety and he did not live to take part in the rehabilitation which followed the victory of 1819, a task for which he would have been admirably qualified. After a vain effort to recover his health in the milder climate of the South he returned to Hanover in June 1820, his death occurring a few weeks later. Brown's portrait, now in the possession of the college, is chiefly expressive of the gentle and scholarly character of the youthful teacher and clergyman but the artist has also caught something of the shrewdness, courage, and determination of the Federalist leader and executive, ready to fight to the death against what he regarded as Democratic encroachment on private rights.

Brown's son, Samuel Gilman Brown [q.v.], was for many years a professor at Dartmouth and later president of Hamilton College; his grandson, Francis Brown [q.v.], became president of Union Seminary.

[Henry Wood, *Sketch of the Life of President Brown* (1834), first published in *Am. Quart. Reg.*, Nov. 1834; John K. Lord, *Hist. of Dartmouth Coll., 1815–1909* (1913); Benj. Chase, *Hist. of Old Chester* (1869); manuscript letters and miscellany in Dartmouth Coll. archives.]   W.A.R.

BROWN, FRANCIS (Dec. 26, 1849–Oct. 15, 1916), theological professor, and president of Union Seminary, was born in Hanover, N. H., the son of Sarah (Van Vechten) and Samuel Gilman Brown [q.v.]. He graduated from Dartmouth in the class of 1870 and after teaching for four years entered Union Theological Seminary, graduating there in 1877. Awarded a traveling fellowship he spent the next two years in study in Berlin. He was the favorite pupil and most devoted disciple of Dr. Charles A. Briggs [q.v.] and he followed him in making the Old Testament his special subject of study. In 1879 he married Louise Reiss of Berlin and returned to America to become instructor and later associate professor of Biblical philology in Union

Seminary. In 1890 when Dr. Briggs was transferred to the chair of Biblical theology Brown succeeded him as professor of Hebrew and the cognate languages, a position he held until his death. For some years he taught in the Seminary not only Hebrew and Greek but also Aramaic and Assyrian. In Berlin he had studied Assyrian—which was then beginning to attract the attention of Old Testament scholars—under Eberhard Schrader and he was the first person in America to give instruction in the language. In 1885 he published a little book on *Assyriology, its Use and Abuse,* declaring that "The root of the misuse of Assyriology in Bible study" was "an ill-directed and excessive Apologetics." In 1907 he gave a course of public lectures at the Seminary (the Ely Lectures) on the relations of Israel with Babylonia and Assyria, but unfortunately the lectures were never published. In 1884 he issued with President Roswell D. Hitchcock the first American edition of the newly discovered *Teaching of the Twelve Apostles,* republished the following year in an enlarged form and with extensive notes for which he was chiefly responsible, as he was also for the translation. In 1907–08 he served as director of the American School of Oriental Study and Research at Jerusalem.

From the beginning Brown displayed those qualities as a scholar which were to make him eminent—untiring diligence, painstaking accuracy, absolute fairness, maturity of judgment, careful weighing of evidence, caution in drawing and stating conclusions. He was not a rapid worker like his teacher Dr. Briggs, and he was not given to venturesome hypotheses, but his scholarship was solid and sound. As a teacher his influence was invigorating and wholesome and he had the unqualified respect of his students. No one could come under him without having his ideals of scholarship heightened and his conscience as a scholar quickened.

The lasting monument of his scholarship is the great *Hebrew and English Lexicon of the Old Testament,* completed in 1906, of which he was the editor-in-chief and to which he devoted more than twenty years. During all those years it consumed the major part of his time and attention and kept him from publishing many other works which he had planned. It was in recognition of his work on the lexicon that he was given the honorary degree of Litt.D. by the University of Oxford.

While primarily a scholar, he became interested in ecclesiastical affairs as a result of the controversy over Dr. Briggs. Throughout the struggle he was Briggs's right hand man and supported him loyally, and after the latter left the Presbyterian Church Brown became a recognized leader of the liberal Presbyterian group. He was a man of strong convictions, but with all the firmness which these gave him he was yet considerate of the opinions of others and was always slow to express dissent. It was quite in accord with his general spirit and attitude that he interested himself in the cause of church unity. In company with Dr. Briggs he worked actively in its behalf for a number of years.

In 1908 upon the death of Charles Cuthbert Hall he succeeded him as president of Union Seminary and though he retained his professorship and continued his teaching, his days of productive scholarship were over. His great-grandfather, John H. Mason, had been president of Dickinson College, his grandfather, Francis Brown [q.v.], of Dartmouth, and his father of Hamilton, so that he came of presidential stock. He himself was called to the presidency of Dartmouth but declined, preferring to remain at Union. His administration there was notable. In 1910 the Seminary moved to its new site on Morningside Heights opposite Columbia University, and the affiliation between the two institutions became even closer than it had been. Under him the endowment of the Seminary was greatly increased and both the faculty and student body were enlarged by more than a half.

Brown had a massive frame and great personal dignity. Many thought him unapproachable and it is true that he was not a man of easy intimacies. It was often difficult to get beyond the barrier of his reserve, but no one ever had a kinder heart or readier sympathy. He was a tower of strength yet extraordinarily gentle, full of generosity and quick to help where help was needed.

[*Memorial Service in Honour of the Rev. Francis Brown* (1917); Henry Preserved Smith, "Francis Brown—An Appreciation" in the *Am. Jour. of Semitic Languages and Literatures*, Jan. 1917; G. L. Prentiss, *The Union Theol. Sem. . . . Another Decade of its Hist.* (1899); obituary in *N. Y. Times*, Oct. 16, 1916.]

A. C. M.

BROWN, FREDERIC TILDEN (Oct. 7, 1853–May 7, 1910), surgeon, the son of David Tilden Brown the alienist by his wife, Cornelia Wells Clapp, was born in New York City. From his father Frederic inherited a bold and enterprising nature. He was graduated from Harvard College in the class of 1877. During his early years he rowed on several victorious crews and was believed to have strained his heart in his efforts. He received his M.D. from the College of Physicians and Surgeons in New York

in 1880 and became house surgeon in the same year at Mt. Sinai Hospital, New York. He became associated shortly afterward with the Bellevue Hospital (attending surgeon) and subsequently with the Presbyterian, Nassau, and Mineola Hospitals as consulting surgeon. He was later made professor of genito-urinary diseases at the University and Bellevue Hospital Medical College, and as teacher and lecturer enjoyed great popularity.

Brown's most important professional contributions lay in the introduction of delicate instruments for use in genito-urinary surgery. His improvements in the lamp-bearing cystoscope made possible better visual definition than had any earlier instrument (*Annals of Surgery*, XXXV, 642–43). He also made a special study of infections of the urinary tract ("A Case of Cystitis, Pyelonephritis, and Pyonephrosis due to Colon-Bacillus Infection," etc., *Journal of Cutaneous and Genito-Urinary Diseases*, XIII, 133–42). In addition to his numerous papers in his special field one finds that he reported two cases of amputation at the hip-joint by a new method (*Annals of Surgery*, XXIII, 153–62); indeed he prided himself upon being a general surgeon as well as a specialist. Through his exceptional operative skill as well as through invention of instruments of precision, Brown "became one of the conspicuous landmarks in his specialty" (Kelly). He was a tremendous worker and throughout his active career was an exponent of vigorous exercise. His avocations were shooting, natural history, and art.

He married in 1884 Mrs. Mary Crosby (Renwick) Strong and there were two children, a boy and a girl. A nervous breakdown which was the direct result of over-work led him to go to Bethel, Me., for his health in the spring of 1910. He died there by his own hand on May 7, 1910.

[Several short notices of Brown's death appeared in the N. Y. medical journals but no obituaries were published. The above material is taken chiefly from H. A. Kelly's account in H. A. Kelly and W. L. Burrage, *Am. Medic. Biogs.* (1920). See also *Harvard Coll. Class of 1877, Report No. 5* (1897) for an autobiographical sketch, and *Report No. 7* (1917) for a memorial. Paul M. Pilcher, *Practical Cystoscopy* (1915) gives descriptions and diagrams of Brown's instruments.]

J. F. F.

BROWN, GEORGE (Apr. 17, 1787–Aug. 26, 1859), pioneer railroad promoter, was born in Ballymena, County Antrim, Ireland, the second son of Grace (Davison) and Alexander Brown [q.v.]. With his brothers, James and John A. Brown [qq.v.], he followed his father to Baltimore in 1802, and in time became a member of the firm of Alexander Brown & Sons. On Feb. 12, 1827, twenty-five leading citizens of

Baltimore called together by George Brown met at his house in Baltimore to consider the best means of restoring to the city trade which had been diverted by the introduction of steam navigation and the opening up of the Erie and other canals in the West. At this meeting the plan of the Baltimore & Ohio Railroad, the first passenger steam railroad in the United States, was conceived. Stock subscription books were opened on Mar. 20, 1827, and 41,781 shares of stock almost immediately subscribed. George Brown was made treasurer of the Baltimore & Ohio Railroad Company and, with his father, virtually supervised the construction of the road, which was begun on July 4, 1828. In 1831–32 he stimulated Ross Winans [*q.v.*] to design and construct the first eight-wheel car, the forerunner of the modern railway car, to supersede the modified stage coaches then in use. George Brown held the position of treasurer, declining to accept any compensation, until 1834, when Alexander Brown died, and George, as the ranking member of the firm in this country, was required to undertake the heavy responsibility of directing the banking affairs of the Browns. To do this he had to give up all outside interests.

Of all the lessons George Brown had learned from his pioneer father, the one he had learned most thoroughly was the lesson of conservatism. Under his guidance, therefore, the Brown firms curtailed rather than expanded their activities. The intrepid pioneers of the profitable but hazardous field of international mercantile banking began to withdraw from the business of shipping and trading, and to devote themselves more exclusively to banking. The independent fortunes of the Browns had been made by the elder Brown's shrewd piloting past the rocks of early nineteenth-century trade, and it was a big job merely to conserve those fortunes. This the sons, advised by George, elected to do to the exclusion of most other activities, and they did it successfully.

George Brown was a leader in every important civic movement in Baltimore in his time, and gave liberally of his money to worthy institutions. He was the first president of the first systematized charitable organization in Baltimore, and among his especial interests outside of business were the House of Refuge and the Peabody Institute of Baltimore. A marble shaft erected to his memory commemorates his tireless and unselfish work for the House of Refuge. Brown Memorial Presbyterian Church erected by his widow, Isabella (McLanahan) Brown, whom he had married in 1818, is another of his city's monuments to him.

[Wm. P. Smith, *A Hist. and Description of the B. & O. R. R.* (1853) ; Edward Hungerford, *The Story of the B. & O. R. R. 1827–1927* (1928) ; John C. Brown, *A Hundred Years of Merchant Banking* (priv. printed, 1909) ; Frank R. Kent, *The Story of Alexander Brown and Sons* (1925) ; Mary E. Brown, *Alexander Brown and his Descendants* (priv. printed, 1917) ; obituary in the *Sun* (Baltimore), Aug. 27, 1859.]   F. R. K.

BROWN, GEORGE (Oct. 11, 1823–May 6, 1892), physician, educator of the feeble-minded, was descended from Thomas and Bridget Brown who settled in Concord, Mass., in 1638. He was the son of Ephraim Brown, a man of unusual mechanical gifts, and of Sarah (King) Brown, and was born at Wilton, N. H. After attending Phillips Academy, Andover, Mass., and the University of Vermont, he began the study of medicine with Dr. Norman Smith of Groton, Mass., matriculated at Jefferson Medical College, Philadelphia, and took his medical degree in 1850 from the University of the City of New York. In this year he went to Barre, Mass., to practise there and immediately became interested in the Elm Hill School, a small private institution for feeble-minded children, the first of its kind in America, established two years before by Dr. Hervey B. Wilbur. On Nov. 28, 1850, he married Catherine Wood who also became a devoted worker in this school. In the summer of 1851, Dr. Wilbur left to take charge of the New York State Institute for Feeble-minded at Albany, and Brown decided to take over the superintendency of the Elm Hill School and make it his life-work. He threw himself into the problem with a scientific skill which was completely modern, and a spirit as fine as any his profession has ever produced. The institution consisted at this time of an ordinary house with space for fifteen children. These ranged in age from five to thirteen years. The types varied from simply retarded mental development to the purely idiotic. At this early period there were twenty acres of land for playgrounds, walks and gardens. Various simple games were taught, one hour before school was devoted to gymnasium work, the older boys were instructed in the management of horses and cattle, the smaller ones in the care of poultry, rabbits, and squirrels. They used tools and learned ordinary trades. Under Brown's supervision the institution grew to have several buildings, and an estate of 250 acres of land, and became the largest private institution of its kind in the United States. Its purpose, as expressed in an early report, was, "to solve the great problem, whether the idiot could be developed to take rank in the scale of our common humanity, and be fitted not only for useful employments but for general observation, comparison, and judgment." Brown was an active participant in the development of Barre. He was one of the founders of the library association, and twice a member of the school board. A founder also of the Glen Valley Association, he was its president until his death. For years he was a leading member of and liberal contributor to the Congregational Church. Originally a Whig, he joined the Republican party when it was formed. After his death his son, Dr. George A. Brown, succeeded to the superintendency of the Elm Hill School.

[*Elm Hill Private School for Feeble-Minded Youth, Barre, Mass., Report,* 1853; *Gen. Alumni Cat. N. Y. Univ. 1833–1907, Medic. Alumni* (1908); *Gen. Cat. of the Univ. of Vt.* (1901); A. A. Livermore and Sewall Putnam, *Hist. of the Town of Wilton, Hillsborough County, N. H.* (1888); *Biog. Rev. . . . of Worcester County, Mass.* (1899), pp. 78–81.]   M.A.K.

BROWN, GEORGE PLINY (Nov. 10, 1836–Feb. 1, 1910), educator, was born in Lenox township, Ashtabula County, Ohio. His father was William P. Brown and his mother was Rachel (Piper) Brown. He was educated in the common schools of Lenox township and at the Grand River Institute, Austinburg, Ohio, a small preparatory school established on a sound basis in 1831. Ill health prevented him from completing a college course. Beginning his career as an educator at the age of sixteen when he taught a rural school in Cherry Valley Township, Ohio, he advanced steadily in his chosen profession. In 1854 he taught in a small academy of Geauga County, and from 1855 to 1860 he was principal of the school at Waynesville. It was in 1860 that he went to Indiana to fill the position of superintendent of schools at Richmond. There he remained until 1865 when he became the head of the New Albany, Ind., schools. The next year saw him back in Richmond holding his former position. He resigned after two years.

Brown had been studying law during his leisure for a number of years, and thinking he would like the legal profession, he established himself as a lawyer. He practised law until 1871. That year, his first love, the school, took him to Indianapolis. After two years as principal of the Indianapolis High School, he was promoted to the superintendence of the system. It was as superintendent of the Indianapolis public schools that Brown received recognition which placed him as an educational leader of the state. His articles and editorials in the *Indiana School Journal* of which he was associate editor for a time (vols. XX, XXI, XXII) reveal his conception of the public school as an institution. He firmly believed and emphatically contended that "the school is a spiritual and not a material entity" (*Indiana School Journal,* February 1876). At the end of the school year in 1878 Brown ac-

cepted a position with D. Appleton & Company, publishers, intending to forsake the teaching profession. During the summer of 1879, however, he was elected president of the Indiana State Normal School at Terre Haute. In this position he became nationally known as an educator of vision. James H. Smart, a former superintendent of public instruction in Indiana, and a contemporary of Brown, expressed a widely accepted estimate of the latter when he said, "He has proven himself to be one of the ablest educators in the West." Brown resigned as president of the Indiana State Normal School in 1886 and moved to Bloomington, Ill. In 1888 he purchased the *Illinois School Journal* which was published there, changed its title to *Public School Journal* and later to *School and Home Education,* and devoted the rest of his life to it as editor. Brown was tall, well formed, of remarkably fine address, ready in decision and prompt in action, a gentleman of heart and intellect whom both teachers and children respected. He died at Bloomington survived by his wife, Mary Seymour Brown, whom he had married in 1855, and four sons.

[Files of the *Ill. School Jour.* and its successors, and of the *Ind. School Jour.;* John W. Cook, *Educ. Hist. of Ill.* (1912); Jas. H. Smart, *The Ind. Schools and the Men Who Have Worked in Them* (1876); obituary in the *Daily Pantagraph* (Bloomington, Ill.), Feb. 2, 1910.]   H.N.S.

BROWN, GEORGE WILLIAM (Oct. 13, 1812–Sept. 5, 1890), lawyer, judge, was the eldest son of George John and Esther (Allison) Brown. Baltimore, Md., his birthplace, and the fitting environment of his eventful life, had been selected in 1783 by his grandfather, Dr. George Brown, a physician, as the most promising home for the American branch of an old Irish family (*The Sun,* Baltimore, Sept. 8, 1890). George William Brown entered Dartmouth at the age of sixteen, and, later, Rutgers, where he graduated in 1831 with the highest honors. After a short preparation in Baltimore, he was admitted to the practise of law, and, in 1839, formed a partnership with Frederick W. Brune, Jr., whose sister he later married. Four years earlier he had actively identified himself with the forces for orderly government when he joined the body of citizens organized under Gen. Samuel Smith to suppress the riots attending the failure of the Bank of Maryland (*Johns Hopkins University Circulars,* vol. X, no. 83, p. 8). This incident was typical of his life. Throughout his career he was a fearless independent in the interests of an orderly democratic government. The energies of such a man were constantly called to action during that chaotic decade in American politics preceding the Civil War, when the Know-Nothing party fixed its hold on Baltimore and maintained it by the methods of mob rule. This hold was not broken until November 1859 when Brown was elected mayor by a large majority on an independent platform. (L. F. Schmeckebier, *History of the Know-Nothing Party in Maryland*, 1899, pp. 41–42, 112–113). His feelings during the Civil War can be taken as representing the feelings of the state, and they are well presented in his *Baltimore and the 19th of April, 1861, a Study of the War* (1887). "The problem of slavery" he says, "was to me a Gordian knot which I knew not how to untie, and which I dared not attempt to cut with the sword" (p. 115). Though opposed to slavery he thought the eventual decay of the system and the arts of persuasion would certainly, in time, bring the states of the Confederacy back to the Union. His brave action in protecting against a mob the 6th Massachusetts Regiment when it marched through Baltimore on Apr. 19, 1860, and his burning of the bridges north of the city to prevent worse bloodshed, are matters of common historical record. On Sept. 11, 1861, Secretary of War Cameron issued an order to prevent the passage of any secession act by the Maryland legislature even at the cost of arresting all the members. Acting ostensibly under this order, Gen. Dix, on Sept. 12, included Brown with those arrested and the latter spent fifteen months in imprisonment.

Brown's long legal career culminated in 1872 with his appointment as judge of the supreme bench of Baltimore, which position he held until 1888. His published addresses, though they show no keen penetration or great original thinking, mark Brown as a liberal who was constantly thinking and acting for the good of society. They are scholarly and worth reading. His usefulness as a public man is apparent from the many positions which he held at the time of his death. He was one of the founders of the University of Maryland and a trustee, one of the original trustees of Johns Hopkins University, a trustee of the Peabody Institute, of Saint Johns College, of Enoch Pratt Library, and of other institutions which need not be noted.

[See *Johns Hopkins Univ. Circulars*, vol. X, no. 83, pp. 6–8; the *Sun* (Baltimore), Sept. 8, 1890; F. A. Richardson and W. A. Bennett, *Baltimore, Past and Present* (1871), pp. 199–206; J. T. Scharf, *Hist. of Md.*, vol. III (1879). Brown's Addresses are deposited in the Peabody Lib., Baltimore. See also *Official Records (Army)*, ser. 1, esp. vols. II. and V.] C.W.G.

BROWN, GOOLD (Mar. 7, 1791–Mar. 31, 1857), grammarian, was born in Providence, R. I., the son of Smith and Lydia (Gould) Brown. (His mother's name is given here in the spelling of the Providence records.) His parents were Quakers. His father, a school-teacher and essayist, began to instruct him in Greek and Latin at an age when even children with quick minds are only learning to read their mother tongue; but after making a brilliant record in the Friends School Brown was compelled to forego a college education and to aid in supporting the family. He is said to have engaged first in "mercantile pursuits" and to have found the work thoroughly repugnant to him. He next taught a district school near Providence and in 1811 was appointed to a position in the Nine Partners Boarding School at Mechanic, Dutchess County, N. Y. Two years later he became a teacher in John Griscom's school in New York. Finally he opened an academy of his own and conducted it for about twenty years. He published the *Child's First Book* (1822); *Institutes of English Grammar* (1823); *First Lines of English Grammar, Being a Brief Abstract of the Author's Larger Work* (1823); *Key to the Exercises for Writing Contained in the Institutes of English Grammar* (1825); and a *Catechism of English Grammar; with Parsing Exercises* (1827). Although his text-books never enjoyed the enormous vogue of Lindley Murray's or Samuel Kirkham's, the *Institutes* and the *First Lines* sold well from the beginning and gained steadily in popular esteem. Twice revised by later hands, they were still in use in 1929 in many Catholic parochial schools and in some of the public schools of New York City. Of English grammars only William Cobbett's has enjoyed so long a life. Brown seems to have been active, though not especially prominent, among New York Friends: in the autumn of 1830, as a member of a joint committee of the New York and Philadelphia Yearly Meetings, he approved a circular urging the support of a proposed school (Haverford School) that in time became Haverford College. In 1835–36 his name appears for the last time in the New York *City Directory*, his residence then being 374 Pearl St.; but whether he moved immediately to Lynn, Mass., where he spent his last years, is uncertain. Possessed of a sufficient income, he was free to devote himself to his favorite subject. He studied grammar after his own fashion with religious fervor and in 1851 published that leviathan of school books, the *Grammar of English Grammars*, an awe-inspiring octavo of over 1,100 pages. Like all grammarians, he professed to base his work on actual usage; in fact, however, he disdained the spoken language altogether and gave his approval only to such constructions as met his rigid notions of logic and propriety. One of the features of the book was the hundreds of examples of "false syntax" culled from the works of rival grammarians. Brown had a real gift for defining terms and for discriminating usage, but the merits of his book are buried under a heap of pedantic rubbish. As a scientific student of the English language he has no standing whatever, but over the methods of teaching grammar and over the content of later American text-books he has exercised a strong and not entirely happy influence. The *Grammar of English Grammars* went into its tenth edition in 1880; in 1929 a sound copy was still worth ten dollars in antiquarian book stores. Brown finished reading the proof sheets of the second edition just three weeks before he died in his home on South Common St. in Lynn. His wife and two adopted daughters survived him. In conventional phrases but with probable truth the local newspaper spoke of the many nameless acts of kindness and of love that had endeared him to his fellow townsmen.

[*Alphabetical Index of the Births, Marriages, and Deaths Recorded in Providence 1636–1850* (1879); *Longworth's Am. Almanac, N. Y. Reg. and City Dir.* (1816–36); *Hist. of Haverford Coll. for the First Sixty Years* (1892), p. 67; *Bull. of Friends' Hist. Soc. of Phila.*, vol. X, no. 1 (1920), p. 14; *Bay State* (Lynn, Mass.), Apr. 2, 1857; R. L. Lyman, *English Grammar in Am. Schools before 1850* (Dept. of the Interior, Bureau of Educ., *Bull.*, 1921, no. 12; pub. also by Univ. of Chicago Libraries, 1922).]   G.H.G.

BROWN, HENRY BILLINGS (Mar. 2, 1836–Sept. 4, 1913), jurist, was born at South Lee, Berkshire County, Mass. His parents, Billings and Mary (Tyler) Brown, were well-to-do, his father being a prosperous merchant and manufacturer, and he received an excellent private education after which he entered Yale University, graduating there in 1856. He then spent a year in Europe, traveling and studying, and on his return entered a law office in Ellington, Conn. He also attended the Law Schools at Yale and Harvard, but did not complete his course at either. In December 1859 he went to Detroit, Mich., continued his legal studies there, and was admitted to the Wayne County bar in July 1860. Commencing practise in Detroit, he was early in 1861 appointed deputy United States marshal. The port of Detroit was at that time one of the most active on the Great Lakes, and much of the litigation there concerned commercial and maritime matters, to which he specially devoted himself. Two years later he became assistant United States attorney for the eastern district of Michigan which included the city of Detroit. He held this position till May 1868, and in July of that year was appointed a circuit judge for the county of Wayne to fill a vacancy. He remained on the bench only till his successor was elected, when he resumed private practise in Detroit. He

became recognized as the leading authority on admiralty law in the Lakes region, and was constantly retained in important shipping cases. In March 1875 he was appointed by President Grant United States judge for the eastern district of Michigan, a position which he was peculiarly fitted to fill, inasmuch as a large proportion of the suits which came before him were maritime. In 1876 he compiled and published *Reports of Admiralty and Revenue Cases, Argued and Determined in the Circuit and District Courts of the United States for the Western Lake and River Districts,* embracing the cases between 1859 and 1875. This was the first volume of an intended series, but no more were published. In court he was dignified almost to austerity, and displayed remarkable readiness in grasping and deciding any point of law which was raised before him. In the conduct of the proceedings he was expeditious, at the same time displaying great patience in examining the merits of every case. Having served on the district court bench for fifteen years with great distinction, he was appointed by President Harrison an associate justice of the Supreme Court of the United States, Dec. 29, 1890. In this larger sphere his legal attainments found full scope, and during his tenure of office he was one of the dominant figures of the Court. Its volume of work was at that time very heavy, the calendar being four years in arrears, and the circuit court of appeals not having been created. His opinions in extradition appeals were always accorded the greatest respect, and he was regarded as the highest authority in the country in points of admiralty law. His outstanding opinion, however, was that in which he expressed his dissent from the majority of the Court in their decision that sections 27–37 of the Income Tax Act of 1894 were unconstitutional (*Pollock* vs. *Farmers Loan & Trust Company,* 158 *U. S.,* 601 at p. 686). He was a majority member of the Court before whom the "Insular Cases" were argued, including *Downes* vs. *Bidwell* (182 *U. S.,* 244). This latter case decided that the island of Porto Rico is not a part of the United States within that provision of the Constitution which declares that all duties, imports, and excises shall be uniform throughout the United States. Though concurring in the decision, Brown's process of reasoning was fundamentally at variance with that of his colleagues, his opinion being that no territory is part of the United States, and that the constitutional rights which the constitutional limitations create do not belong to the citizens of any territory, whether incorporated or not, until by Act of Congress they have been extended to them

(*Ibid.,* p. 247). These propositions have been the subject of severe criticism.

In 1890 he experienced an attack of neuritis and lost the sight of one eye, being threatened for a time with total blindness. Though his vision subsequently improved, he was thereafter compelled to rely in a large measure upon assistance in his judicial work. He resigned from the bench May 28, 1906, on attaining the age of seventy, and lived thenceforth in comparative retirement at Bronxville, N. Y. He was twice married: in 1864 to Caroline Pitts of Detroit, and in 1904 to Mrs. Josephine E. Tyler of Crosswicks, N. J., widow of Lieut. F. H. Tyler, U. S. N. In private life he was somewhat reserved and inclined to formality. "Whether afoot or on horseback he was almost painfully neat in his appearance."

Though a fine classical scholar and great reader, his sole contributions to general literature were a paper on *Judicial Independence,* read before the American Bar Association at Chicago, May 28, 1889, and subsequently published; *A Biographical Sketch of Samuel Tyler* (1909); and an address on Woman Suffrage to the Ladies Congressional Club, Washington (1910).

[Chas. A. Kent, *Memoir of Henry Billings Brown* (1915), contains autobiographical material. An excellent appreciation of his career from the legal standpoint, by Chas. H. Butler, appeared in the *Green Bag,* XVIII, 321. See also *Case and Comment,* II, 79; *Am. Law Rev.,* XXV, 99 and XL, 548; *Green Bag,* I, 207, and III, 91; and the *N. Y. Times,* Sept. 5, 1913.]

H. W. H. K.

BROWN, HENRY CORDIS (Nov. 18, 1820–Mar. 6, 1906), capitalist, was the son of Polly (Newkirk) Brown and Samuel Brown, a New Englander who fought in the battle of Bunker Hill and late in life moved to Ohio. Henry was born near St. Clairsville, Belmont County. The mother died when the boy was two years old; the father five years later. Bound out to work on a farm until he was sixteen, the boy had meager opportunities for an education; such as he had were in the local district school and at Brook's Academy in St. Clairsville. He learned the carpenter's trade and followed it in Wheeling, Va., and after 1844, in St. Louis. In 1852 he yielded to the lure of the West and set out on a journey that took him to the Pacific Coast and around South America. He drove an ox-team to California, but not finding a satisfactory opening went on to Oregon and Washington. For eight months he was interested in a saw-mill on Bellingham Bay. He returned to California and for three years worked as contractor and builder in San Francisco. His restless spirit carried him next to Peru, but after nine months he took passage on a ship bound for the eastern coast of

the United States. In May 1858 he was back in St. Louis. After a few months he went to Sioux City, Iowa, and there joined the Decatur (Nebr.) Town Company. He built a hotel in the new town of Decatur but that venture soon proved a failure. After a few months in St. Joseph, Mo., he again turned his face to the Far West. He arrived in Denver in June 1860, realized the possibilities of this straggling frontier town, and settled there. He followed his trade and invested his money in real estate. The basis of his fortune was laid when he secured by preëmption 160 acres of land on the outskirts of Denver. Within that tract are now located the State Capitol—on a beautiful site donated by Brown for that purpose in 1867—and some of the best business and residence lots in Denver. By 1870 he was one of the wealthiest men in Colorado, and was in position to take an active part in the various business enterprises of a growing city. From 1870 to 1875 he was the owner of the *Denver Tribune;* he was active in the organization of the Denver Pacific Railway, the Denver Tramway Company, and the Bank of Denver. The climax of his business career was reached in the construction in 1889 of the Brown Palace Hotel, which soon became and remains one of the most famous hostelries of the West. Large financial obligations incurred in the building of a hotel that cost more than a million dollars, and the panic of 1893 that followed soon after its completion, seriously impaired Brown's financial power. He was land poor, and became involved in litigation that lasted until his death in San Diego, Cal., in 1906. He was three times married: in 1841 to Anna L. Inskepp at St. Clairsville, Ohio; in 1858 to Jane C. Thompson at Decatur, Nebr.; late in life to Helen Mathews in Denver. He devoted his life to business, but there was something of the dreamer and the poet in his nature; he had a vision of a beautiful city at the gateway to the Rockies, and did much to make that vision a reality.

[J. C. Smiley, *Semi-Centennial Hist. of the State of Colo.* (1913), II, 160–65; obituaries in the *Denver Republican, Rocky Mt. News,* and *Denver Post,* for Mar. 7, 1906.]

C. B. G—z.

BROWN, HENRY KIRKE (Feb. 24, 1814–July 10, 1886), sculptor, was a descendant of Charles Brown, one of the early settlers of Connecticut, and the son of Elijah Brown and Rhoda (Childs) Brown. He was born and brought up on a farm in Leyden, Mass., and received an academic education. Arriving on the New England scene a little after the Concord philosophers, he outlived Emerson, and with a year or two more would have outlived the venerable Alcott also. He himself was accounted a philosopher, in his own vein. When he was about fourteen years old, his artistic imagination was stirred by an itinerant artist who made silhouettes. The boy practised this art by himself until he gained confidence, and then, without seeking paternal consent, started for Albany, paying his way by cutting silhouettes. When almost in sight of the city he was overtaken by his father, with whom he returned to the family fold. One of the neighbors was a blind old man named Parker, who had something of a library. Young Henry, made welcome to its shelves, read Swedenborg aloud to his host, who would sometimes stop him to explain the text. Parker's head was of noble type, and inspired the imaginative lad to attempt a portrait in color. On a canvas prepared from sheeting, with brushes made of hair from the head of an ox, and with colors obtained from a house painter, Henry Brown made a creditable portrait. His parents, recognizing the inevitable, declared that if he must be an artist he should be a good one, and apprenticed him in 1832 to Chester Harding, then the leading portrait painter in Boston. The youth worked diligently, making many friends. In 1836, he went to Cincinnati, planning to establish himself there as a portrait painter. But in Cincinnati he modeled his first head in clay. It was called the best portrait ever modeled in that city, and he became so fascinated with this new mode of plastic endeavor that he turned from paint to clay, choosing definitely a sculptor's career. For him as for previous aspirants, beyond the sea lay Italy. To reach that goal he must earn the necessary money. Fortunately he had the pioneer's gift of a versatile hand, and through Christopher Armes, then state engineer for Illinois, he found work as a surveyor on the state railroads. In this service his target-boy was fifteen-year-old George Fuller, destined to win fame as a painter. Fuller became Brown's pupil in art, and a life-long friendship was begun. Brown's earnings enabled him to study in Cincinnati, where for a brief period he and Shobal Vail Clevenger pursued their chosen art together, each assisting the other, student-fashion, and both profiting by the criticism of a German modeler. In that city, in 1837, the year when Hiram Powers sailed for Italy, Brown produced his first bust in marble, an ideal female head. Returning to the East, he spent a winter in Boston. Among influential New Englanders who gave him encouragement and assistance was Judge James Udall of Hartford, Windsor County, Vt., in whose home the young sculptor was always welcome. In 1839 he married the Judge's daughter, Lydia Louise Udall, and for the next three years the couple re-

sided in Troy and in Albany, Brown meanwhile devoting himself with the utmost diligence to sculpture, until in 1842 he was at last enabled through the help of sympathetic friends to go to Italy. Among many portrait busts made by him during his stay in Albany and its neighborhood are those of Erastus Corning, Silas Dutcher, Eliphalet Nott, William B. Sprague. He is said to have produced at this time no less than forty busts, as well as several figures. Doubtless many of these works showed facility rather than felicity, and seemed "topographical" rather than "artistic," but all in all, they must have proved to Brown's sponsors his ardent determination as well as his considerable manual skill.

His wife accompanied him to Rome, where they made their home. Under Italian skies, the young man's industry was unabated. During his four years' stay, surrounded as he was by classic masterpieces and their imitators, he busily produced for the culture of his countrymen the customary marble statuettes and reliefs. Among his works of this period are his "David," "Rebecca," "Adonis"; also the "Ruth" and the "Boy and Dog" belonging to the New York Historical Society. The work last cited has its "real chain," a prized sculptural adjunct of that day. But Brown was not by nature the typical pseudo-classicist. He was not content with what was then called "the spiritual quality of the pure white marble." He longed to make some more robust expression of his plentiful ideas. Later in his career, he preceded his pupil, John Quincy Adams Ward, in denying the value or necessity of a lengthy sojourn in Italy. On his return to his own country in 1846, he set up a studio in New York City. His first enterprise was characteristic. Breaking away from "real chains" and the like, he produced a bronze group of native inspiration, an "Indian and Panther." "That Mr. Brown installed a miniature foundry in his studio," writes Taft in his *History of American Sculpture*, "and successfully carried into the ultimate metal many small works, speaks volumes for his courage and his ingenuity. It is Mr. Ward's recollection, however, that on account of its size, the group of the 'Indian and Panther' was cast outside, by a Frenchman, but that the finishing was done in the studio." Besides the "Indian and Panther," there was an "Aboriginal Hunter." Even when established in his New York studio, and later in his Brooklyn studio (1850), Brown sometimes refreshed his mind by visits and studies among the Indians, as has often since been done by sculptors weary of academic subject-matter, and interested in primitive man or in animal form. And in animal form, Brown was both interested and competent. His sculpture in this branch compelled the interest of others. In 1851, his election to full membership in the National Academy of Design showed the regard in which his work was held by his fellow-artists; both painters and sculptors appreciated his fine draftsmanship. Among his commissions at this time were a large bas-relief for the Church of the Annunciation in New York City, and many portrait busts of famous men, including those of his warm personal friends, Dr. Willard Parker and William Cullen Bryant.

The commission for what proved to be Brown's highest achievement, the equestrian statue of Washington, had been projected by Greenough, who had planned to execute it in collaboration with Brown, but who later withdrew, leaving the field to his friend (Tuckerman, *Book of the Artists*). The funds for payment came chiefly from a group of New York business men and art patrons, who were to subscribe $500 each. There were delays, changes in contract, withdrawals of contributors. In February 1853, two months after Greenough's death, Brown began the Union Square group. On July 4, 1856, it was unveiled, meeting with applause from artists, critics, and laymen. A still larger appreciation was accorded in after years. In 1856, naturally enough, most Americans knew little about those two equestrian masterpieces of the Italian Renaissance, Donatello's "Gattamelata" in Padua, Verrocchio's "Colleoni" in Venice. Had the writers of Brown's day been familiar with those groups, they would have noted that the American's work is founded on the same principles of art that sustain the two others. It achieves nobility through poise rather than pose, through unity of action in horse and rider, through an adequate feeling for drama, through a wise interpretation of heroic human character, and through an unemphatic, harmonious modeling of form. The very absence of purple passages in the group gives it longer life. Washington is shown in an attitude of native majesty, his arm uplifted in the act of recalling his troops. Simplicity rules both the bronze and its pedestal. A replica of this work has been erected at West Point, in beautiful surroundings.

Brown produced three equestrian statues, the second less good than the first, the third less good than the second. Yet the second, a group cast from cannon captured in the Mexican War, and portraying Gen. Winfield Scott, soldier in three wars, has much to admire in its adequate composition and its fine four-square dignity of man and horse. Unveiled in Washington in 1874, it is perhaps the most generally popular of all Brown's sculptures. His third equestrian monument, erected in the same city three years afterward, in long-delayed pursuance of a vote of the Continental Congress thus to honor Gen. Nathanael Greene, falls far short of the artist's attainment in 1856. Its conscientious modeling does not inspire emotion, and its overdone naturalism in the type and action of the horse and in the pose of the rider lets it down into the purlieus of the commonplace,—a commonplace just touched with eccentricity. In 1858 the state of South Carolina commissioned Brown to make a large pedimental group for the new state house in Columbia (Tuckerman, *Book of the Artists*). A colossal central figure of "South Carolina" was to be flanked by "Justice" and "Liberty"; the industries were to be celebrated by sculptured forms of workers in rice and cotton fields. The "South Carolina" was far advanced when the Civil War put a stop to the whole work. When Sherman's soldiers passed through Columbia in 1865, they destroyed this figure, because they regarded it as a typical statue of Secession. Brown made a host of friends in the South; in vain they urged him to cast in his lot with theirs. Stanch to the Union, he was an officer in the United States Sanitary Commission. During 1859 and 1860, he served on an art commission appointed by Buchanan, and submitted a report designed to spread correct ideas on art among senators and congressmen. From 1861 until his death in 1886, he lived and worked in Newburgh, N. Y. Here he executed four figures destined for Statuary Hall, in the Capitol at Washington,—Gen. Nathanael Greene, marble (1869), Gov. George Clinton, bronze (1873), Brigadier-General Philip Kearny, bronze (1875), and Richard Stockton, marble (1886). From the Newburgh studio came other works, including the equestrian groups, Scott and Greene, already mentioned; an "Angel of the Resurrection," Greenwood Cemetery (1877); and the bronze statue of Lincoln, erected in Union Square in 1868, by popular subscription under the auspices of the Union League Club.

Brown's influence on his pupils was valuable and enduring. At one time they had the privilege of an evening drawing-class, in which master and students worked together from the living model; his kindness in such matters was long remembered. Ward, his most famous apprentice, spoke often of his goodness, and described him as a tall, bearded, fine-looking man, of genially philosophic speech. Among his later assistants was his nephew, Henry K. Bush-Brown.

A lover and knower of horses, a student of the processes of bronze casting, he was the first American to disclose the possibilities of dignity and power in the monumental bronze equestrian statue. His talent was frequently defeated by its own versatility. Moreover, that very quality of unemphatic balance which had helped to make his equestrian statue of Washington a work of high rank led him at times into a commonplace pedestrian interpretation of great themes. He was the first of our sculptors to make any serious attempt to shake off the "real chains" of the contemporary Italianate pseudo-classicism, but he came too early to profit by the vigorous new naturalism taught in the French schools.

[Lorado Taft, *Hist. of Am. Sculpture* (1903); Henry T. Tuckerman, *Book of the Artists* (1867); Monograph by Jas. Lee, *The Equestrian Statue of Washington in Union Square* (1864); C. E. Clement and L. Hutton, *Artists of the Nineteenth Century* (1879); S. G. W. Benjamin, *Art in America* (1879); A. G. Radcliffe, *Schools and Masters of Sculpture* (1902); Chas. H. Caffin, *Am. Masters of Sculpture* (1903); Adeline Adams, *John Quincy Adams Ward, an Appreciation* (National Sculpture Society, 1912). Fremont Rider's *Washington* (1922) gives information as to Brown's sculpture in that city, and Charles Edwin Fairman's *Art and Artists of the Capitol of the United States of America* (1927) includes a sketch of Brown, with mention of his chief works.]   A. A—s.

BROWN, ISAAC VAN ARSDALE (Nov. 4, 1784–Apr. 19, 1861), Presbyterian clergyman, founder of Lawrenceville School, was born at Pluckemin, Somerset County, N. J. The son of Abraham R. and Margaret Brown, he was of Huguenot descent. He took his degree at Princeton in 1802, and was tutor there during the year 1805–06. In the meantime he had studied theology under Dr. John Woodhull of Freehold, N. J., and was licensed and ordained by the New Brunswick Presbytery in 1807. He was given the pastorate of the church at Lawrenceville, known until 1816 as Maidenhead. He married in 1807 Mary Wright Houston of Philadelphia. Three years later he established Lawrenceville Classical and Commercial School, first called the Maidenhead Academy. He was its principal until 1833. For eleven years he continued as pastor of the church in Lawrenceville and during the remainder of the period of his residence here was carried on the minutes of the Presbyterian Church as minister of that denomination. In 1842 he moved to Mount Holly, N. J., where he was instrumental in organizing a Presbyterian church. He also preached occasionally at Plattsburg, N. J., and organized a church there. Various records report him as living at Trenton, Somerville, Bordentown and New Brunswick, N. J., for the remaining years of his life, in all of which places he preached at various times. He was one of the founders of the American Colonization Society and also one of the original members of the American Bible Society. It was

said of him that he was a man of "rare talents and learning, enterprising and public spirited, a warm friend, a liberal and zealous supporter and defender of what he felt was the right." He was a trustee of Princeton College from 1816 and of Princeton Seminary from 1822 until his death. Lafayette College conferred the degree of D.D. on him in 1858. After he left Lawrenceville he devoted some time to literary work, and published a *Historical Vindication of the Abrogation of the Plan of Union by the Presbyterian Church* (1855); and *Slavery Irreconcilable with Christianity and Sound Reason; or, An Anti-Slavery Agreement* (1858; republished in 1860 under the name of *White Diamonds Better than "Black Diamonds"; Slave States Impoverished by Slave Labor*). A *Sermon on the Work of the Holy Spirit delivered before the Synod of New Jersey* had been published in 1837. The *Memories of Robert Finley* (1819) were written during the period of his pastorate and the early years of the School in Lawrenceville. Finley, who seems to have been much the same type of man, interested in the same movements, made a great appeal to Brown, who says of the book in the preface that "the memorial . . . is an act not less of justice than of kindness to ourselves."

[*Princeton Gen. Cat., 1746–1906* (1908); E. M. Woodward and J. F. Hageman, *Hist. of Burlington and Mercer Counties, N. J.* (1883); F. B. Lee, *Geneal. and Personal Memorial of Mercer County* (1907); *Encyc. of the Presbyt. Ch. in the U. S. A.* (1884), ed. by Alfred Nevin; *Minutes of the Gen. Assembly of the Presbyt. Ch. in the U. S. A.,* 1809–1861. A letter from R. J. Mulford, Princeton, N. J., gives Jan. 14, 1782, as the date of Brown's birth, quoting his great-great-grand-daughter who gives as her authority "a pencilled note and a newspaper clipping found in my Father's desk" which agrees with the date "sent to the Sons of the American Revolution by some member of the family." The tombstone and the Trenton Vital Statistics give his age as 77 in 1861.]   M. A. K.

BROWN, JACOB JENNINGS (May 9, 1775– Feb. 24, 1828), soldier, was born in Bucks County, Pa., the son of Samuel Brown and his wife, Abi White. His ancestors were among the earliest settlers in the colony, and Quakers all. His father, originally a prosperous farmer, was ruined by the failure of commercial ventures, and at the age of eighteen the son found himself thrown on the world to earn his own living. He taught school in New Jersey for some three years, and then spent two years in surveying near Cincinnati. Returning east in 1798 he again taught for a few months in New York City, also writing political articles for the newspapers. His stay in New York was short, however, for his residence in Ohio had impressed him with the possibilities of enterprise in a new country. By 1799 he had arranged the purchase of several thousand acres of wilderness on the shore of Lake Ontario, and to this place he removed, founding the village of Brownville, near Watertown. Successful in farming and land operations, he soon found himself in comfortable circumstances. In 1802 he married Pamelia Williams. In 1809 he received the command of a militia regiment. His military knowledge at this time was practically nil, but his energy made amends for many deficiencies. In 1811 he was appointed brigadier-general of militia. At the outbreak of the War of 1812, he was put in command of a section of the frontier, and was present at a skirmish at Ogdensburg. During the winter and spring, Chauncey, the American naval commander, made strenuous preparations to gain control of Lake Ontario, to frustrate which the British moved against Sackett's Harbor, the American base. Called upon to take charge of the defense, Brown found a force of 400 regulars and 500 militia to meet the attack, which was made on May 29, 1813. The British force was slightly inferior in numbers, but superior in quality, being mostly regulars. With thoughts, perhaps, of Guilford and Cowpens, Brown placed his militia in front, expecting them to break but to inflict some damage first. They scattered unexpectedly early, but the British then found themselves facing the unshaken regulars of the second line, who checked the advance with heavy loss. Meanwhile Brown in person rallied part of the militia and harassed the enemy's flank, until the British withdrew to their ships. The successful defense of this important post caused Brown's appointment, on July 19, 1813, as a brigadier-general in the army. He participated in the miserable fiasco of Gen. Wilkinson's expedition directed against Montreal in November, but his own reputation was unimpaired. On Jan. 24, 1814, he was appointed major-general, and assumed command in western New York, with two able brigadiers, Scott and Ripley, under him. "The major-general, though full of zeal and vigor, was not a technical soldier: that is, knew little of organization, tactics, police, etc." (Winfield Scott, *Memoirs*, 1864, I, 118). But he was a natural leader of men and a determined fighter, while Scott, who possessed all the technical knowledge which Brown lacked, was placed in immediate charge of the training of the troops, —still raw and undisciplined, though regulars in name. The American plan of campaign contemplated an advance of Brown's army across the Niagara River and around the end of Lake Ontario against York (Toronto), to be made in conjunction with Chauncey's flotilla. The crossing was made on the night of July 2–3, and Fort

Erie, at the southern end of the river, surrendered at once. Moving northward on the Canadian side, toward the Chippewa River, Scott's brigade was attacked, late in the afternoon of July 4, by a somewhat superior force, and a sharp battle ensued. The remainder of the American army was brought up, but before it was seriously engaged Scott delivered an attack which drove the British from the field. Advancing north toward Lake Ontario, Brown discovered that Chauncey had not left Sackett's Harbor, and that no naval coöperation could be expected. There was now no hope of a successful issue to the campaign. Brown remained on Canadian soil, however, and on July 25 fought the fierce battle of Niagara, or Lundy's Lane. Again Scott's brigade first made contact with the enemy, but this time the other regular brigade (Ripley's) and the militia were in line early in the fight. The British position was carried by assault, and their guns taken, but it was found impossible to carry them off. Brown himself was severely wounded. Though able to claim a tactical victory, the Americans could not continue the campaign, and the next day fell back to Fort Erie. To this day, though the contending forces numbered less than three thousand men each, Niagara is one of the famous battles of our army. During this same summer the militia at Bladensburg dissolved into thin air after a loss of one-half of one per cent, while the regulars, led by Brown and disciplined by Scott, sustained at Lundy's Lane a loss of one-third their number, with organization and morale unimpaired. The British assaulted Fort Erie on Aug. 15, and were repulsed with great loss, while the defenders suffered little. Siege operations continued for a month, and then, on Sept. 17, Brown made a sortie, disabling guns and inflicting other destruction which compelled the British to raise the siege. This ended the campaign, and so far as the northern border was concerned, the war also. Of Brown's operations Admiral Mahan says: "Barring the single episode of the battle of New Orleans, his career on the Niagara peninsula is the one operation of the land war of 1812 upon which thoughtful and understanding Americans of the following generation could look back with satisfaction" (*Sea-Power in its Relations to the War of 1812*, 1905, II, 317–18). In 1815 Brown became the senior officer in service, and in 1821 was regularly assigned to the command of the United States Army, which he retained until his death.

[Brief accounts of Brown are in John S. Jenkins, *Generals of the Last War with Gt. Brit.* (1849), pp. 13–60, and Chas. J. Peterson, *Mil. Heroes of the War of 1812* (1848), pp. 141–58. See also W. H. H. Davis,

"Five Bucks County Generals," and Elizabeth Wager-Smith, "Jacob Jennings Brown, the 'Fighting Quaker' of Bucks County," in *A Collection of Papers read before the Bucks County Hist. Soc.*, vol. III (1909). For Brown's military career, consult the standard works on the War of 1812. A. T. Mahan's work cited above has an exceptionally clear account of the land campaigns. B. J. Lossing, *Pictorial Field Book of the War of 1812* (1869) is full of detail. See also Henry Adams, *Hist. of the U. S.* (1891), vols. VII, VIII. For detailed study, Ernest A. Cruikshank, *Doc. Hist. of the Campaigns on the Niagara Frontier* (1896).]   T. M. S.

BROWN, JAMES (Sept. 11, 1766–Apr. 7, 1835), senator, diplomat, was born near Staunton, Va., the son of John and Margaret (Preston) Brown and brother of John [1757–1837, *q.v.*], Samuel [*q.v.*], and Preston W. Brown. He attended an academy at Lexington, Va., which later developed into Washington College (now Washington and Lee University), and available evidence seems to warrant the conclusion that he attended and graduated from William and Mary College. He later studied law, was admitted to the bar, and began practise in Kentucky. In 1789 he settled in Lexington, Ky., and two years later commanded a company of Lexington riflemen in a war against the Northwest Indians. While living at Lexington he married a Miss Hart, sister of Mrs. Henry Clay and daughter of Col. Thomas Hart. With the formation of a state government and the admission of Kentucky to the Union, in 1792, he became secretary of state under Gov. Shelby, which necessitated his removal to Frankfort, the capital. Soon after the purchase of Louisiana, Brown settled in New Orleans, and during his residence in the Southwest accumulated a comfortable fortune in the practise of his profession. He was appointed secretary of the Territory of Orleans, Oct. 1, 1804, and subsequently became district attorney. The Legislative Council of the Territory at its first session passed an act, approved Apr. 19, 1805, for the establishment of a university, and James Brown was named one of its regents. This institution did not materialize. In 1806 he and Moreau Lislet were appointed a commission to prepare a civil code for the use of the Territory. Their work, entitled, *A Digest of the Civil Laws Now in Force in the Territory of Orleans with Alterations and Amendments Adapted to the Present System of Government*, published in both English and French, was adopted in 1808, and became known as the code of that year. It required amendment after a few years, and was replaced by the Livingston code. Brown was a member of the convention which framed the first constitution of Louisiana, in 1812, and the next year was elected to the United States Senate to fill a vacancy caused by the resignation of J. N. Detrehan. He served from

Feb. 5, 1813, to Mar. 3, 1817. He was defeated for reëlection, but with the death of his successor, W. C. C. Claiborne, he was again elected to the United States Senate, and served from Dec. 6, 1819, until his resignation, Dec. 10, 1823, to accept an appointment from President Monroe as minister to France. Here he succeeded Albert Gallatin, and remained through the remainder of Monroe's second term and through the administration of John Quincy Adams. He died of apoplexy at Philadelphia. John Quincy Adams described him as "a man of large fortune, respectable talents, handsome person, polished manners, and elegant deportment."

[Chief sources are the *Annals of Cong.*, and the *Memoirs of John Quincy Adams* (12 vols., 1874–77), ed. by C. F. Adams. The *Official Letter Books of W. C. C. Claiborne, 1801–16* (6 vols., 1917), ed. by Dunbar Rowland, have been found useful, and the alumni records of Washington and Lee Univ. have supplied a few facts. See also *The Works of Henry Clay* (6 vols., 1855–57), ed. by Calvin Colton; F. X. Martin, *Hist. of La.* (1882); A. Fortier, *Hist. of La.* (4 vols., 1904); C. Gayarré, *Hist. of La.* (3rd ed., 4 vols., 1885); R. H. and L. Collins, *Hist. of Ky.* (1874), vol. II; and G. W. Ranck, *Hist. of Lexington, Ky.* (1872). Obituary notices are published in *Niles' Weekly Reg.*, Apr. 11, 1835, and in the *Bee* (New Orleans), Apr. 28, 1835.]
M. J. W.

BROWN, JAMES (Feb. 4, 1791–Nov. 1, 1877), banker, was the youngest of the four sons of Alexander Brown [*q.v.*] and Grace (Davison) Brown. He came to America in 1802, with his brothers George and John [*qq.v.*] "They landed on a hot Sunday morning in July, dressed in thick woolen Irish suits and heavy plaid stockings and they created quite a sensation among the good people of Baltimore, quietly wending their way to church. Thither their mother took them, with a heart thankful for their safe arrival, after she had borrowed from her neighbors thinner clothing better suited to the American climate" (John Crosby Brown, *A Hundred Years of Merchant Banking*, 1909, p. 9).

Like his brothers, James Brown became a member of the firm of Alexander Brown & Sons. In 1825 Alexander Brown began to feel that the time had come to establish a branch in New York. This was the year the Erie Canal was opened for service. James Brown was sent up to begin business under the firm name of Brown Brothers & Company. The Boston branch grew out of the New York branch, and was given the same name. James Brown made his firm one of the most influential houses in the country. Its business, like the business of the other Brown firms in London, Philadelphia, Boston, and Baltimore, grew to such proportions that eventually it became wise to break the ties and let it stand alone. Inheriting his father's rare business ability, as, indeed, had his brothers, he guided the New York house through many financial crises, notably those of 1837 and 1857, and the critical period of the Civil War. James Brown was the most influential member of the family during that struggle, and spent much of his time in Europe during 1861, in close touch with the American minister in Paris, W. L. Dayton. His many letters on the subject of the war, not only to his elder brother, William, but to the other partners on both sides of the ocean, helped the Brown firms to ride the storm safely.

He was a member of the chamber of commerce of New York State in 1827, and was active in its affairs until his death a half century later. He was one of the earliest trustees of the New York Life Insurance Company; was trustee for the Bank for Savings, and was connected with several railroad companies. Like his brothers, interested in local philanthropies, he was one of the founders of the Association for Improving the Condition of the Poor; among the founders of the Presbyterian Hospital; president of the board of trustees of the New York Orthopedic Dispensary and Hospital; and, from its beginning, a trustee of Union College. He was made a director of Union Theological Seminary, and many churches were beneficiaries of his liberal contributions to religious work. He was married twice: in 1817 to Louisa Kirkland Benedict, and in 1831 to Eliza Maria Coe. At his death the mayor of New York ordered all flags on public buildings to be placed at half-mast.

[Old letter books preserved in the vaults of Alexander Brown & Sons in Baltimore, pamphlets and booklets issued by the Brown houses; Mary E. Brown, *Alexander Brown and his Descendants* (1917); Frank R. Kent, *The Story of Alexander Brown and Sons* (1925).]   F. R. K.

BROWN, JAMES (May 19, 1800–Mar. 10, 1855), publisher, bookseller, was born at Acton, Mass., the eleventh of thirteen children of Capt. Joseph Brown, a Revolutionary veteran. The mother, Abigail Putnam, a second wife, was a woman of excellent understanding who encouraged this willing son to make good use of such schooling and books as a country town afforded. In 1815 he became a servant of Levi Hedge, professor at Harvard College, who gave him some instruction and directed his avid reading. It was a natural step when in 1818 he entered the employment of William Hilliard, publisher and bookseller at Cambridge. After several upward movements, in 1837 Brown formed a copartnership with Charles C. Little, which later became Little, Brown & Company. They dealt in standard books, especially law and importations.

Among their publications were works by Bancroft, Bowditch, Child, Dana, Greenleaf, Lieber, Parkman, Prescott, Sparks, Story, the *United States Digest* and *United States Statutes at Large,* the collected works of John Adams and Webster, a law review, and reprints of famous English authors. Brown's special charge was the importations. He went abroad five times (1842–53) to make personal selections, becoming acquainted with John Murray, Pickering, Rodd, the Didots, Tauchnitz, and other great publishers and booksellers. The catalogues of the firm show the high quality of his choosing. That of 1846 states that the "editions are generally those best fitted for Libraries, printed in large types and substantially bound—avoiding in these respects, the extremes of cheapness and extravagance." There were imprints as early as 1657, and specially-bound books are also listed "in morocco by Hayday." The 1854 catalogue gives 826 titles in foreign languages. This activity established Brown not only as a tradesman, but as a bibliophile; his store became the gathering place of those who made the Boston of that period a literary center. In the collecting of his own large private library his tastes were catholic, but his greatest interest was in Burnsiana and ornithology. He was a patron of the Boston Athenæum, and the Natural History Society, a member of the Agricultural Society, and he bequeathed $5,000 to the Harvard College Library.

Brown was twice married: first in May 1825, to Mary Anne Perry, who died in October 1844, and then to Mary Derby Hobbs in April 1846. His business brought him wealth, and in his later years he developed a country estate at Watertown, where he dispensed "becoming hospitality." Brown is described as of "vigorous tread, erect bearing and ample presence," dignified, of perfect good temper, cheery, fond, when young, of practical jokes, and "remarkable for his insatiable love of knowledge."

[See G. S. Hillard, *A Memoir of Jas. Brown* (1856); Edwin M. Bacon, sketch in *Bookman,* V, 373. The catalogues of Little, Brown & Co., are the best source on his business career.]   D. M. M.

BROWN, JAMES SALISBURY (Dec. 23, 1802–Dec. 29, 1879), inventor, manufacturer, was the only son of Sylvanus [*q.v.*] and Ruth (Salisbury) Brown, of Pawtucket, R. I. His youth was spent in an industrious home environment, as evidenced by the fact that when he was fifteen he had not only finished the school curriculum but also had partially completed his apprenticeship of pattern-making under the instruction of his father. This he accomplished in spite of the fact that he had the use of but one eye, the other having been almost totally destroyed in an accident when he was six years old. In 1817 Brown began work at his trade in the cotton-machinery manufactory of David Wilkinson at Pawtucket and remained there for two years, leaving to go to work in the plant of Pitcher & Gay, another firm of cotton-machinery manufacturers. Within a year, when eighteen, he patented an improvement for the slide rest invented by his father, which permitted the height of the tool to be adjusted while the lathe was in motion. Four years later upon the retirement of Gay from the firm, Brown was taken into partnership and as Pitcher & Brown they continued in business until 1842 when Pitcher retired and Brown continued alone until his son was old enough to join him. Pitcher & Brown had a successful and constantly growing business which did not, however, prevent Brown from pursuing his inventive bent. Thus in 1830 he devised another useful tool—a cutter for cutting bevel gears. Its feature was that it required no change of the head stock to make the proper taper in going once around the wheel. Again in 1838 he patented a specialized drilling machine, and in 1842 devised a number of improvements on the Blanchard lathe for turning irregular forms. Shortly after gaining control of the business in 1842, Brown planned and built an entirely new establishment, the first unit of which, the foundry, was completed in 1847. Two years later the main machine shop was erected, being 400 by 60 feet in size, and in 1859 a pattern house was added. To man the plant fully required three hundred men and it was recognized in 1860 as one of the largest and most complete establishments of its kind in the United States. An interesting fact in connection with the construction of his mill and indicative of Brown's thoroughness is that, not finding the proper quality of bricks suited to his purpose, he bought an island in the Pawtucket River having a fine bed of clay, erected a plant, and made his own bricks. The two outstanding contributions which Brown made to the textile industry were his adaptation to American practise of the Sharpe and Roberts self-acting mule, originally imported from England in 1840, and his improvements of the American long-flyer roving machine, both cotton-manufacturing machines. To supply the demand for these taxed to the limit the capacity of his new plant, and, in fact, after he had devised and patented his speeder in January 1857, and it went into production, he was compelled to abandon for a time the building of mules. Practically all of the tools used in the construction of these machines

were devised by Brown and many were in use years after his death. Thus he changed the planing machine for fluting rolls, increasing its capacity four-fold, and patented a grinding machine for the making of spindles. Upon the outbreak of the Civil War Brown turned his whole plant over to the manufacture of guns and gun-making machinery, using particularly to turn gun barrels his improved lathe, originally designed for the turning of rolls for cotton machinery. His later inventions included a machine for grinding file blanks, a tempering furnace for files, and finally an improved spinning mule, patented on Mar. 7, 1876. About five years before his death Brown became nearly blind, but otherwise enjoyed to the very end the most robust health. His business relations were of the best, and he had the reputation of making every sacrifice to produce the best tools and machines. In 1829 Brown was married to Sarah Phillips Gridley. By her he had two daughters and one son, James, who inherited and carried on the Brown Machine Works.

[J. Leander Bishop, *Hist. of Am. Manufactures from 1608 to 1860*, vol. III (1866); J. W. Roe, *Eng. and Am. Tool Builders* (1916, new ed. 1926); R. M. Bayles, *Hist. of Providence County, R.I.* (1891), vol. II; Robt. Grieve, *An Illustrated Hist. of Pawtucket, Central Falls and Vicinity* (1897); Massena Goodrich, *Hist. Sketch of the Town of Pawtucket, R. I.* (1876).]

C. W. M.

BROWN, JOHN (Jan. 27, 1736–Sept. 20, 1803), son of James and Hope (Power) Brown, was the third of the four brothers (Nicholas [*q.v.*], Joseph [*q.v.*], John, and Moses [*q.v.*]) who formed the mercantile house of Nicholas Brown & Company of Providence. About the year 1770, John, who has been described as "a man of magnificent projects and extraordinary enterprises," withdrew from the firm headed by the more conservative Nicholas and set up business on his own account. His service to the American cause in the Revolution was begun spectacularly enough by his leadership in 1772 of the party that boarded and burned the British armed schooner *Gaspee* as she lay aground in Narragansett Bay. A reward of £1,000 was offered for proof of the identity of the leader of the expedition, and John Brown was arrested on suspicion. He was released from imprisonment and saved from the more unpleasant consequences of his action by the influence of Moses Brown, who, though the youngest of the brothers, seems to have been their helper in all times of serious trouble. Afterward John Brown and his brother Nicholas served the cause by supplying the continental troops with clothing and munitions of war. The records of their dealings with a secret committee of the Continental

Congress show that their ships and their foreign connections were put to good service in the American cause. He was interested in the development of the "Furnace Hope" and during the Revolution made it the chief business of the furnace to manufacture cannon for the army and navy. In his public life, John Brown seems to have supported the American contentions from the beginning. He was active in the Assembly of his state in opposition to the Stamp Act, in support of the non-importation proceedings in 1769 and 1775, and in all crises throughout the Revolutionary period that called for determination and ability. His vigorous efforts in behalf of the adoption of the Constitution were instrumental in bringing Rhode Island into accord with the other federated states. He was elected to Congress twice, in 1784 and 1785, but failed to put in an appearance at either session. He served one term in Congress, however, from 1799 to 1801. In 1787 the firm of Brown & Francis, composed of John Brown and his son-in-law John Francis (husband of Abby Brown), sent out the first Providence vessel to engage in the East India and China trade, only three or four years after this trade had been begun by a shipmaster of Salem, Mass. In December of that year the *General Washington* cleared for the East, carrying a cargo valued at $26,348, composed of anchors, cordage, sail cloth, cannon, bar iron, sheet copper, steel, spars, liquors, cheese, and spermaceti candles. A year and a half later she returned to Providence, loaded with tea, silks, china, cotton goods, lacquered ware, and cloves to the amount of $99,848. This was the auspicious beginning of a trade that continued to bring fortune to Rhode Island for more than half a century.

With his brothers, John Brown was forward in the movement to bring Rhode Island College to Providence from its first location at Warren. It was his hand that laid in 1770 the corner-stone of the first building, the present University Hall of Brown University, and his care as treasurer of the institution during twenty uneasy years helped to establish it on an enduring financial basis. The house he built on Power St. in 1787, probably designed by his brother Joseph, was said in 1800 to be the finest residence in New England, and it remains to-day one of the most strikingly beautiful examples of eighteenth-century architecture in the country. Modern historians have not always approved the character and actions of John Brown. When Congress provided for the building of two ships of war in Rhode Island, he was named one of the committee to oversee the work. It is said that in

this capacity he permitted work on the vessels to be held up so that his own privateersmen might earlier be fitted for the sea, and that in other particulars he allowed self-interest to guide his actions to a degree disapproved of by his fellow-townsmen. There seems to be evidence that he rode the wave of patriotic fervor to his own advantage, but even those who criticize specific actions concede him a life of courageous and vigorous commercial activity which brought wealth and prestige to his community. He was the Elizabethan merchant-adventurer type in a new setting. Of his appearance, it is on record that he was a man of such "large physical proportions" as to take up a whole chaise seat ordinarily occupied by two persons. He married, Nov. 27, 1760, Sarah, daughter of Daniel and Dorcas (Harris) Smith, by whom he had six children.

[For bibliography see list following the sketch of Nicholas Brown (1729–91), and also *State of R.I. and Providence Plantations at the End of the Century: A Hist.* (1902), ed. by Edward Field; Wm. B. Weeden, "Early Oriental Commerce in Providence," *Proc. Mass. Hist. Soc.*, Dec. 1907.]   L. C. W.

BROWN, JOHN (Oct. 19, 1744–Oct. 19, 1780), Revolutionary soldier, was born in Haverhill and grew up in Sandisfield, Mass., where his parents, Daniel and Mehitabel (Sanford) Brown, settled about 1752. He graduated from Yale in 1771, studied law in Providence with his brother-in-law, Oliver Arnold, and in December 1772 was admitted to the bar in Tryon County, N. Y. (Archibald M. Howe, *Col. John Brown of Pittsfield,* 1908, p. 2). He began to practise in Johnstown, N. Y., where he is said to have held the post of king's attorney, but in 1773 removed to Pittsfield, Mass. Here he served on the town's Committee of Correspondence (appointed June 30, 1774), and on the committee which drafted the non-intercourse resolutions adopted by the Berkshire convention at Stockbridge on July 6, 1774. After the suppression of the county courts he was a member of the board of arbitrators appointed to settle civil disputes, and he represented his town in the Provincial Congress from October 1774 to February 1775. In the latter month he volunteered to go to Montreal as agent for the Boston Committee of Correspondence, and set out, charged with the double task of discovering Canadian sentiment toward the revolutionary cause, and of "establishing a reliable channel of correspondence" with the sympathetic element. On Mar. 29, his mission accomplished, he reported to Adams and Warren from Montreal. In crossing the New Hampshire Grants he had been impressed by the strategic importance of Fort Ticonderoga, which, he wrote, "must be seized as soon as possible, should hostilities be committed by the king's troops"; he added that the people of the New Hampshire Grants were ready for "the job" (letter to Adams and Warren, published in L. E. Chittenden, *The Capture of Ticonderoga*, 1872, App.). On May 10, Brown and a little group of Pittsfield men were present with the Connecticut forces when Ticonderoga was taken, and Brown was detailed to carry the news to the Continental Congress (see *Pennsylvania Packet*, May 22, 1775).

He was commissioned major in Easton's regiment on July 6, 1775, and from July 24 to Aug. 10 scouted into Canada, reporting to Schuyler at Crown Point and by letter to Gov. Trumbull of Connecticut (*American Archives*, 4 ser., III, 135). In command for a time of the flotilla on Lake Champlain and discovering that the enemy were preparing gunboats, he counseled immediate advance, volunteering to lead (*Ibid.*, p. 468), and on Sept. 15 commanded the detachment of 134 men which initiated the invasion of Canada. The next week, away from headquarters enlisting recruits, he encountered Ethan Allen on the same business, at Longueuil. Brown had 200 men, Allen had eighty, so they decided to capture Montreal. The attack failed and Allen was taken prisoner (*A Narrative of Col. Ethan Allen's Captivity*, 1807, pp. 28 ff.). On the night of Oct. 19 Brown and James Livingston [*q.v.*], in command of fifty New Englanders and 300 Canadian boatmen, floated guns on bateaux down the rapids of the Sorel (Richelieu), and surprised and captured Fort Chambly with six tons of the powder which the Continentals sorely needed. After the fall of St. Johns (Nov. 3), Brown and Easton started down the Sorel, driving before them Allen Maclean and his irregulars. At the mouth of the stream they stopped to complete fortifications begun by Maclean and there on Nov. 19 by audacity as much as by force they intimidated the British fleet coming down the river from Montreal, and caused it to surrender (see *The Journal of Charles Carroll of Carrollton During His Visit to Canada in 1776*, 1876, p. 97). Before Quebec, in December, Brown was involved in a bit of insubordination due to distrust of Benedict Arnold, but was won back to duty by Montgomery (*American Archives*, 4 ser., IV, 464). After the latter's death Brown claimed a promotion which Arnold refused, charging Brown with plundering the baggage of the officers captured at Sorel (*Ibid.*, p. 907). The quarrel thus precipitated lasted for months, during which, his attempts to obtain a court of inquiry repeatedly thwarted, Brown began to make charges against the character and conduct of Arnold (*Ibid.*, 5 ser., II, 143) and finally resigned his commission in February 1777. (He had been commissioned lieutenant-colonel in Elmore's Connecticut Regiment on July 29, 1776). Returning to Pittsfield, he published there on Apr. 12 a handbill appealing to the public and vigorously attacking his enemy. (There seems, however, to be little evidence to support the story told by W. L. Stone in his *Life of Joseph Brant*, 1838, II, 116 ff., that in 1776–77 Brown published an attack on Arnold predicting Arnold's treason.)

Elected colonel of the middle regiment of Berkshire militia, Brown was called into the field at the time of Burgoyne's advance in the autumn of 1777. Leading a picked detachment of light troops from Pawlet (Oct. 13–18), he captured Fort George, destroyed the British stores there, and, surprising the enemy's outworks along the Lake, took 293 prisoners but was without sufficient strength to take Ticonderoga. Returning to Pittsfield, he resumed his law practise, in 1778 was elected to the General Court, and in February 1779 was commissioned judge of the county court of common pleas. In the summer of 1780 he entered the field once more, with the Massachusetts levies summoned to oppose Brant and Sir John Johnson in the Mohawk Valley. On the morning of Oct. 19, leaving Fort Paris with 300 men to join Gen. Van Rensselaer, he was drawn into an ambuscade near Stone Arabia, N. Y., and killed. Some time after his death, his widow, Huldah Kilbourne, married Jared Ingersoll of Pittsfield.

[F. B. Dexter, *Biog. Sketches Grads. Yale Coll.*, vol. III (1903) lists other sources and mentions literary and legendary references to Brown. J. E. A. Smith, *Hist. of Pittsfield (Berkshire County), Mass.*, vol. I (1869) follows most of his career and gives the best account of the quarrel with Arnold. Justin H. Smith, *Our Struggle for the Fourteenth Colony* (1907) covers the Canadian episodes. The two last-named works contain footnote references to sources, for which see also *Am. Arch.*, 4 and 5 ser., and *The Jours. of Each Provincial Cong. of Mass. . . . with the Proc. of the County Conventions, etc.* (1838). Brown's mother's name is given on p. 237, vol. II, of "Pittsfield Families," MS. in possession of New Eng. Hist. and Geneal. Soc.]

E. R. D.

BROWN, JOHN (Sept. 12, 1757–Aug. 28, 1837), senator, Kentucky legislator, came of distinguished ancestry. His father, having the same name, was for almost half a century a Presbyterian minister in Rockbridge County, Va., and his mother, Margaret, was a daughter of John Preston, a connection which related him to the Clays and Breckinridges. He was born in Staunton, Va., one of four brothers (John, James [1766–1835, *q.v.*], Samuel [*q.v.*], and Preston

W.). He entered Princeton College and being there when the Americans retreated through New Jersey, he joined Washington's forces and later became one of the Rockbridge soldiers under Lafayette. After his military career he continued his education at William and Mary College and then studied law under the supervision of Thomas Jefferson. In 1782 he moved to Kentucky, and settled first at Danville, the political center at that time, but soon removed to Frankfort where he lived thereafter. He readily adapted himself to the Western country and soon became its most outstanding supporter and spokesman. He promoted the material growth of Frankfort and was responsible for securing the machinery for the Kentucky Manufacturing Society which was organized in Danville in 1789 for the manufacture of cotton goods.

He was one of the principal leaders in Kentucky's tortuous course toward statehood, assuming at times an attitude toward the Union which brought against him charges of plotting with the Spaniards for the independence of Kentucky. In 1787 he had conversations with Don Gardoqui, the Spanish minister, which led him to advocate the immediate separation of Kentucky from Virginia and the nation, for the purpose of taking advantage of Spain's offer of the free navigation of the Mississippi River. He represented Kentucky in the Virginia legislature in 1787, and as a means of pacifying Kentucky that body appointed him a representative in the Confederation Congress. He returned to Kentucky in 1788 and was immediately elected a delegate to the Kentucky constitutional convention of that year. Soon afterward he was elected one of Kentucky's delegates to the Virginia convention called to consider the new Federal Constitution, where he voted against its ratification. In 1789 upon the establishment of the new government, he represented the Kentucky district of Virginia in Congress and was reëlected for a second term, but on the entry of Kentucky into the Union as a state in 1792 he became a United States senator and continued in that position until 1805. In 1803–04 he was president *pro tempore* of the Senate. When Aaron Burr came west on his mysterious journeys he stayed in the home of Brown at Frankfort. Though he was thus friendly with Burr, Brown was a constant supporter of Jefferson and had stood for his election to the presidency in 1800–01. He was widely acquainted and was on intimate terms of friendship with the first five presidents of the United States, though he never accepted proffered favors from any of them. In 1799 he married Margaretta, a daughter of John Mason of New York who was Lafay-

ette's chaplain in the Revolution, and the same year he built in Frankfort "Liberty Hall," his residence, from plans drawn by Jefferson.

[See *Lawyers and Lawmakers of Ky.* (1897), ed. by H. Levin, and R. H. and L. Collins, *Hist. of Ky.* (1874), I, II. Various papers relating to Brown's public career may be found in Innes MSS. in the Lib. of Cong. For his Spanish dealings the following are valuable: Wm. Littell, *Political Transactions in and Concerning Ky. from the First Settlement Thereof, until It Became an Independent State, in June 1792* (1806, repr. 1926 as Filson Club Pub. no. 31); T. M. Green, *Spanish Conspiracy: A Review of Early Spanish Movements in the South-West* (1891), a hostile account; J. M. Brown, *Political Beginnings of Ky.* (1889), a friendly account; and Humphrey Marshall, *Hist. of Ky.* (1824), I, II.]   E. M. C—r.

BROWN, JOHN (May 9, 1800–Dec. 2, 1859), "Old Brown of Osawatomie," is now chiefly remembered for his raid on Harper's Ferry. He was born at Torrington, Conn., the son of Owen and Ruth (Mills) Brown. His biographers have pointed out with much satisfaction that he came of the best New England stock, with only slight dilution of the strain from a Dutch ancestor on the maternal side. They have passed over lightly much more significant facts of inheritance. John Brown's mother, who died when he was only eight years old, was insane for a number of years before her death and died insane, as had her mother before her. A sister of Ruth Mills had also died insane, while three sons of her brother Gideon Mills became insane and were confined in asylums (affidavit of Gideon Mills). Two sons of another brother were also adjudged insane. Owen Brown plied various trades in the Connecticut villages in which he sojourned. By his own admission he was "very quick on the moove." One of these moves took him to Hudson, Ohio, where John passed his boyhood. Owen Brown was twice married and became the father of sixteen children. He was a man of much piety, an abolitionist, and an agent of the underground railroad.

John's schooling was scanty, and reading formed the principal part of his early education. As he himself said, school always meant to him, even in later life, confinement and restraint. More to his liking was the free life of the wilderness. He delighted in the long journeys with droves of beef cattle with which he was sent to supply troops in the War of 1812. Later he worked at the tanner's trade, acting as his father's foreman (letter to Henry L. Stearns, July 15, 1857, in F. B. Sanborn's *Life and Letters of John Brown*, ch. I). In 1820 he married Dianthe Lusk, who in the twelve years of her married life bore him seven children. She, like her husband's mother, suffered from mental aberration in her later years and died in 1831. Two of her sons were of unsound mind. Within a year John Brown married Mary Anne Day, a girl of sixteen, of robust physique, who in twenty-one years bore him thirteen more children.

In 1825 Brown moved to Richmond, Pa., where he cleared the land of timber and set up a tannery. This was the first of ten migrations before his adventures in Kansas, in the course of which he established and sold tanneries, dabbled unsuccessfully in land speculation, and incurred debts. Then he turned shepherd, buying Saxon sheep on credit. One sum advanced by the New England Woolen Company he seems—apparently without any dishonest intent—to have diverted to his own use, but he was treated with leniency by his creditors after he had declared himself a bankrupt. He earnestly hoped that "Devine Providence" would enable him to make full amends—but it never did. His family also changed its abode frequently as he changed his pursuits; but he was often absent for long stretches of time. The story of his business career is a tale of repeated failures, complicated by law-suits which aggrieved parties instituted to recover money loaned on notes or to secure damages for non-fulfilment of contracts. Many of these were decided against the defendant, proving clearly enough his utter incapacity for business. His last business venture was a partnership with one Simon Perkins to raise sheep and to establish a brokerage for wool-growers. Brown went to Springfield, Mass., and opened an office, but failure soon overtook this enterprise. Prolonged litigation followed; and one suit involving $60,000 for breach of contract was settled out of court by Brown's counsel (O. G. Villard, *John Brown*, p. 66). As his various ventures came to naught and his inability to earn a livelihood for his numerous progeny became manifest, he began to take more thought about the affairs of others, particularly about those who were or who had been in bondage. He determined to settle with his family in a newly-founded community of negroes at North Elba, N. Y., on lands donated by Gerrit Smith. His purpose was "to aid them by precept and example," avers his latest biographer without any intentional humor. Within two years, however, he had again moved, to Akron, Ohio, followed by his family.

Brown was well over fifty years of age before the idea of freeing the slaves by force dominated his mind. He had always been an abolitionist; he had made his barn at Richmond a station on the underground railroad; he had formed a League of Gileadites among the negroes in Springfield, to help them protect themselves and fugitive slaves. Now he began to have visions of a servile insurrection—the establishment of a stronghold somewhere in the mountains whence fugitive slaves and their white friends could sally forth and terrorize slaveholders (*Ibid.,* pp. 53–56). These visions were never very clear or very coherent, and they were overcast by events in Kansas where protagonists of slavery and free-soilers from the North were contending passionately for possession of the territorial government and where a condition bordering on civil war was soon to exist. In the spring of 1855, five of his sons went to Kansas to help win the territory for freedom and incidentally to take up lands for themselves. In May John Brown, Jr., sent a Macedonian cry to his father for arms to fight the battle for free soil (*Ibid.,* pp. 83–84). Brown then transferred what was left of his family to North Elba again, and in August set out for Kansas in a one-horse wagon filled with guns and ammunition. Ostensibly he was to join the colony on the Osawatomie as surveyor. At once, however, he became their leader and captain of the local militia company. As such he commanded it in the bloodless Wakarusa War, whose indecisive outcome left him ill at ease. The ensuing disorders, particularly the sack of Lawrence in May 1856 by the pro-slavery forces, preyed upon his mind. The cause of free-soil took on the aspect of a crusade. Members of his company met and resolved that acts of retaliation were necessary "to cause a restraining fear" (*Ibid.,* p. 152). A list of victims was made out and on May 23, Capt. John Brown with a party of six, four of whom were his sons, set out for the Potawatomi country to discharge their bloody mission. During the night of May 24 they fell upon their five hapless victims without warning and hacked them to pieces with their sabers. Probably Brown killed no one with his own hand, but he assumed full responsibility for the massacre, asserting as he was wont to do that he was but an instrument in the hands of God. From this time on the name of "Old Osawatomie Brown" became a terror to pro-slavery settlers. Eventually, however, he and his men were beaten and dispersed, while in revenge Osawatomie was sacked and burned. In this guerrilla warfare, Frederick, one of the sons whose mind had become unbalanced, was killed.

Old acquaintances who saw Brown after his return from Kansas, in the autumn of 1856, commented on the change in his appearance and manner. With his gray hair and bent figure he looked like an old man. His inability to talk about anything except slavery, and that always with abnormal intensity, left many with the impression that he had become a monomaniac (affidavits). One keen observer, who did not know Brown's family history, detected "a little touch of insanity about his glittering gray-blue eyes" (*Letters and Recollections of John Murray Forbes*, 1899, I, 179). Upon less keen observers in Massachusetts—less keen perhaps, because more preoccupied with the struggle for Kansas —he made a happier impression. Emerson spoke of him as "a pure idealist of artless goodness." It is charitable to suppose that the Concord philosopher was at this time ignorant of the murders on the Potawatomi; but another ardent resident of Concord, Frank B. Sanborn, could hardly have been so ignorant, nor his friends, G. L. Stearns, T. W. Higginson, Theodore Parker, and S. G. Howe, who were members of the Massachusetts State Kansas Committee and who gave Brown some supplies and arms, a little money, and many assurances of moral support in the fight for freedom in Kansas. When Brown returned to Kansas in the late autumn of 1857, he found both parties disposed to have recourse to ballots instead of bullets, and therefore had no opportunity to employ his peculiar methods of persuasion. He now began to recruit a body of men for a new enterprise. He proposed to transfer his offensive against slavery to a new front. In the following spring, at an extraordinary convention of his followers and negroes at Chatham in Canada, he divulged his plans for the liberation of slaves in the Southern states. He and his band were to establish a base in the mountains of Maryland and Virginia, to which slaves and free negroes would resort, and there—beating off all attacking forces whether state or federal—were to form a free state under a constitution. A provisional constitution was then adopted by the convention and Brown elected commander-in-chief (Villard, pp. 331–36).

Brown's funds were now exhausted and he turned again to Gerrit Smith and to his Massachusetts friends. That they were aware of the wide reach of his new plans cannot now be doubted; yet they encouraged him with promises of financial support in what was essentially a treasonable conspiracy. For the immediate present, however, they counseled delay; and in the early summer of 1858 Brown returned to Kansas to resume operations under the name of Shubel Morgan. His chief exploit was a descent upon some plantations across the border in Missouri, in the course of which one planter was killed while defending his property and some eleven slaves were liberated. In the eyes of the government he was now no better than a dangerous outlaw. The president of the United States and the governor of Missouri offered rewards for his arrest; but Brown and his men, appropriating horses, wagons, and whatever served their purpose, eluded pursuit and finally succeeded in reaching Canada with the liberated slaves. Even this exploit did not cost Brown the confidence of his supporters. He made public speeches at Cleveland and at Rochester, and no one attempted to arrest him. Gerrit Smith declared him "most truly a Christian" and headed a subscription list with a pledge of $400. From the Massachusetts group Brown received $3,800, "with a clear knowledge of the use to which it would be put" (Sanborn, p. 523).

In the early summer of 1859, Brown fixed upon Harper's Ferry as the base of his operations in Virginia and rented a farm about five miles distant where he could collect his arms and his band of followers. By midsummer his little army of twenty-one men had rendezvoused secretly at Kennedy Farm; but it was not until the night of Oct. 16 that the commander-in-chief gave the order to proceed to the Ferry. Even after all these weeks of preparation he seems to have had no coherent plan of attack. That he should have fixed upon this quiet town of mechanics, many of whom came from the North, as the place for an assault upon slavery, is inexplicable on any rational grounds. Neither it nor its environs contained many slaves; and it is one of the tragic ironies of the affair that the first man killed should have been a respectable free negro who was discharging his duty as baggage-master at the railroad station. When morning dawned, Brown and his men were in possession of the United States armory and the bridges leading to the Ferry, had made many inhabitants prisoners, among them one slaveholder from a plantation five miles away, and had persuaded a few slaves to join them; but there Brown's initiative failed. For some unexplained reason he did not make off to the mountains as he might easily have done. Meantime the news of the raid spread through the country-side. By mid-day local militia companies from Charlestown had arrived on the scene and had closed Brown's only way of escape. Desultory firing followed, with some casualties on both sides, while Brown with the remnant of his forces, the slaves, and some of his prisoners were shut up in the engine-house of the armory. During the following night a company of United States marines arrived under the command of Col. Robert E. Lee; and at dawn, upon Brown's refusal to surrender, carried the building by assault. Brown fought with amazing coolness and courage over the body of his dying son but was finally overpowered with four of his men. Seven had already been taken prisoner and ten had either been killed or mortally wounded, including two of Brown's sons. Brown himself was wounded but not seriously. Next morning he was taken to Charlestown and lodged in the jail. One week later he was indicted for "treason to the Commonwealth, conspiring with slaves to commit treason and murder." His trial was conducted with expedition but with exemplary fairness and decorum. It ended inevitably in the sentence of death; and on Dec. 2, John Brown was hanged.

From the moment of his capture to his execution Brown conducted himself with a fortitude and dignity that commanded the respect of his captors and judges. To all questions regarding his motives he had only one answer: he had desired to free the slaves—he believed himself an instrument in the hands of Providence to this end. When confronted with the bloody consequences of his acts and with the designs he had entertained to incite a slave insurrection, he would recognize no inconsistency. It was this obsession regarding his mission and his unaccountableness to anybody but his Maker that created doubts as to his sanity. Before his execution seventeen affidavits from neighbors and relatives who believed Brown to be insane were sent to Gov. Wise, but he decided for some reason not to follow his first inclination and have an alienist examine Brown. These remarkable affidavits with their unimpeachable testimony as to Brown's family history and his own erratic behavior constitute prima facie evidence which no modern court of law could ignore.

It is significant of the passions aroused by the Harper's Ferry raid that Brown was hailed both as a noble martyr in a great cause and as a common assassin. Probably Abraham Lincoln anticipated the final verdict of history when he said in his Cooper Union speech (Feb. 27, 1860): "That affair, in its philosophy, corresponds with the many attempts, related in history, at the assassination of kings and emperors. An enthusiast broods over the oppression of a people till he fancies himself commissioned by Heaven to liberate them. He ventures the attempt, which ends in little else than his own execution. Orsini's attempt on Louis Napoleon, and John Brown's attempt at Harper's Ferry were in their philosophy precisely the same."

[The first biography of John Brown was written by James Redpath: *The Public Life of Capt. John Brown,* published in 1860 with a preface dated Dec. 25, 1859. It is valuable only as reflecting the contemporary opinion of Brown's partisans. Equally partisan but valuable for its letters, documents, and personal recollections is F. B. Sanborn's *The Life and Letters of John Brown* (1885). The references in the text are to the fourth edition (1910). Richard J. Hinton in his *John Brown and His Men* (1894) also holds a brief for his hero. Of the later biographies O. G. Villard's *John Brown* (1910) is by far the best and most extensive. It contains much new material on the earlier career of Brown, drawn from widely scattered sources. Considering the undisguised admiration of the author for Brown as "a great and lasting figure in American History," he has written with commendable fairness. The question of Brown's insanity, however, he dismisses too readily. A valuable bibliography of the literature concerning John Brown is appended to the book. The affidavits relating to Brown's alleged insanity are in the possession of Mr. Edwin Tatham of New York, who has permitted the writer to examine them.] A.J.

BROWN, JOHN A. (May 21, 1788–Dec. 31, 1872), banker, was the third son of Grace (Davison) Brown and Alexander Brown [*q.v.*]. He was born in Ireland, received his elementary schooling there, and in 1802 with his brothers, George and James [*qq.v.*], followed his father to America. Receiving his business training from his father, in time he became a member of the firm of Alexander Brown & Sons, merchant bankers of Baltimore. In 1818 he went to Philadelphia to establish the first American branch of the house. In October of that year the following advertisement appeared in the *Union, United States Gazette,* and *True American* of Philadelphia: "John A. Brown & Company take this opportunity of informing those who have been in the habit of purchasing the linens imported by Alexander Brown & Sons of Baltimore, that the above firm is a branch of that concern and that both houses will import a constant supply of Cheap Linens." The name was changed later to Brown & Bowen and finally to Brown Brothers & Company, but the firm has continued to do business from its foundation to the present day.

John was the most conservative of the four sons of Alexander Brown, yet he had good judgment, shrewd knowledge of men, and alertness in seizing opportunities for the use of capital, and his wise investments at a time when American railroads were first developing enabled him to amass an ample fortune which he used in furthering leading philanthropic enterprises in Philadelphia. He retired from the Philadelphia firm after the panic of 1837 had impaired his health, but continued his philanthropies, which concerned church work mainly. He organized and contributed to the erection of a building for Calvary Presbyterian Church, Philadelphia, and became interested in the work of the New School branch of the Presbyterian Church. Through his influence and assistance and that of his friend and neighbor, Matthias W. Baldwin, that branch of the church became the owner of the Presbyterian House on Chestnut St. He was also a member of and contributor to the American

Sunday School Union, and a short time before his death, made a gift of $300,000 to the Presbyterian Hospital.

The middle "A" in John Brown's name really stood for nothing at all. He adopted it as an initial in order to avoid confusion with another John Brown whose mail frequently had become mixed with his while he lived in Baltimore. His first wife, Isabella Patrick of Ballymena, whom he had married in 1813, died in 1820, and in 1823 he married Grace Brown, a daughter of Dr. George Brown of Baltimore.

[The chief sources of information are the letters, papers, and privately printed biographies of the Brown family, in the vaults and offices of Alexander Brown & Sons, Baltimore; see also J. C. Brown, *A Hundred Years of Merchant Banking* (1909) and Mary E. Brown, *Alexander Brown and his Descendants, 1764–1916* (1917).]

F. R. K.

BROWN, JOHN APPLETON (July 12, 1844–Jan. 18, 1902), landscape painter, was the son of George Frederick Handel and Asenath Lyons (Page) Brown, who were living in West Newbury, Mass., at the time of their son's birth. Early developing a taste for art, Brown studied as a youth with a certain Mr. Porter then well known as a portrait painter. At the age of twenty-one he came to Boston to open his first studio in 1865. Two years later he sailed for Paris for further study under Émile Lambinet, returning to Newburyport to marry Agnes Bartlet, daughter of Edmund and Louisa S. Bartlet of that city. His wife also was an artist, though less widely known than her husband. Brown was ever a mild, lovable man, his temperament showing in the gentle treatment of nature in his paintings. Though he spent some months in England in the early eighties, working with Edwin Abbey and Parsons, and painting in Italy and along the Riviera, most of his work was done in his native New England. The marsh lands and orchards, the scenes of his childhood in his own state of Massachusetts, he immortalized on canvas. Neither realistic nor detailed in his work he portrayed forcibly and directly his subject, realistic outline merging into vagueness. When he painted the sea he caught its cold, grey color, even the weight, density, and mass of the water being preserved and emphasized in his tints. "He had the felicity to utter the right word with just the right accent, never forcing the note. He made us think not of the painter, but of the thing painted" (William Howe Downes in *American Magazine of Art*, August 1923). Brown painted nocturnal scenes; marine pieces; flower gardens; cattle pieces; and architectural compositions; but it is as a painter of apple orchards that he is best

known. He was never fatigued, blasé, or disillusioned in a world of trees, blossoms, grass, flowers, running water, and blue skies. Among his better-known paintings are "Springtime" painted in 1899; "Summer" and "A View at Dives Calvades, France," which were accepted by the Paris Salon in 1875; and "November" exhibited in the Boston Museum of Fine Arts. His work was never impulsive or impassionate, but of an even quiet, having a definite note of serene cheerfulness, typical of the artist's own nature. Though his work shows the influence of Corot he was imitative of none, developing the rural scene into a symbolic reflection typically American in its unquenchable optimism, hopefulness and buoyancy. For many years Mr. and Mrs. Brown lived in the famous Quincy mansion in Boston, returning to Newburyport for their summers, where most of Brown's painting was done directly from nature. Brown never grew old; to his joyous spirit each spring appeared entirely new. He died in New York City.

[C. E. Clement and L. Hutton, *Artists of the Nineteenth Century* (1879); John Currier, *Hist. of Newburyport, Mass.* (1909); *Atlantic Mo.*, Dec. 1877; *Art Jour.* (London), XXXI, 74. Although *Who's Who in America*, 1899, gives the date of Brown's birth as July 24, the *Vital Records of West Newbury, Mass.* (1918), give July 12.]

J. T. M., Jr.

BROWN, JOHN CALVIN (Jan. 6, 1827–Aug. 17, 1889), governor of Tennessee, was born in Giles County, Tenn., and died at Red Boiling Springs, Tenn. His parents, Duncan Brown and Margaret Smith Brown, both of Scotch-Irish descent, were strict Presbyterians and belonged to the small-farmer class of western North Carolina. His grandfather, Angus Brown, had emigrated from Scotland and had fought in the American Revolution under Francis Marion. An older brother, Neill S. Brown [q.v.], was governor of Tennessee in 1847–49. John Calvin Brown was known by his contemporaries as one of the best-educated men of his section. He attended the country schools and later Jackson College at Columbia, Tenn., where he was graduated in 1846. It is said that he spoke both Latin and French. He studied law with his brother Neill, was admitted to the bar in Pulaski in 1848, and soon had a good practise in Giles County and in the surrounding counties. Though a Whig, like his older brother, and a follower of John Bell, Brown was never a candidate for office before 1860 when he was an elector on the Bell and Everett ticket and made a vigorous canvass in opposition to secession and Republicanism, occupying, like nearly all Whigs, a middle ground between the extreme Democrats and the Republicans.

His health becoming impaired by too much hard work, he decided to travel and made a tour of North America, England, the Continent, Palestine, and Egypt, returning just before the Civil War began. At the beginning of the war, though he had been opposed to secession, Brown enlisted in the Confederate service as a private, was soon made captain, and on May 16, 1861, became colonel of the 3rd Tennessee Infantry. Captured at Fort Donelson, he was for a time imprisoned in Fort Warren, Boston Harbor, but was exchanged in August 1862. He was then made a brigadier-general and in 1864 a major-general. His command was engaged in the Kentucky and Tennessee campaigns under Bragg, and in the Georgia and later Tennessee campaigns under Johnston and Hood. He was wounded in the battle of Perryville, had a horse killed under him at Missionary Ridge, and while leading a charge in the battle of Franklin was again seriously wounded. For a time he was disfranchised under the Brownlow régime in Tennessee, but his Whig antecedents gave him influence with the moderate Unionists and his war record aided him with those Democrats who were permitted to vote. In 1869 he was elected to the state legislature, and in 1870 was made president of the state constitutional convention where he exerted a strong influence in the making of a new constitution for Tennessee. Largely on account of his work in the constitutional convention Brown was elected governor of Tennessee on the Democratic ticket in 1870 and was reëlected in 1872. His task was to reduce to order the economic and political chaos following war and reconstruction. He secured the payment of the floating debt of $3,000,000, and reduced the bonded debt, but had to leave unsolved the problem of what bonded debts were legal and what were fraudulent. While governor he sponsored a constructive railroad policy and secured legislation authorizing the consolidation of the smaller lines. Among other constructive measures of his administration were the reorganization of the state prisons, the revision of the system of Chancery courts, the establishment of a state system of public schools, a better apportionment of the state into congressional and legislative districts.

His stand on the state debt brought him defeat in 1875 when he was a candidate for the United States Senate against Andrew Johnson. He then returned for a short time to his law practise, but soon entered the railroad business in which he remained until his death. Immediately after the close of the war he had become interested in some of the short lines in Middle Tennessee and was president of the Nashville Railway. This experience and the railroad legislation framed by him when governor caused him to be made vice-president of the Texas & Pacific Railway in 1876, in charge of the construction, the politics, and the legal interests of the road in Washington, D. C., and in Texas. He built the road east to New Orleans and west to the Rio Grande. One of his chief opponents in railway policy was C. P. Huntington. When Jay Gould acquired the Texas & Pacific in 1880, Brown was retained in charge, and in 1881 he was made general solicitor of the half-dozen Gould roads west of the Mississippi. He was made receiver of the Texas & Pacific in 1885, and three years later president; he practically rebuilt the road. A few months before his death in 1889, he returned to Tennessee as president of the Tennessee Coal, Iron & Railroad Company. He was married twice: first to Ann Pointer of Pulaski, who died leaving no children; and second to Elizabeth Childress of Murfreesboro, by whom he had four children.

Brown was a moderate in his political views, and frank and outspoken on all public questions, but he was not a successful politician. He made a good business governor and gave the state a constructive administration. He was a man of strong and attractive personality. As a lawyer his arguments were notable for ability, learning, and eloquence. His claim to remembrance rests upon his military career and upon his constructive work as governor of Tennessee and as a western railroad builder.

[*Hist. of Nashville, Tenn.* (1890), ed. by John Wooldridge; J. W. Caldwell, *Sketches of the Bench and Bar of Tenn.* (1898); *Tenn., the Volunteer State 1769-1923* (1923), ed. by John T. Moore; *Jour. of the Proc. of the Convention of Delegates, etc.* (1870); *Official Records* (1880-1902); obituary in the *Daily American* (Nashville), Aug. 18, 1889.]   W. L. F.

BROWN, JOHN CARTER (Aug. 28, 1797-June 10, 1874), book collector, was the youngest son of Nicholas [*q.v.*] and Ann (Carter) Brown, and the grandson of John Carter, the second printer of Providence. After learning the details of the family business, he was sent to the Ohio country to select land for purchase, and though he met with experiences distasteful to his youthful fastidiousness, he acquired an interest in the section that led him later to interest himself in its problems and to contribute gifts of money to its struggling societies and institutions. His tastes were for travel and the amenities of life rather than for the restraints of business, and though he never lost touch with the large responsibilities he had inherited, he gave his greatest care to the correct enjoyment of his fortune and to the collection of books. In the beginning as a collector of the type common enough in the first half of the century, he brought together a library of works printed at the Aldine presses, a series of the magnificently printed polyglot Bibles, a few fine editions of the classics, and some notable sets of extra-illustrated books. He possessed an inherited and a trained appreciation of relative cultural values united to the zeal of a real collector. He was not satisfied long with his gentleman-collector's library, and sometime in the early 1840's he found his interest turning toward early books on America. He came into touch with the bookseller Obadiah Rich, and later with Henry Stevens, a young Yale graduate in process of becoming a great London bookseller. In the course of the early dealings with Stevens, Brown arrived at a comprehensive conception of what the scope of his collection was to be; that is, that he was to buy for it printed books dealing with the Western Hemisphere from the Discovery to the year 1801. With this field marked out he set about an intensive cultivation, remarkable in its results. Though James Lenox [*q.v.*], his summer neighbor at Newport and great rival in the collection of American books, excelled him in the pursuit of the rare and elusive variant editions of familiar treasures, yet Brown's training and association led him to give to his American collection a comprehensiveness not attained by the other. These two collectors and their London agent, Henry Stevens of Vermont, created in the purchase and sale of Americana a new branch of the antiquarian book business. The collection was famous among scholars before 1865, when the first volume of a catalogue, compiled under the direction of John Russell Bartlett [*q.v.*], was printed. This was completed in 1871, in four volumes, describing 5,600 titles of books printed before the year 1800, which relate in some way to the Americas. When Brown died his collection numbered about 7,500 volumes, many of them of very great rarity, and the whole forming a well-rounded collection as useful to the scholar as to the bibliographer and bookman.

Brown made substantial gifts in continuation of his inherited obligations, but he drew out of active connection with some of those which had come to rely perhaps unduly upon his support, transferring his special attention to the Butler Hospital, of which his father was in a measure the founder, and to the Rhode Island Hospital, to which he gave largely in his lifetime. His gifts to Brown University in the form of books, land, and buildings, including a new building for the University Library, equalled in amount the benefactions of his father for whom the institution had been named. He was chosen a trustee of the University in 1828 and from then until his death he maintained an effective interest in its affairs. He served one term in the state legislature as representative from Newport. On June 23, 1859, he married Sophia Augusta, daughter of the Hon. Patrick Brown, member of the Council and associate justice of the General Court of the Bahama Islands. His widow transferred the title of the John Carter Brown collection to her elder son, John Nicholas Brown (1861–1900), by the terms of whose will it passed to trustees who deeded it to Brown University, with an endowment fund of $500,000, and $150,000 to erect a special building for it on the campus.

[Henry Stevens, *Recollections of Mr. James Lenox of N. Y. and the Formation of his Library* (London, 1886) contains much information about the formation of Brown's collection, which is supplemented by the correspondence and bills preserved at the library. These were used in G. P. Winship's *The John Carter Brown Library, a History* (1914). See also sketches in the *Providence Jour.*, June 11, 24, 1874.]   L. C. W.

BROWN, JOHN GEORGE (Nov. 11, 1831– Feb. 8, 1913), genre painter, was the son of Ann and John Brown, the latter a poor lawyer of Durham, England. As a boy he knew little of home life, being apprenticed at an early age to a glass-cutter in Newcastle-on-Tyne. There he remained an apprentice seven years, earning the sum of six dollars a week. Half of this amount was sent to his mother and the other half was used to live on; he received no financial aid from his father. The lad early developed a taste for art, doing a portrait of his mother and sister when he was nine years old. While learning the glass-cutting industry, he studied in his spare time with the well-known English artist Scott Lowdes. After leaving Newcastle-on-Tyne he continued the study of art in Scotland under William D. Scott. In 1853, when he was twenty-two years of age, he went to London and there supported himself by drawing and by the painting of portraits. One night he chanced to hear Henry Russell, then a well-known music hall singer, sing of the immigrants that came to the States. The youth was so impressed with the vivid pictures of American life as painted by the singer's words, that he came almost immediately to America, supporting himself in Brooklyn, N. Y., by his trade of glass-cutting. His employer was a benevolent old gentleman by the name of William Owen. Sketches made for stained glass work and decorations so impressed Mr. Owen with Brown's artistic ability that he enabled him to study in New York with Thomas Cummings.

In 1856 Brown married Mary Owen, the eldest daughter of William Owen. After her death he married her younger sister, Emma A. Owen, in 1871. His natural sympathy and kindness for all children was definitely demonstrated in the love he bore his own family of seven.

Opening a studio in the Old Studio Building of New York City in 1860, he started painting street urchins, and in the beginning received for his pictures from five to thirty dollars apiece. A painting of a small boy called "His First Cigar," first brought Brown's work into national consideration, this painting selling for $150 and being exhibited in the Academy of Design of New York in 1860. Another painting, "Curling in Central Park," caused him to be made an Academician. Nine years later he was made president of the National Academy. Although never high art, his paintings of American town and country types were always true to nature and are an invaluable addition to the history of his generation. His work was essentially American, cleverly executed, and intensely realistic. To quote his own words, "I do not paint poor boys solely because the public likes them and pays me for them, but because I love the boys myself, for I was once a poor lad." He died at the age of eighty-two, a wealthy man, his paintings in the latter part of his life having yielded him an annual income of from forty to fifty thousand dollars, which he had invested to a large extent in New York real estate.

[C. E. Clement and L. Hutton, *Artists of the Nineteenth Century* (1879); G. W. Sheldon, *Am. Painters* (1881); *Mag. of Art,* Apr. 1882; *Am. Art News,* Jan. 6, 1906, and Feb. 15, 1913; *N. Y. Herald,* Feb. 9, 1913; Notes of Philip Gilbert Hamerton on "American Exhibition of Paintings" in Paris Exhibition of 1878.]

J. T. M., Jr.

BROWN, JOHN MIFFLIN (Sept. 8, 1817–Mar. 16, 1893), bishop of the African Methodist Episcopal Church, was a mulatto born at what is now called Odessa, Del. There he spent the first ten years of his life. He then moved to Wilmington, Del., where he lived with a Quaker family. These Friends gave him religious instruction at home and sent him to a private school. He had the opportunity for further instruction under a Catholic priest, but declined it for the reason that he desired to adhere to the principles of the Methodist Church. He next found friends in Philadelphia, where he lived in the home of Dr. Emerson and Henry Chester, who continued his education. For a number of years he attended the St. Thomas Protestant Episcopal Church, but in 1836 united with the Bethel African Methodist Episcopal Church. There he attended an evening school and began his preparation for the minis-

try. He made several efforts to obtain advanced training, but had his first such opportunity when he entered the Wesleyan Academy at Wilbraham, Mass. He studied there from 1838 to 1840, when he had to leave on account of poor health. After recovery, he studied further at Oberlin, but did not complete a course. Much better educated than most of his fellows, however, he began a private school in Detroit in 1844. At the same time he was engaged in religious work, for he had charge of a church in that city the following three years. He next served as a pastor in Columbus from 1844 to 1847. From this position he was called to the most significant work with which he had ever been connected. He was chosen the principal of Union Seminary, organized as a result of a vote of the African Methodist Episcopal Conference in 1844. This is often referred to as the original Wilberforce University. It was started in the African Methodist Episcopal Chapel in Columbus; but, being unsuccessful, it was soon moved twelve miles from the city and established on a farm of 120 acres. This was the first national educational effort of the African Methodist Episcopal Church. Being in need of educated ministers, the conference established this institution on the manual labor plan by which poor students could work at some useful occupation to earn what they learned. Brown started the school with three students and left it with 100. Eventually Union Seminary was merged with the actual Wilberforce University founded by the Methodists in 1856 at Tawawa Springs, near Xenia.

Prior to this time, however, Brown had resumed his work in the church. In 1853 he had married Mary Louise Lewis of Louisville, who bore him eleven children. He became a pastor in New Orleans and served at various other places in the South. In 1864 he was chosen editor of the *Christian Recorder,* the organ of the African Methodist Episcopal Church, which still exists as the oldest negro newspaper in the United States. Brown did not remain in this position long. During the same year he was made director of the rapidly expanding missionary work of the church, which required systematization and stimulus. He continued in this capacity for four years. In 1868, the unusual growth of the church after the emancipation of the freedmen necessitated his advancement to the highest post in the denomination, and he was ordained bishop. In this position he toiled successfully for twenty-five years, contributing to the urgent needs of belated people who now had their first opportunity for intellectual and spiritual uplift. To him belongs the credit for establishing Payne

Institute, now Allen University, at Columbia, S. C.; and for founding Paul Quinn College at Waco, Tex. He died at his home in Washington, D. C.

[Sketches of Brown appear in Wm. J. Simmons, *Men of Mark* (1887) and in the *A. M. E. Ch. Rev.*, July 1893; for additional facts see Daniel A. Payne, *Recollections of Seventy Years* (1888); and B. T. Tanner, *Outline of Our Hist. and Govt. for African Meth. Churches.*]   C.G.W.

BROWN, JOHN NEWTON (June 29, 1803–May 14, 1868), Baptist clergyman, was the son of Charles and Hester (Darrow) Brown. His early home was in New London, Conn., where he was born. He graduated from Madison College (now Colgate) in 1823, standing at the head of his class. The next year he was ordained to the Baptist ministry at Buffalo, N. Y., and he preached there for a year before going to New England for his principal pastorates. In 1827 he was settled at Malden, Mass., and two years later went to Exeter, N. H., for a ministry of nearly ten years. During that time he compiled a single-volume religious encyclopedia, *Fessenden and Company's Encyclopedia of Religious Knowledge* (1837). It has been superseded by later and larger works, but for a time it was used widely. In 1838 Brown's scholarly attainments brought him the appointment of professor of theology and church history in the Academical and Theological Institution of New Hampton, in central New Hampshire, where he remained for seven years. In 1845 ill health sent Brown south, and he became pastor at Lexington, Va., for four years. At the end of that time he was made editorial secretary of the American Baptist Publication Society, and also editor of their journals, the *Christian Chronicle* and *National Baptist*. A number of books notable in their time were published under his direction, including the works of the English Baptists, Bunyan and Fuller, and Fleetwood's *Life of Our Lord and Saviour, Jesus Christ* (1866). Brown was himself the author of *Emily and Other Poems* (1840), and he translated the medieval hymn *Dies Irae*. His most permanent work was the preparation of the *New Hampshire Confession of Faith* in 1833. Nearly a century earlier the Philadelphia Association of Baptist churches had adopted a confession based on a seventeenth-century confession of English Baptists, which itself was adapted from the famous Westminster Confession of the English Presbyterians. This was strongly Calvinistic in character, and, while it suited most of the American Baptist churches, it was not entirely satisfactory as an expression of Baptist theology, especially where the Baptists were in contact with the Freewill Baptists of northern

New England. Brown was appointed one of a committee to draw up a briefer statement which would be more moderately Calvinistic. This was accepted by the New Hampshire convention as a satisfactory declaration, and came into general use in the North by a denomination that has had little liking for creeds. Brown's part in the work appears to have been most constructive, and his name remains associated with its history. Never very robust in body or in spirit, he was inclined to mysticism in his religion. The New Hampshire Confession has been characterized as "like the mild Dr. Brown."

[Wm. Cathcart, *Bapt. Encyc.* (1881); L. C. Barnes and others, *Pioneers of Light* (1924), p. 301; Wm. Hurlin and others, *The Baptists in New Hampshire* (1902); *The First Half Century of Madison Univ. 1819–69* (1872); obituaries in the *Press* and *Pub. Ledger* of Phila., May 18, 1868; Conn. Vital Records, State Lib., Hartford.]   H.K.R.

BROWN, JOHN PORTER (Aug. 17, 1814–Apr. 28, 1872), diplomat, Orientalist, was born at Chillicothe, Ohio, the son of an obscure tanner and of Mary (Porter) Brown, daughter of David Porter, a captain in the American navy during the Revolution. Navy Department records do not confirm the statement of Admiral David D. Porter that Brown was in 1829 an acting midshipman in the navy. In 1832 he joined his uncle, Commodore David Porter, minister-resident at Constantinople, where he began the study of Turkish and Arabic. He became assistant dragoman of the legation the following year and was then successively commissioned consul (1835), dragoman (1836), consul-general (1857), and secretary of legation (1858). He was nine times chargé d'affaires *ad interim*. In 1850 he helped to secure the first Turkish mission to the United States, by suggesting to the Grand Vizier, Reshid Pasha, the advisability of sending an agent to inspect American military and naval establishments, Brown having in mind the eventual displacement by Americans of the British in the service of the Sultan. Without credentials, Amin Bey was brought to the United States in the U. S. S. *Erie,* received by the president and cabinet, entertained by Secretary Webster at Marshfield, and with his suite, accompanied by Brown, toured the United States as the guest of the nation. The mission was featured by the widely copied denunciation of Brown that characterized Amin Bey as an impostor (*New York Morning Express*, Dec. 2, 1850). Characteristically Brown attempted to secure the appropriation of entertainment money by Congress through his friend Lewis Cass, without consulting the Department of State. This independence and audacity was even more strikingly exemplified in the Koszta affair. A certain Martin Koszta, a Hungarian refugee and an adherent of Kossuth's insurrection against Austria, came to the United States in 1851 and in the following year declared his intention of becoming an American citizen, in the New York court of common pleas. After a residence of nearly two years he went to Turkey, where he traveled by means of *tezkerehs* (Turkish passports) procured by the American consul in Smyrna and by Brown in Constantinople. He was seized at Smyrna by order of the Austrian consul and imprisoned on the Austrian brig *Hussar*. Although not subject to Brown's instructions, Capt. Ingraham of the United States sloop of war *St. Louis* appealed to the chargé for counsel. Brown advised him to demand Koszta's surrender, and if it were not complied with, to *"take him out of the vessel"* (sic). Ingraham served his ultimatum on the Austrian commander at eight o'clock on the morning of July 2, 1853, and demanded a reply by four o'clock in the afternoon, in the meantime clearing the decks and preparing to fight it out in Smyrna harbor. The Austrian consul-general prevented bloodshed only by delivering Koszta in chains into the custody of the French consul-general. After months of negotiation he was released and returned to the United States. The action of Brown and Ingraham, while highhanded and of questionable legality, was fully upheld by the United States Government. Although admitting that Koszta was not an American citizen, President Pierce declared that he was "clothed with the nationality of the United States" (*Congressional Globe,* 33 Cong., 1 Sess., p. 8).

Brown attained a considerable reputation as an Orientalist among his contemporaries. His translations of the Turkish version of al-Tabari's "Conquest of Persia by the Arabs," Muhammad Misri's "On the Tesavuf, or Spiritual Life of the Soffees" (*Journal of the American Oriental Society,* vols. I, II and VIII), and of Patriarch Constantine's Greek guidebook to Constantinople and its environs (*Ancient and Modern Constantinople,* London, 1868), while interesting, are now of little value. His best translation was Ahmad bin Hamdan Suahili's "Wonders of Remarkable Incidents and Rareties of Anecdotes," a seventeenth-century Turkish collection of Arabic and Persian fairy tales, published under the title of *Turkish Evening Entertainments* (1850). *The Dervishes, or Oriental Spiritualism* (London, 1868; new edition, edited by H. A. Rose, London, 1927) is a fairly accurate account based on first hand knowledge.

After forty years of official life in the Orient Brown died at Constantinople of heart disease, so poor that his widow, Mrs. Mary A. P. Brown, was able to return home only through the generosity of the Sultan.

[*Senate Ex. Doc. No. 43,* 31 Cong., 1 Sess.; *House Ex. Doc. No. 78,* 32 Cong., 1 Sess.; *Senate Ex. Doc. No. 40* and *No. 53* and *House Ex. Doc. No. 1* and *No. 91,* 33 Cong., 1 Sess.; *House Ex. Doc. No. 82,* 34 Cong., 3 Sess.; *Senate Ex. Doc. No. 54,* 35 Cong., 1 Sess.; *House Ex. Doc. No. 63,* 35 Cong., 2 Sess.; *Senate Ex. Doc. No. 1,* 37 Cong., 2 Sess.; *House Ex. Doc. No. 1,* 38 Cong., 2 Sess.; *House Ex. Doc. No. 1,* 42 Cong., 3 Sess.; *Senate Report No. 357,* 33 Cong., 1 Sess.; *Senate Report No. 359,* 34 Cong., 3 Sess.; *Senate Report No. 135,* 36 Cong., 1 Sess.; *House Report No. 40,* 42 Cong., 3 Sess.; *Cong. Globe,* 31 Cong., 1 Sess., pp. 1872-73, 1930; *Ibid.,* 33 Cong., 1 Sess., p. 313; Francis Dainese, *The Hist. of Mr. Seward's Pet in Egypt* (1867); *Daily National Intelligencer* (Washington, D. C.), Sept. 23, 1850; *Boston Courier,* Nov. 5-7, 1850; *Scioto Gazette* (Chillicothe, Ohio), Nov. 26-27, 1850, May 1, 1872; *Daily Commercial* (Cincinnati), Dec. 16, 1850; *The Levant Times* and *The Levant Herald* (both Constantinople), Apr. 30, May 1, 1872; manuscript letters and records in the Dept. of State, Washington, D. C.]

L.H.G.
F.E.R.

BROWN, JOHN YOUNG (June 28, 1835– Jan. 11, 1904), congressman, governor of Kentucky, was the son of Thomas Dudley and Elizabeth (Young) Brown and was born in Elizabethtown, Hardin County, Ky. His father was a man of some note, serving in the state legislature five terms and being a member of the constitutional convention of 1849–50. Thus, his son at an early age heard much speaking and oratory and developed a strong desire to excel in this art. He entered Centre College when sixteen years of age and according to his classmate, W. C. P. Breckinridge, was the outstanding member of his class. He was graduated in 1855 and immediately began the study of law in Elizabethtown where he commenced practise the following year. His interest in politics led him to attack the Know-Nothings with such vigor as to draw threats on his life from that group. In 1859 while attending the Democratic convention at Bardstown he was nominated for Congress despite his protestations of being a year too young. Nevertheless, he entered vigorously into the campaign and was elected, though he was not allowed to take his seat until the meeting of the short session by which time he had reached the constitutional age.

In 1860 he was a supporter of Douglas and a presidential elector, entering into a joint campaign with W. C. P. Breckinridge, who was supporting his kinsman, John C. Breckinridge. About this time (September 1860) he married Rebecca, a daughter of Archibald Dixon, a former United States senator and a conservative Union man. Brown's sympathies for the Union were so alienated during the Civil War by the régime of the Federal army in Kentucky and his support of the war became so infinitesimally small that when in 1867 he was elected to Congress from the 2nd district he was not allowed to take his seat. In 1872 he was elected again by a vote of 10,888 to 457 for his Republican opponent and served for the next four years, refusing to run thereafter. In 1875 he made a withering speech against Benjamin F. Butler, for which he was censured by the House. A subsequent Congress expunged the resolution of censure.

Brown now resumed his law practise in Henderson, whither he had moved about the time of the outbreak of the Civil War, and apparently retired from politics. But his desire to be governor was too strong. In 1891 he sought and secured the nomination, over the protests of the Farmers' Alliance delegates. He won by a majority of 28,000 votes over his Republican opponent and entered in December upon a four-year term characterized by many veto messages brought forth by loose legislation incident to putting into effect the new constitution of 1890. On the expiration of his term, he began again the practise of law in Louisville, but the following year (1896) he ran for Congress and was defeated. In 1899 his hostility to Gobel, the Democratic nominee for governor, led him to run on an independent Democratic ticket. He received 14,000 votes and greatly contributed to the disputed election which resulted in Gobel's assassination. Later he acted as attorney for the defense of Caleb Powers, who was charged with the crime.

[H. Levin, ed., *Lawyers and Lawmakers of Ky.* (1897); Richard H. and Lewis Collins, *Hist. of Ky.* (1874), vol. I; *Lexington Morning Herald*, Jan. 12, 1904; *Courier-Jour.* (Louisville, Ky.), Jan. 12, 1904.]
E.M.C—r.

BROWN, JOSEPH (Dec. 3/14, 1733–Dec. 3, 1785), manufacturer interested in scientific investigation, son of James and Hope (Power) Brown, was the second of the "Four Brothers," of whom Nicholas, John, and Moses [*qq.v.*] were the others. Following the precedent of the elder brother, Nicholas, he entered the paternal store which, in the next generation, was to become a mercantile establishment of international standing. He remained in business with his three brothers, trading as Nicholas Brown & Company, only until he had acquired a competency. His interest in physical science was stronger than his mercantile instinct, and soon after the middle of the century he was living in Providence the life of an investigator and student, while the brothers continued their successful careers in commerce. It was perhaps because of his interest in physical science that he was given charge at its beginning of the iron manufactory controlled by the firm, the "Furnace Hope" at Scituate, R. I. His influence on the conduct of this industry did not cease when he withdrew from the firm, for he remained until his death a partner in the venture and its technical adviser in important undertakings. His interest in physics led him in the direction of electrical experimentation, while his study of mechanics bore fruit in the mastery of the practical problems of house building and architecture. He was associated with James Sumner in the building of the beautiful First Baptist Church of Providence, constructed after a design by James Gibbs. It is said that he was the architect of his own residence on South Main St. in Providence, of the notably fine Power St. house of his brother John, of the Market House, all of which are still standing, and of other buildings that have helped to give Providence a peculiarly distinguished architectural character. In public life, Brown served for several years in the Rhode Island Assembly, but it is probable that he is best remembered for his scientific interests, and locally at least for his connection with the observation of the Transit of Venus made in Providence under Benjamin West on June 3, 1769, an astronomical experiment that has given the name Transit St. to one of the thoroughfares of that city. West's pamphlet, published in Providence in 1769 by John Carter, recorded this early American astronomical observation and his paper on the subject in the *Transactions of the American Philosophical Society*, I, gave the event wider importance. In 1769 Brown became a trustee of Rhode Island College, which was brought to Providence chiefly through the enterprise of himself and his brother Nicholas. In 1770 this institution conferred upon him the honorary degree of Master of Arts, and in 1784 invited him to fill its chair of natural philosophy. One-half of his first subscription to the college in 1769 had been allocated by the donor to the purchase of "philosophical apparatus." Brown was married on Sept. 30, 1759, to Elizabeth Power.

[*The Chad Browne Memorial* (1888) comp. by Abby Isabel Brown Bulkley; Gertrude S. Kimball, *Providence in Colonial Times* (1912); Benjamin West, *An Account of the Observation of Venus upon the Sun* (1769).]
L.C.W.

BROWN, JOSEPH EMERSON (Apr. 15, 1821–Nov. 30, 1894), lawyer, statesman, was of Scotch-Irish descent. His father, Mackey Brown, and his mother, Sally Rice, were of Virginian ancestry. He was born in Pickens District, S. C., but during his early boyhood his parents removed to Union County in the mountainous country of northern Georgia. This section of the state was in the remote interior, without railroads or good schools and far from the plantation areas, which were the centers of the aristocracy, wealth, and political power of Georgia. Until near manhood Brown led the life of a day laborer on the farm, acquiring meanwhile the rudiments of an education in the neighborhood rural schools. In his nineteenth year he left home and attended an excellent school in Anderson District, S. C. After two or three years there he returned and settled at Canton, in northern Georgia. There he had charge of the town academy (1844), and read law. After being admitted to the bar (1845) he entered the Yale Law School (October 1845) and was graduated the following year. He returned to Canton and settled down as a practitioner. He was a Democrat in politics, and a member of the Baptist Church. In 1847 he was married to Elizabeth Grisham, the daughter of a Baptist preacher. Two years later his political career was begun with his election to the state Senate. Close application to the business of the state quickly brought him recognition as a man of force. He was made a Pierce elector in 1852 and in 1855 was elected judge of the Blue Ridge circuit—a position he was holding when he received the Democratic nomination for governor in the convention of 1857. Brown was a compromise candidate, his nomination coming as a result of a deadlock involving five strong and well-known politicians. He defeated the Know-Nothing candidate, Benjamin H. Hill, in the subsequent election, and was reëlected in 1859, 1861, and 1863, and thus became Georgia's war governor.

Brown's predecessors in office had been for many years men of distinguished family—wealthy, well educated, and experienced in political life; Brown, on the contrary, was unknown and untried. The legislature was full of men who considered themselves his superiors in statecraft. Under the circumstances it was expected that he would be guided by the recognized leaders and not be disposed to press his own opinions. The politicians were mistaken. He was frequently in conflict with the legislature and freely exercised the veto power. He opposed measures looking to the relief of banks from the penalties provided by law for the suspension of specie payments (this was the most important political issue in his first term); he vetoed measures seeking by legislative enactment to pardon criminals; in vigorous messages he advocated the establishment of free schools and the endowment of the state university, then struggling for its existence.

One of his most noteworthy accomplishments was the reform in the administration of the state-owned Western & Atlantic Railroad. Under Brown's administration the net profits from the operation of the road were increased four-fold. An ardent state rights and pro-slavery man, Brown correctly read the signs of the time, and, in anticipation of war, carried through important reforms in the militia system. He held that Congress had no right to restrict slavery in the Territories and advocated secession as the only remedy for northern aggressions. But throughout the Civil War Brown, while complying with all demands for troops, was in conflict with the Confederate government. The trouble arose from the fact that he was almost fanatical in his adherence to the doctrine of state sovereignty, while the exigencies of war forced President Davis to move in the direction of centralization of government. Whenever Brown considered that the acts of Davis or of the Confederate Congress transcended the powers granted by the Confederate constitution, he protested vigorously. Thus the state government and the Confederate authorities quarrelled over Davis's accepting state troops without reference to Brown's authority, and over the appointment of officers to command Georgia troops in the Confederate army, Davis maintaining that military efficiency demanded that all officers be named by himself, Brown that the constitution conferred on enlisted men the power to elect their own company officers—the President's right to appoint field and staff officers not being contested. Brown opposed the practise of allowing substitutes after conscription had commenced; he disputed both the wisdom and constitutionality of the conscription law and at times obstructed its operation; he protested against the seizure of property without compensation by agents of the Confederacy; he opposed the suspension of *habeas corpus*.

On Lee's surrender in 1865 Brown was paroled by Gen. Wilson, but shortly thereafter his parole was ignored. He was taken to Washington and imprisoned for a short while. Pardoned by President Johnson, he returned to Georgia and, finding the state controlled by military authorities, resigned the governorship (June 1865). It will be recalled that the Johnsonian reconstruction was carried out by the President at a time when Congress was not in session. When Congress met in December 1865 it refused to seat Southern representatives and Senators elected under the Johnson plan, declared the President's course illegal, and required the Southern states to adopt the Fourteenth Amendment as a condition of readmission to the Union. This amendment guaranteed civil rights to the negro, disfranchised the Confederate leaders, and placed before the Southern states the alternatives of enfranchising the negroes or of having their congressional representation proportionately reduced. At this stage of affairs the Southern leaders were confronted with a momentous decision. Should they advocate acceptance of the amendment, thus conferring on their former slaves full political rights, but thereby escaping the evils of bayonet rule, or should they follow their natural inclinations and refuse to yield? In Georgia the old line leaders were practically unanimous in their opposition to the congressional program. Brown stood almost alone in counselling compliance with the will of Congress. The state, he held, was helpless to resist. Opposition would serve only to inflame the Republican leaders, to prolong military control, and to delay the restoration of normal conditions. This attitude brought down on the ex-governor's head the bitter hatred of his former associates and friends. He was denounced by the conservatives and the press as a renegade to every principle that a Southern man should hold dear.

Abandoning the Democratic party and affiliating with the Republicans, Brown assisted in putting through the Congressional Reconstruction measures. A new state constitution was drafted by the convention of 1868; the negroes were enfranchised; and in the subsequent election, Rufus B. Bullock, a Republican, became governor. The legislature elected at the same time was dominated by Republican carpet-baggers, negroes, and a number of native white Republicans. Before this legislature Brown became a candidate for the United States Senate and was defeated, this being the only defeat he ever suffered in a campaign. Shortly thereafter (1868) Gov. Bullock appointed him chief justice of the supreme court of Georgia. Bullock's administration became involved in charges of corruption, and as the election of a new legislature in 1870 had resulted in returning a majority hostile to him, the Governor fled from the state. At a special election in 1871 a Conservative Democrat, James M. Smith, was elected governor and normal political conditions were restored. At this juncture Brown withdrew from his Republican affiliations, reëntered the Democratic party, and assisted in the Smith campaign.

Meanwhile, in 1870, he had resigned from the court to accept the presidency of the Western & Atlantic Company, a corporation organized to take over on lease the state-owned railroad. Benjamin H. Hill and Alexander H. Stephens were

also members of this company. Brown developed remarkable business ability, made a great success of the road, entered the coal and iron mining industries, invested largely in Atlanta real estate, and became a wealthy man. In 1880 Gen. John B. Gordon, United States senator, suddenly resigned within three weeks of the end of a session. Gov. Colquitt appointed Brown to fill the unexpired term. Immediately all the old fires of hatred were rekindled. When Colquitt came up for reëlection the opposition to him centered on his appointment of Brown to the Senate. Brown threw himself into the campaign, assisted in the reëlection of Colquitt, and offered himself for reelection to the Senate before the new legislature. He was successful (1880), was twice reëlected, and served until Mar. 3, 1891.

As to the wisdom of Brown's conduct during the Reconstruction period there would seem to be little argument, but even now, a half century after the event, the older people of the state strongly question his motives. A recent historian of the Reconstruction era, while refraining from adverse criticism, points out that "He was first in secession, first in reconstruction and very nearly first in the restoration of Democratic home rule. Consequently he came up on top at every revolution of the wheel of destiny" (Thompson, p. 223). The impression is left by this statement that his conduct was distinctly opportunist, but the ultimate verdict of history will probably be otherwise.

[Herbert Fielder, *A Sketch of the Life and Times and Speeches of Joseph E. Brown* (1883) is the only comprehensive biography. Fielder was Brown's contemporary and life-long friend. The inclusion of copious extracts from Brown's messages and other official papers adds greatly to the value of his work. An appendix contains most of Brown's speeches in the Senate. *Confederate Records of the State of Georgia* (1909–10), vols. I–III, give in full Brown's messages to the legislature, and other papers. R. P. Brooks, "Conscription in the Confederate States," *Military Historian and Economist*, vol. I, no. 4, and A. B. Moore, *Conscription and Conflict in the Confederacy* (1924) discuss Brown's relations with the Confederate authorities. C. M. Thompson, *Reconstruction in Ga.* (1915) is a detailed critical study of the Reconstruction period.]
R.P.B—s.

BROWN, JOSEPH ROGERS (Jan. 26, 1810–July 23, 1876), inventor, manufacturer, was the eldest son of David and Patience (Rogers) Brown. He was born in Warren, R. I., where his father was modestly established as a manufacturer and dealer in clocks, watches, jewelry, and particularly silverware. Brown, as a youth, obtained the limited education which the district school afforded and at the same time, after school and during summer vacations, assisted his father in the conduct of the manufactory. When barely seventeen years old he left home to learn the general machinist's trade in Valley Falls, R. I. Within three months he was entrusted with the making of the finest and most important parts of cotton machinery. After a second short term with another manufacturer, in 1829 he joined his father who was then established at Pawtucket, R. I., in the manufacture of tower clocks. The construction and installation of clocks in churches of towns both in Rhode Island and Massachusetts kept Brown busy for the next two years, but, upon reaching his majority, he went into business for himself in Pawtucket, manufacturing lathes and small tools for machinists. After conducting this business in a modest way for two years he rejoined his father in Providence as partner, to engage in the manufacture of watches, clocks, and surveying and mathematical instruments. For eight years father and son continued in their chosen profession and when the elder Brown retired in 1841 the son continued alone for twelve years. The highest degree of mechanical accuracy and perfection seems to have been their goal, as evidenced by the tower clocks built by them and still in use. This same incentive led the younger Brown early in his career to design a linear dividing engine which he finally perfected and built in 1850. It was, so far as is known, the first automatic machine for graduating rules in the United States and is, together with two more built in 1854 and 1859, in use to-day, meeting all modern requirements for accuracy. Following the graduating machine, Brown brought out in 1851 the vernier caliper reading to thousandths of an inch, applied the vernier to protractors in 1852, and introduced the micrometer caliper in 1867. By 1853 Brown's business had grown to the point of employing fourteen persons, and it was then that Lucian Sharpe was taken into partnership and the firm became J. R. Brown & Sharpe. Fifteen years later they incorporated under the name of Brown & Sharpe Manufacturing Company. In 1855 Brown invented a precision gear cutter to make clock gears and to supply his jobbing customers with gears. The machine was capable not only of producing accurate gears but also of drilling index plates and doing circular graduating. Several of them were built and sold and one is still preserved for its historic significance. The introduction of these several precision tools and their acceptance both in this country and abroad, coupled with a contract in 1861 to make Wilcox & Gibbs sewing machines, marked a turning point in Brown's life in that he stopped making clocks and gave his whole time and thought to his manufacturing interests and the development of machine tools. The Civil War proved a stimulus to this development because of ordnance requirements. Thus Brown in 1861 designed and built a turret screw machine for a company manufacturing muskets. He also invented and built during this and the following year a universal milling machine which embodied such important advantages in all types of manufacturing that the demand taxed to the limit the facilities of his plant. Ten machines were sold in 1862 and seventeen were made for as many gun factories during the remaining three years of the war. By 1870 twenty machines had been distributed abroad into twelve different countries. For this invention Brown received Patent No. 46,621 on Feb. 21, 1865, and so far as is known, it was always respected. Brown's greatest achievement, probably, was the invention of the universal grinding machine, Patent No. 187,770, Feb. 27, 1877, issued after his death. In this he introduced an entirely new conception of manufacturing procedure in that articles could be hardened first and then ground with the utmost accuracy and the least waste. This is the universal practise to-day in all modern manufacturing and tool plants. It was the result of over ten years' constant thought and experimenting, beginning about the time he started making sewing machines and ending just before his death. It was also during this most productive period in Brown's career, namely, 1860 to 1870, that he invented the formed gear cutter which could be sharpened on its face without changing its form. This improvement on earlier gear cutters had a marked influence in the general adoption by manufacturers of the involute form for cut gearing as well as for the use of diametral pitch. Brown had always the respect and love of his employees. He had a contagious enthusiasm about his inventions which was shared by all of his associates and his whole-souled affection for each new mechanism was most genuine. His death was very unexpected, occurring at Isles of Shoals, N. H., while he was taking a short vacation.

In 1837 Brown was married to Caroline B. Niles, who died in 1851; in 1852 he was married to Jane Frances Mowray, who with one daughter survived him.

[J. W. Roe, *Eng. and Am. Tool Builders* (1916); Van Slyke, *Representatives of New England* (Boston, 1879); *Sci. Am.,* 1855; *Representative Men and Old Families of R. I.* (1908); *Machinery,* July 1910; *Am. Machinist,* Jan. 5, 1911; Patent Office Records.]

C. W. M.

BROWN, MATHER (Oct. 7, 1761–May 25, 1831), portrait painter, was a son of Gawen Brown, clock-maker, and Elizabeth (Byles) Brown, a daughter of Rev. Mather Byles of Boston [*q.v.*]. He was descended on his mother's side from Cotton Mather, Increase Mather, and John Cotton. His mother dying in his infancy, the boy was brought up by his aunts, the Misses Mary and Catharine Byles, for whom he had a life-long affection. He had lessons in painting from his Aunt Mary, an amateur, and from Gilbert Stuart, of whom he wrote, Aug. 22, 1817, "I wish to know particularly how Mr. Stewart goes on. He was the first person who learnt me to draw at about 12 years of age at Boston." In 1777 he painted miniatures and sold wine in a trip extending through Worcester and Springfield to Peekskill, whence he wrote to his aunts, "The Yankeys are going to Philadelphia; I believe I shall follow them." He returned, however, to Boston and with money earned from his miniatures he went in 1780 to Paris, carrying letters of introduction from Byles to Benjamin Franklin and Copley, the latter already in London. In 1781 Brown became a pupil of West, making good progress and influential friends. He wrote, in 1783: "I have exhibited four Pictures at the Exhibition (Royal Academy). The King and Queen were to see it yesterday. . . . I spent three weeks at Windsor where I often hunted with the King, and I have a bow from him."

Brown rented (1784) a house, 20 Cavendish Square, and set up as portrait painter. He was styled, perhaps originally self-styled, "Historical Painter to His Majesty and the Duke of York." Among his portraits of members of the royal family was the very fine full length of the Prince of Wales, later George IV, now at Buckingham Palace. His most important American portraits are of this period, as of Presidents John Adams and Thomas Jefferson; of Charles Bulfinch, Sir William Pepperell, and Thomas Paine. In 1784 he designed two historical pieces for a new church in the Strand. His "Marquis Cornwallis Receiving as Hostages the Sons of Tippo Sahib" was exhibited, admired, and engraved. He was among those invited to contribute paintings for the Boydell Shakespeare Gallery.

Despite a large practise Brown found his fashionable establishment too expensive. He wrote in 1801: "Every possible exertion which human Industry could do, I have done; and I have adopted the greatest Prudence in my Affairs, and yet have scarcely been able to live." He never married. He failed to inherit, as he had expected to do, a considerable fortune from his father in Boston. In 1809, his lease having expired, he gave up his London studio. He painted for thirteen years at Manchester, Liverpool, and other provincial towns whence he wrote letters vividly descriptive of depressed conditions in the Napo-

leonic era. At the age of fifty he painted, to send home to his aunts, the excellent self-portrait formerly owned by Frederick L. Gay and now in the possession of the American Antiquarian Society, Worcester, Mass. From July 20, 1824, Brown's letters were again dated from London, 23 Newman St., where, living upon a small annuity, he continued to paint industriously and to exhibit regularly at the Royal Academy. He was much interested in politics and in the Church of England. He was taken suddenly ill while visiting an art exhibition, dying soon afterward, May 25, 1831. He was buried at St. John's Wood, Marylebone.

Mather Brown is well represented in the royal collections, in the National Portrait Gallery, London, and in several American collections. Interest in Brown as painter and person has notably revived in the present century, and the sterling qualities of his art are now better appreciated than at any time since his death. Those familiar with his unpublished correspondence resent the imputation of "imbecility," into which he has been said to have fallen in old age. His later letters reveal a disappointed but not embittered man of keen mentality, always industrious, courteous, and intensely interested in professional, political, and religious affairs.

[Letter-books of Mary and Catharine Byles (transcripts in Mass. Hist. Soc. Lib. of originals at Halifax, N. S.); F. W. Coburn, "Mather Brown," *Art in America*, Aug. 1923; Wm. Dunlap, *Hist of the Rise and Progress of the Arts of Design in the U. S.*, ed. by Frank W. Bayley and Chas. E. Goodspeed (1918).]

F. W. C.

BROWN, MORRIS (Feb. 12, 1770–May 9, 1849), bishop of the African Methodist Episcopal Church, was born in that unusual circle commonly referred to as the "free people of color" in Charleston, S. C. Whereas negroes in other parts of the state were handicapped by various restrictions looking toward rigid slave control, this particular group in the largest city of the state had such close relations with the aristocratic whites with the most of whom they were connected by ties of blood, that they were, legally or actually, exempted from such restrictions. As these free people of color were always permitted to maintain schools and churches for their uplift, Morris Brown acquired what was considered a good education for that day. Early converted in the African Methodist Episcopal Church, and being free, too, he secured a license to preach as soon as he professed religion. He was ordained deacon in 1817 and elder the next year, became a traveling minister, and exercised much influence in and around Charleston. In his work as a preacher, however, he soon faced obstacles. Although free himself he could not forget those of his race who were enslaved. He did for their uplift all that the custom of the times permitted a freeman to do for the oppressed, and occasionally he went beyond the limit set by law and public opinion. He was once imprisoned for manifesting too much sympathy for slaves. His career as a preacher in Charleston was abruptly brought to a close when the Denmark Vesey Insurrection broke out there in 1822. This plan to liberate the slaves of South Carolina by killing off the whites remaining in the city, while the majority of the aristocrats were away at summer resorts, so startled the authorities that almost any negro of influence among his people was suspected of being implicated in the plot. An investigation showed that in the freedom of the African Methodist Episcopal Church, which was an organization conducted independently of the whites, there was offered an opportunity for fomenting such plots as that of this projected uprising; although, in spite of the connection of some members with it, there was no evidence that the church had officially instigated this plot. Coming under the ban, however, and subjected to unusual persecution, suspected free negroes had to take measures for saving their lives. Morris Brown escaped, and finally reached Philadelphia in 1823. There he was not exactly a stranger, having been north before to attend conferences of the church and having made a favorable impression upon his co-workers. He quickly took rank as a leader in every movement of concern to negroes. In the decline of Bishop Allen, who was then becoming incapacitated for the strenuous services which had characterized the first years of his life, Brown rose to the actual leadership of his church. Recognizing his services, the African Methodist Episcopal Conference of 1828 elevated him to the episcopate. Upon him, therefore, fell the important task of carrying forward the expansion of this church. He had to travel in various parts of the country where the body which he represented was unknown and was not welcomed. Despite these handicaps, however, he prosecuted the work with great success, and attained such control that when he became the sole bishop of the church, after the death of Bishop Allen in 1831, the denomination suffered no diminution of interest or loss of prestige. Under Brown the influence of the church was extended to states which had not hitherto been touched, and fields already invaded were evangelized more intensively. To administer the affairs of his ever-growing constituency, it was necessary to associate with him Bishop Edward Waters in 1836.

[R. R. Wright, Jr., *Centennial Encyc. of the A. M. E. Ch.* (1916), pp. 47–48; Daniel A. Payne, *Recollections of Seventy Years* (1888), pp. 64, 73–74, 76–77, 80; A. W. Wayman, *Cyc. of African Methodism* (1882), pp. 2–3. For date of birth see obituary by Bishop Daniel A. Payne in the *Pub. Ledger* (Phila.), May 12, 1849.]
C. G. W.

BROWN, MOSES (Sept. 12/23, 1738–Sept. 7, 1836), manufacturer and philanthropist, was born in Providence, R. I., the youngest of the four distinguished sons of James and Hope (Power) Brown, the others being Nicholas, John, and Joseph [qq.v.]. James Brown died in 1739, leaving his boys to be brought up by their mother, a woman "of rare force of mind and character." At thirteen, Moses left school and went to live with his uncle, Obadiah Brown, part of whose fortune he inherited. In 1763 he was admitted to the firm of Nicholas Brown & Company, established by his brothers, but retired in 1773. In 1764 he married his cousin, Anna Brown, by whom he had three children,—Sarah, Obadiah [q.v.], and a daughter who did not survive infancy. Mrs. Brown's death in 1773 was a crushing blow to her husband, temporarily turning his mind away from worldly matters. A year later he became a Quaker, freed his slaves, and helped to start the Rhode Island Abolition Society. After the Revolutionary War, he was one of the first in this country to become interested in cotton manufacturing and in 1789 he purchased a carding machine, which he set up under the management of his son-in-law, William Almy, and a young relative, Smith Brown, the firm name being Brown & Almy. Having made some experiments with a jenney and spinning frame which operated by hand, in the manner of Arkwright's famous invention, Moses Brown induced Samuel Slater [q.v.], one of Arkwright's men, to come to America, writing him (Dec. 12, 1789), "Come and work our machines, and have the credit as well as advantage of perfecting the first water mill in America." Slater evaded the stringent British laws and came to Rhode Island, where, under Brown's patronage, he built from memory, without plans or drawings, a frame of twenty-four spindles and put it into sucessful operation. The venture was prosperous from the beginning, and added to Brown's already large estate. Although he was troubled with attacks of vertigo, Brown was able, by living quietly, to keep his health, and all his senses were alert up to the time of his death near the close of his ninety-eighth year. In 1779 he married Mary Olney, who died in 1798, and a year later he took a third wife, Phœbe Lockwood, who died in 1808.

In 1770 Moses Brown took the leading step toward moving Rhode Island College (founded at Warren, R. I., in 1764) to Providence, where it was later, because of the benefactions of his family, renamed Brown University; and in 1771 he gave $1,000 to its endowment. In 1780 when subscriptions were solicited for a Friends' School, he contributed £115 and, when it was opened at Portsmouth, R. I., in 1784 under Isaac Lawton as principal, he became its treasurer. Owing to lack of funds, the school was discontinued four years later, but it was reopened in 1819 in Providence, its property having accumulated in Brown's hands to $9,300. Brown provided regularly for the school from that time on, and gave it in his will the sum of $15,000, with some land and his library. It is to-day known as the Moses Brown School.

Brown was a member of the Rhode Island General Assembly from 1764 to 1771, and was the founder of many societies, including the Providence Athenæum Library, the Rhode Island Bible Society, and the Rhode Island Peace Society. His punctuality in business became proverbial. Although he was retiring by nature, he had many interests and left behind him an enormous private correspondence. He was a man of sound judgment, unblemished integrity, and liberal spirit.

[The best and fullest account of Brown's career is a sketch read, Oct. 18, 1892, before the R. I. Hist. Soc. by Augustine Jones, principal of the Friends' School, and later printed under the title *Moses Brown; His Life and Services*. See also J. N. Arnold, *Vital Record of R. I.*, vol. II (1892), pt. I, p. 214, and obituary in *Mfrs. and Farmers Jour.* (Providence), Sept. 7, 1836.]
C. M. F.

BROWN, MOSES (Oct. 2, 1742–Feb. 9, 1827), merchant, philanthropist, was the youngest of thirteen children of Joseph, Jr., and Abigail (Pearson) Brown, of Newbury, Mass. As a mere boy he was apprenticed to a chaise-maker, and, on reaching manhood, started in business himself as a carriage manufacturer. Eventually he turned to commerce, developing a large foreign and domestic trade, especially in sugar and molasses with the West Indies. He increased his investments until he was the owner of several wharves, warehouses, and distilleries, as well as of extensive real estate in Newburyport and vicinity. In 1772 Brown married Mary Hall, of Newburyport, who died, without issue, in 1778. Eight years later he took a second wife, Mary White of Haverhill, who had a large amount of property. She died, Aug. 11, 1821. When Brown died, in Newburyport, he was survived by one daughter, Mrs. William B. Bannister, and no one of his direct descendants is living to-day.

At the time in the early nineteenth century when a project for a Calvinistic theological institution in New England was being discussed

as a means of counteracting the strongly Unitarian influence of Harvard College, Moses Brown, encouraged by his wife and persuaded by his pastor, Dr. Samuel Spring, gave, in 1808, $10,000 to the "Associate Foundation" of Andover Theological Seminary, the other donors being William Bartlet of Newburyport, and John Norris of Salem. When the Seminary was opened, Brown contributed $1,000 to start a library, and in 1819, after a period of prosperity in mercantile affairs, turned over an additional sum of $25,000 to establish a professorship of ecclesiastical history. In 1843, Brown's granddaughter, Sarah (Bannister) Hale, who had inherited much of his property, completed the family benefactions to the Seminary by providing a dwelling house on Andover Hill for the Brown professor. In his will Moses Brown left to the inhabitants of Newburyport the sum of $6,000, to be kept at interest until it reached $15,000, when the capital was to be used "as a fund for the use and support of a grammar school in said town forever."

Moses Brown was a thin wiry person, of vigorous constitution and energetic manner. Through force of character and the rectitude of his life he won the respect of his neighbors and associates. A methodical and progressive business man, he organized many enterprises and kept alert and active to the end of his career. Through the years of his financial success he remembered his own less prosperous young manhood and never refused aid to those who had not been so fortunate as he. He gave cheerfully and liberally to all deserving causes; indeed he was described by a fellow townsman as "always engaged in doing good." He was equally remarkable for his modesty, and he never told others of his charities. It was said of him at his funeral, "He pursued business as though the gains therefrom were not for his use alone, and he distributed them as a trust for the good of others."

[John J. Currier, *Ould Newbury: Hist. & Biog. Sketches* (1896); Leonard Woods, *Hist. of Andover Theol. Seminary* (1884).]
C. M. F.

BROWN, NEILL SMITH (Apr. 18, 1810–Jan. 30, 1886), lawyer, politician, was born near Pulaski, Giles County, Tenn., and died in Nashville, Tenn. His grandfather, Angus Brown, came from Scotland to America in time to fight under Francis Marion in the American Revolution. His parents, Duncan Brown and Margaret (Smith) Brown, emigrated from Robertson County, N. C., to Tennessee, in 1809. The Browns in America were small farmers and strict Presbyterians. Neill S. Brown began work on a farm at the age of seven years and with his small savings managed to attend school now and then, but before his seventeenth year he had learned little more than reading and writing. He was then able to spend two sessions at the Manual Labor Academy in Maury County. Securing funds for further education by teaching school, he next studied law with Chancellor Bramlett, was admitted to the bar in 1834, and began the practise of law in Pulaski. A year later he moved to Texas, opening a law office in Matagordo, but, disappointed, soon returned to Tennessee, and is next heard of when he enlisted in Robert Armstrong's brigade of Tennessee troops for service against the Seminoles in Florida.

Joining the anti-Jackson movement, which was led by those in the state whom Jackson had discomfited in politics, Brown was nominated elector on the Whig presidential ticket in 1836, and in 1837 was elected to the state legislature, where he was the youngest member. Defeated for Congress in 1843 by Aaron V. Brown, Democrat, in the so-called "Brown" race, he was elected governor over the same competitor in 1847, the youngest governor of the state up to that time. Again defeated by a Democrat in 1849, he was sent as minister to Russia in 1850. After three years he returned to the state legislature as speaker of the House. The Whig party of the state was now disintegrating, as its old anti-Jackson leaders disappeared, and Brown, though taking no active part in politics after 1856, allied himself with the Democrats. Though opposed to secession, he took office in 1861 under the state government of Tennessee as a member of the military and financial board. When the Union forces captured Nashville in 1862, he was imprisoned for a time by Andrew Johnson, the military governor. During the remainder of the conflict he was neutral in action but with Southern sympathies.

Brown was "one of the most amiable characters and brightest minds in Tennessee history," but failed of opportunity to round out his public career on account of the decline of the Whig party after he reached the age of forty. His administration as governor was not notable and his best work, which extended throughout his life, was his unvarying and constructive support of the public schools before and after the Civil War. He aided in securing grants from the Peabody fund, upon which Peabody College was later established. He was a successful lawyer for fifty years except for the frequent diversions into politics which he made in early life. His fame and influence were due in large part to effective oratory. He said of himself: "I had a native ambition to rise from obscurity and to make myself useful in the world, to shine and be distinguished. . . . My poverty pushed me on. I started life on nothing, was as poor as any man in Tennessee who ever became at all known." His last public service was as delegate to the Tennessee constitutional convention of 1870, of which his younger brother, John Calvin Brown [q.v.], was president. Brown married in 1839 Mary Ann Trimble, daughter of Judge James Trimble of Nashville, who was a man of position and influence and opposed to secession. There were eight children.

[John Allison, *Notable Men of Tenn.* (1905); J. T. Moore, *Tennessee, The Volunteer State* (1923); W. W. Clayton, *Hist. of Davidson County, Tenn.* (1880); H. S. Foote, *Bench and Bar of the South and Southwest* (1876); Joshua W. Caldwell, *Sketches of the Bench and Bar of Tenn.* (1898); W. S. Speer, *Sketches of Prominent Tennesseeans* (1888); obituary in the *Daily American* (Nashville), Jan. 31, 1886; executive and legislative docs. in the State Capitol.] W. L. F.

BROWN, NICHOLAS (July 28, 1729 o.s.– May 29, 1791), merchant, was the son of James and Hope (Power) Brown and the eldest of the four brothers (Nicholas, Joseph [q.v.], John [q.v.], and Moses [q.v.]) who became in the closing years of the eighteenth century the leading merchants and citizens of Rhode Island. James Brown and his brother Obadiah had established a general store in Providence, and in 1739 controlled the movements of eight vessels in the West India trade. In that year James Brown died. The business was carried on by Obadiah, at first alone, and then, as they grew up, with four of the sons of James as assistants and partners under the firm name Obadiah Brown & Company. At the death of the uncle in 1762, the four brothers continued the business as Nicholas Brown & Company. The firm attained international standing during the years between 1762 and the Revolution. Its ventures were extended from the West Indies to London, Marseilles, Nantes, Copenhagen, and Hamburg, while at home its members were active in the development of local manufactures. It is credited with having brought about the change in the spermaceti candle business from the household to the factory stage of development by the gathering of all who had been previously working at the manufacture in their homes into a building erected for the purpose on the outskirts of Providence. When the increase in the business there and in Newport brought about a scarcity of head matter and spermaceti oil, a competitive struggle for this choice product of the whale ensued between the Brown interests and the wealthy Jewish manufacturers of Newport. Useless competition was avoided by the formation in 1761 of a "union" or United Company of spermaceti-candle manufacturers of Providence and Newport, with associates in Boston and Philadelphia. In 1763 the combination was renewed and the Browns were the leading members of the organization. The agreements fixed the price of purchase, provided for preventing the establishment of new manufactories, and designated and limited the dealers in oil to be patronized by the associates. These documents are said to record the earliest monopolistic combination made in America. The effort on the part of the brothers in or soon after 1764 to establish an iron manufactory in Rhode Island to utilize the ore dug from the pits at Cranston resulted in the buildings of the "Furnace Hope" at Scituate, where until the last decade of the century a successful industry was carried on by the firm and certain associates. Pig iron and articles for their trading cargoes were made at the furnace, and in the Revolution cannon of all sizes up to eighteen pounders were cast for the Congress. The firm was interested in distilling; and in the French Wars and later, Nicholas and John Brown were large shareholders in various successful privateering ventures. Though the Newport merchants who were their contemporaries were successful in the Guinea trade, yet the interest of Nicholas Brown & Company in the "triangular voyage" seems to have been only occasional in its character. During the non-importation proceedings in 1769 Nicholas Brown was prominently engaged in the American interest; in the Revolution he served a secret committee of Congress by using his ships and foreign connections for the importation of clothing and munitions for the soldiers; in the struggle in Rhode Island over the Constitution he exercised a strong influence in favor of adoption. In 1767 it was the personal contributions and the guarantee of the pledges of their fellow citizens by Nicholas and his brother Joseph that determined Providence as the location of Rhode Island College, afterward, because of the benefactions of a later member of the family, to be known as Brown University. It was under the oversight of the firm that the first college building, now University Hall, was erected on a piece of ground formerly a Brown family possession. Nicholas was a prominent benefactor, too, of the Baptist Society of Providence.

He married first, on May 2, 1762, Rhoda Jenckes, who died Dec. 16, 1783, survived by two of their ten children, Nicholas [q.v.] and Hope, who married Thomas Poynton Ives. Brown maried second, on Sept. 9, 1785, Avis Binney. He died May 29, 1791. His tombstone records the otherwise forgotten fact that "His stature was large; his personal appearance manly and noble."

[*The Chad Browne Memorial* (1888), comp. by Abby Isabel Brown Bulkley; Reuben A. Guild, *Hist. of Brown Univ.* (1867); Gertrude S. Kimball, *Providence in Colonial Times* (1912); Wm. R. Staples, *Annals of the Town of Providence* (1843); "Commerce of R. I., 1726–1800," in *Colls. Mass. Hist. Soc.*, ser. 7, vols. IX, X (1914–15); Irving B. Richman, *Rhode Island* (1905); Wm. B. Weeden, *Early R. I.* (1910).]   L. C. W.

BROWN, NICHOLAS (Apr. 4, 1769–Sept. 27, 1841), merchant, philanthropist, was the son of the preceding Nicholas Brown and his wife, Rhoda Jenckes. After graduating in 1786 from Rhode Island College, which afterward assumed his name, he went into his father's counting house, and three years later when he became of age the firm was reorganized with the father and son and George Benson as Brown & Benson. In 1792, after the death of the elder Nicholas Brown, the latter's son-in-law, Thomas Poynton Ives, was admitted into the firm, and his name added to that of the partners. Four years later, when Benson withdrew, the younger men, trading as Brown & Ives, the name under which part of the family interests are still managed, set out upon a career notable in the history of American commercial activity. The earlier energies of the firm were devoted at first to the development of the East India and China trade, just then becoming an important element in American commercial life. Seven years after John Brown, uncle of Nicholas, had inaugurated in 1787 a trade between East India and Providence by sending the *General Washington* with a cargo to India, the firm of Brown, Benson & Ives built the *John Jay* and launched her in the eastern trade. Thereafter until the sale of their last ship, the *Hanover,* in 1838, many vessels, the *Ann and Hope,* the *Rising Sun,* and others, kept the name of Brown & Ives constantly on the distant seas, and this in spite of depredation by English and French, of embargo by our own government, and of shipwreck, and a failing trade. With the foresight and caution that characterized his father and himself, Nicholas Brown waited until the manufacturing of cotton had been well established by his uncle Moses Brown [q.v.] before his firm bought in 1804 its first water rights on the Blackstone River. When the Embargo of 1812 put a temporary check on shipping, the firm was found well established in the cotton manufactory and in control of a large part of the Blackstone River water power. With the formation of the Lonsdale Company in the thirties, the character of the firm's business had definitely changed to its present interest. With a similar caution, and a like reward, Brown &

Ives did not at once follow John Brown in his purchase, late in the eighteenth century, of lands in western New York, but ten years afterward they invested a part of their surplus in large tracts on the Ohio. In the years following the Civil War the Ohio farm-land holdings of the successors of the firm attained great value as urban properties in growing middle-western cities.

The relations of Nicholas Brown with the University which bears his name were not simply those of a wealthy benefactor to a chosen object of charity, for family pride and personal affection engaged his interest. He was educated in the building erected for the old Rhode Island College by the efforts of his father and his uncles; he was a trustee by the year 1791, and treasurer from 1796 until 1825. In 1804 he gave $5,000 for the endowment of a professorship of oratory and belles lettres, a gift that resulted in the change of the college's name to Brown University as a recognition of the beneficence of himself and of other members of his family. In 1823 he erected as a gift from him and his nephews, Hope College, named after his sister, Hope (Brown) Ives, and in 1834 he built Manning Hall. Gifts to the library and the laboratories and to other building funds brought his benefactions to the college to the amount of $160,000. Great in amount for those days, his gifts came furthermore at a time in the life of the college that determined its future as an important American educational institution. Nicholas Brown was for many years a member of the Rhode Island General Assembly. He was one of the founders of the Providence Athenæum, and a generous contributor to the Baptist Society and to other local charities. The $30,000 left in his will for the care of the insane resulted in the building and maintenance of the Butler Hospital for the Insane, in the management of which his descendants have continuously had an active part. In him was found in special degree the mingling of shrewd business sense, respect for things of the mind and spirit, and sense of responsibility to his community that have always characterized this family of merchants and philanthropists. President Wayland said of him that his success "testified that boldness of enterprise may be harmoniously united with vigorous and deliberate judgment." In the same *Discourse,* Wayland observes: "In his ample brow and well-developed forehead, you could not but observe the marks of a vigorous and expansive intellect; while his mouth indicated a spirit tenderly alive to human suffering, and habitually occupied in the contemplation

of deeds of compassion." Brown married twice: first on Nov. 3, 1791, Ann, daughter of John Carter, long the leading printer of Providence; and second, Mary Bowen Stelle on July 22, 1801. The younger of the two sons by the first wife was John Carter Brown [*q.v.*]

[Francis Wayland, *A Discourse in Commemoration of the Life and Character of the Hon. Nicholas Brown* (1841); Abby Isabel Brown Bulkley, *The Chad Browne Memorial* (1888); obituary in the *Providence Journal,* Oct, 4, 1841.]   L. C. W.

BROWN, OBADIAH (July 15, 1771–Oct. 15, 1822), merchant and philanthropist, was born in Providence, R. I., the only son of Moses Brown [*q.v.*] and Anna (Brown) Brown. He was sent by his father, who had become a Quaker in 1774, to the Friends' Yearly Meeting School at Portsmouth, R. I., in 1787, but this institution closed in October 1788, because of lack of funds, after four years of existence. Obadiah had almost no other formal schooling, but went directly into business.

About this time his father formed a firm, consisting of William Almy (Moses Brown's son-in-law), together with Slater and Smith Brown, whose place was taken in 1792 by Obadiah Brown. This company, known later as Brown & Almy, produced the first pure cotton goods made in the United States, all the previous warps having been linen. The Brown mills, located at Pawtucket, were immediately prosperous, and the Embargo Act of 1808 furnished an additional stimulus to manufacturing, whereby Obadiah Brown and his partners accumulated a considerable fortune. In 1798, Brown married Dorcas Hadwen, daughter of John and Elizabeth Hadwen, of Newport.

When, early in the nineteenth century, it was proposed to reëstablish the Friends' Yearly Meeting School, the Brown family took up the project. In 1814 Moses Brown offered a suitable tract of land, located in Providence, and when, in 1815, subscriptions were solicited, Obadiah Brown contributed $2,000 for construction, $500 for furnishings, and $1,000 annually for five years toward the school's maintenance. Obadiah Brown and William Almy took the contract for erecting the main hall, and the former drove every day in his chaise to superintend the laborers. In 1817, when the available funds were exhausted, he and Almy agreed to provide half of the additional $7,500 required, on condition that other Friends supply the remainder. The stipulation was met, and the building was completed. After the school was formally opened in 1819, Obadiah and his wife, Dorcas, regularly attended meeting there, and it became his custom to present each scholar at graduation with a book as a token of his personal regard. Although his father was actually treasurer of the school, Obadiah watched over its affairs with a zealous care as a valuable member of the school committee. When he died in 1822, after a brief illness, he left to the school the sum of $100,000, the largest single bequest made to any institution of learning in the United States up to that time, and also a fine library of books and maps. The will, signed in 1814, was drawn up in his father's handwriting. The school thus founded has grown and prospered, and in 1904 was renamed the Moses Brown School. The original building, since much enlarged, still stands as the central feature of the campus.

Personally Brown was gracious and urbane, with an unostentatious and conciliating manner. When decisions were made, he was firm in standing by them, but he instinctively tried to avoid disputes. He was a patient and industrious man, with much public spirit and a genius for wise philanthropy.

[See *Moses Brown: a Sketch by Augustine Jones, Read before the R. I. Hist. Soc., Oct. 18, 1892*; R. W. Kelsey, *Centennial Hist. of the Moses Brown School, 1819–1919* (1919). There are interesting manuscript letters of Obadiah Brown in possession of the R. I. Hist. Soc. For date of birth see J. N. Arnold, *Vital Record of R. I.*, vol. II (1892), pt. I, p. 214.] C.M.F.

BROWN, OLYMPIA (Jan. 5, 1835–Oct. 23, 1926), feminist, was born in a log cabin at Prairie Ronde, Mich. Her parents, Asa B. and Lephia Brown, were New Englanders, having moved to Michigan from Plymouth, Mass. In later life, Miss Brown stated that from early childhood she remembered her mother taking the unpopular view of public questions and it was from her that she received her first ideas of equal rights for men and women. Olympia desired to attend the University of Michigan, but it would not admit women. She therefore entered Antioch College, at Yellow Springs, Ohio, from which she received a degree of bachelor of arts in 1860. While there she decided that the ministry held golden opportunities for women, so she enrolled in the Theological School of St. Lawrence University, at Canton, N. Y. She was graduated in 1863 and ordained to the ministry of the Universalist Church in the same year, the first woman in America to be ordained to the ministry of a regularly constituted ecclesiastical body. She served pastorates at Weymouth, Mass., 1864, Bridgeport, Conn., 1869, and subsequently at Racine, Mukwonago, Neenah, and Columbus, Wis. In 1866 she met Susan B. Anthony at an Equal Rights meeting in New York City and from a passive believer in woman's rights, became an ardent advocate. The following year, when a Republican legislature in Kansas submitted to the vote of the people of that state a proposition to amend the state constitution by striking out the word "male," suffrage leaders selected her to campaign for the cause in Kansas. It was the first time that the men of any state had been asked to vote on such a measure. So thorough was the campaign that, notwithstanding the fact that the Republican party, which had fathered the amendment, refused to aid in its support and even sent out circulars opposing it, the election showed one-third of the votes in its favor. When the campaign was over Miss Brown returned to preaching in New England, but continued actively interested in woman suffrage and all matters affecting women workers and the homes of the nation. In April 1873 she married John Henry Willis, a printer and newspaper-man. By agreement with her husband she retained her maiden name and in all her public work was known as the Rev. Olympia Brown. She became president of the Wisconsin Woman's Suffrage Association in 1887 and continued as such for thirty years. When her husband died in 1893, she became manager of his daily and weekly newspaper and job printing office in Racine, Wis. For many years she traveled from state to state lecturing and campaigning for woman suffrage until at last equal suffrage was made nation-wide by the Federal Constitution. In 1914 she decided to make Baltimore her home and live with her daughter, Gwendolen B. Willis. In the presidential campaign of 1924, she was an ardent supporter of Robert M. La Follette. In 1925, at the age of ninety, she accompanied her daughter on a trip to France and Italy. When she died in Baltimore, an editorial in the Baltimore *Sun* said of her, "Perhaps no phase of her life better exemplified her vitality and intellectual independence than the mental discomfort she succeeded in arousing, between her eightieth and ninetieth birthdays, among conservatively-minded Baltimoreans." She published a book in 1911, entitled *Acquaintances, Old and New, Among Reformers,* which is her own account of her life and activities with many references to her contemporaries. She also published a memorial sketch of Clara B. Colby, in 1917, called *Democratic Ideals.*

[A biography of Olympia Brown is found in the *Hist. of Woman Suffrage,* by Elizabeth Cady Stanton, Matilda Gage, and Susan B. Anthony, vol. III (1886); see also *Who's Who in America,* 1914–15; *Equal Rights,* Oct. 30, 1926; the *Sun* (Baltimore), Oct. 24, 25, 1926.] M.S.

BROWN, PHŒBE HINSDALE (May 1, 1783–Aug. 10, 1861), an early American hymn writer, though of New England ancestry, was born in Canaan, N. Y., the seventh and youngest child of George and Phœbe (Allen) Hinsdale. It is commonly stated that when two years old she was left an orphan, but the sketch of her life in the *Hinsdale Genealogy* (1906), based on an autobiography then in the hands of her grand-daughter, gives the date of her father's death as Mar. 20, 1784, and that of her mother as Apr. 17, 1791. She was early taken in charge by a pious grandmother, Mrs. Allen, who gave her religious instruction, and before she was nine, it is said, she had read the Bible through three times. From her ninth till her eighteenth year she lived with her married sister, Chloe Noyes. The latter's husband proved a hard taskmaster, and Phœbe was deprived of instruction, forbidden books, and made to work like a slave. Later she got a few months' schooling, and on June 1, 1805, at Canaan, N. Y., she married Timothy Hill Brown, a carpenter and painter. They removed to Connecticut where they lived at East Windsor for eight years, then at Ellington for five. From 1818 until Mr. Brown's death in 1853, their home was at Monson, Mass. Both became members of the Congregational Church. Four children were born to them, one of them, Samuel Robbins Brown [*q.v.*], destined to become a well-known educator and missionary. Mrs. Brown's life was one of comparative poverty and some hardship. Her deep religious devotion found expression in simple but sincere verse. At Ellington she was accustomed at each day's close to make her escape from household cares and repair to a quiet spot for meditation. Unkind interpretations of this habit led her to write "Apology for My Twilight Rambles Addressed to a Lady." From this was taken one of her best known hymns, still sung in the churches, "I Love to Steal Awhile Away." It appeared with three others by her in Nettleton's *Village Hymns* (1824). In 1853 it was incorporated in the *Leeds Hymn Book,* and thus came into use in England. Two additional hymns from her pen were published in Hastings's *Spiritual Songs* (1831). Others appeared in *Mother's Hymn Book* (1834), Linsley and Davis, *Select Hymns* (1836), and *Parish Hymns* (1843). Some of these have had wide use in this country and abroad. Two now forgotten prose works were also written by her and published in 1836; *The Tree and Its Fruits,* a collection of little homilies, directed against intemperance, gambling, and infidelity; and *The Village School,* describing the religious instruction given by a teacher, and its effects.

[Herbert C. Andrews, *Hinsdale Genealogy, Descendants of Robt. Hinsdale* (1906) ; Sam. W. Duffield, *English Hymns* (1886) ; John Julian, *A Dict. of Hymnology* (1891) ; Wm. E. Griffis, *A Maker of the New Orient, Samuel Robbins Brown* (1902).]   H.E.S.

BROWN, SAMUEL (Jan. 30, 1769–Jan. 12, 1830), physician, was born in a rural section of what is now Rockbridge County, Va., to Rev. John Brown, Presbyterian minister, and Margaret Preston. His education began in the grammar school which his father conducted in addition to his pastoral duties. Later, he attended a seminary conducted by Rev. James Waddell in Louisa County, Va., followed by two years at Dickinson College at Carlisle, Pa., where he graduated in 1789 with the degree of bachelor of arts. He began the study of medicine with his brother-in-law, Dr. Humphrey, at Staunton, Va., later becoming a private pupil of Dr. Rush in Philadelphia. After two years at the University of Edinburgh and a short time at the University of Aberdeen he obtained his degree of doctor of medicine from the latter institution. Returning to America, he began the practise of medicine at Bladensburg, Md., but in 1797 he left to join his brother James [*q.v.*], who was practising law in Lexington, Ky. He gave up his practise here to follow his brother again, this time to New Orleans, in 1806. In 1809 he married Catherine Percy of Natchez, Miss., and went to live upon a plantation near that city, relinquishing the practise of his profession. The death of his wife a few years later caused him to give up his Natchez home and to establish himself upon a plantation adjacent to that of his brother-in-law, Col. Thomas Percy, near Huntsville, Ala. Here he lived until 1819, devoting himself to the education of his two surviving children. Brown had long had in mind the idea of starting a medical school in his section of the country, and in 1819 he entered into an agreement with Dr. Daniel Drake for the establishment of such a school at Cincinnati. While Drake was obtaining the charter for the Ohio school, however, the trustees of Transylvania University at Lexington offered Brown the chair of theory and practise of medicine in the medical school recently organized there. He accepted this position and held it until 1825 when he resigned and retired to his former home in Alabama. His remaining years were spent largely in travel in America and Europe. He suffered a stroke of apoplexy in 1826 and died from a succeeding stroke at the home of his brother-in-law near Huntsville.

Brown was a man of attractive personality and of unusual scholarship for his time. His portrait shows a round, full, smoothly shaven face, suggesting boundless benevolence. His personality made him a popular practitioner wherever he located. He was, however, a dilettante in medicine as in his other interests. Though he introduced vaccination for smallpox at Lexington as early as 1802, its interest for him lay in its novelty. His lectures were rambling discourses full of interesting even though unrelated facts. He was averse to continued effort and incapable of pursuing any inquiry to its conclusion. His medical writings were sketchy case reports and his few contributions to scientific journals were mere notices of striking or curious phenomena, such as his paper on "Nitre Caves of Kentucky" in the first volume of *Bruce's Journal*. The Kappa Lambda Society of Hippocrates, a society of medical men pledged to professional ideals, was founded by him, and under its auspices, the *North American Medical and Surgical Journal* was started in Philadelphia in 1825. Two treatises often credited to him, *An Inaugural Dissertation on the Bilious Malignant Fever* (1797), and *A Treatise on the Nature, Origin and Progress of the Yellow Fever* (1800), were really written by Dr. Samuel Brown of Boston (1769–1805).

[The sketch of Brown by R. La Roche in Samuel D. Gross, *Lives of Eminent Am. Physicians and Surgeons* (1861), is the undiscriminating eulogy of a warm personal friend. The obituary in the *Western Jour. Medic. and Phys. Sci.*, vol. III (Cincinnati, 1830), and "Dr. Samuel Brown as an Author" by L. P. Yarnell in the *Western Jour. of Medicine and Surgery*, vol. II (Louisville, 1854), give a better idea of Brown's qualities and defects. In the *Ky. Medic. Jour.*, vol. XV (1917) there is a brief sketch of Brown's career.]   J.M.P.

BROWN, SAMUEL GILMAN (Jan. 4, 1813–Nov. 4, 1885), college president, was a descendant on both sides of Calvinist stock, distinguished in the ministerial and educational life of New England. His father was Francis Brown [1784–1820, *q.v.*], Congregational pastor at North Yarmouth, Me., at the time of the son's birth, and later the third president of Dartmouth College. His mother, Elizabeth Gilman, was a woman trained in the sturdiest Puritan traditions. To her, on the untimely death of her husband, fell the bringing up of the seven-year-old boy, the only surviving child.

Brown's boyhood and youth were passed in Hanover, N. H. Here he attended Dartmouth College, graduating in 1831 at the age of eighteen. For the following two years he taught in the high school of Ellington, Conn., and then entered Andover Theological Seminary, acting at the same time as principal of the local Abbot Academy. Following his graduation from Andover in 1837, he devoted two years to travel in Europe and the East. On his return in 1840 he was called to the faculty of Dartmouth, where he taught for twenty-seven consecutive years, occupying successively the chairs of oratory and belles lettres and of intellectual philosophy and political economy. His broad and cultivated taste found expression in many articles and reviews contributed to periodicals, chiefly on literary and biographical topics. His most ambitious undertaking, an edition of *The Works of Rufus Choate, with a Memoir of His Life* (2 vols., 1862), was favorably received (*North American Review*, XCVI, 194–220; *Atlantic Monthly*, XI, 139–142) and remains the standard work on the subject. The *Memoir*, with some additions, was reprinted separately in 1870. Brown married, in February 1846, Mrs. Sarah (Van Vechten) Savage of Schenectady, N. Y. To them were born seven children. In 1867 Brown accepted the invitation to become president of Hamilton College and to fill the related chair of Christian evidences on its faculty. The new president brought scholarly rather than executive gifts to his office, and a winning rather than forceful personality. His conservative administration of fourteen years was unmarked by significant change of educational policy or important development within the college. He relinquished the office in 1881, feeling that the needs of the institution, then in serious financial straits, called for executive qualities which he did not possess. For a few years following his resignation he gave occasional instruction in mental and moral philosophy, first at Dartmouth (1882–83) and then at Bowdoin (1883–85). He died suddenly, in his seventy-third year, at Utica, N. Y., his home since quitting Hamilton, leaving his eldest son Francis [1849–1916, *q.v.*] to carry into the third generation the distinguished ministerial and educational heritage of the family.

Brown's most impressive work was done in the pulpit and on the platform. While he never held a pastorate, he was ordained to the Congregational ministry in 1852, and throughout his career was much in demand as a preacher. As a lecturer, he appeared before the Lowell Institute of Boston in 1859, and was frequently chosen for commemorative orations and for addresses on important occasions. Almost a score of these discourses, separately published, testify to the breadth of his interests and to his command of a graceful and felicitous style. In his well-rounded humanism, gracious and unassuming personality, and high religious purpose, he was representative of the best traditions in American educational life of his time.

[*Memorial of Samuel Gilman Brown* (1886) contains portrait, biographical sketch, memorial addresses, obituary notices, bibliography of publications, etc. See also Arthur Gilman, *The Gilman Family* (1869), and J. K. Lord, *Hist. of Dartmouth Coll. 1815–1909* (1913).]   F.H.R.

BROWN, SAMUEL ROBBINS (June 16, 1810–June 20, 1880), missionary, educator, was born in East Windsor, Conn., the son of Timothy Hill and Phœbe (Hinsdale) Brown [*q.v.*]. Due in no small part to the religious faith and missionary zeal of his parents, though, he states, they never suggested the course to him, he had from childhood but one plan for the future, namely, "to get a liberal education, to study for the sacred ministry, and then to be a missionary to some heathen people." His preliminary education was received at Monson Academy, Monson, Mass., where after 1818 the Browns resided. His father's income as a carpenter and painter was too meager to afford Samuel a college education, but he succeeded in graduating from Yale in 1832, having supported himself by sawing wood, instructing fellow students in music, and ringing the college bell. For more than three years he taught in the New York Institute for the Deaf and Dumb. An attack of pneumonia led him to go South in 1835, and for two years he studied at Columbia Theological Seminary, Columbia, S. C., and later at Union Seminary, New York. He was accepted by the American Board for appointment to China, but seized an immediate opportunity to go there as a teacher for the Morrison Educational Society. On Oct. 10, 1838, he married Elizabeth, daughter of Rev. Shubael Bartlett of East Windsor, Conn.; on Oct. 14, he was ordained by the Third Presbytery of New York; and on Oct. 17, he began a one hundred and twenty-five days' voyage to Macao.

His life embraced two distinct and influential missionary careers: one in China (1839–47); and one in Japan (1859–79). In both countries he was a pioneer in secular education combined with religious instruction. The school he established for the Morrison Society, and conducted, first at Macao, then at Hong Kong, was the parent of its kind. When forced to return in 1847, owing to his wife's ill health, he brought with him three of his students. Their coming marks the beginning of Chinese education in America. One of them, Yung Wing, was the first Chinese graduate of Yale, and through his influence the Chinese government later sent more than a hundred boys to this country.

In Japan, where he went in 1859 as one of the first three members of the Dutch Reformed Mission, he occupied himself largely with teaching, first at Kanagawa, then at Yokohama. Scores of his students became prominent in the Empire. He was a founder and president of the Asiatic Society of Japan and was also (1874–79) chairman of the committee which translated the New Testament into Japanese, his own contributions being translations of Acts, Philippians, Philemon, and Revelation. He prepared the Canton

Colloquial portion for James Legge's Lexilogus, and also published *Colloquial Japanese* (1863); *Prendergast's Mastery System Adapted to the Japanese* (1875); a translation, published in the *Journal of the North-China Branch of the Royal Asiatic Society* (n.s., vols. II, III, 1865–66), of Arai Hakuseki's *Sei Yo Ki-Bun;* biographies of Yung Wing, Wong Shin, and Wong Fun, in Japanese, intended to stimulate young men in Japan to become benefactors of their country—and a number of articles in the *Chinese Repository.* Ill health compelled him to return to America in 1879, and he died at Monson the following year.

In the interim between his Chinese and his Japanese missions, he contributed to the educational progress of his own country. From 1848 to 1851 he conducted a school in Rome, N. Y., and while pastor of the Reformed Dutch Church, Owasco Outlet, N. Y. (1851–59), he was one of the most active of the founders and directors of Elmira College.

[Wm. E. Griffis, *A Maker of the New Orient* (1902); Edward T. Corwin, *A Manual of the Reformed Church in America* (1902); Evarts B. Greene, *A New Englander in Japan, Daniel Crosby Greene* (1927); Yung Wing, *My Life in China and America* (1909); *Biog. Memoranda Respecting . . . Members of the Class of 1832 in Yale Coll.* (1880), ed. by E. E. Salisbury; *Obit. Record Grads. Yale Coll.*, 2nd ser., 1870–1880.]

H. E. S.

BROWN, SIMON (Nov. 29, 1802–Feb. 26, 1873), agricultural editor, was born in Newburyport, Mass., the son of Nathaniel and Mary (Sleeper) Brown. In 1811 Nathaniel Brown's property was destroyed by fire and he was reduced from comparative wealth to poverty. He moved with his family to a farm near Chester, N. H. It was necessary for the children to help their father on the farm; at the early age of nine Simon received his first training in practical agriculture, and soon developed a keen interest in the work. He attended the common schools for a few weeks each year and for the rest of the year devoted his entire time to farming. While residing on his father's farm he attended Pembroke Academy, at Pembroke, N. H., for six months. This was the extent of his education. In 1818 he entered a printing-office in Concord, N. H., as an apprentice. He worked in this shop for several years and then spent a year traveling in the South studying southern agriculture and observing the relations existing between master and slaves. When he returned in 1826 he settled in Hingham, Mass., and commenced the publication of a newspaper called the *Hingham Gazette.* He was married in 1828 to Ann Caroline French of Chester, N. H. A year afterward he sold his interest in the Hingham paper and returned to Chester where he opened a printing-office and published the *New Hampshire Law Reports.* In 1830 in company with his brother-in-law, B. B. French, he purchased a printing-office and a newspaper called the *New Hampshire Spectator,* in Newport. He remained in Newport for the next five years, then moved to Concord, Mass., and established himself as a book and job-printer. In 1838 he received an appointment in the office of the clerk of the House of Representatives at Washington. Within a short time he was appointed librarian to the House and he kept this position until 1848. He had at last saved enough money to realize a life-long dream, which was to live on a farm of his own. He purchased a small, almost worthless place near Concord, Mass., and went there to live for the rest of his days. While working relentlessly to make the farm successful he found time to publish a paper in Concord called the *Concord Freeman,* for one year. In 1858 he became editor of the *New England Farmer,* an agricultural newspaper published in Boston. At various intervals he wrote articles for other periodicals and government agricultural reports. For several years he served on the Massachusetts State Board of Agriculture. In 1855 he was elected lieutenant-governor of Massachusetts. He was a modest, affable man seeking success in the thing which interested him most, agriculture. At the time of his death, which occurred at his home, his farm was known to be very valuable, and many farms in the neighborhood had been materially improved through suggestions made by him.

[*Memoirs of Members of the Social Circle in Concord,* 3 ser. (1907) ; *New Eng. Farmer,* Mar. 8, 1873.]

                                  M.S.

BROWN, SOLYMAN (Nov. 17, 1790–Feb. 13, 1876), poet, teacher, clergyman, dentist, and one of the founders of dentistry as an organized profession, was born in Litchfield, Conn., a son of Nathaniel and Thankful (Woodruff) Brown. Educated with a view to the ministry in the Morris Academy at Litchfield and Yale College, he graduated from the latter in 1812 and received its A.M. in 1817. In 1813, after a year of special preparatory study, he was licensed as a Congregational minister for four years, and occupied several pulpits in northern Connecticut during that period. A renewal of his license was refused through the opposition of the Rev. Lyman Beecher [*q.v.*], who held that two years of special study were necessary for a minister. During the controversy that followed, Brown published *An Address to the People of Litchfield County* (1818) ; *Second Address ...* (1818) ; and

Servile Spirits and Spiritual Masters (1820) ; all three containing biographical data. In 1818 he also published *An Essay on American Poetry* (a long poem), together with *Miscellaneous Pieces* (most of which had appeared originally in the *New Haven Herald*). Failing to obtain a renewal of his license, he removed in 1820 to New York City, where he was engaged as a classical instructor in several fashionable private schools for the next twelve years. In 1822 he embraced Swedenborgianism, and preached in the New Jerusalem Church in New York for many years. During his school-teaching period he published *The Birth of Washington; a Poem* (1822) ; *A Comparative View of the Systems of Pestalozzi and Lancaster* (1825), and *Sermons* (Swedenborgian, 1829).

His later career was largely influenced by his close friendship with an eminent dentist of New York City, Eleazar Parmly [*q.v.*]. They lived together for six years, until Parmly married (1828), and in 1832 and 1833 were again together in Parmly's house, where Brown studied dentistry and wrote his best known work, *Dentologia* (1833). It is the only dental didactic poem in English, a real literary curiosity, which was favorably received by reviewers, and has been quoted frequently by dental writers. It was reprinted five times; it "had a great influence in elevating dentistry as a profession," and the author has been called "The Poet Laureate of the Dental Profession" (B. K. Thorpe, "Solyman Brown," in C. R. E. Koch's *History of Dental Surgery,* 1909, vol. II). Brown left the Parmly house, and practised dentistry with Samuel Avery in 1834, in which year (Dec. 23) he married Elizabeth, a daughter of Amos Butler, editor and proprietor of the *Mercantile Advertiser* of New York. During the previous two years a dozen of his poems appeared in the *New York Mirror,* the earliest being signed "Mynalos," an anagram of Solyman. In the *Mirror* for 1834 he published *The Hermit of the Baikal,* a long prose poem; and in the same year he and Parmly were the prime movers in the organization of the world's first dental association, the Society of Surgeon Dentists of the City and State of New York (L. Parmly Brown, "New Light on Dental History," in the *Dental Cosmos,* August 1920). In 1837 he received his brother, Augustus Woodruff Brown, as student-assistant, and they were associated in dentistry till 1844. To this brother Solyman Brown dedicated his *Dental Hygeia: a Poem* (1838), and about the same time he wrote a novel of the American Revolution, "Elizabeth of Litchfield," published posthumously in the *Litchfield Enquirer* (1917–18), with an Introduction containing the only published account of his early life, by his grandson, L. Parmly Brown.

Among Solyman Brown's numerous contributions to dental literature, ten articles and various editorials appeared in Volumes I and II (1839–42) of the world's first dental periodical, the *American Journal of Dental Science,* of which he was one of the promoters and editors; while his *Treatise on Mechanical Dentistry,* one of the first practical works on the subject, ran serially through Volumes II and III of the same journal and was reprinted in 1843 with J. B. Savier's translation of F. Maury's *L'Art du Dentiste.* In 1840 he published *Llewellen's Dog; a Ballad,* and in the same year he was one of the organizers of the first national dental association, the American Society of Dental Surgeons, from which as a member he received one of the original degrees of Doctor of Dental Surgery. His essay on *The Importance of Regulating the Teeth of Children* (1841) was the earliest treatise on orthodontia published in America, and on the title page the author first appears with his M.D. (honorary). In 1842 he received the honorary D.D.S. of the Baltimore College of Dental Surgery, and published his *Cholera King, and Other Poems.*

In 1844 Brown was preacher, teacher, and dentist in a short-lived Fourieristic "phalanx" at Leraysville, Pa. He practised dentistry and preached in the Swedenborgian churches at Ithaca and Danby, N. Y., from 1846 to 1850; and then returned to New York City, where he opened a dental supply depot and published his *Semi-Annual Dental Expositor* (1852–54). He was one of a group that conducted the New York Teeth Manufacturing Company from 1854 to 1860, and at the time of the World's Fair in the Crystal Palace, 1853, he edited and published the *Citizens' and Strangers' Pictorial and Business Directory for the City of New York.* His *Union of Extremes: a Discourse on Liberty and Slavery* followed about 1858.

Returning to Danby in 1862, he served as a Swedenborgian minister till 1870, when he retired. He died in his eighty-sixth year at the home of a married daughter in Dodge Center, Minn., and was buried with Masonic honors, having been a Mason some sixty years. He was survived by his wife and six of their eight children, one of whom, E. Parmly Brown (1844–1916), was a prominent dentist of New York for nearly fifty years.

Solyman Brown was a typical tall New Englander. A forceful public speaker, with marked mechanical ability and literary talent, he did much for the elevation of dentistry; but his pre-

dominant interests were always religious, and he was seldom without a pulpit. Poetry was his chief hobby; he made frequent contributions of verses to newspapers and periodicals, and has a section in C. W. Everest's *Poets of Connecticut* (1843), with a biographical sketch. He also had talent as a sculptor and painter in oil, his bust and portrait of Eleazar Parmly being his best-known art works.

[See sources of information cited above; also F. B. Dexter, *Biog. Sketches of Grads. of Yale Coll.,* vol. VI (1912); Jas. A. Taylor, *Hist. of Dentistry* (1922); *New Jerusalem Messenger,* Mar. 1, 1876; *New Ch. Messenger,* Mar. 10, 1909 and Apr. 11, 1917.]   L. P. B.

BROWN, SYLVANUS (May 24, 1747 o.s.–July 30, 1824), inventor and millwright, was born at Valley Falls, R. I., the first son of Philip and Priscilla (Carpenter) Brown and a descendant in the sixth generation of John Browne [*q.v.*], of Plymouth Colony. Philip Brown mined ore and coal and manufactured iron at the blast furnace which had been operated by the family since its erection very early in the history of Rhode Island. At Philip's death the furnace was discontinued, and Sylvanus, then ten years old, was placed in the care of an uncle, a millwright, whose trade he learned and followed until he reached twenty-one, when he engaged in business for himself. At the outbreak of the Revolution he enlisted in the Navy and served as master-at-arms on the *Alfred,* flagship of Esek Hopkins, first commodore of the Colonial navy. At the end of his naval service he was engaged at Providence by the State of Rhode Island to stock rifles made by the State, and afterward, by the governor of New Brunswick to superintend the construction and erection of the machinery for several grist and sawmills at St. John, N. B. After the completion of this commission, followed by a short trip to Europe, Brown returned to Pawtucket where he established his machine shop and rapidly earned a reputation as a clever millwright. In 1790 Samuel Slater [*q.v.*], the English millwright, was engaged by William Almy and Smith Brown of Pawtucket to construct replicas of the Arkwright series of spinning machines. Sylvanus Brown was selected to assist Slater, and Brown's shop was used for the work. Brown agreed to work for one dollar a day and furnished bond not to divulge any of the secrets of construction. Slater then, from memory, traced on timbers the outlines of the machine members which Brown cut out and assembled. Within the year the machines were completed and in successful operation in the Almy & Brown mill, the first instance of practical spinning by power in the United States. Slater for this work is now known as the "father of American textile manufactures," while most of the recognition of Sylvanus Brown is merely incidental in stories and accounts extolling Slater. It is a fact, however, that the skill of Brown was a large factor in the success of the machines, and many records credit him with finding and correcting the faults in the card teeth, a weak spot which gave Slater much trouble and nearly caused him to give up the undertaking. Of great importance to the growth of the industry of Brown's development of the tools and machinery necessary to manufacture textile machinery rapidly and cheaply enough to supply the mills. In this connection he constructed and used a slide-crest lathe for turning straight rolls of uniform size some three years prior to the invention of the slide-rest by Maudslay who is generally credited with this achievement. Brown also built a practical machine for fluting the rolls mechanically and rapidly. From 1796 to 1801 he superintended furnaces at Scituate, R. I., for John Brown, manufacturer of cannon, returning then to Pawtucket where he continued his millwright business until his death. He was married to Ruth Salisbury of Westport, Mass. James Salisbury Brown [q.v.] was his only son.

[J. N. Arnold, *Vital Record of R. I.*, vol. III, pt. 5, p. 86; *Representative Men and Old Families of R. I.* (1908); Wm. R. Bagnall, *Samuel Slater and the Early Development of the Cotton Manufactures in the U. S.* (1890); R. M. Bayles, *Hist. of Providence County, R. I.* (1891); *Cotton Centennial 1790–1890* (1890); Jos. W. Roe, *Eng. and Am. Tool Builders* (1916).]

F. A. T.

BROWN, WILLIAM (1752–Jan. 11, 1792), physician, belonged to a Maryland family strikingly devoted to medicine. His grandfather, Gustavus Brown of "Rich Hills," Charles County, his uncle, Gustavus Richard Brown of Port Tobacco, his brother, Gustavus Brown of St. Mary's County, and his own son, Gustavus Alexander Brown, were all medical men. A child of Richard and Helen (Bailey) Brown, he was born in Haddingtonshire, Scotland, where his father was studying for the ministry. His early education was obtained in King and Queen Parish, St. Mary's County, Md., and his academic and medical education in the University of Edinburgh where he received his M.D. degree in 1770. After graduation he returned to America and settled in Alexandria, Va., where he soon established a reputation as a physician. He was a man of culture and was well acquainted with the American leaders of the day, particularly with Washington, Jefferson, and Madison. On the outbreak of the Revolutionary War he was appointed surgeon to the 2nd Virginia Regiment (Col. Woodford). After serving with this regiment about a year he was appointed by Congress, on the recommendation of Dr. Hugh Mercer, to succeed Dr. Benjamin Rush as surgeon-general to the middle department of the Revolutionary army. In February 1778, he was promoted to the office of physician-general to superintend the practise of physic in the army hospital of the middle department. This position he held until July 21, 1780, when he resigned and returned to practise in Alexandria. The physicians who served in the Virginia regiments during the Revolutionary War were entitled by a law of the state not only to their pay but also to a land bounty, provided they served for a period of three years. As Brown resigned after serving with a Virginia regiment for only a year he forfeited his rights, but the esteem in which he was held was so high that in a special act passed on Oct. 21, 1782 he was given not only his back pay but also his land bounty.

While he was serving in the Revolutionary army, in 1778, Brown brought out the first pharmacopeia ever published in the United States, a pamphlet of thirty-two pages, written entirely in Latin. This pharmacopeia was designed to serve the military hospitals and was based on the Edinburgh Pharmacopeia of that day, modified to suit the exigencies of the times, since the pressure of war made certain standard supplies unobtainable. Brown's career as a general practitioner both before and after the Revolutionary War amply demonstrated his efficiency and popularity. He was chairman of the trustees of Alexandria Academy, a position which he accepted at the direct request of George Washington. His tombstone, now in the churchyard of the Old Pohick Church, near Alexandria, Va., sets forth his patience, diligence, and skill as a physician, and his benevolence and integrity as a man. He was married to his cousin, Catherine Scott, of Kalorama, near Washington, D. C., by whom he is said to have had a large family.

[J. M. Toner, *The Medical Men of the Revolution* (1876); W. W. Hening, *Statutes at Large of Va.* (1823), XI, 106; *The First Century of the Phila. Coll. of Pharmacy, 1821–1921*, ed. by Jos. W. England (1922); Bessie Wilmarth Gahn, in *Jour. Am. Pharmaceutical Ass.*, vol. XVI, no. 11 (1927); F. B. Heitman, *Hist. Reg. of the Officers of the Continental Army* (new ed., 1914).]

G. B.

BROWN, WILLIAM CARLOS (July 29, 1853–Dec. 6, 1924), railroad executive, was born in Norway, Herkimer County, N. Y., a son of Charles E. Brown, a Baptist clergyman, and Frances (Lyon) Brown. With but a limited education in the public schools of Iowa he began his railroad career at the age of sixteen as track laborer on the Chicago, Milwaukee & St. Paul

Brown

Railroad. His work included the physical handling of wood for locomotives and he soon transferred to train service as a locomotive fireman. While thus employed he taught himself telegraphy and became an operator. From 1872 to 1875 he was train dispatcher on the Illinois Central Railroad, returning in the latter year for a few months to the Chicago, Milwaukee & St. Paul in the same capacity. He was married, on June 3, 1874, to Mary Ella Hewitt, at Lime Springs, Iowa. His long and successful service with the Chicago, Burlington & Quincy Railroad began in 1876 when he became train dispatcher. His progress was steady: chief train dispatcher in 1880, trainmaster in 1881, assistant superintendent in 1884, superintendent in 1887, general manager of parts of the system in 1890, and general manager of the entire system in 1896. During that period the mileage and business of the Burlington increased rapidly.

His work with the Burlington system had come under the observation of W. H. Newman, president of the Lake Shore & Michigan Southern Railroad. When the latter road passed to the control of the New York Central & Hudson River Railroad, of which Newman was made president, he induced Brown to leave the Burlington and take charge of the Lake Shore as vice-president and general manager. A year later Brown was transferred to New York as senior vice-president of the New York Central System, a newly-created position. Newman gradually turned over more and more of his responsibilities to Brown and when Newman retired from the presidency, in 1909, Brown succeeded him. When responsibilities began to weigh too heavily, Brown transferred a part of the burden to Alfred H. Smith, who had followed him from the Lake Shore to the New York Central, and finally, sensitive over the affliction of growing deafness, he resigned from the presidency on Jan. 1, 1914. With his retirement from railroad service, he gave up nearly all business activities and led a quiet life, part of the time in Iowa, where he had farming interests, and during his last years, in Pasadena, Cal., where he died.

With comparatively little school training in youth, Brown later gave evidence of consistent and continuous self-education in economics, finance, and government. While general manager of the Burlington he studied grammar with his secretary. By extensive reading, he broadened his view-point, and he was well informed on the current literature in his own and bordering subjects. Although his practical training up to the time he moved to New York had been in the

technique of operation, he began a program for improving the relations between the New York Central and the public, issuing a series of addresses and pamphlets, evidencing a broad grasp of economics. These were published in a bound volume of over 200 pages, which also included an effective document called "The Freight Rate Primer." At that time the railroads were endeavoring to convince the Interstate Commerce Commission that an increase in freight rates was justified by the growing costs of operation, —and the public attitude toward railroads was unfriendly. Brown had to combat not only the nation-wide lack of confidence in railroad management but also certain adverse traditions attaching specifically to the New York Central. To the work of creating an attitude of friendly understanding, he gave himself energetically, and by his forward-looking policy of publicity, —a painstaking effort to broadcast in simple terms the fundamental economic facts concerning the interdependence of railroads and their patrons—he achieved a measure of success. At the same time, he met the heavy demands upon him for executive guidance in the expansion of the company's facilities and business. During his period of service with the New York Central its revenues and traffic doubled in volume, and engineering works of large proportions were successfully carried on. Among them were the reconstruction of the Grand Central Terminal in New York City and the electrification of the lines in and near that city.

Personally Brown was courteous and modest. A moderate disciplinarian, he was kind-hearted and considerate. He displayed a keen interest in the work of the Railroad Y. M. C. A. Toward labor unions he was not as uncompromising as many of his contemporaries, although he was not lacking in firmness when, as a superintendent, he did more than his part in keeping the Burlington road open during the great strike of 1888. He had strong organizing ability and the faculty of harmonizing departmental differences. His qualities were thus summarized by an editorial writer for the *Railway Age Gazette*: studious, clear-headed, possessed of retentive memory, able to learn new things quickly, an accurate judge of men and subjects.

[*Who's Who in America*, 1914–15; obituaries in *Ry. Age* and *Ry. Rev.*, Dec. 13, 1924; *N. Y. Times* and *Sioux City* (Iowa) *Jour.*, Dec. 9, 1924; other sketches in railroad journals (1900–24); correspondence with business associates, and personal recollections.]

W. J. C—m.

BROWN, WILLIAM GARROTT (Apr. 24, 1868–Oct. 19, 1913), author, was the son of Wilson Richard and Mary Cogdale (Parish) Brown.

Chiefly of English strain, his ancestors were of Virginia and North Carolina, with a Connecticut branch. His family settled in Alabama in 1832–33. Brown was born at Marion, Ala., and remained there until 1889. After good preparatory schooling, he graduated from Howard College in 1886. He devoted the next year to reading, with occasional contributions to the *Montgomery Advertiser,* after which followed two years of teaching. He then entered Harvard, where he spent thirteen years: three, as student, receiving the degrees of A.B., 1891, and A.M., 1892; nine, as assistant in the college library; one, as lecturer in American history. Increase of deafness, an affliction from youth, prevented an academic career, and he turned exclusively to writing. His principal books appeared between 1902 and 1905. During that period he traveled much in the South, although Cambridge remained his permanent residence. In 1905 he moved to New York, the immediate purpose being to study material about Gen. Grant, whose biography he had engaged to prepare. Finding he had tuberculosis, from 1906 to 1913 he fought a losing battle for health (see "Some Confessions of a 'T. B.,'" *Atlantic Monthly,* CXIII, 747), during a part of which period he wrote editorials for *Harper's Weekly,* working in bed for two and a half years. He died in New Canaan, Conn.

His best books are *Andrew Jackson* (1900), *The Lower South in American History* (1902), *Stephen Arnold Douglas* (1902), *The Foe of Compromise and Other Essays* (1903), and *A Continental Congressman; Oliver Ellsworth* (1905). Posthumously some papers on political topics were gathered from periodicals into *The New Politics and Other Essays* (1914). His *Lower South* is a picture of the Cotton States from 1820 to 1860. He called it "thin and fragmentary"; yet if he had written nothing else, that alone should perpetuate his memory. His most impressive essay, *Foe of Compromise,* expresses what perhaps stood uppermost in his character: willingness to fight on despite certainty of defeat. In *Jackson* and *Douglas* he illustrated how, without confusing detail, a political figure can be made to live again in the imagination. His *Ellsworth,* by telling clearly Ellsworth's part in establishing the government, rescued the third Chief Justice for the average reader from unmerited obscurity. His lesser writings include: *History of Alabama* (1900); *Golf* (1902); *A Gentleman of the South* (1903) and numerous magazine articles.

Born during the poverty of Reconstruction, Brown credited his opportunity to two brothers

who, as he stated, "stood aside to let me pass." Though away from Alabama over half his life, he carried to the end the mark of his own section. In person he was tall, angular, spare, with high forehead and the orator's long lips. With a genius for friendship, he was chivalric, eager for truth, painstaking for facts, scholarly, and lucid of statement. On a worthy theme he wrote with compelling eloquence and always with distinction. While his passion was history, it is a question whether "man of letters," "essayist," or "historian" more nearly describes him. James Bryce said, "Mr. Brown's mind was singularly fair, penetrating and judicious. He was an admirable critic, seeing clearly and deep; and to his capacity for a discriminative appreciation there was joined a remarkable gift of fine expression. In point of style and diction, he seemed to me to stand in the front rank of the men of his generation, and he would doubtless, had his life been prolonged, have been an ornament to American literature."

[For estimates see *Nation,* XCVII, 389; *Outlook,* CV, 461; *Harvard Alumni Bull.,* XVI, 88; *Harvard Grads. Mag.,* XXII, 255; *South Atlantic Quart.,* XIII, 69, XVI, 97; *Hist. of Ala. and Dict. of Ala. Biog.,* III, 237.]   F. G. C.

BROWN, WILLIAM HENRY (Feb. 29, 1836–June 25, 1910), civil engineer, was born in Little Britain Township, Lancaster County, Pa. His parents, Levi K., and Hannah C. (Moore) Brown, were Quakers and people of limited means. William was sent to the district public school and later to the Central High School in Philadelphia, but was unable to go to college. He was determined, however, to become a civil engineer. As a boy he had collected sticks to make axe handles, selling them to procure money to buy books on engineering. Eventually he saved enough money to purchase the most primitive of surveyor's instruments, a Jacob's staff, and he taught himself surveying by practising on the neighbors' farms with their deeds to guide him. On Oct. 15, 1863, he married Sarah A. Rimmel in Pittsburgh.

At the close of the Civil War, in which Brown had rendered effective work of an engineering nature for the Union forces, he entered the employ of the Pennsylvania Railroad Company to which he gave over forty years of continuous service (1864–1906). For the last twenty-five years of that time he was chief engineer. His work included everything that pertains to the construction of a railroad—the building of great stations, tunnels, bridges, railroad shops and yards, piers and docks. He believed that the most important operation he ever undertook was the construction of the Broad Street Terminal and Station in Philadelphia. He was especially proud of the construction of the train-shed there with sixteen tracks under one roof which was supported by twenty trusses set in pairs nine feet apart. It was almost twice the size of any train-shed in existence at the time of its construction. No railroad chief engineer of his time had as much money at his disposal as Brown had as chief engineer for the Pennsylvania Railroad Company, especially after A. J. Cassatt [*q.v.*] became president of the company in 1899. Brown was a great believer in stone bridges, and wherever it was possible built them to take the place of steel ones. Among the important bridges he constructed is the one across the Susquehanna River five miles west of Harrisburg—one of the longest bridges in the United States, and at the time of its construction the largest stone-arched bridge in the world. Some of the other operations of which Brown had charge were: improvements of the Company's terminals in Jersey City; rebuilding the Jersey City Station four times and the Jersey City Elevator; a bridge across the Hackensack River; the elevated road through Newark, New Brunswick, and Elizabeth; the Delaware River Bridge and Railroad, the grade-crossing tunnels at the Zoological Gardens, the piers and docks on the Delaware River front, and the Forty-first St. and Grand Avenue bridges, in Philadelphia, and a practically new line all the way from that city to Harrisburg. He erected two new stations at Harrisburg and built the tunnel through the Alleghany Mountains at Gallitzen, Pa. His services during the Johnstown Flood should not be forgotten. At the risk of his own life he personally took charge of the work that opened up the railroad to bring relief to the sufferers.

Brown's death, due to heart failure, occurred at Belfast, Ireland, where he was visiting with Mrs. Brown. His home, for many years, had been in Philadelphia. He was a member of the Historical Society of Pennsylvania and of the Pennsylvania Society of Sons of the Revolution.

[*Engineering News Record*, vol. LIII, no. 9; *Engineering News*, vol. LXIV, no. 2; *Railroad Gazette*, vol. XL, no. 9, vol. XLIX, no. 1.]   E. Y.

BROWN, WILLIAM HUGHEY (Jan. 15, 1815–Oct. 12, 1875), coal operator, was born in North Huntington Township, Westmoreland County, Pa., the son of James and Sarah Brown. His education was limited to the usual courses taught in the common schools of that day. By turns, he was employed as a laborer on the old Portage Canal, worked on a farm in the summer, and dug coal in the winter. While working as a coal digger, the idea occurred to him that many people would rather buy their coal than come to the mines and dig it. So he bought a horse and wagon and began to peddle coal. In a short time, he had a number of other men with teams hauling coal for him. Next (1845–56) he began to float coal down the Monongahela River, and sold it in Pittsburgh. His profits soon enabled him to buy a coal mine of his own; two years later, he formed a partnership with the owners of the Kensington Iron Works in Pittsburgh. The firm, under Brown's direction, began mining and operating in coal at the Nine-Mile Run on the Monongahela. They furnished coal to passenger boats and steamboats. Also, they established a few coke ovens at the mines.

In 1858 Brown attempted an experiment that places him among America's business pioneers, that of towing coal by steamers down the Ohio River. Prior to this, coal had been floated down in barges, a class of large keel-boats. But the expenses absorbed all the profits. Brown conceived the plan of towing a number of flatboats with steamers. He collected twelve boats, loaded some 230,000 bushels of coal on board, attached the steamer *Grampus* on one side and the *General Larimer* on the other, and started them down the river in charge of his son Samuel S. Brown. The venture succeeded beyond all expectation. There was now no limit to the future coal industry of the Pittsburgh district. In the same year Brown entered the firm of Reis, Brown & Berger, and bought a large rolling-mill at New Castle, Pa. On this occasion he is said to have given his personal check for $100,000 in order to complete the deal,—ample evidence of the wealth he had accumulated.

At the outbreak of the Civil War, Brown secured contracts for supplying coal to the fleet of the Federal forces at Cairo, Memphis, and Vicksburg. During this period he also shipped coal to St. Louis for the gas works of that city. These were years of great activity and responsibility; also of great risks and personal danger. Many times he barely escaped capture by regular armed forces and also by guerrilla bands, but so far as is known, he never lost a single cargo of coal. At the time of his death in 1875, he had fifteen steamboats in operation on the Ohio River. In his obituary notices he was described as "a mental and physical giant," but he broke down from overwork. He retired from active business in 1873, suffered a paralytic stroke, and died in the Kirkbride Asylum, Philadelphia. On Sept. 3, 1840, he had married Mary Smith, daughter of Samuel and Elizabeth Smith of Minersville, Pa.

[Brief sketches of Brown are found in *Hist. of Allegheny County, Pa.* (1889) ; and in the *Century Cyc. of Hist. and Biog.* (1910), vol. II ; obituary notices in the Pittsburgh newspapers of Oct. 13, 14, 1875, relate several incidents of interest.]   J. W. O.

BROWN, WILLIAM WELLS (*c.* 1816–Nov. 6, 1884), negro reformer, historian, was born in Lexington, Ky. The year is variously given as 1814, 1815, and 1816. His mother was a slave, his father is said to have been one George Higgins, a white slaveholder. When a youth Brown was taken to St. Louis and was hired out on a steamboat. He was next employed in the printshop of Elijah P. Lovejoy, then editor of the *St. Louis Times*. Working in this capacity, Brown got his start in education; but he was hired out on a steamboat again at the close of the next year. In 1834 he escaped into Ohio, intending to cross Lake Erie into Canada. On the way he was sheltered by a Quaker, Wells Brown, whose name he assumed in addition to the name William which he had borne as a slave. He now took up steamboating on Lake Erie and obtained the position of steward in which he was able to help many a fugitive to freedom. In the year of his escape he married a free colored woman by whom he had two daughters. Profiting by school instruction and some help from friends, he acquired considerable knowledge of the fundamentals. In the North he soon learned to speak the English language so fluently that he could easily present the claims of the negro for freedom. During 1843–49 he was variously employed as a lecturer of the Western New York Anti-Slavery Society, and the Massachusetts Anti-Slavery Society. He was also interested in temperance, woman's suffrage, and prison reform, and was associated with the most ardent abolitionists like William Lloyd Garrison and Wendell Phillips. In 1849 he visited England and represented the American Peace Society at the Peace Congress in Paris. Highly recommended by the American Anti-Slavery Society as an apostle of freedom, he was welcomed by famous Europeans such as Victor Hugo, James Haughton, George Thompson, and Richard Cobden. He remained abroad until the autumn of 1854. During these years of his activity as a reformer Brown found time also to study medicine. Like many of the physicians of his time, he did not undergo formal training in this field. He attended lectures in medical science and obtained privately other knowledge requisite to service as a practitioner. But although he knew sufficient medicine to be useful in the profession, the urgent need for fighting the battles of the negro kept him in the work of reform. Brown's reputation rests largely on his ability as an historian. His writings covered various fields. The first to appear was his *Narrative of William W. Brown, a Fugitive Slave* (1847). His next important book was *Three Years in Europe* (1852). In 1853 he published *Clotel, or the President's Daughter, a Narrative of Slave Life in the United States*. He next wrote a drama entitled *The Dough Face*, which was well received and was followed by another play, *The Escape or A Leap for Freedom*. In 1863 he published his first history entitled, *The Black Man, His Antecedents, His Genius, and His Achievements*, including an autobiographical memoir, which ran through ten editions in three years. *The Negro in the American Rebellion, His Heroism and His Fidelity* (1867) also made a favorable impression and supplied the need for an account of the part played by the negroes in the Civil War. The last work of importance which he wrote was *The Rising Son: or, the Antecedents and the Advancement of the Colored Race* (1874). In this treatise he undertook to trace the history of the negro from Africa to America. The abolitionists gave the author unstinted praise and widely circulated his books in this country and Europe. Although, like most historians of his day, he did not approach his subject scientifically, he passed for many years as the outstanding authority on the negro. At the time of his death his home was in Chelsea, Mass.

[In addition to Brown's autobiographical writings, see Josephine Brown, *The Biog. of an Am. Bondman, by His Daughter* (1856) ; memoir by Wm. Farmer in *Three Years in Europe* (1852) ; memoir by Alonzo D. Moore in *The Rising Son* (1874) ; W. J. Simmons, *Men of Mark* (1887), pp. 447–50 ; C. G. Woodson, *The Negro in Our History* (4th ed., 1927), pp. 266–69 ; obituary in the *Boston Transcript*, Nov. 8, 1884.]
                                         C. G. W.

BROWNE, BENJAMIN FREDERICK (July 14, 1793–Nov. 23, 1873), druggist, author, was born in Salem, Mass., the son of Benjamin and Elizabeth (Andrew) Browne, and was baptized in the East Church that same day by the Rev. William Bentley [*q.v.*]. On his father's side he was a descendant in the seventh generation of John Browne, who joined the First Church in Salem in 1637, and on his mother's side of the Rev. Francis Higginson, the first minister of the First Church. He entered the shop of E. S. Lang, an apothecary, Aug. 3, 1807, and completed a five years' apprenticeship just as the outbreak of war with England destroyed the commerce of the port and made it impossible for Browne to find gainful employment on land. Though short of stature and delicate of health, he shipped in September 1812 as surgeon's assistant on the privateer *Alfred*. The cruise began auspiciously with the capture of two brigs laden with cotton, sugar, and dye stuffs, but thereafter the captain was inexplicably timid and ended the venture suddenly at Portsmouth, N. H., Jan. 7, 1813. Browne next enlisted on the privateer *Frolic.* This schooner, with her wedge-shaped bottom and reedy masts, was a freak of marine architecture and behaved so alarmingly in the first white squall that the crew returned their bounty money and the captain put back to port. Rebuilt, the *Frolic* set forth again, with Browne acting as captain's clerk, purser, and sergeant of marines. On Jan. 25, 1814, after a plucky attempt to escape, she was captured by the English man-of-war *Heron* and the crew carried as prisoners to Barbados. In August of the same year Browne, with the other enlisted men, was shipped to England and marched across the hills from Plymouth to Dartmoor, where he was incarcerated until May 1, 1815. The scanty fare and other hardships of the prison so told on his health that at the time of his discharge he weighed only ninety-four pounds. He returned to Salem and to fifty-eight years of humdrum. On Jan. 1, 1823, he set up a drug store of his own. On Jan. 23, 1825, he married Sally Bott. He was representative to the General Court in 1831, state senator in 1843, postmaster of Salem 1845–49. For fifty years he attended the Independent Congregational Church in Barton Square. On Jan. 1, 1860, he retired from business, but until stricken with paralysis three months before his death he returned daily to the store to occupy his old chair, watch his erstwhile partner compound prescriptions, and exchange gossip with droppers-in. Sometime in middle life, however, he wrote out the story of his three years of sailing, fighting, and imprisonment. As the "Papers of an Old Dartmoor Prisoner, Edited by Nathaniel Hawthorne," these reminiscences appeared serially in the *United States Magazine and Democratic Review* during 1846. The author had the faculty of presenting just those details about which a reader will be curious, and he wrote with admirable sureness, vigor, and humor. "A careful comparison of the original manuscript with the printed copy shows that the narrative owes nothing whatever to the accomplishments of the editor except some slight use of the pruning knife" (Memoir, p. 88). With the addition from Hawthorne's manuscript copy of some chapters on life in Barbados, the account was republished in 1926 as *The Yarn of a Yankee Privateer.* The publishers did not know the name of the author and offered a reward of $500 for his identification.

["Memoir of Benj. Frederick Browne" in *Essex Inst. Hist. Colls.,* XIII, 81–88; *N. Y. Times,* Mar. 6, 20, 1927.]
G. H. G.

BROWNE, CHARLES FARRAR (Apr. 26, 1834–Mar. 6, 1867), humorist, better known under his pen-name of "Artemus Ward," was the son of Levi and Caroline (Farrar) Brown. The Browns (Charles himself added an "e" to the name) were a pioneer New England family. The father of Artemus was a substantial citizen of Waterford, Me., a civil engineer of sorts, at one time a member of the state legislature. "Charley" was born on a farm just outside of Waterford but his family during his infancy moved into the town itself and occupied the house still shown as "Artemus Ward's home." When the boy was thirteen his father died, and Charley Brown, following in the wake of an elder brother, Cyrus, went to work to learn the printer's trade under a Mr. John Rix of the *Weekly Democrat* in Lancaster, N. H. A year later he got a place with the *Norway Advertiser,* edited by his brother. On this and various other local journals young Browne set type, wrote news items, and learned the general work of a country newspaper. He presently found his way to Boston where he spent three years in the printing trade. His first genuine literary production was published in the (Boston) *Carpet Bag,* Apr. 17, 1852, under the title, "The Surrender of Cornwallis." From Boston, Charley Browne, now a lanky sandy-haired youth of a queer and melancholy countenance, following the fashion of his day and his trade, wandered westward. He worked in Cincinnati, Toledo, and various places of the rising "West." "I didn't know," he said, "but what I might get as far as China." But his errant steps took him instead to Cleveland, Ohio.

It was at Cleveland that young Browne made his real start in the world. He secured a post on the *Plain Dealer* (at ten dollars a week) which gave him his first opportunity to develop his peculiar vein of comic humor. Here he appears as "Artemus Ward,"—a name selected for fancy's sake from certain old records of land surveyed by a bygone member of his family (Seitz, *post,* p. 25). In the pages of the *Plain Dealer* he created (beginning Feb. 3, 1858) the quaint fiction of a traveling showman who signs himself "Artemus Ward," or "A. Ward" and who is anxious to exhibit wax works, tame bears, and a kangaroo, and is apparently approaching nearer and nearer to the city. The wax works are said to include "figgers of G. Washington, Gen. Taylor, John Bunyan, Capt. Kidd and Dr. Webster in the act of killing Dr. Parkman, besides several miscellanyus moral wax statoots of celebrated piruts & murderers &c ekalled by few and exceld by none." This whimsical idea led to the publication of a series of Artemus Ward letters and became the basis of Browne's literary work. Henceforth, as his reputation grew, he was known to the world only as Artemus Ward.

While still at Cleveland, Artemus had already become a contributor to *Vanity Fair,* a newly established illustrated journal of New York, intended to rival the London *Punch.* This connection led him to leave Cleveland for New York (1859), the process of migration itself involving several weeks of wandering. On the staff of *Vanity Fair* at No. 100 Nassau St., Artemus received regular employment at twenty dollars a week and to this paper he contributed some of the most brilliant of his "goaks" and sketches and burlesque romances. These were presently (1862) gathered into a little volume with the title *Artemus Ward: His Book.* A sale of 40,000 copies indicated its immediate popularity. Meantime the idea of being in some sort "a showman" had made a real as well as imaginative appeal to the young man. On a vacation trip to the westward he fell in with E. R. Hingston, the well-known manager of entertainments, then conducting a tour, and arranged with him that he would some day "manage" Artemus as a "moral lecturer." On his return to New York, Ward gathered together from his writings a collection of random material which he strung together as a lecture, under the title "The Babes in the Wood." It was delivered first at New London, Conn. (Nov. 26, 1861), was pronounced by the local press a "decided success," and was repeated in various New England towns including Boston. "Mr. Browne," said the *Boston Post,* "is a young man of some twenty-eight years, with a pleasant genial face, a keen, humorous eye, and a countenance suggestive of close powers of observation, and a fresh, live intellect." Finally the lecture on "The Babes in the Wood" was given in Clinton Hall, New York, on Dec. 23, 1861. Bad weather prevented a large attendance, but in the month following Artemus "spoke his piece" in various cities (including his adopted Cleveland) with huge success. It was characteristic of him that this lecture on "The Babes in the Wood" concerned neither babes nor woods. At the end of it he was wont to add in a sort of reverie of afterthought: "I suppose that you want to hear something about the children in the wood. They were good children, they were unfortunate and, as far as I have been able to ascertain, entirely respectable."

It was a lecture trip to Washington which led to the imaginary personal contact between Artemus Ward and Abraham Lincoln, as described in the sketch, "Artemus Ward in Washington."

In reality they never met. But Lincoln knew and admired Artemus Ward's work and it is a matter of history that at the cabinet meeting of Sept. 22, 1862, the President read aloud Ward's "High Handed Outrage in Utica," laughed heartily over it amid the anxious silence of his advisers, and then, with a sigh, opened and read the draft of the Emancipation Proclamation. The circumstance recalls the fact that Artemus Ward's comic and humorous work was carried on during the stress and struggle of the Civil War. His sympathies were all with the Union; he is said to have given many thousand dollars to the cause. Many of his "pieces" ("Interview with President Lincoln," "The Show is Confiscated," etc.) reflect this attitude, in his own humane way; and his admiration for the President was early and abiding.

Ward's restless nature sought a farther field. A San Francisco theatre manager had telegraphed to him "What will you take for forty nights in California?" and Artemus had wired back, "Brandy and water." The project was fulfilled in the spirit if not to the letter. Under the management of Hingston, Artemus sailed from New York for Panama, Oct. 3, 1863, and on Nov. 1 reached San Francisco. The Pacific tour which followed was from the start a wild and hilarious success. The receipts for "The Babes in the Wood" lecture in San Francisco ran in a single night to $1,465. Ward lectured all through California and Nevada, in cities, in mining camps, in theatres, churches, and billiard saloons, and everywhere with triumphal success and with fatal conviviality. He met all the rising literary stars of the Pacific Coast including, as the most intimate friendship of all, a gaunt young newspaper man of Virginia City, Nev., then known only as Sam Clemens.

The tour was carried on as far as Salt Lake City and Denver. In the former place, Artemus met the Mormons who became for the future his favorite topic of discourse.

On his return from the West, Ward again took the lecture platform in New York (1864), in the eastern states, and in Canada. The principal subject was now "Artemus Ward among the Mormons," and the lecture was illustrated after the fashion of the day by a panorama, itself presently reduced by the comic genius of Artemus to a sort of caricature. The "program" covering four pages was a masterpiece of comic art. In June 1866 Ward sailed for England. The reception awarded to him in London was the crowning triumph of his brief life. The Savage Club became his headquarters. His contributions to *Punch* excited the laughter of all England, while the delivery of his "Mormon" lecture in the Egyptian Hall was an overwhelming success of which the tradition still lingers. But the end was near. His audiences were laughing at a dying man, whose assumed accents of melancholy reflected only too truly the approaching decline. Stricken with consumption Artemus was compelled after six weeks of lecturing to abandon his work and died at Southampton Mar. 6, 1867.

The humor of Artemus Ward on the platform depended in large part on his peculiar personality, on his whimsical assumptions of distress and ignorance, on his sudden flashes of apparent interest, fading rapidly again into despair, not to be reproduced in mere words. In his writings the comic effect is connected on the surface with the use of queer spelling, verbal quips, and puns, long passed out of use and distasteful to the reader of to-day. Had this been all, Artemus Ward would long since have been forgotten. But beneath the comic superficiality of his written work, as behind the "mask of melancholy" of the comic lecture, there was always the fuller, deeper meaning of the true humorist, based on reality, on the contrasts, the incongruities, and the shortcomings of life itself.

[Artemus Ward's works include sketches, etc., in the *Carpet Bag* (Boston), 1852–53, in the Cleveland *Plain Dealer* (1858–59), in *Vanity Fair* (N. Y., 1860–62); *Artemus Ward: His Book* (first ed., N. Y., 1862); *Artemus Ward: His Travels* (first ed., N. Y., 1865); contributions to *Punch* (London), Sept., Nov., 1866. Of the many critical works and notices mention may be made of "Artemus Ward" in A. S. Nock, *On Doing the Right Thing* (1928), and D. C. Seitz's *Artemus Ward* (1919) as admirable as it is complete, and containing an exhaustive bibliography.]   S.L.

BROWNE, DANIEL JAY (b. Dec. 4, 1804), agricultural and scientific writer, was born in Fremont, N. H., the son of Isaac and Mary Browne. He was bred and educated a practical farmer. It is not known what schools he attended except that he took some courses at Harvard University. He began his literary career at the age of twenty-six by publishing a monthly journal called *The Naturalist*. When only twenty-eight he published two books, *Sylva Americana* and *Etymological Encyclopaedia of Technical Words and Phrases Used in the Arts and Sciences*. The years 1833–35 he spent mostly in foreign travel in the West Indies, Cuba, Canary Islands, Spain, France, Sicily, Madeira, Cape Verde Islands and South America, being part of the time on the United States ships *Vandalia* and *Erie*. During 1836–42 he was engaged in various engineering projects in New York State and Cuba. For the next few years his time was largely devoted to his literary work. He served at this time as the first corresponding secretary of the American Agricul-

tural Association and as a member of the Board of Agriculture of the American Institute in New York. From 1845 to 1851 he was employed in the agricultural warehouse of R. L. Allen & Company, New York, and assisted in the editing of their paper, the *American Agriculturalist*. During this period he also published four books, *Trees of America* (1846), *American Bird Fancier* (1850), *American Poultry Yard* (1850), and *American Muck Book* (1851).

In 1852 he was appointed to a position in the United States Census Office where he was chiefly occupied with agricultural statistics. In June 1853 he was appointed as Agricultural Clerk in the United States Patent Office. He edited the agricultural reports of that office for 1854 to 1859 and prepared numerous articles. In 1854 and 1855 he was sent to Europe by the Patent Office to obtain information on agricultural subjects and to make arrangements for procuring seeds and cuttings, probably the first instances of the use of government funds for such purposes. Browne may therefore be regarded as the first official United States agricultural explorer. During his later years in the Patent Office his activities, particularly in the distribution of seeds, were the subject of much controversy and criticism in the agricultural press. The complaints reached the Agricultural Committee of the House of Representatives, which instituted an investigation. The results were published in the *Washington Union* for June 8, 1858, and reprinted as a separate pamphlet entitled *Vindication of the Agricultural Division of the Patent Office*. (This pamphlet contains practically the only available biographical information regarding Browne.) The Committee, at the end of its investigation, stated that it believed Browne to be "fully qualified for the important duties committed to him." Nevertheless the criticism of his administration and of the seed distribution continued, and later resulted in the appointment by the Secretary of the Interior of an "Advisory Board of Agriculture of the Patent Office," of which Marshall P. Wilder was chairman. The Board approved the general plan of operations of the Patent Office but Browne's appointment was terminated on Oct. 10, 1859, due probably to the criticism which was leveled against him. On May 1, 1861, he was appointed by the Patent Office to visit Europe to investigate the cultivation and manufacture of flax. The results of his investigations are given as the leading article in the *Patent Office Report for 1861* (pp. 21–83). This is the last contribution from his pen which has been found. Whatever errors he may have committed, the fair-minded critics of his day seemed to believe that he was sincerely and earnestly devoted to the advancement of the agricultural interests of the country. Much of the most bitter criticism against him emanated from persons connected with the seed business and naturally opposed to government seed distribution. Other critics were those opposed to any national agricultural department. Browne's literary productions were mostly compilations but nevertheless useful in their day, particularly the agricultural books, each of which ran through two or more editions.

[For the adverse and favorable criticism of Browne in the agricultural press, see *Am. Agriculturist*, XVII, 40, 72, 104, 198–99, 230–31 (1858); XVIII, 103, 104, 326 (1859); *Am. Farmers' Mag.*, XI, 151–53, 182, 467–73 (1858); *Cultivator*, VII, 66, 67, 76 (1859); IX, 226 (1861). For summary of transactions of Advisory Bd. of Agric. of the Patent Office, see Washington *States and Union*, Jan. 4–12, 1859. and the *Patent Office Report for 1858*, pp. iv–v.]   C.R.B.

BROWNE, FRANCIS FISHER (Dec. 1, 1843–May 11, 1913), editor, was of direct Puritan descent. He was born at South Halifax, Vt., the son of William Goldsmith Browne and Eunice (Fisher) Browne. He inherited the love of personal freedom and the literary tendency which dominated his life. Early in his childhood the family moved to western Massachusetts where the boy went to school and learned the printing trade in his father's newspaper office at Chicopee. In 1862 he enlisted and served one year with the 46th Massachusetts Regiment. After leaving the army he went to Rochester, N. Y., to work in a law office, later deciding to enroll in the law department of the University of Michigan. He soon abandoned the law course and returned to Rochester to follow his printing trade. In 1867 he married Susan Seaman Brooks. To this union nine children were born. Soon after his marriage he moved to Chicago with the definite intention of following literary pursuits. He found an opening with the *Western Monthly,* a newly established periodical, gradually gained control of the magazine, and at the end of two years, rechristened it the *Lakeside Monthly.* He enlisted the best writers of the West and for the next six years slaved to produce a creditable and distinguished magazine. Just as the *Monthly* was practically self-sustaining Browne suffered a complete physical breakdown and retired for a few years, and the *Monthly* went out of existence. While searching for health, Browne wrote special editorials for some of the leading Chicago newspapers and for a time acted as literary editor of the *Alliance,* then an influential weekly journal, but his mind was preoccupied with plans for a new periodical. In 1880 under the imprint of Jansen, McClurg & Company, Browne's mag-

azine appeared, named *The Dial*. It was a monthly review and index of current literature. His task was a difficult one,—especially in a city such as Chicago, which was concerned almost entirely with commercial interests, but he succeeded in establishing the foremost American journal of literary criticism of that time and the only one of its class which has survived. For several years he contributed a large portion of the writing in the *Dial,* and still edited the magazine at the time of his death which occurred in Santa Barbara, Cal. It was courage and persistency which enabled him to succeed, for he battled against poverty, ill health, and many personal disasters. Along with his literary interests he possessed a marked analytical insight which enabled him to realize the essential truth of a situation or problem, because of which he invariably found himself with the minority. He was not blinded by the sophistries with which American newspapers sought to justify the war with Spain, and he protested from the first against the United States policy in the Philippines. Scarcely one of his judgments on the political events of his time has not since been verified. A student of Burns, Byron, Wordsworth, Arnold, and Tennyson, it is said that he was able to recite by heart almost all of Tennyson's poems and a great quantity of the work of the other poets. He has been likened to Arnold in his habits of thought. During the years that he edited the *Dial* he compiled and edited several anthologies among which are *Golden Poems by British and American Authors* (1881); *The Golden Treasury of Poetry and Prose* (1883); *Bugle Echoes* (1886); and seven volumes of *Laurel Crowned Verse* (1891–92). He was also the author of a small volume called *Volunteer Grain* (1895), a collection of poems none of which are distinguished. Probably his best work was *The Everyday Life of Abraham Lincoln,* published in 1886. It deals with the human-interest side of Lincoln, the material for which was collected from some five hundred persons who were living at that time and had personally known him.

[*Who's Who in America,* 1912–13; *Dial,* May 1, June 1, 16, 1913; *Book Buyer,* May 1900; *Bookman,* May 1900; *Public* (Chicago), May 30, 1913; *Rev. of Revs.* (N. Y.), July 1913.]   M.S.

BROWNE, IRVING (Sept. 14, 1835–Feb. 6, 1899), legal writer, was born at Marshall, Oneida County, N. Y., the son of two persons of strongly contrasting personality, Lewis C. Browne, a Universalist clergyman of austere character, and his wife, Harriet Hand, a lady of attractive personality and social charm. He was educated in the common schools at Nashua, N. H., and Norwich, Conn., leaving at the age of fourteen in order to learn the printing trade. In his leisure he studied telegraphy and was employed for a time in a telegraph office at Boston. In 1853 he went to Hudson, N. Y., and there commenced the study of law, which he continued in New York City, finally entering the Law School at Albany, where he graduated in 1857. He was admitted to the bar the same year and commenced practise at Troy, N. Y., joining the firm of M. R. & I. Townsend. There he remained for twenty-one years, first as office manager and then as counsel for his firm, which conducted a wide and diversified business. He early evinced the possession of unusual gifts of lucid statement and his arguments in the appellate courts were considered models (Kirchwey, *post*). From his youth he had always been a student of literature and in 1876 he published a book of slight sketches termed *Humorous Phases of the Law,* followed two years later by *Short Studies of Great Lawyers.* In 1878 he retired from the firm, intending to practise alone, but on the death in 1879 of J. J. Thompson, the founder and editor of the *Albany Law Journal,* he was offered and accepted the position of editor, and took up his residence in Albany. He had read widely, and being endowed with great determination, facility of expression and capacity for incessant work, he quickly brought the *Albany Law Journal* to a foremost place among the legal periodicals of the day. He was a prolific contributor to its pages, giving to its contents a lightness of touch which made it eminently readable. In 1880 he published *National Bank Cases, Federal and State Courts, 1878–80.* This was followed by *Judicial Interpretation of Common Words and Phrases* (1883) and *Index-Digest of New York Court of Appeals Reports Volumes 1–95, Keyes, Abbott and Transcript Appeals, 1847–84* (1884), the latter being found of great utility by the profession. His text-books, *Elements of the Law of Domestic Relations and of Employer and Employed* (1883) and *Elements of Criminal Law: Principles, Pleading and Procedure* (1892) met with a cordial reception. Concurrently with the preparation of these books, and his editorial work, he was engaged in completing *American Reports: Decisions, Courts of Last Resort of the Several States,* volumes 28 to 60 of which were edited by him, the last volume appearing in 1888. He was continuously at work, contributing largely each week to the *Journal* and also to other periodicals. In 1893 he resigned his editorial position and removed to Buffalo, but did not resume practise. He had, while at Albany, for eleven years been professor of criminal law and the law of domestic relations

at the Law School there, and he now joined the faculty of the Buffalo Law School, delivering also special courses of legal lectures at Cornell and Boston. In 1896 he was appointed librarian of the supreme court at Buffalo. His subsequent contributions to legal literature included *Admissibility of Parol Evidence in Respect of Written Instruments* (1893); *Elements of the American Law of Sales of Personal Property* (1894); *Short Studies in Evidence* (1897); and *Elements of the Law of Bailments and Common Carriers* (1902). In addition he edited and annotated an edition of the *New York Reports,* volumes 16–100, and assumed editorial charge of the American edition of the English *Ruling Cases,* a work which was uncompleted at his death. Despite the volume of his output it is doubtful if he contributed anything of permanent value to the store of legal literature, and his annotations were never profound, though the clarity of his style caused him to be widely read. His causeries were always delightful. Apart from his legal writing, he was an attractive essayist, with a vein of real humor appealing to a wide audience. His published works in addition to the legal volumes before-mentioned were an English translation of Racine's *Les Plaideurs* (1871); *Our Best Society* (1876), a parlor comedy; *Iconoclasm and Whitewash* (1885); *Rhyminiscenses of Travel* (1891), in verse; *In the Track of the Bookworm* (1897); and *The House of the Heart* (1897), verse. He married, first, in 1858, Delia, daughter of Richard F. Clark of Hudson, N. Y., and, second, in 1894, Lizzie B. Ferris, daughter of Frederick Buell of Buffalo, N. Y.

[Biographical sketch by Geo. W. Kirchwey, in *Albany Law Jour.,* Feb. 18, 1899, p. 212; a more critical article in *Am. Law Rev.,* XXXIII, 271. See also *Green Bag,* Dec. 1889, Apr. 1890, Aug. 1897; *Chicago Legal News,* May 2, 1896, Feb. 18, 1899; obituary in *Buffalo Morning Express,* Feb. 7, 1899. *A Cat. of the Lib. of Irving Browne* (1878) contains an introduction and notes valuable as an indication of Browne's wide literary interests.]

H. W. H. K.

BROWNE, JOHN (d. Apr. 10, 1662), Plymouth Colony magistrate, brought his family to America about 1634. He was led to settle in Plymouth Colony by a pleasant acquaintance formed years before with John Robinson's congregation at Leyden (Nathaniel Morton, *New-England's Memoriall,* 1669). Browne was a man of gentle birth, as "Mr." prefixed to his name in the colony records indicates. Chosen one of the Governor's Assistants in January 1635/36, he was reëlected annually (with the exception of the year 1646) for nineteen years, was a member of the Council of War in 1642, 1646, and 1653, and a Commissioner of the United Colonies of New England from 1644 to 1656. Removing from Plymouth to Cohannet, he was a proprietor when that settlement was incorporated as the town of Taunton in 1639. He had the respect and confidence of the Indians and was frequently the Colony's agent in dealings with them. In 1641 he and Edward Winslow [*q.v.*] were appointed to purchase from Massasoit the land comprising the present towns of Seekonk, Rehoboth, East Providence, and Pawtucket. Two years later he was an incorporator of Rehoboth. Going to Providence in 1645, on behalf of Plymouth Colony he opposed putting into effect Roger Williams's charter. He then proceeded to Shawomet where the outcast Samuel Gorton and his followers had settled, and forbade some twenty families from Massachusetts Bay to interfere with Gorton, claiming that the land belonged to Plymouth. Again in 1651 by setting Plymouth Colony's claim to jurisdiction in opposition to that of Massachusetts Bay he created a deadlock, the result of which was that Gorton retained his land. In October 1645, pursuant to a vote of a Rehoboth town meeting, Browne advanced money to purchase from the Wampanoags a tract known as Wannamoiset, lying between the Pawtucket River and Narragansett Bay. Here he settled permanently. One of the well-to-do among the colonists, he was characterized by a sturdy liberalism already exhibited in his championing of Gorton. He opposed the persecution of the Quakers and favored religious toleration, in 1655 pledging his estate to cover possible deficiencies in voluntary contributions so that Rehoboth need not be subjected to taxation for church support. In 1656 he went to England to take charge of the estate of his friend Sir Henry Vane, returning some four years later to his Wannamoiset home, where he died in 1662. His wife, Dorothy, died in 1674/75, aged about ninety. Browne had descendants through two sons and a daughter, the latter married to Thomas Willett, first English mayor of New York City.

[Wm. Bradford, *Hist. of Plymouth Plantation* (Mass. Hist. Soc. ed., 1912); *Winthrop's Journal*, ed by Jas. K. Hosmer (1908), II, 228–29, 261; Samuel Gorton, "Simplicities Defence against Seven-Headed Policy" with notes by Wm. R. Staples, *R. I. Hist. Soc. Colls.*, II (1835), 167 f., 249; Adelos Gorton, *The Life and Times of Samuel Gorton* (1907), pp. 18, 62, 64, 69; *New Eng. Hist. and Geneal. Reg.*, XXXVI, 368; *Mass. House Report No. 801*, Jan. 1915. The best account of Browne is by John A. Goodwin, in *The Pilgrim Republic* (1888), pp. 517–21. Many of the references to Browne in the *Records of the Colony of New Plymouth* and other publications have been compiled by Geo. Tilden Browne in *John Browne, Gentleman, of Plymouth* (privately printed, 1919).]   E. R. D.

BROWNE, JOHN ROSS (Feb. 11, 1821–Dec. 8, 1875), traveler and author, was born in Dublin and came to the United States with his parents, Thomas Egerton and Elana Buck Browne, in 1832 or 1833. He was the third of four children. The family settled in Louisville, Ky., and there John Ross spent the next half dozen years. The advantages of college training were denied him, but the direction of intelligent parents and his own easy acquisition of knowledge gave him a fund of information which he used to practical advantage. He wrote easily and was clever at caricaturing people and things about him. Both of these talents were cultivated from his early boyhood. At the age of eighteen he determined to travel. In order to secure funds necessary to gratify his desire, he deemed it wise to prepare himself for work in which competition was limited. With this in mind he studied shorthand. In November 1841 he went to Washington and had no difficulty in securing a position as reporter in the United States Senate. This lasted until the summer of 1842. He saved little money during the interval, but he accumulated quantities of contempt for the "big men" in Congress. Leaving Washington on July 5, he went to New Bedford, Mass., and shipped as a common sailor on a whaling vessel. The next quarter of a century was spent very largely in travel. He told a son years later that on one of his trips he had covered a hundred thousand miles. Observations made during these wanderings, and presented usually in a humorous vein, are found in *Etchings of a Whaling Cruise, with Notes of a Sojourn on the Island of Zanzibar* (1846); *Yusef; or, The Journey of the Frangi: A Crusade in the East* (1853); *Crusoe's Island: A Ramble in the Footsteps of Alexander Selkirk; With Sketches of Adventures in California and Washoe* (1864); *An American Family in Germany* (1866); *The Land of Thor* (1867); and *Adventures in the Apache Country: A Tour through Arizona and Sonora* (1869). He published numerous sketches in *Harper's Magazine*, many of which were later assembled in book form. (For a complete list see the Index to *Harper's New Monthly Magazine*, vols. I–XL.) Pen drawings of his own frequently accompanied his narratives. There are several reports that came from his pen while he was engaged in the government service, among which *Resources of the Pacific Slope* (1869) has been one of the most widely used. He was the official reporter for the convention that drew up California's first state constitution in 1849, and received $10,000 for his services. In 1868 he was appointed minister to China, but soon after arriving there expressed opinions which were contrary to the ideas of the Government as embodied in the Burlingame Treaty, and was recalled. In 1870 he settled in Oakland, Cal., a place he had called "home" since 1855, and entered the real estate business with offices in San Francisco. He was engaged in this at the time of his death. Browne had married, in 1844, Lucy Anna Mitchell, daughter of Dr. Spencer Cochrane Mitchell of Washington. Eight of his ten children reached maturity. Browne had a keen sense of humor, was versatile, modest, good-natured, cordial, and generous.

[A short sketch was published in *Harper's Weekly*, Feb. 22, 1868, later copied in the *Daily Alta California*, Mar. 21, 1868; *San Francisco Chronicle*, Feb. 13, 1881; H. H. Bancroft, *Hist. of Cal.*, VI (1888), 286, note 65. Obituaries in the *Oakland Daily Evening Tribune* and in the San Francisco *Evening Bulletin* for Dec. 8, 1875; in the *San Francisco Chronicle* and the *Sacramento Daily Record-Union* for Dec. 9, 1875; and in *Daily Alta California* for Dec. 9 and 12, 1875; additional information from Ross E. Browne, of Oakland, Cal.]   C. G.

BROWNE, JUNIUS HENRI (Oct. 14, 1833–Apr. 2, 1902), journalist, was born in Seneca Falls, N. Y. His boyhood was spent in Cincinnati, where he received his education at St. Xavier College. At sixteen he went into his father's banking house but two years later left it for journalism. He served on several papers in Cincinnati and when the Civil War broke out became a war correspondent for the *New York Tribune*. For two years he followed the campaigns in the Southwest, witnessing several battles and the activities of the Union gunboat flotilla on the Mississippi. On May 3, 1863, with two other journalists, he accompanied an expedition which tried to run the Vicksburg batteries. The boat was sunk, and the journalists were captured by the Confederates. One of them, Richard T. Colburn of the New York *World*, was promptly paroled but Browne and his *Tribune* colleague, Albert D. Richardson, were not so fortunate. Apparently because of their connection with that paper and their presumed abolitionist convictions they were kept in prison with no prospect of release before the end of the war. Lieutenant-Colonel William H. Ludlow, agent for the exchange of prisoners, sought repeatedly, under special instructions from President Lincoln and Secretary Stanton, to obtain their liberation, but in vain (*Official Records*, Army). During a year and a half they were passed from prison to prison in Vicksburg, Jackson, Atlanta, Richmond—where they were incarcerated both in the famous Libby Prison and in Castle Thunder—and Salisbury. Their privations and sufferings in these institutions are told by Browne in his book, *Four Years in Secessia* (1865) with complete naiveté and the quiet assumption that adherence to the Con-

federate cause was in itself enough to turn ordinary human beings into creatures addicted to injustice, cruelty, and bad faith. Browne and Richardson finally escaped from Salisbury with three companions and traveled four hundred miles through the enemy's country. They suffered greatly from cold, hunger, and fatigue but with aid received from negroes, bushwackers, and Union sympathizers they succeeded in reaching the Union lines at Knoxville. After the war Browne was connected with the editorial staffs of the *New York Times* and the *Tribune* and acted as correspondent for many other newspapers throughout the country. He contributed to a number of magazines and wrote several books, including *The Great Metropolis; a Mirror of New York* (1869), *Sights and Sensations in Europe* (1871), and a series of small volumes on the French Revolution. He died in New York City.

[Obituaries in the *N. Y. Tribune* and *N. Y. Evening Post*, for Apr. 3, 1902.]   H. H.

BROWNE, THOMAS (d. Aug. 3, 1825), was one of the most noted Tory partisan commanders in the South, during the Revolutionary War. The date and place of his birth are unknown, but he is described as a young man residing in Augusta, Ga., at the beginning of the war. He early declared his opposition to the Revolution, and ridiculed the Continental Congress in toasts given at dinner. Following this action he fled from the town, but was brought back; he was tarred, feathered, and carried for several miles in a cart, but refused to retract. Vengeance for this treatment was henceforth a controlling motive with him. He began raiding in 1776, and took part in an attack on Fort McIntosh in the southeastern part of the state in 1777. His importance began with his organization in Florida in 1778 of a regiment called the King's Rangers; of this regiment he was lieutenant-colonel, and he was soon notorious for his raids in Georgia. In the following year he was defeated in two engagements near Waynesboro by an inferior force led by Col. Twiggs, Col. Benjamin Few, and Col. William Few. He was present at the successful defense of Savannah. In 1780 he occupied Augusta, a strategic point on the Savannah River, banished the Whigs, and sequestrated their property. Here he was repeatedly attacked by Col. Clarke in September of that year. Browne, whose force comprised Florida Rangers, Creeks, and Cherokees, showed bravery, skill, and determination in the defense. He was wounded, and nearly on the point of surrender, when the siege was raised by the arrival of British forces under Col. Cruger. This period of irregular partisan warfare in the South abounded in atrocities, and Browne had an unenviable preëminence in this respect. After the successful defense of Augusta, some of his prisoners were hanged in his presence, and others were given to the Indians to be tortured to death. In 1781 he repulsed a night attack by Col. Harden, and soon afterward he was again besieged in Augusta by Pickens and Lee. By the use of a tower of logs which commanded his defenses, they compelled his surrender with about 300 men, June 5, 1781. So intense was the hatred felt toward Browne that he was especially guarded from avenging Whigs on his journey to the coast. That he was treated as a prisoner of war and exchanged was probably due to the British threat of hanging six Whig captives. After his release he was colonel of Queen's Rangers of South Carolina and superintendent of Indian Affairs in the South. His last conflict was on May 21–22, 1782; in an attempted sortie from Savannah he was defeated in a night attack by Wayne, who charged with the bayonet. Browne's rangers were dispersed in Florida and elsewhere, his estates in South Carolina and Georgia were confiscated, and he went to the Bahamas. From there in 1786 he wrote a criticism of Ramsay's history of the war which had severely condemned his cruelty (George White, *Historical Collections of Georgia,* 3rd ed., 1855, pp. 614–19). He received a grant in the island of St. Vincent in 1809, and died there in 1825. According to Charles C. Jones, *History of Georgia,* he was convicted of forgery in London in 1812 (doubted, with good reasons, by Sabine in his *Loyalists*). Browne undoubtedly had the qualities of bravery and good discipline, but he was revengeful and cruel. One biographer says, "Of all the human characters developed during this abnormal period . . . none can be named more notorious than Thomas Brown."

[Hugh McCall, *Hist. of Ga.* (1811–16); Chas. C. Jones, *Hist. of Ga.* (1883); Wm. B. Stevens, *Hist. of Ga.* (1847); Lorenzo Sabine, *Biog. Sketches of the Loyalists of the Am. Revolution* (1864); David Ramsay, *Hist. of the Revolution of S. C. from a British Province to an Independent State* (1785) and *Hist. of the Am. Revolution* (1793); Chas. Shephard, *Hist. Acct. of the Island of St. Vincent* (1831); obituary note in *Gentleman's Mag.,* Oct. 1825, p. 382.]   E. K. A.

BROWNE, WILLIAM (Mar. 5, 1737–Feb. 13, 1802), Loyalist, judge of the superior court of Massachusetts, governor of Bermuda, was born in Salem. His father, Samuel Browne, a graduate of Harvard in the class of 1727, was a member of a mercantile family, "the most respectable that has ever lived in the town of Salem, holding places of the highest trust in town, county, and State, and possessing great riches"

(*The Diary of William Pynchon,* 1890, p. 94n). His mother, Catherine Winthrop, daughter of John and Ann (Dudley) Winthrop, was descended from four colonial governors. William was brought up presumably by his mother and his step-father, for Samuel Browne died in 1742 and two years later his widow married Col. Epes Sargent, himself the founder of a distinguished family. William graduated from Harvard in 1755, valedictorian of his class (*The Holyoke Diaries,* 1911, p. 14) and third in order of social position. He studied law, but abandoned practise to attend to the increase of his already considerable estate.

In 1762 he was elected to the Assembly, and two years later was appointed collector of the port of Salem. At this time he was in sympathy with those who resented the imposition of taxes by Parliament, and his leniency in enforcing the odious Sugar Act caused his dismissal from the collectorship in the winter of 1766–67 (Joseph B. Felt, *Annals of Salem,* 1849, II, 262 f.). Later, however, his inherent love of order made him unwilling to offer resistance to established authority, and in 1768 when the Massachusetts legislature received instructions from England to rescind its resolutions expressing protest against the Townshend Acts, Browne voted with the minority of seventeen in favor of rescinding. This action lost him his seat at the succeeding general election. In 1770 he became judge of the court of common pleas of Essex County, and in 1771 was commissioned by Gov. Hutchinson colonel of the Essex militia. In May 1774 Gov. Gage nominated him as judge of the superior court; the nomination met with opposition and was not confirmed until June. In August he was one of those appointed to the Governor's Council by writ of *mandamus,* a proceeding bitterly resented by the more radical colonials. Of the thirty-six appointees only ten, Browne among them, took the required oath. He was approached on Sept. 9 by a committee of the patriot convention then meeting at Ipswich who asked him to resign both of the offices he held under the Crown. This he declined to do, stating that "neither persuasions can allure me, nor shall menaces compel me to do anything derogatory to the character of a councillor of his majesty's province of the Massachusetts Bay" (*Journals of Each Provincial Congress of Massachusetts, etc.,* 1838, p. 618). On Oct. 4 the officers of his militia regiment resigned their commissions, refusing to serve under him, and within the month he left Salem. He went to Boston, where he remained until March 1776, when the British forces under Lord Howe evacuated the city, then went to England by way of Halifax, bearing Howe's dispatches to the home government and reaching London about the first of May (*The Journal and Letters of Samuel Curwen*, 4th ed., 1864, p. 58). Here he resided for the next five years, continuing to draw £200 per annum as judge of the superior court of Massachusetts Bay. His name was included in the Banishment Act passed by the Massachusetts legislature in 1778, and in 1779, by the Conspiracy Act, his property was declared forfeit.

Early in 1781, possibly through the influence of Benjamin Thompson (later Count Rumford), whom as a youth Browne had befriended (*Pynchon*, p. 94n), he was appointed governor of Bermuda, entering upon his new office in January 1782. Because of his own colonial birth and experience he understood the view-point of the island colonials as none of his home-born predecessors had been able to do, and won favor by his first speech to the legislature. He opened the whale-fishery, which for years had been restricted by high gubernatorial license, encouraged cotton culture, and promoted ship building. At his coming the public finances had been in bad condition; he reorganized them and left them flourishing. In 1788 he returned to England, his departure sincerely regretted (William Frith Williams, *An Historical and Statistical Account of the Bermudas*, 1848, pp. 97–101). For the rest of his life he made his home in Percy St., Westminster. His wife, Ruth Wanton, daughter of Gov. Joseph Wanton of Rhode Island, died on May 13, 1799 (*Gentleman's Magazine*, May 1799), and he survived her less than three years.

Browne was characterized by his classmate, John Adams, as "a solid, judicious character." Adams continued, "They made him a judge of the superior court and that society made of him a refugee. A Tory I verily believe he never was" (*Works of John Adams*, 1856, X, 195–96). He retained the esteem of his Salem neighbors throughout his life, and was cordially welcomed when he paid them a visit in 1784 while governor of Bermuda.

[In addition to sources cited see *The Diary of Wm. Bentley*, II (1907), 425; *The Diaries of Benj. Lynde and of Benj. Lynde, Jr.* (1880), esp. p. 145; *Essex Inst. Hist. Colls.*, XLIII, 290 ff.; Emory Washburn, *Sketches of the Judicial Hist. of Mass.* (1840); John Russell Bartlett, *Hist. of the Wanton Family of Newport, R. I.* (1878), esp. p. 78; *New Eng. Hist. and Geneal. Reg.*, V, 49, 51; obituary note in *Gentleman's Mag.* (London), Mar. 1802, p. 275. Ezra D. Hines, "Browne Hill and Some History Connected with It," in *Essex Inst. Hist. Colls.*, vol. XXXII (1896), presents an incomplete account and Dean Dudley, *Hist. of the Dudley Family* (1886–94), pp. 682, 1035, 1057, is inaccurate in some details.]

E. R. D.

BROWNE, WILLIAM HAND (Dec. 31, 1828–Dec. 13, 1912), author, educator, was born in a house on Paca St., Baltimore. His father,

William Browne, descendant of an old family on the Eastern Shore of Maryland, had moved to Baltimore and was a member of a firm of commission merchants, trading largely with the West Indies. His mother, Patience Hand, had come to Baltimore in 1794 with her father, Moses Hand, an artist of commendable ability as a painter of landscapes and portraits, who upon settling in Baltimore continued the pursuit of his profession. William Hand Browne obtained all of his education in Baltimore, first in the private school of T. P. Carter, later in a local college no longer existing, and finally in the University of Maryland, where he received the degree of M.D. in 1850. The practise of medicine, however, was distasteful to him, and he never entered upon it. For the next ten years he was associated with his cousin, T. J. Hand, in the commission business. When this firm was dissolved in 1861 Browne's literary career began with the publication in the *South*, a Baltimore daily, of a translation from the German of a story entitled "The Armourer," which owing to the state of the public mind attracted wide attention. This was followed by a period of travel and observation in the South. In June 1863, Browne married Mary Catherine Owings, daughter of Dr. Thomas Owings of Baltimore, and removed his residence to Baltimore County. After the close of the Civil War he came into prominence, in the work of restoring the cultural conditions of the South, through his connection with various literary periodicals. In January 1867 he joined with Alfred Taylor Bledsoe in founding the *Southern Review*, and remained as editor for two years, after which he became co-editor with Lawrence Turnbull of the *New Eclectic Magazine*, later called the *Southern Magazine*, with which he remained till 1875. During part of this time he was also editor of the *Statesman*, a weekly paper devoted to politics, literature, and art, started in 1868, but lasting only a year and a half. He was also joint editor of text-books on English literature and the history of Maryland, and of a concise English dictionary. With Richard Malcolm Johnston he brought out a *Life of Alexander H. Stephens* in 1878. In 1879 he became librarian of the Johns Hopkins University and remained with that institution in various capacities until the time of his death as professor emeritus of English literature. During this academic period Browne rendered important services to the history of Maryland. In 1882 an act of the General Assembly placed the provincial records in the charge of the Maryland Historical Society with provision for publication. Browne was chosen editor and carried out his task with expert knowledge and meticulous care. At the close of his life he had brought out thirty-two of the large quarto volumes of these *Archives of Maryland.* Further historical contributions included volumes on *Maryland: the History of a Palatinate* (Commonwealth Series, 1884); and *George Calvert and Cecilius Calvert, Barons Baltimore of Baltimore* (1890). Browne also edited the first two parts of the "Calvert Papers" (*Maryland Historical Society Fund Publications,* vols. XXVIII and XXXIV, 1889–94) and the *Writings of Severn Teakle Wallis* (1896). Upon the establishment by the Historical Society of the quarterly *Maryland Historical Magazine* he was made editor and became responsible for the first five volumes (1906–10).

Browne's activities as a teacher began after he had passed his fiftieth year. Of medium height, of vigorous frame, but slightly stooping in carriage, his twinkling eyes set in a full bearded face, his careful enunciation and moderated tones were marked with the playful humor of the cultivated gentleman. His broad scope of information and his artistic skill made him a recourse for colleagues in difficulty about almost any subject from bibliography or cryptograms to heraldry and music, and to every one his office door was hospitably open. The wide range of his learning in classical as well as modern literature made deep impression upon serious students, although his lectures were too much like polished essays to attract the indifferent. His devotion to Scottish poetry as a theme of instruction resulted in the publication of *Selections from the Early Scottish Poets* (1896), and *The Taill of Rauf Coilyear* (1903). His literary monuments, however, are to be found in the field of American colonial history.

[Biographical sketch by J. W. Bright, with tributes by other writers, in *Johns Hopkins Univ. Circulars,* 1913, No. 2, under the title "In Memoriam, William Hand Browne, 1828–1912."]   J. M. V.

BROWNELL, HENRY HOWARD (Feb. 6, 1820–Oct. 31, 1872), poet, was born in Providence, R. I. His father was Dr. Pardon Brownell, a physician, brother of Bishop Thomas Church Brownell [*q.v.*]; his mother, Lucia de Wolf. In 1862 he published in the Hartford (Conn.) *Evening Press* a rhymed version of Farragut's "General Orders" which brought him to the commander's attention; and that the author's desire to witness a naval battle might be gratified, Farragut secured his appointment as master mate in the navy, from which position he was advanced to ensign with special duties on the *Hartford* as the commander's secretary. He was in the battle of Mobile Bay and several other en-

gagements, and wrote, almost in the smoke of them, a number of descriptive poems of great vividness and force. In 1864 he published *Lyrics of a Day, or Newspaper-Poetry by a Volunteer in the U. S. Service.* He was one of the most popular of the war poets. Oliver Wendell Holmes dubbed him "Our Battle Laureate" (*Atlantic Monthly,* May 1865). After the war he accompanied Admiral Farragut on his European tour. again acting as ensign and secretary.

His naval service was the one great episode in a comparatively short life. He came of seafaring ancestors, loved the sea, and a spirit of adventure was in him; yet he was of modest, retiring disposition, preëminently a scholar. Holmes called him one of the "most highly endowed persons" he had ever met, and Thomas Bailey Aldrich, in two poems bearing Brownell's name, pays high tribute to his worth as a man and poet (*Ibid.,* May 1873, April 1888). He lived a quiet bachelor's life inu East Hartford, Conn., to which place his family had moved when he was a child. Summers he found recreation sailing his cat-boat on Narragansett Bay. He had graduated from Washington (now Trinity) College, Hartford, in 1841, and had taught in Mobile, Ala., for a period, but returning to Hartford, had been admitted to the bar in 1844. He soon turned from practise to literary work, in which he was associated with his brother. In 1851 he published *The People's Book of Ancient and Modern History,* and in 1853 *The Discoverers, Pioneers, and Settlers of North and South America.* As early as 1847 he had published *Poems,* and in 1855 appeared *Ephemerson,* so called from a poem it contains dealing with conditions leading up to the Crimean War. His career ended in his fifty-second year after he had bravely endured a lingering death from cancer of the face.

Considered as a whole, his poems are often tediously long, frequently imitative, and sometimes crude in form. His war poems, however, have high merit. Accuracy of observation is recorded in vivid descriptions, the language of which is vigorous and sometimes racy, while through them all burn passionate loyalty and invincible faith in the Union cause. A selection from these, entitled *Lines of Battle,* by M. A. De Wolfe Howe was published in 1912, and has an informing introduction.

[In addition to references above see Richard Burton, *Literary Likings* (1898); *Cambridge Hist. of Am. Lit.* (1918), II, 277–78; *Atlantic Mo.,* C, 588–93; Ferris Greenslet, *Thos. Bailey Aldrich* (1908), 156–57; C. E. Norton, *Letters of James Russell Lowell,* II, 350–51; *Hartford Courant,* Nov. 9, 1872.]   H. E. S.

BROWNELL, THOMAS CHURCH (Oct. 19, 1779–Jan. 13, 1865), Episcopal bishop, college president, was descended from Thomas, son of Sir Thomas Brownell, who came from England about 1650 and made his home in Little Compton, R. I.; and he was the son of Sylvester and Nancy (Church) Brownell, who lived in Westport, Mass. Here Thomas Church Brownell was born. His early training was that of a farmer's boy, and his education was that of the district school. When he was about eighteen years old, on the advice of the village pastor, with whom he had studied for a time, he went to Bristol Academy in Taunton to prepare for admission to the College of Rhode Island, now Brown University. He entered that institution in the fall of 1800. He remained there only two years, however, for when the then president, the Rev. Dr. Maxcy, accepted the presidency of Union College, Brownell followed him to Union, where he graduated with high honors in the class of 1804. On Apr. 5, 1805, he became tutor in the Latin and Greek languages in Union College and two years later was made professor of belles lettres and moral philosophy and, again after two years, professor of chemistry and mineralogy. The latter was a new department at Union, and Brownell was given a year's leave of absence in Europe to study similar departments there. His marriage in August 1811 to Charlotte Dickinson of Lansingburg, N. Y., an ardent Episcopalian, changed the course of his life. For some time he had been interested in theological matters. He had investigated the doctrines of Calvinism professed by his family, but had been unable to accept them, even in the "mitigated form" presented by the Rev. Eliphalet Potter, whose guidance he had sought. Further study had convinced him of the historical and scriptural grounds of Episcopacy. Now, under his wife's influence, he became an Episcopalian and began the study of theology with the ministry in view. On Apr. 11, 1816, he was ordained deacon by Bishop Hobart in Trinity Church, New York City, and on Aug. 4 of that year was advanced to the priesthood by the same bishop. On June 11, 1818, he was nominated by the rector of Trinity Church, New York, as an assistant minister, and was working in that capacity when the Diocese of Connecticut unanimously elected him to be the successor of Bishop Jarvis. He was consecrated bishop in Trinity Church, New Haven, Oct. 27, 1819. His advancement was remarkable, for it was only three years and a half since he had been made a deacon.

The first year of his episcopate Brownell lived in Hartford, serving as rector of Christ Church in addition to performing his duties as bishop.

The General Theological Seminary, at first located in New York City, was in 1820 removed to New Haven, and Brownell took up his residence there to be in close touch with the Seminary. But in less than two years it went back to New York, and the Bishop again made his home in Hartford. Connecticut Episcopalians had long had it in mind to establish in Connecticut a college of their own. They had vainly tried to enlarge the charter of the Episcopal Academy of Connecticut, so that it might confer degrees. With the adoption of the new state constitution in 1818, and the consequent loosening of the grip of the Congregational standing order, their chance had come, and a charter was granted in 1823 to Washington, now Trinity, College. It was located in Hartford, and Brownell became its first president. He was essentially an educator, and he threw himself heart and soul into the task of placing the newly organized college upon a firm foundation. The diocese, however, soon felt that his whole time and energy should be given to his episcopal duties, and in 1831 he relinquished the presidency, though he continued to hold the office of chancellor. In 1829, in response to the request of the Missionary Society, he made an extensive tour through the states of Kentucky, Mississippi, Louisiana, and Alabama, and again in the winter and spring of 1834–35 he visited this region, and as a result of his journeys an impetus was given to the Episcopal Church throughout the entire section. He compiled a Commentary on the Book of Common Prayer, which in its day was highly regarded. He also compiled other works of a religious character, and many of his addresses and charges to his convention were printed in pamphlet form. On the death of Bishop Philander Chase in 1852, Brownell became the presiding bishop by right of seniority. For the ten years immediately preceding his death his physical condition was such that he could do but little work, and his life slowly and wearily dragged to its end. He died in Hartford and was buried there.

[Brownell's autobiography, printed in E. E. Beardsley, *Hist. of the Episc. Ch. in Conn.*, vol. II (1868); *Calendar*, Jan. 1865; *Ch. Rev.*, July 1865; various memorial sermons and addresses; information from a grand-daughter, Mrs. Thomas Brownell Chapman.]

W.A.B.

BROWNELL, WILLIAM CRARY (Aug. 30, 1851–July 22, 1928), critic, was descended on both sides from early New England settlers. His father, Isaac Wilbour Brownell, a commission merchant in New York City, was born at Westport, Mass., on the border of Rhode Island; his mother, Lucia Emilie (Brown) Brownell, was born near-by in the town of Little Compton,

R. I. His maternal grandmother belonged to another branch of the Brownell family which included Bishop Thomas Church Brownell [*q.v.*], author of a commentary on the Prayer Book, and his nephew Henry Howard Brownell [*q.v.*], a Civil War poet. Thus the future critic's New England inheritance was flavored with Episcopalianism and a tradition of literary achievement. He was born in New York City, but when he was five years old the family moved to Buffalo and there remained for another five years. An only child, he first attended a dame's school, and then Miss Gardner's school for larger children, where Platt Rogers Spencer [*q.v.*], inventor of the Spencerian penmanship, was visiting writing master and doubtless helped to develop the habits of precision later so notable in his pupil. From this period also dated Brownell's love of France, first inspired by his drawing teacher, M. Liard. Always an absorbed reader, during these early years he was especially devoted to the stories of the Old Testament, his familiarity with which is attested by the unusual number of Biblical quotations in his works. Precociously interested in politics and religion, he was already at the age of ten a confirmed Democrat, an Abolitionist, and an Episcopalian.

On the death of his mother Brownell was taken to live with her parents at Adamsville, R. I., where he attended a country school for two years, after which he went to Mr. Fay's boarding-school in Newport until the age of sixteen when he entered Amherst College. After his graduation in 1871, he became a reporter on the New York *World,* and at the age of twenty-one was made city editor. Journalism was then still a literary art; the *World's* staff included such writers as Manton Marble, Montgomery Schuyler, Andrew Carpenter Wheeler, and David Goodman Croly [*qq.v.*]. Brownell's life, always mainly constituted by his friendships for men and books, became unusually rich in intellectual contacts. At this time he began to frequent the art studios of Homer Martin, Thomas Eakins, John La Farge, Olin Warner, and John Quincy Adams Ward [*qq.v.*]. From 1879 to 1881 he was on the staff of the *Nation,* where again he was associated with a brilliant group, headed by Edward Lawrence Godkin [*q.v.*]. Married in January 1878 to Virginia Shields Swinburne, daughter of Daniel T. Swinburne of Newport, Brownell sailed with his wife in October 1881 for a three years' residence abroad, mainly in Paris. He and his wife returned to America in August 1884 and then lived for nearly two years in Philadelphia, where he was employed on the staff of the *Philadelphia Press.* In January 1888 he became editor and literary adviser in the firm of Charles Scribner's Sons, a position which he was to retain until his death more than forty years later. His first wife died in 1911, and in January 1921 he married Gertrude Hall, poet and translator of Verlaine and Rostand.

During the long years with Scribner's, Brownell's rich humanity lifted the editorial work far above the level of routine. He was uncompromising in his standards, but his critical severity was tempered by kindness and quiet geniality. "In spite of the great dignity of Mr. Brownell's bearing and expression, which might have made people stand in awe of him, he was in human touch with all the employees in the building. . . . He was truly, instinctively democratic,—one who knew that the largest elements in men are shared by all of them—that distinctions of intellect and education are comparatively trifling ones" (Robert Bridges, *A Companionable Colleague,* pamphlet, 1929).

Above financial need and devoid of zeal for fame, writing carefully and unhurriedly, Brownell brought out, at comparatively long intervals, a series of critical volumes notable for their polished Latinized style and serious content. His work, even when it dealt with foreign themes, was fundamentally a criticism of American culture as expressed in manners, art, and letters. Thus his first volume *French Traits* (1889), bearing as a sub-title, "An Essay in Comparative Criticism," elaborates a series of antitheses between Gallic idealization of reason and honor, Gallic respect for institutions, Gallic social instinct, and American idealization of emotion and duty, American distrust of institutions, American individualism. As a study of racial characteristics the book ranks with Emerson's *English Traits.* Finding the central evil of American life in its excessive individualism, self-condemned by the astonishing number of eccentrics, fanatics, and ill-mannered bores which it has bred, Brownell was still well aware of the value of the individual creative energy released by the romantic ideal, and in his criticism here as always he strove for sanity and the mean. The same orientation governed his second work, *French Art* (1892) which, probably more than any other critical writing, brought to America due recognition of the value of modern French painting and sculpture. At the same time it revealed certain limitations in the critic's sympathies. Brownell shared his generation's antipathy to England: this prevented his acknowledging the influence of Constable and Turner on French painting; he also shared, though in slighter measure, his generation's antipathy to radical experiment or self-expression, and thus, although he accepted Rodin enthusiastically because of his poetic quality, he entirely missed Daumier, Renoir, and Cézanne. After *Newport* (1896), a charming descriptive sketch of the city of his youth, Brownell's next three works, *Victorian Prose Masters* (1901), *American Prose Masters* (1909), and *Criticism* (1914) embodied a defense and exemplification of judicial criticism. Every work of art being the concrete expression of a personality, the task of criticism, according to Brownell, is the interpretation and evaluation of this personality according to the norms of beauty or "reason expressed in form." The application of this criterion led in *Victorian Prose Masters* to eulogistic judgments of Thackeray and Arnold, a cool appraisal of George Eliot and Meredith, and derogatory estimates of Carlyle and Ruskin; in *American Prose Masters* it resulted in a glorification of Emerson, a rehabilitation of Cooper, a much qualified respect for Hawthorne and Lowell, an absolute refusal to accept Poe as a great writer, and a rather puzzled attitude toward Henry James. The basis for the evaluation in each case was a ruthless analysis of the author's content and manner, conducted with such thoroughness as to give an appearance of objective finality to Brownell's conclusions even in this dangerously subjective field. In *Standards* (1917) he pointed out the contemporary decline of public taste and of literary style, due, he thought, to the disintegrating individualism and sensationalism of the day; in *The Genius of Style* (1924) he enlarged upon the same theme, contrasting the ideal of disciplined inspiration consciously directed toward impersonal ends with the current surrender to personal impulse, egotism, and anarchy. Finally, in what he knew was to be his last book, *Democratic Distinction in America* (1927), he made his peace with the world in a reiteration of faith in the organic spirit of society as competent in the long run to curb individual extravagance and levity.

Brownell was the last of the Victorians. Brought up in a period of expanding industry, he never questioned the virtues of industrialism and had less than his usual patience with its radical critics, such as Carlyle and Ruskin; hence its inevitable but less desirable social consequences seemed to him merely wilful and to be overcome by a simple change of heart. He had little of the philosopher's skepticism; indeed, he considered "a smattering of philosophy" sufficient for the critic; for this reason he never examined the ethical presuppositions upon which his theoretical universe was constructed. Thus he quite

failed to understand the naturalistic basis of the passionate revolt whose echoes disturbed his later years. On the other hand, if he was unable, fundamentally, to justify the Victorian attitude theoretically, he illustrated it in his practise most attractively. The quiet self-respect and reticence of his style were in themselves a rebuke to contemporary vulgarity; his devotion to high, even though often vaguely defined ideals, gave the cast of nobility to his work; his instinct for the avoidance of extremes, accompanied by a gracious worldly wisdom and a kind of enlightened common sense, lent weight to his judgments. He may be regarded as a connecting link between the Sainte-Beuve–Arnold tradition and the New Humanism of Irving Babbitt, Paul Elmer More, and Stuart Sherman: but he was too well disciplined to share the later school's excessive praise of discipline. While neither the most profound nor learned of American critics he was, perhaps, the sanest.

[*Amherst College Biog. Record* (1927), p. 307 ; *N. Y. Times, N. Y. Herald-Tribune*, July 23, 1928 ; *Who's Who in America*, 1928–29 ; information as to specific facts from Mrs. Gertrude Hall Brownell, N. Y. City.]

E. S. B.

BROWNING, JOHN MOSES (Jan. 21, 1855–Nov. 26, 1926), inventor, was born in Ogden, Utah, of Mormon parentage, son of Jonathan Browning, a gunsmith, and Elizabeth Caroline (Clark). From childhood Browning displayed a remarkable talent for invention. At the age of thirteen he made his first gun of scrap iron in his father's gunshop. In 1879 he secured his first patent for a breech-loading single-shot rifle. He, with his brother Mathew, made about 600 of these rifles, one of which was brought to the attention of the Winchester Repeating Arms Company who were so impressed with the simple and effective design of the arm that they paid the brothers large royalties to allow the Winchester Company to produce this rifle, which is still being made by them. Browning's association with the Winchester Company led him into the field of repeating rifles and shotguns. He designed many types of sporting firearms, such as the Remington Auto-loading shotguns and rifles; the Winchester repeating shotguns; single-shot and repeating rifles; the Stevens rifles; and the Colt automatic pistols. The repeating rifle was patented in 1884; the box magazine in 1895; and numerous other patents were secured on rapid-fire guns. From all of these Browning drew large royalties. With his brother, he organized the J. M. & M. S. Browning Company, and the Browning Brothers Company, branching out from gun-making to banking and stock-raising, until their estates, at the time of his death, were rated in many millions.

In 1890 a machine gun of Browning design, but known as the Colt, was adopted by the United States Army. The first machine gun turned out by Browning was made famous during the Spanish-American conflict through its effective work in both land and naval engagements around Santiago. It became known as the "Peacemaker." Browning produced in 1896 the automatic pistol, later improved and used by the United States Army in the World War. The manufacturing rights for this weapon were obtained by the Colt Patent Firearms Manufacturing Company of Hartford, Conn.

In May 1917, when the secretary of war ordered a Machine Gun Board to test all machine guns and automatic rifles submitted to it, Browning submitted through the Colt Company two guns, one, the heavy water-cooled machine gun, and the other the light Browning automatic rifle, demonstrating these guns himself. They proved to be superior to anything else tested or known, and were so declared by the Board. The Browning Machine Gun, Model of 1917, the Browning Automatic Rifle, Model of 1918, and the Automatic Pistol, Model of 1911, were supplied to the United States Army in large numbers. The Browning Aircraft Machine Gun, which is the Browning heavy type machine gun modified for use in aircraft, has a rate of fire of 1150–1250 shots per minute and can be used with a synchronizer to fire through propeller blades, being fired from a special aircraft mounting. One of Browning's machine guns, adopted by the United States Army in 1918, at its official trial fired 39,500 rounds before a breakage developed.

Browning's inventions never lacked a market. From the time he manufactured his first gun until the World War made him more widely known, he received flattering offers for his ideas and inventions almost as soon as they had taken definite shape on the work bench. No design of Browning's ever proved a failure, nor was any arm produced by him ever discontinued. At the time of his death he was working on an "over and under" double-barrelled shotgun. He always avoided publicity and his name was used in one establishment only, the Fabrique National at Liège, Belgium, and only on his last machine gun and automatic rifle. He was made a Chevalier of the Order of Leopold and was decorated by King Albert of Belgium on the occasion of the completion of the millionth automatic pistol at Liège. His longest and last association in this country was with the officials of the Colt Patent Firearms Company, with whom he worked for

many years. He was considered one of the greatest inventors of small arms in history and was foremost in the field of automatic weapons. He was a man of sterling character, a cheerful companion, modest, quiet, and unassuming. He died suddenly of heart disease at Herstals, near Liège, Belgium, where he had gone on a mission to Belgium's national armament factory, in which he was interested. When his remains were brought to this country they were received with military honors and forwarded to his home at Ogden, Utah. He was married in 1879 to Rachel D. Child.

[*Who's Who in America*, 1926–27; Patent Office Records; *Army Ordnance*, vol. VII; *New Internat. Year Book*, 1926; *Salt Lake Tribune*, Nov. 27, 1926.]

C.F.C.

BROWNING, ORVILLE HICKMAN (Feb. 10, 1806–Aug. 10, 1881), lawyer, politician, was born in Harrison County, Ky., the son of Micaijah Browning and Sally Brown. He attended Augusta College, but financial reverses in his family compelled him to leave before receiving his degree. He studied law at Cynthiana, Ky., and in 1831 settled in Quincy, the county seat of Adams County, Ill. Here he soon engaged in politics, and was elected state senator as a Whig in 1836. He gained momentary unpopularity by refusing to support the internal improvement scheme espoused by Abraham Lincoln which almost wrecked the state financially. In 1842 he was elected to the lower house in the General Assembly and in 1843 he contested the seat in Congress with Stephen A. Douglas. The district had been formed by a Democratic legislature with the express intention of giving Douglas a seat but Browning ran him so strenuous a race that both men broke down physically on the eve of Douglas's election. In 1850 and 1852 Browning was again defeated. Like many conservative Illinois Whigs, he was slow to cast in his lot with the Republican party. In the state convention of 1856, he drafted the platform, helping to give it the conservative slant that would attract the old Whigs to the new party. It is quite possible that Browning felt some jealousy at the rapid rise of his old associate, Abraham Lincoln, although the two had been most intimate friends for many years. He was suspected, probably not without reason, of lukewarmness in the cause of Lincoln's presidential aspirations. As a member of the state delegation to the Republican Convention of 1860, however, Browning took a prominent part in winning over other delegates to accept Lincoln as a second choice. His own choice for the nomination was Judge Edward Bates of Missouri and he had endeavored in the earlier part of 1860 to line up the state of Illinois for him.

Lincoln showed Browning in advance the copy of his inaugural address and Browning suggested some important changes, regarding the new president's attitude toward federal property in the South, which Lincoln incorporated. On the death of Stephen A. Douglas, Browning was appointed by Gov. Yates to fill the unexpired term. This brought him to Washington for the special session of 1861 and the regular session of 1861–62. In the Senate, for a while, he was the spokesman of Lincoln's Border State policy but gradually as Lincoln moved on in the direction of emancipation, he and Browning drifted apart. Browning took his political life in his hand by opposing the second Confiscation Act and made no secret of the fact that he regarded the Emancipation Proclamation as a calamity. His backward attitude in the election of 1862 was partly responsible for the election of a Democratic legislature in Illinois, which in turn promptly elected William A. Richardson senator in his room.

In the course of 1863 Browning returned to Washington to establish what was ostensibly a law partnership with Thomas Ewing, ex-Senator Cowan, and Britton Hill. Actually, Ewing and Browning traded on their influence with the leaders of the Republican party in securing special favors for contractors. Browning renewed his old intimacy with Lincoln and in connection with James W. Singleton, an old Illinois Whig who had become something of a copperhead, planned to secure special permission to bring Confederate produce through the Federal lines with huge profits to himself and his associates. The collapse of the Confederacy prevented him from reaping his profits.

As Browning was the advocate of the old Border State policy, he naturally turned with disgust from the radical reconstruction policy that followed the assassination of Lincoln. Accordingly, he became a supporter of Andrew Johnson. In May 1866 he was installed as Johnson's adviser on the Illinois patronage. He took an active part in the Philadelphia Convention and on Sept. 1, 1866, became secretary of the interior in Johnson's cabinet. For a few months he also held the office of attorney-general. He had for some time foreseen the impeachment of Johnson and stood loyally by the President during his struggle. Along with Johnson, he left office on Mar. 4, 1869. On his return to Illinois he was elected on the Democratic ticket to the state constitutional convention of 1869–70. His influence was mainly responsible for the adoption of the principle of minority representation. It is interest-ing to note that he had willingly pledged himself to oppose the principle of negro suffrage.

Browning and his partner, Nehemiah Bushnell, had been engaged in a steadily expanding legal business since the fifties. Both men took a warm interest in the railroad development, Browning becoming one of the special attorneys for the Chicago, Burlington & Quincy. He argued before the Supreme Court the case of *Chicago, Burlington & Quincy* vs. *Iowa* which was one of the leading Granger cases. He was consistently a lawyer defending vested interests against the principles of government regulation. In person, he was tall, well-built, of stately carriage, bald in later years, and with a ruddy complexion. He had the suave and formal manners of a Kentucky gentleman of the old school and wore ruffled shirts to the end of his life. He was married, in 1836, to Eliza Caldwell.

[Browning's diary, written intermittently from 1850 to 1881, is being published in the *Ill. State Hist. Lib. Colls.* Aside from this, the obituary in *Proc. Ill. State Bar Ass.*, 1882, is the best life of Browning available. There is also an obituary in the *Chi. Daily Tribune*, Aug. 12, 1881.]   T.C.P.

BROWNLEE, WILLIAM CRAIG (1784– Feb. 10, 1860), Presbyterian clergyman, was the fifth child of James Brownlee, a farmer of Lanarkshire, Scotland, and his wife Margaret Craig. He graduated and took his M.A. with honors at the University of Glasgow, studied theology under Rev. Dr. Bruce and was licensed by the Presbytery of Sterling in 1808. He came to America at about this time and became pastor of the Associate Church, Mount Pleasant, Pa. From 1813 to 1816, he was pastor of the Associate Scotch Church, Philadelphia. From 1816 to 1819, he had charge of the Queen's College (Rutgers) Academy, New Brunswick, N. J. From 1819 to 1825 he was pastor of the Presbyterian Church, Basking Ridge, N. J., and principal of a classical academy there. In 1825 he became a professor of languages at Rutgers, and on June 18, 1826 he was installed associate pastor of the Collegiate Church, New York City, his particular charge being the Middle Church on Lafayette Place. On Sept. 23, 1843, while in Newburgh to fulfil a lecture engagement, he was stricken down with paralysis which incapacitated him for all further work. He lived however till Feb. 10, 1860. He received the degree of D.D. by unanimous vote of the Senate of Glasgow University, Dec. 6, 1824, in recognition of his *Inquiry into the Principles of the Quakers* (1824).

Brownlee was an orthodox Calvinist. His sermons were doctrinal and scriptural and were characterized by a clear, finished, extemporaneous style, with much use of the imagination. He was an eloquent preacher with a strong Scotch brogue. He was one of the earliest of the Protestant clergy of America to take a firm anti-Catholic stand and he at times incurred personal danger therefrom. He was also an uncompromising foe of Unitarianism and Universalism. All his convictions were strong and he held them with an unswerving tenacity inherited from generations of Covenanter ancestry. His scholarship was exact and his learning extensive. From 1826 to 1830 he edited the *Magazine of the Reformed Dutch Church of America,* writing many of its articles himself. He was the author of several anti-Catholic works, such as *Letters in the Roman Catholic Controversy* (1834), *Popery an Enemy to Civil and Religious Liberty* (1836), *The Doctrinal Decrees and Canons of the Council of Trent* (1836), *Romanism in the Light of Prophecy and History; its Final Downfall and Triumph of the Church of Christ* (1854) ; a number of general religious and theological subjects; and is credited with a novel, *The Whigs of Scotland; a Romance.*

There is a very impressive portrait of Brownlee in gown and bands, at the Collegiate Church of St. Nicholas, Fifth Ave., N. Y. He had a fresh, open countenance and a kindly expression. In 1807, he married at Kilsyth, Scotland, Maria McDougall who lived till September 1849.

[Shortly after Brownlee's death, a volume was issued entitled *Memorial of the Rev. Dr. Brownlee,* which contains much biographical material. Corwin's *Manual of the Reformed Ch. in America* (4th ed. 1902) contains a good article, with a complete list of Brownlee's publications. Another sketch is found in the *Collegiate Ch. Year Book,* 1896.]   F.T.P.

BROWNLOW, WILLIAM GANNAWAY (Aug. 29, 1805–Apr. 29, 1877), governor of Tennessee, was born in Wythe County, Va. His parents, Joseph A. Brownlow and Catharine (Gannaway) Brownlow, were among the many Virginians who migrated to eastern Tennessee in the early nineteenth century and developed in that somewhat isolated region a community distinct in culture and opinion. Some five years after the birth of their son they settled near Knoxville. Joseph Brownlow died in 1816, and the death of his wife three months later left the boy to grow up in the care of his mother's relatives. He had little schooling, but, while learning the carpenter's trade, studied the common branches and acquired a fair education, especially in English literature and the Bible, and subsequently prepared for the Methodist ministry, which he entered in 1826. For ten years he served as an itinerant preacher, but his intense interest in public questions, and a natural gift of pungent speech soon led him into political as well as religious controversy. In his speeches and in a pamphlet defending his political activity, he avowed beliefs and displayed a fearlessness that were to make him a national figure thirty years later. This pamphlet, a controversy with a Calvinistic preacher named Posey (October 1832), contained his first published utterance on the slavery question. He said that he expected to see the day when slavery, not the tariff, would shake the government to its foundations, and that when such a day came he, though no opponent of slavery, would stand by the government. He became in 1838 the editor of the *Tennessee Whig* (Elizabethton), and the following year, of the *Jonesboro Whig and Independent* which he edited until 1849. In that year he entered upon his editorship of the *Knoxville Whig,* which under his hand was soon the most influential paper in eastern Tennessee and before the Civil War had a circulation larger than that of any other political paper in the state. He was a candidate against Andrew Johnson for nomination to Congress in 1843 and in 1850 was one of several commissioners appointed by President Fillmore to carry out the improvement of the Missouri River for which Congress had made provision. He had always been a "Federal Whig of the Washington and Hamilton type," always a "national" man, an unconditional advocate of the preservation of the Union. On Nov. 17, 1860, he declared editorially that Lincoln, though elected by a sectional vote, "is chosen president, and whether with or without the consent and participation of the South, will be and ought to be inaugurated on the 4th of March, 1861." His was the last house in Knoxville over which the Union flag was displayed, and the *Whig* was the last Union paper in the South. Until it was suppressed (Oct. 24, 1861) every issue contained arguments and appeals to the Union men of the South and defiance of and contempt for the leaders of secession. In the last issue Brownlow declared that he would rather be imprisoned than "recognize the hand of God in the work of breaking up the American Government." After he had refused allegiance to the Confederate government his arrest was imminent and on Nov. 5, 1861 (*Congressional Record,* 42 Cong., 2 Sess., pp. 1038–40), he fled to the mountains on the North Carolina border. His press and types were destroyed. He was found by Confederate scouts, returned to Knoxville, and notified that he would be given a passport beyond the Confederate lines into Kentucky. But on Dec. 6 he was arrested and placed in jail under suspicion of having had a hand in the state-wide burning of railway bridges on Nov. 6, and charged with treason because of his final editorial in the *Whig*. He suffered from typhoid during his imprisonment and after a month was allowed to go to his home, where he was kept under guard for nearly eight weeks. On order of Judah P. Benjamin, Confederate secretary of war, he was sent inside the Federal lines on Mar. 3, 1862. Going at once to Ohio, he spent some time regaining his health and writing his *Sketches of the Rise, Progress, and Decline of Secession; With a Narrative of Personal Adventure Among the Rebels* (1862), after which he made an extensive lecture tour through the North where he was shown distinguished attention by public officials and large audiences. His ideas in regard to slavery changed and he supported President Lincoln's emancipation policy (*Cincinnati Gazette*, Apr. 30, 1877).

Returning to eastern Tennessee with Burnside's army in the fall of 1863, he again became a leader among the Unionists of that section, was among those who called a nominating convention for May 30,—preliminary to restoring civil government in the state,—and was a member of the Union central committee until elected governor by acclamation in 1865. His first message gave a remarkably comprehensive view of conditions and needs in the state, and outlined closely the course afterward followed by legislation. He was determined to disfranchise all who had fought against the United States, and asked the legislature for a military force to make such a measure effective. The Ku Klux Klan became a dangerous power after the franchise law had been made more severe, and when the protection of federal troops was denied, Brownlow gathered 1,600 state guards and proclaimed martial law in nine counties. He was afflicted with palsy and unable to make an active campaign for reëlection, but was returned by a large majority. Before the close of his second term he was elected to the United States Senate to succeed David T. Patterson, and took office on Mar. 4, 1869. His career in the Senate was not distinguished. He usually acted with the Republicans, and for a while spoke often and vigorously in debate. His health was failing, however, and although he attended regularly until toward the end of his term, he became unable to speak, and several addresses, mainly defenses against attack, were read by the clerk. The last bill introduced by him was for the purchase of a site for Fisk University. At the end of his term, he returned to Knoxville, bought control of the *Whig*, which he had sold in 1869, and edited it with something of his old-time vigor until a short time before his death.

Brownlow was of robust figure, six feet in height, and weighed 175 pounds. He had, he said, as strong a voice as any man in east Tennessee. When not in controversy he was a peaceful and charming man, but his fearless and ruthless honesty in expressing his opinions made him always a storm center. Besides the book already mentioned, he wrote *Helps to the Study of Presbyterianism* (1834); *A Political Register, Setting forth the Principles of the Whig and Locofoco Parties in the United States, with the Life and Public Services of Henry Clay* (1844); *Americanism Contrasted with Foreignism, Romanism, and Bogus Democracy* (1856); *The Great Iron Wheel Examined, and an Exhibition of Elder [J. R.] Graves, its Builder* (1856). He was married to Eliza, daughter of James S. and Susan Dabney (Everet) O'Brien.

[The chief sources are the works mentioned above, especially *Sketches of the Rise . . . of Secession.* See also *Parson Brownlow and the Unionists of East Tenn.: with a Sketch of His Life* (1862); *Portrait and Biog. of Parson Brownlow, the Tenn. Patriot, Together with His Last Editorial in the Knoxville Whig; Also His Recent Speeches, Rehearsing His Experience with Secession and His Prison Life* (1862); Jas. Walter Fertig, *The Secession and Reconstruction of Tenn.* (1898); J. T. Moore and A. P. Foster, *Tenn. the Volunteer State* (1923); O. P. Temple, *Notable Men of Tenn.* (1912); John R. Neal, *Disunion and Restoration in Tenn.* (1899). W. F. G. Shanks compared Brownlow and Andrew Johnson in *Putnam's Mag.*, April 1869, pp. 428 ff. Obituaries were published in the *Public Ledger* (Memphis, Tenn.), May 1, 1877, and in the *Evening Post* (N. Y.), *N. Y. Tribune,* and *N. Y. Times,* the *Cincinnati Gazette,* and other papers of Apr. 30, 1877.]   F.W.S.

BROWNSON, ORESTES AUGUSTUS (Sept. 16, 1803–Apr. 17, 1876), author, was born at Stockbridge, Vt., of an old Connecticut family. The death of his father, Sylvester Augustus Brownson, left the widow, Relief Metcalf, in straitened circumstances, and after six years of unsuccessful struggle against poverty she was obliged to leave to charitable neighbors the care of her two youngest children, Orestes Augustus and Daphne Augusta (twins). Brought up on a small farm, the boy grew into a stalwart youth over six feet tall with no education save that supplied by omnivorous reading largely of a religious character. In 1822 he joined the Presbyterian Church but, repelled by its doctrines of election and reprobation, he left it after two years to become a Universalist, and on June 15, 1826, was ordained as a Universalist minister. He was married on June 19, 1827, to Sally, daughter of John Healy of Elbridge, N. Y. During the next few years he preached in various churches in Vermont, New Hampshire, and northern New York, and in 1829 became editor of the *Gospel Advocate*, published in Auburn, N. Y. The expression of his increasingly liberal views in regard to the inspiration of the Scriptures, the divinity of Jesus, and the future life offended his fellow-Universalists and he gradually withdrew from their communion and became a kind of ministerial free lance, preaching and writing as opportunity permitted. For a time he associated with Robert Dale Owen and Fanny Wright in their socialistic schemes, acted as corresponding editor of the *Free Enquirer,* and helped to organize the short-lived Workingmen's Party. Always identified in sympathy with the laboring classes, he nevertheless hoped to ameliorate their condition by moral suasion rather than by political action, and at length drifted back into the Church, this time as a Unitarian, serving parishes at Walpole, N. H. (1832–34) and at Canton, Mass. (1834–36). In 1836 he organized his own church among the laboring men of Boston, calling it the Society for Christian Union and Progress, and during the same year published his first book, *New Views of Christianity, Society and the Church,* in which he condemned both Catholicism and Protestantism, and celebrated the "Church of the Future." Eloquent and irascible, Brownson had now become a force both on the platform and in the press. In January 1838 he established the *Boston Quarterly Review,* an influential Democratic organ which in July 1840 made itself notorious by attacking, in the interest of the common man, organized Christianity, the inheritance of wealth, and the existing penal code. In 1840, also, he published *Charles Elwood; or, the Infidel Converted,* a semi-autobiographical romance, in which the infidel hero is converted, through Cousin's philosophy, to a rather tepid unitarianism. Two years later *The Mediatorial Life of Jesus* showed that the position of the author had shifted to a virtual trinitarianism. In 1842 the *Boston Quarterly Review* was merged with the *Democratic Review* of New York to which Brownson contributed a series of articles on "Synthetic Philosophy" and on "The Origin and Constitution of Government" (revised and republished in 1865 as *The American Republic; its Constitution, Tendencies and Destiny*). Brownson's hostility to the extreme political theories of popular sovereignty offended his constituents so that he soon severed his connection with the *Democratic Review* and in January 1844 resumed the publication of his own journal in Boston with its named changed to *Brownson's Quarterly Review.* During these years he had become closely associated with Channing, Thoreau, Bancroft, George Ripley (with whose Brook Farm experiment he sympathized to the extent of sending his son Orestes

to join the community), and J. C. Calhoun (whom he supported for the presidency in 1844). He was still so much identified, in men's minds, with New England liberalism that his conversion to Catholicism in October 1844 came with much of the same shock that the conversion of Newman was to bring just a year later. Less subtle and profound than Newman, Brownson reached the same goal by much the same path, acceptance of the divine mediatorial power of Jesus seeming to both to involve necessarily the acceptance of the divine mediatorial power of the church. As with Newman, though less startlingly so, Brownson's conversion involved a sacrifice of worldly prosperity. It cost the *Review* a large number of its New England supporters and almost all its Southern constituency. He continued to publish it, however, until January 1865, when it was suspended until October 1872. Meanwhile he changed his residence in 1855 to New York City and again in 1857 to Elizabeth, N. J. A polemicist by nature, he chiefly devoted his pen, after his conversion, to an uncompromising assertion of the claims of the Catholic Church and to trenchant attacks upon her enemies. In *The Spirit-Rapper; an Autobiography* (1854), really a fantastic romance, he traced the spiritualistic phenomena of the day to Satanic influence. In his more important *The Convert; or, Leaves from my Experience* (1857) he gave a valuable, if inevitably partisan, account of his own religious development. He died on Apr. 17, 1876, in Detroit, Mich., whither he had removed in the previous year. His complete works were published in twenty volumes (1882–87), ably edited by his son, Henry F. Brownson.

[The standard biography is *Orestes A. Brownson's Early Life, Middle Life, Latter Life* (3 vols., 1898–1900), by Henry F. Brownson, who also has a sketch of his father in the *Cath. Encyc.* An interesting dissertation on *The Critical Principles of Orestes A. Brownson,* by Virgil G. Michel (Cath. Univ., Washington, 1918), contains a full list of important magazine articles on the man and his work.]   E.S.B.

BRUCE, ARCHIBALD (February 1777–Feb. 22, 1818), physician, mineralogist, was born in New York City. His father, William Bruce, a native of Dumfries, Scotland, was a medical officer in the British Army stationed in New York, where he married Judith (Bayard) Van Rensselaer, a widow, and where their son was born. William Bruce was later transferred to Barbados where he died of yellow fever. The young Archibald was left in New York with his mother, who sent him to Halifax to the care of Dr. William Almon, a friend of his father. He remained there but a short time when, returning to New York, he was placed in a private school conducted by Peter Wilson at Flatbush, Long

Island. Thence he proceeded to Columbia College. For reasons of his own, his father had been strongly opposed to the idea that his son should follow him in the study and practise of medicine and the boy's mother and her friends had been charged with carrying out the father's wishes. Even while a student of the school of arts, however, the young man was attending the medical lectures of Dr. Nicholas Romayne, a popular instructor of the time. Later he attended the private medical school of Dr. David Hosack and pursued the several courses of instruction given by the Medical Faculty of Columbia College. After his graduation with the A.B. degree in 1797, he went to Europe and in 1800 he was given the degree of M.D. from the University of Edinburgh. His thesis on that occasion was entitled *De variola vaccina*. While taking medical instruction from Dr. Hosack in New York, he had learned to share the latter's interest in mineralogy. Therefore, after finishing at Edinburgh, he went to the Continent where during two years spent in France, Switzerland, and Italy he pursued the study of minerals and the assembling of a mineralogical collection. Returning to England, he was married in London, and in the summer of 1803 he returned to New York to take up the practise of medicine. With Dr. Romayne and others, he organized the state and county medical societies and in 1807 secured a charter for the College of Physicians and Surgeons of the State of New York. He was given the chair of materia medica and mineralogy in the new faculty, the first professorship of these branches created in America. A reorganization of the school in 1811 deprived him of his professorship and the post of registrar. Again associated with Romayne and others, he organized a new medical faculty where again he lectured on materia medica and mineralogy, but the new organization was soon disbanded. He was at one time (1812–18) connected with the faculty of Queens (now Rutgers) College. In 1810 he established the *American Mineralogical Journal,* the first purely scientific journal in America. It completed but one volume.

It is probably as a mineralogist that Bruce will be longest remembered. His name is given to the metal brucite, a native magnesium hydroxide, which he discovered in New Jersey. He also discovered the deposits of zinc oxide in Sussex County, N. J., and published a paper *On the Ores of Titanium Occurring Within the United States.* There is no record of any medical writing other than the inaugural thesis. The biographer of his day credits him with "conciliating social habits and disposition" together with "dig-

nity of character and urbanity of manner." His portrait shows a round, full, smooth-shaven face with bovine eyes. His appearance was that of one who enjoyed his food and drink. He died from apoplexy, at the age of forty-one, in his native city.

[In the *Am. Jour. of Sci.,* vol. I, 1819, there is a biographical sketch with portrait, which is apparently the basis for all subsequent biographies. See also the *Gen. Catalogue* of Columbia Univ.]   J.M.P.

BRUCE, BLANCHE K. (Mar. 1, 1841–Mar. 17, 1898), negro senator, was born in Farmville, Prince Edward County, Va. At an early age he moved to Missouri. For two years he attended Oberlin College where he pursued a special course in the fundamentals. He then in 1868 started life as a planter at Floreyville, Miss., and accumulated considerable property. For a while he engaged in teaching and at the same time he entered politics. By judgment, tact, and executive ability, he easily made himself a leader of a large constituency which rewarded him with many political honors. He served the state Senate of Mississippi as sergeant-at-arms in 1870, secured the appointment of assessor of Bolivar County in 1871, became its sheriff in 1872, and the same year obtained a seat in the Board of Levee Commissioners of the Mississippi. To give him the opportunity to crown these efforts with a service for the whole country, his constituents elected him to the United States Senate in 1874. On June 24, 1878, he was married to Josephine B. Wilson of Cleveland. He served creditably in the Senate for six years from 1875 to 1881. Although he spent much time and energy in the debates on election frauds, Southern disorders, and civil rights, he was equal to the occasion in dealing with other important problems. He fearlessly opposed the Chinese exclusion policy, he forcefully combated our selfish attitude toward the Indians, and he worked for the removal of the disabilities of men who had opposed the emancipation of the race to which he belonged. He showed statesmanlike foresight, too, in his advocacy of the improvement of the navigation of the Mississippi. He not only labored to prevent the periodical inundation of that stream, but endeavored so to improve the waterway as to furnish increased facilities for interstate and foreign commence. Deprived of further political preferment as the result of the overthrow of the Reconstruction governments in the South, he settled in Washington. At the expiration of his term in the Senate, President Garfield made him Register of the Treasury, a position which he held for four years. In 1889, President Harrison appointed him Recorder of

Deeds in the District of Columbia when the position meant much more than it does to-day. President McKinley called him back to the office of Register of the Treasury in 1895. He served in this capacity until his death.

[*Jour. of Negro History*, vol. VII (1922); *Biog. Dir. of the Am. Cong.* (1928); W. J. Simmons, *Men of Mark* (1887); *Evening Star* (Washington, D. C.), Mar. 17, 1898.]   C. G. W.

BRUCE, GEORGE (June 26, 1781–July 5, 1866), typefounder, was born in the outskirts of Edinburgh, Scotland. He was the son of a tanner, and was educated in the public schools. Before he was fifteen he gained the consent of his family to join his older brother, David, in Philadelphia, Pa. There he became an apprentice in book-binding, but, chafing under the direction of a tyrannical and exacting master, he apprenticed himself to Thomas Dobson, a Philadelphia printer by whom David was also employed. The destruction of the Dobson plant by fire in 1798 and the prevalence of a fever in Philadelphia, led the brothers to leave the city. Traveling by foot, George was stricken with the yellow fever at Amboy, N. J., and was nursed by David. For a time both worked in a printing office at Albany, N. Y., but the firm there failed, and they followed the Post Road on foot to New York City. George was employed in various offices until 1803, when he was made foreman on the *Daily Advertiser,* to which he had contributed articles, and in the same year he became the printer and publisher of that newspaper for the proprietor, David being associated with him in this venture. In 1806 the brothers opened a book-printing office at the corner of Pearl St. and Coffee House Slip, and in the same year brought out an edition of Lavoisier's *Chemistry* on their own account, doing all the work with their own hands, with borrowed type and press. Their industry and zeal soon brought them abundant commissions, and, in 1809, when they removed to Sloat Lane, near Hanover Square, they were running a veritable battery of presses. In 1812, David brought from England the secret of stereotyping, but their attempt to introduce the process here encountered many difficulties which it required all of their ingenuity to surmount. The type of that day was cast with so low a beveled shoulder that it was not suitable for stereotyping, since it interfered with the moulding and weakened the plate. The brothers found it necessary, therefore, to cast their own type. At the same time they added several important improvements to the English process. Their first stereotyped works were school editions of the New Testament in bourgeois, and the Bible in nonpareil, about 1814–15, and they subsequently stereotyped the earlier issues of the American Bible Society, and a series of Latin classics. In 1816 they sold their printing business and bought a building in Eldridge St. for their foundry, and two years later they erected their own foundry in Chambers St. George gave his attention not alone to the typemaking end but to the enlargement and development of the business. The partnership was dissolved in 1822. Soon thereafter, George relinquished stereotyping to give his whole attention to type-founding. He introduced valuable improvements into the business, cutting his own punches, making constantly new and tasteful designs, and graduating the size of the body of the type so as to give it a proper relative proportion to the size of the letter. In connection with his nephew he invented the only type-casting machine that has stood the test of experience, and which is still in general use. His scripts early became famous among printers, and he was the first to take advantage of the Act of Congress of 1842 protecting designs. At the age of nearly fourscore he cut punches for a primer script. He was for several terms president of the Mechanics Institute of New York and of the New York Typefounders' Association; an officer in the General Society of Mechanics and Tradesmen and in the Apprentices' Library; a patron of the New York Typographical Society and of the Printers' Library, and a member of the New York Historical Society and of the St. Andrew's Society. His death called forth memorials from the various printing industries in New York. Bruce was twice married: on Jan. 1, 1803 to Margaret Watson of Schenectady, who died of yellow fever in October of that year, and in 1811 to Catherine Wolfe.

[The life and work of Bruce are mentioned in a variety of papers of the old Printers' Lib., now a part of the collection of the N. Y. Pub. Lib. The "Horace Greeley Papers" also contain occasional reference to him and to his relations with the editor of the *Tribune*. Obituaries were published in the *N. Y. Evening Post*, July 7, 1866, and *N. Y. Tribune*, July 10, 1866, the latter being the Typographical Soc. memoir. See also sketch in Wm. N. MacBean, *Biog. Reg. of the St. Andrew's Soc. of the State of N. Y.*, vol. I (1922), p. 383.]   R. R. R.

BRUCE, ROBERT (Feb. 20, 1778–June 14, 1846), Presbyterian clergyman, educator, believed to have been a descendant of King Robert Bruce, was born in the parish of Scone, Perthshire, Scotland. He studied theology for five years in Associate Hall under A. Bruce, and was licensed to preach in 1806 by the Presbytery of Perth Associate Church. Adventurous, filled with missionary zeal, he declined the preferment awaiting him in his native country, and committed himself to the crude life of new America.

Two years in Pennsylvania and the Carolinas, preaching to congregations as opportunity offered, brought him definitely to the decision to make the frontier village of Pittsburgh his future home. On Dec. 14, 1808 he was ordained and became pastor of the Associate Church in Pittsburgh (and at Peter's Creek also, relinquishing this charge in 1813). For thirty-eight years he was pastor of this church, now the First United Presbyterian, until his death. As early as 1810 he was prominent enough to be moderator of the Synod. He became a strong preacher, an influential presbyter, a leader in his denomination, and one of Pittsburgh's most distinguished citizens. Of gentle voice and gracious manner he was a man of intense convictions and fearless conscience. In 1818 bitter controversy arose in his congregation over giving out two lines instead of one in the service of praise; and in 1822 charges were laid against him of too great liberality in respect to other communions. In 1829 he published a volume of discourses on Christian doctrine and practise (J. B. Scouller, *Manual U. P. Church,* 1887, pp. 249–50; *Glasgow's Manual,* 1903, pp. 60–61). Meanwhile the Pittsburgh Academy, chartered in 1787, was in 1819 rechartered as the Western University of Pennsylvania. A new curriculum and a new faculty were necessary. Bruce was elected principal and his associates in the faculty were John Black of Glasgow University, a Covenanter, Joseph McElroy of Jefferson College, Associate Reformed, Elisha P. Swift of Williams College, Presbyterian, and Charles B. Maguire, educated in Belgium, Roman Catholic, all scholarly men and destined to eminence in years to follow. This faculty was installed with picturesque and brilliant ceremony in the First Presbyterian Church May 10, 1822. Except for one year Bruce held his office of principal until 1843. Under his guidance the Western University took high rank and sent out many graduates later distinguished in church and state. After Bruce resigned as principal of the University in 1843 he was instrumental in establishing Duquesne College which was chartered in February 1844. That year it had seventy-two students, graduating a class of six young men (Isaac Harris, *Business Directory of Pittsburgh,* 1844, p. 71). While the life of this college was brief it did excellent educational service particularly in the vicissitudes of the University after the fire of 1845. Its alumni were later made alumni of the University. The portrait of Bruce in the possession of the University of Pittsburgh reveals a dignified personality, benign, refined, forceful; a fine face, a noble head, crowned with abundant white hair.

His son, David D. Bruce, who died in 1907, became one of the eminent lawyers of Pittsburgh.

[Wm. J. Reid, *Hist. of the First United Presbyt. Ch., Pittsburgh 1801–1901* (n.d.) ; *125th Anniversary Univ. of Pittsburgh* (1912), pp. 112–115; minutes Session First United Presbyt. Ch., Pittsburgh.]   S.B.M.

BRÜHL, GUSTAV (May 31, 1826–Feb. 16, 1903), physician, author, was born in the village of Herdorf, Rhenish Prussia. His father, owner of mines and smelting works, was able to provide for him a classical education at the gymnasia of Siegen, Münster-Eifel, and Trier. Following upon this, Gustav studied medicine, philosophy, and history at the universities of Munich, Halle, and Berlin. The so-called "emigration fever" of the revolutionary period of 1848–49 and the overcrowded condition of the medical profession at home induced the young man to lend a willing ear to the alluring letters of his uncle John Gerlach Brühl, who had settled in Missouri. Gustav came to the United States in 1848, and was on his way to Missouri, when a period of low water on the Ohio compelled him to stop over in Cincinnati. There a relative on the maternal side persuaded him to tarry longer, and a very successful beginning as a medical practitioner soon encouraged him to settle down and cast in his lot with the thriving city of Cincinnati. For several years he was practising physician at St. Mary's Hospital, and also lectured on diseases of the throat and laryngoscopy in Miami Medical College, Cincinnati. He wrote scientific articles for medical journals, and was an active participant in the numerous scientific, educational, historical, and philosophical societies that sprung up about him. He was one of the founders of the Peter Claver Society for the education of negro children, and a member of the board of examiners of the public schools. Subsequently he became a member of the council of the newly organized University of Cincinnati. As a public-spirited citizen of untiring energy he advocated reforms in education and politics. He stood for Tilden in 1876 and was one of the presidential electors in that memorable conflict. He was nominated by the Democratic party for the position of state treasurer, but was not elected, though he won the distinction of running ahead of his ticket.

In spite of his public service and heavy professional duties, Brühl found time for an avocation. This was the study of American archæology. For this he made extensive trips to Mexico, Central and South America, as well as the far western sections of the United States, and embodied the results of his studies in lectures and books. The following publications, written in German, are noteworthy: *Die Culturvölker Alt-Amerikas* (Benziger Brothers, New York, Cincinnati, St. Louis, 1875–87); *Aztlan-Chicomoztoc. Eine ethnologische Studie* (same publishers, 1879); *Zwischen Alaska und Feuerland. Bilder aus der Neuen Welt* (A. Ascher & Company, Berlin, 1896). The last is a popular work descriptive of the natural wonders of the Far West, in Arizona, New Mexico, California, Wyoming, and Alaska, giving special attention to the American Indian in his home, and passing on to a portrayal of the land of the Montezumas and the Incas and of conditions then existing in the South American republics.

Intimately connected with his archæological and ethnographical studies were Brühl's writings in German verse. He was a passionate lover of nature in her grand moods, and these he photographed in such lyrics as: *"Auf dem Corcovado," "Im Thale von Jucay," "Am See von Atitlan," "In den Anden";* or he would embody some Indian legend in heroic or elegiac stanzas, as: *"Die Heldin des Amazon," "Winona (eine Dakota Sage)," "Tupac-Amaru."* Still more numerous were his poetical dedications to the German pioneers in American colonial history, such as: *"Pilgerzug der Mährischen Brüder," "Das Feuerschiff," "Die Frau des Pioniers," "Regina"* (the child kidnapped by Indians identified by her mother's singing a German hymn), *"Vinum, linum textrinum"* (the motto of the Germantown settlers), *"Leisler," "Christian Schell," "Capt. Hiester," "Steuben," "De Kalb," "Herckheimer,"* etc. All of these lyrics and ballads first appeared in the volumes of the Cincinnati monthly *Der Deutsche Pionier*, 1869–87, published to record the history of German pioneers in the United States. Of this journal Brühl was editor during 1869–70, after which he continued to contribute over the signature *Kara Giorg* (a Serbian pen-name, meaning Black George). A collection of his poems was published in Cincinnati under the title *Poesien des Urwalds* in 1871, and a second volume was prepared about 1878. There appeared also: *Charlotte: Eine Episode aus der Colonialgeschichte Louisianas* (Cincinnati, 1883). A photograph of the author reveals a massive frame and large features radiating virility, intelligence, and energy. A long, shaggy beard and the professional man's spectacles cannot altogether conceal gentler aspects of expression. Brühl was married to Margarete Reis, by whom he had two sons and one daughter.

[*Der deutsche Pionier: Erinnerungen aus dem Pionier-Leben der Deutschen in Amerika* (1869–87); *Deutsch-amerikanisches Conversations-Lexicon*, by Prof. Alex. J. Schem (1869–74), vol. II; *Cincinnati, Sonst und Jetzt*, by Armin Tenner (1878); *Deutsch in Amerika*, by Dr. G. A. Zimmermann (1892).]   A. B. F.

BRULÉ, ÉTIENNE (*c.* 1592–1632), French explorer, was born in Champigny and came in 1608, when a mere lad, with Champlain to New France. He took part in the building of the "habitation" at Quebec, escaped the scurvy, which destroyed so many of its colonists, and in 1610 at Champlain's suggestion went to the wilderness with the Algonquin chief Iroquet. The next year he came back, clad like a native, speaking the Indian language, equipped with a superior knowledge of woodcraft. As an interpreter, therefore, he was useful to Champlain and as an explorer he described the hinterland of Canada. In 1612 he went with the Huron tribesmen to their home on Georgian Bay. He would seem thus to have been the first white man to see any of the Great Lakes. He accompanied Champlain in his voyage of 1615 to Huronia and was sent by him on a perilous mission to the Andastes, dwelling on the headwaters of the Susquehanna River. Later in the same year he explored that stream to its outlet, and probably coasted Chesapeake Bay to the ocean. These explorations he related to Champlain in 1618, describing also his capture and torture by the Iroquois, and his rescue by a seemingly miraculous storm.

Champlain sent him back to the Hurons, where he lived thereafter, and where he received a salary of one hundred pistoles per year for his services to the fur trade company. He explored widely, but the extent of his voyages is uncertain. There is evidence to show that he visited Lake Superior in 1622 and saw its copper mines: he was also in the Neutrals country in 1624, and probably saw Lake Erie. In that case, he traversed first of any European four of the five Great Lakes—Huron, Ontario, Superior, and Erie.

Coming with the Indians to Tadoussac in 1629 Brulé sold his services to the English invaders, for which act of treason Champlain bitterly reproached him. During the English occupation (1629–32) he lived among the Hurons, where his life was so dissipated and licentious that the Bear clan of that tribe killed him in a quarrel and ate his remains. Champlain refused, on his return in 1633, to take vengeance for Brulé's murder, declaring that because of his treason he was no longer a Frenchman.

Brulé was one of that class of wanderers who, while brave and adventurous, became among savages more savage than the aborigines. His life was scandalous, and his only title to remembrance rests on his early discoveries in interior North America.

[The sources for Brulé's career are Samuel de Champlain's *Voyages*, of which there are many editions; see W. L. Grant, *Voyages of Samuel de Champlain* (1907). Gabriel Sagard-Theodat, *Le Grand Voyage du Pays des Hurons* (Paris, 1632) and *Histoire du Canada* (Paris,

1636), reprinted in 1865 and 1866, give the reports concerning the exploration of Lake Superior. Brulé's death is noted in *Jesuit Relations* (Thwaites edition, 1896–1902), Index. Modern works are Consul W. Butterfield, *Hist. of Brulé's Discoveries and Explorations, 1610–26* (1898); Benjamin Sulte, "Étienne Brulé," in *Proc. and Trans. of the Canada Royal Soc.*, 1907, sec. I, 97–126; Louise P. Kellogg, *The French Régime in Wisconsin and the Northwest* (1925).]   L.P.K.

BRUMBY, RICHARD TRAPIER (Aug. 4, 1804–Oct. 6, 1875), educator, son of Thomas and Susannah (Greening) Brumby, of English and Swiss ancestry, was born in Sumter District, S. C. When he was six years old his father died, leaving a large family with barely more than a scant livelihood. Young Brumby's education was begun in a small "academy" about four and a half miles from his home, a distance which he walked daily. From there in January 1821 he went to the classical school of the Rev. John Marshall at Statesville, N. C., paying for his passage on this "pedestrian tour of thirteen days" by assisting the wagon driver whom he accompanied. He continued his studies at Statesville and later Lincolnton, N. C., until October 1822, when he entered the junior class of the South Carolina College. By supplementing his slender resources with money earned through teaching school during vacation, he managed to meet the expenses of the course, and was graduated with first honors in the class of 1824. While tutoring in the family of Richard Singleton, he read law under the direction of Stephen D. Miller, later governor of South Carolina, and William C. Preston, from whom he probably derived the ardent state's rights views which he entertained throughout the rest of his life. With Preston he entered into partnership at the time of his admission to the bar (December 1825), but in 1827 he was forced to withdraw from this connection on account of ill health induced by his excessive labors. After a year's sojourn in the western country, with his health temporarily restored, he recommenced the practise of law at Lincolnton, N. C. There he married Mary Isabelle Brevard (Apr. 22, 1828), daughter of Capt. Alexander Brevard, veteran of the Revolutionary War. From Lincolnton Brumby removed in 1831 to Montgomery, Ala., and subsequently to Tuscaloosa where he edited the *Expositor,* a newspaper established to advance the cause of Nullification. On Aug. 12, 1834, though apparently without special qualifications for the position, he was elected to the chair of chemistry, mineralogy, and geology in the University of Alabama; and here he found occupation both agreeable to his tastes and, as it proved, well adapted to his talents. He had soon added physiology, conchology, and agricultural chemistry to the curriculum of his department, and in 1838 he prepared the first sys-

tematic report of the mineral resources of Alabama (published in *Barnard's Almanac,* 1839; an abstract in W. B. Jones, "Index to the Mineral Resources of Alabama," *Geological Survey of Alabama*, Bulletin No. 28, 1926). In January 1849 he resigned in order to accept a professorship in his alma mater, where Preston, his former law partner, had been made president. He filled this position until July 1855, when his health again failed and he took up his residence at Marietta, Ga., the home of his brother Arnoldus. He does not appear to have returned to active life. During the Civil War he converted practically all of his property into Confederate bonds and sent his five sons into the Southern army.

[The best account of Brumby's life up to the time of his retirement from teaching is contained in the *Hist. of the S. C. Coll.* (1859, rev. ed. 1874), by Dr. Maximilian La Borde, one of his colleagues. The sketch of him in the *Hist. of Ala. and Dict. of Ala. Biog.* (1921), vol. III, by Thos. M. Owen, is based upon this but introduces new material.]   J.H.E—y.

BRUMIDI, CONSTANTINO (July 26, 1805–Feb. 19, 1880), painter, was born in Rome, his father a Greek and his mother an Italian. As a young boy, he showed great talent for drawing and became a pupil of the Academy of Fine Arts. When thirteen years old, he was admitted to the Academia di San Lucca, studying painting under Baron Camuccini and modeling under Canova and Thorwaldsen. During the pontificate of Pius IX, he was commissioned with three other Roman artists to restore the Raphael frescoes in the Loggia of the Vatican. He also painted the Pope's portrait for the Vatican Gallery, for which he received a gold medal. He was made a captain of the papal guards, and in 1848 when Rossi was assassinated and the Pope fled to Gaeta, Brumidi was ordered to turn the guns of his command upon the people. This he refused to do, with the result that he was arrested and thrown into prison, where he remained fourteen months. When the Pope was restored to power, he had the artist released and advised him to leave Italy forever. He decided upon America as the haven of his exile and arrived in New York in 1852. He at once received recognition and painted an altar piece, "The Crucifixion," for St. Stephen's Church. Later he went to Mexico where he painted "The Holy Trinity" in the Cathedral at Mexico City. Upon his return, he secured his naturalization papers in Washington, and there became inspired by the possibilities of the Capitol as adapted to fresco. At his first meeting with Capt. Meigs, superintendent of the Capitol, who was apparently interested in examples of Roman grandeur, Brumidi's services were accepted. His first work was the decoration of the Agricultural Committee room, where he selected as his subject "Cincinnatus at the Plough." This was painted in 1855, being the first example of fresco in America. His work in the Capitol, from then on, extended over thirty years. In the corridors, Washington at Valley Forge, the battle of Lexington, the death of Gen. Wooster, the storming of Stony Point, and the Boston Massacre, were all graphically portrayed. In the committee rooms, Brumidi painted symbolic figures, typifying History, Geography, Arts and Sciences, Mechanics, Commerce and War; also portraits of Robert Fulton, Franklin, Morse, and John Fitch. When he began his work he received only $8 a day; later Jefferson Davis had this increased to $10. The decoration of the Rotunda was his great ambition. He knew that the tremendous height and width of the vaulted room would lend themselves to mural decoration, and at every spare moment he worked on the cartoons for the decoration of the canopy and the frieze. The frieze was done in imitation of sculpture, in alto-relievo. The belt upon which the frieze is painted is one hundred feet from the floor. When Brumidi began his work on the frieze he was over seventy years old, but he planned and rigged the scaffolding, a sliding affair, and every day the striking figure of the old man, his hair and beard snow white, might be seen being hoisted by a system of pulleys to what he called his "shop." He worked from ten in the morning until three in the afternoon, and his descent from the lofty height was an event of the day to the visitors, who watched anxiously the slowly moving ropes until his cage was safely landed. He was three years on this work and received $30,000, the only decoration for which he was paid a lump sum. In January 1880 he was taken ill, as the result of a partial fall, and never recovered. The decoration was left unfinished. Brumidi painted many portraits of distinguished men and was painting a portrait of Clay at the time of his death, but he was essentially a decorative artist, knowing well the technical side of his craft: how to draw and paint large figures in distemper on curved plaster surfaces. Many years after his death, original studies of some of his ceiling frescoes were discovered; also paintings which were acquired by distant relatives. Brumidi was twice married before leaving Italy, and late in life he married a Washington woman, said to be a great beauty, Lola V. Germon. He left one son, who also became an artist.

[Chas. E. Fairman, "Art and Artists of the Capitol of the U. S. A.," *Senate Doc., No. 95,* 69 Cong., 1 Sess., and "Works of Art in the U. S. Capitol Bldg.," *Senate Doc., No. 169,* 63 Cong., 1 Sess.; *Fine Arts Jour.,* Aug. 1910; *Jour. Am. Institute of Architects,* Sept. 1914; *Washington Post,* Feb. 20, 1880; Phila. *Evening Telegraph,* Feb. 19, 20, 1880; Washington *Sunday Star,* Apr. 15, 1928.]   H. W.

BRUNNER, ARNOLD WILLIAM (Sept. 25, 1857–Feb. 12, 1925), architect and city planner, son of William Brunner and Isabella Solomon, was born in New York City. He received his education in the New York public schools, in the schools of Manchester, England (where the family was resident for a while in connection with the elder Brunner's business), and then again in the New York City public schools. In 1877 he entered the earliest-developed academic school of architecture in the United States, that of the Massachusetts Institute of Technology, then under the brilliant leadership of William R. Ware [*q.v.*], where he graduated in 1879. He then entered the office of George B. Post in New York City, remaining there for five years; the next three, 1883–85, were spent in extensive travelling in Europe, sketching and studying intensively. Soon after his return to New York, he formed a partnership with Thomas Tryon, under the name of Brunner & Tryon. It was this partnership which, in 1888, designed the studio of Daniel Chester French on Eleventh St., and in 1890, Temple Bethel, at Fifth Ave. and Seventy-sixth St. In 1898, shortly after the partnership of Brunner & Tryon had been dissolved, Brunner won the competition for the Mt. Sinai Hospital; in 1901 the competition for the Federal Building of Cleveland; and in 1910, the competition for a proposed building for the Department of State in Washington, unfortunately never constructed. The winning of these competitions in which the best of the profession participated, gave Brunner a nation-wide fame. Outside of New York the two chief centers of his activity were Harrisburg, Pa., and Cleveland, Ohio. At Harrisburg, in his conduct of the work under his charge, the Capitol Park State Office Buildings, the Plaza between them, and the first design for the Memorial Bridge (not constructed), he set a high standard of honesty and professional idealism, even refusing a salary that would have brought his total receipts up to an amount greater than the usual fee. In recognition of his important work in connection with the Cleveland Civic Centre, he was appointed in 1902 a member of the Board of Supervision of Public Buildings and Grounds, of which he became chairman in 1912. He was also member of the city planning commissions of Baltimore, Denver, and Rochester, and was appointed to the National Council of Fine Arts by President Roosevelt. In 1913 and 1914 he was architect for the improvement of the water front of the City of Albany, creating out of what had been a dreary chaos, a beautiful composition of river walls, piers, and parked open spaces.

In 1923 Mayor John Hylan of New York City,

seeking for someone to put into concrete form his ideas of an art center in Central Park, just north of Fifty-ninth St., appointed Brunner as his architect for this, and a monumental scheme was developed and published. There was an immediate storm of public protest at the proposed use of park land for great buildings, and the scheme was accordingly abandoned. At the time of his death, Brunner was working on another of those great inclusive schemes so dear to him, a layout for Denison University, Granville, Ohio.

Brunner's art was preëminently large in conception, monumental, often severe. His sense of monumental planning was complete; he always attempted to gain an almost rugged simplicity of general idea. In style, his taste was toward an ever-increasing Roman classicism, for he never returned to the brilliant originality of his first great achievement, the square domed Temple Bethel, whose detail is somewhat reminiscent of the modified Romanesque of Richardson. Although the Mt. Sinai and Columbia buildings are somewhat French in their Renaissance feeling, it was in such purely classic work as that at Harrisburg and Cleveland that Brunner's personality found most complete expression; the square masses at Cleveland with their heavy rusticated basements and ranked orders above being peculiarly characteristic in their almost stark strength. In his work for Denison University, however, there is greater lightness and delicacy; Georgian influence is noticeable.

Brunner was the author, in collaboration with Thomas Tryon, of *Interior Decoration* (1887); in collaboration with Charles Downing Lay, landscape architect, of *Studies for Albany* (1914), prepared at the request of the Mayor of Albany; and in collaboration with Frederick Law Olmstead and Bion J. Arnold, of the *City Plan for Rochester* (1911). He was married in 1906, to Emma B. Kaufman of San Francisco. He was for many years a member of the American Institute of Architects, and president of its New York chapter, 1909–10, and of the Architectural League, 1903–04. He was made a member of the National Institute of Arts and Letters in 1913, and was its treasurer, 1914–25. He was also a member of the National Sculpture Society, and of the Fine Arts Federation of New York, vice-president of the American Civic Association; associate of the National Academy of Design, 1910, and member, 1916; member of the New York Board of Education, 1902, and of the New York Fine Arts Commission, 1908–10.

[R. I. Aitken and others, *Arnold W. Brunner and His Work* (1926), with many illustrations of his work, and a reproduction of an excellent portrait by Irving R. Wiles; *Who's Who in America,* 1922–23; *N. Y. Times,*

Feb. 15, 1925; *Arch. Record,* LVII, 461; *Am. Mag. of Art,* XVI, 253; *Am. Architect,* CXXVII, 167; *Architect,* IV, 33; *Arch. Forum,* XLII, 49; *Architecture,* LI, 124.]   T.F.H.

BRUNTON, DAVID WILLIAM (June 11, 1849–Dec. 20, 1927), mining engineer, inventor, was born at Ayr, Ontario, son of James and Agnes (Dickie) Brunton, both of whom had come from Scotland, where the families are historically known along the border. After attending public school, he went to Toronto at the age of twenty-one and worked as an apprentice under J. C. Bailey, a prominent civil engineer. Three years later he came to the United States, and in 1874–75 he took courses in geology and chemistry at the University of Michigan. Going then to Colorado, he held a variety of jobs for different companies and assisted James Douglas, the Guggenheims, and other pioneers to develop mines and treat the complex ores in the new metal-mining districts then being opened. With F. M. Taylor, in 1880, he built the first custom-mill at Leadville, where he also became manager of the largest mine in the district, the Colonel Sellers. In 1888 he was made manager of a group of mines at Aspen, and distinguished himself by driving under Smuggler Mountain the difficult Cowenhoven tunnel, two and one-half miles long, for draining and opening the principal Aspen mines. Brunton's account of this achievement, for the (British) Institution of Civil Engineers, published in their *Proceedings* for 1898, won him the Telford Premium. The Cowenhoven initiated him in what became his greatest specialty, driving long tunnels. At Aspen he also designed an early electric hoist which was for many years the largest in the world. Later he was associated in the driving of the Roosevelt tunnel at Cripple Creek, where the new Leyner water-feed hammer-drill attracted attention. While continuing his Colorado engagements, he was retained through the 1890's by the Anaconda interests of Butte, Mont., as consulting engineer in litigation over mining rights and the geology of the apex law. He made visits to Butte to testify and to organize the technical part of the suits, becoming also technical adviser in general to Marcus Daly and H. H. Rogers. When this work increased, he secured Horace V. Winchell as chief geologist for the Anaconda company, and a staff was developed which greatly influenced American mining by applying geology systematically to mining. This technique is described in the *Transactions of the American Institute of Mining Engineers* for July 1905. Brunton opened an office in Denver with F. M. Taylor, and the firm of Taylor & Brunton became noted for skilful and reliable sampling of ores such as smelters buy and mix;

for this important work, special machinery had to be designed and plants erected at strategic centers, and a reputation for integrity was essential. Brunton had invented a mechanical sampler as early as 1884. These developments in sampling were described by him in the *Transactions of the American Institute of Mining Engineers* for 1896.

The Brunton pocket-transit for engineers, patented in 1904, became popular all over the world because of its simplicity and lightness; during the World War military variations of it were adopted by the United States army and thousands of the instruments were used in France. Brunton was chairman of the War Committee of Technical Societies and an active member of other governmental boards to develop inventions to be used in the war. Other inventions of his own include a mine pump, a velocipede tunnel-car, a car coupling, improvements in revolving ore-roasters and in leaching ores, and a system of round-timber framing for mines. In 1922 he was made chairman of the board of consulting engineers for the Moffat railroad tunnel in the Rockies. In 1909–10 he was president of the American Institute of Mining Engineers and in 1927 he received the first Saunders gold medal, given by the Institute for "achievement in mining." Besides many technical papers, he was author of *Safety and Efficiency in Mine Tunneling* and *Modern Tunneling*, both published in 1914. Though he lived in Denver, he traveled extensively and made examinations of mines in all parts of the world for the Exploration Syndicate of London. He was later called upon to advise on mining methods by many companies, including the Rio Tinto in Spain. He was married on Feb. 11, 1885, to Katherine, daughter of John C. Kemble, a merchant of Stone Ridge, Ulster County, N. Y., and they had four children.

[*Mining and Scientific Press*, May 28, 1921; *Engineering and Mining Jour.*, Feb. 18, 1928; *Rocky Mt. News*, Dec. 21, 1927; *Who's Who in America*, 1926–27; *Who's Who in Engineering*, 1922–23; *Who's Who in Science*, 1912–14; *Am. Men of Science* (1927).]

P. B. M.

BRUSH, GEORGE JARVIS (Dec. 15, 1831–Feb. 6, 1912), mineralogist and executive, son of Jarvis Brush and his wife, Sarah (Keeler) Brush, was born in Brooklyn, N. Y., being the seventh in line of descent from Thomas Brush who settled in Southold, Long Island, in 1653, and who is believed to have been the first of the family in America. At the time of his son's birth, Jarvis Brush was in business as a commission and importing merchant, but in 1835 he retired and moved to Danbury, Conn., where the boy George began his education in private schools. In 1841

the family returned to Brooklyn, but five years later, when he was fifteen years of age, the boy was sent to the private school of Theodore S. Gold at West Cornwall, Conn. Aside from being an admirable teacher, Gold was an enthusiast in mineralogy and other of the natural sciences. It was undoubtedly while here that the boy got his first insight into the studies that were to occupy his future life. Not long after his return from school, however, he took a position with a mercantile house where he remained some two years, only occasionally indulging in mineralogical excursions. Ill health forced him to give up this position, and he decided to try farming. With this in view, he went to New Haven in 1848 to attend lectures in practical chemistry and agriculture under J. P. Norton and Benjamin Silliman. In October 1850 he left New Haven for Louisville, Ky., to become an assistant to Benjamin Silliman, Jr., who was instructor in chemistry and toxicology in the medical department of the University of Louisville. This position he held until the spring of 1852, though in the meantime making a trip to Europe in company with the elder Silliman. Notwithstanding these absences from New Haven he was able to pass the necessary examinations and graduate, as a member of the first class, from what was later to become the strong and flourishing Sheffield Scientific School.

The college year of 1852–53 was passed as an assistant in chemistry in the University of Virginia where he was associated with the well-known mineral chemist, J. Lawrence Smith, and with him made a series of mineralogical studies, the results of which were published in 1853–55, under the caption of "A Reëxamination of American Minerals," in the *American Journal of Science*. Becoming convinced of the need of further studies, after spending the summer of 1853 as an assistant in the department of mineralogy in the Crystal Palace at the International Exposition in New York, he went to Germany, passing the years 1853–55 with Liebig, von Kobell and Pettenkofer, and going later to the celebrated mining school at Freiberg, Saxony. On his return to America in 1855, he was elected professor of metallurgy in the Sheffield Scientific School. To fit himself for his new duties he went once more abroad, studied at the Royal School of Mines in London, and visited the principal mines and smelting works of both Great Britain and the Continent, finally entering upon his duties in New Haven, in January 1857. In 1864 he was married to Harriet Silliman Trumbull. In the same year his professorial position was broadened to include mineralogy. Later it was limited to mineralogy only. In 1872 he was made director of the Sheffield Scientific School, holding that position until 1898, when he resigned, though continuing to act as secretary and treasurer of the Sheffield Trustees until 1900, when he was elected president of the board. It is stated by his biographer and collaborator, Prof. E. S. Dana, that Brush's labors in connection with the development of the Sheffield Scientific School showed him to possess the faculty of "quick, sure judgement, firmness of resolution and great energy." In all of his work there he was remarkably successful, as he was also in the management of the affairs of the Peabody Museum of which he was a trustee. For many years he was a director in the Jackson Iron Company of the Lake Superior district and in the New York, New Haven & Hartford Railroad Company. He was elected a member of the National Academy of Sciences in 1868; an honorary member of the Mineralogical Society of England, a foreign member of the Geological Societies of London and Edinburgh, and of the Royal Bavarian Academy of Sciences of Munich.

Brush was an associate editor of the *American Journal of Science* and also an important contributor to J. D. Dana's *System of Mineralogy.* His *Manual of Determinative Mineralogy* (1874) was for many years (and its revised edition still is) the standard work on the subject. He developed a wonderfully keen eye for recognition of the essential features of mineral species and in the course of his career built up a collection, numbering some 15,000 specimens, unexcelled at that time in the number of type specimens and in value for scientific study. This collection, since widely known as the Brush Collection, he, in 1904, presented to the Sheffield Scientific School together with an endowment of $10,000, the income of which was to be utilized in its increase and maintenance.

He was of medium height, stocky build, and ruddy complexion, with long mustache, according to the fashion of those days. He is stated to have been of a very kindly disposition, although in his earlier days he could occasionally show a sharp temper. It is told of him that when matters were unusually irritating he would go into the room behind his office in the old Scientific School building, and, pulling out a drawer in which he kept his collection, spend some time looking over his specimens. This would serve to comfort and quiet him: the "minerals would not talk back," and he would shortly recover his normal temper. He was an entertaining talker, with a good sense of humor.

[Sketch by E. S. Dana, in *Memoirs of the Nat. Acad. of Sci.,* XVII, 105–12, containing full bibliography of Brush's publications.]   G. P. M.

BRUTÉ DE RÉMUR, SIMON WILLIAM GABRIEL (Mar. 20, 1779–June 26, 1839), theologian and first Catholic bishop of Vincennes, was born in Rennes, France, where his father, Simon Gabriel Bruté, was superintendent of the royal domains in Brittany and his mother, Jeanne Renée le Saulnier, managed a former husband's printing establishment. The elder Bruté died in 1787 leaving an entangled estate, due to loans and back rentals, which the mother straightened out with business skill, paying off all debts and caring for her family. Simon attended the local school until the Revolution closed its doors. Then he was taught by private tutors, stressing the classics, literature, and mathematics in preparation for the Polytechnical School. During the Terror, the boy worked for two years as a typesetter in his mother's shop. In his home there was dread but a high degree of courage. A private chapel was maintained; hunted priests were given an asylum; Simon disguised as baker's boy attended trials and visited prisons carrying the host to the dying and running messages for condemned priests and royalists. Mere suspicion of these activities would have meant the death penalty. When the red danger passed, he commenced the study of medicine in Rennes and later went to Paris where he was graduated (1803) from the Medical School with the highest prize in a contending class of 1,100. Bruté's reaction from the radicalism and materialism of faculty and fellow students was so sharp that he turned from a promising medical career to enter the Seminary of St. Sulpice.

In the seminary, Bruté became as profound a student of theology and scripture as he had been of science. On ordination (1808), he declined an assistant chaplaincy to Napoleon and joined the Sulpicians. It was as a professor in their College of Rennes, that he met Bishop Flaget of Bardstown, Ky., in search of missionary priests for America. Bruté listened to the appeal and on approval of his superior sailed for the States with Flaget. For two years he taught in St. Mary's Seminary, Baltimore, when he was called by President Dubois to St. Mary's College, Emittsburg, as a teacher of moral philosophy, science, and Scripture. He soon won renown for scholarship and self-sacrificing goodness. Despite his humility, he was soon regarded as an oracle by the American hierarchy. In 1815, he returned to France but friends in high places could not induce him to remain. He brought back several priests and seminarians and his library of 5,000 volumes which was unusually rich in medical, philosophical, and scientific books. He was now appointed rector of the Baltimore seminary where he also bore his burden of teaching. His health failing, he was transferred to Emittsburg (1818) where he taught for sixteen years, improving the school and serving as spiritual director of the neighboring Sisters of Charity. When St. Mary's became a secular institution (1826), he still continued on its faculty until he was named first bishop of Vincennes at the suggestion of Bishops Flaget and Chabrat.

Bruté was alarmed at the appointment, for he had the Sulpician aversion to a mitre and no money for the westward trip. His friends collected a purse of $200, and he journeyed to St. Louis where he was consecrated by Bishop Flaget in the new cathedral. Vincennes was an outpost with 25,000 Catholics, largely illiterate French and half-breeds, scattered over an area of 6,000 square miles. There were only three priests and a few small log chapels. Bruté was an organizer and a business man. A physician in a land of "doubtful doctors," he could cure physical as well as spiritual ills. Soon Vincennes became the site of the bare brick Cathedral of St. Francis Xavier, a seminary, a college, a convent, an orphan asylum, and a Catholic cemetery, though the last institution met local opposition. On his visits to Rome and France, Bruté enlisted a number of priests for his diocese and obtained financial aid from the Leopoldine Association and the Society for the Propagation of the Faith. With the coming of Irish and Bavarian immigrants, the diocese grew in population, and the bishop and his score of priests saw no idleness as mission chapels were widely separated and travel was arduous. Bruté succumbed to consumption brought on by exposure on long stage-coach journeys (1837).

[J. R. Bayley, *Memoirs of the Rt. Rev. Simon Wm. Gabriel Bruté* (1876); *Vie de Mgr. Bruté de Rémur* (Rennes, 1887); Rev. John McCaffrey, *Funeral Discourse* (1839); H. J. Alerding, *Hist. of the Cath. Ch. in the Diocese of Vincennes* (1883); R. H. Clarke, *Lives of the Deceased Bishops of the Cath. Ch. in the U.S.* (1872), II, 1-43; C. G. Herberman, *The Sulpicians in the U.S.* (1916); J. G. Shea, *Hist. of the Cath. Ch. in the U.S.* (1886-90); T. O'Gorman, *Hist. of the Roman Cath. Ch. in the U.S.* (1895); C. I. White, *Life of Mrs. Eliza A. Seton* (1853); P. Guilday, *Life and Times of John England* (1927); J. R. G. Hassard, *Life of the Most Rev. John Hughes* (1866); *Cath. Encyc.*; J. O'K. Murray, *Lives of Catholic Heroes and Heroines of America* (1880).]   R.J.P.

BRYAN, GEORGE (Aug. 11, 1731–Jan. 27, 1791), jurist, politician, was born in Dublin, Ireland, the son of Samuel Bryan, a merchant, and his wife, Sarah Dennis. He came to America in 1752, settling in Philadelphia and entering a partnership with one James Wallace in the importing business. In 1755 the partnership was dissolved and Bryan continued in business alone; two years later, on Apr. 21, 1757, he married Elizabeth, daughter of Samuel Smith. As a Pres-

byterian he early became associated with the Scotch-Irish Presbyterians of Philadelphia, who were a distinct political faction, and gradually rose to prominence in their ranks. He was fined five pounds, in 1758, for refusing to serve as constable (*Passages from the Remembrancer of Christopher Marshall*, 1839, App., p. v) but in 1762 he accepted office as member of a commission to apply receipts from tonnage dues to the improvement of Philadelphia harbor. In 1764, Bryan and Thomas Willing were elected by the conservative party to represent Philadelphia in the Assembly. They defeated Benjamin Franklin and Joseph Galloway, the leaders of the party desirous of substituting Royal for Proprietary government, although the Anti-Proprietary forces carried the rest of the provinces. In the same year Gov. John Penn reorganized the judiciary, appointing new judges from among the conservatives, and Bryan was made judge of the orphans' court and the court of common pleas. He continued at the same time to serve in the Assembly, and in 1765 was a member of the committee which drafted instructions for Pennsylvania's delegates to the Stamp Act Congress to meet in New York on Oct. 1 of that year. On Sept. 11, Bryan, Dickinson, and John Morton were chosen as delegates to the congress. During their absence in New York the Philadelphia elections took place, Franklin's party won, and Bryan was defeated. He returned from the congress, signed the non-importation agreements, and resumed his judicial service. He was recommissioned judge in 1770 and again in 1772, by which time he had retired from a failing business. He was appointed naval officer of the port of Philadelphia in 1776. After the adoption in that year of the new Pennsylvania constitution, with a share in the framing of which—though not a member of the convention—he had been credited (Alexander Graydon, *Memoirs of a Life, etc.*, 1811, p. 266), he was elected to the Supreme Executive Council and by it chosen vice-president. In this capacity he served from Mar. 5, 1777 until Oct. 11, 1779, acting as president between the death of Wharton and the election of Joseph Reed (May 23–Dec. 1, 1778). In 1779 he was a member of a commission to settle the boundary dispute with Virginia.

Elected to the Assembly on Oct. 12, 1779, he was given the chairmanship of several committees on special bills, notably those which framed the "Divesting Act," transferring title in the proprietary estates to the Commonwealth of Pennsylvania, the act revoking the charter of the College of Philadelphia and vesting its property in a new institution, the University of the State of

Pennsylvania, and the act for the gradual abolition of slavery. The authorship of the last-named law is usually attributed to Bryan as his major claim to remembrance. He was commissioned a judge of the supreme court of Pennsylvania on Apr. 3, 1780, and held the office until his death. For some years he acted as trustee of the University of the State of Pennsylvania. In 1784 he was elected to the septennial Council of Censors. A stout (state) constitutionalist, he opposed every tendency toward nationalism, even attacking the Bank of North America. When the Federal Constitution was submitted to the states in 1787 he fought it earnestly, and after its ratification by Pennsylvania was a member of the Harrisburg convention of irreconcilables which met Sept. 3, 1788 to urge a revision of the Constitution by a new federal convention. But resistance, however stubborn, was of no avail against the inevitable; the old order passed, and Bryan outlived it only a little time, dying in 1791, two years after the inauguration of the federal government and five months after the adoption of a new state constitution by Pennsylvania.

[The Hist. Soc. of Pa. has five boxes of Bryan MSS., and the Lib. of Cong. has several of his letters to Justice Atlee and a "memorandum of events" of the years 1758–64 entered in the back of an almanac. There are letters to and from Bryan in Wm. B. Reed, *Life and Correspondence of Joseph Reed* (1847), and official communications in the *Pa. Archives.* Burton Alva Konkle, *Geo. Bryan and the Constitution of Pa.* (1922) contains previously unpublished biographical material but overestimates Bryan's importance. An obituary in *Dunlap's Am. Daily Advertiser,* Jan. 31, 1791, was copied by other Phila. papers.]   E. R. D.

BRYAN, MARY EDWARDS (May 17, 1842– June 15, 1913), journalist, author, the daughter of Maj. John D. and Louisa Critchfield (Houghton) Edwards, was born near Tallahassee, Fla. The family later moved to Thomasville, Ga., and Mary received her education at the Fletcher Institute at Thomasville. While yet in school, at the age of fifteen she married I. E. Bryan, a wealthy Louisianian. Her first experience in the literary field was as literary editor of the *Literary Crusader* at Atlanta, Ga., in 1862. For a time she was a regular correspondent of *Southern Field and Fireside.* In 1866 she became editor of the *Natchitoches* (La.), *Tri-Weekly.* She was associate editor of the *Sunny South* from 1874 to 1884. To these papers she contributed sketches, poems, stories, and, not infrequently, political articles. In 1880 she published her novel called *Manch,* which is a shortening of the Indian proper name "Comanche." The next year she published *Wild Work,* a novel dealing with the reign of the carpet-baggers and the Ku Klux Klan in the South. Eight other novels and three volumes of verse followed in due time. She wrote all her books at night. *His Legal Wife,* her favorite novel, is said to have been written in a week and a half (*Atlanta Constitution,* June 17, 1913). Her stories were very sensational, invariably reaching many dramatic climaxes. In spite of being produced according to a general formula, they covered a wide variety of settings, including the Western frontier, the South, and New York City. Invariably they brought out the moral lessons which would appeal to the undiscriminating readers of popular novels. Several of her books ran through a number of editions. She went to New York in 1885 to superintend the publication of her novels and was engaged as assistant editor of the *New York Fashion Bazaar* and the *Fireside Companion.* In 1887 she edited *Munroe's Star Recitations for Parlor, School, and Exhibition.* G. Munroe was for some time her principal publisher. She was also one of the early writers for Street & Smith. In 1895 she returned to Georgia to work on the *Sunny South* which subsequently merged into *Uncle Remus' Magazine.* In the latter she conducted a popular page entitled "Open House" in which she made editorial comments on current issues and in turn published individual letters sent to the paper. She was also an editor of the *Half Hour Magazine.* At the time of her death she was writing for the *Golden Age,* a magazine published in Atlanta.

[*Who's Who in America,* 1912–13; *Atlanta Constitution,* June 15, 17, 1913; Mary T. Tardy, *The Living Female Writers of the South* (1872); *Men and Women of America* (1910).]   M. S.

BRYAN, THOMAS BARBOUR (Dec. 22, 1828–Jan. 25, 1906), lawyer, was born in Alexandria, Va., and died in Washington, D. C. His parents, Daniel and Mary Barbour Bryan were both representatives of Virginia families accustomed to public leadership. At the age of twelve he delivered a sermon before a large congregation; at seventeen he did his part toward the war in Mexico by giving of his oratory as an aid to recruiting; at twenty-one he published a grammar for the use of Germans desiring to learn English; at twenty-two, he married Jane Byrd Page, the daughter of an army chaplain. He attended a Southern school, and in 1849 was graduated in law at Harvard. He practised law in Cincinnati from 1849 till 1853, when he removed to Chicago, partly to find a more lucrative practise and partly to avail himself of financial opportunities in real estate. Both of these objectives were realized. He became a leading "office-counsellor," and in business his enterprises ranged from the promotion of auditoriums to cemeteries. A brisk, energetic little man, capable in affairs, he had the reputation of being widely erudite in languages and literature. He wrote poems and epigrams, adapted fables, translated sermons to read aloud in his private chapel, entertained sumptuously, and spoke brightly at many banquets. Chicago twice refused to elect him mayor, but otherwise accepted him without reservation, overlooking the "old-Virginian haughtiness" which, cropping out at times, it was complained, made him not altogether agreeable. During the 1860's he was ardently pro-Union. He devoted his resources liberally to the Northern cause, and, indorsing the view that the Southern leaders were "arch traitors, alone responsible for the war" (Bryan, *Stephen A. Douglas*, p. 1), made frequent speeches to enhearten troops. At the conclusion of hostilities he went with his family for an extended residence in Europe, in order to rest himself, but before leaving, as newly elected president of the Old Soldiers' Home, he purchased and gave to his wounded veterans the original copy of the Emancipation Proclamation. In 1875–78 he was a commissioner of the District of Columbia, but it was in the years 1889–93 that he was most generally known. He was among the first to suggest bringing the World's Fair to Chicago, and in January 1890, he presented before a committee of the Senate in Washington the claims of his city as the fittest place for the projected celebration. His speech is generally regarded as having governed the committee in its decision. As vice-president of the great Fair, he was tireless and effective, going twice to Europe as its advocate and interpreter. He had two children, several palatial residences, and countless close friends.

[T. B. Bryan, *Englische Sprachlehre* (1849); *Stephen A. Douglas on the Cause and Effect of the Rebellion* (1863); *Arguments in support of the Application of Chicago for the Location of the World's Exposition* (1890); anonymous, *Biog. Sketches of the Leading Men of Chicago* (1868); *Biog. Dict. of Chicago* (1892); C. Dean, *World's Fair City* (1892); *Who's Who in America*, 1906–07; *Harvard Univ. Quinquennial Cat. 1636–1915* (1915); Washington *Evening Star*, Jan. 26, 1906.]   J. D. W.

BRYAN, WILLIAM JENNINGS (Mar. 19, 1860–July 26, 1925), political leader, was born in Salem, Ill., the son of Silas Lilliard and Mariah Elizabeth (Jennings) Bryan. The elder Bryan was of Virginia farmer stock, a Democrat, and in 1872 an unsuccessful candidate for Congress. He was an ardent believer in education, and sent William Jennings to Jacksonville to stay at the Academy and College for six years. Bryan graduated from Illinois College in 1881, and for the next two years read law at the Union College of Law in Chicago. Here he came to know Lyman Trumbull, a political friend of his father, and spent much of his time reading law

in Trumbull's office. In college and law school he took a prominent part in school debates but little part in athletics, though he excelled in broad jumping. He was industrious and obedient to discipline, but he was not noted for originality of thought. His college orations have an easy direct manner of statement, though the thought in them is commonplace.

From 1883 to 1887 he practised law in Jacksonville, Ill. He opened his office on July 4, influenced, as he says, by a certain hankering for important dates (*Memoirs*, 62). In the beginning he saw very severe days, but by virtue of his economy he ended the year with as much success as a young lawyer without influential friends had a right to expect. In 1884 he was doing well enough to venture on matrimony. The bride was Mary Baird, daughter of a merchant in a near-by town. She was a woman of unusual mind. After her marriage she read law under her husband's instruction, and in 1888 was admitted to the bar in Nebraska. In the autumn of 1887 Bryan moved to Lincoln, Nebr., where he had to begin again at the bottom. He understood the law of small-town courts; he had much of that resourcefulness which enables a lawyer to win such cases; he had a ready and convincing manner with a jury; and he had much of that fair and generous conduct that brings to a young lawyer the good will and assistance of the older lawyers. Yet he had not attained a position at the bar which pointed to a great career when he was drawn into politics and gave up his practise. The ease with which he threw over the law indicates that he was not deeply interested in it, and, if not interested, he could hardly have been deeply versed in its principles.

In 1890 he became a Democratic candidate for Congress. The district was normally Republican, but he carried it by 6,713 majority. In 1892 he was reëlected but the state had been redistricted and his majority was only 140. In 1894 he announced his candidacy for the United States Senate, and made speeches with the hope that his friends would carry the legislature. The effort was unsuccessful; and so, without office, he had to find a way of making a living. He turned to journalism and became editor-in-chief of the *Omaha World-Herald* at a fair salary. By this time he had developed a vogue as a lecturer and was employed in that capacity by the Chautauquas. He kept in close touch with public questions, and when the monetary problem came to the fore he was in much demand as an advocate of the free coinage of silver. During his four years in Congress Bryan had lived simply and quietly at 131 B St., S. E. He did not try to go into society and there is not much reason to think that he came into close contact with the leaders of his party. His father had been a friend of William M. Springer of Illinois, however, and by that means he got a position on the Ways and Means Committee, of which Springer was chairman. It was an unusual beginning for a new member. The Ways and Means Committee was at that time a committee of special importance, for the tariff was the livest political question before the country. But there is nothing to show that Bryan took special interest in the tariff. He made some effective speeches on the floor, but they were more notable for fluency of expression than for grasp of the subject. He identified himself with the silver men in Congress; voted against the repeal of the silver-purchase law of 1890; and made a brilliant speech in which he used violent language against President Cleveland for demanding its unconditional repeal. The silver men now set out to control the next Democratic national convention in 1896, and conducted in 1894 and 1895 a vigorous campaign with that end in view. They sent speakers into all parts of the country in which there was a considerable amount of silver sentiment, winning the support of the voters and laying plans for electing silver men to the next national convention. Into this movement Bryan threw himself with enthusiasm. He was the most popular of the speakers and probably the most energetic. When the convention met in Chicago in 1896 the free-silver men were in control. They used their power without sympathy for their opponents. The New York leaders, who for many years had controlled the party, were brusquely thrown aside and a new alignment, composed of Western and Southern men was set up. In discussing the platform, Bryan made his notable "Cross of Gold" speech, in which he narrated the history of the silver movement, declaring that silver Democrats had gone from victory to victory and were now assembled "not to discuss, not to debate, but to enter upon the judgment already rendered by the plain people." "Having behind us the producing masses of this nation and the world, supported by the commercial interests, the laboring interests, and the toilers everywhere, we will answer their demand for a gold standard by saying to them: You shall not press down upon the brow of labor this crown of thorns, you shall not crucify mankind upon a cross of gold" (Bryan, *First Battle*, 199). This speech swept the silver ranks like fire and won him the presidential nomination on the fifth ballot, despite the fact that he was only thirty-six years of age (*Chicago Daily Tribune*, July 10, 1896).

Bryan was honestly in favor of the free coinage of silver. His speech of acceptance, delivered in Madison Square Garden, read to the large audience, and perhaps well revised under the inspection of other Democrats, has the ring of sincerity. His enemies called him a demagogue and a deceiver. They made fun of his youth, of his oratory, and of his slips of speech. Dignified Eastern newspapers abused him in terms falling little short of Billingsgate. In all this torrent of abuse, Bryan, two years earlier only an inconspicuous newspaper editor in a rural state, carried himself with composure. His speeches, though based on an economic fallacy, were clear and easily understood by his auditors. His magnificent voice was a perfect medium of expression. He went everywhere, spoke to hundreds of audiences, and carried home his ideas to the country as no other candidate had done since the days of Henry Clay. While his opponent remained snugly at his home and uttered truthful platitudes to trainloads of excursionists which an over-rich campaign committee sent to his front door, Bryan, fighting brilliantly in behalf of error, traveled 18,000 miles, kept his poise, always was on the aggressive, and never broke down physically or mentally. It was a remarkable achievement. The campaign was also a social and sectional struggle. Bryan told his hearers that it was a conflict between Wall Street and the great "toiling masses," between the rich men and the poor men. His defeat in this campaign, however, was on the silver issue, not on the class issue. At the time little attention was paid to the two-fold nature of Bryan's position. Probably he himself was not greatly conscious of it. He looked on himself as a crusader for silver.

The outcome of this extraordinary campaign was a popular majority for McKinley over Bryan of about 600,000 in a total vote of 13,600,000. The electoral vote stood 271 to 176. Bryan's defeat was hailed by his enemies as the end of his public career. Had he stood solely on the money question, the prediction would probably have been realized. But the basis of his fight, the people vs. the power of wealth, was more permanent. To all who wished to free the party from the domination of the New York group, itself in close association with the so-called money power, Bryan was still the leader. The alliance between the South and West was a salient fact in his career. Then the Spanish-American War intervened. In 1898 he was made a colonel by the governor of Nebraska and raised a regiment for service in the war with Spain, but did not serve outside the United States. He resigned the day the treaty with Spain was signed, after serving five months. The only military glory that he won was the title of colonel.

As the year 1900 approached he was seen to be as strongly entrenched in party affection as in 1896. The organization of 1896 was now in control and it was thoroughly committed to Bryan. A move started by his Eastern opponents to drop the silver plank from the platform failed because he refused to be the candidate on that basis. At the same time he was willing to consider "expansion" and not silver the "paramount issue," and on that basis made the campaign against McKinley. He had used his influence with Democratic senators to get the treaty with Spain ratified, and defended that action on the ground that the people wanted the war ended, that other nations would oppose a Philippine Republic and that it would be easier to accept the Philippines and then urge the United States to make them independent. It was not a convincing argument. Bryan's opponents charged that he got the treaty accepted in 1899 so that he could make a campaign in 1900 out of anti-expansion. He miscalculated the feeling of the country. Flushed with victory, the voters looked on the Philippines as its fruits and felt no hesitation in taking them for national dependencies. The election showed that Bryan was less popular in 1900 than in 1896, and he received only 155 of the 447 electoral votes, whereas he had had 176 four years before. His strength was confined to the South and the states of Idaho, Colorado, Montana, Nevada.

In 1903 Bryan became involved in a lawsuit known as the Bennett Will Case. In that year Mr. Philo S. Bennett, of New Haven, died, leaving $80,000 at Bryan's disposal: $30,000 for charity and $50,000 for himself if he wanted it—otherwise he was to give it also to charity. This will had been written at Lincoln, Nebr., by Bryan, on a visit of the testator to his home. It was contested on the ground of being imperfectly drawn. Bryan then decided not to accept the $50,000 for himself but insisted on his right to administer the fund. The decision was entirely in his favor, and the money was distributed for charitable purposes. This incident caused much comment at the time, although there were few who believed that Bryan had acted dishonestly. He was a man of personal integrity and by this time he had materially improved his financial position by lecturing. Moreover, he frequently lectured for nothing. On Jan. 23, 1901, appeared the first issue of the *Commoner*, a weekly newspaper in which Bryan sought to carry on his fight against the influence of wealth in politics. It started with 17,000 advance subscribers, and was suc-

cessful from the first. It was widely quoted by the local Bryan papers, thus keeping the ideas of the editor before the country. It was also bitterly denounced by his opponents, who continued to consider him a demagogue who set the poor against the rich. Bryan wrote its leading articles until he entered Wilson's cabinet in 1913. The paper was thereafter conducted merely as a monthly.

As the election of 1904 approached the anti-Bryan Democrats began to take courage. Roosevelt was unpopular with the "business men" of the East, and it was hoped that they would aid the election of a conservative Democrat if Roosevelt, as was expected, got the Republican nomination. The Eastern Democrats believed, therefore, that they had a chance of success, provided they had a "safe and sane" candidate. After much consideration they united on Judge Alton B. Parker of New York, who was conservative enough for the business men of the East and whose character and legal ability were of the highest order. The party was to be rescued from the wild leaders of the past eight years, Bryan was to be thrown over, and the ship *Democracy* was to return to her old tack. To the Bryan men it soon became evident that their position in the party was at stake, and they decided to fight to retain it. They could not present a Bryan man who would make a better candidate than Bryan himself, but they could exert themselves to control the nominating convention and keep it out of the hands of their enemies. In this spirit they chose delegates to the convention of 1904. At that convention the extreme Bryan men were in the minority, and Parker was nominated as a "compromise candidate." Senator David B. Hill of New York directed the convention, and Bryan found the platform already made when he arrived in St. Louis, and the candidate picked out. He fought until the platform was changed. William Randolph Hearst had the support of the extreme radicals, but Bryan, in one of his best speeches, seconded the nomination of Senator Cockrell of Missouri, although he says in his *Memoirs* (1925) that ex-Governor Pattison of Pennsylvania would have been a more acceptable candidate. The Parker men offered a platform in which were expressions that the Bryan men thought offensive, among them a gold plank. Through a long night session of the platform committee Bryan got one plank after another modified, until he could say at last, "I kept out of the platform everything to which I objected." When it was known that a platform was adopted which the Bryan men no longer opposed, there was a feeling of relief and the convention proceeded to nominate Parker on the first ballot. The sense of security was suddenly disrupted by the receipt of Parker's famous telegram, announcing himself in favor of a gold standard.

The prolonged contest had left Bryan ill and he was sent to bed by an attending physician who warned him of pneumonia. On hearing of Parker's telegram he rose instantly and a few minutes later stalked down the aisle of the convention hall, to assume the leadership of the fight. His face was pale, his brow was wet with perspiration, but his mouth was clinched and his eye gleamed. Gasping for breath, he climbed to the platform and took part in the discussion. He made motion after motion trying to get an expression of free-silver opinion into the records. They were voted down, his friends standing by him bravely, but the men of expediency voting for the indorsement of Parker and the action that had been taken. Bryan left the convention with the full conviction that he had been beaten but with his friends in the party more strongly bound to him than ever before. A month's rest restored his health, and he took active part in the campaign, though he could not put much heart into his advocacy of the man whom he had denounced as a man of "the money power." The election showed the effects. Parker received only 140 electoral votes while Roosevelt had 336. Parker lost every Northern and Western and one Southern state, and it was a more overwhelming defeat than Bryan ever sustained. The defeat of Parker, "safe and sane" candidate, proved that the Democratic party could not win with a conservative at its head. Bryan quickly regained control of the party organization and in the nominating convention of 1908 he was named presidential candidate on the first ballot. If Bryan's policies were to be followed Bryan was undoubtedly the strongest candidate. But the country was under the Roosevelt spell, and Taft, Roosevelt's selection to carry out the Roosevelt policies, was elected. Bryan did better than Parker in 1904, but he received only 162 of the 483 electoral votes. "Three times and out," exclaimed the country in baseball language. Bryan knew it. In his home in Nebraska he continued to appeal to the country in the *Commoner* and through his lectures, and he did not give up his grasp on the Democratic organization; but he realized that he would never be president.

When the next presidential election came around the Republicans were hopelessly split. The party found that it could no longer exist with the most conservative and the most radical of the large political groups within its fold. The

two wings were divided, and there was good opportunity for the Democrats to win, for they were ordinarily less radical than the Roosevelt wing and less conservative than the Taft wing. In the party, however, the old division reappeared. The New York conservatives, directed by Charles F. Murphy, Tammany leader, supported Gov. Judson Harmon of Ohio, who had been a conservative Democrat in 1896. There were several other candidates who had been recommended in the primaries as progressives, among whom were Gov. Woodrow Wilson of New Jersey, and Champ Clark of Missouri, speaker of the House of Representatives. The New York group was in a strong position in the convention. The national committee put forward Judge Alton B. Parker for temporary chairman. Bryan took this step as a challenge, and endeavored to unite the progressive delegates on John W. Kern of Indiana, but Kern insisted upon nominating Bryan himself as chairman. Thus the convention had to choose between Parker and Bryan, and it named Parker. In this contest many of the Clark men voted for Parker, while most of the Wilson men supported Bryan. Bryan's defeat was heralded by the Eastern papers as conclusive. Yet Bryan was offered the chairmanship of the platform committee and also the permanent chairmanship; but he refused both posts, declaring that he would not be responsible for what the convention did until it took some step to show that it was not controlled by the reactionaries (*Baltimore American,* June 26, 1910). He served as a member of the committee on resolutions, however, and was not seriously opposed. The platform reported was a series of planks chiefly taken from the three preceding Democratic platforms.

In order to draw the attention of the country to the situation in the convention, Bryan opened an attack on August Belmont of New York and Thomas F. Ryan of Virginia. He offered two resolutions, one regretting their appearance in the convention, and the other demanding their withdrawal (*Memoirs,* p. 174). This action was truly described as "a bombshell." The air was full of protests; Bryan was denounced as a marplot. Yet the first resolution passed by a vote of 899 to 196. As the vote was about to be taken on the second resolution Bryan withdrew it. In defending his belligerent course Bryan told the delegates that there was not one of them who did not know that "an effort was being made to sell the Democratic party to the predatory interests of the country." He received showers of approving telegrams, and he succeeded in calling the attention of the country to the fight going on in the convention between the conservative and progressive forces. When the balloting began, New York led the Harmon forces, which amounted to 148 votes on the first trial. Clark had 440½ and Wilson had 324, while other candidates had 173½. Altogether 1,085 votes were cast, and 725 were necessary for the nomination. On the tenth ballot New York did what had been expected, transferred her 90 votes from Harmon to Clark. The uproar that followed brought Bryan into the convention hall. He had been using his personal influence for Wilson, although his delegation had been instructed for Clark as long as there was hope of a nomination. On the fourteenth ballot Bryan announced that he no longer felt himself bound by his instructions. Clark, he said, was supported by Nebraska with the understanding that he was a progressive, but his support by New York showed that he did not deserve that designation. He said that he, Bryan, would not vote for any man whose selection depended on the vote of New York. The result was to check any further defection to Clark, and for many ballots the situation remained the same, Clark having about 550 votes, and Wilson about 400. Clark issued a statement repudiating the charge that he was or would be under the control of Wall St., and pronouncing Bryan's accusations "false and infamous." To this Bryan replied in a circular letter disclaiming personal feelings against Clark, but asserting that the same forces that had ruled at the Republican convention were seeking to control at Baltimore. On the twenty-fifth ballot Wilson led Clark, gaining slowly as delegates came under the influence of a strong back-fire of opinion from the country. On the forty-sixth ballot he was nominated. The Illinois delegation had broken away from Murphy's grasp on the forty-third ballot and precipitated the victory. In this remarkable contest Bryan perhaps reached the summit of his career. In courage and honesty, in the wise mastery of a political convention, he has not been surpassed in our political history. It was something like irony that he fought better when fighting for another than when fighting for himself. During the severest hours of the crisis his friends came to urge that he would allow them to put his own name into nomination. It was a time when many a man's judgment was distorted by excitement, but Bryan's judgment remained true, though in the realm of ideas it had so often gone astray. Had he yielded, the glory of his fight would have faded.

Wilson's election carried Bryan into the State Department where he served from Mar. 4, 1913,
to June 9, 1915. The appointment was not popular, for nothing in his training prepared him to direct our foreign policy. He knew nothing about international law, which, however, might have been said of some of his predecessors in the office. More important still, his range of thought was narrow. He had been to Europe and once around the world, but he had not shown that it broadened his concept of policies. On the other hand, his appointment had deep political significance. He was head of the strongest faction in the Democratic party and he had been responsible for the nomination of Wilson. It was natural to give him his choice of offices, and it was natural for him to choose the best. In itself Wilson's action was politically wise. Bryan made it even better. He served Wilson faithfully and used his large political influence to carry administration measures through Congress, a principal instance being his aid in framing and passing the bill for the Federal Reserve Bank. The program of reform that made the first seventeen months of President Wilson's administration remarkable was carried through Congress largely through Bryan's influence. A selfish man could have exacted his price for such efforts. Bryan asked for nothing and took no credit for what he did. Persons in the State Department were impressed with his honest desire to understand foreign affairs, and, as the months passed, with his increasing grasp on policies and the justness of his views about them. The Mexican policy of the administration was approved by him thoroughly; he was in complete accord with the decision not to continue government support to the Six-Power Loan to China; and he gave aggressive aid to those who opposed "dollar diplomacy" in Latin-American countries. In April 1913 the President sent Bryan to California to do what he could to dissuade the legislature of that state from passing a bill prohibiting the holding of land by aliens—the point of the bill being directed against the Japanese. No one expected him to do much, but what could be done was done, and it was largely due to Bryan's good nature that a somewhat less offensive bill was substituted and passed.

His long and steady devotion to peace was more personal, and it expressed itself in the negotiation of arbitration treaties with nations situated in all parts of the world. He considered these treaties the most notable thing in his service at the head of the State Department. His plan for international arbitration was formulated in his own mind as early as 1905 (*Commoner*, Feb. 17, 24, 1905), and he had advocated it on several occasions before becoming secretary of state. He took his appointment to that office as an opportunity to give his plan practical application. Soon after he took office he laid it before the Conference of the Diplomatic Corps in Washington. Its distinctive feature was the creation of a Commission of Five by the two nations accepting it, one member chosen by each country from its own citizens, one member chosen by each country from the other country, and the fifth member chosen by the other four. When diplomacy failed to settle a dispute this Commission was to function and to reach a decision within a year during which time neither side should begin hostilities. But at the end of that time either party was to take such action as it chose. The strength of the plan was in the hope that no states would begin war if they had to wait a year while investigation was in progress. Bryan prudently submitted his plan to the Senate Committee on Foreign Relations and got its approval. He then took it up with the nations separately and found no opposition. Thirty states signed such treaties with the United States, but the Senate refused to sign with Panama or the Dominican Republic (*Treaties for the Advancement of Peace, negotiated by William Jennings Bryan,* 1920).

In the crisis of 1914 the Bryan treaties proved ineffective. Germany had not accepted the Bryan arbitration treaty when the war began, but she did so immediately afterward. The United States Senate, however, had not acted on the matter when the *Lusitania* was sunk, May 7, 1915. Bryan thought that Germany should be given the benefit of the doubt and that a commission should be set up to investigate the quarrel, with the assurance that it would have a year to come to a decision; but the President and the cabinet were against using Bryan's treaties. The Secretary had also convinced himself that it was against the spirit of neutrality, international law to the contrary notwithstanding, to allow neutral ships to carry ammunition to a belligerent. Rather than dispatch the second *Lusitania* note which President Wilson had drafted he resigned his post, to take effect the day the note was sent, June 9. Bryan's resignation was made necessary by the very nature of his views. He was a pacifist at heart, and in the struggle then going on had a fixed idea that the United States by preserving strict neutrality would be in a position to make peace between the other nations and thus in some hazy way tremendously enhance her own glory and happiness.

Of all the causes which he led this plea for peace during the World War was the most futile. The people were too much excited to heed him

—all but a few pacifists. Moreover, the warmth with which the pro-Germans received his plea but added to his unpopularity. He was dubbed pacifist and pro-German, and little short of disloyal. This impression of pro-Germanism was increased by a report circulated soon after he retired from the State Department that the careless manner in which Germany took Wilson's first *Lusitania* note, if not his second, was due to verbal assurance given by Bryan to Dumba, Austrian ambassador, that the strong tone of the note was merely intended for home consumption. Bryan denied the charge and produced notes of his conversation with Dumba, in which no such sentiment appeared. Dumba testified to the correctness of the notes and said that his report had been "misinterpreted" in Europe. The responsibility for this "misinterpretation" has never been fixed. Bryan was, however, loyal to Wilson, and out of the cabinet he refused to criticize him. He supported him in 1916, speaking chiefly in the West and Southwest, and when the country entered the war he offered his services in any capacity desired. But he was not the man for war.

Bryan's last fight in politics was in the Democratic national convention in New York, 1924. He was a supporter of William G. McAdoo, around whom rallied the men who held the old progressive doctrines and who represented most of the "dry" sentiment in the party. The faction next strongest was that of Gov. Smith of New York. The convention was very turbulent, due to the fact that a vast number of Smith's followers gained admission and howled down the speakers who displeased them. This element vented its wrath against Bryan, interrupting his speaking and filling the air with insulting epithets. When he began a sentence, saying, "This is probably the last convention of my party to which I shall be a delegate," some of them began to applaud. Bryan's good humor came to his aid and he shouted back, "Don't applaud. I may change my mind." It was, in fact, his last convention. He was not broken in health, but his frame, his nerves, and his energies were worn out.

J. S. B—t.

[Since Prof. Bassett had not given his article a final revision before his death, the editor has added the following paragraphs.]

For thirty years Bryan had been probably the most popular lecturer on Chautauqua platforms. "Each year," wrote Mrs. Bryan (*Memoirs,* p. 286), "when he returned from his tours he had not only spoken to, but had listened to, the mind of America." It was this insight into the minds of his auditors that made him seem a leader when he was often only a follower. He could think their thoughts, divine their aspirations, and give simple and cogent expression to their half-formed convictions. It was thus that he became the champion of many causes which he did not originate. The public came to think of him as a champion of national prohibition; but as late as 1908 he was arguing in favor of local county option in the control of the liquor traffic in Nebraska (*Memoirs*, p. 290). He had been a total abstainer since boyhood and he had always deplored intemperance; but he was only slowly converted to the notion of making men temperate by a national prohibitory law. An incident while he was secretary of state gave newspaper men their chance to make him appear ridiculous as champion of this new cause. Before taking office he had asked President Wilson "whether he would regard the exclusion of intoxicating liquors from our table as an insurmountable objection to my assuming the duties of the office." He was assured that he might follow his own wishes, whereupon followed the farewell luncheon for Ambassador Bryce when thirsty diplomats were given the alternative of drinking water or grape juice. "Not that we thought of drawing a contrast between wine and grape juice," explains Bryan in his *Memoirs,* "but because the glasses for plain and mineral water looked a little lonesome."

Bryan had joined the Presbyterian church as a boy and had always maintained his connection with it. After 1900, when there was no certainty of being a candidate again, he felt "no longer justified in avoiding religious activity" (*Memoirs*, p. 451). He became an elder in the church at Lincoln and began to accept more and more invitations to address religious gatherings. He was troubled by the sceptical attitude of young men, never having himself experienced any doubts regarding Christian dogmas and creeds. To meet these frequent calls for addresses, he prepared his lectures on "The Prince of Peace" and "The Value of an Ideal." Holding firmly with childlike faith to a literal interpretation of the Bible, as he grew older he became more and more hostile to the teachings of biological science which he had never had the inclination to study. Theories of evolution seemed to him to contradict flatly the straightforward words of Genesis and to cheapen the significance of man's earthly career.

In 1924 he drafted the text of a resolution passed by the legislature of Florida which declared it improper and subversive of the best interests of the people of the state for any public

teacher "to teach as true Darwinism or any other hypothesis that links man in blood relationship to any other form of life." He was interested also in a bill under consideration by the legislature of Tennessee, which declared it unlawful for any public teacher "to teach the theory which denies the story of the divine creation of man as taught in the Bible, and to teach instead that man has descended from a lower order of animals." His lecture "Is the Bible True?" was circulated in pamphlet form among the members of the legislature and was believed to have aided the supporters of the bill in securing the necessary votes for its passage (*Memoirs,* p. 481). When, then, a teacher in Dayton, Tenn., was indicted for violation of this statute and Bryan was invited to join the prosecuting attorneys, he accepted the call as a summons to battle. In the course of the trial Bryan was summoned as a witness and subjected to a relentless cross-examination by Clarence Darrow, one of the counsel for the defense. So far as Bryan was concerned, the trial only revealed the naïveté of his religious faith and his want of familiarity with the trend of biological science. Five days after the conclusion of the trial, he was found dead in his bed, having passed away quietly in his sleep.

[*The Memoirs of Wm. Jennings Bryan* (1925) were begun by himself and finished by Mrs. Bryan after his death, with the aid of his correspondence and her own diary. The value of the book lies in its unconscious revelation of personal habits and modes of thought. Bryan had already published three books bearing on his political career: *The First Battle: A Story of the Campaign of 1896* (1896); *The Second Battle or The New Declaration of Independence 1776–1900: An Account of the Struggle of 1900* (1900); and *A Tale of Two Conventions* (1912), containing his account as special correspondent of the national conventions of 1912. *Speeches of Wm. Jennings Bryan Revised and Arranged by Himself,* with a biographical introduction by Mary Baird Bryan, had appeared in two volumes in 1909. Several biographies have been written, all by ardent admirers: H. E. Newbranch, *Wm. Jennings Bryan* (1900); A. L. Gale and G. W. Kline, *Bryan the Man* (1908); G. F. and J. O. Herrick, *The Life of Wm. Jennings Bryan* (1925). More discriminating appraisals are those by C. E. Merriam, in *Four Am. Party Leaders* (1926) and Albert Shaw in the *Rev. of Revs.* (N. Y.), Sept. 1925. The latest biography, *Bryan* (1929), by M. R. Werner is a readable account of his career but adds little that is new.] A. J.

BRYANT, GRIDLEY (Aug. 26, 1789–June 13, 1867), inventor, civil engineer, was born at Scituate, Mass., the son of Zina and Eunice (Wade) Bryant. His father dying poor, the boy reeived only a meager common school education. He early displayed a mechanical bent, and, at fifteen, was apprenticed by his mother to a Boston contractor. By 1808 he was in complete charge of his employer's affairs and two years later himself became a contractor. On Dec. 3, 1815, he married Maria Winship Fox, of Boston, by whom he had ten children. He was for a time a contractor for the United States Government and in 1823 built the branch of the United States Bank in Boston, at which time he invented the portable derrick that afterward came into general use. In 1825 he suggested to the Bunker Hill Monument Association that a railroad be built for the transportation of granite over the rough country from the Quincy quarry to the Neponsit River, a little less than three miles. Bryant and his associates, chief among whom was Thomas H. Perkins, received a charter from the Massachusetts General Court, Mar. 4, 1826, which incorporated them as the Granite Railway Company, although the enterprise was popularly known as the Quincy Railroad. Work was begun Apr. 1, 1826, Bryant acting as engineer. Wooden rails, six inches thick and twelve inches in height, were laid on stone sleepers, which were placed eight feet apart. The rails were covered with iron plates, four inches wide and one-fourth of an inch thick. At crossings stone rails were used. Bryant then built four-wheeled trucks, each with a projecting platform, two trucks being joined to form an eight-wheeled car, and erected a switch and a turntable. These inventions he never patented. He had, as he later declared, "abandoned [them] to the public." Others improved the inventions and they became standard railroad equipment. The road was completed at a cost of $50,000 and was opened Oct. 7, 1826, by a train of horse-drawn cars (*Boston Daily Advertiser*, Oct. 9, 1826). It was one of the pioneer American railroads, but it was not, as is alleged, the first railroad in the United States, although it was probably the first American railroad to cover wooden rails with iron plates.

Bryant's later years, devoted to the care of the Quincy quarry and the Granite Railway Company, were featured by the eight-wheeled car controversy. In 1859 he declared that, "Every railroad in the country is now using my eight-wheeled car, and I have never received one cent for the invention" (Stuart, *post*, pp. 120–21). Ross Winans [*q.v.*] adapted the eight-wheeled car to high-speed freight and passenger transportation, and for his adaptation he received a patent in 1834. Sometime after the renewal of the patent in 1848 Winans began suit against the railroads for violation of patent rights. Litigation continued for years, during which Bryant assisted the railroads, whose chief defense consisted of the Bryant car used on the Quincy Railroad. In 1858 the Supreme Court of the United States refused to sustain the Winans patent on the ground that it was too broad (21 *Howard*,

88). Bryant never received the promised financial settlement from the railroads and he died poor at Scituate at the age of seventy-eight.

[Percy Bryant, "Descendants of John Briant, Sen., of Scituate, Mass.," *New Eng. Hist. and Geneal. Reg.*, Jan. 1894; Henry T. Bailey, "An Architect of the Old School," *New Eng. Mag.*, Nov. 1901; *Laws of the Commonwealth of Mass.*, 1826, ch. CLXXXIII; "Internal Improvements," by Agricola, in the *National Aegis* (Worcester, Mass.), Nov. 29, Dec. 6, 1826; Wm. H. Brown, *The Hist. of the First Locomotives in America* (1871); Chas. B. Stuart, *Lives and Works of Civil and Military Engineers of America* (1871); Angus Sinclair, *Development of the Locomotive Engine* (1907); Seymour Dunbar, *A Hist. of Travel in America* (1915).]

F. E. R.

BRYANT, JOHN HOWARD (July 22, 1807– Jan. 14, 1902), Illinois pioneer, the youngest child of Dr. Peter and Sarah (Snell) Bryant and brother of William Cullen Bryant [*q.v.*], was born at Cummington, Mass. In the spring of 1831 he went to Jacksonville, Ill., clerked there for a year, and then squatted on land just south of Princeton. There he lived for seventy years while the untenanted prairie became a populous farming country. His brothers, Austin, Arthur, and Cyrus, settled in the same neighborhood. On June 7, 1833, he married Harriet Elizabeth Wiswall, who had come with her parents from Norton, Mass., to Jacksonville. In 1835, when the land he occupied was thrown on the market, he entered a half section, to which he later added tracts of 160 and 80 acres. Like his friend Lincoln he was large, powerful, and of great endurance, able in the course of a day to split a hundred rails, labor sixteen hours about the farm, or ride seventy-five miles across country on horseback. In temper and interests he was of much the same stuff as his brother, William Cullen, to whom he was devoted. Although farming was his chief occupation, he built roads and bridges, manufactured brick for a time, and edited a local newspaper. He was probably the most useful citizen in his community. He was instrumental in getting Bureau County organized and in erecting at Princeton the first township high school in Illinois, took an active part in the Illinois State Agricultural Society, was recorder of deeds, chairman of the county board of supervisors, census taker of the county in 1840, member of the legislature in 1842 and in 1858, and collector of internal revenue for the fifth Illinois district 1862–66. In politics he began as a Democrat, and became in turn a member of the Liberty party, a Free-Soiler, a Republican, a Liberal Republican in 1872, and a Democrat. He prided himself on having been a member of the Republican conventions at Pittsburgh in 1856 and at Chicago in 1860. He gave hearty support to Owen Lovejoy [*q.v.*], and, as a maintainer of the "Underground Railroad," lodged as many as fifteen fugitive negroes under his roof at one time in 1854. Though his education had been scanty and irregular, he had a cultivated mind and was fond of writing verse, publishing *Poems* in 1855 and *Life and Poems* in 1894. In his preference for simple stanza forms, a diction tinctured with eighteenth-century classicism, and themes drawn from nature, he resembles his greater brother.

[*Who's Who in America*, 1901–02; H. C. Bradsby, ed., *Hist. of Bureau County, Ill.* (Chicago, 1885); *Current Lit.*, Apr. 1902, pp. 488–89; P. Godwin, *Life of William Cullen Bryant* (1883); J. A. Boutelle, "Stephen Bryant and His Descendants," in *New Eng. Hist. and Geneal. Reg.*, July 1870. Examples of his poems are to be found in the later editions of Rufus Griswold's *Poets and Poetry of America* (1842).]   G. H. G.

BRYANT, JOSEPH DECATUR (Mar. 12, 1845–Apr. 7, 1914), surgeon and medical educator, the only child of Alonzo Ambrose Bryant, by his wife, Harriet Adkins, was born in East Troy, Walworth County, Wis. His ancestors on both sides were English, his mother being of the family of Adkins who took part in the Crusades. His father was one of twelve children, none of whom died before the age of seventy. Joseph was brought up on a farm and received his early education at the public school in his native town, and was later sent to Norwich Academy (New York). He began the study of medicine under Dr. George Avery of New York and received his degree in 1868 from the Bellevue Hospital Medical College. He served as a surgical interne at Bellevue Hospital during 1869–71. His success was immediate and outstanding. He became visiting and consulting surgeon to the Bellevue, St. Vincent's, and other hospitals in New York City. In 1884 he increased his reputation by the publication of his successful two-volume *Manual of Operative Surgery*, which passed through four editions, the last appearing in 1905. He became a friend and the private surgeon of Grover Cleveland, and during Cleveland's presidency performed an heroic operation upon him for a malignant growth (sarcoma) of the left upper jaw in which almost all bony structures were removed except the floor of the orbit. The major part of the operation, which proved life-saving, occurred on July 1, 1893, on Commodore E. C. Benedict's yacht, the *Oneida*, which at the time lay at anchor in New York harbor. The public was not informed of the operation until 1917, after the death of both the President and the surgeon. It was described by W. W. Keen in a paper entitled "The surgical operations on President Cleveland in 1893" which appeared in the *Saturday Evening Post*, Sept. 22, 1917.

Many of Bryant's students have testified to his gifts and deep enthusiasm for teaching (see J. A. A. Sutcliffe, *Indianapolis Medical Journal*, XVII, 248). He made his ward rounds attractive and his lectures were always anticipated with much pleasure by his students. It was also his custom during the six winter months to hold an evening "quiz" class in surgery, as he termed it, for those who were preparing for graduation. On these occasions he often surprised his students by his complete familiarity not only with his immediate subject but with the fundamental sciences of physiology, biological chemistry and anatomy. As a leader in public health, he served for six years in the New York Health Department and became at various times both City and State Commissioner of Health. He championed crusades against pulmonary tuberculosis, secured systematic enforcement of the tenement laws against overcrowding, and acted energetically when New York was threatened with an epidemic of cholera (1892). Political pressure was brought to bear upon him at the time of the cholera epidemic because his quarantine measures threatened commercial activities. He was unmoved, however, and within a short time had the epidemic completely under control.

As a writer Bryan was always lucid and painstaking, but apart from his text-books his surgical contributions were few. The most noteworthy were his paper on "The Treatment of penetrating gun-shot wounds of the cranium" (*New York Medical Journal*, May 5, 1888), and "The relation between the gross anatomy of the appendix and appendicitis" (*Medical News*, Mar. 3, 1894). He also rendered important service to surgery by becoming the senior editor (with A. H. Buck [*q.v.*]) of the *American Practice of Surgery* which appeared in eight volumes between 1906 and 1911. He was an indefatigable worker, painstaking and conservative as a surgeon, a keen observer and a remarkable diagnostician. He studied his patients with exceptional care and was noted for his generosity to the poor. In 1874 he married Annette Amelia, daughter of Samuel Crum. They had one child, Florence, who married Frederick Augustus de Peyster. For many years Bryant was the victim of diabetes but he continued his professional activities until a few days before his death.

[The obituaries and appreciations of Bryant are numerous and are listed in the *Index Cat. of the Surgeon-General's Lib.*, 3 ser. Those in the *N. Y. State Jour. of Medicine*, 1914, XIV, 229–30, the *N. Y. Times*, Apr. 8, 1914, and the *Indianapolis Medic. Jour.*, 1914, XVII, 248–51 (by J. A. A. Sutcliffe) are the most adequate. The N. Y. Acad. of Medicine possesses a scrap-book of newspaper-cuttings, photographs, and other documents relating to Bryant's operation upon Cleveland, compiled by Dr. Kasson C. Gibson, the dentist who devised the rubber jaw for the President.]   J. F. F.

BRYANT, WILLIAM CULLEN (Nov. 3, 1794–June 12, 1878), poet, editor, was descended from Stephen Bryant, who settled in the Plymouth colony in 1632 and became a town officer of Duxbury, Mass. For several generations the Bryants were farmers, but the poet's grandfather, Philip Bryant, and his father, Peter Bryant, were physicians. The latter settled at Cummington, in western Massachusetts, married Sarah Snell, who traced her ancestry back to the *Mayflower,* and carried on a laborious and ill-paid practise. He was a skilful surgeon, who had been trained under the French refugee, Leprilète; he had traveled widely as a surgeon in a merchant vessel; he had musical taste, playing much on the violin; and he was a lover of poetry, possessing a well-stocked library and writing light verse in both Latin and English. His strength was such that he could easily lift a barrel of cider over a cartwheel. The poet's mother was tall, strong, known for her common sense and stern moral qualities, and with certain literary habits; she kept a diary in which she concisely noted the occurrences in the neighborhood. Bryant's health in early childhood was delicate, his head seemed excessively large, and he was of a painfully nervous temperament, but by a stern regimen, including daily cold baths, his father made him a sturdy boy. The mother took pride in his precocity, teaching him the alphabet at sixteen months. The future poet was fortunate in his natural surroundings. His birthplace was a farmhouse surrounded with apple-trees, standing amid fields which sloped steeply down to the north fork of the Westfield River. In his fifth year the family removed to a place of still greater attractiveness, the homestead of his maternal grandfather, Ebenezer Snell, also of Cummington. The boy delighted in the brooks, the river, the rocky hillsides, and the deep forests, as yet only partly invaded by settlement, and enjoyed nutting, gathering spearmint, fishing, and other outdoor pastimes. He was fortunate also in the fact that his father's political interests—Dr. Bryant represented Cummington first in the lower and later the upper branch of the legislature—kept the door of the farmhouse partly open upon the wider world of Boston.

Measured in years of formal tuition, Bryant's education was limited. The district schools gave him a training in reading, writing, arithmetic, geography, and the Westminster Catechism. At the age of twelve, his parents having decided that he deserved a college education, he was sent to live with the Rev. Thomas Snell, an uncle in North Brookfield, to learn Latin, and the following year was transferred to the care of the Rev.

Moses Hallock to acquire Greek. Both were men of great dignity, elevated moral standards, and austere influence. In the eight months with his uncle, Bryant showed a remarkably acquisitive mind, reading Virgil, the select orations of Cicero, and the colloquies of Corderius, while after two months with the Rev. Mr. Hallock "I knew the Greek New Testament from end to end almost as if it had been English" (Godwin, *Bryant,* I, 33). Meanwhile poetical ambitions had awakened in the boy. He owed much to his early and ingrained familiarity with the Scriptures, and when he was ten or eleven his grandfather Snell gave him the whole book of Job to turn into verse. A more important incentive came from his father's library, a collection ultimately numbering about 700 volumes. "In the long winter evenings and stormy winter days," Bryant wrote later, "I read with my elder brother. . . . I remember well the delight with which we welcomed the translation of the *Iliad* by Pope when it was brought into the house. I had met with passages from it before, and thought them the finest verses ever written" (*Ibid.,* I, 24). In childhood he often prayed "that I might receive the gift of poetic genius, and write verses that might endure" (*Ibid.,* I, 26). Before he was in his teens he had scribbled on many subjects, with the encouragement and also the sharp criticism of his father. Taken to Williamstown in September 1810, Bryant passed an easy examination for entrance to the sophomore class of Williams College. The institution was small and poverty-stricken, with a faculty of four who taught a meager curriculum for ill-prepared country lads. Bryant's chief amusements were woodland rambles, participation in the meetings of the Philotechnian literary society, and a course of miscellaneous reading, in which he profited particularly by his study of the Greek poets. Classmates remembered him later as modest, unobtrusive, studious, inclined to choose sober and bookish friends, and competent but not brilliant in the classroom. But his college career was brief. Withdrawing from Williams to prepare himself to enter the junior class at Yale, he worked at his books all summer (1811), only to have his father declare that his means were insufficient for the step.

Already Bryant had appeared, in a way which he later regretted, in print. In 1808, catching the indignant spirit of the Federalists about him, he had written a satire called "The Embargo," which in five hundred lines or more assailed President Jefferson as unpatriotic, a cowardly truckler to the French, an eccentric dabbler in science, and a man of low personal morals. Dr. Bryant unwisely carried this production up to Boston and had it published under the title of *The Embargo: or Sketches of the Times, a Satire; by a Youth of Thirteen.* It sold well, was praised by some reviewers, and attracted so much attention that in 1809 Dr. Bryant had it republished with several other pieces taken from the Hampshire *Gazette,* and placed his son's name on the title-page. Not a line of the volume was ever included by Bryant in his later writings, and he spoke of the pamphlet with testy disgust as "stuff." But it proved the precursor of a really great poem. The autumn after he left Williamstown witnessed the composition of the first form of "Thanatopsis," a work written under several clearly traceable influences. His father had brought home the melancholy poetry of Henry Kirke White, and Bryant, hanging over it eagerly, read also Blair's *Grave,* and Bishop Porteus's poem upon *Death.* Simultaneously he was captivated by the fine blank verse of Cowper's *Task.* Under these circumstances—imbued with the mortuary meditations of Blair and Kirke White, watching the onset of the dark Berkshire winter, and supplied by Cowper with a superior and fascinating metrical form—he began the poem which was to make him famous; a great Puritan dirge, the first fine poetic expression of the stern New England mind. But after completing the poem he was content to stuff it into a corner of his desk. It was necessary for him to turn seriously to a career, and guided largely by his father, he determined to study for the bar. In December 1811 he entered the office of a Mr. Howe of Worthington, four or five miles distant, and there remained until June 1814, an unhappy period. He had no liking for legal study, and was troubled by the fear that his sensitive nature was unfitted for the controversies of the law courts. Meanwhile he made the acquaintance, momentous for his future work, of Wordsworth's *Lyrical Ballads.* For the first time he understood the true character of the impulses which had caused him to pray to be a poet, and realized that they were inextricably bound up with his intense love of natural beauty. As yet, however, he was still groping for an authentic poetic expression. An unfortunate and obscure love affair was reflected in conventional verse, much of it callow in thought and hackneyed in imagery. In the late spring of 1814 he transferred his legal studies to the office of William Baylies in Bridgewater, and there completed them, passing his preliminary examination for the bar in August. These were the years of the second war with England, which awakened no enthusiasm in Bryant. His letters attack the conflict vehemently, and show that he, like other New England Federalists, was thinking seriously of the possibility of secession from the Union and of conflict with the Southern States.

Bryant was fully admitted to the bar in August 1815. While the young lawyer would have liked to embark upon practise in Boston, his purse was too thin to support him in a large city, and he somewhat hastily decided to hang out his sign in Plainfield, a village seven miles from his Cummington home. In December 1815 he walked over to make some preliminary inquiries. While striding along the highway he saw in the afterglow of sunset, flooding the western sky with gold and opal, a solitary bird winging along the horizon; his mind was filled with the beauty of the scene, and at his lodgings that night he wrote the finest of his lyrics, "To a Waterfowl." This also went into his drawer. After eight months in Plainfield, he found a larger opening in Great Barrington, in partnership with a young established lawyer whose practise was worth $1,200 a year. Bryant's experience as a lawyer in Great Barrington endured till the beginning of 1825. There were then three grades of lawyers in the state, entitled respectively to plead in the lower courts, to manage cases in the supreme court, and to argue before the supreme court bench; and Bryant by the fall of 1819 had been admitted to the third category. His name appears four or five times in the supreme court reports, indicating a practise larger than that of most young lawyers. But he found the contentious life of the bar uncongenial, while the frequent miscarriages of justice offended him. Tradition ascribes his final decision to relinquish practise to a decision of the state supreme court in 1824 reversing upon a flimsy technical quibble a judgment for $500 which Bryant had obtained for a plaintiff in a libel suit. But the basic reason was financial. On June 11, 1821, Bryant married Frances Fairchild, daughter of a neighboring farmer—the beginning of a union of singular harmony and devotion; and shortly afterward a daughter was born. As head of a family he required a larger income, and fortunately his pen enabled him to find it.

His fame as a poet dates from the almost accidental publication of "Thanatopsis" in the *North American Review* in 1817. One of the editors, Willard Phillips, had told Dr. Bryant that he wished William Cullen to contribute; Dr. Bryant found in his son's desk the manuscript of "Thanatopsis," "To a Waterfowl," and a briefer piece; and Phillips excitedly carried them at once to his Cambridge associates. "Ah, Phillips, you have been imposed upon," said R. H. Dana; "no one on this side of the Atlantic is capable of writing such verses." When in September the first abbreviated version of "Thanatopsis" was published, its effect was somewhat blunted by four weak stanzas on death which were accidentally prefaced to it; but thereafter Bryant's position in the narrow American literary world was secure. He contributed several other poems and three prose essays, one on American poetry, to the *Review*. Four years later, in 1821, he was invited to read the Phi Beta Kappa poem at the Harvard Commencement to a distinguished audience, and wrote "The Ages," one of his longest productions, which contains many fine passages but is deplorably uneven. His Boston acquaintances prevailed upon him to publish it and some of his other verse, and the result was a pamphlet of forty-four pages, containing twelve pieces in all (*Poems:* Cambridge, 1821). Besides the final version of "Thanatopsis," to which he had added a stately exordium and conclusion, it contained three lyrics of unmistakable genius—"Green River," "To a Waterfowl," and "The Yellow Violet"; and it was warmly praised not merely by American reviewers, but by *Blackwood's*.

Among the fruits of this literary success were a visit to New York (1824) at the invitation of Henry Sedgwick of Stockbridge, and an engagement to furnish an average of one hundred lines a month to the *United States Literary Gazette* of Boston for $200 a year. This ushered in a period of unexampled productivity in Bryant's career, for in about eighteen months (1824–25) he wrote between twenty and thirty poems for the *Gazette,* including some of his finest work—"Rizpah," "An Indian at the Burial Place of his Fathers," "Monument Mountain," "Autumn Woods," and the "Forest Hymn." By 1825 he had clearly emerged as America's one great poet. The result was an invitation (January 1825) to assume the co-editorship with Henry J. Anderson of the monthly called the *New York Review and Athenæum Magazine,* at $1,000 a year. Bryant accepted, left his wife and baby in Great Barrington, and for a little more than a year was exclusively employed upon a magazine of precarious and declining fortunes. He made the acquaintance of the literary circle of New York—Halleck, S. F. B. Morse, Verplanck, Chancellor Kent, and others; he wrote for the *Review* a few fine poems, notably "The Death of the Flowers," as well as much hack work. But he was increasingly worried by poverty and had obtained a license to practise law in the city courts when he was rescued by an offer from the *Evening Post*. Its editor, William Coleman [*q.v.*], had been injured in an accident, and Bryant stepped in (June 1826) as assistant.

For the next three years Bryant was sub-editor of the *Evening Post,* and upon the death of Coleman in July 1829 he assumed the editorial chair which he was to hold for almost a half-century. He quickly acquired a one-eighth share in the journal, which in 1830 became one-fourth, and in 1833 one-third. From the standpoint of material gain the step was fortunate. For the first time it lifted Bryant above financial anxiety, giving him an annual income during the first four years of between $3,300 and $4,000, sums then counted large in New York. He became at one step a public figure of prominence and influence, for the *Evening Post,* founded under the auspices of Alexander Hamilton, had long been one of the country's leading newspapers. But as a poet he unquestionably suffered by the new demands upon his time. Of the whole quantity of verse which he wrote during his long life, about one-third had been composed before 1829. During 1830 he wrote but thirty lines, during 1831 but sixty, and in 1833 apparently none at all. Newspaper staffs were small, and for the first fifteen years of his control Bryant had but one permanent editorial assistant. He wrote editorials, clipped exchanges, reviewed books, and sometimes gathered news. Usually he was at his desk soon after seven in the morning and remained till nearly five. This confining labor irked him, he cared little at the outset for journalism as a career, bracketing it with the law as "a wrangling profession," and his letters show that at first he meant to escape from it to find "leisure for literary occupations that I love better." Meanwhile he gave the *Evening Post* increased strength as a Jacksonian and free trade organ, enlarged its news, and improved its format. But he relied more and more heavily upon his able, aggressive, and highly radical assistant, William Leggett, and after 1830 spent much time out of the office. He enjoyed excursions to the Catskills, Berkshires, and Alleghanies; in 1832 he made a journey to Illinois, where the prairies delighted him, and where he is said to have met Abraham Lincoln; and in 1833 he went on a Canadian tour. In June 1834 he sailed for Europe with his wife and children, intending to leave the *Post* forever and live upon his one-third share. He was absent during the whole of 1835 and was spending the winter of 1835–36 in Heidelberg when news reached him that Leggett was dangerously ill and the *Evening Post* in financial difficulties. He arrived in New York in March 1836, to find the journal without an editor, its business manager just dead, and its circulation, advertising revenue, and influence disastrously injured by the ill-temper and lack of judgment with which Leggett had asserted a Locofoco Democracy, attacked monopoly and inflation, and harried the Whigs. It was necessary to plunge in and labor with unwearying assiduity to rescue the paper. Leggett's connection with it was severed, and Bryant became half-owner. During 1837 and 1838 he worked again from dawn until dark, alarming his wife by his neglect of his health. As editor he had been taught a sharp lesson, and for three decades thereafter his primary allegiance—at times his sole allegiance— was to the *Evening Post*.

By 1840 he had become one of the leading Democratic editors of the nation, and had begun to take advanced ground against slavery. He supported Jackson and Van Buren, demanded a low tariff, opposed the use of public money for internal improvements, and advocated a complete separation between government and banking. He vigorously championed the workingman against judges who held that labor unions were a conspiracy to obstruct trade. When J. Q. Adams defended the right of petition against Calhoun and the South, the *Evening Post* stood with him; it opposed the annexation of Texas; and it assailed Van Buren for pledging himself to maintain slavery in the District of Columbia. Bryant was able in 1840 to wage a whole-hearted campaign against Harrison, and four years later still kept the *Evening Post* on the Democratic side, though in his revulsion against Polk and the annexation of Texas he considered bolting the ticket. His chief aid during these years was Parke Godwin [*q.v.*], later his son-in-law, who assisted in a steady expansion of the news features. To the editorial page Bryant gave dignity and moderation; in vivacity, cleverness, and force it was not equal to the *Tribune* or *Springfield Republican,* but in occasional bursts of noble eloquence it was far superior, and his stately, elevated style was a model for American journalism.

In 1832 he had brought out a collection called *Poems* containing eighty-nine pieces in all; the most notable additions to his previous work being "To the Fringed Gentian" and "The Song of Marion's Men." It was a slender sheaf to represent the entire production of a man who had written "Thanatopsis" twenty-one years earlier, but the *North American Review* rightly pronounced it "the best volume of American verse that has ever appeared." So marked was the American success of his work that Bryant sent a copy to Irving, who was then abroad, asking him to find an English publisher. The English edition came out (London, 1832), with a dedication to Samuel Rogers and an introduction by Irving which made in too unqualified terms the generally valid claim that "the descriptive writings of Mr. Bryant are essentially American"— a claim which some reviewers at once challenged. Irving also slightly displeased Bryant by altering a line of "The Song of Marion's Men" from "The British foeman trembles" to "The foeman trembles in his camp." The English reception of the poems was friendly, and John Wilson wrote an extended and for the most part eulogistic review for *Blackwood's*. This same year Bryant edited a prose collection called *Tales of the Glauber Spa* which was published anonymously, and which contained several stories, creditable but by no means distinguished, from his own pen. This line of endeavor, a fruit of his contacts with Robert Sands and others, he wisely abandoned.

After the first heavy labor of restoring the *Evening Post* was accomplished Bryant resumed his pen, and the half-dozen years following 1838 evinced a partial renewal of his poetic energy. He wrote some fifteen poems in this period, and the fresh material enabled him to issue *The Fountain, and Other Poems* (1842) and *The White-Footed Doe, and Other Poems* (1844), the former containing fourteen pieces, and the latter ten. A prefatory remark in the first volume shows that he had in contemplation a long reflective and descriptive poem somewhat resembling Wordsworth's *Excursion* and Cowper's *Task;* for he says that some of the poems are presented "merely as parts of a longer one planned by the author, which may possibly be finished hereafter." His friend R. H. Dana, Sr., had for years been insistently urging him to compose an extended poem; but it is probable that Bryant found when he attempted it that he did not have a sufficiently fertile and broad imagination, and that his art lacked flexibility and variety. The real value of the project was in furnishing him a much-needed incentive to write the brief lyrics which he hoped to fit into a larger scheme. The reason usually assigned for the slenderness of his output, his preoccupation with the conduct of the *Evening Post,* has partial, but only partial, validity. After the early forties he was free to take long vacations from the office, and did take them. The journal prospered, its annual average dividends during the forties being almost $10,000, while in the fifties it rapidly became a veritable gold-mine. From beginning to end of his life the poet-editor lived with a simplicity that was in some respects almost Spartan. But Bryant's growing wealth enabled him to buy in 1843 an old farmhouse and forty acres of land at Roslyn, Long Island, on the shores of an inlet of the Sound. Here, following the outdoor pursuits he always loved, he was able to spend week-ends and even whole weeks together in summer and fall. He delighted to work in his garden, to take long walks, to swim, and to botanize. He collected a large library, in which he spent much time. He could continue, moreover, those extensive travels which he loved, and which he partially described in correspondence to the *Evening Post* collected under the title of *Letters of a Traveller* (1850)—a wide tour of the South, four trips in close succession to Europe, and a jaunt to Cuba. Had it been only leisure and peace that were lacking, Bryant might have written as much in these years as Longfellow; and his keen professional interest in current events might, had he possessed a different temperament, have inspired his pen as passing history inspired Whittier's.

Yet despite increased leisure and frequent absences, Bryant devoted much hard labor to the *Evening Post* and after 1848 gave it a leading place in the national discussion of the slavery question. It broke sharply with the Democratic party in 1848, supporting the Free-Soil candidacy of Van Buren against Zachary Taylor with such ardor as to be the most efficient advocate of the new party. Two years later it opposed Clay's compromise bill, urging the free states not to give up a single principle. In 1852 it reluctantly indorsed the Democratic nominee, Franklin Pierce, but the following year its utterances against slavery were so radical that the Richmond *Enquirer* called it "abolitionist in fact." Bryant's disgust with the subserviency of Pierce to the South, and his resentment at the Kansas-Nebraska bill, made him quickly and completely dissever the *Post* from the Democratic party. In 1856 he enthusiastically allied the paper with the new Republican organization, while his assistant editor, John Bigelow [*q.v.*], was one of the men instrumental in bringing Frémont forward as its candidate. In the four heated years which ensued Bryant made the *Evening Post* one of the most vigorous of the "Black Republican" organs. He encouraged the despatch of settlers and rifles to Kansas, denounced the Dred Scott decision as an unallowable perversion of the Constitution, and called John Brown a martyr and hero. When Lincoln made his Cooper Union speech in 1860, Bryant introduced him, and the poet-editor was heartily glad to see him defeat Seward for the nomination. After secession began, Bryant never wavered in denouncing all plans for compromise, and in demanding that rebellion be put down by the sword. Many of his editorial utterances for these years display a grandeur of style, and a force and eloquence not to be matched elsewhere in the press of the period, and they produced an effect out of all proportion to the slender circulation of the *Evening Post*.

Throughout the Civil War Bryant belonged to the radical faction which demanded greater energy in its prosecution and assailed Lincoln for his moderation and his reluctance to emancipate the slaves. He was indignant at the modification of Frémont's proclamation. The *Evening Post* repeatedly urged the President to act, and pointed out that Antietam furnished a favorable opportunity. In his criticism of many administration policies Bryant was in close contact with Salmon P. Chase, whose appointment to a cabinet position he had urged upon Lincoln; but the editor objected warmly to some of Chase's own fiscal policies, notably the inflation of the currency by the issue of treasury notes as legal tender. For a time in 1864 the *Evening Post* hesitated to advocate the renomination of Lincoln, but in midsummer Bryant fell into line, and thereafter his praise of the Chief Executive lacked nothing in fervor. After the close of the war he broke from his former radical associates upon the issue of reconstruction in the South, the *Evening Post* maintaining an unflinching advocacy of President Johnson's mild policy, and attacking the harsh measures of Congress. Bryant regretted the impeachment of Johnson, and rejoiced when the Senate failed to convict him. After Grant's inauguration his active interest in the management of the *Evening Post* materially relaxed. The death of Mrs. Bryant on July 27, 1865, had been a heavy blow. In 1866 he tried to escape from his depression of mind by beginning a translation of the whole of Homer, completed in 1871, and showing a fine mastery of blank verse; and in 1866–67 he made a dispirited tour, his sixth and last, of Europe. He had been everywhere regarded for many years as the first citizen of New York, and he was unweariedly at the service of all good causes. In civic, social, and charitable movements his name took precedence of all others. But he was never in any sense popular; austere, chill, precise, and dignified, his demeanor made familiarity impossible, and even in small gatherings he was not a clubbable man. Though he was a polished and impressive orator, and spoke often, his immense influence as a public leader was almost wholly an indirect influence; he reached the minds of those who in turn could reach the masses. His volume of original writing in this period was not large, but it maintained the even merit which had usually marked his production since the appearance of "Thanatopsis." In 1876 he harked back to the subject of mortality in the noble poem "The Flood of Years," and followed it by his retrospective meditation, "A Lifetime," the last of all his works. To the end of his life, always athletic and active, he continued to give several hours daily when in town to the *Evening Post,* walking to and from his home. He was estranged from the Grant Administration by its blunders, its tariff policy, its course at the South, and its low moral tone, and he regarded the Liberal Republican movement with guarded approbation. Had the Liberal Republican convention in 1872 nominated Charles Francis Adams he might have supported him, but he regarded Greeley's candidacy as preposterous. Four years later, associates urged him to side with Tilden (an old personal friend) against Hayes, but he kept the *Evening Post* Republican. He labored as usual in the office on the day (Apr. 29, 1878) when he delivered an oration under a hot sun at the unveiling of the Mazzini statue in Central Park. Returning after the ceremonies to the home of James Grant Wilson, he fell on the steps, sustained a concussion of the brain, and shortly lapsed from partial consciousness into coma. His death in June was followed by a funeral in All Souls' Unitarian Church and burial in Roslyn Cemetery.

Bryant holds a double place in American history. He brought to his editorial chair some qualities which no editor of his time possessed in equal degree. In culture and scholarship he surpassed Raymond, Bowles, and Greeley, while in dignity and adherence to moral principle he was far in advance of Bennett and Dana. Few men of his time did half so much to lift journalism from a vulgar calling to a place of high honor and national influence. The literary correctness of the *Evening Post,* controlled by Bryant's fastidious taste—his *index expurgatorius* is still quoted—was famous. But, preoccupied with the great aims of his editorial page, he lacked the faculty of Bowles and Greeley for creating a broad newspaper which would appeal by enterprise in newsgathering and by special features to a great popular audience. He was responsible for few innovations in journalism, and they were not of high importance. His journalistic vein had something of the narrowness which marked his poetic genius, and though the *Post's* editorials, political news, literary articles, and foreign correspondence were of the highest merit, they were for the few and not the many. As a poet he holds a position in American letters akin to that of Wordsworth in English. He is our great poet of nature, with which more than one hundred of his total of about one hundred and sixty poems deal. He had certain clear limitations: he lacked warmth of emotion, and especially human emotion, while his imagination was restricted in range, and he

seldom revealed intellectual profundity. But he possessed a sensitively artistic perception of what was lovely in nature, and a capacity for its imaginative interpretation, which are not equaled by any other American writer. It is not nature in general, but the untouched nature of the New World, and of New England in particular, which his verse pictures with definiteness and accuracy. With this descriptive power are joined an elemental piety, a pervading sense of the transiency of all earthly things, and a meditative philosophy which, while melancholy, is also peaceful and consoling; qualities which give to much of his work a religious depth, and make his poetry as cool and restful as the deep forests he loved. His range was not wide nor high, but within that range he wrought with a classical love of restraint, purity, and objectivity, chiseling his work as out of marble; and he produced a small body of poetry which may be called imperishable.

[The standard life is Parke Godwin's *A Biography of Wm. Cullen Bryant, with Extracts from His Private Correspondence* (1883), in two large volumes. Godwin also edited Bryant's *Poetical Works* and *Complete Prose Writings* (1883, 1884). The latter includes a selection of articles from the *Evening Post,* but the paper's editorial pages contain additional material of value which has never been collected. Godwin also made a selection from Bryant's travel writings, but these are found more fully in Bryant's own *Letters of a Traveller* (1850), dealing with his European, Western, and Southern wanderings. John Bigelow's brief volume in the American Men of Letters series, *Wm. Cullen Bryant* (1890), reflects the author's intimacy with the poet, as does also Jas. Grant Wilson's *Bryant and His Friends* (1886). The aim of Wm. Aspenwall Bradley's *Bryant* (1905) in the English Men of Letters series is critical rather than biographical. A note by Carl Van Doren on the origin of "Thanatopsis" may be found in the *Nation,* CI, 432–33. Some light is thrown upon Bryant's work as editor by Geo. Cary Eggleston, *Recollections of a Varied Life* (1910), and by Allan Nevins, *The Evening Post: A Century of Journalism* (1922), while a sharply critical sidelight is furnished by a manuscript volume of memoirs by J. Ranken Towse, in the possession of the *Evening Post.* The best brief critical studies are by E. C. Stedman in *Poets of America* (1885), and Wm. Ellery Leonard in the *Cambridge Hist. of Am. Lit.* (1917), I, 260 ff. The last-named volume contains a full bibliography.]
A. N.

BRYCE, LLOYD STEPHENS (Sept. 20, 1851–Apr. 2, 1917), politician, author, was born at Flushing, L. I., the son of Joseph Smith Bryce and Elyzabeth (Stephens) Bryce. His father, whose name was originally Joseph Brice Smith, graduated from West Point in 1829, was assistant professor of mathematics at the Academy for the next two years, became a successful lawyer in New York, reëntered the army at the outbreak of the Civil War, was stationed most of the time in or near Washington, and rose to the rank of brevet major of volunteers. His mother was a sister of John Lloyd Stephens [*q.v.*]. Bryce spent his boyhood at Georgetown, D. C., the home of the Smith family. He received his schooling there from the Jesuits of Georgetown College and in New York from Charles Anthon [*q.v.*]. In 1867 he traveled in Europe and copied pictures in the Louvre. He was matriculated at Christ Church, Oxford, on Jan. 28, 1870, and graduated in 1874. Well educated and well connected, more than comfortable financially, a member of the best clubs and the best society, Bryce interested himself in a number of things, always acquitted himself well, but did not persist with anything long enough to attain eminence. Home again in New York he studied law but never practised. He entered politics as a Democrat, and in 1886 Gov. Hill appointed him paymaster-general of the state with the rank of brigadier-general. That autumn he ran for Congress from the seventh district on an anti-single-tax platform and was elected. Discovering in Washington that the single tax was not imminent, he devoted himself during the Fiftieth Congress to the improvement of New York harbor and to the copyright laws, in which he had recently acquired a personal interest. In 1887 had appeared his first novel, *Paradise*. The next year he was defeated for reëlection. Subsequently he published *The Romance of an Alter Ego* (1889), which was reissued as *An Extraordinary Experience* (1891); *Friends in Exile* (1893); and *Lady Blanche's Salon* (1899). His novels were amusing but have no claim to remembrance. He also wrote shorter fiction, magazine articles, and reviews. In 1889 his friend Allen Thorndike Rice [*q.v.*] died suddenly and left him a controlling interest in the *North American Review*. Bryce hastened home from Europe, assumed the editorship with the issue for September 1889, bought the other interests in the magazine, and conducted it until 1896. In his editorial policy he followed the lines laid down by Rice, secured able and eminent contributors, and showed a canny regard for timeliness. On President Taft's appointment Bryce served as United States minister to the Netherlands and Luxembourg from August 1911 till September 1913. He was a delegate to the Opium Conference of 1913, was an honorary vice-president of a Conference on Bills of Exchange, and furthered the building of the Peace Palace at The Hague. His wife was Edith Cooper, daughter of Mayor Edward Cooper of New York and grand-daughter of Peter Cooper.

[*Who's Who in America*, 1916–17; *Who's Who in N. Y. C.*, 1904; *Rev. of Revs.* (N. Y.), May 1891; J. Foster, ed., *Alumni Oxonienses, 1715–1886*, vol. I (1887); G. W. Cullum, *Biog. Reg.* (3rd ed., 1891), I, 424–25; *Biog. Cong. Dir. 1774–1911* (1913); *N. Y. Times*, Apr. 3, 1917; information from Peter Cooper Bryce, Esq. (son).]
G. H. G.

BUCHANAN, FRANKLIN (Sept. 17, 1800–May 11, 1874), naval officer, was born at "Auchentorlie," Baltimore, the eighth of eleven children. His father was Dr. George Buchanan, son of a distinguished Scotch physician who came to Maryland in 1723; his mother, Laetitia McKean, was the daughter of the Pennsylvania "Signer" Thomas McKean, who was of Scotch-Irish descent. Young Buchanan, becoming a midshipman Jan. 28, 1815, served first on the *Java*, Commodore Oliver Hazard Perry. After five years on various ships, chiefly in the Mediterranean, he made, with the permission of the Navy Department, a fifteen months' voyage to China as mate on a merchant vessel. He then spent six strenuous years in the West India Squadron, suppressing piracy in the Caribbean. Meanwhile, becoming a lieutenant Jan. 13, 1825, Buchanan in July following, delivered at Rio de Janeiro the frigate *Baltimore*, to the Emperor of Brazil. After another Mediterranean cruise in the *Constellation*, he went in 1833 as first lieutenant on the ship of the line *Delaware* which carried the United States minister Edward Livingston to France, and among other officers he was invited to dine with King Louis Philippe. He was afterward ordered to shore duty, during which he tested guns at the Philadelphia Navy Yard and then commanded the receiving ship at Baltimore. This service was followed by a cruise in the Pacific, April 1839–June 1840, in the frigate *Constitution* and the sloop *Falmouth*. Promoted to commander Sept. 8, 1841, he was early the next year placed in command of the steam frigate *Mississippi;* but after a few months he was transferred to the sloop *Vincennes*, which he commanded for nearly two years. While cruising in this ship in search of pirates and slave-traders, he assisted two British merchantmen in peril in Galveston Harbor, for which service he received the official thanks of Great Britain. On Aug. 14, 1845, having submitted, in obedience to Secretary of the Navy Bancroft, a plan for organizing the new Naval School at Annapolis, he was appointed its first superintendent, which position he filled, from the formal opening of the School, Oct. 10, 1845, until his detachment, Mar. 2, 1847, after "renewed" application for active service in the Mexican War. Buchanan initiated the high standards of discipline and efficiency for which the Naval Academy is famous; Bancroft commended his "precision and sound judgment" and his "wise adaptation of simple and moderate means to a great and noble end" (*Annual Report*, Dec. 1, 1845). Throughout the Mexican War Buchanan commanded the sloop

Germantown, which coöperated in the operations against Tuxpan, Apr. 18, and Tabasco, June 16, 1847. In 1852, after some years of shore duty chiefly at Baltimore, he took command of the steam frigate *Susquehanna,* the flagship of Perry's squadron in the expedition to Japan. When on July 14, 1853, the President's letter was presented with due ceremony to representatives of the Emperor at Uraga, Buchanan was the first officer to set foot on Japanese soil. On his return home, he became a member of the Board of Officers to Promote Efficiency of the Navy, and was afterward made commander of the Washington Navy Yard, meanwhile becoming captain Sept. 14, 1855. Under the impression that Maryland would secede from the Union, he resigned from the navy Apr. 22, 1861; but soon thereafter becoming convinced that there would be a reconciliation between the North and the South, he wrote to the Navy Department requesting to withdraw his resignation. On May 14, 1861, however, he was "dismissed" from the service. Going to Richmond soon afterward, he joined the Confederate States Navy, with the rank of captain, Sept. 5, 1861. He was chief of the Bureau of Orders and Detail until Feb. 24, 1862, when he was placed in command of the Chesapeake Bay Squadron, with his flag on the reconstructed U. S. S. *Merrimac,* renamed the C. S. S. *Virginia.* On Mar. 8, he surprised the Union squadron in Hampton Roads, and destroyed the frigate *Congress,* of which his brother McKean was purser, the sloop of war *Cumberland,* and three small steamers. Having been seriously wounded, however, in the left thigh by a Minié ball from the shore batteries during the engagement, he was prevented from commanding his ironclad in the *Monitor-Merrimac* battle of the following day. He was "promoted for gallant and meritorious conduct" (*Official Records,* 1 ser., VII, 62) to admiral, Aug. 26, 1862, thus becoming the ranking officer, and was then made commander of the naval forces at Mobile. In the battle of Mobile Bay, Aug. 5, 1864, he commanded the Confederate squadron, his flagship being the ram *Tennessee.* His smaller vessels having been captured or driven to cover, "Old Buck" made a heroic attack single-handed against Farragut's entire squadron. In the furious engagement, the *Tennessee's* rudder chain jammed, she became unmanageable, and other injuries forced her to surrender. Her commander, seriously wounded again, remained a prisoner of war until exchanged in February 1865. Returning to his home, "The Rest," Talbot County, Md., he became president of the Maryland Agricultural College, September 1868–June 1869. After about

a year in Mobile where he was secretary of the Alabama Branch of the Life Insurance Company of America, he returned again to his Maryland home where he died May 11, 1874. He was buried in the cemetery of the Lloyd family at Wye House, four miles distant from "The Rest." In appearance Buchanan was slightly below middle stature, but he was compactly built and had great physical strength, being in his prime the third strongest man in the navy, according to his brother McKean. He moved with grace and had an affable, courteous bearing; while his magnetism and great personal courage gave him a remarkable influence over men. He was married at Annapolis on Feb. 19, 1835, to Ann Catharine, daughter of Gov. Edward Lloyd of Wye House.

[See *Official Records (Navy)*; the *Navy Register,* 1821–62; letter-books, ships' journals, etc., in U. S. Naval Acad. Lib.; other manuscript letters and papers access to which may be had through Franklin Buchanan Owen, Cleveland, Ohio, and Wm. W. Gordon, Savannah, Ga. Information is to be found also in Roberdeau Buchanan, *McKean Genealogy* (Lancaster, Pa., 1890); *Battles and Leaders of the Civil War,* vols. I, IV, and "Narrative of the Expedition of an American Squadron to the China Seas and Japan, 1852–1854, under the command of Commodore M. C. Perry, U. S. Navy," in *House Ex. Doc. No. 97,* 33 Cong., 2 Sess. An obituary appeared in the *New Eng. Hist. and Geneal. Reg.,* XXVIII, 364.]   C.L.L.

BUCHANAN, JAMES (Apr. 23, 1791–June 1, 1868), fifteenth president of the United States, was born near Mercersburg, Pa. His ancestors —Buchanans, Russels, Speers, and Pattersons— were all North-Ireland Scottish Presbyterians who emigrated to south-central Pennsylvania. His father, James Buchanan, who came to America in 1783, was a successful, hard-headed storekeeper, who wisely invested in farm lands. His mother, Elizabeth Speer, was a hard-working frontier wife, with a taste for good reading. James had a good classical preparation at a school in Mercersburg, and in the fall of 1807 entered the junior class of Dickinson College, of which his memories were not complimentary. In 1809 he graduated. There followed three years of diligent reading for the bar at Lancaster, and admission to the bar in 1812. His rise in his profession was so rapid that within three years his income was $11,297. This legal success was founded on Buchanan's knowledge of the law, and also upon his capacity for oratorical presentation, which had been developed in the society debates then so prominent a feature of college life, and which he had assiduously cultivated by the habit of speech-making when walking. His debating power soon made him an available figure for politics. Politics also appealed to him because of the close personal associations that it made possible. His nature was adapted to friendships, and those which he made were lasting and satisfying to him.

In 1814 he entered the Pennsylvania House of Representatives as a Federalist of the middle-states type. He had opposed the declaration of war with England but he believed it his duty to support the administration when once war began; and he enrolled as a volunteer in a company of dragoons. On July 4, 1815, he delivered an oration before a branch of the Federalist Washingtonian Society of Lancaster, in which the phraseology used by President Monroe in his famous message of 1823 was almost anticipated by the words: "We are separated from the nations of Europe by an immense ocean. We are still more disconnected with them by a different form of government, and by the enjoyment of true liberty. Why, then, should we injure ourselves by taking part in the ambitious contests of foreign despots and kings?" (*Works*, I, 9). In 1815 he was reëlected and exerted himself to protect the banks by delaying the return to specie payment. It was his intention to retire from politics at the close of this term, but there fell upon him a calamity, from which he never fully recovered. He was engaged to be married. Some mischief-makers spread tales, which caused the young lady to break the engagement. It seems to have been a trivial lovers' quarrel, which he fully expected to heal. Before this happened, however, the young lady died. This irremediable sorrow put away all thought of marriage, and he turned for consolation to the associations of politics. In 1820 he was elected to Congress, and his devotion to his political duties is indicated by his dwindling professional income. Buchanan, however, was never poor. His savings were judiciously invested, and his fortune grew to the comfortable sum of three hundred thousand dollars. He was elected as a Federalist, but his positions were those of a moderate, and he had friends on both sides of the house.

As the election of 1824 approached it was plain that the Federalist party was dead; what would become of its members was a problem which excited much discussion. Ultimately the majority, because of a general similarity of views, became Whigs. Buchanan was of the smaller number who went the other way. But it was not long before the relations which he formed with Gen. Jackson and his following were temporarily imperiled. In December 1824 Buchanan had an interview with Jackson in which he mentioned a conversation which he had had with a friend of Clay. In 1827 Jackson stated that Buchanan had come to him with a proposal from the friends of Clay for a political bargain. This put Buchanan

in a very awkward position, for the statement was important and untrue, while Jackson's sensitiveness to personal differences was well known. Buchanan both denied the statement, and maintained his relations with Jackson—no small achievement. During the Adams administration he was active in opposition to the administration and in particular disapproved the Panama mission. In the course of a debate on the latter subject he made his first public statement on slavery, to the effect that it was a moral and political evil, that it was irremediable, and that he recognized his duty to help the Southern whites in case of a servile insurrection. In 1828 he played a prominent part in the Jackson campaign. It may have been as a reward for his party services that his brother, George W. Buchanan, was appointed district attorney while he, himself, became chairman of the committee on judiciary, in which position he enhanced his reputation for solid legal attainment and sound judgment, although he failed to bring about the success of an impeachment brought against Judge Peck in 1831. On the positive side he saved the appellate jurisdiction of the United States Supreme Court based on writs of error.

Having served ten years in the House of Representatives, Buchanan once more determined to retire from politics and to resume his law practise. He was now, however, a well-known political figure in the dominant party. He was even mentioned for the vice-presidency, and he was finally offered the ministry to Russia. In June 1831 he accepted the latter, and by the next June he was in St. Petersburg. The mission was not important, but it gave his mind a slant toward international affairs, and he achieved some small successes and a considerable popularity. His successes were sufficient to cause him to be mentioned in 1833 as a successor to Edward Livingston in the secretaryship of state. On his return to the United States, he was elected to the Senate, from Pennsylvania, first for an unfinished term, and then in 1837 for a full one, and again in 1843. Here he took his stand as an administration man, a full-fledged Democrat, and came to be relied upon as one of the chief supporters of the measures of Jackson and Van Buren. In 1839 he was offered by Van Buren the position of attorney-general, but he preferred to remain in the Senate.

The slavery question had now begun to divide parties, and to test the quality of every man aiming at a national career. Buchanan stood the test well so far as consistency was concerned. He shared the Pennsylvania opinion against slavery in the abstract; he fully recognized the constitutional defenses of slavery and the duty of the national government to protect slavery where it existed: he expressed strongly his sympathy with the Southern whites, in their fear of the harmful effects of agitation upon the negroes and the peril which it might bring to Southern homes; he denounced the abolitionists as dangerous fanatics; but at the same time, as a constitutionalist, he defended the right of petition, and besought the Southerners not to create the impression "that the sacred right of petition and the cause of the abolitionists must rise or must fall together." He joined with the Southerners, however, in supporting a bill which made it unlawful for postmasters to distribute any material touching slavery, where the circulation of such material was forbidden by state laws.

Under the Tyler administration Buchanan continued to be one of the leaders and spokesmen of his party. As the election of 1844 approached he was mentioned for the presidency as "Pennsylvania's favorite candidate." He wrote friends on the Pennsylvania delegation in the Democratic convention at Baltimore that his support was pledged to Van Buren, but that should the latter's nomination become impossible, he would be willing to have his name used. The choice of the convention was neither Van Buren nor Buchanan but James K. Polk of Tennessee, whose nomination was considered by many an affront to better-known men such as Buchanan. The latter, however, bore himself with dignity, accepted the inevitable, and gave Polk his support, writing privately that Polk had "greatly improved, since he had been a member of congress.' He exerted himself in the campaign particularly to prevent the anti-tariff views of the Southern Democrats from being so expressed as to alarm the protectionist Democrats of Pennsylvania, for he considered the outcome in the Keystone State very doubtful.

When, then, the Pennsylvania electors cast their votes for Polk, and recommended Buchanan as secretary of state, the President-elect could hardly ignore his claims. He offered him the position, but at the same time sought to exact from him a promise that if he should become a candidate for the presidency or vice-presidency, he would retire from the cabinet (Curtis, I, 548). Buchanan replied that he could not promise not to become a candidate in 1848, but that he would not agitate the question, and if he were presented as a candidate by a state or national convention, he would retire from the cabinet. Actually he served the full term of four years. During this term he greatly enhanced his reputation and provided himself for the first time with a definite program, though his chief policies and methods were those directed by the President. He was fortunate in many of his diplomatic agents, though whether this was his own work or that of Polk it is difficult to say. What he did contribute was laborious study of the history of cases, careful writing of dispatches, and a certain oratorical appeal to patriotism. These notes were read by the public; and made him a popular figure. His habitual tact, discretion, and moderation were generally recognized. The Texan situation was the chief interest of the new administration, and was one of unusual complexity. Congress had voted to annex Texas, but Texas had not yet accepted annexation. Great Britain and France were anxious to prevent acceptance. Mexico refused to recognize the independence of Texas, and hoped that the Oregon question might involve the United States and Great Britain in difficulties which would enable her to insist strongly on her position. The speedy settlement of the Oregon question was, therefore, earnestly desired by President Polk and his advisers. Buchanan's contribution was a powerful statement of the American claim to the whole of Oregon, with a refusal of arbitration, while he kept the road open to negotiation.

To Mexico Buchanan sent a note which Webster regarded as "mild and conciliatory," but which held firmly that the annexation of Texas must be considered as an accomplished fact. His confidence was not misplaced. In July 1845 a Texas convention accepted annexation. The administration now started two lines of action in dealing with Mexico. One was the occupation of Texan territory by United States troops; this occupation including certain regions claimed by both Mexico and Texas. The second was the sending of a minister to Mexico in the person of John Slidell of Louisiana, a close friend of Buchanan. He was instructed to refuse negotiation on the Texan boundary, since the United States supported the claims of Texas in their entirety. He was to insist on certain claims of United States citizens against Mexico which had been violently pressed by President Jackson in a message of 1837. These had been accepted by Mexico, but had remained unpaid. Slidell was to demand payment, but to accept as payment the territory between Texas and the Pacific, to the acquisition of which many in the United States had long looked forward, and which Polk had determined to secure during his presidency. The instructions were Buchanan's; and his was the skilful delay of negotiations until a revolutionary change in Mexico gave a new chance of settlement. The negotiation was the work of Slidell.

It resulted in an *impasse* which President Polk considered, when the dispatches reached Washington in April 1846, as justifying a war message to Congress. It so happened that this diplomatic crisis practically coincided with a military skirmish on the Texan border. The two incidents were combined in Polk's message to Congress which declared that war existed by act of Mexico. In the midst of these events Buchanan concluded a treaty with the British ambassador which put an end to the Oregon question by a sensible compromise of territorial claims. In the negotiation of the treaty of peace which ended the Mexican War, the President played a larger part than his secretary of state.

It was the Secretary of State, however, who shaped the policy of the administration in many other matters of international importance. It seems that it was by Buchanan's advice that President Polk in his first message made a vigorous restatement of the Monroe Doctrine, which was intended to discourage suspected British designs in California. He was largely responsible, too, for Polk's second statement on the Monroe Doctrine, in his annual message of 1848. He was keenly interested in all Central American affairs. On his advice President Polk recommended in a message of Apr. 29, 1848, that Congress take action to prevent the acquisition of Yucatan by Great Britain. Buchanan was so much disturbed at the foothold which Great Britain had already acquired in Nicaragua by a protectorate over the Mosquito Indians that in June 1848 he sent a chargé, Mr. Hise, to Guatemala, instructed to promote the reformation of the Central American Confederation, and to oppose the designs of the British. Peculiarly his own policy, however, was his attempt to secure the island of Cuba. The ultimate annexation of this island had long been in the minds of American statesmen, but it had been held that this was an affair of the future, and that in the meantime Spanish rule should be supported. Buchanan believed that the hour had now struck, and he made a proposal to Spain for its purchase for $120,000,000. The offer was refused, but Buchanan to the end of his career continued to insist upon this program.

On retiring from office in 1849, Buchanan gave up his house in Lancaster and bought a country estate near-by, called Wheatland. His domestic interest was centered in his orphan niece, Harriet Lane, of whose upbringing he took entire charge. Her charm brought about him the most exclusive society of the day. In his retirement a vigorous campaign was pressed to give him the presidential nomination of 1852, the three other leading candidates being Lewis Cass, William L. Marcy, and Stephen A. Douglas, but on the forty-ninth ballot a much less prominent man, Franklin Pierce of New Hampshire, was nominated. If Buchanan was disappointed, he successfully disguised his feelings and gave Pierce his cordial support. His speech at Greensburgh, Pa., in October, in which he traversed the career of the Whig candidate, Gen. Winfield Scott, was generally regarded as a campaign document of the first importance. That he would receive some important post in the new Democratic administration was a foregone conclusion. Disappointed he must have been, however, when the post offered was the ministry to Great Britain, instead of the state department which was given his rival and intimate, William L. Marcy. Buchanan accepted with the understanding that he should be allowed to conduct a general negotiation in London, whereby he hoped to combine a reciprocity treaty, an agreement on the fisheries, and a check to British influence in Central America, which he considered to have been too liberally recognized by the Whigs in the Clayton-Bulwer Treaty of 1850. Marcy, however, kept the first two matters in his own hands at Washington, and without these for trafficking Buchanan was unable to accomplish anything on the third during his two years in London.

His mission, however, was very agreeable. It began with a curious episode. Secretary Marcy had issued a circular to the effect that our ministers abroad should appear only in the "simple dress of an American citizen" in place of the uniform previously prescribed, unless such rule would seriously interfere with the conduct of their business. Buchanan, rather amused, determined to adhere to the rule, perhaps in order to prevent his friend Marcy from reaping Democratic laurels at home, and for a time it seemed that he might be excluded from court functions. In the end he was accepted as he chose to appear in "frock-dress" with the addition of a plain dress sword, and seems to have gained by the episode. At least he was popular in society, and when Miss Lane visited him, the mission became one of the most generally popular the United States has had in England. The most interesting episode of his stay occurred when Secretary Marcy requested Pierre Soulé, minister at Madrid, to consult with the United States ministers at Paris and London, John Y. Mason and Buchanan, on the Cuban question. The three met first at Ostend and then at Aix-la-Chapelle in October 1854, and drew up a document which became known as the "Ostend Manifesto" (*House Ex. Doc. No. 93,* 33 Cong., 2 Sess.). It included an historical discussion of the Cuban problem, and set forth the danger of European interference, particularly with reference to the possible emancipation of slaves. It recommended that an offer be made to Spain for the purchase of the island. What made it remarkable was its discussion of what should take place if Spain refused. "We should . . . be recreant to our duty . . . should we permit Cuba to be Africanized and become a second St. Domingo, with all its attendant horrors to the white race, and suffer the flames to extend to our neighboring shores, seriously to endanger or actually to consume the fair fabric of our Union. We fear that the course and current of events are rapidly tending towards such a catastrophe." "Self preservation is the first law of nature, with States as with individuals. . . . We must, in any event, preserve our own conscious rectitude and our own self-respect." Should Cuba become necessary to our safety, then "by every law, human and divine, we shall be justified in wresting it from Spain if we possess the power."

Buchanan was, therefore, more than ever a presidential possibility when he returned in April 1856, having made these appeals to Southern and to Democratic feeling. By his absence, moreover, he had escaped the domestic conflicts over the Kansas-Nebraska bill. He was again presented for the presidency by the Pennsylvania Democracy, with the strong support of his close friends, Schell of the "Hard" New York Democracy and Slidell of Louisiana, and with that of his old party associates in Virginia. Most of his support, however, came from the North. He led from the first ballot, and on the seventeenth was unanimously nominated, John C. Breckinridge of Kentucky being chosen as candidate for vice-president. The platform contained a statement of the finality of the compromise of 1850, and an indorsement of the principle of non-interference by Congress with slavery in the territories. Buchanan did little speaking during the campaign, and when he did speak he was most emphatic in his denunciation of the abolitionists. He failed of a popular majority vote, receiving 1,800,000 to 1,300,000 for Frémont, the Republican candidate, and about 900,000 for Fillmore, on the American and Whig tickets. Of the electoral votes he received 174 to 114 for Frémont, and 8 for Fillmore. He carried Pennsylvania, New Jersey, Indiana, Illinois, California, and all the slaveholding states except Maryland.

Buchanan's inaugural address was emphatic in its statement of his conversion to the principle of strict construction. Nevertheless, he recommended, for military purposes, the construction of a national railroad to the Pacific. He stood for economy, for the payment of the public debt, but for a small increase in the navy. Most important was his statement that the question of slavery in the territories was one for judicial decision, and he referred to the Dred Scott Case, then pending, of the progress of which he had somewhat irregularly informed himself (*Works,* X, 106–08), as destined to give a solution to which all good citizens would cheerfully submit. His individual opinion he stated to be that popular sovereignty, or local control, began with the formation of a state constitution. He reiterated his well-known belief that a president should not be reëlected. On taking office he made an appeal to democratic sentiment by enunciating the principle of rotation in office, which meant that although succeeding a Democratic president, he would re-man the civil service. The selection of his cabinet was directed by another principle, which he maintained with reference to all important appointments; that of giving, as far as possible, equal representation to slave and non-slaveholding states—"the sacred balance." Lewis Cass became secretary of state, and the other most important appointments were those of Howell Cobb, the Georgia Unionist, as secretary of the treasury, of John B. Floyd of Virginia as secretary of war, and of the Pennsylvania lawyer, his personal friend, Jeremiah S. Black, as attorney-general. With Miss Lane as mistress of the White House, the administration was one of the most successful, socially, in our history. Its height was marked by the visit in 1860, of the Prince of Wales. The tone of Washington society at the time was set by a group of brilliant women from the South, such as Mrs. Roger Pryor of Virginia, Mrs. Chesnut of South Carolina, and Mrs. Clay of Alabama. The Gwins, formerly of Mississippi and now of California, entertained lavishly. One of the closest intimates at the White House was Senator Jefferson Davis of Mississippi.

It was Buchanan's intention that his administration should be chiefly characterized by a vigorous foreign policy. In this he had some success, which seems to have been due for the most part to his own careful and minute attention. He was instrumental in the conclusion of arrangements between Great Britain and Nicaragua and Honduras, which, in his opinion, neutralized some of the dangerous features of the Clayton-Bulwer Treaty, and he checked the activity of the British fleet in searching vessels suspected of being engaged in the slave trade in American waters. He secured reparation from Paraguay for the firing on the *Water Witch,* a United States naval vessel, surveying La Plata. He made an advantageous treaty with China, and cemented our relations in the Far East by his reception of embassies from Japan and Siam. His main purpose, however, the annexation of Cuba, was blocked by the impossibility of securing from Congress the appropriation necessary to initiate negotiation. The same was true of his policy with regard to Mexico. Whether he looked to acquisition of Mexican territory is uncertain. It is certain, however, that his avowed purpose was to prevent European intervention by aiding the Liberal party of Juarez to establish order. In 1859 he had negotiated a treaty of "Transit and Commerce" and a convention "to maintain order and security in the territory of the Republic of Mexico and the United States," the main point of which was the payment of $2,000,000 by the United States to Mexico, with which it was hoped that Juarez would be enabled to establish himself. These were not ratified. The most dramatic diplomatic episode was the checking of a filibustering expedition to Nicaragua of the well-known William Walker, by Commodore Paulding under direction of Isaac Toucey, the secretary of the navy. This vigor in dealing with such irregular activities of Americans was new. It was supported by conservative Southern opinion, but it did little to convince the North that Buchanan was not striving to expand the United States to the south for the benefit of the slave states (William O. Scroggs, *Filibusters and Financiers,* 1916, pp. 333–67).

On the subjects of finance and the tariff Buchanan did not assume leadership, presenting them as subjects which belonged to Congress. This left the executive direction to Howell Cobb, the secretary of the treasury, at whose suggestion a tariff bill was passed in 1857. However this act may be judged from an economic point of view, it was one of the worst political blunders ever committed in the United States, uniting as it did the influence of the South and New England, an alliance of no political potentiality, and alienating from the Democrats the protectionist interests of the President's own Pennsylvania and of the Northwest, and thus giving the Republicans an opportunity of which they took immediate advantage. In the financial crisis of 1857, the President was stopped by his accepted principles from taking any policy except that of protecting the government. The credit even of the government did not recover during his administration. The attempt of the opposition to convict the President of maladministration by means of the "Covode Investigation" failed to re-

veal any condition of unusual laxity in the administration.

The main subject of discussion, however, was the territories. In Utah the President firmly but peacefully established the authority of the United States government by a military expedition. So far as the status of slavery in Kansas and Nebraska was concerned, Buchanan accepted the Dred Scott decision as final. In administration he showed apparent wisdom and strength. To the territory of Kansas, where something very like civil war prevailed between the Free-State party and the Slave-State party, he sent Robert J. Walker, one of the ablest men at his disposal, whose conduct now receives the general approval of historians. It was not, however, a situation calling for wise administration only, but for Congressional action. When the Lecompton convention in January 1858 presented its request for statehood under the pro-slavery constitution which it had drawn up, the President at once presented it to Congress with his recommendation. He argued that it was republican in form, that opportunity had been given for a popular vote on the all-important question of slavery, that acceptance would banish the question of slavery from Congress, and that once admitted as a state the people of Kansas could decide as they saw fit. This stand at once brought about a break between the two factions of the Democratic party. It identified the administration with the Southern wing, and caused the revolt of the supporters of Stephen A. Douglas. Both factions still claimed to be in good party standing, but from now on the full powers of the administration, including that of the patronage, were thrown against Douglas. In the campaign of 1860, the sole public part taken by Buchanan was a speech delivered at the White House, on July 9, 1860, beginning "I have ever been the friend of regular nominations. I have never struck a political ticket in my life," and giving a vigorous support to John C. Breckinridge as Democrat candidate.

The election of Lincoln in November 1860 brought Buchanan to the most critical portion of his career. In October Gen. Scott had advised the President that the result of the election might well be an attempted dissolution of the Union, and that certain preparatory steps be taken, such as the adequate garrisoning of the Southern ports. This advice Buchanan refused to consider. By the end of November it was obvious that secession, at least in South Carolina, would soon follow. The President prepared his message with care, taking legal advice from his attorney-general, Black. It contained a strong denial of the right of secession, but a confession of helplessness in dealing with actual secession, since the federal officers in South Carolina through whom the national executive could enforce the law had resigned. Aside from the collection of the customs and the defense of the property of the United States in South Carolina, the Executive had no authority to act. Congress alone had the power to decide whether the present laws could or could not be amended so as to carry out the objects of the Constitution. The President violently attacked the abolitionists and recommended the repeal of the personal-liberty laws by the Northern states. He also urged an "explanatory amendment" of the Constitution giving express recognition of the right of property in slaves in the states where it existed or might exist, declaring it the duty of the national government to protect this right in the territories, and giving a like recognition of the right to recover fugitive slaves.

In the meantime he exerted his personal influence to keep the peace. He sent Caleb Cushing to Gov. Pickens of South Carolina "to state to you the reasons which exist to prevent, or to delay, the action of the state" (Curtis, *Buchanan*, p. 368). On Dec. 8 he met the South Carolina members of Congress, the result of the conference being an understanding on their part that no violence should be used by the government or people of South Carolina until "an offer has been made through an accredited representative to negotiate for an amiable arrangement of all matters between the State and the Federal Government." Buchanan subsequently declared that he had refused to pledge himself, but on Dec. 15 again refused the advice of Gen. Scott that the forts in Charleston harbor be reinforced. On Dec. 20, 1860 the South Carolina convention voted secession. On Dec. 22 three commissioners were appointed to go to Washington. On Dec. 25 Maj. Anderson, in charge of the United States forces at Charleston, removed his troops from the indefensible Fort Moultrie to the defensible Fort Sumter. This was immediately taken by the South Carolina commissioners to be a change in the *status quo* to the maintenance of which they considered the President committed.

In the meantime Buchanan's administration had begun to fall to pieces. On Dec. 12, 1860, Secretary Cass resigned on the ground that the Charleston forts should be reinforced. Already on Dec. 2, Secretary Cobb had resigned because of the President's denial of the right of secession. Black was immediately appointed secretary of state, his place as attorney-general being taken on Dec. 19 by another Pennsylvania Democrat, Edwin M. Stanton. This changed the balance among the President's advisers during the critical days of Dec. 26 to 31, days in which by the evidence of such observers as Stanton the President lived through an agony of indecision. On Dec. 31 Buchanan replied to the South Carolina commissioners in a letter conciliatory in character, but sustaining the action of Maj. Anderson. Meantime on Dec. 29 the Secretary of War, John B. Floyd of Virginia, resigned, it was said, as a result of financial irregularities. On Jan. 8, 1861, Jacob Thompson of Mississippi, Secretary of the Interior, and on Jan. 11, Philip F. Thomas of Maryland, who had succeeded Howell Cobb as secretary of the treasury, resigned. These resignations were followed by appointments of John A. Dix of New York, as secretary of the treasury, of Joseph Holt of Kentucky, as secretary of war, and Horatio King of Maine, as postmaster-general.

The policy of the administration now changed. The *Star of the West* was sent to Charleston with reinforcements for Fort Sumter. On Jan. 9 it was fired upon by the South Carolina batteries. This resulted in an interchange of notes between Maj. Anderson, who threatened to use his guns on all vessels in and out of Charleston, and Gov. Pickens, who demanded the surrender of Fort Sumter. The matter was referred to Washington. The administration stated its intention to hold Fort Sumter and reinforce it if necessary, but also its intention to keep the peace until "the question shall have been settled by competent authority." In the case of Fort Pickens at Pensacola an agreement was authorized that it should not be reinforced, if not attacked. Meantime the President sponsored bills for a popular referendum on certain proposed amendments to the Constitution, to give the President power to call the militia under certain circumstances, and to provide for the collection of duties at Charleston. None of these bills were passed. Further executive acts were confined to the bringing to Washington of a small force to insure the tranquillity of Lincoln's inauguration. Buchanan took his part in the inauguration, and on Mar. 9 left for Wheatland (J. F. Rhodes, *History of the United States,* chs. XIII and XIV).

Buchanan continued to reside at Wheatland until his death. On Mar. 18, 1861, he wrote John A. Dix, "There is a general desire for peace," but on Apr. 19, 1861, he wrote, "The present administration had no alternative but accept the war instigated by South Carolina or the Southern Confederacy. The North will sustain the administration almost to a man; and it ought to be sustained at all hazards." He supported the administration throughout the war as a Union Democrat. Much of his time he devoted to the preparation of a careful defense of his administration.

Buchanan's career has been viewed almost entirely from the point of view of the last months of his administration. The estimates of his conduct at this time have been colored by the fact that it was pleasing to neither the North nor the South. This came from his sharing in part the views of both, but neither completely. He hated the Abolitionists whom he regarded as the chief cause of dissension; he liked the Southerners personally; he became a strict constructionist; and he favored a laissez-faire policy for the national government. His chief public policy was expansion, which, under the circumstances, meant expansion southward. His administration was undoubtedly strongly influenced by Southern interests. He trusted men who, to some degree at least, were working for the South, and he left the government less prepared for a vigorous enforcement of the laws than he could have done had he exercised a stricter administrative control. The Southern leaders, however, failed to perceive that his devotion to the preservation of the Union was the strongest of his convictions, and were bitterly disappointed when they found that, his effort to content the South having failed, he reverted to the other side. The Northern criticism, that by vigor he might have prevented secession and the formation of the Southern Confederacy, is quite unjustified. The United States did not possess the military force to accomplish such a result. Unlike Lincoln, he failed to find the legal authority to meet secession, but action by Buchanan would probably only have begun the war earlier. There is nothing in his conduct, at the time, however, which indicates political wisdom. He was primarily a constitutional lawyer, confident that the mechanics of law, as established in the United States by the divine voice of the people, was sufficient to solve all problems, and his most distinct emotion was irritation with those who failed to consider legal solutions all-sufficient. He was fitted neither by nature nor by self-training to "ride the whirlwind and command the storm," to which test he was put by an unkind fate.

[Numerous Buchanan MSS. are in the Lib. of Cong., and letters from him are frequent in the papers of many of the men of his time. *The Works of Jas. Buchanan* (1908–11), ed. by J. B. Moore in twelve volumes, contains many public papers and speeches, as well as private correspondence. G. T. Curtis, *Life of Jas. Buchanan* (1883) is a substantial biography, containing many papers by and to Buchanan; it is distinct-

ly a defense. J. F. Rhodes, *Hist. of the U. S.* (1900), vols. II and III, is the most complete historical account yet written of Buchanan's administration. Buchanan's own book, *Mr. Buchanan's Administration on the Eve of the Rebellion* (1866), is an unusually careful document. Extracts from the diary of William L. Marcy, *Am. Hist. Rev.*, XXIV, 641–53, are of some importance. R. G. Horton, *Life and Public Services of Jas. Buchanan* (1856) and C. Jerome, *Life of Jas. Buchanan* (1856) are campaign biographies. Horatio King, *Turning on the Light* (1895) contains letters.]

C. R. F.

BUCHANAN, JOHN (1772–Nov. 6, 1844), Maryland jurist, was born in Prince Georges County, the son of Thomas Buchanan, an English emigrant who settled in Maryland about 1760 and married Mary Cook, a daughter of William and Eliza (Tilghman) Cook. Death having claimed both parents while he was yet a child, he was sent to Charlotte Hall Academy in St. Marys County, and later to the office of Judge Robert White of Winchester, Va., to study law. He remained there but a short time when he found an opportunity to complete his studies with John Thompson Mason of Hagerstown, Md. He served in the lower house of the state legislature, 1797–99, and in 1806 received the appointment as chief judge of the fifth judicial district, by virtue of which he became an associate justice of the Maryland court of appeals. On Oct. 4, 1808 he was married to Sophia, daughter of Judge Eli Williams. Upon the resignation of Judge J. T. Chase he became chief justice of the appellate court, July 27, 1824. He served in that capacity in every session of the court until his death, except for a brief period in 1837 when he was sent to England as one of the commissioners on the part of Maryland to negotiate the sale in London of $8,000,000 of state-secured railroad and canal stocks. The commissioners failed in England (message of Gov. T. W. Veazey, *Maryland Senate Journal*, December Session, 1837), but they did succeed in getting the Chesapeake & Ohio Canal Company and the Baltimore & Ohio Railroad Company to agree, conditionally, to take $6,000,000 of the state stock before they set out for Europe—an arrangement that resulted in heavy losses to both companies (*Maryland Senate Journal*, "Document O," December Session, 1837).

Buchanan has been called one of Maryland's greatest jurists. His diction was polished and unlabored; he was not given to copious citations of authorities; he sought his decisions in an analysis of the social and economic factors which produced the cause rather than in a compilation of obsolete legal precedents. Among his important decisions were those in the cases of *Chesapeake & Ohio Canal Company* vs. *Baltimore & Ohio Railroad Company* (4 *Gill and Johnson*), argued by Daniel Webster and Reverdy Johnson, determining the railroad's privileges conferred by its charter (*Acts of 1826*, ch. 123); and *Calvert* vs. *Davis* (5 *Gill and Johnson*), a leading case in Maryland on testamentary capacity.

[See Wm. McSherry, "The Former Chief Justices of the Court of Appeals of Md." in *Md. State Bar Ass. Report*, 1904; T. J. C. Williams, *Hist. of Washington County, Md.*, vol. I (1906); A. W. P. Buchanan, *The Buchanan Book* (1911); *Laws of the General Assembly State of Md.*, 1836–38; *Baltimore Clipper*, Nov. 8, 1844; *Green Bag*, VI, 229; *Torchlight and Public Advertiser* (Hagerstown, Md.) Nov. 7, 1844. Buchanan's decisions are found in 7 *Harris and Johnson; 1–2 Harris and Gill; 1–12 Gill and Johnson; 1–3 Gill*.]

T. D. M.

BUCHANAN, JOSEPH (Aug. 24, 1785–Sept. 29, 1829), philosopher, educator, inventor, was born in Washington County, Va., the son of Andrew and Joanna Buchanan. His boyhood, spent in Tennessee, was marked by unusual hardships, poverty, and illness. Despite the scantiest opportunities for education, in 1804 he entered Transylvania University. Proficiency in mathematics and critical skepticism of mere authority compensated for his rusticity and diffidence. His empiricism early led him to experiment with devices for improving mills and for producing a color symphony from glasses of different chemical composition—"the music of light," as he called it. Putting aside these experiments without perfecting them, he began the study of medicine, and in 1807, while at Port Gibson, Miss., wrote a volume on fever. He took this with him to Philadelphia, but although Dr. Benjamin Rush is said to have spoken highly of the manuscript, Buchanan was too poor to publish it, or to remain for the medical lectures in Philadelphia. Hence, in 1808, he returned by foot to Lexington, Ky., determined to devote himself to the medical department of Transylvania University, which had only a nominal existence. He was appointed by the trustees as professor of the institutes of medicine, and, in his twenty-fourth year, began the preparation of a course of introductory lectures for medical students. These lectures were published as the *Philosophy of Human Nature* (Richmond, Ky., 1812). For his emphasis on matter rather than on mind and his attempt to construct a materialistic monism he has been called "the earliest native physiological psychologist" (Woodbridge Riley, *American Philosophy: The Early Schools*, 1907, p. 395). He appears later to have modified his views by postulating the spiritualization of matter, although he did not abandon his fundamental monism.

A true pioneer, Buchanan left to others the development of the medical school and went to Philadelphia to study the Pestalozzian system of education, in order to introduce it into Kentucky. While teaching and popularizing this method he prepared *A Practical Grammar of the English Language* (Lexington, 1826). Educational work could no more hold his undivided attention than medicine or philosophy, however, and after studying law, he delivered a course of lectures to a private law class, and entered the field of journalism. After association with the Lexington *Reporter*, the Frankfort *Palladium*, and the *Western Spy and Literary Gazette*, he edited at Louisville, from 1826 till his death, the *Focus*. Although this journal was rather a literary and scientific than a controversial organ, it opposed Jackson and supported Clay (William Henry Perrin, *The Pioneer Press of Kentucky*, 1888, p. 72). Buchanan's early interest in invention continued, and in 1821–22 he constructed a spiral boiler which, because of its superior lightness and efficiency, he hoped might be applied to aerial navigation. In 1824–25 he applied his engine, which seems to have been a prototype of the exploding tubular boiler, to a wagon, with sufficient success, apparently, to astonish "a throng of spectators" in Louisville.

He was married to Nancy Rodes Garth and inculcated in their son, Joseph Rodes Buchanan [*q.v.*], many of his own interests. An admirer remembers the father for his "slender form, massive head, and thoughtful, intellectual face" (Dr. Robert Peter, *The History of the Medical Department of Transylvania University*, 1905, p. 14). His manners were simple and amiable, and his spirit, though ardent and enthusiastic, was critical. Doubtless his great and varied mental powers were dissipated by desultory labors, and by his inability to concentrate on a single task. Essentially an intellectual pioneer working in an environment which encouraged versatility rather than specialization and profundity, he contributed substantially to the development of culture in the Ohio River Valley.

[In addition to references given above, see sketch of Buchanan by his son in Lewis Collins, *Hist. Sketches of Ky.* (1847), pp. 559–60, and compare Lewis and R. H. Collins, *Hist. of Ky.* (1874), II, 218.] M. E. C.

BUCHANAN, JOSEPH RAY (Dec. 6, 1851–Sept. 13, 1924), labor agitator, was born in Hannibal, Mo., the son of Robert Sylvester and Mary Ellen (Holt) Buchanan. After leaving the public schools he was for a time variously employed. About 1876 he obtained work on a Hannibal newspaper, where he learned typesetting. Two years later he went to Denver, where he set type on a daily newspaper, later becoming its managing editor. With a partner he started a printing office, but he soon gave it up and went to prospecting, from which he turned again to typesetting, this time on a newspaper in Leadville, Colo. On Dec. 16, 1879, he was married to Lucy A. Clise. The entrance of the first railway into Leadville, in the summer of 1880 brought to the town hundreds of men in search of work, glutting the labor market. The mine-owners thereupon ordered a reduction of wages, and a strike followed. The contest was carried on with great bitterness, and the leaders of the striking miners were fiercely assailed. Buchanan had made his first acquaintance with the labor movement in Denver, where he had joined the Typographical Union. He had become an ardent trade-unionist and soon became prominent in the strike. A vigilance committee ordered him to leave town; he resisted the order for a time, but on his friends' advice obeyed, and in the spring of 1881 returned to Denver, where he resumed work as a typesetter. In 1882 he was the Denver representative at the convention of the International Typographical Union, and in December, with Samuel H. Laverty as partner, he started a weekly newspaper, the *Labor Enquirer*. In the brief but successful strike of the Union Pacific shopmen against a wage reduction in May 1884, he acted as adviser, as also, about the same time, in the strike of the Colorado coal miners. He was further active in the strike of the shopmen on the Gould lines and later on the Denver & Rio Grande Railroad in the spring of 1885. In the growing conflict between the Knights of Labor and the American Federation of Labor he essayed the futile rôle of peacemaker. He had joined the former organization in 1882 and two years later had been elected to its general board. In 1886 he was a delegate to its convention in Richmond, where, against his protests, action was taken which brought on an open warfare between the two bodies and caused the ruin of the Knights of Labor. His newspaper had been a financial failure from the start and had been maintained only by great personal sacrifice. In 1887 he turned it over to others and moved to Chicago. Here he was active in the unsuccessful effort to obtain a commutation of the sentences of the men convicted of the Haymarket bomb-throwing. In 1888 he moved to New York, subsequently making his home in Montclair, N. J. For many years he was the labor editor of the plate service furnished by the American Press Association. Twice an unsuccessful candidate for Congress in the Montclair district, he each time made an active campaign. From 1904 to 1915 he was the labor editor of the *New York Evening Journal,* and from February 1918 to

July 1921 a member of the conciliation council of the Department of Labor. His last years were inactive. He died at his home in Montclair.

In labor politics Buchanan was an opportunist. His policy of "seeking the line of least resistance" carried him into and out of many radical and reform organizations. A Socialist in principle, he belonged for a time to the Socialist Labor party, but he did not join the newer organization, the Socialist party. He was one of the organizers of the People's (Populist) party, which held its first convention in Omaha in 1892, and he served on its national committee in 1892, 1896, and 1900. He was also a member of Hearst's Independence League, and in his Denver years had been a member of the International Workmen's Association. To the end he was a devoted trade-unionist. He was an eloquent and forceful speaker. Tall, somewhat slender, with a shock of unruly hair that even in his middle years had become white, and bearing himself with a native grace of manner, he was an impressive figure on the platform. His personality was attractive, his character was honest, and in the fierce conflicts that from time to time divided the labor and radical movements he retained the esteem even of those who strongly opposed him.

[*Who's Who in America,* 1924–25; *The Story of a Labor Agitator* (an autobiography, 1903); recollections of the writer, based on an acquaintance of thirty-nine years.]

W.J.G.

BUCHANAN, JOSEPH RODES (Dec. 11, 1814–Dec. 26, 1899), erratic physician and writer, was born in Frankfort, Ky., of a Virginia family which had early moved to Kentucky. He was the son of Joseph Buchanan [*q.v.*] and Nancy Rodes (Garth) Buchanan. From his father, an intellectual jack-of-all-trades, philosopher, educator, physician, and journalist, he seems to have inherited an unstable disposition and a brilliant mind which the eager parent over-stimulated in childhood. An infant prodigy, the boy was versed in geometry and astronomy at the age of six, then took up sociology, and at the age of twelve began to study law. After the death of his father in 1829, he supported himself for a time first as a printer, then as a school-teacher. Becoming interested in phrenology and cerebral physiology, he entered the Medical School of the University of Louisville where he graduated in 1842. While still in college he laid the foundations for two new so-called sciences which he later elaborated, "psychometry" and "sarcognomy," the former demonstrating the excitability of cerebral tissue by the aura of another person, the latter dealing with the sympathetic relations between other parts of the body and the indwelling soul. The trained psychometer, he held, could diagnose any disease at sight of the patient or even by letter, while the sarcognomist could heal all diseases by making dispersive passes over the body, particularly if the patient sat with his feet in a tub of water. Buchanan lectured upon his alleged discoveries with great success throughout both the North and the South, and established a periodical, *The Journal of Man,* in which for many years he promulgated his extraordinary views. On Mar. 25, 1846, he joined the faculty of the Eclectic Medical Institute of Cincinnati, and during the next decade his truculent disposition made him a prominent figure in the turbulent history of that institution. Forced out in 1856, he at first started a rival institution, the Eclectic College of Medicine, but, soon disagreeing with his colleagues, he removed to Louisville, and in 1863 unsuccessfully ran for Congress as the Peace party candidate. Later he removed to Syracuse, N. Y., and manufactured salt. In 1867 he became professor of physiology in the Eclectic Medical College of New York City, where he remained until 1881 when he established his own college of therapeutics in Boston. On account of his health he removed in 1892 to Kansas City, Mo., and in 1893 to San José, Cal., where he resided until his death. He was married three times: in 1841 to Anne Rowan of Louisville; in 1881 to Mrs. Cornelia H. Decker, a clairvoyant of New York City; in 1894 to Elizabeth S. Worthington of Denver. His highly original medical theories, which may have influenced the later career of the notorious Albert Abrams [*q.v.*] were set forth in a series of volumes of which the most important were *Therapeutic Sarcognomy* (1884) and *Manual of Psychometry* (1885). His last production was a two-volume semi-spiritualistic work entitled *Primitive Christianity* (1897–98), including lives of the Apostles which he said had been dictated to him by the Apostles themselves. He was a man who loved humanity in general, who hated his neighbors, and who throughout his long life remained peculiarly gifted with self-confidence, expressed in his erect carriage, lifted head, and smile of infinite condescension.

[Harvey Wickes Felter, *Hist. of the Eclectic Medic. Institute* (1902), containing sketch and numerous references; less full accounts in *Allibone's Dict. of Authors, Supp.* (1891) and in Kelly and Burrage, *Am. Medic. Biogs.* (1920).]
          E.S.B.

BUCHANAN, ROBERT CHRISTIE (Mar. 1, 1811–Nov. 29, 1878), Union soldier, was born in Baltimore, Md. His paternal ancestry dated back to Dr. George Buchanan, an immigrant from Scotland to Maryland as early as the year

1698, whose son, Andrew Buchanan, was a brigadier-general of the Maryland militia during the American Revolution. The father of Robert Christie Buchanan was Andrew Buchanan of Baltimore; his mother was Carolina Virginia Marylanda Johnson, daughter of Joshua Johnson, Esq., and sister of Mrs. John Quincy Adams (Roberdeau Buchanan, *Genealogy of the McKean Family of Pennsylvania,* 1890). When but fifteen years of age, young Buchanan received appointment to the United States Military Academy from the District of Columbia,—his legal guardian at the time being Mr. Nathaniel Frye, Jr. He graduated Number 31 in a class of forty-two members, and on July 1, 1830, received his commission as second lieutenant, 4th Infantry. Upon graduation, he participated in the Black Hawk War of 1832, and commanded the gunboats in the engagement of Bad Axe River. He served as adjutant of his regiment from 1835 to 1838,—having been promoted first lieutenant, Mar. 16, 1836, and captain, Nov. 1, 1838. In 1837–38 he took part in the arduous campaign against the Seminole Indians.

Buchanan entered the war with Mexico as a captain in the 4th Infantry, Ulysses S. Grant being a lieutenant in the same organization. He went through the campaigns of both Generals Taylor and Scott, and was brevetted major, May 9, 1846, for gallant and distinguished services at Palo Alto and at Resaca de la Palma; and lieutenant-colonel Sept. 8, 1847, for gallant and meritorious services at the taking of Molino del Rey, where it is said Buchanan forced the doors of the stronghold with his own hands (J. C. Ropes, *The Army under Pope,* 1881, p. 140). Shortly after the war with Mexico he married Miss Winder, a grand-daughter of Gov. Lloyd of Maryland. He received his majority in the regular army, Feb. 3, 1855, his lieutenant-colonelcy Sept. 9, 1861, and during the decade preceding the Civil War, was associated in the old 4th Infantry, with such distinguished officers as Grant, Sheridan, Judah, Crook, Alvord, and D. A. Russell.

At the outbreak of the Civil War, Buchanan's regiment formed part of the defense of Washington; and from November 1861 to March 1862 during McClellan's Peninsular Campaign he commanded with distinction a brigade in Gen. Sykes's famous "Regular Division." On June 27, 1862, he was brevetted colonel for services at Gaines's Mill, and was brevetted brigadier-general, Mar. 13, 1865, for similar distinguished service at Malvern Hill, where his brigade drove a portion of the enemy from the field and captured a flag. In the much discussed withdrawal of McClellan's army to Harrison's Landing, following the battles before Richmond, Buchanan had the difficult responsibility of covering much of the movement with his brigade. And of the Second Battle of Bull Run, which followed, Gen. John Pope has said: "Porter's Corps . . . was pushed to the support of our left, where it rendered distinguished service, especially the brigade of regulars under Colonel (then Lieutenant-Colonel) Buchanan" (*Battles and Leaders of the Civil War*, II, 487, and *The Army under Pope*, p. 142). Buchanan was made a brigadier-general of volunteers, Nov. 29, 1862, and commanded his brigade in the bloody battle of Antietam, and in front of the famous "stone wall" at Fredericksburg, where his command suffered serious casualties. His commission as brigadier-general having expired, Mar. 4, 1863, he was placed in command of the defenses of Fort Delaware, and attained his colonelcy in the regular army, Feb. 8, 1864. On Mar. 13, 1865, as the war was about to end, he received the brevet of major-general for his distinguished services in the battles of Second Bull Run (Manassas) and Fredericksburg.

Late in the year 1865, Buchanan was a member of an important military commission, investigating complaints by the government of Prussia regarding enlistments, and in the year 1867 was a member of the Iowa Claims Commission. In 1868, after serving for a short period as an assistant commissioner in the Freedman's Bureau, he was placed in command of the important Department of Louisiana, where the work of reconstruction and the problems attendant upon the readmission of Louisiana to the Union were beset with many difficulties. On Apr. 16 and 17, 1868, the state voted for state officers, as well as for a constitution which would permit of entrance into the Union; and while the election passed off quietly, many controversies subsequently followed and much ill-feeling resulted. Acting under instructions from Gen. Grant, Buchanan installed into office the newly elected Gov. H. C. Warmoth, and Lieut.-Gov. Oscar J. Dunn (a negro), and later, upon the ratification by Louisiana of the Fourteenth Amendment, Buchanan declared military law no longer existent in the state (J. R. Ficklen, *History of Reconstruction in Louisiana*, 1910, pp. 199–204, and *Appleton's Annual Cyclopedia*, vol. VIII, 1878, p. 431). Buchanan commanded Fort Porter, New York, during 1869–70, was retired from active service, Dec. 31, 1870, and died in Washington, D. C., Nov. 29, 1878. He was affectionately known to Civil War soldiers as "Old Buck," and his brigade of regular soldiers proved always a dependable reserve in many of the earlier battles of

the war. That such was the case was largely due to his wide experience, fine attainments, and high sense of duty and of discipline.

[In addition to references given above, see F. B. Heitman, *Hist. Reg.* (1914) ; Justin H. Smith, *The War with Mexico* (1919) ; C. M. Wilcox, *Hist. of the Mexican War* (1892) ; *Battles and Leaders of the Civil War* (1887–88), vols. II, III.]
C.D.R.

BUCHANAN, THOMAS (Dec. 24, 1744– Nov. 10, 1815), merchant, descended from a line of prosperous Scotch merchants, was born at Glasgow, the son of George and Jean (Lowden) Buchanan. His father was a man of liberal education and young Thomas studied at the University of Glasgow in addition to acquiring experience in his father's counting-house. In 1763 he went to New York where he soon entered into partnership with his father's cousin Walter, who was already established in business there. This firm of W. & T. Buchanan owned several ships and their extensive trade with the British ports gave them a place among the foremost New York commercial houses. Thomas Buchanan married Almy, the daughter of Jacob Townsend of Oyster Bay, on Mar. 17, 1766. He signed the original non-importation agreement in 1766 and was elected a member of the Chamber of Commerce at its second meeting in 1768. Two years later, he was active in the attempt to restore normal trade (*Post Boy*, July 23, 1770). There seems to be no authority for the frequently repeated statement that Buchanan, who had dissolved the partnership with his cousin in 1772, was the consignee of the New York tea ship *Nancy* in 1773 (Francis S. Drake, *Tea Leaves*, 1884, p. 305). In 1775, he was a member of the local Committee of One Hundred (Carl L. Becker, *The History of Political Parties in the Province of New York, 1760–1776*, 1909, p. 198), but a year later he signed the Loyalist address to Howe. During the war, he continued active business, maintaining a fairly neutral stand, for his own Loyalist position was counterbalanced by the activity of his wife's family on the other side. He served as vice-president of the Chamber of Commerce from 1780 to 1783 when he was elected president. He prudently declined to serve, for the Chamber was soon reorganized with "patriot" officers who had been absent from the city during the British occupation. His property escaped confiscation and his Tory stand did not prevent him from carrying on an extensive foreign trade, principally with Scotland and Jamaica, for more than thirty years after the Revolution. His son George was later taken into partnership. Like many American firms, the Buchanans suffered from the suspension of trade during the embargo and the War of 1812. In 1815, the year of his death, Thomas

Buchanan's estate was valued at $50,000 (*Valentine's Manual*, 1864, p. 756). He had a residence and counting-house on Wall St. and a country seat on the East River near Hell Gate. He was a member of the First Presbyterian Church and the St. Andrew's Society, and a director of the United Insurance Company. He is described as of middle height, slender in youth but quite corpulent later, with sandy hair, light-blue eyes, and a florid complexion. He died at his home on Wall St. Nov. 10, 1815, not Sept. 10, as has been frequently stated (*Commercial Advertiser*, Nov. 11, 1815).

[Short biographical sketches appear in John Austin Stevens, *Colonial Records of the Chamber of Commerce of the State of N. Y.*, 1768–84 (1867), pp. 125–28; Wm. M. MacBean, *Biog. Reg. of the St. Andrew's Soc. of the State of N. Y.* (1922), I, 96; and A. W. Buchanan, *The Buchanan Book* (1911), p. 457. These incorporate some of the half-dozen errors found in the scattered remarks concerning Buchanan in Jos. A. Scoville, *The Old Merchants of N. Y.* (1863–66). The extent of Buchanan's trade may be judged by the advertisements of his firm which appeared regularly in the N. Y. newspapers of the period. A few of his business letters are preserved by the N. Y. Hist. Soc.]
R.G.A.

BUCHANAN, WILLIAM INSCO (Sept. 10, 1852–Oct. 16, 1909), business man, amusement-manager, diplomat, was descended from a Scotch family which had been settled in Virginia since the second half of the eighteenth century. His grandfather, Col. George Buchanan, in 1806 moved to Miami County, Ohio, where, near the town of Covington, William Insco Buchanan was born, the son of George Preston and Mary Elizabeth (Gibson) Buchanan. Left an orphan before he was nine years old, William received his only schooling from the country schools. Before he was thirty he had learned the trade of edge-tool making, had nibbled at politics (he was engrossing clerk of the Indiana legislature, 1874–75), and had been for half a dozen years a commercial traveler. He was married on Apr. 16, 1878, to Lulu Williams of Dayton, Ohio. In 1882 he settled in Sioux City, Iowa, and there, after a venture in wholesale trade as a jobber of crockery, he opened a theatre. In this enterprise, and in promoting the four "corn-palaces" of that city (1887–90), of which he was the moving spirit—serving as manager of the last and most elaborate—he revealed rare talents as an amusement-manager and executive, which led to his appointment as the Democratic member of the Iowa commission to the World's Columbian Exposition held in Chicago in 1893. In this he was chief of the department of agriculture (1890–93) and organizer of the departments of live stock and forestry (1891), and was remarkably successful. In these varied callings he found opportunity to exercise the social sense and judgment of men that were

essential factors in his achievements in the diplomatic service which filled the rest of his life.

Buchanan's diplomatic career began with his appointment by President Cleveland in 1894 as envoy extraordinary and minister plenipotentiary to the Argentine Republic. One evidence of his felicitous discharge of his duties in this post, which he held for six years, was his designation by Chile and Argentina as umpire of a commission appointed by those countries to settle their extreme northern boundary line in the desert of Atacama. After an interim of one year's service as director-general of the Pan-American Exposition held in Buffalo in 1901, Buchanan represented his country, successively, as one of the delegates to the Second International Conference of American States (at Mexico City, October 1901); as its first envoy extraordinary and minister plenipotentiary accredited, first on special mission (Dec. 12, 1903) and then on regular appointment, to Panama (Dec. 17, 1903–05); as chairman of its delegation to the Third International Conference of American States (at Rio de Janeiro, July 1906); as one of its commissioners to the second Peace Conference at The Hague (June–October, 1907); as its representative in attendance upon the Central American Peace Conference held in Washington in 1907 (November–December); as high commissioner at the installation of the Central American Court of Justice at Cartago, Costa Rica (May 25, 1908); as high commissioner charged with the renewal of diplomatic relations with Venezuela (Dec. 21, 1908–09) after the overthrow of President Cipriano Castro; and as agent of the United States in the prospective arbitration before the international court of arbitration at The Hague of the only claim against Venezuela that he had failed to settle diplomatically. He was also a member of a Pan-American committee appointed by Secretary of State Elihu Root in 1907 to stimulate Pan-American comity, and was appointed chairman (Feb. 21, 1908) of another Pan-American committee charged with the preparation of the Fourth International Conference of American States. His discharge of his diplomatic duties was unvaryingly felicitous, as the mere list of his appointments indicates. He gained tariff concessions for United States commodities, settled old claims, consummated long-pending negotiations. Particularly notable were his services at the Central American Peace Conference and in settlement of our distempered relations with Venezuela. He was extremely well informed on Latin-American affairs, and seemed to possess an intuitive understanding of Latin-Americans. Upon his retirement from the Argentine post

Buchanan became the representative of the New York Life Insurance Company in the adjustment of differences arising between it and foreign governments, particularly those of South America, and remained in the Company's service until his death. About 1902 he also joined the Westinghouse interests, serving from 1903 to 1905 as managing director of the British Westinghouse Company and an officer of the French Westinghouse Company, and through life continuing otherwise to serve the parent American company. In these very important business duties his success was as uniform as in his governmental service. In both he showed a broad and liberal spirit, "basing his claims upon justice and pressing them with courtesy and with proper regard for the rights and customs of the people with whom he dealt" (resolutions of the New York Life Insurance Company, Oct. 20, 1909); and in both fields his country reaped the legitimate fruits of a sound diplomacy, an increase of commercial intercourse and a better international understanding.

[See A. W. P. Buchanan, *The Buchanan Book* (1911), and the *Buffalo Morning Express,* the *Evening Star* (Washington, D. C.), the *N. Y. Tribune,* the *Chicago Daily Tribune,* the *Sioux City Jour.,* all of Oct. 18, 1909; *Hist. of the Counties of Woodbury and Plymouth, Iowa* (1890–91), pp. 92, 746; *Who's Who in America,* 1908–09. Buchanan's diplomatic career can be traced through the *Monthly Bulletin of the International Bureau of the American Republics* and in the Department of State's lists of its diplomatic representatives. The year of his birth, sometimes given as 1853, was really 1852 according to Buchanan's daughter.]
F.S.P.

BUCHER, JOHN CONRAD (June 10, 1730– Aug. 15, 1780), German Reformed clergyman, soldier, was born at Neunkirch, Switzerland, six miles west of Schaffhausen, the third of the six children of Hans Jacob and Anna Dorothea (Burgauer) Bucher. He was sixth in descent from Claus Bucher of Lindau, who became a citizen of Schaffhausen in the first half of the sixteenth century. His father was made *landvogt* of Neunkirch in 1745. Bucher studied at the gymnasium in Schaffhausen, at St. Gall, and at the University of Marburg, where he matriculated July 14, 1752. While a student he paid several visits to some friends stationed at Namur as officers of Swiss troops, and these visits are thought to have awakened in him a desire for military experience. He was last in Marburg, according to his album book, in April 1755. The circumstances under which he came, shortly after, to Pennsylvania are unknown. According to John Christian Stahlschmidt's *Pilgerreise zu Wasser und zu Land* (Nuremberg, 1799, p. 287) Bucher was an officer of Dutch troops that were sent to America to serve as mercenaries under Braddock; and the date of his landing at Philadelphia is sometimes given as Nov. 1, 1755; but

the first authenticated fact about his American career is that on Apr. 11, 1758, he was commissioned ensign in the 1st Battalion of the Pennsylvania Regiment. He took part in the expedition against Fort Duquesne in that year and was stationed over winter at Carlisle. During the next two winters he commanded the garrison at Carlisle. He was commissioned lieutenant of the 2nd Battalion Apr. 19, 1760, participated in the War of Pontiac's Conspiracy, and was commissioned adjutant July 12 and captain July 31, 1764. He was a trusted and capable officer. When the war ended next spring he resigned.

Meanwhile, on Feb. 26, 1760, he was married at Carlisle to Mary Magdalena, daughter of John George Hoke (Hans Georg Hauk). She and four of their six children survived him. While still in the militia Bucher began to preach; his earliest sermon notes and records of ministerial acts date from March 1763. In 1766 the Coetus of Pennsylvania, in applying to the Classis of Amsterdam for authority to ordain him, described Bucher as one "made willing by the Lord to serve these people, who devotes himself with all diligence to learn the truth and to expound it to others, and is also content to share the poverty of his hearers" (*Minutes,* p. 244). The Classis authorized his ordination in a letter of June 20, 1767. Until 1768 he served congregations at Carlisle, Middletown, Hummelstown, and Falling Spring (Chambersburg). From time to time he made missionary trips westward to Bedford near Fort Cumberland, Redstone (Brownsville), Big Crossings of the Yiogheny, and Fort Pitt, riding hundreds of miles through the forest and over rugged mountains. He was the first minister to preach in German beyond the Alleghanies. After 1770, however, he seldom crossed the Susquehanna. Making Lebanon his headquarters, he ministered to about eleven scattered little congregations, including Quittapahilla, Manheim, Weisseichenland, Hummelstown, and Lancaster. In 1775 he was secretary of the Coetus. At the outbreak of the Revolution he was a chaplain in the "German Regiment" under Baron von Arnt, but ill health caused him to resign Aug. 1, 1777. A backwoods missionary, he kept up his scholarship; several hundred sermon outlines, with citations from Latin, Greek, and Hebrew, have been preserved among his papers. He died at Annville of a heart attack during the festivities attendant on a wedding. His body was carried to Lebanon for burial.

[H. Harbaugh, *The Fathers of the Ger. Ref. Ch.,* vol. II (1857); T. C. Porter, "The Bucher Album" in *Proc. and Addresses Pa. Ger. Soc.,* V, 133–40 (1895); G. B. Ayres, "Rev. Capt. J. C. Bucher" in W. H. Egle's *Notes and Queries Hist. and Geneal.,* II, 411–16 (1895); W. H. Agle, *Pa. Genealogies* (1886; 2nd ed., 1896);

Pa. Archives, 5 ser., vols. I and VII; A. Stapleton, "Rev. John Conrad Bucher" in the *Pa. German,* IV, 291–308 (1903); *Minutes and Letters of the Coetus of the Ger. Ref. Congregations in Pa. 1747–92* (1903): F. B. Heitman, *Hist. Reg. of Officers of the Continental Army* (new ed., 1914); an unpublished article on Bucher by Prof. Wm. J. Hinke of Auburn Theological Seminary, who has also given his personal assistance in the preparation of this article.]   G.H.G.

BUCHTEL, JOHN RICHARDS (Jan. 18, 1820–May 23, 1892), business man, philanthropist, son of John and Catharine (Richards) Buchtel, was born in Green Township, then in Stark County, now a part of Summit County, Ohio. His boyhood was spent in hard work on his father's farm. Educational advantages were meager. In his later teens he sold clocks and bought and sold horses, but these ventures proved unprofitable and he returned to farming. In 1844 he married Elizabeth Davidson. In 1854 he became a salesman for Ball, Aultman & Company of Canton, Ohio, manufacturers of mowers and reapers. He was largely instrumental in persuading the firm to build an Akron branch ten years later, and became the first president of the Buckeye Company, as the Akron branch was popularly known. In 1877, with other capitalists, he undertook the development of the mineral resources of the Hocking Valley. The extent of this project may be guessed from the fact that in 1880 alone the company paid the Hocking Valley Railroad a million dollars for freight charges. For several years Buchtel had the active management of this enterprise, and its remarkable success was due largely to his energy and wisdom. He was keenly interested in civic affairs, and gave generously of time and money to whatever he believed was for the public good. In 1872 he was a presidential elector; in 1874, candidate for secretary of state on the Prohibition ticket; and for several years a trustee of the State Agricultural College.

In 1887, while in the Hocking Valley, he was stricken with paralysis, and was never again able to take an active part in business. Buchtel's greatest monument is Buchtel College (now the University of Akron). While tolerant of all religious faiths, he was an ardent Universalist, and when in 1870, the Universalists of Ohio undertook to found a college, his gift of $31,000 brought the college to Akron. Thenceforward he and Mrs. Buchtel, being childless, lavished upon the new college their affection and generosity. By 1882 their gifts had reached $138,828 and eventually nearly half a million. Buchtel was one of the incorporators of the college, and was president of the Board of Trustees until his death. His leading characteristics were energy, sincerity, bluntness of manner with sympathy and kindness of heart.

[Samuel Lane, *Fifty Years and Over of Akron and Summit County* (1892); A. I. Spanton, ed., *Fifty Years of Buchtel, 1870–1920* (1922).]   A.I.S.

BUCK, ALBERT HENRY (Oct. 20, 1842–Nov. 16, 1922), otologist and medical historian, was one of five children of Gurdon Buck [*q.v.*], surgeon of New York, by his wife, Henriette Elisabeth Wolff of Geneva, Switzerland. He received a part of his early education near his mother's native haunts in Switzerland and there laid the foundation of the linguistic powers for which he became subsequently distinguished. He was graduated from Yale in 1864 and obtained his M.D. from the College of Physicians and Surgeons of Columbia in 1867. After an internship in the New York Hospital he spent several years in Germany and Austria studying the physiology and diseases of the ear. He was married in 1871 to Laura S. Abbott, daughter of John S. C. Abbott [*q.v.*]. In 1872 he was made aural surgeon at the New York Eye and Ear Infirmary, with which institution he remained associated until his death. From 1888 to 1904 he held the post of clinical professor of diseases of the ear in the College of Physicians and Surgeons of Columbia University. Throughout his life he was a prolific writer and made numerous contributions to otological journals. One of his early literary accomplishments was the editing of the American edition of H. W. Ziemssen's *Cyclopædia of the Practice of Medicine* in fifteen volumes, published between 1874 and 1880; a second edition appeared in 1890. In association with Joseph Decatur Bryant [*q.v.*], he edited the *American Practice of Surgery* in eight volumes, published between 1906 and 1911. Smaller works were his editions of Salomon Stricker's *Manual of Histology* (1872) and of the two-volume *Treatise on Hygiene and Public Health* (1879). His most important contribution was his *Diagnosis and Treatment of Ear Diseases* (1880), which passed through three editions. This last work represented the results of his own observation and study and was for many years the *vade-mecum* of students and otologists. Buck's studies on the physiology of the ear were also important. His first published paper (1870) was entitled "An Essay on the Mechanism of the Ossicles of the Ear," and three years later he edited the New York edition of Helmholtz's classic work bearing the same title.

After Buck resigned his professorship in 1904 he gradually withdrew from private practise, and about 1910 began an intensive study of the history of medicine. His first contribution in this field, *The Growth of Medicine from the Earliest Times to about 1800* was published in 1917 under the auspices of the Williams Memorial Publication Fund of Yale University. The book is admittedly a compilation chiefly from secondary sources, but Buck's gift for writing and his energetic style made the volume attractive and stimulating. His second historical work, *The Dawn of Modern Medicine,* was published in 1920 and was intended as a sequel to the first. For it the sources were thoroughly studied and advantage was taken of the rich collection of early nineteenth century medical works in the library of Transylvania College at Lexington, Ky. The chapters on Bichat and Laennec are particularly attractive.

[See A. H. Buck, *The Bucks of Wethersfield, Conn.* (1909); *Hist. of the Class of 1864, Yale Coll.* (1895); obituary by R. Lewis and E. B. Dench in the *N. Y. Medical Jour.,* CXVII, 48. Extensive lists of Buck's papers are given in the *Index Cat. of the Surgeon-General's Library,* 1, 2, 3 ser.]   J.F.F.

BUCK, DANIEL (Nov. 9, 1753–Aug. 16, 1816), lawyer, legislator, was the second son of Thomas and Jane Buck. He was born in Hebron, Conn., and while young emigrated to Thetford, Vt., which was largely settled by emigrants from Hebron. During the American Revolution, he lost an arm in the battle of Bennington. In 1784 or 1785 he removed to Norwich, Vt., where he was one of the first settlers. He studied law and was the first lawyer to open an office in Norwich. In 1791 he represented Norwich in the convention called to determine whether Vermont would ratify or reject the United States Constitution. The chief opposition came from a group of Windsor County towns and Buck was its leader and spokesman, but he finally voted for immediate union with the new nation. That his opposition to statehood did not prejudice Vermonters against him is shown by his election as speaker of the Assembly in 1793 and 1794. He served one term in Congress as a Federalist (1795–97), making the journey to the seat of government on horseback with his fellow townsmen accompanying him to the border of the neighboring town. He made one of the ablest speeches delivered in defense of the position of the Washington administration on the Jay Treaty, opposing the attempt to compel the executive department to deliver to Congress its instructions to the American envoy (*Annals of Congress,* 4 Cong., 1 Sess., pp. 430–35, 703–17), but he was defeated for reëlection. He served as a member of the Council of Censors (1792), as attorney-general of the state (1794), and as state's attorney of Windsor County (1802–03). In 1806 he was again in the legislature and was active in establishing a state bank. He was married on Sept. 22, 1786 to Content Ashley of Norwich by whom he had eleven children. The eldest son, Daniel A. A. Buck, became a member of Congress.

[M. E. Goddard and H. V. Partridge, *Hist. of Norwich, Vt.* (1905); Leonard Deming, *Cat. of the Principal Officers of Vt.* (1851); *Biog. Cong. Dir.* (1903); W. H. Crockett, *Vt., the Green Mt. State* (1921), vols. II, III.]   W.H.C.

BUCK, DUDLEY (Mar. 10, 1839–Oct. 6, 1909), composer, organist, was born in Hartford, Conn., the son of Dudley and Martha Church (Adams) Buck, and grandson of Daniel Buck, also of Hartford. His earliest American ancestor was Emanuel Buck, who, soon after his arrival at Plymouth Colony from England, became one of the original settlers of Wethersfield, Conn., in 1647. There is no evidence of musical ability in any of his immediate ancestors. His mother, however, had a deep love of poetry and it was her custom to read aloud her favorite poems to her son during his early years. Young Dudley had been destined for a business career by his father, who was a prominent shipping merchant and owner of a line of steamships plying between Hartford and New York City. But he early displayed an unusual aptitude for music, and, although he was self-taught until he was sixteen years old, he finally obtained, with some difficulty, the consent of his parents to prepare himself for a professional career in music,—a procedure directly athwart the New England prejudices of the time. In 1855 he took his first piano lessons of W. J. Babcock of Hartford, and at the same time entered Trinity College, where he remained three years. He applied himself to his music with such ardor and revealed such unmistakable talent that his father sent him to Europe in 1858 for extended study,—eighteen months (1858–59) at the Leipzig Conservatory with Hauptmann and Richter (harmony and composition), Plaidy and Moscheles (piano), and J. Rietz (orchestration); later at Dresden with Rietz and Johann Schneider (organ); and one year (1861–62) in Paris. On his return to Hartford in 1862 he was appointed organist of the North Congregational Church. He was married on Oct. 3, 1865, to Mary Elizabeth van Wagener of Burlington, N. J., and in 1869, heeding the call of the West, he went to Chicago to become organist at St. James's Episcopal Church. After the great fire of Oct. 9, 1871, which destroyed his home with valuable library and manuscripts, he removed to Boston (1872) as organist of St. Paul's Church and, soon after, of Music Hall, the highest honor a Boston musician of that period could attain. In 1875 he was official organist of the Cincinnati May Festival and on his return to Boston accepted the invitation of Theodore Thomas to be assistant conductor of his orchestral concerts at Central Park Garden in New York. He removed his family to Brooklyn and began his long musical career there as organist in various churches, while from 1877 to 1903 he was conductor of the Apollo Club (male chorus). In 1903 he resigned all positions and retired to private life, dividing his "playtime," as he called it, between travel and composition. His death occurred at Orange, N. J.

Buck was one of the first American composers to possess musicianship of genuine solidity, with respect both to technical equipment and creative ability. American organ-music practically begins with him. As a concert-organist of imposing ability, his extensive tours during the first fifteen years of his public life helped greatly to uplift standards of organ-playing and organ-music, both of which were in dire need of improvement. He was the first American composer to gain wide recognition in this field. His best organ works include two Sonatas (in E-flat and G-minor), Concert Variations on "The Star Spangled Banner," and several shorter pieces (as "At Evening"); also a valuable handbook, *Illustrations in Choir Accompaniment, with Hints on Registration*. His first published compositions were written to supply the needs of his own choir in Hartford. When his first *Motet Collection* appeared in 1864 (a second book followed later), it met with immediate success, which led him to give increasing attention, as composer, to church-music. Indeed, his influence in this field was probably stronger and more lasting than in any other to which he contributed, for the needs of American Protestant church-music could not be met, as could those of choral societies and organists, by mere importation of foreign-made music. His many excellent anthems, solos, hymns, *Te Deums*, etc. (there are about 140 of these),— fluent, attractive, well-constructed, and many of them of real depth and fervor—offered a refreshing contrast to the insipid and trivial music in general use in American churches of this period and produced a marked improvement in public taste. His versatility led him to write also in the large forms: *Serápis* (1895), text by himself, an unperformed grand opera on an Egyptian subject; *Deseret* (1880), a comic opera on a Mormon theme; "In Springtime," a symphony; "Marmion," a symphonic overture (first performed by the Thomas Orchestra, 1881); some chamber music, etc. By far the most important of his large works, however, are his concert cantatas. Of these, five are for male chorus and twelve for mixed chorus. Of the former group the best probably are "The Nun of Nidaros" and "Paul Revere's Ride." Of the latter group especial mention must be made of "The Centennial Meditation of Columbia," written for the Centennial Exposition and performed at Philadelphia,

May 10, 1876, under Theodore Thomas's direction by a chorus of 1,000 and an orchestra of 200, by which Buck's reputation as a composer was firmly established; "The Golden Legend," which won the prize offered by the Cincinnati May Festival Association for the best work by an American and was first performed at the Festival in 1880; "The Light of Asia," his largest and most pretentious choral work (first English performance at St. James's Hall, London, Mar. 19, 1889); and "The Christian Year," a series of five effective cantatas for the important church festivals. Mention must be made of his wide influence as a teacher, for he was the direct source of inspiration to a large number of pupils. In disposition he was genial and warm-hearted; and he combined tact and practical wisdom in dealing with his public.

[A. H. Buck, *The Bucks of Wethersfield, Conn.* (1909); *Grove's Dict. of Music and Musicians* (Am. Supp., revised ed., 1928), pp. 146–47; *Baker's Biog. Dict. of Musicians* (3rd ed., 1919); Rossetter Cole, *Choral and Ch. Music* (1916), pp. 218–20, 498; R. Hughes and A. Elson, *Am. Composers* (1914), pp. 165–74; G. P. Upton, *The Standard Cantatas* (1888), pp. 101–22; Louis C.Elson, *The Hist.of Am.Music* (1904), pp. 230–32.]

R.G.C.

BUCK, GURDON (May 4, 1807–Mar. 6, 1877), surgeon, was the son of a New York merchant bearing the same name, by his cousin, Susannah Manwaring, who, like her husband, was a grandchild of Gov. Gurdon Saltonstall of Connecticut. Buck received his preliminary education at the Nelson Classical School where he prepared for higher studies, but instead of going to college he yielded to his father's wishes and became a clerk in the house of G. & D. Buck. Soon developing an interest in medicine, however, he left his position and entered the office of Dr. Thomas Cock, under whom he completed his medical studies. In 1830 he obtained his M.D. from the College of Physicians and Surgeons at New York. After eighteen months in the New York Hospital (1832) he had the advantage of two years' study in the hospitals of Paris, Berlin, and Vienna. On a second trip to Europe in 1836 he married (July 27), Henriette Elizabeth Wolff of Geneva, Switzerland. When he finally settled in New York (1837) he became visiting surgeon to the New York Hospital, and later to St. Luke's (1846) and to the Presbyterian Hospital (1872); in addition he was associated from 1852 to 1862 with the New York Eye and Ear Infirmary.

Buck was one of the great American surgeons of the pre-Lister era. A scholarly anatomist and a bold operator, he was at the same time rapid, skilful, and humane. He studied his cases with a diligence that was rare in those early days, and especially praiseworthy was the attention which he bestowed upon post-operative treatment. He kept careful case histories and his surgical publications always reflected his painstaking methods. His chief contributions relate to his methods of managing fractures and to plastic surgery. His advocacy of treatment of fractures of the thigh by means of weights and pulleys received prompt recognition in other parts of the world. The device which he introduced is still used and is known as "Buck's extension." His methods were well described in a pamphlet published in 1867 entitled *Description of an Improved Extension Apparatus for the Treatment of Fracture of the Thigh*. As early as 1842 Buck had performed a successful excision of the olecranon process of the elbow joint (*American Journal of Medical Science,* April 1843, pp. 297-301). He was also a pioneer in plastic surgery of the face, and the year before his death he published *Contributions to Reparative Surgery* (1876), an admirable monograph describing his own experience in this field. It was excellently illustrated from photographs of his cases and attracted wide attention, being translated into three foreign languages. A complete bibliography of his numerous contributions to medical and surgical journals is given in the *Transactions of the Medical Society of the State of New York* for 1877, pp. 370-74. His son, Albert H. Buck [*q.v.*] was a physician.

[A. H. Buck, *The Bucks of Wethersfield* (1909); F. A. Castle, obituary in the *Trans. Med. Soc. of the State of N. Y.* (1877), pp. 367-70; *Medic. Record,* Mar. 10, 1877, p. 158; Buck's introduction to his *Reparative Surgery* (1876).]   J.F.F.

BUCK, LEFFERT LEFFERTS (Feb. 5, 1837–July 17, 1909), civil engineer, was born at Canton, N. Y., the third son of Lemuel and Elizabeth (Baldridge) Buck. He inherited the courage and dexterity as well as the gaunt frame and swarthy countenance of his New England ancestors who had participated in every conflict that had arisen since Emanuel Buck settled at Wethersfield, Conn., in 1647 (Cornelius B. Harvey, *Origin, History and Genealogy of the Buck Family,* 1889, pp. 25-28). He had spent nearly five years in a machine shop and two years at St. Lawrence University, before he left college to enlist in the Union army. When he was discharged as captain with the rank of brevet major, he selected engineering as the field for which he was best adapted by temperament and training and entered Rensselaer Polytechnic Institute, from which he received the degree of civil engineer in 1868. After an apprenticeship in the Croton Aqueduct department of New York City, he secured his first retainer in South America. During two years in which he was engaged on the

Oroya Railroad, in Peru, he erected the original Verrugas Viaduct, in its day the highest and, possibly, the most remarkable bridge in the world. In 1875 he constructed several bridges on the Chimbote & Huarez Railroad. Seven years later he designed a number of bridges in Mexico; and, in 1890, he built the second Verrugas Viaduct, of the cantilever type. From 1890 to 1908 he represented Peru and Ecuador upon the International Railway Commission. On his return from his first trip, he spent two years in the shops of the Toledo & Wabash Railroad; and, in 1880–81, he served as resident engineer of the Central Railroad of New Jersey, for which he constructed the Lake Hopatcong Division. Except for this interruption, he devoted himself almost exclusively to the design and construction of bridges. As early as 1873 he supervised the manufacture of material for the Louisiana Railroad Bridge. In 1883 he built several bridges for the Northern Pacific Railroad. Between 1886 and 1888 he designed for it those across the White River, the Yakima River, and the Columbia River. For the Great Northern Railroad he drew plans for the Nooksack Drawbridge (1892).

Like many civil engineers of the nineteenth century, Buck was a wanderer. Although he was associated with George McNulty during 1883–88, he did not establish himself in independent practise until 1902. In the same year he married Myra Rebecca Gould of Paducah, Ky. Wide as was the range of his work, he is remembered primarily for his achievements at Niagara Falls and New York. His connection with the Falls began in 1877, when he repaired the cables in the Railway Suspension Bridge. Three years later he replaced the wooden superstructure; and, in 1886, he substituted iron towers for the stone towers. This feat, which, as in previous alterations, he accomplished without interrupting traffic, has been described as "the most difficult, delicate, and daring piece of bridgework ever undertaken" (*Transactions of the Society of Civil Engineers,* LXXIII, 495). Again, in 1896, he erected, without interrupting traffic, the present spandrel-braced arch. In Rochester, N. Y., where he had constructed the Platt Street Bridge, he had also constructed the Driving Park Avenue Bridge of the three-hinged type; and it was through a study of the vibrations of this bridge that he eliminated the central hinge at the Falls. There he rebuilt the Niagara and Clifton Suspension Bridge in 1888–89 and, in 1896–87, replaced it by the longest steel arch span in the world, once more maintaining traffic without material interruption. He was also consulting engineer for the Lewiston and Queenston Suspension

Bridge (1899). In New York, although he promoted the development of the metropolitan tunnels, his name is linked more closely with the bridges of the district. As one of a committee of three, he recommended that the New York and Brooklyn Suspension Bridge be opened to surface and elevated trains (*Report of the Board of Experts*, Feb. 8, 1897). His chief monument, however, is the Williamsburg Bridge, which is distinguished for its vast reach and massive symmetry. Although he is known as one of the great bridge-builders of his time, his career must be considered in connection with the history and influence of Rensselaer Polytechnic Institute; for, from the beginning, he drew constantly upon its graduates for aid in design, manufacture, and supervision. He received the Norman Medal in 1881 and the Telford Premium in 1901.

[The most detailed accounts of Buck's career are those in Henry B. Nason's *Biog. Record Officers and Grads. Rensselaer Polytechnic Inst.* (1887) and Wm. R. Cutter's *Geneal. and Family Hist. of Northern N. Y.* (1910). C. D. Christie's *Notes on the Central and Southern Railways of Peru* (1917) touches his life in South America. The memoir by Richard S. Buck in the *Trans. Am. Soc. Civil Engineers*, LXXIII, 493–97, is a personal impression stressing his military services and his achievements at Niagara Falls and New York. His work at the Gorge is treated in his *Report on the Renewal of the Niagara Suspension Bridge* (1880) and in his papers in the *Trans. Am. Soc. Civil Engineers*, X, 195–224, and the *Minutes of the Proc. of the Inst. of Civil Engineers*, CXLIV, 69–94. Several points are amplified in the *Engineering News*, Dec. 10, 1887, and in Richard S. Buck's study of the Niagara railway arch in the *Trans. Am. Soc. Civil Engineers*, XL, 125–50. Buck's most important work in New York is described in the *Engineering Record*, Dec. 19, 1903, and in Edward Hungerford's *The Williamsburg Bridge* (1893). In Ray Palmer Baker's *A Chapter in Am. Education* (1924), Buck's accomplishments are related to the tradition of bridge-building at Rensselaer Polytechnic Institute. Among obituaries are a pamphlet published by the Loyal Legion of the United States, Sept. 10, 1909, and an appreciation by Albert Shaw in the *Rev. of Revs.* (N. Y.), XL, 175–76.]   R. P. B—r.

BUCK, PHILO MELVIN (May 15, 1846–Sept. 8, 1924), Methodist missionary, was born in Corning, N. Y., the son of Ethal Curry Buck and Mariam (Underwood) Buck. His parents moved West and finally settled in Kansas, where their son's educational opportunities were meager and most of his early reading was necessarily self-directed. When he was seventeen he began to preach and two years later he joined the Kansas Conference of the Methodist Episcopal Church. In 1868 he married Angie M. Tibbott who died the next year. Having volunteered for foreign mission service, he was sent to India in 1870. In 1872, in India, he was married to Caroline Louisa MacMillan of Gettysburg, Pa. His earliest appointment in India was at Shahjahanpur where he remained from 1871 to 1876. During 1876–78 he studied in Drew Theological Seminary, Madi-

son, N. J., graduating in the latter year. He returned to India and was successively stationed at Kumaun (1879–84), Cawnpore (1885), and Mussourie (1889–92), where he was principal of Philander Smith Institute. But it was as superintendent of the Meerut District (1893–1914) that he first had full scope for his exceptional qualities as a missionary. He traveled continually over the district, using a bicycle for the most part, everywhere making friends with persons of every caste and religion. As his work prospered, he acquired property, secured funds, and trained Indian men and women to meet his needs. Under his leadership a great movement toward Christianity, known as the "Mass Movement," began. The new converts were from the lowest, "untouchable" groups, Tanners and Sweepers, and utterly illiterate. The training of a large number of pastors and teachers to care for them became necessary. Buck's workers were drawn, mostly, from the "untouchable" groups. Since no literature was available for use in the training of these workers, he began to write books. His first catechism was prepared for the quarterly conferences in his own district and for his summer schools. Then to meet the growing needs of his workers he prepared books to serve all classes from beginners to members of annual conferences. His district became an example for other superintendents and his books had a very wide use. For nearly a quarter of a century, he conducted a department in the *Kaukab-i-Hind*, a religious weekly published in Roman Urdu at Lucknow. Through the columns of this paper he became the teacher of preachers throughout the Urdu-speaking areas of India. The usefulness of his literary work, as well as of his preaching, was due, in no small measure, to a remarkable and idiomatic use of Urdu, and, late in life, of Hindi. Of his numerous works the most important was *Christianity in Doctrine and in Experience* (1914), which first appeared in Urdu and was translated into Hindi, Marathi, Gujurati, Chinese, Korean, and even Spanish—for use in Latin America.

[J. M. Reed, *Missions and Missionary Soc. of the M. E. Ch.* (3 vols., 1895–96); *Who's Who in America*, 1924–25; files of the minutes of the North India Conference, of the North-West India Conference and of the Central Conference of Southern Asia; also files of the *Kaukab-i-Hind* and of the *Indian Witness*.] G. W. B.

BUCKALEW, CHARLES ROLLIN (Dec. 28, 1821–May 19, 1899), senator, was descended from a branch of the Buccleugh family which emigrated from Scotland to France in the sixteenth century and later, during the Huguenot persecutions, emigrated to America. By 1775 one branch of the family, changing its name to

Buckalew, had pioneered to Muncy, Pa. In 1808, one John McKinney Buckalew acquired a large tract of land in Columbia County, where he married Martha Funston, by whom he became the father of Charles Rollin Buckalew. The latter's academic education was mainly at Harford Academy, Harford, Pa. His early career included school-teaching, selling goods in a local store, and the study of law in a local attorney's office. His wife, Permelia Stevens Wadsworth, was a member of a Connecticut family notable in colonial history. Entering politics at the age of twenty-four, by the traditional route of the local prosecuting attorney's office, he rapidly assumed local political leadership and within five years was elected as Democratic state senator. This position he retained from 1850 to 1858, supporting such policies as the reform of the penal code and the relinquishment by the state of its transportation facilities to private corporations. In 1854 he served as one of the United States commissioners to ratify a treaty with Paraguay. His position as a lawyer and as a party leader was recognized by his appointment in 1857 by Gov. Packer as a member of a commission to revise the penal code of the state. This position, as well as the chairmanship of the state Democratic committee, and his office as state senator, he resigned in 1858 to accept appointment by President Buchanan as minister to Ecuador (letter to Buchanan, June 29, 1858). After his return in 1861, his leadership in his party was recognized by his election in 1863 as United States senator. His career in the Senate, though dignified and creditable, was not distinguished. His position was a most difficult one, due in part to the turbulent character of national politics, when Democrats generally were subjected to the harshest criticism; and in part to the fact that his party in Pennsylvania was in a measure out of sympathy with the national party, especially on tariff questions. Furthermore, his modesty, moderation, and disinclination to depend on the arts of political maneuvering, qualities admirable no doubt in themselves, unfitted him for effective participation in the troubled course of events. He opposed the extreme war powers of the Government, the Freedman's Bureau, the impeachment of President Johnson, and other distinctively Republican policies. He advocated, alike for the nation and the state, a system of proportional representation (see his speeches in Congress on the subject and his book, *Proportional Representation,* 1872), and he was influential in minor matters of a noncontroversial nature, as in much-needed improvements in Congressional buildings (*Congressional Globe,* 1863–69).

Upon the expiration of Buckalew's term as federal senator, Pennsylvania was under Republican control. He returned to the state Senate, where his chief activity was as chairman of the committee on constitutional reform. In 1872 he was the unsuccessful Democratic candidate for governor. He was also a delegate to the convention which rewrote the state constitution in 1872–73, and although an outstanding member of the convention, was unable to secure the inclusion of provisions which he particularly favored. A modified form of his view of minority representation was, however, included in the constitution (see his *Examination of the Constitution of Pennsylvania,* 1883). His later career was marked by his return to national politics as Congressman in 1887. After the expiration of his second term as Congressman in 1891, he spent the remainder of his life in retirement at his home in Bloomsburg, Columbia County.

[Buckalew's work in the state legislature may be studied in the *Journal* of the state Senate, the *Legislative Journal,* and the *Daily Legislative Record.* For his career in the federal Congress, see *Cong. Globe* and *Cong. Record.* There are brief estimates in the memoirs of such men as J. G. Blaine and G. W. Julian. For his work in the state constitutional convention, see the *Debates* (9 vols.) and the *Journals* (2 vols.) of the convention; and A. D. Harlan, *Pa. Constitutional Convention* (1873). Some of his letters are preserved in the manuscript collections of the Pa. Hist. Soc.]   W. B.

BUCKHOUT, ISAAC CRAIG (Nov. 7, 1830–Sept. 27, 1874), civil engineer, descended from an old Knickerbocker family and the son of Jacob and Charlotte Eveline (De Val) Buckhout, was born in Eastchester, N. Y., on the old Gouverneur Morris estate of which his father was manager. As a boy he was of a studious nature and was considered to be somewhat of a mathematical genius. Early in life he decided to become a civil engineer and by hard work got enough money together to take an engineering course under a Prof. Davies. When he was seventeen he began the practical experience which was to lead him into engineering prominence in spite of his short life. He was fortunate in the tutelage through which he laid the foundations of his profession. In 1848, when he first entered the employ of the Harlem Railroad as a rodman, he worked under Allan Campbell, a civil engineer who later became president of the railroad. Shortly afterward he engaged in surveying at Paterson, N. J., where his chief was Col. J. W. Allen. In a short while Buckhout rose to the position of engineer and superintendent of the waterworks at Paterson but he gave this up to return to New York as city surveyor. In 1853, however, he returned to the employ of the Harlem Railroad and it was in railroad work that he achieved outstanding prominence in his day. His earlier work included the construction of an aqueduct over the Harlem flats and of a bridge over the Harlem River. But he will chiefly be remembered for the old Grand Central Depot, which he designed, and the "Fourth Avenue Improvement," the name given at the time to a new line to run from the Harlem River to Forty-second St., New York City. A board of four engineers was appointed by the state legislature when the charter for this "Improvement" was granted, and Isaac Buckhout was put in charge of the work. He resigned his position as superintendent of the New York and Harlem Railroad in order to give his time completely as engineer in charge of the new work. It was his literal devotion to duty here that caused his untimely death. Standing day after day in the marshland that is now New York's exclusive East Sixties, he contracted acute rheumatism and typhoid fever which resulted in his death at his home in White Plains.

Buckhout also drew up plans for an underground railroad to run from Grand Central Depot to City Hall, and for another underground road in Brooklyn. He had been appointed a member of the Committee on Rapid Transit shortly before his death. He was an engineer whose advice was sought not only because of his innate practical ability and the indefatigable care which he took with details but also because of the qualities of manhood which made him a warm personal friend and inspired trust and confidence in those with whom he came in contact. In personal appearance he so much resembled Henry Ward Beecher that he was often mistaken for him.

[The files of the Am. Soc. of Civil Engineers, especially their *Proceedings,* vol. I; *Railroad Gazette,* Oct. 3, 1874; *Sun* (N.Y.) and *N. Y. Tribune,* Sept. 29, 1874.]

E.Y.

BUCKINGHAM, JOSEPH TINKER (Dec. 21, 1779–Apr. 11, 1861), editor, was born in Windham, Conn., the son of Nehemiah Tinker—whom he believed to be a descendant of the Thomas Tinker who came over in the Mayflower—and of Mary (Huntington) Tinker. The family name of his maternal grandmother was Buckingham, and he records that "By request of a relative and intimate friend of my mother's, I was baptized by the name of Joseph Buckingham." (In 1804, for reasons concerning which his usually frank and detailed *Memoirs* are reticent, he secured a legal change of name to Joseph Tinker Buckingham). When he was little more than three years old, his father died, leaving a wife and ten children in indigent circumstances. After various vicissitudes the fam-

ily was broken up, and Joseph was bound out to a farmer until he was sixteen. His schooling was very slight and desultory. After leaving the farm he served an apprenticeship to the printer's trade in Walpole, N. H., Greenfield, Mass., Northampton, and Boston. During one summer he traveled with a theatrical troupe, and at a later time he taught school for a year and a half; but during most of his active career he was printer, publisher, and editor. He carried on the *Polyanthos,* a monthly, 1806–07 and 1812–14; the *Ordeal,* a Federalist weekly, 1809; the *New England Galaxy* (for a time the *New England Galaxy and Masonic Magazine*), a non-political weekly, 1817–28; the *Boston Courier,* a daily founded to advocate protectionist principles in 1824; and the *New England Magazine,* an ambitious and not discreditable attempt to give Boston a literary monthly, 1831–34. The last-named periodical was established in part to give an opportunity to the proprietor's son, a young man of promise who performed many of the editorial duties for the first two years, but who died at the age of twenty-three. Buckingham continued as editor of the *Boston Daily Courier* until 1848. At that time he felt himself unable to support Gen. Taylor, the Whig nominee for the presidency, and rather than inflict on his financial backers the loss that would follow if the paper repudiated the Whig ticket he withdrew from the editorship. For the rest of his life he is said to have been an occasional contributor to various journals, and he wrote and compiled *Specimens of Newspaper Literature, with Personal Memoirs, Anecdotes, and Reminiscences* (1850) and *Personal Memoirs and Recollections of Editorial Life* (1852).

As an editor Buckingham had qualities that led his eulogists to describe him as "a terrible opponent," and "the most independent editor of his time." He not only engaged other editors in ferocious word-combats, which was the custom of his age and often led to no serious break in personal friendship, but he often became involved in troubles with others who resented his outspoken comments. The first of these difficulties that he records came in the days of the *Polyanthos,* when Mr. Poe, father of Edgar Allan Poe, called to chastise him for his strictures on Mrs. Poe as an actress. He was later the defendant in several libel suits, and he had quarrels with many who did not wish to resort either to personal violence or to the law. It was no doubt partly because of his fearless aggressiveness that none of his publications was highly successful financially; and he seems to have felt keenly the lack of a substantial reward for his labors. With all his readiness to open an attack on anything that he regarded as false he was never seriously accused of intellectual dishonesty, and he was usually on the side of reforms that time has approved. Both he and his periodicals commanded the respect and support of New Englanders of importance. Mrs. Rowson, William Austin, Edward Everett, and others of equal note in their day wrote for the *Galaxy*. The list of contributors to the *New England Magazine* included Frothingham, Edward Everett, Story, Hildreth, Longfellow, Holmes, and many more. The columns of the *Boston Courier* were open to contributors and correspondents of all opinions; and prominent New Englanders, particularly those of liberal views, often took advantage of the liberty extended them. It was in the *Courier* that Lowell printed "The Present Crisis" and the first series of the "Biglow Papers," and it was to "Mister Buckinum," personally, that the letters of Hosea Biglow which introduced some of the numbers were addressed.

Buckingham was for seven years a representative and for four years a senator in the Massachusetts legislature. For the earlier terms he was elected as a Whig, but after his refusal to support Taylor in 1848 he was nominated by the Free Soil and the Democratic parties as a union candidate for state senator. In the address issued at this time he denied that he had changed his views, and characteristically exclaimed: *Left the Whig party! . . . the party left me.*"

[The chief sources of information regarding Buckingham's early life and active career are the *Memoirs* mentioned above, which all subsequent sketches seem to have followed. Obituary notices and tributes appeared in the *Boston Transcript*, Apr. 11, 1861 (reprinted, *Living Age*, LXIX, 447), and the *Boston Courier*, Apr. 12, 1861. Interesting bits of self-revelation are found in many of his published editorials and addresses to his readers. He touched the life of his time in many ways, and anecdotes and personal estimates are found in the biographies, letters, and personal memoirs of other New Englanders.]

W. B. C.

BUCKINGHAM, WILLIAM ALFRED (May 28, 1804–Feb. 5, 1875), governor of Connecticut, senator, was born in Lebanon, New London County, Conn., the son of Samuel and Joanna (Matson) Buckingham. He attended the local schools and afterward the Bacon Academy in Colchester. Until he was twenty, he worked on the home farm. Then he clerked in a Norwich dry-goods shop; was employed for a brief time in a wholesale establishment in New York; and finally in 1826 opened at Norwich a dry-goods store of his own. In 1830 he also took up the manufacture of ingrain carpet, then much in vogue. In the same year he was married to Eliza Ripley. Both the dry-goods business and carpet-weaving he relinquished in 1848 to help organize the Hayward Rubber Company. Its

plant for the making of India-rubber goods was situated in Colchester and he became its treasurer. Twice—in 1849–50 and again in 1856–57—he served as mayor of Norwich. In 1858 he was elected governor on the ticket of the newly-formed Republican party. Reëlected seven consecutive times, he was in office eight years, the longest period of service of any Connecticut governor since the days of Oliver Wolcott (1817–27).

In 1860 his opponent was Thomas H. Seymour, sometimes called "the Democratic war-horse," who had been governor in 1850–53. The contest was watched with peculiar interest, particularly in the South. Buckingham won by the close margin of 541 votes. Abraham Lincoln, already known to the East through his Cooper Union speech of Feb. 27, 1860, visited Connecticut in March of that year and met the man who was to be one of the relatively small group of distinguished "war governors," and who was to render him much the same kind of support that Trumbull had given Washington. Of Buckingham it has been said, "The military and civil history of Connecticut during the war of 1861–65, is almost wholly the story of his administration" (*Representative Men of Connecticut*, 1894, p. 6). On Jan. 17, 1861, Buckingham issued to the state militia a proclamation of warning, advising readiness for "any exigency." Nevertheless when the President on Apr. 15 summoned to arms 75,000 three months militia, so far from ready were the Connecticut forces that the State could not furnish even the one regiment fixed as her quota. Buckingham on his own responsibility had already ordered equipments for 5,000 men; and although without due authority, he now called for a regiment of volunteers. In May the General Assembly met, ratified what Buckingham had done, and voted $2,000,000 for military purposes. Connecticut's first regiment did not arrive in Washington until May 13, but it arrived fully prepared for active duty. Two more regiments followed. Though he did not resort to the draft, Buckingham eventually furnished during the period of the war no less than 54,882 volunteers—this at a time when the population numbered but 461,000 and the voters only about 80,000. The governor's concern for the welfare of Connecticut troops was unfailing. Both the national administration and the citizens of his state had particular confidence in his ability and spirit.

After two years of private life, he was elected (1868) to the United States Senate, to serve from Mar. 4, 1869. There, respected for his personal qualities, he was also valued for his services —especially as a conscientious and hardworking member of the committees on commerce and on Indian affairs (chairman). He died shortly before his term would have expired. His associate John J. Ingalls said of him, "While the powers of his intellect were upon a high plane, yet were I called upon to define the impression that remains strongest with me, I should say it was that of incomparable rectitude and dignity" (*Memorial Addresses . . . Delivered in the Senate and House of Representatives*). Buckingham was a corporate member of the American Board of Commissioners for Foreign Missions and the moderator of the first National Council of the Congregational Churches (1865); and he became president of the American Temperance Union. He was among the founders of Norwich Free Academy (1856) and the benefactors of the Yale Divinity School. In him strong convictions and a high ideal of public service were united to a winning temperament and an old-school dignity and courtesy. On June 18, 1884, a badly-placed bronze statue of him, modeled by Olin L. Warner, was unveiled in the battle-flag vestibule of the capitol at Hartford.

[S. G. Buckingham (a brother), *The Life of Wm. A. Buckingham* (Springfield, Mass., 1894); F. W. Chapman, *The Buckingham Family* (Hartford, 1872); W. A. Croffut and J. M. Morris, *The Military and Civil Hist. of Connecticut during the War of 1861–65* (1868); Alexander Johnston, *Connecticut* (1887); F. C. Norton, *The Governors of Connecticut* (1905); I. N. Tarbox, *Sketch of Wm. Alfred Buckingham* (1876), reprinted from the *Cong. Quarterly* for April 1876. The date of Buckingham's death is sometimes given as Feb. 3, but this is erroneous.]　　　　　　　　G. S. B.

BUCKLAND, CYRUS (Aug. 10, 1799–Feb. 26, 1891), inventor, was born at East Hartford (now Manchester), Conn., the youngest in the family of eleven children belonging to George and Elizabeth Buckland. His youth was that of the farmer's son of the period: his time was spent in attending school a few months each year and in helping with the farm work. An older brother was practising his trade of wheelwright in the neighborhood, and in helping him Cyrus gained considerable mechanical knowledge and experience by the time he came of age. When twenty-two he left home and went to Monson, Mass., where he obtained employment in a cotton-machinery manufacturing plant. This kind of work apparently appealed to him for he continued in it for the next seven years both in Monson and in Chicopee Falls, Mass. A slump in the cotton business in 1828 necessitated his finding work elsewhere and he entered the Government Armory at Springfield, Mass., as a pattern maker. He continued here for twenty-nine years until poor health compelled him to give up all active work. During the first ten years of his service Buckland rose to the position of proof-master and inspector of barrels but as early as 1833 a note appears on the pay-roll opposite his name as "making patterns for new machines." The system of interchangeability of parts was being especially applied in firearms manufacture during this period and afforded many opportunities to Buckland to apply his inventive powers and mechanical skill. In 1843 he was instrumental in the manufacture of an eccentric bit and auger used in cutting the lock, guard plate, side plate, breech plate, rod spring, and barrels to gunstocks. He perfected a change in the form of the cone for percussion muskets in 1847, and devised the machines and tools to alter flintlock muskets to percussion on Dr. Edward Maynard's plan in 1848. In 1846 Buckland made improvements in Blanchard's system of making gun-stocks which resulted in doubling the previous production and in a fourfold gain in output over hand-made stocks. This increase was effected by building thirteen machines each one of which had a special function to perform in the process which transformed the lumber as it came from the mills into gunstocks, completed save for final rubbing. In 1854 Buckland devised the machines to manufacture a lock and chamber breech for altering rifles to the Maynard percussion type. In no single instance up to this time had he applied for a patent on any of the improvements which he had made, and private manufacturers of firearms both in the United States and other countries availed themselves of his devices. When, therefore, he was called upon in 1855 to design a rifling machine to cut a groove of a regularly decreasing depth from the breech to the muzzle, he decided, upon designing such a machine, to patent it, and so notified the secretary of war. This was his only patent and it was a year after his retirement in 1857 that Congress, on the recommendation of the secretary of war, J. B. Floyd, paid Buckland $10,000 for the government rights to his invention. He relinquished his duties in the armory in November 1857, as inspector of arms and master machinist, but continued to reside in Springfield until his death thirty-four years later. He was married at Monson on May 18, 1824, to Mary A. Locke, and the two lived to observe their sixty-sixth wedding anniversary, surviving their three children and leaving two grandchildren.

[Sources of information on Cyrus Buckland are original correspondence and reports of the U. S. War Dept., and the *Springfield Daily Republican*, Feb. 27, 1891.]　　　　　　　　C. W. M.

BUCKLAND, RALPH POMEROY (Jan. 20, 1812–May 27, 1892), lawyer, soldier, was the grandson of Stephen B. Buckland, of East Hartford, Conn., a Revolutionary artillery captain who died on a British prison ship, and the son of Ralph B. and Anna (Kent) Buckland. He was born in Ravenna, Ohio, whither his parents had recently moved from Massachusetts, and where his father died not long afterward. His mother marying again, Ralph Pomeroy, as the eldest of a numerous family, was, while quite young, thrown partly upon his own resources, living much of the time with an uncle, helping upon the farm, and acquiring the rudiments of an education in the country school. At the age of eighteen he descended the Ohio and Mississippi Rivers with a boatload of western produce. Finding employment at New Orleans, he remained there for three years; then, returning to Ohio, he attended Kenyon College for a year, afterward reading law under attorneys at Middlebury and Canfield until admitted to the bar in 1837. Beginning practise at Fremont almost penniless, he prospered, married Charlotte Boughton, who traced descent from William Bradford, won the confidence of his neighbors, and held a succession of local offices. In 1848 he went as delegate to the Whig national convention which nominated Gen. Taylor for the presidency. During the Free-Soil controversies he was carried from his old party moorings into the incipient Republican organization. In 1855 he was elected to the state Senate, serving for two terms. He organized the 72nd Ohio Volunteer Infantry in the autumn of 1861, was mustered into the United States service early in 1862, and was soon assigned to the command of the fourth brigade of Sherman's division. This brigade was the only unit of its size in Sherman's army that retained its organization during the hard fighting at Pittsburg Landing and Shiloh, and by many critics is credited with preventing a complete disaster to the Union forces. Buckland was especially commended by Sherman in his report on these engagements (*Official Records*, Army, I ser. X, pt. I, 266–69). He continued field service till January 1864 when he was placed in command of the District of Memphis. In August 1866 he was commissioned brevet major-general, United States Volunteers, for meritorious service. Meantime his friends at home had elected him to Congress, and in January 1865, he had resigned from the army preparatory to taking his seat. After two consecutive terms he resumed his law practise at Fremont, but continued to participate in public affairs. In 1870 he became president of the Ohio Soldiers' and Sailors' Orphans Home, at Xenia; in 1876 he was a delegate to the Republican national convention which nominated Hayes; and from 1878 to 1881 he held the post of government director of the Union Pacific Railroad. In early manhood he was slender and somewhat dyspeptic, but systematic out-of-door exercise resulted in robust health in middle life. Although a semi-invalid during his last few years, he continued active to the day of his death, going to his home from his office only two or three hours before his demise. Rutherford B. Hayes, a law partner from 1846 to 1849, thought that Buckland's appearance was "against him" (Charles R. Williams, *Diary and Letters of R. B. Hayes*, I, 191); but a post-war portrait gives no such impression. On the morning following Buckland's death Hayes entered in his diary this estimate: "a strong and conspicuous figure for more than forty years, at the bar, as a citizen, as a public man, and especially as a soldier. His traits . . . were honesty, amazing industry, tenacity of purpose, and perseverance, and a courage, physical and moral, unsurpassed" (*Ibid.*, V, 86–87).

[There are biographical sketches of Buckland in *The Biog. Cyc. of the State of Ohio*, vol. I (1883–91); Geo. I. Reed, *Bench and Bar of Ohio* (1897); and Basil Meek, ed., *Twentieth Century Hist. of Sandusky County, Ohio* (1909). Buckland's military career may be traced in the *Official Records* (Army), and is briefly summarized in Whitelaw Reid, *Ohio in the War* (1868). Many allusions to him are to be found in C. R. Williams, ed., *Diary and Letters of R. B. Hayes* (1922–26).]

H. C. H.

BUCKLER, THOMAS HEPBURN (Jan. 4, 1812–Apr. 20, 1901), physician, son of William Buckler, a merchant who emigrated from Warminster, England, in 1783, and his wife, Anne Thomas Hepburn, was born at "Evergreen," near Baltimore, Md. He was educated at St. Mary's College (Baltimore) and in 1835 obtained from the University of Maryland his degree of M.D., for which he presented a thesis on Animal Heat. After spending a short time in the office of his brother, Dr. John Buckler, who had a large practise in Baltimore, he left in 1836 for Europe on a sailing vessel, and spent six months in the clinics of Paris where he studied under Louis, Chomel, and Ricord. After his return to Baltimore he became physician to the City and County Almshouse for some years. During the period from 1850 to 1855 his practise rapidly increased; he attended Chief Justice Taney and President Buchanan, and was consulted by Gen. R. E. Lee (*Recollections and Letters of Gen. Robert E. Lee*, 1904, pp. 412, 419–20). His sympathies during the Civil War were with the South and at the close of the conflict, partly as a result of the outcome, he moved to Paris where he remained from 1866 to 1890 practising under license from the French Government. His medical writings, which are fully listed by Quinan, were bold and original. He was an early advocate of laparotomy for intestinal obstruction (*American Journal of the Medical Sciences,* Jan. 1869), recommended the use of ammonium phosphate for the treatment of rheumatism (*Ibid.,* Jan. 1846) and wrote extensively on the pathology of uterine affections (*Boston Medical and Surgical Journal,* Jan. 15, 22, Sept. 16, Oct. 28, 1880). His most important contribution, however, was to the study of cholera and other epidemic infections. In 1851 he wrote *A History of Epidemic Cholera, as it appeared at the Baltimore City and County Almshouse, in the Summer of 1849, with Some Remarks on the Medical Topography and Diseases of this Region.* "If the history of epidemic cholera," he said, "as it first appeared throughout the country in 1832 be compared with the invasion of 1849, it will be remarked, as one of the most striking facts connected with this disease, that it returned to every place which it had visited during the first epidemic, unless, during the interval, the locality had undergone some marked change or entire renovation." From this he argued that sanitary improvement of the districts which had been revisited was urgently needed. He proposed the filling of the "basin" or inner harbor of Baltimore with the earth from "Federal Hill," and was of opinion that the waters of the Gunpowder River should be used to supply the city, a suggestion not carried out until 1875 (see W. T. Howard, Jr., *Public Health Administration . . . in Baltimore,* 1924, pp. 128, 132). In 1853 he also published a useful monograph *On the Etiology, Pathology and Treatment of Fibro-bronchitis and Rheumatic Pneumonia.* Owing to his trust in *vis medicatrix Naturæ,* Buckler preferred to the use of drugs, whenever possible, diet, exercise, baths, mineral water (especially at the Virginia "Healing Springs"), and residence in sea or mountain air. He was thus in the fifties among the first to treat tuberculosis by no other means than life in the open air, rest, and nourishment (especially with cod-liver oil). Drugs he believed in only for some specific purpose. Personally independent and somewhat eccentric, he was much sought after on account of his wide reading, charm of manner, and brilliant conversational powers. He was twice married: in 1861 to Anne, daughter of the Rev. Richard Fuller, who died within a year; and on Nov. 21, 1865, to Eliza, daughter of John Ridgely, and widow of John Campbell White, who died in 1894.

[*Baltimore News,* Apr. 22, 1901; W. T. Howard, in *Trans. Medic. and Chir. Fac. Md.,* 1903, pp. 46–49; J. R. Quinan, *Medic. Annals of Baltimore,* 1884, pp. 71–72; E. F. Cordell, *Medic. Annals of Md.,* 1903, pp. 338–39; personal information.]   J.F.F.

BUCKLEY, JAMES MONROE (Dec. 16, 1836–Feb. 8, 1920), Methodist clergyman, was born in Rahway, N. J., the son of the Rev. John Buckley. The latter, a native of Lancashire, England, emigrated to this country in 1827, became a Methodist preacher, married Abbie Lonsdale Monroe, and soon died of consumption, as had both his parents, leaving behind James, not yet six, and another son still younger. The boys were brought up in the home of their grandfather, Judge Monroe, at Mount Holly, N. J., their mother helping to support them by teaching. James early displayed a restless energy, quickness of mind, varied interests, ability as a public speaker, and skill in debate, but also a tendency to the family malady. Because of his slender means and poor health, his schooling was limited to several years of preparatory work at Pennington Seminary, and a year in Wesleyan University where he enrolled in 1856. So effective a speaker had he become by this time, however, that he went about stumping for Frémont in the presidential campaign of that year. After having taught several schools, and supplied a Wesleyan Methodist church at Exeter, N. H., in 1859 he was admitted to the New Hampshire Conference of the Methodist Episcopal Church, and was immediately appointed to the church at Dover, one of the largest in the state. His advancement was rapid and his reputation steadily increased. After pastorates in Manchester, N. H., Detroit, Stamford, Conn., and Brooklyn, in 1880 the General Conference elected him editor of the *Christian Advocate,* which office he held for thirty-two years, during which time the paper became one of the best-known religious journals in the country.

He was married three times: first, on Aug. 2, 1864, to Eliza A. Burns of Detroit; second, on Apr. 22, 1874, to Mrs. Sarah Isabella (French) Staples, a widow of Detroit; and, third, on Aug. 23, 1886, to Adelaide Shackford Hill of Dover, N. H. He was small of stature and slight of frame, but had a massive head, almost entirely bald. Dark, thin whiskers and mustache covered his face. His eyes were round, dark, and steady. When a young man the doctors told him his days were numbered, but by keeping much in the open air and by taking long walks and breathing exercises, he held the disease in check. Requirements of health, calls for lectures, and an acquisitive mind, made him a traveler, and he visited almost every place of interest in the United States, Canada, and Europe, and parts of Asia and Africa. Though but twenty-seven when he first went abroad, in 1863, his patriotic addresses had made him known to national leaders, and he carried letters from Horace Greeley, Charles Sumner and others to members of the British Parliament, certifying his fitness to explain the Constitution with reference to the Civil War. Many accounts of his travels appeared in his own and other periodicals, and he published *The Midnight Sun, the Tsar, and the Nihilist* (1886) and *Travels in Three Continents* (1895). His meager schooling was no handicap. Possessing a virile and versatile mind, a retentive memory, and the ability to read with great rapidity, he acquired knowledge of extraordinary extent and variety. A resourceful, logical debater, well informed on everything pertaining to Methodism, he was a power in ecclesiastical councils, being a member of eleven General Conferences, and of the Ecumenical Conferences at London (1881), Washington (1891), and Toronto (1911). Although a conservative and opposed to many changes that were finally effected, he left a decided impress upon the laws and institutions of his church. In addition to the works mentioned, his principal publications include *Christians and the Theater* (1875) in which he holds that, "No habit which does not imply a positive renunciation of morality is more pernicious than that of theater going"; *Oats or Wild Oats?* (1885), containing much sane discussion of the problems of young men; *Faith Healing, Christian Science, and Kindred Phenomena* (1892); *A History of Methodists in the United States* (1896), being vol. V in the American Church History Series; *The Fundamentals and Their Contrasts* (1906); *The Wrong and Peril of Woman's Suffrage* (1909); *Theory and Practice of Foreign Missions* (1911); *Constitutional and Parliamentary History of the Methodist Episcopal Church* (1912).

[Geo. P. Mains, *Jas. Monroe Buckley* (1917); *Who's Who in America*, 1918–19; *N. Y. Times*, Feb. 9, 1920; *Christian Advocate*, Feb. 19, 1920; *Outlook*, Feb. 18, 1920.]
H. E. S.

BUCKLEY, SAMUEL BOTSFORD (May 9, 1809–Feb. 18, 1883), botanist, field naturalist, was born at Torrey, in Yates County, N. Y. He graduated from Wesleyan University, Middletown, Conn., in the class of 1836, studied medicine at the College of Physicians and Surgeons in New York, 1842–43, and received the degree of Ph.D. from Waco University, Tex., in 1872. After leaving college he taught for a time in Illinois and Alabama and for two years was principal of the Allenton Academy in Wilcox County in the latter state. In 1842 he visited various parts of Alabama, collecting plants, and secured a skeleton of a zeuglodon seventy feet in length. He also made collections in the mountains of Tennessee, North Carolina, and South Carolina, where he obtained twenty-four new species of plants and a new genus which bears his name. In 1843 he went to Florida to collect plants and shells. The following twelve years were passed on the homestead farm, and then for a time in 1855 and 1856 he was employed in a bookstore at Yellow Springs, Ohio. The summer of 1858 was spent in the mountains of North Carolina and Tennessee in the determination of the elevation of some of the higher peaks in the southern Alleghanies, and in the following years he traveled through the South collecting material for a Supplement to Michaux and Nuttall's *Sylva.*

In 1860–61 he was assistant geologist and naturalist on the Texas Geological Survey and began his labors in the state which became the scene of his activities during his later years. With the outbreak of the Civil War he returned North and from 1862 to 1865 occupied the position of chief examiner in the Statistical Department of the United States Sanitary Commission. After the close of the War Buckley returned to Texas and succeeded in securing appointment as state geologist, but the work of the Survey was terminated in 1867. Upon the organization of the Second Geological Survey of Texas he again received appointment as state geologist from 1874 to 1877 during which time he issued two reports.

After his retirement from office he devoted his time largely to literary work. In 1871–72 he was agricultural and scientific editor of the *State Gazette* in Austin, and for some years he was engaged in preparing a work on the geology and natural history of Texas. He also prepared several articles in 1881 for the *Library of Universal Knowledge.* His more important papers included his description of the skeleton of zeuglodon and of his new plants, several entomological contributions, and the account of his work in determining elevations in the mountains of North Carolina and Tennessee. Apparently the narrative of his botanical trips and his natural history of Texas were never published. His field work in the South is commemorated in the names of the black-backed rock squirrel of Texas (*Citellus variegatus buckleyi*) and the peculiar parasitic shrub *Buckleya*, and in "Buckley's Peak," one of the highest elevations in the Great Smoky Mountains in Tennessee. He was married three times: (1) in

1852 to Charlotte Sullivan of Naples, N. Y., who died in 1854; (2) in 1855 to Sarah Porter of Naples who died in 1858; and (3) in 1864 to Libbie Myers of Elbridge, N. Y. His death occurred in Austin, Tex.

[Geo. P. Merrill, *First One Hundred Years of Am. Geology* (1924), pp. 401–02; sketch by S. H. Wright in *Bull. of the Torrey Bot. Club*, XI, 46; *Am. Jour. of Sci.*, 3 ser., XXIX, pp. 171–72; *Bull. 109, U. S. Nat. Museum*, pp. 474–80; *Alumni Record of Wesleyan Univ.*, 1883, containing a chronology, p. 10, and a bibliography, pp. 547–49.] T. S. P.

BUCKMINSTER, JOSEPH STEVENS (May 26, 1784–June 9, 1812), Unitarian clergyman, author, descended in the seventh generation from Thomas Buckminster of Scituate and Brookline who came to America about 1640, was the son of the Rev. Joseph Buckminster and his wife Sarah Stevens, daughter of the Rev. Benjamin Stevens of Kittery Point, N. H. He was born in Portsmouth, N. H., during his father's pastorate of the North Church in that city. Educated largely at home by his father, he went to Phillips Exeter Academy at eleven, finished his preparation in a year, and in 1797 entered the sophomore class of Harvard College, where he took his first degree in 1800 at the age of sixteen. During the next two years, which he spent as an instructor at Exeter, he suffered the first of a series of epileptic attacks, which foreshadowed an early death. In 1803 he returned to live as a tutor in the family of his relative Theodore Lyman of Boston and Waltham, where his duties left him ample time to continue his reading, both in general literature and in theology, to which he now turned. With several generations of devoted service to the church behind him, Buckminster's choice of the ministry as his profession was natural, and his association at this time with Dr. James Freeman, minister of King's Chapel in Boston, influenced his decision to break away from his orthodox inheritance and join the Unitarian movement, then well under way, although no break had yet occurred in the Congregational ranks. After a year of further study, he preached his first sermon as a candidate for the ministry, in the spring of 1804, at York, Me., and shortly afterward was called to the pulpit of the Brattle Street Church in Boston, where he was ordained and installed, Jan. 30, 1805. His defection from the orthodox creed had bitterly disappointed his father, but the latter nevertheless consented to preach the ordination sermon (published in Boston, 1805), a composition of unusual tenderness and pathos. After a brilliant year in Brattle Street, Buckminster's health failed, and he went to Europe in the spring of 1806, remaining over

a year. He traveled part of the time with his friend Rev. Samuel Cooper Thacher, preached occasionally in Great Britain, and, having familiarized himself with British and Continental scholarship, brought home a library of some three thousand volumes, unique in New England at that time for its size, rarity, and scholarly character. The introduction of Biblical scholarship into this country must be credited in large measure to the efforts of Buckminster after his return (letter of Edward Everett, his successor at Brattle Street, in W. B. Sprague, *Annals of the American Pulpit,* VIII, 1865, 400; H. B. Adams, *Life and Writings of Jared Sparks,* I, 104). His preaching was also an innovation, combining the results of his critical studies and a deep interest in human affairs with enthusiasm and a freshness of point of view which drew to him eager support and great popularity. Although his pastoral duties were exacting, Buckminster by no means confined his efforts to his congregation. He secured the publication of, and saw through the press, the American edition of Griesbach's Greek Testament (2 vols., 1809), and he delivered the Phi Beta Kappa oration at Harvard in 1809 (*Monthly Anthology,* Sept. 1809, VII, 145–58). He was a member during its entire existence of the Anthology Club of Boston, a small group of literary men who met weekly to dine and discuss original contributions, which were later published in the *Monthly Anthology.* From this circle grew the Boston Athenæum, of which Buckminster was a founder, in 1807. When the Dexter Lectureship on Biblical Criticism was established at Harvard in 1811, Buckminster was given the first appointment, but he had scarcely begun his preparation for these duties when death came to him in a severe epileptic attack at the parsonage on Court Street, Boston, in the twenty-eighth year of his age. Two identical Stuart portraits of Buckminster, painted about 1810, show a fine and unusually intelligent face, but betray a lack of physical strength (L. Park, *Gilbert Stuart,* I, 184–86; III, 78). His stature was somewhat below the medium, a defect amply compensated by his grace and dignity of carriage.

[Mrs. Eliza Buckminster Lee, *Memoirs of Rev. Jos. Buckminster, D.D., and of his son Rev. Jos. Stevens Buckminster* (1849); Wm. B. Sprague, *Annals of the Am. Pulpit, VIII* (1865), pp. 384–406; Jas. Savage, *Mass. Hist. Soc. Colls.,* 2 ser., II, 271–74; Andrews Norton, *General Repository,* Oct. 1812, II, 306–14; and Rev. Samuel Cooper Thacher's memoir, prefixed (pp. xi–lxii) to the first collection of Buckminster's sermons (1814). Buckminster's only separate publications in his lifetime were funeral sermons on Gov. Jas. Sullivan and Rev. Wm. Emerson, and a hymn book edited for his congregation, the earliest collection of Unitarian character published in this country, which was the subject of considerable controversy (cf. *The Panoplist and Missionary Mag.*, Sept. and Nov., 1808, n.s. I, 170–77, 275–82). Two volumes of collected works by and about Buckminster were published in Boston by Jas. Munroe & Co. in 1839. *The Jour. of the Anthology Soc.* (1910) records Buckminster's activities in the society, and identifies his contributions to the magazine. He also contributed articles, reviews, and translations to the *Literary Review* and the *General Repository*. A catalogue of his library was printed previous to its sale at auction in August 1812. For Buckminster's part in the development of American Unitarianism, see H. C. Goddard, *Studies in New Eng. Transcendentalism* (Columbia doctoral dissertation, 1908), p. 27.]   M. H. T.

BUCKNELL, WILLIAM (Apr. 1, 1811–Mar. 5, 1890), business man, philanthropist, was born near Marcus Hook, Delaware County, Pa., the son of William and Sarah (Walker) Bucknell. His father, one of the pioneer settlers of Delaware County, had been a Lincolnshire farmer and carpenter. The boy's education consisted only of a short period in a country school. He then learned the trade of a wood carver and as he had been taught thrift at home was soon able, with some small savings, to start a business of his own. Even as early as this, through the teachings of his father, he set aside a tenth of his earnings for philanthropic and religious purposes. At twenty-five he married Harriet Ashton. Soon after, he found speculation in real estate more profitable than following a trade. By purchase of outlying land, by building, and by taking contracts for constructing gas and waterworks in various cities and accepting stock as payment, he made a fortune. Later in his life he was a broker in Philadelphia and dealt in securities and improvement of real estate. He was a large owner in railroads, various coal and iron mines, and other property. He was not desirous of political office nor was he a member of clubs, but he took a great interest in his church and in religious and educational philanthropies. His many gifts included over $140,000 to the University of Lewisburg, renamed in 1887 Bucknell University, and over $525,000 to missions and churches of the Baptist denomination. His ability to carry out his policy of giving away one-tenth of his fortune developed as that fortune grew until toward the end of his life his gifts averaged $1,000 a week. At his death he had given a total of a million dollars for public purposes. A man of strong likes and dislikes and independent in all his activities, he showed these characteristics by withdrawing from connection with the University of Lewisburg although his name was continued on the list of trustees until 1863, because he disapproved of the financial management. When David Jayne Hill was elected president of the college in 1879 he reënlisted

Bucknell's interest on a thoroughly businesslike basis. Bucknell became chairman of the board of trustees and remained so until his death. He had married in 1839 Margaret Crozer, and at her decease Emma Ward.

[H. Hall, *America's Successful Men of Affairs* (1896), vol. II; J. H. Harris, *Thirty Years as President of Bucknell, with Baccalaureate and Other Addresses* (1926); *Appleton's Annual Cyc.* (1890); *Phila. Press*, Mar. 7, 1890.]   M. A. K.

BUCKNER, SIMON BOLIVAR (Apr. 1, 1823–Jan. 8, 1914), Confederate soldier, was born of English ancestry near Munfordville in Hart County, Ky., the son of Aylett Hartswell Buckner and Elizabeth Ann (Morehead) Buckner. His father was a farmer and iron manufacturer, who had taken part in the second war with Great Britain and who was present at the battle of the Thames. Simon received whatever education Hart County could afford and when seventeen years old he was appointed to West Point Military Academy. Four years later (in 1844) he finished the course there in a class not conspicuous for subsequent greatness and was immediately made brevet second lieutenant of the 2nd Regiment of Infantry and stationed at Sackets Harbor, N. Y. The next year he was appointed assistant professor of ethics at West Point but in 1846 on the outbreak of the war with Mexico he was released at his own request to enter active service. He was now attached to the 6th Infantry as second lieutenant where he served as regimental quartermaster from August until December 1847. At first he was attached to Gen. Taylor's army and was with him at Saltillo. He was then joined to Gen. Scott's command and was actively engaged at the siege and capture of Vera Cruz. He was in almost every engagement from the sea to Mexico City, and for bravery at Churubusco he was brevetted first lieutenant and for gallantry at Molino del Rey he was promoted to the rank of captain. Before leaving Mexico he visited the volcano of Popocatepetl and wrote an account of his trip which was published in *Putnam's Magazine* (April 1853).

He returned to West Point in August 1848 as assistant professor in infantry tactics and filled this position until January 1850 when he was ordered to New York harbor. He remained here only a few months before going to Fort Snelling in Minnesota Territory. In September 1851 he was moved to Fort Atkinson on the Upper Arkansas River. Here he came in contact with the wild life of the Indians for a year, after which he was ordered back to New York where he served as captain in the subsistence department.

Seeing no great future in the army and no private fortune whatever, he resigned in 1855 to enter business, engaging in work which led him to short residences in Nashville, Tenn., and in Chicago. At the latter place he was made superintendent in charge of the construction of the Chicago customs house, and while here he laid in city real estate the beginnings of a small fortune. When the difficulties with Brigham Young and his Mormons arose in Utah, Buckner was made colonel in a regiment of Illinois volunteers, who were, however, never called into service. In 1858 he removed to Louisville.

Buckner had shown good business sense and had accumulated a considerable amount of wealth, but he could never quite forget his love and regard for military affairs. As the dangers of a civil war approached he showed no disposition to take part in politics and in the sectional debate as did many others; he chose rather to express his energies in the way of military preparedness for Kentucky. In 1860 he drew up an elaborate militia bill which the legislature adopted in March of that year. By its provisions all able-bodied men between eighteen and forty-five years of age were made to constitute what was termed the enrolled militia, from whom should be selected the active militia or state guards. The legislature at the time made him inspector-general with the rank of major-general. He now feverishly set to work to develop a well-trained and well-armed force which he hoped might play an important part in any war that might come. With funds that he secured from private sources he held an encampment in the summer of 1860 near Louisville, which was made to assume much the purpose of an officers' training camp. By the beginning of 1861 he had developed a well-organized army of sixty-one companies. For the purpose of further arming the state, he advocated the expenditure of $3,500,000, but by this time the interplay of the various forces of party desires and ambitions led many Kentuckians to fear for the outcome if the state guards were enlarged and armed under the command of Buckner. The result was that most of the money spent for military purposes by the state during the summer of 1861 went to another force called the home guards, over whom Buckner had no control.

Out of the initial confusion came the state's neutrality doctrine which was fully adopted by May 24, 1861. In the meantime Gov. Beriah Magoffin, hoping to avert war, attempted to set up a League of Neutrality among the border states, North and South in the Mississippi Valley, and sent Buckner to the states of Missouri and Tennessee to secure their adherence. Buckner succeeded in his mission, but the league was never organized because of the attitude of the states north of the Ohio River. Kentucky alone having declared her neutrality, Buckner in June entered into negotiations with Gen. George B. McClellan, who commanded Federal troops north of the Ohio, and secured an agreement wherein the latter promised to respect Kentucky's position. On June 24, carrying out the pact agreed upon, Buckner sent six companies of troops to Columbus, on the Mississippi River, to relieve the danger of invasion by the Confederates; but a little later when Federal forces from Cairo invaded Kentucky and when Buckner called on Mc-Clellan to act, he refused. This ended the agreement and strongly inclined Buckner toward the Confederates. During the summer of 1861 Gov. Magoffin sent Buckner to Washington to secure Lincoln's adherence to Kentucky's neutrality. Accompanied by John J. Crittenden he saw the President but received a cautious and equivocal answer, though the President offered him a commission as brigadier-general in the Federal army. Still bent on maintaining Kentucky's neutrality Buckner declined the offer.

By July the Union leadership in Kentucky had become so strong and had so hampered the military power that Buckner resigned his command, and in September visited Richmond, the capital of the Confederacy, where he was offered a commission in the Confederate army. This, too, he declined. On his return he heard at Nashville of Gen. Leonidas Polk's invasion of Kentucky and seizure of Columbus. He considered it a great political blunder and sought without avail to have the Confederates withdraw. When the state legislature officially abandoned neutrality, he issued an address in which he bitterly denounced that body for betraying the state. He forthwith joined the Confederates, receiving a commission as brigadier-general. His control over the state guards and his popularity with them had been so complete that many had already left to join the Confederates and now most of those remaining departed to join their comrades. Bitterly disappointed, the Union leaders declared Buckner a traitor and in November the Federal army seized his estate in Hart County.

On joining the Confederates Buckner was attached to Gen. Albert Sidney Johnston's command and stationed at Bowling Green. On the retreat of the Confederates out of Kentucky he was ordered with eight regiments in February 1862 to go to the rescue of Fort Donelson. After Gen. Grant's forces had surrounded the fort Buckner sought to cut his way through the Federal lines, but did not succeed, owing to the failure of Generals Floyd and Pillow to coöperate.

When capture seemed inevitable, Floyd and Pillow escaped and left Buckner in command. Soon thereafter the latter was forced to surrender unconditionally to Grant. He was taken as a prisoner first to Camp Morton in Indianapolis, and soon afterward to Fort Warren in Boston harbor where he was kept in solitary confinement until his exchange in the following August (1862). While Buckner was in prison, Garret Davis, a United States senator from Kentucky, sought unsuccessfully to have him turned over to the civil authorities to be tried for treason. After Buckner's return to the Confederacy he was promoted to be a major-general and was assigned to Gen. Bragg's army in Chattanooga. He took part in Bragg's invasion of Kentucky in the fall of 1862, commanding the 3rd division of infantry under Gen. Hardee. For a time he was detached at Lexington for recruiting service but took his regular command again in time to be present at the battle of Perryville on Oct. 8. In December he was sent by President Davis to build the defenses of Mobile and after four months' work he succeeded in creating a strongly fortified city. In the summer of 1863 he was placed in command of east Tennessee and in September of that year he joined Bragg in northern Georgia. In the battle of Chickamauga which followed he commanded a corps of the left wing. The next year he was put in command of the Department of Louisiana and was made a lieutenant-general. Little fighting took place there, and after Lee's surrender at Appomattox Buckner and General Sterling Price negotiated terms of capitulation with Gen. Canby for the trans-Mississippi armies.

Being denied by the terms of surrender the right to return to Kentucky, Buckner settled in New Orleans where he engaged in newspaper work and in insurance business. In 1866 he became the head of an insurance company. By 1868 the Confederate element in Kentucky had become so completely dominant that Buckner thought it would be to his advantage to return. He received wide applause and immediately became editor of the Louisville *Courier*, a newspaper which during the war had been driven out of the state by the Federal régime. For a number of years Buckner was busied with efforts to regain various properties which had been confiscated. When he had joined the Confederates in 1861 he had deeded some valuable property in the heart of Chicago to a brother-in-law who joined the Federal army, and who before his death willed it back to Buckner. After a long-drawn-out litigation Buckner succeeded in recovering the property, which he sold for $500,000. As a

record of service in the Confederate army was now a great political advantage in Kentucky he received the Democratic nomination for governor in 1887 and was elected by a large majority. His four years' term as governor was creditable but not brilliant. In 1891 he was elected a delegate to the constitutional convention and was instrumental in making the Kentucky constitution of that year. He then returned to his estate, "Glen Lily," near Munfordville, where he carried on farming operations, often engaging in manual labor himself. He visited Louisville frequently and was a familiar figure at the historic Galt House, where he might often be seen in the lobby smoking his corn-cob pipe. In 1896 when the Democrats embraced free silver he bolted the party and was himself nominated for the vice-presidency on a national Democratic ticket headed by John M. Palmer, another native-born Kentuckian. Buckner was active in the campaign and so completely was the Democratic party split in Kentucky that McKinley received the state vote, the first time the Republicans ever received the electoral vote of the state. Buckner died near Munfordville in 1914, the last of the lieutenant-generals of the Confederacy, and was buried in the Frankfort Cemetery.

He was married twice: first in May 1850 to Mary Kingsbury, who died soon after the Civil War, and then in 1885 to Delia H. Claiborne of Richmond, Va. Tall and manly in appearance, he was friendly and considerate to the most lowly, and was always unassuming in whatever position he occupied. He maintained a life-long friendship with Gen. Grant, which began at West Point and was not broken even when he surrendered to Grant at Fort Donelson; he was one of those who offered to come to Grant's assistance in his financial difficulties, and he acted as a pallbearer at Grant's funeral.

[For Buckner's military career as well as a sketch of his earlier career see E. P. Thompson, *Hist. of the First Ky. Brigade* (1886); *Hist. of the Orphan Brigade* (1898); Jos. Cross, *Papers from the Portfolio of an Army Chaplain*; and E. M. Coulter, *Civil War and Readjustment in Ky.* (1926). The *Official Records* (Army), contain his official military dispatches, and the documents relating to his governorship are in the state library in Frankfort. Obituaries containing appreciations of his life may be found in Louisville *Courier-Journal*, *Lexington Leader*, *Lexington Herald*, and *N. Y. Times*, for Jan. 9, 1914.]

E. M. C—r.

BUDD, JOSEPH LANCASTER (July 3, 1835–Dec. 20, 1904), pioneer in horticulture, was born near Peekskill, N. Y. His early life was spent on the farm and he was prepared to take a college course. This plan, however, he was obliged to abandon. In 1857 he moved to Rockport, Ill., where he spent two years in teaching. Then, first at Wheaton, Ill., and soon after at

Shellsburg, Ia., he entered on a successful career as a nurseryman, orchardist, and instructor in horticulture. He was made secretary of the Iowa Horticultural Society and for twenty-one years prepared its annual reports. In 1876 he became professor of horticulture and forestry in the Iowa Agricultural College. Old-world methods and foreign text-books were of subordinate value for the American climate and agricultural conditions. For the great Northwestern states a very different horticultural practise had to be developed. Budd became the leader in this work and one from whom many in this field received their first training and enthusiasm. Following a journey to Russia in 1882, he imported into the Northwest from that country hardier varieties of fruit trees to withstand the severe winters. This work proved to be of the greatest value to the Northwestern states. In Dakota and Manitoba practically the only varieties of apples grown are of Budd's introduction, and hundreds of orchards and groves in the colder parts of the Northwest bear testimony to his great service. His work extended successful fruit-growing much further north than had ever before been possible. Assisted by N. E. Hansen he published in 1902–03 a *Manual of American Horticulture* in two volumes. He was a man of sterling integrity, buoyant nature, considerable literary ability, and great enthusiasm and energy. In 1869, his health broken by his strenuous life, he resigned his active professorship, remaining emeritus professor. He was married on Jan. 26, 1861, to Sarah M. Breed. He died at Phœnix, Ariz.

[*Proc. Iowa Park and Forestry Ass.*, Dec. 1904, p. 116; L. H. Bailey, ed., *Cyc. of Am. Ag.*, vol. IV (1909); Clarence Ray Aurner, *Hist. of Ed. in Iowa*, vol. IV (1916); B. F. Gue, *Hist. of Iowa*, vol. IV (1903).]
E. H. J.

BUEHLER, HUBER GRAY (Dec. 3, 1864–June 20, 1924), educator, was of German descent through his father, David A. Buehler, lawyer, journalist, and president of Pennsylvania College, while through his mother, Fanny Guyon, he traced his ancestry back to the French Huguenot settlers of Staten Island. From both sides came a strong religious heritage which led him to enter the ministry of the Lutheran Church (1889). He was born in Gettysburg, Pa., and except for two years spent in teaching at St. James' College, Maryland (1883–85), he lived in his native town until his twenty-eighth year. Gettysburg provided him an education in its Preparatory School (1877–79), in the Pennsylvania College (1879–83), which granted him its B.A. in 1883 and its M.A. in 1886, and finally in its Lutheran Theological Seminary (1885–89). It offered him also experience in teaching and

administration (1887–92) as professor of Latin and Greek in the College and as principal of the Preparatory School.

Meantime in 1891 he received an invitation from Edward G. Coy to join the faculty of the newly-founded Hotchkiss School for boys at Lakeville, Conn. His acceptance ended his connection with Gettysburg except for his return to marry Roberta Wolf in 1892 and for occasional visits with his family. At the formal opening of Hotchkiss in October 1892 he began his new duties as master in English. Of medium height, rather slender build, and somewhat diffident manner, he did not reveal his real power to the casual observer. But his students soon recognized in him a precision and orderliness of thought and an ability to present facts clearly which brought him a wide reputation with the publication of three little books that grew out of his teaching—*Practical Exercises in English* (1895), *A Modern English Grammar* (1900), and, in collaboration with Caroline W. Hotchkiss, *Modern English Lessons* (1903). These qualities were turned to new uses when, after Coy's death, he was appointed headmaster of Hotchkiss (1904) after a year as acting headmaster. His genius for organization brought new vigor and efficiency to the school, whether directed toward enlarging the buildings, beautifying the grounds, or building up a strong teaching staff and attracting able students. His achievement was recognized by election to the presidency of the Headmasters' Association (1914–15). Thoughtful always of the atmosphere of dignity he believed should characterize a great school, he had a handsome study built in the headmaster's house commanding a splendid view of lake and mountains, and arranged carefully every detail of the entertainment of guests and the formal ceremonial of school life. With his enthusiastic support, plans were laid out for the eventual replacement of the old buildings by others at once more beautiful and permanent. As the years passed, his whitening hair and the gradual filling out of his figure made him more and more impressive in appearance, and his natural shyness became overlaid with a certain formality of manner that led his boys to call him "the King," though it failed to conceal from them the essential kindliness, simplicity, and genuine humor of the man. A fine portrait in the school library records his appearance during these years. After nearly twenty years of service as headmaster, he was warned by a series of heart attacks that he needed rest. Arrangements were made for a year's leave of absence during 1924–25, but death intervened less than a week after the school commencement.

[Material about Buehler's parentage, his father's connection with Pennsylvania College, and his own life there as a student is to be found in the *Pennsylvania College Book* (1882). For his life at Hotchkiss much material is available scattered through the weekly *Hotchkiss Record* and the *Mischianza*, the school annual. The issues of the latter during his headmastership contain a brief biographical sketch listing his various accomplishments, with dates for each. The *Hotchkiss Alumni Bulletin* issued a Memorial number in August 1924 with eulogies and estimates of his services to the school. MSS. in the possession of Mrs. Buehler, and the records of the school and college at Gettysburg and those of Hotchkiss contain further material about him.]   G. V–S.

BUEL, JESSE (Jan. 4, 1778–Oct. 6, 1839), agriculturist, the youngest of the fourteen children of Elias Buel, farmer and Revolutionary major, was born in Coventry, Conn. In 1790 the family moved to Rutland, Vt., where two years later Jesse was apprenticed to a printer. Learning the trade in four years instead of the customary seven, he worked for a year as a journeyman printer, and then successively, with various partners, started three weekly newspapers in Troy and Poughkeepsie. In the meantime, in 1801, he married Susan Pierce of Troy. In 1803, Buel's accumulations were wiped out by business losses. Undiscouraged, however, he immediately founded the *Kingston Plebeian,* which he ran for ten years, serving also for a time as judge of the Ulster county court. In 1813 he moved from Kingston to Albany, where he founded his fifth weekly newspaper, the *Argus.* He published the *Argus* for seven years, during the last six of which he was also printer to the State. He had already begun to be interested in farm problems, and devoted space in his paper to agricultural articles. In 1821, having achieved a competence, he disposed of his publishing interests and began the agricultural efforts that were to make him widely known both in the United States and abroad. He bought for $30 an acre a tract of eighty-five acres lying in the "Sandy Barrens," west of Albany. Unhampered by the prejudices of the traditional farmer, Buel applied scientific practises to his own farm—drainage, deep plowing, destruction of weeds, maintenance of livestock, application of manure and plowing under of green crops for fertilizer, and crop rotation instead of the customary naked-fallow system. As a result, his farm became a show place and by 1839, eighteen years after he had purchased it, was yielding returns on a valuation of more than $200 an acre (Preface to *The Farmer's Companion,* 1893). From his entrance into farming, he devoted tireless energy to the improvement of agriculture and rural life. In 1822 he became recording secretary to the State Board of Agriculture, and two of the three volumes issued by that body in its six years of existence were apparently edited by him (*Memoirs of the Board of Agriculture of the State of New York,* vol. II, 1823; vol. III, 1826). In 1823 he was elected from Albany County to the New York Assembly. Immediately this unassuming, quietly dressed, smooth-faced printer-farmer became the leading spokesman for agriculture. He was a member of the committee on agriculture, and offered a resolution looking to the establishment of a state agricultural school (*New York Assembly Journal,* 1823, p. 796). For the next thirteen years, in and out of the legislature, he advocated this educational enterprise, and, finally, under pressure of a state agricultural convention, in 1836, over which he presided, the legislature acted. The money, however, was to be raised by public subscription rather than by legislative appropriation, and efforts by Buel and others to enlist support were discouraging. In the meantime, under the auspices of the State Agricultural Society, Buel had in 1834 established the *Cultivator,* one of the first popular agricultural journals. Although a number of other farm periodicals were being published, their subscription prices ranged from $2 to $4 a year, while the *Cultivator* charged but fifty cents. Notwithstanding this fact, the magazine was markedly superior to other farm journals of the time. In it Buel emphasized not only scientific farm practises but also the need for professional schools of agriculture and for agricultural instruction in the district schools. In 1836, running as a Whig, Buel was defeated for the governorship of New York by William L. Marcy, but he made no mention of his candidacy or any other party matter in his magazine. His interest in education led to his appointment as a regent of the University of the State of New York. The Massachusetts Board of Education urged him to prepare a book for school and rural libraries, which he did under the title of *The Farmer's Companion.* First published in 1839, this book went through at least six editions. A two-volume work, *The Farmer's Instructor,* made up chiefly of reprints from the *Cultivator,* was issued in the same year. Buel also edited an edition of *A Treatise in Agriculture,* by John Armstrong. He had planned still another book, to deal with grain crops, gardening, and similar topics, but his unexpected death at Danbury, Conn., intervened (see Note to *The Farmer's Companion,* 2nd edition, p. 4). Buel is properly considered by Bidwell and Falconer "to typify the movement for agricultural improvement in the East from 1820 to 1840" (*History of Agriculture in the Northern United States, 1620–1860,* 1925). This simple, self-educated man not only exerted powerful influence on the rural thought of his own time, but laid out an educational program which was in large measure adopted in the late nineteenth and early twentieth centuries.

[Authoritative information as to Buel's views and agricultural activities is obtainable from his books and from the files of the *Cultivator*, 1834–39. Two speeches, *Address Before the Berkshire Ag. Soc.* (1837), and *Address Delivered Before the Ag. and Hort. Soc. of New Haven County, Conn.* (1839) are also of interest. *A Eulogy on the Life and Character of the Late Judge Jesse Buel* (1840), delivered by Amos Dean before the N. Y. State Ag. Soc. embodies a biographical sketch. This is reprinted in the 6th edition of *The Farmer's Companion*, pp. vii–xxiv. The *Cultivator* for November 1839 contains a brief obituary.]   N. A. C.

BUELL, ABEL (Feb. 1, 1741/42–Mar. 10, 1822), silversmith, typefounder, and engraver, the son of John Buell of Killingworth, Conn., served his apprenticeship with the silversmith Ebenezer Chittenden and about the year 1762 set up on his own account in his native town of Killingworth. Almost his first action was to employ his craftsman's skill in raising a series of five-shilling Connecticut notes to the more comfortable denomination of five pounds. For this error in judgment and conduct he was tried at Norwich in March 1764 and sentenced to branding, imprisonment, and confiscation of property. Released from prison by the Assembly some months later, "from a compassionate regard and pity on his youthful follies," Buell succeeded in gaining a restoration of civic rights by the construction of a lapidary machine of his own invention for the cutting and polishing of crystals and precious stones. He next applied his ingenious mind to learning the art of typefounding. In May 1769, Edes & Gill of Boston printed the proof of an advertisement set in types of Buell's design and casting. A copy of this "first Proof struck by American Types" as Gale described it remains to-day in the Yale University Library, the first crude specimen sheet of an English-American typefounder. In October 1769, as the answer to a printed petition set in another font of his own making, Buell was granted a subsidy of £100 by the Connecticut Assembly to aid him in the establishment of a type foundry in New Haven, but he took no further steps toward the immediate realization of this enterprise. About the year 1770, he began to exercise his clever fingers in the art of copperplate engraving. In 1773 or 1774 he engraved the Chart of Saybrook Bar drawn from surveys made by Abner Parker to render the entrance to the Connecticut River easier of navigation. In March 1784 he achieved his chief work as engraver in the publication of a large wall map of the territories of the United States according to the Peace of 1783. Crude in some respects and soon outmoded, this map of 41 x 46 inches yet has distinction in that it was the first map of the new political division to be compiled and engraved by one of its citizens. It was probably while employed as an engraver on the Bernard Romans charts of the Florida coast that Buell fell in debt to James Rivington, the New York printer of the Romans maps, and it was probably, too, this work that gave rise to the tradition that Buell surveyed for Romans the Pensacola section of the Florida coast. It is not certain that Buell was ever in Florida or that he came in contact with Romans until the surveys for the charts were completed and the eccentric engineer had come to New York to arrange for their publication. The debt to Rivington and the unreturned £100 he had received from the Connecticut Assembly forced Buell to abscond from New Haven and to remain outside the Connecticut jurisdiction from 1775 until 1778. He was enabled to return through the loyalty and industry of his wife Aletta, who kept his silversmith establishment, "At the Sign of the Coffee Pot," in operation during the period of his absence and ultimately discharged his indebtedness to the government. The claim of the "inhuman varlet" Rivington, as Aletta called him, lapsed because the printer had joined the British and could no longer prosecute in the Connecticut courts.

At last in 1781 Buell began to supply type in quantity to the Greens of New Haven and New London. Meanwhile typefounding had become an established industry in Germantown, Pa., and thus, though Buell was the initiator of the art in English America, he had forfeited the distinction of being the first to put it on a practical commercial basis. Until the end of the century he remained in New Haven busily employed as a man of affairs. He operated a line of packet boats, helped develop a marble quarry, conducted a regular vendue, owned or had an owner's interest in two privateersmen, fashioned silver and jewelry, cast type, practised the art of engraving, made plans, drawings and models for all sorts of engineering work, invented a machine for planting corn, exhibited a negro in the process of turning white, and in many directions turned his hand to things interesting and useful to his community but rarely profitable to himself. In 1785 he invented a machine for coining money and formed a company that made copper coins under the supervision of the state for the ensuing two or three years. In 1789 he went to England to learn cotton manufacturing and in 1793 is found for a short time at "the cotton manufactory near New York." Two years later he built at New Haven a cotton mill which drew a prophecy of success from President Stiles, but like most of his projects this seems to have failed soon after its beginning operations. In 1799 he removed to Hartford and began his life anew as silversmith, armorer, and engraver of printers' ornaments. About 1805 he is found as a silversmith in Stockbridge, Mass., where under the influence of the religious revival of 1813 he abjured the doctrines of Thomas Paine, which he had previously held, and threw himself into the practise of Christianity with the fervor that characterized all his actions. He died in the Alms House in New Haven at the age of eighty-one years, described in the newspaper notice of his death as "an ingenious mechanic." He was married first in 1762 to Mary (Parker); second, probably in 1771, to Aletta Devoe; third in 1779, to Mrs. Rebecca (Parkman) Townsend; fourth, to Sarah ——, who died in 1803.

[Lawrence C. Wroth, *Abel Buell of Conn., Silversmith, Type Founder and Engraver* (1926); E. G. Jones, *Stockbridge, Past and Present* (1854); J. W. Barber, *Conn. Hist. Colls.* (1836).]   L. C. W.

BUELL, DON CARLOS (Mar. 23, 1818–Nov. 19, 1898), Union soldier, descended from William Buell, a Welshman who settled in Windsor, Conn., about 1639, was born near Marietta, Ohio, the son of Salmon D. and Eliza (Buell) Buell. When he was five years old his father died, and the boy was taken to his uncle, George P. Buell of Lawrenceburg, Ind., where he remained—barring five years passed with his stepfather in Marietta—until 1837 (M. R. Martin, *History of Marietta and Washington County, Ohio,* 1902, pp. 697 ff.). In the latter year he was appointed cadet at West Point, and four years later he graduated as second lieutenant, 3rd Infantry. He participated in the Seminole War. In 1846 he joined Taylor's army in Texas. Promoted first lieutenant, he was brevetted captain for gallant and meritorious conduct at Monterey on Sept. 23, 1846. Transferred to Scott's army, he was again brevetted in the following year for gallant conduct at the battles of Contreras and Churubusco. After the Mexican War he became an adjutant-general, and at the commencement of the Civil War was a lieutenant-colonel in the Adjutant-General's Department.

He was appointed brigadier-general United States Volunteers, on May 17, 1861, and aided in organizing the Army of the Potomac. Selected by Gen. McClellan to organize and train the Federal forces in Kentucky, he arrived at Louisville early in November, assuming command of the Army of the Ohio. The mission assigned this army was to invade and liberate east Tennessee, largely Union in sentiment. Buell foresaw the difficulties of moving from Louisville toward Knoxville, in a country lacking roads and railroads, especially in view of the presence of large Confederate forces then at Bowling Green, and on Nov. 27, profiting by the suggestion of an engineering officer, he recommended to McClellan an advance by the Cumberland and Tennessee Rivers toward Nashville, as auxiliary to the desired advance toward east Tennessee. Both McClellan and President Lincoln strongly disapproved of this plan, but Buell stuck to his recommendation, and urged the abandonment of the East Tennessee project. On Feb. 6, 1862, he was authorized to march on Bowling Green, in support of an advance under Grant up the Cumberland and Tennessee Rivers.

With 50,000 men, Buell started out. Due to Grant's victories at Forts Henry and Donelson, he met no opposition, and reached Nashville on Feb. 24. On Mar. 11, President Lincoln placed Buell under the orders of Gen. Halleck, and the latter ordered him to advance on Savannah, twenty-two miles north of Corinth on the Tennessee River. Nothing being said about haste, Buell marched very leisurely. As late as Apr. 4, he was advised by Grant that there was no need to hurry. By good luck, the leading division of Buell's army arrived on the Tennessee River on Apr. 6, the first day of the Confederate attack at Shiloh. Ferried across the river, this division by its presence restored the sinking fortunes of the Federal troops. During that night two more divisions came up and crossed the river. On Apr. 7, Buell attacked the Confederates. He had fresh troops and superior numbers, and forced the enemy back until they abandoned the field. No effort was made to pursue them.

Buell had been promoted on Mar. 21 to be a major-general, United States Volunteers. He accompanied Halleck's army to Corinth, but on June 10 was detached with four divisions, and ordered to proceed to Chattanooga following the railroad to that place. He was directed to repair this railroad as he advanced, an order which caused the failure of his expedition. The work was interrupted by raiding parties, and constant repairing so delayed Buell that he never arrived at his destination. On July 28, Morgan's cavalry completely stopped his advance by destroying railroad communications, and on Aug. 6 Buell knew that Bragg's Confederate army had reached Chattanooga. Buell then concentrated his forces near Murfreesboro, Tenn. On Sept. 2, Buell learned that the Confederate general, Kirby

Smith, advancing by Cumberland Gap, had defeated the Federal forces at Richmond, Ky. Knowing also that Bragg had started north from Chattanooga, he suspected that the latter was en route to join Kirby Smith. Buell therefore decided to leave a small force to cover Nashville, and to march at once with the greater part of his forces into Kentucky. Arriving at Bowling Green on Sept. 14, he found Bragg ahead of him at Glasgow, and between him and his base at Louisville. He decided not to attack on a field chosen by his antagonist, and soon Bragg moved away and left the road to Louisville open. Buell arrived at that city on Sept. 25.

On Oct. 1, Buell marched out to seek battle, and on Oct. 8, three divisions of his army found Bragg's forces at Perryville. A severe battle was fought, with indecisive results. Bragg however withdrew, leaving the battlefield in Buell's possession. The latter followed slowly for four days, when he discontinued the pursuit. Disappointed in the escape of Bragg's army, the Federal government relieved Buell on Oct. 24, and on Oct. 30, he surrendered the command of his army to Rosecrans. The army did not regret the change. It was the general opinion that Bragg should have been forced to a decisive battle, and relentlessly pursued thereafter. Buell's explanation that his failure to pursue was due to his inability to live off the country has been questioned, as Bragg subsisted his army in that way, and the Federal forces were better supplied than the Confederates. A military commission was convened in November 1862 to investigate Buell's conduct. On Apr. 15, 1863, the commission reported the facts without recommendation. The government, however, after keeping him for a year in waiting orders, discharged Buell as a major-general of volunteers, and he thereupon immediately resigned his regular commission on June 1, 1864. Grant later recommended his restoration to duty, but no action was taken. After the war Buell settled in Kentucky and engaged in mining; for a time he was a pension agent. He died at Rockport, Ky.

Buell was an excellent organizer and disciplinarian. He utterly disregarded politics. A friend of McClellan, to whom he owed his first important assignment, he was charged with being opposed to the administration. His reserved and studious character emphasized this belief, and led to the difficulties of the Kentucky campaign not being rightly estimated. His campaigns showed no military genius, but they were as good as those of other generals in the West. The early departure of Buell from military life prevented the development of what might have been a good general. Grant evidently thought so, and he was probably correct. Buell was of medium stature, wore a full beard, and had a stern, determined appearance. His wife was Margaret (Hunter) Mason of Mobile (*Courier-Journal*, Louisville, Sept. 4, Nov. 20, 1898).

[*Official Records* (*Army*), 1 ser., X, XVI, XX, XXIII; Jas. B. Fry, *Operations of the Army under Buell . . . and the "Buell Commission"* (1884); J. C. Ropes, *The Story of the Civil War* (1894–1913); *Battles and Leaders of the Civil War* (1887–88); *Thirtieth Annual Reunion Ass. Grads. Mil. Acad.* (1899), pp. 105–18; Jas. B. Hudnut, *Commanders of the Army of the Cumberland* (1884).]   C. H. L.

BUFFALO BILL. [See CODY, WILLIAM FREDERICK, 1846–1917.]

BUFFUM, ARNOLD (Dec. 13, 1782–Mar. 13, 1859), Quaker, anti-slavery lecturer, was the grandson of Joseph Buffum, of the second or third generation of his family in America, who moved from Massachusetts to Smithfield, R. I., in 1715. There Arnold, second son among eight children of William and Lydia (Arnold) Buffum, was born. William Buffum was a farmer and merchant, a Quaker, and a member of the Providence Society for Promoting the Abolition of Slavery. Fugitive slaves sheltered in his household enlisted his son's sympathies for anti-slavery. Without extensive education, Arnold became a hatter; but having an inventive mind, he conceived and patented various mechanical contrivances. Until he was fifty he was but partially successful at his trade, residing now at Smithfield or Providence, now in Massachusetts or Connecticut. Between 1825 and 1831 business led him twice to Europe, where he met Thomas Clarkson, Amelia Opie, and Lafayette. Returning, he established in Fall River certain "infant schools," based on some foreign educational theory.

As president of the New England Anti-Slavery Society from its organization in January 1832, Buffum was commissioned as its lecturing agent, thereafter devoting what time he could to forwarding emancipation. This meant personal danger and sacrifice of friends and business interests, but his moral courage, eloquence, and telling appeals for the negro's freedom made a deep impression. He was one of the founders of the American Anti-Slavery Society in Philadelphia in 1833. Thither he moved about 1834, establishing himself in the hatting industry. In 1840–41 he aroused serious reflection, ripening into anti-slavery sentiment, throughout Ohio and Indiana by lecturing and by editing at New Garden (now Fountain City), Ind., the *Protectionist*. Rejecting Garrison's and Phillips's radical principles, Buffum, by voice and vote, supported successively the Liberty, Free-Soil, and Republican parties. He also exerted himself in behalf of temperance.

Buffum married (1803) Rebecca Gould, from near Newport, R. I. His daughter, Elizabeth (Buffum) Chace [*q.v.*], became a Garrisonian anti-slavery worker, his younger son, Edward Gould Buffum, Paris correspondent of the *New York Herald*. Muhlenberg, Arnold Buffum's fellow passenger on a European trip (1843), thus describes him: "An Old Hickory Abolitionist . . . a tall, gray-headed, gold-spectacled patriarch . . . a very sharp old fellow [who] has all his facts ready, . . . abuses his country outrageously" as being pro-slavery, but still a "genuine democratic American." Buffum was of religious nature, and had high literary tastes. In 1854 he entered the Raritan Bay Union, Perth Amboy, N. J., where he died.

[Lillie B. C. Wyman and Arthur C. Wyman, *Elizabeth Buffum Chace* (1914); W. P. and F. J. Garrison, *Wm. Lloyd Garrison* (1889); Anne Ayres, *The Life and Work of Wm. A. Muhlenberg* (1880); information from Mrs. L. B. C. Wyman, Buffum's grand-daughter.]

R. S. B.

BUFORD, ABRAHAM (July 31, 1749–June 30, 1833), Revolutionary soldier, was descended from Richard Beauford who emigrated from England about 1635 and some years later received grants of land along the Rappahannock River. He was born in Culpeper County, Va., the son of John and Judith Beauford. In the first year of the Revolution he raised a company of minutemen from his county, and had a share in the operations which resulted in the expulsion of the royal governor, Lord Dunmore. He served throughout the war, in the earlier years with the army in the North, and later under Morgan. He was commissioned major of the 14th Virginia Nov. 13, 1776, lieutenant-colonel 5th Virginia Apr. 1, 1777, and colonel May 15, 1778, taking command of the 11th Virginia Sept. 14, 1778, and of the 3rd Virginia Feb. 12, 1781. Early in 1780 the condition of affairs at Charleston became precarious. Buford enlisted recruits for its relief, marched southward, and had reached a point on the Santee River when he learned that the city had capitulated. He was ordered by Gen. Huger to return to North Carolina, removing or destroying the military stores. His little army numbered about 300 to 400 men. To intercept him, Lord Cornwallis dispatched 270 men under Col. Tarleton, and by forced marches this famous cavalry commander overtook Buford at the Waxhaws, a locality nine miles from Lancaster, near the state boundary. A parley ensued; the events following are a matter of controversy. American historians have usually charged Tarleton with treachery. His own account is: "A report

among the cavalry that they had lost their commanding officer (when his horse was shot) stimulated the soldiers to a vindictive asperity not easily restrained" (Tarleton, quoted in H. B. Carrington, *Battles of the American Revolution*, 1876, p. 498). John Marshall gives the common American view: Tarleton "demanded a surrender on the terms which had been granted to the garrison of Charleston. This was refused. While the flags were passing, Tarleton continued to make his depositions for the assault, and the instant the truce was over, his cavalry made a furious charge on the Americans, who had received no orders to engage, and who seem to have been uncertain whether to defend themselves or not. In this state of dismay and confusion, some fired on the assailants, while others threw down their arms and begged for quarter. None was given" (*Life of Washington*, 1884–87, I, 337). The Americans lost 113 killed, and about 200 prisoners, of whom about 150 were badly wounded. All the stores were captured, and Buford with a remnant of his force was saved only by rapid flight. "Tarleton's Quarter" became proverbial; "Buford" was the countersign of the day of the frontiersmen who a few months later stormed King's Mountain (Theodore Roosevelt, *The Winning of the West*, 1889–96, II, 272). Tarleton himself defended his course, as we have seen, and Cornwallis in a dispatch to Clinton recommended him for especial favor. But the contemporary English historian, Stedman, observed, "The virtue of humanity was totally forgot."

After the war, Buford received warrants for land grants, and bought the claims of his brother. In October 1788 he was married to Martha, daughter of Judge Samuel and Mary (McClung) McDowell. Migrating to Kentucky, he became a deputy surveyor, and located his grants in the Blue Grass region and elsewhere. He settled near Georgetown in Scott County, where he possessed a fine estate, entertained many persons of prominence, and died.

[M. B. Buford, *Hist. and Genealogy of the Buford Family* (1903), revised and enlarged by G. W. Buford and M. B. Minter (1924); T. M. Green, *Historic Families of Ky.* (1889).]

E. K. A.

BUFORD, ABRAHAM (Jan. 18, 1820–June 9, 1884), Confederate soldier, stock-raiser, belonged to a family which was originally of French origin and which later held large estates in England and Scotland. The first American Bufords settled in Virginia, descendants later migrating to Woodford County, Ky., where William B. Buford, formerly of Culpeper County, Va., became noted as a breeder of blooded horses and cattle. Abraham Buford, the son of William B. and Frances Walker (Kirtley) Buford, was born in Woodford County. He received his earlier education under Verpyle Payne, a teacher of some note, and at Centre College; and was graduated from the Military Academy at West Point in 1841, with such men as D. C. Buell, Z. B. Tower, H. G. Wright, A. P. Howe, and Thomas J. Rodman. Upon graduation, young Buford was assigned to the First Dragoons, and saw immediate service in Kansas and Iowa, then part of the frontier. Promoted to a first lieutenancy in 1846, he participated in the war with Mexico, and was brevetted captain for gallant and meritorious services in the battle of Buena Vista. From the years 1848 to 1851 he was stationed in New Mexico; and, after being promoted to captain in 1853, was assigned to duty the year following at the cavalry school for practise at Carlisle. His resignation from the army followed, Oct. 22, 1854, and he retired to his stock farm, Bosque Bonita, near Versailles, Ky., where for some years he specialized in the breeding of thoroughbred horses and short-horn cattle. With the outbreak of the Civil War, he was appointed in 1862 a brigadier-general in the Confederate army. His command of Kentucky troops covered the retreat of Gen. Bragg to Knoxville, Tenn., and thereafter he commanded a brigade of Loring's division until the spring of the year 1864. He was then assigned to a cavalry brigade of Gen. Forrest's command, consisting of the 3rd, 7th, and 8th Kentucky Cavalry, and participated with this noted leader in numerous engagements and raids. He was severely wounded at Lindville, Dec. 24, 1864, and was unable to resume active command until the spring of 1865. After the war, he returned to his stock farm, which became a great social-center in the Blue-Grass region, where he became one of the best known turfmen in Kentucky. He acquired ownership of the celebrated horses, Crossland, Nellie Gray, Selena, Inquirer, Hollywood, Marion, and Versailles, and delighted in lavish entertaining of noted sportsmen from all over the country. Himself a man of marked force of character and mentality, with magnificent physique, he took a deep interest in politics; and although originally strongly espousing state rights and having reluctantly yielded to secession, he subsequently used his best efforts for a united country. In the year 1845, he had married Amanda Harris of New York, from which union he had one son William, who died in 1872. With the loss of this son, and the loss of his wife afterward, came severe financial reverses also, resulting in the eventual loss of his home. Crushed by grief and advancing years, Buford ended his life by his own hand at Danville, Ind.

[M. B. Buford, *Hist. and Geneal. of the Buford Family in America* (1903); J. M. Armstrong, *Biog. Encyc. of Ky.* (1878); *Official Records (Army)*; *Army Register of the U. S. for One Hundred Years (1779–1879)*; *15th Ann. Report, Ass. Grads. U. S. Mil. Acad.* (1884); Louisville *Courier-Journal*, June 10, 1884. Although certain authorities give Buford the name "Abram," he matriculated at West Point as "Abraham," and this is confirmed by the President of the Woodford Sun Co., Versailles, Ky. (letter of Feb. 10, 1927), who furthermore confirms the date of Buford's death as June 9, 1884, and not 1864, as mistakenly given in certain biographies.]

C. D. R.

BUFORD, JOHN (Mar. 4, 1826–Dec. 16, 1863), Union soldier, was eighth in descent from Richard Beauford, who came from England in 1635, at the age of eighteen, and settled in Lancaster County, Va. Members of the family became extensive landowners, devoted themselves to horse raising and the cultivation of tobacco, and furnished many soldiers in the early Indian wars and in the Revolution. A change was made in the spelling of the name as a result of the troubles with the mother country. John was the son of John and Anne (Bannister) Watson Buford, widow of John Watson. He was born in Woodford County, Ky., was appointed to the West Point Military Academy from Illinois, and graduated in 1848, standing sixteenth in a class of thirty-eight members. On May 9, 1854 he married Martha McDonald Duke. After a year as brevet second lieutenant he was promoted to second lieutenant in the 2nd Dragoons, and to first lieutenant on July 9, 1853. He saw frontier service in Texas, New Mexico, and Kansas and was appointed regimental quartermaster in 1855 at the time when the Sioux expedition was organized to punish the Indians who had massacred Lieut. Grattan's party. In the winter campaign which followed, ending with the defeat of Little Thunder's band, near Ash Hollow, Nebr., on Sept. 3, he won the approval of Col. Philip St. George Cooke, the commanding officer. The expedition was broken up in July 1856, and the troops hastened to a new field of action in the Kansas troubles of that year. Just then the danger point shifted to the difficulties with the Mormons in Utah. The 2nd Dragoons were recalled in haste from duty in Kansas, on three or four days' notice, and ordered to make a march of 1,100 miles in the dead of winter through an uninhabited wilderness, under the conditions of war. During this march the quartermaster was the hardest-worked man in the command, and Col. Cooke reported Buford as a "most efficient officer." Next came the troublous times of 1861. The regiment marched overland for sixty days to Fort Leavenworth, and made its camp in Washington in October 1861. More than a year after the war began, Gen. Pope came to Washington to take a high command. He was surprised to find Buford there in an unimportant position, and at once asked for his advancement. Buford was accordingly promoted brigadier-general on July 7, 1862. Two days later he took command of the reserve brigade of cavalry and within less than ten days was in action at Madison Court House. Pope's movement had been delayed too long and Lee's Manassas Campaign had begun. Finding the enemy on his front, flank, and rear, Buford extricated his command and retreated toward Sperryville. When Jackson appeared in Pope's rear on Aug. 28, McDowell sent Buford beyond Thoroughfare Gap for observation. Buford captured fifty of Jackson's stragglers, struck the head of Longstreet's column, delayed him for several hours, and counted seventeen regiments of infantry, five hundred cavalry, and a battery of artillery. He then made his report, retreated, and acted as rear guard for Ricketts's Division. When Pope's army retreated to Centerville on the 30th, Buford's brigade covered the withdrawal across Bull Run at Lewis Ford, on the extreme left. The pursuing cavalry attacked, and Buford was so severely wounded that he was at first reported to be dead. The Confederate commander claimed a victory.

Buford was disabled by his wound and on sick-leave until Sept. 10, 1862, when he was announced as chief of cavalry of the Army of the Potomac. The position had only nominal importance on the staff of the commanding general. Buford seems to have still been suffering from his wound, as he served in this minor capacity under McClellan and Burnside at the battles of South Mountain, Antietam, and Fredericksburg. When Gen. Hooker in February 1863 consolidated the cavalry into an army corps, Buford resumed command of the reserve brigade, and rendered effective service both in Stoneman's raid toward Richmond and in covering the retreat of Hooker's army after Chancellorsville. When Lee began his second invasion of the North, well covered by Stuart's cavalry on his right, the efforts of the Federal cavalry to penetrate the screen brought on daily combats and considerable actions at Aldie Gap, Upperville, Middleburg, and Ashby's Gap. Buford, now in command of a division, crossed the Potomac on June 27, reached Gettysburg on June 30, and drove back the advance of Hill's corps which was approaching from Cashtown. On July 1 the Confederate advance on the Cashtown road was opposed by a single brigade of Buford's cavalry, dismounted at about one man to a yard of front, with one battery against two of the enemy. Hill was delayed for about two hours, at the end of which

time Buford was relieved by the arrival of Reynolds's corps. Later in the afternoon the cavalry was withdrawn to Seminary Ridge where it was opposed to McGowan's South Carolina brigade. Meanwhile Buford's other brigade was doing equally good work on the other roads which entered Gettysburg further to the north and east; it reported the advance of Ewell's corps, and held its ground until relieved by Howard's corps. On July 3 Buford was sent to Westminster ostensibly to guard the trains but more probably to relieve the fears of Washington concerning an enemy raid. His absence from the battlefield gave Longstreet the opportunity to surprise and defeat Sickles's corps on the 3rd. From Westminster Buford was sent to Williamsport on the Potomac to capture Lee's retreating trains, but when he arrived on July 6 he found the Confederates there, with cavalry, infantry, and artillery, trains parked and intrenched. Cavalry actions were fought at Westminster, Boonsboro, Beaver Creek, and Funkstown. When the opposing armies got back into Virginia a season of maneuvering began and lasted for months. Buford's division was heavily engaged at Manassas Gap, Chester Gap, Morton's Ford, and Rixeyville. Toward the latter part of November, Buford received leave of absence owing to failing health. He went for treatment to Washington where he died on Dec. 16. His commission as major-general was put in his hands just before his death. He was buried at West Point.

[*Official Records* (*Army*); G. W. Cullum, *Biog. Reg.* (3rd ed., 1891); J. C. Ropes, *The Army under Pope* (1881) and *The Story of the Civil War* (1894-1913); *Battles and Leaders of the Civil War* (1887-88); obituary in the Washington *Evening Star*, Dec. 17, 1863; M. B. Buford, *Genealogy of the Buford Family in America* (1903).]   E. S.

BUFORD, NAPOLEON BONAPARTE (Jan. 13, 1807–Mar. 28, 1883), Union soldier, half-brother of John Buford [*q.v.*], was born on a plantation in Woodford County, Ky., the second child of John Buford by his first wife, Nancy Hickman. He was a grandson of Simeon Buford, who migrated from Virginia to Kentucky in 1790 and settled in what was to become Woodford County. Napoleon Buford graduated sixth in his class in the United States Military Academy, July 1, 1827, and was commissioned a lieutenant of artillery. He attended the artillery school at Fortress Monroe, Va., 1827–28; was on topographical duty along the Kentucky River and at the Rock Island and Des Moines Rapids of the Mississippi, 1828–29; was in garrison at Fort Sullivan, Me., 1830–31 and 1832–34; studied on leave of absence at the Harvard University Law School during 1831; was assistant professor of natural and experimental philosophy at West Point 1834–35; and resigned from the Army, Dec. 31, 1835. For the next seven years he was in the service of his native state as engineer in charge of the Licking River improvement. He then followed his family to Rock Island, Ill., where he was successively a merchant, iron founder, railroad promoter, and banker. In 1850 he was a member and secretary of the board of visitors of the Military Academy. The outbreak of the Civil War ruined him financially, for his bank had invested heavily in the bonds of Southern states. Making over his entire property to his creditors, he helped raise the 27th Illinois Volunteers, was commissioned its colonel, Aug. 10, 1861, and was presently in action.

At Belmont, Mo., Nov. 7, 1861, the 27th Illinois was left behind in the retreat and might easily have fallen into the hands of the enemy; Buford, with a cool head and accurate information about the terrain, took his men down a by-road to the river and got them aboard a gunboat without mishap. In a subsequent parley over the exchange of prisoners he met his classmate, Leonidas Polk [*q.v.*], who wrote of him to Mrs. Polk: "He is as good a fellow as ever lived, and most devotedly my friend; a true Christian, a true soldier, and a gentleman, every inch of him." Buford took part in the demonstration on Columbus, Ky., Feb. 23, 1862, and was in command of the town, Mar. 4–14, after its evacuation by the Confederates. He was in the siege of Island No. 10 Mar. 14–Apr. 7, and commanded the garrison after its capitulation. During the siege he took a small detachment and fell on Union City, Tenn., early in the morning of Mar. 31, taking the town by surprise and capturing a number of prisoners, one hundred horses, and a quantity of munitions and stores. For this exploit he was promoted to brigadier-general of volunteers, Apr. 15, 1862. He participated in the expedition to Fort Pillow, Tenn., Apr. 10–20, and served in the Mississippi campaign of the following summer. During the pursuit after the second day's fighting at Corinth, Miss., Oct. 4, 1862, he suffered a sunstroke. While recuperating he was sent to Washington on court-martial duty and was a member of the court that convicted Gen. Fitz-John Porter [*q.v.*]. On his return to the West he was in command of Cairo, Ill., Mar.–Sept., 1863, and of the District of East Arkansas, with headquarters at Helena, Sept. 12, 1863–Mar. 9, 1865. There he did his most notable work. He coped successfully with smugglers, guerrilla parties, and lessees of plantations (some of whom, he declared, were as bad as the enemy), organized a freedmen's department of 5,000 men,

established an orphan asylum and an industrial school for liberated slaves, and prosecuted dishonesty among his own subordinates. In spite of an inadequate force of men and much illness, he gave an excellent account of himself. The state of his health finally compelled him to ask for a change of duties. He was relieved of his command by an order of Mar. 6, 1865, was brevetted major-general of volunteers, Mar. 13, "for gallant and meritorious service during the Rebellion," and was on leave of absence from Mar. 9 until Aug. 24, 1865, when he was mustered out of the volunteer service.

He was superintendent of the Federal Union Mining Company in Colorado June 1–Dec. 1, 1866, special United States commissioner of Indian affairs, Feb. 7–Sept. 1, 1867, and special United States commissioner to inspect the completed Union Pacific Railroad, Sept. 1, 1867–Mar. 10, 1869. The latter years of his life were spent in Chicago, where he was one of the founders of the Chicago Society of the Sons of Virginia and was a social favorite. He was twice married: first, to Sarah Childs of Cazenovia, N. Y.; and second, to Mrs. Mary Anne (Greenwood) Pierce. He died in Chicago and was buried at Rock Island.

[*Official Records*, ser. I, II, III; G. W. Cullum, *Biog. Reg.*, I, 389–90 (3rd ed., 1891); T. M. Eddy, *The Patriotism of Ill.*, II, 53–57 (1866); *Battles and Leaders of the Civil War* (1884–88); W. M. Polk, *Leonidas Polk, Bishop and General* (1893); M. B. Buford, *Geneal. of the Buford Family in America* (San Francisco, 1903; rev. ed. by G. W. Buford and M. B. Minter, LaBelle, Mo., 1924); *Biog. Encyc. of Ill.* (1875); *Quinquennial Cat. Harv. Univ. Law School 1817–1924* (1925); *Chicago Daily Inter-Ocean*, Mar. 29, 31, 1883.]
           G. H. G.

BULFINCH, CHARLES (Aug. 8, 1763–Apr. 4, 1844), architect, public official, was descended from Adino Bulfinch, a sail maker, who was surveyor of highways in Boston in 1706. The son of Thomas Bulfinch and his wife Susan Apthorp, Charles came of a wealthy and cultivated Boston family. He graduated at Harvard in 1781, and early cultivated a taste for architecture which was greatly stimulated during a tour of England and the Continent in 1785–87. He saw the monuments of Paris under the suggestions of Jefferson, whose classical tendency influenced his young compatriot, and he then followed Jefferson's route through Southern France and Northern Italy, pressing on to Florence and Rome. On his return to Boston his talents were soon laid under contribution by friends, to whom he gave gratuitous advice in architecture. He was married on Nov. 20, 1788 to Hannah Apthorp, by whom he had eleven children, one of them Thomas Bulfinch [*q.v.*], the author. March and April following his marriage were passed by

Bulfinch in a visit to Philadelphia and New York. The observations of this tour were quite as influential in forming his style as were those of foreign travel. His first design, submitted in November 1787, soon after his return from abroad, had been for a new State House, but this project remained for a time in abeyance. In 1788 the old Hollis Street Church was built from his plans, and was followed by designs for churches at Taunton and Pittsfield. The Beacon monument of 1789, a Doric column sixty feet high, testified to his classical interests, as did the triumphal arch erected the same year for Washington's reception in Boston. The State House at Hartford, begun in 1792 from his plans, was on the most ambitious scale yet attempted in New England. He was one of the projectors of the Boston Theatre and gave the design for the fine building erected in 1793 (burned, and rebuilt by him, 1798). His public work of this first period was crowned by the building of the Massachusetts State House on Beacon Hill, with its portico and the famous dome, later gilded, which served Oliver Wendell Holmes as "the hub of the universe." Although the Capitol at Washington, which inaugurated the prevailing domed type of American governmental buildings, had been begun on a still larger scale in 1793, it remained long unfinished, so that the Boston State House was at its completion in 1800 the most conspicuous public building in the United States. In the same period Bulfinch inaugurated likewise a reformation of the domestic architecture of New England, where he introduced the delicate detail of the Adam style. His first houses, from 1792, were those for Joseph Coolidge, and, more important, the one for Joseph Barrell in Charlestown. This had an oval parlor projecting on the garden side in the manner of the design adopted the same year for the president's house at Washington. Above was a semicircular portico with tall columns. In these houses curved staircases were adopted for the first time in New England. The scheme of the Barrell house was soon followed in the famous mansion of Elias Hasket Derby in Salem (design by Bulfinch, modified and executed by Samuel McIntire). Bulfinch's public services had led to his election in 1791, at the age of twenty-seven, to the board of selectmen of the town of Boston, on which he was to serve, with one interval, for twenty-six years. Here he was active on committees which for the first time lighted the streets of the town in 1792, admitted children of both sexes to the public schools, and attempted to secure the adoption of a form of city government. Events meanwhile brought about a tragic

change in Bulfinch's situation in life. In 1793, following models seen in England, he had projected for the first time in America a row of houses of coherent design, the Tontine or Franklin Crescent, which still gives the line to Franklin St. in Boston. It consisted of sixteen houses with an arch in the center, over which were rooms assigned to the Boston Library Society and the Massachusetts Historical Society. The houses at the ends and others opposite were adorned with tall pilasters. Enthusiastic for the success of the project, Bulfinch took over the shares of less sanguine backers. In 1795 he declined his reëlection as a selectman to devote himself to the State House and to his own affairs, but in the financial depression of that year he became so deeply involved that in January 1796 he was adjudged bankrupt and the large monetary rewards were later reaped by others. His talents in architecture, hitherto so generously exercised for others by the amateur and gentleman of fortune, now became the basis of a professional practise by which he gradually reëstablished a modest livelihood. In these years he built the first of three houses for Harrison Gray Otis which is still standing on Cambridge St., the Morton house in Roxbury, a court house at Dedham, and other buildings. In 1799 he was reelected to the board of selectmen of which he now acted as chairman until his departure for Washington in 1817. This service was unpaid, though when a police system was created Bulfinch was also appointed superintendent of police at a salary of $600. The years of his chairmanship were those of the great development of old Boston, the form of which is due in large degree to Bulfinch in his dual capacity of official and architect. The neglected Common was turned into a park and fronted on three sides with fine buildings of uniform character: Park St., 1803-04; Colonnade Row on Tremont St., 1809-11; and Beacon St., from about 1800. Bulfinch also laid out on regular plans the lands on Boston Neck, those in South Boston (1804), and those on the site of the Mill Pond (1808). He designed India Wharf with its admirable warehouses, and also designed for the town the fine almshouse, two school-houses, the enlargement of Faneuil Hall (1805), the Boylston Market (afterward Public Library), and the Court House (later City Hall, demolished 1862). During this period his architectural practise included a number of public buildings elsewhere in Massachusetts, the State Prison at Charlestown, the Massachusetts General Hospital (1817-20), several banks, as well as many churches and private houses. Of the churches the most notable were the Cathedral of the Holy Cross (1805) and the New South Church (1814), both in Boston, and Christ Church in Lancaster (1816–17). Following in general the schemes of Wren's churches in London, Bulfinch gave great attention to the varieties of the type, which are illustrated in a series of his manuscript drawings.

In December 1817, on the resignation of Latrobe, the architect of the Capitol in Washington, President Monroe offered the post to Bulfinch, who removed with his family to Washington and remained in charge until the building was finished in 1830. Essentially he was called on to complete the wings and construct the central part according to the lines already established by the earlier architects, Hallet, Thornton, and Latrobe. His principal contribution was the detailed form of the western front. His mildness of temper enabled him to avoid the controversies which had enmeshed Latrobe, on whom had fallen the burden of establishing professional standards, and led Bulfinch to compromise in certain matters such as the excessive height of the central and lateral domes. Meanwhile he had found time to design the Unitarian Church in Washington (demolished in 1900), the state capitol at Augusta, Me. (1828–31), and several institutional buildings. After his return to Boston at the age of sixty-seven he lived in retirement, with occasional visits elsewhere, until his death in 1844.

Bulfinch exercised a wide influence on the architecture of New England, where his version of the Adam style became characteristic of the early republican period. His earliest and most gifted follower was Samuel McIntire of Salem who remodeled his style after seeing the Barrell and Derby designs. Alexander Parris similarly followed Bulfinch's style in his houses in Portland. Asher Benjamin made its forms widely accessible through his early publications, and it remained dominant in New England until the advent of the Greek revival about 1820.

[C. A. Place, *Chas. Bulfinch, Architect and Citizen* (1925) assembles the material on Bulfinch's life, for which the principal source is the *Life and Letters* (1896) by his grand-daughter Ellen S. Bulfinch. Additional detail on various phases of his work may be gleaned from Thos. A. Fox, "A Brief Hist. of the Boston State House" in the *Am. Architect,* XLVIII, 127; C. A. Place, "From Meeting House to Church in New England" in *Old-Time New Eng.,* vols. XIII, XIV, and "The New South Church," *Ibid.,* vol. XI; Fiske Kimball, *Domestic Architecture . . . of the Early Republic* (1922), and "The Derby Mansion" in *Essex Inst. Hist. Colls.,* LX, 273; Glenn Brown, *Hist. of the U. S. Capitol* (1900–03); and *The Documentary Hist. of the U. S. Capitol* (1904). Bulfinch's library and a number of his manuscript drawings are preserved by the architectural department of the Mass. Inst. of Technology, other drawings by the Essex Inst., Salem.]   F. K.

BULFINCH, THOMAS (July 15, 1796–May 27, 1867), author, was one of the eleven children of Charles Bulfinch [*q.v.*] and Hannah Apthorp, and was born at Newton, Mass. His education was obtained at the Boston Latin School, Phillips Exeter Academy, and Harvard University, where he was graduated in 1814, having W. H. Prescott as a classmate. After graduation he taught for a year in the Boston Latin School and was then for a short time an assistant in the store of his elder brother. In 1818 he accompanied his family to Washington, D. C., where his father had been appointed architect of the Capitol, and was in business there for six years. In 1825 he returned to Boston and attempted various business enterprises, without success. In 1837 he received a clerkship in the Merchants' Bank of Boston, which he held until his death. He seems to have lacked initiative in the world of affairs and to have been content with the small position which insured him a livelihood and left him considerable leisure, which he devoted to study and writing. Natural history interested him and he was for six years secretary of the Boston Society of Natural History. He cared little for politics and hated controversy but supported William Lloyd Garrison in the anti-slavery movement. Literature was his chief interest and a number of books resulted from his hours of study: *Hebrew Lyrical History* (1853), *The Age of Fable* (1855), *The Age of Chivalry* (1858), *The Boy Inventor* (1860), *Legends of Charlemagne* (1863), *Poetry of the Age of Fable* (1863), *Shakespeare Adapted for Reading Classes* (1865), and *Oregon and Eldorado* (1866). *The Boy Inventor* is a memoir of his brilliant pupil Matthew Edwards who died early. *Oregon and Eldorado* was suggested by his father's connection, as an organizer, with a sea expedition to the Northwest coast, which had much to do with the discovery of the Columbia River. Bulfinch's best-known work is *The Age of Fable*. It is a successful attempt to make mythology interesting, has gone through several editions, and is still widely used as a reference book by students. Greek and Roman mythology receive the most attention but chapters are devoted to Scandinavian, Celtic, and the various Oriental mythologies. *The Age of Chivalry* is a similar but less successful attempt to popularize the Arthurian and early Welsh legends. At the time of his death Bulfinch was at work on *Heroes and Sages of Greece and Rome*. He always remained a bachelor and lived with his parents, to whom he was devoted. His short experience in teaching had interested him in boys and he was helpful to them on many later occasions. His was a gentle, modest personality. The excitement which his material life lacked he supplied by his mental absorption in the deeds of heroes and adventurers. He died in Boston and his funeral was held in King's Chapel.

[The chief source of information is an appendix to a sermon preached by the Rev. Andrew Preston Peabody at King's Chapel, Boston, the Sunday following the decease of Bulfinch, and published under the title *Voices of the Dead* (1867). This appendix gives the facts of Bulfinch's life, taken from the class-book of his Harvard class, of which he was secretary; a genealogy of the direct descendants of Adino Bulfinch; and an appreciation of Thos. Bulfinch by Mr. Peabody. *Memorials of the Dead in Boston; Containing Exact Transcripts of Inscriptions on the Sepulchral Monuments in the King's Chapel Burial Ground* (1853), by Thos. Bridgman, contains chapters on the Bulfinch and Apthorp families. Obituaries were published in the *Boston Commonwealth*, June 1, 1867, and the *Boston Daily Advertiser*, May 28, 1867.]   S. G. B.

BULKELEY, MORGAN GARDNER (Dec. 26, 1837–Nov. 6, 1922), governor of Connecticut, senator, was born in East Haddam, Conn., the son of Judge Eliphalet Adams Bulkeley (1803–1872) and Lydia S. (Morgan) Bulkeley. His ancestry went back to Peter Bulkeley [*q.v.*], the first pastor of the church at Concord, Mass., and included the Rev. Gershom Bulkeley (1636–1713), clergyman, physician, magistrate and publicist. Judge Bulkeley moved to Hartford when Morgan was nine years old. President of the Aetna Life Insurance Company, judge of the police court, commissioner of the school fund, and a founder of the Republican party in Connecticut as well as its first speaker of the House, Judge Bulkeley was a man of considerable moment. At the age of fifteen Morgan left the Hartford Public High School to take a job as errand boy in an uncle's store in Brooklyn, N. Y. There he became in turn confidential clerk and partner. His work was interrupted by the Civil War. He enlisted with the 13th New York Regiment and was with Gen. McClellan in the Peninsular campaign. Later he was to be commander of the Grand Army of the Republic in Connecticut and war memories were always to color his political views. On the death of his father in 1872 he returned to Hartford. There he helped to found the United States Bank and was its first president. In 1879 he became the third president of the Aetna Life Insurance Company and continued as such until his death. Under his management the Aetna became one of America's soundest financial institutions; its assets rose from twenty-five million dollars to over two hundred million dollars and the number of employees increased from twenty-nine to fifteen hundred. Bulkeley was responsible for the establishment of two subsidiary companies, the Aetna Casualty and Surety Company, and the Automobile In-

surance Company of Hartford, and was also instrumental in merging the Aetna National and the Hartford National banks, as well as the Charter Oak and the Phœnix National banks. He was a trustee and director in many corporations; his financial interests covered a wide field.

He early entered politics. In Brooklyn he served on the Republican general committee for Kings County. In Hartford, starting as councilman, he passed from alderman to president of the court of common council. Elected mayor in 1880, he served for four terms, 1880–88, and then was nominated on the Republican ticket for governor. Luzon B. Morris, the Democratic candidate received 75,074 votes to Bulkeley's 73,569, but five thousand scattering votes made it so that neither candidate had a "majority of all the votes cast," as was required by the constitution. The Republican legislature accordingly seated Bulkeley. The next election, that of 1890, was the first to be held under a new secret-ballot law, and it proved to be much more complicated than that of 1888. Morris, Democrat, received 82,787 votes to 76,745 for Merwin, Republican. There were, however, enough scattering votes to prevent a clear majority, providing all the ballots cast were counted. But in the counting, Morris sympathizers had thrown out certain "specked" ballots though the defects were purely mechanical. The two branches of the legislature were of opposite political faiths and could not agree on what should be done. The Democratic Senate held that the "specked" ballots were illegal and that Morris was accordingly clearly elected; consequently they refused to concur with the Republican House in a legislative election. There resulted a deadlock and Gov. Bulkeley held over. A Democratic comptroller, Staub, had, however, been unquestionably elected and was seated. As custodian of the capitol he tried to recognize Morris as his superior. Locking the governor's office he detailed special officers to keep Bulkeley out. The Governor, thereupon, called a superior force and sending for a crowbar pried his way into office. A decision by the supreme court upheld him but a legislative deadlock continued throughout his term; no laws, appointments, or appropriations were made. For two years the state was financed from the private funds of Bulkeley and the Aetna.

Elected governor in 1892, Morris had all the acts and accounts of his predecessor validated, and a constitutional amendment instituted plurality elections, but the larger question of Connecticut's system of representation smoldered till the legislative session of 1901. At that time it was possible for twenty per cent of the voters of

Connecticut to elect a clear majority of both branches of the legislature. Gov. George P. Mc-Lean called attention to this fact and when remedial legislation was blocked a movement for a constitutional convention was inaugurated. This movement Ex-Governor Bulkeley vigorously opposed. He debated the matter before the legislative committee with James G. Batterson, president of the Travelers Insurance Company. (See *The Debate on Constitutional Amendments, Session 1901,* by James G. Batterson and Morgan Gardner Bulkeley.) He was defeated, the question went to the voters, and the convention was authorized. There Bulkeley decided to kill the proposed revision with kindness. A final resolution of the convention (No. 253) discloses his hand: "Whereas, Ex-Governor Morgan G. Bulkeley and the Honorable Delegate Lewis Sperry have correctly revised . . . the original Constitution of 1818, . . . be it Resolved by this honorable body that we extend to them our thanks." The proposed constitution was submitted to the people and, as Bulkeley had anticipated, was overwhelmingly defeated.

During 1905–11 Bulkeley was United States senator and was often out of sympathy with President Roosevelt. He joined Senator Foraker in fighting the President's order which summarily discharged—in dishonor—a whole battalion of colored troops of the 24th Infantry, because some of its individual members had been charged with "shooting up" the town of Brownsville, Tex. He also opposed Roosevelt on the Philippine tariff issue. He strenuously objected to placing the tobacco growers of Connecticut in competition with the labor standards of the Filipino and when the President sent for him on this matter he frankly informed the President that he was in Washington to represent the interests of the Commonwealth of Connecticut. Roosevelt's "New Nationalism" ran squarely counter to all of Bulkeley's principles. Perhaps no other matter so vitally affected the Senator as did insurance. Insurance affairs came to a head in 1905. Roosevelt's nationalistic idea was immediately in evidence and there was much talk of federal regulation. Bulkeley was extremely active and the idea did not get very far in the Senate. The question was referred to the Judiciary Committee and on June 25, 1906, that body reported that it was unanimously of the opinion "that the Congress is without authority under the Constitution to supervise and regulate the business of marine, fire, and life insurance, except in the District of Columbia, the Territories, and the insular possessions of the United States."

Greatly interested in sports, Bulkeley was con-

nected with the National Trotting Association for thirty years. He organized numerous baseball teams and was president of the National League when it was founded in 1876. He was also an antiquarian and collector. He arranged for the restoration of the Nathan Hale School-House in East Haddam and led the movement of private citizens for the preservation of the Bulfinch Old State House in Hartford. He was married to Fannie Briggs Houghton in 1885.

[*Hartford Courant,* Nov. 7, 1922; *Hartford Times,* Nov. 7, 1922; *Hartford Telegram,* July 2, 1888; *The Aetna-Izer,* vol. VII, no. 13, special issue, Dec. 1922; *Life Insurance Sales Training Course for Aetna-Izers* (Hartford, 1925), Bk. II, sections on "The Early Development of Life Insurance in Conn." and "Hist. of the Aetna Life Insurance Co."; *Commemorative Biog. Records of Hartford City* (2 vols., 1901); F. C. Norton, *Governors of Conn.* (1895); F. W. Chapman, *The Bulkeley Family* (1875); J. H. Trumbull, *Memorial Hist. of Hartford County, Conn., 1633–1884* (1886).]
E. F. H.

BULKELEY, PETER (Jan. 31, 1582/3–Mar. 9, 1658/9), Puritan clergyman, son of Edward and Olyff (Irby) Bulkeley, was born at Odell in Bedfordshire, England, and died in Concord, Mass. Both his parents were of distinguished ancestry. His father, a man of independent means, was a Church of England clergyman somewhat touched with dissent. At about sixteen, Peter entered St. John's College, Cambridge, where he remained for a long time as student (M.A., 1608) and fellow, acquiring an education to be approved of later by Cotton Mather as "Learned, . . . Genteel, and which was the top of all, very Pious" (*Magnalia,* 1702, Bk. III, p. 96). In January 1619/20, upon the death of his father, he succeeded to a considerable fortune and to his father's position as rector of Odell. He was married twice. His first wife, Jane Allen, after giving birth to twelve children, died in 1626. "A thundering preacher and a judicious divine" (Daniel Neal, *The History of the Puritans,* 1754, p. 585), he was clear in his disapproval of ritualism and of men with long hair, but not so clear that his recalcitrance could not be overlooked by ecclesiastical superiors who were themselves often of his view-point. But on the accession of Laud to the archbishopric, recognizing the divergence between himself and those in control of the Church, Bulkeley determined in 1634 or 1635 to emigrate to Massachusetts. His second wife, Grace Chetwode, whom he had but recently married, and his many children and servants came with him in 1636. After a short residence in Cambridge, he went up "further into the Woods" (Mather, *Magnalia,* Bk. III, p. 96) and established a new town, with a church of which he was officially made "teacher." He was from that time head of the theocracy of Concord, diligently and with substantial results, so far as one can judge, furthering the interests of his followers in both this world and the next. His chief participation in affairs away from Concord was in 1637, when, with Thomas Hooker, he served as moderator of a church council held in Cambridge, to determine among other things, whether for salvation one should look more confidently to grace or to works. Himself a partisan of works, he denounced Anne Hutchinson as a "Jezabell whom the Devill sent over thither to poison these American Churches with her depths of Satan" (*New England Historical and Genealogical Register,* XXXI, 157). His *Gospel Covenant,* made up of a number of his sermons, was published in London in 1646, and again in 1651—"one of those massive, exhaustive, ponderous treatises, into which the Puritan theologians put their enormous Biblical learning, their acumen, their industry, the fervor, pathos, and consecration of their lives" (M. C. Tyler, *History of American Literature during the Colonial Time,* 1897, I, 217).

[Additional references: *New Eng. Hist. and Geneal. Reg.,* vol. X; F. W. Chapman, *Bulkeley Family* (1875); J. W. Bailey, *Paternal Pedigree* (1907).]   J. D. W.

BULKLEY, JOHN WILLIAMS (Nov. 3, 1802–June 19, 1888), educator, was descended from the Rev. Peter Bulkeley [*q.v.*], an emigrant from Bedfordshire, England, in 1636 and one of the early settlers of Concord, Mass. One branch of the family spread into Connecticut, in which state, at Fairfield, John Bulkley was born. It was his father's intention that his son on leaving the common school should take up an occupation of a mechanical nature. Intellectual pursuits appealing more to the youth, however, he betook himself to Clinton, N. Y., where he entered upon a study of the classics and mathematics with a view to entering Hamilton College in an advanced class. Although intending to enter the ministry on graduation, he was forced to make a temporary digression in favor of a sea voyage to restore his health which had become impaired during his studies. In 1825, after his return, he took up "school keeping" but only as a temporary expedient. He found the work so congenial, however, that he made a permanent profession of it. After teaching for six years in his home town, he was called to Troy, N. Y., where as teacher and principal he was so successful that his services were sought by numerous academies and public schools. In 1838 he accepted a position in a new public school in Albany, N. Y. Williamsburg secured his services in 1850 and when Williamsburg, Bushwick, and Brooklyn united into a single municipality, he was chosen

as the first superintendent of schools. It was Bulkley's fortune to spend his most productive years during the period commonly known as the American "common school revival," a period during which education was becoming popularized and a professional consciousness was being developed among teachers. His early reports as superintendent of schools in Brooklyn were definite attempts to stimulate his board of education and his community to espouse the cause of educational improvement. He early advocated teacher training and Pestalozzian object teaching. His chief contribution, however, lay in his activities in organizing teachers' associations. While he was still in Troy, he aided in the organization of the Troy Teachers' Society, one of the first in the state. He assisted in projecting the convention at Syracuse in 1845 which launched a New York state teachers' association, the first of its kind in the country. As the first president of the association and as president again in 1851 he continued his leadership of the convention. He was one of the eleven original founders of the National Teachers' Association, now the National Education Association. He served this great organization as its first secretary and fourth president. In 1873 he was made assistant superintendent of schools. This unusual demotion seems to have been made because of his advanced age and in lieu of dismissing so old and tried a public servant. In 1885 he declined reëlection for the triennial period on account of failing health, and three years later he died at the age of eighty-six.

[The principal sources of biographical material are Henry Barnard's *Am. Jour. of Ed.,* XIV, 28, XV, 349; and the *N. E. A. Jour. of Proc. and Addresses,* 1888, p. 677. An obituary appeared in the *N. Y. Times,* June 21, 1888. Bulkley's reports to the Brooklyn Board of Education also are of interest for the period 1855–73. The *Brooklyn Daily Eagle,* July 9, 1873 contains an account of his election as assistant superintendent.]

J. S. B—r.

BULKLEY, LUCIUS DUNCAN (Jan. 12, 1845–July 20, 1928), physician, was born in New York City, the son of Henry D. and Juliana (Barnes) Bulkley. His father was a prominent general practitioner with a special interest in skin diseases, and his own career was largely a continuation of his father's dermatological activity. Having graduated in arts at Yale in 1866 and in medicine from the College of Physicians and Surgeons in 1869, he studied dermatology in Europe under such masters as Von Hebra and Neumann of Vienna, and Hardy of Paris, and in 1872 settled in his native city with the aim of limiting his practise to dermatology. On May 28, 1872, he was married to Katherine La Rue Mellick. His father was now dead, but aided by the professional support of the latter's friends, he soon laid the foundations of a large and select practise. In the conviction, however, that a practise cannot be self-perpetuating but requires incessant publicity to thrive, he plunged into many professional activities beginning with a translation of Isidor Neumann's *Lehrbuch der Hautkrankheiten* (1872), which he had begun while in Vienna. With others he organized the clinical activity of the Demilt Dispensary into a teaching force and thus laid the foundation for systematic post-graduate teaching which culminated in the New York Post-Graduate Medical School and the New York Polyclinic. He founded (1874) and for eight years edited the *Archives of Dermatology* and was throughout his career a contributor to medical journal literature, and published many text-books. He took an active part in the work of the then new local and national dermatological societies, but as his aggressiveness made enemies he failed in two of his aims,— the presidency of the American Dermatological Association and the chair of dermatology in his alma mater. He became, however, professor of dermatology in the Post-Graduate Medical School and Hospital, was from 1887 to 1900 chairman of the section on dermatology of the American Medical Association, and in 1897 was president of the American Academy of Medicine. Beginning in 1877, he gave free courses of instruction in dermatology at the New York Hospital, later transferred to the New York Skin and Cancer Hospital which he founded in 1882. He traveled much in the interest of his special work, attending many congresses both in this country and Europe and studying exotic diseases in their habitat, and he accumulated an unrivaled collection of books, pamphlets, plates, models, etc., pertaining to his special work. On retiring from dermatological activity he astonished the profession by coming out for the non-surgical treatment of cancer, at first with reservations but eventually limiting it to diet, hygiene, and drugs. He published books and journal articles on his attitude, established a free clinic, and founded a special society and a quarterly journal, *Cancer*. The reaction of the profession was on the whole very unfavorable, his motives were impugned, and he was forced to sever some of his society and hospital affiliations. But his motives were certainly not mercenary, for he was worth a large fortune and his crusade cost him thousands of dollars. He had an instinctive horror of the knife (never forgetting the death of his father from incision of a carbuncle, now regarded as bad surgery); he was a religious mystic who believed that his life had often been spared for some

special end which might well have been the conquest of cancer; he loved controversy, especially when on the weak side; and he needed an outlet for his energies, old as he then was. His mentality was highly extroverted and he was unequal to reflection and self-criticism; but, while he often blundered, he usually won his case by sheer energy and persistence. He did not abandon his work until blinded by double cataract and did not long survive his enforced rest. *Eczema* (1882, 3rd edition, 1901); *Acne* (1885); *Manual of Diseases of the Skin* (1882, 6th edition, 1912); *Syphilis in the Innocent* (1894), the Alvarenga Prize Essay; are the best-known of his writings, but he published a number of smaller works on dermatology and several volumes on the medical treatment of cancer which were not convincing to the profession: *Cancer, its Cause and Treatment* (2 vols., 1915–17); *Cancer and Its Non-Surgical Treatment* (1921; a second edition in press at the time of his death); and *Cancer of the Breast* (1924).

[*N. Y. Times* and *N. Y. Herald-Tribune*, July 21, 1928; *Archives of Dermatology and Syphilology*, Nov. 1928; *Jour. of the Am. Medic. Ass.*, July 28, 1928; Herman Goodman, "A Pioneer of Am. Dermatology," *Medic. Life*, Aug. 1928; *Who's Who in America*, 1924–25; personal information.]   E. P.

BULL, EPHRAIM WALES (Mar. 4, 1806– Sept. 26, 1895), horticulturist, was born in Boston, Mass., the son of Epaphras Bull of Bullsville, N. Y., and Esther Wales of Dorchester, Mass. He was a studious child, winning the Franklin medal for scholarship in the Boston public schools at the age of eleven, but was also given to strenuous physical work in his father's vineyard. Though from the first interested in grape raising, he was when a boy apprenticed to Louis Lauriat, a Boston chemist, to learn the trade of goldbeating, and this, until his reputation as a horticulturist was established many years later, was his profession. While practising it, he raised grapes in his garden on Fayette Street in Boston, and later on a more extensive scale at Concord, Mass. He worked chiefly with native stock, rather than the European wine grape, and was led to the use of sexual propagation by reading the classic treatise of Van Mons on raising pears from seed. At that time the "Isabella" was the earliest-ripened grape in the country; yet early as it was it did not always escape an early frost. Having discovered an extraordinarily early-ripening specimen of *Vitis labrusca,* the northern fox grape, Bull planted the grapes whole, and nursed the seedlings for six years. On Sept. 10, 1849, he picked the first fruit of these seedlings. For five years more he cared for the vines, reproducing them by cuttings, and continuing to replant the seeds. He obtained an astonishing number of variations by this method, even white grapes appearing from black parents. It is not certain just when Bull realized the superiority of one of the new strains that was to become the famous "Concord." He exhibited it on Sept. 3, 1853, at Massachusetts Horticultural Hall. Through a mishap the specimens almost failed to be noted by the judges; when brought to light, however, the new variety proved to be earlier than the "Isabella," extremely hardy, prolific, and phenomenally heavy, handsome, fragrant and juicy; it was both a good table grape and a wine grape. Bull sold this new grape at five dollars a vine, and the first year obtained $3,200 net income, but when nurseries bought the stock and propagated it for sale, he received almost no further income from the "Concord." For this reason he hated commercial grape culture, and died embittered. He produced also the white "Esther," the "Rockwood," the "Iona," and the "August Rose." He is said to have raised 22,000 seedlings, and to have saved only twenty-one as worthy of preservation. A member of the Massachusetts House of Representatives in 1855, he was chairman of the committee on agriculture, and the ensuing year occupied the same position in the Massachusetts Senate. From 1856 to 1858 he was a member of the Massachusetts State Board of Agriculture. Personally he was eccentric, and a lover of homely philosophy. His intimates included Louis Agassiz and Nathaniel Hawthorne. He was married on Sept. 10, 1826, to Mary Elden Walker of Dorchester, Mass.

[Sketch by Wm. Barrett in *Memoirs of Members of the Social Circle in Concord*, 4th ser. (1909); *Am. Breeder's Mag.*, I, 238–42; *The Story of Concord told by Concord Writers* (1906), ed. by Josephine Latham Swayne, pp. 157–58.]   D. C. P.

BULL, WILLIAM (1683–Mar. 21, 1755), lieutenant-governor of South Carolina, was the son of Stephen Bull, a man prominent in the first settlement of South Carolina and a deputy of Lord Ashley, a proprietor. Stephen was a member of the Council and engaged extensively in the Indian trade. His son, William, followed his father's example in both politics and trade. He was a member of the Commons House, 1706–19. During the Tuscarora and Yemassee wars he served as a captain of the militia. He was appointed Lord Proprietor's Deputy in 1719; and when the proprietary government was overthrown in the same year by the people with the connivance of the Crown, he was loyal to the proprietors. Despite his support of the defeated faction he was so prominent that he was made a member of the Council in 1721 under the new government and

served in that capacity until 1737. Also in 1721 he was chosen one of the three commissioners to manage the colony's lucrative Indian trade (*South Carolina Statutes*, III, 141–46), and his knowledge of colonial conditions led to his selection in 1733 as adviser to Oglethorpe in locating his first settlement in Georgia. Savannah was chosen, and Bull furnished laborers who worked for a month in building the new town. When Lieut.-Gov. Broughton died in 1737 Bull as senior member of the Council became acting governor and in 1738 lieutenant-governor, an office which he held until his death. His active administration lasted from 1737 until the arrival of Gov. Glen in 1743. From 1740 to 1742 his son, William Bull II [*q.v.*], was speaker of the House, and the laws of the province were authenticated by the signatures of father and son during this period. Bull's administration was notable for three constitutional advances. The governor was excluded from the Council's legislative sessions; the House secured control of money bills; and it obtained the right of electing a treasurer without the consent of the governor and Council. The colony was ready for these changes, but they were perhaps more easily obtained under a native-born governor who could readily understand the temper of the people. During Bull's administration the colony was menaced by war with Spain and by servile insurrection. In the handling of both situations he showed resource and decision. He persuaded the Assembly to vote 600 men and £120,000 paper money to aid Oglethorpe in an attack on St. Augustine, which failed because of Oglethorpe's incompetence. Bull himself sounded the alarm of the slave outbreak. On his way to Charleston he saw the negroes plundering, murdering, and compelling others to join the insurrection. Avoiding them, he hastened to his destination, gave the alarm, raised the militia, and succeeded in ending the revolt before it gained great headway. In addition to Ashley Hall and other property which he inherited from his father he obtained large grants in the province and settled on the Sheldon estate, adding materially to the family fortune. He was married to Mary, daughter of Richard Quintyne, who died on Mar. 19, 1738/39.

[A short sketch of Bull is in the *S. C. Hist. and Geneal. Mag.*, Jan. 1900. Some information regarding his public career may be found in Edward McCrady, *S. C. under the Proprietary Govt., 1670–1719* (1897), and *Hist. of S. C. under the Royal Govt., 1719–76* (1899). Source material is contained in the Commons House Jours.; the Council Jours.; the Pub. Records, and the *S. C. Hist. Soc. Colls.* (1858).]   H. B–C.

BULL, WILLIAM (Sept. 24, 1710–July 4, 1791), colonial governor of South Carolina, the second son of Lieut.-Gov. William Bull [*q.v.*], and of Mary (Quintyne) Bull, was born at Ashley Hall, South Carolina. He studied medicine at Leyden and was the first native-born American to receive the degree of Doctor of Medicine. After his return to South Carolina he did not practise his profession but devoted himself to agriculture and politics. His own ability, combined with the advantages of wealth and social position, made him important in the colony. He was a member of the Commons House in 1736–49, and was speaker, 1740–42 and 1744–49. In the war with Spain he was captain of one of the South Carolina companies. In 1748 he was appointed to the Council and served with distinction until he became lieutenant-governor in 1759. While in this position, he acted five times as governor, 1760–61, 1764–66, 1768, 1769–71, 1773–75, a total of eight years. In his relations with the Indians he showed moderation, but when forced to action against them he was energetic and determined. He was sent as commissioner to an Indian conference at Albany, in 1752, where peace was concluded between the Catawbas of South Carolina and the Iroquois of New York, allies of the English but at war with each other. He tried to avert the Cherokee war in 1759, counseling patience and further conferences with the Indians. His advice was not taken by Gov. Lyttleton, and for more than two years South Carolina was embroiled in Indian warfare. Once Bull took part in an active campaign, and after he had replaced Lyttleton as acting governor in 1760, he secured British and colonial aid, and finally in 1761 subdued the Indians. While Bull was primarily concerned with politics he was also interested in education. He contributed £150 to the College of Philadelphia (forerunner of the University of Pennsylvania) and in 1770 recommended that the colony establish public schools and a college for higher education, thus foreshadowing a public school system. His plan for free schools was lost because the colony was becoming absorbed in opposition to England. Bull's last four administrations as acting governor occurred during the critical period, 1764–75, and his tact and ability were tried to the utmost. Born and reared in the colony, he had a true understanding of colonial prejudices, but he was loyal to the British government and vainly endeavored to stem the growing revolutionary sentiment. At the time of the Stamp Act, he had the stamps landed at Fort Johnson at Charleston and prevented a clash with the mob in its first attempt to destroy the paper. When the tea ships arrived at Charleston, he acted with his usual dispatch and, before a hostile populace expected the move, he ordered the Collector to seize the tea and store it. In the summer of 1774 despite his efforts South Carolina ad-

vanced rapidly toward colonial union. Delegates were appointed by the people of Charleston to the First Continental Congress. A sympathetic House would have confirmed this action had not Bull kept it prorogued. Finally a meeting was contrived for an early hour in the morning, and, before the governor could order the House prorogued, the Charleston election was ratified, and £1,500 were appropriated for the delegates' expenses. By the summer of 1774 practically all power had passed out of the Governor's hands into those of the Provincial Congress, and when Bull was replaced by Lord William Campbell in 1775, his public career closed and royal authority ended in South Carolina. Bull retained the love and respect of the people, and his extensive estates were exempted from the act confiscating the property of royalists. He left the colony with the British troops in 1782 and spent the remaining nine years of his life in London. He had married on Aug. 17, 1746, Hannah, daughter of Othneal Beale.

[An outline of Bull's life is in the *S. C. Hist. and Geneal. Mag.*, vol. I. E. McCrady's *Hist. of S. C. under the Royal Government* (1899) and W. R. Smith's *S. C. as a Royal Province* (1903) give an account of his public career as identified with the colony's history in the period before the Revolution.]   H. B–C.

BULL, WILLIAM TILLINGHAST (May 18, 1849–Feb. 22, 1909), surgeon, the son of Henry B. Bull by his wife, Henrietta Melville, was born in Newport, R. I. The Bulls were descended from Henry Bull, one of the founders of the Roger Williams settlement at Newport (Aquidneck), who later was twice made governor of the colony. William was graduated from Harvard College in 1869 and in 1872 received the degree of M.D. from the College of Physicians and Surgeons of the City of New York. Following his internship at the Bellevue Hospital he studied for two years in the leading clinics of Vienna, Berlin, Paris, and London and then returned to New York City where he passed the rest of his life engaged in an active surgical practise. At various times he was associated with the New York Dispensary (1875–77), the Chambers Street Hospital (1877-78), the New York Hospital (1883), St. Luke's Hospital (1880–83), the Hospital for the Ruptured and Crippled, the Woman's and the Roosevelt hospitals. In these several positions he was active as teacher, consultant, and surgeon. From 1889 to 1904 he was professor of surgery at the College of Physicians and Surgeons.

Bull specialized upon the surgery of the abdomen, and his important contributions concern procedures which he studied and later advocated for treatment of gunshot wounds of the abdomen, for hernia, and for cancer of the breast. It is related that during his service at the Chambers Street Hospital a woman died following an abdominal bullet wound. At the autopsy Bull became convinced that through prompt laparotomy with suture of the damaged intestines such cases might be saved. A few months later (Nov. 2, 1884) a man was brought in with a similar wound and was promptly operated upon with complete success even though the intestines had to be sutured in seven places. Since then Bull's procedure for such emergencies has been adopted by all surgeons. With William B. Coley he published "Observations on the Mechanical and Operative Treatment of Hernia at the Hospital for Ruptured and Crippled" (*Annals of Surgery*, May 1893), in which he pointed out the inadequacy of the methods then employed and suggested improvements. With Coley also he wrote the sections on hernia in F. S. Dennis's *System of Surgery* (1896) and in the *International Textbook of Surgery* (1900). In 1894 he published a noteworthy paper on "Cases of Cancer of the Breast treated by Radical Operation, with a Report of 118 Cases" (*Medical Record*, N. Y., Aug. 18, 1894) which was the most valuable contribution by an American surgeon up to that time. With W. Martin he edited the translation of Bergmann, Bruns, and Mikulicz's *System of Practical Surgery* in five volumes which appeared in 1904. Early in 1908 he developed cancer of the neck, and as surgery and X-ray proved of no avail, he succumbed, February 22, 1909. He was married on May 30, 1893, to Mary, widow of James G. Blaine, Jr., and daughter of Col. Richard Nevins of Ohio.

Bull, like A. T. Cabot [*q.v.*], was deeply impressed by the early papers of Lister, with the result that he became one of the first in America to adopt antisepsis, and the large measure of success which immediately came to him on his return from Europe was undoubtedly due to this fact. He had in addition remarkable technical skill, great acumen in diagnosis, and a broad understanding of human problems. He is said to have been the first American who devoted himself entirely to surgery from the beginning of his practise. His avocations were music and art.

[There are numerous obituaries, but that by his co-worker, W. B. Coley, in the *Trans. Am. Surgic. Ass.*, 1909, XXVII, pp. 29–30, is the most complete and authentic; see also *N. Y. Times*, Feb. 23, 1909, and obituaries listed in the *Index Cat. of the Surgeon-General's Lib.*, 3 ser.]   J.F.F.

BULLARD, HENRY ADAMS (Sept. 9, 1788–Apr. 17, 1851), jurist, was born at Pepperell, Mass., the son of John and Elizabeth (Adams) Bullard. His father was a Congregational clergyman, his mother a member of the distinguished Adams family. He was sent to Harvard University where he took his A.B. degree in 1807. The Harvard alumni records also show that the degree of M.A. was conferred upon him in 1836. After graduating from the university he studied law, first in Boston and later in Philadelphia, and, at the same time, indulged a fondness for the modern languages by studying French, Spanish, German, and Italian, all four of which he is said to have been able to read and to speak with fluency. Soon after completing his legal studies, but before practising, he enlisted with Toledo, a Mexican revolutionary general who was in Philadelphia gathering recruits for an expedition into Mexico, then strongly affected by the liberation movement taking place in Latin-America. Toledo was so impressed by the young man, especially by his ability to speak Spanish, that he made him his secretary and aide-de-camp. They departed for the West, spent the winter of 1812–13 in Nashville, Tenn., and in the spring made their way to the frontier town of Natchitoches, La. From here they entered Spanish territory where, on Aug. 13,1813, their force was defeated and scattered by Spanish troops in an engagement near San Antonio, Tex. Bullard, and a few companions, after great hardships and dangers, managed to return to Natchitoches, where he decided, since he was friendless and destitute, to remain and open a law office. His ability to speak French and Spanish soon enabled him to form acquaintances with members of the leading families, most of whom were of French or Spanish origin; his education and culture, his handsome face, his musical voice, and his kindly sympathy created a favorable impression; he made himself familiar with the Napoleonic Code and with the Louisiana code of 1808; his practise increased and he prospered. On Oct. 24, 1816, he married at Natchitoches Sarah Maria Kaiser, a native of Lexington, Ky. Between 1822 and 1830 he twice served as state district judge. In 1830 he was elected, on the Whig ticket, to represent the Western District of Louisiana in the Twenty-second Congress. Reëlected to the Twenty-third Congress, he served until 1834, when he was appointed a judge of the supreme court of Louisiana. With the exception of a few months in 1839, when he was secretary of state of Louisiana, he remained upon the state supreme bench until 1846, when the judiciary was remodeled under a new constitution and the old bench replaced by a new. With Judge Curry he undertook to make a digest of the laws of the state, but only one volume was published because they knew that the constitutional convention, which was about to assemble, would necessarily change or abrogate many of the important laws. From 1847 to 1850 Bullard was professor of civil law in the University of Louisiana (now Tulane University). In 1850 he was elected to the state House of Representatives, but had served only a short time when he was elected to the Thirty-first Congress, as a Whig, to fill a vacancy in the 2nd Louisiana Congressional District caused by the resignation of Charles M. Conrad, appointed secretary of state in the cabinet of President Fillmore. Bullard was probably the founder of the Louisiana Historical Society in 1836, and was its first president. It fell into decay, was revived in the summer of 1846, and Judge Martin, the historian, was made president. The next year the society was incorporated. When Judge Martin died in December 1846, Bullard was again chosen president, and continued in that office until the time of his death. He was also a corresponding member of the Massachusetts Historical Society. He died in New Orleans, and is buried in the Girod Street Cemetery.

[B. F. French, *Hist. Colls. of La.*, pt. II (1851), pp. 5–8, including resolutions passed by the members of the New Orleans bar at the time of Bullard's death; *De Bow's Rev. of the Southern and Western States*, vol. XII (n.s., vol. V), pp. 50–56; New Orleans *Daily Picayune*, Apr. 22, 1851; inscription upon the tombstone in the Girod Street cemetery; Harvard University alumni records; records of Tulane University; information from Mr. Arthur Lastrapes, great-grandson, and Mrs. Robert Strother Moore and Mrs. O. W. McNeese, great-grand-daughters of Bullard.]   M.J.W.

BULLARD, WILLIAM HANNUM GRUBB (Dec. 6, 1866–Nov. 24, 1927), naval officer, the son of Orson Flagg and Rebecca Ann (Huston) Bullard, was born in Media, Pa., and graduated from the United States Naval Academy in 1886. He became ensign July 1, 1888; lieutenant, junior grade, Sept. 5, 1896; lieutenant Mar. 3, 1899; lieutenant commander Jan. 1, 1905; commander Feb. 1, 1909; captain July 1, 1912; rear admiral (temporary rank) July 1, 1918; and permanent rear admiral Oct. 20, 1919. Throughout the service he was known for his accomplishments, his poise of mind, and his invariable courtesy. In the Spanish-American War he served on the U. S. S. *Columbia*, and in 1905–06 and 1906–07 on the U. S. S. *Maine*, the first year as navigator and then as executive officer. During the following four years he was on duty at the Naval Academy, where he reorganized the department of electrical engineering, in which subject he was considered an expert. His *Naval Electricians' Test and Hand Book*, published in 1904, proved so useful that it has been reissued in several editions. In 1911 and 1912 he was commandant of the naval station at San Fran-

cisco, and from 1912 to 1916 superintendent of the naval radio service. He commanded the battleship *Arkansas*, 1916–18, his ship forming part of the American division of the British Grand Fleet in the World War. Later he commanded the American forces in the Eastern Mediterranean, and became a member of the Inter-Allied Commission to put into effect the naval terms of the armistice with Austria-Hungary, effecting, with notable tact and forbearance, the surrender of the Austro-Hungarian fleet. In January and August 1919, he was a member of the Inter-Allied conference on radio, and from 1919 to 1921 served as director of communications in the Navy Department. He commanded the Yangtze Patrol Force, U. S. Asiatic Fleet, in 1921–22, and retired Sept. 30, 1922.

Bullard has, with some show of justice, been called "the father of American radio," and there can be no doubt that his extraordinary knowledge of this subject, added to his firm stand for his country's rights, preserved to the United States her prestige in this field. The decisive turning point of his activities came in 1919, when, by his persistence and the convincing presentation of his views, he prevented the sale to foreign interests of the patent rights in the Alexanderson alternator. At the same time he counseled the formation of an independent company which developed into the Radio Corporation of America, the foremost body of the kind in the world. At his death he was chairman of the Federal Radio Commission. He was married to Beirne Saunders of Baltimore on Oct. 30, 1889, and had one son, a naval officer.

[*Who's Who in America*, 1926–27; Navy Registers, 1887–1927; "Admiral Bullard," by Capt. Edwin T. Pollock, *Army and Navy Reg.*, Dec. 24, 1927; "Admiral Wm. H. G. Bullard," in the *Outlook*, Dec. 7, 1927.]
E.B.

BULLITT, ALEXANDER SCOTT (1762–Apr. 13, 1816), lieutenant-governor of Kentucky, the son of Cuthbert and Helen (Scott) Bullitt, was of Huguenot descent, the first of the line in America having come from France in 1685 and settled at Port Tobacco, Md. The family later moved to Dumfries, Va., where Alexander Scott Bullitt was born. His father was a judge of the supreme court of Virginia and an uncle, Capt. Thomas Bullitt, was one of the first explorers of Kentucky. Alexander Scott Bullitt was educated for law and in 1783 was elected to the Virginia House of Delegates. During the same year, however, he was induced by the lure of frontier life to move to Kentucky where he settled on Bull Skin Creek in Shelby County. Being too much exposed to the Indians there, he removed in two years to Jefferson County and settled about eight miles from Louisville on an estate which he named "Oxmoor" from Tristram Shandy (T. W. Bullitt, *post*, p. 16).

Bullitt was one of the outstanding men of Kentucky from the beginning. In 1786 he was appointed county-lieutenant of Jefferson County and the next year was made a trustee of Louisville (*History of the Ohio Falls Cities and their Counties,* 1882, I, 200). He entered state politics in 1788 as a member of the convention to secure statehood and in 1792 became a member of the convention which drafted the first constitution (B. H. Young, *History and Texts of the Three Constitutions of Kentucky,* 1890, p. 31). One of the electors for selecting the governor under the first constitution, he was also chosen as one of the first state senators. He remained in the Senate by successive reëlections until 1800 and throughout this period was its speaker (Lewis and R. H. Collins, *History of Kentucky,* 1874, II, 357). In 1799 he was president of the convention which drafted the second constitution for Kentucky, and the next year he was elected lieutenant-governor, in which capacity he continued to preside over the Senate. At the expiration of his term he was again elected to the Senate in 1804 where he remained until 1808, at which time he retired to private life. His long service in the Senate was without brilliance or special incident. The undoubtedly great influence he exerted was due to his reputation for probity and integrity. He was greatly honored by his contemporaries and Bullitt County was named for him. He was twice married: first, in October 1785 to Priscilla Christian, daughter of Col. William Christian, one of the best known of early Kentuckians; second, after her death, to Mary (Churchill) Prather, a widow.

[Thos. Walker Bullitt's *My Life at Oxmoor* (Louisville, 1911) is a book of reminiscences by A. S. Bullitt's grandson. Much the same ground is covered by E. H. Ellwanger, "Oxmoor—Its Builder and Its Historian" in the *Reg. of the Ky. State Hist. Soc.,* Jan. 1919. Kathleen Jennings, *Louisville's First Families* (1920) supplies some collateral facts. See also H. E. Hayden, *Va. Genealogies* (1891). The *Jours. of the Ky. Senate* give glimpses of Bullitt as a presiding officer.]
R. S. C.

BULLITT, HENRY MASSIE (Feb. 28, 1817–Feb. 5, 1880), physician and teacher of medicine, of Huguenot descent, a son of Cuthbert Bullitt and his wife Harriet Willit, was born in Shelby County, Ky. At the age of seventeen he began the study of medicine in the office of Dr. Coleman Rogers, Sr., of Louisville, subsequently entering the University of Pennsylvania, where he graduated with distinction in 1838. He thereupon returned to Louisville and prac-

tised his profession until 1845 when he went to Europe for further study. A year later he returned to America to accept a professorship at the St. Louis Medical College where he lectured on the practise of medicine during the academic years 1846–47 and 1847–48. In 1849 he became professor of materia medica at Transylvania University at Lexington, Ky., the medical department of which institution (founded 1819) was the best known as well as the oldest school in the Ohio Valley. In the following year he founded the Kentucky School of Medicine at Louisville. He gave his attention to the new school until 1866 when he was called to the chair of the principles and practise of medicine at the University of Louisville. In the next spring he became, in addition, professor of physiology. In 1868 he established the Louisville Medical College, remaining connected therewith until his death, which occurred in that city following a long and painful illness borne with brave cheerfulness. He was married first on May 26, 1841, to Julia Anderson of Louisville, who died on Jan. 16, 1853, leaving seven children, but two of whom survived childhood. His second wife was Mrs. Sarah Crow Paradise whom he married on Sept. 14, 1854. Of the second marriage there were a son and five daughters.

Bullitt is best known as a teacher, though he labored under the handicap of extreme deafness which necessarily limited his teaching in his last years. He was successively professor in no less than five medical schools, of two of which he was a founder. As these two have since his death become a part of the University of Louisville, he may properly be considered one of the fathers of that institution. His best-known contributions to medical literature are: "The Art of Observing in Medicine," *St. Louis Medical Journal,* 1847; "On the Pathology of Inflammation," "Medical Organization and Reform," and other articles in the *Transylvania Journal of Medicine.* He was associate editor of both of these journals as well as of the *Louisville Medical Record* which he helped to found. Perhaps his best-known paper was a reply (published in the *Medical Examiner,* Philadelphia, 1844) to Dr. Charles Caldwell, who had claimed that to understand Southern and Western diseases, a physician must have been trained in the South or West. This paper is an excellent example of the controversial medical writing of the period, and in it Bullitt held his own against Caldwell then firmly established as the dean of medical teachers west of the Alleghanies.

[See sketch of Bullitt's life by his colleague Dr. Jas. Morrison Bodine of Louisville in Burrage and Kelly, *Am. Medic. Biogs.* (1920). Bullitt's editorials and articles in the journals of which he was editor throw light on his life, character, and attainments.]

E. E. H.

BULLOCH, ARCHIBALD (1729/30–February 1777), first president of the Provincial Congress of Georgia, was born at Charleston, S. C., the son of a Scotch clergyman and planter, James Bulloch, and his wife, Jean Stobo. After the family had moved to a plantation on the Savannah River, Georgia (*c.* 1750), he studied law and was admitted to practise. He remained both lawyer and planter until his removal to Savannah in the early seventies. On Oct. 9, 1764, he was married to Mary de Veaux, daughter of Judge James de Veaux of Shaftesbury, Ga. Elected to the Commons House in 1768, he served continuously until 1773, when he declined the seat to which he had been chosen. He was a member of the committee that corresponded with Benjamin Franklin, the colonial agent in London, and in April 1772 he was chosen speaker—an empty honor when Acting-Governor James Habersham dissolved the Assembly immediately after his election. Consequently Bulloch allied himself more firmly with the irreconcilable colonial party and his name was one of four signed to the first call, June 14, 1774, for an assemblage of patriots in Savannah. From July 4, 1775, until his death Bulloch was president of the Provincial Congress, was a delegate in occasional attendance in the Continental Congress, and in April 1776, on the flight of Sir James Wright the royal governor, he was made "President and Commander-in-chief of Georgia."

In official life Bulloch disclosed something of the energy and vivid conception of patriotic duty that characterized his descendant Theodore Roosevelt. His personal popularity and vigorous espousal of the cause of liberty made him influential in molding public opinion in the early years of the war. In his efforts to defeat the enemy he was not to be limited to his numerous civil offices : he led the party of militia and Creek Indians that destroyed the British and Tory base on Tybee Island, Mar. 25, 1776; and, in case the sins of Georgians should have been responsible for the late military reverses suffered by the colonies, he issued a proclamation against swearing in the streets of Savannah, "especially on the Sabbath," and set aside a day of prayer "to implore his divine goodness to restore our Adversaries to reason and Justice, and thereby to relieve the United States from the distresses of an Unnatural War" (*Revolutionary Records,*

State of Ga., I, 1908, p. 304). An ordinance of the council of safety, Feb. 22, 1777, recognized an established fact when it conferred upon him "the whole executive power of government." The gesture came too late, for he died before the end of the month.

[A. D. Candler, ed., *Rev. Records, State of Ga.* (1908) and *Colonial Records, State of Ga.* (1904–16); J. G. B. Bulloch, *Biog. Sketch of Hon. Archibald Bulloch,* n.d.; W. F. Northen, *Men of Mark of Georgia,* vol. I (1907); L. L. Knight, *Georgia's Landmarks, Memorials and Legends,* vol. II (1914), p. 642.]

T. D. M.

BULLOCH, JAMES DUNWODY (June 25, 1823–Jan. 7, 1901), naval officer, Confederate agent, was descended from a distinguished Georgia family of Scotch-Irish and Huguenot extraction. His great-grandfather, Archibald Bulloch [*q.v.*], held many important positions under the colonial government, and his father, Maj. James Stephens Bulloch was a member of the company under whose auspices the *Savannah* made her famous voyage across the Atlantic from Savannah to Liverpool. His mother, Hester Amarinthia, was a daughter of Senator John Elliott and his wife Esther. His half-sister, Martha Bulloch, was married in 1853 to Theodore Roosevelt, Sr., and was the mother of President Roosevelt. James Dunwody Bulloch was born near Savannah, Ga. His later home was "Bulloch Hall" at Roswell near Atlanta. In 1839 he became a midshipman in the United States navy. He served first on board the *United States* and later on board the United States sailing sloop of war *Decatur,* on the Brazil station, first under command of Henry W. Ogden and later under command of David G. Farragut. In 1842 he was transferred to the battle-ship *Delaware,* cruising in the Mediterranean. After a brief attendance at the navy school at Philadelphia in 1844–45 he returned to active service, on the Pacific coast. In 1849–51 he served in the coast survey. He succeeded Lieut. (later Admiral) D. D. Porter in command of the *Georgia,* the first subsidized mail steamer to California, and subsequently he commanded various vessels in the Gulf mail service. He was one of a small number of lieutenants of the United States navy who were detailed by the government to enter the mail service to enlarge the school for experience in steam navigation. Later, influenced by the demand of the growing packet and mail service for commanders and by the slowness of promotion in the navy, he retired and entered private mail service, becoming identified with the shipping enterprises of New York. Immediately after the opening of the Civil War, he accepted from Secretary Mallory the foreign mission as agent of the Confederate navy, especially to buy or build naval vessels in England. Arriving at Liverpool in June he promptly began operations, aided by the generous confidence of Fraser, Trenholm & Company. Under his instructions were dispatched and equipped all Confederate cruising ships except the *Georgia*. After laying the keel of the *Oreto* (the later *Florida*) and arranging for the construction of *No. 290* (the later *Alabama*) he returned to the Confederacy on the blockade-runner *Fingal* sailing via Nassau and carrying much-needed supplies to Savannah. In February 1862 he returned to Liverpool on a steamer blockade-runner of Fraser, Trenholm & Company, sailing from Wilmington. Soon thereafter he dispatched the cruiser *Florida* and later another cruiser the *Alabama* to seize United States merchant vessels. All these operations he claimed were justified under English law and the rules of war. In March 1863, following the manifest intention of the British ministry to enforce the Foreign Enlistment Act more strictly, he went to Paris, having received intimations that French authorities would not interfere with the departure of Confederate vessels built in French ports.

After the War he decided to establish his residence at Liverpool, partly because he belonged to a class which was excluded from pardon under the post-bellum amnesty proclamations, and partly influenced by friendships formed in England. At Liverpool he entered the mercantile (cotton) business. He was regarded as an accomplished scholar with a thorough knowledge of maritime and international law. He had a distinguished personality, magnetic courtly manners, and was courteous and kind. In 1881–83 he wrote the history of his secret service in Europe during the Civil War. He was, however, very reserved in talking of himself and his achievements. He was married twice: on Nov. 19, 1851, at Richmond, to Elizabeth Euphemia Caskie who died at Mobile, Jan. 23, 1854; and in January 1857 to Mrs. Harriott Cross Foster, a daughter of Brigadier-General Osborne Cross of Maryland.

[Jos. Gaston B. Bulloch: *A Hist. and Geneal. of the Families of Bulloch and Stobo* (1911); Jas. D. Bulloch, *The Secret Service of the Confed. States in Europe* (2 vols., 1884); J. M. Callahan, *Diplomatic Hist. of the Southern Confederacy* (1901); Clement A. Evans, *Confed. Mil. Hist.*, vol. I (1899); *Official Records* (Navy), 2 ser., II, III; newspaper clippings lent by Martha Louise Bulloch of Liverpool.]   J.M.C.

BULLOCK, RUFUS BROWN (Mar. 28, 1834–Apr. 27, 1907), Reconstruction governor of Georgia, the son of Volckert Veeder Bullock and his wife Jane Eliza Brown, was born in Bethlehem, N. Y. After securing a high school education, he became interested in telegraphy, in which art he became an expert. He developed executive talent and for several years was employed in supervising the building of telegraph lines between New York and the South. The year 1859 found him located at Augusta, Ga., as the representative of the Adams Express Company. He organized the express business in the South and became an official of the Southern Express Company. On the outbreak of the Civil War he offered his services as a telegraph expert to the Confederacy and was used in the establishment of telegraph and railroad lines on interior points. At the close of the War he had reached the rank of lieutenant-colonel and was paroled at Appomattox as acting assistant quartermaster-general. He then returned to Augusta, resumed his connection with the express business, organized a bank, and became (1867) president of the Macon & Augusta Railroad.

Bullock's entrance into politics was as a Republican member of the constitutional convention of 1868. Congress had overthrown the state government set up by President Johnson, had reestablished military control, and had required as the condition of readmission the adoption of the Fourteenth Amendment, already rejected by the Johnson government. Congress ordered the adoption of a new state constitution, and, by disfranchising the responsible native white element and empowering the negro to vote for members of the convention and to sit in it, assured the election of a convention which would carry into effect the will of Congress. To this convention Bullock, who heartily favored the Congressional plan of reconstruction, was elected. Being a man of considerable ability, large, handsome, pleasant-mannered and popular, he at once became the leader of the carpet-bag and negro element of the convention. Under his leadership the constitutional convention was turned into a party nominating convention and he was nominated as the Republican candidate for governor in the election shortly to be held. The reviving Democratic party nominated Gen. John B. Gordon, but was defeated in the November 1868 election.

As governor from 1868 to the fall of 1871 Bullock was charged by the contemporary Democratic newspapers and other partisan opponents with every known form of political rascality,—with almost wrecking the state-owned Western & Atlantic Railroad by placing its control in the hands of incompetent and venal carpet-baggers (it piled up a debt of three-quarters of a million dollars during Bullock's administration instead of yielding a steady net revenue to the state as it had done during the previous administration);

with seeking to prolong military control for personal and party ends; with the sale of pardons; with purchasing the influence of the press by wasteful publications of public documents; with allowing the state penitentiary to be plundered; with gross corruption in the payment of subsidies to railroads; with selling state bonds and appropriating the proceeds; with general extravagance and corruption in every department of his administration. Two years of misrule were enough for the state, and in 1870 the conservatives returned an overwhelming majority to the legislature. The Governor saw that his rule was over; fearing criminal indictment, he resigned, on Oct. 23, and fled from the state. On the restoration of Democratic control the legislature appointed a committee to investigate his official conduct. The report, covering 166 pages, pronounced Bullock guilty of various charges of corruption and mismanagement. Bullock undertook to defend himself in October 1872, in an *Address to the People of Georgia*. The historian of the Reconstruction period (C. M. Thompson, *Reconstruction in Georgia,* 1915) says of the defense that it "fails to bring conviction that he disproved a single charge of the investigating committee." Bullock eluded efforts to capture him until 1876, when he was arrested, brought back to Georgia, tried on an indictment charging embezzlement of public funds, and acquitted for lack of evidence. At a much later period he again published a defense, this time in the *Independent,* Mar. 19, 1903. It is wholly unconvincing. The truth appears to be that Bullock and his crew "instituted a carnival of public spoliation" (U. B. Phillips, *Life of Robert Toombs,* 1913, p. 262). Through the device of issuing state bonds (later repudiated) to subsidize railroad corporations, they poured public money into their own pockets. During the fight over the matter of repudiating these bonds, Henry Clews & Co. of New York, who acted as Bullock's financial agents, published a card in the *Atlanta Constitution* in which they admitted that the proceeds of the bonds were misapplied and that the state had failed to receive value for them, but urged that they be not repudiated, as this would hurt the credit of the state.

After his acquittal by the jury, Bullock remained in Atlanta and rehabilitated himself, at least in the contemporary business world. He became president of the Atlanta Cotton Mills, president of the Chamber of Commerce, vice-president of the Piedmont Exposition, and a director of the Union Pacific Railroad. He was married to Marie Salisbury of Pawtucket, R. I., and was a vestryman in St. Philip's Church.

[A definitive history of the Reconstruction period in Georgia has been written by C. Mildred Thompson, now professor of history in Vassar College: *Reconstruction in Georgia* (1915). The most interesting contemporary account of the period is to be found in I. W. Avery, *Hist. of Georgia, 1850–81* (1881). Avery was editor of the *Atlanta Constitution* from 1869 to 1874 and was thus in a position to keep a close watch over events. A condensed account of the Reconstruction period is in R. P. Brooks, *Hist. of Georgia* (1913), chapters XXIII, XXIV. The *Atlanta Constitution* of Apr. 28, 1907, contains a long and highly flattering account of Bullock's career.]   R. P. B—s.

BULLOCK, WILLIAM A. (1813–Apr. 12, 1867), inventor, manufacturer, was born in Greenville, N. Y., of parents of whom nothing is known. At the age of eight he was an orphan. An elder brother in Catskill gave him a place in which to live and put him to work immediately to learn the trade of iron founder and machinist. Bullock seems to have shown great aptitude in these crafts, becoming expert even before completing his apprenticeship. At the same time he taught himself pattern-making and devoted his leisure time to the study of all books on mechanics that he could secure. When twenty-three years old he left his brother's home and started a machine shop of his own in Prattsville, N. Y. Besides the varied work that he could pick up he devised several mechanical contrivances amongst which was a shingle-cutting machine. Armed with this, perfected during the two years in Prattsville, Bullock went to Savannah, Ga., to engage in shingle manufacture. This venture was not successful, however, and in a short time he returned North, this time to New York City where he set up shop and made hay and cotton presses of his own design and also artificial legs. He gave up this business in 1849 and began a patent agency and shop in Philadelphia. The only products known from this shop were three of his own invention,—a grain drill, a seed planter, and a lath-cutting machine, for which he received patents between 1850 and 1854. In connection with his agency Bullock started printing a daily newspaper, *The Banner of the Union,* which he continued from 1849 to 1853. This experience turned his attention to printing-machinery and the balance of his life was devoted to improving the press. He worked simultaneously on three ideas,—a mechanical paper feed, a more rapid cutting method, and the printing of both sides of the paper. By the time he was satisfied with his improvements and undertook the manufacture of a single press embodying all of them, fifteen more years had passed. During this time he was at work in Philadelphia, then in New York, and finally after 1859 in Pittsburgh where the presses were made under U. S. Patent 38,200, issued Apr. 14, 1863. The Bullock Press, when eventually marketed in 1865, revolutionized the art of press building. It was the first to print from a continuous roll of paper, to print both sides of the sheet, and to cut it either before or after printing. The speed of printing, too, was phenomenal. For the next two years Bullock devoted himself to the manufacture and installation of presses for which there was a great demand and, as might be expected of a mechanical genius, he was constantly working on improvements which were to be added as they were perfected. One of these installations was for the Philadelphia *Public Ledger,* and just as the last test on the press was being made Bullock's foot was caught in the driving belt and so badly crushed that he died nine days after the accident at the age of fifty-three years. It is said that he had imparted many of his ideas for improvements to one of his faithful employees and that after Bullock's death these ideas were brought to perfection and incorporated in the later presses. According to report, Bullock was married and had a daughter living in Pittsburgh, but no definite information can be found concerning his surviving family.

[J. Ringwalt, ed., *Encyc. of Printing* (1871); W. W. Pasko, ed., *Am. Dict. of Printing and Bookmaking* (1894); *Public Ledger* (Phila.), Apr. 3–16, 1867; U.S. Patent Office Records.]　　　　　　　　　　C.W.M.

BUMSTEAD, FREEMAN JOSIAH (Apr. 21, 1826–Nov. 28, 1879), surgeon, perhaps the first reputable practitioner in America to limit himself to the specialty of venereal diseases and hold a professorship of the same, was born in Boston, the son of Josiah Freeman Bumstead and Lucy Douglas Willis. His father, engaged in mercantile business, was also an author of school text-books and a member of the department of education of Boston; his brother Horace Bumstead [*q.v.*] was a prominent educator and college president; his mother was a sister of N. P. Willis and "Fanny Fern." Bumstead was educated in the Chauncey Hall School, English High, and Latin Schools of his native city, and entered Williams College in 1843, graduating in the arts in 1847. Although his father was prosperous, the son resolved to pay his own way and taught school in Roxbury while attending lectures and dissections at the Tremont Medical School. He entered Harvard Medical School in 1849 but interrupted his course to visit Europe, as surgeon on a sailing vessel, to study disease in the London and Paris hospitals. On his return he served as house surgeon in the Massachusetts General Hospital and received the degree of M.D. from Harvard in 1851. He then made a second voyage to Europe where he sojourned for a year, set-

tling on his return in New York City as a general practitioner. His first appointment (1853), which he held for two years, was as surgeon to the Northern Dispensary. In the meantime he seems to have begun to specialize on the eye and ear and in 1857 obtained the appointment of surgeon to the New York Eye and Ear Infirmary, resigning in 1862. His first public connection with venereal diseases goes back to 1853, in which year he published a translation from the French of Philippe Ricord's translation and amplification of John Hunter's *Treatise on the Venereal Diseases,* which went through a second edition in 1859. He had also been appointed surgeon to the venereal wards of Charity Hospital. About 1860 he decided to limit his practise to venereal including male genito-urinary diseases and in 1861 appeared his classical *Pathology and Treatment of Venereal Diseases,* which received the honor of an Italian translation and went through new editions in 1864, 1870, and 1879, the last in collaboration with R. W. Taylor. He served as professor of venereal diseases in the College of Physicians and Surgeons from 1867 to 1871 when, owing to overwork, he was obliged to resign and spend two years abroad. He traveled extensively, visiting the principal schools and hospitals of Great Britain and the Continent, and thus did much to strengthen his European reputation. In 1868 he had added to his reputation at home by bringing out an English edition of A. F. A. Cullerier's *Précis iconographique des maladies vénériennes.* From 1871 until his untimely death eight years later we hear but little from him. He was a tremendous worker, often sitting up all night, but this was offset in a measure by his long summer vacations which were devoted to the study of botany and ornithology. He made a complete collection of the bird life of Massachusetts which he presented to the Natural History Society of Boston. A duplicate collection remained in his possession, and his skill in taxidermy and mounting made these exhibits works of art. His collection of plants and flowers, of equal value, was presented to his alma mater, Williams College. In 1861 he married Mary Josephine White of Boston. He was a man of the highest character and integrity. His relatively early death must be charged chiefly to overwork. He lived barely long enough to see the fourth edition of his book through the press.

[G. A. Peters, *In Memory of Freeman J. Bumstead* (1880); *Medic. Record,* XVI, 551, Dec. 6, 1879; *N. Y. Medic. Jour.,* XXXI, 110, Jan. 1880.]　　　E. P.

BUMSTEAD, HENRY ANDREWS (Mar. 12, 1870–Dec. 31, 1920), teacher, physicist, was born in the small town of Pekin, Ill., close to

Peoria. His father was Samuel Josiah Bumstead, a physician of local prominence, and his mother, Sarah Ellen Seiwell. His elementary education was obtained in the high school of the neighboring city of Decatur, from which he went to Johns Hopkins in 1887 with the intention of preparing himself to follow his father's profession. There he came under the influence of Rowland, who so stimulated the interest which he had already shown in physics that he decided to specialize in that subject. In 1893 he went to New Haven as instructor in the Sheffield Scientific School and received his doctor's degree in physics from Yale in 1897. The year before, he had married Luetta Ullrich of Decatur, Ill., who survived him. In 1900 his success as a teacher was recognized by promotion to an assistant professorship. In spite of his heavy teaching schedule he always found time for research. Among his earlier investigations were: a theoretical discussion of the reflection of electric waves at the free end of a parallel wire system (*American Journal of Science*, November 1902, p. 359), and two papers with L. P. Wheeler on radioactive gases in surface water (*Ibid.*, October 1903, p. 328, and February 1904, p. 97). With R. G. Van Name he edited the *Scientific Papers of J. Willard Gibbs* in 1906.

The first Silliman lectures at Yale were given by J. J. Thomson in 1903. Bumstead was greatly interested in the investigations in progress at the Cavendish Laboratory and decided to spend the year 1904–05 at Cambridge in research. His experiments there (*London, Edinburgh and Dublin Philosophical Magazine*, February 1906, p. 292) led to the surprising conclusion that the heat developed by the absorption of X-rays in lead is double that produced in zinc, which seemed explicable only on the ground that the rays effected a disintegration of the lead atoms through which they passed, liberating energy which was then converted into heat. Unfortunately later work by Angerer and by Bumstead himself (*Ibid.*, April 1908, p. 432) failed to confirm the earlier result, which was shown to be due to faulty heat insulation of the metals under investigation. On his return to New Haven, Bumstead succeeded A. W. Wright as professor of physics in Yale College and director of the Sloane Laboratory. These positions, with occasional leaves of absence, he held until his death from heart failure at the age of fifty.

Since the preparation of the critical survey of electro-magnetic theories which had constituted his doctor's thesis, Bumstead had maintained a keen interest in theoretical physics. In 1908 he published a critical comparison of the scientific view-points of Einstein and Lorenz (*American Journal of Science*, November 1908, p. 493) in which he made an attempt to extend Einstein's methods to gravitational problems. He is best remembered, however, for the experimental investigations of the properties of delta rays emitted by metals under the influence of alpha rays which he began in 1911 and continued with some interruptions during the remainder of his life (*Ibid.*, December 1911, p. 403, October 1912, p. 309, August 1913, p. 91). The later of these researches (*Physical Review*, December 1916, p. 715) showed that fast-moving electrons are produced when alpha rays collide with gaseous molecules.

During the early stages of the World War Bumstead was a member of the national committee appointed to examine the merits of proposed anti-submarine devices. Early in 1918 he went to London as scientific attaché of the American Embassy. While there his tact and wide acquaintance among men of science enhanced his services as a clearing house for scientific information of military value. On his return to New Haven a few months after the Armistice he took an active part in the reorganization of the University then in progress. Before the end of the academic year he was called to succeed James Rowland Angell, president-elect of Yale, as chairman of the National Research Council. For many years a fellow of the American Physical Society, he had been an editor of its official publication, the *Physical Review*, and president of the Society. As retiring vice-president of the American Association for the Advancement of Science he delivered the annual address at the meeting in Pittsburgh in December 1917 on "Present Tendencies in Theoretical Physics" (*Science*, Jan. 18, 1918, p. 51). In 1913 he was elected a member of the National Academy of Sciences.

[Obituaries in the *Yale Daily News*, Jan. 4, 1921 and *Science*, Jan. 28, 1921, and sketches of Bumstead's life in the *Am. Jour. of Sci.*, June 1921, p. 469, and *Yale Alumni Weekly*, Mar. 18, 1921.]   L. P.

BUMSTEAD, HORACE (Sept. 29, 1841–Oct. 14, 1919), Congregational minister, educator, was the son of Josiah Freeman Bumstead, a Boston merchant, author of a series of text-books, and for many years before the Civil War superintendent of a negro Sunday-school. Nathaniel Willis, his maternal grandfather, was founder, publisher, and editor of the *Boston Recorder*, said to be the earliest of religious periodicals, and of the *Youth's Companion*. His mother, Lucy Douglas (Willis) Bumstead was sister to the poet Nathaniel Parker Willis. Bumstead was prepared for college at the Boston Latin School, and in 1863 was graduated with honor from Yale College. He then entered a training school for officers and, after passing an examination before a military board at Washington, was commissioned major of the 43rd Massachusetts Regiment of colored troops. His military service extended from April 1864 to December 1865. Although only twenty-three years old and with scant preparation for such responsibility, he was during most of the time in command of the entire regiment and had active service around Petersburg and Richmond. In the fall of 1866 he entered Andover Theological Seminary and completed the course there in 1870. For fourteen months he traveled and studied in Europe, spending the greater part of two semesters at the University of Tübingen. In January 1872 he married Anna M. Hoit, daughter of Albert G. Hoit, portrait painter. He was ordained a Congregational minister and for three years was pastor of a church in Minneapolis. A classmate in Yale, Edmund Asa Ware, was president of Atlanta University, recently organized for the higher education of negro youth. After accepting an invitation to join in this work, Bumstead moved to Atlanta in October 1875 and became an instructor in natural science. He continued in this department till 1880, was professor of Latin from 1880 to 1896, acting president 1886–87, and president from 1888 to 1907 when he retired and was given a pension by the Carnegie Foundation. He was a man of dignity, courtesy, and of high devotion to the educational work for which he considered himself "almost foreordained." While he believed in industrial education for negro youth he maintained that the leaders and teachers of the race should have opportunity for the broadest culture and to this conviction Atlanta University became committed. Bumstead and Atlanta University are in this respect to be contrasted with Booker T. Washington and Tuskegee Institute. As president Bumstead spent much of his time in the North raising funds (about $30,000 yearly) with which to carry on the work of the institution.

[*The Hist. of the Class of 1863, Yale Coll.* (1905), pp. 47–56, contains a sketch of Horace Bumstead written by himself. The account in the *Nat. Cyc. of Am. Biog.*, V, 381, was written by his wife. The *Atlanta University Bull.* of July 1917 contains an address by Bumstead in commemoration of the semi-centennial of the charter of Atlanta University. The January 1920 number of the same bulletin gives extracts from letters, articles, and addresses called forth by his death.]

E. H. J—n.

BUNCE, OLIVER BELL (Feb. 8, 1828–May 15, 1890), author, publisher, was born in New York City, of English stock. After attending Rand's Academy he became while still young a clerk in the stationery firm of Jansen & Bell, of which his uncle was a partner. He read avidly in his leisure hours and developed a competent literary style, his first play *The Morning of Life* being produced at the Bowery Theatre, Aug. 30, 1848, while he was still selling foolscap and blank books over the counter. The play is no longer extant, but A. H. Quinn infers from the cast of characters that it was a rural comedy. Bunce wrote three other plays: *Marco Bozzaris,* also lost, a dramatization of recent Greek history, produced at the Bowery Theatre, June 10, 1850, with J. W. Wallack, Jr., in the hero's part; *Fate, or the Prophet* (1856), a romantic tragedy in verse, which Wallack is also said to have produced, although Quinn has found no record of its production; and *Love in '76,* one of the best of the Revolutionary comedies, produced at Laura Keene's Theatre, Feb. 28, 1857, with Miss Keene in the part of Rose Elsworth. His theatrical work bringing him nothing more tangible than a certain name as a man of letters, Bunce turned to publishing, starting out for himself at the age of twenty-five years under the name of Bunce & Brother. The firm had little capital and lasted only a few years. He then became manager of the publishing house of James C. Gregory. His two conspicuous achievements at this time were a notable edition of Cooper's novels with illustrations on steel and wood by F. O. C. Darley and the discovery, now become commonplace, that highly embellished editions of favorite poems will enjoy a brisk sale at Christmas time. He began this sort of enterprise with a volume called *In the Woods with Bryant, Longfellow, and Halleck,* with illustrations by John A. How. After a short period with Harper & Brothers he became literary manager of D. Appleton & Company, with whom he remained for the rest of his life. He edited *Appleton's Journal* and had much to do with the policy of the house. He took a keen interest in his authors, often sending one a four-page letter, criticizing his manuscript unmercifully for three pages and accepting it on the fourth. Similar treatment, kindly meant but sometimes frightening, was meted out orally to writers who called at the office. His Sunday evening suppers were a happy institution among many New York literary men. His most ambitious undertaking for the Appletons was *Picturesque America* (1872–74), two handsome volumes, sumptuously illustrated, which were sold in parts by the old subscription method. The work was nominally under the editorship of William Cullen Bryant, but the conception and execution were really Bunce's. It cost a fortune to produce, but was an enormous success, and was followed by *Picturesque Europe* (1875–79) and *Picturesque Palestine* (1881–84). In all 600,000 sets of these works were sold. *Don't* (1884), a little book on etiquette and grammar, was in its way equally successful. His own books were: *The Romance of the Revolution* (1852); *A Bachelor's Story* (1859); *Life before Him* (1860); *Bensley* (1863); *The Opinions and Disputations of Bachelor Bluff* (1881); *My House, an Ideal* (1885); and *The Adventures of Timias Terrystone* (1885). He also compiled an anthology, *Fair Words about Fair Women* (1884). The last twenty years of his life were a brave battle with tuberculosis. He died, as he claimed that he wished to, in harness, working in his office till a week before the end, and taking manuscripts home with him to read for his employers on his deathbed. He was survived by a wife and four children.

[Obituaries in *Publisher's Weekly*, XXXVII, 649–50, *Critic*, XVI, 262, *N. Y. Times* and *Tribune*, May 16, 1890; A. H. Quinn, *Hist. of the Am. Drama* (1923); J. C. Derby, *Fifty Years among Authors, Books, and Publishers* (1884), pp. 158, 184, 600–01; S. G. W. Benjamin, *Life and Adventures of a Freelance* (1914), pp. 303–04. *Love in '76* is accessible in M. J. Moses, *Representative Plays by Am. Dramatists*, III (1920).]

G. H. G.

BUNCE, WILLIAM GEDNEY (Sept. 19, 1840–Nov. 5, 1916), painter, was born in Hartford, Conn., the son of James M. and Elizabeth Chester Bunce. Before entering seriously into art studies he enlisted during the Civil War in the 1st Connecticut Cavalry. Here he served two years, retiring from the Union army upon receiving a wound in one of his legs, which caused him to limp during the remainder of his life. His early art education was obtained at the Cooper Union School of New York and from the artist William Hart of that city, with whom he continued to study until he sailed for Europe in 1867 to become an artist resident of Paris. His studio there joined that of the famous sculptor Saint-Gaudens, who became his intimate friend and materially influenced the work of the young artist (*American Art News*, Nov. 11, 1916). Later he studied art technique under Achenbach in Munich, taking still further studies with the well-known marine painter P. J. Hays in Antwerp. A painting by Ziem led Bunce to go to Venice to live, study, and paint. Here he did his greatest amount of work. When asked to whom he owed most of his training, he replied, "Titian is my master." He worked in oil, water-color, and pastel, using oil most extensively. His early work was done with a brush, but later he developed a method entirely his own, gaining delightful color effects by the use of finger and scraping

knife, several of his most striking works being done in this manner. He was of the impressionistic school though never an extremist. Painting with a total disregard for minute detail in his desire to produce effects, he emphasized the sentiment of a scene rather than the photographic reproduction. Placing the emotional emphasis of his work in the color compositions rather than in the design, he caused nature, which he loved so well to paint, to awaken the artistic appreciation that the artist himself must have felt. His greatest subjects were nearly all Venetian. Attracted to Venice by its moist atmosphere, he made of Venice a dream city, being little influenced by its architecture, but preserving its poetry and its spirit. This is clearly demonstrated in such paintings as "Venice" (in the Montclair, N. J., Art Museum) and "On the Lagoon" (in the Rhode Island School of Design, Providence, R. I.). "Though unified in subject, the work of Bunce is always varied in expression, his skies, clouds, and water being never the same. His work shows exquisite aerial perspective and his use of life is ever varied and always charming" (Charles D. Warner in *Century Magazine*, August 1900). A few of his more important paintings are "Morning View in Venice" and "Early Morning," both of which are now in the Metropolitan Museum of Art in New York City; "Sunset, San Giorgio, Venice," in the National Gallery, Washington, D. C., and "A Venice Night" awarded the Paris Salon prize in 1870. One of his paintings, a Venetian landscape, was ordered by Queen Victoria and now hangs in Osborne House. He never married, but made his home with one of his sisters, Mrs. Archibald A. Welsh. In 1916 as the result of an automobile accident he died in a hospital in Hartford. The popularity of his work was in a great measure due to the interest of Stanford White, the American architect, and Daniel Cottier, the art dealer.

[C. E. Clement and L. Hutton, *Artists of the Nineteenth Century*, vol. I (1879); *Am. Mag. of Art*, Jan. 1917; *Century Mag.*, Aug. 1900; *Am. Art News*, Nov. 11, 1916; *Art in America*, Feb. 1926; Mantle Fielding, *Dict. of Am. Painters, Sculptors and Engravers* (1926).]

J. T. M. Jr.

BUNDY, JONAS MILLS (Apr. 17, 1835–Sept. 8, 1891), journalist, was born at Colebrook, N. H., and while still young went with his parents to Beloit, Wis. After graduating from Beloit College in 1853 he studied law at the Harvard Law School and in the office of United States Senator Matthew H. Carpenter. He did not pursue the practise of the law, however, but became a reporter on the Milwaukee *Daily Wisconsin*. He created for the paper a new department of market reports. Later he joined the staff of the

Milwaukee Sentinel. During the Civil War he joined the Federal army and in the early part of 1865 was appointed major of the 3rd Regiment United States Volunteer Infantry. At the close of the war, going to New York, he secured the position of dramatic, musical, and literary critic on the *Evening Post* under William Cullen Bryant. Three years later he joined in founding the *New York Evening Mail* and became its editor-in-chief. In 1879 the *Mail* passed into the ownership of Cyrus W. Field, who two years later bought the *New York Evening Express,* in order to obtain an Associated Press franchise, and consolidated it with the *Mail* under the title of the *Mail and Express.* He continued Bundy as editor-in-chief as did Elliott F. Shepard, who bought the paper in 1887. In 1871, when the "Executive Committee of Citizens and Taxpayers for the Financial Reform of the City and County of New York," popularly known as the "Committee of Seventy," was organized to fight the Tweed Ring, Bundy was made chairman of the Committee on Address. The "Appeal to the People of the State of New York" adopted by the Committee of Seventy was prepared under his leadership. Although the youngest member of the Committee, he proved to be one of its real working members. In 1880 he was selected by James A. Garfield to write his campaign biography and went to Mentor, Ohio, the candidate's home, where he completed the task in six weeks. He was a consistent Republican in politics and his advice was sought by many of the party's leaders, including three presidents, Grant, Garfield and Arthur. He was recognized by those about him as a valuable associate, a loyal and devoted friend, and a stout antagonist in matters of public concern. In July 1891 he went to Europe for a vacation and died suddenly in Paris.

[Obituaries appeared in the *Weekly Mail and Express,* Sept. 16, 1891 ; *Evening Post* (N. Y.) and *Evening Wisconsin* (Milwaukee), Sept. 9, 1891 ; *Milwaukee Sentinel,* Sept. 10, 1891.]   H.H.

BUNNER, HENRY CUYLER (Aug. 3, 1855–May 11, 1896), author, the son of Rudolph and Ruth (Tuckerman) Bunner, was born in Oswego, N. Y. His father belonged to an old New York family; his mother was of New England stock, being a sister of Henry T. Tuckerman; and it was in the ample library of this uncle that Bunner browsed in his boyhood and acquired his intimate acquaintance with English literature. He went to school in New York; he was prepared for Columbia College; but—like that earlier New Yorker, Washington Irving—he had to forego the advantages of college. After a brief stay in an office, he became a newspaper man,

contributing to a short-lived weekly, the *Arcadian,* and soon joining the staff of *Puck,* the earliest American comic weekly to establish itself. In 1886 he was married to Alice Learned. He remained with *Puck* until his death, and into its columns he poured a profusion of prose and verse, jokes, parodies, lyrics of all sorts, brief stories, character-sketches, and editorials. He often suggested the cartoons; and he was responsible (in 1884) for what is perhaps the most famous of all American cartoons,—that of Blaine as the Tattooed Man. His editorials were directed to the intelligence of his readers; they were effective because they were always simple, sincere, straight-forward, and because they were never aggressive, domineering, or abusive. To him his work as a journalist was as important as his work as a man of letters; and he gave to his newspaper articles the polish which characterized his more ambitious and less ephemeral efforts.

Although he never weakened in his allegiance to *Puck,* Bunner began early to contribute poems and stories to the magazines. His first volume of poems, *Airs from Arcady and Elsewhere,* appeared in 1884; it was followed in 1892 by a second collection, *Rowen;* and after his death these two volumes (enriched by later lyrics and by half-a-dozen "Ballads of the Town") were issued as *The Poems of H. C. Bunner* (1896). He had the lyric gift; his blithe and cheerful verse sang itself into the memory; and few of those who have once read "The Way to Arcady" are likely to have forgotten its lilting lyric quality, its grace, and its charm. But he was seen at his best in a department of poetry in which the literature of our language is more abundant than the literature of any other tongue and which has in English no exact name, for to call it *vers de société* is both inadequate and unsatisfactory, since it is not mere society verse. Perhaps the best name for it is that which Cowper gave it—"familiar verse." Bunner's work in this form has had the good fortune to please both the critical and the uncritical. It has the finish, the flavor of scholarship which the cultivated recognize and relish; and it has also the freshness, the spontaneity, the heartiness, and above all the human sympathy without which no poetry has ever won a welcome outside the narrow circle of the dilettants. Many of his more comic lyrics Bunner regarded as too broadly and boldly humorous to deserve inclusion in either of the volumes of verse by which he wished to be judged as a poet. He was a facile and fecund parodist; but in his collected poems he reprinted only one evidence of his mastery of this difficult art—

"Home, Sweet Home" as it might have been written by Pope and Goldsmith, Horace and Austin Dobson, Swinburne, Bret Harte, and Walt Whitman—in which he recaptured the essential spirit of these various bards as skilfully as he echoed their external mannerisms. He had profited by his intimacy with these poets and with many others; but in his own lyrics he was himself with a pungent individuality of his own.

Beginning as a journalist Bunner was also a story-teller, adventuring successfully in both fields of prose fiction, the short-story and the novel. His prose was the prose of a poet in that it was pure and pellucid. As a teller of tales he had rich invention and adroit construction. He was a devoted student of the craft of story-telling, analyzing the processes of the masters of fiction, especially Boccaccio and Hawthorne and Maupassant. He worked with ease within the rigid limits of the short-story where selection and compression are of the essence of the contract. His two novels, *The Midge* (1886) and *The Story of a New York House* (1887) might almost be called short-stories writ large; and his delightfully fantastic tale of varied adventure, *The Runaway Browns* (1892) has for its sub-title "a story of small stories." *In Partnership: Studies in Story-telling* (1884) contained two stories written by Bunner in collaboration with Brander Matthews and three other tales by each of the two partners. Other volumes for which Bunner was solely responsible were *Short Sixes* (1890), "stories to be read while the candle burns"; *Zadoc Pine* (1891); *More Short Sixes* (1894); and *Made in France* (1893), in which he retold half a score of Maupassant's stories, frankly readjusting their incidents to American life and character,—an experiment as daring as it was successful. No anthology of the American short-story is likely to appear which shall fail to include at least one example of Bunner's mastery in this form. And it will matter little whether the chosen specimen shall be "Love in Old Cloathes" or "Zadoc Pine" or "As One Having Authority."

It remains only to be noted that while Bunner sat at the feet of many European masters of prose and of verse, spying out the secrets of their art, he was himself intensely an American and specifically a New Yorker. His subjects were almost always chosen from the life of his own country—and most of them from the life of his own city. He was one of the first American writers of fiction to find a fertile field in the sprawling metropolis so multiplex in its aspects and so tumultuous in its manifestations; and here he was truly a pioneer, driving a furrow of his own in soil scarcely scratched before he tilled it.

[Brander Matthews, "H. C. Bunner" in *The Hist. Novel and Other Essays* (1901); "The Uncollected Poems of H. C. Bunner" in *The Recreations of an Anthologist* (1904); sketch in *Scribner's Mag.*, Sept. 1896; Benj. W. Wells in *Sewanee Rev.*, Jan. 1897; H. G. Paine in *Critic*, May 23, 1896; Laurence Hutton in *Bookman*, July 1896.]   B. M—s.

BURBANK, LUTHER (Mar. 7, 1849–Apr. 11, 1926), plant breeder and originator of many new cultivated varieties of fruits, flowers, vegetables, grains and grasses, was born in Lancaster, Worcester County, Mass. His ancestry was chiefly English, with some Scotch and a dash of both French and Dutch. He was the thirteenth child of Samuel Walton Burbank, a farmer, a maker of brick and pottery, and a level-headed business man. Luther's mother, Olive Ross of Sterling, Mass., was the third wife of Samuel, and Luther was the third of her five children. Although Burbank's New England ancestors included no men or women of illustrious names they were an eminently respectable lot of whom he has been able to say: "All my ancestors and all my relatives on both sides, as far as known, without exception have been industrious, happy, prosperous, respected, self-supporting citizens in their several communities. Not one of them, either on the Burbank or the Ross side, has been deaf, blind, imbecile, insane, incompetent, intemperate, or addicted to the use of drugs or liquor" (Beeson, pp. 17–18). In a word, Luther Burbank's was a sound heredity; although one looks at the records of his ancestors in vain for an indication of the precise source from which he might have derived by particular inheritance his absorbing, almost passionate, love of plants; unless, perhaps, that indication lies in a statement by his sister, Emma Burbank Beeson: "Olive, the mother of Luther Burbank . . . was especially fond of nature even as a little child. She used to bring into the house so many wild flowers, bright-colored leaves and pretty stones that the busy mother would be compelled to sweep these treasures from chairs and floor, much to the sorrow of the little girl. She loved the robin, bluebird and wren, their plumage as well as their notes of joy, and her first effort with pencil was to sketch the birds that flew about the door" (*Ibid.*, pp. 31–32). But this sounds rather more like a trait of artistry than one of close study, which was Burbank's special possession. Burbank had, however, not a little of the artistic temperament in his make-up. He had much imagination—as have most of the greater scientific men—and he was extremely sensitive. He would burst into tears when some one praised him too strongly to his face, and, also, when some one said something too unkind to him. This very sensitiveness, a sensitiveness to plant behavior as well as to human behavior, was important in that group of traits which enabled him to succeed so unusually as a plant breeder.

Burbank's early environment was not unfavorable to the development of his love and study of plant life. To be sure, it included almost nothing in the way of formal education and nothing at all of a scientific education, in the usual acceptation of that phrase. Of schooling he had only that which he obtained from a simple New England district school until he was fifteen, and then what he got from four winters in Lancaster Academy, which seems to have been, however, a rather unusually well-conducted academy, with special lecturers of some eminence brought from various places to take part in its "forum." One of these, who made "a deep and lasting impression upon Luther's life," according to his sister, was a certain Prof. Gunning, a German, who gave a series of lectures on astronomy, physical geography, geology, mineralogy, paleontology, and still other scientific subjects.

There was a good public library in Lancaster, and Burbank made use of it. In a letter written in January 1909, he made the following interesting statements: "When I was about nineteen, in 1868, probably the turning point of my career in fixing my life work in the production of new species and varieties of plant life was fixed by the reading of Darwin's *Variation of Animals and Plants under Domestication* which I obtained from the library at Lancaster, Mass., my old home. Well do I remember reading that work of Darwin's—that the whole world seemed placed on a new foundation. It was without question the most inspiring book I had ever read, and I had read very widely from one of the best libraries in the state on similar scientific subjects. I think it is impossible for most people to realize the thrills of joy I had in reading this most wonderful work. At once, as soon as I was able, I purchased other books written by Charles Darwin, and today I have still one to read, which probably influenced the general public more than all the rest of his writings—*Origin of Species*. I have been so busy producing living forms from the thought inspired by Master Darwin's conclusions that I have never, to the present date, had time to read his *Origin of Species*. However, I imagine I could write the *Origin of Species* myself from what I have read of his other works. The second book which I purchased of Darwin's was *Cross and Self-Fertilization in the Vegetable Kingdom*" (Ibid., pp. 74–75).

But outside of district school, academy, and books, young Burbank obtained a special educa-

tion very much to the point in connection with his later career. This special education came from his opportunities and experiences as a boy on the New England farm. Here he gained knowledge at first hand of the life of plants. This knowledge together with his innate love of plants led him, two or three years after his father's death in 1868, deliberately to take up the business or profession of market gardening. With a little money obtained from his father's estate, and by the help of a mortgage, he purchased, when he was just twenty-one years old, a tract of seventeen acres of land in or adjoining the small town of Lunenburg where the Burbank family then lived. Original and practical in his methods, Burbank made a modest success of his gardening from the very outset, bringing vegetables of special quality into the neighboring city of Fitchburg earlier than other gardeners were able to bring inferior ones there. It was in this garden, too, that he produced his first "new creation," the Burbank potato, and thus began the lifework that made him famous.

The fact that Burbank's three elder brothers, George (in 1854), David (in 1859), and Alfred (in 1870), had all gone to California and were living there,—added to the fact that he and a certain Mary had a falling out—probably accounts more for Luther's removal from Massachusetts to California than any reasoning on his part with regard to the relative advantages of the two regions as locations for a market gardener and plant breeder. Whatever the reason, however, he continued his gardening at Lunenburg for but four years, and in the summer of 1875, sold his land, paid his mortgage, and bought a ticket for California. The $140 which this ticket cost was, according to the sister's account, taken from the $150 he had been paid by J. J. H. Gregory, the seedsman of Marblehead, for the total rights in the Burbank potato. Gregory, however, generously allowed him to retain ten potatoes of the new variety with which to get a start in California. These ten potatoes constituted most of his capital to support the new venture.

The trip West was made in October 1875 and took nine days and nights with Burbank sleeping in a day coach and living on the contents of the large lunch basket packed by his tearful mother and sister. His daily letters to the Massachusetts home during the course of the journey are of much interest. They reveal a mind eagerly open to new impressions and eyes quick and happy to see the beauties of mountains, plains, and desert. Once arrived at Santa Rosa, which was the Californian town that had been decided on in Massachusetts as goal of the journey, the enthusiastic newcomer burst into a dithyramb: "I firmly believe from what I have seen," he wrote, "that it is the chosen spot of all this earth as far as Nature is concerned. . . . The climate is perfect—all must like it. The air is so sweet that it is a pleasure to drink it in. The sunshine is pure and soft; the mountains which gird the valley are lovely. The valley is covered with majestic oaks placed as no human hand could arrange them for beauty. I cannot describe it! I almost have to cry for joy when I look upon the lovely valley from the hillsides" (*Ibid.*, p. 93).

In this paradise Burbank settled down in a little nursery garden with greenhouse which was soon to become famous the world over, and in which, with certain added acres near another town a few miles away, he was to carry on uninterruptedly his experimental and creative work for fifty years. This work was on the grand scale. It involved experimentation with thousands of kinds of plants, and the experimental rearing of hundreds of thousands of plant individuals. It was not conducted to prove or test any particular scientific theories or to make scientific discoveries, but it had for its sole aim the production of more and better varieties of cultivated plants. "I shall be contented if because of me there shall be better fruits and fairer flowers," he said. By the very nature of his experimenting he inevitably accumulated masses of data of scientific value, if he had cared to preserve them. But he did not. Almost all of his delicate work was done by himself, and, never strong and always overworked, he simply had no time or energy left to assemble and preserve these data. He kept for as long as he needed them the records necessary to be before him during the course of a given experiment, but when the experiment was concluded and the "new creation" established, the records were, in most cases, destroyed. Tangible results in the way of new varieties produced and taking their place in agriculture and horticulture were what he sought. Scientific results in the way of contributions to the knowledge of such subjects as variation, heredity, selection, hybridization, acquired character, and mutations were not his goal. One notable effort, to be sure, was made to collect and preserve some of the scientific data that sprang to light during his long observing and experimenting. In 1905 the Carnegie Institution of Washington made an arrangement with him by which he was to receive $10,000 a year for ten years, partly as salary and partly for expenses, with the understanding that the Institution was interested in collating such scientific data as might become available during the course of Burbank's work. To effect this, Dr. George

H. Shull, a scientific botanist, and member of the Carnegie Institution's staff, was sent to Santa Rosa to devote himself, with Burbank's coöperation, to this work of collation. The arrangement, however, was not, on the whole, a successful one, and was terminated by mutual agreement at the end of five years.

Before reference is made to any of the many new plant varieties produced by Burbank, it may be well to attempt to analyze, in general terms at least, the various processes which, either singly, or in combinations of two or three, or all together, were used by him in his work. These processes, or means, may be roughly classified.

First, there was the importation from foreign countries, through many correspondents, of a host of various kinds of plants, some of economic value in their native land and some not, any of which grown under different conditions might prove especially vigorous or prolific or hardy, or show other desirable changes or new qualities. Among these importations were often special kinds particularly sought for by Burbank to use in his multiple hybridizations; kinds which were closely related to American native or already cultivated races and which, despite many worthless characteristics, might possess one or more valuable ones needed to be added to a race already useful in order to make it more useful. Such an addition makes a new race.

Second, the production of variations, abundant and extreme, by various methods, as (a) the growing under new and, usually, more favorable environment (food supply, water, temperature, light, space, etc.) of various wild or cultivated forms; and (b) by hybridizations between forms closely related, between others less closely related and, finally, between those as dissimilar as may be (not producing sterility), this hybridizing being often immensely complicated by multiplying crosses, *i.e.*, the offspring from one cross being immediately crossed with a third form, and so on. These hybridizations were made sometimes with very little reference to the actual useful or non-useful characteristics of the crossed parents, but with the primary intention of producing an unsettling or instability in the heredity; of causing, as Burbank sometimes said, "perturbation" in the plants, so as to get just as wide and as large variation as possible. Other crosses were made, of course, in the deliberate attempt to blend, mix, to add together, two desirable characteristics, each possessed by only one of the crossed forms. Some crosses were made in the attempt to extinguish an undesirable characteristic.

Third, there was always, immediately following the unusual production of variations, the recognition of desirable modifications and the intelligent and effective selection of them, *i.e.*, the saving of those plants to produce seed or cuttings which showed the desirable variations, and the discarding of all the others. In Burbank's gardens the few tenderly cared for little potted plants or carefully grafted seedlings represented the surviving fittest, and the great bonfires of scores of thousands of uprooted others, the unfit, in this close mimicry of Darwin and Spencer's struggle and survival in nature.

It was precisely in this double process of the recognition and selection of desirable variations that Burbank's special genius came into particular play. Right there he brought something to bear on his work that few, if any, other men have been able to do in similar degree. This was his extraordinary keenness of perception, his delicacy of recognition of desirable variations in their (usually) small and to most men imperceptible beginnings. Was it a fragrance that was sought? To Burbank in a bed of hundreds of seedlings scores of the odors of the plant kingdom were arising and mingling from the fresh green leaves, but each from a certain single seedling or perhaps from a similar pair or trio. To the visitor until the master prover pointed out two or three of the more dominant single odors, the impression on the olfactories was simply (or confusedly) that of one soft elusive fragrance of fresh green leaves. Similarly Burbank was a master at seeing, and a master at feeling. And besides he had his own unique knowledge of correlations. Did this plum seedling with its score of leaves on its thin stem have those leaves infinitesimally plumper, smoother, or stronger, or with more even margins and stronger petiole or what not else, than any other among a thousand similar childish trees? Then it was saved, for it would bear a larger, or a sweeter, or a firmer sort of plum, or more plums than the others. So to the bonfires with the others and to the company of the elect with this "fittest" one. It was this extraordinary knowledge of correlations in plant characters, developed through many years of testing and perfecting that was perhaps the most important single new thing which Burbank brought to his work. He had enormous industry, utter concentration and single-mindedness, deftness in manipulation, and fertility in practical resource. So have other plant breeders. But in his special perception of variability in its forming, his keen recognition of its possibilities of outcome, and in his scientific knowledge of correlations Burbank had a special advantage over his fellow-workers.

But let us follow our saved plum seedling. Have we now to wait the six or seven years before a plum tree comes into bearing to know by actual seeing and testing what new sort of plum we have? No; and here again was one of Burbank's contributions (not wholly original to be sure, but original in the extent and perfection of its development) to the scientific aspects of plant-breeding. This saved seedling and other similar saved ones (for from the examination of 20,000 seedlings, say, Burbank would find a few tens or even scores in which he had faith of reward) would be taken from their plots and grafted on to the sturdy branches of some full-grown vigorous plum tree, so that in the next season or second next our seedling-stem would bear its flowers and fruits. Here are years saved. Twenty, forty, sixty, different seedlings grafted on to one strong tree (in a particular instance Burbank had 600 plum grafts on a single tree!); and each seedling-stem certain to bear its own kind of leaf and flower and fruit. (It has long been known that the scion is not modified radically by the stock nor the stock by the scion, although grafting sometimes increases or otherwise modifies the vigor of growth and the extent of the root system of the stock.) If now the fruit from our variant seedling is sufficiently desirable; if it produces earlier or later, sweeter or larger, firmer or more abundant, plums, we have a new race of plums, a "new creation" to add to the catalogue of results. For by simply subdividing the wood of the new branch, *i.e.*, making new grafts from it, the new plum can be perpetuated and increased at will.

Although Burbank's experimental and creative work ranged over a long list of plant kinds his most intensive and long persisting work was done with plums, berries, and lilies. He originated no less than two score new varieties of plums and prunes, some of which are among the best known and most successful kinds now grown. Most of these new plum and prune varieties are the result of multiple crossings in which Japanese plums played an important part. Hundreds of thousands of seedlings, the results of these crossings, were grown and carefully worked over in the forty years of plum experimentation. Next in extent, probably, to Burbank's work with plums and prunes was his long and successful experimentation with berries. This ran through about thirty-five years, involved the use of over fifty different species of *Rubus,* and resulted in the origination and commercial introduction of ten or more new varieties mostly obtained through various hybridizations of dewberries, blackberries, and raspberries.

An interesting feature of Burbank's brief account, in his *New Creations* catalogue of 1894, of the berry experimentation, is a reproduction of a photograph showing "a sample pile of brush 12 ft. wide, 14 ft. high, and 22 ft. long, containing 65,000 two and three-year-old seedling berry bushes (40,000 blackberry x raspberry hybrids and 25,000 Shaffer x Gregg hybrids) all dug up with their crop of ripening berries. . . . Of the 40,000 blackberry x raspberry hybrids of this kind 'Phenomenal' is the only one now in existence. From the other 25,000 hybrids, two dozen bushes were reserved for further trial."

Burbank's work with lilies came to culmination after sixteen years of steady experimentation in which he used more than half a hundred varieties in his hybridizings and produced a brilliant array of new forms. His love of his work and the satisfaction and thrill he found in it are well revealed in a brief paragraph in the account of the work with the lilies written for his *New Creations* catalogue for 1893. "Can my thoughts be imagined," he said, "when, after so many years of patient care and labor, as walking among them on a dewy morning I look upon these new forms of beauty on which other eyes have never gazed? Here a plant six feet high with yellow flowers, beside it one only six inches high with dark red flowers, and further on one of pale straw or snowy white, or with curious dots and shadings; some deliciously fragrant, others faintly so; some with upright, others with nodding flowers; some with dark green, woolly leaves in whorls, or with polished, light green, lance-like scattered leaves."

Among Burbank's other better-known new flowers are numerous roses, several callas, including a fragrant variety, several poppies and clematises, the two giant Shasta and Alaska daisies, several Nicotianas, and a wax myrtle. The famous Shasta daisy—one of Burbank's special prides—is the result of a multiple crossing between an American and a European species of field daisy and then between these hybrids and a Japanese form. The fragrant calla, known as "Fragrance," is descended from a single individual found by Burbank while critically examining a block of "Little Gem" calla seedlings. He was surprised to note a fragrance resembling that of violets or water lilies, and found that it came from a single individual. This little seedling was removed and tenderly taken care of. No further selecting was done; this single plant was the immediate ancestor of the fragrant new race. The blue Shirley poppy was obtained solely by long selection from the crimson field poppy of Europe, but the Fire poppy, a brilliant flame-colored new variety is the result of hybridizing a butter-colored species and a pure white species in the ancestry of which there was red of a shade much less bright than that characteristic of the new race.

Burbank's new fruits, besides his numerous new plums and prunes, make a list too long to be recorded here. They include notable varieties of apples, peaches, quinces, and nectarines, and certain interesting although not profitable crosses of the peach and almond and of the almond and plum.

Of new vegetables Burbank introduced, besides the Burbank and several other new potatoes, new forms of tomatoes, sweet and field corn, squashes, asparagus, peas, etc. One of his most extensive and interesting experiments was that extending through sixteen years and resulting in the production of a series of luxuriantly growing spineless cactus useful for feeding cattle in arid regions. In this work selection was first made from three hardy northern cactus forms. These selected plants were then crossed with three southern forms, one from Southern California, one from Central America, and one from Spain. On the whole pure selection proved to be more efficacious than hybridization in getting the desired results in this cactus work. The cross-bred forms tended constantly to revert to the ancestral spiny condition.

Burbank's home life during the fifty years in which he lived and worked in California was extremely simple. In 1877, only two years after he had removed from Massachusetts to California, his mother and sister joined him in Santa Rosa. The mother was then sixty-four years old but with hair still black and eyes still wide open to the beauties of nature. She died in the Santa Rosa home in 1909, at the age of ninety-six. Burbank was twice married but there were no children; and he loved children. "I love sunshine, the blue sky, trees, flowers, mountains, green meadows, sunny brooks, the ocean when its waves softly ripple along the sandy beach or when pounding the rocky cliffs with its thunder and roar, the birds of the field, waterfalls, the rainbow, the dawn, the noonday and the evening sunset—but children above them all" (*Ibid.,* p. 93).

Many will ask if Burbank did not make a great deal of money from his plant creations. The answer is, he did not and, in fact, could not. He could get a fairly good price from the nurseryman for his single sale of the new plum or berry or flower, and the nurseryman could sell the offspring or the grafts from the new plant for a season or two—and then the control was gone.

Reproduction and distribution of the new thing were now possible to any of the buyers. So Burbank made no money beyond that needed for a comfortable simple living. But that was all he cared to make. Various attempts by friendly, or self-interested business men to make his work reap larger financial returns all resulted only in troubles for him, and were put aside. He found his reward in his work and in its results. "Becoming tired with the years, he now rests beneath the Cedar of Lebanon by the vine-covered cottage."

[The printed records of Burbank's life and work, and of the many and various new plant varieties produced by him are to be found in newspapers, magazines, and books. They vary a great deal as regards authenticity. Burbank suffered both in reputation and spirit because of the unauthentic and absurdly exaggerated character of certain newspaper and even magazine accounts of him and his work. So intent were some of the writers of these accounts on making a wizard out of Burbank that they led some persons to believe him a faker. In addition, in the very last months of his life he expressed certain opinions about religious dogmas and creeds that brought down on him the displeasure of many theologians of the fundamentalist type. The bitterness of these attacks both surprised and pained him. Among the books about his life and work may be mentioned *The Early Life and Letters of Luther Burbank* (1927), by his sister, Emma Burbank Beeson; W. S. Harwood, *New Creations in Plant Life* (1905); H. de Vries, *Comments on the Experiments of Nilson and Burbank* (1907); David Starr Jordan and Vernon Kellogg, *The Scientific Aspects of Luther Burbank's Work* (1909); H. S. Williams, *Luther Burbank, His Life and Work* (1915); Luther Burbank and Wilbur Hall, *Harvest of the Years* (1927). Written under Burbank's immediate direction are twelve beautifully illustrated volumes entitled *Luther Burbank, His Methods and Discoveries and Their Practical Application* (1914-15); and another set of eight volumes, entitled, *How Plants are Trained to Work for Man* (1921). Of peculiar interest is Burbank's brief series of descriptive catalogues entitled, *New Creations* (1893-1901).]   V. K.

BURBRIDGE, STEPHEN GANO (Aug. 19, 1831–Dec. 2, 1894), Union soldier, was the grandson of Capt. George Burbridge (a Revolutionary soldier who settled in Kentucky during her early history), and the son of Capt. Robert Burbridge (a soldier in the War of 1812) and his wife, Eliza Ann Barnes of Mississippi (*History of Bourbon, Scott, Harrison, and Nicholas Counties,* 1882, edited by W. H. Perrin). He was born in Scott County, Ky., attended Georgetown College and Kentucky Military Institute, and then studied law, but did not practise. When the Civil War began he was a farmer in Logan County. Entering the Union Army as colonel of the 26th Kentucky Infantry, a regiment he himself had raised, he served with the Army of the Ohio at the battle of Shiloh. He was appointed brigadier-general of volunteers, June 9, 1862, and commanded a brigade of the 13th Corps at the taking of Arkansas Post and in the Vicksburg campaign. On Feb. 15, 1864,

he was assigned temporarily to the command of the District of Kentucky, with extensive civil as well as military powers. The post was one of extreme difficulty, for Kentucky was a border state; its people were divided in sentiment, and its territory was constantly subject to raids from the east and south. On the whole, his military operations were successful, forwarding the Union cause and reflecting credit upon himself. He defeated and dispersed Gen. John Morgan's forces in June 1864, thus turning into disaster a raid which had been highly successful in the beginning. An advance into southwestern Virginia in October, for the purpose of destroying the salt works and lead mines which were of vital importance to the Confederacy, failed to accomplish its purpose; but a second attempt, in December, made in conjunction with Generals Stoneman and Gillem, was more fortunate. As civil official, however, Burbridge was shortsighted and injudicious, making no attempt to conciliate the disaffected, and actually antagonizing the moderate Union men by his severe and seemingly arbitrary measures. He sought to control the election of 1864 by the free use of the military, making numerous arrests (it was charged) of persons whose only offense was that they had opposed Lincoln. He involved himself in what the people of the state regarded as a deliberate swindle when by orders issued Oct. 28, 1864, and later, he practically forced the farmers to sell their hogs only to the Federal agents and at a price considerably lower than that offered in the Cincinnati markets. The injustice of the action was recognized by Lincoln and upon instruction from the War Department Burbridge revoked his orders (Nov. 27, 1864). He suppressed the "Home Guards" and disbanded the state troops raised to resist guerrillas, but the policy which won him the ardent hatred of the majority of the people of his state was the system of reprisals inaugurated as a means of suppressing guerrilla warfare—a system so rigorous that he was accused of the "murder" of many citizens (Basil Duke, *Reminiscences,* 1911, p. 478). Complaints of Burbridge's policies were made by the civil governor, Thomas E. Bramlette [*q.v.*], and others, to Lincoln and to Grant—the latter as early as November 1864 earnestly advocated his removal—but at first his ruthless punishment of guerrillas was approved at Washington and for a time Stanton seems to have hesitated to yield to the Bramlette party in effecting his removal. In December 1864, however, the Assistant Inspector General reported that though "his administration has been mainly a good one," nevertheless "the substitution of a man stronger in capacity and character would be an advantage." He was relieved from his command in January 1865, and resigned from the army in December. He was ostracized for the rest of his life. In 1867 he wrote that he was not "able to live in safety or do business in Kentucky"; and again, "my services to my country have caused me to be exiled from my home, and made my wife and children wanderers." He applied for appointment as marshal of the District of Columbia, and later as commissioner of internal revenue, but without success. He died in Brooklyn, N. Y., where he had resided for some time, and only one of the Louisville papers contained a notice of his death. He was married twice: first, to Lizzie Goff; second, to Sara R. Burbridge, who survived him.

[See Lewis and R. H. Collins, *Hist. of Ky.* (1874), vol. I; E. M. Coulter, *The Civil War and Readjustment in Ky.* (1926); F. B. Heitman, *Hist. Reg.* (1890); *Official Records* (Army), ser. I, vols. XVI (pt. 2), XVII (pt. 1), XXIV (pts. 1, 2), XXVI (pt. 1), XXXII (pts. 2, 3); XXXVIII (pt. 5), XXXIX (pts. 1, 2, 3), XLV (pts. 1, 2), XLIX (pt. 1), LII (pt. 1); ser. II, vol. VII; ser. III, vol. IV. In response to attacks made upon him in the *Cincinnati Commercial* and the Louisville *Courier-Journal*, Burbridge published a defense of his conduct as commander of the district of Ky., *Louisville Commercial*, Feb. 5, 1882.]   T. M. S.

BURCHARD, SAMUEL DICKINSON (Sept. 6, 1812–Sept. 25, 1891), Presbyterian clergyman, was born in Steuben, Oneida County, N. Y., the son of Jabez and Lucina Burchard. The first Burchard in America was Thomas, who came over in the ship *True Love* in 1635. Jabez Burchard served in the Revolutionary War in the so-called Hampshire regiment of Massachusetts under Capt. David Barton. After the Revolution he married the captain's daughter and the two families made the long trek to Western New York and settled in Oneida County. Jabez Burchard bought the land for his farm from Baron Steuben, general in the Continental army, to whom a large grant of land had been made by the State of New York. On this farm Samuel was born. After receiving a common-school education, he taught school himself for a time but when he was eighteen moved to Kentucky where he entered Centre College. In 1832 during an epidemic of cholera in Kentucky he was the only student who did not leave the college. He was indefatigable in nursing the sick and became known as "the student nurse of Danville." On his graduation in 1836 he became a lecturer, attracting large audiences to hear him speak on abolition and temperance. He received his license to preach the same year from the Transylvania Presbytery, but did not accept a call to a pastorate until three years later. Then he became the pastor of the Houston Street Presbyterian Church in New York City, a position which he held for forty years. In 1846 a new church building was erected in Thirteenth St., which was destroyed by fire nine years later. It was rebuilt and Burchard continued to preach in it until 1879. His second and last pastorate was of the Murray Hill Presbyterian Church, where he served six years, becoming pastor emeritus in 1885. In 1866 he was made chancellor of Ingham University and continued in this position for eight years, making semi-annual visits to the institution. Later he accepted the presidency of Rutgers Female Academy.

The most dramatic event of Burchard's life had far-reaching consequences. It came in the closing days of the bitterly fought presidential campaign between Grover Cleveland and James G. Blaine. On Oct. 29, 1884, Burchard was the spokesman—selected at the last moment in the absence of the Rev. Dr. McArthur, the designated leader—of a body of several hundred clergymen of all denominations who called upon Blaine at the Fifth Avenue Hotel in New York to assure him of their support. Burchard's address to the candidate contained these words: "We expect to vote for you next Tuesday. We have higher expectations, which are that you will be the President of the United States and that you will do honor to your name and to the high office you will occupy. We are Republicans and don't propose to leave our party and identify ourselves with the party whose antecedents are rum, Romanism, and rebellion. We are loyal to our flag. We are loyal to you." Blaine either did not take in the words "rum, Romanism, and rebellion" or did not realize the danger involved in them, for he made no comment. But the Democrats did not treat them so carelessly. They were seized upon as campaign material, printed on leaflets which were spread broadcast, and displayed on flaring posters. It was inevitable in the crowded closing hours of a hard-fought campaign that the words should be attributed to Blaine himself, and there were plenty of his opponents to accuse him of being an announced and bitter anti-Catholic. There is good reason to believe that in New York State sufficient votes were alienated by the phrase to turn the election to Cleveland. The Democratic plurality in the state was only 1,047 so that a change of less than six hundred votes would have reversed the result. New York's electoral vote decided the election. Burchard suffered much annoyance and recrimination after the election but he made no apology for his words, declaring that if he had been an instrument in the hands of Providence against his own will he was content to abide by the consequences. He died at Saratoga, N. Y.

[Obituaries in the N. Y. papers of Sept. 26, 1891; accounts of the "Rum, Romanism, and Rebellion" incident in *Life and Public Services of Hon. Jas. G. Blaine* (1893) by Henry Davenport Northrop, in *An American Statesman, the Works and Words of Jas. G. Blaine* (1892) by Willis Fletcher Johnson, and in the life by Edward Stanwood (1908) in the American Statesmen Series.]   H.H.

BURDEN, HENRY (Apr. 22, 1791–Jan. 19, 1871), ironmaster, inventor, was born in Dunblane, Stirlingshire, Scotland, the son of Peter and Elizabeth (Abercrombie) Burden. As a youth, while working for his father, a small farmer, he is said to have given evidence of marked inventive talent. He attended the local school of William Hawley, a mathematician, and afterward studied mathematics, drawing, and engineering at the University of Edinburgh. In 1819, bearing letters from the American minister at London to Stephen Van Rensselaer and Senators Benton and Calhoun, he came to America. At Van Rensselaer's suggestion he went to Albany, where he found work in making agricultural implements in the establishment of Townsend & Corning. He invented an improved plow, which took the first premium at three county fairs, and a cultivator which is said to have been the first to be put into practical operation on this side of the Atlantic. On Jan. 27, 1821, he was married in Montreal to Helen McOuat, whom he had known in Scotland. The next year he moved to Troy to become the superintendent of a small and ill-equipped plant, the Troy Iron and Nail Factory, and by his executive ability and his inventive skill he gradually transformed it into one of the largest iron factories in the country. In 1825 he received a patent for a machine for making wrought iron spikes. An improvement was added to the machine in 1834, and another in 1836 (patented in 1840), by which it was altered to make the hook-headed spike, which soon came into general use in track-laying on all American railways. The patent was bitterly contested in litigation lasting for twenty years between Burden and the Albany Iron Works, but in the end Burden won a complete victory. The most widely known of his inventions was the horseshoe machine, first patented in 1835, and successively improved in 1843, 1857, and 1862, which produced virtually all the horseshoes used by the Federal armies in the Civil War. In 1840 Burden patented the "rotary concentric squeezer," for rolling puddled iron into cylindrical bars, a machine declared by the commissioner of patents to be the most important invention in the manufacture of iron which had been reported to the patent office. From the beginning of Burden's connection with the Troy Iron and Nail Factory, and as rapidly as his means would permit, he bought its stock, so that by 1835 he owned half of it and by 1848 was sole owner. He thereupon established the partnership of H. Burden & Sons, which continued till his death. He had early shown a deep interest in steam navigation, and in 1825 had made suggestions to the Troy Steamboat Association that later were largely adopted in the building of the *Hendrick Hudson,* which in 1845 made the trip from New York to Albany in seven and a half hours. One of the innovations credited to Burden is the placing of sleeping berths on the upper decks. In 1833 he built for the Hudson traffic a passenger and freight boat of two cigar-shaped hulks, with a thirty foot paddle-wheel in the center. It was lost, however, in an accident the following year. He was an advocate of larger and faster boats for the Atlantic trade, and in 1846 was instrumental in the formation by Glasgow capitalists of Burden's Atlantic Steam Ferry Company, of which nothing came. His later years were passed in the general supervision of his immense and ever-growing establishment. He died of heart disease in his suburban home of Woodside, and the body was interred in the family vault in the Albany Rural Cemetery. Burden is described as a tall and well-made man, with a large head, prominent though regular features, a wide and high forehead, deep-set eyes, and a mouth which betokened a kindly and cheerful disposition. As an inventor his rank is high; and he had the good fortune, rare among inventors, to reap the rewards of his creations, by reason of his ownership of a factory. In his closing years he was doubtless Troy's most prominent citizen; and his death evoked from all classes a chorus of exceptional tributes.

[Margaret Burden Proudfit, *Henry Burden; His Life, and a Hist. of His Inventions* (1904); *A Memorial of Mrs. Henry Burden* (N. Y., 1860).]   W.J.G.

BURDETTE, ROBERT JONES (July 30, 1844–Nov. 19, 1914), humorist, Baptist clergyman, the son of Frederick Edwin and Sophia Eberhart (Jones) Burdette, was born in Greensboro, Pa., of Welsh and French Huguenot ancestry. In later life he turned to literary account the sentimental memories of a boyhood spent in the villages of Cumminsville, Ohio, and Peoria, Ill. In 1862 he enlisted with the 47th Illinois Regiment from Peoria. His first battle was fought before Vicksburg in May 1863. Returning to Illinois in 1866, he taught district school near Peoria for a few months, was a United States railway mail clerk, and then went to New York to study French, German, and art at Cooper Institute. While there he embarked (1869) for Cuba on the blockade runner *Lillian* and was wounded while landing a consignment of arms for the Cuban insurgents. He went West in 1869 to work on the *Peoria Daily Transcript*. His first interview was with Horace Greeley. In 1871 he assisted in founding the Peoria *Review*. Upon its collapse in 1874 he joined the staff of the *Burlington Daily Hawk-Eye*. His "Hawkeyetems of Roaming Robert, the Hawkeye man," were for many years a biweekly feature of the *Hawk-Eye* and earned for it a national circulation.

Gradually Burdette became absorbed in the work of a platform lecturer, though he kept always his newspaper connections. His first lecture (Keokuk, Iowa, December 1876), "The Rise and Fall of the Moustache," was afterward delivered nearly five thousand times and in almost every state of the union. He had many close friends among his lyceum associates, notably Henry Ward Beecher, H. W. Shaw (Josh Billings), Bill Nye, Mark Twain, Robert Ingersoll, Sol Smith Russell, and James Whitcomb Riley. In 1883 he removed to Ardmore, Pa. From this headquarters he continued to arrange lecture tours, and to contribute to his regular column on the *Brooklyn Daily Eagle* verse parodies, and skits on Master Bilderback, Mr. Dresseldorf, the rooster who expected to die "necks tweak," and other homely creatures of his fancy.

In 1888, while living at the "Robin's Nest" at Bryn Mawr, Burdette was licensed to preach in Baptist pulpits. His "one-day" pastorates while on lecture tours, were scattered from Maine to Texas. Upon his removal to California in 1898 he was for some months supply pastor of the First Presbyterian Church of Pasadena. In 1903 he became the first pastor of the Temple Baptist Church of Los Angeles. Under his pastorate the roll increased from a charter membership of two hundred and eighty-five to a church of one thousand and sixty-nine, with an average attendance of three thousand at the two Sunday services. In six years the Sunday-school was enlarged from one hundred and seventy-five to nearly a thousand pupils. Burdette's later life was given to his church work, occasional addresses, contributions to newspapers, and the editing of various manuscripts and addresses for book publication. A spinal injury, incurred through a fall in 1909, brought on a lingering semi-invalidism, and finally death. He was married twice: on Mar. 4, 1870 to Carrie S. Garrett, and on Mar. 25, 1899 to Mrs. Clara (Bradley) Wheeler-Baker.

"The physician of the merry heart," as Burdette was often called, embodied his philosophy in several volumes of humorous sketches: *The Rise and Fall of the Moustache and Other Hawkeyetems* (1877); *Hawk-Eyes* (1879); *Schoon-* ers that Pass in the Dark (1894); *Chimes from a Jester's Bells* (1897); *Old Time and Young Tom* (1912). Of the verse parodies scattered among his prose contributions, *Smiles Yoked with Sighs* was collected and published in 1900, and *The Silver Trumpets* was assembled in 1912 from poems first printed in the *Temple Herald*. Several of his later sermons were circulated in pamphlet form. He contributed a *Life of William Penn* (1882) to Henry Holt's series of the Lives of American Worthies, and supervised the California edition of *American Biography and Genealogy* (2 vols.). In his last year he saw the publication of *The Drums of the 47th* (1914) an account of his Civil War experiences which had appeared serially in the *Sunday School Times*.

[The standard biography is *Robt. J. Burdette, His Message* (1922), by his wife, Clara B. Burdette.]

J. R. T.

BURDICK, FRANCIS MARION (Aug. 1, 1845–June 3, 1920), legal writer, son of Albert G. and Eunetia Yale (Wheeler) Burdick, was a descendant of Robert Burdick, a freeman of Newport, R. I. in 1655 and one-time member of the Assembly. He was born at De Ruyter, N. Y., where his father was a farmer, and his early education was obtained at De Ruyter Institute and Cazenovia Seminary, whence he proceeded to Hamilton College, where he graduated in 1869. He then for a short time became a classical teacher at Whitestone Seminary (New York) and in 1871 joined the editorial staff of the Utica *Herald*. Later in that year he returned to Hamilton to study law under Prof. Theodore Dwight, was graduated LL.B., and was admitted to the bar in 1872. He commenced practise in Utica and soon acquired a substantial connection, identifying himself with all matters of civic interest. In 1882 he was elected mayor on a reform platform. His inclinations had always been academic, and, in that year the Maquard King Professorship of Law and History at Hamilton becoming vacant, he accepted an invitation to occupy the chair. In this position he was an unqualified success, thorough scholarship being united in him with an innate capacity for imparting knowledge and attracting students. In 1887 on the establishment of a college of law in connection with Cornell University he was appointed one of its first professors. "He was an important factor in establishing the new school on a firm basis," and while there "began to make use of original sources as the basis of class room instruction, a method which has come to be somewhat inaccurately and quite incompletely described as the 'case system'" (Harlan F. Stone). Four years later the trustees of Columbia University reorganized its law school, and appointed him Theodore Dwight Professor of Law. This position he occupied for twenty-five years, in the course of which he lectured on a number of subjects. His lectures, prepared with meticulous care, systematic in arrangement and development, admirably illustrated, and delivered with unusual lucidity and simplicity of exposition, invariably drew large, appreciative audiences. His attention was particularly directed to torts, sales, and partnership, and for the elucidation of these special topics he prepared a number of text-books and collections of cases. His first book, *Cases on Torts,* was published in 1891. *The Law of Sales of Personal Property* and a companion volume of *Selected Cases on the Law of Sales of Personal Property* appeared in 1897. They were followed by *Selected Cases on the Law of Partnership including Limited Partnerships* (1898), *The Law of Partnership* (1899), and *The Law of Torts* (1905). Designed for class study, in connection with the curriculum, these works were welcomed by the profession and student body alike and passed through a number of editions. In 1907 Burdick was appointed one of the commissioners on uniform laws. In this capacity he took a leading part in drafting the uniform laws which were indorsed by the commission, recommended for adoption, and subsequently enacted in the various states. He resigned his professorship in 1916, being appointed emeritus professor, and lived in comparative retirement till his death, which occurred at De Ruyter. He was married, on June 8, 1875, to Sarah Underhill, daughter of Gustavus A. Kellogg of Utica.

In addition to the works already mentioned, Burdick wrote *The Essentials of Business Law* (1902) and *The Uniform Sales Act of 1908, with Annotations* (1908). He contributed the articles "Law and Jurisprudence" to the *American Year Book* for 1910, 1911, 1913, and 1915. As a trustee of the *Columbia Law Review* he took a lively interest in its progress, regularly contributing book reviews of a general character in addition to articles of legal interest. He also wrote largely for other periodicals on matters of law, history, and jurisprudence.

[The "Memorial" in *Ass. of the Bar of the City of N. Y., Yearbook* 1921, p. 159, by Judge Harlan F. Stone of the U. S. Supreme Court, at that time dean of the Columbia Law School, and the same author's article in *Columbia Law Rev.,* Nov. 1920, contain an authoritative summary of Burdick's career and a competent appraisal of his academic achievements. The latter article also gives a complete bibliography, listing all Burdick's contributions to periodicals, prepared by Prof. F. C. Hicks. See also *Case and Comment,* Sept. 1916; *Green Bag,* Nov. 1889.]
                                              H. W. H. K.

BURGESS, ALEXANDER (Oct. 31, 1819– Oct. 8, 1901), Episcopal bishop, was descended from Thomas Burgess, who came from England about 1630, and ultimately established himself in Sandwich, Mass. One of Thomas's descendants, who also bore the name Thomas, made his home in Providence, R. I., and in 1803 married Mary Mackie of Scotch descent, whose home was in Wareham, Mass. These were the parents of Alexander Burgess, who was born in Providence.

Following in the footsteps of his father, Alexander prepared himself for admission to Brown University, and graduated in the class of 1838. He then went to the General Theological Seminary, New York, to fit himself for the Episcopal ministry, graduating from that institution in 1841. He was ordained deacon Nov. 3, 1842, by the Rt. Rev. Alexander Viets Griswold, bishop of what was then known as the Eastern Diocese, which included all of New England except Connecticut, and was advanced to the priesthood, Nov. 1, 1843, by the Rt. Rev. John P. K. Henshaw, bishop of Rhode Island, that part of the Eastern Diocese having within the year elected its own bishop. On Dec. 11, 1842, Burgess took charge of St. Stephen's Church, East Haddam, Conn., remaining there about a year, when he was called to the rectorship of St. Mark's Church, Augusta, Me. After serving over ten years in this charge he completed a rectorship of nearly thirteen years in St. Luke's Church, Portland. From there he went to be rector of St. John's Church, Brooklyn, L. I., but remained only three years, when he assumed the rectorship of Christ Church, Springfield, Mass. In whatever diocese he served he was chosen for positions of importance and responsibility. In the dioceses of Maine, Long Island, and Massachusetts he was almost continuously from 1845 to 1877 a member of their respective standing committees. He was elected as a deputy to eight general conventions from the Diocese of Maine, and to three from the Diocese of Massachusetts. At the last convention in which he served as a deputy, that of 1877, he was made the president of the House of Deputies. Before this convention there came an application from the Diocese of Illinois asking that two additional dioceses might be set up within the limits of the State of Illinois. This application was granted, and one of these dioceses became the Diocese of Quincy. At a special convention held Feb. 26, 1878, Burgess was elected bishop on the forty-fourth ballot, and on May 15, 1878, in Christ Church, Springfield, Mass., he was consecrated the first Bishop of Quincy.

It was a difficult field to which Bishop Burgess had been called, and the work was pioneer work.

He was an Eastern man by birth and education, and all his ministry hitherto had been in the East. But he adapted himself to the new conditions, and by his strong scriptural preaching, by his faithful and sympathetic labors, and by his broad-mindedness, he started the new diocese well on its way. He was especially skilled in the canon law of the Church, and an able parliamentarian. Though possessed of rich intellectual gifts, yet in his busy life as pastor and bishop he found little time for literary work. In 1869 he published a Memoir of his brother, George Burgess [q.v.], the Bishop of Maine, which, however, was more a compilation of the impressions of others than an original production. Bishop Burgess was twice married: in September 1845 to Mary Williams Selden, who died Apr. 22, 1856; and on June 1, 1858, to Maria Annette Howard, daughter of the Hon. Joseph Howard of Portland, Me., who died Jan. 4, 1899. He died in St. Albans, Vt., and was buried there.

[H. G. Batterson, *A Sketch Book of the Am. Episcopate* (1878); Wm. Stevens Perry, *The Episcopate of America* (1895); E. Burgess, *Burgess Genealogy* (1865); *Jour. of Convention, Diocese of Quincy*, 1902; information from Bishop Burgess's daughter, Miss Caroline Howard Burgess.]   W. A. B.

BURGESS, EDWARD (June 30, 1848–July 12, 1891), yacht designer, entomologist, was born in West Sandwich, Mass., the son of Benjamin F. and Cordelia (Ellis) Burgess. His father was a wealthy Boston merchant in the West Indian trade. After a preparatory course in a private Latin school the son in 1866 entered Harvard, from which he graduated in 1871, with the degree of A.B. He left college with two well-developed hobbies, entomology and boating. His attachment to the former prompted him to accept the secretaryship of the Natural History Society of Boston in 1872, and his attachment to the latter led him, during his travels in Europe, to make some study of yacht building. Through his father's failure in business in 1879 he was left without means. He returned to Harvard as an instructor of entomology in the Bussey Institution and remained there four years. At the request of the United States Entomological Commission, he and Charles S. Minot contributed a paper "On the Anatomy of Aletio" (published as Chapter V of *House Miscellaneous Documents, No. 39*, 48 Cong., 2 Sess.). Other scientific papers were published by him in *Science* and in the *Proceedings of the Boston Society of Natural History*. In the fall of 1883 he and his younger brother Sidney started in business as yacht designers under the firm name of Burgess Brothers. There were few orders, and Sidney, discouraged, left the firm and went abroad. A revival of English interest in the contest for the *America's* Cup brought about a challenge for another race, which was accepted by a syndicate of Boston yachtsmen headed by J. Malcolm Forbes, and Burgess was chosen to design the American contender. The undertaking was one before which he might well have faltered, for his previous experiments in designing could help him little in the planning of a vessel such as the one now demanded. "He had nothing to guide him—no yacht from which to obtain any data," writes McVey. Nevertheless he resolutely set to work and in the end produced the *Puritan*, which in the race of 1885 defeated the English cutter, the *Genesta*. The victory brought him instant fame and a favorable turn in fortune. In the next year he designed the *Mayflower*, which outsailed the English *Galatea*, and in 1887 the *Volunteer* which defeated the English *Thistle*. His services were now in great demand among wealthy yachtsmen. In the short period of his professional career he designed over two hundred vessels. In 1887 he was appointed a member of the United States Naval Board to award prizes for the designs of cruisers and battle-ships, and in 1888 permanent chairman of the board of life-saving appliances of the United States Life-Saving Service. He died of typhoid fever in his home in Boston.

Burgess was married to Caroline L. Sullivant, of Columbus, Ohio, who with two sons survived him. He was a man of cultivation and refinement, in manner quiet and reserved and in speech reticent. His tastes were intellectual and artistic, and his home, largely designed by himself, is said to have been a characteristic expression of his personality. Among his intimate friends his studied reserve was doffed; he was capable of jesting and could play the boy; and it is recorded of him that he signalized every victory by turning a double somersault on the deck of his vessel. As a naval architect he is celebrated less for being an originator than for being an effective combiner. His genius, writes one of his eulogists, lay in his remarkable powers of observation and selection; though he did not discover any new element of speed, as did some of the others of his time, he still excelled his rivals in uniting known elements of speed as they had never before been combined.

[*Burgess Genealogy* (1865); *Eleventh Report of the Class of 1871 of Harvard College* (1921); A. G. McVey, "Edward Burgess and His Work," *New Eng. Mag.*, Sept. 1891; Samuel H. Scudder, "The Services of Edward Burgess to Natural Science," in *Proc. Boston Soc. Natural Hist.*, vol. XXV, containing bibliography of Burgess's writings; Thos. W. Lawson, *The Lawson Hist. of the America's Cup* (1902); H. L. Stone, *The "America's" Cup Races* (1914); Edward Burgess, "Yachts and Yachting" in *Am. and Eng. Yachts* (1887); obituaries in the *Boston Daily Advertiser*, the *Boston Herald*, and *N. Y. Times*, July 13, 1891.]   W. J. G.

BURGESS, GEORGE (Oct. 31, 1809–Apr. 23, 1866), Episcopal bishop, was born in Providence, R. I., the second son of Thomas and Mary Mackie Burgess, and an older brother of Bishop Alexander Burgess [*q.v.*]. As a young lad he was exceptionally studious, and possessed a remarkable power of concentration, so that he was ready for college before he was twelve years old. But his father was averse to his entering so young, and kept him back for a year. In 1822, he entered Brown University, and after a brilliant academic career graduated with high honors in the class of 1826. His father was a lawyer of prominence in Providence, and young Burgess after his graduation studied law in his office and completed his preparation, though he never applied to be admitted to the bar. His family were Congregationalists, and in that faith had been his early training. But his study and reading led him into the Episcopal Church, and even while he was working in his father's law office he began to experience a drawing toward the ministry. From 1829 to 1831 he served as tutor at Brown, at the same time studying theology under the guidance of his rector, the Rev. Dr. Nathan B. Crocker. The three years following he spent abroad attending lectures at the Universities of Berlin, Bonn, and Göttingen, and in traveling. Upon his return he was ordained deacon in Grace Church, Providence, by Bishop Alexander Viets Griswold, and was advanced to the priesthood, Nov. 2, 1834, in Christ Church, Hartford, Conn., by Bishop Thomas Church Brownell. He was immediately made rector of Christ Church, Hartford. Under his wise administration the parish grew, and his work there was congenial. But he was destined for promotion. Maine, which had been a diocese since 1820, had continued under the bishop of the Eastern Diocese, that is, of all New England except Connecticut. But the time had now come when Maine desired its own bishop, and so at a special convention held in Portland, Oct. 4, 1847, Burgess was unanimously elected to that office. He was consecrated in Christ Church, Hartford, Oct. 31, 1847. When he went to Maine he made his home in Gardiner, assuming the rectorship of the church there, which position he held until his death, performing his duties as rector in conjunction with and in addition to his duties as bishop, such doubling of duties being necessary because of the inadequacy of the support available for the episcopate. His diocese was weak, but by his steadfast devotion and saintly life, by his unwearying energy and convincing preaching, he had the satisfaction of seeing it develop and increase in influence under his guidance.

Bishop Burgess possessed a well-informed mind, and the ability to give clear expression to his thoughts. As a result he wrote much, in spite of the demands which his work as bishop made upon him. There was a poetic strain in his nature, and *The Poems of the Rt. Rev. George Burgess* (1868), published after his death, constituted, perhaps, his chief literary production. He translated the Book of Psalms into verse (1840), wrote *Pages from the Ecclesiastical History of New England between 1740 and 1840* (1847), and *The Last Enemy, Conquering and Conquered* (1850), and in addition published numerous sermons and addresses in pamphlet form. Trouble with his throat began to show itself, and early in 1865 the suggestion was made to him that he visit Hayti and look over the missionary work there. Toward the end of the year he undertook the journey, with the double purpose of seeking benefit to his health and studying the conditions of the mission stations at Hayti. It was on this journey that he died on board ship as he was going from Port au Prince to the port whence he was intending to sail for home. His body was taken to Gardiner, Me., and buried in the churchyard there. He was married on Oct. 26, 1846, to Sophia, daughter of Leonard Kip.

[Alexander Burgess, *Memoir of the Rt. Rev. Geo. Burgess* (1869); *Am. Quart. Ch. Rev. and Ecclesiastical Reg.*, July 1867; Calvin R. Batchelder, *A Hist. of the Eastern Diocese* (1876).]   W.A.B.

BURGESS, NEIL (June 29, 1851?–Feb. 19, 1910), actor, was born in Boston, his mother's name being Ellen A. Lunt. He was educated in the public schools of Cambridge, and, after a brief time in business, made his professional beginning, at the age of nineteen, with Spaulding's Bell Ringers, and in the vaudeville theatres. One evening in Providence, while he was stage manager with a company on tour playing *The Quiet Family,* the actress who had been impersonating Mrs. Barnaby Bibbs was unable to appear, and Burgess took her place, for that performance only, as he thought. Although he disliked his task, he found favor with the audience, and his destiny was thereby settled. After that his entire life on the stage was spent in grotesque impersonations in which he burlesqued rather than interpreted the eccentric personalities of elderly women. For his effects, and for the laughter across the footlights, he relied largely upon extravagances of feminine costume. He starred first in 1879 in *Vim, or, a Visit to Puffy Farm.* Interspersed with his experiences in this play were appearances, beginning in 1879, in *Widow Bedott, or, a Hunt for a Husband,* a dramatization of *The Widow Bedott Papers.* But his most popular part was Abigail Prue, and his most popular play *The County Fair,* written by Charles Barnard, and produced in Burlington, N. J., Oct. 6, 1888, and at Proctor's Fifth Avenue Theatre, New York, Mar. 5, 1889, after which it was acted more than five thousand times during the ensuing seasons. In it was utilized the treadmill device for a horse race later used effectively and with great spectacular effect in the chariot race in *Ben Hur.* In San Francisco, Sept. 7, 1880, Burgess had married a member of his company, Mary E. Stoddart, a niece of James H. Stoddart, the actor. She accompanied him on his tours through many seasons, and died in 1905, leaving one son. When not on the road they made their home at Atlantic Highlands, N. J., during the years of Burgess's prosperity. As a reward for his stage success, he acquired considerable wealth, but lost the greater part of it through injudicious investments and unprofitable theatrical ventures. He was essentially a single character performer, doing his one specialty with an individual ingenuity that brought him, for a considerable period, unbounded popularity. He attempted a tour of England with *The County Fair* in 1897, but the English public failed to understand and appreciate his peculiar type of humor. During his last years on the stage he gave a condensed version of *The County Fair* in vaudeville.

[A. D. Storms, *The Players Blue Book* (1901); J. B. Clapp and E. F. Edgett, *Players of the Present* (1899–1901); *Boston Morning Jour.,* Apr. 2, 1892, Feb. 13, 1893; *Providence Daily Jour.,* Feb. 16, 1903; *Illustrated American,* Jan. 14, 1893; *Boston Evening Transcript,* Feb. 19, 1910; *N. Y. Dramatic Mirror, N. Y. Dramatic News, N. Y. Clipper,* Feb. 26, 1910. The year of birth was either 1851 (Storms and the *Transcript*) or 1846 (*Mirror, News, Clipper*).]   E.F.E.

BURGEVINE, HENRY ANDREA (1836–June 26, 1865), adventurer, was the second of four children born to Gen. Andrea and Julia (Gillette) Burgevine. His father had been one of Napoleon's officers who, subsequent to the Peninsular campaign, served with the king of Spain, and was granted an extensive tract of land in Florida on which he spent many years surveying and vainly trying to secure recognition of the claim. His headquarters were at New Bern, N. C., in the French colony there. For a few months in 1836 he was a professor of modern languages at Chapel Hill, and possibly Henry was born there. The latter was educated in the public schools, but when still young went forth to adventure. After some service in the Crimea he wandered about and eventually appeared on the China coast. When, in 1860, Frederick Townsend Ward [*q.v.*] was recruiting a foreign company to recapture Sungkiang from the Taiping rebels he enrolled Burgevine as an officer. The young

leader showed dash and gallantry in a fruitless attack on Tsingpu, leading a charge after Ward was wounded. In the "Ever Victorious Army" which emerged from this nondescript company, Burgevine was third in command. Ward's untimely death in September 1862 precipitated a British-American rivalry for the command of the army which now numbered about 4,000. Li Hung Chang, Governor of Kiangsu, despite misgivings regarding Burgevine's character and aims, awarded him the post, deferring to the representations of the American minister, Anson Burlingame [*q.v.*], whom the British authorities eventually supported. The governor soon had cause to rue his compliance. Early in November, the Taiping forces in full strength challenged their besiegers outside Nanking. The imperialist cause stood in dire peril. His superior requested Li Hung Chang to send Gen. Ch'en to the rescue, but, owing to complications, Burgevine was offered instead,—an offer reluctantly accepted. To the governor's intense chagrin Burgevine, advancing various excuses, failed to move until at last the danger disappeared. Insult was added to injury when, early in January, December payments being overdue, Burgevine quelled an incipient mutiny in Sungkiang by promising to make payments within a limited time and proceeded to fulfil the promise by leading an armed guard to the home of the paymaster in Shanghai, there to seize forty thousand *taels,* wounding an official slightly in the mêlée. Li Hung Chang was fairly beside himself with anger, and would have executed the offender but for the latter's extraterritorial status. Dismissal and refusal to reinstate naturally followed, although Burgevine went to Peking and secured powerful support, including that of Burlingame.

Undaunted by his failure, Burgevine enrolled a hundred or more kindred spirits whom he led to join the insurgents in Soochow. Becoming dissatisfied there, he made overtures in October to come over with his entire following to Charles George Gordon, now in command of the "Ever Victorious Army." Li Hung Chang made no objections, but warned Gordon not to trust the man. Most of the company actually changed sides during a battle, but Burgevine himself was too closely watched. Gordon thereupon negotiated for his release,—the rebels apparently happy to be rid of him—and he was delivered to the United States consul at Shanghai, charged with treason. Eventually he was released on promising to leave China permanently. There was general relief at his departure. Nevertheless, shortly before the fall of Nanking, he was again in China attempting to join the insurgents, but was hindered by imperialist vigilance. In May 1865 he appeared in Fukien on his way to join the last unconquered Taiping chief. Being recognized by a foreign military instructor attached to the imperialists, he was arrested, together with a British companion. Once more Li Hung Chang sought to secure his execution, chafing at treaty restrictions that precluded direct action. He did not show undue grief when news came that the small boat conveying the prisoners had capsized, drowning them both. Shanghai foreigners suspected foul play, but it could not be proved and is improbable.

[Burlingame's reports to the State Dept. in *Foreign Relations of the U. S., 1863–66;* files of the *North China Herald;* Gen. Edward Forester, "Personal Recollections of the Tai-Ping Rebellion" in the *Cosmopolitan,* Oct., Nov., Dec., 1896; Gerald Browne, "Last Months of the Taeping War," *Harper's,* 1866; Wm. J. Hail, *Tseng Kuo-Fan and the Taiping Rebellion* (1927).]

W.J.H.

BURGIS, WILLIAM (fl. 1718–1731), artist and engraver, came from London to New York about 1718, and published by subscription "A South Prospect of ye Flourishing City of New York," sending it to London to be engraved by John Harris. Having been successful in New York, he went to Boston and, with his associates, William Price and Thomas Selby, ran a series of advertisements in James Franklin's *New England Courant* from Oct. 8, 1722, to Jan. 6, 1723/24, which resulted in the publishing, by subscription, of "A South East View of the Great Town of Boston," also engraved in London by John Harris, which gives the first known portrayal of a two-masted schooner in a view originating in America. One of his said associates, Thomas Selby, Senior Warden of King's Chapel, and keeper of the Crown Coffee House, where Burgis resided, died rather suddenly, and his widow, Mehitable, who had inherited £659-10-4 from him, and had an estate of her own besides, married William Burgis on Oct. 1, 1728. From that time on he is variously referred to in the records as draftsman, painter, innholder, taverner, and gentleman, until Feb. 11, 1730/31, when he was defaulted in a civil suit, having apparently left town. This is confirmed by his wife's unsuccessful petition to the Governor's Council on July 20, 1736, for a divorce, on grounds that he had got what he could of her estate into his hands, about five years since, had left her, and "has never returned into the Province again . . . and that whether he be living or dead she knows not, and no further trace has as yet been found of him." Besides the two works mentioned above (only one copy of the first state of each being known) he is associated with the following engraved works as delineator, engraver or publisher: "A

Prospect of the Colledges in Cambridge in New England," issued July 14, 1726, just too late for commencement (only one copy known, in the Massachusetts Historical Society, Boston); "A Draught of the Meeting-House of the Old (First) Church in Boston with the New Spire & Gallery," issued June 5, 1727 (no copy known); "Plan of Boston in New England," issued about July 3, 1729 (only three copies known, one in possession of R. T. H. Halsey of New York, another belonging to the estate of the late Dr. John Collins Warren of Boston, and the third in the Library of Congress); "Boston Light," issued Aug. 11, 1729, engraved in "mezzotinto," possibly the second plate so done in America and the only known work that carries Burgis's name as engraver (only one copy known, in possession of the United States Light House Board, Washington, D. C.); "View of the New Dutch Church (New York), founded A. D. 1727 and finished A. D. 1731" issued between July 31, 1731, and Aug. 1, 1732 (only one copy known, lately in possession of William Loring Andrews of New York).

[The principal sources of information are the *Boston News-Letter,* 1718–32; *Boston Gazette,* 1719–32; *New Eng. Courant,* 1721–26; *New Eng. Weekly Jour.,* 1727–32; *Reports of the Record Commissioners of the City of Boston* (1876–1909); Suffolk Court Files and Records, MS., 1718–32, Court House, Boston; John H. Edmonds, "The Burgis-Price View of Boston" in *Mass. Colonial Soc. Pubs.,* vol. XI (1910), and "The Burgis Views of N. Y. and Boston," in *Proc. Bostonian Soc.,* 1915.]

J. H. E—s.

BURK, FREDERIC LISTER (Sept. 1, 1862– June 12, 1924), educator, was born in Blenheim, Ontario, Canada, of an American father, Erastus, and an English mother, Matilda Turner. At the age of seven he was brought to California, the family settling in the town of Coloma, El Dorado County, a spot made famous by the discovery of gold there in 1848. Graduating from the Sacramento City High School, Burk entered the University of California and was graduated with the degree B.L. in 1883. When Stanford University opened in 1891, he became one of the first candidates for the M.A. degree which was conferred upon him in 1892. In the immediate years following, he was successively teacher in a country school and in a military academy, and then became a writer of feature articles for various San Francisco journals. The latter experience colored his whole career, giving him access to the press and also a sense of news values.

As a writer he became interested in psychology, and in 1896 he went to study under G. Stanley Hall at Clark University, where he received the Ph.D. degree in 1898. During the same year he was married to Caroline Frear (B.S., Wellesley, M.A., Stanford). In the following year he became president of the State Normal School at San Francisco. This office made him automatically a member of the California State Board of Education in which capacity he served until the Board's reorganization in 1911. In his normal school for a number of years everything was subordinated to psychology. Later, becoming disappointed in the results obtained, he threw out psychology, not to take it up again until tests and measurements came to his attention.

Burk became a challenger of accepted opinion in educational matters. He held that no subject should be put into the curriculum unless a case could be made out for it. First, let the subject prove its educational value, then add it to the course of study. His greatest contribution to educational progress was his theory of motivated individual instruction. Pioneering in that field, he held to his course in spite of criticism and indifference. As a public speaker he was unusual. Full of wit and sudden turns of thought, he depended on the intellectual force he could put back of his ideas rather than on persuasion. From the standpoint of inspiration he was a notable leader—especially in the loyalties he developed. There can be no doubt that his inspiring of a small group of men and women, including Carleton Washburne of Winnetka and Willard Beatty of Bronxville, will perpetuate his name and methods into the years ahead. He was the author of *From Fundamental to Accessory in the Development of the Nervous System and of Movements* (1898), his doctoral dissertation; *A Study of the Kindergarten Problem in the Public Kindergartens of Santa Barbara, Calif., for the Year 1898–99* (1899), in collaboration with his wife; *A Simplified Course of Study in Grammar* (1912); *In Re Everychild, A Minor vs. Lockstep Schooling* (1915).

[*Who's Who in America*, 1924–25; *Bulls. of the San Francisco State Normal School;* articles in the *Sierra Ed. News* and the *Western Jour. of Ed.* (both published in San Francisco); personal acquaintance; interviews with members of the family.]　　　　W. W. K.

BURK, JOHN DALY (*c.* 1775–Apr. 11, 1808), dramatist, was born in Ireland and came to America in 1796, evidently a political refugee. He had, he said, been a student at Trinity College, Dublin, and was reputed to have attempted the rescue of a condemned political prisoner and then himself escaped the country in woman's clothes, supplied by a Miss Daly, whose name he added to his own in gratitude. He settled first in Boston, where, on Oct. 6, 1796, he started a newspaper, the *Polar Star and Boston Daily Advertiser*. This venture lasted only six months.

From Boston he went to New York and attempted the publication of another paper, the *Time Piece*. This also failed. He then went to Petersburg, Va., where he finally settled. Here, on April 11, 1808, he was killed in a duel with a Frenchman named Coquebert. Burk's hot temper was probably the cause of the quarrel (*Some Materials to Serve for a Brief Memoir of John Daly Burk,* by Charles Campbell, Albany, 1868).

Burk was the author of *A History of the Late War in Ireland* (Philadelphia, 1799), "An Historical Essay on the Character and Antiquity of Irish Songs" (*Richmond Enquirer*, May 27, 1808), and a four-volume *History of Virginia* (vol. I, 1804; vols. II, III, 1805; vol. IV, completed by others, 1816). It was as a playwright, however, that he chiefly figured in American letters. He was among the earliest to put an American battle scene on the stage, in *Bunker Hill, or the Death of General Warren,* produced first at the Haymarket Theatre, Boston, Feb. 17, 1797, and at the John Street Theatre, New York, the following September. Burk apparently earned $2,000 from the Boston engagement, a very considerable sum for a playwright in those days, and the play remained popular on such holidays as the Fourth of July for almost fifty years. A full and interesting description of how the battle scene was staged will be found in a letter from Burk to the manager of the New York theatre (Brander Matthews's introduction to the reprint of the play, Dunlap Society, New York, 1891). The play was full of inflated rhetoric and bombastic blank verse, to-day highly ludicrous. One character refers to nightingales singing in Boston. President Adams saw the play in New York, and said to the manager, "My friend Gen. Warren was a scholar and a gentleman, but your author has made him a bully and a blackguard." Of course Burk had no intention of doing this, and to tastes less fastidious than Adams's it did not seem that he had done so. The public of the day at any rate forgave the inflated rhetoric (if they did not enjoy it!) for the sake of the battle scene. In 1798, at the Park Theatre, New York, Burk's *Female Patriotism, or the Death of Joan d'Arc* was produced. Professor Quinn (*A History of the American Drama from the Beginning to the Civil War*, 1923, pp. 117–18) calls this play one of the best of all our early American dramas. Joan, he says, is a human character and the verse rises to a respectable level of eloquence. Other plays by Burk were *The Death of General Montgomery in Storming the City of Quebec* (1797); *Bethlem Gabor, Lord of Transylvania, or the Man-hating Palatine* (published in 1807, in Petersburg, Va., where it had been acted by Burk and other amateurs, as well as by the professional company at Richmond) ; *The Innkeeper of Abbeville;* and (attributed to Burk by some writers) a lost play called *Which Do You Like Best, the Poor Man or the Lord?* Burk had an undoubted love for freedom and this was reflected in his plays, however crude. He also appealed to the patriotic emotions of the day, and by making a stage pageant out of national history helped our infant drama to identify itself with the national life.

[In addition to the sources cited above, see Oscar Wegelin, *Early Am. Plays* (1900) ; Wm. W. Clapp, Jr., *A Record of the Boston Stage* (1853) ; Wm. Dunlap, manuscript journals in the N. Y. Hist. Soc.]

W. P. E.

BURKE, ÆDANUS (1743–Mar. 30, 1802), congressman, jurist, was born in Galway, Ireland, and was the grandson of an officer under James II in the Irish uprising of 1689–90. A letter of Dec. 2, 1769, shows him at that time hard at work studying law in Stafford County, Va. (*State Records of North Carolina,* XV, 676–78). In February 1778 he resigned a lieutenant's commission in the 2nd South Carolina Continental Regiment (*Year Book, City of Charleston,* 1893, p. 209), and a month later was appointed one of the associate judges of the state. In his charge to the grand jury of Ninety Six District in May, he set forth the democratic basis of the new state government, and rejoiced in the abolition of the "unnatural distinctions of nobleman and commons." On the fall of Charleston two years later the courts were suspended not to be opened until 1783 (D. J. McCord, *Statutes of South Carolina,* VII, 206), and the judge again took the field, this time as captain of the militia. He was representative in the legislature in 1781 and 1782, and from 1784 to 1789. The leading issue in South Carolina during the years immediately following the Revolution was the treatment of the Loyalists. Burke always voted for leniency. In 1783 he published an admirably written pamphlet, *An Address to the Freemen of South Carolina,* in which he appealed for amnesty on grounds of humanity, public policy, and legal principle. He flayed John Rutledge as the originator of the confiscation policy. In another pamphlet of the same year he gave full vent to his distrust of the forms of nobility. His *Considerations on the Order of the Cincinnati* (1783) had a wide circulation in the United States, and was translated by Mirabeau into French under his name. English and German translations of this then appeared. In the South Carolina convention for ratifying the Federal Constitution Burke appeared as a representative of a back-country district, and voted against adoption. He declared that the eligibil-

ity of the President to succeed himself was dangerous to the liberties of the people, and moved an amendment to prohibit it. He was elected to the First Congress and there continued his fight for the qualification of the general powers of the government, to keep, he said, "our liberties from being fooled away." He opposed the excise tax and the establishment of the United States Bank. But the assumption of state debts he vigorously urged, as a measure of justice, both because the debts were incurred in the common cause, and because South Carolina, deprived by the Constitution of her import duties, would become bankrupt without it. Likewise he spoke and voted with the majority on paying the Continental obligations at par, basing his argument on public policy. He was a firm proponent of slavery. He did not return to Congress, and devoted the rest of his life to his judicial duties. In 1785 an act of the legislature appointed him, with Justices Grimké and Pendleton, on a commission to revise and digest the South Carolina law. The digest was reported in 1789. It was not adopted as a whole, but it had an influence on the Constitution of 1790, and portions were enacted as separate statutes (Thomas Cooper, *Statutes of South Carolina,* I, 435). In December 1799 Burke was elected chancellor of the court of equity. He never married, but lived in comfortable quarters in Charleston. He was first and foremost the judge, his solid legal learning and careful reasoning determining his conduct in all important matters. He was, next, the ardent democrat. But neither principle nor policy obscured his courage, his Irish wit, or his irascible temper.

[Jos. Johnson, *Traditions of the Am. Rev.* (1851) ; J. B. O'Neall, *Bench and Bar of S. C.* (1859) ; *S. C. Hist. and Gen. Mag.,* XIII, 146, XXVII, 45–48 ; *Am. Hist. Ass. Report,* 1896, I, 885–87.]

R. L. M—r.

BURKE, CHARLES ST. THOMAS (Mar. 27, 1822–Nov. 10, 1854), actor, dramatist, was the son of Thomas Burke, an actor of some repute, and Cornelia Frances Thomas, a capable actress of French ancestry who, after the death of her first husband, became the wife of the second Joseph Jefferson and the mother of the third and most celebrated actor of that name. Burke's career on the stage began in infancy, his early childhood experiences in the theatre culminating in his appearance at the National Theatre, New York, on Sept. 3, 1836, as the Prince of Wales to the Richard III of Junius Brutus Booth. Later in the same season he was seen as Prince John in *Henry IV* with James H. Hackett as Falstaff, and as Irus in Talfourd's tragedy *Ion* with George Jones. At this time he began the singing of comic songs in a manner that gained him an added popularity throughout his career. Toward the end of 1837, Mr. and Mrs. Jefferson, accompanied by their family, began journeys through the west and south which gave Burke intimate acquaintance with the life and hardships of the wandering actor. His aunt, Elizabeth Jefferson, says of him during this period that "he grew up to be one of the best actors we ever had," that "as a boy he was full of promise," and that "a more talented and kind-hearted man never lived." He returned to the east in 1847, and the rest of his short life was passed mainly in the theatres of New York and Philadelphia, notably in association with William E. Burton. Joseph Jefferson refers to them as "these two great artists," and in the course of his *Autobiography* mentions Burke again and again in the most affectionate terms. Burke acted many of the favorite heroes of comedy, including Paul Pry in John Poole's comedy, Dickory in *The Spectre Bridegroom,* Ichabod Crane, Solon Shingle, Touchstone, Sir Andrew Aguecheek, Bob Acres, Caleb Plummer, and Rip Van Winkle. He made his own version of the Washington Irving story, and portions of it were later utilized by Joseph Jefferson, who at one time acted Seth the innkeeper to his half-brother's Rip. The famous line, "Are we so soon forgot when we are gone?" is Burke's. He was twice married, first to Margaret Murcoyne of Philadelphia, and upon her death to Mrs. Sutherland, who survived him. A stepdaughter, Ione Sutherland, took his name, and had a brief career on the stage as Ione Burke. He had many of the appealing physical and mental attributes of the comedian. His figure was slender, graceful, and lithe, and his features though plain were notably expressive. He was a typical example of the born actor to whom the stage is a world of reality as well as of illusion, and the results of whose work come from intuition rather than from study. William Winter says that his "art concealed every vestige of effort." He died in New York in his thirty-third year, almost at the outset of what might have been a great career.

[T. A. Brown, *Hist. of the N. Y. Stage* (1903); J. N. Ireland, *Record of the N. Y. Stage* (1866–67); Wm. Winter, *The Jeffersons* (1881); Jos. Jefferson, *Autobiography* (1890); the *Era* (London), Dec. 2, 1899; *Lippincott's Mag.,* July 1879.]   E. F. E.

BURKE, JOHN G. [See BOURKE, JOHN GREGORY, 1846–1896.]

BURKE, STEVENSON (Nov. 26, 1826–Apr. 24, 1904), lawyer, railroad promoter, was the son of two Scotch-Irish immigrants from the North of Ireland, David and Isabella Burke, who in 1825 landed at New York and proceeded to a farm near Ogdensburg in Lawrence County, N. Y. Nine years later they moved to North Ridgeville, Ohio. Stevenson was the oldest of four children. For several years he attended the local school for a short time in the winter and worked on his father's farm in the summer. He also went to private schools at Ridgeville Center and Elyria. At the age of seventeen he began teaching in the district schools. In 1846 he entered Ohio Wesleyan University, but soon left to take up the study of law. He was admitted to the bar on Aug. 11, 1848. From 1848 to 1862 he practised law at Elyria. In 1861 he was elected common pleas judge, an office he held until 1869. He then moved to Cleveland to resume the practise of law in a larger field. He had a conspicuous part in the Oberlin-Wellington slave rescue case, but more representative of his practise, which was usually concerned with corporation law, particularly after his removal to Cleveland, were the Utah silver mine cases (the "Nez Percés" and the "Old Telegraph" mining companies) involving title to the properties; the Butzman and Mueller case testing the constitutionality of the Scott liquor license law of Ohio; and the series of cases connected with the foreclosure of mortgages on the Indianapolis & St. Louis Railway. For many years Burke was the general counsel of the Cleveland, Columbus, Cincinnati & St. Louis Railway and also for the Cleveland & Mahoning Valley Railway Company (Erie). From the practise of law he easily turned to the actual management of railway affairs. One of his early ventures in the railroad world was the consolidation of three lines into one company, the Columbus, Hocking Valley & Toledo Railway (about 1881). He was led into this merger in order to care for his coal properties in the Hocking Valley. In 1882 he negotiated the purchase of the New York, Chicago & St. Louis Railway ("Nickel Plate") for William H. Vanderbilt. In 1880 he became president of the Cleveland & Mahoning Valley Railway Company. After the organization of the Columbus, Hocking Valley & Toledo Railway, he was actively connected with its financial management. The "Big Four" Railway had his services as director, as chairman of the financial and executive committee, as vice-president, and later as president. Extensive as were his interests in the railroad world, however, Burke found time and energy to enter into other forms of business, among them iron manufacture, and coal and nickel mining. In his later years he gradually withdrew from active business management, although he remained president of the

Cleveland & Mahoning Valley Railway until the time of his death. In two fields, as a corporation lawyer and as an organizer and owner of railroads, he was distinguished among men of the Middle West. He was always interested in current affairs and was unusually well-read on a wide range of subjects, including art, education, finance, and government. A patron of the Western Reserve Historical Society, he was also the leading spirit in the foundation of the Cleveland School of Art, president of its board of trustees, and one of its foremost benefactors. He was married twice: on Apr. 26, 1849, to Parthenia Poppleton of Bellville, Ohio, who died on Apr. 7, 1878; and on June 22, 1882, to Mrs. Ella M. Southworth of Clinton, N. Y.

[Manuscript biography in the Western Reserve Hist. Soc.; sketch in the *Mag. of Western Hist.*, 1885–86, III, 296–306, by a local historian, J. H. Kennedy; another in the *Bench and Bar of Ohio* (1897), II, 360–66; articles including a resolution of the Cleveland Bar Association of Apr. 26, 1904, with estimates of character, as given by various members; *Cleveland Plain Dealer*, Apr. 25, 26, 1904; *Cleveland Leader*, Apr. 25, 27, 1904.]   E. J. B.

BURKE, THOMAS (*c.* 1747–Dec. 2, 1783), governor of North Carolina in the period of the Revolution, also a member of the Continental Congress, was born in County Galway, Ireland, of Norman-French descent. He was the son of Ulick Burke and his wife Letitia Ould. He attended one of the universities, probably Dublin, and after a family quarrel emigrated to America, settling first in Accomac County, Va., later in Norfolk. In Virginia he began the practise of medicine which he soon relinquished for law. In 1771 he removed to North Carolina and located in Orange County, about two miles north of Hillsboro, calling his estate "Tyaquin," the name of the Burke family seat in Ireland. He was licensed to practise law in the superior court of Orange in 1772 and soon became active in the political affairs of the county and of North Carolina.

In Virginia Burke had written and spoken against the Stamp Act and in North Carolina he represented Orange County in all of the provincial congresses save the first. In the third congress which met at Hillsboro in August 1775 he was very active, being a member of the committee which framed the test oath and also of the committees to prepare an address to the people, to conciliate the disaffected, and to provide ways and means. In the next congress, which met at Halifax in April 1776, he was a member of thirteen committees. Of these the most important was that on Usurpations and Grievances, which on Apr. 12 reported a resolution, unanimously adopted, empowering the delegates of

North Carolina in the Continental Congress to concur with the delegates from the other colonies in declaring independence—a measure which gave North Carolina a distinct priority in the movement for separation from Great Britain. Of barely less importance was the committee to report a frame of government for North Carolina. The committee, and also the congress, was divided into two groups, conservatives and radicals. Burke belonged to the latter group, advocating sovereignty of the people, annual elections, the separation of the organs of the government, the separation of church and state, and ratification by the people. Division of opinion was so strong that no decision could be reached, and the problem of constitutional principles was referred to the next congress, called to meet at Halifax in November 1776. The ensuing election was warmly contested; Burke and other candidates of like political creed in Orange County were defeated, but the congress, when it assembled, unseated the delegates chosen and ordered a new election in which Burke was successful. He then took his seat on Dec. 16, 1776. The constitution which was adopted was a compromise, but it embodied the principles of sovereignty of the people, separation of powers, separation of church and state, and annual elections. According to tradition the final draft of the Constitution and also of the bill of rights was the work of Burke, Richard Caswell [*q.v.*], and Thomas Jones. Burke's prominence in these political agitations resulted in his election to the Continental Congress by the Halifax Convention in December 1776. He appeared in Congress the following February and continued to represent North Carolina until June 1781, with the exception of the period from April to August 1778. He had no sympathy with the secrecy of the proceedings in Congress and was very critical whenever the military power seemed to infringe on civil rights. He was a severe critic of the Articles of Confederation while that document was in process of formation and after it was completed, and he was responsible for the final form of Article II of the Articles, which guaranteed to each state the powers not specifically delegated to Congress.

In the spring of 1778 Burke gave a practical demonstration of his conception of state sovereignty. A certain group in Congress hostile to Washington secured the adoption of instructions which interfered with a cartel which he was negotiating. Washington wrote Congress asking for a modification of the instruction and intimated that his sensibilities were wounded. The reply of Congress, as drafted by a committee, contained language which Burke did not approve, and, after a prolonged debate on the night of Apr. 10, seeing that his presence was necessary to make a quorum, he left the hall. Congress then summoned him to return. Believing that the message was from an individual, Burke refused. The next day when Congress attempted to discipline him, Burke declared that such action was an unwarranted exercise of power and that in his official actions he was responsible to the State of North Carolina. He therefore left Philadelphia, laid his case before the North Carolina Assembly, was exonerated and reëlected. This incident probably saved his political career, for in April 1778 he had been defeated for reëlection because he had favored the appointment of a Pennsylvania military officer as brigadier over North Carolina troops; but the issues of the instruction to Washington and responsibility to the State brought about his return to Congress in August.

In October 1779, Burke was officially thanked by the Assembly for his services in Congress. In the summer of 1780 he was in Hillsboro and he soon assumed a leadership in state affairs. The Continental Army, under command of Gen. Horatio Gates, was in the neighborhood. Complaint and dissatisfaction were aroused by the arbitrary seizure of supplies for military purposes. Burke became the spokesman of the people, declaring that the policies of the military warranted resistance. He entered into correspondence with Gates and the President of Congress and soon secured a satisfactory revision of policy. In June 1781 he was elected governor of North Carolina. It was a time of utmost demoralization because of the British invasion. Troops and supplies had to be mobilized quickly. Burke undertook the direction of this task with such vigor that he came into conflict with the board of war, to which state military administration had been entrusted in 1780; the outcome was the establishment of his authority as supreme executive. He was so active in rallying the people and in assembling soldiers and supplies that British and Tory leaders decided that he must be captured, and this was accomplished by a Tory raid on Hillsboro on Sept. 12, 1781. He was taken first to Wilmington, N. C., where he was held as prisoner of state, then to Sullivan's Island in the harbor of Charleston, S. C., where he was placed in close confinement. In November he was paroled to James Island. There he was treated with consideration and respect, but in a few weeks refugees were also admitted to the island and the resulting disorder became so great that Burke believed his life was

in danger. He therefore asked for a parole to the American lines; the reply was that he was held as a hostage to secure the life of David Fanning, notorious Tory leader. Acting on the theory that the British had violated the terms of parole and that he was thereby released from its obligation, he managed to escape and took refuge at the headquarters of Gen. Greene. On Greene's advice he notified Gen. Leslie, British commander at Charleston, of his escape, and offered to secure an exchange or to return within the British lines if the terms of parole would be guaranteed. Receiving no reply, he returned to North Carolina and resumed his official duties, but refused to be considered for reëlection in the spring of 1782. So ended his public career. He died at "Tyaquin" the next year, being survived by his wife, Mary Freeman, whom he had married in 1770, and by a daughter Mary. Burke County, N. C., created in 1777, was named for him.

[Marshall D. Haywood, sketch in *Biog. Hist. of N. C.*, vol. II (1905); J. G. de R. Hamilton, sketch in *N. C. Booklet* (Oct. 1906); *Colonial and State Records of N. C.* (vols. X–XXII); "Letters of Members of the Continental Cong." being *Carnegie Inst. of Washington Pubs.*, No. 229 (1921); and the *Jours. of the Continental Cong.* (L. C. ed. 1904–22).]   W. K. B.

BURKE, THOMAS (Dec. 22, 1849–Dec. 4, 1925), lawyer, was born in Clinton County, N. Y., the son of James Burke, an Irish immigrant, and his wife, Bridget Delia Ryan. He obtained a smattering of education at the Clinton public school, but in 1862 his mother died and the family removed to Iowa, where for the following four years he worked on a farm and in a store, earning money which enabled him to attend school intermittently. In 1866 he went to Michigan, and, pursuing the same method, saved sufficient to defray a year's attendance at Ypsilanti Academy, where he graduated in 1870. He then entered the law department of the University of Michigan, teaching school in vacations. In 1872 he studied in a law office at Marshall, Mich., and in 1873 was admitted to the Michigan bar, being immediately afterward elected city attorney. Business conditions, however, were not promising, and he borrowed money to travel to the Pacific Coast, arriving in Seattle, Wash., May 3, 1875. There he opened a law office, and for the remainder of his life—a period of fifty years—his career was synonymous with the history of the city. He was married in 1876 to Caroline E., daughter of J. J. McGilvra of Seattle. In the same year he was elected probate judge of King County, and, being reëlected, served till 1880 but declined a third term. A strong Democrat, he was the party nominee for delegate to Congress in 1880 and 1882, but was unable to overcome the Republican majority. He was prominent as a successful advocate, but gradually withdrew from court work, confining his professional work to consultations and associating himself more with business enterprise. When the anti-Chinese troubles arose in 1886 he defended the Chinese at the risk of his life, narrowly escaping being lynched by an excited mob. In 1888 he temporarily accepted the appointment of chief justice of the supreme court of Washington Territory in order to relieve a critical situation which had arisen owing to the sudden deaths of two successive occupants of that position, but retained office only until April 1889. He organized the Seattle & Walla Walla Railway and the Seattle, Lake Shore & Eastern Railway to connect with the Union Pacific and the Canadian Pacific railroads, the accomplishment of which in 1892 gave Seattle the transportation facilities she needed. In 1893 when J. J. Hill was planning to extend the St. Paul, Minneapolis & Manitoba Railway to the Pacific Coast as the Great Northern Railroad, Burke was retained as general western counsel to the company. He became the intimate friend and adviser of Hill, and it was mainly due to his efforts that Seattle was made the Pacific terminus of the new trans-continental line. He conducted for the Great Northern Railroad all the negotiations relative to the acquisition of real estate, the tunnel under Seattle, and the right of way through the state. He also actively interested himself in stimulating trade between Seattle and China and Japan, paying several visits to those countries and acting as counsel for the Nippon Yusen Kaisha Steamship Company. In politics he refused to follow Bryan in 1896, was active in campaigning throughout the state on behalf of McKinley, and shortly afterward joined the Republican party. In 1907 he withdrew from practise. He was one of the originators of the Alaska-Yukon Exposition and went in 1908 as commissioner on its behalf to Japan and China. The following year he was offered by President Taft the position of minister to China but declined. He was a candidate for the Senate at the ensuing election, but suffered defeat in the general Republican débâcle. In 1910 he was appointed a trustee of the Carnegie Endowment for International Peace. He died Dec. 4, 1925, in New York City. Burke was a sound lawyer, but his professional success was largely due to his great business ability and foresight. His services to the city of Seattle were fundamental, and he was recognized as preëminently her foremost citizen. Small of stature, unassuming and genial in company, he had great

force of character and an infinite capacity for hard work, which, joined to a natural felicity of speech and intense earnestness, made him a dominating figure in public affairs.

[The chief source of information is *Thos. Burke 1849–1925*, (1926), comp. and ed. by Chas. T. Conover. See also "Judge Thos. Burke" by S. B. L. Penrose in *Whitman Coll. Quart.*, June 1926, and *Sketches of Washingtonians* (1907), p. 125.]   H. W. H. K.

BURLEIGH, CHARLES CALISTUS (Nov. 3, 1810–June 13, 1878), abolitionist, was a son of Rinaldo and Lydia (Bradford) Burleigh, and a member of a family of reformers. Born in Plainfield, Conn., he received his schooling at Plainfield Academy, and while continuing to help with the work of his father's farm, began the study of law. But early in 1833 an attack on the Connecticut "Black Law" which he had published in the *Genius of Temperance* attracted the attention of the Rev. Samuel J. May [q.v.], through whose instrumentality he became editor of Arthur Tappan's new paper the *Unionist,* published at Brooklyn, Conn., in defense of Prudence Crandall [q.v.] and her negro school. Burleigh— later assisted by his brother, William Henry [q.v.],—edited the *Unionist* for some two years during which he won a reputation for fearless and forceful writing. He had continued his study of law, and in January 1835 was admitted to the bar, but again the Rev. S. J. May and the call of reform intervened, and Burleigh turned his back on a professional career to become agent and lecturer for the Middlesex Anti-Slavery Society. In the same year he was in the company of William Lloyd Garrison when the latter was mobbed in Boston, wrote the account of the mob published in the *Liberator* (Oct. 24, 1835), and helped conduct that journal during Garrison's absence from the city. His name appeared frequently in the *Liberator* thereafter, and his long thin figure, "flowing beard and ringlets and eccentric costume" (Garrison, III, 298) became familiar on lecture platforms throughout the northeastern states. In 1838 he was a witness of another mob when Pennsylvania Hall in Philadelphia was burned. At this time and for some years he was editor of the *Pennsylvania Freeman,* after 1844 the regular organ of the Eastern Pennsylvania Anti-Slavery Society. As a member of the business committee of the American Anti-Slavery Society he introduced at the meeting in 1840 a resolution stating that the constitution of the society should not be interpreted as requiring members either to exercise or refuse to exercise their political votes; this resolution led to the repudiation by the society of both Harrison and Van Buren as candidates for the presidency. In 1859 Burleigh succeeded Sydney H. Gay as corresponding secretary of the American Anti-Slavery Society, and in that capacity prepared its twenty-seventh annual report, published under the title, *The Anti-Slavery History of the John Brown Year* (1861). He also prepared the introduction to *Reception of George Thompson in Great Britain* (1836); and an appendix to *Discussion on American Slavery between George Thompson, Esq., and Rev. Robert J. Breckinridge* (1836); and was the author of *Slavery and the North* (Anti-Slavery Tracts, No. 10, 1855); and an address, extracts from which appeared in *No Slave-Hunting in the Old Bay State* (Anti-Slavery Tracts, new series, No. 13, 1859).

Burleigh's zeal in the anti-slavery cause led him indirectly into another crusade. Twice jailed in West Chester, Pa., for selling anti-slavery literature on Sunday, he plunged into Anti-Sabbatarianism, joining with others in a call for a convention, held in New York in March 1848, at which he was prominent among the speakers. He also dabbled from time to time in other reforms: opposed capital punishment in a pamphlet, *Thoughts on the Death Penalty* (1845) and on the platform in Philadelphia (*A Defence of Capital Punishment by Elder Frederick Plummer in a Discussion of Six Evenings with Charles Burleigh*, 1846); and supported woman suffrage, notably by his speeches in the conventions at Cleveland and New York in 1853 and at the first annual meeting of the American Equal Rights Association at New York in May 1867 (Susan B. Anthony and others, *History of Woman Suffrage*, 1881–82, I, 148, 549, II, 194). He later followed his brother William Henry into the field of temperance reform (*Centennial Temperance Volume*, 1877, p. 83).

Burleigh's personal appearance, his eccentricity of dress and manner, were against him, in the opinion of Samuel J. May, who nevertheless reckoned Burleigh among his ablest associates, characterizing him as "a single-minded, purehearted, conscientious, self-sacrificing man," who often "delighted and astonished his hearers by the brilliancy of his rhetoric and the surpassing beauty of his imagery" (May, p. 66). The son of William Lloyd Garrison said that as a close debater Burleigh "was easily first of all the abolition orators" (Garrison, IV, 319). During his later years he made his home at Northampton, Mass., where he died in 1878 from injuries received in a railroad accident at Florence, Mass. On Oct. 24, 1842, he had married Gertrude Kimber of Chester County, Pa., who bore him three children.

[Chas. Burleigh, *Genealogy of the Burley or Burleigh Family of America* (1880); Ellen D. Larned,

Hist. of Windham County, Conn., vol. II (1880), p. 497; Samuel J. May, *Some Recollections of Our Antislavery Conflict* (1869); W. P. and F. J. Garrison, *Wm. Lloyd Garrison* (1885–89); J. T. Scharf and T. Westcott, *Hist. of Phila.* (1884), III, 2015; files of the *Liberator* (Boston); obituary in *Boston Transcript,* June 14, 1878.]   E. R. D.

BURLEIGH, GEORGE SHEPARD (Mar. 26, 1821–July 20, 1903), poet, reformer, was born at Plainfield, Conn., the youngest child of Rinaldo and Lydia (Bradford) Burleigh. His father, a graduate of Yale College, had been principal of the local academy, but became blind from excessive study, and had to betake himself to a farm. Owing to the straitened circumstances of the family, none of the children received much of an education, but they were all influenced by various aspects of Transcendentalism—religious, educational, philanthropic, ethical—then permeating New England culture, and the home became a veritable seed-bed of reformers, five of the six brothers—Charles Calistus, William Henry [*qq.v.*], Lucian, Cyrus, and George Shepard—attaining some note in the anti-slavery or other causes. The father himself was one of the early abolitionists and sympathized with his fellow townswoman, Prudence Crandall [*q.v.*], in her brave attempt (1832–34) to provide school facilities for negro children. George received a common school education and until well on in life was engaged in farming. He also wrote verses and went about the country lecturing on the slavery question. In 1846 he published an *Elegiac Poem on the Death of Nathaniel Peabody Rogers,* an abolitionist so devoted to personal liberty that he objected to having a presiding officer at anti-slavery gatherings and quarreled irreconcilably with William Lloyd Garrison. The poem, both in thought and phrasing, owes much to *Lycidas* and *Adonais.* The year 1846–47 Burleigh spent at Hartford as editor of the *Charter Oak,* an abolitionist paper. On one of his lecture trips he met Ruth Burgess of Little Compton, R. I., whose father was one of the helpers on the "Underground Railroad." He married her Mar. 17, 1849. In that year he published at Philadelphia *The Maniac and Other Poems.* The title poem has some interest as an attempt at Wordsworthian narrative, but in general Burleigh has little claim on posterity as a poet. He shows a preference for elaborate stanza forms and sententious or ornate, not to say turgid, language; much too frequently he hides his fundamental image behind a mass of opaque metaphor. As a tribute to John C. Frémont, then Republican candidate for president, he issued in 1856, without his name, *Signal Fires on the Trail of the Pathfinder,* a poetical campaign tract, more dashing—as befitted its subject—than his other work. He also contributed verse to magazines and in 1874 published privately a translation of Victor Hugo's *Légende des Siècles*. He made his home for about fifty years at Sakonnet Point, R. I., spending the winters latterly with his son in Providence.

[*Who's Who in America*, 1903–05; *Providence Jour.*, July 22, 24, 1903; Chas. Burleigh, *Geneal. of the Burley or Burleigh Family of America* (1880).]

G. H. G.

BURLEIGH, WILLIAM HENRY (Feb. 2, 1812–Mar. 18, 1871), journalist, reformer, was the fourth of the six sons of Rinaldo Burleigh, a Yale graduate and a classical teacher until failing sight forced him to retire, and his wife Lydia Bradford, a descendant of Gov. William Bradford. He was born at Woodstock, Conn., but spent most of his boyhood on his father's farm at Plainfield, Conn., where he early became a sharer in the family responsibilities, which meant hard work and few recreations. His education was received at the district school and the Plainfield Academy, of which his father was in charge until William was eleven. Winter schooling and summer work alternated for a number of years. He was apprenticed to a dyer, then to a printer, in order that he might quickly become self-supporting. In 1830 he became a journeyman on the *Stonington Phenix,* where he was soon setting up articles of his own composition. In 1832 he was printer and contributor to the *Schenectady* (New York) *Cabinet* and in 1833 assisted his brother, Charles Calistus Burleigh [*q.v.*], in editing the *Unionist,* Brooklyn, Conn., a paper founded to support Prudence Crandall's colored school in which William Burleigh also taught for a time. He was married to Harriet Adelia Frink of Stonington, Conn., by whom he had seven children. He early felt interest in reform causes, especially anti-slavery, temperance, peace, and woman suffrage, and in 1836 began lecturing for the American Anti-Slavery Society. At about the same time he was editor of the *Literary Journal,* Schenectady, but left that in 1837 to become editor of the *Christian Witness* and afterward the *Temperance Banner,* in Pittsburgh. In 1843 he went to Hartford at the invitation of the Connecticut Anti-Slavery Society, to take charge of its organ, the *Christian Freeman,* afterward the *Charter Oak.* In 1849 he was employed by the New York State Temperance Society, with headquarters at Albany and Syracuse, as corresponding secretary, lecturer, and editor of the *Prohibitionist.* He remained in this position until 1855, when he was appointed harbor master of the port of New York and went to live in Brooklyn.

Later he was made a port warden, but in 1870 was displaced for a Democrat. His first wife died in 1864 and in 1865 he married Mrs. Celia Burr of Troy, a teacher, prominent in woman suffrage work, and afterward a Unitarian minister. Burleigh's fiery tilts against the evils of his day often made life hard for himself and his family. He denounced the Mexican War, as waged in the interest of the slave power, and for this and on other occasions narrowly escaped mob violence. Yet he really disliked controversy and preferred purely literary work. Poetry was the form he chose for personal literary expression, apart from editorial and lecture composition. A volume of *Poems* was published in 1841 and enlarged editions appeared in 1845 and 1850. After his death his wife collected these poems in a new edition (1871). His poetry is not without beauty and vigor and shows his longing for the quiet, studious life which, because of his goading conscience, he was never able to enjoy. This conscience also dictated a certain amount of propaganda verse, such as *The Rum Fiend and Other Poems* (1871). His picture, taken shortly before his death, shows a worn, kindly face, with high cheek bones, unusually alert dark eyes, heavy, drooping, white mustache, and white hair worn long and brushed straight back. He was brought up by his parents a strict Presbyterian but later became a Unitarian. He died in Brooklyn, N. Y., as a result of what were called epileptic attacks, and his funeral was held at the Second Unitarian Church, where Samuel Longfellow had preached and where John White Chadwick was then pastor. His old friend John G. Whittier visited him shortly before his death.

[The chief source of information about Burleigh is the memoir by his wife Celia Burleigh, which forms the preface to his collected *Poems* (1871). A long obituary appeared in the *N. Y. Tribune*, Mar. 20, 1871, and an obituary notice in the *N. Y. Times*, Mar. 19, 1871. See also Chas. Burleigh, *The Genealogy of the Burley or Burleigh Family of America* (1880), p. 141.]

S. G. B.

BURLESON, EDWARD (Dec. 15, 1798–Dec. 26, 1851), soldier, frontier leader, was born in Buncombe County, N. C. He was descended from Aaron Burleson, who emigrated from England to North Carolina in 1726. His father was James Burleson who had married Elizabeth Shipman. James Burleson moved to Tennessee about 1812 and commanded a company of Tennessee volunteers under Andrew Jackson in the Creek War in Alabama. Young Edward accompanied him and seems to have acquired a taste for military life. At the age of seventen he married Sarah Owen of Madison County, Ala. In 1816 he moved to Howard County, Mo., and became a captain and then a colonel of militia. He moved back to Tennessee in 1823 where he again became a militia colonel. In 1830 he visited Texas, and the next year he moved his family there and settled on the Colorado River about eleven miles below the town of Bastrop. This was on the extreme frontier and subject to frequent incursions of hostile Indians. Burleson, who was a natural leader, took the principal part in repelling the raids, and in December 1832 he was made lieutenant-colonel of his municipality. When the revolution broke out, he joined the Texans who besieged the Mexican general, Cos, in San Antonio; and when Stephen F. Austin resigned the command of the besieging army, Burleson was elected by the men to succeed him, Nov. 24, 1835. San Antonio was stormed and Cos surrendered on Dec. 10. Soon afterward Burleson returned to his farm, but the news of Santa Anna's approach the next spring again brought him into the field. He was made colonel of a regiment that was organized at Gonzales and commanded it, under Gen. Sam Houston, in the retreat which ended in the victory of San Jacinto and the capture of Santa Anna. Burleson played a conspicuous part in that battle and afterward commanded the forces that followed the Mexican divisions under Filisola to the Rio Grande. In 1836 he was elected to the first Senate of the Republic of Texas. In 1838 he discovered, from papers captured from Mexican raiders in the vicinity of Austin, that the Mexicans and the Cherokee Indians, with other tribes, were planning a hostile combination against the Texans. In January 1839 he was made colonel of a regiment of regulars and commanded them in the Cherokee War the following summer until the Cherokees were expelled from Texas. In the same year he took part in the fight on Brushy Creek with the Comanches, and in 1840 he was in command in the great fight at Plum Creek with the same fierce tribe. He resigned his commission in the army and in 1841 he was elected vice-president of the Republic over Memucan Hunt. Burleson presided over the Senate with great dignity and fairness and won the respect of all parties. In 1844 he was a candidate for the presidency, but was defeated. He supported the movement for annexation to the United States, and when war broke out with Mexico he went with the troops raised in Texas to the support of Gen. Zachary Taylor. He was at the battle of Monterey as aide to Gen. J. P. Henderson. After he returned, he removed from his old home to the site of the present town of San Marcos. He was elected to the state Senate and died in Austin while in attendance upon that body. Though he had but little formal education, he was a man of unusual gifts, and these, with his unaffected simplicity, dignity, honesty, and fearlessness, had made him one of the loved figures of Texas.

[There is a good sketch of Burleson's life in the *Texas Almanac for 1859*, pp. 197–204. Other material may be found in the *Papers of Mirabeau Buonaparte Lamar* (1921–24); John Henry Brown, *Hist. of Texas* (1892–93); J. W. Wilbarger, *Indian Depredations in Texas* (1889); *Jour. of the Senate of the Republic of Texas* and *Jour.* of the 3rd and 4th Leg.; Memorial Proc. of the Senate and House of the 4th Leg., Dec. 26, 27, 1851 (published in *Texas State Gazette*, Jan. 3, 1852); and *A Brief Hist. of the Burleson Family* (1889). There is much also in various early Texas newspapers, especially the *Telegraph and Texas Register* of Houston.]

C. W. R.

BURLESON, RUFUS CLARENCE (Aug. 7, 1823–May 14, 1901), Baptist clergyman, educator, was descended from Aaron Burleson, who emigrated from England to North Carolina about 1726. His father, Jonathan Burleson, was a native of Kentucky and commanded a volunteer company in the Creek War. His mother, Elizabeth (Byrd) Burleson, also a native of Kentucky, was descended from the Byrd family of Virginia. Jonathan Burleson and his wife settled in Morgan County, northern Alabama, in 1813, where Rufus, their sixth child, was born. He attended the local schools and academies, and spent one year in a college at Nashville. Then his health became impaired by over-zealous study and he returned to his father's farm. In the meantime he had been ordained as a Baptist preacher. After teaching for two or three years in Mississippi, he began preaching and took part vigorously in the theological controversies of the period. In January 1846 he entered the Western Baptist Theological Seminary at Covington, Ky., where he graduated in June 1847. He had determined to go to Texas and received an appointment to that field from the mission board of his church. Soon afterward he was elected pastor of the Baptist church in Houston. He arrived there early in January 1848, and remained for more than three years. In June 1851 he was elected to the presidency of Baylor University, then a small school at Independence, Tex., which had been founded by the "Baptist Education Society" in 1845. The task of building a college in a new country whose people were generally poor was one of extreme difficulty. There were only two small buildings at the college in 1851 and only fifty-two students. The salaries of the faculty were very small and had not been paid in full. Burleson set himself to his task with energy and enthusiasm. Through the arduous labors of himself and the agents more buildings were erected, more equipment and more money for salaries were procured, standards were raised, and a competent law faculty added. But a controversy arose in the school and church between Burleson and the head of the "female department," which was virtually a separate institution, and in 1861 Burleson resigned. The entire faculty and the senior class of the "male department" went with him to Waco where they took over a school which they renamed Waco University. It was feebly supported by the Waco Baptist association and struggled on through the Civil War. From 1861 Burleson's career was identified with that of the school in Waco. At Baylor he had been opposed to coeducation but now he came to favor it, and it was established at Waco in 1865. Waco and Baylor remained rival institutions until 1886. During this period Waco grew steadily in size and importance, for it was in a section of the state which was increasing rapidly in population and wealth. After 1868 it received the official support of the Baptist General Association of Texas, which covered the greater part of northern Texas. Meanwhile Baylor had declined in attendance, as Independence was not on a railroad. About 1870 a movement for the consolidation of the two schools began, but their partisans could not agree and nothing was done until 1886, when the older institution was moved from Independence to Waco; the old name, Baylor, was given to the consolidated school; and Burleson was made president. He remained in that position until 1897, despite some controversies with the trustees, when he was retired as president emeritus on full salary. At this time Baylor was the largest of the denominational colleges in Texas. Burleson was a man of high ideals, devoted to the promotion of education and of his church. He was of a kindly disposition and a playful humor; but he was noted also for a naïve egotism and great tenacity of opinion, traits which sometimes involved him in unprofitable controversy. He was married in 1853 to Georgia Jenkins of Independence.

[The most complete account of Burleson, rather fulsome and badly arranged, is *The Life and Writings of Rufus C. Burleson* (1901) containing a biography by Harry Haynes, comp. and pub. by Mrs. Georgia J. Burleson. There is a useful sketch in the *Quarterly of the Tex. State Hist. Ass.*, V, 49. Other material may be found in J. M. Carroll, *A Hist. of Tex. Baptists* (1923); Frederick Eby, *The Development of Ed. in Tex.* (1925); J. J. Lane, *Hist. of Ed. in Tex.* (1903); and *A Brief Hist. of the Burleson Family* (1889).]   C. W. R.

BURLIN, NATALIE CURTIS (Apr. 26, 1875–Oct. 23, 1921), student of Indian and negro music, was born in New York City, the daughter of Edward and Augusta Lawler (Stacey) Curtis and niece of George William Curtis. She first studied in the National Conservatory of Music,

New York, with Arthur Friedheim; later, in Europe, with Busoni at Berlin, Giraudet in Paris, Wolf in Bonn, and Julius Kniese at the "Wagner-Schule" in Baireuth. On returning to America it was evidently her purpose to continue her career as pianist, but while visiting her brother in Arizona she became so much interested in the Indians of that region and in their music that she visited many different encampments, taking down their songs by word of mouth. From that time on, her great interest lay in this sort of research. The first tangible result of these studies came in the form of *The Indians' Book* (1907), a collection of two hundred songs gathered from eighteen different tribes of North American Indians, mostly those of the Southwest, the Plains and the Pueblo tribes.

As indicative of her deep and genuine interest in her subject and her ability to communicate this interest to others, it may be noted that when she began her studies the Indians were not allowed to sing their native songs in the government schools and that her earnest appeal to Theodore Roosevelt, then president, had the effect not only of revoking this rule, but also of giving the Indians every encouragement in the performance of their own music. The publication of *The Indians' Book* aroused so much enthusiasm that an urgent request came that she should do for the negro music what she had so successfully accomplished for the Indian. This request resulted in her making at Hampton Institute a thorough study of negro songs. In 1918–19 she published four volumes of *Hampton Series Negro Folk-Songs* for male quartet, retaining the instinctive harmonization of the singers themselves with no retouching on her part. This artistic restraint naturally gives to these volumes great historical value. Percy Grainger, in the *New York Times*, Apr. 14, 1918, said: "When I peruse these her strangely perfect and satisfying recordings of these superb American negro part songs, I cannot refrain from exclaiming: How lucky she to have found such noble material, and it such an inspired transcriber!" Mrs. Burlin,—she had been married in 1917 to Paul Burlin, painter, of New York—obtained the material for her last published book, *Songs and Tales from the Dark Continent* (1920) from two native-born African students at Hampton Institute who gave her freely of the songs and stories of their native land. In 1921 she died as the result of an automobile accident in Paris. In addition to the works noted above she published, *Songs of Ancient America* (1905), *Songs from a Child's Garden of Verses by Robert Louis Stevenson* (Wa-Wan Press), and various other songs and choruses. A new edition of *The Indians' Book,* with added material and new drawings made by Indians especially for the purpose, was issued in 1923.

[A. Eaglefield Hull, *Dict. of Modern Music and Musicians* (1924); *Outlook,* Nov. 23, 1921; Preface to *The Indians' Book* (edition of 1923).]   W. T. U—n.

BURLINGAME, ANSON (Nov. 14, 1820–Feb. 23, 1870), congressman, diplomat, the son of Joel Burlingame, a Methodist exhorter and lay preacher, and his wife, Freelove (Angell) Burlingame, was born at New Berlin, Chenango County, N. Y. As a small child he went with his parents to Seneca County, Ohio, and thence ten years later to Detroit. His early education was in the common schools and his undergraduate days were concluded in the Detroit branch of the then very young University of Michigan. Although in his later years he displayed an urbanity not usually bred in frontier life there was also in him a marked freedom and directness of manner characteristic of the environment in which he was reared. At the age of twenty-three he came eastward to the Harvard Law School and then settled in Massachusetts where he became a junior law partner in Boston with George P. Briggs, son of Ex-Governor George Nixon Briggs. On June 3, 1847, he married Jane Cornelia Livermore, a daughter of Isaac Livermore of Cambridge.

Burlingame's gift of oratory together with his exceptional personal charm led him quickly into politics where he found ample opportunities in the tumultuous fifties. He was elected to the Massachusetts Senate in 1852 and in the following year was a member of the Massachusetts constitutional convention. In 1855 he was elected to Congress where he served three terms, being defeated in 1860 by William Appleton. A Free-Soiler and one of the organizers of the Republican party in Massachusetts, he was also an outspoken admirer of Kossuth and was at one time associated with the Know-Nothing party. Few records remain of his Congressional career. His speeches were unwritten and the reports in the *Congressional Globe* are fragmentary. He usually voted with his New England colleagues, he was a faithful representative of his constituents, and he was quickly responsive to appeals of justice and humanity. As the result of a stinging speech in castigation of Preston Brooks [*q.v.*], the assailant of Sumner, he was challenged to a duel by Brooks. Burlingame formally accepted, but named as the place the Canadian side of Niagara Falls, which was difficult for Brooks to reach with safety. Brooks declined to go and the duel was averted. Burlingame's ostensible acceptance gained him great popularity in the North. (For the fullest and most recent account of this affair, see James E. Campbell, "Sumner, Brooks, Burlingame, or the Last of the Great Challenges," *Ohio Archæological and Historical Quarterly,* XXXIV, 1925, 435–73; for an earlier account, more favorable to Burlingame, see John Bigelow, *Retrospection of an Active Life,* I, 1909, 165–70.)

In the campaign of 1860 Burlingame did yeoman service for the Republican party and was rewarded by the appointment of minister to Vienna. Because of his previous sympathy for Kossuth and for Sardinian independence he was unacceptable to the Austrian court and his appointment was changed to Peking, a capital in which his former constituents maintained a lively interest because of the large share of Massachusetts in the China trade. Although by the treaties of 1858 the powers had at last attained the right of resident diplomatic representation in Peking, they had overreached themselves in China in more than one important respect. The imperial government was by no means able to carry out all of the provisions of the treaties because of the semi-autonomous character of the local governments. The treaty-port merchants, long held back from direct participation in the interior trade were both jubilant at the recent chastisement administered to China and truculent in claiming their new treaty rights. The situation was ominous when Burlingame arrived. Further military conflicts with the provinces seemed very possible and there was even the prospect that either by conquest or penetration the European nations would assert and seek to maintain full sovereign rights at least in the treaty-ports where they had been granted the right of residence and trade. While even the prospect of a partition of China presented itself to the American Government, practically all naval forces had to be withdrawn from the Far East because of the Civil War. Burlingame had to meet his problem single-handed.

With a sagacity singularly in contrast with the temerity of some of his other foreign policies at the outbreak of the war, Secretary Seward had instructed Burlingame to coöperate closely with the powers in China. Almost immediately, Burlingame assumed the leadership among the diplomatic representatives in Peking, although they were all far more experienced than he, and coöperation under his direction involved the agreement among the ministers to withstand the pressure of the treaty-port merchants and to assume toward the imperial government a tolerant attitude. This policy in turn gave to Burlingame great influence among the Chinese officials who sought his advice on a variety of problems such as the Lay-Osborn flotilla fiasco, the appointment of Robert Hart to the Foreign Inspectorate of Maritime Customs, and the suppression of the Taiping Rebellion. To Burlingame much credit is due for thwarting the early efforts of the foreign merchants to set up in the treaty-ports government wholly independent of the imperial authority. He developed a great admiration for and confidence in the Chinese and during a visit to the United States in 1865–66 he sought by speeches and personal conference to spread his enthusiasm and confidence among American mercantile houses. He also sought to promote the practise, which became common in later years, of placing American technical advisers in the employ of the Chinese Government. One may sum up the policy of Burlingame in China in the words of Raphael Pumpelly, who for a time was the guest of the American Legation in Peking and subsequently engaged in some surveys of the Chinese mineral resources, as a policy "based upon justness and freed from prejudice of race."

Among other projects which Burlingame urged upon China was the sending of diplomatic representatives to the western powers, an innovation which Japan had already adopted with some success in 1860. Very likely because of Burlingame's suggestion, Seward, on Dec. 15, 1865, instructed him to urge such a course upon China. The idea seems to have met also with the approval of Robert Hart and it came about very naturally, when Burlingame let it be known in Peking in November 1867 that he was about to resign as minister, that the Chinese Government offered him the post as the head of an official delegation with two Chinese colleagues to visit the western powers, both to observe western civilization and also to plead with the governments not to press their demands for a revision of the treaties of 1858.

Burlingame set out promptly, visiting first the United States, then Europe. While the so-called Burlingame Mission met with unqualified hostility in China and was relatively barren of results on the Continent it fully accomplished its purpose in America and measurably succeeded in England. On July 28, 1868, Burlingame had signed with Secretary Seward a convention supplementary to the American treaty of 1858, which convention pledged the American Government to respect Chinese sovereignty and stated that the Chinese emperor by granting foreigners certain rights of trade and residence in China had "by no means relinquished his right of eminent domain or dominion." It contained other provisions which were also mere amplifications of

rights granted ten years before. There was added also a bilateral immigration clause, designed to promote the importation of Chinese laborers to the Pacific Coast, particularly for work on the construction of the Union Pacific Railroad which had been experiencing labor difficulties. This article subsequently proved to be most ill-advised and was a fundamental cause of friction which brought the two governments twenty-five or more years later to a prolonged state of diplomatic non-intercourse. It may be questioned whether the treaty itself did not in the end do more harm than good but the immediate effect was beneficial to China and to Chinese-American relations. Supported by the most emphatic approval of the American Government, Burlingame visited London, arriving just on the eve of the inauguration of the first Gladstone ministry. From Lord Clarendon he secured not a treaty but a declaration that China was "entitled to count upon the forbearance of foreign nations," and this was followed by an instruction from London to Peking which clearly revealed that the new government in London was not disposed to support the extravagant demands of the foreign merchants in China for the revision of the treaties. After London, Burlingame visited Paris, Berlin, and other European capitals, reaching St. Petersburg in February 1870, where he was stricken with pneumonia and died on the twenty-third of that month. His diplomatic career may fairly be described as brilliant. With the exception of the bilateral immigration clause in the treaty of 1868, for which Seward was at least as much responsible as Burlingame, few Americans in the Far East have served their own country so beneficially and certainly none has given to China a more sincere friendship.

[The most extensive bibliography with reference to Burlingame is to be found in *Anson Burlingame and the First Chinese Mission to Foreign Powers* (1912) by Frederick Wells Williams. While less a biography than an interpretation of Burlingame's services with respect to China, it is appreciative and yet judicial in purpose. The contemporary estimates of Burlingame vary with the nationality of the writers. For the British point of view see Alexander Michie, *The Englishman in China* (1900); J. Barr Robertson, "Our Policy in China," *Westminster Rev.*, Jan. 1870; *Blackwood's Edinburgh Mag.*, Feb. 1869. J. Von Gumpach, in his *The Burlingame Mission; a Political Disclosure* (1872), seeks to demonstrate from documentary sources that the Burlingame Mission greatly exceeded its powers and misrepresented many important facts. Of a very much more favorable character are the appreciations of Burlingame by Jas. G. Blaine, *Atlantic Mo.*, Nov. 1870; W. A. P. Martin, *A Cycle of Cathay* (1896); Raphael Pumpelly, *Across America and Asia* (1870), and *My Reminiscences* (1918).]   T.D.

BURLINGAME, EDWARD LIVERMORE (May 30, 1848–Nov. 15, 1922), editor, was the son of Anson Burlingame [*q.v.*], and Jane (Livermore) Burlingame. The surroundings and contacts of his formative years were Boston and Cambridge. His father was an eminent congressman from Massachusetts, and his mother belonged to an old Cambridge family. With such a parentage it was natural for Edward to go to Harvard where he entered the class that was graduated in 1869. President Lincoln had appointed Anson Burlingame minister to China in 1861, and his son left Harvard College in the first year of his course to become his father's secretary in China. Later, when Anson Burlingame was made Ambassador Extraordinary of China to negotiate treaties with the United States and European powers, Edward followed him in that most interesting pilgrimage, and, though still a very young man, found abundant opportunity to study in Paris, Heidelberg, Berlin, and St. Petersburg. At Heidelberg he received the degree of Ph.D. in 1869. His father's position opened to him the doors of many people eminent in literature, art, and statesmanship. This cosmopolitan training, of which he made the most by reason of his fluent knowledge of French and German, gave his natural aptitude for letters just the right nourishment for an ambitious youth. The European sojourn was abruptly ended by the sudden death of his father in 1870 while negotiating a treaty with Russia. Soon afterward, the son came home and began his long literary and editorial career. He was on the *New York Tribune* in 1871 and there formed a life-long friendship with John Hay. In the same year he was married to Ella Frances Badger. For four years, 1872–76, he was associated in the making of the *American Cyclopedia.*

In 1879 he became one of the literary advisers of the publishing house of Charles Scribner's Sons, and for the rest of his life was associated with it. When Charles Scribner, the son of the founder of the house, formulated a plan for *Scribner's Magazine* in 1886, Burlingame became the editor from the first number (January 1887) until his resignation in 1914. As an editor, his aim was "a magazine of good literature in the widest sense." During the many years of his editorship, he formed lasting literary friendships with Stevenson, Meredith, Barrie, Page, Hopkinson Smith, Brander Matthews, Edith Wharton, Robert Grant, F. J. Stimson, Bunner, E. S. Martin, Henry van Dyke, and many others. He was keen in discernment of new talent and a discriminating and severe critic of the output of new and old writers. His wide knowledge of international affairs and acquaintance with celebrated people gave his editorial judgment authority and unusual foresight. He had a particular *flair* for

what was of permanent interest in letters, and his acquaintance with several literatures made him impatient of the casual and unimportant. He edited *Current Discussion; a Collection from the Chief English Essays on Questions of the Time* (2 vols., 1878), *Stories by American Authors* (10 vols., 1884–85), and *Stories from Scribner's* compiled after the magazine had been running for many years. In 1875 he published *Art Life and Theories of Richard Wagner, Selected from his Writings and Translated by Edward L. Burlingame,* one of the earliest books on Wagner to be published in this country.

[Robt. Grant, "Edward Livermore Burlingame," *Harvard Grads. Mag.,* Mar. 1923; *Boston Evening Transcript,* Nov. 17, 1922; *N. Y. Times,* Nov. 17, 1922; *Scribner's Mag.,* Jan. 1923.]   R. B.

BURNAM, JOHN MILLER (Apr. 9, 1864– Nov. 21, 1921), educator, was born at Irvine, near Richmond, Ky., the son of Edmund Hall Burnam, a Baptist minister, and Margaret Shackelford (Miller) Burnam. His mother died when he was about two years old, and he was brought up by a kind stepmother. Until he was thirteen he received most of his education from his father. In 1877 he entered Central University, then at Richmond, Ky., and in 1878 Washington University, St. Louis, where he remained until 1880, when, at the age of sixteen, he entered Yale College. Here he was distinguished for regular attendance at classes, diligence, and ability. He received the degree of A.B. with honors in 1884. Remaining at Yale University as a graduate student in Sanskrit and Latin, he gained the degree of Ph.D. in 1886. Then followed nearly three years of study in Europe. He was professor of Latin and French in Georgetown (Kentucky) College, 1889–91, and assistant professor of Latin in the University of Missouri, 1891–99. After a year in Europe he became, in 1900, professor of Latin at the University of Cincinnati in the College of Liberal Arts, a position which was later changed to that of research professor of Latin and Romance palæography in the Graduate School. He was devoted to pure scholarship, and when he was relieved from the duty of teaching undergraduates he looked forward joyously to a future rich in scholarly achievement. He spent many summers in Europe working in libraries containing important manuscripts. His knowledge of Latin was profound, he possessed unusually perfect command of French, Spanish, and Italian, and read with ease all the languages of Europe, including Russian; but his chief interest was in palæography. His published writings include, in addition to numerous contributions to periodicals, monographs on *The Paris Prudentius* (1900), *The So-Called Placidus Scholia of Statius* (1902), *Glossemata de Prudentio* (1905), *Technologia Lucensis* (1919). His greatest work, *Palæographia Iberica,* was written in French and was to consist of eighteen parts. The first part appeared in 1912, the second in 1920, the third, completed by Prof. Rodney Potter Robinson, in 1925. The graduate students found him an inspiring teacher whose scholarship combined love for his chosen work, the authority which resulted from years of training and research, the independence of a vigorous and original mind, and the modesty of a sincere and gentle nature. He had no love of ostentation and no yearning for wide popularity, but his friends regarded him with deep and lasting affection. He was never married. On Aug. 26, 1921, while on a vacation in California, he received a paralytic stroke from which he suffered until his death, which occurred nearly three months later at Pomona, Cal.

[*Who's Who in America*, 1922–23; *Classical Journal,* Feb. 1922; Leonard M. Daggett, *A Hist. of the Class of Eighty-four, Yale Coll.* (1914); *Regular Baptist*, Dec. 1922; *Yale Univ. Obit. Record* (1922).]
H. N. F.

BURNAP, GEORGE WASHINGTON (Nov. 30, 1802–Sept. 8, 1859), Unitarian clergyman, writer, a lineal descendant of Isaac Burnap, one of the founders of Reading, Mass., was born in Merrimac, N. H., where his father, Jacob, was for almost fifty years pastor of the Congregational Church. He was the youngest of thirteen children. His mother, Elizabeth Brooks, sister of Gov. John Brooks [*q.v.*] of Massachusetts, died when he was seven years old, and he was brought up under the supervision of a sister. The size of the family and the meagerness of his father's salary put difficulties in the way of the boy's schooling, but with the help of relatives he secured sufficient education at Groton Academy and an academy at Thetford, Vt., to enable him to enter Harvard as a sophomore in 1821. Though the state of his finances compelled him to teach more or less during his course, he graduated in 1824, and then spent three years at the Harvard Divinity School. A careful study of the whole Bible pursued while in college had made him a Unitarian, and immediately upon his graduation from the divinity school he was called to the pastorate of the First Independent Church of Baltimore, Md., as successor to Jared Sparks. Here he was ordained, Apr. 23, 1828. On July 18, 1831, he married Nancy, daughter of Amos Williams, who had married his cousin, Nancy Williams.

Until the end of his life, thirty-two years later,

Burnap was the pastor of the Baltimore church. Although performing his professional duties acceptably and taking active part in public enterprises, he was preëminently a student, and gave much of his time to writing and lecturing. The fact that Unitarianism was widely misunderstood and misrepresented, rather than zest for controversy, he states, made him an aggressive exponent and vindicator of its doctrines. More than twenty-five thousand copies of his books were sold during his lifetime. He was of the conservative wing of his church, basing his arguments upon a none too critical acceptance of the authority of the Scriptures, and betraying a rather limited intellectual range. His *Lectures on the Doctrines of Christianity in Controversy between Unitarians and Other Denominations of Christians,* published in 1835, was followed by *Lectures on the History of Christianity* (1842); *Expository Lectures on the Principal Passages of the Scriptures which Relate to the Doctrine of the Trinity* (1845); *Discourses on the Rectitude of Human Nature* (1850); *Popular Objections to Unitarian Christianity Considered and Answered* (1848); *Christianity, Its Essence and Evidence* (1855). Two works of a different character which had a large circulation were *Lectures to Young Men* (1840) and *Lectures on the Sphere and Duties of Women* (1841). He was a regent of the University of Maryland, one of the original trustees of the Peabody Institute, and a founder of the Maryland Historical Society. Among his other writings are *A Life of Leonard Calvert,* Sparks's Library of American Biography, 2nd series, vol. IX (1846) and a *Memoir of Henry Augustus Ingalls* (1846).

[*Memorial Biographies of the New Eng. Hist. and Geneal. Soc.,* vol. III (1883), which lists thirty separate publications by Burnap; *Mo. Religious Mag.,* XXII, 313; Jos. Palmer, *Necrology of Alumni of Harvard Coll.* (1864); S. A. Eliot, ed., *Heralds of a Liberal Faith,* vol. III (1910).]
H. E. S.

BURNET, DAVID GOUVERNEUR (Apr. 4, 1788–Dec. 5, 1870), Texas politician, was born at Newark, N. J., the son of William Burnet [*q.v.*], and Gertrude (Gouverneur) Burnet. His parents died when he was very young and he was reared by his elder brothers and given a good education. One of these brothers, Jacob Burnet [*q.v.*], became a justice of the supreme court of Ohio and United States senator from that state. Another became mayor of Cincinnati. When seventeen years old David became a clerk in a counting-house in New York; but the firm soon failed. In 1806 he joined, as a lieutenant, Francisco de Miranda's expedition to Venezuela to free that country from Spain. The expedition failed and Burnet barely escaped with his life.

But he joined Miranda again in the abortive attempt of 1808. On his return Burnet went to his brothers in Ohio. In 1817 he purchased a mercantile business in Natchitoches, La.; but having developed tuberculosis, he sold his business and went to live among the Comanche Indians on the upper Colorado River in Texas. Then, his health being completely restored, he returned to Ohio. His visit to Texas resulted in a series of articles for the Cincinnati papers descriptive of the region he had seen. He studied and practised law for a time, but drifted back to Louisiana and Texas. In the summer of 1826, bearing letters from Henry Clay and Stephen F. Austin, he went to Saltillo and obtained from the Mexican government an empresario's contract to settle three hundred families near Nacogdoches. But the enterprise proved beyond his means and he sold the contract to a firm in New York. In 1831 he married a Miss Estis of New York and, returning to Texas, settled on the San Jacinto River. In 1833 he was a member of a convention at San Felipe, the capital of Austin's colony, which was called to petition the central authorities of Mexico for the separation of Texas and Coahuila. Burnet drew the petition, which was rejected in Mexico. In 1834 he was appointed judge of the municipality of San Felipe de Austin. The Texas Revolution was brewing. On Aug. 8, 1835, Burnet drew a set of very able and conservative resolutions for the San Jacinto community in which the rights of the citizens of Texas were firmly declared but desire for separation from Mexico was denied. Later in the same year he was a member of the General Consultation at Washington on the Brazos, which was called to protest against the measures of Santa Anna; and he was made a member of the committee of vigilance and safety. Hostilities had begun at Gonzales and San Antonio, and Burnet was gradually won over to the cause of independence. In the spring of 1836 he was a member of the convention at Washington which issued the Texas Declaration of Independence. Two weeks later he was elected by the convention president *ad interim* of the infant Republic of Texas. Burnet's administration, which lasted only until the following October, was as troubled as it was short. Santa Anna's forces had destroyed the Texan garrison at the Alamo and all the other small commands in the west except the little army under Gen. Sam Houston, and Houston was in retreat. As the Mexicans swept nearer, panic seized the people and a stampede began toward the Sabine. Deeming Washington unsafe, Burnet moved the seat of government to Harrisburg, near the present

city of Houston; later he removed again to Galveston Island, and after the battle of San Jacinto, to Velasco. About all his government could attempt in the meanwhile was to allay the fears of the people, increase the army, and procure supplies. Burnet was not conspicuously successful in these efforts. The people paid little attention to his assurances; recruits came in slowly; and the agents in New Orleans whom Burnet appointed to forward supplies failed miserably. After San Jacinto, fresh troubles arose over the disposition to be made of the captive dictator, Santa Anna, and the command of the Texan army. The government was too weak to enforce its will upon the undisciplined spirits who came in from the United States. Burnet also became involved in a quarrel with Houston. In September Houston was chosen president; and on Oct. 22 Burnet resigned his office. He retired to his farm, but two years later he was elected vice-president. During part of the administration of Lamar he acted as secretary of state, and later as president because of Lamar's illness and absence from the Republic. In 1841 Burnet ran for the presidency against Houston, but was defeated. The campaign had been marked by rancorous personalities which developed in Burnet a hatred of Houston that never abated. From this time on Burnet was only intermittently interested in politics. He lived on his farm, which he cultivated with his own hands, and struggled unsuccessfully against poverty. During 1846 and 1847 he served as secretary of state under the first governor, J. P. Henderson. He had lost all his children except one; and his wife died in 1858 leaving him disconsolate. He opposed secession, but his only son was killed in battle at Mobile in 1865. In 1866 he was elected by the first Reconstruction legislature to the United States Senate, but was not allowed to take his seat. In 1868 he was a delegate to the national Democratic convention in New York and was a presidential elector. This was his last contact with public affairs. During the final years of his life he was too feeble to work his farm and lived with friends in Galveston, where he died. That Burnet was a man of ability his public papers show, but he evidently was not a successful administrator. He was of unyielding temper, quick to resent offense, and prone to controversy: while his inflexible honesty and high sense of self-respect made it impossible for him to cultivate the arts of popularity.

[A. M. Hobby, *The Life and Times of David G. Burnet*, is a pamphlet published shortly after Burnet's death. Hobby also wrote a sketch for the *Texas Almanac* for 1873. Considerable material may be found in F. W. Johnson and E. C. Barker, *A Hist. of Texas and Texans*, vol. I (1916); John Henry Brown, *Hist. of Texas*; Chas. A. Gulick, ed., *The Papers of Mirabeau Buonaparte Lamar* (1921–24); E. C. Barker, ed., *The Austin Papers* (1924); D. G. Burnet, *Review of the Life of Gen. Sam Houston*, pamphlet (1852); and various early Texas newspapers, especially the *Telegraph and Texas Register* (Houston). The most complete study of Burnet's administration is an unpublished M.A. thesis by Sallie E. Sloan, "The Presidential Administration of David G. Burnet" in the Lib. of the Univ. of Texas.]

C.W.R.

BURNET, JACOB (Feb. 22, 1770–May 10, 1853), lawyer, senator, was a son of William Burnet [*q.v.*], and of Mary Camp, daughter of Nathaniel Camp. He was born in Newark, N. J., graduated at Nassau Hall in 1791, and studied law. In 1796 he settled in Cincinnati, where in 1800 he married Rebecca Wallace of Kentucky. When he first came to the Old Northwest, there were only a few scattered settlements along the watercourses. In the work of building modern commonwealths there, young Burnet was to play a leading part, as he was able and practical, with exceptionally fine judgment. Although he disliked public office, the record of his service is a long one, beginning in 1799 when he was appointed a member of the Legislative Council in the newly organized territorial government. For this office he was eminently qualified by his legal training and also by many professional trips throughout the territory. Soon he was called upon to help straighten out the legal tangle left over from the régime of the judges, and he drew up a number of laws that were to become of basic importance in the Ohio code. In his next public office, as a member of the state legislature, 1812–16, he gave important aid to the Federal government during the Western campaigns.

As president of the Cincinnati branch of the second National Bank, he keenly appreciated the distress caused by the sale of public lands on credit under the Act of 1800. Many settlers were hopelessly in debt to the government and were threatened with the loss of their lands with all improvements. This situation Burnet clearly explained in a memorial to Congress, copies of which he sent to influential men throughout the Western country. By this means public opinion was aroused, and strong pressure was brought to bear upon Congress. The sequel was the Land Act of 1820 which followed essentially the plan of relief proposed by Burnet, and really prevented a catastrophe in the Western settlements. Appointed judge of the supreme court of Ohio in 1821, he resigned in 1828, and almost immediately was chosen to fill the vacancy in the United States Senate, caused by the resignation of William Henry Harrison. Burnet

served until the end of the Twenty-first Congress, interesting himself especially in measures that concerned the West. Of utmost importance to Ohio was an extensive grant of public lands to aid the Miami Canal from Dayton to the Maumee. Unfortunately the act as first passed imposed impossible conditions, but by persistent efforts Burnet secured such favorable terms that the construction of the canal became possible. Equally important was his work to secure permission for the erection, by the State of Ohio, of toll-gates along the National Road. Although a maintenance fund was an obvious necessity, the proposed grant of this authority threatened to arouse an extended debate upon the general subject of Internal Improvements. By arguments that skilfully avoided controversies, Burnet secured the necessary act, and saved the National Road in Ohio (Register of Debates in Congress, 21 Cong., 2 Sess., pp. 287–92). In the Hayne-Webster Debate, he took only a very minor part, but it has been asserted, upon plausible grounds, that his notes on Hayne's speech on the first day formed the basis for a part of Webster's reply. In 1831 the legislature of Kentucky elected Burnet to be one of the commissioners to settle certain territorial disputes with Virginia. His last notable public act was the speech at the Harrisburg Convention in 1839 which nominated his friend, William Henry Harrison, for the presidency.

In an active professional life Burnet found time for a leading part in the intellectual and social movements of Cincinnati, serving as president of the local Astronomical Society, the Colonization Society, the Cincinnati College, and the Medical College of Ohio. These intellectual interests received notable recognition when he was elected a corresponding member of the French Academy of Science upon the nomination of Lafayette. In politics, Burnet took special pride in calling himself a Federalist, considering this the party of Washington and the one that was loyal to the Federal Union. This political conservatism was characteristic. Disdaining half-way measures he never hesitated to express his opinions in no uncertain terms. His very appearance was indicative of the tenacity of his views. Tall and dignified, he retained the style and manners of an older generation, wearing a queue long after it had been generally discarded. In 1847 he published his *Notes on the Northwestern Territory*, a work that is essentially autobiographical, and is still one of the most important historical sources for the period of transition in Ohio from a territorial government to statehood.

[*Cincinnati Daily Commercial*, May 11, 1853; G. A. Worth, *Recollections of Cincinnati, 1817–21* (1851), p. 61; *Hist. of Cincinnati and Hamilton County, Ohio* (1894), pp. 165–67; C. T. Greve, *Centennial Hist. of Cincinnati* (1904), vol. I, *passim*.]   B. W. B—d.

BURNET, WILLIAM (March 1688–Sept. 7, 1729), colonial governor, who was born at The Hague during his father's temporary residence there, was the son of Gilbert Burnet, the celebrated Bishop of Salisbury, and his second wife, Mary Scott. The Bishop was not only a man of intellectual distinction himself but had a wide acquaintance among men both of mind and action so that the atmosphere of the home into which the young William was born was one to stimulate his own abilities and ambition. He was, however, by no means a model student, and, although he entered Trinity College, Cambridge, at thirteen, he was soon removed for "idleness and disobedience." He then received private instruction from tutors and was subsequently called to the bar. About May 1712 he made an imprudent love-match with a daughter of Dean Stanhope, his wife dying within three years from a broken heart, it was said, due to a previous attachment.

Burnet was a man of ability who had his own way to make in the world. Fortunately, he was the godson of King William and Queen Mary and had numerous friends in high places. On Apr. 19, 1720, he was appointed governor of New York and New Jersey. He promptly sailed from England on July 10 and arrived at New York on Sept. 16. Both at this post and at his subsequent one in Massachusetts, his record was an honorable one.

New York, owing to its geographical position with relation to the French in Canada by way of Lake Champlain, and to the Indian fur trade routes to the westward through the Mohawk Valley, was the key colony in regard to the entire colonial Indian policy. Burnet at once sensed the importance of the Indian problem. The English were able to import the goods used in the Indian trade to purchase furs at much lower prices than could the French at Montreal, and this should have given them a great advantage in dealing with the savages. But although the New Yorkers held a powerful weapon in their hands in the cheapness of their trading goods, this was blunted to a great extent by the fact that there were important merchants who found it more profitable and easier to sell their goods to the French than to trade them with the Indians. Burnet realized that by this French trade the English were handing their strongest weapon to their enemies. It was his endeavor to prevent this and to rectify the Indian policy of the English which furnished the main-spring of his policy as governor. In his first year he secured the passage of a law prohibiting the Canadian trade and subsequently established a trading post at Tirondequot where goods were sold to the savages at half the price at which the French sold them. His Indian policy was not without mistakes in detail but was wise and farsighted in principle. He at once, of course, came into conflict with powerful mercantile forces which cared more for their private gain than for the public benefit. His struggle with certain mercantile groups and with the Assembly became increasingly bitter. He made enemies of such powerful families as the Philipses and De Lanceys, and his action in setting up a court of chancery was roundly denounced by the Assembly in 1727. The English government transferred him to Massachusetts and he left for Boston soon after the arrival of his successor on Apr. 15, 1728.

The few months which were left to him before death were marked by the culmination of the contest between the Massachusetts Assembly and governor over the salary question. The argument took constitutional ground and both sides stated their positions, which were irreconcilable, with greater clearness and fulness than at any other point in the interminable wrangle (see E. B. Greene, *The Provincial Governor in the English Colonies of North America*, 1898, pp. 171 ff.). Burnet's stand was honorable throughout and in no way dictated by avarice, from which vice he was entirely free. Worn out by the work of his office, he died Sept. 7, 1729. While governor of New York, he had married Anna Maria (Mary) Van Horne, daughter of Abraham Van Horne and Mary Prevoost of that city.

Burnet was distinctly above the average of colonial governors. He was able, cultivated, charitable, just, genuinely solicitous to promote the welfare of the provinces he governed and not unwilling to make personal sacrifices for their good. His struggles with the Assemblies were always for principles and not for personal advantage.

[Some facts as to Burnet's early life may be found in *A Life of Gilbert Burnet* (1907), by T. E. S. Clarke and H. C. Foxcroft. His will and some other documents were printed by Wm. Nelson in *Original Papers Relating to Wm. Burnet* (1897). For his career in N. Y. and N. J. much material may be found in the *N. J. Archives*, 1 ser., IV, V, VI, and in *Docs. Relating to the Colonial Hist. of N. Y.* as stated in the index volume. Wm. Smith, *Hist. of N. Y.* (London, 1757) may also be consulted. For Mass. see Thos. Hutchinson, *Hist. of Mass. Bay* (London, 1828), vol. III; *A Collection of the Proc. of the Great and General Court of His Majesty's Province of the Mass. Bay* (1729); Greene's *Provincial Governor* as cited above, and the general histories.]   J. T. A.

BURNET, WILLIAM (Dec. 2, 1730 o.s.–Oct. 7, 1791), member of the Continental Congress, surgeon-general, was the son of Dr. Ichabod and Hannah Burnet, both natives of Scotland. He was born at Lyon's Farms, a hamlet between Elizabethtown and Newark, and was brought up in a home in which the father was one who took the popular side in the political controversies of the time. Educated at the College of New Jersey under the presidency of the Rev. Aaron Burr, he was a member of its second class, 1749, which was graduated before the College was removed to Princeton. Thereafter he studied medicine under a Dr. Staats of New York and then established himself in Newark where he lived and practised, except for the interruption due to the Revolution, until his death. At the outbreak of hostilities, although an extensive and lucrative practise had made him a man of means, he took an active part with those organizing opposition to royal authority. In May 1775 he became chairman of the committee of public safety for Newark and a little later chairman of the Essex County committee of safety, both committees laboring to keep the powerful Loyalist element under control. In June 1776 by direction of Washington he took measures for securing the person of Gov. William Franklin, who, after having given his parole, had issued a proclamation reconvening the defunct Loyalist legislature. Meanwhile in March 1776, at the call of Lord Stirling, Burnet collected and dispatched several military companies in aid of the defense of New York, his eldest son, Dr. William, Jr., going as surgeon attached to these companies. In addition Burnet was shortly made presiding judge of the Essex County courts, having as an early duty the sentencing of Loyalist neighbors and friends for furnishing aid to the enemy. The exercise of dictatorial and judicial powers did not interfere with the establishment, in 1775, on his own responsibility and largely at his own expense, of a military hospital located at Newark, to which he and his son gave personal supervision. In the winter of 1776–77 New Jersey sent him to the Continental Congress, which shortly after elected him physician and surgeon-general of the Eastern District. In 1780 he was again a member of the Continental Congress. As one result of his connection with Washington's headquarters there was formed between him, his sons, and the young Lafayette a lasting attachment, of which a memento in the brace of pistols worn by the Marquis at the Yorktown surrender is still in the possession of descendants. Since he was the chief suppressor of Loyalist activities in eastern New Jersey his property was the object of especial attack during times of British successes. Among other losses his medical library, spoken of as one of the most extensive in the colonies, was carried off. Following the cessation of hostilities he returned to an extensive practise in Newark, being described as a skilful and successful physician, and engaging also in agricultural pursuits. He was shortly after appointed presiding judge of the court of common pleas as well as chosen president of the New Jersey Medical Society, of which years before he had been one of the founders. On taking the chair at a meeting in Princeton he revived the custom of delivering the inaugural address in Latin. He died suddenly at the age of sixty-one. He was married twice: first, in 1754 to Mary, daughter of Nathaniel Camp, by whom he had eleven children; second, to Gertrude, daughter of Nicholas Gouverneur and widow of Anthony Rutgers by whom he had three children.

[Jos. P. Bradley, *Biog. Sketch of Wm. Burnet, M. D.* (n.d.); Jacob Burnet, *Notes on the Early Settlement of the Northwestern Territory* (1847); Samuel W. Fisher, *The Unfolding of God's Providence* (1853); Stephen Wickes, *Hist. of Medicine in N. J.* (1879); C. T. Greve, *Centennial Hist. of Cincinnati*, vol. I (1904); Gen. Wm. Fitzpatrick, "Letters" in *N. Y. Times*, Nov. 7, 1926; J. H. Clark, *Medical Men of N. J. in Essex District 1666–1866* (1867); *N. J. Provincial Cong. Jours. for 1775–76*; *Jours. of the Continental Cong.* (L. C. ed. 1904–22, 25 vols.); *Colls. N.J.Hist. Soc.*, vol. VI, suppl. (1866); *Geneal. and Memorial Hist. of the State of N. J.* (1910); John Livingston, *Portraits and Memoirs of Eminent Americans* (1854), p. 153.]

D. B.

BURNETT, CHARLES HENRY (May 28, 1842–Jan. 30, 1902), otologist, son of Eli Seal Burnett and Hannah Kennedy Mustin Burnett, was born in Philadelphia and received his preliminary education in that city. He graduated from Yale College in 1864 and from the Medical Department of the University of Pennsylvania in 1867. After serving as resident physician in the Episcopal Hospital of Philadelphia, he went abroad, spending ten months in post-graduate work. Returning to Philadelphia he practised for a year. In the course of his studies abroad he had become much interested in diseases of the ear, and in 1870 he gave up his practise and went to Vienna to pursue his otological studies under Politzer and to Berlin where he worked with Virchow and Helmholtz. He continued his friendship with these scientists in later life. It was in Helmholtz's laboratory in 1871 that Burnett conducted his very valuable investigations into the condition of the membrane of the round window during the movements of the auditory ossicles and upon the results of changes in intralabyrinthine pressure. These were published in the *Archives of Ophthalmology and Otology* in 1872. On his findings Burnett based the operation which he subsequently devised and performed in many cases for the relief of progressive deafness in chronic catarrhal otitis media, consisting in the performance of tympanotomy and removal of the incus. Burnett later advocated the same procedure for the relief of vertigo in chronic catarrhal otitis media. In 1872 he entered into practise once more, now devoting his energies solely to diseases of the ear. On June 18, 1874, he was married to Anna L. Davis. In spite of the exacting claims of a very large practise, throughout his life he was able to devote much time to laboratory research and became known as one of the foremost investigators into the physiology of hearing. He was for many years professor of otology in the Philadelphia Polyclinic and served on the staff of several hospitals. Most of his operative work was done in the Presbyterian Hospital.

Burnett was of frail physique and suffered much from ill health. He was an indefatigable worker and must often have overtaxed himself with the combined labors of his practise and his scientific work. In addition to his very frequent contributions to periodical medical literature he edited the department of progress of otology in the *American Journal of Medical Sciences*. In 1877 he published *The Ear; Its Anatomy, Physiology, and Diseases* and in 1879 *Hearing, and How to Keep It*. In 1893 he edited a *System of Diseases of the Ear, Nose and Throat*. He also contributed the sections on otology in Keating's *Cyclopedia of the Diseases of Children* (1888–89) and in the *American Textbook of Surgery* (1892) and the *American Year-book of Medicine and Surgery*. In 1901 in conjunction with Dr. E. Fletcher Ingalls of Chicago, and Dr. James E. Newcomb of New York, he edited a *Textbook of Diseases of the Ear, Nose and Throat*. On Jan. 15, 1902, he attended the meeting of the Section of Otology and Laryngology of the College of Physicians of Philadelphia and participated in the discussion of the papers read on that occasion. A few days later he developed pneumonia and died on Jan. 30, at his home in Bryn Mawr. He was a fellow of the College of Physicians of Philadelphia, a member of many other medical societies, and at one time president of the American Otological Society.

[Chas. G. Rockwood, *Hist. of the Class of 1864, Yale Coll.* (1895) and *Supplement* (1907); *Trans. of the Lehigh Valley Medic. Ass.* (1902); F. R. Packard, memoir in *Trans. of the College of Physicians of Phila.*, ser. 3, vol. XXV (1903), containing complete bibliography of Burnett's writings.]   F.R.P.

BURNETT, FRANCES ELIZA HODGSON (Nov. 24, 1849–Oct. 29, 1924), author, born at Cheetham Hill, Manchester, England, and reared until her sixteenth year in her native city, was thoroughly English even to the end of her life. Her father, Edwin Hodgson, a small shopkeeper, had died at thirty-eight, leaving the mother, Eliza Boond Hodgson, with a family of four small children and with inadequate means of support. Heroically she attempted to carry on the small shop, but with steadily decreasing income until soon the family was forced to move into the tenement district of Islington Square. Here amid the mill population with their broad dialect and their narrow horizon Frances Hodgson spent her formative years. She was a highly imaginative child, living in a world of her own creation, dramatizing always her environment and her experiences into fairy creations, and all her life long she kept vividly alive this childhood accomplishment. The Civil War, which stopped the supply of cotton, closing the mills and bringing disaster and want to the city of Manchester, brought ruin to the mother's business and the prospect of starvation to the family. A brother of the mother, William Boond, had early migrated to America, settling at Knoxville, Tenn., where he had succeeded as the proprietor of a general store, and, following his advice, the family in the spring of 1865 set sail on the steamer *Moravian* for the new world, settling finally near Knoxville. Life in the new environment seems to have made small impression upon the sensitive girl. Though she lived for more than eight years in the Tennessee mountain region, there is no trace of the fact in her later writings. She was dwelling in a world of her own. At seventeen she was writing stories, and to obtain the money required for paper and for postage to editors she was gathering and selling wild grapes. *Godey's Lady's Book* was the first to publish her work, then came *Peterson's*, and in 1872 *Scribner's Monthly*, with her story in broadest Lancashire dialect "Surly Tim's Trouble." All of this early work was essentially English in tone, language, and setting, so English indeed that it was often viewed by editors with suspicion. In 1873 she was married to Dr. Swan Moses Burnett [q.v.], who in 1875 took her to Europe, where for the next two years he studied diseases of the eye and throat in England and France. Returning, he settled in Washington, D. C., where he became widely known as a specialist in ophthalmic and aural surgery.

Two years later came Mrs. Burnett's first literary success, the publication in *Scribner's Monthly* (August 1876–May 1877) of her Lancashire story "That Lass o' Lowrie's," issued as a volume in 1877. Wide-spread popularity was immediate. In England a first edition of 30,000 was quickly exhausted and in America the sale was vastly greater, edition following edition. Following it came a rapid series of fictions, first a republication of earlier work, then a succession of novels keyed to the popular demand,—*Haworth's* (1879), *Louisiana* (1880), *A Fair Barbarian* (1880), *Through One Administration* (1883), and her second sensational success *Little Lord Fauntleroy,* issued as a book in 1886. Quickly the latter became a best-seller despite a loud chorus of humorous comment and sarcastic criticism. Fauntleroy, a study of Mrs. Burnett's own son, undoubtedly was made too perfect. As he is represented, he is an insufferable mollycoddle, and even a prig. Chiefly is he made up of wardrobe and manners. The story was at once dramatized, and largely through the genius of Elsie Leslie, who took the title rôle, it became the dramatic success of the season. Other plays from Mrs. Burnett's pen followed, all of them successful: *Esmeralda* (October 1881) in collaboration with William Gillette; *The First Gentleman of Europe* (January 1897) produced by Daniel Frohman; and *The Lady of Quality* (1896), perhaps Mrs. Burnett's best dramatic effort. Her pen was busy to the last: the titles of her novels mount up to forty or more. Perhaps the most significant of her later stories are *Sara Crewe* (1888), *The Pretty Sister of José* (1889), *Little Saint Elizabeth* (1890), *In Connection with the De Willoughby Claim* (1899), *The Shuttle* (1907), *T. Tembarom* (1913). Much of her later life she spent in England. She was divorced from her first husband in 1898, and two years later was married to Stephen Townesend, an English physician and litterateur, a man many years her junior. For a time she made her home at Maytham Hall, in Kent, his residence, but, soon leaving him, spent the rest of her life near Plandome Park on Long Island. Her novels had all the characteristics of mid-nineteenth-century feminine fiction; over-emotionalism, sentiment even to sentimentality, ultra-romanticism; but her sense of the dramatic and her power to throw into her narratives something of the vividness of her own personality begot sympathy and interest in her readers. To her own generation she seemed advanced in realism and in daring, especially in her first novel which introduced coarse characters and scenes from the mill areas of Lancashire with all the dialogue in broadest dialect, yet over even this novel she threw thickly an atmosphere of the romantic. Unquestionably she was at her best in her stories for juveniles, work that has been termed "fairy tales of real life." It is her juveniles like *Little Lord Fauntleroy, Sara Crewe,* and *Little Saint Elizabeth,* that will keep her name alive in future years.

[Mrs. Burnett's autobiographic study, *The One I Knew Best of All, A Memory of the Mind of a Child* (1893), brings her life with minuteness up to her eighteenth year. Her biography entitled "Dearest," by her son Vivian Burnett, the Little Lord Fauntleroy of the novel and the play, was published in *McCall's Mag.,* May–Sept. 1927, and in book form, with additions, under the title *The Romantick Lady* (1927). The titles of two biographical articles, one in the *Bookman,* Feb. 1925, "Frances Hodgson Burnett: 'Romantic Lady,'" and one in the *Outlook,* Nov. 12, 1924, "A Portrayer of Lovable Children" sufficiently characterize her and her work.]   F.L.P—e.

BURNETT, HENRY LAWRENCE (Dec. 26, 1838–Jan. 4, 1916), Union soldier, lawyer, was born in Youngstown, Ohio, the son of Henry and Nancy (Jones) Burnett, and a descendant of William Burnet, colonial governor of New York, 1720–28. At fifteen, determined upon getting an education, he stole away from home, equipped with a bundle of clothing, forty-six dollars, and copies of *Thaddeus of Warsaw* and *The Lady of Lyons,* and walked about one hundred miles to Chester Academy. Admitted to the school, he remained for two or three years, when he entered the Ohio State National Law School, from which he graduated with the degree of LL.B. in 1859. In the same year he began the practise of law at Warren. On the outbreak of the Civil War he became active in support of the Union. At one of these meetings he was challenged by a man in the audience with the question, "Why don't you enlist?" "I will," he promptly replied. He at once volunteered in Company C of the 2nd Ohio Cavalry, of which he was chosen captain on Aug. 23. With his regiment he was sent to Missouri and saw service in the actions at Carthage, Fort Wayne, and Gibson, later taking part in the campaigns in southern Kentucky. In the fall of 1863, with the rank of major, he was appointed judge-advocate of the Department of the Ohio. A year later at Gov. Morton's request, he was sent to Indiana to prosecute members of the Knights of the Golden Circle and later took part in the cases growing out of the Chicago conspiracy to liberate the Confederate prisoners at Camp Douglas. In these trials he obtained seven convictions. He was also prominent in the trial of L. P. Milligan for treason before a military commission. He was brevetted a colonel of volunteers Mar. 8, 1865, and in the omnibus promotions of Mar. 13 was brevetted a brigadier-general. In the prosecution of the assassins of Lincoln he served under Judge-Advocate Joseph Holt [*q.v.*] with Gen. John A. Bingham [*q.v.*] as a special assistant, and seems to have borne a major part in the preparation of the evidence. After the trials he moved to Cincinnati, where he practised law with Judge T. W. Bartley until 1869, and then with Ex-Governor J. D. Cox and John F. Follett until 1872. He then moved to New York, where at various times he was in partnership with E. W. Stoughton, with B. H. Bristow, William Peet, and W. S. Opdyke, and with Judge James Emott. He was for a time counsel for the Erie railroad, and was engaged in many noted cases, including the litigation over the Emma mine, in which he acted as attorney for the English bondholders. Probably his greatest case was that of the Rutland Railroad Company against John B. Page: in the closing argument he spoke for sixteen hours with a "consummate ability" that stamped him "the peer of the greatest advocate of the age" (D. McAdam and others, *Bench and Bar of New York*, 1899, II, 64). He was an organization Republican, a participant in the party councils, and was on especially close terms with McKinley who used to call him "Lightning Eyes Burnett." In January 1898 McKinley appointed him federal district attorney for the southern district of New York, and on the completion of his four-year term he was reappointed by Roosevelt.

Burnett was married three times. His last wife was Agnes Suffern Tailer, of a prominent New York family, who survived him. In his later years he spent much of his time at his country home, Hillside Farm, Goshen, N. Y., where he kept a large stable of harness horses which he drove on the track of the Goshen Driving Club. In the middle of November 1915, while at the farm, he was taken ill with pneumonia. Despite his serious condition he insisted on being taken by train to his city home, where, two months later, he died.

[Burnett's article, "Assassination of President Lincoln and the Trial of the Assassins," in *Hist. of the Ohio Soc. of N. Y.* (1906); David Miller DeWitt, *The Assassination of Abraham Lincoln* (1909); *The Conspiracy Trial* (3 vols., 1865–66), ed. by Benj. Perley Poore; *Official Records* (Army); *Who's Who in America*, 1912–13; obituaries in the *N. Y. Times* and *N. Y. Tribune*, Jan. 5, 1916.]   W.J.G.

BURNETT, JOSEPH (Nov. 11, 1820–Aug. 11, 1894), philanthropist, manufacturing chemist, the son of Charles and Keziah (Pond) Burnett, was born in Southborough, Mass., and educated in the district schools there. The name Burnett appears among those of the pioneer citizens of the town. John Burnett was the founder of the family in New England. At fifteen Joseph went to the English and Latin School in Worcester, but never attended college. The study of medicine, which, however, he never practised, gave him the title of Doctor. At seventeen he established with Theodore Metcalf a perfumery

and extract manufacturing business,—one of the earliest in America—from which he made a fortune. In 1854 he sold his interest and started a firm of his own, Joseph Burnett & Company, manufacturing chemists. This firm became so successful that its products are now known the world over. Burnett was also a pioneer in the raising of high-bred stock in New England and started in 1847 the well-known "Deerfoot Farm" at Southborough. He married in 1847 Josephine Cutter, the daughter of Edward and Ruth Cutter of Boston, by whom he had eleven children. He was devoted to Southborough and until he was fifty-five years old and business took him to Boston, he spent every winter there. He showed his love for the town in benefactions of every kind. As early as 1860 he built a small stone church, the first Episcopal church in Southborough. Services had been held ten years before in the schoolhouse at Southville with ten or twelve people present. After a decade of only occasional services at Southborough, St. Mark's Parish was organized and received help from other places for a year or two. Burnett then gave the parish a lot in the center of the township on the condition that the church to be built here was to be free to all with no distinction as to wealth, color, race, or station. The cost of building it was paid by Burnett. His religious interests were an unusually large factor in his life and led later to the founding of St. Mark's School. He had sent his oldest son, Edward, to St. Paul's, the first church school in New England. This had been founded in 1855, and ten years later was so successful that it had a long waiting list. When he was entering another son, Harry, the head master, Dr. Coit, suggested to him that as he had four sons it might be a good thing to start a church school in Massachusetts. The great success of St. Paul's probably encouraged Burnett in carrying out the suggestion. In 1865 the school was started. Its founder gave it the benefits of his wide business experience, his time, and his wealth, and spared no pains to make it in every way successful. Until his death, as a result of an accident in 1894, he was treasurer of the corporation and his son then succeeded him. One of his greatest gifts, according to historians of the school, was the example set by his own life of Christian reverence, unselfishness, and modesty. He "was at the school *every afternoon* the first year" wrote one boy of the class of 1871, "and not only took an intense interest in the school itself as a whole, but also in each boy, in fact, he looked after the younger boys as if he were their father, and perhaps more than some of their fathers ever had." Records of the meetings of the Board of Trustees show the constant growth of the school and its founder's interest. Burnett found opportunity also to give his services in various other channels of usefulness during his life. He was member of the school board of Southborough, vestryman of St. John's Church, Framingham, of St. Paul's, Hopkinton, and was one of the original incorporators of the Church of the Advent in Boston. Gov. Alexander H. Rice appointed him prison commissioner and he became chairman of that body when it was entrusted with the erection of a reformatory for women at Sherborn. He was the first road commissioner appointed by the town, and to him it largely owes its excellent roads and beautiful trees.

[Obituary in *Boston Evening Transcript*, Aug. 13, 1894; A. E. Benson, *Hist. of St. Mark's School* (1925).]

                     M.A.K.

BURNETT, PETER HARDEMAN (Nov. 15, 1807–May 17, 1895), Oregon and California pioneer, was born in Nashville, Tenn., the eldest son of George and Dorothy (Hardeman) Burnet. When about nineteen he added the second *t* to the surname to make it "more complete and emphatic," and his brothers followed his example. Burnett's father, a carpenter and farmer, came of a humble family, while the mother's family was distinguished. When the boy was about four his parents moved to a farm, and in the fall of 1817 to Howard County, Mo. Nine years later the youth returned to Tennessee, where for a time he was clerk in a hotel at $100 a year, and, afterward, at double the wages, clerk in a store. On Aug. 20, 1828, he married Harriet W. Rogers. In the following spring he bought out his employer, but after three years of unsuccessful storekeeping gave up and went back to the Missouri frontier, settling at Liberty. Though he had received little schooling, he had read widely and had made some progress in the study of law; and in the spring of 1839, after becoming heavily in debt through the failure of several efforts in business, he turned to the law for a livelihood. In the following winter he was appointed prosecuting attorney for the Liberty district. Two years later, deeply concerned over the continued illness of his wife and hopeless of earning enough money in Missouri to pay his debts, he decided to move to Oregon. Consulting his creditors and receiving their approval, he set out with his family on the historic migration of 875 men, women, and children that left the vicinity of Independence, Mo., May 22, 1843. On June 1 he was elected captain of the expedition, but a week later resigned. Reaching Whitman's Mission on Oct. 14, he went on to Fort Van-

couver, subsequently taking up a farm near the mouth of the Willamette and later another farm near the present town of Hillsboro, Ore.

He at once became prominent in the affairs of the new colony. He was chosen one of the nine members of the legislative committee of Oregon in 1844, in 1845 judge of the supreme court, and on the preliminary establishment of a territorial government in 1848 was elected to the legislature. In August of the last-named year, on the passage by Congress of the territorial organization bill, he was appointed by President Polk one of the territory's supreme court justices—an honor of which he was not to learn for many months. In September, leading a company of 150 men, he started for the California goldfields, arriving at the Yuba mines on Nov. 5. Six weeks later he left the mines to become the attorney and general agent of John A. Sutter, Jr. In July 1849 he left the employ of Sutter and on Aug. 13 was appointed by Gen. Bennet Riley judge of the superior tribunal of California. In the movement for statehood that year he took an active part, and in the election of Nov. 13, which ratified the constitution, was chosen governor by a vote almost equal to the combined vote of the four other contestants. The government thus set up in December of that year was legitimized by the admission of California, Sept. 9, 1850, but by the time the news arrived Burnett had tired of his post and on Jan. 9, 1851, he resigned. For several years thereafter he practised law. In the beginning of 1857 he was appointed to fill a vacancy in the supreme court of the state, serving until October 1858. During his early years in California he succeeded in paying off the indebtedness incurred in Missouri. From San José, which he had made his home since about 1854, he moved to San Francisco in 1863 and with Sam Brannan and Joseph W. Winans founded the Pacific Bank, of which he was made president. In 1880 he retired from business and the same year brought out his *Recollections and Opinions of an Old Pioneer*. He died of old age in his San Francisco home.

Hittell describes Burnett as tall and spare, but strong and rugged, and adds that he was of a cheerful disposition, with a fondness for reminiscences and anecdotes. Bancroft rates him as a man of no particular force, but with an ability to accommodate himself to circumstances and to make friends and avoid making enemies. Though his life was crowned by no great or noble achievement, continues Bancroft, it was marked by not a single conspicuous error. Gray, in his *History of Oregon* (1870), makes some strictures upon Burnett as lacking in candor and disinterestedness, but the censure seems captious and prompted by personal dislike. Certainly the man revealed in the *Recollections,* a book written with almost childish *naïveté,* has the virtues of straightforwardness and strict integrity.

[Theodore H. Hittell, *Hist. of Cal.* (1885–97); H. H. Bancroft, *Hist. of Cal.,* vol. VI (1888); *San Francisco Chronicle,* May 15, 18, 1895.]   W. J. G.

BURNETT, SWAN MOSES (Mar. 16, 1847–Jan. 18, 1906), physician, was born in New Market, Jefferson County, Tenn., the son of Dr. John M. and Lydia (Peck) Burnett. His medical education was begun in the Miami Medical College, Cincinnati, Ohio, which he attended in 1866–67, and was continued at the Bellevue Hospital Medical College in New York City during 1869–70, from which institution he received his degree in medicine. He first located in Knoxville, Tenn., where he was a general practitioner from 1870 to 1875. In 1873 he married Frances E. Hodgson, who subsequently became well-known as the author of *Little Lord Fauntleroy.* In 1875, tiring of the demands made upon him by general practise, Burnett left Knoxville and went abroad, spending the major portion of two years in London and Paris preparing himself in ophthalmology and otology, in which he specialized upon his return to America in 1876. He now located in Washington, D. C., with which city the rest of his professional activities were connected. In 1878 he was appointed lecturer in ophthalmology and otology, and in 1883, clinical professor in these subjects in the Medical School of Georgetown University, attaining full professorship in 1889. He was likewise connected with the teaching staff of the Washington Postgraduate Medical School. He was a member of the staff of the Dispensary & Emergency Hospital, and of the Children's, Providence, and Episcopal Eye, Ear & Throat Hospitals. With Dr. Louis Marple, Dr. James E. Morgan, and others he founded the Emergency Hospital in 1881, and established the Lionel Laboratory as a memorial to a son who died in childhood. He was a skilful operator and a teacher of no mean ability. At the time of his death he possessed the largest individually owned medical library in Washington. He contributed several books to medical literature, including a translation of E. Landolt's *Manual of Examination of the Eyes* (1879); *A Theoretical and Practical Treatise on Astigmatism* (1887); *The Principles of Refraction in the Human Eye, based on the Laws of Conjugate Foci* (1904); *Study of Refraction from a New Viewpoint* (1905); the section on "Diseases of the Conjunctiva and Sclera," in W. F. Norris and C. A. Oliver, *System of Ophthalmology* (1898); the sec-

tion on "Diseases of the Cornea and Sclera" in De Schweinitz and Randall, *American Textbook of Diseases of the Eye, Ear, Nose and Throat* (1899). Burnett was also associated with Dr. John S. Billings in the production of the *National Medical Dictionary* (1889). He devised an ophthalmoscope with a rack for holding the correcting lenses of the observer while making an examination. The large ophthalmic field among the colored population of Washington afforded him countless opportunities for making original observations among these people, and his minor writings contain diagnostic and therapeutic points concerning the negro that heretofore had not been recorded. He also wrote extensively on his hobby, Japanese art, for the *International Studio,* the *Craftsman,* and the *Connoisseur.* The first Mrs. Burnett obtained a divorce from him in 1898, and in March 1904 he married Margaret Brady of Washington.

[Sketch by H. V. Würdemann, in *Ophthalmic Record,* Feb. 1906 (repr. in *Ophthalmology,* Apr. 1906); *Ophthalmic Year Book,* 1907; Casey A. Wood, ed., *Am. Encyc. and Dict. of Ophthalmology,* vol. II (1913); *Index Cat. of Lib. of Surgeon-Gen.;* *Washington Post,* Jan. 19, 1906; *Who's Who in America,* 1906–07.]   L. W. F.

BURNHAM, CLARA LOUISE ROOT (May 26, 1854–June 20, 1927), author, descendant of two families of musical ability through several generations, was the daughter of George F. Root, composer, and Mary O. Woodman, musician. George F. Root was descended from a Puritan settler of Connecticut in 1640. Clara Louise was born in Newton, Mass., and passed her early childhood there and in North Reading, Mass. When she was nine, the family removed to Chicago which was thereafter her home. There she attended public and private schools and studied music, which she intended to make her profession. Before she was twenty, she married Walter Burnham, a lawyer. Soon after her marriage she began to write, under the influence of a brother, who said she should make a good fiction writer because she had a vivid imagination, not too much hampered by truth, and playfully locked her in a room with pad and pencils, telling her to stay until she had produced a story. Her first efforts, novelettes, were rejected, with the advice to give up writing. Her first accepted work was a poem, published in *Wide Awake,* and her first published novel *No Gentlemen* (1881). She wrote easily and fluently and produced many novels, stories, and poems, besides librettos for her father's cantatas. Her stories and poems were frequently contributed to *Wide Awake, St. Nicholas,* and the *Youth's Companion.* Her novels include: *A Sane Lunatic*

(1882); *Dearly Bought* (1884); *Next Door* (1886); *Young Maids and Old* (1889); *The Mistress of Beech Knoll* (1890); *Miss Bagg's Secretary* (1892); *Dr. Latimer* (1893); *Sweet Clover* (1894); *The Wise Woman* (1895); *Miss Archer Archer* (1897); *Miss Pritchard's Wedding Trip* (1901); *The Right Princess* (1902); *Jewel* (1903); *Jewel's Story Book* (1904); *The Opened Shutters* (1906); *The Leaven of Love* (1908); *Clever Betsy* (1910); *The Inner Flame* (1912); *The Right Track* (1914); *A Great Love* (1915); *Instead of the Thorn* (1916); *Hearts' Haven* (1918); *In Apple-Blossom Time* (1919); *The Key-Note* (1921); *The Queen of Farrandale* (1923); *The Lavarons* (1925).

Through ill health, Mrs. Burnham became interested in Christian Science as early as 1902 and her later novels have a strong Christian Science flavor, which sometimes suggests propaganda. In *A View of Christian Science* (1912) she explains how her own early antagonism was changed to adherence and says: "One after another of the conditions which hampered my life slipped away." In appearance she was tall, slender, and blonde, with expressive blue eyes. She enjoyed people and had many social contacts; her vivacity and conversational gift made her generally popular. Her fiction is not notable, but shows a certain cleverness in plot situations, realistic characterization and dialogue, and a simple, unaffected style. It is of a type known as perfectly "safe" for young people. Shortly before her death Mrs. Burnham returned from a visit to Hollywood, Cal., where she sold the motion picture rights of *The Lavarons*. She died at her summer home, "The Mooring," Bailey Island, Casco Bay, Me.

[*Root Genealogical Records 1600–1870* (1870), by Jas. Pierce Root; a biographical sketch by Lydia Avery Coonley in the *Writer*, Sept. 1895, p. 133; *Who's Who in America,* 1926–27; obituaries in the *N.Y. Times, Boston Transcript,* and *Boston Herald,* all June 22, 1927.]

S.G.B.

BURNHAM, DANIEL HUDSON (Sept. 4, 1846–June 1, 1912), architect, was born at Henderson, N. Y., a small town near Lake Ontario, in a substantial stone house still shown as a memorial of him. The Burnham family in America began in Ipswich, Mass., in 1635, and there continued for a century and a quarter, undertaking the duties and enjoying those honors in church, town, and colony which were a part of life in a Puritan community. Then two John Burnhams, father and son, made their way first to Connecticut and next to the inchoate state of Vermont, with whose beginnings both were conspicuously identified. In 1785 the younger John established himself at Middletown, Vt., and in a valley still

known as Burnham's Hollow built a forge and foundry, and mills of various kinds, including a distillery. In 1811, a freshet having swept away the labor of years, Nathan, the eldest son of the family, removed to the New York frontier, where speculation in lands was rife. In 1832 Nathan's son Edwin married Elizabeth Keith Weeks, of Pilgrim ancestry on both sides of her family. The daughter of a Swedenborgian minister, she was deeply imbued with the poetic qualities of that religion and imparted them to her seven children, of whom Daniel Hudson was the sixth.

In 1855, Edwin Burnham removed his family to the fast growing city of Chicago, where he established himself as a wholesale merchant in drugs. Daniel was destined by his parents for the ministry, and after a year or more in the Chicago High School he was sent to the New Church School of the Worcesters at Waltham, Mass., to be fitted for Harvard. He had a marked propensity for drawing but no aptitude for study; and his tutor, Tilly B. Hayward of Bridgewater, was unable to get him into Harvard, and he failed also to pass the Yale examinations. Both universities afterward bestowed upon him honorary degrees.

Returning to Chicago he tried business, but a mercantile life did not interest him. So he was placed in an architect's office, whence he was lured by the prospect of finding gold in Nevada. After a sorry experience in that field he again returned to Chicago and settled down to his life work in architecture. In 1872, at the age of twenty-six, he entered the office of Carter, Drake & Wight. Among his fellow draftsmen with that prosperous firm was John Wellborn Root, of Vermont antecedents and Southern birth. The two became first friends, then partners in an office of their own. After months that seemed years of struggle, success came with a commission to build a house for the influential manager of the Chicago Stock Yards, John B. Sherman, whose daughter, Margaret, Burnham married before the house was completed. The devastation caused by the Chicago fire of 1871, and the subsequent rebuilding, gave to the young firm opportunities they were not slow to seize. Burnham's facility with his tongue and with pencil sketches engaged the interest of clients; and Root's early education in England (whither he was taken in one of his father's blockade-runners) and his architectural training in the New York office of James Renwick made a combination of talents that quickly won success. Root was versatile, romantic, and inventive; Burnham was practical and business-like, he had a keen appreciation of the points that make an office-building a paying enterprise, and his clients were not led into heavier expenditures than they had planned to make.

The term "sky-scraper" is said to have been first applied to Burnham & Root's Montauk Building, ten stories in height, the first distinctly tall building in Chicago. Its commercial success made it the forerunner of tall fire-proof buildings throughout the United States. Here for the first time the iron floor-beams were encased in fire-clay tiles, in order to overcome the defects caused by the bending and giving way of exposed iron beams when subjected to fire. This general form of protection, afterward highly developed by the firm, proved to be successful even in the combined earthquake and fire in San Francisco.

The Chicago firm of Holabird & Roche was one of the first to erect a building having a complete riveted steel frame above the foundations. Burnham & Root saw that this construction was good and immediately adopted it for all their tall buildings. In 1890 they built the Masonic Temple at the northeast corner of State and Randolph Sts.—in its day famous as "the tallest building in the world," and famous also for its beauty of design according to the standards of that era, an achievement that gave Root fame among architects. In 1902, Burnham's Flatiron Building, New York's first sky-scraper, broke the record for "the tallest building in the world." It was a nine years' wonder. Meanwhile Burnham's theory that above all architecture should express the uses to which a building is to be put found expression in his Monadnock Building, austere, but abounding in such subtleties of proportion as to make it a work of art. During their partnership from 1873 to 1891, Burnham & Root erected, in cities from Detroit to San Francisco, buildings that cost upwards of forty million dollars—a record unprecedented in those days.

Congress having decreed that the celebration of the four-hundredth anniversary of the discovery of America should center in Chicago, the State of Illinois, on Apr. 9, 1890, licensed the corporation known as the World's Columbian Exposition, of which Lyman J. Gage (afterward secretary of the treasury) became the president. Due to the insistence of James W. Ellsworth, Frederick Law Olmsted was entrusted with the selection of site and the design of the land and water features. He was ably assisted by his partner, Henry Sargent Codman, a young man of rare discernment and taste in matters of adapting landscape to buildings.

After the usual delays, in October 1890 the construction force was organized, with F. L. Olmsted & Company, consulting landscape architects; A. Gottlieb, consulting engineer; J. W. Root, consulting architect; D. H. Burnham, chief of construction, with autocratic powers. By December a tentative scheme of canals, lagoons, and islands had been worked out by Olmsted, Codman, Root, and Burnham in coöperation. Jackson Park, then a sandy waste, was selected as the location, and improvements were designed to fit the area ultimately for use as a park. Supplementary buildings were to be erected on the lake front near the center of Chicago. Then five outside and five local firms of architects were selected to design the principal buildings: Richard M. Hunt, McKim, Mead & White, and George B. Post of New York; Peabody & Stearns of Boston; Van Brunt & Howe of Kansas City; and Burling & Whitehouse, Jenney & Mundie, Henry Ives Cobb, S. S. Beman, and Adler & Sullivan of Chicago. It was no small achievement on Burnham's part to secure the promise of effective and interested coöperation on the part of the reluctant eastern architects, unacquainted as they were with the energy, resources, and spirit of Chicago.

During the first meeting of the architects, in January 1891, Root died suddenly, leaving on Burnham's shoulders the responsibility of securing and maintaining the team-work necessary to accomplish the opening of the Fair by 1893, an achievement seemingly impossible. At a meeting in New York the eastern architects determined that the buildings surrounding the Court of Honor should be classical in design, with a uniform cornice line; and this scheme was adopted in spite of the fact that up to this time no building of classical design had been erected in Chicago. In the East Richardson had died in 1886, leaving Trinity Church in Boston as the supreme enduring product of his genius. Because the style he adopted fitted the temperament of the times, it was eagerly seized upon; but by 1890 round arches and great wall spaces were found lacking in respect of providing light and air. Also, in the hands of men of small artistic sense, the revived Romanesque became lawless and altogether lacking in those elements of strength and bigness which expressed Richardson the artist. Richardson's death left Richard M. Hunt the undisputed leader among American architects. Hunt was made chairman of the board of architects for the Fair. Both Hunt and Richardson had been trained at the École des Beaux Arts; but Hunt had brought from France a respect for authority and tradition, which had been strengthened by work on the buildings connecting the Louvre with the Tuileries and by employment under Walter on the extension of the United States Capitol. In his own practise, however, he inclined to the French style expressed in their chateaux, and his greatest remaining monument is at Biltmore, N. C. It is commonly said that, had John Root lived, his authority, versatility, and strong predilection for the romantic in architecture would have given an altogether different and picturesque character to the general appearance of the Chicago Fair. Possibly and probably this is so, in a measure. It is to be considered, however, that the domination of the classic motives for the Court of Honor had been decided upon while Root was living, with his and Burnham's assent. Moreover, the minds of both men were attuned to the new architectural notes which had already been struck in the east, notably by McKim, Mead & White in plans based on classical precedents, for the Boston Public Library, accepted in 1887,—a building to face Richardson's masterpiece across Copley Square.

To Burnham, left without professional support, the sense of orderliness and the largeness of the conception involved in a series of related public buildings strongly appealed. Denied the advantages of European training or even travel, Burnham instinctively was drawn to the big conception representing power, dominating vast spaces, and withal arranged as one organism. Moreover, he was then and to the end of his life an assiduous student of architecture, ever seeking to supply those early deficiencies against which his practise brought him. Never for a moment did he abdicate the architectural throne. Trained and brilliant draftsmen came and went, but every design bore his individual stamp both in conception and in execution. His own mind meeting the mind of his clients solved the fundamental problems. His was the vision; he made others see it.

It was at this critical time in the development of the plans for the World's Fair that Burnham met Charles F. McKim. Between the two men a friendship gradually grew up, not without sharp conflicts and misunderstandings. This friendship kept them together in public service and in ideals for the future, and will keep their names associated both in the plans for the development of the national capital and in the school for the training of artists known as the American Academy in Rome. Burnham's tremendous energy, his grasp of details, and his ability to handle clients on the one hand, and on the other to build up the organization for carrying out great undertakings, obscured during his lifetime the purely artistic side of his character; and yet his power to dream dreams, and to make

others see with him, was the direct cause of his success. To him the Chicago Fair far transcended the mere bringing together of displays of American prowess in manufactures, invention, and production, important as was that side of the undertaking. In the project he realized the opportunity to express to the world the capacity of this country in architecture, in sculpture, in painting, each art contributing its full share to bring a unified result. Happily the time was ripe for such a combination. During the decade and a half since the Philadelphia Exposition which marked the first century of our life as a nation, the sense of permanence, of wealth and power, of appreciation of national heroes—explorers, founders and preservers—had developed a body of artists the like of which this country had never before known. It was Burnham's opportunity to call together this band and to bring them into one united service to secure one unified result.

In the associations created and fostered during the two years of the construction period, Burnham found his greatest pleasure. His large and generous nature led him to give full credit to those who under his leadership and his management found opportunity to express each his own individuality. Nor were they unappreciative. At a dinner given to Burnham in New York, Mar. 25, 1893, on the eve of the opening of the Chicago Fair, their appreciation found full expression. The event, arranged "in recognition of the great benefit to architecture, sculpture and painting that had resulted from Mr. Burnham's connection with the World's Columbian Exposition," was participated in by artists, men of letters, leaders in business and at the bar, from all parts of the country.

The immediate results of the success of the Chicago Fair were honorary degrees bestowed on Burnham at the following commencement by Harvard and Yale; election as president of the American Institute of Architects; and membership in the Century Club of New York, where he ever after, among congenial companions, made headquarters when in the metropolis.

The winding up of the World's Fair at the end of 1893 left Burnham with a practise broken by the loss of his partner and two years of interrupted work, a debt of some $20,000 incurred by becoming involved in the venture of a friend, and the reputation of being the best-known architect in America. He called into partnership with himself three of his associates at the Fair: Ernest R. Graham, the assistant chief of construction; E. C. Shankland, the chief engineer; and Charles Atwood, a designer of unusual taste and refinement, whose achievements in the Peristyle and the Art Gallery were the more conspicuous of many successes. His arrangements with his partners made him dominant in the office; also he was left free to do public work, and to engage in underwriting the finances of large buildings, then becoming a profitable form of enterprise. The work done by the firm assumed colossal proportions—in New York, Boston, Pittsburgh, San Francisco, Washington, and many another city besides Chicago. Living much on trains and in clubs and hotels, Burnham nevertheless found opportunity to indulge his propensity for the quiet home life in the midst of a growing family of children, who regarded him as their best friend.

In the spring of 1901, the United States Senate Committee on the District of Columbia, by virtue of a resolution offered by Senator James McMillan of Michigan, was directed to report a plan for the development of the national capital, with authority to employ experts. The chairmanship of the commission of experts was offered to Burnham; and Charles McKim, Augustus Saint-Gaudens, and Frederick Law Olmsted, Jr., were selected as the other members. At the first meeting Burnham insisted that studies be made of those European capitals which had furnished precedents for the original plan of Washington, drawn by the French engineer Pierre Charles L'Enfant in 1792, under the direction of President Washington and approved by him. The Senate Park Commission became convinced that, first, the L'Enfant plan should be taken as the basis of their work; and, secondly, that that plan was inspired by the plans made for Versailles and Paris by the architects of Louis XIV, and especially by André Le Nôtre, greatest of landscape architects. While the Commission was visiting European cities, studies of the topography of the District of Columbia were in progress. On Jan. 15, 1902, Senator McMillan reported the completed plan to the Senate, with illustrative models, drawings, and photographs. This report was the beginning of the city-planning movement in the United States.

The essential features of the Le Nôtre design were long, tree-lined vistas, stretching even to the horizon and adorned with fountains and basins; and also focal points with radiating avenues. These features L'Enfant brought to Washington from Versailles, then the capital city of his native country. It was the aim of the Burnham Commission to restore the unity of the Mall, which had been cut into sections; to revert to the main axis of the original central composition, by drawing a new axis from the

dome of the Capitol through the Washington Monument and prolonging it to the bank of the Potomac, where a location was created for the Lincoln Memorial. Thus both historical and artistic considerations would be subserved. The obstacle to the Mall restoration was the fact that railroad tracks divided the area, and the removal of them was fundamental to success.

Fortunately, even before the Park Commission was created, Burnham had been commissioned by the Pennsylvania Railroad to design their new Washington station. While in London, Burnham secured the consent of President Cassatt to withdraw the tracks from the Mall and to build a station in an entirely new location. The present Union Station was the result. This station and the adjoining Post Office Building were planned to be subordinate to the Capitol, while still under the domination of that structure. In this subordination, no less than in the monumental character of the group, Burnham achieved a result which marks his sense of proportion and his desire for team-work, to use his favorite phrase.

Burnham thus became the recognized leader and authority in the new field of city-planning. His services were sought by Cleveland and San Francisco, for both of which cities his ideas of orderliness, dignity, and beauty found expression in the plans for civic development. Unfortunately, in neither case were his plans carried out without serious modification. In 1904 the secretary of war, William H. Taft, asked Burnham to undertake a plan for Manila, and one for a summer capital in the hills at Baguio. In this work he was assisted by Peirce Anderson of his office. In Manila the French idea of turning outgrown fortifications into boulevards was successfully carried out. On Burnham's return, the execution of both plans was placed in the hands of William E. Parsons, who interpreted them in buildings, parks, and driveways in accordance with the Burnham spirit and climatic and topographical requirements.

In 1906, all conditions were favorable to carrying out ideas long cherished in Burnham's mind for creating a plan to make Chicago the finest commercial city in the world—a city in which people should labor and live under the most perfect conditions. For the production of this plan the men of the city met in council week after week for three years. Building a workshop on the roof of the Railway Exchange, his own business building of seventeen stories, Burnham had spread before his far vision the great expanse of land and water and sky, and the city of Chicago at his feet. With the aid of

Edward H. Bennett and a band of assistants, and with the strong and steady support of the Commercial Club, he made the Plan of Chicago, and in 1909 presented it to the public in compelling fashion. After the inevitable pause for explanation and mental expansion to allow the people to rise to an appreciation of so stupendous an undertaking, the City of Chicago took up with enthusiasm the Burnham conception. They taught the plan to the children in the public schools. They appointed and financed an influential committee to carry it out. By taxation and bond issues voted by the people, they purchased thousands of acres for an outer park system, cut broad thoroughfares through blighted districts, filled in miles of parkways along the lake front, built recreation piers out into the lake, adorned the parks and created playgrounds. The leadership, unfaltering, enthusiastic, inspiring, was Burnham's; and his, too, was the conception, and the faith that a great plan adequately recorded would so take hold on the imagination of men that they would find the means to carry it out.

On June 15, 1910, President Taft appointed Burnham chairman of the National Commission of Fine Arts, an organization then created by Congress to give advice to the president, to the executive officers, and to committees of Congress, on matters of art for which appropriations are made from the federal treasury. The creation of a body of precedents and the overcoming of prejudice against the exercise of authority in matters of taste, even though such authority is disguised as advice,—such were the intangible problems which the commission successfully met under Burnham's wise and tactful guidance. One of its first duties was to advise the Lincoln Memorial Commission (of which President Taft was chairman) as to the location for that monument. The fact that a site had been fixed in the Burnham Report (as it is frequently called) did not preclude Burnham from giving serious consideration to other proposed sites, only to find that logic and history combined to determine the location on the main axis, where the Memorial now stands with such appropriateness that long controversy now seems inconceivable. No less important was the choice of architect. For a decade the tentative plans made by Charles McKim and presented in the Burnham Report had been before the public, and had come to be tacitly accepted as fulfilling the requirements of intrinsic impressiveness and harmony with the Capitol and the Washington Monument, with which structures it was to stand in relationship. In his own mind Burnham had

selected Henry Bacon as the man peculiarly fitted by habit of thought and technical training to design the Lincoln Memorial. This conviction was formed from experience gained at the World's Fair, where Bacon acted as the interpreter and executive in carrying out the designs of McKim, Mead & White in the construction of their monumental buildings. Time has justified the choice of Bacon by the Commission of Fine Arts.

In Burnham's thought and speech, standards of taste in this country had their origin in the association of architects, landscape architects, sculptors, and mural painters which produced the Chicago Fair. He realized that these men based their work firmly on precedents drawn from the great work done in the past. To provide for the adequate training of American artists for future tasks of even greater importance, due to the increase in wealth and taste, seemed to him a matter of the first consequence. Therefore he joined heartily with McKim, Hunt, Saint-Gaudens, French, La Farge, Blashfield, and the other artists who organized, immediately after the World's Fair of 1893, the American School of Architecture in Rome, which broadened into the American Academy in Rome. So keen was his interest, and so steady were his money contributions to this enterprise during its early years of uncertainty and struggle, that he has come to be recognized as a founder second only to McKim in this work of training successors to carry on the tradition of patriotic service.

For his public work in Washington, San Francisco, the Philippines, and Chicago, Burnham would accept no compensation. He declined to place himself in the position of working for and under a client, when that client was the public. He felt it requisite to the success of his studies and the presentation of them to be absolutely free from the always unsatisfactory necessity of compromise. He would make the finest design his mind could conceive, and would present it in the most adequate and convincing manner possible. He required freedom, and he took to himself the text selected by President Eliot for the Water Gate at the World's Fair: "Ye shall know the truth, and the truth shall make you free."

To the very end he was a keen student. His visits to Europe, which came to be annual, were periods snatched from a busy life and devoted to the enjoyment of family intercourse and to the training of himself and his sons. It was on one such visit in 1912 that the infirmities which had been gathering for several years overcame him at Heidelberg, where he died suddenly on June

1. He was buried on an island in Graceland Cemetery, Chicago. His continuing monument is the Burnham Architectural Library at the Chicago Art Institute.

[D. H. Burnham and F. D. Millet, *World's Columbian Exposition* (1894) uncompleted; "The Improvement of the Park System of the District of Columbia," ed. by Chas. Moore, *Senate Report No. 166*, 57 Cong., 1 Sess. (1902); *Report on a Plan for San Francisco* (1905), by D. H. Burnham assisted by Edward H. Bennett, ed. by Edward F. O'Day; *The Group Plan of the Public Buildings of the City of Cleveland* (2nd ed. 1907), . . . by D. H. Burnham, John M. Carrère, Arnold W. Brunner; *Plan of Chicago* (1909), by D. H. Burnham and Edward H. Bennett, ed. by Chas. Moore; *Daniel H. Burnham, Architect, Planner of Cities* (2 vols., 1921), by Chas. Moore.]   C. M.

BURNHAM, SHERBURNE WESLEY (Dec. 12, 1838–Mar. 11, 1921), astronomer, son of Roswell O. and Marinda (Foote) Burnham, was born at Thetford, Vt., where, too, his graduation from the Academy marked the end of his schooling. During the Civil War he was stationed with the Federal army in New Orleans as shorthand reporter. He had practised shorthand by himself and had gone to New York in 1857 or 1858. After the war he went to Chicago and acted as official court reporter for more than twenty years, winning, at the same time, with his tireless energy, a world-wide reputation as an astronomer. His days were fully occupied in taking down the court reports and writing them out in long hand; at night, he carried out a full program of observing. In 1868 he was married to Mary Cleland. Twenty years later he went to the Lick Observatory as a member of the staff and remained there until 1892, when he returned to Chicago, serving from then until 1902 as clerk of the United States circuit court. From 1897 to 1902 he acted as receiver for the Northern Pacific Railway. From 1897 until his retirement in 1914, he was senior astronomer at the Yerkes Observatory.

Burnham's first interest in astronomy seems to have been aroused by reading Barritt's *Geography of the Heavens,* purchased in New Orleans. He soon began to trace out the constellations pictured in the book. A small, cheap telescope, which he purchased, was soon exchanged for a better one. In 1869 he ordered from Alvan Clark & Sons a six-inch telescope which was to be the best that they could make, especially in respect to its defining power, for by this time his interest had become focused on the observation of double stars. He brought to this work an exceptionally keen eye, a tireless industry, and boundless enthusiasm. His discoveries with the six-inch telescope number over four hundred double stars, some of them difficult objects with much larger telescopes. The six-inch had no driving clock, but this difficulty he overcame by a contrivance of his own. He had no micrometer, but he soon secured the sympathetic interest of the Polish astronomer, Baron Dembowski, who devoted much of his time to measuring the new Burnham stars. Burnham dedicated the "General Catalogue" of his own double stars (*Publications of the Yerkes Observatory,* Volume I) to this staunch friend.

The major part of his astronomical library, at this time, consisted of a copy of Webb's *Celestial Objects for Common Telescopes.* The literature of double stars was scattered through periodicals and observatory publications, few of which were easily accessible to him. The need of a single catalogue was very insistent. In the interests of his own work he felt compelled to make manuscript copies from various libraries, some of them at a considerable distance, of all the material bearing on the subject. This material, brought together in a manuscript catalogue, contained the data on every known double star within 121° of the north pole, and enabled Burnham quickly to discriminate between known and new double stars. This catalogue passed into a second and a third edition, and finally appeared as *A General Catalogue of Double Stars,* published in 1906 by the Carnegie Institution of Washington. The manuscript edition was continued and kept up to date with all published observations. It is now being carried forward by Prof. Aitken. The preparation of this catalogue constantly suggested the necessity of re-observation of many stars, and Burnham's observations at the forty-inch Yerkes telescope, from 1900 to 1906, were mainly devoted to supplying this need. His later observations were chiefly the measurement of double stars with reference to faint stars in their vicinity, with a view to the eventual knowledge of their proper motions.

His work on double stars was begun at a time when it was generally supposed that the Struves and the Herschels had left no more double stars to be found. Burnham's keen eye detected many double stars with a separation of only a small fraction of a second of arc, and other close pairs in which the difference in brightness of the two components made the discovery extremely difficult. His keen insight kept his attention on these pairs as having a large probability of orbital motion. An occasional measurement was sufficient for the more widely separated pairs. His observations, which were of the highest accuracy, were made with great rapidity. He is said to have measured as many as one hundred double stars, with the forty-inch telescope, in a single night.

After he resigned his position as court clerk he

still preferred to live in Chicago and travel out to the Yerkes Observatory for the two nights a week, Saturday and Sunday, during which the forty-inch was entirely reserved for his use. The round trip involved a distance of about 160 miles on the railroad and a three-mile walk. In winter he often had to break his own path through the snow between the railroad station and the Observatory. He is described by Prof. Barnard as a man of slight, wiry build, tough as iron, with not an ounce of surplus flesh. Among his greatest pleasures was a tramp in the rough country about Mt. Hamilton, or a bicycle ride near the Yerkes Observatory. His camera always went with him and his photographs were almost always works of art. His professional associates had a high opinion of him as an astronomer; he had many friends among the judges and lawyers with whom he came in contact in his daily life, and other friends who knew him only during his wanderings and recreations.

[The very intimate story told by E. E. Barnard (*Pop. Astronomy*, June–July 1921) is of especial interest. The history of Burnham's early life is related by John Frazer in the *Century Mag.*, June 1889. See also *Astrophysical Jour.*, July 1921; *Observatory*, XLIV, 154–58, 163–64; *Pubs. of the Astronomical Soc. of the Pacific*, 1921, pp. 85–90; *Astronomische Nachrichten*, CCXIII, 141–44; *Monthly Notices of the Royal Astronomical Soc.*, Feb. 1922; *Populär Astronomisk Tideskrift*, 1921, pp. 178–80; *Science*, Apr. 22, 1921; *Pubs. of the Yerkes Observatory*, vol. I (1900), intro.; *A Gen. Cat. of Double Stars, Carnegie Inst. of Washington, Pub. No. 5* (1906), intro.]   R.S.D.

BURNS, ANTHONY (May 31, 1834–July 27, 1862), fugitive slave, was born in Stafford County, Va. It is said, but without certainty, that his father, who died when the child was very young, had been a freeman and had come from the North. Certainly the boy from the beginning showed unusual independence and character. At six, in return for little services he did them, he learned the alphabet from white children with whom he was thrown in contact. He was converted while a youth to the Baptist faith and two years later became a "slave preacher." As a young man he was sent to take a position in Richmond, for which his master was to be paid. A transfer of positions left him free to escape, and in February 1854 he fled from Richmond on a vessel on which he had a friend. On May 24, he was arrested in Boston on the charge of theft. The excitement in Boston during the following week was said to have been without parallel since the days of the Revolution. The abolitionists and the woman suffragists were holding anniversary conventions at the time but people poured in also from neighboring suburbs. A mass meeting two days after the arrest was addressed by Wendell Phillips and Theodore Parker. An attack was made on the Court House, in which one of the deputy marshals was killed. President Pierce and the Mayor of Boston brought together military forces to prevent a second attack. Burns was defended by R. H. Dana and others, but without success. He had been immediately identified by his master. To prevent his release, he was taken down State St. between armed troops. The Grand Jury was charged by Judge B. R. Curtis to indict Parker, Wendell Phillips, and Higginson for their Faneuil Hall talks on "obstructing the process of the United States," but the indictments were quashed on technical grounds. The cost to the United States of sending this one fugitive back to Virginia was $100,000. A sum of money had been raised to purchase Burns's freedom but this was not possible at the time. A few months later he fell into the hands of a friendly master, who sold him to individuals in Boston interested in setting him free. He attended the preparatory department of Oberlin College, 1855–56, and is supposed to have attended Fremont Academy, 1856–57. From 1857 to 1862, through the generosity of a Boston woman, he was able to study at Oberlin College. For a short time in 1860 he was in charge of a colored Baptist church in Indianapolis, but was forced to leave. Later he went to Canada, and became pastor of the Zion Baptist Church at St. Catherines, where he died.

[*Boston Slave Riot and Trial of Anthony Burns* (1854); C. E. Stevens, *Anthony Burns, A Hist.* (1856); M. G. McDougall, *Fugitive Slaves* (1891); Wm. Lloyd Garrison, *The Story of His Life, Told by His Children* (1885–89); the *Liberator*, June, July 1854, Aug. 22, 1862; Fred Landon, "Anthony Burns in Canada," in *Ontario Hist. Soc. Papers and Records*, vol. XXII (1925).]   M.A.K.

BURNS, OTWAY (1775?–Oct. 25, 1850), privateer, shipbuilder, legislator, born in Onslow County, N. C., near the present village of Swannsboro, was the son of Otway Burns whose father, Francis, came to North Carolina from Glasgow in 1734. He early went to sea and at the outbreak of the War of 1812 was in command of a merchantman plying between New Bern, N. C., and Portland, Me. Learning of the declaration of war he sold his vessel in New York and for eight thousand dollars bought the *Levere*, a Baltimore clipper noted for her speed. He took her to New Bern where books of subscription were opened to equip her as a privateer. She was renamed the *Snap-Dragon* and carried six guns and a crew of a hundred. For three years Burns was a terror to the enemy. He preyed on British commerce from Greenland to Brazil. The command of a privateer gave him every opportunity to display his reckless courage and skilful seamanship. His daring exploits were many: he dashed into the midst of armed convoys to seize his prey; he pounced on British commerce under the guns of Halifax. He attacked British men-of-war; at St. Thomas he escaped from five of them; at other times capture semed so inevitable that the crew packed their baggage for the long journey to England and to Dartmoor. There are no estimates of the total damage he did to British shipping, but in a single cruise of about three months in 1813 he captured or destroyed commerce of over two and a half millions (*North Carolina University Magazine*, April 1856, p. 131). The profits of these ventures were enormous; they would have been greater but for his miserable set of prize masters who allowed many of the most valuable prizes to be retaken. The British government offered a prize of $50,000 for his capture, dead or alive. In June 1814 through a skilful stratagem the *Leopard* captured the *Snap-Dragon* but Burns was not in command; rheumatism had kept him in port.

After the war he returned to shipbuilding. In 1820 he built the *Prometheus,* the first steamer that plied the waters of Cape Fear, three years later the *Warrior,* and in 1831 the brig *Henry.* Elected to the General Assembly in 1821 he represented Carteret County, in the Commons or in the Senate, until 1835. His career as a legislator was independent and enlightened. In the historic Eastern and Western controversy Burns played an important part, acting with a sense of justice unintelligible to the narrow interests of his constituency. His vote in the Senate in January 1835 carried the measure calling the Constitutional Convention, and ended his political career. Reckless extravagance and heavy investments in the Dismal Swamp Canal dissipated his large fortune and in 1835 his friend, Andrew Jackson, appointed him keeper of the Brant Island Shoal Light. He settled in the village of Portsmouth and there sank into his anecdotage. He was fond of his brilliant naval uniform and cocked hat, he liked good whiskey, and he liked a good fight, whether on the water-front or in the legislature. The figure of this picturesque patriot early became wrapped in legends from which his biographers have not wholly disengaged themselves. He was married three times: first, to a Miss Grant; second, in 1814, to Jane Hall of Beaufort, N. C.; and, third, in 1842, to Jane Smith of Smyrna, N. C.

[*N. C. Univ. Mag.,* IV (1855), 407–13, 461–67; V (1856), 126–31, 205–08; *Capt. Otway Burns* (1905), ed. by W. F. Burns; S. A. Ashe, *Biog. Hist. of N. C.,* I (1905), 200–02; John H. Wheeler's *Reminiscences* (1884), pp. 102–03; Edgar Stanton Maclay, "The Exploits of Otway Burns, Privateersman and Statesman," in *U. S. Naval Inst. Proc.,* May–June, 1916; private information.]

F. M—n.

BURNSIDE, AMBROSE EVERETT (May 23, 1824–Sept. 13, 1881), Union soldier, was born at Liberty, Ind., the son of Edghill and Pamelia (Brown) Burnside. His great-grandfather, Robert Burnside, came from Scotland to South Carolina about 1750; some of the later generations settled in Kentucky but his branch went to Indiana. Until the age of eighteen he was educated in the seminary at Liberty whose principal was a ripe scholar and born teacher, where he received an education that prepared him well for college work. At this time, however, his father was unable to give him further assistance as he was in moderate circumstances with a large family. Young Burnside was therefore apprenticed to a tailor and a year later with a partner opened a shop in Liberty. Shortly thereafter his father became a member of the state Senate of Indiana and through friends secured for his son an appointment to the United States Military Academy, which he entered July 1, 1843, and from which he graduated four years later, entering the army as a lieutenant of artillery. He joined his battery in Mexico but was too late to see much active service. On Apr. 27, 1852, he was married to Mary Richmond Bishop of Providence, R. I. Before he resigned his commission in October 1853 he had served on the frontier and in garrison.

While in the army he invented a breech-loading rifle and he resigned to engage in its manufacture. His last post was Fort Adams, R. I., and at Bristol, R. I., he formed a company to manufacture his new arm. He had counted on the support of the government in his new venture, but in this he was disappointed, and in 1857 he was obliged to turn over his works to his creditors and begin life anew. During these years, however, due to his pleasing personality, genial manners, and the interest he showed in local military organizations, he made many friends, was appointed major-general of the state militia, and was nominated for Congress on the Democratic ticket. Gen. McClellan, who was then connected with the Illinois Central Railroad, secured for him a position in its land department, and he was later made treasurer of the company.

In April 1861, at the request of the governor, he organized the 1st Rhode Island Regiment and became its colonel; it was among the first regiments to reach Washington. The promptness with which Burnside had responded to the call, his imposing person, pleasing manners, and the fine condition of his regiment made for him a strong friend in President Lincoln who often visited his camp. In the Bull Run campaign he commanded the brigade which opened that battle. On Aug. 6, 1861, he was commissioned brigadier-general of volunteers, and that autumn was engaged in organizing at Annapolis, Md., a division of New England troops for coastal operations. In January 1862 this force, with a fleet under the command of Flag Officer Goldsborough, sailed from Hampton Roads to Hatteras Inlet on the coast of North Carolina to secure a base of operations and destroy a small Confederate fleet in Albemarle and Pamlico Sounds. The expedition was eminently successful. Roanoke Island, which had been fortified to prevent entrance into Albemarle Sound, was captured in February with 2,600 prisoners and thirty-two guns. In March the Confederates were driven from their lines covering New Bern and that town occupied. Beaufort was next seized and Fort Macon, a permanent fortress on the coast, was besieged and taken in April. In the meantime the Confederate fleet was captured and destroyed by the naval vessels. This completed the program of the expedition. Although one of the minor operations of the war, it excited great interest at the time. Burnside was commissioned major-general on Mar. 18, and received a sword from Rhode Island and the thanks of the legislatures of Massachusetts and Ohio.

In July it was decided to withdraw some troops from both North and South Carolina and send them under Burnside to reinforce the Army of the Potomac. At this time he was offered the command of that army and declined. When it was decided to withdraw the army from the vicinity of Richmond, Burnside's troops were sent to Pope, but as Burnside ranked Pope they went under the command of Reno. Before the opening of the Antietam campaign Burnside was again offered the command of the Army of the Potomac but again declined.

In the Antietam campaign he was assigned to the command of the right wing, consisting of the 1st Corps under Hooker and his own 9th Corps. His command was in advance and was charged with the attack on the Confederate position on South Mountain where Lee planned to check the advance of the main Union column. This position was carried by the 1st and 9th Corps on Sept. 14, 1862, and the Confederates retired across Antietam Creek. In the advance from South Mountain, Hooker's corps was temporarily detached from Burnside's command and at Antietam was engaged on the extreme right while the 9th Corps was on the extreme left. Burnside accompanied the latter but refused to assume command as he still considered himself the commander of a unit composed of two corps. This militated against proper preparation for the coming battle. The 9th Corps reached its position in the line on the night of Sept. 15, and the following day should have been employed in making a careful reconnaissance of the creek in its front and in the preparation of a plan of attack. This was not done as Burnside did not consider himself in command, the corps staff was absent attending the funeral of Gen. Reno, killed on the preceding day, and the senior division commander remained with his division as he considered Burnside the commander of the corps. McClellan visited Burnside in person that day and assigned the duties to the various divisions, but he relied on Burnside to make the necessary reconnaissances. The consequence was that on the 17th, the day of the battle, much time was lost in attacking the strongest position of the enemy's defense at the Burnside bridge, which might easily have been turned by crossing the stream at a lightly guarded ford a mile below. After the stream was crossed, about 1.00 P. M., the 9th Corps made a spirited attack, but it was too late to have the influence on the course of the battle that McClellan had expected.

After the Confederate Army recrossed the Potomac there was a period of inaction during which the two armies were reorganized and reequipped. Toward the end of October the Army of the Potomac crossed the river and advanced on Warrenton, Va. En route, Burnside received the President's order assigning him to the command of the Army. It was a responsibility which he did not seek, for which he felt himself incompetent, but which he now felt it his duty to accept. When McClellan left the Army on Nov. 10 the situation was as follows: the main body of the Army of the Potomac was in the vicinity of Warrenton with a cavalry screen some ten miles in advance; one corps and part of another were guarding the Potomac against operations from the Shenandoah Valley; the two Confederate corps were widely separated, Longstreet at Culpeper and Jackson in the Shenandoah Valley near Winchester with one division in the mountain pass on the road connecting the two towns. Burnside was not long in deciding on his plan of operations and on Nov. 9 sent it to Gen. Halleck for the consideration of the President. It was to march the army to Fredericksburg where supplies were to meet him, cross the river on ponton bridges, and make a rapid march on Richmond. It was not the plan the President desired; he wanted Burnside to pursue the Confederate army. On Nov. 12 he sent Halleck to Burnside to confer with him. Burnside adhered to his plan and gave practically the same reasons that induced Grant to move on a parallel line from

Culpeper in 1864. On the Fredericksburg-Richmond line it would be easier to supply the army, the lines of supply would be more easily protected, and it was a shorter line. Had the Army of the Potomac been equipped with mobile bridge trains as in 1864, the first phase of the operation, the concentration south of the Rappahannock at Fredericksburg, would have been effected without difficulty, but unfortunately in 1862 the Army was not equipped with such trains. The bridge equipment of the Army was in charge of an engineer brigade with a depot in Washington, and at this time the available boats were in the two bridges over which the army had crossed the Potomac below Harper's Ferry. Burnside knew that McClellan had issued an order on Nov. 6 to have these bridges dismantled and the material taken to Washington where a mobile train was to be organized. On this order he based his plan, but he did not know that the order was delayed in transmission and was not delivered until Nov. 12.

On Nov. 14 Burnside received the following message from Halleck: "The President has just assented to your plan. He thinks it will succeed if you move rapidly, otherwise not." Burnside immediately gave the order to start the movement on the following day, and at the same time had inquiries made of the commander of the engineer brigade as to the status of the ponton train. On Nov. 15 he learned that the last of the boats would reach Washington that day but that it would be several days before the train could start.

Burnside was now confronted with the choice of adhering to his original plan and waiting for the pontons or of crossing the river above Fredericksburg by fords as Halleck had recommended to him. On Nov. 17 Sumner's grand division of two corps reached the north bank of the Rappahannock and finding no pontons but the river above still fordable, requested permission to cross over, but Burnside would not consent. Hooker's grand division arrived shortly after, and on Nov. 19 he informed the Secretary of War that the fords were available and also requested permission to cross. Lee was early informed of the movement, and as the Union troops did not cross the river, Longstreet was started for Fredericksburg on Nov. 18, and several days before the pontons arrived, he was in possession of the heights of Fredericksburg. Toward the end of the month Jackson joined him and the armies faced each other across the river.

From this situation there resulted the battle of Fredericksburg in which the Army of the Potomac crossed the river under the protection of its artillery, and on Dec. 13 made a frontal attack on the Confederates in their well-chosen position, and was repulsed with heavy loss. On Dec. 15 the Army was withdrawn across the river. To silence the rumors that he had been directed from Washington to make this attack, Burnside on Dec. 17 in a manly letter to Halleck assumed the entire responsibility: "The fact that I decided to move from Warrenton on this line, rather against the opinion of the President, Secretary of War, and yourself, and that you left the whole movement in my hands, without giving me orders, makes me responsible."

In the latter part of the month Burnside decided to make an attempt to cross the river at the fords above Fredericksburg, but in a letter to the President said that none of his grand division commanders approved his plan. In his discouragement he wrote, "It is my belief that I ought to retire to private life." After an interview with the President he wrote him that he had decided to carry out the plan, and inclosed the resignation of his commission to relieve the President of embarrassment should he not approve. The President approved the plan and wrote that he could not yet see any advantage in a change of commanders of the army and in any case would not accept his resignation. The movement was begun in the latter part of January but had to be abandoned because of unfavorable weather. Burnside was opposed in his plans by Gen. Hooker and others. He decided that he must have a clear field if he retained the command so he prepared General Order No. 8, Jan. 23, 1863, in which he dismissed from the United States Army Gen. Hooker, Gen. Brooks and Gen. Newton, while two other major-generals, two brigadier-generals and a lieutenant-colonel were relieved from their duties and ordered to report to the adjutant-general at Washington. Burnside went to Washington and asked Lincoln either to sanction the order or to relieve him of the command. Lincoln relieved him and gave the command to Gen. Hooker. Order No. 8 was never officially issued (*Official Records (Army)*, 1 ser., XXI, 998).

In March 1863 Burnside was assigned to the command of the Department of the Ohio which included the states of Ohio, Indiana, Illinois, Michigan, and Kentucky. It was Lincoln's great desire to send military protection to the loyal inhabitants of East Tennessee and he now proposed to reinforce the troops in Kentucky by the 9th Corps so that Burnside could advance on Knoxville when Rosecrans moved on Chattanooga. On taking command of his department, Burnside learned that military operations had been greatly hampered by disloyal persons within the lines who gave information and aid to the enemy. To break up these practises he issued his General Order No. 38 in which after giving a list of the acts considered treasonable, he said, "The habit of declaring sympathies for the enemy will no longer be tolerated in this department. Persons committing such offenses will be at once arrested with a view to being tried as above stated or sent beyond our lines into the lines of their friends." The most noted case that came under this order was that of Clement L. Vallandigham who had been a member of Congress from Ohio from May 1858 to March 1863 and had made himself conspicuous in that body by his attacks on the government from the beginning of the war. On May 1, 1863, at Mount Vernon, Ohio, he made a speech in which he characterized Lincoln as a tyrant and reminded his hearers that "resistance to tyrants is obedience to God." This speech the loyalty of Burnside for the President could not tolerate: Vallandigham was promptly arrested and when his appeal to the United States courts for a writ of *habeas corpus* was denied, he was tried by a military commission for "declaring disloyal sentiments and opinions with the object and purpose of weakening the power of the government in its efforts to suppress unlawful rebellion." The commission found him guilty and sentenced him to be imprisoned until the close of the war, but the sentence was commuted by the President who directed that Vallandigham be sent to Gen. Rosecrans to be passed through the lines to the Confederate Army in his front. Under this same General Order No. 38, on June 1, 1863, by Order No. 84, Burnside suppressed the *Chicago Times* and forbade the circulation of the *New York World* in his department. By the President's direction this Order No. 84 was soon revoked.

The advance into East Tennessee was delayed by various causes until the middle of August when Rosecrans maneuvered Bragg out of Chattanooga and Burnside advanced on Knoxville, which he entered on Sept. 2; at Cumberland Gap on Sept. 9 he received the surrender of the main Confederate force left in East Tennessee. On the following day he was informed by Rosecrans that Bragg was in full retreat, and he immediately wrote the President that as the rebellion seemed pretty well checked he would like to resign his commission. The President, however, did not think it advisable to permit his resignation at that time.

After the battle of Chickamauga, Sept. 19–20, Bragg invested Chattanooga, held by Rosecrans, and early in November when Union reinforcements had reached there and Bragg gave up hope of capturing it, he decided to send Longstreet's veteran corps of the Army of Northern Virginia reinforced by a large body of cavalry to capture Burnside. Such a movement had been expected by the latter and he called up all his available forces from Kentucky and fortified Knoxville to withstand a siege. When Longstreet made his appearance in his front about the middle of November, Burnside had the option of abandoning the Tennessee Valley or of retreating to Knoxville. He decided on the latter as he would thus, by drawing Longstreet so far north that he would be unable to return to take part in the battle, assist Gen. Grant who was preparing to attack Bragg as soon as sufficient troops had arrived. Burnside withdrew his troops to Knoxville in what Longstreet called a very cleverly conducted retreat, and there awaited the assault. The position was so strong that for ten days Longstreet could not make up his mind where to attack. In the meantime Grant had defeated Bragg in the battle of Chattanooga, Nov. 24–25, and the latter was retreating. Immediately after the battle Sherman was directed to march to the relief of Knoxville and was en route when Longstreet made his assault on Nov. 29 and was repulsed. On Dec. 4, on the approach of Sherman, Longstreet raised the siege and moved eastward. Shortly thereafter Burnside turned over his command to his successor who had been appointed Nov. 16 but was unable to reach Knoxville until after the siege.

In preparation for the operations of 1864 it was decided to bring the 9th Corps back to the East and recruit it to full strength. This was work which it was felt could be best done by Burnside, and in January he was assigned to its command and the corps was reorganized at Annapolis, Md. It now consisted of four divisions, one of which was composed wholly of colored troops. The 9th Corps reinforced the Army of the Potomac as an independent unit under the command of Grant, and as such took part in the battles of the Wilderness and Spottsylvania. After the latter battle, as Burnside consented to serve under his junior, Gen. Meade, it was made a corps of the Army of the Potomac and as such took part in the battle of Cold Harbor and in the operations leading up to the investment of Petersburg. While Burnside was intrenched before Petersburg a mine was driven under the Confederate works in his front, and Grant determined to take advantage of the favorable opportunity to make a strong assault on the enemy's position. The 9th Corps was to take the lead and to be supported by the corps on either side. The task assigned to the 9th Corps was one requiring fresh troops and able leadership. Unfortunately, with the exception of the colored division which had not hitherto been engaged, the corps had no fresh troops, and the commander of the division selected by lot to lead the attack proved hopelessly inefficient. Burnside wanted to employ the colored division to lead but was overruled. The mine was blown up early on the morning of July 30 and produced a crater 150 feet long, 60 wide, and 25 deep, the Confederates abandoning the trenches for a considerable distance on either side. The leading division of the 9th Corps, which was to seize a ridge some 500 yards beyond the crater, got no farther than the crater itself and before other troops arrived the Confederates had recovered from their surprise. The result was that the 9th Corps lost 4,000 in killed, wounded, and prisoners. Meade held Burnside largely responsible and asked Grant for a court martial for him, which the latter refused. Meade then ordered a court of inquiry, which blamed Burnside for the failure. Shortly thereafter Burnside left the army on leave and was not recalled. Toward the close of the war he resigned his commission.

In the years following his active service in the war, because of his experience as a leader and his reputation for integrity, Burnside was elected to important positions in railroad and other corporations. In 1864 he became a director of the Illinois Central Railroad Company; in 1865, president of the Cincinnati & Martinsville Railroad Company; in 1866, president of the Rhode Island Locomotive Works; in 1867, president of the Indianapolis & Vincennes Railroad Company and director of the Narragansett Steamship Company. Although he held some of these offices for years, he was nevertheless elected governor of Rhode Island in 1866 and was reëlected in 1867 and 1868. In 1870 he was abroad on business connected with one of his corporations and while there became a voluntary and trusted medium of communication in the interests of conciliation between the French and Germans then at war. In 1874 he was elected United States senator from Rhode Island and served as such from March 1875 until his death which occurred at Bristol, R. I., Sept. 13, 1881.

[B. P. Poore, *The Life and Public Services of Ambrose E. Burnside* (1882); Augustus Woodbury, *Maj.-Gen. Ambrose E. Burnside and the Ninth Army Corps* (1867); G. W. Cullum, *Biog. Reg.* (3rd ed., 1891); *Personal Memoirs of U. S. Grant* (1885–86); Jas. Longstreet, *From Manassas to Appomattox* (1896); *Battles and Leaders of the Civil War* (1887–88); *Senate Report No. 108*, 37 Cong., 3 Sess. and *Senate Report No. 142*, 38 Cong., 2 Sess. (covering congressional investigations of the battles of Fredericksburg and Petersburg).]   G. J. F.

BURR, AARON (Jan. 4, 1715/16–Sept. 24, 1757), Presbyterian clergyman, college president, son of Daniel and Elizabeth Burr, was the descendant of a family distinguished in the early history of the American colonies and the father of a son who was to be even more famous in their later history—Col. Aaron Burr [*q.v.*]. His great-grandfather, Jehu Burr, had come from England with Winthrop's fleet in 1630 and had assisted William Pynchon in the founding of Springfield, Mass., settling eventually in Fairfield, Conn. His grandfather, Jehu the younger, had been one of the Proprietors under the Fairfield Patent of 1685, a deputy to the General Court, a lieutenant in the Fairfield train-band, and a member of the Standing Council. His father was, at the time of Aaron's birth, a wealthy landholder in Fairfield. From his earliest childhood Aaron displayed an extraordinary quickness of intellect and a strong inclination for learning. He was graduated from Yale College with highest honors at the age of nineteen, and, being particularly proficient in Latin and Greek, won a Berkeley scholarship for advanced work in the classics. During this period of graduate study he underwent a marked religious experience which turned him to theological study, and in 1736 he was licensed to preach. After short pastorates at Greenfield, Mass., and at Hanover, N. J., he was called on Dec. 21, 1736, to the First Church of Newark, N. J. Here he engaged in extensive religious revivals and started his career as educator, very early in his pastorate gathering in his parsonage a class of eight or ten pupils for the study of English and the classical languages. Soon he became identified with a movement to establish a college in the Middle Colonies to rank with Harvard and Yale in New England and William and Mary in Virginia, and he was named one of the seven trustees of the College of New Jersey (later Princeton University) in its first charter which passed the seal of the Province on Oct. 22, 1746. The college was opened May 1747, at Elizabethtown (now Elizabeth), N. J., in the parsonage of Jonathan Dickinson, its first president. Less than six months later Dickinson died, and Burr became acting president. He was formally elected the second president of the college on Nov. 9, 1748, and the college was moved to his parsonage in Newark.

Burr paused in his labors long enough to marry, on June 29, 1752, Esther Edwards, daughter of Jonathan Edwards [*q.v.*]. He was thirty-six at the time of his marriage, his bride only twenty-one. Meantime he had made of the College of New Jersey a reality. He drew up its first entrance requirements, its first course of study, its first code of rules for internal government; he created its first treasury and supervised the erection of its first building in the Borough of Princeton where the college was to find a more adequate and permanent home. On the completion of Nassau Hall in the autumn of 1756, he and seventy students moved to Princeton. Here he set himself to the task of organizing the college life under its new and improved conditions. But the new building required funds for upkeep and money was needed for the instruction of a growing student body, so Burr was obliged to make frequent trips through the Colonies in an effort to interest the wealthy in his college. Returning from an arduous journey through New England in August of 1757, he learned that Gov. Belcher, his close friend and ally, and patron and benefactor of the college, had died. He spent nearly the whole of a night preparing a funeral sermon and the next morning, nearly delirious with fever, traveled to Elizabeth where he presided at the Governor's funeral. Less than a month later, on Sept. 24, 1757, he died and was buried in the Princeton Cemetery.

[There are biographical sketches in Wm. A. Packard, *The Princeton Book* (1879) and Chas. Burr Todd, *A Gen. Hist. of the Burr Family* (4th ed., 1902). Other sources are: F. B. Dexter, *Biog. Sketches Grads. Yale Coll.*, ser. I (1885); John Frelinghuysen Hageman, *Hist. of Princeton and its Institutions* (1879); John De Witt, "Hist. Sketch of Princeton Univ." in the *Memorial Book of the Sesquicentennial Celebration of the Founding of the Coll. of N. J. and of the Ceremonies Inaugurating Princeton Univ.* (1898); Varnum Lansing Collins, *Princeton* (1914); and Caleb Smith, *Diligence in the Work of God, and Activity During Life, A Sermon Occasioned by the Much-Lamented Death of the Rev. Mr. Aaron Burr* (1758).] A. L.

BURR, AARON (Feb. 6, 1756–Sept. 14, 1836), Revolutionary soldier, lawyer, United States senator, and third vice-president of the United States, came of an ancestry remarkable as well for its ecclesiastical eminence as for its intellectual vigor. His father was Aaron Burr [*q.v.*], scholar, theologian, and second president of the College of New Jersey; his mother was Esther Edwards, daughter of Jonathan Edwards [*q.v.*], the greatest of the New England divines. Burr and his sister Sarah, or "Sally," were born at Newark, N. J., where for some years the elder Burr had acted as pastor of the First Presbyterian Church. Shortly after the birth of his son, however, he moved to Princeton, where he died in September 1757. After the death of Burr's mother and of her parents within a few months, a maternal uncle, Timothy Edwards, became guardian of the children, essaying to rear them in the family tradition. Tapping Reeve, who subsequently became judge of the supreme court

of Connecticut, and a famous preceptor in law, served for a time as their tutor and later married Sally Burr (Davis, *post,* I, 25, 26).

From all accounts Burr was an attractive boy, fair of face, sprightly and merry, but not readily submissive to the discipline of his austere uncle. There was always in him a certain independence and audacity of spirit that carried him over or around artificial barriers. Yet he could apply himself to the task that engaged his interest. He prepared for college as a matter of course, ambition here coinciding with the wishes of his family; and he entered the sophomore class of the College of New Jersey at the age of thirteen. Tradition has it that he was a brilliant student but dissipated. Brilliant he was in whatever enlisted his interest, but Parton doubts that he was guilty of serious dereliction in these early years, arguing that part of his dissipation in college was "merely a dissipation of mind in multifarious reading." Be this as it may, Burr graduated with distinction at the age of sixteen. He is described as a youth of winning presence, rather short in stature but graceful in manner, who made friends easily among both sexes. A fondness for adventure and intrigue, however, gave a certain instability to his character, and a degree of waywardness to his life. He hesitated for a time over the choice of a career. During his college course a revival that had stirred many of his mates had awakened his curiosity and led him to consult the president of the college. That conservative mentor, John Witherspoon [*q.v.*], expressed disbelief in revivals, and thus reassured, Burr did not yield to the zealous expostulations of his fellows. Some months later, however, motivated by curiosity fully as much as by a pious desire to follow in the footsteps of his fathers, he entered upon the study of theology. But his curiosity was too much for his teacher, and in 1774 he left theology for law.

Less than a year later, the clash at Lexington summoned him to arms. After a few weeks with the motley host that beleaguered Boston, he joined the expedition against Quebec. On the difficult march thither, in the unsuccessful attack on the city (during which he is credited with an attempt to rescue the body of the commander, Montgomery), and during the gloomy winter that followed, he showed marked soldierly qualities. In the spring of 1776, having served Arnold as staff officer with the rank of captain, he was sent to New York. Here he served with the rank of major in the official household of Gen. Washington, but Burr's want of regard for military decorum, and perhaps occasional impertinence, antagonized his chief, and the intimacy of a few weeks led only to mutual dislike and distrust. Transferred to the staff of Gen. Putnam, Burr gave a good account of himself in the battle of Long Island and in the evacuation of New York—and had time to indulge in one of his numerous amatory intrigues. In July 1777 he was appointed lieutenant-colonel in the Continental line and assigned to a regiment stationed in Orange County, N. Y., and as its virtual commander established a commendable reputation for discipline and daring.

Throughout his life Burr displayed an unfortunate tendency to follow impulses which were prompted by personal likes or dislikes, as, for example, at Valley Forge where he narrowly missed inclusion in the notorious "Conway Cabal," and again at Monmouth where he suffered a repulse -a misfortune that led him to sympathize openly with Gen. Charles Lee. Following Monmouth, he spent the winter on patrol duty with his regiment in Westchester County, N. Y., where he maintained his reputation for vigilance and discipline. The hardships of this service, plus the exertions of the previous summer's campaign, eventually forced him to resign from the army in March 1779 (*Ibid.*, I, ch. V–XI).

He desired to enter upon professional training at once, but ill health forced a long wait. In the fall of 1780 he took up the study of law at Raritan, N. J., with William Paterson, an older friend of college days, but later transferred to an office in Haverstraw, N. Y. By means of this transfer and through the favor of Judge Robert Yates, of the state supreme court, he hastened his training and early in 1782 was licensed as attorney and counselor-at-law. In preparing for a profession Burr, as usual, had preferred to follow his own bent and was not averse to short cuts (Parton, *post*, 130–34).

In July 1782, he married Mrs. Theodosia (Bartow) Prevost, some ten years his senior, the widow of a former British officer. Though possessed of little fortune and of no great beauty, she was a woman of charm and intellectual vigor, and despite the disparity in their ages, her invalidism, and his exacting temperament, their twelve years of married life were apparently stimulating to both. Burr has been charged with more than one intrigue before his marriage and with many more after his wife's death, but he seems to have been true to her, if not as passionately devoted to her as she was to him, and he was an affectionate and zealous parent to their one daughter, Theodosia [*q.v.*]. His circle of stimulating regard included his stepsons, Frederick and Bartow Prevost, and numerous protégés, who, like his daughter, were always his devoted admirers.

In the fall of 1783 Burr moved to New York. Here he soon shared with Alexander Hamilton the pick of legal practise and for six years stuck closely to the law. In pleading he was noted for clarity and conciseness of utterance. He never ranted nor lost his temper, but as a contemporary noted, "He is more remarkable for dexterity than sound judgment or logic." Burr's practise brought him a substantial income which he tried to increase by extensive speculations. Generosity as well as self-indulgence made an incurable spendthrift of him. His carelessness in money matters was often a cause of grief to clients as well as to friends.

Burr's attempts to enter politics during his early residence in New York were uniformly unsuccessful. His professional rival, Hamilton, was the leader of one group, and Gov. George Clinton, who headed the opposing forces, at first made no bid for his support. But in September 1789 Clinton made him his attorney-general. From that office, after participating in a questionable deal in state lands, he was transferred, in 1791, to the United States Senate. He owed his elevation to his own finesse in fusing the Clinton and Livingston factions in opposition to the financial plans of Hamilton. The coalition defeated the latter's father-in-law, Gen. Philip Schuyler, and thereby gained for Burr Hamilton's persistent enmity.

During his term as senator (1791–97) Burr was twice mentioned for the governorship and in 1797 received thirty electoral votes for president. He took his membership seriously, applied himself to routine tasks, did nothing unseemly, and accomplished nothing of great repute. He attracted public attention and gained some worthwhile friends, including Gallatin and Jackson, but was not really accepted by either of the major party groups then being formed. He was defeated for reëlection to the Senate but in April 1797 was elected to the state Assembly. Here he introduced a measure to choose presidential electors by separate districts and was influential in the passage of a bill to aid the Holland Land Company in which he himself had a financial interest (Paul D. Evans, *The Holland Land Company*, 1924, pp. 180, 212–13). These measures, coupled with efforts in obtaining a charter for the Manhattan Company, a banking corporation disguised as a water company, led to his defeat in April 1799.

For some years past Burr had been gathering about himself a band of enthusiastic young helpers, who by letter urged their leader's claims to high office and directed operations at "Martling's Long Room," where met St. Tammany's Society. Burr did not openly affiliate with the mechanics and small householders who largely made up this organization but through henchmen kept informed of their activities and around them built up his political machine. With this, he proposed to make himself a power in local politics and force Jefferson and his associates to recognize his leadership. He first secured his election to the state assembly from Orange County and then in New York City brought about the selection of a strong legislative ticket headed by Clinton, Brockholst Livingston, and his own friend, Gen. Horatio Gates. With this coalition ticket and using the "Martling Men" as a nucleus, he definitely listed and organized the voters of the city and in April 1800 roundly defeated Hamilton. The city returned a Republican delegation which gave that party control of the legislature by a narrow majority, and thus assured it the entire vote of New York in the electoral college. Then through a clever by-play, Burr procured his own indorsement for vice-president (*American Historical Review*, VIII, 512) and later journeyed to Philadelphia and secured from the Republican members of Congress a pledge to support him equally with Jefferson.

Owing to this agreement Burr tied with Jefferson for the presidency, each receiving seventy-three votes. The Federalists, who controlled a slight majority in the House of Representatives, determined to vote for him rather than Jefferson. Burr at once disclaimed competition for the office and his letter to that effect was published (Davis, II, 75). He also wrote a vigorous disclaimer to one of the Virginia group (Burr to John Taylor, Dec. 18, 1800, manuscript in the Pennsylvania Historical Society). Later he kept quiet, in part, perhaps, because he learned that his local party associates were preparing to repudiate him and that Jefferson favored them rather than himself in the prospective division of patronage (P. L. Ford, ed., *Writings of Thomas Jefferson*, VIII, 102). He issued no more disclaimers, but apparently repelled all direct attempts of the Federalists to bargain with him. "Had Burr done anything for himself," wrote one of them in the midst of the balloting to break the tie, "he would long ere this have been president" (Davis, II, 113), and that, too, we may add, despite the bitter secret opposition of Hamilton. But he did nothing and on the thirty-sixth ballot the Federalists permitted the election of his rival. The share of patronage accorded to him was not wholly satisfactory

but he helped in the reëlection of Gov. Clinton and presided over the convention that in 1801 amended the state constitution. He alienated both Republicans and Federalists by his vote when the Senate was evenly divided over the Judiciary Act and further antagonized the Republicans by taking part in the Federalist celebration of Washington's birthday. He was also attacked for suppressing a lengthy scurrilous pamphlet against the administration of John Adams. From this the editors who directed it passed to the more serious charge that Burr had intrigued with the Federalists to supplant Jefferson. Then followed two years of unstinted newspaper abuse. A pamphlet by Van Ness in rejoinder gave the presidential group a pretext for finding another running mate. Accordingly, at the party caucus on Feb. 25, 1804 George Clinton replaced Burr on the Republican ticket.

Burr's friends in the New York legislature had already nominated him on Feb. 18 for the governorship. In this contest there was some prospect of receiving Federalist aid through those New England leaders who were looking forward to a Northern confederacy. Burr refused to commit himself to their disunion schemes, but in spite of his attitude and Hamilton's renewed opposition, the rank and file of the Federalists voted for him and helped him carry the city and some outlying counties. Nevertheless, the regular Republican candidate, Morgan Lewis, supported by the Clinton and Livingston factions and countenanced by Jefferson and Hamilton, defeated him by a heavy majority.

Following this contest came the fatal duel with Hamilton. For fifteen years in contests for the Senate, the presidency, and the governorship the latter had filled his private correspondence with invective against Burr's public and private character. Their personal relations during all this time had generally been friendly. Now Burr regarded himself for the third time as the peculiar victim of Hamilton's malevolence. "These things," he significantly stated in the correspondence that preceded the fatal encounter, "must have an end." In the course of the campaign there had been published three compromising letters in which Hamilton was represented as stating publicly that Burr was a "dangerous man and one who ought not to be trusted with the reins of government." This ill-considered remark ended with reference to a "still more despicable opinion which Gen. Hamilton had expressed of Mr. Burr" (Wandell and Minnegerode, I, 274). These statements provoked Burr's challenge. They must be interpreted in connection with Hamilton's long-continued secret abuse, which the other had certainly not repaid in kind. The correspondence that preceded the duel favors Burr. His demands were peremptory, and Hamilton's replies were evasive. As the latter was unwilling to repudiate his previous harsh judgments, he reluctantly accepted the challenge (Davis, II, ch. XXI). In addition to settling past grievances, however, Burr may have wished to forestall further unwelcome rivalry, either in a possible Northern confederacy or on the Southwestern border. The latter was the more probable field, for both Burr and Hamilton cherished the ambition to lead an army thither in an effort to free the Spanish colonies. Viewed in this light the duel with Hamilton may be regarded as the opening move in the "Conspiracy," as well as the lurid finale to Burr's local political career. The meeting itself took place on the morning of July 11, 1804, at Weehawken, N. J., a circumstance that permitted two states to bring indictments against the survivor. Each man fired a single shot; Hamilton fell mortally wounded and died the next day. Burr fled, first to Philadelphia and thence southward, while his enemies took revenge on his heavily encumbered property and reputation.

Burr's journey was not an aimless one. Both before and after the duel he had conferred with Gen. James Wilkinson [q.v.], a friend of long standing who had just come northward from New Orleans. The two had evidently agreed upon a plan of action in case war should break out with Spain. As a preliminary step Burr was to visit East Florida; but much to the relief of his prospective hosts, a series of destructive tempests prevented him from reaching his destination (East Florida Papers, Casa Yrujo to Enrique White, Aug. 12; Burr to White, Sept. 22, 1804). Apparently he saw enough to convince him that the way to Mexico did not lie in that direction. Before leaving Philadelphia he had requested the British minister, Anthony Merry, to aid financially and otherwise in bringing about the separation of the Western states from the Union. This proposal was distinctly treasonable, but Burr probably never seriously intended to carry it out. Wilkinson may have told him how successfully he had used the lure of separatism with the Spaniards and had suggested that Burr approach Merry with a similar proposal. Merry readily listened to the project, which was broached to him through an intermediary, but his superiors refused to countenance it (H. Adams, II, 395).

At the next session of Congress, 1804–05, it fell to Burr's lot to preside over the impeachment of Justice Samuel Chase of the Supreme Court. Because Jefferson was anxious to have the latter removed, the administration leaders showed the retiring vice-president unusual attention and gave two of his family connections and his friend Wilkinson lucrative territorial appointments (Beveridge, *Marshall*, II, 182). Nevertheless Burr conducted the trial "with the dignity and impartiality of an archangel, but with the rigor of a devil," and at the end his most bitter critics commended his rulings and also gave him a general vote of appreciation for the "impartiality, dignity and ability with which he had presided over their deliberations" (Plumer, 312; Adams, *Memoirs*, I, 365; *Annals of Congress*, 8 Cong., 2 Sess., col. 72). This vote followed his valedictory address to the Senate on Mar. 2, a remarkable address that moved some of the senators to tears.

During this winter in Washington, Wilkinson and Burr frequently conferred over maps of the Floridas, Louisiana, and adjacent regions. Their purpose may be inferred from a letter of John Adair to the former, which ends thus: "Mexico glitters in our Eyes—the word is all we wait for" (Julius W. Pratt, *Expansionists of 1812*, 1925, p. 62). Burr accordingly planned to journey westward with Wilkinson when the other went to take over his new post in St. Louis. But other projects besides the invasion of Mexico occupied Burr's attention. There was the possibility of being returned to Congress from one of the western districts, or of obtaining a territorial appointment. Moreover he and a number of his friends were concerned in a dubious project to construct a canal around the falls of the Ohio. Inspired by these various possibilities Burr left Washington in the middle of March 1805 on his westward journey. His first stop was at Philadelphia, where he brought his separatist project once more to Merry's attention, reinforced it with reference to discontent among the French Creoles of Louisiana, and definitely asked for a half million loan and the use of a British fleet at the mouth of the Mississippi. Merry could only transmit these proposals to his government.

In this westward journey Burr touched all the important river towns of the Mississippi Valley from Pittsburgh to New Orleans and coursed over the connecting trails. He everywhere received marked public attentions while his movements continually provoked surmise and inquiry. In the Creole capital his faith in the invasion of Mexico was confirmed by the so-called "Mexican Association"—a loose aggregation of persons that vaguely planned to make that country independent. Press reports spoke of his appointment as governor of Orleans in place of W. C. C. Claiborne and mentioned other projects of pecuniary or political character. But if his journey had any purpose aside from putting himself in touch with those who would be helpful in case of war with Spain, it was apparently a failure. He had aroused in many quarters an unfortunate suspicion as to his own motives and loyalty, which the Spanish minister, Casa Yrujo, fully cognizant of his proposals to Merry, took care to disseminate widely.

Burr passed the following winter and spring in the East. He tried to interest Jefferson in giving him a diplomatic appointment but the President told him that the country had lost confidence in him. Then he sought to persuade either the British or the Spanish minister, or both, to finance his inchoate western plans. When Merry could report no response from his superiors, the conspirators—for Ex-Senator Jonathan Dayton [q.v.] of New Jersey was now actively associated with Burr—approached Casa Yrujo for ready funds and future pensions. The attempt to persuade Spain to finance an expedition that might be aimed at her own colonies came to nothing (McCaleb, ch. III).

Early in 1806 Burr asked a dissatisfied and idle friend, Commodore Thomas Truxtun [q.v.], to command a phantom naval contingent. Truxtun later testified that Burr's statements to him were wholly concerned with Mexico, but when he learned that the government was not immediately behind the undertaking he refused to entertain Burr's offer (Pickering Papers, January and February 1807). Far different was the testimony of William Eaton [q.v.], an adventurer then also unemployed, who had both a claim and a grudge against the administration. He later testified—when assured that his claim would be paid—that Burr mentioned in addition to the above invasion, a hare-brained plot to seize the president and cabinet and establish himself as dictator in Washington, or, failing in this, to loot bank and arsenal, seize vessels in the navy yard, and sail for New Orleans, where the independence of the West was to be proclaimed. Burr occasionally gave evidence of mental aberration, but uttered nothing like this drivel.

Unable to get money elsewhere, Burr next approached his friends and family connections. His plan was to take over a part interest in the Bastrop grant, lying on the Washita River, and convey thither young men who might serve as settlers in peace and soldiers in war. To this plan his supporters in New York, his son-in-law, and friends in Kentucky ultimately contributed the modest sums with which he contracted for the building of boats, the gathering of provisions, and for making the first payment on the contract.

Burr and his associates had hoped that the administration would be forced into a war with Spain. When instead it resorted to diplomacy under the "Two Million Act"—an appropriation for the purchase of the Floridas—and when the death of the younger Pitt early in 1806 removed all hope of aid from England, they fell back upon the prospect of hostilities being provoked along the border. Dayton tried to stimulate Wilkinson to precipitate a clash, by warning him that he was to be supplanted in the army, and Burr sent a longer cipher letter to the same effect (Adams, III, 252–55; McCaleb, 73–75).

In the first week in August 1806, Burr again started westward. The simultaneous advance of the Spaniards east of the Sabine seemed to promise a belated chance to realize his dream of conquest, but rumors of the last twelve months had done their work and suspicion everywhere greeted him. Alarming reports of his movements began to rain in on Washington. Harman Blennerhassett [q.v.], a wealthy expatriated Irishman living near Marietta, helped Burr finance the Bastrop speculation, provided for gathering and transporting settlers thither, and also contributed to a local paper a series of articles which frankly discussed the probability of a separation of the Western states from the Union. The cause now became publicly associated with Western separatism and on this basis Burr was twice arraigned before a federal grand jury in Kentucky. Thanks in part to his own frank bearing, he was triumphantly cleared on both occasions. Nevertheless the reiterated charges were now working out their natural result. Jefferson and his advisers were finally convinced that something serious was afoot and late in October had sent an observer on Burr's trail; and on Nov. 27, after receiving alarming communications from Wilkinson, who had made a border settlement with the Spaniards and was preparing to betray Burr, the President issued a proclamation, announcing that a group was illegally plotting an expedition against Spain and warning all citizens not to participate.

Following the two arraignments in Kentucky, Burr went to Nashville and then late in December to the mouth of the Cumberland, where his followers joined him. Hostile manifestations had driven these presumptive settlers from the rendezvous at Blennerhassett Island. With the opening of the new year Burr with his modest array of nine boats and some sixty men recruited at the various stopping points, was on the Mississippi, totally ignorant of the hostile reception that his whilom friend and confederate Wilkinson was preparing for him. That general was now in New Orleans, intriguing to apprehend Burr and his Washita colonists and to send the former eastward as a tangible exhibit of his charges. Burr first learned of this meditated treachery, when on Jan. 10, 1807, he reached the settlements in Mississippi Territory. He immediately submitted to the authorities, was indicted before another federal jury, and was again triumphantly acquitted. This fiasco added to Burr's popularity, but the judge refused to release him from bond. Burr suspected with only too much truth, that Wilkinson was planning to kidnap him and bring him before a pretended court martial, and, after vain attempts to change the court decision, he fled toward Mobile. When within a few miles of the border, he was detected, apprehended, and within a few days was being escorted back to the region he had shortly before renounced forever.

On Mar. 30, 1807, Burr was brought before Chief Justice Marshall in the United States Circuit Court of the district of Virginia for a preliminary examination. After three days of discussion by counsel and deliberation by the court, he was held for a misdemeanor in organizing an expedition against Spanish territory. The question of treason was left for a grand jury to determine, and it proved difficult to select that tribunal. The panel finally obtained consisted of fourteen Republicans and two Federalists headed by John Randolph as foreman. The trial formally began on May 22, 1807. Burr was present with an array of distinguished counsel, and was faced by others, able but distinctly inferior to his own. The audience was generally hostile to the prisoner. The rulings of the court and the influence of the President—unseen but distinctly felt through his constant communication with the district attorney—determined that the proceedings should take on a political character. These were delayed at first by the absence of Wilkinson. Finally, after the General reached Richmond and gave his testimony—upon which he himself narrowly escaped indictment—the grand jury established a charge of treason against Burr. This was based largely upon a mistaken interpretation of Marshall's previous ruling in the hearing of J. Erich Bollman and Samuel Swartwout [qq.v.], Burr's luckless messengers to Wilkinson, who by falling into the General's hands had experienced something of the treatment he had reserved for Burr. The outcome of the trial depended largely upon the article of the Constitution defining treason. Marshall ruled

that "levying war" as there mentioned could only be established by an overt act in which the accused actually participated. The assemblage on Blennerhassett's Island was selected to meet this requirement. It was definitely shown that Burr was not present, nor near enough to affect actual proceedings. The theory of "constructive treason" which would have made him "contributory" to that assemblage and equally guilty with those who were present, was rejected. Hence it was impossible to establish the "overt act" necessary to convict. This failure meant the exclusion of much testimony as to collateral events, which, indeed, was mostly hearsay. The jury, on Sept. 1, basing its decision on the "evidence submitted," acquitted Burr and his associates of treason. Jefferson urged the district attorney to press the charge of misdemeanor against him but upon this charge also the jury decided in his favor. Burr and Blennerhassett, however, were remanded to trial in the district court of Ohio, but the prisoners did not appear within the state nor did the government press the suit further.

Late in October 1807 Burr was free but no less a fugitive. In Baltimore a mob hanged him in effigy along with Blennerhassett, Marshall, and Luther Martin, his chief defender, while he and the faithful Swartwout fled to Philadelphia, where numerous creditors besieged him. In June 1808 he sailed for England, still hopefully pursuing his plan to revolutionize Mexico. In England he became acquainted with many of the leaders of thought and letters—notable among them Jeremy Bentham and William Godwin—but failed, through the interference of the American minister and consuls, to gain official support, and was later ordered to leave, perhaps on the request of the Spanish junta, then allied with England (Parton, p. 535).

He spent several months in Sweden, Denmark, and Germany, and in February 1810 went to Paris, hoping to lay before Napoleon his projects for freeing the Spanish colonies and Louisiana and inciting war between the United States and England which should result in the acquisition of Canada by France. In March he presented to the Ministry of Relations Extérieures, through an affable young deputy, M. Roux, several memoranda embodying his schemes. In one of the wildest of these (Archives Nationales, no. 37, post) he stated that the people of the United States were discontented with their form of government, but that the majority would oppose a change. However, he continued, there is "a third party, superior in talent and in energy; they desire something grand and stable, something which in giving occupation to active spirits will assure the tranquillity of reasonable men. This party has a recognized head; they ask only to follow him and obey him." This head was Burr himself, who, as the ministry evidently inferred (Archives Nationales, no. 36, *post*) "inclines toward monarchy" and was ready to use the 40,-000 sailors that he had represented as idle on account of the embargo, "to overthrow the republican government. The declaration of war against the English would follow this change." Another proposal according to an anonymous report (Dec. 10, 1811, Madison Papers, New York Public Library), was to bring about a reconciliation between England and France, and to use their combined forces against the United States. These proposals reached the chief of the foreign office who forwarded them to the Emperor with the comment that Mr. Burr apparently could initiate nothing except in Florida or Louisiana and that "he could not be employed without giving great offense to the United States" (Archives Nationales, no. 106, *post*). Burr, continuing to call upon M. Roux and trying to obtain the interest of other officials, was constantly met by the statement that there was no reply from the Emperor, and after four or five months he abandoned his effort to be heard. His attention then was given to getting a passport so that he might return to the United States and to Theodosia, but for one whole year his requests were persistently refused, by the French officials and by the American consul and chargé d'affaires. He fell into dire poverty—even pawning one after another the books and "pretty things" he had bought for Theodosia and his grandson—but his buoyant spirit remained unchecked, hopefully considering various expedients to gain ready cash or possibly a fortune. In July 1811 he was at last granted his passport, but the French ship on which he sailed was captured and taken to England, he was detained there, and it was not until \May 1812 that he reached the United States.

He had little difficulty in reëstablishing his legal practise in New York, but before he had been at home two months he received news of the death of his grandson. In December of the same year Theodosia, sailing from Charleston harbor, was lost at sea. For more than a score of years he survived these crushing blows. During the greater part of this period he had a good law practise, but never abandoned his ingrained amatory habits or his carelessness in money matters. He also kept his interest in the Spanish colonies but when asked to take part in their struggle for independence, was unable to accept (Davis, II, 442–45). In July 1833, when he was

seventy-seven, he married the widow of Stephen Jumel [*q.v.*], some twenty years his junior. After four months of domestic wrangling over finances, for Burr threatened to run through her substantial property, his wife brought suit for divorce in July 1834. The decree confirming her request bore the date of his death. The latter occurred at Port Richmond, Staten Island, on Sept. 14, 1836 (Wandell and Minnegerode, II, 323–40). To the bitter experiences of his later years as to the ephemeral successes of his earlier life he had presented the same unruffled serenity that had so often disarmed opponents and captivated followers. Shortly before his death he had again protested that he had never designed the separation of the West from the Union.

[The most important printed sources for Burr are Matthew L. Davis, *Memoirs of Aaron Burr* (2 vols., 1836–37) and *The Private Jour. of Aaron Burr During His Residence of Four Years in Europe* (2 vols., 1838, repr. 1903, from the MS. in library of Wm. K. Bixby of St. Louis, Mo.). The printed works of many of Burr's contemporaries are important, especially those of Jefferson (Ford, ed.), Hamilton, and King. For the trial consult "Reports of the Trials of Col. Aaron Burr," reported by David Robertson (2 vols., 1808) ; *Annals of Cong.*, 9 Cong., 2 Sess., 1008–19, and 10 Cong., 1 Sess., 385–778; and *Am. State Papers Misc.* (1834), I, 468–645. Jas. Wilkinson, *Memoirs of My Own Times* (1816) is necessary but unreliable. For events in Mississippi and Orleans territories the most significant source is Dunbar Rowland (ed.), *Letter Books of Wm. C. C. Claiborne*, vols. I–III (1916). For nearly a score of years contemporary newspapers contained frequent references to Burr's political career, some items of which under the names of Jas. Cheetham and W. P. Van Ness appeared also in pamphlet form. Casual but important references to Burr occur in E. S. Brown (ed.), *Wm. Plumer's Memorandum* (1923), and in C. F. Adams (ed.), *Memoirs of John Quincy Adams*, vol. I (1874). The manuscript sources are also valuable. Of chief importance are the Papers of Jefferson, Madison, and Monroe, in the Lib. of Cong., and the Papers of Harry Innes, vol. XVIII, Papers in Relation to Burr's Conspiracy, and the East Florida Papers, in the same repository. The Papers of Jas. Wilkinson in the Chicago Hist. Soc., the Durrett Papers in the Univ. of Chicago, the Pickering Papers in the Mass. Hist. Soc., and the collections of the Miss. Dept. of Archives and Hist., and of the La. Hist. Soc. are also worthy of attention. For material in Spanish the Bexar Archives in the Univ. of Texas and the general archives in Mexico City, Madrid, and Seville are especially important. Some MSS. relating to Burr were discovered by Dr. Waldo G. Leland in the Archives Nationales: AF iv, 1681 A, Nos. 36–40 and Nos. 106, 107, 110, 114, 115. Among the earlier biographies Jas. Parton, *The Life and Times of Aaron Burr* (1858) is a sympathetic account. The most recent life, S. H. Wandell and Meade Minnegerode, *Aaron Burr* (1925), is a sprightly narrative that is often too favorable to its subject. It is, however, based on much patient and long continued investigation by the first-named author. Isaac Jenkinson, *Aaron Burr, His Personal and Political Relations with Thos. Jefferson and Alex. Hamilton* (1902) is likewise an overly favorable interpretation of some disputed phases of his career. W. F. McCaleb, *The Aaron Burr Conspiracy* (1903) and Henry Adams, *Hist. of the U.S.*, vols. II and III (1889–90), present opposing views of the conspiracy, of which that of the former is the more substantial and convincing. A. J. Beveridge, *The Life of John Marshall* (1916–19), vol. III, ch. VI–IX is the best account of the trial at Richmond. Edward Channing, *Hist. of the U. S.*, vol. IV (1917), is excellent for bibliographic references and John B. McMaster, *Hist. of the People of the U. S.* (1891), vol. III, presents an unfavorable summary of the events of the conspiracy.]

I. J. C.

BURR, ALFRED EDMUND (Mar. 27, 1815–Jan. 8, 1900), editor, was descended from Benjamin Burr, who came to the shores of the Connecticut river from Newtown, Mass., with the earliest settlers in 1636. Alfred's mother, before her marriage Lucretia Olcott, was also a descendant of the first settlers in Connecticut. The eighth of fourteen children of James Burr, Alfred at the age of twelve began to earn his own living at the printer's trade in the office of the *Hartford Courant*. At the age of twenty he was foreman of the composing room and at twenty-four he rejected an offer to become part owner of the paper because it was conditional on his joining the Whig party and attending the Congregational church. Thus early he showed the independence in opinion evident throughout his life of nearly eighty-five years. Accordingly, in 1839 he turned his attention to the *Hartford Weekly Times* established in 1817. The *Weekly Times* had fought for religious toleration under John M. Niles (United States senator 1835–39 and 1842–48, and postmaster-general under President Van Buren). On Jan. 1, 1839, Judge Henry A. Mitchell accepted Burr's offer to buy a half interest in the paper on advice of Gideon Welles, a frequent contributor from 1824 until he became a member of President Lincoln's cabinet. On Jan. 1, 1841, Burr became sole owner, and on Mar. 2 the first issue of the *Daily Times* appeared. From the start Burr took a lively interest in national issues and this led to many antagonisms in the sharp political controversies that raged prior to and during the Civil War. He believed that the war might have been avoided by a spirit of conciliation and adherence to the Constitution. He made the *Daily Times* a steadfast democratic newspaper and vigorously opposed the movement to repeal the Missouri Compromise. His influence in Connecticut was shown by the result of the election in 1860, when 16,493 Democrats voted for Breckinridge whom he had supported, 17,374 for Stephen A. Douglas and 3,291 for Bell. In other New England states the vote for Breckinridge was proportionately much smaller. He did not swerve from his course of opposing the conflict and, in 1864, 42,285 Connecticut voters supported the policy advocated by the *Daily Times* or 48.61 per cent of the total vote. No one at that time or later questioned his motives as other than pure and patriotic. Another example of his independence was afforded in the three campaigns of William Jennings Bryan for the presidency, opposed in each case by the *Daily Times*, which re-

pudiated free silver heresies and stood for sound money. Burr's only elective office was as representative in the Connecticut legislature, two terms, in 1853 and 1866. He stood high in the state and national councils of the Democratic party, however, and was repeatedly a delegate to national conventions. For many years no Democratic platform was adopted in Connecticut which was not wholly or in part prepared by him. He was a pioneer in shaping the Democratic party's tariff-reform policy so that due allowance should be made for the difference between the wages of American and foreign labor. He refused a seat in President Cleveland's cabinet. His leadership in local affairs was indicated by his choice as chairman of the commission that built the state capitol, and by his influence in pushing park projects and in enlarging Hartford's water supply and school facilities. In appearance he was tall and spare, and he often walked from his home to the office carrying his editorial copy in his tall silk hat. In April 1841 he married Sarah A. Booth. His son, Willie Olcott Burr, succeeded his father as editor of the *Daily Times*. The service of the father was sixty-one years, that of the son sixty years, a total given to the *Hartford Daily Times* by both of 121 years, a record probably unequaled in newspapers of the United States.

[Wm. F. Moore, ed., *Representative Men of Conn.* (1894), pp. 30–32; N. G. Osborn, *Men of Mark in Conn.*, I (1906), 265; A. E. Burr, *Founder of the Hartford Daily Times* (1900); *Hartford Daily Times*, Jan. 8, 1900.]

C. L. S.

BURR, ENOCH FITCH (Oct. 21, 1818–May 8, 1907), Congregational minister, the son of Zalmon and Mary (Hanford) Burr, and descended from Jonathan Edwards, was born at Greens Farms, near Westport, Conn. He prepared for college at the local academy and at Wilton, Conn., under Dr. Hawley Olmstead, entering the same class at Yale with Zalmon B., his older brother. He graduated with the distinction of "class orator" in 1839 and continued for a year in the Divinity School, then led by Nathaniel W. Taylor [*q.v.*]. Two further years were spent at the college in scientific study, but failing health kept him for the next three at home. On his mother's death he returned to New Haven and devoted nearly four years to higher mathematics and physical astronomy, his studies resulting in an application of calculus to the theory of Neptune entitled *Results of Analytical Researches in the Neptunian Theory of Uranus* (1848).

Renewed religious interest interrupted the scientific career thus auspiciously begun. Burr had been licensed to preach in 1842. On Oct. 3, 1850, he was ordained pastor of the village church of

Hamburg, Conn., part of the ancient town of Lyme. Ten months later he married Harriet A., daughter of Peter Lord of Lyme. Save for a year of travel abroad in 1855, accompanied by his wife and brother Zalmon, Hamburg remained Burr's home for life.

But his energies sought wider outlet. A theological essay, *Christ the Revealer of God* (1854), was followed (1857–62) by a series of tracts and sermons, and finally, after an interval of five years, by a volume destined to give him wider reputation. *Ecce Coelum, or Parish Astronomy* (1867) met so well the popular demand for science in the service of apologetics as to pass through sixteen or more editions. It also led to his appointment at Amherst from 1868 to 1874 as lecturer on The Scientific Evidences of Religion, with further invitations to lecture in New York and Boston, and at Yale and Williams. Two volumes, *Pater Mundi* (1870) and *The Doctrine of Evolution* (1873), contain these lectures, and show, together with two successors of similar type, *Celestial Empires* (1885) and *Universal Beliefs* (1887), the reaction of New England orthodoxy to the inroads of science. Three later volumes of sermons, *Ad Fidem* (1871), *Toward the Strait Gate* (1875), *In the Vineyard* (1876); a book of verse, *Thy Voyage* (1875); and two biblico-historical novels, *Dio, the Athenian* (1880) and *Aleph the Chaldean* (1891) may be mentioned.

Literary pursuits so absorbing could scarcely fail to remove the spare, austere, and often Quixotic minister from his farmer parishioners. Among his conservative ministerial associates Dr. Burr loomed up as the scientific champion of the ancient faith. To his flock also he seemed a great man, but increasingly removed from common life. Nevertheless, when, after fifty-six years of service, the aged pastor resigned his charge the church declined to accept his resignation, continuing him as pastor until his death.

[*Quarter-Century Record of the Class of 1839, Yale Coll.* (1865); *Obit. Record Grads. Yale Univ.* (1907), pp. 669 ff.; *Who's Who in America*, 1906–07; *Hartford Courant*, May 9, 1907.]   B. W. B—n.

BURR, THEODOSIA (June 21, 1783–January 1813), daughter of Aaron Burr, was born in Albany, but passed most of her girlhood in New York City. Her education, under the careful direction of her father, included mental discipline such as did not fall to the lot of many girls of her generation. "If I could foresee," Aaron Burr wrote once to his wife, "that Theo would become a mere fashionable woman, with all the attendant frivolity and vacuity of mind, adorned with whatever grace and allurement, I would earnestly pray God to take her forthwith hence. But I yet hope by her to convince the world what neither sex appears to believe—that women have souls" (Pidgin, 165). So, in addition to the customary French, music, and dancing, Theodosia began early to apply her mind to arithmetic, Latin, Greek, and English composition—the last in the form of letters to her father which were promptly returned with detailed criticisms. After the death of her mother, when Theodosia was eleven, her father gave his personal attention to her social education, instructing her—and few other teachers were so competent—in the arts and artifices of getting on with people. At fourteen she was beginning to be hostess for him at Richmond Hill. The story is told that in 1797, while Burr was away, at his request she entertained Joseph Brant, chief of the Six Nations, giving a dinner in his honor to which she invited, among other guests, Dr. Hosack, Dr. Bard, and the Bishop of New York (W. L. Stone, *Life of Joseph Brant*, 1838, II, 455–56). At sixteen she was one of the belles of New York society, but without "the attendant vacuity of mind." The following year (Feb. 2, 1801) she was married to Joseph Alston [*q.v.*], and became prominent in South Carolina social circles. This step some of her friends thought to be a political move on the part of her father, and bewailed her "sacrifice" to "affluence and influential connections" (Maria Nicholson to Mrs. Gallatin, Henry Adams, *Life of Albert Gallatin*, 1879, pp. 244–45). But her letters show that Theodosia was attached to her husband, and the birth of their son in 1802 gave her a new interest so overwhelming that the comments of friends mattered naught. The next few years were broken by trips to Saratoga and Ballston Spa in the effort to restore Theodosia's health—very delicate since the birth of the boy—and by visits to her father in New York. In the summer of 1806, she took Aaron Burr Alston and went with Burr to Blennerhassett's Island in the Ohio, where she completely captivated both the proprietor and his wife. She was joined by Alston in October, some weeks later returning with him to South Carolina. Burr was arrested the following spring, and during his trial Theodosia was with him in Richmond, sharing his anxiety, her graciousness and charm exerting a potent influence in his favor (Blennerhassett's journal, W. H. Safford, *Blennerhassett Papers*, 1861, p. 469). In June 1808 Burr took passage for Europe, under an assumed name. Theodosia, also under an assumed name, went north to bid him farewell. The night before he embarked she met him for the last time, and received his papers and final instructions.

During the four years of his exile she was his agent in America, raising money—whenever she could—and sending it to him, and transmitting messages. On her own initiative she wrote to Gallatin and to Mrs. Madison, in an attempt to smooth the way for his return. But when in July 1812 Burr was once again established in New York, Theodosia was unable to go to him immediately. She had been in feeble health, and the death of her son of fever, on June 30, had nearly prostrated her. It was not until December that she was ready to undertake the voyage. Gov. Alston's public duties prevented his accompanying her, so she was escorted by "a gentleman with some medical knowledge" whom her father sent down from New York. On Dec. 30, 1812, they embarked on the *Patriot,* and sailed out of Georgetown Harbor, but the *Patriot* never reached port. Whether, as seems most probable, it foundered in the terrific storm which struck the Carolina coast early in January, or whether, as some legends have it, the *Patriot* was captured by pirates and the passengers forced to walk the plank, or was driven ashore by the storm to be the prey of the notorious Carolina "bankers," is a question which has never been settled.

The mystery attending her fate has so enveloped Theodosia that in the many forms in which her story has been told she has usually appeared as the shadowy heroine of romance rather than as the vital young woman one sees in her letters. She is most interesting in her relations with that erratic father, to whom, through all the vicissitudes of his career, she was passionately devoted. She was his confidante, whom he did not try to deceive. But she seems to have been blind to his frailties. When he was in the deepest disgrace,—already an exile from home, he had been asked to leave England,—she wrote to him: "You appear to me so superior, so elevated above other men; I contemplate you with such strange mixture of humility, admiration, reverence, love and pride, that very little superstition would be necessary to make me worship you as a superior being. . . . I had rather not live than not be the daughter of such a man" (Parton, II, 188).

[Biographies of Aaron Burr, especially Jas. Parton, *Life and Times of Aaron Burr* (enl. ed., 1885) and S. H. Wandell and Meade Minnigerode, *Aaron Burr* (1925) contain material on Theodosia. Perhaps the most comprehensive recent sketch is that by Meade Minnigerode, "Theodosia Burr, Prodigy, An Informal Biography," in the *Sat. Eve. Post,* Sept. 6, 1924. Chas. Felton Pidgin, *Theodosia* (1907) is useful chiefly as a compilation of documents. See also Virginia T. Peacock, *Famous Am. Belles of the Nineteenth Century* (1901); and Gamaliel Bradford, *Wives* (1925). The most commonly reproduced portrait is from a miniature by Vanderlyn, but the previously unpublished portraits, contained in Wandell and Minnigerode, of the child by Stuart and of the young matron by Vanderlyn, accord more fully with the tradition of striking beauty, aristocratic features, and remarkable dark eyes. There are photostat copies of some of Theodosia's letters in the Lib. of Cong.]

E.R.D.

BURRAGE, HENRY SWEETSER (Jan. 7, 1837–Mar. 9, 1926), editor, historian, was descended in the seventh generation from John Burridge of Norfolkshire, who was imprisoned for refusing to pay ship money demanded by Charles I. and who migrated by 1637 to Charlestown, Mass. He was also seventh in descent from Maj. Simon Willard, the founder of Concord. His father, Jonathan Burrage, a varnish manufacturer, married Mary T. Upton. Henry was born at Fitchburg and prepared for college at Pierce Academy in Middleton, being graduated from Brown University in 1861. He was admitted to Phi Beta Kappa, while his literary ability was recognized in his election as class poet. After one year at Newton Theological Institution, he enlisted as a private in the 36th Massachusetts Volunteer Infantry and rose to the rank of major. Wounded in the shoulder at Cold Harbor, he was captured at Petersburg soon after his return from the necessary furlough and spent some time in Libby Prison. At the close of the war he resumed his theological studies at Newton, being graduated in 1867. The year 1868–69 he spent at the University of Halle, living in the home of Prof. Tholuck, enjoying associations which he ever cherished. His first and only pastorate was at the Baptist Church in Waterville, Me., 1869–73. He then became editor of *Zion's Advocate,* residing in Portland for the thirty-two years he held this position. Although this paper was most specifically devoted to the Baptist interests in Maine and factors of local circulation remained economic necessities, in its broad appeal and with its high literary and spiritual standards, it ranked among the best of the provincial religious journals. Although Burrage had no assistant in his editorial task, he kept in constant touch with the religious movements and workers in all parts of the state, making more vital his editorials which maintained a high degree of scholarship. While positive in his convictions, he did not display the dogmatic and disputative temper which marred much contemporary religious journalism. His avocational interests and services were many and valuable. He was recording secretary of numerous organizations, including the American Baptist Missionary Union, which brought him into close touch with foreign mission affairs. His educational judgment was sought as trustee of Colby College, 1881–1906, of Newton Theological Institution, 1881–1906, and of Brown University, 1889–1901, and as Fellow of Brown from 1901. He kept in close touch with the interests of the Civil War veterans, serving as recorder of the Maine Commandery, Loyal Legion, 1889–1912, and as chaplain of the National Soldiers' Home at Togus, 1905–12. His historical work may be considered avocational until his appointment as state historian of Maine in 1907, but for sixty years his pen turned frequently to historical themes and he greatly stimulated the development of the Maine Historical Society. A large part of his published works deal with the history of Maine and with that of the Baptists. Of the more extensive works may be mentioned: *The Act of Baptism in the History of the Christian Church* (1879); *History of the Anabaptists of Switzerland* (1882); *Baptist Hymn Writers and Their Hymns* (1888); *History of the Baptists in New England* (1894); *History of the Baptists of Maine* (1904); *The Beginnings of Colonial Maine, 1602–1658* (1914); *Maine in the Northeastern Boundary Controversy* (1919); *Maine Historical Memorials* (1922). As state historian, he examined and arranged the correspondence of the governors of Maine during the Civil War.

He was married twice: first, in 1873 to Caroline Champlin, who died in 1875; and, second, in 1881, to Ernestine Maie Giddings.

[Private papers at Burrage's late home, Kennebunkport, Me.; *Who's Who in America*, 1924–25; *Portland Press Herald*, Mar. 10, 1926.]   W.H.A.

BURRALL, WILLIAM PORTER (Sept. 18, 1806–Mar. 3, 1874), lawyer and railroad executive, was born at Canaan, Conn., the son of the Hon. William M. Burrall by his wife Abigail Porter Stoddard of Salisbury, Conn. He was educated in the public schools and by private tutors and entered Yale College, graduating in the class of 1826. Immediately upon graduation he began the study of law with his father. After one year he entered the office of the Hon. Samuel Church (afterward chief justice of the State of Connecticut) in Salisbury, subsequently attended a course of lectures at the Litchfield Law School, and was admitted to the bar of Litchfield County in April 1829. In May 1831 he was married to Harriet Holley. He practised law in Canaan, Conn., until October 1839 at which time he was elected president of the Housatonic Railroad Company which was just organized. He held this office until his resignation due to press of other business in 1854, during which time he lived in Bridgeport, Conn. In 1856 he was made vice-president of the Hartford and New Haven Railroad Company then being constructed and held the position until 1867 when he was elected president, which office he occupied until

the road was consolidated with the New York, New Haven and Hartford Railroad Company in 1872. At this time he was made vice-president of the consolidated corporation which position he held until his death. He was also connected with the Illinois Central Company having been elected treasurer in 1852 and president in 1853, and holding this office until 1855 when he resigned but continued in the service of the company as advisory counsel until 1857. In 1859 he made his permanent home in Salisbury, Conn., and took an active part in local politics, representing that town in the General Assembly in 1861. He died from apoplexy in Hartford, Conn.

Burrall was considered one of the ablest railroad executives of his time, particularly in the legal phases. As a negotiator of railroad contracts he was most successful and his services were of very great value in consolidations. Under his management the Hartford and New Haven Railroad Company was known as one of the best paying roads in the country. In manner he was quiet and reserved, a practical business man, admirably fitted for an executive position requiring coolness, forethought, and decision.

[*Yale Univ., Class of 1826 Biog. Sketches* (1866); *Obit. Record of Grads. of Yale Coll.* (1874); obituaries in the *N. Y. Herald, N. Y. Times,* and *Hartford Courant,* Mar. 4, 1874.]   J.H.F.

BURRELL, DAVID JAMES (Aug. 1, 1844–Dec. 5, 1926), clergyman, pastor of Presbyterian and Reformed Dutch churches, was born in Mount Pleasant, Pa., the son of David and Elizabeth (Felgar) Burrell. His great-grandfather, John Burrell, a descendant of French Huguenots who had been driven out of Alsace by the revocation of the Edict of Nantes, had emigrated from County Armagh, Ireland, in the middle of the eighteenth century, and had settled in Westmoreland County, Pa. His mother was the daughter of Ludwig and Catharine (Dunn) Felgar, the latter having been born on the ocean while her parents were coming to America from the north of Ireland. Having prepared for college in the high school, Freeport, Ill., to which place his family had moved, and later at Phillips Academy, Andover, he graduated from Yale in 1867; and from Union Theological Seminary in 1870. After a brief period of mission work in New York (1870–71) he went to Chicago and took charge of the Peoria Street Chapel of the Third Presbyterian Church. On Oct. 18, 1871, he married Clara DeForest, daughter of George F. and Caroline (Sergeant) DeForest of Freeport, Ill. His ordination occurred on Apr. 9, 1872. The chapel he served became the Westminster Presbyterian Church, and of this he was pastor until 1876. From 1876 to 1887 he was pastor of the Second Church, Dubuque, Iowa, and from 1887 to 1891 of the Westminster Church, Minneapolis. These churches had remarkable growth under his ministry. In 1891 he accepted a call to the Marble Collegiate Church, Reformed Dutch, of New York, with which he remained connected till his death.

From his college days he was noted for proficiency in rhetoric and for oratorical ability. His sermons grounded in the old-fashioned evangelical theology, which he championed, were well-planned, direct, fervent, copiously illustrated, and effectively delivered. For several years, beginning in 1903, he was acting professor of homiletics in the Princeton Theological Seminary. He also served as associate editor of *The Presbyterian*, Philadelphia, and *The Christian Herald*. From 1909 to 1913 he was president of the World's Council of the Reformed and Presbyterian Churches. He was active in behalf of temperance and Sunday observance, being long a manager of the American Sabbath Union, later the Lord's Day Alliance of the United States, and one of the seven incorporators of the Anti-Saloon League of New York. Of the latter he was a director (1905–24), and president (1921–23). He was also a director of the Anti-Saloon League of America. His publications were numerous. They are mostly books of a religious nature, popular rather than scholarly, and of passing value. Among them are: *The Religions of the World* (1888); *The Early Church: Studies in the Acts of the Apostles* (1897), in collaboration with his brother, Rev. Joseph Dunn Burrell; *Christ and Progress* (1903); *The Verilies of Jesus* (1903); *Teachings of Jesus Concerning the Scriptures* (1904); *The Evolution of a Christian* (1906); *The Sermon, Its Construction and Delivery* (1913); *The Apostles' Creed* (1915); *Why I Believe the Bible* (1917); *Paul's Campaigns* (1918); *Paul's Companions* (1921); *Paul's Letters* (1921).

[*Gen. Cat. of Union Theol. Sem.* (1919); *Who's Who in America,* 1926–27; *Yale Univ. Obit. Record,* 1926–27, which lists forty-two of his publications; *N. Y. Herald-Tribune, N. Y. Times, N. Y. Evening Post,* Dec. 6, 1926; *Presbyterian,* Dec. 16, 23, 1926; David De Forest Burrell, *David James Burrell* (1929).] H.E.S.

BURRILL, ALEXANDER MANSFIELD (June 19, 1807–Feb. 7, 1869), lawyer, author, was a member of the well-known Burrill family of Lynn. George Burrill, probably of Boston, England, was one of the proprietors of Lynn, Mass., in 1638 and his descendants were very prominent in the early colonial days. Sixth in the direct line from him was Ebenezer Burrill, a prosperous business man, who married Phebe,

daughter of Capt. James Cahoone of Newport, R. I., and moved to New York City in 1802 where their son, Alexander Mansfield Burrill, was born. His early education was received at the hands of private tutors, and he entered Columbia College in 1820, graduating in 1824 with the highest honors. He then took up the study of law under Chancellor Kent, and was admitted to the New York bar in 1828. He commenced the practise of his profession in New York City, but did not achieve any measure of success. His temperament was not such as to fit him for litigation, and he had a natural aversion to the sharp contests inevitable in court work. In consequence he withdrew from active practise in order to devote himself to legal authorship. His first publication was *Practice of the Supreme Court of the State of New York in Personal Actions* (2 vols., 1840). The reception accorded to it by the profession was so favorable that a second edition was quickly called for. It was followed by a *New Law Dictionary and Glossary* in two parts (1850–51), a work of a very high standard, which at once took its place as perhaps the best book of its kind so far produced. *Law and Practice of Voluntary Assignments for the Benefit of Creditors* followed in 1853, and was equally well received. His last work, *The Nature, Principles and Rules of Circumstantial Evidence, Especially That of the Presumptive Kind, in Criminal Cases* (1856) deals with a difficult and very technical branch of the law, in a scientific spirit alien to previous treatises on the subject. All his books were distinguished for their graceful style and a scholarly precision and finish which earned the unstinted commendation of the judiciary. In addition their accuracy of statement and definition was fully recognized at the time by the profession at large. He also assisted in the preparation of *Worcester's Dictionary*.

Refined in his nature and tastes, he made his immediate circle of intimates, in the main, from men of similar scholarly attainments and interests. Endowed with keen intellectual perception and high ideals he had no inclination for the public life of the day. With the members of the bar his reputation was of the highest and he enjoyed universal respect.

[Ellen Mudge Burrill, *The Burrill Family of Lynn* (1907), containing full details of ancestry; Paul C. Burrill, *Burrill Lineage* (1910); brief obituary in the *Am. Law Times,* II, 77.] H. W.H.K.

BURRILL, JAMES (Apr. 25, 1772–Dec. 25, 1820) lawyer, Rhode Island politician, and senator, was born in Providence, the son of James and Elizabeth (Rawson) Burrill. He prepared for college in the school of William Wilkinson, at that time a celebrated classical and mathematical teacher in Providence. After graduating from Rhode Island College (now Brown University) in 1788, he began the study of law in the office of Theodore Foster, a Providence lawyer of extensive practise. When Foster, elected to the Senate in May 1790, relinquished his law practise, Burrill went into the office of David Howell, a prominent Rhode Island politician, where he remained until he was admitted to the bar in September 1791. He then began the practise of law in Providence. In the summer of 1795 he served as secretary of protest against a new apportionment of state taxes that had been ordered by the General Assembly, and in August 1797 served on the committee of three that welcomed President John Adams to the town of Providence. In the following month (Oct. 8, 1797) he married Sally Arnold. Although little more than a youth Burrill now became attorney-general of Rhode Island, which post he held from October 1797 to May 1813. During the next seven years he served as trustee of Brown University. In politics he was a Federalist. On June 7, 1813, he was elected to the General Assembly, and in May 1814, was chosen speaker of the House, which office he held until he resigned from the House in October 1816. At the May session of the latter year he was elected chief justice of the supreme judicial court of Rhode Island. A contemporary, writing in after years, speaks of Burrill at this time as the acknowledged head of the Rhode Island bar (Henry L. Bowen, *Memoir of Tristam Burges,* 1835, p. 38). On June 21, 1816, the General Assembly, in grand committee, unanimously elected Burrill to the Senate. He declined to serve, on the ground that there was some doubt as to the constitutionality of his election (*Rhode Island Acts and Resolves,* Feb. Sess., 1817, p. 5). The General Assembly, however, unanimously confirmed his election Feb. 19, 1817, and Burrill represented his state in the Senate from December 1817 until his death, during which time he came to be recognized as one of the leading orators in that body. The *Annals of Congress* and the *Senate Journal* testify to his activity. He served on the committees on commerce and manufactures and on the judiciary. His first important effort was on Nov. 26, 1818, when he unsuccessfully attempted to obtain an increase in the salaries of the chief justice and the associate justices of the Supreme Court of the United States (*Annals of Congress,* 15 Cong., 2 Sess., col. 27). The most important questions before the Senate were those of the admission of Maine and Missouri to the Union. Although a member of the committee that reported

the resolution, Burrill vigorously opposed the bill in two important speeches. In the first, Jan. 13, 1820, he opposed binding the two questions together and urged that each be considered separately on its merits (*Ibid.,* 16 Cong., 1 Sess., col. 94–97). The second speech, delivered Dec. 7, 1820, was an attempt to prevent the passage of the resolution. He urged that Section 26, Article 3, of the Missouri constitution, which made it the duty of the Missouri legislature to prevent free negroes and mulattoes from settling in Missouri, was ". . . entirely repugnant to the Constitution of the United States . . ." on the ground that it distinguished between classes of citizens (*Ibid.,* 16 Cong., 2 Sess., col. 45–50). The resolution passed the Senate Dec. 12, 1820. Burrill died in Washington and was given a memorable funeral in the Senate chamber (*Daily National Intelligencer,* Washington, D. C., Dec. 27, 28, 1820).

[Wm. R. Staples, *Annals of the Town of Providence, from its First Settlement, to the Organization of the City Govt., in June 1832* (1843); Wm. G. Goddard, "Biog. Notices of Early Grads. at Brown Univ.," *Am. Quart. Reg.,* May 1839, p. 360; *Biog. Cong. Dir.* (1928); *R. I. Am. and General Advertiser,* Jan. 2, 5, 9, 1821.]

F. E. R.

BURRILL, THOMAS JONATHAN (Apr. 25, 1839–Apr. 14, 1916), botanist, horticulturist, was of Irish and Scotch descent, the son of John and Mary (Francis) Burrill. He was born on a farm near Pittsfield, Mass., and while still a child went to work in a cotton-mill. When he was nine his family moved to Stephenson County, in northwestern Illinois, where in the time that was not occupied at school or in farm chores the little boy was busy at the loom. His education was in log school-houses until he went to high school in Freeport at nineteen, whence shyness and consciousness of his country clothes and manners drove him home. He returned to school, however, at Rockford, working at chores to earn his board, and in 1862 he entered the State Normal School where the museum of the State Natural History Society was located. In his attachment to natural history he gravitated to the museum, where he made the acquaintance of B. D. Walsh the entomologist and George Vasey the botanist. These men guided his studies in the natural sciences. He graduated from the Illinois State Normal School in 1865, and in 1865–68 was superintendent of schools in Urbana. On July 22, 1868, he was married to Sarah H. Alexander of Seneca Falls, N. Y. In the same year he became assistant professor of natural history in the University of Illinois, and in the following year he conducted with his students a natural history survey and collecting trip from Cairo to

Chicago, in other words from the southern extremity of the state and its austral life zones to the northern end where it borders Lake Michigan. The next year he began contributing articles to the Illinois Horticultural Society's publications, and continued to write with vigor and precision on subjects horticultural, botanical, and pathological up to 1915, some eighty-two articles in all, practically every one of which has an integral place of importance in its subject. He was for nearly fifty years the moving spirit in the Illinois Horticultural Society and in the Agricultural School of the University of Illinois; beside this he threw himself into administrative duties, was long the vice-president of the University (acting president 1891–94 and again in 1902), and held, when he died, the presidency of the Society of American Bacteriologists.

He was among the first of the modern microscopists. One of his publications was on the rusts and mildews of Illinois, part of a survey of the cryptogamic flora of his state which was never completed. In 1877 he announced his suspicion that the terrific epidemic of "fire blight" of pears then sweeping the Middle West was caused by bacteria, which had previously been supposed to cause disease only in animals. His views were cautiously regarded in America and received with scorn in Europe, but by 1880 his intensive microscopical investigations and his inoculations of healthy pears with the virus of fireblight, causing the appearance of fire-blight symptoms, had gone far toward proving his contention, though he still offered his views with orthodox modesty and tentativeness. His prediction that many mysterious diseases, such as the mosaic blights, would prove to be bacterial, has been fully justified, so that he may be said to have been the pioneer American in perhaps the most economically important branch of botany in the last fifty years, that of the bacterial diseases of plants. His pathological investigations were extended constantly and included such important crop diseases as ear rot of corn, potato scab, blackberry rust, peach yellows, and, especially, bitter rot of apples. When the first news of the appearance of this last disease in Illinois reached him he sat up all night preparing a circular for farmers on methods of combating it, rushed it through the printing, and had it distributed in a few hours. In the meantime he had telegraphed warnings to every corner of the state. His last work was an attempt to domesticate or cultivate the beneficial wild bacteria of the soil. He was not what is known as an inspiring teacher, if personal magnetism and eloquence make a teacher inspiring, for his manner was deliberate, even

somewhat rustic, but he had those qualities of the sterling scientist which most appeal to the modern laboratory student. In 1876 Northwestern University conferred the degree of A.M. upon him, and in 1893 the degree of LL.D. The latter degree was given him also by his own university in 1912, and he had previously (1881) received a Ph.D. from the old University of Chicago. His private life was marked by uprightness, kindness, and sincerity. It has been said of him that he acknowledged but one God, never loved but one woman, and had but one ideal in his work, the spirit of true science.

[The "Memorial Address" by E. Davenport, *Trans. Ill. State Hort. Soc.*, n.s., L, 67–97, with bibliography, is decidedly the fullest and most valuable; it draws liberally upon some reminiscences by S. A. Forbes, *Alumni Quart. of the Univ. of Ill.*, July 1916. Other notices are Wm. Trelease in *Bot. Gaz.*, LXII, 153–54, and J. Barrett in *Phytopathology*, VIII, 1–4. See also "Scientific Writings of T. J. Burrill" in *Trans. Ind. State Hort. Soc.*, n.s., LI, 195–201, and Erwin F. Smith's estimate of his work in the historical introduction to his *Bacterial Diseases of Plants* (1920). For list of administrative positions held by Burrill see *Who's Who in America*, 1916–17.]   D. C. P.

BURRINGTON, GEORGE (*c.* 1680–February 1759), colonial governor of North Carolina, belonged to a family of good standing in the county of Devon, and was probably born in that shire. One member of his family is accredited by English historians as being the first gentleman of consequence to join the standard of William of Orange when that prince invaded England in 1688 (Sir James Mackintosh, *History of the Revolution in England in 1688*, 1834, ch. XV). The favor in which his family was held by the House of Hanover gained for Burrington a captain's commission in the British army before he was sent to America as governor of North Carolina. In 1732 he proudly declared: "I have served the crown in every reign since the Abdication of King James, & always was allowed to behave as became a Man of Honour, and the Family whose name I bear; their Services at the Revolution and during the life of King William of glorious memory I hope are not yet in Oblivion" (*Colonial Records of North Carolina*, III, 375). At a session of the Royal Council on Feb. 26, 1723, King George the First gave his approval to the appointment by the Lords Proprietors of Burrington, as governor of North Carolina. The latter took the oath of office at Edenton, the colonial capital, on Jan. 15, 1724. His first administration was of short duration, ending, after about a year and a half, when he was superseded by Sir Richard Everard, Baronet, who took the oath of office on July 17, 1725. Burrington had attempted to assault Chief Justice Christopher Gale, and, when that gentleman barricaded his house, had threatened to burn it or blow it up with gunpowder. Gale thereupon went to England to prefer charges, substantiated by the written statements of seven members of the Provincial Council, and Burrington was displaced in consequence. When his successor arrived, Burrington challenged the newcomer to single combat, and denounced him as a "calf's head," "noodle," and "ape, no more fit to be governor than a hog in the woods or Sancho Panza." For this outbreak he was indicted, but left Edenton before the case was tried, and it was later nolle-prossed. Notwithstanding his violent conduct, he had many strong friends in the colonial assembly. At the end of his first administration, and after Everard had qualified, the assembly in an address referred to "the great happiness which this Province lately enjoy'd" under Burrington, and referred to "his Carryage & behaviour being very Affable & courteous, his Justice very Exemplary & his care and Industry to promote . . . the welfare of this Province being very Eminent and Conspicuous" (*Ibid.*, II, 577–78).

After North Carolina became a royal province in 1729, governors were appointed by the king. One of King George's secretaries of state was the Duke of Newcastle. Some bond of friendship existed between Newcastle and Burrington in consequence of which Burrington was again appointed governor of North Carolina in 1731. In this second administration he rendered services of the greatest value to the colony. He laid out roads and built bridges, making personal inspections from time to time to see that they were kept in proper repair. He pushed to completion a highway from New Bern to the settlements further south; and another, of still greater length, running from the Virginia boundary to the banks of the Cape Fear River, was undertaken at his instance. He was largely instrumental in developing the Cape Fear section of North Carolina. Three different times he went on expeditions for the purpose of taking the soundings of the inlets, bars, and rivers of the province. He discovered and made known the channels of the Cape Fear River and Beaufort or Topsail inlets, theretofore unused and unknown. Often he made journeys on foot through dense forests and dangerous morasses, accompanied by only one man, finally arriving at some frontier settlement with the clothing almost entirely torn from his body. Once he lived on a single biscuit for three days. On these journeys he often carried considerable sums of money for distribution among the poorer families to relieve the hardships incident to their new location. Hugh

Williamson truly says of him: "He is not charged, nor was he chargeable, with fraud or corruption; for he despised rogues, whether they were small or great" (*History of North Carolina*, 1812, II, 14). He spent his private fortune in carrying on his work in North Carolina, never receiving a penny of salary, though he had the King's order for its payment. Nor was he reimbursed for his large personal expenditures in the interest of public works. He himself declared that the only reward he ever received was a vote of thanks from the colonial assembly. He was finally relieved from office at his own request in 1734. After his return to England he was the author of at least two works: *Seasonable Considerations on the Expendiency of a War with France* (1743) and *An Answer to Dr. William Brakenridge's Letter Concerning the Number of Inhabitants within the London Bills of Mortality* (1757). In February 1759 he was mysteriously murdered in the Bird Cage Walk, St. James's Park, London, and his body thrown in the Canal (*London Evening Post*, Feb. 24–27, 1759).

[The chief sources of information about Burrington are in the *Colonial Records of North Carolina*, especially those cited in the monograph *Gov. Geo. Burrington* (1896) by M. DeL. Haywood.]   M. DeL. H.

BURRITT, ELIHU (Dec. 8, 1810–Mar. 6, 1879), "The Learned Blacksmith," reformer, linguist, was born in New Britain, Conn. Named after his father, an eccentric shoemaker and farmer, he also derived from him an enthusiasm for impracticable ventures. From his mother, Elizabeth Hinsdale, who bore nine other children, he learned self-denial and whole-hearted devotion to the ideal of service. If, as a child, he tried to persuade her to borrow fewer sermons and more histories from the meager church library, he nevertheless made her deep religious feelings his own. Neither the district school nor a term at his brother's boarding-school satisfied his appetite for knowledge, and hence he imagined and solved quaint problems of mental arithmetic and learned Greek verbs while blowing the bellows at the smithy where he was an apprentice. At the age of twenty-seven he made in his Journal this entry, a typical one: "June 19, Sixty lines of Hebrew; thirty pages of French; ten pages of Cuvier's Theory of the Earth; eight lines of Syriac; ten lines of Danish; ten ditto Bohemian; nine ditto of Polish; fifteen names of stars; ten hours' forging." Overwork undermined the health of this narrow-chested, stouthanded youth, and for his entire life he paid the price in acute suffering. Awkward as he was, and in spite of excessive shyness, his clear blue eyes, his broad, sloping forehead, and his fine mouth compelled sympathy. With scarce a dollar in his pocket he set out from his native village in the year 1837 seeking work and a chance to further his self-education. Worcester, Mass., offered both. His attainments in all the European and several Asiatic languages reached the ear of Gov. Edward Everett, who referred to them in an address and offered him the advantages of Harvard, which Burritt refused. Although chagrined at such undesired publicity, he did, however, bring himself to accept lecture invitations.

While preparing a lecture on "the anatomy of the earth," he was so struck by the unity and interdependency of its parts that he ended by writing a plea for international peace. Into that cause, which had just lost its chief apostle by the death of William Ladd in 1841, Burritt now threw himself heart and soul. With the help of a business partner he founded at Worcester, in 1844, a weekly newspaper, the *Christian Citizen*. This truly international pacifist publication dragged Burritt deeply into debt before, in 1851, he was forced to abandon it.

During the Oregon crisis, when Burritt was also editing the *Advocate of Peace and Universal Brotherhood,* he besieged Congress with peace propaganda and cooperated with Friends in Manchester, England, in a picturesque exchange of "Friendly Addresses" between British and American cities, merchants, ministers, and laborers. According to Burritt eight hundred newspapers printed these "Friendly Addresses" (*Advocate of Peace and Universal Brotherhood,* February 1846, p. 56). He himself carried the "Friendly Address" from Edinburgh, with its impressive list of signatures, to Washington, where Calhoun and other senators expressed much interest in this "popular handshaking" across the Atlantic (Burritt, Manuscript Journal, Mar. 31, 1851).

This cooperation with British friends of peace led Burritt to cross the Atlantic in June 1846, and during that autumn he formed there the League of Universal Brotherhood. By 1850 this "world peace society" had, through his efforts, twenty thousand British and as many American signatures to its pledge of complete abstinence from all war. It sponsored a "Friendly Address" movement between British and French cities when war seemed imminent in 1852, Burritt personally delivering the friendly interchange of opinion to appropriate municipal officials in France. He also induced the League to sponsor "The Olive Leaf Mission," through which peace propaganda was inserted in forty influential Continental newspapers. This work was financed by woman Leaguers whom Burritt organized into sewing circles. Between 1850 and 1856 he estimated that the *Olive Leaves* reached monthly one million European readers.

Almost single-handed this enthusiast organized in 1848 the Brussels Peace Congress, which inaugurated the series held in the following years at Paris, Frankfort, London, Manchester, and Edinburgh. Burritt's Journals exhibit incredible activity which included traveling widely in Germany to enlist delegates and soliciting and gaining the cooperation of Victor Hugo, Lamartine, and distinguished French economists and philanthropists. To bring the American peace movement into this truly international peace organization, Burritt in 1850 organized eighteen state peace conventions, with the result that forty Americans attended the Frankfort Congress that year. These peace congresses won increasing attention from the European and British press, and Burritt's name was celebrated in popular periodicals like those of Douglas Jerrold, Charles Dickens, and Thomas Chambers, and ridiculed in *Blackwood's* and the influential London *Times*. At each Congress Burritt ably pled for such a Congress and Court of Nations as William Ladd had advocated.

The Crimean War interrupted this European peace work, and Burritt devoted more time to the related scheme of cheap international postage, and to plans for preventing civil war in his own country. Urging by pen and lecture the utilization of the public domain for compensated emancipation, he also organized a convention to stimulate interest in this plan, and during one winter traveled 10,000 miles from Maine to Iowa in its behalf.

Burritt, who had identified himself with the thoroughgoing anti-war group, opposed the Civil War on pacifist grounds, but he was appointed by Lincoln in 1863 as consular agent at Birmingham. In several volumes he described industrial and rural England with insight, vigor, and charm. From 1870 until his death in 1879 he lived in New Britain, devoting himself to the improvement of a few stony acres of land, to writing, and to teaching languages. He never married, but his entire life was rich in friendships.

Almost uniquely in the America of his generation, Burritt was capable of thinking in international terms. Deprecating sectarianism, he found solace in Quaker meetings and the Anglican ritual as well as in his own Congregationalism. His sympathies with free trade and labor were intelligent and realistic. Only two years after the publication of the *Communist Mani-*

festo (1848) he was advocating, in *Olive Leaves* printed in the German press, a strike of the workers of the world against war as the only alternative to a Congress and Court of Nations. In his numerous writings in behalf of peace he used statistical evidence skilfully, though his chief appeal was to the brotherhood of man. This maker of horseshoes and a Sanscrit grammar endured the most irksome poverty and physical suffering in order to devote himself to the greatest value he found in life, "the capacity and space of labouring for humanity."

[The chief sources of information about Elihu Burritt are his manuscript Journals, 28 vols. (1837–60) in the Lib. of the Inst. of New Britain, Conn., and his newspaper, the *Christian Citizen*, Worcester, Mass. (1844–51), a complete file of which is in the Am. Antiquarian Soc. A small portion of the Journals was included in the uncritical compilation of Chas. Northend, *Elihu Burritt: a Memorial Volume containing a Sketch of His Life and Labors* (1879). Of Burritt's sixteen published volumes the most characteristic are, *Sparks from the Anvil* (1846); *Thoughts of Things at Home and Abroad, with a Memoir by Mary Howitt* (1854); *Lectures and Speeches* (1866); *Walk from London to John O'Groat's* (1864); and *Ten Minute Talks* (1873).]   M. E. C.

BURROUGHS, JOHN (Apr. 3, 1837–Mar. 29, 1921), author, was descended from early seventeenth century settlers in New England. Ephraim Burroughs, his great-grandfather, born in 1740, removed to a farm in Delaware County, N. Y., and Eden, son of Ephraim, in 1795 settled near the village of Beaver Dam (later called Roxbury). Among the children of Eden was Chauncey A. Burroughs, farmer, the father of John Burroughs. The latter's maternal grandfather, Edmund Kelly, of Irish descent, born in Dutchess County, N. Y., in 1767, was with Washington at Valley Forge; his maternal grandmother, Lovina Liscom, was a practical housewife. Among their children was Amy Kelly, the mother of John Burroughs; like the father, she was an Old-School Baptist. In his own view Burroughs derived from his paternal ancestry his love of peace and solitude and his intellectual impetus, and from his maternal, his love of nature and introspective habit and idealism. The seventh of ten children, he was born on a farm near Roxbury. Among his brothers, "homebodies, rather timid, non-aggressive men . . . the kind of men that are so often crowded to the wall" (as he described them), he felt himself closest to Hiram, "who was curious about strange lands, but who lost heart and hope as soon as he got beyond the sight of his native hills" (*Life and Letters*, I, 17). It is impossible to exaggerate Burroughs's own love of his native hills, the lower pastoral ranges of the Catskills, where he lived and wrote during most of his long life. He early took delight in exploring the fields and woods and especially in watching the birds, the passenger pigeons that came in armies, or the beautiful wood-warblers whose names he did not know.

After some schooling in the neighborhood, he went to teach, as a youth of seventeen, at Tongore, in Ulster County, and saved enough money to study for a time in the Ashland Collegiate Institute in Greene County; then returned to teach at Tongore. About this time he began writing essays, Johnsonian in style. In 1856 he studied at Cooperstown Seminary, where his literary enthusiasms included Wordsworth, Saint-Pierre's *Studies of Nature,* and especially Emerson, whom he read "in a sort of ecstacy. I got him in my blood, and he colored my whole intellectual outlook" (*Ibid.*, I, 41). For six months he taught school near Polo, Ill. On Sept 12, 1857, when but twenty years old, he married Ursula North, whom he had come to know at Tongore, "A self-complacent, thrifty, and forceful young woman, thirteen months his senior" (*Ibid.*, I, 44), whom he informed, a week after the wedding, "If I live, I shall be an author. My life will be one of study" (*Ibid.*, I, 80). It was nearly two years before a teaching post at East Orange, N. J., enabled them to set up housekeeping. At the age of twenty-three he wrote an essay, "Expression," so Emersonian in thought and manner that Lowell, before printing it in the *Atlantic Monthly* (Nov. 1860), looked through Emerson's writings for it. Unsigned, it went into *Poole's Index* as Emerson's work. His self-reliance thus challenged, Burroughs now began to write for the *New York Leader* a series of nature essays entitled "From the Back Country." The necessity of securing a livelihood, however, kept him at his task of teaching, except when he abandoned it for the study of medicine, and that in turn, on one occasion, to write "Waiting," a poem first published in *Knickerbocker's*, March 1863, and frequently reprinted in later years. In the spring of 1863 he began to take a livelier interest in the study of wild flowers, owing partly to the influence of a friend, a botanist named Eddy; and by summer he was so enthusiastic over the study of birds that he said he could think or talk of nothing else—such was the effect of his chancing upon Audubon's book in the library at West Point. Breaking away from his home country in October 1863, he went to Washington, where for nearly ten years he was to sit at a desk in the Currency Bureau of the Treasury Department. In Washington he formed the most important friendship of his life, and wrote his first books. The friendship was with Walt Whitman, in whose poetry he had become interested at least two years before their meeting in the autumn of 1863, when Burroughs was twenty-six and Whitman forty-four. They had walks and talks together, and oyster-eating orgies, and sometimes Burroughs accompanied Whitman in his hospital rounds. "I loved him," said Burroughs, "as I never loved any man. We were companionable without talking. I owe more to him than to any other man in the world. He brooded me; he gave me things to think of; he taught me generosity, breadth, and an all-embracing charity" (*Ibid.*, I, 113). His complete acceptance of Whitman found expression in his first published book, *Notes on Walt Whitman as Poet and Person* (1867), to which Whitman contributed the title, some of the chapter-titles, a large part of the notes in the second edition (1871), passages of the text itself, and much detailed revision: "I have no doubt," Burroughs conceded in 1920, "that half the book is his" (*Ibid.*, I, 129).

Meantime, in the spring of 1865, he published the first of his *Atlantic* essays on nature, "With the Birds," which became the initial chapter of his first book on nature. It was followed by "In the Hemlocks" and other essays. The rebound from his clerical work, from the iron door of the Treasury vault, was sending Burroughs back to the fields and woods of his boyhood. His love of his Northern home country, his fresh poetic feeling for the beauty and eager life of birds, united with an accuracy of observation superior to that of Thoreau, and a gift for expression neither too homespun nor too cultivated, resulted in writing that he probably never excelled in all his subsequent career as an author. As early as 1866, however, he informed Benton, "I think I have had my say about the birds, for the present, at least. Sometimes I may make a book of these, and other articles, but am in no hurry" (*Ibid.*, I, 118). He was in no hurry chiefly because Whitman as poet and person was absorbing his energies; it was five years before the book on the birds, *Wake-Robin* (1871), so named by Whitman, actually appeared. It was favorably received, William Dean Howells, for example, writing, "The dusk and cool and quiet of the forest seem to wrap the reader . . . It is sort of summer vacation to turn its pages. It is written with a grace which continually subordinates itself to the material" (*Atlantic Monthly*, August 1871). In the same year Burroughs was sent by the Treasury Department to England, where he incidentally gained the matter of four essays published in *Winter Sunshine* (1875). Reviewing this book in the *Nation* (Jan. 27, 1876), Henry James described the author as "a sort of reduced, but also more humourous, more available, and more sociable Thoreau" and conceded his possession of

"a style sometimes indeed idiomatic and unfinished to a fault, but capable of remarkable felicity and vividness." Burroughs was now safely launched upon his literary career; a third nature book soon followed, *Birds and Poets* (1877), and for the rest of his long life he published at the average rate of one book every two years.

Upon leaving Washington in 1873, Burroughs returned to his native mountain country, with which he became associated as intimately as Wordsworth with the English Lakes. He purchased a farm and built a house, which he named "Riverby," near Esopus, on the west shore of the Hudson about eighty miles from New York, and there cultivated fruit-trees, berries, and grapes. In 1895 he built, in the hills about a mile from his river home, a secluded bar-covered cabin which he called "Slabsides." The summers following 1908 he was accustomed to spend at a farmhouse, "Woodchuck Lodge," on the old home farm near Roxbury, using the hay-barn as his literary workshop. In these several retreats he read and wrote, observed wild life, and welcomed friends and admirers; in his last years, indeed, when he was regarded not only as a naturalist but also as a sage and prophet, all manner of persons made the pilgrimage to "Slabsides," and many of them reported their experience in magazines and newspapers. Through innumerable photographs, his erect, substantial figure, steady eyes, long rustic beard, and pervasive air of repose, formed an image familiar to readers throughout the country, an image that blended easily with a background of woods and pastures and long sloping hills. Despite his attachment to his home region, however, Burroughs traveled extensively—in the Western and Southern states, to Jamaica and Bermuda, to Hawaii, in Canada, in the Maine woods, in Europe (*Fresh Fields*, 1885). He cruised with the Harriman Expedition to Alaska (*Far and Near*, 1904). He camped in the Yosemite with John Muir, and in the Yellowstone with President Roosevelt (*Camping and Tramping with Roosevelt*, 1907). He was associated with Roosevelt also in a campaign against the "Nature Fakers,"—writers who colored and embroidered the facts of natural history —a campaign opened by his *Atlantic* paper, "Real and Sham Natural History" (1903) and brought to a climax by the President four years later in an interview given to *Everybody's Magazine*. Among the friends of his last years were Thomas Edison and Henry Ford. Honorary degrees were conferred upon him by Yale (1910), Colgate (1911), and the University of Georgia (1915).

The interval between the departure of Burroughs from the Capital in 1873 and his death in 1921 was almost a half century, a period in which his outward life pursued an even tenor, while his inner life, recorded in his books, was undergoing significant changes. The title of his 1877 volume, *Birds and Poets,* is symbolical; he had had his say about the birds, and had reached the end of his most poetic epoch. His next epoch, which may be said to begin with *Locusts and Wild Honey* in 1879 and to close with *Leaf and Tendril* in 1908, was one in which his main passion was "Straight Seeing and Straight Thinking," that is, deliberate, faithful observation accompanied by reasonable inference, as opposed to the careless use of the senses and the hasty guessing that characterize most people in their contact with nature. His poetic feeling for nature was less, his scientific study of fact greater, both in his reading and in his saunterings afield. Yet he did not adopt the method of science; he wanted the facts in so far as he could secure them without method, by the simple expedient of random and affectionate observation. When Maeterlinck called Fabre "the insects' Homer," Burroughs pointed out that he was really the insects' Sherlock Holmes; and he himself was assuredly a Sherlock Holmes, the most proficient detective of nature in American literature.

Gradually, however, Burroughs drifted into what may be designated as another period in his literary history, a period of lively enthusiasm for science that accompanied, rather than supplanted, his detective observation. More and more he was reading books of science; in 1883, for instance, *The Origin of Species* and *The Descent of Man,* and in 1887 the work of John Fiske. The next year he asked Benton, "Can you still read the great poets? I cannot. I have not looked in Shakespeare for years, and do not care to . . . I read Wordsworth a little, and Tennyson, but expect by and by I shall read none of the old poets" (*Ibid.,* I, 294). Though not wholly inconsistent in enjoying field observation and scorning laboratories and museums, he made himself a little absurd by celebrating the results of modern science while deploring the methods necessarily employed in the attainment of those results. Earnestly did he welcome the results offered by geology and biology, including the "cosmic chill," because he believed exact objective knowledge to be better than the shifting subjectivity of the poets and the "pretty little anthropomorphic views of things" that religion proposes. His writings in this period express the same time spirit that actuated John Fiske, who by 1885 had substantially secured American recognition of the Darwinian theory of life; though it was not until

1900, when he published *The Light of Day,* that Burroughs fully and enthusiastically set forth his indorsement of the results of Victorian science. The light of day is reason, which demolished the authority of revealed religion and establishes the only true interpretation of the universe. Seeking truth, science is, indeed, profoundly religious: "Think you the man of science does not also find God? that Huxley and Darwin and Tyndall do not find God, though they may hesitate to use that name? Whoever finds truth finds God, does he not? whoever loves truth loves God?" Literature and religion, in the old sense, are passing away, but science is probably only "in the heat of its forenoon work." Great will be its high noon!

But when, a dozen years later, it seemed to Burroughs that science had reached the meridian, his glad faith in reason had departed and he had come to a fresh period in his inner history. "In the Noon of Science," an essay in *The Summit of the Years* (1914), while conceding the achievements of natural science, is in the main a criticism of science on the ground that the civilization it creates is "like an engine running without a headlight": it may draw us to our destruction. The salvation of society depends upon "vision," or "intuitive perception of the great fundamental truths of the inner spiritual world," and for this we must look not to those who are intent upon explaining life in terms of physics and chemistry but to "the great teachers and prophets, poets and mystics." To one of these, Walt Whitman, he had long been devoted, without, however, being able to reconcile the spiritual *aplomb* of *Leaves of Grass* with the rational certitude of the successors of Darwin and Huxley. In his mature book on his friend, *Whitman, A Study* (1896), Burroughs had asserted that Whitman "does not have to stretch himself at all to match in the human and emotional realm the stupendous discoveries and deductions of science." To match science by emotionally absorbing the whole of nature is not, of course, to enter into the point of view of science and proceed to spiritual conquest from that point of view. In Bergson, however, whom Burroughs began reading in 1911, it seemed that modern thought had its most acceptable leader, a man at once scientist, philosopher, poet, and a prophet of the soul, proving at last that such words as "soul" and "spirit" stand "for real truths." Where Whitman only felt, Bergson demonstrated the immanence of spirit in nature and so enabled us to enter joyously into the fellowship of creation. The exhilarating influence of this new master dominates *Time and Change* (1912), *The Summit of the Years* (1913),

The Breath of Life (1915), and *Under the Apple-Trees* (1916).

Under the apple-trees in the years of the World War, Burroughs brooded less upon Bergson and the fellowship of creation, and more upon Germany and the fellowship of destruction. "The gods of science," whom he had always sought loyally to serve, were, he thought, with Germany; "the gods of the moral law," whom he had comparatively neglected, with the Allies. He now ranged his mind and heart with the latter, believing that "our blended inheritance from Greece and Judea and the meditative Orient" faced the prospect of extinction; although he had never largely availed himself of this humanistic and religious inheritance, in the hour of crisis it seemed to him of supreme importance. He was frankly savage in his hatred of the Germans on the ground that they were savage. "When told [1918] that if the war lasted much longer, he could qualify as one of Whitman's 'race of savage old men,' he admitted it was so; that the war poisoned his blood and allowed to come to the surface feelings that had seldom found expression through all his life" (*Ibid.*, II, 208, 267).

Between 1919 and 1922 came his last four books, in which he sought, with an increasing melancholy, to make the best of a dubious universe. "I am trying again," he confessed, "to read Bergson's *Creative Evolution,* with poor success. . . . Bergson's work now seems to me a mixture of two things that won't mix—metaphysics and natural science." Faced anew with the necessity of choosing between a philosophy of intuition and scientific reason, Burroughs showed the fundamental bent of his mind by remarking that if the heart often knows what the head does not, it is because the intellect tells it so. "The animals live by instinct, and we live largely in our emotions, but it is reason that has placed man at the head of the animal kingdom." By reason he means essentially the reason of science, which knows nothing of the gods of the moral law but insists that, "Hedge or qualify as we will, man is a part of Nature. . . . Can there be anything in the universe that is not of the Universe? Can we make two or three out of the one?" Finally, in "Facing the Mystery," the last essay in his last book, Burroughs with admirable integrity recants the greatest emotional enthusiasm of his life, his devotion to Whitman, poet of immortality, and accepts the prospect of personal extinction. At the time of his death, and, indeed, for the last four decades of his life, Burroughs may plausibly be said to have had "more of a personal following, more contacts with his readers, both through correspondence and in person, than any other American author has had, and, probably, more than any other author of modern times" (*Ibid.,* I, 247). The Sage of "Slabsides" was a national figure, picturesque in his simplicity of life, exact and sympathetic in his observation of nature, friendly alike to the voice of science and of essential religion; he was poet, detective, and priest of nature, and the greatest of these, in the public mind, was the priest, the wise man who in a time of decaying creeds expounded a way of life that could free men from Mammon, frivolity, and insincerity and render them content to accept the universe with all its beauty, wonder, and apparent evil. He continued the work of the three authors of the nineteenth century whom he most admired,—Carlyle, Emerson, and Whitman—bringing to his spiritual quest a far more scientific frame of mind than any one of them had possessed, but also, it must be admitted, a far smaller moral and spiritual endowment and an inferior order of literary talent. In the decades beginning with 1870, when American literature was feeling the scientific impulse, the desire to be faithful to locality, to the facts of human life, and to the phenomena of nature, Burroughs served his time by showing how blunt the eyes and ears of writers generally are, and thus he played a part in the rise of that latter-day movement in our literature known as realism. Passing beyond the bounds of literature, his influence extended to a popular impulse of the epoch,—"nature study," both within and without the schools. He was an inspiration to immense numbers of people who with more or less seriousness pursued the study of birds and flowers in the field, and of geology and biology in the library. If the scientists were unable to think of him as one of themselves, he assuredly served their ends by stimulating popular interest in the facts of nature.

Time will doubtless adjudge Burroughs most significant, however, not as a sage or observer of nature, but as a writer by whom the American "nature essay" was definitely established as a literary *genre*. This form of expression emerged, in the American romantic movement, by means of the Transcendental emotional interest in nature and the scientific interest manifested by naturalists and travelers. Both interests were marked in Thoreau. Thoreau was followed by Lowell, Wilson Flagg, T. W. Higginson, and many others, but it was Burroughs who employed the form with the greatest frequency and most thoroughly exploited its capacities. His debt to Thoreau was probably much greater than he was willing to acknowledge, and he may have been under obligations to other predecessors; but to him belongs what measure of credit may attach to bringing the nature essay into widespread vogue (a vogue declining since the World War) and of contributing to American literature a long series of essays marked by delicate feeling, fine observation, honest thought, and a style simple and natural without affront to the traditions of English prose.

[There is much autobiography in the writings of John Burroughs, with which should be included the "Autobiographical Sketches" in Clara Barrus's *Our Friend, John Burroughs* (1914) and the first 132 pages of the volume entitled *My Boyhood* (1922). To the latter, Julian Burroughs contributed a concluding chapter entitled "My Father." Clara Barrus has written, in addition to the book named above, *John Burroughs, Boy and Man* (1920), and the official biography in two volumes, *The Life and Letters of John Burroughs* (1925), and has edited *The Heart of Burroughs' Journals* (1928). Associated with Burroughs for the last twenty years of his life, she faithfully accumulated an immense amount of material, "heavily taxing," as she conceded, her "powers of selection"; believing her subject "worthy of immortal regard," she made her work a Boswellian record. Clifton Johnson, after many interviews, published a readable and generally accurate work, *John Burroughs Talks: His Reminiscences and Comments* (1922). Accounts of others' interviews, in magazines and newspapers, are innumerable. The correspondence of *John Burroughs and Ludella Peck* (1925) covers the years 1892–1912. There is much matter relating to Burroughs in Horace Traubel's *With Walt Whitman in Camden* (3 vols., 1906–14). Of works of scholarship and criticism, two may be mentioned: Norman Foerster's *Nature in Am. Lit.* (1923), ch. IX, and Philip M. Hicks's dissertation on *The Development of the Natural Hist. Essay in Am. Lit.* (1924), ch. VI.]   N.F.

BURROUGHS, JOHN CURTIS (Dec. 2, 1817–Apr. 21, 1892), Baptist clergyman, educator, was born in Stamford, Delaware County, N. Y. He entered Yale at twenty-two, graduated three years later (1842), and was married to Elvira S. Fields of New Haven the following year. He was a divinity student at Hamilton Literary and Theological Institution until 1846. After a year as a Baptist clergyman in the little town of Waterford, N. Y., and five years in a pulpit in West Troy, he left New York state for the rapidly growing city of Chicago (1852), to become pastor of the First Baptist church. It was here that his career of distinction in education took definite form. The community itself was swiftly changing and expanding, and Burroughs took active interest in its educational problems. Three years after his arrival, he was offered the presidency of Shurtleff College, which he declined. But in the following year he gave up his pastorate to engage in the movement which resulted, largely through his own tireless industry, in the establishment of the (old) University of Chicago. Stephen A. Douglas had given impetus to the undertaking in 1855 by his gift of a ten-acre tract. Burroughs was elected the first president of the University in 1857 and remained in this position until 1873. For the next four years he was its

chancellor. Financial difficulties forced the institution to close its doors in 1886, and the buildings were torn down. Burroughs, who lived in the immediate neighborhood, never thereafter allowed himself to look at the spot where they had stood. He served on the Chicago Board of Education, with special supervision over the high schools, from 1880 to 1883, when he was made assistant superintendent of schools, a position he held until his death.

[T. W. Goodspeed, *A Hist. of the Univ. of Chicago* (1916); *Obit. Record Grads. Yale Univ.*, 1890–1900; *Colgate Univ., Gen. Cat., 1819–1919*; *Univ. of Chicago, Annual Register*, 1925–26; *Chicago Tribune*, Apr. 22, 1892.]   M.A.K.

BURROWES, EDWARD THOMAS (July 25, 1852–Mar. 19, 1918), manufacturer and inventor, was born at Sherbrooke, Canada, the son of Ambrose and Jane (Hall) Burrowes. He removed with his parents shortly before his fifteenth birthday to Portland, Me., which became his residence until his death. After working several years with Hayes & Douglas, dealers in crockery, he entered in 1873 the Maine Wesleyan Seminary at Kent's Hill. Upon graduation he matriculated at Wesleyan University in 1876, but left during his freshman year. While at seminary and college he had supported himself through his own efforts, chiefly by the manufacture of screens. After leaving school he turned naturally to the production of screens and through intense industry and business capacity built up the largest screen factory in the world. He was a man of considerable inventive capacity as well as a business executive. His first patent, that of a window screen, was taken out in 1878, and between that date and 1919 over forty patents were either secured by him or assigned to him. These patents fall into four main divisions: (1) window screens; (2) spring actuated curtains and shades; (3) automobile accessories; (4) folding tables, particularly card and billiard tables. Burrowes built up a large manufacturing business in curtains and shades and is credited with inventing the first curtains used in passenger cars, and of manufacturing ninety per cent of those used (1918) in railroad and street cars. These were manufactured by the Curtain Supply Company of Chicago of which he was president. The E. T. Burrowes Company of Portland produced not only screens but billiard and pool tables, folding card tables, and folding chairs.

Outside of his business affairs Burrowes was noted for his sustained interest in charitable and educational projects, especially those connected with the Methodist Episcopal Church. His grandfather had been a class leader under

Wesley, and he, himself, was an active member of the Chestnut Street Church of Portland. He practically built a church in the Italian section of that city, was a trustee of the Maine Wesleyan Seminary at Kent's Hill, and of Boston University (1901–18). He is described as "quiet in manner, reticent in conversation, genial and pleasant to his intimate friends. His qualities best shone in his home life and among his business associates" (Minutes of the Board of Trustees of Boston University, Apr. 11, 1918). He was married on Oct. 4, 1880, to Frances E. Norcross of Portland.

[*Zion's Herald*, Mar. 27, 1918; *Bostonia*, Mar. 1918; *Daily Eastern Argus* (Portland), Mar. 20, 1918; *Who's Who in America*, 1918–19.]   H.U.F.

BURROWES, THOMAS HENRY (Nov. 16, 1805–Feb. 25, 1871), politician, educator, was born at Strasburg, Pa., the son of Thomas Bredin Burrowes, an Irish immigrant, and Anne (Smith) Burrowes. His education was more noteworthy for its varied sources than for any great profundity: private tutors, Trinity College, Dublin, a Quebec classical school, and Yale College, are supposed to have assisted in the project that Amos Ellmaker, a Lancaster lawyer, completed when Thomas Henry was admitted to the bar in 1829.

Burrowes was a politician by choice and an educator by accident. He was elected to the lower house of the Pennsylvania legislature in 1831 and 1832, where, as a member of the Whig minority, he distinguished himself only by acquiring influence in his state party such that he could give valuable aid in the election of Joseph Ritner as governor in 1835, and secure for himself an appointment as secretary of the commonwealth, to which were attached the duties of state superintendent of schools. Burrowes, Thaddeus Stevens [*q.v.*], and Theophilus Fenn became the "Kitchen Cabinet" of the Ritner administration, and under their leadership every public and private measure was shaped to serve political ends. So well satisfied was the triumvirate with their administration that as the days of office-holding waned they became more and more loath to surrender their scepters to the incoming Porter régime. The Anti-Masonic Whig party, of which Burrowes was state chairman, was defeated by alleged frauds at the Philadelphia polls. Instead of submitting the evidence of fraud to the legislature, the secretary, in a proclamation dated Oct. 15, 1838, called on "the good people" of the state to "treat the election of the 9th instant as if we had not been defeated" (*Pennsylvanian*, Dec. 8, 1838)—an invitation to revolution that precipitated the bloodless Buckshot War. In an attempt to seat the defeated Anti-Masonic Whigs of Philadelphia in the House of Representatives Ritner called in the state militia and appealed to President Van Buren for aid, while the tainted but victorious Democrats brought a mob of thugs from their constituency to aid them in the organization of the legislature. The militia, recruited largely from the City of Brotherly Love, refused to assist the defeated governor; the President of the United States was not interested; and the threatening mob was in possession of the senate galleries, so Burrowes left office through a window in the rear of the senate chamber to take up the more peaceful pursuit of agriculture. The charge of treason, although seriously considered, was never pressed.

Paradoxically, a man, totally ignorant of the requirements of a state educational system, and who had voted against the free school measure, was destined to play a leading rôle in the establishment of Pennsylvania's public schools. Burrowes, during the Ritner administration, revised the school law of 1834 and organized the free school system of the state, the most distinctly creditable feature of the régime. Although he insisted in his *Report* of Feb. 19, 1837, that only the "elements of a good business education—reading, writing, and arithmetic" should be taught in the common schools, and that any individual who had not learned his "three R's" before he reached the age of fifteen could not learn them afterward, he became and remained the oracle of the Pennsylvania educational crusade until his death. He gave advice on almost every important school measure brought before the legislature after 1836, founded the *Pennsylvania School Journal* in 1852 and edited it for eighteen years, served as state superintendent of schools, 1860–63, organized the Soldiers' Orphans' Schools after the Civil War, and died as president of Pennsylvania Agricultural College. None of Burrowes's projects were cut from whole cloth, for his strength was in his sagacious sifting of practical ideas from the mass of suggestions proffered by his contemporaries. Hence he could set the public school system in motion during 1835–38, but in 1860, when the system had passed the formative stage, he was unable to contribute further to the growth of his creation.

He was married on Apr. 6, 1837, to Salome Jane Carpenter, by whom he had fifteen children.

[Burrowes, the politician, appears in W. H. Egle, "The Buckshot War," *Pa. Mag. Hist. and Biog.*, July 1899, pp. 137–56, and in the files of the *Nat. Gazette and Lit. Reg.*, and the *Pennsylvanian* (both Phila.) for the period Oct. to Dec. 1838; the educator is discussed in *Pa. Sch. Jour.*, Apr. 1871, pp. 281–85, and in J. P. Wickersham, *Hist. of Educ. in Pa.* (1886), pp. 346–53.]   T.D.M.

BURROWS, JULIUS CÆSAR (Jan. 9, 1837–Nov. 16, 1915), senator, son of William and Marie Burrows, was born in Northeast, Erie County, Pa. As a boy of seven years he heard Daniel Webster speak and the impression made by the great orator mastered the youthful auditor. Later, when the Burrows family removed to Ashtabula County, Ohio, Burrows came under the influence of Benjamin F. Wade and Joshua R. Giddings, whose children attended the school he taught. In 1859, he secured the principalship of a female seminary at Richland, Mich. In 1861 he was admitted to the bar, formed a partnership with A. A. Knappen, an able and successful lawyer, and began practise in Kalamazoo, which city ever after was his home. He came into local prominence by his stump speeches in the first Lincoln campaign, and Gov. Blair commissioned him a captain in the 17th Michigan Infantry, a position given primarily for recruiting ability. On Aug. 22, 1862, the regiment left for the front, on Sept. 4 it took part in the bloody battle of South Mountain, and three days later it fought at Antietam. The arduous and disastrous battles at Fredericksburg sapped Burrows's strength, and when the 17th was sent to the western army he was transferred to staff duty. After three more engagements, his failing health and the value of his services on the stump led to his resignation. He became the law partner of Henry F. Severens, afterward United States district judge. He spoke in the second Lincoln campaign, when, to use his own phrase, "Sheridan's guns were knocking every plank out of the Chicago platform." In 1865–67 he was prosecuting attorney for Kalamazoo County. Entering the national House of Representatives in 1873, he found the Republican party broken by dissensions and by the Crédit Mobilier scandals. He ranged himself with the reform element in the earliest efforts to subject the railroads to government control. Having been trained from youth in the camp of the abolitionists, and having fought to preserve the Union, he naturally worked in Congress with those who believed in securing civil rights to the negro by federal bayonets if necessary. Defeated for the nomination in 1874, he was reëlected to Congress in 1878, and continuously thereafter (except to the 48th Congress, 1883–85) until elected to the Senate in 1894. In the House he was an influential member of the small group (including Thomas B. Reed, William McKinley, and Joseph G. Cannon) that dominated the Republican side. With eloquence he supported party policies when in the majority; and with all the resources of an alert and trained parliamentarian he obstructed or defeated the aims of the Democrats when that party was in control. As a member of the Committee on Ways and Means he had an active share in arranging tariff schedules. On the stump he attained such a reputation as a vote-winning speaker that wherever the political battle raged most fiercely, from Maine to California, he was called to defend or to expound Republican policies. His honorable military service took the sting out of his advocacy of the Harrison "Force Bill." He marched with his party through the wilderness of silver coinage and came to victory for "sound money" in the McKinley campaign of 1896. If he was not a leader, he was an effective supporter of leaders.

When he was elected to the Senate in 1894, his work in the House was permitted to count in the matter of committee assignments. As chairman of the Committee on Privileges and Elections, he established a precedent by causing the Senate to exclude Senator Matthew S. Quay, who had been appointed by the governor of Pennsylvania to fill the vacancy caused by the failure of the state legislature to elect. While able constitutional lawyers, like George F. Hoar, took issue with Burrows (maintaining that a state should not be suffered to go without full representation in the Senate) the arguments of the latter prevailed, and the case was decided against seating Senator Quay, in spite of his political prestige. In both House and Senate Burrows worked to make effective the laws against polygamous marriages in Utah. After three years' investigation of the case of Senator Reed Smoot, Burrows reported from the Committee on Privileges and Elections a resolution unseating that senator; but the Senate voted otherwise. The decision, however, was influenced largely by the belief that polygamy had ceased to be practised among the Mormons. Also the personality and manifest ability of Senator Smoot had much to do with the vote in his favor. Burrows attained the height of senatorial ambition by being assigned a place on the Committee on Finance, a position to which his House service on Ways and Means gave him claims over those of Senator Thomas A. Platt of New York, who was Burrows's senior in senatorial service. The Finance Committee, under the able leadership of Nelson A. Aldrich, was considering the methods of changing the financial system so as to avert money panics by broadening the basis of note circulation. The Vreeland-Aldrich Act of 1908 was a preliminary step. That act created the Monetary Commission, of which body Burrows became an active member. The Commission made a study of the general subject of the currency, and the years of investigation and discussion prepared the way for the present Federal Reserve Act. When Burrows came up for reëlection in 1910, the younger element of the party had been brought into prominence by the intensity of the first McKinley campaign against the free coinage of silver. Michigan had enacted a law whereby the people might indicate to the legislature their preference for senators. Burrows announced his adherence to this method. Defeated by Charles E. Townsend he retired from the Senate Mar. 3, 1911; but as a member of the Monetary Commission he served until the submission of the Commission report, Jan. 9, 1912. After a public life covering half a century, he spent his remaining years in retirement at Kalamazoo. His career may be summed up in Joseph G. Cannon's laconic phrase: "You always found Burrows nearest the load."

Burrows was married twice: on Jan. 29, 1856 to Jennie S. Hibbard of Harpersfield, Ohio; and on Dec. 25, 1867, to Frances S. Peck of Richmond, Mich.

[Wm. Dana Orcutt, *Burrows of Mich. and the Republican Party* (1917); *Who's Who in America*, 1914–15; *Detroit Jour.*, Nov. 17, 1915.]   C.M.

BURROWS, WILLIAM (Oct. 6, 1785–Sept. 5, 1813), naval officer, was born at Kinderton, near Philadelphia. His father was Lieut.-Col. W. W. Burrows, first commandant of the United States Marine Corps, after its reorganization as such in 1798 (Richard S. Collum, *History of the United States Marines*, 1890), who afforded his son an excellent education, both in the classics and in modern languages. William was warranted a midshipman in November 1799 and joined the 24-gun ship *Portsmouth* in the following January, under the gallant though eccentric Capt. Daniel McNeill. After a cruise to France, during which two French privateers were captured, he obtained a furlough of several months, for the purpose of perfecting himself in navigation and the French language. In 1803, as acting lieutenant, he joined the *Constitution,* serving in her throughout the Tripolitan war. In 1808 he commanded a gunboat in the Delaware flotilla, engaged in enforcing the embargo law. In 1809 he was transferred to the *President,* Capt. Bainbridge, and then to the *Hornet,* Capt. Hunt, as first lieutenant, in which vessel he gave proof, during a violent gale, of intrepidity and sound seamanship.

Discovering that he was outranked by certain of his former juniors, Burrows sent in his resignation, which, however, was not accepted by Secretary Hamilton, who instead offered the young officer a furlough of nearly a year. This was accepted and spent in a voyage to India and China as officer of a merchant ship, the *Thomas Pen-*

rose, which on the return voyage was captured by a British ship and taken into Barbados. Paroled shortly afterward, Burrows returned home and was given command of the sloop-of-war *Enterprise,* 16 guns. Sailing from Portsmouth on Sept. 5, 1813, he fell in the next day with the British brig *Boxer* of about equal strength, which, with colors nailed to the mast, fired several shots in challenge and closed with the American ship. A sharp action of some forty-five minutes at close quarters ensued, in which Burrows gave proof of great gallantry and tactical resourcefulness. At 4 p. m. the fire of the *Boxer,* which had been repeatedly raked and had lost her main-topmast, ceased, and the vessel was surrendered. Burrows, who had been wounded but had remained on deck to direct the fight, was later mortally wounded by a canister shot, and lived only long enough to receive the surrender of the British ship, whose brave commander, Capt. Blythe, had been cut in two by a cannon ball. The *Enterprise* and her capture were brought into Portland, Me., where the two commanders were buried side by side. As this was the first American naval success since the loss of the *Chesapeake,* it was hailed with delight, and Congress passed a resolution of praise and regret, and presented a gold medal to Burrows's next of kin. He died unmarried.

[J. Fenimore Cooper, *Hist. of the Navy of the U. S.* (1839); John Howard Brown, *Am. Naval Heroes* (1899); *Analectic Mag.,* II, 396–403; *Port Folio,* 3 ser., III, 114–26.]   E.B.

BURSON, WILLIAM WORTH (Sept. 22, 1832–Apr. 10, 1913), inventor, manufacturer, was born on his father's farm near Utica, Venango County, Pa., the son of Samuel and Mary (Henry) Burson. When he was nine years old his parents migrated in stages to McDonough County, Ill., and a year later settled in Fulton County where young Burson passed most of his boyhood and early manhood, sharing the experiences of pioneer life which included a limited education. This he augmented later when, with his own savings, he entered Lombard University, Galesburg, Ill., graduating with the first class in 1856. Reared to the occupation of farming and early developing considerable mechanical ingenuity, Burson became much interested in the improvement of farm machinery, his first work in this field being the designing of a self-rake reaper in 1858. He then turned to grain binders and on June 26, 1860, received a patent for a twine binder. This was attached to his self-rake reaper and operated by hand. Twine, however, was not easily obtained, and Burson adapted his machine to use wire. On Feb. 26, 1861, he obtained a patent on this improvement and that year twenty-

337

five binders were made and used in the harvests from Vandalia, Ill., as far north as Red Wing, Minn. The following year fifty more were made, one of which was entered in the great reaper trial at Dixon, Ill., and proved a decided sensation. Emerson & Company of Rockford, Ill., manufacturers of the Manny reaper, immediately contracted to build 1,100 binders for Burson who in 1863 moved with his family from Yates City, Knox County, Ill., to Rockford. In the course of building these machines he devised and patented two improvements, Mar. 3 and Aug. 11, 1863, respectively. Prejudice against wire binders, however, developed, and their cost at war prices operated against them; while the machines were eventually sold, a profitable market could not be established and their manufacture was discontinued. Burson then returned to twine binders, patenting certain improvements in 1864–65 which resulted in a practical machine. The following year he began experimenting with automatic knitting machinery and in the succeeding twelve years devised and patented a number of machines for the manufacture of knit goods and hose. On Apr. 23, 1870, the first hose were knit on his machine in Rockford, and in 1872, with the perfection of his parallel row machine, Rockford's great knitting industry was definitely launched. In 1878 Burson withdrew from the knitting business to devote his whole time to invention, and in the succeeding thirteen years made many improvements in knitting and grain harvesting machinery, totalling about fifty patents. In 1892 he organized the Burson Manufacturing Company for the manufacture of knitting machinery and accepted the vice-presidency of the Burson Knitting Company, manufacturer of knit goods. He married Emily S. Wilson of New Jersey, Oct. 5, 1856, who with three children survived him at the time of his death in Rockford.

[R. L. Ardrey, *Am. Ag. Implements* (1894); Newton Bateman, *Hist. Encyc. of Ill.* (1916), vol. II; *Hist. of Winnebago County, Ill.* (1877); Chas. A. Church, *Past and Present of the City of Rockford and Winnebago County, Ill.* (1905); *Textile World*, May 19, 1913; *Am. Inventor*, Aug. 1, 1901; Patent Office Records.]
C. W. M.

BURT, JOHN (Apr. 18, 1814–Aug. 16, 1886), inventor, capitalist, was the eldest of the five sons born to William Austin and Phebe (Coles) Burt, at that time residents of Wales, Erie County, N. Y. The first ten years of his life were spent in the rather settled community in which his father was justice of the peace, school inspector, postmaster, land surveyor, and builder of saw and grist-mills, but in 1824 the elder Burt took his little family to Michigan, settling in the township of Washington, Macomb County. In this virgin territory John shared the characteristic life of all pioneers, helping in the hard labor of clearing land; attending school spasmodically; and, in addition, receiving from his father instruction in surveying, mill construction, and engineering. He developed an aptitude along mechanical lines and from the age of sixteen assisted his father in his millwright work. When he came of age he acquired a farm of his own near his father's and for five years thereafter cleared and developed it. In 1840, however, when his father was deputized by the federal government to survey the upper peninsula of Michigan in conjunction with the Geological Survey then in progress, John and his four brothers were taken along as assistants. A year later, on May 18, 1841, John was appointed a deputy surveyor and in this capacity continued in the work for the next ten years. While his father made the original iron discovery in this area, John, in 1848, subdivided the Jackson Mine District and discovered amongst other deposits, the Republic and Humboldt Mines. He gradually became thoroughly familiar with the whole area and its iron ores. When the survey was completed in 1851, after receiving an opinion from the United States attorney-general that iron ore lands did not come under the head of mineral lands, he purchased 15,000 acres, which later formed part of the lands of the Lake Superior Iron Company. After being unsuccessful in interesting any other men in purchasing shares in his acquisition, he returned to the Carp River, where the city of Marquette is now located, and built a dam and a saw-mill, preparatory to the erection of a forge for the manufacture of iron blooms. Shortly thereafter, with the cooperation of Heman B. Ely of Cleveland, he began the construction of a railroad from Marquette to Lake Superior, which was completed in 1857. Meanwhile, foreseeing the need of a ship canal around the Sault Ste. Marie rapids, Burt, aided by his father and friends, induced Congress to aid his state in building such a canal. On its completion in 1855 he was made the first superintendent. With the resolve to devote his life to the industrial development of the upper peninsula, Burt spent his time in organizing companies, building additional railroads,—looking toward a complete transportation system for the whole peninsula—engaging in extensive lumbering activities, and organizing ore mining companies and steel works. In each of these enterprises he served actively as an officer or director. In addition, he found time to devise a number of improvements for the manufacture of pig and wrought iron, involving methods of effecting carbonization, for which he obtained patents in 1869. Again, as early as 1867, when the ship canal needed to be enlarged, he devised and patented a type of canal lock which was incorporated in the enlarged structure completed in 1881. Finally, in the seventies and early eighties, Burt obtained patents for purifying blast furnace gases; for a ventilating system; and for a by-product charcoal burning process. Burt also for four years (1885–89) published the first newspaper in Marquette, known as the *Marquette Mining Journal*. He was little interested in public life but did serve as Republican elector-at-large in 1868, delivering in Washington the Michigan vote for President Grant. At the time of his death he was president of the Lake Superior & Peninsula Iron Companies and the Burt Freestone Company. He was married on Dec. 3, 1835 to Julia A. Calkins, who with two sons and a daughter survived him at the time of his death in Detroit where he made his home for many years.

[Henry M. Burt, *Early Days in New Eng. Life and Times of Henry Burt of Springfield, and Some of his Descendants* (1893); Silas Farmer, *Hist. of Detroit and Mich.* (1889), vol. II; La Verne W. Spring, *Non-Technical Chats on Iron and Steel* (1917); *Detroit Free Press*, Aug. 17, 1886; Patent Office Records; U. S. Nat. Mus. Records.]   C. W. M.

BURT, MARY ELIZABETH (June 11, 1850–Oct. 17, 1918), educator, author, was the daughter of Roswell and Rotalana Burt. She was born at Lake Geneva, Wis., and received her earliest education in the public schools there. She then went to Anna Moody's Academy and for one year to Oberlin College. Unable to continue her college course, she completed its equivalent with private teachers. In the year 1870–71 she began her teaching career at the River Falls (Wisconsin) Normal School and for twenty-two years thereafter was a teacher in the Chicago public schools, three years of that time in the Cook County Normal School. She was also for three years a member of the Chicago Board of Education. In 1893 she went to New York, taught for a time in a private school, and became the editor of the Scribner School Reading Series. She had already had considerable experience in the editing of school texts and brought to this work a knowledge of the needs and tastes of children, as well as a firm belief in the value of the best literature as a means of character education. She wrote several books of literary criticism, *Browning's Women* (1887), *Literary Landmarks* (1889), *The World's Literature* (1890), but most of her literary work was editing, and she wrote in the introduction to one of her texts: "There

is more religion in *editing* one *good* book that shall carry forth and hand down the torch of life, than in *writing* a dozen of indifferent merit." Her more important texts are a school edition of John Burroughs's *Birds and Bees* (1888), *Seed Thoughts for the Growing Life from Robert Browning* (1885), *The Story of the German Iliad* (1892), *The Eugene Field Book* (with M. B. Cable) (1898), *The Cable Story Book* (with L. L. Cable) (1899), *The Lanier Book* (1904), *Poems Every Child Should Know* (1904), and *Prose Every Child Should Know* (1908). The last two volumes show excellent selection, adapted to the memorizing of good literature by children, and are widely used in schools. Miss Burt's *Bird Song Phonetic Charts* (1913) have value in nature study. She wrote articles and lectured on educational subjects at various times, before the National Education Association, the Illinois State Teachers' Association, and in 1911 before the College for the Training of Teachers in Cambridge, England. In educational practise she believed in the Socratic and Froebelian methods, in manual training, and in psychological methods of teaching reading. She was active in the contest for equal pay for primary teachers and favored woman suffrage, but found little time for organization work. Her personality was a very earnest one, with all its enthusiasms devoted to children, whom she loved and understood well. During the last few years of her life she was something of an invalid and lived in retirement at her home, Englewood Cliffs, Coytesville, N. J., where she died.

[*Who's Who in America*, 1916–17; *The Woman's Who's Who of America*, 1914–15; *N. Y. Tribune*, Oct. 20, 1918; information from Miss Burt's brother, Dr. J. C. Burt, of Lake Geneva, Wis.]   S. G. B.

BURT, WILLIAM AUSTIN (June 13, 1792–Aug. 18, 1858), inventor, surveyor, was the son of Alvin and Wealthy (Austin) Burt, and of the seventh generation descended from Richard Burt who settled in Taunton, Mass., about 1634. He was born in Petersham, Mass., on his father's farm. When he was ten years old his family moved to Freehold, N. Y., and within a year again moved to Broadalbin, N. Y. Burt was able to attend school from the time he learned his alphabet until he was nine years of age and for three weeks when he was fourteen. This was the extent of his schooling. Circumstances compelled him to assist his father and at an early age his mechanical skill was well developed. In writing of his early youth, "Judge Burt," as he came to be known in later life, stated that his mother had instructed him early in "piety and virtue" and that his whole life had been influenced by her teachings. He was always a student but had small means for acquiring information through books or from individuals. Access to a book on navigation, however, when he was about sixteen years of age, had a marked influence on him and seemingly led him into his loved occupation of surveying. (It is interesting to note, in this connection, that his ancestor, Richard Burt, in 1658, was appointed "Surveyor of Highways.") A continuous home study, whenever possible, of astronomy, mathematics, navigation, and mechanics, using whatever books he could secure, coupled with a natural mechanical skill which he religiously cultivated, brought him recognition and enabled him to earn a living by the time he was seventeen, in the neighborhood of his father's home in Erie County, N. Y., not far from Buffalo. When he was twenty-one he married Phœbe Cole and settled in Wales, about twenty miles from Buffalo. During the succeeding ten years he practised the trade of millwright, and also served as justice of the peace, postmaster, and county surveyor. A desire to know the West caused him to undertake a journey alone in 1817 from his home to Pittsburgh and St. Louis, and then north through Illinois and Indiana to Detroit and back to Buffalo. A second trip in 1822, this time to Michigan Territory, resulted in his purchasing a tract of land in Macomb County, not far from Detroit, and in 1824 he moved his family there. For a time he engaged in his usual occupation and took contracts for the construction of saw and grist-mills. It was during this time that he conceived the idea of a writing machine. This he perfected and called "The Typographer," receiving United States Patent No. 259 on July 23, 1829. This invention is recognized to-day as the ancestor of the typewriter. In 1831 he was elected surveyor of Macomb County, and also served as district surveyor through appointment by the governor. In 1833 he was appointed an associate judge of the circuit court, being at the same time postmaster of Mt. Vernon, and was selected by the General Land Office in Washington as United States deputy surveyor, in which latter capacity he continued to serve till within three years of his death. While executing a surveying contract in the vicinity of Milwaukee, Wis., in 1834, he encountered difficulties due to magnetic attraction, which made the surveyor's compass needle unreliable. This difficulty suggested to him the need of a solar device and with his knowledge and skill he eventually constructed an instrument which he named the "solar compass," for which he received letters patent of the United States in 1836. This instrument, which de-

termines the true meridian by a single observation, the sun being on the observer's meridian, was adopted by the United States Government for use in surveying the public domains and has been so used to the present time. In his capacity of deputy surveyor Burt ran the course of the fifth principal meridian in Iowa, and with the assistance of his five sons, all of whom he trained to be surveyors and who successively became deputy surveyors, he surveyed the upper peninsula of Michigan between 1840 and 1847. At the same time a geological survey was in progress and, upon the sudden death of the geologist Douglass Houghton [q.v.], Burt took over his notes, completed the work, and prepared the report (*Senate Executive Document No. 1*, 31 Cong., 1 Sess., Pt. III). In the course of this survey Burt made the first discovery of iron ore in Marquette County, Mich., on Sept. 19, 1844. This survey demonstrated the great value of the solar compass, without which it could not have been completed with any degree of accuracy. Franklin Institute in 1840 awarded Burt the Scott medal and twenty dollars in gold for the invention of the solar compass. His lifetime interest in navigation caused him, on a return voyage from England in 1851, to take passage on a sailing vessel especially to observe the accuracy of the course laid by the ship's compass. As a result of these observations Burt began working on his third invention, that of the equatorial sextant (Patent No. 16,002 granted on Nov. 4, 1856; Burt's description of invention in *Senate Executive Document, No. 53*, 34 Cong., 3 Sess.). He was elected as one of two members of the Territorial Legislative Council of Michigan for 1826–27; was a member of the House of Representatives in the state legislature of 1853; and served as chairman of the Committee on Internal Improvements. In this connection he is recognized as one of the prime movers for the construction of what is now known as the Sault Ste. Marie Canal. He wrote *Key to the Solar Compass and Surveyor's Companion*, first published in 1855, with a second edition in 1858.

[Henry M. Burt, *Early Days in New Eng. Life and Times of Henry Burt of Springfield and Some of his Descendants* (1893); Horace E. Burt, *Wm. Austin Burt* (1920); John Burt, *Hist. of the Solar Compass invented by Wm. A. Burt* (1878); *Mich. Pioneer and Hist. Soc. Colls.*, vols. V, XXVIII, XXXVIII; Silas Farmer, *Hist. of Detroit and Mich.* (1889); Records of the General Land Office; Records of the United States Patent Office.]   C. W. M.

BURTON, ASA (Aug. 25, 1752–May 1, 1836), Congregational clergyman, was the son of Jacob and Rachel Burton and was born in Stonington, Conn. When he was sixteen years of age, the family removed to Norwich, Vt., where he spent a number of years in severe pioneer labor. He prepared himself for Dartmouth in eight months, entered college on his twenty-first birthday, and graduated in 1777. He studied divinity with the Rev. Levi Hart of Preston, Conn., and was ordained in January 1779 at Thetford, Vt., where he became pastor for life. From very unpromising beginnings he built up a strong church and lifted the life of the entire region. Though rigid in his doctrinal and moral standards, he received nearly five hundred members into the church. Through his monthly conferences with the youth of the town, he became a pioneer in young people's work. Although a believer in evangelism he opposed the Methodists and kept out of Thetford all denominations but his own.

Burton was best known as a teacher of theology. The number of candidates for the ministry which he trained wholly or in part, is variously estimated at from sixty to a hundred. He was a great promoter of education and was a founder of Thetford Academy and of Kimball Union Academy at Meriden, N. H. He was also a founder and trustee of the University of Vermont and a member of the corporation of Middlebury College. In 1804 he received the degree of D.D. from Middlebury, but declined its presidency in 1809. He was honored with many prominent offices by the churches of Vermont. Beginning in January 1809, he edited for several years the *Adviser; or Vermont Evangelical Magazine*. In addition to about twenty sermons, he published one book, *Essays on Some of the first Principles of Metaphysics, Ethicks and Theology* (1824). In it he sets forth his "taste" scheme of theology which holds that regeneration consists in the impartation to the disposition of a new relish or "taste" for good, in opposition to the "exercise scheme" of Nathaniel Emmons (Williston Walker, *A History of the Congregational Churches in the United States,* 1894, p. 303). In this work also, he foreshadows many things in the modern psychologies. In a sermon on *The Works of God* (1811) he seems to anticipate the theory of evolution, and he predicted a foreign missionary society twelve years before the American Board, and a theological seminary ten years before the founding of Andover (E. A. Park, *Memoir of Nathaniel Emmons,* 1861, p. 176).

Burton's only known portrait, copies of which were once found in many Thetford homes, is reproduced in the *American Quarterly Register* for May 1838. It represents a rugged face with a pronounced aquiline nose, but was not considered a good likeness. He lived a laborious and self-sacrificing life. He was not sociably in-

clined and was not a wide reader except in theology and metaphysics. He was a preacher of marked originality, and was a clear and able reasoner rather than an orator. He was married three times: in 1778 to Mercy Burton, his half-cousin, who died in 1800; in 1801 to Polly Child of Thetford, who died in 1806; in 1809 to Mrs. Rhoda (Braman) White of Randolph, Mass., who died in 1818.

[Burton left a brief autobiography in MS. This is the basis of a rather full biographical article by Rev. Thos. Adams, in the *Am. Quart. Reg.* for May 1838. Other sketches are found in Wm. B. Sprague, *Annals Am. Pulpit,* II (1857), and in A. M. Hemenway, *Vt. Hist. Gazeteer,* II (1871). There is also an excellent survey of his life and work in "Churches and Ministers of Vt., 1762–1830," by P. H. White and A. W. Weld, which exists in MS. in the Congreg. Lib. in Boston. The writer is also indebted to the Rev. Wm. Slade of Thetford, Vt., who has contributed much valuable information.]   F. T. P.

BURTON, ERNEST DE WITT (Feb. 4, 1856–May 26, 1925), college president, the son of the Rev. Nathan Smith Burton and his wife Sarah J. Fairfield, came of distinguished Virginia and Vermont ancestry. He was born in Granville, Ohio, and was educated at Griswold College, Davenport, Ia., and at Denison University, Granville, Ohio, where he graduated in 1876. In Denison, he had as teachers, E. Benjamin Andrews [*q.v.*] and W. A. Stevens [*q.v.*] a future colleague. After brief teaching at Kalamazoo, Mich., and serving in executive places in high schools in Xenia, Ohio, and in Norwood, a suburb of Cincinnati, he entered Rochester Theological Seminary (Baptist) in 1879. Graduating in 1882, he was in the following year ordained to the Baptist ministry, married to Frances Mary Townson of Rochester, N. Y., and elected professor of New Testament Greek in Newton (Mass.) Theological Seminary, the historic seminary of the Baptist Church. Promoted presently to the full chair, he remained until 1892 when he was elected by the University of Chicago as head of its department of New Testament and Early Christian Literature. This department was coördinate with the department of Oriental Languages and Literatures, of which President Harper was the head. In this chair, Burton continued till chosen president of the University, July 12, 1923 (after a service of six months as acting president). As president he served until his death. For thirty-three years he was an officer of the University.

To his professorships in both Newton and Chicago, Burton brought qualities intellectual, ethical, religious, personal, of the highest order. He was learned in classical and in New Testament Greek. While serving as professor in Chicago, he edited the *Biblical World* and the *Amer-*

ican *Journal of Theology,* and wrote numerous books on New Testament questions, including his widely studied *Harmony of the Gospels* (1894) in collaboration with W. A. Stevens. He served as director of the university libraries. He was chairman, also, of the China Educational Commission of 1921–22 to inquire into the whole educational condition in China in its broadest relationships.

To his presidency, Burton brought the qualities and elements embodied in his professorship, and more. He was gifted with imagination and vision. His personality represented leadership without autocracy and with real affection for his associates. His power of work, like that of his two predecessors, Harper and Judson, was tireless. The results of less than two years of his presidency were great and apparently enduring. A reorganization of various departments was made, especially of the Medical School to which Rush Medical School was joined. A new medical center was established. A great building plan, including graduate and undergraduate halls, was adopted. The endowments were largely increased,—to fifty-four millions,—and the standards of scholarship were advanced.

[Thos. Wakefield Goodspeed, *Ernest DeWitt Burton* (1926); Harold R. Willoughby, ed., *Christianity in the Modern World, Papers and Addresses by Ernest De Witt Burton* (1926), containing full bibliography; *Univ. Record* (Chicago), July 1925; *Christian Century,* June 4, 1925.]   C.F.T.

BURTON, FREDERICK RUSSELL (Feb. 23, 1861–Sept. 30, 1909), composer, student of Indian music, was born at Jonesville, Mich., the son of a Universalist clergyman, the Rev. William S. Burton. His mother was Sarah Evelyn (Mason) Burton. He was fitted for college at West Newton English and Classical School and graduated from Harvard in 1882, *summa cum laude,* receiving at the same time the highest honors in music, which he had studied throughout his college course with John Knowles Paine. He had always felt a deep, personal interest in Longfellow's poem *Hiawatha,* which he regarded as one of the world's real epics. Indeed, it is a tradition in his family that he had read the poem when but seven years old and pronounced it good! This poem he set to music while at college and it was sung by the Glee Club in 1882. About the same time he published a number of songs: *Sea-Weed, The Engineer, My Cigarette, Kitty Bahn.* After graduation he taught music until January 1883 when he became a reporter on the *Boston Globe,* being made night city editor in 1884. He went to Troy, N. Y., in June 1884 to write editorials for the *Daily Telegram* and was made city editor soon after his arrival.

In the following September he went to Fall River, Mass., as editor of the *Fall River Daily Herald,* but remained there only one month when he secured city editorship of the *Boston Post.* Later he was on the staff of the New York *Sun* under Dana and he also at one time did considerable journalistic work in London, England. In 1885 he married Winifred Baxter, who died in 1892. In 1895 he married Susan M. Carr. In 1896 he organized the Yonkers Choral Society which in 1898 performed his cantata *Hiawatha.* Its chief interest lay in the fact that he had tried to reproduce in its music the Indian mood of the text; and to this end he had made use of a true Indian melody, jotted down by Henry E. Krehbiel when heard at some tribal dance. This was undoubtedly one of the earliest instances of the use of an authentic Indian melody in legitimate music. In 1900 Burton published a second cantata, *The Legend of Sleepy Hollow;* in 1901 an *Inauguration Ode* (for the inauguration of President McKinley); in 1904 a *Carnegie Library Dedication Ode.*

By far his most important work, however, was to come in the logical development of his interest in and knowledge of Indian music. This he obtained at first hand, both in Canada and the United States, by spending long periods in intimate association with the Indians, particularly the Ojibways, who lived round about Lakes Huron and Superior. This intensive study resulted in the publication in 1903 of *Songs of the Ojibway Indians,* later amplified and developed into *American Primitive Music,* which has been generally accepted as "one of the most important contributions to the literature of American folk music" (*Art of Music,* IV, 347). This work was posthumously published in 1909. An interesting opportunity for Burton to make constructive use of his authoritative knowledge of Indian music came in the summer of 1902 when he was asked to supervise the music in the production of the Indian play of *Hiawatha* which had already been given annually for some time at Desbarats, Ontario, on the shore of Lake Huron. (This play is not to be confused with Burton's cantata of the same name.) He threw himself with enthusiasm into the task, writing certain incidental music himself, based upon Indian *motifs,* while he helped the Indians in their choice of original material. So successful was the result that, with the permission of the Canadian government, the group of Indian players accompanied Burton to England, where the play was presented at Earl's Court, London.

Burton also published the following narratives: *The Mission of Poubalov* (1897); *Shift-*

ing Sands (1898); *A Seven Days' Mystery* (1900); *The Song and the Singer* (1902); *Her Wedding Interlude* (1902); *Strongheart* (1908); and *Redcloud of the Lakes* (1909). He died suddenly on Sept. 30, 1909, at his summer home on Lake Hopatcong, N. J.

[Grove's *Dict. of Music* (*Am. Supp.*, 1920); *Class of 1882, Harvard Coll., 6th Report of the Sec.* (1907); N. Y. *Sun*, Oct. 2, 1909, quoted in *Musical Courier*, Oct. 6, 1909; Wm. E. Brigham, in the *Boston Evening Transcript*, Nov. 27, 1925; Hughes and Elson, *Am. Composers* (new rev. ed., 1914); Eugene E. Simpson, *America's Position in Music* (1920).]   W. T. U—n.

BURTON, HUTCHINS GORDON (*c.* 1774–Apr. 21, 1836), governor of North Carolina, was the son of John and Mary (Gordon) Burton. There is a conflict of opinion as to his birthplace, with statements that he was a native of Virginia and on the other hand that he was born in Granville County, N. C. It is certain that while he was still a youth his parents died and that he was reared and educated in the household of his uncle, Robert Burton, of Mecklenburg County, N. C. He attended the University of North Carolina as a student, 1795–98, was trained in the law, and achieved an early success in his profession, becoming ultimately a leader of the state bar. There is evidence that his genial personality and social gifts made him a general favorite. His marriage to Sarah, a daughter of Willie Jones, a man distinguished in politics and society, contributed to his success. His political career began with his election to the House of Commons in 1809. For six years (1810–16), by election of the General Assembly, he served as attorney-general of the state, resigning to reënter the Commons in 1817. From 1819 to 1824, he was a representative in Congress. His service was inconspicuous; he remained silent through most of the proceedings; his speeches on vaccination and the bank were modestly apologetic. His participation in the work of the committees on the judiciary and on military affairs, however, appears to have been more active. In 1824, he resigned to become governor, being elected by the Assembly. Twice reëlected, he served from December 1824 to December 1827. His administrations were uneventful. Perhaps the most colorful happening was the visit and reception of Gen. Lafayette in 1825. Burton's messages were concerned, in the main, with the advocacy of internal improvements,—development of resources, deepening of watercourses, and construction of roads —and with educational reform. (His three messages on education appear in C. L. Coon, *The Beginnings of Public Education in North Carolina*, 1908, I, 263–64, 294–95, 362–64.) He also

interested himself in an effort to modify the criminal code. One act, passed in 1827, authorized the directors of the Literary Fund to sell a lottery for $50,000, $25,000 of which was to aid Archibald D. Murphey in the preparation and publication of a history of the state. This measure was one of several attempts to raise funds by means of a lottery. Some notice was taken of a resolution of the legislature of Ohio looking toward gradual emancipation of slaves and their colonization. Although leaving the matter to the Assembly for disposal, Burton commented on it, calling Ohio's attention to the eleventh commandment: "Let every one attend to his own concerns."

Burton was not a Jackson man; so although he was nominated at the end of John Quincy Adams's term to be territorial governor of Arkansas, this nomination was not confirmed by the next administration. His remaining years were spent in retirement.

[A short sketch of Burton by Marshall DeLancey Haywood appears in S. A. Ashe, ed., *Biog. Hist. of N. C.*, IV (1906), 68 ff. A brief, but authoritative review of his administration as governor may be found in S. A. Ashe, *Hist. of N. C.*, II (1925), 295–312. His speeches in Congress are reported in *Annals of Cong.* (16 Cong., 2 Sess., and 17 Cong., 1 Sess.). His official correspondence may be consulted in his manuscript Letter-Book and Correspondence (2 vols.), N. C. Hist. Commission.]   W. W. P.

BURTON, MARION LE ROY (Aug. 30, 1874–Feb. 18, 1925), Congregational clergyman, college president, was born in Brooklyn, Iowa. He was the son of Ira John Henry Burton and Jane Adeliza (Simmons) Burton. After spending a part of his boyhood in Minneapolis, he entered Carleton College (Minnesota) where he graduated in 1900. On June 14, 1900 he was married to Nina Leona Moses of Northfield, Minn. His public life was divided into three parts, unequal in importance as well as in length. Its first third was occupied in teaching in the Academy of Carleton College (1899–1900), in the principalship of Windom Institute, Minnesota (1900–03), and in an assistant professorship of theology at Yale (1907–08). At the Yale School of Divinity he had studied, and received the degree of B.D., *summa cum laude,* in 1906 and of Ph.D., in 1907. The second part of his career, and briefest, lay in the pastorate of the Church of the Pilgrims, Brooklyn, N. Y. (1908–09), a pulpit occupied for fifty years by the eloquent Richard Salter Storrs [*q.v.*]. The third and most important part covered three university presidencies. The first, preceded by a visit to European universities, in special preparation for his administration, was at Smith College (1910–17); the second was at the University of Minnesota (1917–20); the third was at the University of Michigan (1920–25). Burton possessed unique ability in the raising of funds and in influencing legislatures. He secured a one million dollar endowment for Smith, ten millions for the University of Minnesota, and fourteen millions for the University of Michigan. He was endowed with a gift of flowing and persuasive speech before either a political or a popular audience, making the nominating speech for Calvin Coolidge at Cleveland in 1924. He published *The Problem of Evil; a Criticism of the Augustinian Point of View* (1909); and *Our Intellectual Attitude in an Age of Criticism* (1913). His educational policy was twofold, to build up the physical side of the institution and also to raise its intellectual standards. To his service as administrator, he gave great qualities of personal character—enthusiasm, friendliness, vigor—both intellectual and physical, a just union of humility and of self-respect, optimism, and a distinct charm of manner.

[*Ann. Report of the President of Smith Coll.,* 1910–17; *Univ. of Minn., President's Report,* 1917–20; *Univ. of Mich., President's Report,* 1920–25; *Detroit Free Press* and *N. Y. Times,* Feb. 19, 1925; *Mich. Alumnus,* Feb. 26, 1925; *Yale Univ. Obit. Record,* 1925.]

C. F. T.

BURTON, NATHANIEL JUDSON (Dec. 17, 1824–Oct. 13, 1887), Congregational clergyman, came of old Connecticut stock, his family having settled in that state in the seventeenth century, and was born in Trumbull, Conn., the son of the Rev. Henry and Betsy (Porter) Burton. As a boy he shared the fortunes of an itinerant Methodist preacher, and in one of his lectures ("Parish Inconveniences," *Yale Lectures,* p. 152) he speaks of the period as one when "my clothes were not as expensive as I would have liked, and my spending money was limited, and when my father had offers from well-to-do childless women to adopt me for their own." He prepared for college at Wilbraham Academy, a Methodist school in Wilbraham, Mass., and graduated from Wesleyan University in 1850. After a year of teaching in Newark, N. J., he entered the Yale Divinity School, from which he graduated in 1854. On July 20, 1853, he was ordained and made pastor of the Second Congregational Church of Fairhaven, Conn., now Pilgrim Church, New Haven. The same year, Sept. 14, he married Rachel, daughter of Rev. Henry and Rachel (Pine) Chase of New York. In October 1857 he became pastor of the Fourth Congregational Church, Hartford, Conn., and in March 1870 succeeded Horace Bushnell as pastor of Park Church, Hartford, where he remained until his death.

During his thirty years' residence in Hartford, he became known as one of the leading preachers of New England. He resembled Bushnell in his originality of thought and his poetic imagination. He was a man of broad culture, fine social qualities, practical common sense, and engaging humor, and was intimate with members of the literary and clerical coterie of Hartford, which included Charles Dudley Warner, Mark Twain, and Joseph Twichell. In 1884 he delivered the Lyman Beecher Lectures at Yale, and in the two following years was a special lecturer at the Yale Divinity School. From 1882 until his death he was a member of the Yale Corporation. He never said or did anything in order to attract attention, was careless with respect to perpetuating his influence, and was strongly disinclined to publish. Letters on his travels in Europe were printed in the *Hartford Evening Post* in 1868 and 1869. Extracts from these, his lectures at Yale, and some of his sermons and addresses were published by his son, Richard E. Burton, under the title, *Yale Lectures on Preaching, and Other Writings by Nathaniel J. Burton, D.D.* in 1888. His lectures were republished in 1925 with the title *In Pulpit and Parish.* They are written in an attractive literary style, and their content, the result both of keen thought and of long experience, is of permanent value.

[*Congreg. Year-book* (1888); *Hartford Courant,* Oct. 14, 18, 1887; Timothy Dwight, *Memories of Yale Life and Men* (1903).]

H. E. S.

BURTON, WARREN (Nov. 23, 1800–June 6, 1866), Unitarian and Swedenborgian clergyman, the son of Jonathan and Persis (Warren) Burton, was born at Wilton, N. H. While still young, he lost his mother, whose memory he later celebrated in the character of Mary Smith, in *The District School as it Was.* His early home training was in the circle of his grandparents, and with no additional schooling, he prepared, by private study and with the occasional help of a minister, to enter Harvard (1817), whence he graduated with distinction in 1821. After an apprenticeship in school-keeping, he entered the theological school at Cambridge, studied three years, was ordained, and settled at East Cambridge in 1828. The same year he married Sarah Flint; and, in 1845, his second wife, Mary Merritt of Salem, Mass. After a year's ministry at East Cambridge, he withdrew to engage in various reforms, by speaking and writing, preaching only occasionally. Later, he was minister at South Hingham, 1833–35; at Waltham, 1835–37; and at Boston, irregularly, 1844–48. He rendered public ministerial service as chaplain in Worcester prison, 1849; in the state Senate, 1852; at the constitutional convention, 1853; and in the House of Representatives, 1853 and 1860. Though at first in the Unitarian ministry, in later life he became a Swedenborgian. With the movements of his day, such as transcendentalism, phrenology, Pestalozzianism, he identified himself closely. From 1841 to 1844, he was associated with the Brook Farm experiment. In education he saw the chief means of effecting the reforms ardently desired in society. One or another of these contemporary interests runs throughout his books; it was to improve society in general, the home and the school in particular, that most of his lectures, books, and periodical articles were prepared. His chief works in the order of their appearance were: *My Religious Experience at my Native Home* (1829); *Cheering Views of Man and Providence* (1832); *The District School as it Was* (1833), which was republished in New York and London; *Essay on the Divine Agency in the Material Universe* (1834); *Uncle Sam's Recommendations of Phrenology to His Millions of Friends in the United States* (1842); *The Scenery-Shower or Word-Paintings of the Beautiful, Picturesque, and the Grand in Nature* (1844); *Helps to Education in the Homes of Our Country* (1863); and *The Culture of the Observing Faculties in the Family and the School* (1855). As representative of his shorter essays may be named: "A Supplication," a plea for pure English, "A Traveller's Story for the Perusal of Parents," and "Emulation, as a Motive to Study," which was delivered before the American Institute of Instruction, in 1834.

The influence of Burton was widespread, due to popularity as a lyceum lecturer, and the circulation of his major works, *The District School as it Was* and *Helps to Education*. The former, by its charm, attracted many to a knowledge of their schools, who would not have read a formal treatise; the latter, by its practical suggestions could not fail to open to parents a new view of their responsibilities and opportunities. Burton was an early promoter of the parent-teacher association idea, being convinced that "all the improvements in schools and modes of teaching" amounted to little, as long as home education was comparatively neglected. To remedy this defect, he advocated that "during the more leisure season of the year, meetings of parents, teachers, and others, should be held, from week to week, for the discussion of questions appertaining to family discipline, to the relation of the home to the school, and to education generally."

[*Salem Reg.*, June 11, 1866; *Salem Observer*, June 9, 1866; *Boston Evening Transcript*, June 7, 1866, Mar. 20, 1897; *Barnard's Am. Jour. of Ed.*, II, 333–36, XVI, 430; Abiel A. Livermore and Sewall Putnam, *Hist. of the Town of Wilton, N. H.* (1888).]   T. W.

BURTON, WILLIAM (Oct. 16, 1789–Aug. 5, 1866), physician, governor of Delaware, was the son of John Burton, farmer in Sussex County, Del., and of Mary (Vaughan) Burton. After receiving an elementary training he studied medicine in the office of Dr. Sudler in Milford, Del., and at the University of Pennsylvania, where he graduated with the degree of M.D. After beginning his profession in Lewes, Del., he soon removed to Milford, where he built up a good practise, living on a farm near the town. Here he delighted in dispensing a gracious hospitality and enjoyed a wide circle of friends. He was married twice, his first wife being Mrs. Eliza Wolcott, daughter of William Sorden of Kent County, his second, Ann C. Hill, daughter of Robert and Rhoda (Davis) Hill. Active in state politics, first as a Whig, he was elected sheriff of Kent County in 1830. In 1848, like so many other Whigs, he joined the Democratic party, and in 1854 was nominated for the office of governor of the state, but was defeated by the candidate of the Know-Nothing party, Peter F. Causey. Nominated again for the governorship in 1858 he defeated the candidate of the People's party and was inaugurated on Jan. 18, 1859. A Democratic legislature was likewise elected. Burton served his state the full constitutional term of four years, retiring in January 1863 in favor of William Cannon, the candidate of the Union party.

Although Delaware was a slave state and the Breckinridge Democrats had carried it in 1860, the state administration proved loyal to the Union, while at the same time it endeavored to conciliate those elements of the population who were strongly opposed to the war. Delaware's answer to Mississippi's invitation to join the Southern Confederacy was an "unqualified disapproval." On the other hand, Delaware sent five delegates to the Peace Convention in the following month of February, and a large peace meeting was permitted to assemble in Dover in June of the same year. When Lincoln called upon Delaware for its first quota of troops in April, however, Burton complied immediately by issuing a proclamation calling for volunteers (there being no state militia to order into the Federal service), and by his subsequent measures acted in harmony with the Federal authorities except on occasions when he felt that the Federal power was encroaching too much upon the rights of Delaware, *e.g.*, when making what he, and the Democrats in general, regarded as illegal arrests. The so-called invasion of the state by Federal troops at the general election in November 1862 and the consequent victory of the Lincoln candidate for governor brought forth from Burton in his last message to the legislature in January 1863 severe strictures upon the methods of the Union party.

[J. T. Scharf, *Hist. of Del.* (1888), I, 328 ff.; Henry C. Conrad, *Hist. of the State of Del.* (1908), I, 194 ff., III, 843; Records of Executive Acts for years 1859 ff., in the Governor's office, Dover; *Official Records*, 1, 3, 4 ser.; Senate Jours., Nos. XIX, XX, XXI and House Jours. Nos. XIX, XX, XXI for the years 1859 to 1863 inclusive, in the State Lib., Dover.]   G.H.R.

BURTON, WILLIAM EVANS (Sept. 24, 1804–Feb. 10, 1860), actor, author, was the son of a London printer, William George Burton, who was the author of a work entitled *Researches . . . Illustrative of the Sacred Scriptures, etc.* (2 vols., 1805). This title suggests why the son was sent to St. Paul's School, and destined for the Church. His father died, however, when young Burton was eighteen, and the boy had to leave school to run the printing business. Like many other young men of the period, he took part in amateur plays, and in 1825 joined a professional company in the provinces. After six years of this training, in which he developed a natural aptitude for comedy, he appeared in 1831 at the London Pavilion, as Wormwood in *The Lottery Ticket.* The following year he succeeded Liston as comedian at the Haymarket, when the latter left that company in a huff. But presently Liston decided to come back, so Burton was once more out of steady employment, and readily consented, in 1834, to accept an offer from America. As early as Apr. 10, 1823, he had married an actress but apparently was divorced from her, as on July 18, 1834, he was married to Caroline Glessing of London (T. A. Brown, *History of the New York Stage,* vol. I, 1903, pp. 358–59). On Sept. 3, 1834, he appeared as Wormwood, and as Dr. Ollapod in *The Poor Gentleman,* at the Arch Street Theatre, Philadelphia, then one of the leading playhouses of the country. He remained four years in Philadelphia, playing such parts as Goldfinch in *The Road to Ruin,* Sir Peter Teazle, Dogberry, and Bob Acres. Meanwhile he also wrote numerous magazine sketches later collected in a volume called *Waggeries and Vagaries* (1848). He also started the *Gentleman's Magazine* (1837–40) a monthly publication, of which Edgar Allan Poe was editor during the last year, but the two men did not get on together. Meanwhile Burton visited other cities as a traveling star, acting first in New York in October 1837, at the National Theatre, for the benefit of Samuel Woodworth, author of "The Old Oaken Bucket." In 1841 he essayed management in New York, but the theatre burned down and he returned to Philadelphia, managing not only two theatres there but the

Front Street Theatre in Baltimore and a theatre in Washington. He also acted constantly himself. Evidently a man of tireless energy, on July 10, 1848, he again entered the New York field, opening a small, intimate house on Chambers St., rechristened Burton's Theatre, which soon became and remained for eight years, the most popular playhouse in New York, if not in America. It was regarded with much the same affection that Manhattan later bestowed on the intimate little Weber and Fields Music Hall. It was a theatre where more or less serious plays, including the classics, alternated with hilarious broad comedy, or even burlesque, where the company was composed of a happy family of excellent players, and where the audience was always sure of a well-produced entertainment and a good time. It was a school for actors, for in the company during its eight years were Henry Placide, John Brougham, Lester Wallack, Lawrence Barrett, George Holland, Charles Fisher, and many more who later became leaders on the stage. Here were acted stage versions of *Dombey and Son* and *David Copperfield,* with Burton as Cap'n Cuttle and Micawber (two or his most famous parts), here Shakespeare was carefully revived with Burton as Falstaff, Bottom, Sir Toby, and even Caliban, and here he made the town roar as Sleek and Toodle. In his company was Miss Jane Hill, wife of James Hilson, stage-doorkeeper; after April 1853 she appeared under the name of Mrs. Burton (Brown, *op. cit.,* p. 342; Ireland, *Records of the New York Stage,* 1867, II, 235). In 1856 Burton moved to a larger house uptown, but the intimacy was gone in the new surroundings, and the venture failed in two years. He then toured the country with much success. At Mechanics Hall, Hamilton, Canada, in December 1859, he made his last appearance, returning to New York exhausted, and dying of heart disease on Feb. 10, 1860. He was a born comedian, with a broad, genial face which could assume any expression, and a joyous, hearty nature which always infected an audience with good humor. Everybody loved him. He was also a painstaking, intelligent impersonator, in spite of the somewhat broadly exaggerated style of acting he had learned from Liston, and he had a high ideal of ensemble playing and careful stage direction. His New York company set a standard of all-round excellence which materially affected the American theatre for good. Having a large income, Burton collected a very considerable library, especially of Shakespeariana, which was housed in his residence on Hudson St., New York, and he enjoyed the reputation of a scholar and gentleman, thus helping to stabilize the actor's profession in this country. His three daughters are mentioned pleasantly by Jefferson in his *Autobiography*. Besides the literary work mentioned above, Burton was the author of two domestic farces, *Ellen Wareham* (1833) and *The Toodles*; an adaptation of R. J. Raymond's *The Farmer's Daughter of the Severn Side*; *The Court Fool*; and *Burton's Comic Songster* (1837). He contributed a series of papers called "The Actor's Alloquy" to the *Knickerbocker Magazine* and edited *The Literary Souvenir* (1838–40) and *The Cyclopædia of Wit and Humor* (1858).

[In addition to sources cited above see W. L. Keese, *Wm. E. Burton, Actor, Author and Manager* (1885), and "Wm. E. Burton," *Dunlap Soc. Pub. No. 14* (1891); and *Actors and Actresses of Gt. Britain and the U. S.*, vol. III (1886), ed. by Brander Matthews and Lawrence Hutton.]   W.P.E.

BUSH, GEORGE (June 12, 1796–Sept. 19, 1859), Presbyterian clergyman, later a Swedenborgian, prominent in his day as a scholar, writer, and controversialist, was born in Norwich, Vt., where his grandfather, Timothy, immigrating from Connecticut, had settled. He was the son of John and Abigail (Marvin) Bush. The former, a graduate of Dartmouth, had studied law but never practised. George Bush graduated from Dartmouth in 1818, studied theology and served as tutor at Princeton, preached for a time in Morristown, N. J., and in 1824 went as a home missionary pastor to Indiana. Here he was ordained by the Salem Presbytery, Mar. 5, 1825, and installed pastor of the church in Indianapolis. The same year he married a daughter of Hon. Lewis Condict of Morristown, who died Nov. 9, 1827. A statement which he made in the pulpit to the effect that there was not a shadow of Scriptural authority for the Presbyterian form of church government caused a controversy with his session, which in 1828 brought about a termination of the pastoral relationship. From 1831 to 1847 he was professor of Hebrew language and literature in New York University, also serving, 1836–37, as instructor in sacred literature at Union Theological Seminary. In 1845 he associated himself with the Church of the New Jerusalem, and for the remainder of his life, as a writer, lecturer, and preacher, promulgated the doctrines of Swedenborg. Although opposed to all ecclesiastical rites he consented to be re-ordained to the New Church ministry privately in August 1848.

His knowledge was encyclopedic. As a boy his sole interest had been in books. Put into a printing office that he might not injure his health by too much study, he was tolerated there but a short time because he would become so interested in reading the manuscripts that he forgot to set the type. Before his second marriage, Jan. 4, 1849, to Mary W. Fisher, he had a study in the third story of a building on Nassau St., described as a "perfect den of learning," where barricaded with books he might be found at almost any time of day or night. Even those who were not able to accept the theological conclusions of his later days, professed great admiration for his scholarship. A modest, kindly man, he made no display of learning, but without regard for personal interests, stubbornly contended for what he believed to be the truth. His first important publication was *The Life of Mohammed* (1830), constituting Volume X in Harper's Family Library. This was followed in 1832 by *A Treatise on the Millennium*. In 1835 he published *A Grammar of the Hebrew Language*, a second edition of which appeared in 1838. Between 1840 and 1858 he issued a number of commentaries on books of the Old Testament. A work of his which was widely read and created much controversy was *Anastasis: or, the Doctrine of the Resurrection of the Body, Rationally and Scripturally Considered* (1844) in which he opposed the doctrine of the physical construction of the body in the future life. In 1846 he published *Statement of Reasons for Embracing the Doctrines and Disclosures of Emanuel Swedenborg*, and the same year edited *The Memorabilia of Swedenborg*. Another work which occasioned discussion was his *Mesmer and Swedenborg* (1847), in which he attempted to show that what is involved in mesmerism tends to support Swedenborg's teachings. His most radical treatise perhaps was his *Priesthood and Clergy Unknown to Christianity, or The Church a Community of Co-equal Brethren* (1857). Besides these more important works he published many others, including pamphlets, letters and compilations. He also issued from June 1842 to May 1843, the *Hierophant*, a monthly journal of sacred symbols and prophecy, and beginning in 1848 edited for a number of years the *New Church Repository and Monthly Review*.

[*Gen. Cat. Dartmouth Coll.* (1900); *Gen. Cat. Princeton Univ.* (1908); *Princeton Theolog. Sch. Biog. Cat.* (1909); W. M. Fernald, *Memoir and Reminiscences of the Late Prof. Geo. Bush* (1860); H. A. Edson, *Contributions to the Early Hist. of the Presbyt. Ch. in Indiana* (1898); R. W. Griswold, *Prose Writers of America* (1847).]   H.E.S.

BUSHNELL, ASA SMITH (Sept. 16, 1834–Jan. 15, 1904), governor of Ohio, was reputed to be the descendant of Francis Bushnell of Surrey, who came to New Haven in 1639 as one of the original signers of the plantation covenant. He was born at Rome, N. Y., where his father, Daniel Bushnell, taught school. His mother, Harriet (Smith) Bushnell, was a woman, according to the son, of "great energy," whose "house was a model," whose "life was a benediction," and whose "presence was always an inspiration." When the boy was eleven years old the family removed to Cincinnati; but six years later, after a limited attendance at school, he went to Springfield where for several years he struggled as clerk and bookkeeper. In 1857 he married Ellen Ludlow, and the outbreak of the Civil War found him engaged in the drug business in partnership with his father-in-law. This he left for service as captain of Company E of the 162nd Ohio Volunteer Infantry, which was assigned in 1864 to guard and picket duty in the Shenandoah Valley. After the war Bushnell's fortunes rose rapidly. Becoming a partner in 1867 in a concern in which he had formerly been an employee, he promoted its incorporation as the Warder, Bushnell & Glessner Company, becoming its president in 1886. This corporation was engaged in the manufacture of harvesting machinery; but other banking and public service enterprises also enlisted Bushnell's attention, and he speedily acquired both wealth and reputation as a keen and progressive man of affairs.

Although in politics from 1885 to 1900, a political career seems always to have been a secondary matter with him. His first venture in this sphere was as Joseph B. Foraker's manager in his successful gubernatorial campaign of 1885. He served for four years as quartermaster-general under Gov. Foraker, but resisted the importunities of his friends, in the years that followed, to become a candidate for elective office. In 1895, however, he was nominated for governor as a result of the factional strife within the Republican party in Ohio. The Foraker forces gained control of the state convention in that year and signalized their victory by nominating Bushnell. He was elected by a plurality of 92,622, the largest that had been received by an Ohio governor since John Brough's war-time defeat of Clement L. Vallandigham. In 1897 the candidacy of Senator Marcus A. Hanna to succeed himself became the issue of the state legislative campaign, and Bushnell, reëlected governor, was believed to have sought to frustrate Hanna's plan. Whether or not the ill-feeling engendered by this episode influenced Bushnell's career is a question; at any rate, he virtually abandoned politics when his term expired. Notwithstanding the Hanna incident, his administrations were less notable for political maneuvering than for efficient handling of the state's business, for which his experience fitted him well. The management of the finances was improved to such a degree that many thousands of dollars were saved; and the merit system in the civil service, which he advocated, was introduced so far as he could do it without legislation to support him. His energy as governor is well illustrated by the fact that, in the Spanish-American War, the Ohio troops were mobilized and placed in the field before those of any other state. On Jan. 11, 1904, he was stricken with apoplexy while attending the inauguration of Gov. Herrick, and died in a Columbus hospital four days later.

[A sketch of Bushnell, written in 1882, while he was president of the Springfield City Council, is given in *The Biog. Cyc. . . . of the State of Ohio*, vol. I (1883). A recent study is that in G. F. Wright, *Representative Citizens of Ohio* (1918). B. F. Prince, ed., *A Standard Hist. of Springfield and Clark County, Ohio* (1922), contains an appreciation, and numerous notes on Bushnell's part in Springfield's industrial development. An obituary by the Rev. J. W. Atwood appeared in the *Ohio Archæol. and Hist. Quart.*, Apr. 1904, and a "Sketch and Genealogy," by Geo. W. Knight, was published in the *Old Northwest Geneal. Quart.*, July 1904. The Hanna-Foraker factional contest and Bushnell's relation to it is told from the two points of view, respectively, by H. D. Croly, *Marcus Alonzo Hanna* (1912), and J. B. Foraker, *Notes of a Busy Life* (1916).]

H.C.H.

BUSHNELL, DAVID (*c.* 1742–1824), inventor, a descendant of Francis Bushnell, an Englishman, who in 1639 joined the New Haven Colony and subsequently helped to found Guilford, Conn., was born on his father's farm in Saybrook, Conn. The home was located in an extremely secluded portion of the township and here young Bushnell grew up, helping his father with the farm duties, devoting his leisure moments to reading, and shunning all society. When he was twenty-seven his father died, and, as his mother had died some years before, the farm descended to David and his brother. David immediately sold his inheritance, moved into town, and began to prepare for college, securing as tutor, the Rev. John Devotion, pastor of the local Congregational church. Two years later Bushnell entered Yale, and completed the four-year course in 1775. On one occasion as a result, presumably, of a discussion with members of the faculty, he demonstrated, in a small way, the fact that gunpowder could be exploded under water. This is thought to have suggested to him the idea of a submarine mine or torpedo. Apparently he gave much time and attention to this during his college years, for in 1775 he completed at Saybrook a man-propelled submarine boat on the outside shell of which was attached a wooden magazine containing gunpowder and a clock mechanism for igniting it at any particular time. The boat, built entirely of heavy oak beams, had the shape of a top. In fact, its exterior appearance was said to resemble a structure which would result from joining together the upper shells of two turtles and weighting the whole so that the tail end pointed downward and the head skyward. For this reason it was called "Bushnell's Turtle." The vessel was equipped with a vertical and horizontal screw propeller and rudder, operated by hand from the interior; a water gauge to indicate the boat's depth; a compass for direction, lighted up with phosphorus; a foot-operated valve in the keel to admit water for descending; and two hand-operated pumps to eject the water for ascending. The magazine, or torpedo, was located above the rudder and was connected by a line with a wooden screw, turned from within, which could be driven into a ship's hull. A further arrangement was contrived so that as the submarine moved away the clockwork in the mechanism was set in motion, having been previously set to ignite the charge at a certain time, the maximum being twelve hours. Bushnell successfully demonstrated his idea to the governor and Council of Safety of Connecticut who approved of his plan and suggested that he proceed with further experiment if necessary, with the expectation of a proper public reward. During 1776–77 Bushnell attempted to blow up British ships but was never successful, owing entirely to his inability to obtain a skilled operator, he personally being too frail. Attempts were made in Boston Harbor; off Governor's Island, N. Y.; and in the Delaware River above Philadelphia. After the failure at Philadelphia, in December 1777, Bushnell gave up further attempts amidst general popular ridicule, although to-day he is recognized as the father of the submarine. His inability to prove the merits of his invention in actual warfare, however, did not entirely discredit him, for when Gen. Washington in 1779 organized companies of sappers and miners, Bushnell was made a captain-lieutenant. He was promoted to captain in 1781, and was stationed at West Point in command of the Corps of Engineers on June 4, 1783. In November of that year he was mustered out of service, receiving the commutation of five-years' pay in lieu of one-half pay for life. During the following ten or twelve years it is believed that he went to France. In 1795, however, he appeared in Columbia County, Ga., as a school teacher, under the name of Dr. Bush. He lived with a fellow soldier, Abraham Baldwin [q.v.] who was the only person who knew his real identity, and through him Bushnell became head of a private school. Several years later he settled in Warrenton, Ga., and began the practise of medicine which he continued until his death at the age of eighty-four. As far as is known he never married.

[F. B. Dexter, *Biog. Sketches of the Grads. of Yale Coll.*, vol. III (1903); Henry Howe, *Memoirs of the Most Eminent Am. Mechanics* (1844); D. Bushnell, "General Principles and Construction of a Submarine Vessel," in *Trans. Am. Phil. Soc.*, vol. IV (1799), No. 37; *Beginning of Modern Submarine Warfare,* arranged by Lieut.-Col. Henry L. Abbot (1881); contemporary account of submarine (1775) in *Conn. Hist. Soc. Colls.*, vol. II (1870); contemporary account of attempts to destroy British vessels in *Am. Jour. of Sci.*, Apr. 1820; Geo. White, *Hist. Colls. of Ga.* (3rd ed., 1855), pp. 406–09.]   C. W. M.

BUSHNELL, GEORGE ENSIGN (Sept. 10, 1853–July 19, 1924), tuberculosis specialist of the United States army, born in Worcester, Mass., a descendant of Francis Bushnell, a Connecticut pioneer, was the son of the Rev. George Bushnell by his wife, Mary Elizabeth Blake. He attended Beloit College for one year, entered Yale as a sophomore, and graduated in 1876 in the class with President Hadley. As undergraduates these two young men distinguished themselves by their linguistic attainments and were the only two undergraduates of the class to study Sanskrit. In 1880 Bushnell received his M.D from the Yale Medical School. Pulmonary symptoms developed a few months later while he was serving as an interne in the German Hospital, New York City, but he regarded them lightly, and in February 1881 was made first lieutenant and assistant surgeon in the United States army. During the next few years he received a series of appointments of various army posts in the middle west and obtained a wide experience. At the time of the Spanish-American War he worked in the surgeon-general's office, but the strain provoked a recrudescence of his pulmonary symptoms and he passed a six-months' sick leave under the care of Dr. Charles L. Minor at Asheville, N. C. Later he was cared for by C. E. Edson of Denver, and from these two physicians he learned the value of rest in the treatment of pulmonary tuberculosis. From 1904 until 1917 Bushnell was commanding officer of the army tuberculosis hospital at Fort Bayard, N. Mex. There he had extensive experience and an unusual measure of success in treating the disease. He made the surroundings of the patients extremely attractive but maintained vigorous discipline for which he became widely known. His views concerning tuberculosis were at the time new and in part original. He maintained that in adults active tuberculosis was caused by infection from within. He minimized the value of the tuberculin test as a diagnostic measure and was a strong advocate of moderate eating and drinking for those afflicted. He attempted to introduce the Carton diet, but his judgment on this point proved less sound than in his other measures. During his years at Fort

Bayard, he kept abreast of medical literature, reading widely in all the foreign journals, and he even conducted classes in medical German for his officers. His greatest services were rendered during the World War. He introduced measures for rapid examination of large numbers of men and did much to quell the popular alarm concerning the high incidence of tuberculosis in the army. He established a school of diagnosis to train officers in the rapid detection of tuberculosis, and at the end of a year had turned out 450 examiners. The local tuberculosis boards during the war examined 3,288,699 men, of whom 23,991, or 0.73 per cent, were rejected. Bushnell's activity at this time was so strenuous that by the end of 1918 his health had again broken and he was forced to turn his work over to others. As soon as he had regained his strength he began to write his well-known book, *A Study in the Epidemiology of Tuberculosis,* which was published in 1920, and immediately this was completed he began another, *Physical Diagnosis of Diseases of the Chest,* in conjunction with Dr. Joseph H. Pratt of Boston, which did not appear until 1925, after Bushnell's death. In 1922–23 he was professor of military science and tactics in the Harvard Medical School. He spent his last years on his farm at Bedford, Mass., but was taken suddenly ill in California whither he had gone for his health, and finally succumbed to pulmonary tuberculosis, at the age of seventy, after a life-long fight. He was married twice: on Aug. 22, 1881, to Adra Vergilia Holmes, who died in 1896; and on Dec. 24, 1902 to Ethel Maitland Barnard.

[An excellent estimate of Bushnell by "E. H. B." in the *Am. Rev. of Tuberculosis,* June 1925, pp. 275–91; *Military Surgeon,* Sept. 1924; *Yale Univ. Obit. Rec. of Grads.* (1925); additional information from Dr. Jos. H. Pratt.]   J. F. F.

BUSHNELL, HORACE (Apr. 14, 1802–Feb. 17, 1876), Congregational minister, theologian, descended from Francis Bushnell, one of the founders of Guilford, Conn., in 1639, was the grandson of Abraham and Molly (Ensign) Bushnell. His grandmother was a woman of forceful character. Unable to torture her religious experience into the Calvinistic system held by the Congregational churches of New England of that day she heard with gladness a Methodist preacher and joined that denomination. Her grandson saw her but twice in his childhood, yet her vivid personality made so deep an impression on him that in after years he wrote: "Somehow she has been always with me, felt as a silent subtly-operative presence for good." Her son, Ensign, married Dotha Bishop, and the first of their six children was Horace, who was born

in Bantam, Conn. When he was three years old the family moved to a farm in New Preston some fourteen miles away; here the boy grew up. The father was a sagacious, industrious, cheerful man who gave his children of his best; yet it was to the uncommon character and ability of his mother that Bushnell felt he owed the greatest debt. "She was the only person I have known," he wrote, "in the close intimacy of years who never did an inconsiderate, imprudent, or any way excessive thing that required to be afterwards mended. In this attribute of discretion she rose even to a kind of sublimity. I never knew her to give advice that was not justified by results. Such wisdom, as I look upon it, marks a truly great character." She interested herself in her children's studies, trained them in correct habits, refused to be broken by drudgery, and kept the atmosphere of the home genially religious. Bushnell's sensitive spirit was also moulded by the unusual beauty of the neighboring country, a locality notable for its rounded hills, its frequent lakes, its extended and pleasant views. The love of nature and respect for her laws were early awakened within him and profoundly influenced the thought of his maturer years.

He attended the schools of the town, united with the Congregational church when he was nineteen, and worked on the farm under no eight-hour law, "but holding fast the astronomic ordinance in a service of from thirteen to fourteen hours." Clad in homespun, he entered Yale College in 1823 when he was twenty-one years of age. Here he worked hard and achieved both athletic and intellectual eminence in his class. Graduating in 1827, he taught school for a few months in Norwich, Conn., and for ten months served on the editorial staff of the New York *Journal of Commerce.* He next studied for the bar at the Law School in New Haven, having given up, on account of religious doubts, his earlier intention of entering the ministry. Accepting an appointment as tutor in Yale College, he still continued his law studies, passed his examinations, and was ready for admission to the bar when his course of life was suddenly changed. In the winter of 1831 a revival of spiritual interest developed in the college. Bushnell for a while stood aloof, but feeling his responsibility for the students who looked to him for guidance, he changed his attitude, silenced his doubts by religious activities, and in the following autumn entered the Divinity School at Yale. Here he came into the invigorating atmosphere of Nathaniel W. Taylor, the champion of the "new divinity," whose independent and courageous spirit he admired, but from whose methods and conclusions he reacted sharply. Taylor was a vigorous dialectician, promulgating and defending a theological system by formal logic. Bushnell's intuitive, imaginative mind was ill at ease in the iron cage of Calvinism, even when interpreted by the ablest thinker of its broadest school: so he turned to Coleridge, whose *Aids to Reflection,* deeply pondered at this time, opened to him "a whole other world somewhere overhead, a range of realities in a higher tier." In old age he affirmed that to this book he owed more than to any other save the Bible.

On May 22, 1833 he was ordained pastor of the North Church of Hartford, Conn., and on Sept. 13, 1833 he wedded Mary Apthorp of New Haven, a descendant of John Davenport. Bushnell entered the ministry at a time when the Old and New School of New England theologians were in fierce debate, but he sided with neither, having little sympathy with their spirit and none with their dialectical methods of reaching the truth. In a sermon preached on the twentieth anniversary of his ordination, he thus describes his position and purpose: "I was just then passing into a vein of comprehensiveness, questioning whether all parties were not in reality standing for some one side or article of truth ... accordingly my preaching never was to overthrow one school and set up another, neither was it to find a position of neutrality midway between them, but as far as theology is concerned, it was to comprehend, if possible, the truth contended for in both." From the first his thought was mature and his language had the "beauty and high solemnity" which characterized all his later writings. His sermon on "Every Man's Life a Plan of God," delivered in those early years, was later ranked by a writer in the *New York Tribune* as one of the three most notable of modern times, the other two being Canon Mozley's "Reversal of Human Judgments" and Phillips Brooks's "Gold and the Calf."

In 1840 Bushnell declined a call to be president of Middlebury (Vt.) College. In July 1845, broken in health, he sailed for a year's sojourn in Europe. On his return he published *Christian Nurture* (1847). Two years later there came to him a mystical experience which profoundly influenced his after life and thought. It was a spiritual birthday, such as came to Augustine and Luther and Wesley—a vision of truth whose light lingered permanently on his soul and whose power gave him perfect freedom. His daughter thus describes the event: "On an early morning in February his wife awoke to hear that the light they had waited for, more than they that watch for the morning, had risen indeed. She asked, 'What have you seen?' He replied, 'The Gospel.' It came to him at last, after all his thought and study, not as something reasoned out, but as an inspiration—a revelation from the mind of God himself." Referring to it in his closing years, he remarked: "I seemed to pass a boundary ... from ... partial seeings, glimpses and doubts, into a clearer knowledge of God and into his inspirations, which I have never wholly lost. The change was into faith—a sense of the freeness of God and the ease of approach to him." Made a new man in the joy and power of his vision, he naturally incorporated its meaning in a book, issued from the press within a year, entitled *God in Christ* (1849). But his glorious intuition was uncongenial to the rigid orthodoxy of the day, and from New Haven, Bangor, Princeton there came immediately severe reviews. Repeated efforts were made by the conservative ministers of the state to bring the author to trial for heresy, but the fellowship of the Congregational churches was organized for conference and fraternal helpfulness, not for dogmatic overlordship of faith, and the common sense of the ministers of the General Association forbade them putting restraint upon a mind that was so evidently rooted in the essentials of religion. Bushnell answered his critics and redefined his position in a new publication, *Christ in Theology* (1851).

Unfortunately the invalidism which was to afflict Bushnell's subsequent life now made its appearance. What had been at first a minister's sore throat took a deeper hold until increasing bronchial trouble compelled Bushnell to seek a milder climate and 1856 found him in California. This new country greatly stimulated those more mundane faculties which had lain dormant during his theological controversies. Being a man of robust common sense with the talents of an engineer, he took keen interest in the problems of this developing region. He predicted a railroad across the continent, studied all feasible entrances into San Francisco, and selected the one ultimately adopted. Interesting himself in the establishment of a college in this state whose greatness he foresaw, he examined seven proposed sites and finally designated Berkeley as having the proper requirements of situation, soil, and water supply. Here the college was founded which afterward became the University of California. He was offered the presidency of the young institution but declined. Returning to Hartford, he gathered up the fruits of twenty-five years of his ministry in a volume of *Sermons for the New Life* (1858). Despairing of regaining his health, he resigned his pastorate in April

1861. Yet to such an extent did his vigorous mind triumph over his growing weakness that nearly half of his published works were issued after his retirement from active service. *Christian Nurture* came from the press in its final form in 1861; *Work and Play*, a volume of essays and addresses, in 1864; and in the same year another book of sermons, *Christ and his Salvation*. In 1866 was given to the world the most permanently significant of his works, *The Vicarious Sacrifice*, in which is set forth at length his conception of the atoning work of Christ, now commonly known as the "moral influence" theory of the Atonement. This was followed in 1868 by a collection of essays entitled, *Moral Uses of Dark Things* which reveal Bushnell's breadth of culture and his mastery of literary form. In 1869 he declared against woman's suffrage in a small treatise whose central thought is shown in its title, *Women's Suffrage; The Reform against Nature*, and in 1872 he issued a final volume of sermons bearing the title, *Sermons on Living Subjects*. He continued his discussion of the Atonement, somewhat modifying his previous restatement of that doctrine, in *Forgiveness and Law* (1874). Although his health was rapidly failing, he projected a new book to be called "The Inspirations." "I do not expect," he said, "to live the labor through. I undertake it, in fact, to get a *sense of being* from it." On the morning of Feb. 17, 1876, he died, in his seventy-fourth year. Two days before his death he received news from the Common Council of Hartford that the park in which the capitol now stands had been named Bushnell Park in his honor. After his death a group of his essays and addresses were published under the title *Building Eras in Religion* (1881), and in the same year a uniform edition of his works was issued. In 1903 *Nature and the Supernatural, Sermons for the New Life, Work and Play* were reissued; also a volume of sermons and selections under the title *The Spirit in Man*.

In national questions Bushnell adhered to his principle of seeing the truth on both sides. He strenuously opposed the fugitive slave law, yet he was not an abolitionist. His faith in Lincoln was pronounced from the first for he believed that wisdom dwelt in a mind so simply honest, and this confidence he maintained during the dark days which followed. At the Commemorative Celebration held in honor of the men of Yale who died in the Civil War he was chosen to deliver the oration, which he entitled "Our Obligation to the Dead" (1865). In this oration his forward-looking spirit saw a nobler future coming out of the tragic sacrifices of the war. He predicted a new birth of literature such as had followed the wars of Elizabeth and Anne and Napoleon. "Henceforth," he said, "we are not going to write English but American. We have gotten our position, we are now to have our own civilization, think our own thoughts, rhyme our own measures . . . make our own canons of criticism. . . . In place of politicians we are going to have, at least, some statesmen; for we have gotten the pitch of a grand, new, Abrahamic statesmanship, unsophisticated, honest and real. . . . We seem, as it were, in a day, to be set in loftier ranges of thought, by this huge flood-tide that has lifted our nationality." The scope of Bushnell's public interests may best be shown by naming some of his contributions to the discussions of his day: *The True Wealth and Weal of Nations* (1837); *Barbarism the First Danger* (1847), a paper which had immense influence in founding Christian colleges in the West; *Common Schools* (1853); and *Popular Government by Divine Right* (1864). On his return from Italy, in 1846, having been profoundly impressed by the evidences of misgovernment in the Papal States, he wrote a *Letter to His Holiness, Pope Gregory XVI*, recounting the iniquities he had seen and urging reform both ecclesiastical and political. The letter was written and published in England; was translated into Italian and widely circulated, was placed on the *Index Expurgatorius* and specified by proclamation as one of the seditious publications to be suppressed by the police. *The Age of Homespun* (1851), one of the finest pieces of historical writing produced by Bushnell, is a vivid picture of early New England life when strong men enjoyed religion and enlarged their minds by profound metaphysical discussions.

He was not a popular preacher, but his was one of the most original and deeply penetrating minds which ever uttered itself from the pulpit in America. He reasoned, not with his intellect merely, but with his whole nature, and his solid thought moved steadily forward with a mastery of energetic words, a majesty of statement, a glow of spiritual passion which have given his sermons what appears to be a permanent place in the literature of the Church. George Adam Smith rightly classified him when he stated that as Spenser was the poet's poet, so Bushnell was the preachers' preacher; "his sermons are on the shelves of every manse in Scotland." Essentially a poet with a mystic's high vision he spoke with all the fervor and authority of a seer, yet a seer of profound and practical realities.

His daughter thus describes his personal appearance in his prime: "The spare sinewy figure, tense yet easy in its motions; the face, then smoothly shaven, showing delicate outlines about the cordial, sweet-tempered mouth; the high, broad forehead, straight to the line where it was swept by the careless hair, just streaked with gray; the kindling gray eyes, deep-set under beetling eyebrows; and, above all, the abrupt yet kindly manner, indicating in its unaffected simplicity a fund of conscious power."

It now remains to state the distinctive character of the service Bushnell rendered to his times and to the future. In New England Jonathan Edwards had reshaped the Calvinistic system of theological thought with such astonishing ability and urged it with such impressive fervor that it became the intellectual and spiritual home of the leading religious thinkers of the country. Yet they were not quite comfortable in it. It limited them in too many places. Hopkins, Bellamy, Emmons, Taylor, Hodge each changed a little this marvelously constructed house. They shared its grandeur and they were involved in its tragic error—a conception of human nature which ran athwart the best instincts of the heart. Disagreeing in many respects, they were at one in their method. Theology to them was essentially an intellectual system and was to be established by processes of exact logical deduction. Defining words with utmost care, they fashioned their statements of doctrine with meticulous precision. All being dialecticians, they differed violently and ranged themselves into distinct schools of thought. Now into this group of dialectical rationalists came a poet, a mystic, who apprehended truth by intuition, who gave the instincts of the heart full hearing, and whose appeal was to life rather than to logic. The theologians did not understand him for he belonged to a different order. What was still more puzzling, he used language in a manner quite incomprehensible to them. Interested in metaphysical speculation they endeavored to employ words as precise instruments to express nicest distinctions in thought. Bushnell denied that this was possible, and so cut under the very foundations of their work. He used language, not as the logicians, but as the common people and the poets have always done, as suggestive of truth, as a symbol of thought. This theory of the limitation of speech he early adopted and set forth with great care in his introductory chapter on language in the volume *God in Christ,* and in a more popular form in the essay, "Our Gospel a Gift to the Imagination." Spiritual things, he contended, cannot be precisely expressed in formal statements. Words are suggestive of religious truth but cannot be definitive. The gospel yields its

secrets to the disciplined imagination—the eye of the soul—rather than to severe intellectual processes. Such use of language, of course, discredited all theological attempts at exact system building.

At four points he broke decidedly with the prevailing theological views and became the pioneer of a new order. First, he protested against the common view of the relation of children to the church. The Puritan churches were depending for their growth largely on revivals, and revivals aimed at the conversion of adults. In their scheme of thought there was no place for children which was satisfactory to the mind and heart. The criticism is well taken that they reversed the gospel precept so that it read, "Except ye become as grown men and be converted, ye shall not enter into the kingdom of heaven." Over this perversion of nature and Christianity Bushnell brooded for ten years before he attacked the prevalent system in his book *Christian Nurture*. Its main thesis is that "the child is to grow up a Christian, and never know himself as being otherwise." This little volume turned the attention of the churches toward the training of the young, gave them a clearly defined doctrine of Christian growth, and suggested a working method in the religious training of children.

Of less permanent importance, but of real service to his day, was the relief he brought to orthodox Christians in respect to the doctrine of the Trinity. The audacious speculations of the theologians regarding the triune nature of God had issued in a conception which was practically tritheistic and caused much intellectual bewilderment. In this as in all things, Bushnell appealed to life. We experience, he argued, the one God under three different expressions. But that these three aspects of the divine revelation represented eternal distinctions in the Godhead, he refused to affirm, for here was a mystery which the human mind could not penetrate.

The third point at which he broke from the accepted opinion of his day was in his interpretation of the meaning of the cross. He repudiated both the penal and the governmental theories of the Atonement then in vogue, and affirmed that God's holy love was not satisfied until it was so revealed and brought to men in Christ that the love and power of sin in them is conquered and they are united in living spiritual union with God. This explanation is known in theology as "the moral influence theory" and has been widely approved because it shows that the atoning work of Christ falls under a law of self-sacrifice which is of universal validity.

A final service he rendered by recalling men

from the fatal dualism into which their philosophy had led them. According to Calvinism, human nature and nature itself were involved in the fall of Adam, humanity was alienated from God and was fast moving toward the fires of everlasting burning. This monstrous view of nature had caused theologians to draw a sharp line between nature and the supernatural, it divided further reason and revelation, the sacred and the profane. It was not original with New England, or even with Calvinistic theology, it was equally pronounced in the thought of medieval Catholicism. Already Bushnell had reacted against this perverted conception in his *Christian Nurture,* and he attacked it more explicitly in his volume entitled *Nature and the Supernatural as Together Constituting the One System of God.* This exaltation of nature his biographer, Dr. Theodore T. Munger, finds to be the key to Bushnell's thinking. "Bushnell," he writes, "outrunning his day, conceived of God as immanent in his works—the soul and life of them. Their laws were his laws. Therefore if one would know how God feels and thinks and acts, one must go to nature, and to humanity as its culmination. God is the spiritual reality of which nature is the manifestation." This book brought great help to the younger men in the ministry of that day on the vexing question of miracles. The prevalent notion was that a miracle implied the suspension of natural law. Bushnell affirmed that a miracle is not a violation of law, but is under law, the law of the supernatural which works through the order of nature.

His place in the history of religious thought may be stated as follows. He was the exponent on this side of the Atlantic of that spiritual movement in theology which was represented in Germany by Schleiermacher and in England by Coleridge. Like them he revolted against the dry rationalism of the times and endeavored to restate the truths of religion in terms of human experience. Like them he would give the emotions and intuitions their due recognition. Like them he saw nature and humanity filled with the divine presence and expressive of its purpose. Many were feeling the inspiration of this liberalizing movement, but Bushnell was the first notable theologian in New England to apprehend the full meaning to religion of that conception of nature which was finding such memorable utterance in the literature of the century, especially in Wordsworth, and to translate the doctrines of the church in harmony with the laws of life. His contemporaries in England embodying the same tendency were Maurice and Robertson, in America his essential message reached

the people through the more widely acclaimed ministries of Beecher and Brooks. Emerson was, indeed, a more conspicuous herald of this enfranchising movement which was sweeping through Europe and was disturbing our shores; and he had his own audience and his own peculiar work. Bushnell's appeal was to the more conservative religious mind of the churches, first of New England and then of the country. He brought to the interpretation of the supreme doctrines of Christianity a sense of the divine in nature, of life as the superlative test of truth, of the heart as a means of spiritual knowledge, of language as suggestive, not precise, in the realm of the spirit; thus his coming marked the end of that school of thought which began with Edwards and is known as the New England Theology; it ushered in new habits of thinking and new methods of expression.

[The chief sources of information are an excellent biography, *Life and Letters of Horace Bushnell* (1880, 1903), prepared by his daughter, Mary Bushnell Cheney, with the help of others. Very valuable is Dr. T. T. Munger's analysis of Bushnell's genius and work in *Horace Bushnell, Preacher and Theologian* (1899), and also his essay, "The Secret of Horace Bushnell," in *Essays for the Day* (1904). In 1902 the General Association of Connecticut held a meeting in Bushnell's honor in Hartford, and the addresses were published in a pamphlet entitled *Bushnell Centenary* (1902). *My Four Religious Teachers* (1903), by H. C. Trumbull; "Horace Bushnell and Albrecht Ritschl," by G. B. Stevens in *Am. Jour. Theol.,* Jan. 1902; "Horace Bushnell and His Work for Theology," by C. F. Dole in *The New World,* Dec. 1899, are valuable. See also Frank Hugh Foster, *A Genetic Hist. of the New Eng. Theology* (1907), *passim.* A list of Bushnell's published articles, the replies they evoked, references to him in books and periodicals including the year 1903, was assembled by Henry B. Learned, *Bibliography of the Writings of Horace Bushnell* (n.d.); it takes slight account, however, of Bushnell's pamphlets and books published in Great Britain, and only of editions involving some alteration of the text.]　　　　　　　　　　　　　　C.A.D.

BUSSEY, CYRUS (Oct. 5, 1833–Mar. 2, 1915), Union soldier, was born at Hubbard, Trumbull County, Ohio, the son of Amos Bussey, a Methodist minister, and his wife Hannah Tylee. Four years later the family moved to Indiana. Cyrus went to work in a dry-goods store at the age of fourteen, and at sixteen started a small business for himself at Dupont, Ind. He was married to Ellen Kiser of Rockford, Ind., on May 15, 1855. In the same year he removed to Bloomfield, Ia., continuing in business and entering politics. He was elected to the Iowa Senate in 1858, as a Democrat, and in 1860 was a delegate to the Democratic national convention which met at Charleston and Baltimore and nominated Stephen A. Douglas for the presidency. Early in 1861 the governor of Iowa appointed him as one of his aides in charge of the defense of the state. Invading Missouri with a force of Iowa militia,

Bussey dispersed a body of secessionists in a skirmish at Athens, and assisted in saving Missouri to the Union. Appointed colonel of the 3rd Iowa Cavalry, he was mustered into the volunteer service of the United States on Sept. 5, 1861. At the battle of Pea Ridge, where his regiment was first engaged with the enemy, he was in charge of a small force of cavalry, with three guns, in addition to his own men. He commanded a brigade of cavalry in the Army of the Tennessee (Grant) during the Vicksburg campaign of 1863. He was appointed brigadier-general of volunteers, Jan. 5, 1864, and commanded a brigade and division, employed in minor operations and on garrison duty in the southwest, until his muster out, Aug. 24, 1865, with the brevet rank of major-general of volunteers. After the war he resumed business as a commission merchant, first in St. Louis and later in New Orleans. He was president of the chamber of commerce of the latter city for six years, and was chairman of a committee which secured the appropriation for the construction of the Eads jetties to improve navigation at the mouth of the Mississippi River. In 1881 he removed his business to New York. The war having made him a Republican in politics, he was elected a delegate to the national convention of that party in 1868 and again in 1884. President Harrison appointed him assistant secretary of the interior in 1889, and he held that office until 1893, his administration being marked by a lavish policy in the award of pensions. He then established a law office in the city of Washington, where he spent the remainder of his life. He was buried in Arlington National Cemetery.

[*Who's Who in America*, 1914–15; *Annals of Iowa*, 3rd ser., vol. V (1901–03), pp. 81–92, and vol. XII (1915), pp. 153–54; *Official Records*, ser. I, vols. III, VIII, XXIV (pts. 2, 3), XLI (pts. 2, 3), XLVIII (pts. 1, 2); F. B. Heitman, *Hist. Reg.* (1903), I, 268.]

T.M.S.

BUTLER, ANDREW PICKENS (Nov. 18, 1796–May 25, 1857), lawyer, senator, was the fifth child of William Butler [*q.v.*], the Revolutionary soldier, and his wife Behethland Foote Moore, who when seventeen years old had made a celebrated midnight ride of warning to the Continental troops, through which she first met her future husband. Andrew attended Moses Waddell's academy in Abbeville District—the training school of Calhoun, McDuffie, and other men famous in state history—and then entered South Carolina College, graduating in 1817. Two years later he was admitted to the bar. After a brief residence in Columbia he moved to Edgefield and soon built up a wide practise in the courts of the state. In 1824 he was elected to the legislature where he became recognized as a leader of the

Calhoun faction and a champion of nullification. From 1829 until the end of his legislative term, he was a trustee of South Carolina College. After a brief service as circuit judge in 1833, he was advanced in the same year to the bench of the court of appeals where he remained for thirteen years. Judicial responsibilities were not particularly congenial to him and he welcomed an opportunity, in December 1846, to go to the Senate as successor to McDuffie, who had resigned. He was reëlected in 1848 and again in 1854, both times without opposition.

Partly because of Calhoun's influence, the younger senator early assumed a place of measurable prominence; in 1849, for example, he was elected by the Senate chairman of the Judiciary Committee, defeating Seward and Chase. Standing necessarily somewhat in the shadow of his conspicuous colleague, Butler was vigorous in the debates and active in routine work. He devoted himself faithfully to the interests of his slaveholding constituency, opposing the admission of California, supporting the fugitive-slave law, and reaching the climax of his senatorial career in the forensic battle over Kansas. His speech on this topic in part drew forth Sumner's address on May 19, 1856, in which the Massachusetts senator attacked Butler in a vituperative manner. Three days later, while Sumner was seated at his desk in the Senate chamber, Preston Brooks [*q.v.*], congressman from South Carolina and nephew of Butler, beat him over the head with his cane until he was insensible. The following year, Butler, who had been in weak health for some time, died at his Edgefield home, "Stonelands."

Within the councils of his own state, Butler was more temperate than many of his contemporaries. He represented in the main the upcountry point of view as opposed to the more radical attitude of the coastal leaders. In the early fifties he resolutely opposed the secession agitation, and argued strongly against any form of separate state action. He was known for his wit, sometimes caustic, and for his qualities of good comradeship. Gov. Perry, who was in the opposing political camp, thought him too impatient and sarcastic for highest judicial excellence and reported his speaking as rather dull; but even Perry freely conceded to him force of intellect and character. Butler was impressive in personal appearance, tall, clean-shaven, with a mass of fine hair on a large head. His domestic life was sad. His first wife, Susan Anne Simkins, lived after marriage only a few months, and his second wife, Harriet Hayne, died in 1834 after two years of marriage. Through the long period of his loneliness, Butler's mother kept his house until her death in 1851. By his second wife he had one child, Nancy, who married Johnson Hagood, a general of the Confederate army.

[Sketches of Butler are in John Belton O'Neal, *The Bench and Bar of S. C.* (1859), in B. F. Perry, *Reminiscences of Public Men* (1883), and in U. R. Brook, *S. C. Bench and Bar* (1908). Many of his speeches in the Senate are in the *Cong. Globe* for the decade of his tenure. Records of the Butler family are in "The Butlers of S. C.," in *S. C. Hist. and Geneal. Mag.*, Oct. 1903.]

F.P.G.

BUTLER, BENJAMIN FRANKLIN (Dec. 14, 1795–Nov. 8, 1858), lawyer, politician, was descended from Jonathan Butler, who settled at Saybrook, Conn., in 1724. Jonathan's grandson Medad migrated from Branford, Conn., to Kinderhook Landing (Stuyvesant) in Columbia County, N. Y. Here he married Hannah Tylee in 1794, and here their eldest son, Benjamin, was born the next year. After completing the scanty education offered by the district school, he studied law and was admitted to the bar in 1817. For four years thereafter he was a partner at Albany in the office of Martin Van Buren, for whom he retained a life-long admiration and affection. The year after his admission to the bar he married Harriet Allen, whose parents (the mother a Quaker related to Benjamin Franklin) had moved from Nantucket, Mass., to Hudson, N. Y., about the same time that his own father had left Branford. As Butler rose in his profession, honors and duties came to him rapidly. He was district attorney of Albany County from 1821 to 1824, and the next year was associated with John Duer and John C. Spencer in the important commission for the revision of the statutes of the State of New York. From 1827 to 1833 he was a member of the state legislature, which would have elected him to the United States Senate had he given his consent. At the same time he declined an appointment by Gov. Marcy to the supreme court of the state. He did, however, yield to the urgent invitation of his former law partner, Van Buren, now vice-president of the United States, to enter President Jackson's cabinet as attorney-general in the autumn of 1833,—perhaps on Van Buren's assurance that his acceptance would not interfere with his continued practise in the courts of New York and Albany, the former of which cities might be reached in fifteen hours and the latter in a day and a night from Washington, "next season, when the railroad is completed." Butler held the office of attorney-general for five years, and added to its duties the secretaryship of war in the closing months of Jackson's administration (October 1836–March 1837) when Lewis Cass retired from the cabinet to become minister to France. He might have

had his pick of cabinet posts under Van Buren, but the practise of law appealed more strongly to him than political office. Nor could President Polk persuade him seven years later to reënter the cabinet as secretary of war. He did, however, accept both Van Buren's and Polk's appointments as United States attorney for the southern district of New York (1838–41, 1845–48), a position which was less incompatible with his professional duties. The last ten years of his life (1848–58) he devoted entirely to the law, withdrawing more and more from general practise to the management of a small group of corporation cases involving very large sums of money. His rank among the leaders of the New York bar was firmly established. Chancellor Kent spoke of him as "this remarkable lawyer whose memoranda the student finds in all his books." Butler's interest in the law as a science led him to organize the department of law in the University of the City of New York in 1838 and to serve for several years as its leading professor. In politics he was a staunch Jacksonian Democrat. He headed the electoral college of New York which cast its vote for Polk in 1845. As the contest over slavery grew more heated, however, he began to waver. He supported his old chief, Van Buren, who ran on the Free-Soil ticket in 1848, but he returned to the Democratic fold in 1852 to vote for Pierce and the finality of the compromise acts of 1850. The Kansas-Nebraska Act of 1854, however, drove him out of the Democratic ranks. With thousands of other Anti-Nebraska Democrats he joined the new Republican party, and he cast his last presidential ballot for Frémont in 1856. He appeared at a mass meeting in City Hall Park, New York, on May 13, 1854, to denounce the repeal of the Missouri Compromise. But he did not live to see the Republican victory in 1860 and the civil strife which followed. In the summer of 1858 he went to Europe to recuperate from his heavy labors and died at Paris of Bright's disease. His body was brought back to New York and buried from the Mercer Street Presbyterian Church, of which he had been a devoted member, although he would never accept any office in the church, because there were articles in the Westminster Confession of Faith to which he could not subscribe. Aside from his legal opinions and arguments, the work in collaboration with Duer and Spencer in the revision of the statutes of New York, and the convention (approved by Act of Congress in June 1834) by which he and five associated commissioners settled the controversy of fifty years' standing over the boundary line between New York and New Jersey, Butler left but a scanty literary legacy. His grasp of history and power of lucid exposition, however, are amply shown in his "Outline of the Constitutional History of New York" (1847), an address on the occasion of the forty-third anniversary of the founding of the New York Historical Society, tracing the changes in government in New York from the days of the Dutch rule down to the adoption of the Constitution of 1846 (published in the *Collections of the New York Historical Society*, 2 ser., II, 1848, 9–75).

[Wm. Allen Butler (B. F. Butler's son), *A Retrospect of Forty Years, 1825–1865*, ed. by Harriet Allen Butler (1911) ; *Procs. and Addresses on the Occasion of the Death of Benj. Franklin Butler*, a memorial privately printed for the family (1889) ; Wm. Lyon Mackenzie, *The Lives and Opinions of Benj. Franklin Butler . . . and Jesse Hoyt* (1845) ; L. B. Proctor, *Bench and Bar of N. Y.* (1870).]   D.S.M.

BUTLER, BENJAMIN FRANKLIN (Nov. 5, 1818–Jan. 11, 1893), Union soldier, congressman, governor of Massachusetts, was born at Deerfield, N. H. His family was largely of Scotch-Irish stock, settled on the New England frontier before the Revolution. His father, John, was captain of dragoons under Jackson at New Orleans, traded in the West Indies, and held a privateer's commission from Bolivar. His mother was Charlotte Ellison, of the Londonderry (N. H.) Cilleys, or Seelyes. After Capt. Butler's death she ultimately settled, in 1828, at Lowell, Mass., running one of the famous factory boarding houses there.

Benjamin was sent to Waterbury (now Colby) College in Maine to continue the family Baptist Calvinism ; but he rejected Calvinism altogether. He graduated in 1838, and returned to Lowell where he taught school and studied law. He was admitted to the bar in 1840 and began a successful practise which continued until his death. At first he was chiefly occupied with criminal cases in which he built up a reputation for remarkable quickness of wit, resourcefulness, and mastery of all the defensive devices of the law. His practise gradually extended so that he maintained offices in both Boston and Lowell. He was shrewd in investment, and in spite of rather lavish expenditures built up a fortune. On May 16, 1844, he married Sarah Hildreth, an actress. Their daughter Blanche married Adelbert Ames, who during the period of Reconstruction was senator from Mississippi, and governor of that state. After the Civil War, Butler maintained residences at Lowell, Washington, and on the New England coast. He was interested in yachting, and at one time owned the famous cup-winner *America*.

Butler early entered politics, as a Democrat, being elected to the Massachusetts House of Representatives in 1853, and the Senate in 1859. He was an effective public speaker. His method, which seems to have been instinctive with him, was to draw attack upon himself, and then confute his assailants. He made friends of labor and of the Roman Catholic element in his home district, whose support he always retained. In the legislature he stood for a ten-hour day, and for compensation for the burning of the Ursuline Convent. He took great pains to be in the intimate councils of his party, but was seldom trusted by the party leaders. His talent for biting epigrams, and his picturesque controversies made him one of the most widely known men in politics from 1860 till his death. In the national Democratic convention of 1860 he advocated a renewal of the Cincinnati platform, opposed Douglas, and voted to nominate Jefferson Davis. With Caleb Cushing and other seceders from the adjourned Baltimore meeting he joined in putting forward Breckinridge and Lane. It was characteristic of him that in thus supporting the Southern candidate, he advanced as his reason for leaving the Douglas convention the fact that the reopening of the slave-trade had there been discussed. As was the case with so many Northern supporters of Breckinridge, Butler was a strong Andrew Jackson Unionist. He had always been interested in military affairs, and to the confusion of the Republican majority in Massachusetts had been elected brigadier-general of militia. At the news of the firing on Fort Sumter he was promptly and dramatically ready, with men and money, and left Boston for Washington with his regiment on Apr. 17, 1861.

Thereupon began one of the most astounding careers of the war. Butler was, until Grant took control, as much a news item as any man except Lincoln. He did many things so clever as to be almost brilliant. He moved in a continual atmosphere of controversy which gradually widened from local quarrels with Gov. Andrews of Massachusetts until it included most of the governments of the world ; in which controversies he was sometimes right. He expected the war to advance his political fortunes and the financial fortunes of his family and friends. His belief in the Union and in his own ability were both strong and sincere. He had hopes of the Unionist presidential nomination in 1864. A thorn in the side of those in authority, his position as a Democrat fighting for the Union and his prominence in the public eye, made it impossible to ignore or effectively to discipline him.

At the beginning of the war, his relief of blockaded Washington by landing at Annapolis with the 8th Massachusetts, and by repairing the railroad from that point, was splendidly accomplished. Probably because of his Southern connections, he was chosen to occupy Baltimore, which he did on May 13, 1861, peacefully, with but 900 troops. On May 16 he was nominated major-general of volunteers. His next command was at Fortress Monroe. Here he admirably administered the extraordinary provisions necessary for increased numbers. The problem of how to deal with slaves fleeing from Confederate owners to the Union lines he solved by declaring these slaves contraband; and the term "Contraband" clung to them throughout the war. He undertook a military expedition which ended disastrously in the battle of Big Bethel. On Aug. 8, 1861, he was replaced by the venerable Gen. Wood. He was then given command of the military forces in a joint military and naval attack on the forts at Hatteras Inlet, and took possession of them on Aug. 27 and 28. He then returned to Massachusetts with authority to enlist troops; which led to a conflict with the state authorities. His plan was to use his independent command to reduce the peninsula of eastern Virginia, but he was attached instead to the expedition against New Orleans, again commanding the land forces. On May 1, 1862, he entered the city, which lay under the guns of the fleet. He was assigned the difficult task of the military government of this hostile population.

Butler's administration of New Orleans is the most controversial portion of his career. It is at least evident that he preserved the peace and effectively governed the city, improving sanitation, and doing other useful things. It is equally evident that his conduct of affairs was high-handed. Ignoring the United States government, he assumed full financial control, collecting taxes, and expending monies. He hung William Mumford for hauling down the United States flag. He seized $800,000 in bullion belonging to Southern owners, which had been left in charge of the French consul; thereby bringing upon the United States government protests from practically all the governments of Europe. A portion of the bullion was not turned over to the United States government until the whole country had become excited over its fate. Still more sensational was his Order No. 28. It certainly was true that the women of New Orleans had rendered themselves unpleasant to the occupying troops. To meet this situation Butler ordered that . . . "When any female shall, by word, or gesture, or movement, insult or show contempt for any officer or soldier of the United States, she shall be regarded and held liable to be treated as a woman of the town plying her avocation." To the international storm of indignation which

this aroused, it could only be replied that no violence was intended. In addition to these overt acts, there hangs about Butler's administration a cloud of suspicion of financial irregularity, popularly characterized in the tradition that he stole the spoons from the house he occupied. That corruption was rampant there can be no doubt. It seems that his brother was implicated. In so far as Gen. Butler is concerned the historian must be content to recognize that if he were guilty, he was certainly too clever to leave proofs behind; a cleverness somewhat unfortunate for him, if he were indeed not guilty. On Dec. 16, 1862, he was removed.

In 1863 he was given command of the districts of eastern Virginia and North Carolina, and was put in command of the Army of the James, consisting of two corps. In this position Grant, the next year, used him as commissioner for the exchange of prisoners, perhaps hoping (it being contrary to Grant's policy to exchange) that the Confederate commander would refuse to recognize him, as President Davis had issued a proclamation declaring that his conduct at New Orleans had placed him outside the rules of war. Butler, however, conducted some exchanges, and forced the Confederacy to recognize the military status of the United States negro troops. He encouraged trade in his districts, almost violating the orders of the government. Having made an independent advance, this resulted in the bottling of his army at Bermuda Hundred, where they remained blocked by a greatly inferior number of Confederates. In November 1864 he was sent to New York to preserve order during the election, riots being anticipated. His adroitness and his popularity with the Democrats prevented all disorders; if any were indeed brewing. On Jan. 7, 1865, he was ordered by Grant to return to Lowell.

He had by this time become identified with the Radical element among the Republicans. In the elections of 1866 he was elected to Congress, as a Republican, serving until 1875. He lived at Washington lavishly, the Radicals were the dominant element, and he became prominent among them. In the management of the Johnson impeachment for the House of Representatives he was, owing to the feebleness of Thaddeus Stevens, the most impressive figure. After Stevens's death in 1868 he seems to have aspired to succeed him as Radical chief, taking a drastic stand on all questions of reconstruction as they came up during the Grant administration. At this stage, his influence with Grant seems to have been strong. In the Democratic wave of 1875 he lost his seat.

In the meantime he had been having difficulties with the ruling element in the Republican party in his own state. He was hardly more hated in Louisiana than by the conservative elements of both parties in Massachusetts, because of his radical proposals, his unconventionality, and their questioning of his honesty. This hostility he took as a challenge, and determined to become governor of the Bay State. In 1871 he ran for the Republican nomination for governor, and was defeated. In 1872 he ran again, and was again defeated. After his defeat for Congress in 1875 he actively took up the cause of the Greenbacks, which indeed he had supported from the beginning. In 1878 he was again elected to Congress, as an independent Greenbacker. In the same year he ran for the governorship, with the support of the Greenbackers and a portion of the Democrats. Defeated, he ran again in 1879, as Democratic candidate, but there was a split in the party, and again he was defeated. In 1880 he attended the national Democratic convention and supported Gen. Hancock, who received the nomination. In 1882 he at length succeeded in obtaining the undivided support of the Democratic party of his state, and had the advantage of the general reaction against the Republicans. His persistency, also, appealed to many, who felt that he was unduly attacked and should have a chance. He was elected, alone of his ticket, by a majority of 14,000. His position gave him no power, as in Massachusetts no executive steps could be taken without the assent of the council, which was controlled, as were both Houses of the legislature, by his opponents. He attacked the administration of the charitable institutions of the state, especially the Tewkesbury State Almshouse; but the investigation which he instigated led to no results. He characteristically attended with full military escort the Commencement at Harvard, after that institution had decided to break its tradition and not award a degree to the governor of the commonwealth. His drastic Thanksgiving proclamation created a scandal, until he pointed out that it was copied complete from that of Christopher Gore in 1810, with the addition of an admonition to the clergy to abstain from political discussion. In 1883 he was defeated for reëlection. In 1884 he was an avowed candidate for the presidency. He was nominated on May 14, by a new party called Anti-Monopoly, denouncing national control of interstate commerce and the eight-hour day. On May 28 he was nominated by the National [Greenback] party. He was a delegate to the Democratic convention, where he sought to control the platform and secure the nomination; but was defeated. In the election he received 175,370 votes, scattered in all but nine states, and most numerous in Michigan, where he received 42,243. This was his last political activity. He died at Washington, Jan. 11, 1893.

[Butler's autobiography, *Butler's Book*, 2 vols. (1892), is entertaining and valuable as a reflection of the man. *The Private and Official Correspondence of Gen. Benj. F. Butler, during the Period of the Civil War*, 5 vols. (1917), is a fascinating collection of all varieties of material, but not complete with respect to any. His speeches and public letters outside of Congress have not been collected, and exist scattered in newspapers and pamphlets. He is constantly referred to in the letters and reminiscences of the men of his time. There is no standard life. Among the sketches are: Blanche B. Ames, *The Butler Ancestry of Gen. Benj. Franklin Butler* (1895); Jas. Parton, *Gen. Butler in New Orleans* (1864); Edward Pierrepont, *Review of Defence of Gen. Butler Before the House of Representatives, in Relation to the New Orleans Gold* (1865); *Life and Public Services of Maj.-Gen. Butler* (1864); J. F. McLaughlin, *The American Cyclops, the Hero of New Orleans, and the Spoiler of Silver Spoons, Dubbed LL.D. by Pasquino* (1868); M. M. Pomeroy, *Life and Public Services of Benj. F. Butler* (1879); T. A. Bland, *Life of Benj. F. Butler* (1879); *Record of Benj. F. Butler Compiled from the Original Sources* (1883). For Butler's military career see also the *Official Records* (Army).]   C.R.F.

BUTLER, CHARLES (Jan. 15, 1802–Dec. 13, 1897), lawyer, philanthropist, the son of Medad and Hannah (Tylee) Butler and brother of Benjamin Franklin Butler [*q.v.*], was born at Kinderhook Landing (now Stuyvesant), Columbia County, N. Y. In June 1819 he became a clerk, at a salary of $100 a year, in the office of Martin Van Buren at Albany, and later studied at Kinderhook and Albany in the offices of Judge James Vanderpoel and of Benjamin Franklin Butler, who had renewed a partnership with Van Buren. In 1822 he was made deputy clerk of the state Senate, an appointment which gave him the opportunity to become acquainted with many of the leading men in New York politics. He was admitted to the bar in 1824, and, after practising for a few months at Lyons, moved to Geneva to become a partner of Judge Bowen Whiting, a state senator and the district attorney of Ontario County. On Oct. 10, 1825, Butler married Eliza A. Ogden of Walton, N. Y., niece of his uncle William Butler's wife. At Geneva he took an active part in the establishment of Hobart College, and, in the long absences of his partner at Albany, he not only conducted a large part of the law business of the firm but also acted as assistant district attorney of the county. It was in this latter capacity that he prosecuted the kidnappers of William Morgan the Free Mason, in 1826–27, a case which attracted nation-wide attention and deeply stirred the political waters of the country.

In 1833 Butler made a journey to the West, "attended with great privations, fatigue, exposure, and difficulty," which had an important influence on his subsequent activities and laid the basis for his large personal fortune. He bought real estate both at Toledo and at Chicago, and later acquired large interests in the Michigan Southern, the Rock Island, and the Chicago & Northwestern railroads. "There is to-day," says his biographer F. H. Stoddard, "scarcely a railroad leading to or from Chicago, east, west, north, or south, with which he did not have important association and to which he did not render efficient service, so that his acts are written in lines of steel all over the west." In 1834 he moved to New York, where he resided for the remaining sixty-three years of his life. Always interested in the development of the West, as agent of the New York Life Insurance & Trust Company he loaned the farmers of western New York large sums of money for the development of the lands to which the opening of the Erie Canal in 1825 had given enhanced prospective values, and for the conversion of their leaseholds from the large land-grant companies into estates in fee simple. Meanwhile his extensive real estate interests in Chicago were looked after by his brother-in-law, William B. Ogden, who became the first mayor of Chicago upon its incorporation into a city in 1837. When several of the Western states threatened to repudiate their bonds (Mississippi actually did so) during the hard times which followed the over-confident extension of canal and railroad construction in the early thirties, Butler performed a service which won him lasting gratitude both in this country and abroad. As agent for the domestic and foreign holders of the bonds of Michigan and Indiana, he spent weeks in Detroit (spring of 1843) and Indianapolis (winter of 1845–46) laboring to convince the legislators and governors of their responsibility for preserving the plighted faith of their states, in the face of public sentiment, "shared by 99 persons in 100," that there was "no obligation resting on them to recognize or pay any of the bonds." In the end Butler succeeded in getting the bills passed and signed for the preservation of the public credit in both of the states. The letters written to his wife from Detroit and Indianapolis, often at midnight, after fifteen hours of work with wabbling legislators and obstinate officials, furnish an interesting combination of childlike trust in Providence and shrewd political manipulation.

Butler's services in the promotion of education were constant and conspicuous for a period of more than threescore years. He was one of the twenty-four "Founders" of the Union Theological Seminary in 1836, a member of its first board

of directors, and president of the board from 1870 to his death in 1897. Until his ninety-third year he was constant in his attendance at the meetings of the board and distributed the diplomas to the graduating class of the Seminary. In 1836 he became a member of the Council of the University of the City of New York, on which he served for more than half a century. He was a man of singular charm and sterling character, unheralded in his large charities, fond of books and works of art, simple and sincere in his religion. He made frequent trips abroad and numbered among his friends some of the most eminent men of England and the Continent. J. A. Froude, Goldwin Smith, Charles Kingsley, and Matthew Arnold were among the guests who enjoyed the unostentatious hospitality of his house in Fourteenth St., and his beautiful country estate at Fox Meadows in Westchester County.

[Francis H. Stoddard, *The Life and Letters of Chas. Butler* (1903) ; Geo. L. Prentiss, "A Sketch of the Life and Public Services of Chas. Butler," being pt. V of *The Union Seminary in the City of N. Y.* (1899) ; *Letter of Chas. Butler, Esq., to the Legislature of Indiana and Other Docs. in Relation to the Public Debt* (1845).]

D. S. M.

BUTLER, EZRA (Sept. 24, 1763–July 12, 1838), congressman, governor of Vermont, was the fifth of seven children born to Asaph and Jane (McAllister) Butler in the town of Lancaster, Mass. When he was a child of seven years the family emigrated to West Windsor, Vt. The mother died and the lad was bound out to service. He had only six months' schooling, and in his youth was a hunter and trapper. For six months he was a soldier in the American Revolution. He settled in Weathersfield, Vt., and with a brother removed to Waterbury, Vt., when there was only one family in the new township. He married Tryphena Diggins of Weathersfield, built a log cabin, and later erected the first frame house in Waterbury. Active in organizing the town, he was elected its first town clerk. He served as town representative from 1794 to 1807 with the exception of the years 1798 and 1805. Ordained to the Baptist ministry in 1801, in his subsequent political activity he continued his church duties when he was not absent from home. He was an active Republican in politics, was elected a member of Congress in 1812, and entered that body in 1813 with Daniel Webster. He delivered a speech in opposition to Webster's resolution calling for information from the President concerning Napoleon's revocation of decrees against American shipping. Elected governor in 1826, he was reëlected in 1827, declining to be again a candidate. While governor he was active in curbing the lottery and in promoting a more liberal system of education. He was a presidential elector in 1804, 1820, 1828, and 1832. In the last-named year, Vermont was the only state to cast its electoral vote for the candidates of the Anti-Masonic party. Butler also served on committees to locate the first state house, the state arsenal, and the state prison. His public career included service on the bench, as a member of the governor's council, the council of censors, and the constitutional convention of 1822. He was a trustee of the University of Vermont (1810–16). In personal appearance he was slightly stooping, and had a dark and sallow complexion and penetrating black eyes. He is numbered among the influential governors of the state during the first half of the nineteenth century.

[*Hist. of Waterbury, Vt.* (1915), compiled by Theo. G. Lewis; sketch by Rev. C. C. Parker in A. M. Hemenway's *Vt. Hist. Gazetteer*, IV (1882), 816; W. H. Crockett, *Vt. the Green Mt. State* (1921), vols. II, III.]

W.H.C.

BUTLER, HOWARD CROSBY (Mar. 7, 1872–Aug. 13?, 1922), archeologist, son of Edward Marchant and Helen Belden (Crosby) Butler, was born at Croton Falls, N. Y. His mother, a woman of great talent, devoted to music and literature, taught him his Latin and exercised a lifelong influence upon his development. Early letters reveal his love of farm life, of flowers and trees, of gentle hills and meadows. The whole course of his education was singularly fortunate. Aided by private tutors at the Lyons Collegiate Institute and the Berkeley School, New York, he entered the class of 1892 at Princeton University as a sophomore. His moderate scholarship in sophomore and junior years gave slight promise of the coming powers of his senior and graduate years. His studies lay in history, Greek and Latin languages, ancient and modern art; starting with a thorough grounding in classical history and English literature, he gained a command of French and Italian and, subsequently, a working knowledge of Arabic, Turkish, and modern Greek which served him well throughout his extensive exploration in the Near East. In art and architecture he came under the genial influence of Prof. Allen Marquand, founder of the Princeton departments of art and architecture. He had a prominent share in reviving the original drama at Princeton through the now well-known Triangle Club, himself playing the part of Bianca in John Kendrick Bangs's *Katharine* and of Portia in *The Hon. Julius Cæsar*, by Post Wheeler and Booth Tarkington. Throughout his life the plays of Shakespeare were his favorite reading, next to the daily reading of his Bible. Having received the degrees of A.B. (1892) and A.M. (1893) from Princeton, he then pursued post-graduate studies in the Columbia School of Architecture, became lecturer on architecture at Princeton (1895–97), and was Fellow in Archeology at the American Schools of Classical Studies in Rome and Athens (1897–98). In 1899–1900 he organized an archeological expedition to the deserts of north-central Syria. The next year he returned to Princeton where he became professor of art and archeology (1901–22), first master in residence of the Graduate College (1905–22) and director of the School of Archæology (1920–22). He published *Scotland's Ruined Abbeys* (1899) and *The Story of Athens* (1902) and was contributing editor of *Art and Archeology* (1906–22). His major work, however, was in connection with two later expeditions to Syria (1904–05, 1909). It was the sterling integrity, as well as the consummate skill, of Butler's work there which led to the highest distinction ever offered to an American and Christian explorer by a Mohammedan government, namely, the unsolicited invitation to enter and take command of the excavation of Sardis. The Turks knew they could trust Butler; they knew that he was absolutely honorable. The difficulties of Sardis exploration had seemed insurmountable to others; the great period of civilization and culture of Asia Minor, just older than the Syrian and extending back to the Lydian and beyond, was buried fathoms deep. These deeply buried ruins were entered under Butler's leadership between 1910 and 1922. His splendid Syrian and Sardis monographs were published as *Archæology and Other Arts* (1903) and *Sardis* (1922). He died in the American Hospital at Neuilly, France on either Aug. 13, 1922 (Collins), Aug. 14 (*New York Herald*, Aug. 16), or Aug 15 (*New York Times*, Aug. 16, and *Who's Who in America*, 1924–25). His remains were brought back to Croton Falls, N. Y., to be interred beside the quiet country church of his boyhood. He was unmarried.

[The chief sources of information are the tribute by Henry Fairfield Osborn, *Impressions of Great Naturalists* (1924), pp. 206–12, and *Howard Crosby Butler, 1872–1922* (1923), a memorial volume from the Princeton Press which contains a biography by V. Lansing Collins, pp. 3–41, tributes by President Hibben, Edward Robinson, and others, and a complete bibliography of Butler's writings by H. S. Leach (reprinted separately as *A Bibliography of Howard Crosby Butler*, 1924).]

H.F.O.

BUTLER, JOHN (1728–May 1796), Loyalist, soldier, Indian agent, was born in New London, Conn., the son of Capt. Walter and Deborah Butler. In 1742 his father moved his family to the Mohawk Valley, where he had been for many years commandant at Fort Hunter and at Oswego. Commissioned captain, John served under

Sir William Johnson in the expedition against Crown Point (1755), under Abercromby at Ticonderoga, under Bradstreet at the capture of Fort Frontenac, and in 1759 accompanied Johnson as second in command of the Indian auxiliaries in the campaign against Fort Niagara, becoming leader of the Indian allies during the siege when Johnson took over the command-in-chief. In the conduct of Indian affairs he was a trusted agent of Sir William Johnson. With the outbreak of Revolution he and his son Walter [q.v.], together with Guy Johnson and Col. Daniel Claus, fled to Canada. Stationed at Niagara by Guy Johnson as deputy Indian commissioner, Butler was instructed by Sir Guy Carleton to preserve the good will of the Indians and to keep them neutral. In the spring of 1777, acting under orders from Carleton, he collected as many Indians as possible and joined St. Leger in his unavailing march down the Mohawk Valley, during which Claus, Sir John Johnson, and Butler issued an appeal to the Loyalists of Tryon County. After the battle of Oriskany he obtained permission from the Governor-General to recruit a battalion of rangers to serve with the Indians, which he should command with the rank of major. This body of troops, known as Butler's Rangers, he recruited from the refugee Loyalists at Niagara, and in the spring and summer of 1778 he undertook his famous invasion of the Wyoming Valley in Pennsylvania, aided by a detachment of the King's Royal Regiment of New York (Sir John Johnson's Loyalist regiment) and a large number of Indians led by the Seneca chief Old King (Sayenqueraghta). Two forts were captured easily and Butler sent a summons to Forty Fort. The Continental forces, led by Lieut.-Col. Zebulon Butler [q.v.], determined to leave the fort and attack the invaders, which unwise decision the British commander reported "pleased the Indians highly, who observed they should be on an equal footing with them in the woods." In the battle of July 3, 1778 the Indians made a flank attack and the Continentals, outnumbered, fled to Forty Fort, which capitulated on July 4. Maj. Butler attempted to restrain his dusky allies, but failing, there followed a number of atrocities, which historians with imagination have depicted as a general massacre, rendered immortal by Thomas Campbell in his famous poem Gertrude of Wyoming (London, 1809). The caustic strictures on Butler by the historians of Wyoming, on the ground of inhumanity, seem to be wholly unjustified. With the invasion of the Iroquois country by Maj.-Gen. John Sullivan [q.v.] in 1779, Butler opposed him with his Rangers and a number of

Indians led by the famous Mohawk chief, Joseph Brant (Thayendanegea), but was defeated in the battle of Newtown (Elmira), Aug. 29, 1779. Commissioned lieutenant-colonel, Butler joined Sir John Johnson in his raid upon the Mohawk and Schoharie valleys (1780). His wife Catherine and the younger children, held as hostages at Albany, were exchanged for Cherry Valley captives by his son Walter and joined him at Niagara. Attainted by the New York Assembly and his property confiscated, Butler received a grant of land and a pension from the British government at the close of the war and served as His Majesty's commissioner of Indian affairs at Niagara and as a member of the land board for the district of Nassau. He is described as being short and fat but very active. He died at Niagara, respected as an honorable and faithful servant of his King, and was buried on May 15, 1796.

[Ontario Hist. Soc. Papers and Records, vols. III (1901), XXIII (1926); Report of the Bureau of Archives for the Province of Ontario, 1904–05; Docs. Relative to the Colonial Hist. of . . . N. Y. (1850–61); House Doc. No. 203, 25 Cong., 3 Sess.; The Papers of Sir Wm. Johnson (1921 . . .); Buffalo Hist. Soc. Pubs., vols. I (1879), IV (1895); Jour. of the Mil. Exped. of Maj.-Gen. John Sullivan (1887); Orderly Book of Sir John Johnson (1882); "Diary of Joshua Hempstead of New London, Conn.," Colls. of the New London County Hist. Soc., I (1901), 401; Mich. Pioneer and Hist. Soc. Colls., XIX (1892); E. A. Cruikshank, The Story of Butler's Rangers, etc. (1893); J. Carnochan, Hist. of Niagara (1914); Wm. Kirby, Annals of Niagara (2nd ed., 1927); F. M. Caulkins, Hist. of New London, Conn. (1852); Wm. W. Campbell, Annals of Tryon County (1831); Wm. L. Stone, Life of Jos. Brant-Thayendanegea (1838); Chas. Miner, Hist. of Wyoming (1845); Wm. M. Reid, The Story of Old Fort Johnson (1906); Butler's report of the battle of Wyoming to Lieut.-Col. Mason Bolton, dated July 8, 1778, printed in Geo. Peck, Wyoming (1858) and in Proc. and Colls. of the Wyoming Hist. and Geol. Soc., vol. XVI (1918).]   F. E. R.

BUTLER, JOHN WESLEY (Oct. 13, 1851–Mar. 17, 1918), Methodist missionary, was born in Shelburn Falls, Mass., the son of Julia (Lewis) Butler and William Butler, founder of the missions of the Methodist Episcopal Church in India (1856) and Mexico (1873). On his father's departure for India, he was put in a boarding school at Wilton, Conn. Rejoining his father on the latter's return (1865), he had two years in the Chelsea (Mass.) High School and a year in the Boston Latin School, and graduated from the Passaic (N. J.) Collegiate Institute (1871). His delicate health making a college course inadvisable he went to the Boston University School of Theology for three years of study (1871–74). While a student in theology he held small pastorates in the city of Boston. He was ordained at the age of twenty-two, and appointed to Mexico for missionary service, arriving May 9, 1874. He reported to his father who was superintendent of the mission. For almost forty-four years he held his residence continuously in Mexico City, and was at death one of the best known and most influential men in the capital, for he was not an ardent denominational ecclesiastic, but a broad-souled and eager lover of men. As pastor and "preacher in charge" (1874–88); as publishing agent (1886–90, 1898); as overseer of schools and acting-president of the Mexico Methodist Institute (1895–97) and of the Mexico Methodist Theological School (1897); as editor of *El Abogado Cristiano* and other religious publications (1892–1907); as presiding elder or district superintendent (Mexico or Central District, 1889–1918 with exception of the year 1891 when he was in charge of the Hidalgo District); as president of the Mexico Annual Conference (1911); as treasurer and attorney for the Mission; and as author of books, pamphlets, and articles on Mexico he rendered long and notable service. In addition, he was delegate to two Ecumenical Conferences (1901, 1911), and to eight successive quadrennial General Conferences of the Methodist Episcopal Church (1888–1916). He represented his church at the Congress on Christian Work in Latin America (Panama, 1916). His principal books are *Sketches of Mexico* (1894), *Mexico Coming into Light* (1906), and *The History of the Methodist Episcopal Church in Mexico* (issued on the very day of his death in 1918). He wrote the article "Christianity in Mexico" for the *New Encyclopædia Americana* (1907). He was married on Aug. 13, 1878 to Sara A. Aston, who also became a writer on Mexican themes.

The work of the Methodist Episcopal Church in Mexico stands as his enduring monument. He lived to see some 30,000 communicants and adherents and 5,000 children in schools. He aided the beginnings of interdenominational cooperation; the Union Hymn Book and Union Theological Seminary. Greater than these, however, was the regard of Mexicans for this humble Protestant missionary. He had the interests of Mexico at heart and Mexicans knew it. He enjoyed personal and friendly relations with every president from Lerdo de Tejada on. No Mexican ever harmed him in his frequent travels. Many Roman Catholic priests were among his acquaintances. He kept outside of national politics. In Mexico he pleaded for popular education, and in America for a free hand for Mexico in her own internal affairs.

[*Annual Reports of the Mexico Annual Conference of the M. E. Ch.* (1885–1919); *Reports of the Board of Foreign Missions of the M. E. Ch.* (1874–1918); C. Butler, *Wm. Butler, the Founder of Two Missions of*

the *M. E. Ch.* (1902); files of *Mexico*, especially Apr. 1918; article by C. Butler in *Missionary Rev. of the World*, June 1918.]   O. M. B.

BUTLER, MATTHEW CALBRAITH (Mar. 8, 1836–Apr. 14, 1909), Confederate soldier, senator, was the son of Dr. William Butler, naval surgeon, and Jane (Perry) Butler, sister of Commodores Oliver Hazard and Matthew Calbraith Perry. He was born in Greenville, S. C., the eleventh of sixteen children. He attended the male academy in Greenville and then in 1848 went with his father to Fort Gibson, where Dr. Butler, who had previously served a term in Congress, took up his work as agent to the Cherokees. On the death of his father in 1850, young Butler returned to live with his uncle, Senator A. P. Butler [*q.v.*], and his grandmother, Behethland Butler, at Edgefield. After more study at a local academy, he entered South Carolina College in 1856 as a junior but did not remain through his senior year. He was admitted to the bar in 1857, having studied law with his uncle, and the following year married Maria, daughter of Gov. F. W. Pickens. Having returned to Edgefield, he was elected in 1860 to the legislature but resigned at the coming of war in order to become captain of the Edgefield company of cavalry, which formed part of the Hampton Legion. Six of his brothers also bore arms for the South. After the first battle of Manassas, in which Butler had a part, he was made major. After Williamsburg he was commended for bravery; and in August 1862 he was named colonel of the 2nd South Carolina Regiment. He lost his right foot at the battle of Brandy Station. In September of this year, 1863, he was promoted to be brigadier-general when only twenty-seven years old. He saw much fighting around Richmond, his most important engagement being the clash at Trevilian Station. In September 1864 he was advanced to the rank of major-general. The close of the war found him in South Carolina where he had come in the spring of 1865 to oppose Sherman's progress.

Financially ruined by the war, Butler returned to the practise of law in Edgefield. In 1865 he was chosen for the legislature; and from this time he was throughout the period of Reconstruction a prominent figure in the political life of the state. Feeling at first that the best hope lay in a fusion of the honest elements, white and colored, he was a member of the Union Reform Convention of 1870, to which he submitted the platform and from which he received the nomination for lieutenant-governor. He waged a vigorous but fruitless campaign. For the next year or two, he was active in behalf of the tax-payers who were seeking improvement of fiscal conditions. He was a member of the convention of May 1871 and was one of a committee which waited upon President Grant. Finally convinced that the only resource was in Democratic control of the state, he renounced his allegiance to any fusion party and became one of the most energetic promoters of the "straightout" movement. When the convention met in August 1876 he nominated Wade Hampton for governor. Meantime, he had been connected with several race riots, one in Edgefield where the residence on his own plantation had been burned, and one, far more notable, at Hamburg, where he had gone to represent the whites in civil action against a company of negro militia. When questioned later by a senatorial committee, he insisted that his connection with the Hamburg disturbance had been merely that of an attorney. Foremost among the campaigners in behalf of the Hampton ticket, in December 1876, he was elected to the Senate without opposition, by the Democratic legislature. It seemed an empty compliment, since the Republican legislature, sitting in competition, declared D. T. Corbin, conspicuous in the prosecution of Ku Klux cases, duly elected. The contest between Butler and Corbin hung fire for a year until Butler was sworn in, Nov. 30, 1877. Well-authenticated historical gossip attributes Butler's triumph to the secret influence of Senator James Donald Cameron of Pennsylvania who was thus paying a debt of gratitude for a kindness rendered by A. P. Butler, years before, to Simon Cameron. Butler served three terms in the Senate. He secured many improvements for his state, notably public buildings and enlargement of the Charleston harbor. Instinctively friendly and wholly free from inflammatory rhetoric, he did much to conciliate more stubborn Northern sentiment concerning the South. In 1894 he went down in defeat before Ben Tillman. This political reaction was partly a kind of agrarian revolt and partly an expression of the temper of a new generation of voters, which, coming into power twenty-five years after the Civil War, no longer reverenced the heroes of that conflict and sought new leaders. After his retirement, Butler practised law in Washington until the Spanish-American War, when he was appointed by McKinley major-general of volunteers. Later he served as a member of the commission for the Spanish evacuation of Cuba. Then he returned to Washington. In 1903 he was elected vice-president of the Southern History Association. In the next year he undertook new business ventures as president of the Hidalgo Placer Mining

and Milling Company of Mexico. In 1906 he married Mrs. Nannie Whitman of New York, his first wife having been dead for several years. The second Mrs. Butler was a descendant of Pierre Robert, first pastor of the Carolina Huguenots. Butler's death occurred in Washington but his body was brought to the old home place in Edgefield for burial.

In war Butler was a striking figure. Handsome, graceful, cool, he personally led his soldiers to battle, with only a silver-mounted riding whip in his hand. Solicitous of the welfare of his men, he was regarded by them with affection. In peace he manifested uncommon gifts for political success. He possessed a remarkable memory for names and faces; he was affable in manner; he adapted himself easily to almost any social group.

[For records of Butler's military service see U. R. Brooks, *Butler and His Cavalry in the War of Secession* (1909), Ellison Capers's account in *Confed. Mil. Hist.*, vol. V (1899), and E. L. Wells, *Hampton and His Cavalry in '64* (1899); for sympathetic narratives of his career during Reconstruction days see John S. Reynolds, *Reconstruction in S. C.* (1905), and H. T. Thompson, *Ousting the Carpet-Bagger* (1927); for brief biographical sketches see J. C. Hemphill, *Men of Mark in S. C.*, vol. III (1909), J. C. Garlington, *Men of the Time* (1902), and B. F. Perry, *Reminiscences of Public Men* (1889); for senatorial investigation and for Butler's career in this body, see *Cong. Record* for the years involved. Full obituaries were published in the papers Apr. 15, 1909, notably the Charleston *News and Courier*, the Columbia *State*, and the Greenville *News*.]

F. P. G.

BUTLER, PIERCE (July 11, 1744–Feb. 15, 1822), senator, was born in County Carlow, Ireland, the third son of Sir Richard Butler, Baronet, Member of Parliament for County Carlow 1729–61, and of Henrietta (Percy) Butler (*Burke's Peerage*). He became major of H. M. 29th Regiment, but on Jan. 10, 1771 married Mary, the daughter of Thomas Middleton, of Prince William's Parish, in South Carolina, and there made his home thenceforward. In 1773 he resigned his commission and devoted himself to planting and politics. In 1779 he was adjutant-general of the state (Edward McCrady, *The History of South Carolina in the Revolution, 1775–80*, 1901, p. 366). From 1778 to 1782 and from 1784 to 1789 he was a representative in the state legislature. His failure to act with the planter-merchant group in state politics may have been due to the enmity of Christopher Gadsden (*State Gazette*, Sept. 9, 1784), to his political ambition, or to his independent, impulsive nature. Whatever his motives, this wealthy, somewhat dictatorial aristocrat championed the inadequately-led democracy of the back country, and pushed its enterprises for the reform of representation, removal of the state capital, and re-valuation of property. In 1786 he was elected by the legislature to commissions to fix the boundaries of the state. On Mar. 6, 1787, he was elected delegate to the Congress of the Confederation, and two days later to the Federal Convention. There his proposals were for a strong central government, with property as part of the basis for representation. He was author of the fugitive slave clause. He returned to South Carolina in time to defend the Constitution in the Assembly, but did not sit in the ratifying convention. He was elected to the United States Senate as a Federalist in 1789, and was reëlected in 1792, but refused to observe party lines. During the first session he voted for the funding bill and the assumption of state debts, but opposed the tariff and judiciary bills. He later opposed the Jay treaty. In October 1796 he resigned and repaired to his state, apparently intending to become candidate for governor (*American Historical Review*, July 1909). At the time of the election, however, though the Federalist Harper said that he was still strong in the back country and had "no inconsiderable support" in the tidewater, he refused to allow his name to be used (*City Gazette*, Dec. 10, 1796). But in 1802 he was elected to fill an unexpired term in the Senate. He denounced the Twelfth Amendment, and charged that the Republican party was abusing its powers as the Federalists had done. In January 1806 he resigned. He died in Philadelphia in 1822.

[Sketch of Butler in Jos. Johnson, *Traditions and Reminiscences, Chiefly of the Am. Rev. in the South* (1851); *Biog. Cong. Dir.* (1903); *Franklin Gazette* (Phila.), Feb. 16, 1822; C. Jervey, *Inscriptions on the Tablets and Gravestones in St. Michael's Church and Churchyard, Charleston, S. C.* (1906); *S. C. Hist. and Geneal. Mag.*, Jan. 1900; *Assembly Jours.*; *Annals of Cong.*; Max Farrand, ed., *The Records of the Federal Convention of 1787* (1911).]   R. L. M——r.

BUTLER, PIERCE MASON (Apr. 11, 1798–Aug. 20, 1847), governor of South Carolina, was born at Mount Willing in Edgefield District, the sixth child of William Butler [*q.v.*], a Revolutionary soldier, and his wife, Behethland Foote Moore. Like his older brother, Andrew Pickens Butler [*q.v.*], Pierce was trained at Moses Waddell's academy in Abbeville. Evincing ambition for a military career, he was, through Calhoun's influence, appointed in 1818 lieutenant in the United States army. By 1825 he was a captain. Much of his service was at Fort Gibson, where he met his future wife, Miranda Julia Duval of Maryland who was visiting her brother, Edward, agent to the Cherokees. Shortly after his marriage, Butler resigned from the army in 1829 and settled in Columbia. In civil life again, he chose banking as his field and became in a few

years president of the state bank of South Carolina. He had more than passing interest in public affairs, however, and manifested particular enthusiasm for nullification, signing the ordinance of November 1832. Particularly active in behalf of education, he was elected a trustee of South Carolina College in 1833.

When the excitement of the Seminole War was at its height, he accepted a commission as lieutenant-colonel of Godwyn's South Carolina regiment. Returning to Columbia, he was elected governor in 1836, though, true to his declared conviction that the office should seek the man, he made no campaign. Earnestly seeking to give a practical and helpful administration, he endeavored to eliminate the residual bitterness from the long discussion of tariff and nullification and to initiate beneficial measures. He had a vision —rare in the ante-bellum South—of a public school system for the whole state, and appointed a commission headed by Stephen Elliott to make surveys and recommendations. He threw his influence in favor of the proposed Louisville, Cincinnati & Charleston Railway, believing that better commercial and political relations between the South and West would follow. Shortly after he left office in 1838, he was named agent to the Cherokees and returned to Fort Gibson where he remained until ill health prompted his resignation in 1846. According to a tribute published in an Indian journal (Tahlequah *Advocate*, Sept. 30, 1847) he was just with and showed sympathy for the Cherokees. At the outbreak of the Mexican War he was called to be colonel of the Palmetto Regiment. He was killed at Churubusco while leading this regiment in the face of what Gen. James Shields, writing to Gov. Johnson (Sept. 2, 1847), called "one of the most terrific fires to which soldiers were ever subjected." Wounded in the early stages of the conflict, Butler had continued to advance until a musket ball through the head caused instantaneous death. His body was brought back to Edgefield. Many tributes in verse were written at the time of his death, one of them being by the youthful Paul Hamilton Hayne.

Tall and distinguished in personal appearance, Butler was by temperament more of a military officer than a politician. He was marked, however, by broad social interests and at the time of his death was a member of many fraternal organizations in his state. Shields bears witness to the Carolinian's popularity in the brigade to which he was attached.

[A brief sketch of Butler is in "The Butlers of S. C." by T. D. Jervey in *S. C. Hist. and Geneal. Mag.*, Oct. 1903. A brief summary of his administration is in Yates Snowden, *Hist. of S. C.*, vol. II (1920). The fullest collection of material is a file of newspaper clippings, drawn largely from the Charleston *Mercury* and *Courier,* now in the possession of Mrs. Elizabeth Butler Carson of Greenville, a niece of P. M. Butler.]

F. P. G.

BUTLER, RICHARD (Apr. 1, 1743–Nov. 4, 1791), Revolutionary soldier, Indian agent, was born in the parish of St. Bridget's, Dublin, Ireland, the son of Thomas and Eleanor (Parker) Butler. His father later came to America and settled in Lancaster, Pa. Richard served as an ensign with the Bouquet expedition of 1764, after which he and his brother William ventured a partnership as Indian traders at Chillicothe, Ohio, and at Pittsburgh. Richard married Mary (or Maria) Smith and had numerous descendants. During the dispute between Pennsylvania and Virginia he raised a company of men to resist the authority of the Virginia commandant sent to Pittsburgh by Lord Dunmore. In 1775 he became an Indian agent but in the following year entered into active military service as major and in 1777 became lieutenant-colonel of Morgan's Rifles. He took part in the battle of Saratoga, commanded Wayne's left column at the storming of Stony Point and later aided Wayne in quelling the mutiny of the Pennsylvania line. After Yorktown he went with Wayne to Georgia and was brevetted brigadier-general (1783). Appointed Indian commissioner by Congress, he negotiated, together with Oliver Wolcott and Arthur Lee, an important treaty with the Iroquis confederacy defining their western boundary (Oct. 22, 1784). In the following year, Butler, Lee, and George Rogers Clark negotiated a boundary treaty with the Wyandot, Delaware, Chippewa, and Ottawa nations (Jan. 21, 1785). The most striking feature of Butler's career as an Indian agent was the negotiation of the famous treaty with the Shawnees (Jan. 31, 1786). With Clark and Samuel H. Parsons as fellow commissioners he met the Shawnees at the mouth of the Great Miami, and so overawed them that they signed a treaty ceding a great area of land to the United States and yielding hostages. In response to an inquiry from Congress, Butler and Parsons reported, June 19, 1786, that the western tribes were distinctly hostile and were encouraged in their continued depredations by the British (Papers of the Continental Congress, No. 56, pp. 283–85, in the Library of Congress). On Aug. 14, 1786, Congress elected Butler superintendent of Indian affairs for the Northern District. He served as state senator, as judge of the court of common pleas, and as president of the court of inquiry *re* Gen. Josiah Harmar [*q.v.*]. In 1791 he was appointed second in command, with the rank of

major-general, of the army under Gen. Arthur St. Clair [*q.v.*] sent into the Ohio country to avenge the ill-fated Harmar expedition. In reply to the protests of army officers against Butler's appointment, President Washington wrote to Col. William Darke, Aug. 9, 1791, admitting that because of illness Butler wasn't what he should be but appealing to Darke's loyalty to suuport him (Jared Sparks, *The Writings of George Washington,* X, 183). Nowhere is Butler's military incompetence better exemplified than in his change of St. Clair's order of march while he was in command during St. Clair's absence, Butler's order of march requiring that a forty-foot road be cut. The expedition finally reached the Indian country north of the Ohio River and was attacked by the Indians on Nov. 4, 1791. Butler, commanding the right wing, fought bravely, but was mortally wounded and carried to the middle of the camp, where he was soon joined by his wounded brother, Maj. Thomas Butler. St. Clair ordering a retreat, Capt. Edward Butler came to remove his brothers. As he could save only one, Gen. Butler urged him to take his brother Thomas. Edward Butler did so, writing to his brother Percival in Kentucky that, "We left the worthiest of brothers . . . in the hands of the savages . . . nearly dead."

[*Jours. of Cong.,* May 16, 1776, June 3, 1785, Apr. 17 and Aug. 14, 1786; *Minutes of the Supreme Exec. Council of Pa.*; *Pa. Archives*; *Am. State Papers, Military Affairs,* vol. I and *Indian Affairs,* vol. I (both 1832); *Mil. Jour. of Maj. Ebenezer Denny* (1859); *Diary of Col. Winthrop Sargent . . . during the Campaign of 1791* (1851); *Olden Time,* Mar.–Dec. 1847; *Hist. Reg.* (Harrisburg), Jan. 1883; *Pa. Mag. of Hist. and Biog.,* Apr. 1883; Jas. A. James, *Life of Geo. Rogers Clark* (1928); Wm. H. Smith, *The St. Clair Papers* (1882); Chas. J. Stillé, *Maj.-Gen. Anthony Wayne and the Pa. Line in the Continental Army* (1893); Chas. S. Hall, *Life and Letters of Samuel Holden Parsons* (1905); Wm. D. Butler and others, *The Butler Family in America* (1909).]

F. E. R.

BUTLER, SIMEON (Mar. 25, 1770?–Nov. 7, 1847), publisher, was probably the oldest son of Josiah and Martha (Ranney) Butler, and was probably born at Wethersfield, Conn. He migrated about 1790 from Hartford to Northampton, Mass., where he had been preceded by two cousins, William and Daniel Butler, both of whom were already prominent in that town, the former having established in 1786 the *Hampshire Gazette* for the purpose of opposing the malcontents of the Shays Rebellion, while the latter for many years (1817–49) operated the paper-mill built by his brother, William, in 1795. Immediately upon his arrival Simeon established himself as a bookbinder and bookseller. For a short time (1793) he was in partnership with William Butler, but after 1794 seems to have conducted the business alone. The bookselling speedily became subordinated to publishing and binding, and the shop of Simeon Butler became famous not only as the first, but for a half century the most important publishing house in western Massachusetts. According to William Allen, his fellow townsman and contemporary, "he published the first volume of the Massachusetts Reports and two or three hundred thousand other volumes of valuable books" (Allen's *American Biographical Dictionary,* 3rd ed., 1857, pp. 177-78). Although his interests were chiefly centered upon publishing books, for a time he manufactured paper in partnership with his brother, Asa, in Suffield, Conn., and, it is believed, produced the first American letter paper used in the United States Senate. In 1800 he was appointed postmaster of Northampton, an office which he held for six years. He was a man of force of character and distinct individuality, the autocrat of his household and of his business. Endowed with great business capacity he amassed a considerable fortune for his day. Shortly after his arrival in Northampton he married in 1795 Mary Hunt (1774–1829), a member of a prominent local family, by whom he had ten children; after her death he married Charlotte McNeill of New York (1833). His book-shop, to-day operated under the firm name of Bridgman & Lyman, is still doing business on the same spot, one of the two or three oldest bookstores in the country.

[The *New Eng. Hist. and Geneal. Reg.,* Jan. 1862, contains items concerning the Wethersfield Butlers, and the Judd MSS. in the Forbes Lib. of Northampton contain the local genealogical records. The *Centennial Hampshire Gazette* (1886) contains some information. An unsigned article by Clifford H. Lyman in the *Hampshire Gazette* of Jan. 22, 1927, gives a short history of the business founded by Simeon Butler, and *Theodore Bliss, Publisher and Bookseller* (Norwalk, Ohio, 1911), tells of the life of an apprentice in the store during the days of Simeon's son, J. H. Butler. The Forbes Lib. contains an oil portrait of Simeon Butler, and books containing his imprint.]   H.U.F.

BUTLER, THOMAS BELDEN (Aug. 22, 1806–June 8, 1873), jurist, was born in Wethersfield, Conn., the son of Frederick and Mary (Belden) Butler. His elementary schooling completed, he decided to study medicine. For two years he attended the Yale Medical School, graduating in 1828. He afterward settled in Norwalk, Conn. (then a town of less than 4,000 inhabitants), where he was married (Mar. 14, 1831) to Mary Phillip Crosby and where he practised for a number of years. In 1835 he determined to forsake medicine and essay the law. He thereupon studied in the office of Judge Clark Bissell [*q.v.*] of Norwalk, who later was to become a professor in the Yale Law School; and in

1837 he was admitted to the Fairfield County bar and began practise in Norwalk. Thaddeus Betts, Orrin S. Terry, and Josiah M. Carter were successively his partners. For him, as for many another in those days, the law was a stepping-stone to a career in politics. In his case the career began in 1849 with an election as representative in the United States Congress, where he served one term. His later political services were in the General Assembly of his state. No less than five times he was chosen from Norwalk to the state House of Representatives; and in 1848, 1852, and 1853 he was a member of the state Senate. It was not, however, in the legislature, but in the judiciary that he was to become best known. In 1855 he was appointed by the General Assembly to the bench of the superior court and in 1861 to that of the supreme court of errors. Upon the death of Joel Hinman of Waterbury, chief justice of the supreme court, he was selected to fill the vacancy thus created; and he was chief justice for the remainder of his life. Butler found a hobby in examining weather phenomena. After years of research, he published *The Philosophy of the Weather, And a Guide to Its Changes* (1856). In 1870 he reissued this compendium of weather-wisdom in a revised and enlarged form as *A Concise, Analytical, and Logical Development of the Atmospheric System* (Norwalk) and *A Concise Analytical and Logical Development of the Atmospheric System as God Made It* (Hartford). These copious works have now only a historical interest. *The Slave Question,* a speech delivered by Butler in the House of Representatives on Mar. 12, 1850—five days after Webster's great Senate speech on the Constitution and the Union,—was officially printed (Washington, 1850). He was esteemed for his good mind in matters judicial; and as a "natural philosopher" he possessed considerable native ability. He likewise had a Yankee fondness for mechanics, and is said to have obtained patents on several of his inventions.

[S. W. Adams and H. R. Stiles, *The Hist. of Ancient Wethersfield, Conn.* (1904); C. M. Selleck, *Norwalk* (Norwalk, 1896); D. Loomis and J. G. Calhoun, *The Judicial and Civil Hist. of Conn.* (1895); *Obit. Record Grads. Yale Coll.* (1873); *Hartford Courant,* June 10, 1873.]   G.S.B.

BUTLER, WALTER N. (d. Oct. 30, 1781), Loyalist, soldier, was born near Johnstown, N.Y., the son of Lieut.-Col. John Butler [*q.v.*] by his wife Catherine. He studied law at Albany but with the outbreak of the Revolution he joined his father and the other Loyalist leaders of the Mohawk Valley in flight to Canada. Accompanying St. Leger on his march down the valley in 1777, Ensign Butler was active in exhorting the

Loyalists to rise. Soon after his father, Col. Daniel Claus, and Sir John Johnson had issued a proclamation to the inhabitants of Tryon County, he was captured while attending a nocturnal conference at the house of a Loyalist. He was ordered court-martialed by Arnold and was condemned as a spy, but, upon the intercession of Continental officers whom he had known while a law student in Albany, he was reprieved and imprisoned in that town. When he became ill, his friends prevailed upon Gen. Lafayette to place him under guard in the home of a family with secret Loyalist sympathies, from which he escaped by eluding a conveniently inebriated sentinel. Governor-General Sir Frederick Haldimand approving the plan, Capt. Butler, commanding his father's Loyalist troops (Butler's Rangers) and accompanied by a number of Indians led by the famous Mohawk chief Joseph Brant (Thayendanegea), made an attack on Cherry Valley, Nov. 11, 1778, in which he is generally alleged to have shown great cruelty, suffering his Indian allies to commit many atrocities. To Gen. Schuyler he declared that "I have done everything in my power to restrain the fury of the Indians from hurting women and children, or killing the prisoners who fell into our hands," and he wrote to Gen. James Clinton that "the inhabitants killed at Cherry Valley do not lay [sic] at my door—my conscience acquits me." His mother and the younger children, held as hostages at Albany, he exchanged for Cherry Valley captives (1779). In October 1781 he accompanied Major Ross in a raid on the Mohawk Valley, with regular troops, Rangers, and Indians. Repulsed by Col. Marinus Willett, the British forces retreated, Butler commanding the detachment covering the retreat. They had succeeded in crossing West Canada Creek when the fog that hung over the stream lifted and Butler was shot from the opposite bank by the pursuing Continental scouts.

Historians of the Revolution have invariably depicted Butler as a fiend incarnate because of the Cherry Valley massacre. It is quite possible that he may not have been able to prevent it (like his father in his attack on Wyoming Valley), but it is also true that he was a sterner man than John Butler, and is described as morose, vindictive, and governed by strong passions.

[Jas. F. Kenney, "Walter Butler's Journal . . ." in the Canadian Hist. Rev., Dec. 1920; Wm. W. Campbell, Annals of Tryon County (1831); Wm. L. Stone, Life of Jos. Brant-Thayendanegea (1838); Docs. Relative to the Colonial Hist. of . . . N. Y., VIII (1857), 721; Wm. M. Willett, A Narrative of the Military Actions of Col. Marinus Willett (1831); J. R. Sims, The Frontiersmen of N. Y. (1882–83); Lorenzo Sabine, The Am. Loyalists (1847); Butler's report of the attack on Cherry Valley to Lieutenant-Colonel Mason Bolton, dated Nov. 17, 1778, printed in part in Ernest A. Cruikshank, The Story of Butler's Rangers and the Settlement of Niagara, published in 1893 by the Lundy's Lane Hist. Soc.]
F. E. R.

BUTLER, WILLIAM (Dec. 17, 1759–Sept. 23, 1821), Revolutionary soldier, congressman, was the son of James Butler of Prince William County, Va., who with his wife Mary Simpson and eight children moved to Ninety Six District, S. C., about 1772. James Butler served in several campaigns of the first half of the Revolution, but in 1781 he and his second son, James, were killed at Cloud's Creek by "Bloody Bill" Cuningham, the notorious Loyalist leader. William Butler, the eldest son, was in the battle of Stono, and several other actions of 1779 and 1780. He was lieutenant of militia before he was of age (Accounts Audited, State Archives). In November 1781 he was appointed captain in the militia under Gen. Pickens, but was usually on detached service. His most noted exploit was the surprise and dispersing of Cuningham's force, in May 1782. He appears to have been elected to the state House of Representatives in 1786. In 1788 he opposed the calling of the convention to ratify the Federal Constitution, and in that convention voted against ratification. In the legislature he consistently opposed leniency to the Loyalists, and in this as in other important matters accurately reflected the dominant sentiment of the back country. In 1791 he was elected sheriff of Ninety Six District, and held the office for many years. In 1794 he was made brigadier-general of militia, and later became major-general. In 1796 he was candidate for Congress against R. G. Harper, the Federalist lawyer, but was defeated by a vote of more than two to one. In 1800 Harper did not run (City Gazette, Oct. 31, 1800), and Butler gained the seat which he held until 1813. In Congress he seems never to have debated but to have attended faithfully. He voted against the anti-slavery motions, but supported proposals for the removal of judges on address of both houses of Congress, and for removal of senators on address of legislatures. He steadily supported the embargo. In 1810 he was chairman of the committee which investigated the charges against Gen. Wilkinson. He is described as a tall, handsome man, and a lover of fine horses. His home was in Edgefield County. On June 3, 1784, he married Behethland Foote Moore and they had eight children: James, George, William, Frank M., Andrew P. [q.v.], Pierce M. [q.v.], Emmala, and Leontine, several of whom were distinguished in the later history of the state.

[See esp. *The Memoirs of Gen. Wm. Butler* (1885), based largely on a manuscript by A. P. Butler. In Joseph Johnson, *Traditions and Reminiscences Chiefly of the American Revolution in the South* (1851) and in Alexander Garden, *Anecdotes of the Revolutionary War in America* (1822), there are brief sketches. T. D. Jervey in *S. C. Hist. and Geneal. Mag.*, Oct. 1903, 296–311, gives a genealogy of the family. Butler's public career may be followed in the journals of the bodies in which he sat. There was a trader James Butler among the Cherokees,—*e.g.*, S. C. Council Jour., Mar. 29, 1748, *S. C. Gazette*, Nov. 29, 1760,—but he was not the James Butler of this sketch.]   R.L.M—r.

BUTLER, WILLIAM (Jan. 30, 1818–Aug. 18, 1899), Methodist missionary, was born in Dublin of English parentage. Orphaned soon after birth he was reared by a great-grandmother who instilled into him permanent religious ideals which were realized through Methodist channels. In young manhood he became a Methodist and entered the Hardwick Street Mission Seminary (Wesleyan) of Dublin to prepare for the ministry. Upon graduation he was given a charge in Lisburn and later went to a Donegal circuit. Eager for further training he went over to Didsbury College, Manchester, England, but returned to Ireland after finishing the course, bringing a Manchester lady as his wife. In 1850 he and Mrs. Butler and their three sons crossed to America, which was to be thenceforth the land of their citizenship. On May 5, 1851, he was admitted to the New York East Conference. He served churches in Williamsburg, Shelburne Falls, and Westfield. His first wife died suddenly at Westfield, and on Nov. 23, 1854, he was married in Portland, Me., to Clementina Rowe of Wexford, England, whom he had met in her father's house, and who came at his persuasion by letter to be his bride. On Oct. 10, 1856, while pastor of a church in Lynn, Mass., he accepted a call to the superintendency of the proposed India Mission of his Church. With his wife and two of his sons he sailed on Apr. 9 to "lay broad and deep foundations for Methodism in India." After five weeks of enquiry he decided to open the Mission in Oudh and Rohilkhand (the Northwest Provinces). He could find no quarters in Lucknow, the capital of Oudh, and therefore moved on to Bareilly in the next province. Hardly had he settled at his task when the Mutiny broke out, compelling him to flee for his life. After the Mutiny he resumed work in Bareilly and also began work in Lucknow. At Bareilly the first official meeting of the Mission was held on Aug. 20, 1858. The foundation of the Mission was a girls' orphanage, established in Bareilly, and a boys' orphanage, in Lucknow. In time, but under other hands, there developed in the former place a theological seminary and in the latter two standard colleges.

In 1864 Butler fell ill in Calcutta and was obliged to leave India for home, after trying in vain to recuperate by a voyage to Burmah. On arrival in America he was given a charge in Chelsea, Mass. Thence he removed to Dorchester Street Church, Boston, from which he retired to take the secretaryship of the American and Foreign Christian Union (organized for work in Papal lands), and to make his headquarters in New York City, while living in Passaic, N. J. He took time in his new post to write his useful volume, *The Land of the Veda* (1872).

When the Methodist Church decided upon a mission in Mexico, Butler, at the age of fifty-five, was given the superintendency. He sailed for Vera Cruz on Feb. 4, 1873, and proceeded to Mexico City, where he soon found quarters for the new work. The evangelical message and the open Bible proved welcome to many. Butler also established a Union Church, and acted for a time as its pastor; and took steps toward the founding of a Mission Press. In 1879, however, lung trouble developed and he was forced to return home.

After serving for a time the Freedman's Aid Society, he took a pastorate at Melrose, Mass., from which he was invited to visit India again. Accordingly, he sailed from New York in May 1883, bound for India by way of Great Britain and the Suez Canal. He included in his India itinerary all the points at which the Mission was operating and was cordially greeted everywhere. He returned home in 1885, including a trip through the Holy Land on the way.

In 1887 he made another journey to Mexico, this time by rail, and spent the winter there. On his return he gave himself to the "Million and a Quarter for Missions" campaign of his Church. But failure of health caused him shortly to retire to Newton Center, Mass., where increasing invalidism held him for eight years. His end came in the Missionary Rest Home, Old Orchard, Me. He willed the proceeds of his insurance to the seminary and to the Press in Mexico City. In addition to his *Land of the Veda* he wrote the article on "Methodist Missions" in *Newcomb's Encyclopædia*; *From Boston to Bareilly and Back* (1885); and *Mexico in Transition* (4th ed., 1892).

[*Wm. Butler, the Founder of Two Missions of the M. E. Church* (1902), by his daughter, Clementina Butler; *Official Minutes, New Eng. Conf. of the M. E. Ch.* (1900).]   J.C.A.

BUTLER, WILLIAM ALLEN (Feb. 20, 1825–Sept. 9, 1902), lawyer, author, son of Benjamin Franklin Butler, 1795–1858 [*q.v.*], and Harriet (Allen) Butler, was born at Albany, N. Y. He was eight years old when the family moved to Washington on his father's acceptance of the attorney-generalship in President Jackson's cabinet. The journey from Albany to Washington took four days of travel by water, rail, and stagecoach. From January to June 1834, young "Allen" went to a select school kept by Silas Hill at Georgetown, where the staggering bill presented to his father for the six months' tuition, books and supplies, and fuel came to $25.56. The next year he was sent to school at Hudson, N. Y., and in the winter of 1837 he studied at the Grammar School of the University of the City of New York. It was only natural that he should go to the University, near which the family lived after his father's retirement from the cabinet and Washington, and with which both his father and his uncle Charles were intimately associated. He graduated in the class of 1843, studied law in his father's office, and was admitted to the bar in July 1846. His practise became extensive and varied, including important cases in bankruptcy, insurance, partnerships, contracts, and patents, and he was a sound authority on admiralty law. His interest in this branch of the profession was undoubtedly due in large measure to his marriage on Mar. 21, 1850, to Mary Russell Marshall, daughter of Capt. Charles H. Marshall, agent and part owner of the famous Black Ball line of Liverpool packets. Capt. Marshall was a member of the Board of Pilot Commissioners, a voluntary association formed by the Chamber of Commerce and the Marine Underwriters of New York. When the legislature of the state passed an act (1853) legalizing this voluntary association, the statute was attacked as conflicting with the mode of appointment prescribed in the state constitution and with the powers of Congress to control interstate and foreign commerce, as enumerated in the Federal Constitution. Butler successfully defended the constitutionality of the act of 1853 (and incidentally confirmed his father-in-law's position) in the case of *Sturgis* vs. *Spofford* (45 *N. Y.* 446). In the case of *People* vs. *Vanderbilt* (26 *N. Y.* 287) he performed a lasting service to the general shipping interests of New York by preventing the monopoly of the piers in the North River by private steamship lines. Three gifts were combined in Butler's mentality to make his legal arguments unusually effective: a faculty of memory which enabled him to repeat poems or addresses almost verbatim after a lapse of several years; a power of analysis which moved Chief Justice Waite of the Supreme Court to speak of his argument in the case of *Hoyt* vs. *Sprague* (103 *U. S.* 613) as "the most lucid statement of complicated facts that I have

ever heard"; and a keen sense of humor which never failed to relieve a dull case or refresh a jaded jury. Though he never held any political office, Butler found time in the midst of his busy practise for many activities that testified to his strong spirit of public service. He was closely identified with the University of the City of New York for nearly sixty years from his graduation to his death, lecturing at times on admiralty law in the new department of law created by his father's efforts, serving as a member of the Council from 1862 on, and as its president after the death of his uncle Charles Butler [*q.v.*] in 1897. He was a member of the board of trustees of the New York Public Library, was president of the American Bar Association in 1885 and of the Bar Association of New York in 1886 and 1887, and was one of the speakers, with Grover Cleveland, Chief Justice Fuller, and Justice Field, at the celebration at the Metropolitan Opera House, New York, in 1890, of the hundredth anniversary of the organization of the Supreme Court of the United States. When he moved to Yonkers in 1865, he immediately became one of the leading citizens of the town, helping to improve the school system, contributing to the establishment of hospitals, and making possible the organization of the Women's Institute. As a staunch Republican and Presbyterian (though, like his father, he never consented to hold office in the church), he was active in the political and religious life of the town, until the increasing blindness of his last years confined him to his home at "Round Oak." Somewhat to his chagrin, he believed that his "chief, if not only, claim to public recognition was the writing of a few pages of society verse." Gifted with a nimble wit and a faculty for rhyming which reminds one often of Lowell's, he wrote a number of satirical poems (*Two Millions*, 1858, "The Sexton and the Thermometer" in the *Literary World*, Mar. 24, 1849, *Dobbs, his Ferry*, 1875, etc.), one of which, *Nothing to Wear; an Episode of City Life* (1857), has become an American classic. William Dean Howells said of him, in a notice of the 1899 edition of his poems, "But for the professional devotion of this able lawyer, we might have counted in him the cleverest of our society poets." Butler's attempts at novel writing (*Domesticus; a Tale of the Imperial City*, 1886, and *Mrs. Limber's Raffle; or, a Church Fair and its Victims*, 1876) were less successful. He was the author also of *Martin Van Buren, Lawyer, Statesman and Man* (1862); *Memorial of Charles H. Marshall* (1867); *Lawyer and Client: their Relation, Rights, and Duties* (1871); *Evert Augustus Duyckinck* (1879); *Samuel J. Tilden*

(1886); *The Revision of the Statutes of the State of New York and the Revisers* (1889); *Oberammergau* (1891). It has been said of him that, while there were greater lawyers and greater literary men than Butler, perhaps "no man of his time, either in England or America, held an equally high rank, both as lawyer and a literary man."

[Wm. Allen Butler, *A Retrospect of Forty Years, 1825–65* (1911), ed. by Harriet Allen Butler, with appendices containing the Memorial Addresses of Geo. C. Holt, John E. Parsons, and Alton B. Parker; also a sketch of Butler's legal career by Geo. C. Hoyt in *Annual Report, Ass. of the Bar of the City of N. Y.*, 1904.]

D.S.M.

BUTLER, WILLIAM ORLANDO (Apr. 19, 1791–Aug. 6, 1880), soldier, lawyer, congressman, vice-presidential candidate, was of Irish descent, the second of four brothers, all destined to become men of note, and a son of Percival Butler, who with three brothers played a prominent part in the Revolution and won the attention of Washington and Lafayette. Percival Butler moved to Kentucky in 1784, and marrying Mildred Hawkins, a sister-in-law of Col. John Todd, a victim of the battle of the Blue Licks, settled in Jessamine County, where William O. Butler was born. In 1796 he removed to the mouth of the Kentucky River and established there the famous Butler estate. William O. Butler attended Transylvania University where he graduated in 1812. He immediately began the study of law in Lexington under the celebrated Robert Wickliffe, but on the declaration of war against Great Britain in June he volunteered as a private. He well maintained the traditional military glory of the Butler family, for it was his war record that gave him his greatest claim to remembrance. He was attached to Winchester's army and was sent to the relief of Fort Wayne. He took part in the battle at the River Raisin, Jan. 18 and 22, 1813. At the second engagement he was wounded and captured but escaped the massacre that was meted out to many of his comrades. He was taken to Fort Niagara and after many sufferings and hardships was exchanged. Making his way back to Kentucky, he won a commission as a captain, and raised a company which he led under Andrew Jackson against Pensacola. He took part in the battle of New Orleans, leading the attack on Pakenham on the night of Dec. 23, 1814, thereby making it possible to throw up the defenses at Chaumette. He also took a prominent part in the battle on Jan. 8. His bravery and resourcefulness won him the unstinted praise of Jackson, a brevet majorship, and in 1816 a position on Jackson's staff, succeeding his brother Thomas B. Butler. He came eloquently to the defense of

Jackson in his conflict with the New Orleans authorities following the battle.

Butler showed unmistakable military genius and he greatly disappointed Jackson when he resigned from the army in 1817 to finish the study of law. He chose to practise his profession in Carrollton (Port William), his father's home, and soon became one of the most prominent and best-liked Democrats in the state. On the declaration of war against Mexico in 1846 he was appointed by President Polk major-general of volunteers and assigned to Gen. Taylor's command. He took an important part in the campaign, being second in command at Monterey, where, in the street fighting, he was wounded in the leg. After spending some time at home recuperating, he joined Gen. Scott in 1848 and was present at the capture of Mexico City. Shortly before the treaty of peace was made he succeeded Gen. Scott in command of the army in Mexico. For his bravery at Monterey he was voted a sword by Congress and also by Kentucky. On returning home he gave up the practise of law to engage in farming.

Butler's military record from the beginning gave him outstanding political opportunities. In 1817 and 1818 he represented Gallatin County in the legislature and in 1839 took his seat in Congress, being reëlected for the following term. He refused to stand for a third term. With a successful congressional career back of him, he was drafted by the Democrats as their candidate for governor in 1844. Although the state was almost impregnably Whig at this time he reduced the majority against him to less than 5,000. In 1848 when both parties were capitalizing war records the Democrats nominated him for vice-president to run with Lewis Cass. In addition to his military record, as a Southern slaveholder he gave strength to the ticket. In 1851 the Kentucky Democrats attempted without success to elect him to the United States Senate, and in the following year, encouraged by his friends, he developed ambitions for the presidency. In 1855 President Pierce offered him the governorship of Nebraska but he declined it.

Butler, though a slaveholder, was opposed to the extension of slavery and in 1861 stood staunchly for the maintenance of the Union. He was one of Kentucky's delegates to the Washington Peace Congress in February of that year. He was a Union Democrat during the Civil War, too old to serve in the army. He had some literary ability and often wrote poetry, published in the state press. A book of his poems was published called, *The Boatman's Horn and Other Poems*. He was tall, dignified, and refined, not a brilliant orator but an able speaker. He died in Carrollton.

[Short sketches may be found in R. H. and L. Collins, *Hist. of Ky.* (1874), vols. I, II. More extensive accounts are Francis P. Blair, Jr., "Biog. Sketch of Gen. W. O. Butler," *Graham's Mag.*, Jan. 1848; and *Life of Gen. Lewis Cass: Comprising an Account of His Military Service in the North-West During the War with Gt. Brit., His Diplomatic Career and Civil Hist. To Which Is Appended a Sketch of the Public and Private Hist. of Maj.-Gen. W. O. Butler, of the Volunteer Service of the U. S.* (1848). For Butler family see J. A. Murray, "The Butlers of the Cumberland Valley" in *Hist. Reg.* (Harrisburg), Jan. 1883; T. M. Green, *Hist. Families of Ky.* (1889); *Pa. Mag. of Hist. and Biog.*, Apr. 1883.] \   E. M. C—r.

BUTLER, ZEBULON (Jan. 23, 1731–July 28, 1795), soldier, was born at Ipswich, Mass., the son of John and Hannah (Perkins) Butler and the grandson of Lieut. William Butler of Ipswich. His youth was spent in Lyme, Conn., where his parents settled in 1736 and where he is usually alleged to have been born. Here he engaged in the West India trade, owning one or more sloops. In the French and Indian War he saw service as ensign (1757), lieutenant and quartermaster (1759), and captain (1760). Ordered to Cuba in 1762, he was shipwrecked during the voyage but arrived in time to participate in the latter part of the siege of Havana. Returning to civilian life at the close of the war he led a band of Connecticut settlers to the Wyoming Valley (now Luzerne County, Pa.), where they settled along the Susquehanna (1769) on land claimed by Connecticut by virtue of her charter and through purchase from the Indians. In the ensuing Pennamite Wars between Connecticut and Pennsylvania, Butler acted as leader of the Connecticut settlers, serving as director of the Susquehanna Company and representing Wyoming in the Connecticut Assembly (1774–76). In July 1771 he laid siege to Fort Wyoming, garrisoned by Pennsylvania troops, forced its capitulation, and later repulsed Col. Plunkett's invasion of the valley in a battle at the Nanticoke Gap (1775). With the outbreak of the Revolution he was commissioned colonel of the Connecticut militia. He later became lieutenant-colonel (1776) and colonel (1778) of the Continental line. In March 1778 invasion of the valley became imminent, and Butler, acting on behalf of the "Town of Westmoreland," appealed to the Board of War for its protection, the Wyoming regiments then being with the Continental army. Before aid arrived, the valley was invaded by the New York Loyalist leader, Maj. John Butler [*q.v.*], with an army consisting of Rangers, a detachment of Sir John Johnson's loyalist regiment (the King's Royal Regiment of New York), and several hundred Indians led by the Seneca chief Old King

(Sayenqueraghta). Lieutenant-Colonel Zebulon Butler, home on leave, on assuming command of the Continental forces, found himself at the head of barely sixty regulars and about 300 militia consisting largely of "the undisciplined, the youthful, and the aged." He wished to await reinforcements but was overruled by his council of war, and it was decided to leave Forty Fort and seek battle, an unfortunate decision that made victory for the invaders almost a certainty. Outnumbered, and the Indians making a flank attack, the Continental forces fled to the fort (July 3, 1778), which capitulated on the following day, Butler fleeing to prevent capture. While there were many atrocities committed, there was not the wholesale massacre so vividly described by Thomas Campbell in *Gertrude of Wyoming* (London, 1809). After the departure of the invaders Butler returned to Wyoming as commandant, where he remained during the Sullivan expedition of 1779 against the Iroquois confederacy. The expedition detached by Gen. Sullivan, Sept. 20, 1779, to destroy the Indian villages east of Cayuga Lake, frequently credited to Col. Butler, was commanded by Lieutenant-Colonel William Butler of the 4th Pennsylvania regiment. On Dec. 29, 1780, Butler was recalled from Wyoming by Washington at the request of Congress to prevent any recurrence of friction between Connecticut and Pennsylvania, and he was then stationed at West Point, retiring from the army at the close of the Revolution. He was married three times: first, on Dec. 23, 1760, to Anna Lord, who died in 1773; second, in August 1775 to Lydia Johnson, who died on June 26, 1781; third, in November 1781 to Phebe Haight. He died at Wilkesbarre at the age of sixty-four leaving children by each of his three wives.

[*House Doc. No. 203*, 25 Cong., 3 Sess.; *Minutes of the Provincial Council of Pa.*; *Pa. Archives*; *Jour. of the Military Exped. of Maj.-Gen. John Sullivan* (1887); *Proc. and Colls. of the Wyoming Hist. and Geol. Soc.*, vols. II to XVI *passim*; *Buffalo Hist. Soc. Pubs.*, vols. I (1879), IV (1896); *Vital Records of Ipswich, Mass.* (1910); Geo. A. Perkins, *The Family of John Perkins of Ipswich, Mass.* (1889); H. E. Hayden, *The Massacre of Wyoming* (1895) and *Geneal. and Family Hist. of the Wyoming and Lackawanna Valleys, Pa.* (1906); Thos. J. Rogers, *A New Am. Biog. Dict.* (3rd ed., Easton, Pa., 1824); Wm. L. Stone, *Life of Jos. Brant-Thayendanegea* (1838); Chas. Miner, *Hist. of Wyoming* (1845); Geo. Peck, *Wyoming* (1858); O. J. Harvey, *A Hist. of Wilkes-Barre, Luzerne County, Pa.* (1909); *Conn. Mag.*, Mar.–Apr. 1900; Butler's report of the battle of Wyoming to the Board of War, dated July 10, 1778, printed in John Marshall, *Life of Geo. Washington* (2nd ed., 1832, I, 281).]   F. E. R.

BUTTERFIELD, DANIEL (Oct. 31, 1831–July 17, 1901), Union soldier, the third son of John [*q.v.*] and Malinda Harriet (Baker) Butterfield, was born in Utica, N. Y. He inherited from his father, a genius for organization, an indomitable will, and a natural ability for promoting large enterprises. After preparatory work in private schools and the Utica Academy, he entered Union College, where he made a fair scholastic record and from which he graduated in 1849 at the age of eighteen, with the degree of Bachelor of Arts. He then studied law, but finding himself too young for admittance to the bar, traveled extensively through the South, and incidentally became convinced of the certainty of conflict between the states over slavery. Soon after, he established himself in New York City as superintendent of the eastern division of the American Express Company. Having in mind, however, the inevitability of civil war, he entered the New York militia as a captain in the 71st Regiment, and after rising through intermediate grades, became colonel of the 12th Regiment, an organization in which he had a peculiar interest during his entire life. On Apr. 14, 1861, Fort Sumter was evacuated, and official records show that within two days, Butterfield was appointed first sergeant of the *Clay Guards,* a battalion of three hundred prominent citizens of Washington, hastily recruited to defend the city from expected attack. Butterfield's 12th New York Regiment was mustered into the Federal service on May 2, 1861, and on May 24 crossed the historic Long Bridge, the first Union regiment to enter Virginia. The regiment was soon ordered to reinforce Gen. Patterson's command at Martinsburg, W. Va., and participated in many early operations in that vicinity, with Butterfield temporarily in command of a brigade of New York regiments. The coming of army reorganization brought to him appointment as a brigadier-general of volunteers, Sept. 7, 1861, and assignment to command of the 3rd Brigade, 1st Division (Morrell), 5th Army Corps (Fitz-John Porter).

As a brigade commander, Butterfield participated most creditably in McClellan's Peninsular campaign, and was wounded at the battle of Gaines's Mill, June 21, 1862. Thirty years later, Congress awarded Butterfield a medal of honor for distinguished gallantry on this occasion, the citation reading, "where he seized the colors of the 83rd Pennsylvania Infantry Volunteers at a critical moment, and under galling fire of the enemy led the command." His brigade covered the important withdrawal of the Army of the Potomac to Harrison's Landing, when it changed base to join Pope, and at the end of October, Butterfield assumed command of Morrell's division, succeeding by virtue of seniority to command of the 5th Army Corps, Nov. 16, 1862. On Nov. 29, he received his appointment as

major-general, and on Dec. 13, commanded the 5th Corps in the Central Grand Division at the battle of Fredericksburg. On Dec. 16, his corps covered Burnside's withdrawal.

When Gen. Hooker succeeded Burnside in command of the Army of the Potomac, Jan. 26, 1863, Butterfield became Hooker's chief of staff, and served as such during the battle of Chancellorsville. At about this time he devised a system of corps badges, which gained immediate popularity with officers and men. He remained as chief of staff of the army after assumption of command by Gen. Meade, and was severely wounded at the battle of Gettysburg, July 3, 1863, by the Confederate shell fire which preceded Pickett's charge. Following this decisive battle, both Gen. Meade and Gen. Butterfield were parties to a controversy which lasted long after the Civil War as to Meade's real intentions on the critical morning of July 2, 1863,—Meade contending that a preparatory order covering the withdrawal of the Army of the Potomac from the field of Gettysburg was merely tentative and precautionary; while Butterfield and certain other generals regarded the order as positive and mandatory on Meade's part to surrender the field without further battle (*Battles and Leaders of the Civil War,* III, 243–97, 410–11).

The following October, Butterfield joined the Army of the Cumberland as Hooker's chief of staff, in time to act as such at the battle of Lookout Mountain. In Sherman's march to the sea he commanded the 3rd Division, 20th Army Corps, under Generals Thomas and Hooker, and was engaged at Buzzard's Roost, at Resaca (where his troops captured the first guns lost by Johnston in the Atlanta campaign), at Dallas, New Hope Church, and at Lost and Kenesaw Mountains. Before the Atlanta campaign ended, he was seriously stricken with fever and was never able to rejoin his old command. When convalescent, he was ordered on special duty at Vicksburg, and later went to New York City, where on Aug. 24, 1865, he was mustered out of the volunteer service, but was retained as superintendent of the general recruiting service, by virtue of his appointment, July 1, 1863, as colonel of the 5th Infantry, Regular Army. On Mar. 13, 1865, he was honored with brevet appointment as brigadier-general, United States Army, for gallant and meritorious services during the war; and on the same date with the brevet of major-general, United States Army, for similar services in the field during the war.

In January 1866, at the suggestion of Alexander T. Stewart of New York, Butterfield became the prime mover in raising a testimonial fund amounting to $105,000 from patriotic citizens of New York, which was presented to Gen. Grant, Feb. 15, 1866.

On Mar. 14, 1870, Butterfield's resignation from the army was accepted, that he might become assistant United States treasurer at New York City, under President Grant. Various considerations induced Butterfield's resignation from the military service, chief among which was the death of his father and the constant attention required in the administration of a large estate. After retirement to private life, Butterfield became associated with many important business enterprises, and exhibited the same tireless energy and sound judgment in these affairs which had marked his army career. He constructed a railroad in the republic of Guatemala; was president of the Albany & Troy Steamboat Company; and was financially interested in the Apartment Hotel Company, the Butterfield Real Estate Company, and the National Bank of Cold Spring, N. Y. He was also owner of the Brooklyn Annex steamships, connecting with the Pennsylvania Railroad, and was a director of the Mechanics & Traders Bank of New York. In 1870, he visited Europe, where he made an exhaustive study of the London and Paris post-office systems, the subject of a report to the Postmaster-General of the United States. On June 4, 1877, he lost his wife to whom he was married on Feb. 12, 1857; and on Sept. 21, 1886, he was married in London, to Mrs. Julia Lorillard (Safford) James, of New York City and Cold Spring. On two subsequent trips to Europe, he visited Russia with a view to securing concessions to build a Siberian railroad, in which his efforts were unsuccessful. During these visits, he received many social attentions and honors from the Emperor of Russia. At the Washington Centennial Celebration in New York City, in May 1889, he acted as grand marshal of the parade, where over 100,000 men passed in review. In the year 1892, he established a course of thirty lectures at Union College, on popular topics of the day. He was during this period of his career at one time or another, president of the Society of the Army of the Potomac, member of the Grand Army of the Republic, and chancellor of the New York Commandery of the Loyal Legion. On July 2, 1893, at Gettysburg, he acted as grand marshal of the dedication exercises of the New York State Memorial Monument, attended by over 10,000 veterans. As a testimonial to his war service, he was, at various times, made the recipient of a sword of superb workmanship, set with emeralds; a 5th Corps

Badge, set with diamonds; and badges of the 20th Corps and of the Army of the Potomac, set with precious stones,—all presented by former comrades of the Civil War. In politics, he was a Republican, and in 1892, rather against his will, consented to become a candidate for Congress, but was defeated. He was actively interested in military preparedness, and in 1900 framed legislation for submission to Congress which contemplated uniform organization and training for the militia of the country, and for the organization of army reserves. In this connection Gov. Roosevelt appointed him a delegate to a conference called by the Governor of Florida, to consider plans for the rapid mobilization of troops in time of war.

Early in April 1901, Butterfield suffered a stroke of paralysis, and two months later was taken from his home in New York City to "Cragside," his country residence at Cold Spring. Here he passed away, in the seventieth year of his age. By special authority of the War Department, the interment took place at West Point, where his remains received the major-general's salute of thirteen guns and where the escort of honor included his old regiment, the 12th New York. Over his grave a magnificent white marble monument has been erected, thirty-five feet in height, consisting in the main of sixteen slender columns upon which rests an ornate superstructure. Butterfield died, honored and mourned by a host of friends in both military and civil life.

[A very complete account of Butterfield's life and services is to be found in Julia Lorillard Butterfield, *A Biog. Memorial of Gen. Daniel Butterfield* (1904). See also *Battles and Leaders of the Civil War* (vols. II, III, IV), and the *Official Records* (Army).]

C. D. R.

BUTTERFIELD, JOHN (Nov. 18, 1801–Nov. 14, 1869), expressman, financier, was descended from Benjamin Butterfield, who brought his family to the Bay Colony in 1638. His grandfather saw service in the American Revolution, while others of his kinsmen participated in the French and Indian War. His father, Daniel Butterfield, was a native of Berne, near Albany, N. Y., and here it was that John Butterfield was born. Brief periods of attendance at the primitive schools in the Helderberg provided his meager formal training, while the broader education of his practical career was begun as a stage driver. He rose from the driver's seat to a share in the proprietorship and soon most of the stage lines of western New York were under his control. He became interested in packet-boats on the canal, steamboats on Lake Ontario, and plank roads in the region; he originated the street railway of Utica and aided in the promotion of railroads. With Wells, Livingston, and others he established the New York, Albany & Buffalo Telegraph Company. He was not the originator of the express business but was one of the first to see the possibilities of such service. In 1849 he formed the express company of Butterfield, Wasson & Company. The year following there was effected at his suggestion a consolidation of his firm and two others to create the American Express Company. When in 1857 Congress provided for the establishment of the first great transcontinental stage line Butterfield and his associates were awarded the contract at $600,000 per year. It was to be the longest stage-coach line in America, extending from St. Louis via El Paso, Tucson, and Los Angeles to San Francisco. The route was nearly 2,800 miles long and coaches were to be run semiweekly each way on a twenty-five day schedule. As president of the Overland Mail Company Butterfield displayed his executive ability in planning and establishing this service. Upon arrival of the pioneer eastbound stage at St. Louis he telegraphed the good news to Washington and President Buchanan replied: "I cordially congratulate you upon the result. It is a glorious triumph for civilization and the Union." This overland service was maintained with outstanding success. In Utica, his home city, Butterfield continued to be an important factor. He was director of the Utica City National Bank, was builder of the Butterfield House and the Butterfield Block, and was interested in land investments and development. He was elected mayor of the city in 1865. His portrait reveals a man of regular features and rather handsome appearance, with aggressive ability and determination written on his face. He was married to Malinda Harriet Baker in February 1822, and to them were born nine children; of these, their third son, Daniel [*q.v.*], was a general in the Union army in the Civil War. In 1867 he was stricken by paralysis, from the effects of which he lingered until Nov. 14, 1869. His wife survived him, living until Aug. 20, 1883.

[Julia Lorillard Butterfield's *A Biog. Memorial of Gen. Daniel Butterfield* (1904) is devoted primarily to the son of John Butterfield but presents considerable data upon the father. Mention of Butterfield's express service is found in *Harper's Mag.*, August 1875, and a fuller treatment in LeRoy R. Hafen's *The Overland Mail* (1926). For ancestry see Geo. A. Gordon's "The Butterfields of Middlesex" in *New Eng. Hist. and Geneal. Reg.*, Jan. 1890.]   L. R. H.

BUTTERICK, EBENEZER (May 29, 1826–Mar. 31, 1903), inventor of standardized paper patterns for clothes, was the seventh child of Francis and Ruhamah (Buss) Butterick. His father was a carpenter in the small town of Sterling, Mass. There Ebenezer was born and became a tailor and shirt-maker. About 1859, either he or his wife Ellen conceived the idea of a set of graded shirt patterns, by which it would be possible to reproduce these garments in unlimited quantities. Experiments on such patterns were continued for several years, until, on June 16, 1863, the first patterns, cut from stiff paper, were placed on the market. The cheapness and practical utility of these patterns made them instantly successful, and the demand for them was so widespread that Butterick removed, later in 1863, to the larger town of Fitchburg, where there were better facilities for manufacture and distribution. At the suggestion of his wife that mothers would welcome patterns from which to make clothes for their children, he added to his shirt patterns a graded set of patterns for boys' suits. At this time, Giuseppe Garibaldi was an international hero, and these first juvenile patterns were for "Garibaldi" suits, modeled after the uniform worn by him and his men. These garments, picturesque, and easily made at home from these simple patterns, became immensely popular throughout the country. The demand for his patterns so increased that Butterick removed his factory from his home to a disused academy in Fitchburg. The desirability of a metropolitan office became evident, and in 1864 quarters were opened at 192 Broadway, New York City. The patterns, now made from tissue paper, were chiefly for children's suits, and especially for the "Garibaldi." Butterick sold his patterns largely through agents, and one of these, J. W. Wilder, reported a demand for similar patterns for women's garments. The suggestion was at once adopted, and with this step the business expanded to enormous proportions. In 1867, Wilder and A. W. Pollard were associated with Butterick as E. Butterick & Company, and two years later the factory was removed from Fitchburg to Brooklyn. Wilder, an aggressive and imaginative business genius, became the active and controlling member of the firm. One of his inspirations was a magazine with fashion reports to stimulate the sale of the patterns, and the *Metropolitan* was established in 1869. This later became the *Delineator*. In 1871 the company sold 6,000,000 patterns, and by 1876 branches had been placed in London, Paris, Berlin, and Vienna. The business was reorganized in 1881, and was renamed The Butterick Publishing Company, Ltd., with J. W. Wilder as president, and Ebenezer Butterick as secretary. Butterick held this position until 1894, when he retired from active participation in the business. It may be noted that Butterick's priority as inventor of paper patterns has been disputed and that the credit has also been given to Mrs. John Ellis, of Manchester, England. Investigation has shown, however, that Mrs. Ellis made her first patterns in 1866, and that they were for her own use only. Butterick patterns, whether first conceived by Ebenezer, or by Ellen, his wife, were undoubtedly the first to be practically and commercially utilized.

[Data for the life of Ebenezer Butterick have been obtained from the files of The Butterick Company, and from the recollections of G. W. Wilder, now president of that company. Obituaries were pub. in the *Brooklyn Times, Brooklyn Eagle, N. Y. Evening Post*, and *N. Y. Times*, all for Apr. 1, 1903.]   A. L. C.

BUTTERWORTH, BENJAMIN (Oct. 22, 1837–Jan. 16, 1898), lawyer, politician, came of Quaker stock on both sides. His grandfather, Benjamin Butterworth, a planter of Campbell County, Va., and a member of the Society of Friends, in 1812 migrated to Ohio, taking up a homestead in Warren County. His father, William Butterworth, a school-teacher and farmer, married Elizabeth, daughter of Nathan Linton of Clinton County, also a member of the Society of Friends, and Benjamin was born in Hamilton township, Warren County. He received an excellent preparatory schooling, completing his education at Lebanon Academy and Ohio University (Athens). He then studied law at Cincinnati, graduating from the Cincinnati Law School and being admitted to the bar in 1861. Serving during the war in an Ohio regiment he later commenced practise at Lebanon and quickly obtained an extensive clientele, owing to his attractive personality and powers of speech. In 1870 he was appointed United States district attorney for Southern Ohio but shortly resigned in order to resume practise. From 1873 to 1875 as a Republican he represented the district of Butler and Warren Counties in the state Senate. In 1875 he moved to Cincinnati, which city offered a wider scope for legal talent, and he rapidly acquired a prominent position at the bar. At the call of party, however, he practically sacrificed his professional career and reëntered politics, being elected in 1878 to the 46th Congress as Republican representative for the 1st District of Ohio. Reëlected in 1880, he retained his seat until 1882, when he was defeated. Returning to practise, he was retained by the attorney-general of the United States as special counsel in the South Carolina election cases and also acted as commissioner to investigate certain phases of the Northern Pacific Railway. President Arthur had desired to appoint him post-

master-general but the exigencies of local politics would not permit, and he accepted, June 1883, the commissionership of patents, a position where his legal ability found adequate scope. He resigned, however, Mar. 23, 1885, having been elected as representative from his old district to the 49th Congress. Reëlected in 1886 and 1888, he ranked among the party leaders in the House, though noted for the independent standpoint from which he was wont to view questions of the day. In 1890, he retired from Congress and opened a law office in Washington. In 1892 President Harrison appointed him president of the commission to the European governments in the interests of the Columbian Exposition, and the fine foreign exhibits at Chicago were in great measure due to his labors. He was a close personal friend of President McKinley and in April 1897 at the latter's request, he again became commissioner of patents. He died at Thomasville, Ga. He married, Nov. 2, 1863, Mary E., daughter of Jacob Seiler of Harrisburg, Pa. "During the last quarter of a century [1875–1900] no more picturesque and charming personality occupied the position of Representative from Ohio than Benjamin Butterworth" (F. Starek, *post*). Broad-minded, tolerant and genial, he was popular with all members, irrespective of politics.

[Butterworth's ancestry is traced in *Hist. of Warren County, Ohio* (1882), p. 939. A contemporary review of his earlier career appeared in *Biog. Cyc. and Portrait Gallery of the State of Ohio*, III (1884), 661. There are sketches of his life in *Appleton's Annual Cyc. and Register*, 1898, p. 528, and in W. A. Taylor, *Ohio in Cong. from 1803 to 1901* (1900), p. 264. See also article by F. Starek in O. O. Stealey, *Twenty Years in the Press Gallery* (1906), p. 288, and obituaries in *Cincinnati Times-Star, Cincinnati Enquirer, Cincinnati Commerical Tribune, Washington Post* and *Evening Star*, Washington, D. C., Jan. 17, 1898.]
     H. W. H. K.

BUTTERWORTH, HEZEKIAH (Dec. 22, 1839–Sept. 5, 1905), journalist, author, was born at Warren, R. I., of a substantial New England family whose ancestor had emigrated from England to Massachusetts before the middle of the seventeenth century. His father, Gardiner M. Butterworth, was a "good-natured, Bible-reading farmer," while from his mother, Susan (Ritchie) Butterworth, he inherited a poetic temperament. We are told that Hezekiah was different from the five other children of the family, a nervous, timid, superstitious boy, with a love for ghost stories. He never lost his keen interest in the traditions of the locality in which he was brought up. As a child, he was prevented by poor health from any extended schooling. He intended to go to Brown University after graduation from the high school at Warren, but never got beyond studying under the direction of one of the Brown professors. He evinced quite early a taste for journalism, writing for a local paper and contributing to periodicals. Having attracted the attention of the owner and editor of the *Youth's Companion* through a series of articles on self-education, he came into prominence through his connection with that periodical,—a connection which was maintained for almost a quarter-century (1870–94). It is said that during 1877–87, when his influence was the strongest, the circulation of the *Youth's Companion* increased from 140,000 to 400,000. Authorities differ in regard to the amount of foreign travel in which he was engaged throughout his life. It is certain that he went to Europe at least once and took one voyage to South America, but his travels were perhaps never so extensive as his seventeen volumes of *Zig Zag Journeys* to various parts of the world would indicate. He was known especially as a juvenile and patriotic writer, and while the literary value of his works may be questioned, there is no doubt of their wholesome moral influence. In his journal in 1885 he wrote: "Resolved, it is my purpose to give my whole heart and thought to my work with the pen and to write only that which will tend to make my readers better in heart and life and richer in spiritual knowledge." Most of his writings and his lectures took on a moral or religious tone, and he became especially known for his interest in church music. His book *The Story of the Hymns* received in 1875 the George Wood Gold Medal awarded to the book of the year which had exerted the best influence. He was also a popular religious lecturer the character of whose lectures is indicated by two of his favorite topics, "Men Who Overcame Obstacles to Spiritual Success" and "The Religious Experiences of Famous Men."

Much of his work was characterized by an exaggerated sentimentality. In literature his critical standards were affected by his kindliness and ready sympathy; he was, as a personal friend has said, "very hospitable to poets, good and bad." Prolific in output, he lacked the ability to criticize himself. He was very charitable, both with his money and with his interest, and the honesty and geniality which were expressed in his "transparently good" face won him the sincere affection of hosts of friends, especially among the poor. He never married, and there is very little reference to love and marriage in his books. The "touch of medieval asceticism" which his friends noted in him became very marked in his later years.

[Very little has been written about Hezekiah Butterworth although he was for many years a familiar figure to hosts of Americans. Most of the information in the above sketch came by word of mouth from his former associates on the *Youth's Companion,* such as C. A. Stephens and M. A. DeWolfe Howe. Ralph Davol in the *New England Mag.* of Jan. 1906 shortly after Butterworth's death wrote an appreciation of his work and personality and M. B. Thrasher reproduces in the *National Mag.,* X, 530, a personal interview with him. There is a tribute in an article by Nixon Waterman in the *Boston Evening Transcript,* Sept. 6, 1905. For bibliography of his writings see *Who's Who in America,* 1903–05.]   J. L. M.

BUTTRICK, WALLACE (Oct. 23, 1853–May 27, 1926), Baptist clergyman, educator, was born in Potsdam, N. Y. His father, Charles Henry Buttrick (1823–77), was a direct descendant of William Buttrick who came from Kingston-on-Thames in 1640 and settled at Concord, Mass. His mother, Polly Dodge Warren (1828–1919), was descended from Richard Warren who came over in the *Mayflower* in 1620. Buttrick attended Ogdensburg Academy and the Potsdam Normal School between 1868 and 1872. On Dec. 1, 1875, he married Isabella Allen of Saginaw, Mich. Early possessed of a desire to enter the ministry, his hopes were deferred by the necessity of earning a livelihood, and for a time he was employed as a clerk in the railway mail service. Subsequently he entered the Rochester Theological Seminary and was graduated there in 1883. The same year he became pastor of the First Baptist Church of New Haven, Conn., where he served until 1889. He then accepted a call to a pastorate in St. Paul, Minn., and after three years there became pastor of a Baptist church at Albany, N. Y. Ten years later he was invited to become secretary and executive officer of the General Education Board which had just been established by Mr. John D. Rockefeller for the promotion of education in the United States. While money had been provided by Mr. Rockefeller for the administrative needs of the new organization, no endowment funds had then been received, the policy of the Board and its founder being to make first of all a thorough survey of the educational needs of the country with a view to discovering the strategic points to which the efforts of the Board could be most wisely directed, and the methods by which private funds could best be used, so as to stimulate the efforts and the self-reliance of each community. To the study of this great problem Buttrick devoted himself with wisdom, tact, and assiduity. Although he neither possessed nor claimed to possess the formal qualifications of an educational expert, his firm grasp of the essential purposes of education, his abundant common sense, and a remarkable understanding of human nature, equipped him admirably to take a fresh view of the educational field and to discover the points at which reinforcement was needed. While the work of the Board, soon supported by generous endowment, covered many aspects of education, its main efforts were exerted in two directions: first, to promote the better endowment of those colleges in different parts of the country which, by reason of their location, by the evidences of vitality already manifested, and by their possession of constituencies capable of carrying the main burden of future support, gave promise of permanent usefulness; the second point to which the Board directed its attention was the general condition of education in the Southern states. While the needs of higher education in this section were not overlooked, the improvement and extension of primary and secondary schools were recognized as of more urgent importance. Economic development was the indispensable means of providing the resources necessary for education. Accordingly, Buttrick's efforts turned in the direction of popular education to increase the productivity of the land through the demonstration on a wide scale of improved agricultural methods. Fortunately, a beginning had been made by Dr. Seaman A. Knapp of the Department of Agriculture. In cooperation with that Department, farm demonstration was extended and maintained for many years under the guidance of the General Education Board. The merit of this work, however, was that while it entailed a moderate expense in the employment of agricultural experts and demonstrators, the chief contribution was that of guidance and stimulus. With land, equipment, and labor furnished by the farmers themselves, the expense incurred by the Board was insignificant as compared with returns in increased productivity of the land. While these efforts were under way, the Board, through its agents, was studying the problem of secondary education in the South so that, with gradually increasing resources, improvements in the number and quality of schools could be financed by the Southern communities themselves. Buttrick lived to see these improvements largely realized. The special problems of negro education, as well as those which the negroes shared with the whites, also largely engaged his attention, and he contributed much to their solution, exhibiting a tact, sympathy, and understanding which won the confidence of both races. In his later years he turned his attention to the needs of education for the professions, especially in medicine; and his Board assumed large responsibilities in this field for the expenditure of the sums placed at its disposal by Mr. Rockefeller. In 1914 he assumed the direction of the China

Medical Board of the Rockefeller Foundation in addition to his activities as executive officer of the General Education Board. He spent some weeks of the year 1917 in Great Britain, meeting leaders of public opinion, addressing large popular gatherings on the subject of American participation in the war, and interpreting to the British public the sentiments and aims by which that participation was inspired. In 1917 he was made president of the General Education Board and held that office until 1923 when he became chairman. He was also a trustee of the Rockefeller Foundation and a member of the International Health Board, the China Medical Board, the Peking Union Medical College, and the International Education Board. To the discharge of these responsibilities he brought great wisdom, a passionate devotion to his work, an ever-present sense of humor, geniality, and a kindliness that found spontaneous expression in his close personal relations with men of every station and calling. He died in Baltimore on May 27, 1926.

[*Who's Who in America*, 1903–05; *Gen. Ed. Board: an Account of its Activities, 1902–14* (1915); *Annual Report of the Gen. Ed. Board*, 1925–26; *N. Y. Times*, May 28, 1926.]   J.D.G.

BUTTS, ISAAC (Jan. 11, 1816–Nov. 20, 1874), newspaper editor, the son of Nicholas and Elizabeth (De Witt) Butts, was born in Dutchess County, N. Y. When twelve years old he went with his parents to Irondequoit, Monroe County, N. Y. The death of the father within four years left the management of the farm to the six children, of whom Isaac was the second in age. There was no opportunity for any formal education beyond what was offered by the district school. In spite of handicaps, young Butts made steady progress. Before he was thirty he had become the owner of the *Daily Advertiser*, published in the neighboring city of Rochester and said to be the oldest daily paper west of Albany. At a time when personal journalism in New York State was in the ascendant, with Greeley, Bryant, and Bennett setting the pace in the metropolis, Butts quickly found his place as a writer of political editorials. Rochester already had a newspaper-reading public of more than ordinary discrimination. Butts developed a pungent, terse, editorial style that won readers in a day when the editor's opinions on public questions received attention and respect in proportion to his independence of judgment and the forcefulness with which he gave it expression. Butts measured up to both criteria in an exceptional way. He was a Democrat and his advocacy of the Wilmot Proviso led to his taking an advanced position in the party on the slavery question. In 1848 he was among the Democratic editors of New York who went over to the "Barnburner" wing of the party and came out for the Van Buren ticket. The triumph of the "Hunkers," or conservative Democrats, in that election caused his retirement, for a brief season, from editorial responsibilities, but he was soon back in harness. In 1852, after the election of President Pierce, Butts became one of the owners of the Rochester *Daily Union* and continued as the political editor of that journal for twelve years (the *Advertiser* having in 1857 been consolidated with the *Union*). He was a leading exponent of the Douglas, or Squatter Sovereignty, idea and upheld the Missouri Compromise. He consistently opposed the Lincoln administration in its conduct of the Civil War and his final withdrawal from journalism in 1864 has been attributed to his conviction that the war was wholly wrong and that nothing but evil could result from it, so far as the nation was concerned. He was a life-long enemy of protective tariffs for home industry. A treatise on free trade that he had written in the last year of his life was published after his death (*Protection and Free Trade*, 1875). He had become independently rich through the success of the Western Union Telegraph Company, in which he was interested at an early stage of its development. In 1844 he was married to Mary Smyles, who with two sons and three daughters survived him.

[Rochester *Evening Express*, Nov. 20, 1874; Wm. F. Peck, *Semi-Centennial Hist. of Rochester* (1884); the *World* (N. Y.), Nov. 22, 1874.]   W.B.S.

BUTTZ, HENRY ANSON (Apr. 18, 1835– Oct. 6, 1920), Methodist clergyman, educator, was born at Middle Smithfield, Pa. He attended the village school there and at fifteen taught a district school. Then there followed alternate periods of attending school and teaching, until 1858, when he was graduated from Princeton University. His theological studies were pursued in the Theological Seminary of the Reformed Church at New Brunswick, N. J. His ecclesiastical affiliations were with the Newark Conference of the Methodist Episcopal Church, in which he served as pastor of several churches during the ten years of his public ministry, before being called to the work of the newly opened Drew Theological Seminary in Madison, N. J., to which he gave a most fruitful half-century of distinguished service. He was adjunct professor of Greek and Hebrew 1868–70; professor of Greek and New Testament Exegesis 1871–1918; president of the faculty 1880–1912, and president emeritus 1912–20. While primarily not an administrator, his tastes and training being along other lines, his presidency was a notable one, for

when he resigned in 1912 every new building on the campus, six in all, had been secured by him, and practically the entire endowment had been built up through his efforts. Nearly three thousand students of almost every nationality had come under his influence. It was said of him that he *was* Drew Theological Seminary. In this he lived and moved and had his being. No other opportunity appealed to him. He declined an election to the editorship of the *Methodist Review*. He was indifferent to a possible election to the bishopric of the Church. Essentially a teacher, a scholarly, ardent, interpretative teacher of the Greek New Testament, he was himself an example of the interest he sought to awaken in others. Various works were edited by him: *Epistle to the Romans in Greek* (1876); *The New Life Dawning* (1873), by B. H. Nadal; and *The Student's Commentary—The Book of Psalms* (1896), by Dr. James Strong. He was a member of various societies such as the American Exegetical Society and the American Philological Association, and of several ecclesiastical organizations, but his voice was seldom heard in debate. Never dogmatic, even though a man of strong convictions, he was urbane without obsequiousness, gentle without effeminacy, and, when necessary, firm without harshness. He was married, on Apr. 11, 1860, to Emily Hoagland.

[*Henry Anson Buttz, His Book: Lectures, Essays, Sermons, Exegetical Notes* (2 vols.), ed. by Chas. Fremont Sitterly (1922); the *Methodist Rev.*, Mar.–Apr. 1921; E. S. Tipple, *Drew Theol. Sem. 1867–1917* (1917); *Minutes of the Newark Conference of the M. E. Ch.* (1921).]   E.S.T.

BYFORD, WILLIAM HEATH (Mar. 20, 1817–May 21, 1890), gynecologist, descended from a family of Suffolk, England, was the eldest child of Henry T. and Hannah Byford. He was born in the village of Eaton, Ohio, where his father worked as a mechanic. In 1821 the family moved to the Falls of the Ohio River, now New Albany, Ind., and later moved to Hindostan, in the same state, where the father died when William was nine years old. With but three or four years of elementary schooling, William was forced to give up his studies and help his mother in the support of the family. When he was twelve years old, the family went to live with Mrs. Byford's father on a farm near Palestine, Ill., and two years later William began an apprenticeship with a tailor in that village. Later he went to Vincennes, Ind., to finish learning his trade. While serving his apprenticeship, he was acquiring an education. By diligent study, he mastered the structure of his native tongue and gained a useful knowledge of Latin, Greek, and French. With an eye to a medical career, he also studied physiology, chemistry, and natural history, and, during the last year of his apprenticeship, associated himself with Dr. Joseph Maddox of Vincennes. At the age of twenty-one he was able to pass the required examination, and began practise in Owensville, Ind. In 1840 he moved to Mt. Vernon, Ind., where he associated himself with Dr. Hezekiah Holland, whose daughter he afterward married. He remained at Mt. Vernon until 1850, during which time he pursued a course at the Ohio Medical College and, in 1845, obtained his medical degree. In 1850 he was appointed to the chair of anatomy at the Evansville Medical College and in 1852 was transferred to the chair of theory and practise of medicine. In 1857 he was called to the professorship of obstetrics and diseases of women and children in Rush Medical College in Chicago. Two years later he was transferred to a similar chair in the newly organized Chicago Medical College of which he was one of the founders. In 1879, Rush Medical College created especially for him a chair of gynecology, which he held until his death. In 1870, he was active in the organization of the Woman's Medical College of Chicago.

As a pioneer in gynecology and a medical teacher for nearly forty years, Byford made a deep impression upon the profession of his time. Good judgment combined with patient industry and singleness of purpose gave him leadership. His name is associated with many important innovations in gynecological practise, some of which have subsequently given way to improved methods while others remain as permanent contributions. He will be longest remembered, however, as a systematic writer on the subjects of obstetrics and gynecology. His most ambitious work was his *Treatise on the Theory and Practice of Obstetrics* (1870) ; others were: *A Treatise on the Chronic Inflammation and Displacements of the Impregnated Uterus* (1864) ; *The Practice of Medicine and Surgery applied to the Diseases and Accidents Incident to Women* (1865), widely used as a text-book; *The Philosophy of Domestic Life* (1869). In these works he also was a pioneer advocate of medical and nursing education for women. Deeply religious and of abstemious habits, he cared little for ordinary diversions and had practically no interests beyond his family life and his professional work. Physically of short and vigorous body, he had a triangular face with high and broad forehead, abundant wavy hair, full beard, and deep-set kindly eyes, with a suggestion of Butler's:

"Grave synod men that were revered
For solid face and depth of beard."

He continued his active practise to the end. Having retired in his usual health on the night of May 20, 1890, in the early hours of the next morning he succumbed to an attack of angina pectoris. He was married twice : on Oct. 3, 1840, at Mt. Vernon, Ind., to Mary Ann Holland, who died in 1864 ; and, in 1873, to Lina Flersheim.

[*Am. Jour. of Obstetrics,* June 1890; *Trans. Am. Gynecological Soc.,* 1890, vol. XV; *Trans. Ill. State Medic. Soc.,* 1891; *North Am. Practitioner,* 1890, vol. II; *Album of Fellows, Am. Gynecological Soc.,* 1918; Kelly and Burrage, *Am. Medic. Biog.* (1920).]

J.M.P.

BYINGTON, CYRUS (Mar. 11, 1793–Dec. 31, 1868), missionary to the Choctaw Indians, one of nine children of Capt. Asahel and Lucy (Peck) Byington, was born at Stockbridge, Mass. His father was a tanner and farmer, industrious and respected, but, the family being in humble circumstances, the future missionary to the Choctaws necessarily received a limited early education. Grown to be a sturdy lad, his career began when Joseph Woodbridge received him into his family and taught him Latin and Greek, a most important aid in his life-work. Apparently law was prescribed by Mr. Woodbridge as a profession for his protégé, and in fact Byington became a lawyer and practised for a few years in his native town and at Sheffield, Mass. The profession of law seemingly would have satisfied him but for the fact that he became, as he said, "a subject of divine grace," and was turned toward the ministry. Entering the Andover Theological Seminary he graduated in 1819, received ordination as a minister of the gospel, and was licensed to preach. Intent upon missionary work and hoping to go to the Armenians of Turkey, he bided his time till an opportunity should offer. Meanwhile he continued to preach in various churches in Massachusetts. At this time (1820) recruits to the number of twenty or twenty-five persons set out from Hampshire County, Mass., under the direction of the American Board, for the Choctaw Indian nation then in Mississippi. With them went Byington, who was placed in charge of the party. They proceeded by land to Pittsburgh, by flatboats down the Ohio and Mississippi to the mouth of the Yalobusha River, and by another land journey of 200 miles to their destination. Byington soon began the preparation of a Choctaw grammar and dictionary. Without the help of modern philological science, he had to take up the subject *de novo*. Assiduously he labored at the grammar and at the time of his death, nearly fifty years later, was making the seventh revision. The dictionary, representing a work of magnitude which he never concluded to his satisfaction, was of good use to him in translating into Choctaw several books of both the Old and New Testament, and in preparing Choctaw almanacs and a Choctaw definer. His grammar was published posthumously, edited by Daniel G. Brinton, in *Proceedings of the American Philosophical Society*, 1871, XII, 317–67, and his dictionary, edited by J. R. Swanton and H. S. Halbert, in *Bulletin 46, Bureau of American Ethnology* (1915). Byington's work is highly regarded by philologists. His portrait shows an alert and enthusiastic face, with clear, piercing eyes and tender mouth. Garbed in a long black coat with broad lapels, a soft collar, and flowing tie, he typified the clergyman of more than a hundred years ago.

[E. F. Jones, *Stockbridge, Past and Present; or, Records of an Old Mission Station* (1854) ; H. B. Cushman, *Hist. of the Choctaw, Chickasaw, and Natchez Indians* (1899) ; *Annual Report Am. Bd. of Commissioners for Foreign Missions*, 1821–59; *Gen. Cat. Theol. Sem., Andover, Mass.*, 1909.]   W.H.

BYLES, MATHER (Mar. 15, 1706/7–July 5, 1788), Congregational clergyman, was the son of Josiah or Josias Byles, a saddler, who came from England late in the seventeenth century and joined the Second Church of Boston in 1696, and of his wife Elizabeth, widow of William Greenough and daughter of Increase Mather. Josiah Byles died in 1708, and Mather Byles was brought up by his mother, aided by her father and by his uncle, Cotton Mather. Probably he attended the Boston Latin School; certainly in 1725 he took his A.B. at Harvard. His life-long friend, Benjamin Franklin, said that in college Byles "distinguished himself by a close application to his studies" (Manuscript Letter in the Massachusetts Historical Society). Probably in part because of his grandfather's expressed wish (H. E. Mather, *Lineage of Rev. Richard Mather*, 1890, p. 67), he prepared himself for the ministry, taking his A.M. in 1728. In 1732 he was ordained minister of the Hollis Street Congregational Church, founded in that year, and continued in office there until the Revolution ended his active career. He associated with the prosperous aristocrats of Boston, with whom he allied himself by marriage, and was a Tory at heart, although he did not air his politics in the pulpit. When the British occupied Boston he stayed in town while the ardent patriots fled. His own church was used by the troops. For a time he preached at the First Church (Manuscript Letter of his daughter, Oct. 4, 1783, in New England Historic Genealogical Society), and throughout the siege he maintained friendships with the "invaders." After the British evacuation, the patriots in his congregation preferred charges and, at a meeting which he held to be illegal, dismissed him

from his pulpit. This was followed by a court trial resulting in a sentence of banishment which was not enforced, though for a time he was imprisoned in his own house. For the rest of his life he lived quietly with his two daughters. The generosity of friends, old and new, saved him from want. In 1783 he had a paralytic shock; five years later he died. He was married in 1733 to Mrs. Anna Gale, whose uncle, Gov. Jonathan Belcher, had been a benefactor of the Hollis Street Church. She died in 1744, and Byles married in 1747 Rebecca Tailer, daughter of William Tailer, an erstwhile lieutenant-governor of Massachusetts. By his first wife he had six children, but only the eldest, a boy, outlived him. By his second wife he had one son who died in infancy and two daughters who survived.

In his own day Byles enjoyed fame as preacher, writer, and scholar. In 1765 the University of Aberdeen gave him the degree of S.T.D. He inherited a large part of the great library accumulated by Increase and Cotton Mather, and formed a curious collection of oddities, scientific and otherwise. His interest in literature developed early, and he wrote admiring letters to several English writers, Pope, Watts, and Thomson among them, and rejoiced at receiving answers from the first two. In the *New England Weekly Journal* and elsewhere he printed much verse, markedly imitative of his English literary idols, and some conventional prose essays. After 1744, when he bade "adieu to the airy Muse" (*Poems on Several Occasions*, Preface), his publications were largely theological.

Most of his best poetry is in his *Poems on Several Occasions* (1744) or in *The Conflagration, Applied to that Grand Period or Catastrophe of Our World, When the Face of Nature is to be Changed by a Deluge of Fire, As Formerly it was by That of Water. The God of Tempest and Earthquake* (1755). The most interesting of his other publications are *A Discourse on the Present Vileness of the Body, and its Future Glorious Change by Christ. To which is added, A Sermon on the Nature and Importance of Conversion* (1732); *Affection on Things Above* (1740); *The Glories of the Lord of Hosts, and the Fortitude of the Religious Hero* (1740); and *The Flourish of the Annual Spring* (1741).

To-day Byles seems undistinguished as a scholar and writer, though his verse is as fluent as that of any of his American contemporaries. Nor does he stand out as a theologian. He remained orthodox in his Calvinism, with neither the narrowness nor the ardor of his Puritan forebears. As a preacher his popularity was aided by his large stature and imposing presence, and

by the fact that he often lived up to his belief
that good sermons demanded "lively Descriptions, a clear Method, and pathetick Language."
It is as an incorrigible punster and amateur of
repartee that he is most marked among divines
of his period. Few of his *mots* are intrinsically
excellent, but in New England they won him ce-
lebrity—and sometimes censure (*Massachusetts
Historical Society Collections,* 1891, 6 ser., IV,
122). They are fairly represented by his remark,
on seeing the British soldiers enter Boston, that
at last the colonists' wrongs were "red(d)ressed,"
or by his calling a sentry, set to guard him, his
"Observe-a-Tory."

Historically Byles has interest as a man reared
in the old Puritan tradition who became not only
a divine but a jester, liked good society and light
verse as well as sound theology, and seemed more
akin to the worldly English parsons of his time
than to the colonial Puritans. He never formally deserted Congregationalism, but his Loyalist sympathies and taste for the society of the
wealthy, associated him with Episcopalians. The
logical development of some of his tendencies appears in his children. His son, Mather, Jr., entered the Anglican ministry. His two daughters
lived in Boston well into the nineteenth century,
loyal to English government and the English
Church, and, like their father, perhaps, more concerned with polite society in this world than with
aspirations toward sainthood in the next.

[The Massachusetts Historical Society has many
manuscripts, originals and copies, bearing on Byles and
his family. The New England Historic Genealogical
Society has copies of letters written by Byles and his
daughters. There is a brief biography in Sprague, *Annals Am. Pulpit* (1857), I, 376–82, and another in E. A.
Duyckinck, *Cyc. of Am. Lit.* (1855), I, 116–20. Some
of Byles's witticisms are in Wm. Tudor, *Life of Jas.
Otis* (1823), and in L. M. Sargent, *Dealings with the
Dead* (1856). A. W. H. Eaton in *The Famous Mather
Byles* (1914) makes use of this and other material, and
the notes give references to further sources of information. Dr. Eaton includes a brief bibliography of Byles's
chief publications. From this should be omitted *Divine
Power and Anger Displayed in Earthquakes* (1755),
which was written by Mather Byles, Jr., according to
his sister's memorandum, a copy of which is in the
Mass. Hist. Soc. The same authority ascribes to the
elder Byles *A Present for Children* (No. 9246 in Chas.
Evans, *Am. Bibliography* 1903–25), which is not included in Dr. Eaton's list. The portraits of Byles are
discussed by John H. Edmonds in his "Account of the
Mather-Byles Portraits" in *Proc. Am. Antiquarian Soc.,*
XXXIII, 285–90. J. H. Tuttle, "The Libraries of the
Mathers" in *Idem,* XX, 269–356, gives data on books
owned by Byles.]   K.B.M.

BYNUM, WILLIAM PRESTON (June 16,
1820–Dec. 30, 1909), jurist, was born in Stokes
County, N. C., whither his grandfather Gray
Bynum had moved from Virginia prior to the
Revolution. William's father, Hampton Bynum,
was a large landowner in the county and married
Mary Colman, daughter of Col. John Martin.

His early education was received at home, but
he subsequently proceeded to Davidson College
where he graduated with distinction in 1843. He
then studied law with Chief Justice Pearson and
was admitted to the bar in 1844. He commenced
practise at Rutherfordton, but removed to Lincoln County when he married Ann Eliza, daughter of Bartlett Shipp and sister of Judge W. M.
Shipp of the supreme court of North Carolina.
He practised at Lincolnton up to the outbreak of
the Civil War, and acquired an extensive legal
connection. Politically a Whig, he strongly opposed the movement for secession, both on the
platform and in the press. When Lincoln called
for volunteers to coerce the South, however, he
threw in his lot with his state, and in 1861 was
appointed lieutenant-colonel of the 2nd North
Carolina Regiment by Gov. Ellis. For two years
he was on active service, participating in the battles in the neighborhood of Richmond and in the
first battle of Fredericksburg. In 1863 he was
appointed by the North Carolina legislature solicitor for the 6th judicial district of the state, and
retired from the army in order to take up his duties. He occupied this position for eleven years,
resigning on his appointment to the supreme
court in 1873. He was a delegate from Lincoln
County to the state constitutional convention
which assembled at Charlotte in October 1865
and held an adjourned session in May 1866. Its
proceedings were important, involving radical
changes in the constitution, and Bynum took an
active part in the discussions, serving on the
Committee on Amendments to the Constitution
not otherwise referred and the Committee on
Acts of the Convention, the Legislature and the
Courts since 1861 (see *Journal of the Convention
of the State of North Carolina,* 1865). In 1866
he was elected state senator for Lincoln, Gaston,
and Catawba Counties, but served only one
term. He was appointed by Gov. Caldrock an
associate justice of the supreme court of North
Carolina, on Nov. 20, 1873, and remained on the
bench till the expiration of his term on Jan. 6,
1879. Possessed of a strong individuality, clear
intellect, and keen analytical powers, he was an
excellent judge. His legal knowledge was exact
and extensive, and his impartiality unassailable.
Though strongly urged to accept nomination for
another term, he declined, and resumed law practise in Charlotte, to which city he had removed.
As he was financially independent, he thereafter
did not concern himself much with either professional work or public affairs. He declined the
Republican nomination for chief justice, and on
several occasions refused to consider nomination
for governor of the state. He died at Charlotte.

[An excellent contemporary review of Bynum's career appeared in Jerome Dowd, *Sketches of Prominent Living North Carolinians* (1888). See also S. A. Ashe, *Hist. of N. C.*, II (1925), 1151; the *Green Bag*, Dec. 1892; *Charlotte Daily Observer*, Dec. 31, 1909.]

H.W.H.K.

BYRD, WILLIAM (1652–Dec. 4, 1704), planter, merchant, Indian trader, was the oldest son of John Byrd, a London goldsmith of moderate means, and Grace, daughter of Capt. Thomas Stegg. He came to Virginia when young, where he at once became a person of influence as the heir of his uncle, Thomas Stegg. Under Stegg's will, which was proved May 15, 1671, he acquired lands on both sides of the James at the present site of Richmond. In 1673 he married Mary, daughter of Warham Horsmanden, a Royalist refugee. Ambitious, possessing great business ability, rich, well connected both by blood and by marriage, his advancement was rapid. In 1675, when twenty-three years old, he was called Capt. Byrd. In 1676 he courted ruin by accompanying Bacon the Rebel on his southern Indian expedition but later made his peace with Gov. Berkeley. He was a member of the House of Burgesses from 1677 to 1682, and on Jan. 11, 1683, entered the Council of State, "the House of Lords of Virginia." Five years later he assumed the post of auditor-general of Virginia. In 1691 he moved his residence to Westover, which was nearer Jamestown and better suited for the home of a wealthy planter than the frontier estate at the Falls. In 1703 he became president of the Council. He died Dec. 4, 1704.

Byrd was one of the most prominent members of that small group of seventeenth-century Virginians who grew wealthy by planting tobacco and trading. Their success depended largely upon their ability to secure slave labor, and Byrd imported large numbers of negroes, some for his own use, some for sale to his neighbors. "If you sent the *Pinke* to Barbadoes on our account, I would have by her 506 negroes," he wrote to Perry and Lane, in 1684 (*Virginia Magazine of History and Biography*, July 1916, p. 232). For his tobacco, hundreds of hogsheads of which he shipped to England, he received all manner of manufactured articles—cloth, hats, iron work, brandy, wire, guns, hoes, powder, chairs, tables, shoes, brushes, horse collars, files, and above all else indentured servants. "If you could send me six, eight, or ten servants (men or lusty boys) . . . they would much assist in purchasing some of our best crops," he wrote his factor (*Virginia Historical Register*, Apr. 1848, p. 63). From Barbados he imported slaves, rum, sugar, molasses and ginger; and sent in return corn, flour, and pipe staves.

He was also deeply engaged in the fur trade. His estate at the Falls was at the head of the 400-mile trail southwest to the Catawba, and along it he sent his rough wood rangers with pack-horses carrying cloth, guns, powder, kettles, knives, and beads, in exchange for deer skins, and beaver and raccoon furs. It was a dangerous business, for in 1684 five traders were killed by the Indians, and in 1686 two more lost their lives. So great was Byrd's knowledge of Indian affairs, that he was often selected to represent the colony in treating with the natives. In 1685 he went to Albany, accompanied by several Virginia Indians, where he signed a treaty with the Iroquois. As the commander of the Henrico County militia, upon him fell the duty of protecting the upper James from Indian raids. Not satisfied with these multiform activities, Byrd was part owner of several merchantmen, and speculated extensively in land. Tobacco planter, merchant, fur trader, slave dealer, importer, speculator, public official, colonel of militia, he typified the spirit of the seventeenth-century Virginia aristocracy.

[There is an excellent biographical sketch in *The Writings of Col. William Byrd* (1901), by the editor, J. S. Bassett. The most important source of information is Byrd's "Letter Book," in the possession of the Va. Hist. Soc., Richmond, Va. Some of these letters are published in the *Va. Hist. Reg.*, Apr., July 1848, Apr., Oct. 1849, others in the *Va. Mag. of Hist. and Biog.*, June 1916 to Jan. 1920. Valuable material is found also in the *Jours. of the House of Burgesses of Va.* (1905–15), *Exec. Jours. of the Council of Va.*, vol. I (1925), *Legislative Jours. of the Council of Colonial Va.* (1918–19), and in the Correspondence of the Board of Trade, in the Public Record Office, London.]

T.J.W.

BYRD, WILLIAM (Mar. 28, 1674–Aug. 26, 1744), planter, author, colonial official, was the son of William Byrd [*q.v.*], and Mary, daughter of Warham Horsmanden. As a frontier plantation, peopled chiefly with negroes, was no place to educate a boy, he was early entrusted to relatives in England. In 1684 he was at school under Christopher Glassock. Six years later he visited Holland, and in 1692 was pursuing his studies at the Middle Temple. Later in the same year he returned to Virginia. Heir to a large estate, well educated, socially charming, enjoying the friendship of prominent men both in England and Virginia, Byrd at once assumed an important position in the colony. The very year of his return he was elected to the House of Burgesses. In 1697 he was back in England, defending Sir Edmund Andros against charges of hostility to the Anglican Church in Virginia. The next year we find him acting as agent for the colony. Upon the death of his father he returned to Virginia. In 1706 he married Lucy, daughter of Gen. Daniel Parke. The same year he was made receiver-general, but did not enter the Council of State until Sept. 12, 1709. The early years of his official career were full of strife. In 1710 Alexander Spotswood came to Virginia as lieutenant-governor. Energetic, forceful, stubborn, Spotswood soon found himself embroiled with the group of wealthy planters whose power centered in the Council. He tried to put an end to the monopolizing of vast tracts of land by enforcing the collection of quit-rents. And then, while Byrd, Ludwell, Carter, Blair, and the others were still angrily resisting this measure, Spotswood delivered a blow at their judicial power. For decades the Council had served as the supreme court in Virginia. Spotswood now announced his intention of setting up a court of oyer and terminer, and of appointing to it others than members of the Council. The Council replied by preferring charges against Spotswood, which Byrd, who was once more in England, pressed before the Board of Trade. It was a serious menace to liberty, he pointed out, for a governor to "take upon him by his own absolute will . . . to appoint judges, who without appeal are to determine concerning not only the lives and liberties, but also concerning the whole estates" of the colonists. Spotswood maintained that his action was necessary if the king's prerogative was to be preserved. The power of the governor had been "reduced to a desperate gasp," he wrote, and unless the Council were curbed, "the haughtiness of a Carter, the hypocrisy of a Blair . . . the malice of a Byrd," would henceforth rule the colony. In 1718 Spotswood attempted unsuccessfully to have Byrd removed from the Council. Byrd returned to Virginia in 1720 with orders to both sides to reconcile their differences, and Spotswood's removal soon after left the Council with powers undiminished.

Byrd's later years were spent in peace, at his beautiful home, which he had erected at Westover, Va. "A library, a garden, a grove, and a purling stream are the innocent scenes that divert our leisure," he wrote. Despite the elegance of his life, he was more than once so oppressed with debt that he had to sell land and negroes to satisfy his creditors. In 1728 he served as one of the commissioners to run the dividing line between Virginia and North Carolina, and in 1736 he surveyed the bounds of the Northern Neck. An extensive landowner on the frontiers, he was deeply interested in western expansion. Decades before the French established themselves on the Ohio, Byrd pointed out the danger from that source. "They may build forts to command the passes," he wrote, "to secure their own traffic and settlements westward

. . . (and) to invade the British colonies from thence" (*Virginia Magazine of History and Biography,* January 1902, p. 226). Byrd was author of "The History of the Dividing Line," "A Journey to the Land of Eden," and the "Progress to the Mines," all of which were first published as *The Westover Manuscripts* in 1841. These works, as well as his private letters, show a grace, wit, and sprightliness unique among the colonists.

Byrd's portrait reveals a well-built man, elegantly attired, with prominent nose, firm mouth, broad forehead, and rather haughty demeanor. He was a Fellow of the Royal Society, and was a warm friend of Charles Boyle, Earl of Orrery. His first wife died in 1716, and later he married Maria, daughter of Thomas Taylor of Kensington. In 1743 he became president of the Council. He died Aug. 26, 1744, and was buried in the garden at Westover. As William Byrd I possessed to a superlative degree the business acumen of the wealthy seventeenth-century Virginians, so William Byrd II typified the grace, charm, the culture, and also the rather lax business methods of the Virginians of the eighteenth century.

[There is an excellent biography by the editor, J. S. Bassett, in *The Writings of Col. Wm. Byrd* (1901). The most important primary sources are: *Correspondence of the Board of Trade,* Public Record Office, London; Spotswood's "Official Letters," in *Colls. of the Va. Hist. Soc.,* n.s., vols. I, II; "Letters of Wm. Byrd II," *Va. Mag. of Hist. and Biog.,* Oct. 1901, Jan. 1902.]

T.J.W.

BYRNE, ANDREW (Dec. 5, 1802–June 10, 1862), Roman Catholic bishop, a pioneer in the establishment of Catholicism in the United States, was born of pious parents in Navan, County Meath, Ireland. He early determined to enter the priesthood, and began his preparation in the Diocesan Seminary of his native town. While a student there he volunteered to come to America with Bishop John England [*q.v.*] who had just been consecrated to the See of Charleston, S. C. He continued his studies under the tutelage of the bishop and was by him ordained, Nov. 11, 1827. The Charleston diocese of this time included North Carolina, South Carolina, and Georgia, and for nearly ten years he ably assisted his superior in the latter's notable administration, serving at various arduous posts, making frequent long and fatiguing journeys, and enduring all the privations of missionary life, until, his health somewhat impaired, he was made pastor of St. Mary's Church, Charleston. For several years he was the bishop's vicar-general, and accompanied him as theologian to the Second Provincial Council at Baltimore. In 1836 he removed to New York where he served as assistant at the Cathedral, and pastor of St. James, of the Church of the Nativity, and finally of St. Andrew's, the fruit of his own zeal and energy. In 1841 Bishop John Hughes [*q.v.*] sent him to Ireland to secure a community of Christian Brothers for New York, a mission which was unsuccessful because of the great demand at that time for the service of these Brothers. While here he became keenly interested in the agitation for the repeal of the union between Great Britain and Ireland, and upon his return publicly advocated it, and became a member of an organization formed in its interests.

His unselfish devotion, administrative ability, and missionary experience, led to his being appointed in 1844 first bishop of the diocese of Little Rock, comprising Arkansas and the Indian Territory, and he was consecrated on Mar. 10, by Bishop Hughes. Here he renewed his earlier strenuous journeyings and labors. He twice visited Ireland to procure priests, nuns, and educators, securing among others a colony of Sisters of Mercy from Dublin who established St. Mary's Academy at Little Rock, a parent institution. He was active also in promoting Catholic immigration to the Southwest. He attended the Sixth Provincial Council at Baltimore in 1846, and the First Provincial Council of New Orleans in 1856. His health gradually failed, and he died in the midst of his labors at the comparatively early age of sixty, leaving important projects unfinished.

[Richard H. Clarke, *Lives of the Deceased Bishops of the Cath. Ch. in the U. S.*, vol. II (1872) ; John G. Shea, *The Cath. Churches of N. Y. City* (1878), and *A Hist. of the Cath. Ch. within the Limits of the U. S.*, vol. IV (1892), which contains portrait ; *Cath. Encyc.*, vol. III (1913).]   H. E. S.

BYRNE, DONN. [See DONN-BYRNE, BRIAN OSWALD, 1889–1928.]

BYRNE, JOHN (Oct. 13, 1825–Oct. 1, 1902), physician, pioneer in electric surgery, was born in the small town of Kilkeel, County Down, Ireland. He was the son of Stephen Byrne, a successful merchant, and his wife Elizabeth Sloane. As a boy he received a classical education, partly under the tutorship of William Craig, a Moravian minister and classical and mathematical scholar. At seventeen he began the study of medicine at the Royal Institute at Belfast under the guidance of Dr. Daniel Murray, a prominent practitioner of that city. He continued his medical studies in Dublin, Glasgow, and finally Edinburgh, where he received his medical degree in 1846. His graduation being contemporaneous with one of the periods of famine and pestilence which scourged Ireland in the nineteenth century, he received an appointment as medical of-

ficer to a fever hospital in his native town and at once showed his mettle. His knowledge of hospital routine and the more advanced sanitary methods of the day, his energy, and his executive ability resulted in a remarkable lowering of the mortality in the institution under his care. In 1848 he left Ireland for the United States and settled in Brooklyn, N. Y., where he spent the remainder of his life. Five years later, feeling perhaps that an American degree would help him, he graduated from the New York Medical College. In 1857 he was prominent in bringing about the merger between the German General Dispensary and the Long Island College Hospital. Later he was appointed a member of the executive board and he was for many years clinical professor of uterine surgery. He was also surgeon-in-chief to St. Mary's Hospital from 1858 to the year of his death.

Byrne was always a student of physics and it was therefore natural that he should become interested in the application of this subject to surgery. His chief claim to distinction lies in his ingenious adaptation of the electric cautery-knife to the surgery of malignant disease of the uterus. His early researches were published in *Clinical Notes on the Electric Cautery in Uterine Surgery* (1872), in which he described in detail the instrument he had devised and the technique of its use. In 1889 he published in the *Transactions of the American Gynecological Society* a report covering twenty years' experience in the treatment of uterine cancer by the cautery-knife. This paper showed that his mortality rates were low and his final results good; in fact, better results were probably obtained by him than by any other method of treatment in the hands of other surgeons at that time.

Byrne's success was due to a sound general and medical education, an energetic disposition, an inquiring mind, and a capacity for hard work and attention to detail. His associate, Dr. Mac-Evett, describes him as of medium height, rather portly in build, with a florid complexion and prematurely gray hair and mustache; the stocky type so often associated with great physical energy and staying power. While his expression was serious he had a fund of kindliness and good nature, the saving grace of humor, and the gift of the raconteur. He exemplified the value of training and interest in the sciences underlying medicine at a time when the importance of such training was not fully appreciated in this country. His death occurred at Montreux, Switzerland.

[*N. Y. Jour. of Gynecology and Obstetrics*, Jan. 1892, p. 42 ; Jas. J. Walsh, *Hist. of Medicine in N. Y.* (1919) ; Wm. B. Atkinson, *Physicians and Surgeons of the U. S.* (1878) ; *Trans. Am. Gynecological Soc.*,

1903, vol. XXVIII; *Album of Fellows, Am. Gynecological Soc.* (1918); obituary in *Brooklyn Eagle*, Oct. 2, 1902.]
                                                    G.B.

BYRNES, THOMAS F. (1842–May 7, 1910), police executive, was born in Ireland and brought as an infant by his parents, James and Rose (Smith) Byrnes, to New York. He had the most meager education. When the Civil War came on he had learned the trade of gas-fitter and was at work in New York City. He enlisted with Ellsworth's Zouaves in 1861 and served two years with that unit. In 1863 he was taken on the New York police force as patrolman, became a roundsman five years later, and a captain in 1870. He gained widespread reputation in 1878 by running down the gang of Manhattan Savings Bank robbers. Two years later, as inspector in charge of the Detective Bureau, he reorganized that branch of the police service, established a Wall Street office, and practically ended the depredations of thieves in that part of the city. As Inspector Byrnes he quickly won national distinction. He increased the detective force from twenty-eight to forty men and soon caused it to be known as the most efficient body of its size and kind in the world. In four years it made 3,300 arrests. Byrnes brought about the conviction of many criminals,—in some cases when the evidence of guilt was far from complete. What became known as the application of "the third degree" in dealing with criminals has been ascribed to him. He acted on the theory that it is not remorse, but mental strain, that leads the hardened criminal to confess his misdeeds. The practise he adopted in procuring confessions involved far more than sheer brutality. Indeed in many cases no physical pain accompanied the process,—not that Byrnes had any scruples against employing bodily torture, but he frequently thought other methods more effective. He was himself a man of powerful imagination. He would reconstruct in his own mind the scene and incidents of a crime and so vividly reproduce them in conversation with the suspect that the average mentality could not withstand the shock. Jacob A. Riis, who as police reporter for the New York *Sun* knew Byrnes well, declared that he was "a great actor" and hence a great detective. All agreed that he was a man of unusual intellectual force. He was thought by his contemporaries to have the common failings imputed to the police of his day. Riis called him an unscrupulous autocrat, a "big policeman," a veritable giant in his time. In 1894 Byrnes testified before the Lexow Committee investigating the New York police that he had made $350,000 through Wall Street "tips" from Jay Gould and other important operators who were among his friends. No personal misdemeanor on his part was disclosed,—and that at a time when graft in high places was characteristic of the police department. Byrnes had stated repeatedly that he was not a member of any political organization. In 1892 he had been made superintendent and three years later became chief of police, retiring in the same month on the reorganization attending the disclosures of the Lexow Committee. Julian Hawthorne, who knew Byrnes intimately, described his personal appearance at the height of his career in these words: "He is a handsome man, large and powerful in every sense of the word. His head is well shaped, with a compact forehead, strong nose, and resolute mouth and chin, shaded with a heavy moustache. His figure is erect, his step light, his bearing alert and easy. His eyes are his most remarkable feature. They are set rather close together in his head, increasing the concentration of his gaze. They have in moments of earnestness an extraordinary gaze. His voice is melodious and agreeable, but he often seems to speak between his teeth, and when aroused his utterance acquires an impressive energy." He was the author of *Professional Criminals of America* (1886). At his death he was survived by his wife Ophelia and five daughters.

[*N. Y. Times, Tribune,* and *Sun,* of May 8, 1910; Jacob A. Riis, *The Making of an American* (1901).]
                                                    W.B.S.

CABELL, JAMES LAWRENCE (Aug. 26, 1813–Aug. 13, 1889), physician, educator, was born in Nelson County, Va., the sixth and youngest child of George and Susanna (Wyatt) Cabell. His father was a physician. The founder of the family was James's great-grandfather, William Cabell, who was born in Wiltshire and is said to have been a surgeon in the Royal Navy. He settled in Virginia about 1724, acquired extensive holdings in land, and practised medicine with success until his death in 1774. James Lawrence Cabell entered the University of Virginia in 1829 and graduated M.A. in 1833. He received the degree of M.D. the next year from the University of Maryland. He continued his studies in the Baltimore Almshouse and in one or more Philadelphia hospitals and went to Paris for further instruction and observation in 1836. While in France he was appointed professor of anatomy, surgery, and physiology in the University of Virginia. To call a man to an important academic post at the outset instead of toward the close of his career has never been customary in the United States, and since Cabell was in addition the nephew of Joseph Carrington

Cabell [*q.v.*] he entered on his duties in the autumn of 1837 amid much unfriendly gossip about "nepotism." But he was undeniably a gentleman and a scholar, and he soon proved to be also an able physician and a distinguished teacher. He gained the respect of the entire University and exercised as great an influence as anyone over the intellectual life of the community. In 1846–47 he was chairman of the faculty. In 1849 a separate chair of anatomy was established, but Cabell continued to teach surgery and physiology until a few months before his death. He kept abreast of his subjects, contributed occasionally to medical periodicals, and was one of the early leaders of the public health movement. During the Civil War he was chief surgeon of the Confederate hospitals in Charlottesville. He was president of the Medical Society of Virginia in 1876 and of the National Board of Health, 1879–84; he also served for one year as president of the American Public Health Association. A man of broad culture, he was almost as well versed in philosophy and pure science as in medicine. At times he seems to have felt that he ought not to confine himself to the teaching of medicine, and in 1846 he was a candidate to succeed George Tucker [*q.v.*] as professor of moral philosophy. He wrote little: his one book, *The Testimony of Modern Science to the Unity of Mankind* (N. Y., 1858; 2nd ed., 1859) attempts to show, from such evidence as was at hand, that the different races of mankind descend from a common ancestor. The essay is especially interesting as an indication of the state of scientific thought in the South just before the appearance of Darwin's *Origin of Species*. The fact that the author was deeply concerned for the truth of the Biblical account of Creation and that he was addressing readers who were fain to regard the negro as a species quite separate from their own makes the book now seem a little quaint but does not disguise its solid merits. Cabell was married on Feb. 5, 1839, to Margaret Gibbons, who died in 1874. They had no children. Cabell died at the home of his friend, Maj. Edward B. Smith, in Albemarle County.

[Alex. Brown, *The Cabells and Their Kin* (1895); P. A. Bruce, *Hist. of the Univ. of Va. 1819–1919* (1920–22); R. M. Slaughter, article in Kelly and Burrage, *Am. Medic. Biogs.* (1920).]   G. H. G.

CABELL, JOSEPH CARRINGTON (Dec. 28, 1778–Feb. 5, 1856), principal coadjutor of Thomas Jefferson in founding the University of Virginia, was born in Amherst (now Nelson) County, in Virginia, to which colony his grandfather, Dr. William Cabell, had emigrated from England in the early eighteenth century. He was the son of Col. Nicholas and Hannah (Carrington) Cabell, both of them of stock socially and politically distinguished in the colony, and was the brother of William H. Cabell [*q.v.*]. After graduating from William and Mary College (1798) and studying law, he resided abroad for more than three years, during which he attended lectures under famous scholars and sojourned at a half-dozen leading universities. He won the friendship of Robert Fulton and Washington Allston, traveled with Washington Irving, and enjoyed the acquaintance of Cuvier, Pestalozzi, Volney, Kosciusko, and William Godwin. On Jan. 1, 1807, he married Mary Walker Carter, of Lancaster, Va., granddaughter of Sir Peyton Skipwith, but had no issue. The next year he returned to Amherst County, entered politics, and was elected to the House of Delegates, where he served two terms and was instrumental in establishing the important Literary Fund. From 1810 to 1829 he was a member of the Virginia Senate, in which body he espoused ardently the cause of state betterment, advocating especially local government, popular education, and internal improvements; from 1831 to 1835 he again served in the House of Delegates, reëntering that branch that he might further the interests of the James River and Kanawha Canal. His labors in behalf of a great state university, helping first to secure legislative sanction therefor and subsequently to obtain financial appropriations toward its construction, have led the institution's historians to designate him as Jefferson's right hand man; nor did he promote merely the material needs of the University, but for thirty-seven years, as visitor and as rector, he helped to shape its destiny. At the same time he used his powers to extend to both sexes general opportunities for modern primary and secondary instruction; won the title of "the De Witt Clinton of Virginia" for his services as pioneer and president of the James River & Kanawha Canal Company; and, himself a progressive and large-scale plantation owner, supported before the Assembly all bills to improve agricultural conditions in the state. Although he held no office of national importance, he won more than sectional recognition for his conspicuous talents, his persuasive oratory, his sense of integrity and justice, his dignity, amenity, conscientiousness, and honor. His personal and political creed is epitomized by his own comment: "I think the greatest service a man can render is to speak the truth and to show that is his only object." He was peculiarly and emphatically "the Virginia statesman," for without thought of self he dedicated deliberately his entire life to his commonwealth, declining the diplomatic posts which Jefferson tendered him, refusing to stand for the governorship or the federal congress though repeatedly solicited, and rejecting cabinet seats probably under Madison and certainly under Monroe.

[The best account of Cabell is that in P. A. Bruce, *Hist. of the Univ. of Va.* (1920), I, 145–57, with innumerable references to him elsewhere in that work. N. F. Cabell, *Early Hist. of the Univ. of Va. as Contained in the Letters of Thos. Jefferson and Jos. C. Cabell* (1856) contains a ten-page sketch in addition to the voluminous correspondence that passed between Cabell and Jefferson. J. S. Patton, *Jefferson, Cabell, and the Univ. of Va.* (1906) and D. M. R. Culbreth, *The Univ. of Va.* (1908) cover more briefly the same ground. For Cabell's ancestry see Alexander Brown, *The Cabells and Their Kin* (1895). There is frequent mention of Cabell in *De Bow's Rev.*, the *Southern Lit. Messenger*, the correspondence of William Wirt, and the various biographies of Jefferson. His letters and manuscripts are in the possession of the Univ. of Va. Lib.]

A. C. G., Jr.

CABELL, NATHANIEL FRANCIS (July 23, 1807–Sept. 1, 1891), author, was most fortunate in his ancestry. His father, Nicholas Cabell, Jr., was a grandson of Dr. William Cabell of England, the emigrant ancestor of a distinguished family of Virginia, and his mother, Margaret Read (Venable) Cabell came from some of the most prominent families of southside Virginia. His father died when Nathaniel was an infant, and his mother reared him amid Presbyterian surroundings. He attended a Presbyterian college, Hampden Sidney, where he graduated in 1825. His great interest in religion in after life was probably due to the atmosphere in which he was reared. In 1827 he received his degree of bachelor of laws from Harvard College. During the next four years, he was located in Prince Edward County, but in 1832 returned to "Warminster," Nelson County, the place of his birth. A few years later he removed to the "Liberty Hall" estate, which he had inherited. The wide range of his interests may be seen in his voluminous writings, especially in the fields of religion, genealogy, and the history of agriculture. Largely through the influence of Richard K. Cralle of Lynchburg, friend and biographer of John C. Calhoun, he became a follower of Emanuel Swedenborg, being baptized into the New Church in 1842. During this period (1840–42) he had written in the *New Jerusalem Magazine* a number of articles, "Excerpts, or Readings with My Pencil," etc. He also contributed to the *New Churchman*. Among his numerous religious writings may be mentioned an article on the New Christian Church in Israel D. Rupp's *An Original History of the Religious Denominations at Present Existing in the United States* (1844); *Reply to Rev. Dr*

Pond's "Swedenborgianism Reviewed" (1848); *A Letter on the Trinal Order for the Ministry of the New Church* (1848, 1857); *The Progress of Literature during the Preceding Century When Viewed from a Religious Standpoint* (only the introductory chapter published, 1868); and papers on the theology of Paul, published under the title "Horæ Paulinæ" in the *New Jerusalem Messenger*, 1873–74. In the meanwhile he was writing in other fields. He edited the *Early History of the University of Virginia as Contained in the Letters of Thomas Jefferson and Joseph C. Cabell* (1856); rearranged and edited in part "The Lee Papers" portions of which reappeared in seventeen numbers of the *Southern Literary Messenger*, 1858–60; and contributed to the *Memoirs of Professor George Bush* (1860). He contributed a number of essays on agriculture and on the history of agriculture in Virginia to the *Farmers' Register* and other magazines. It was his purpose to write a history of agriculture in Virginia. For that purpose he made a valuable collection of manuscripts on the subject. This material annotated by Cabell may now be found in the Virginia State Library. From 1832 until his death he collected much material relating to genealogy and prepared manuscript family memoirs, Cabelliana, Carringtoniana, etc. He was married twice: on Sept. 14, 1831 to Anne Blaws Cocke, and, after her death in 1862, to Mary M. Keller of Baltimore. The last few years of his life were spent in Bedford City at the home of his daughter, Mrs. R. Kenna Campbell. He was buried in the Cabell cemetery at "Liberty Hall."

[Alexander Brown, Cabell's friend and neighbor has the best account, in *The Cabells and their Kin* (1895), pp. 601–05. See also Earl G. Swem, "A List of MSS. Relating to the Hist. of Ag. in Va., Collected by N. F. Cabell and Now in the Va. State Lib." (*Va. State Lib. Bull.*, Jan. 1913), and "An Analysis of Ruffin's Farmer's Reg." (*Ibid.*, July–Oct. 1918).]

R. L. M—n.

CABELL, SAMUEL JORDAN (Dec. 15, 1756–Aug. 4, 1818), Revolutionary soldier, congressman, born in Amherst County, Va., was the son of Col. William Cabell [*q.v.*] and Margaret Jordan, his wife. The former was a prominent Virginian, a member of the Revolutionary Committee of Safety in the colony. At the outbreak of the Revolutionary War, S. J. Cabell left the College of William and Mary to assume command as captain of a company of expert riflemen of Amherst County. Upon his arrival at Williamsburg in March 1776, his company was assigned as light infantry to the 6th Virginia Regiment, in Gen. Andrew Lewis's brigade, and during the same year it was sent to join Gen. Washington in New Jersey. Washington placed it in Gen. Morgan's body of expert riflemen, which he sent to aid Gen. Gates at Saratoga. For his skill and bravery in this campaign, Cabell (not yet twenty-one years old) was commissioned major. He then rejoined Washington's army, was at Valley Forge, and in Washington's campaigns of 1778 and 1779. In the latter year he was made lieutenant-colonel and was dispatched to Gen. Lincoln at Charleston. Here he was made prisoner in May 1780 and remained in prison fourteen months, until paroled. He was married in 1781 to Sally Syme, daughter of Col. John Syme of Hanover County, a half-brother of Patrick Henry. He was, in 1784, county lieutenant of Amherst County, and represented that county in the Virginia legislature of 1785–86, and in several subsequent sessions. He and his father were elected, almost unanimously, to the Convention of 1788. They both followed Patrick Henry in opposing the adoption of the Constitution. In 1795 S. J. Cabell was elected to the federal House of Representatives. He retained his seat until he retired from active politics in 1803. He was an ardent Republican, "an impetuous follower of Jefferson." So active was he in opposition to Federalist policies that the grand jury of the United States district court, in session at Richmond, acting under the spell of Judge Iredell's fiery charge to the jury, brought in the following presentment: "We . . . present as a real evil, the circular letters of several members of the late Congress and particularly those with the signature of Samuel J. Cabell, endeavoring, at a time of real public danger, to disseminate unfounded calumnies against the happy government of the United States. . . ." The Virginia legislature, prompted doubtless by Jefferson, responded with a vigorous protest, a prelude to Madison's famous Resolutions of 1798. (For the protest see *Journal of the House of Delegates,* 1797–98, pp. 64–65.) When Nelson County was created out of Amherst, Cabell, who had served as justice in the latter, became one of the first justices in the former. The last thirty-three years of his life were spent at his home, "Soldier's Joy," in Nelson County. Cabell was one of the original members of the Virginia Society of the Cincinnati. He was impulsive, kind-hearted, hospitable, and fluent in speech.

[Alexander Brown, *The Cabells and Their Kin* (1895) is the best source. Brown had access to numerous Cabell manuscripts, including Col. William Cabell's Diary. See also F. B. Heitman, *Hist. Reg.* (1893) and widely scattered items in the *Va. Mag. of Hist. and Biog.*]   R. L. M—n.

CABELL, WILLIAM (Mar. 13, 1729/30–Mar. 23, 1798), Revolutionary patriot, known as Col.

William, Senior, of Union Hill, Amherst County, was the son of William and Elizabeth (Burks) Cabell. The elder William Cabell, of Bugley near Warminster, in Wiltshire, England, was of ancient lineage and trained in surgery. Migrating to Virginia, he married in 1726 and by 1741 had carried settlements fifty miles westward. As pioneer, Indian fighter, surveyor, deputy sheriff, justice of the peace, vestryman, coroner, trader, planter, and surgeon with a private hospital on the fringe of the forest, from which he dispensed physic, and wooden legs made by his artisans, until he died in 1774, he hastened Virginia's westward growth. This tall, lithe, black-eyed man, audacious in action, liberal in thought, scientific in method, having by 1753 accumulated 26,000 picked acres, tossed his surveyor's mantle to his eldest son, who like his father speedily became a constructive leader of men.

Tradition but no evidence makes the younger William Cabell a student in William and Mary. A vestryman at the age of twenty-one, second sheriff two years later, and settled on 2,700 acres granted him by the Crown in 1753, by 1761 he was first presiding magistrate, first lieutenant, first surveyor and first coroner for Amherst County, vestryman, church warden, and burgess. He held stock in the Hardware River Iron Company and in the James River Canal Company. No evidence shows that as burgess he supported Patrick Henry's Resolutions of May 1765. When the Stamp Act was repealed he hoped for reconciliation. But in May 1769, when rebel burgesses drew up Articles of Association in Raleigh Tavern, Williamsburg, Cabell signed them. A delegate to all Virginia's revolutionary conventions, he stoutly supported the patriot measures, was elected member of the Committee of Safety, when Gov. Dunmore fled the Colony, and was reëlected upon its revision in January 1776. Meanwhile he was chairman of the Amherst County Committee. Owing no debt to English merchants, he risked all for the Revolution. A member of the famous committee which prepared a Declaration of Rights and a form of government for Virginia, he served also on the Committee of Propositions and Grievances. He was first state senator for his district (Buckingham, Albemarle, and Amherst Counties), retiring in 1781 because of Virginia's rule of rotation. Elected delegate immediately thereafter, he served in the House (1781–83, 1787–88) and was a member of the celebrated Virginian Convention in 1788 where he voted against ratification of the Federal Constitution. Probably his last political service was to cast an electoral vote for Washington for first president under the Constitution.

He now retired after some thirty years in public life, but remained a trustee of Hampden Sidney College until his death. He succumbed in 1798, leaving 30,000 acres, many slaves and other property, all free from debt. His wife, Margaret Jordan Cabell (married, 1756), four sons, and three daughters survived him. Six feet high, corpulent, with capacious forehead, he was of superior brain, strikingly liberal in mind and pocket, of ceaseless energy and infinite capacity for work. Of equal caliber perhaps with his nationally significant contemporaries in a great American era, Fate designed him to be primarily a builder of Virginia.

[Alexander Brown, *The Cabells and Their Kin* (1895); *Jours. of the House of Burgesses of Va.* (1905–15); *Jour. of the Senate, 1776–81*; *Jour. of the House of Delegates, 1781–88*; the Cabell papers preserved in the Va. State Lib. in Richmond.]   K. B.

CABELL, WILLIAM H. (Dec. 16, 1772–Jan. 12, 1853), governor of Virginia, was a grandson of Dr. William Cabell, who came to Virginia in the early eighteenth century. The son of Col. Nicholas and Hannah (Carrington) Cabell and brother of Joseph Carrington Cabell [*q.v.*], he was born at "Boston Hill" near Cartersville, Cumberland County, Va. He attended Hampden Sidney College, 1785–89, and then entered the College of William and Mary, from which he received his law degree in 1793. In the fall of that year he moved to Richmond, and was licensed to practise law in the following year. On Apr. 9, 1795, he married his cousin Elizabeth, daughter of Col. William Cabell [*q.v.*] of "Union Hill." He lived for several years in her home, and since there were two other William Cabells there he added the initial "H" to his name. His political career began in 1796, when he was elected to the legislature from Amherst County. He was reëlected four times, and was also presidential elector in 1800 and in 1804. He voted for Madison's famous Virginia Resolutions of 1798. In December 1805 the legislature elected him governor of the state. After reëlecting him twice—the maximum number of times under the constitution of Virginia—the legislature appointed him judge of the general court, a position which he held until appointed by Gov. Monroe member of the court of appeals in April 1811. He was also placed on the governor's council that year. Under the new constitution of 1830, he was reappointed to the court of appeals, and was made president of that body in 1842, in which position he continued until he retired in 1851. He was an advocate of public schools and was deeply interested in higher education. From

1809 to 1830 he was one of the trustees of Hampden Sidney College. He was a member of the board of commissioners appointed by the Virginia Assembly in 1818 to select a site for the University of Virginia and to give a plan for its organization. On Nov. 5, 1801, Elizabeth Cabell, his wife, died, and four years later (Mar. 11, 1805) he maried Agnes S. B. Gamble, daughter of Col. Robert Gamble of Richmond. He had a beautiful summer home overlooking the James River at Montevideo, in Buckingham County, but in 1822 he sold this estate and thenceforward made Richmond his home. He was buried in Shockoe Cemetery in that city. He was vigorous in mind and in body, respected and trusted as a public officer, and loved for his genial spirit.

[Alexander Brown, *The Cabells and their Kin* (1895) contains a sketch of Cabell, including a brief autobiographical account. There is a good sketch in R. A. Brock, a reliable historian, *Virginia and Virginians* (1888), pp. 98–103. Cabell's official papers are in the Va. State Lib. in Richmond. For his messages as governor see *Jour. of House of Delegates*, 1805–08. Note also court records, 1808–51.]   R. L. M—n.

CABELL, WILLIAM LEWIS (Jan. 1, 1827–Feb. 22, 1911), Confederate soldier, lawyer, a descendant of Dr. William Cabell who came to Virginia in the early part of the eighteenth century (see sketch of William Cabell, 1730–98), was born in Danville, Va., the son of Benjamin W. S. and his wife Sarah Epes (Doswell) Cabell. His father was a veteran of the War of 1812, member of the Virginia Assembly, member of the constitutional convention of 1829–30, and a newspaper editor. William graduated from West Point Military Academy in 1850, entered the United States army, and by 1858 had attained the rank of captain. In July 1856 he was married to Harriet A. Rector. He served in Gen. Harney's Utah campaign, and continued in the West until he resigned his commission in 1861. He was commissioned as major in the Confederate army. President Davis sent him to Richmond to organize the commissary and ordnance departments. He was next transferred to Manassas as chief quartermaster on Gen. Beauregard's staff and later served on the staff of J. E. Johnston. He aided Generals Johnston and Beauregard to devise the first Confederate battle flag (W. L. Cabell in *Southern Historical Society Papers*, XXXI, 68–70). In January 1862 he reported to Gen. Albert Sidney Johnston, as chief quartermaster (*List of Staff Officers of the Confederate States Army*, Government Printing Office, Washington, 1891, p. 26). He was placed in the Trans-Mississippi department under Gen. Van Dorn. His excellent record gained for him promotion to the rank of brigadier-general in command of all the troops on White River. After the battle of Elk Horn (March 1862) he successfully transferred the entire Trans-Mississippi army to the east bank within a week. In the battles which followed he distinguished himself for his bravery in attack. He was wounded while leading his men at Corinth and at Hatchers Ridge in October 1862. As a result he was rendered incapable of command in the field. While still disabled, however, he was ordered to inspect the staff department of the Trans-Mississippi army. When he again reported for active duty in February 1863 he was placed in command of all the forces in northwest Arkansas. Here he organized one of the largest and most efficient cavalry brigades west of the Mississippi. This brigade took part in many engagements during 1863 and 1864. While on a raid in Missouri under Gen. Price, Cabell was captured on Oct. 24, 1864. Upon his release from prison on Aug. 28, 1865, he went to Fort Smith, Ark., studied law, and was admitted to the bar. In December 1872 he moved to Dallas, Tex., and in 1874, 1875, 1876, and 1882 was elected mayor of that city. He was a delegate to to the Democratic national conventions of 1876, 1884, and 1892. During Cleveland's first administration he served as United States marshal. He was vice-president and general manager of the Texas Trunk Railway (later the Texas & New Orleans Railway). In 1890 the United Confederate Veterans elected him commander of the Trans-Mississippi department, a position which he held until elected honorary commander-in-chief of the Confederate Veterans.

[Alexander Brown, *The Cabells and Their Kin* (1895); *Who's Who in America*, 1903–05; *Official Records (Army)*, 1, 2 ser.; obituaries in the *Confederate Veteran*, Apr. 1911, and *Dallas Morning News*, Feb. 23, 1911.]
R. L. M—n.

CABET, ÉTIENNE (Jan. 1, 1788–Nov. 8, 1856), communist, reformer, was the fourth and youngest son of a cooper of Dijon, France. In childhood he was strongly impressed by echoes of the great revolution. Unable because of his frail body and his nearsightedness to follow the paternal occupation, he was given a thorough education. At fifteen, he became a lycée instructor under Jacotot. He began the study of medicine in the university, but soon turned to law, where he was influenced by the liberal Proudhon of the Dijon faculty. In 1810 he was licensed and in 1812 took the doctor's degree in law (Jules Prudhommeaux, *Icarie et son Fondateur*, pp. 5–7). For pleading the cause of patriots he was denied access to the courts of his native village for a year. Obtaining a secretaryship in Paris, he identified himself with the Carbonari and other secret societies. He took part in the July Revolution. In 1831, Louis Philippe, in conciliating the proletarian and intellectualist factions, appointed him procureur-général in Corsica. Due to his anti-administration activities, he was soon recalled. Elected to the Chamber of Deputies in July, he joined the extreme radicals. In 1833, he established *Le Populaire* which he used as an organ of the workingmen's cause. Two articles of January 1834 gave a pretext for convicting him as a traitor. In preference to two years in prison, he spent five years in exile in London. There he married Delphine Lesage, who had joined him after the birth of their daughter, Celine. His wife, like himself, was of plebeian origin and a native of Dijon (*Ibid.*, p. 98, n. 3).

Encouraged by his contact with Robert Owen, Cabet wrote the interesting Utopian romance, *Voyage et Aventures de Lord William Carisdall en Icarie*, which he published on his return to France in 1839 (republished in 1840 as *Voyage en Icarie*). Its circulation was tremendous, and adherents of the Icarian doctrine were reported to be 400,000 by 1847. During the years 1843 to 1847, Cabet's annual *Almanach Icarien, astronomique, scientifique, pratique, industriel, statistique,* his *Histoire populaire de la révolution française de 1789 à 1830* (1839–40), and his *Le vrai christianisme suivant Jésus-Christ* (1846) all found a large audience. An article describing the projected community in America appeared in May 1847. Finding several hundred ready for the venture, Cabet, after consulting Owen, contracted for a million acres on the Red River in Texas. The advance guard of sixty-nine persons discovered after a long journey through the wilderness that the land was in half-section tracts widely scattered. Cabet had trusted too utterly the land company's representative. Discouraged, the men retreated to New Orleans, where they met Cabet with the main body of five hundred. Hearing of the abandonment of the community at Nauvoo, Ill., by the Mormons, the Icarians in 1849 leased the land and houses there, and for six years enjoyed a rapid increase in fortune and numbers. In 1852, Cabet went to Paris to vindicate himself of the charges of fraud brought by those who had turned back at New Orleans. In 1854, he became an American citizen. Icaria had its own printing-press and library and operated a mill and a distillery. Freedom of religion was allowed. Cabet was annually reëlected president, but in 1856, dissensions arose involving the Paris office in charge of Madame Cabet. When the civil authorities intervened and confirmed three newly-elected directors of the opposing party, Cabet with 180 followers withdrew to St. Louis. Within the week he died from a stroke of apoplexy and was buried at St. Louis. Chief of the colonies of Icaria were those of Cheltenham, near St. Louis; Corning, Iowa (the successor of Nauvoo), dissolved in 1884; and Cloverdale, Cal., which survived until 1895.

[The best short sketches of Cabet are found in Morris Hillquit, *Hist. of Socialism in the U. S.* (1903), Albert Shaw, *Icaria* (1884), and Adolph Hepner, *Die Ikarier in Nordamerika* (1886). More extensive biographies are those of H. Carle and J. P. Beluze, *Biographie de Étienne Cabet* (1861–62); Felix Bonnaud, *Étienne Cabet et son œuvre* (1900); and Jules Prudhommeaux, *Icarie et son fondateur, Étienne Cabet* (1907), the last being the most complete and up-to-date.]

E. C.

CABLE, GEORGE WASHINGTON (Oct. 12, 1844–Jan. 31, 1925), author, was an unusual blending of diverse elements. His father, George W., was from an old slaveholding family of Virginia, his mother, Rebecca Boardman, was a native of New England, a Puritan of the straitest sect. They met in Indiana and were married there in 1834. Three years later, attracted by a business opening, they removed to New Orleans where was born the future novelist. The hard times of 1837 all but destroyed the family fortunes, but the father struggled on with his business until 1859, when, after a second business reverse, he died, leaving the boy of fourteen head of the family which included several children. For several years the boy was his mother's chief support, finding employment as he could. He was small for his years and physically frail. When in 1863 the family was sent outside the Union lines for refusing to take the "Yankee" oath of allegiance, his sisters had no difficulty in obtaining permission for their "little brother" to accompany them. Immediately, however, he enlisted in the 4th Mississippi Cavalry and with them he served to the end of the war. Despite the headlong activities of a trooper with the enemy never far away, he found time to pursue with intensity self-imposed studies in mathematics, Latin, and the Bible. His troop was in several engagements in one of which he was severely wounded. The war over, he found employment immediately on the state survey of the levees along the Atchafalaya River, but contracting malarial fever, he was for two years almost totally incapacitated for labor.

It was during this period that he began to write, his first product being a weekly miscellany in the New Orleans *Picayune* under the heading "Drop Shot." The success of the column led to its being made a daily feature of the paper, and in 1869 its author was added to the staff as a reporter. His journalistic career, however, was short. Refusing to report theatrical performances, he was summarily dropped. Employment more congenial came quickly in the firm of A. C. Black & Company, cotton factors, who employed him as an accountant and correspondence clerk. Seemingly he was settled now for life. On Dec. 7, 1869, he was married to Louise S. Bartlett of New Orleans, he established a home in the city, and in due time found himself the head of a family of seven children. But the ambition for culture and scholarship which had driven him to study in his army days still kept him restless. He had been denied school and college: he would educate himself. He arose at four in the morning and pored over his books: he wasted not a moment. He made himself master of French and then began to delve among the old records in the city archives, fascinated by the strange true romance that he found in them. At first he had no thought of literary production, but at length he began to put the old records into narratives of his own. "It seemed a pity," he explained in later years, "to let them go to waste." Publication of these narratives and then literary fame came to him seemingly by accident. Edward King, who had been sent by *Scribner's Monthly* in 1872 on a tour of the Southern States for the series of papers later issued with the title *The Great South* (1875), came across the busy young delver, examined his papers, and induced him to send some of them to J. G. Holland, editor of the monthly. The result was a glowing letter from R. W. Gilder, a member of the staff, and the publication in the magazine in October 1873 of the short story "'Sieur George." During the following three years five others were published, and then in 1879 came the volume *Old Creole Days,* containing the six stories and also "Posson Jone" which had appeared in *Appleton's.* The recognition of the work as an American classic in its field was instant and unanimous. Its success, too, came at the moment when the death of Cable's employer and the dissolution of the firm threw him out of employment. He turned at once to authorship as a profession. A year later, after it had run serially in *Scribner's,* he published *The Grandissimes* (1884), an ambitious historical romance, following it with "Madame Delphine," which has been incorporated in later editions of *Old Creole Days; The Creoles of Louisiana* (1884); *Dr. Sevier* (1885); *Bonaventure* (1888); and *Strange True Stories of Louisiana* (1889).

His life now became one of intense activity in many fields. He was a zealous advocate with pen and voice of changed election laws, of reform in prison administration, of abolition of the contract labor system, and of justice for the negro. His outspoken views, especially in the series of papers later collected under the title *The Silent South* (1885), aroused the resentment of his native region against him. It was not this alone, however, that caused him to remove his residence to the North: he would be nearer his work and his literary market. After 1885 Northampton, Mass., became his residence and the radiating center of a remarkable series of reading tours into all parts of the nation. Reading from his own works became for a time his profession. He made tours with Mark Twain; for some years his yearly journeyings averaged more than ten thousand miles. At Northampton he started the Home-Culture Clubs, now the Northampton People's Institute, and to the project he gave for years generously of his time and his enthusiasm (see an account of the Clubs by Cable in the *World's Work,* October 1906). No sketch of his life can omit to mention his work as a philanthropist, a reformer, a religious leader, a Bible-class teacher. The titles of some of his later books show the range of his interests: *The Negro Question* (1888); *The Southern Struggle for Pure Government* (1890); *The Busy Man's Bible and How to Teach It* (1893); *John March, Southerner* (1894); and *The Amateur Garden* (1914).

In later years he applied himself again to the writing of romance, producing some eight volumes: *Strong Hearts* (1899); *The Cavalier* (1901); *Bylow Hill* (1902); *Kincaid's Battery* (1908); *Posson Jone and Père Raphael* (1909); *Gideon's Band* (1914); *The Flower of the Chapdelaines* (1918); and *Lovers of Louisiana* (1918); but, save in rare flashes, the old charm and power are not in them. His hand had lost its cunning, the intensity of his first enthusiasms had evaporated. More and more it is evident that his ultimate literary fame will depend upon a few of his earlier romantic creations. There is a vivacity, a Gallic brilliance, an exotic atmosphere about these creations that make them stand alone among American works of fiction. Coming as they did at the moment that new literary forces were gathering for the new literary period following the Civil War, they were widely influential. With Bret Harte he was one of the causes of the so-called "local color episode" in American fiction. Not without criticism did he gain his place, however. His representation of the Creole was sharply challenged by the South; it was charged that he drew his characters from the lower grade of the Creole population and left the inference that there was no higher grade. It was to correct Cable's picture and to represent the Creole in what she, herself educated in a Creole school, believed to be the true light, that

Grace King in later days wrote her tales of New Orleans life.

[*Geo. W. Cable, his Life and Letters* (1928), by his daughter, Lucy L. Cable Bikle; "The Literary Career of Cable," by E. F. Harkins, in *Famous Authors* (1906); "Geo. W. Cable in Northampton, Mass.," by F. W. Halsey in *Am. Authors and their Homes* (1901).]

F. L. P—e.

CABOT, ARTHUR TRACY (Jan. 25, 1852–Nov. 4, 1912), surgeon, was the third son of Samuel Cabot, surgeon to the Massachusetts General Hospital, by his wife, Hannah Jackson. The traits of the Cabot family, ardently conscientious, scrupulous almost to a fault in their dealings with men, and possessed of an extraordinary sense of personal responsibility to their immediate community, were sublimated in the personality of Arthur Tracy. He entered Harvard College in 1869 and received his A.B. degree from that institution in 1872, having done good work without special distinction. He received his M.D. from the Harvard Medical School in 1876 and entered immediately upon a surgical internship at the Massachusetts General Hospital, at which institution he had previously served as house pupil. In August 1877 he went abroad to study surgical pathology and arrived in London in time to hear Lister's inaugural address (October 1877) at King's College ("On the Nature of Fermentation"), this being Lister's first public appearance in London after leaving Scotland. Soon after this lecture, Cabot became an ardent protagonist of the antiseptic system, and on returning to Boston a few months later he did much to spread the gospel of "Listerism" among his surgical contemporaries. For several years after his return, he occupied himself in building up a general practise in medicine and surgery, in order to approach surgery in its broadest aspects. At the end of ten years he found it necessary to confine himself entirely to surgery. On Aug. 16, 1882, he was married to Susan Shattuck, daughter of George O. Shattuck. From 1886 until 1902 he was visiting surgeon at the Massachusetts General Hospital. H. J. Bigelow [*q.v.*], recognizing the ability of the young surgeon, gradually turned over to him his extensive clinic, and Cabot became in a very short time the leading genito-urinary surgeon of New England. He always prided himself, however, on having been a general surgeon.

Cabot's career of public service began with his instructorship in oral pathology and surgery (1878–80) at the Harvard Medical School; subsequently he was appointed clinical instructor in genito-urinary surgery (1885–96). In 1896 he was elected a Fellow of the University, a position of responsibility demanding much time. Throughout his life he was active in campaigns against tuberculosis and in promoting the cause of public health. His last published work, which appeared in the *Atlantic Monthly* for November 1912, was a plea for the employment of energetic measures in the prophylaxis and treatment of juvenile tuberculosis. In 1907 the governor of Massachusetts appointed him trustee (subsequently he became chairman) of the State Hospital for Consumptives, into the work of which he threw himself with whole-hearted enthusiasm.

Cabot's medical writings were extensive. Between 1886 and 1896 he published in the *Boston Medical and Surgical Journal* a series of eighteen contributions on various aspects of genito-urinary surgery. They were issued in four groups (1886, 1887, 1893, and 1896). In 1891 there appeared from his pen a series of seven papers on abdominal surgery in the same journal. He also published a paper on spina bifida and cephalocele (*Annals of Surgery, Aug. 1892*), and he contributed to W. W. Keen's *Surgery; its Principles and Practice,* vol. IV (1908), the section on stone in the bladder.

[Obituaries in the *Boston Medic. and Surgic. Jour.,* Nov. 28, 1912, 784–86; *Ibid.,* Mar. 20, 1913, 409–15 (H. P. Walcott and others); *Ibid.,* Aug. 28, 1919, 302–04; and in the *British Medic. Jour.,* 1912, pt. II, p. 1775; more extensive memoirs in the *Proc. Am. Acad. of Arts and Sci.,* 1918, III, 793–98 (F. C. Shattuck) and in the *Harvard Grads. Mag.,* Mar. 1913; personal information from Mrs. Arthur Tracy Cabot.]
                                                    J.F.F.

CABOT, EDWARD CLARKE (Apr. 17, 1818–Jan. 5, 1901), architect, was born in Boston, the third of the eleven children of Samuel Cabot and Eliza Perkins, daughter of Thomas Handasyd Perkins, a well-known merchant. Cabot's father, too, was a merchant in Boston, largely interested in the China and East India trade. A somewhat delicate child, Cabot was educated at private schools in Boston and Brookline, spent his early summers at Nahant, and had no university training. At the age of seventeen he went to Illinois, where, in partnership with George Curzon, he engaged in sheep raising. This venture, in which Cabot's father had invested some $12,000, ended disastrously and Cabot returned to the East in 1841. Then for more than four years he had a sheep farm at Windsor, Vt. In 1845 the Boston Athenæum invited designs for a new building, and, from his farm, Cabot submitted a sketch which was accepted with the proviso that he associate himself with George M. Dexter, a civil engineer, as supervisor. Cabot stayed some time in Dexter's office and later opened his own office in Boston. In 1849–58 and 1862–65 he was associated with his brother, James Elliot Cabot, and in 1875 he entered into partnership with Frank W. Chandler, under the firm name of Cabot & Chandler. When, a few years later, Chandler became professor of architecture at the Massachusetts Institute of Technology, two members of the office force were made partners and the firm name was changed to Cabot, Everett & Meade. During the Civil War, Cabot served for less than a year as lieutenant-colonel of the 44th Massachusetts Infantry. His architectural practise consisted largely of country houses of the more informal type, in the picturesque style then in vogue, to which he gave great charm by the restraint and exquisiteness of his taste. His two largest commissions were the Boston Theatre (1852–53), and the hospital of Johns Hopkins University, finally opened in 1889, which was done in association with Chandler. Before working on the Boston Theatre, Cabot spent a year abroad and made an intensive study of La Scala in Milan in preparation for his Boston work. After his retirement in 1888, he devoted the major portion of his time to painting and became an accomplished water-colorist, exhibiting frequently in Boston. He was twice married: first, at Salem, Mass., July 7, 1842, to Martha Eunice Robinson (died Brookline, Mass., Nov. 28, 1871), by whom he had five children; second, at Melrose, Mass., Oct. 13, 1873, to Louisa Winslow Sewall (died Brookline, Mass., Aug. 10, 1907), by whom he had three children. He lived all his life in Boston and its suburbs, building for himself two houses in Brookline, and spending his later summers at Nonquitt.

Cabot's work was distinguished by its delicacy, its restraint, and its schooled originality. The Boston Athenæum is in a fine Italian Renaissance, an extraordinary style for that date, 1845; and still more extraordinary is the beauty with which it was carried out, as it was the work of one till then a mere amateur. But Cabot's influence upon architecture in America was less through his own work than through his personality. His position as president of the Boston Society of Architects was an expression of the general esteem and affection in which he was held, and through it he came in contact with every important architect in Boston for thirty years. He was, says an editorial in the *American Architect and Building News* (Jan. 12, 1901), "a model of kind and gentle dignity."

[There is a tribute by Chas. A. Cummings in *Am. Architect and Bldg. News,* LXXI, 45, and an obituary in the *Am. Art Annual,* IV, 137. L. Vernon Briggs, *Hist. and Genealogy of the Cabot Family* (2 vols., 1927), pp. 686–93, gives an extended notice of some of the more intimate details of Cabot's life.]
                                                    T.F.H.

CABOT, GEORGE (Jan. 16, 1752–Apr. 18, 1823), merchant, senator, was the son of Joseph Cabot, whose father, John, emigrated from the Channel Islands to Salem, Mass., in 1700. Joseph, a successful merchant, married Elizabeth Higginson. George, the seventh of their eleven children, was born in Salem. In the autumn of 1766, he entered Harvard College, and was "placed" seventeenth in a class of forty-two. He took part in the "rebellion of 1766" against bad butter in commons, and was freshman member of a committee elected by the students to deal with the authorities (*Publications of the Colonial Society of Massachusetts*, X, 54–57). He withdrew from college on Mar. 19, 1768, just in time to escape public admonition for "his great Neglect of his Exercises" and "idle Behavior" (MS. Faculty Records). His elder brothers John and Andrew Cabot of Beverly, who were carrying on their father's rum, fish, and iron trade with the Southern colonies and Spain, promptly sent him to sea as cabin-boy under a strict disciplinarian. On his eighteenth birthday he was already skipper of his brothers' schooner *Sally*, taking a load of salt codfish from Beverly to Bilbao. The following year, for a salary of £3 a month and primage, he commanded their new schooner *Premium*, exchanged at the James River a cargo of rum and cider for wheat, which he delivered to his brothers' correspondents at Bilbao, and returned with a cargo of silk handkerchiefs.

In 1774 he was married to his double first-cousin, Elizabeth Higginson, "prudent, energetic, and commanding," who so far overcame his "invincible indolence of disposition" that he acquired one-sixth of the family distillery, and was entrusted with some of their best ships. About 1777 he gave up active seafaring, and was taken into his brothers' firm, which during the war owned at least forty privateers and letter-of-marque ships. Their armed merchantmen continued to trade with Spain, making their headquarters at Bilbao, where all the prizes taken by the firm's vessels were sold, and the proceeds deposited with Gardoqui & Sons. By this means the Cabots, unlike most privateering firms, kept their gains until peace was concluded. In 1784, two of their ships first carried the American flag to St. Petersburg. In the same year George Cabot became director of the Massachusetts Bank, the earliest in the state. He was the leading promoter of two important corporate enterprises of 1788, the Essex bridge and the Beverly cotton manufactory (James S. Davis, *Essays in the Earlier History of American Corporations*, vol. II). In 1785 he formed a partnership with his brother-in-law Joseph Lee which was so successful that within ten years he retired from the mercantile and shipping business with a "reasonable and sufficient fortune."

In 1778 Cabot began taking an active part in politics with the group of Essex County merchants and lawyers who became the nucleus of the Federalist party. As a member of the Concord convention of 1779 on the high cost of living, he argued in vain against price-fixing. As delegate to the adjourned session of the state constitutional convention in 1780 he served on the committee, which so juggled the returns that every clause appeared to have the requisite majority (*Proceedings of the Massachusetts Historical Society*, L, 397). For a few months in 1783 he was state senator for Essex County. Both temperament and interest made him an ardent advocate of a strong federal government. He did not attend the Annapolis Convention to which he was elected, but in the Massachusetts ratifying convention of 1788, while condescending to pose as "one of the people," he acted in close concert with the Federalist leaders. In 1789 he entertained President Washington at Beverly, and in June 1791 was chosen United States senator from Massachusetts.

Of commanding stature and dignified presence, yet easy and gracious in manner, with a good conversational style though an indifferent public speaker, and well informed on all business matters, Senator Cabot was well fitted for useful work in a small house, with closed sessions. He became a trusted follower and adviser of Alexander Hamilton, and, until the end of 1793, a director of the United States Bank. He framed the Act of 1792 granting bounties for codfishing. During the session of 1793–94 he was chairman of the committee on appropriations. He was one of the New England senators who supported Hamilton in urging the Jay mission to England, the results of which he accepted as satisfactory. For the same reason as Hamilton, Cabot abhorred the French Revolution, and wished to maintain peace with England at any price. One of his last acts in the Senate, in 1796, was to strike out the phrase "that magnanimous nation" from a resolution returning thanks to the French Republic for a flag presented by it to the United States. As late as 1807 he favored an offensive-defensive alliance with Great Britain.

Upon retiring from mercantile business, Cabot had sold his house in Beverly and purchased a farm in Brookline, near Boston. Weary of politics at the age of forty-four, he resigned his seat in the Senate (May 1796), retired to private life, and two years later refused an appointment by President Adams as the first secretary of the navy. In 1803, having sold his Brookline estate and moved to 3 Park St., Boston, Cabot became president of the Boston branch of the United States Bank, a director of the Suffolk Insurance Company, and (about 1809) president of the Boston Marine Insurance Company. His real position in Boston was that of Federalist sage. "George Cabot," wrote John C. Hamilton, "was one of those rare men, who, without ambition, without effort, almost without the consciousness of admitted superiority, control, and become the oracles of communities" (*History of the Republic,* 1859, III, 411). Rather than economic power or political wire-pulling, his constant interchange of ideas with other members of the "Essex Junto" explains the hold which that group had on Massachusetts politics and political thought. Socially, the solidarity of those plain, energetic Essex County families of Cabot, Lowell, Lee, Higginson, and Jackson, who moved to Boston after the Revolution, was equally significant. For over a generation they remained a compact social group, frequently intermarrying, and helping one another in business, to such good purpose that eventually they were regarded as typical Boston aristocrats.

After the election of Jefferson, whom he considered an "anarchist," Cabot revelled in pessimism. His very indolence became a virtue when opposed to the secessionist zeal of Timothy Pickering, and led him thrice to intervene in politics in order to exert a moderating and unionist influence: as state councillor during the Embargo, as member of a Federalist corresponding committee to nominate a Clinton for the presidency in 1808 and 1812 (Samuel E. Morison, *H. G. Otis,* 1913, I, 305, 318), and as member of the Hartford Convention in 1814. "Dragged in like a conscript to the duty of a delegate," he was chosen president, where his cool wisdom seconded the cautious leadership of H. G. Otis [*q.v.*], in preventing radical action (C. R. King, *Rufus King,* 1894–1900, V, 476). That was his last public service. In 1821 he was attacked by a disease of the gall-bladder, from which he died on Apr. 18, 1823.

[*Life and Letters of Geo. Cabot* (1877) by Henry Cabot Lodge [*q.v.*], his great-grandson, is the standard authority, but is almost exclusively confined to Cabot's political career and correspondence. The letter of Feb. 14, 1804 to Pickering on pp. 341–44 (also in Henry Adams, *Documents Relating to New Eng. Federalism,* 1877, pp. 346–49), is a succinct expression of Cabot's political views. Additional letters are in Geo. Gibbs, *Memoirs of the Administrations of Washington and John Adams* (1846); in the Pickering MSS., Mass. Hist. Soc. (Calendared in *Mass. Hist. Soc. Colls.,* 6 ser., VIII); the Pa. Hist. Soc.; the Ridgway Library, Phila.; and the Lib. of Cong. His privateering ventures

are described by O. T. Howe in "Beverly Privateers in the Am. Revolution," *Mass. Colonial Soc. Pubs.,* XXIV, 318–435, and his early voyages are treated by L. V. Briggs, *Hist. and Geneal. of the Cabot Family* (1927), I, 119–62. Abundant material on these subjects is in the Dane and Lee-Cabot MSS. (Mass. Hist. Soc.), the Essex Institute, Salem, and the Beverly Hist. Soc.]

S. E. M.

CABRILLO, JUAN RODRIGUEZ (d. Jan. 3, 1543), explorer, was a Portuguese by birth, and a skilled mariner. He went to Mexico in 1520 with Narvaez, took part with Cortés in the capture of Mexico City, joined Orozco's expedition to Oaxaca, and assisted in the conquest of Guatemala. Balboa's discovery of the South Sea in 1513 had set in motion a series of voyages up the Pacific coast of North America. From Panama sailors ran the Central-American shore-line. Cortés founded Zacatula on the western coast of Mexico, and another series of explorations began. In 1533 Lower California was discovered. Interest in the north was stimulated by Cabeza de Vaca's journey across the continent (1528–36), and in 1539 Ulloa, sent out by Cortés, rounded the Peninsula of California. Next year Pedro de Alvarado sailed from Guatemala with a fleet designed for northwestern explorations, with Cabrillo as *almirante*. Alvarado landed on the west coast of Mexico, and there met his death. Viceroy Mendoza now took charge of the vessels and sent Cabrillo with two of them to continue northward explorations. The expedition comprised the flagship *San Salvador* and the fragata *Victoria*. Bartolomé Ferrelo, or Ferrer, a native of the Levant, went as chief pilot, and there was a chaplain on board. The start was made on June 27, 1542, from Navidad, on the western coast of Mexico. Cabrillo reached the southern extremity of the Peninsula on July 3, Magdalena Bay on July 19, and Cerros Island on Aug. 5. On Aug. 22 he anchored and took possession of Port San Quintín. On Sept. 28 he discovered San Diego Bay, naming it San Miguel. Proceeding up the coast, he discovered Santa Catalina Island, San Pedro Bay, Santa Monica Bay, and Santa Bárbara Channel. Here, at San Miguel Island, he fell and broke his leg. Continuing north, nevertheless, he discovered the Santa Lucía Mountains and Point Reyes. Being driven out to sea he neared the shore again, turned south, missed the Golden Gate, discovered Monterey Bay, and returned to San Miguel Island, where he died from illness caused by his fall while previously on the island. The command of the expedition now fell to Ferrelo. From Cabrillo's northern limit he continued up the coast to latitude 44°, according to his observations, which Davidson corrects to 42½°, placing the limit of the voyage near the mouth of the Rogue River, Ore. Wagner concludes that Ferrelo did not get above 42°. On Apr. 14, 1543, the expedition reached Navidad, whence it had sailed the previous June.

[The source of most of what is known of the Cabrillo expedition is the diary commonly, but erroneously, attributed to Juan Paez. This was published in Spanish in 1857 by Buckingham Smith in his *Colección de Varios Documentos para la Historia de la Florida y Tierras Adyacentes* (London), pp. 173–89. Another Spanish version was printed in 1870 by Joaquin Pacheco and Francisco de Cárdenas, in their *Colección de Documentos Inéditos* (Madrid), XIV, 165–91. English translations have been published: (1) by Richard Stuart Evans, in Geo. M. Wheeler, *Report upon U. S. Geographical Surveys West of the One Hundredth Meridian* (1879), VII, 293–314; (2) by Geo. Davidson, in "Report of the Superintendent of the U. S. Geodetic Survey," being *House Ex. Doc. No. 40*, 49 Cong., 2 Sess., pp. 160–241; (3) by Herbert E. Bolton, in *Spanish Exploration in the Southwest* (1916, 1925), pp. 3–29; (4) by Henry R. Wagner, in *Cal. Hist. Soc. Quart.*, vol. VII, no. 1 (Mar. 1929). Mr. Wagner has made a thorough study of the itinerary, reaching conclusions considerably at variance with earlier opinions.]   H. E. B.

CADILLAC, ANTOINE DE LA MOTHE, Sieur (*c.* 1656–Oct. 18, 1730), founder of Detroit, governor of Louisiana, was born in Gascony, son of a minor nobleman, Jean de la Mothe, who owned the seigneury of Cadillac. His mother was Jeanne de Malenfant; and although in his marriage contract of 1687 Antoine declared himself about twenty-six, he was in fact some years older. Like lads of his ancestry he early entered the army, first as cadet, then as lieutenant (1677) in the regiment of Clairembault. In 1683 he came to America and had a home at Port Royal (now Annapolis); after his marriage at Quebec in 1687 to Marie Thérèse Guyon, he lived for a brief time on his grant in what is now Maine, including the island of Mount Desert. In 1689 he visited France, and during his absence his Port Royal place was sacked and burned by the British (1691). He obtained a recommendation to Count de Frontenac, who greatly favored him, and whose anti-Jesuit principles he embraced. In 1694 Frontenac gave Cadillac, whom he calls "a worthy man, good officer, keen witted," the command of the post at Mackinac, the most important position in the western country. Cadillac himself was not pleased with his position; he complained of the climate, the food, and the savages; later he became reconciled and declared his post the healthiest place in the world (memoir in Margry, V, 75–132; translation in *Wisconsin Historical Collections*, XVI, 350–63).

In 1697 the posts in the West were abandoned by order of the crown; Cadillac returned to Canada, and in 1699 went to France, where he laid before the ministry his plan for a post on Detroit River, which would protect the western fur trade from the English. His rank at this time was captain in the troops of the Marine (that is, of the colonies), and he obtained a grant of Detroit and the title of lieutenant of the King. In 1701 he set forth with many colonists to found Detroit; he was also head of a company which had the trade monopoly. Recollet missionaries were part of his colony, and he planned to attract the western tribesmen to the region of Detroit, and to place them under the care of these missionaries. The Jesuits, especially those at Mackinac, bitterly opposed the removal of their neophytes and other Indians. This and other high-handed procedure brought about Cadillac a swarm of enemies. In 1704 he was arrested, tried at Quebec, and acquitted, when he returned in triumph to Detroit. His enthusiasm for his new colony was so great and his communications to the minister in France so diffuse, that the latter rallied him upon his anticipations, writing in 1706, "I am glad to be assured that Detroit will become the Paris of New France" (*Report on Canadian Archives*, 1899, Supplement, p. 391).

Cadillac brought his wife and family to Detroit, and planned to make this place his lifelong home; but in 1711 he was recalled, and appointed to the governorship of the new colony of Louisiana, which was granted in 1712 to a company founded by Antoine Crozat. Cadillac reached Louisiana with his family in 1713 and again expressed in his reports his dissatisfaction with his appointment. He treated the Louisianians haughtily and incurred the ill will of the former governor, Bienville, and his Canadian relatives. During his three years in Louisiana, Cadillac sought every means to enrich himself, and in 1715 made a trip to Illinois in search of silver mines reported to exist there. He was much disappointed at finding only lead.

In 1716 Cadillac, of whose complaints Crozat had tired, was recalled, and is thought to have suffered a short imprisonment in the Bastille, whence he was released in February 1717. Thenceforward he made his home in his native province and died there at Castle Sarrazin. His heirs made several attempts to realize on Cadillac's American grants. Finally in 1787 his granddaughter, Madame Gregoire, visited America, introduced by Lafayette. In a burst of generosity the Massachusetts Assembly confirmed her title to that part of Mount Desert and the neighboring mainland yet unsold, after which she and her family lived there for several years.

Cadillac's name is yet potent in Detroit, where buildings and monuments have been christened in his honor. He seems to have been a typical

Gascon, alternately buoyant and depressed, of inordinate pride and much self-esteem, but withal able and clever. Had he been permitted to remain at Detroit and carry out his plans for that colony, he might have succeeded, although his enmities were stronger than his friendships. He had a wide vision of the French situation in the West, and brilliant plans for expanding French power; but he was covetous and grasping, unable to lend himself unselfishly to broad enterprises. In Louisiana his rule was a failure, by which his last years were embittered.

[The sources for Cadillac's life are scattered. C. M. Burton collected his papers and published them in *Mich. Pioneer and Hist. Colls.*, vol. XXXIII. Several of his reports or memoirs are in Pierre Margry, *Découvertes et établissements des français dans l'Amérique septentrionale* (Paris, 1876–86), vol. V, and E. B. O'Callaghan, *N. Y. Colonial Docs.*, vol. IX. In *Maine Hist. Soc. Colls.*, 1859, pp. 273–89 and 1902, p. 89 are his grants in that state. B. F. French, *Hist. Colls. of La.*, pt. III (1851), gives a contemporary report on his governorship. For a modern work there is *Antoine de la Mothe Cadillac and Detroit before the Conspiracy of Pontiac: a Bibliography* (Detroit Pub. Lib., 1912). C. M. Burton has written several pamphlets on the life of Cadillac; see also *Mich. Pioneer and Hist. Colls.*, XXIV, 303. Chas. Gayarré's account of Cadillac in Louisiana in his *Hist. of Louisiana* (4th ed., New Orleans, 1903), I, 175–89 is incorrect and prejudiced.]   L. P. K.

CADWALADER, JOHN (January 1742–Feb. 10, 1786), Revolutionary soldier, was born in Philadelphia, the son of Dr. Thomas Cadwalader [*q.v.*] and Hannah (Lambert) Cadwalader. He was educated at the College and Academy of Philadelphia (now University of Pennsylvania) but apparently never graduated. Prior to the Revolution he engaged in business with his brother, Lambert Cadwalader [*q.v.*], under the firm name of John & Lambert Cadwalader. A man of considerable wealth and position, he espoused the popular side in the struggle with Great Britain. He was a member of the Philadelphia Committee of Safety, and was captain of a city troop known as the Silk-Stocking Company. He became colonel of a Philadelphia battalion, and was appointed brigadier-general of Pennsylvania militia, Apr. 5, 1777. To his later regret, he twice declined the offer by Congress of a brigadier-generalship in the Continental army.

Cadwalader came into notice in the Trenton campaign. Washington's plan contemplated crossing the Delaware by three columns quite widely separated, his own, Ewing's, and Cadwalader's. The latter could not carry out his part of the program on account of ice, though he exerted himself, and transferred part of the infantry. Two days later with about 1,800 men he crossed from Bristol to Burlington, marching thence to Bordentown, in time to be present at the battle of Princeton. As Sir William

Howe's invasion approached Philadelphia, Cadwalader, at Washington's request, organized the militia on the eastern shore of Maryland. He fought at Brandywine and Germantown, engaged in the irregular warfare of the following season near Philadelphia, and was active in the Monmouth campaign. The winter of 1777–78 was that of the Conway cabal. Cadwalader was a strong supporter of Washington in this attempt to undermine the authority of the Commander-in-Chief, and he challenged Gen. Conway to a duel. The encounter took place near Philadelphia, and Conway fell, severely—and as he at first believed, mortally—wounded. Conway's confession to Washington, his disappearance from the scene, and the collapse of the "cabal" followed. After this year, Cadwalader had no prominent part in affairs, though he served in the legislature of Maryland. He was married twice: first, in October 1768 to Elizabeth Lloyd; second, on Jan. 30, 1779, to Williamina Bond. His death occurred at Shrewsbury, Pa., in 1786.

Cadwalader was a man of "polished manners." He was regarded as a good disciplinarian, and the esteem in which he was held by Washington is shown by two letters, one written from Valley Forge, and the other sent at the time of Arnold's treason. Cadwalader wrote *A Reply to General Joseph Reed's Remarks on a Late Publication in the Independent Gazetteer* (1783), which was part of a controversy dealing with events in the time of the Trenton campaign, Reed having thought that Cadwalader was the author of the so-called "Brutus letter," in 1782, containing innuendos.

[Jared Sparks, *The Writings of Geo. Washington* (1834–37); Thos. J. Rogers, *A New Am. Biog. Dict.* (3rd ed., Easton, Pa., 1824); Chas. P. Keith, *The Provincial Councillors of Pa.* (1883); Wm. S. Stryker, *The Battles of Trenton and Princeton* (1898); "Selections from the Military Papers of Gen. John Cadwalader," *Pa. Mag. of Hist. and Biog.*, Apr. 1908.]

E. K. A.

CADWALADER, JOHN (Apr. 1, 1805–Jan. 26, 1879), jurist, was descended from John Cadwalader, who came from Pembroke, Wales, toward the close of the seventeenth century, settled in Philadelphia, and died there in 1734. Thomas Cadwalader, of the third generation from John, was a lawyer in Philadelphia and later acted as land agent for the Penns and other owners of extensive interests in Pennsylvania. He married Mary, daughter of Col. Clement Biddle, Washington's friend, and their son John was born at Philadelphia. John was educated at the University of Pennsylvania, graduating in 1821, and then entered the law office of Horace Binney, at the same time assisting his father in the management of the Penn estates. He was admitted to the bar Sept. 30, 1825, while still a minor, and commenced practise in Philadelphia. His father was able to influence much important business and John very quickly acquired a large practise, particularly in matters involving the law of real property, in which he became recognized as an expert. In this connection he prepared a history of the title of William Penn's family to their large estates in America (*Pennsylvania Magazine of History and Biography,* April 1899, p. 60). In 1830 he was retained as counsel by the Bank of the United States, and acted as such throughout the extensive and prolonged litigation arising out of its failure. He became vice-provost of the Law Academy of Philadelphia in 1833, continuing as such for twenty years. As an advocate he had early acquired a prominent position through his thorough preparation and exhaustive study of his briefs, and this trait, combined with a forceful style and remarkably wide knowledge of law in general, gave him a professional prestige second to none. Among the many important cases in which he appeared were the "Cloth Cases" in 1839—perhaps the most important proceedings ever instituted by the revenue department—in which he was specially retained by the attorney-general in behalf of the United States. Another was the Girard Will case, where he was associated with Daniel Webster. During the riots of 1844 he raised and commanded a company of city militia. His interests were wide, and he was an active supporter of all schemes which had for their object the improvement of conditions in Philadelphia. He was leader of the movement advocating the consolidation of the city with the surrounding incorporated districts into one municipal corporation, which was carried into effect in 1854. Always a strong constitutional Democrat, he was in 1854 nominated for the office of city solicitor, but was defeated. In the same year, however, he was elected congressional representative for the fifth district by a narrow majority after a bitter contest, and took a leading part in the deliberations of the House during his term but did not seek reëlection. He was appointed by President Buchanan judge of the United States district court for the eastern district of Pennsylvania, Apr. 24, 1858, and retained this position till his death. His tenure of office coincided with the Civil War and Reconstruction periods, and many difficult questions incident thereto came before him for adjudication. One of the most important services rendered by him as a judge was his pioneer exposition of the provisions of the Bankruptcy Act of

1867. Coming to the bench with a wide experience acquired at the bar, and equipped with a knowledge of law in respect of which he "had no contemporary superior," his opinions on difficult or novel points were brilliant, though he had a tendency to over-elaboration. In matters involving no new principles, however, he frequently delivered extempore judgments, a practise which had been seldom adopted in the United States courts up to that time. Counsel frequently found it difficult to present an argument before him owing to his habit of constantly intervening, but this failing was attributed to his innate fairness and scrupulous anxiety to render absolute justice. "In admiralty proceedings he availed himself of the expert assistance of a retired shipmaster, nautical nomenclature being to him an absolutely sealed book, altogether beyond his ability to master" (R. D. Coxe, *Legal Philadelphia,* 1908, p. 82). He died in Philadelphia, Jan. 26, 1879. He was twice married: (1) in 1825 to Mary, daughter of Horace Binney, who died in 1831; (2) in 1833 to Henrietta Maria, daughter of Charles Nicoll Bancker of Philadelphia. In 1907 appeared *Cadwalader's Cases* (2 vols.), comprising his judicial opinions on questions of prize and belligerency arising during the Civil War, together with decisions in admiralty, in equity and at common law, between 1858 and 1879. This work, prepared by his son, included an introductory sketch of the judge's life, and reproduced the proceedings in the circuit court and at the meeting of the Philadelphia Bar on the occasion of his death.

[Sketches of the careers of Cadwalader and his immediate ancestors will be found in Chas. P. Keith, *The Provincial Councillors of Pa.* (1883), pp. 370–96. See also Robt. C. Moon, *The Morris Family of Phila.* (1890), I, p. 198; J. T. Scharf and T. Westcott, *Hist. of Phila.* (1884), II, 1538; F. M. Eastman, *Courts and Lawyers of Pa.* (1922), II, 387; *N. J. Law Jour.,* II, 61; *Legal Intelligencer,* Jan. 31, 1879, p. 46.]   H. W. H. K.

CADWALADER, LAMBERT (1743–Sept. 13, 1823), Revolutionary soldier, was a native of Trenton, and was descended from Welsh and Quaker ancestry, being the son of Dr. Thomas Cadwalader [*q.v.*] and Hannah (Lambert) Cadwalader. He was well educated, studying at the College and Academy of Philadelphia (now the University of Pennsylvania). Prior to the Revolution he engaged in business with his brother, John Cadwalader [1742–1786, *q.v.*], under the name John & Lambert Cadwalader. When the conflict with England began, he was actively patriotic. He signed the non-importation agreement in 1765, was a member of the Committee of Correspondence, of the Provincial Convention of 1775, and of the state constitutional convention of 1776. Like his brother, he was captain of an aristocratic company in Philadelphia, the Greens. He was appointed lieutenant-colonel, 3rd Pennsylvania Battalion, Jan. 4, 1776, and colonel, 4th Pennsylvania, later in the year. He was one of the commanders in the disastrous battle of Fort Washington. After performing his part well in the fighting, he was taken prisoner, Nov. 16, 1776, but was released, and resigned from the army in 1779. He held no further command in the war, but was a delegate to the Continental Congress, 1784–87, and a member of Congress in the lower house, 1789–91, and 1793–95. He was not marked as a debater, but was an efficient worker. In the Continental Congress he was a member of the Grand Committee which received the report of the Annapolis Convention. In 1793 he was married to Mary, daughter of Archibald McCall of Philadelphia. He owned a large estate at Greenwood, near Trenton, where he died in 1823.

[Wm. Henry Rawle, *Col. Lambert Cadwalader* (privately printed, 1878), also in *Pa. Mag. of Hist. and Biog.*, Oct. 1886 ; Chas. P. Keith, *The Provincial Councillors of Pa.* (1883).]   E.K.A.

CADWALADER, THOMAS (1707 or 1708–Nov. 14, 1799), physician, of Philadelphia, was the son of John Cadwalader and his wife Martha Jones, daughter of Edward Jones and Mary Wynne. He was educated at the Friends' Public School, now known as the Penn Charter School. He was then apprenticed to his uncle Dr. Evan Jones. When he was nineteen or twenty, his father sent him abroad to complete his medical education. He is said to have spent a year studying under Cheselden and to have attended courses at the University of Rheims. Returning to Philadelphia, he soon acquired a large practise and distinguished himself by his activity in public affairs. He was associated with Benjamin Franklin in founding the Philadelphia Library in 1731. In 1730 or 1731, according to Dr. Caspar Wistar, he made dissections and demonstrations for the instruction of the elder Dr. Shippen and some others who had not been abroad. At about the same time he is noted as employing inoculation against smallpox. In 1738 he married Hannah, daughter of Thomas Lambert, Jr., a wealthy man who owned a great tract of land on and near where the city of Trenton, N. J., now flourishes. Cadwalader then left Philadelphia to live on his father-in-law's estate, but although he was elected to several minor political offices in New Jersey, he maintained a residence in Passyunk Township in Philadelphia, in which he passed part of each year. He undoubtedly also practised his profession in New Jersey as he was physician to Gov. Belcher, and had at least one pupil. In 1750 he resigned his office of burgess

in Trenton, presenting to the town £500 to found a public library, and again took up his permanent residence in Philadelphia. In 1751 he subscribed toward the founding of the Pennsylvania Hospital and was asked by the board of managers, along with Drs. Graeme, Moore, and Redman, "to assist in consultations on extraordinary cases," in which capacity he continued to give his services until 1779, when he resigned. In 1751 he was elected a trustee of the Academy of Philadelphia (later the College of Philadelphia, and now the University of Pennsylvania). He was very active in the affairs of the American Philosophical Society, being at one time vice-president. He was also prominent in civic and colonial affairs. He was a member of the Common Council of Philadelphia from 1751 to 1774, and of the Provincial Council from 1755 until that body was dissolved at the outbreak of the Revolution. From an early date he rendered himself obnoxious to the Government by the patriotic zeal which he manifested in colonial matters. After Braddock's defeat he was one of twenty citizens who offered to pay £500 each for purposes of defense against the French and Indians, the Governor having refused to allow the Assembly the right to impose a tax for this purpose. In 1765 he affixed his signature to the "Non-Importation Articles" and that year was a prominent participant in a great meeting in the State House yard to protest against the Stamp Act. Although there is no record of his having held any military position during the Revolution there is evidence that he from time to time performed certain duties requested of him by the American authorities. Thus in 1776 he was asked to examine into the health of Gen. Prescott of the British army, then a prisoner of war in Philadelphia, and to report on the sanitary conditions of the jail. Prescott seems to have appreciated his services on this occasion, for, some time later, after his own release, he secured the release of Cadwalader's son Lambert [*q.v.*], who had been taken prisoner by the British. He is also said to have helped Dr. John Morgan in his work as director-general of the American military hospitals.

Cadwalader's only contribution to medical literature was *An Essay on the West-India Dry-Gripes; with the Method of Preventing and Curing that Cruel Distemper; to Which Is Added an Extraordinary Case in Physick. Philadelphia. Printed and sold by B. Franklin, M.DCC.XLV.* The "Dry-Gripes" was the name given to a very frequent complaint in Cadwalader's day, due to the prevalent custom of drinking punch made with Jamaica rum. It was a form of lead-poisoning due to the lead pipes which were used in distilling the rum. The most usual form of treatment consisted in the administration of mercury and drastic purgatives. Cadwalader recommended instead the use of mild cathartics and opium. The "Extraordinary Case" was one of osteomalacia, or as it was then called "mollities osseum." Cadwalader performed an autopsy on the body in 1742, which may be regarded as one of the earliest recorded autopsies in this country. Courteous and kind, he enjoyed the esteem and affection of his fellow-townsmen. Of him it might be said, as Dr. Johnson wrote of the great physician Richard Mead, "No man lived more in the broad sunshine of life." He died while visiting his son Lambert, in Trenton, and was buried in that city.

[Sketch by Chas. W. Dulles, in *Pa. Mag. of Hist. and Biog.*, July 1903; Geo. W. Norris, *The Early Hist. of Medicine in Phila.* (1886); John F. Watson, *Annals of Phila.* (1830); Jas. Thacher, *Am. Med. Biogs.* (1828); T. G. Morton, *Hist. of the Pa. Hospital* (1895).]

F.R.P.

CADY, DANIEL (Apr. 29, 1773–Oct. 31, 1859), jurist, was descended from Nicholas Cady, who, coming probably from Suffolk, England, settled at Watertown, Mass., in 1630. Fourth in the direct line from Nicholas, Eleazer Cady, a Connecticut farmer, married Tryphena, daughter of John Beebe of Kent, Conn. They moved to Columbia County, N. Y., and their son Daniel was born at Chatham (Canaan) in that county. He was educated at the public schools and worked on his father's farm. Later he was apprenticed to a shoemaker, but in 1791 through an accident at the bench lost the sight of one eye. He thereupon became a school-teacher, at the same time studying law at Canaan, and in 1794 entered an Albany law office. He was admitted as an attorney in 1795, "having worn a pair of boots of his own manufacture at the time of his examination" (W. Raymond, *post*). He commenced practise at Florida, Montgomery County, but at the end of a year removed to Johnstown, the county seat, being admitted as a counsellor in 1798. A Federalist in politics, he was elected to the state legislature in 1808, being reëlected in 1809, 1811, 1812, and 1813. For one term, Mar. 4, 1815, to Mar. 3, 1817, he was representative in Congress for Montgomery County, but did not make any mark in the political field, and thereafter devoted his attention to his law practise. In his early years at the bar he had become favorably known as an advocate, and in 1812 had distinguished himself in the trial of Solomon Southwick for attempting to bribe the speaker of the New York Assembly to vote for the incorporation of the Bank of North America, appearing for the defense in association with Aaron Burr and pro-

curing an acquittal. Later on he came to the front as an "ejectment lawyer." He specialized in equity and real property law with its accompanying technicalities and ancient learning, and, practising in a neighborhood where titles were always involved and frequently litigated, acquired a large and lucrative business. Among his clients were the heirs of Sir William Johnson, who were contemplating action against the Government in regard to the confiscation of their ancestor's extensive estate.

Cady's remarkable knowledge of all the intricacies of the most difficult branch of the law was in great measure due to his method of study. "He had no patience with the digest-mongers and book-manufacturers of the day," but invariably went to the fountainhead, reading *Coke upon Littleton, Fearne on Contingent Remainders,* and *Shepard's Touchstone.* Always interested in agricultural problems, he invested largely in wild land contiguous to Johnstown, and expended much time and money in experiments in reclamation and cultivation. In 1847, when seventy-four years old, he was elected an associate judge of the supreme court of New York, as organized under the state constitution of 1846, there being at that date no age limit on office-holders. In 1849 he was reëlected for a term of eight years, and retained his seat on the bench till Dec. 31, 1854, when he resigned, owing to his hearing having become seriously impaired. As a judge he was capable, dignified, and conscientiously painstaking, but had little scope for exhibiting his peculiar learning. Despite his age, his intellectual vigor remained undiminished, and he enjoyed to a remarkable degree the confidence and esteem of the community. "He was more than once retained, after his judicial career was finished, merely to look virtuous; to say nothing and to do nothing but to nod assent to all his associate might say, and wag a vigorous dissent from all the opposition might utter" (Irving Browne, *post*). Somewhat paradoxically he had inherited a strain of Puritan narrowness, and in his everyday contacts was "secretive and taciturn to an extraordinary degree"(Franklin Ellis, *post*). He died at Johnstown, Oct. 31, 1859, having shortly prior thereto become totally blind. He was married on July 8, 1801, to Margaret, daughter of Col. James Livingston, and their daughter Elizabeth later became, as Mrs. Elizabeth Cady Stanton [*q.v.*], the champion of women's rights.

[Details of Cady's ancestry appear in Orrin Peer Allen, *Descendants of Nicholas Cady of Watertown, Mass., 1645–1910* (1910), which also contains an outline of his life at p. 173. The *Green Bag,* June 1890, has a short character sketch by Irving Browne. Other biographical notices will be found in Alden Chester, *Courts and Lawyers of N. Y.* (1925), pp. 1043, 1126; Franklin Ellis, *Hist. of Columbia County, N. Y.* (1878), p. 104; Wm. Raymond, *Biog. Sketches of the Distinguished Men of Columbia County* (1851), p. 44; Peyton Farrell Miller, *A Group of Great Lawyers of Columbia County, N. Y.* (1904), p. 126; the *Green Bag*, Mar. 1897; 18 *Barbour*, p. 659.]   H. W. H. K.

CADY, SARAH LOUISE ENSIGN (Sept. 13, 1829–Nov. 8, 1912), educator, was the daughter of Salmon and Melinda (Cobb) Ensign. Her father was a coachmaker of Northampton, Mass. Family tradition told of a coach built by him for President Pierce, which, beautifully ornamented, lined with tufted gold brocade, was drawn by horses to Philadelphia, rousing great admiration along the way. The family moved to Westfield, where at seventeen Sarah was graduated from the Normal School. Then followed the practical training of teaching in district schools, under customary conditions of pupils older than the teacher, belief in using the rod when necessary, and adventures of "boarding round,"—all excellent means of developing personality. On Oct. 10, 1850, Sarah was married to Henry Stearns Cady, a merchant in Springfield, a second cousin, descended like herself from Samuel Cobb, physician, who came from England in 1630. Left on her husband's death (1863) with only a small life insurance to support three little children, she naturally returned to teaching, and opened a school in Westfield. After two years she was invited to teach in Maplewood Hall (Pittsfield), a large boarding-school for young women, and later became associate principal. In 1870 she established her own school, West End Institute, in New Haven, Conn., attended during twenty-nine years of existence by several hundred pupils. Mrs. Cady's sincere interest and enthusiasm for her profession, and belief in the serious education of girls, made this more than the usual finishing school of the day. It earned a standing which enabled its pupils to enter colleges without examination. The first pupil to enter Vassar from Connecticut was fitted here in the early seventies; no other school in the state gave the necessary instruction. Mrs. Cady was a born teacher and disciplinarian, thorough in her methods, generous in the number and quality of her teachers. They were college graduates, native teachers in foreign languages, special lecturers and instructors. The school also had one of the earliest kindergartens. About 1891 the school moved to a building on the famous Hillhouse Ave. belonging to Yale University, which (1899) refused to renew the lease. The difficulty, at her age, of finding another suitable location, and of moving the establishment, caused Mrs. Cady reluctantly to close the school after graduating the largest class in its history. She spent the rest of her life in New York City with a daughter. Naturally active and a leader, she became a member of various clubs,—Sorosis, Clio, and others— was prominent in the Broadway Tabernacle, and served on executive boards and committees of the Y. W. C. A., W. C. T. U., and so forth.

In appearance stately and handsome, with beautiful coloring, she had unusual talent in reading and elocution. In 1920, as a jubilee gift and memorial to her, the Alumnæ Association established at Connecticut College an annual prize for reading and public speaking.

[School records and information supplied by Mrs. Cady's daughter, Mrs. Charles A. Terry; O. P. Allen, *Descendants of Nicholas Cady of Watertown, Mass., 1645–1910* (1910).]   M. H. M.

CAFFERY, DONELSON (Sept. 10, 1835–Dec. 30, 1906), senator, was born on his father's sugar plantation near Franklin, St. Mary's Parish, La. He was of Scotch-Irish descent. His father was Donelson Caffery, a native of middle Tennessee, who came to Louisiana as a young man in 1811. His mother was Lydia (Murphy) Caffery, who when a child came with her father, John Murphy, from Edenton, N. C., to St. Mary's Parish. Donelson Caffery attended a private school at Franklin and St. Mary's College in Baltimore. He then studied law in the office of Joseph W. Walker at Franklin and at the old Louisiana University in New Orleans. After completing his course, however, he engaged in sugar planting on Bayou Cypremont, bordering on the Gulf of Mexico. Though he did not favor secession, when Louisiana seceded from the Union, he left his business in the hands of his overseer and joined the Crescent Rifles in New Orleans in January 1862. Shortly afterward he was transferred to the 13th Louisiana Regiment and under that command fought in the two days' battle of Shiloh. Later he became a lieutenant and was detailed to the staff of Brigadier-General W. W. Walker, on which he continued until the close of the war.

After the war he engaged in the practise of law at Franklin, and in sugar planting. He was active in the movement to rid the state of carpet-baggers, and with several others was indicted for attempting to drive out J. Hale Sypher, a Republican official. In the trial at New Orleans, his masterly speech before the jury is said to have obtained the verdict of acquittal for himself and the others. In 1869 he was married to Bethia Richardson, daughter of Francis D. Richardson, a prominent sugar planter of Jeanerette, La. Ten years later he was elected to the Louisiana state constitutional convention. The main question before that body concerned the debt that had been incurred by the state during the Reconstruction period. The convention was inclined to repudiate the debt, but Caffery's activity, both on the floor and in personal contact with the members, contributed much toward getting it ratified. In 1892 he was elected to the state Senate and later in the same year he was appointed to the United States Senate to succeed Randall L. Gibson who had died. Two years later he was reëlected and served until the expiration of his term in 1901. As senator he opposed both free silver and the war with Spain. He was particularly active in the formation of the National or "Gold" Democratic party in 1896 after the nomination of Bryan by the Democrats at Chicago on the free silver platform. He was permanent chairman of the convention at Indianapolis that nominated Palmer and Buckner for president and vice-president. In 1900 he was nominated for president by the convention of the National Party, composed chiefly of "Gold" Democrats and Anti-Imperialists, but declined the nomination. On retiring from the Senate he returned to his home in Franklin and resumed the practise of law and the cultivation of his sugar plantation in St. Mary's Parish. Contrary to current reports, he was a man of only ordinary means throughout his entire life. He died while on a visit to New Orleans and was buried at Franklin. He was survived by his wife and eight of their nine children.

Caffery was a man of medium height, rather stockily built, with a flowing beard and large features. The dominant trait of his character was his independence of thought and action. He had strong convictions and obeyed his sense of justice even when it ran counter to his own interests. Though he was himself a sugar planter, he opposed the sugar bounty and so alienated one of the most powerful industrial interests in his own state. His private life was one of great purity and unselfishness.

[There is a brief sketch in Alcée Fortier, *Louisiana* (1914), I, 145–46; New Orleans newspapers (*Daily Picayune* and *Times-Democrat*) for Dec. 31, 1906, contain more or less lengthy but not altogether reliable obituaries.]   E.M.V.

CAFFIN, CHARLES HENRY (June 4, 1854–Jan. 14, 1918), author, was born at Sittingbourne, Kent, England, the son of Rev. Charles Smart and Harriet C. Caffin. He graduated in 1876 from Magdalen College, Oxford, with a splendid background of culture and a finely developed æsthetic sense. The years following his college career were occupied with teaching and theatrical work. The training gained in these pursuits quickened his powers of observation and descrip-

tion. In 1888 he married Caroline Scurfield and in 1892 came to the United States, where he was engaged in the decoration department of the Chicago Exposition. In 1897 he settled in New York and entered upon his profession as an art critic for *Harper's Weekly,* the New York *Evening Post,* the New York *Sun* (1901–04), the *International Studio,* and the *New York American.* His press articles, characterized by ease of style and much individuality, attracted wide attention. In 1897 was published the volume, *Handbook of the New Library of Congress, compiled by Herbert Small; with Essays on the Architecture, Sculpture and Painting by Charles Caffin.* In 1901, Caffin's first of a long series of books, popular in style, was issued under the title of *Photography as a Fine Art.* It was followed by: *American Masters of Painting* (1902); *American Masters of Sculpture* (1903); *How to Study Pictures by Means of a Series of Comparisons of Paintings and Painters* (1905); *The Story of American Painting* (1907); *A Child's Guide to Pictures* (1908); *The Appreciation of the Drama* (1908); *The Art of Dwight W. Tryon* (1909); *The Story of Dutch Painting* (1909); *The Story of Spanish Painting* (1910); *A Guide to Pictures for Beginners and Students* (1910); *The Story of French Painting* (1911); *Francisco Goya Lucientes* (1912); *Art for Life's Sake* (1913); *How to Study the Modern Painters* (1914); *How to Study the Old Masters* (1914); *The A. B. C. Guide to Pictures* (1914); *How to Study Architecture* (1917). This long list of works, written in addition to Caffin's onerous editorial duties, exercised a wide-spread influence. They were suggestive and stimulating to the layman and did much to elicit interest in the various fields of art. The essay, *Art for Life's Sake,* describes Caffin's philosophy. "Art is not confined . . . to painting, or sculpture, or architecture, or music, but is, in its highest and broadest sense, organization—susceptible of application to, or expression through, every kind of human activity, high or humble, practical or idealistic" (*International Studio,* February 1918).

[*Am. Art Annual,* vol. XV (1918); the *Evening Post* (N.Y.), Jan. 14, 1918; *Who's Who in America,* 1916–17.]   L.F.P.

CAIN, RICHARD HARVEY (Apr. 12, 1825–Jan. 18, 1887), negro clergyman and politician, was born of free parents in Greenbrier County, Va., and remained there throughout his boyhood. His parents then moved to Ohio, first to Portsmouth and later to Cincinnati. There he had some opportunity to ground himself in the common school branches. Like so many enterprising negroes of that day, he entered upon the steamboat service on the Ohio River. This was a much more lucrative employment at that time than years later because, prior to the development of the railroad and Pullman service, the sort of travel preferred by the rich and aristocratic was by way of steamboat. Cain began the serious work of his life after he was converted in 1841. Upon moving to Hannibal, Mo., in 1844, he was licensed to preach by the Rev. William Jackson of the Methodist Episcopal Church. Returning to Cincinnati soon after, and dissatisfied with the conditions then obtaining in the Methodist Episcopal Church, he joined the African Methodist Episcopal Church. He was then assigned a church at Muscatine, Iowa, and was ordained deacon by Bishop W. P. Quinn in 1859, but, feeling the need of more learning, he temporarily abandoned the work to study for a year at Wilberforce University. In 1861 he was transferred to the New York Conference to serve four years in Brooklyn. He was ordained elder by Bishop Payne in Washington in 1862. Three years later he was sent to the South Carolina Conference where he had the opportunity to extend the influence of his church and to take the initiative in the reconstruction of the religious work among the freedmen in that state. In this field, he was not only a minister, but rendered valuable service also in the publication of a newspaper entitled the *Missionary Record*.

Being in South Carolina at the time when the enfranchised negroes together with their white friends controlled the politics of the state, Cain was quickly sought to represent them in politics. He was a member of the constitutional convention of 1868 which revised the fundamental law along liberal lines. He next served two years as state senator from the Charleston district. In 1872 he was elected to represent South Carolina in the Forty-third Congress. He was elected also to the Forty-fifth Congress. As a member of that body, he not only manifested interest in those measures which peculiarly concerned the freedmen, but took an active part in all matters pertaining to the general welfare of the country. To eliminate fraud from South Carolina, he joined with others in the organization of the Honest Government League. To keep the federal government out of the mire of corruption, he spoke and wrote fearlessly in behalf of clean politics. In spite of the vituperation and recrimination with which the atmosphere was charged in the conflict of the Reconstructionists and their opponents, he was generally referred to, even by his enemies, as an upright and honest man who deserved the good will of all citizens.

Upon the elimination of the negro from poli-

tics, Cain devoted himself altogether to the work of the church. He was elected bishop in 1880 and was assigned to the Louisiana and Texas diocese. There he had not only the religious work to direct but that of education, as it centered in Paul Quinn College of which he became president. Throughout his career, he made the impression of a man of clear vision, good judgment, strong resolution, and firm convictions.

[Wm. J. Simmons, *Men of Mark* (1887), pp. 866–71; A. A. Taylor, *The Negro in S. C. During the Reconstruction* (1924), *passim*; *Jour. of Negro Hist.*, Apr. 1922, July, Oct. 1924; *A.M.E.Ch.Rev.*, Apr. 1887; L. G. Tyler, *Encyc. of Va. Biog.* (1915), vol. III.]

C.G.W.

CAINES, GEORGE (1771–July 10, 1825), lawyer, author, was a prominent figure in New York legal circles for over thirty years, but no details of his parentage or the place or exact date of his birth have survived. He was practising as a counsellor-at-law in New York City when in 1802 he published anonymously the first volume of *An Enquiry into the Law Merchant of the United States; or, Lex Mercatoria Americana on Several Heads of Commercial Importance*. Marvin (*post*, p. 189) says that other volumes of this work were intended but the indifferent reception accorded to it induced Caines to abandon his project. Up to this time all legal reports in the United States had been private ventures with no official sanction, but in 1804 the New York legislature provided for the appointment by the state supreme court of a reporter of its decisions and Caines received the appointment, being thus the first official reporter on this continent. In this capacity he issued *New York Term Reports of Cases Argued and Determined in the Supreme Court of that State,* in three volumes covering the period May 1803–Nov. 1805 (1804–06), of which a second edition appeared with corrections and additions in 1813–14. These reports were distinguished by brevity and accuracy, and for long enjoyed a high reputation with both bench and bar, but subsequent statutory amendments have deprived them of much of their utility. At the same time he was engaged upon a compilation of *Cases Argued and Determined in the Court for the Trial of Impeachments and Correction of Errors in the State of New York,* two volumes (1805–07), commonly cited as *Caines' Cases in Error*. This work, embracing cases from the court of errors from 1801 to 1805 inclusive and supreme court cases from 1796, contains much important matter, displays much ability, and is esteemed authoritative. Caines also edited a second edition (1808) of William Coleman's *Reports of Cases of Practice Determined in the Supreme Court of Judicature of the State of New York*

1794 to 1800, adding cases up to November 1805, which is generally cited as *Coleman and Caines' Cases,* a later edition appearing in 1883. He was in addition the author of a practical manual, *Summary of the Practice in the Supreme Court of the State of New York* (1808) and *Practical Forms of the Supreme Court [of New York] Taken from Tidd's Appendix* (1808). He retained the position of official reporter for less than three years and after the publication of the two last mentioned works, devoted himself to his practise in New York City, ultimately achieving a prominent position at the New York bar. In 1816 he was counsel for the plaintiff in a suit for assault and battery under unique circumstances, his client complaining that when a passenger on the British ship *Thomas* he had, on the high seas off the Newfoundland Banks, been subjected against his will to ignominious treatment at the hands of Father Neptune and his acolytes impersonated by members of the crew. The trial took place in the Marine Court of New York City and the jury returned a verdict in favor of the plaintiff for $46.00 (*Duffie* vs. *Matthewson et al.,* 2 *American State Trials,* ed. J. D. Lawson, 1914, p. 901). Caines retired from practise in 1825 and shortly afterward died suddenly at Catskill, N. Y., when on his way to take up his residence at Windham.

[D. McAdam *et al.,* ed., *Hist. of the Bench and Bar of N. Y.,* vol. I (1897) ; B. V. Abbott and A. Abbott, *Digest of N. Y. Statutes and Reports* (1860), I, xiv, xv ; J. G. Marvin, *Legal Bibliography* (1847), p. 169 ; Chas. Warren, *Hist. of the Am. Bar* (1911), p. 331 ; *N. Y. Spectator,* July 15, 1825.]   H. W. H. K.

CALDWELL, ALEXANDER (Mar. 1, 1830– May 19, 1917), Kansas politician, business man, was born at Drake's Ferry, Huntingdon County, Pa. He was the son of Jane Matilda (Drake) Caldwell and James Caldwell, who came to America as a child with his parents from County Donegal, Ireland. As a boy Alexander had only very limited advantages but secured a common school education and became a clerk in a store. When the Mexican War broke out he enlisted at the age of seventeen in a company of volunteers of which his father was captain. He took part in all of the principal battles fought by Gen. Scott's army. His father was killed in a skirmish just outside the City of Mexico, Sept. 13, 1847. At the close of the war Alexander became a successful banking official at Columbia, Pa. While living there he married Pace A. Heise, a member of a prominent family of Columbia. In the spring of 1861 he came to Leavenworth, Kan., where he took contracts for transporting military supplies to the army posts west of the Missouri River. His business soon became very large. Five thousand men were employed; an equal number of wagons and many thousand oxen were used. With the coming of railroads in the West, the business of carrying freight in wagons declined and was discontinued by Caldwell in 1870. He now became interested in railway construction and secured the contract for building the Missouri Pacific from Kansas City to Leavenworth. A few years later he extended this line to Atchison, Kan., and became its president until it was sold. His next venture was the organization of the Kansas Central Railroad Company which constructed a line between Leavenworth and Miltonvale, Kan., a distance of one hundred and seventy miles.

In the winter of 1870–71 Caldwell was chosen United States senator for the term beginning Mar. 4, 1871. Serious charges were afterward made as to the methods used to secure his election. The Kansas legislature appointed a joint committee of investigation. On Feb. 24, 1872, a unanimous report was presented in which it was alleged that bribery had been freely used to obtain votes for him (Report of Joint Legislative Committee, *Annals of Kansas,* pp. 570 ff.). On May 11, 1872, the Senate adopted a resolution to investigate his election (*Congressional Globe,* 42 Cong., 2 Sess., pp. 3316–17). This committee later reported unfavorably and offered a resolution that Caldwell was "not duly elected to a seat in the Senate of the United States." They added however that he "was as much sinned against as sinning," owing to the fact that he "was a novice in politics." His defense was that he had done nothing in violation of any laws either state or Federal in securing his election. A long debate ensued (*Congressional Record,* 43 Cong., Special Session of the Senate, pp. 30 ff.). Before any vote was taken on the committee's resolution it was officially announced that Caldwell had resigned. This closed the incident (*Ibid.,* p. 164). His next business venture was the organization of the Kansas Manufacturing Company which made yearly about seven thousand wagons and gave employment to hundreds of men. He was also head of the Idaho & Oregon Land Improvement Company for locating towns and constructing irrigation ditches in the new country made available for settlement by the completion of the Union Pacific Railroad. In 1897 he bought a large block of stock in the First National Bank of Leavenworth and became its president. Under his able and efficient management it soon became one of the largest and most prosperous banks in Kansas. His death occurred just as America was entering the World War and attracted little attention.

[Who's Who in America, 1916–17; Kansas State Hist. Soc. Colls., vol. XII (1912); Daniel W. Wilder, Annals of Kansas (1875); Frank W. Blackmar, Kansas, a Cyc. of State Hist. (1912), vol. I; Portrait and Biog. Record of Leavenworth, Douglas, and Franklin Counties, Kan. (1899); Leavenworth Times, May 20, 1917.]
T. L. H.

CALDWELL, CHARLES (May 14, 1772–July 9, 1853), physician, was the son of Lieut. Charles Caldwell and —— Murray, both of the Presbyterian gentry of County Tyrone, Ulster, who emigrated in 1752 to Newark, Del., and a few years later to Caswell County, N. C. Here the younger Charles Caldwell was born. He received the educational basis for his subsequent training from private tutors and the primitive schools of the state. For several years he taught school to acquire funds for his professional education. He had been designed for the pulpit but after brief study abandoned this career for that of medicine, beginning his medical training in 1791 in the office of Dr. Harris of Salisbury, N. C. In the following year he entered the Medical Department of the University of Pennsylvania where, under Rush, Wistar, Shippen, Barton, Khun, and others he completed his education. Shortly thereafter he obtained a commission as surgeon and served in the bloodless "Whiskey Insurrection" in western Pennsylvania (1794). Thereafter he declined a permanent army commission. Immediately after obtaining his M.D. (1796) he began the practise of medicine in Philadelphia. At first he had been Rush's favorite pupil; later they were estranged; but ultimately they became friends again and after Rush's death Caldwell wrote a sketch of his life for *Delaplaine's Repository* (1813). Due chiefly to the opposition of Rush he never became professor in the Medical Department of the University of Pennsylvania, though made professor in the faculty of physical sciences. He declined invitations to take part in the formation of three medical schools in New York, Baltimore, and Philadelphia respectively. In 1812 he edited the *Port Folio* of Philadelphia. His correspondence with many prominent officers made his record of the events of the War of 1812 prompt and interesting. In 1819 he accepted an invitation to become a founder of the Medical Department of Transylvania University at Lexington, Ky., and professor of the institutes of medicine and clinical practise. With $10,000 contributed by the state he purchased in Europe (1821) books for the Transylvania library, the first collection in the West. After eighteen years of successful work in Lexington, he concluded that industrial Louisville was a more logical city for a great medical center. He became the first professor at the Louisville Medical Institute (now University

of Louisville) founded in 1837, and continued in this capacity until 1849 when he retired on account of advanced age. He was married, first, in 1799 to Eliza, daughter of Thomas Leaming of Philadelphia, and second, to Mrs. Barton, *née* Warner, of Kentucky. He succeeded in his purpose of being "the first introducer of true medical science into the Mississippi Valley." His literary work extended over more than sixty years during which time he wrote more than two hundred books and papers. He was strong in his belief in the power of nature to preserve health and cure disease as opposed to Rush's doctrine of "turning nature out of doors." Sound in the light of our present knowledge in many of his opinions, he nevertheless advocated phrenology, mesmerism, the theory of spontaneous generation, and the like.

[The chief source is the caustic *Autobiography of Chas. Caldwell* (1855) which has been called "the choicest repository of medical scandal in existence." An appendix to that volume lists Caldwell's many publications. Biographies are found in the *Western Jour. of Medicine and Surgery* (1853) and in a notice by B. H. Coates in *Proc. Am. Philos. Soc.*, vol. VI (1859).]
E. E. H.

CALDWELL, CHARLES HENRY BROMEDGE (June 11, 1823–Nov. 30, 1877), naval officer, son of Charles H. and Susan (Blagge) Caldwell, was born at Hingham, Mass. He entered the navy as midshipman on Feb. 27, 1838, and was promoted to lieutenant on Sept. 4, 1852. On Oct. 11, 1858, while on duty in the *Vandalia*, he commanded a detachment from that vessel, defeated a force of cannibal savages at Wega in the Fiji Islands, and burned their town. In 1862 he commanded the gunboat *Itasca* of the West Gulf blockading squadron under Admiral Farragut, and took part in the bombardment of Forts Jackson and St. Philip. On Apr. 20, 1862, Lieut. Caldwell in the *Itasca* and Lieut. Peirce Crosby in the *Pinola*, under Capt. H. H. Bell, were detailed on a night expedition to break a chain which extended from shore to shore below the forts. The movement was detected by the defenders of Fort Jackson, and its fire concentrated on the two vessels, without however preventing the parting of the cable, which left a passageway open on the left bank of the river. On Apr. 24 came the long-prepared execution of the plan to pass the forts, the entire success of which led to the speedy reduction of these important defenses and the capture of New Orleans. During the running fight, the *Itasca,* crippled by a shot which wrecked her boiler, was one of the three vessels of the fleet unable to get by the forts. Caldwell was obliged to drop down the river, out of action, and run his ship, which bore the scars of fourteen shots, ashore. He took part

Caldwell

Caldwell

in the action at Grand Gulf on June 9, 1862. His promotion to commander followed, dating from July 16, 1862, during the autumn of which year he received command of the *Essex* and of the mortar flotilla in the Mississippi squadron, participating in the operations at Port Hudson during the spring of 1863. He was then transferred to the command of the *Glaucus* of the North Atlantic blockading squadron, 1863–64, and of the *R. R. Cuyler* of the same squadron until 1865. He was commissioned captain Dec. 12, 1867, was chief-of-staff of the North Atlantic Fleet in 1870, and was promoted commodore June 14, 1874.

[David D. Porter, *Naval Hist. of the Civil War* (1886); *Official Records* (*Navy*), 1 ser. XVIII; *Hist. of the Town of Hingham, Mass.* (1893), II, 117; *Report of the Secretary of the Navy,* 1862–65, inclusive; Navy Registers, 1824–1877.] E.B.

CALDWELL, DAVID (Mar. 22, 1725–Aug. 25, 1824), Presbyterian clergyman, the son of Andrew Caldwell, a Scotchman who emigrated to America and married Ann Stewart in 1718, was born in Lancaster County, Pa. A farmer's son, David followed the occupation of a carpenter in his early life. After graduation at the College of New Jersey (now Princeton)—where he was a friend of Benjamin Rush—in 1761, he studied for the Presbyterian ministry. He was licensed by the New Brunswick (N. J.) Presbytery in 1763, and ordained at Trenton in 1765. In 1766 he married Rachel Craighead. Becoming a missionary in North Carolina, he was installed pastor of the two churches at Buffalo and Alamance in that province in 1768. Thenceforth for half a century he was foremost in the community. He was a man of varied activities, owning a farm, conducting a classical school which had a high reputation, practising medicine, and reaching eminence as a preacher and as a leader in public affairs. In 1771 the agitation of the North Carolina Regulators reached its climax in civil war near his home. In an attempt to thwart hostilities, he negotiated both with Gov. Tryon and with the Regulators but was unable to prevent the battle of Alamance. He was prominent in the Revolution, being a member of the state constitutional convention in 1776. A few years later Cornwallis offered a reward of £200 for his capture, and he was obliged to remain in hiding for a while. His home was situated near the battlefield of Guilford Court House, and in that campaign his house was plundered by the enemy, and his library and papers were destroyed. After the battle (Mar. 15, 1781), he aided in caring for the sick and wounded. He was a member of the state convention which met to consider the new Federal Constitution, and like many other delegates he was opposed to ratification. One of

the features in the proposed instrument of government to which he objected was the absence of a religious test. Soon after, he declined the presidency of the University of North Carolina on account of his age. He lived, however, many years longer, conducting his school, supporting the War of 1812, and preaching until 1820. He died in North Carolina, having very nearly rounded a century.

[E. W. Caruthers, *A Sketch of the Life and Character of the Rev. David Caldwell* (1842); Wm. H. Foote, *Sketches of N. C.* (1846); S. A. Ashe, *Biog. Hist. of N. C.,* vol. I (1905); Alex. Harris, *A Biog. Hist. of Lancaster County* (1872).] E. K. A.

CALDWELL, EUGENE WILSON (Dec. 3, 1870–June 20, 1918), Roentgenologist, born in Savannah, Mo., was the son of W. W. and Camilla (Kellogg) Caldwell. In his early boyhood, his parents moved to Kansas, in which state he grew up. After attending the public school, he studied electrical engineering at the University of Kansas. During his university studies he assisted Prof. Lucien O. Blake in his experiments on submarine telephony and gained the high praise of his teacher for his ingenuity. After his graduation as an electrical engineer in 1892 he went to New York and entered the service of the New York Telephone Company. In 1898 he had occasion to buy a second-hand Roentgen apparatus. He took such an intense interest in the new branch of sciences, foreseeing its great value for medicine and surgery, that he entered the University and Bellevue Hospital Medical College to study medicine, obtaining the degree of M.D. in 1905. In the meantime he had been appointed director of the Edward N. Gibbs Memorial X-Ray Laboratory which post he held until 1908.

He became one of the foremost Roentgenologists of the country. His inventive genius enabled him to make many valuable improvements on the Roentgen apparatus, among which may be mentioned an electrical interrupter, a new induction coil, an X-ray generator with valve tube rectification, a moving grid for the elimination of secondary radiation in Roentgenography, and various types of X-ray tubes. His work also on the Roentgen examination of the nasal accessory sinuses is of permanent value. In collaboration with Wm. A. Pusey he published *The Practical Application of the Roentgen Rays in Therapeutics and Diagnosis* (1903). During the World War he was commissioned major in the Medical Corps. He died a martyr to science. So intense was his application to the X-ray work that he contracted serious injuries which led to his death in 1918.

He was a member of the New York Academy

407

of Medicine; of the College of Physicians and Surgeons, Columbia University; of the Roentgen Ray Society of London; of the German Roentgen Society; and of a number of other scientific societies. He was married in 1913 to Elizabeth Perkins.

[*Am. Jour. of Roentgenology*, Dec. 1918, V, 575; *Am. Jour. of Electrotherapeutics and Radiology*, June 1918; *N. Y. Medic. Jour.*, June 29, 1918; *Jour. of the Am. Medic. Ass.*, June 29, 1918; *Who's Who in America*, 1916–17.]   A. A—n.

CALDWELL, HENRY CLAY (Sept. 4, 1832– Feb. 15, 1915), jurist, was the son of Van and Susan M. Caldwell of Marshall County, Va., where he was born. His father, a well-known frontier character, moved in 1836 to Davis County on the Des Moines River, at that time part of Wisconsin Territory, and Henry passed his youth there, attending the common schools, where he obtained all the education he ever received. He then entered the law office of Wright & Knapp at Keosauqua, Van Buren County, Iowa, and, on his admission to the Iowa bar in 1852 in his twentieth year, became a partner in the firm. In 1856 he was elected prosecuting attorney for Van Buren County. On Mar. 25, 1857, he was married to Harriet Benton. A year later he became a member of the state legislature, acting as chairman of its judiciary committee during two sessions. In 1860 he was a delegate from Iowa to the Republican convention at Chicago which nominated Lincoln for the presidency. On the outbreak of the Civil War he enlisted in the 3rd Iowa Cavalry, was commissioned major, and subsequently became colonel of his regiment, participating in much heavy fighting in the Mississippi Valley. In June 1864, while yet on active service, he was appointed by President Lincoln United States district judge for the District of Arkansas. The situation at that time in the district was a difficult one, the judicial machinery being disorganized and the population sullen and impoverished. In addition, as an aftermath of the war, the volume of litigation was great, most of the cases involving novel and intricate problems, requiring extreme delicacy of treatment. The people of Arkansas viewed Caldwell at first with suspicion, if not aversion, as a Northern soldier and intruder. Displaying, however, great firmness and courage, and resolutely resisting political pressure, he administered justice with scrupulous impartiality, and by his tact, common sense, and expedition gradually obtained the respect and confidence of the populace. It was said of him that "during the six years that the carpet-bag régime lasted he was the greatest protection that the people of the state had," and it was through his

influence that a subsequent attempt in Congress to reimpose repressive conditions was frustrated. He remained district judge for twenty-five years, and was appointed circuit judge for the eighth Federal district in 1890 by President Harrison. He accepted the new position with reluctance as the district extended from Arkansas north to Minnesota and westward to Wyoming, but the creation of the United States circuit court of appeals ultimately enabled him as presiding judge to concentrate his work in St. Louis. In 1896 his name was prominently mentioned in connection with the Republican nomination for president. Four years later he dissociated himself from the party on its stand in relation to the gold standard, but firmly declined an offer of the nomination for vice-president in conjunction with W. J. Bryan. He resigned from the bench in 1903, retiring into private life, and in 1906 went to California where he passed his last days, dying in Los Angeles. His judicial career was distinguished by practical common sense and sturdy independence. He was identified with numerous important reforms in the Arkansas laws, including the introduction of code pleading, the amendment of the "Anaconda mortgage" law, and the state regulation of the liquor traffic. Standing six feet four inches in height, he had a massive head with a broad forehead and a flowing beard. In manner genial, sympathetic, and eminently approachable, he held strong opinions on most subjects and never hesitated to express them in clear, pungent language. His scrupulous honesty of mind and conduct was exemplified in his declining the appointment of chief justice of the United States Supreme Court, offered him by President Cleveland, assigning as a reason his lack of the necessary qualities of training and legal equipment.

[The article "Henry Clay Caldwell" by Edward H. Stiles in *Annals of Iowa*, 3 ser., VIII, 241, contains an excellent summary of Caldwell's judicial activities and the main incidents of his career. See also *Am. Law Rev.*, XXIV, 299, XXX, 282; *Case and Comment*, IV, 133, XXII, 87; and Fay Hempstead, *Hist. Rev. of Ark.* (1911).]   H. W. H. K.

CALDWELL, JAMES (Apr. 1734–Nov. 24, 1781), was a militant clergyman during the Revolutionary War. The family, traditionally of Huguenot origin, had emigrated from Scotland to Ireland, and thence to America, and James Caldwell, son of settler John Caldwell, was born in Charlotte County, Va. He graduated at Princeton in 1759, and was ordained by the presbytery of New Brunswick, N. J., in 1761. He was settled as pastor of the First Presbyterian Church at Elizabethtown (now Elizabeth), N. J.; his congregation included men of unusual prominence, Gov. Livingston, Col. Francis Barber, Boudinot, Dayton, and others. On Mar. 14, 1763 he was married to Hannah Ogden.

Caldwell belonged to the "muscular type" of Christianity. He was an eloquent preacher, and during the war was very active in his patriotism. In 1776 he was appointed chaplain of Dayton's New Jersey brigade, and for a time was assistant commissary-general, with headquarters at Chatham. Rewards were offered, so it is stated, for his capture, and he often went armed. His church was used as a hospital during the war, but on Jan. 25, 1780 it was burned by a refugee. Caldwell's family, meanwhile, on account of exposure to attack had moved to the neighboring village of Connecticut Farms (Union), where on June 7, 1780 Mrs. Caldwell was killed by a random bullet during Knyphausen's invasion. Two weeks later the battle of Springfield took place (June 23) in which Caldwell—often known as the "Soldier Parson"—according to an often repeated story, urged his men to use the hymn-books in the neighboring church as extemporized wadding, exhorting them, "Now put Watts into them, boys." The following year, at Elizabethtown Point, he was shot and killed by an American sentry. The two men were in dispute over a package which Caldwell carried, and various charges were made regarding the sentinel's conduct; he was eventually tried and executed for murder. A monument to the memory of Mr. and Mrs. Caldwell was erected at Elizabeth. Another, in front of the church at Springfield, commemorates the battle and Caldwell's part therein.

[Nicholas Murray, Notes, Hist. and Biog., Concerning Elizabethtown (1844), and "A Memoir of the Rev. Jas. Caldwell," Proc. of the N. J. Hist. Soc., 1848–49; E. Kempshall, Caldwell and the Revolution (1880); Wm. B. Sprague, Annals of the Am. Pulpit, vol. III (1858); Inscriptions on Tombstones . . . of the First Presbyt. Ch. . . . at Elizabeth, N. J. (1892); Jas. F. Folsom, "Manuscript Light on Chaplain Jas. Caldwell's Death," Proc. of the N. J. Hist. Soc., Jan. 1916.]
E. K. A.

CALDWELL, JOSEPH (Apr. 21, 1773–Jan. 27, 1835), mathematician, college president, the youngest of the three children of Joseph Caldwell and Rachel (Harker) Caldwell, was born in Lamington, N. J., two days after his father's death. The family, in somewhat straitened financial circumstances, moved to Princeton when Joseph was eleven years old. There he entered the grammar school which had the personal attention of Dr. John Witherspoon, for several years the distinguished head of the College of New Jersey (Princeton). His early education was interrupted by the removal of the family to Newark and later still to Elizabethtown (now Elizabeth). But in 1787, when Joseph was four-

teen years old, he reëntered the grammar school at Princeton and a few months later entered the college from which he was graduated in the class of 1791 at the age of nineteen. For a short time he taught in a school for young children and later was assistant in an academy. In 1795 he was made a tutor in mathematics in Princeton, and in 1796 he was called to the professorship of mathematics in the University of North Carolina which had opened its doors in 1795. In 1804 he was elected president. In 1812 he retired from the presidency to resume the chair of mathematics in order to devote more time to study and teaching. In 1817 he was induced to resume the chief office of the institution and in that position he continued during the remainder of his life.

In the spring and summer of 1824 he went to Europe to secure philosophical and scientific apparatus and books for the University library. In 1830 he erected, out of his personal funds, for which he was reimbursed by the University trustees a few days before his death, a building in which use could be made of the telescope and other astronomical instruments which he had brought from Europe. This was the first observatory established in connection with any educational institution in the United States. Caldwell's European experience also aroused his imagination and interest on the subject of internal improvements. His very advanced and practical views, which were set out in a series of articles (1828), over the pen name of "Carlton," in which he urged the state to provide transportation facilities, gained for him the name of the "father of internal improvements" in North Carolina.

He was an early and conspicuous advocate of the cause of common schools. In 1832, three years before his death, he published a series of eleven *Letters on Popular Education Addressed to the People of North Carolina*. In these writings he described the backward educational condition of the state which he charged to the "fatal delusion" that taxation was "contrary to the genius of republican government." He criticized the state for its failure to provide schools and suggested plans for public elementary, secondary, and higher education, provisions for the training of teachers, and other features of a modern school system.

He was married twice: in 1804 to Susan Rowan of Fayetteville, who died three years later; and in 1809 to Mrs. Helen (Hogg) Hooper of Hillsboro, the widow of William Hooper, son of one of the signers of the Declaration of Independence. He was an effective teacher and a scientist of wide and disciplined knowledge. In 1813 he served North Carolina as scientific expert in running the boundary line between North Carolina and South Carolina. He was a man of deeply religious nature, had been licensed to preach by the Presbytery of New Brunswick while he was at Princeton, and was an effective if not eloquent preacher. Dignified and often stern in manner, he was described as "strong of arm and swift of foot," capable of inspiring respect and confidence and, in the disorderly, fear. A spirited and militant controversialist, utterly fearless, and a keen analyst, he was often driven into bitter partisan controversies by attacks upon himself or upon the University for alleged aristocratic views or tendencies. A monument to his memory was erected on the campus of the University of North Carolina in 1858.

[See *The Autobiography and Biography of Rev. Jos. Caldwell* (1860); Walker Anderson, *Oration on the Life and Character of the Rev. Jos. Caldwell* (1835); Kemp P. Battle, *Hist. of the Univ. of N. C.* (2 vols., 1907, 1912); Hope Summerell Chamberlain, *Old Days in Chapel Hill* (1926); *Univ. of N. C. Record*, Apr. 1900; *N. C. Univ. Mag.*, May 1844, Mar. 1860; F. P. Venable, "A College President of a Hundred Years Ago," in *Univ. of N. C. Record*, Apr. 1911; C. A. Smith, "Presbyterians in Educational Work in N. C. since 1813," in *Union Seminary Rev.*, Dec. 1913, Jan. 1914. Caldwell's *Letters on Popular Education* were reprinted in Chas. L. Coon, *The Beginnings of Public Education in N. C.*, vol. II (1908), and are treated briefly by Edgar W. Knight in *Public School Education in N. C.* (1916). Some of his sermons were printed in Colin McIver, *The Southern Preacher* (1824). His *Compendious System of Elementary Geometry* was published in 1822. The manuscript of his *A New System of Geometry* (1806) is in the Univ. of N. C. Lib.]

E. W. K.

CALEF, ROBERT (1648–Apr. 13, 1719), Boston merchant, writer and disputant on the subject of witchcraft, was probably born in England. By 1688 he was settled as a cloth merchant in Boston where he came into prominence in 1693 by accusing Cotton Mather of attempting to stir up a Boston witchcraft delusion in the wake of the Salem tragedy. Calef obtained a copy of "Another Brand Pluckt out of the Burning," Cotton Mather's manuscript account of his efforts to exorcise Margaret Rule, and circulated his own observations concerning the seance, containing unsavory insinuations as to Mather's, and his father's, motives and methods. Cotton Mather caused Calef to be arrested for libel, but dropped the case after receiving a temperate but ambiguous explanation. Calef incorporated "Another Brand," with the correspondence, in a book called *More Wonders of the Invisible World*, which he completed in 1697, but was unable to induce any Boston printer to publish. It was printed in London, in 1700, and caused a great sensation in Boston, for it not only at-

tacked the Mathers, but included a well-documented and devastating account of the Salem trials of 1692. A committee of Cotton Mather's congregation replied in a pamphlet, *Some Few Remarks upon a Scandalous Book* (1701). Increase Mather caused a copy of *More Wonders* to be burned in the Harvard yard.

The controversy between the partisans of Calef and of the Mathers has never ceased. William F. Poole, for instance, declares that Calef was only stirring the ashes of a dead fire, with the purpose of maligning the Boston clergy (*Memorial History of Boston*, 1882, II, 165 ff.), whilst Charles W. Upham asserts, "Calef's book . . . drove the Devil out of the preaching, the literature, and the popular sentiment of the world" (*Salem Witchcraft and Cotton Mather*, 1869, p. 83). The truth no doubt lies between these extremes. That *More Wonders* was a direct and powerful condemnation of the seventeenth century view of witchcraft, written in terms to arouse the most intellectually inert, there can be no doubt. That Cotton Mather failed to reply is significant.

Calef was not a rationalist. He rested his arguments on the Bible, and admitted "That there are Witches . . . but what this witchcraft is, or wherein it does consist, seems to be the whole difficulty." Yet this common basis of thought with his contemporaries made his book the more powerful. One may, however, admit that *More Wonders* occupies an important place in the literature of witchcraft, without sharing Calef's opinion of his opponents. Their counter charges that his motives were political, and that he was assisted in writing the book, have never been substantiated. There is no reason to question his declared motive of discrediting the doctrines that produced the Salem tragedy; and he succeeded, completely.

A persistent belief that *More Wonders* is the work of Robert Calef, Jr. (1676?–1722?) was effectually refuted by George Lincoln Burr. This younger Calef, who generally signed himself Calfe, was one of eight children. The father in later life held several town offices in Boston and Roxbury, where he died on Apr. 13, 1719. The son held several petty offices in Boston.

[*More Wonders*. There are six editions after the first (of which there were two impressions), the best being contained in S. G. Drake, *Annals of the Witchcraft* (3 vols., 1866), and in G. L. Burr, *Narratives of the Witchcraft Cases* (1914), which includes a critical discussion of the question of authorship. See also W. S. Harris, "Robert Calef," *Granite Mo.*, May 1907.] R. L. P.

CALHOUN, JOHN (Oct. 14, 1806–Oct. 13, 1859), politician, was best known for his friendship with Lincoln and his reputed complicity in election abuses in early Kansas. He has sometimes been confused with the John Calhoun (1808–59) who founded the *Chicago Democrat*. Born in Boston, the son of Andrew and Martha (Chamberlin) Calhoun, he studied law in New York state, and settled in 1830 at Springfield, Ill. On Dec. 29, 1831, he was married to Sarah Cutter of Sangamon County, by whom he had nine children. He served in the Black Hawk war and became surveyor of Sangamon County. Being attracted to Lincoln, he assisted him in the study of surveying and made him his deputy, thus forming a friendship which, in spite of Calhoun's prominence as a Douglas Democrat, persisted through life. He was elected to the Illinois legislature in 1838; was made clerk of the Illinois House of Representatives (1839–40 and 1840–41); engaged in the business of constructing a railroad from Jacksonville to Springfield; served as clerk of the circuit court of Sangamon County; and was thrice chosen mayor of Springfield. In contests for Congress, for the state Senate, and for the Democratic gubernatorial nomination, he was unsuccessful. At a state fair at Springfield in October 1854 he joined in a debate in which Lincoln and Douglas were also participants; and Lincoln always had a high regard for his ability as a stump speaker. Through the influence of Douglas, Calhoun was appointed in 1854 by President Pierce as surveyor general of Kansas and Nebraska. He attended the constitutional convention of 1857 at Lecompton as delegate, and was made president of that body. At first he led the fight to have the Lecompton Constitution submitted to the people; but, failing in this, he acquiesced in the program by which the vote of Dec. 21, 1857, was so taken as virtually to deny the ballot to free-state men, and his report of this vote, transmitted to Buchanan, produced a crisis in the Kansas situation. When in 1858 the legislature, then in free-state hands, ordered an investigation concerning alleged frauds in the December election, Calhoun left for Missouri, and his clerk, L. A. McLean, asserted that he had taken the election returns with him. A melodramatic scene followed when a sheriff found the coveted papers where McLean had concealed them, in a candle box buried under a woodpile near the surveyor's office in Lecompton. So intense was the popular indignation that McLean fled, and President Buchanan accommodated Calhoun by removing his office to Nebraska City, as he could not have returned to Kansas. Much of the odium for the Lecompton Constitution was visited upon Calhoun; and he was censured by Gov. Walker when testifying before a committee of Congress. In a vindication by his brother, A. H. Calhoun

(manuscript, cited in *Transactions of the Kansas State Historical Society*, VIII, 1–2) the blame for the candle-box episode is placed upon McLean; and Calhoun is represented as a conservative who opposed the design of the Southern element to fasten slavery upon Kansas in the face of a preponderant free-state sentiment. Calhoun died at St. Joseph, Mo., Oct. 13, 1859, much broken in spirit.

[See G. A. Crawford, "The Candle-Box under the Wood-Pile," *Trans. Kan. Hist. Soc.*, X, 196–204; John Carroll Power, *Hist. of the Early Settlers of Sangamon County, Ill.* (1876), a somewhat inaccurate volume; "The Covode Investigation," *House Report No. 648*, 36 Cong., 1 Sess.; A. J. Beveridge, *Abraham Lincoln, 1809–58* (1928); Paul M. Angle, "The Minor Collection: A Criticism," *Atlantic Mo.* 143:516–25 (Apr. 1929). In the article by Mr. Angle certain supposed Lincoln documents published in the *Atlantic Mo.* (1928–29), including alleged letters from Lincoln to Calhoun, are shown to be forgeries; and "Sally Calhoun" (supposed daughter of John), who is represented as one of the links in the transmittal of the reputed Lincoln material to posterity, is proved never to have existed.]   J.G.R.

CALHOUN, JOHN CALDWELL (Mar. 18, 1782–Mar. 31, 1850), was secretary of war, vice-president, senator, secretary of state, and political philosopher. Three Scotch-Irish brothers Colquhoun, Colhoun or Calhoun, in the unstable spelling of the time, entered Pennsylvania about 1733, and moved southward by stages. By 1746 one of them, James, was dwelling with Catherine his wife, four sons and a daughter in Bath County on the Virginia frontier. Driven thence by the Indian disorders after Braddock's defeat, this family and some of its kinsfolk founded the "Calhoun settlement" in the South Carolina uplands near the Savannah River. James appears to have died in peace, but Catherine was killed by a party of Cherokees in 1760 at a spot which her youngest son Patrick marked with a slab. The four sons clung to their steadings through foul times and fair, supporting the American cause against Great Britain and attaining considerable repute. Patrick in particular was for many years a member of the South Carolina legislature. As a pronounced individualist in political philosophy, he opposed the ratification of the Federal Constitution. Having lost a first wife without surviving issue, he married Martha Caldwell and by her had a daughter and four sons, of whom the youngest but one was named for an uncle whom Tories had murdered, John Caldwell.

After a normal childhood in a family prosperous enough to possess a score or two of slaves when slaves were few in that primitive region, the youth went in his fourteenth year to become a pupil of his brother-in-law, the talented Moses Waddel, in Columbia County, Ga. But Mrs. Waddel's death soon caused the academy to suspend, and young Calhoun returned home, where his father's death in the same year, 1796, cast some of the burdens of the farm upon him. Here he continued at work and at play till the turn of the century. Then an elder brother, who was in business at Charleston, prompted him to prepare for a profession. John returned for a time to Waddel's academy, then entered the junior class at Yale College, graduated in 1804, studied law in Tapping Reeve's school at Litchfield, Conn., and in Henry W. DeSaussure's office at Charleston, was admitted to the bar in 1807, and opened an office at Abbeville near his native home. Though quickly acquiring a substantial practise, he found the pursuit uncongenial and resolved to abandon it as soon as opportunity should permit. This came within a few years through his marriage and his entrance into public life.

John Ewing Calhoun, cousin of Patrick, had attained wealth and distinction in the South Carolina lowlands, partly through his marriage to Floride Bouneau, who inherited from her Huguenot family a plantation on Cooper River. After her husband's death in 1802, the widow continued a practise, fairly common among grandees of the "rice coast," of spending the summers at Newport and the winters at Charleston or on the plantation. John C. Calhoun became a protégé of hers and an intimate of her household. Friendship with her daughter Floride, who was ten years his junior, ripened into love which led to a happy marriage in January 1811. His bride brought him a modest fortune, which, because of his objection to the lowland custom of marriage settlements, was put under his control. This property when added to his own patrimony and savings made Calhoun financially independent, though the increase of his family (nine children all told) kept a degree of frugality expedient. Calhoun enlarged his landholdings and in 1825 established a commodious plantation homestead in his native district. Named "Fort Hill" from its having been a fortified spot in days of Indian warfare, the dwelling still stands on what is now the campus of Clemson College.

Calhoun's interest in public affairs doubtless began at his father's knee, and his Republicanism was intensified by his encounters with Federalists during his years at New Haven and Litchfield. His own political career began in 1807 with a speech at a public meeting in Abbeville denouncing British aggressions upon American maritime rights. In the next year he was elected to the South Carolina legislature, in time to share in the revision of representation to give numerical preponderance in the lower house to the uplands of the state while the control of the Senate was left with the lowlands. This device

of "concurrent majorities" or mutual checks was one which he was eventually to propose for the relief of sectional apprehensions in the United States. But at the time of his election to Congress in 1810, and for long thereafter, his federal program had quite another direction.

Calhoun's service in national halls began with the convening of the Twelfth Congress which the "war hawks" were to make famous. Regardless of consequences in Europe and impatient of opposition from New England, these young men were resolute for war with Britain. Clay as speaker made the most effective use of the copious talent available in committee assignments, and Calhoun soon became acting chairman of the committee on foreign affairs. After months of labor to gain a favorable majority in the House, he presented on June 3, 1812, a report in ringing phrase recommending a declaration of war. Since James Monroe's authorship of this (*American Historical Review*, XIII, 309, 310) was kept secret, the episode spread Calhoun's fame afar.

As long as the war continued he wrought constantly to raise troops, to provide funds, to speed the service of supply, to improve the currency, to regulate commerce, to do everything in short which he thought conducive to military success. Disasters to American arms made him double his legislative efforts to wring victory from defeat. He was in the thick of every important debate, laboring to overcome the obstructionism of Randolph and Webster alike but occasionally separating himself from the bulk of his customary associates to find other allies wherever he might. A. J. Dallas called him, in happy phrase, "the young Hercules who carried the war on his shoulders."

Calhoun was sufficiently a supporter of the administration to indorse the treaty of Ghent; but its inconclusive character as concerned the issues which had provoked the war gave him an expectation that the peace would prove but a truce and left him with a continued zeal for promoting American strength. In a speech of Jan. 31, 1816, he advocated as the first consideration an effective navy, including steam frigates, and in the second place a standing army of adequate size; and as further preparation for emergency "great permanent roads," "a certain encouragement" to manufactures, and a system of internal taxation which would not be subject like customs duties to collapse by a war-time shrinkage of maritime trade (*Works*, II, 135–53). In the further course of the session he spoke for a national bank and again for internal improvements and protective tariff, deprecating sectional spirit and "refined arguments on the constitution" (*Works*, II, 191,

192), and asserting his own preference for "that erectness of mind which in all cases is disposed to embrace what is in itself just and wise." There can be no doubt that in this period Calhoun's early Republicanism in so far as it connoted allegiance to state rights was in eclipse. The word "nation" was often on his lips, and his conscious aim was to enhance national unity which he identified with national power.

Calhoun was at this time described as "the most elegant speaker that sits in the House. . . . His gestures are easy and graceful, his manner forcible, and language elegant; but above all, he confines himself closely to the subject, which he always understands, and enlightens everyone within hearing; having said all that a statesman should say, he is done" (letter of J. C. Jewett, in *William and Mary Quarterly*, XVII, 143). His talent for public speaking seems to have been acquired by systematic effort. A later critic, remarking the sharp contrast between his talking and speaking tones, said that Calhoun "had so carefully cultivated his naturally poor voice as to make his utterance clear, full, and distinct in speaking and while not at all musical it yet fell pleasantly on the ear" (H. S. Fulkerson, *Random Recollections of Early Days in Mississippi*, 1885, p. 63).

But his power in debate did not incline Calhoun to remain always in legislative halls. Before the end of his third term in Congress he accepted appointment as secretary of war in Monroe's cabinet. His conspicuous concern with military affairs made him an obvious choice for this post; and during the seven and a half years of his tenure he discharged its functions with marked capacity, improving the organization of the army in general and establishing in particular the useful bureaux of the surgeon-general, commissary-general, and quartermaster-general.

In the cabinet Crawford and Calhoun were in habitual disagreement, but Adams and he were for some years in close accord. As late as the fall of 1821 Adams wrote in his diary: "Calhoun is a man of fair and candid mind, of honorable principles, of clear and quick understanding, of cool self-possession, of enlarged philosophical views, and of ardent patriotism. He is above all sectional and factious prejudices, more than any other statesman of this Union with whom I have ever acted" (Adams, *Memoirs*, V, 361). But with the Federalist party dead and Monroe reëlected for a final term in the presidency there now began a free-for-all race for the succession. Crawford was the candidate of the reviving state-rights school now styled Radicals; Adams and Clay, Lowndes and Calhoun became rivals for the leadership of the nationalists; while Jackson turned from military to civilian campaigning as the candidate of those who were more interested in popular power than with details of policy. The homes of these candidates lay in an arc reaching from Massachusetts through Kentucky and Tennessee to Georgia and South Carolina. The choice among them must needs lie with the states of the middle seaboard. Lowndes's death left Calhoun the favorite son of his state; Pennsylvania for a while gave promise of support because of his advocacy of tariff protection, and he had hopes also of New York and some lesser states. But the nominating convention in Pennsylvania gave its indorsement to Jackson for the first office and to Calhoun for the second. Thereupon Calhoun lowered his ambition for the time being and was elected vice-president in 1824 by a large majority. For the presidency Jackson had a plurality in the electoral college, but Clay's influence gave Adams the victory at the hands of the House of Representatives. Adams's appointment of Clay as secretary of state in sequel to this gave Jackson a mighty grudge, spurred Randolph to seek new epithets, and caused Calhoun to remark that it created a most dangerous precedent which the people would presumably reprove at the next election (*Correspondence*, p. 231).

In presiding over the Senate Calhoun was meticulous, attending assiduously but confining his participation within the positive specifications of the Constitution. His abstinence from interrupting Randolph's vituperations of Adams and Clay, except when a senator raised a point of order, involved him in a newspaper controversy in which the president himself was his putative opponent. Another episode of some salience arose from a journalist's charge that Calhoun while secretary of war had participated in the profits of a fortification contract. Calhoun asked the House of Representatives to investigate the matter as a "grand inquest of the nation," and he discontinued his attendance upon the Senate until a House committee had cleared him. Conspicuously cherishing his repute, he was shaping his course for the White House, though the Adams-Jackson battle clearly postponed the goal for him for another quadrennium. For the time being he chose the Jackson alliance and was elected in 1828 on the Jackson ticket for a second term as vice-president. His hope now was to succeed to the presidency after a single term of Jackson.

But the next four years brought events great and small which impinged heavily upon Calhoun's career and upon the course of American history. Jackson's predilection for Van Buren whom he put at the head of the cabinet was itself ominous; and Eaton's appointment as secretary of war, followed by his indiscreet marriage and Mrs. Calhoun's exclusion of his wife from social recognition, brought a strain between the President and Vice-President. Close upon this came Crawford's betrayal of the fact that in Monroe's cabinet in 1818 Calhoun had censured the capture of Spanish posts by Jackson during his campaign against the Seminoles. Jackson's egotistic sense of outrage now produced a breach which Calhoun found irreparable.

Meanwhile developments in South Carolina, which for some years had followed an ominous course, were producing a national crisis. Successive measures in Congress enhancing and proposing further enhancement of protection to favored industries caused increasingly stringent opposition, coming as they did in a decade of declining cotton prices. By the middle of the twenties this opposition movement was spreading widely in the South and was becoming linked with a denial of the constitutional power of Congress in the premises. Calhoun was an object of censure in anti-tariff publications because of his formerly conspicuous and still unrecanted protectionism. He confronted a grave dilemma. If he held his course South Carolina would repudiate him, and if he changed it he would lose his following in Pennsylvania. But his personal fortunes, whether as a cotton planter or a presidential aspirant, were of smaller concern than the national prospect. Early in 1827 he defeated the Woollens Bill by his casting vote in the Senate; and before the end of the year he was deprecating the project of a higher-tariff convention as tending to place the great geographical interests in hostile array, to promote political plundering, and eventually "to make two of one nation." He was now finding it "a great defect of our system; that the separate geographical interests are not sufficiently guarded." But these reflections were expressed only in a confidential letter (*Correspondence*, pp. 250, 251). At the beginning of the next year he joined in a jockeying project to divide the eastern and western groups of protectionists to the defeat of both; but the plan was thwarted by Van Buren and the result was the "tariff of abominations" (*Works*, III, 48–51).

During the congressional recess of 1828, which Calhoun spent as usual at his plantation home, he painstakingly informed himself of the South Carolina situation. He was already acquainted with the legislature's resolutions of 1825 and 1827 denying the constitutionality of protective tariffs and with the turbulent writings of Thomas Cooper, R. J. Turnbull, and sundry others. Reaching now the conviction that without mitigation

of grievances desperate recourses were in train, he complied with a request of W. C. Preston and wrote a report for a committee of the legislature. The result, modified by the committee, was the "South Carolina Exposition" (*Works*, VI, 1–57), embodying the doctrine which was to become famous as nullification. After asserting the unconstitutionality of the protective tariff and maintaining the power of a state within its own area to estop the enforcement of an unconstitutional act, the document concluded by recommending that decisive steps be deferred in the hope that reflection by the people and Congress might bring abandonment of the obnoxious policy. The legislature ordered the report printed in a large edition, and it adopted resolutions asking the sister states to express their sentiments in the premises. The Exposition was a warning of what might be done should the protectionist program be pursued. Its promulgation did not commit the state to a course of action; and in particular it committed Calhoun to nothing, for he kept his authorship confidential until the middle of 1831.

Having thus devised a plan for use in a contingency, Calhoun sought in various ways to prevent the contingency from coming. For a while he pinned his faith to Jackson; then he nursed a project for a complete intersectional accord. The West, by a constitutional amendment, was to be given a great public-land fund for internal improvements; the South was to procure a reduction of the tariff in the main to a revenue basis; but the North was to be placated by sundry special tariff concessions (*American Historical Review*, VI, 741–45, conversation reported by J. H. Hammond). But events proceeded otherwise. The systematically protective tariff of 1832 was enacted by Congress and approved by Jackson in July, whereupon Calhoun hastened home to guide proceedings there.

In August he published his famous letter to Gov. Hamilton (*Works*, VI, 144–93), containing the final embodiment of nullification doctrine. This is a superb piece of rigorous reasoning. Premising the possession of sovereignty by the people and the trustee character of all governments, and asserting that in the American federal system the central and state governments alike are mere organs of popular power, it argued, on the basis of the records of the Federal Convention, that "with us *the people* mean *the people of the several states*," whose delegates and conventions framed and ratified the Constitution creating the general government as their common agent. The ratification by any state bound all its citizens to obey the Constitution although some of them might individually have opposed it. The purpose of any constitution is at once to empower and to restrain the government; and if the general government should exceed its powers against the will of the people of a state it is within their legitimate power, by means of a convention though not by act of the legislature, to declare the congressional act null and to require the state government to prohibit enforcement within the limits of the state. "It is the constitution that annuls an unconstitutional act. Such an act is itself void and of no effect." Any court may proclaim such nullity, but the people of a state retain a similar power which no federal agency may override. Indeed, the general government in all its branches must acquiesce in such declaration of nullity, so far as enforcement within the state is concerned; or, as an escape, it may apply to the states to obtain a grant of the disputed power in the form of an amendment to the Constitution. But if the amendment should fail of ratification, "no alternative would remain for the general government but a compromise or its permanent abandonment." Nullification would give no ground for clash of arms; it would be "a conflict of moral, and not physical force," a trial before courts and juries. The rights of nullification and secession inhere in the sovereign states; but the two programs are poles apart in their purposes and effects. The object of secession is to withdraw a member from the Union; while the object of nullification is to confine the general government within its prescribed limits of power in order to perpetuate the Union on an equable basis. Nullification may indeed be followed by secession in case a proposed amendment should be ratified by the sister states to such effect as to defeat the object of the Union so far as the nullifying member is concerned. The power of nullification, it is true, tends to weaken the general government; but the power of amendment is an adequate offset. The two powers establish a system of mutual checks, in effect a system of government requiring agreement by concurrent majorities in critical issues, and as such it is in the line which genuinely free institutions have followed ever since the Tribunate in ancient Rome. Such a system, which inheres in the Federal Constitution as thus interpreted, maintains "the ascendency of the constitution-making authority over the law-making—the concurring over the absolute majority." It maintains a power, essential for liberty and the general welfare, "to compel the parts of society to be just to one another by compelling them to consult the interest of one another."

Affairs now marched rapidly. A legislature was elected in South Carolina with an over-

whelming majority favorable to nullification; this was called into special session and in turn it ordered the election of delegates to a convention of the state; the convention adopted an ordinance nullifying the tariff acts of 1828 and 1832; and the legislature thereupon enacted sundry laws to make the ordinance effective. Thus by the beginning of December 1832 the schedule was complete, though by its own terms the ordinance was not to take effect until the first day of February following.

December brought a battle of proclamations between President Jackson and the governor of South Carolina, and a mustering of military forces. But these things had somewhat of a sham character, for the concrete issue was the tariff, which could only be handled by Congress. In the Senate R. Y. Hayne had proved not letter-perfect in the nullification doctrine, and he was now shifted to the governor's chair to make room for Calhoun who resigned the vice-presidency and appeared on the floor of the Senate at the turn of the year. Jackson soon sent a message to Congress asking to be empowered in case of need to use armed force to execute the laws. A bill introduced in response, commonly known as the Force Bill, brought Calhoun into debate with Webster in which he opposed argument to eloquence with better effect than Hayne had done two years before. Meanwhile Calhoun joined hands with Clay in support of a tariff bill to reduce duties by degrees and put the customs on a revenue basis at the end of a decade. This bill, which repealed the tariff act of 1832, was passed and became law on the same day as the Force Bill.

In South Carolina an informal meeting of the leading nullifiers had postponed the effectuation of the ordinance, and Gov. Hayne had called a second meeting of the convention for Mar. 11, 1833. Calhoun hastened to Columbia to persuade the members to accept the compromise tariff as a settlement of the essential issue. B. W. Leigh as commissioner from Virginia to South Carolina aided these efforts; and the convention repealed the ordinance nullifying the tariff but adopted another nullifying the Force Bill. Thus every one saved his face. The result of the contretemps as a whole was in South Carolina the virtual destruction of Calhoun's opponents and an eclipse of his own lieutenants; in the United States an alignment of new parties with Calhoun holding himself and South Carolina somewhat aloof from both.

For some years the advocates of Clay's "American system" had maintained a rudimentary organization as National Republicans to oppose the administration. And now state-rights adherents in many Southern states reacted so strongly against Jackson's proclamation and the Force Bill that they were disposed to embrace an alliance against the President. Hence the coalition in the middle thirties to form the Whig party opposing the Democratic. It was under this régime that the final phase of Calhoun's career took form. In sequel to the recent clash he retained his repugnance toward Jackson and his favorites. At the same time he distrusted Clay and held Webster in low esteem except for oratory, and he was not disposed to make a "choice of evils" (*Correspondence*, p. 330). He revived his presidential ambitions ere long and acted as an auxiliary of the Whigs. But no sooner was Jackson succeeded in the White House by the mild-mannered Van Buren than Calhoun began to shift to the Democratic side. In the Senate he was constantly attentive to the public business; and whatever were his views upon banking, public lands, or foreign relations, he voiced them in a manner which proved his concern with sound government for the whole country. The growth of his prestige gave him a following in all parts of the South and rehabilitated him in many Northern quarters. But the rise of the abolition agitation made impossible for him any return to nationalistic paths.

In the premises of negro slavery the South was more conspicuously marked as a distinct community with a minority status than in regard to the tariff; and the menace of a hostile domination was reckoned to involve not mere shrinkage of income but destruction of capital and a precipitation of social chaos. Organization and strategy were widely demanded in Southern defense, and Calhoun came to be regarded as the main source of plans, arguments, and inspiration. His devices were manifold: to suppress agitation, to praise the slaveholding system; to promote Southern prosperity and expansion; to procure a Western alliance; to frame a fresh plan of government by concurrent majorities; to form a Southern bloc; to warn the North of the dangers of Southern desperation; to appeal for Northern magnanimity as indispensable for the saving of the Union. A devoted lieutenant, Dixon H. Lewis of Alabama, wrote in 1840: "Calhoun is now my principal associate, and he is too intellectual, too industrious, too intent in the struggle of politics to suit me except as an occasional companion. There is no relaxation in him. On the contrary, when I seek relaxation in him, he screws me only the higher in some sort of excitement" (Hunt, *Calhoun*, p. 228).

Was the conflict irrepressible? Calhoun feared it might prove so, but he hoped and labored unceasingly to find means for its avoidance. If he turned again and again to formulæ, that was the ingrained bent of his mind. He could never consent to mere "muddling through."

Reluctantly he faced the slavery issue. In 1815 he had expressed shame at the record of South Carolina in having caused the Constitution to forbid for twenty years any congressional prohibition of the foreign slave trade (*Works*, II, 133). In 1820 the stringency of debate on the Missouri question caused him to remark that he could "scarcely conceive of a cause of sufficient power to divide this Union, unless a belief in the slaveholding states, that it is the intention of the other states gradually to undermine their property in their slaves and that a disunion is the only means to avert the evil. Should so dangerous a mode of believing once take root, no one can calculate the consequences" (Hunt, *Calhoun*, p. 54). In the next year he expressed relief at the prospect "that a question which has so deeply agitated this country will be settled forever" (*Correspondence*, p. 181). But Garrison's work revived his apprehensions and set his feet upon their final path. At the close of his debate with Webster in February 1833, he said that slavery might give the South greater reason than the tariff to cherish state-rights.

Within the next two years the increase of anti-slavery activities and a turbulent counter-agitation in the South determined him to meet the issue "on the frontier"; and he became the most thoroughgoing advocate of the exclusion of incendiary publications from the mails and of anti-slavery petitions from Congress. His own devices in these premises were too technical to procure much indorsement, though the essential purposes were attained for the time being by other means. There was virtually no Southern dissent from his declaration in 1836 that abolition "strikes directly and fatally, not only at our prosperity, but our existence as a people. . . . The door must be closed against all interference on the part of the general government in any form, whether in the District of Columbia, or in the states or territories. The highest grounds are the safest" (*Niles' Weekly Register*, L, 432).

By the next year he had followed Governors Miller and McDuffie of South Carolina and the Rev. James Smylie of Mississippi toward asserting that slavery was a positive good: "Our fate, as a people, is bound up in the question. If we yield we will be extirpated; but if we successfully resist, we will be the greatest and most flourishing people of modern time. It is the best substratum of population in the world; and one on which great and flourishing Commonwealths may be most easily and safely reared" (*Corre-*

spondence, p. 369; see also *Works,* III, 179, 180). And by 1838 he was even contemplating a separation of the Union, though resolved still to labor for less drastic programs (*Correspondence,* p. 391).

The issue, ramifying endlessly, involved the mathematics of equilibrium in the Senate, the admission of new states, the organization of territories as prospective states, and the cherishing of sectional prestige for the sake of morale. In premises which he considered unessential Calhoun deprecated controversy. Thus he suppressed a movement in South Carolina to nullify the tariff of 1842; and on sundry other matters he was conciliatory in this period when his hopes were high for the presidency through a Democratic nomination. But in the main, and upon every issue which he thought vital, he was disposed to force the fighting, to lead a campaign of aggressive defense of "Southern rights."

He had spoken in favor of the annexation of Texas immediately after the battle of San Jacinto in 1836. But his assertions from the outset that the slaveholding states had a special interest in the question operated rather to delay than to speed the achievement. At length A. P. Upshur, secretary of state under Tyler, negotiated a treaty; and upon Upshur's death a maneuver by H. A. Wise carried Calhoun into that office to complete the proceedings. In the department Calhoun found a note from Mr. Pakenham communicating a dispatch from Lord Aberdeen to the effect that the British government desired to see slavery abolished in Texas and throughout the world, but that it had no purpose to disturb the domestic tranquillity of the slaveholding states of the Union. Calhoun seized the occasion to write and publish a reply to Pakenham saying that abolition in Texas would necessarily impinge upon the domestic security of the states adjacent, and proceeding to praise negro slavery in terms even stronger than he had previously used (*Works,* II, 333–339). This again was bad strategy. The treaty was defeated in the Senate by anti-slavery votes; and only after months of further delay was annexation accomplished by joint resolution of Congress.

Where Calhoun sat in cabinet, there was the head of the table. In this Tyler acquiesced; but Polk, wishing to be chief of his own administration, did not invite Calhoun to continue in office. Most of the year 1845 was accordingly spent by the latter in private life, though not without participation in public projects. He had long desired to see a system of railroads linking the West with the South, preferably a connection from Charleston across Georgia as against Hayne's plan of piercing the Blue Ridge in a line to Cincinnati. As a culmination of similar meetings, a large railroad and waterway convention was held at Memphis in November which Calhoun was persuaded to attend as a delegate from South Carolina. After a journey signalized by thronged public entertainment at every stopping-place, he was chosen to preside over the sessions. The address he delivered urged his railroad program and in addition argued that Congress had constitutional power to improve the navigation of the Mississippi because the Father of Waters, washing the shores of many states, was virtually an inland sea. The splitting of a logical hair seemed expedient in behalf of the desired alliance of sections.

This interlude was abbreviated by a summons once more into the public service. With war clouds lowering on two horizons, Calhoun was urgently needed in the national councils. D. F. Huger willingly resigned his seat in the Senate, and the legislature elected Calhoun unanimously to fill the vacancy. Arrived in Washington, his positions on the Oregon and Texas boundary questions proved much alike, for he advocated conciliation toward both Great Britain and Mexico. The Oregon issue resulted as he wished; but to his dismay and against his vehement opposition, the war with Mexico was precipitated.

Wilmot's proposal to prohibit slavery in all areas to be acquired by this war set Calhoun to spinning his last fine theory and involved him in the most desperate of his struggles. Aware as he was that the region was unsuited to plantation industry and slave labor (*The Diary of James K. Polk,* 1910, II, 283–84), he took the Proviso to be a gratuitous affront to the South, an index of aggressive disposition by Northern Democrats, and a culminating ground of Southern apprehension. To make state sovereignty applicable he framed a new series of syllogisms: that all territories were an estate owned by the states in common, to be administered by the central government only as a trustee for them; that any citizen of any state had full right to emigrate to any territory, carrying with him whatever property he possessed in his own state, and was entitled to Federal protection in the enjoyment of that property in his new home until the community should itself become a state. Therefore, whether his migration be to California, New Mexico, or Oregon, no slaveholder could be debarred from the transport and continued use of his slaves (*Works,* IV, 344–49). In short, notwithstanding the precedents of the ordinance of 1787 and the Missouri Compromise act, which he now considered erroneous, Congress was estopped from restricting the spread of slaveholding. He was perhaps willing to be outvoted in the organization of Oregon if he could carry his point as concerned the more southerly regions; but a sense that this hope was forlorn drove him to two devices which he had held somewhat in reserve. For permanent purposes he sped his pen to complete his treatises on government in general and the Federal Constitution in particular; and to meet the present exigency he strove to rouse and organize the South with a view to its issue of an ultimatum.

His treatises, destined to have only a posthumous publication, embodied his final philosophy. In the "Disquisition on Government" (*Works*, I, 1–107) he declares that society is essential to mankind, and government necessary to preserve and perfect society by curbing individual selfishness. But government itself must be held in check by constitutions in order that public agents may be prevented from abusing their power whether by self-aggrandizement or by promoting majority interests through the spoliation of minorities. The problem here, he said, is extremely difficult. No plan devised abstractly can suffice, but a satisfactory system can arise only as the product of an intelligent community seeking in the light of experience to meet its own conscious needs. On the one hand authority must be adequate to meet external emergencies by summoning the whole strength of the community. In domestic affairs, on the other hand, apparatus must be available by which minorities may compel majorities to compromise issues between them. That the two requirements are not mutually exclusive is shown by the common success of the jury system in forcing unanimous verdicts and by the long duration of the Polish Kingdom despite the possession of a veto by every member of its Diet. Far better designed, however, and therefore more lasting, were the constitutions of ancient Rome and modern England embodying less extreme examples of automatic check upon authority. The elements of aristocracy and monarchy embodied in them were wholesome in correcting the tendency of numerical majorities to tyrannize; but such elements are not indispensable, for a democracy may combine equity with efficiency if it avoid the "great and dangerous error" of considering all people equally entitled to liberty and if at the same time it maintain government by concurrent majorities and avoid the demagogic tendency and the despotic proclivities inherent in control by mere numbers.

In the "Discourse on the Constitution and Government of the United States" these lessons are given specific application, but in a tone of argument rather than of exposition. With elaborate citation of eighteenth-century records he contends that the American system is in no sense national, but purely federal. The people of the several states ordained alike their separate state governments and the general government. "Deriving their respective powers . . . from the same source, . . . the two governments, State and Federal, must, of necessity be equal in their respective spheres" (*Works*, I, 167). Sovereignty, which is indivisible, remains in the people of the several states; but the exercise of "the powers of sovereignty" may be distributed and have actually been divided between the two agencies. To make it efficient the central government was clothed with the attribute of deciding, in the first instance, on the extent of its powers (*Works*, I, 168); but the people of any state may challenge any assumption of undelegated authority in order to preserve the equilibrium of the complex system. The sectionalizing of interests or policies in the Union has made it imperative upon the South as the minority to oppose the concentration of despotic force. Calhoun's contentions of 1832, though he repeats them, now seem to him inefficacious in view of the progress of unconstitutional centralization in the interim. He, therefore, concludes that the domestic tranquillity of the South can be secured and the Union perpetuated only by a new device. To this end he advocates an amendment to the Constitution to replace the single president by a dual executive, each of the two chief magistrates to be chosen by one of the great sections of the country, and the assent of both to be requisite for the validation of acts of Congress (*Works*, I, 392–95).

These writings had influence upon political thought and projects not only at home but in the German Confederation (C. E. Merriam in *Studies in Southern History and Politics*, 1914, p. 336). The North in one case and Prussia in the other were quite unconvinced; but Lord Acton echoed Calhoun by saying that liberty can only be safeguarded by a multiplicity of checks— and the conversion of the British Empire into a "commonwealth of nations" has given practical embodiment to the precepts of decentralization.

But the current crisis could not be solved by a dissertation even if it had been ready for the press. Convinced as he was that the existing political parties were so constituted that the control of both must lie in the North and be used for Southern injury, Calhoun summoned a meeting, in January 1849, of the Southern senators and congressmen to consider an address which he had written for their adoption. This reviewed the history of the slavery issue, foretold disaster from the continuance of the existing scheme of politics, and called for unity in holding Southern rights paramount over party allegiance. The prophecy in this document was amazingly corroborated within two decades; abolition by a dominant North against Southern resistance; hatred between the whites of the two sections; enfranchisement of the negroes and a party union between them and the North to hold the Southern whites in subjection; a carnival of profligacy and a bottomless degradation (*Works*, VI, 310–11). But most of the members attending were unconvinced, and a mere minority signed the address for issue to their constituents. Calhoun next turned to local committees and newspaper agitation to procure a call from some commonwealth for a convention of the slave-holding states, and was rejoiced when Mississippi responded and the convention was scheduled to meet at Nashville (*Correspondence*, pp. 765–79).

Before the end of the year an irregular convention in California applied for statehood with a constitution excluding slavery. This met Calhoun's trenchant opposition on the grounds that the proceedings had not been authorized by an enabling act, and that their validation would at once and forever destroy the Senate equilibrium. Nearing the allotted span of three score and ten, his life was drawing to a close in baffled zeal and unrelaxed strain. His tall frame emaciated by half a decade of intermittent illness, his voice failing but his piercing eyes undimmed, he tottered from his lodgings to the Senate chamber day by day to save the Union if it might be saved upon a basis of comity and to preach Southern resistance to the point of independence if that should prove essential for social security.

The California demand, which put his territorial theorizing to scorn, was clearly not to be denied nor long delayed in its granting. A crisis was at hand, and the South, or its lower half at least, was at length girding its loins. Demonstrations became too vigorous to be longer disregarded. Clay framed the celebrated Omnibus Bill to settle the many pending issues on a give-and-take basis. Calhoun approved the purpose but criticized the text as failing to provide adequate guarantees for the South. To express these views he wrote his last formal speech, which was read to the Senate on Mar. 4, 1850, by Senator Mason while its author sat voiceless in his chair. A few days later he expressed

praise of Webster's great speech of Mar. 7, but still thought it "difficult to see how two peoples so different and hostile can exist together in one common Union" (*Correspondence*, p. 784). At the end of this, his last letter, he wrote: "Kiss the children for their grandfather"; but virtually his last spoken words were "The South, the poor South." Fading out of life, he died at the end of the month. His body was carried in state to Charleston and interred with an outpouring praise and lamentation, for he was first in the hearts of his Carolina countrymen. His course was run, but his work was to have a mighty sequel.

[To promote his presidential prospects, there was published in 1843 a volume of Calhoun's *Speeches*, including sundry public papers; and simultaneously a *Life of John C. Calhoun*. The latter, unusually substantial for a campaign biography, was currently attributed to R. M. T. Hunter, but latterly Calhoun himself has been proved to have been its principal author (*Am. Hist. Review*, XIII, 310–13). Just after Calhoun's death R. K. Crallé edited his *Works* (1851–55), including the "Disquisition on Government" and the unfinished "Discourse on the Constitution" in the first volume, the speeches in the next three, and reports and public papers in the fifth and sixth. In 1857 was published *The Carolina Tribute to Calhoun*, J. P. Thomas, ed., containing the record of obsequies along with the text of many eulogies; and in 1888 *A Hist. of the Calhoun Monument* at Charleston, S. C. with its chief item the notable commemorative address by L. Q. C. Lamar. Biographies have been written by John S. Jenkins (1851), a perfunctory product; Hermann von Holst (1882), censorious and homiletic; Gustavus M. Pinckney (1903), eulogistic; Gaillard Hunt (1908), discriminatingly sympathetic; and William M. Meigs (2 volumes, 1917), elaborate and painstaking. A stout volume of Calhoun's correspondence, J. F. Jameson ed., has been published in the *Annual Report of the Am. Hist. Ass. for the Year 1899*, vol. II, being *House Doc. No. 733*, 56 Cong., 1 Sess.; and a supplementary volume, to consist mainly of letters to Calhoun, is now awaiting publication by the same agency.]   U. B. P.

CALHOUN, WILLIAM BARRON (Dec. 29, 1795–Nov. 8, 1865), lawyer, politician and educator, was the eldest child of Martha (Chamberlain) and Andrew Calhoun, a Scotch merchant of Boston. After a thorough preparation by William Wells of Harvard, he entered Yale College, where he graduated in 1814. Private study of law, carried on at Concord, N. H., and at Springfield with George Bliss, prepared him for admission to the bar in 1818, and the beginning of his practise at Springfield in 1822. In the latter he was not particularly happy or successful. It has been truthfully said that he was "an erudite writer" but not "a great orator"; that he "was lacking in the qualities that shine in a court of law." Bowles insisted that he needed "some pepper injected into his veins." In truth, Calhoun was more interested in economic, social, and political affairs than in his personal fame or prosperity. Though early concerned with problems of public welfare, and honored by numerous offices, he appears to have attended to the former "with the spirit of a philosopher," rather than with the usual self-interest of politicians, and to have made little or no effort to secure the latter. From 1825 to 1835, he was a member of the state legislature, serving as speaker of the House (1828–33) save for one year. In 1834, he was elected to Congress on the Whig ticket and served acceptably till 1843, declining further reëlection because of tubercular and catarrhal trouble. Other offices followed, however, in rapid succession. He was presidential elector for Clay (1844), was elected state senator (1846)—in which position he served as presiding officer—and was secretary of the commonwealth from 1848 to 1851. From 1853 to 1855 he served as bank commissioner; in 1859, he was made mayor of Springfield; and, two years later, was again sent to the legislature. Throughout his mature life he was an interested and effective promoter of public education. As member of the legislature, he presented the report of the select committee on a "Seminary for the instruction of school teachers" (1827), as also the memorial of James G. Carter on the same subject. In reporting a bill to provide for such an institution he made a strong plea: "In what more suitable and rational way can the government interpose than in providing the means for furnishing the schools with competent instructors . . . and in encouraging the establishment of seminaries, whose object shall be to teach the art of communicating knowledge?" (*House Report No. 10*, 1827, p. 5). Calhoun was chairman of the convention which founded the American Institute of Instruction in 1830, served as vice-president, and later, for many years, as president. From 1829 till his death he was a trustee of Amherst and, in 1850, was a lecturer there on political economy. In 1854 he edited the *Connecticut Valley Farmer*. A religious steadfastness, dignified self-respect, and purity of mind marked both his public and private life. He was married, on May 11, 1837, to Margaret Howard Kingsbury. Among his writings which are scattered here and there, a patriotic *Address Delivered in Springfield* (1825), *Addresses at the Dedication of the New Cabinet and Observatory of Amherst College* (1848), an examination into the condition of banks in Massachusetts (1849), and the articles and editorials in the *Springfield Republican* are fair samples. They indicate not a brilliant writer but a careful, logical, exact one.

[Frederick J. Kingsbury, *Genealogy of the Descendants of Henry Kingsbury* (1905); F. B. Dexter, *Biog. Sketches Grads. Yale Coll.*, vol. VI (1912); Chas. W. Chapin, *Sketches of the Old Inhabitants . . . of Old Springfield* (1893); Mason A. Green, *Hist. of Springfield* (1888).]
T. W.

CALHOUN, WILLIAM JAMES (Oct. 5, 1848–Sept. 19, 1916), diplomat, was born in Pittsburgh, Pa., the son of Robert and Sarah (Knox) Calhoun. He was educated at the Union Seminary, Poland, Ohio. His family having removed to Danville, Ill., he was admitted to the bar in that town and practised law there from 1875 to 1898 when he removed to Chicago. While acting as western counsel for the Baltimore & Ohio Railroad, he was the legal opponent of Elbert Gary, later to become head of the United States Steel Corporation. The friendship that was one of the results of this forensic battle had a widening influence upon Calhoun's career, and it was upon Gary's suggestion that in 1897 Calhoun was sent on a special mission by President McKinley to the war-racked island of Cuba to study conditions and to report on the manner in which, under Captain-General Weyler's decree, the civilian population of the war zones was being herded into insanitary reconcentration camps. His reports, which substantiated the inhumanity of the conditions prevailing, reconciled the President to intervention. Shortly after his return from Cuba, early in 1898, Calhoun was appointed by McKinley a member of the United States Interstate Commerce Commission. Here he served acceptably for two years. In 1900 he resigned to return to Chicago and the active practise of law.

In 1905 he was sent to Venezuela as confidential agent of President Roosevelt at a time when the Caribbean republic was in the throes of a revolution which by some was thought to indicate European inspiration and financial support. In 1909 he was appointed by President Taft Envoy Extraordinary and Minister Plenipotentiary to China where he served for four years. Throughout this period of political transition and travail in China, Calhoun was successful in maintaining the traditional American attitude of non-intervention, at the same time demonstrating on many critical occasions a helpful understanding of the long-accumulating problems with which the unprepared Chinese people were confronted.

Calhoun was a graceful speaker as well as a trained, industrious lawyer. He led several reform movements within the Republican party of Illinois and it has been said that the positions of responsibility which he held were due rather to the opposition than to the indorsement of the regular party machine of his state. He was married twice: first, on Dec. 26, 1875, to Alice D.

Harmon, who died in 1898; second, in 1904, to Lucy Monroe of Chicago.

[*Who's Who in America*, 1914–15; obituaries in *Chicago Herald* and *Chicago Daily Tribune*, Sept. 20, 1916; information from Judge John Barton Payne.]
S. B.

CALIFORNIA JOE (May 8, 1829–Oct. 29, 1876), frontiersman, scout, was born near Stanford, Ky. His real name was Moses Embree Milner. In 1849 he journeyed overland to California, later going to the Oregon country and working at various occupations. He came into general notice during the Civil War as a member of Berdan's Sharpshooters. After the war he drifted to the plains, serving in the Indian campaigns, and was with the 7th Cavalry, near Fort Dodge, in October 1868, when Custer reassumed command. His odd appearance, engaging personality, and shrewd comments on Indian warfare attracted the General, who appointed him chief of scouts; but he lost the honor within a few hours by getting uproariously drunk. As an ordinary scout he took part in the Washita expedition, and after the battle of Nov. 27 was chosen by Custer to carry the news to Sheridan. Declining any escort but that of his partner, Jack Corbin, he traversed on muleback the hundred miles of snowbound, hostile country to Camp Supply in eighteen hours. "An invaluable guide and Indian fighter," wrote Sheridan in recording the incident, "whenever the clause of the statute prohibiting liquors in the Indian country happened to be in full force."

In 1875 he guided Col. Dodge's escort to Prof. Jenney's Black Hills expedition, and after his discharge at Fort Laramie returned to the Hills as a prospector. From Deadwood, in July 1876, when news came of Custer's death, he went to Camp Robinson and joined the 5th Cavalry as a guide, serving throughout the campaign and returning with the troops in October. Two days before the time set for his departure with Mackenzie's winter expedition, a civilian, Tom Newcomb, who bore him a grudge, shot him in the back, killing him instantly.

California Joe came into enduring fame through the writings of Custer and his wife. He was more than six feet tall, well proportioned, with lustrous black eyes and dark brown hair, mustache and beard, which he wore long. His face, as far as it was revealed from its hirsute framing, was, according to Custer, "full of intelligence and pleasant to look upon." His dress was conspicuous for its oddity and slouchiness. His mount was usually a mule. He smoked a pipe almost incessantly and usually chewed at the same time, though with an art that permitted neither habit to interfere with his conversation. Though reticent about his personal history, on other matters he was garrulous, especially when well liquored; and his stories, told in a jargon of frontier, gambling, and Indian terms and plentifully adorned with fiction, were listened to with delight. He was brave, self-reliant, and faithful. His skill as a scout, trailer, and marksman is attested by all under whom he served. As a "character" of the frontier he occupies a unique place.

[See "California Joe," *Harper's Weekly*, Aug. 2, 1862; G. A. Custer, *My Life on the Plains* (1874); E. B. Custer, *Following the Guidon* (1890); E. L. Sabin, "California Joe, Good Old Scout," *Frontier Stories*, Apr. 1927; De B. R. Keim, *Sheridan's Troopers on the Border* (1885); Harry Young, *Hard Knocks* (1915); G. W. Stokes, *Deadwood Gold* (1926); J. Brown and A. M. Willard, *The Black Hills Trails* (1924). The scout is several times mentioned in the second volume of Sheridan's *Memoirs*, as well as in various writings that appeared under the name of W. F. Cody, and is made the hero of a number of fantastic adventures in J. W. Buel's *Heroes of the Plains* (1883).]
W. J. G.

CALKINS, NORMAN ALLISON (Sept. 9, 1822–Dec. 22, 1895), educator, author, descended from a Plymouth settler of 1640, was the son of Elisha Deming Calkins and Abigail (Lockwood) Calkins, pioneer settlers of Gainesville, N. Y., where he was born. The family had moved to this community from Connecticut with that general westward expansion of New England population which occurred in the first part of the nineteenth century. The New England school tradition seems to have been carried to Gainesville, for young Calkins not only attended the common schools of the district but also spent several terms at a classical academy. At the early age of eighteen he began teaching during the winter terms in Castile, N. Y., returning to his own studies during the summer and vacation terms. Later he went back to Gainesville where he became principal of the Central School. He was elected county superintendent during the school year 1845–46 but resigned the position in the fall of the latter year to go to New York City to become editor of the *Student*. The monthly issues of this magazine were intended not only as a family miscellany but also as a school reader, for Calkins had a conviction that reading in the schools could be much improved by the frequent introduction of fresh reading matter. The magazine was well received and provided him with an income on which to marry Mary Hoosier in 1854. So successful did the *Student* prove that it encouraged competition in a similar publication called the *Schoolmate* with which it later consolidated under the title of *Student and Schoolmate*. At this juncture, however, Calkins vacated the editorial chair, as he was getting ready for the publication of his most outstanding book. Always interested in new and better methods of teaching, he had studied Robert Owen's experiment at New Harmony, Ind., and thus early became acquainted with Pestalozzian principles of object teaching. These he set forth in 1861 in a volume entitled *Primary Object Lessons for a Graduated Course of Development* which ultimately went through at least forty editions and was translated into several foreign languages. Distinction quickly followed in his election as assistant superintendent of schools in New York City in charge of the primary grades. Reëlection followed reëlection to this post to the year of his death. He further popularized the new educational theory and greatly added to his prestige as lecturer in the methods and principles of education at the Saturday classes held for teachers in New York City for approximately twenty years. Further books followed from his pen, all based on Pestalozzian principles: *Teaching Color* (1877); *Manual of Object-Teaching* (1882); *First Reading, from Blackboard to Books* (1883); *How to Teach Phonics* (1889). He served the National Education Association as president of the department of elementary schools, as president of the department of superintendents, as treasurer, and finally in 1886 as president.

[Obituaries in the *N. Y. Times*, Dec. 23, and *N. Y. Tribune*, Dec. 24, 1895; memorial published in the *N. E. A. Jour. of Proc. and Addresses*, 1896.]

J. S. B—r.

CALKINS, PHINEAS WOLCOTT (June 10, 1831–Dec. 31, 1924), clergyman, was descended from Hugh Calkins, who came from Wales to Gloucester, Mass., in 1640. His parents were James and Sarah Newton (Trowbridge) Calkins. His birthplace was Painted Post, now Corning, N. Y., and his father was the first white child born at Painted Post. Born on a farm, as a boy Calkins was a mechanical genius and throughout his life his avocation consisted in all kinds of mechanical pursuits in which he was an adept. Before entering college he taught for several years in order to pay his expenses. He graduated as valedictorian in the class of 1856 at Yale. Continuing his studies at Union Theological Seminary, 1859–60, and at the University of Halle, Germany, 1860–62, and traveling meantime in Europe, he was ordained to the Congregational ministry, Oct. 22, 1862. After his student days he dropped his first name, Phineas. He was associate pastor of Center (Congregational) Church, Hartford, Conn., 1862–64; pastor of Calvary (Presbyterian) Church, Philadelphia,

1864–66; pastor of the North Presbyterian Church, Buffalo, N. Y., 1866–80; pastor of Eliot (Congregational) Church, Newton, Mass., 1880–95; supplied Clyde Congregational Church, Kansas City, Mo., 1896–98; was pastor of Montvale (Congregational) Church, Woburn, Mass., 1898–1907 and pastor emeritus of the same church until his death. In 1886 he was acting pastor of the American Chapel in Paris and preached frequently in England between 1890 and 1902. On his various visits to Europe he acted as correspondent for the *New York Observer* and *Boston Transcript*. To the periodical press he was a frequent contributor, chiefly on religious subjects. He was author of a sketch of Matthias W. Baldwin published in *Memorial of Matthias W. Baldwin* (1867), and of the following books: *Keystones of Faith* (1888), *Essays* (1890), *Parables for Our Times* (1901). Nearly to the end of his ninety-three years he was characterized by great physical and intellectual vigor. The mathematical mind which made him a prize winner at Yale was of great value in working out all the details of personal and parish administration. His originality of exposition and expression were a feature of his preaching. He was married, on June 6, 1860, in Worcester, Mass., to Charlotte Grosvenor Whiton.

[*Congreg. Year Book*, 1924; *Congregationalist*, CX, 93; *Who's Who in America*, 1924–25; *Reports of the Class of 1856, Yale College*; *Obit. Record Yale Grads.*, 1924–25; personal information from Calkins's son, Dr. Raymond Calkins.]

T. C. R.

CALKINS, WOLCOTT. [See CALKINS, PHINEAS WOLCOTT, 1831–1924.]

CALL, RICHARD KEITH (1791–Sept. 14, 1862), governor of Florida, was born in Prince George County, Va., the third of four children. His father, William Call, fought in the Revolution, and his uncle, Richard Keith Call, friend and aide to Washington, was a charter member of the Order of the Cincinnati. His father died while Richard was a mere lad, and his mother (Helen Mead Walker) soon afterward moved to Kentucky. As in most pioneer families, the Call children had little actual schooling, but after their mother's death (August 1810), Richard attended an academy in Montgomery County, Tenn. This he left in 1813 to join an expedition against the Creeks; and later in the same year volunteered under Jackson. In January 1814, although his whole company mutinied and went home, Call (third lieutenant) served in the ranks until the end of the campaign. This incident and his courage were the basis for Jackson's deep attachment to him. Shortly afterward Call joined the regular army with the rank of lieutenant. For gallantry in Jackson's operations about Pensacola and in the battle of New Orleans he was soon promoted to captain and later became a member of Jackson's staff. He fought in Jackson's campaigns of 1818 and 1820; negotiated with Gov. José Masot at Pensacola in the former year; and in 1821 arranged with Gov. José Callava for the transfer of West Florida. In 1821 he resigned his commission to practise law in Pensacola, but in 1823 he was appointed brigadier-general of militia. The same year, while a member of the municipal board of Pensacola and of the first territorial council, he was appointed delegate to Congress, succeeding Gen. Joseph M. Hernandez. Before going to Washington (1824), he married Mary Letitia Kirkham (died 1836) of Nashville. Returning to the territory in 1825 (his successor in Congress being Joseph M. White, who also defeated him as delegate in 1832), Call removed to Tallahassee, and besides his town house acquired a large plantation on Lake Jackson. In 1829 Jackson sent him to Havana to obtain the documents relating to land grants, surveys, and claims taken thither by the Spaniards in 1821. After his return to the United States he was frequently consulted about these matters and in one case, argued before the Supreme Court, was associated with William Wirt. In 1832–34, he built the third railroad in the United States—the Tallahassee-St. Marks—and as a feeder to it founded the town of Port Leon. He was active in the Indian troubles during the period 1826–42. In 1836 (while governor during his first term, 1836–39), the War Department, at his request, authorized him to conduct a summer campaign; but notwithstanding the soundness of Call's plan and the care exercised by him, the campaign was not a complete success, and Call was superseded in the command. Heatedly, Call accused the War Department of injustice and discrimination; which caused Van Buren, in 1839, notwithstanding that Call had been reappointed governor for three years more, to rescind the appointment. Call retaliated by turning Whig: and after the Harrison-Tyler victory was reappointed governor (1841–44). During his terms the most important issues, aside from the Indian hostilities, were those of the banks and statehood. When the banks failed and Florida repudiated the "faith bonds" issued by the territory, Call was greatly disturbed. He declared for statehood in 1837, but this was not obtained until 1845, although the St. Joseph convention (1838–39) drafted a state constitution. His defeat by a small margin in the first state election caused him to withdraw from active politics. In the Baltimore convention of 1856, he re-

fused nomination for the vice-presidency, and himself nominated Donelson. Being an ardent unionist, though a slaveholder, he attempted unsuccessfully to save Florida from secession; but stood with his state, offered his services to the Confederacy, and was grieved because his military experience was not availed of. He was a man of great integrity and sincerity and was highly regarded as a lawyer and orator. He was somewhat obstinate, loved his friends and hated his enemies with true Jackson fervor, and did not hesitate to challenge when he considered his honor impugned.

[The best printed biography of Call is that by his grand-daughter, Caroline Mays Brevard, in the *Fla. Hist. Soc. Quart.*, July, Oct. 1908. This is based in part upon an uncompleted autobiography in manuscript among the Call papers in Tallahassee. These papers have also many letters and documents of prime importance. The Lib. of Cong. has considerable Jackson-Call correspondence; and the archives of the State Dept., the records pertaining to the mission in Cuba. The *Am. State Papers, Military Affairs*, vols. VI and VII, publish many of the letters and documents relating to Call's campaigns against the Indians. See also C. M. Brevard, *A Hist. of Fla.* (2 vols. 1924–25), ed. by J. A. Robertson.]   J.A.R.

CALLAWAY, SAMUEL RODGER (Dec. 24, 1850–June 1, 1904), railroad executive, was born in Toronto, Ont., the son of Frederick William Callaway of Wiltshire, England, and Margaret (Rodger) Callaway of Crieff, Scotland. The fact that he began railroad work at the early age of thirteen, as an apprentice in the auditor's office of the Grand Trunk, indicates that his formal education was meager. His father, who was a dry-goods merchant, had lost his life and everything he owned in the Toronto fire of 1863. After six years' training in detail, young Callaway became chief clerk to the superintendent of the Great Western, a position which he held from 1869 to 1871. From the latter year to 1874 he was private secretary to the general manager of the same company; and then he became superintendent of the Detroit, Grand Haven & Milwaukee. On June 7, 1875, he was married at Hamilton, Ontario, to Elizabeth Ecclestone. In 1878 he was appointed superintendent of the Detroit, Saginaw & Bay City and in 1881 became general manager of the Chicago & Grand Trunk. These properties, with the exception of the Detroit, Saginaw & Bay City, were affiliated with or were controlled by the Grand Trunk System. In 1884 Callaway accepted the vice-presidency and general managership of the Union Pacific. After three years in this position, he was asked to take charge of the Toledo, St. Louis & Kansas City during the trying period between 1887 and 1895. The company was reorganized and the railroad practically rebuilt under his direction, first as president and then as receiver. Callaway's work attracted the attention of the Vanderbilt interests and in 1895 he became president of the New York, Chicago & St. Louis. About that time he was offered the presidency of the Grand Trunk System, but declined it because he feared that he would not be given a free hand by the English directors. In 1897 he was elected president of the Lake Shore & Michigan Southern and one year later (Apr. 20, 1898) he was selected by William K. Vanderbilt to succeed Chauncey M. Depew when the latter retired from the presidency of the New York Central & Hudson River to become chairman of the board of directors. After three years in the presidency of the New York Central, Callaway was sought as the president of a new company formed to take over the locomotive construction plants at Schenectady, N. Y., Paterson, N. J., Dunkirk, N. Y., Providence, R. I., Manchester, N. H., Pittsburgh, Pa., and Richmond, Va., with other smaller properties. These were all merged into the American Locomotive Company, an undertaking of magnitude in that early period of large industrial combines. The merger, when first discussed, did not inspire the public confidence that was necessary to insure its initial success, and the promoters thought that if Callaway were made the chief executive his prestige would be a valuable asset. Although Callaway's chief interest was in railroads, the financial inducements were so attractive that he could not resist. He had always been on a salary, his investments had not been wisely chosen, and his personal fortune was small. He was elected president of the new company in May 1901. While he never was as happy in that position as he had been in railroad service, he found interesting problems of coördination and wide latitude for the exercise of his ability as an organizer. The success of the American Locomotive Company in later years was due in substantial part to the leadership of Callaway during the period of unification and the formulation of policies of finance, production and sales. Unfortunately he did not live to see the permanency of the structure to which he contributed so much in the formative period, as he died on June 1, 1904.

In the earlier years of his railroad service Callaway displayed unusual capacity for detail as well as broad qualities of leadership. As he progressed to positions of greater responsibility he did not, as so many do who rise from the ranks, carry with him this burden of detail. Instead, he adopted a policy of developing the initiative and resourcefulness of subordinates by insisting that they assume responsibilities, subject only to broad executive supervision and the test of accomplishment. From the time he first became

a railroad president, Callaway would not load himself with departmental minutiæ. He discouraged letter writing, would not sign a letter consisting of more than one page, and would never allow papers to remain on his deck. Instead, he encouraged accomplishment through team work and conference, and granted an exceptional measure of departmental autonomy. These characteristics were frequently criticized at the time as extreme. He would often be wholly out of touch with his office for several days at a time and subordinates were sometimes required to take action in matters which Callaway personally should have directed. One feature of his administration should be noted specifically. He believed that adequate publicity of corporate accounts was one of the best methods of dispelling public suspicion of large combinations of capital. The completeness and frankness of the early annual reports of the American Locomotive Company attracted favorable public attention at the time.

[The foregoing based in the main on correspondence with business associates; other data gleaned from biographical notes in *N. Y. State's Prominent and Progressive Men* (1900), *Railroad Gazette* and *Railway Age*, and an article in *Cassier's Mag.*, Apr. 1902.]

W. J. C—m.

CALLENDER, GUY STEVENS (Nov. 9, 1865–Aug. 8, 1915), economist and historian, was the ninth of ten children of Robert Foster and Lois (Winslow) Callender, both emigrants from New England to the Western Reserve. As a boy on his father's farm in Hartsgrove, Ohio, he showed the active mind, intellectual curiosity, retentive memory, and fondness for argument which characterized his later life and work. "He devoured the contents of all the books he could get hold of, especially history. He was always ready for discussion with his friends or his elders. In an argument he was outspoken, without regard for the feelings of his opponent." The human qualities which later endeared him to his small circle of intimate friends were also evident. His teaching career began at the age of fifteen in the district schools of Ashtabula County. By the savings of several winters of teaching, supplemented by summer earnings, he paid for a college preparatory course at New Lyme Institute. At the age of twenty-one he was ready for Oberlin College. "With the money earned in haying and harvesting he bought himself a suit of clothes, and with $40 in his pocket he said goodbye to his family. When asked how he expected to get through, he replied with tears in his eyes that he didn't know, but he was going just the same."

With the same pluck and ability which had characterized his earlier struggle he put himself through Oberlin, graduating in 1891. For a year his choice of a career was undecided, and he spent the time traveling through the Middle West in the interests of a publishing house. But his thirst for knowledge proved still unsatisfied and in 1892 he entered the senior class of Harvard College, where he remained as undergraduate, graduate student, and finally as instructor in economics until 1900. "He was an outstanding man among our graduate students of his time," writes Professor Taussig. "His high intellectual quality, and the independence and originality of his work, impressed us from the start." In 1900 he was called to Bowdoin College as professor of political economy, but remained there only until 1903 when he accepted a professorship in the Sheffield Scientific School of Yale University which he held until his death. On June 14, 1904, he was married to Harriet Rice in Cambridge, Mass. Just at the beginning of his work he had a complete nervous breakdown from which he never entirely recovered. The daily grind of drilling large classes of undergraduates and the administrative work accompanying the teaching deprived him of the time and energy which he longed to devote to historical research. *Selections from the Economic History of the United States 1765–1860* (1909) was practically his only published work, but it was enough to establish him as the leading authority in his field. Always intolerant of loose thinking and of verbosity, he compressed into the masterly introductory essays which he prefixed to each chapter his entire theory of the progress of the United States from the beginnings of colonization until the Civil War. In his view economic history should not be a chronological recital of events of industrial and commercial importance, but an explanation by the principles of economic science of the economic and social development of communities. He insisted that the economic historian must not shirk the vital task of interpretation of his facts ("The Position of American Economic History," *American Historical Review*, XIX, 80–97). He himself was master of a surprisingly wide range of facts from which he drew conclusions which have illumined the colonial and early national periods of United States history. His analysis of the part played by economic factors in the adoption of the Federal Constitution and his discussion of the economic basis of slavery in the South were two of his outstanding contributions.

[The material for this sketch has been taken from letters from Prof. Callender's family and friends and from a biographical article written by Dr. C. W. Mixter in the *Yale Alumni Weekly* of Oct. 1, 1915.]

P. W. B.

CALLENDER, JAMES THOMSON (1758– July 17, 1803), political writer, was born in Scotland in 1758, acquired by some means a fair classical education, and became in 1792 a messenger at arms and writer in Edinburgh. There his propensity for intemperate political discussion expressed itself in a pamphlet, *The Political Progress of Britain* (Part I), which he termed an impartial history of the abuses of government, but which led to his indictment for sedition in January 1793. Ofttimes called in court, he did not appear and was pronounced a fugitive and outlaw. He found temporary safety, if not peace, in America. Here he was regarded by Jefferson and other lovers of liberty as a man of genius suffering under persecution. Until the spring of 1796 he was a reporter of congressional debates for the Philadelphia *Gazette*. In 1797 appeared his *American Annual Register,* a discursive partisan work. In his *History of the United States for 1796,* his genius as a scandal-monger first became conspicuous. Here he uncovered to public gaze the intimate affairs of Hamilton and forced that statesman to bare his personal shame in the Reynolds affair to vindicate his official honor. In 1798, frightened by the Sedition Law, he fled Philadelphia and took refuge in Virginia. In 1799 he went to Richmond and attached himself to Meriwether Jones of the *Examiner,* who utilized his dangerous talents in connection with that Republican paper. Here, under the secretive patronage of Jefferson, he published in 1800 his most notorious pamphlet, *The Prospect Before Us* (vol. I), which, despite certain palpable hits was more characterized by abuse than valid criticism of Federalist leaders. For remarks about President John Adams in this work, he was tried under the Sedition Law in May and June, fined $200, and sentenced to nine months' imprisonment. No sufferer under this unwise law deserved less sympathy than Callender, but the political aspects of the case gained him strong support from his party, and the bullying tactics of Justice Chase in the trial aroused a storm of indignation in behalf of the eminent Virginia lawyers of the defense and their client. From prison, Callender hurled against the administration two fiery pamphlets, on both of which Jefferson advanced him money. Following the inauguration of his benefactor in 1801, Callender was pardoned and was singled out by the remission of his fine. Irritated, however, because of delay in the receipt of the money, he was already talking of the ingratitude of the President, who appears rather to have been excessively gullible and long-suffering.

Having broken with his old employer, Jones, whom he later attacked, Callender became associated, in February 1802, with Henry Pace in the publication of the Richmond *Recorder*. Now increasingly critical of an administration which had failed to reward him with an appointment, he was openly charged with apostasy. By the autumn of 1802, he was turning the artillery of slander full on his most illustrious patron. Accusing Jefferson of dishonesty, cowardice, and gross personal immorality, he gave currency to most of the scandals which have been associated with the private life of the third President, and, despite the extravagance of the charges, left on him, as he had left on Hamilton, a stain which can never be entirely effaced.

Callender was married and had at least four children, whose needs served at times to stimulate his reckless pen. His wife apparently died before him, and his children were supported during his last years at least by Thomas Leiper of Philadelphia. Toward the end of his life, Callender was destitute, in part because of mistreatment by his partner. Shunned by his former associates, constantly intoxicated, he several times threatened suicide. He was drowned in three feet of water in the James River, July 17, 1803. The coroner's jury pronounced his death accidental, following intoxication.

[The best account of Callender is contained in Worthington C. Ford's *Thos. Jefferson and Jas. Thomson Callender* (1897), where the correspondence between the two men is published. For his indictment in Edinburgh, see T. B. and T. J. Howell, *State Trials* (1817), XXIII, 79–84. For Hamilton's reply to his charges, see Lodge's edition of Hamilton's *Works* (1886), VI, 449–81. For Callender's trial in 1800, see Francis Wharton, *State Trials* (1849), pp. 688–721. For an editorial on his death, see Richmond *Examiner*, July 27, 1803.]

D. M.

CALLENDER, JOHN (1706–Jan. 26, 1748), Baptist clergyman, the son of John Callender, was born in Boston, where his grandfather, the Rev. Ellis Callender, was pastor of the First Baptist Church from 1708 to 1726. At the age of thirteen he entered Harvard College. There he shared in the income derived from benefactions of Thomas Hollis, a London Baptist, who had endowed two chairs and supplied scholarship funds. In the year of his graduation from college he joined the Baptist church in Boston, and a few years later was licensed to preach. He soon was invited to preach for the church at Swansea, the oldest church of the denomination in Massachusetts, and he remained there until 1730. Upon leaving Swansea he married Elizabeth Hardin of that town, by whom he had three sons and three daughters. The next year he was ordained to the regular ministry and became pastor of the Baptist church at Newport, R. I., the second church of that faith in the United States. There he remained until his death.

Callender was a man of pleasing appearance, with fair complexion and a kindly, serious expression. His brilliant blue eyes and high forehead indicated keenness of intelligence. His character was irreproachable, and he had many friends both in and outside of the church. He was highly esteemed in the community, and was a member of a select literary and philosophical society in Newport, having been suggested for membership, it is thought, by Bishop Berkeley, the English philosopher, who resided for a time at Newport. He made an important contribution to Rhode Island history in his *Historical Discourse on the Civil and Religious Affairs of the Colony of Rhode Island and Providence Plantations* (1739). He was also the author of several published sermons. His interest in history led him to collect historical material relating to the colonial history of churches of his own faith, which proved a valuable source of information for Isaac Backus when he wrote his history of the Baptists in New England about sixty years later. Callender was honored among Baptists, even though he declared himself in favor of admitting non-Baptists to the communion table, an act of generosity not often practised. After a long illness he died in 1748 in the forty-second year of his age, and was buried at Newport. The epitaph on his tomb credited him with being "distinguished as a shining and very burning light by a true and faithful ministry."

[Memoir by Romeo Elton in *R. I. Hist. Soc. Colls.*, IV (1888), 9–25.]

H. K. R.

CALVERLEY, CHARLES (Nov. 1, 1833–Feb. 25, 1914), sculptor, of English parentage, was born in Albany, N. Y., where he received his education. He became a marble-cutter and while he was engaged at this trade his ability was noticed by Erastus D. Palmer, the sculptor, who took him as an assistant. He remained with Palmer about fourteen years. At some time in the later sixties he went to New York and opened a studio of his own. In 1872 he was elected an associate member of the National Academy and in 1875 a full academician. "The Little Companions" and "Little Ida" (a medallion) seem to have been comparatively early works. He became known as a maker of busts and particularly of portrait medallions. He did, however, make larger statues on occasion; such are the statue of Robert Burns in Washington Park, Albany, and the bronze figure of "Meditation" on the Boulware Lot in the Albany Rural Cemetery. The latter was one of his last works. He was represented at the Centennial Exposition of 1876 by a bas-relief of Peter Cooper and a large bronze bust of John Brown (1873), the latter of which now belongs to the Union League Club. Among his large busts in bronze are those of Horace Greeley (1876) and Elias Howe (1884), both in Greenwood Cemetery. At the exhibition of the National Sculpture Society in 1895 he showed a portrait bust of himself. He also did busts of Lincoln, Charles Loring Elliott, and the Rev. John MacLean, a former president of Princeton. A bust of Burns by him is in the Metropolitan Museum. Examples of his medallions are preserved in the Historical and Art Society of Albany. He is likewise said to have done some remarkable cameo cutting.

In his busts and medallions Calverley showed fine workmanship and skill in portraiture. Taft calls him "a craftsman of sterling worth," and says: "Mr. Calverley's permanent reputation will rest largely upon his medallions, which, in their precision and firmness of construction, are among the admirable products of the art. A forceful characterization of aged Louis Menand is especially noteworthy."

Calverley lived to an advanced age and in later life photographs show him to have been a man of venerable appearance with mustache and long flowing beard. For the last few years of his life he lived with his daughter, Mrs. Francis Byrne-Ivy, and died at her house in Essex Fells, N. J. He was apparently in good health to within a few days of his death which was caused by acute bronchitis.

[C. E. Clement and L. Hutton, *Artists of the Nineteenth Century* (3rd ed., 1885) ; Lorado Taft, *Hist. of Am. Sculpture* (rev. ed., 1925) ; *Albany Evening Jour.*, Feb. 26, 1914 ; *N. Y. Times,* Feb. 27, 1914.]

E. G. N.

CALVERT, CHARLES (Aug. 27, 1637–Feb. 21, 1715), third Lord Baltimore, second proprietor of the province of Maryland, was the only son of Cecilius Calvert, second Lord Baltimore, and of his wife, Anne Arundell, daughter of Lord Arundell of Wardour. He was commissioned governor of Maryland, Sept. 14, 1661, and served in that capacity until the death of his father, Nov. 30, 1675, when he succeeded to the proprietorship of the province. His task both as governor and as proprietor was beset with many difficulties. He was a Catholic. Protestants in the colony outnumbered Catholics by at least ten to one and the fabrication of a rumor of a "Popish Plot" became a formidable weapon. The ranks of the malcontents were strengthened with recruits from those who had come to the colony as convicts or as indentured servants. The Susquehanna Indians were hostile, and the spirit of Bacon's rebellion in Virginia was contagious. A boundary dispute with William Penn required Calvert's presence in England where his troubles culminated in the Protestant Revolution of 1688 and the hostile attitude of King William toward proprietary charters. Calvert was energetic in his efforts to cope with these difficulties but his efforts were directed, with an irritable temper, chiefly toward the suppression of opposition. He was lacking in the range of vision and personal magnetism so essential to success. In 1670, following a stormy experience with the Assembly the preceding year, suffrage was restricted to such freemen as had a freehold of at least fifty acres or a visible estate of forty pounds sterling, and at the same time there was commenced the practise of summoning to the Assembly only one-half of the delegates who had been elected. Calvert was accused of abusing the privilege of appointing sheriffs to control elections. In 1672 he brought about the election of Thomas Notley, a stalwart supporter, as speaker, and wrote his father that he was resolved to keep him there. Occasionally, when the delegates to the Assembly were stubborn, he called them before him in the council chamber and prevailed upon them to yield. He vetoed acts of the Assembly several years after they had been passed.

Calvert was married four times. By his second wife, Jane, daughter of Vincent Lowe and widow of Henry Sewall, he had five children, and these were married with a view to making the government more and more a family affair. It was successfully administered during a brief visit of Calvert to England in 1676, but it passed to incompetent guardians not long after his departure in 1684 to defend his charter and his territorial jurisdiction from the attacks of William Penn. It was overthrown in 1689 by a Protestant association led by the blasphemous John Coode [*q.v.*], and in 1692 a royal government was established. Until his death, however, Calvert contended successfully against encroachments on his territorial rights.

[The chief sources of information are the *Archives of Md.* and *The Calvert Papers* (1889). For reviews of Calvert's administration of the government see C. C. Hall, *The Lords Baltimore and the Md. Palatinate* (1902), and N. D. Mereness, *Md. as a Proprietary Province* (1901). For family history see John Bailey Calvert Nicklin, "The Calvert Family" in *Md. Hist. Mag.,* vol. XVI (1921).]

N. D. M.

CALVERT, CHARLES BENEDICT (Aug. 23, 1808–May 12, 1864), congressman, was the grandson of Benedict Calvert, earlier known as Benedict Swingate. The latter, of uncertain maternity, was the son of Charles, fifth Lord Baltimore. Benedict's son George Calvert, removed from Mt. Airy to Riverdale, Md., occupying there a large estate which still remains in the family. He married Rosalie Eugenia Stier, of

Belgian parentage (John B. Calvert Nicklin, "The Calvert Family" in *Maryland Historical Magazine*, XVI, 313–16), who became the mother of George Henry Calvert [*q.v.*] and Charles Benedict Calvert. The large Riverdale farm probably induced Charles to study the problems of agriculture, for his whole life was devoted to furthering its development. After attending school in Philadelphia he entered the University of Virginia, graduating in 1827. On June 6, 1839 he married Charlotte Augusta Norris. The Journal of the legislature of Maryland records his appearance at the sessions of 1838, 1843, and 1844, but of his activities therein there is no mention. The project to establish the Maryland Agricultural College must have taken much of his time for he is commonly regarded as the one through whose efforts the college was established. It was finally located on 428 acres of his land which he sold the corporation for $10,000, remaining its creditor. In addition he loaned it over $2,000 cash (*Report of the Trustees of the Maryland Agricultural College to the Legislature of Maryland*, January session, 1864, pp. 13–14). Shortly after the outbreak of the Civil War he appears as a representative in the Thirty-seventh Congress. His ardent unionism was tempered strongly by an inherent sense of justice. At one time he advocated a direct tax on all property, personal and real, saying it would be "not half as odious as this rebellion," and at another time proposed to reimburse loyal owners of escaped slaves at the rate of $1,000 for each fugitive (*Congressional Globe*, 37 Cong., 1 Sess., pp. 212, 272–73; 2 Sess., pp. 1549, 3215).

As a promoter of the Department of Agriculture Calvert's efforts were directed mainly outside of Congress. In 1852 the United States Agricultural Society was organized, which, during the brief eight years of its existence, had a marked influence in congressional circles. At every meeting we find Calvert waging a persistent, determined fight for a department of agriculture. "When a cabinet minister represents agriculture," he said, "the farmer will be appreciated by the government, and proper steps will be taken to advance his noble calling by all means possible; but until such a platform is formed and such a representative takes his seat in the Cabinet, the hope the farmer cherishes that the government will regard agriculture as its chief bulwark and cherish its advance accordingly, is fallacious" (*Journal of the United States Agricultural Society*, 1856, p. 67). The society's influence was concentrated on Calvert's favorite project, and in 1853 it adopted his resolution memorializing Congress to establish a de-

partment of agriculture. When he entered Congress, Calvert was assigned to the Committee on Agriculture, which had under consideration a bill for the establishment of a department. This was reported favorably Jan. 7, 1862, but the House amended it over his protest by changing the word "Department" to "Bureau," in which form it became a law. Although a Department was not established until 1889 the Act of 1862 is generally regarded as the organic law (Henry Barrett Learned, *The President's Cabinet*, 315, 323 ff.; *Congressional Globe*, 37 Cong., 2 Sess., pp. 855–56). Calvert's untimely death at his home, Riverdale, Md., probably deprived the farmers of many interesting ideas on the development of agriculture.

[Chas. Lanman, *Biog. Annals of the Civil Govt. of the U. S.* (1887); *Country Gentleman*, XXIII, May 19, 1864, p. 321; *Jour. of the U. S. Agr. Soc.*, 1852–59 (see references in Learned, *ante*, pp. 321 ff.); personal information.]

C. W. G.

CALVERT, GEORGE (*c.* 1580–Apr. 15, 1632), first Lord Baltimore, projector of the province of Maryland, belonged to a family whose name occurs in the records of Yorkshire, England, as early as 1366. Its unbroken record begins about two centuries later with the marriage of Leonard Calvert, a country gentleman, and Grace Crossland, a lady of gentle birth in the same neighborhood. George, their eldest, if not their only son, was born at Kipling, in the chapelry of Bolton, in 1580 or very close to that year. At the age of fourteen he entered Trinity College, Oxford, where he became proficient in Latin, obtaining his bachelor's degree in 1597 and the honorary degree of Master of Arts in 1605. In 1604–05 he was married to Anne, daughter of George Mynne of Hertingfordbury, Hertfordshire. Shortly after receiving the first degree he traveled on the continent and became familiar with the French, Spanish, and Italian languages. In 1606 he became private secretary to Sir Robert Cecil, principal secretary of state and until his death, in 1612, controller of the policy of King James. Under Cecil's influence Calvert enjoyed rapid advancement and won the confidence of the King. He was made clerk of the crown of assize and peace in County Clare, Ireland, in 1606. He was returned a member of Parliament for Bossiney, in Cornwall, in 1609; was sent on a special mission to France in 1610; and assisted the King in a theological dispute witht Vorstius, a Dutch theologian. He was appointed a clerk of the Privy Council in 1613, and served on a commission to inquire into religious grievances in Ireland. He was knighted in 1617; and in 1619 the King, in opposition to the wishes of the Duke of Buckingham, appointed him a principal secretary of state to serve as a colleague of the less active Sir Robert Naunton. In this office, which made him a member of the Privy Council, Calvert faithfully discharged important diplomatic functions and was a staunch defender in Parliament of the unpopular policy and measures of King James, particularly the negotiations for a marriage alliance with Catholic Spain. Those negotiations failed, and Calvert, in 1624, lost the seat in Parliament which he had held for Yorkshire since 1621. He was immediately returned as one of the members for the University of Oxford, but in the face of pending measures for the persecution of Catholics he announced his conversion to that faith and tendered his resignation of the secretaryship. In accepting the resignation, in January 1625, the King retained him as a member of the Privy Council and created him Baron of Baltimore in the Kingdom of Ireland.

Calvert's interest in American colonization is first disclosed by his membership in the Virginia Company from 1609 to 1620 and by his admission as one of the council of the New England Company in 1622. In 1620 King James granted him an increased duty on silk and the same year he acquired by purchase a portion of the peninsula of Avalon, the southeastern section of Newfoundland. In December 1622 he received from the King a grant of the whole country of Newfoundland. By a re-grant, in March 1623, the territory was restricted to the peninsula of Avalon, and this, by a royal charter, dated Apr. 7 of the same year, was erected into the province of Avalon, modeled after the county palatine of Durham, a great crown fief, the powers of whose lord were regal in kind and inferior only in degree to those of the king. A small colony was established at Ferryland in 1620. There was some building and planting but the colony did not prosper. Lord Baltimore made it a short visit in the summer of 1627 and returned to it in 1628 with his second wife, Joan, and all, except Cecilius, of the children by his first wife. After an engagement with three French ships in the summer of 1628, Lord Baltimore appealed to the King for special protection. In August 1629, he complained of the severity of the weather from October to May, stated that his house had been a hospital all winter, and prayed for a grant of land in the warmer climate of Virginia. Before the King's unfavorable reply had been received he departed for Jamestown where Lady Baltimore had gone in the autumn of 1628. Objecting to Papists, the Virginians treated him harshly and hastened his departure for England by tendering him the oaths of supremacy

and allegiance. Yielding to his appeal, King Charles, in February 1632, granted him the territory extending southward from the James River to the Roanoke and westward to the mountains, as the province of Carolina. Bitter opposition by members of the late Virginia Company resulted in the substitution of the territory between the 40th degree of north latitude and the Potomac River extending westward from the ocean to the longitude of the first source of the river, as the province of Maryland. Lord Baltimore died, Apr. 15, 1632, before the charter, copied from that of Avalon, had passed the great seal, but, bearing date of June 20, of the same year, it was issued to his eldest son, Cecilius.

A portrait of Calvert by Daniel Mytens exhibits an oval face, a mustache and pointed beard, large straight nose, melancholy eyes, and marks of refinement. Although not brilliant, he was an industrious and reliable public servant, zealously intent upon the welfare of England; and in the charter of Maryland he laid the foundation for one of the most successful governments in the American colonies.

[The most important primary source is the *Calendar of* (British) *State Papers*, colonial and domestic series. B. C. Steiner, "The First Lord Baltimore and His Colonial Projects" in the *Ann. Report, Am. Hist. Ass.* for 1905, contains a long list of authorities. Consult also C. C. Hall, *The Lords Baltimore and the Md. Palatinate* (1902); the sketch in H. F. Powell, *Tercentenary Hist. of Md.* (1925); and Anthony Wood, *Athenæ Oxonienses* (1721). For family history see J. B. C. Nicklin, "The Calvert Family" in *Md. Hist. Mag.*, vol. XVI (1921).]

N. D. M.

CALVERT, GEORGE HENRY (June 2, 1803–May 24, 1889), poet, essayist, was the eldest son of George Calvert, and was born on his father's estate, Riverdale, near Bladensburg, Md. His great-grandfather was the fifth Lord Baltimore, and his mother was Rosalie Eugenia Stier, daughter of a Belgian emigré who had settled temporarily in Maryland. He completed his education at Harvard (1819–23), and at eighteen was described by his father as "a very clever fellow . . . a little spoiled by the ladies as he is thought by them very handsome" (*Ancestry of Rosalie Morris Johnson*, 1905, II, 48). In the summer of 1823 he sailed for England, under the care of Stratford Canning, the British Minister at Washington; visited at his uncle's chateau seven miles from Antwerp; and then settled in Göttingen—one of the earliest American students there—for fifteen months' work in history and philosophy. During the summer of 1825 he visited Weimar, saw the aged Goethe, and was welcomed in the society of the Weimar court. The next winter he was in Edinburgh, and during the following year he saw much of the best social life of Antwerp and Paris. Two years after his return from abroad he was married, on Mar. 8, 1829, to Elizabeth, daughter of Dr. James Steuart of Baltimore. For some years, until Aug. 18, 1836, he was an editor of the *Baltimore American*. Upon the marriage and establishment in charge of the family estate of his younger brother, Charles Benedict Calvert [*q.v.*], he again went abroad, 1840–43, spending three days with Wordsworth, Aug. 1–3, 1840, and later sojourning in Germany and Italy. On his return he established his home in Newport, R. I., where, aside from travel, he spent his remaining years. For some time he was chairman of the Newport School Committee, and he was Democratic mayor of Newport, 1853–54. He was once more abroad in 1851–52. One who remembers him in old age describes him as living with his wife a retired life in his Newport home, "a rambling conglomeration of architecture in a setting of somber fir trees." He was "of great courtesy and dignity of manner, interested in spiritualism, tall, dark, gaunt, stooped, steeped in introspection, universally respected and beloved."

Calvert's verse includes many lyric and narrative poems in a diluted Tennysonian strain, such as *Cabiro, a Poem* (1840), *Anyta and Other Poems* (1866), *Ellen, a Poem for the Times* (1867), *Life, Death, and Other Poems* (1882); two comedies laid in Renaissance Italy (*Comedies,* 1856), and the historical closet dramas in respectable blank verse: *Count Julian, a Tragedy* (1840); *Arnold and André* (1864); *Mirabeau* (1873); *Maid of Orleans* (1873); *Brangomar* (1883), a tragedy of Napoleon. In the seventies he published the critical, or in his phrase "biographic æsthetic" studies, *Goethe, His Life and Works* (1872), *Wordsworth* (1878), *Shakespeare* (1879), *Coleridge, Shelley and Goethe* (1880). From time to time throughout his life he delivered public addresses on political, literary, and artistic themes, several of which were put in print. His mild interest in the theories of the French socialists Fourier and Godin appears in his *Introduction to Social Science* (1856). "Essentially a feeble and commonplace writer of poetry, although his prose compositions have a certain degree of merit"—this verdict of Poe on Calvert, though written in 1841 (*A Chapter on Autography*) when Calvert had produced little, will apply without great modification to all his thirty-odd slender volumes of narrative and dramatic verse, travel, criticism, and translation. The prose works, as Poe says, are the better, and of these perhaps the best worth reopening to-day are his essay on manners, *The Gentleman* (1863), which went to three editions, his *First Years in Europe* (1866), and his second

volume of *Scenes and Thoughts in Europe* (vol. I, 1845, vol. II, 1852), which gives an interesting account of the temper of Germany after 1848 and of France under Louis Napoleon. These works reveal the author in his most significant aspect, as a middle-states gentleman of distinguished family and independent means, a devoted American, who gave his life to literature and the translation of old-world culture to the new.

[See E. A. and G. L. Duyckinck, *Cyc. of Am. Lit.* (1855), vol. II, and *A Bibliography of the Works of Geo. Henry Calvert* (1900), by H. B. Tompkins, with biographical sketch and portrait, published by the Redwood Library, Newport, to which Calvert gave his books. Four letters written to John P. Kennedy in 1861–62, one of them expressing his sympathy with the North in the Civil War, are in the Kennedy MSS., Peabody Inst., Baltimore.]

A. W.

CALVERT, LEONARD (1606–June 9, 1647), colonial governor, was the second son of George Calvert [*q.v.*], first Lord Baltimore and of his wife, Anne Mynne. His elder brother, Cecilius (1605–75), was the second Lord Baltimore and the first proprietor of the province of Maryland. As the presence of Cecilius was needed in England to defend his charter from repeated attacks of enemies he never visited the province, as he had planned to do, but entrusted the exercise of his authority there to Leonard who served under a commission as governor. The record of Leonard's early life is obscure. He went with his father to Newfoundland in 1628, at about the age of twenty-one, returned to England with some French prizes, and petitioned the king for letters of marque. With two vessels, the *Ark* and the *Dove,* carrying about three hundred colonists, he sailed from England, Nov. 22, 1633, and landed at St. Clements (now Blackistone) Island, in Maryland, Mar. 25, 1634. Here he immediately took "solemn possession of the Country for our Saviour and for our Sovereign Lord the King of England." The following month, after some days of exploration and friendly intercourse with the Indians, he established the seat of government at St. Mary's, in St. Mary's County. Up to this time he was directed by instructions of Nov. 15, 1633, covering chiefly early proceedings and addressed to himself as governor and to two commissioners who were to assist him. He was particularly enjoined to give no offense to the Protestant members of the colony and to cultivate friendly relations with Virginia. By the first extant commission to him as governor, dated Apr. 15, 1637, he was made commander-in-chief of armed forces by land and sea; was made chief magistrate with large power of appointment; was authorized to call, prorogue, and dissolve the legislative Assembly;

was made chancellor and chief justice with full power to hear and determine all criminal and civil cases not involving life, member, or freehold, and to grant pardons. He was authorized to grant patents for lands and appoint places for ports of entry, fairs, and markets. Instructions for the discharge of these functions were occasionally issued by the proprietor, who also appointed a council to advise him.

Calvert gave early attention to the promotion and regulation of trade with the Indians, and in the summer of 1634 he sent the *Dove* with a cargo of corn to Boston to trade for fish and other commodities. He called the first Assembly of freemen to meet at St. Mary's in February, 1634/35, and the laws which it passed he sent to the proprietor for approval. The proprietor rejected them and sent others for the assent of the second Assembly. In January 1637/38 all members of that body, except Calvert and the secretary of the province, voted against them. To a suggestion that some laws be agreed upon until the proprietor had again been heard from, the governor replied that the Assembly had no power to do this. But he yielded to a proposition that he govern during this period according to the laws of England, or, if necessary, by martial law. Forty-two bills were subsequently passed. The governor signed them and wrote the proprietor, "I am persuaded they will appear unto you to provide both for your honor and profit as much as those you sent us did." The proprietor yielded, and the right of initiative in legislation passed to the Assembly. It was the first important step in the transition to popular government in Maryland. In February 1637/38, Calvert, at the head of a small force, reduced to submission a trading post on Kent Island which had been established there in 1631 by William Claiborne. In April 1643 he sailed for England to confer with his brother. Shortly after his return, in September 1644, Claiborne and Richard Ingle incited an insurrection of Protestants against Catholics. St. Mary's was seized and the governor took refuge in Virginia. Two years later he returned with a force of Virginians and Marylanders, recovered possession, and restored order. He died June 9, 1647, leaving two children: William and Anne, whose mother, Anne (Brent), had died some time before. He made his sister-in-law, Margaret Brent [*q.v.*], his executrix. Calvert was industrious and faithful to his brother's interest but was lacking in tact and personal magnetism. He governed by force rather than by leadership.

[The chief primary sources are the *Archives of Md.*, vols. I, III, and the *Calvert Papers* (1889). The best secondary sources are B. C. Steiner, *Beginnings of Md.*

(1903) and W. H. Browne, *Md., the Hist. of a Palatinate* (1884). For family history see J. B. C. Nicklin, "The Calvert Family," *Md. Hist. Mag.,* vol. XVI (1921).]
N. D. M.

CALVIN, SAMUEL (Feb. 2, 1840–Apr. 17, 1911), geologist, was born of Scottish parents, Thomas and Elizabeth Calvin, in Wigtonshire, Scotland, where he lived until eleven years of age. The family was one of only moderate means, and his early schooling limited. Among his school associates was James Wilson, who in after years became secretary of agriculture in the United States.

When Samuel was eleven years old the family emigrated to the United States, living for three years near Saratoga in New York State and then moving on to the open prairie lands of Buchanan County, Iowa. The country was then largely a wilderness scantily peopled by a few hardy pioneers, and, owing to a lack of qualified teachers, educational facilities were few and poor. At the age of sixteen, Calvin was himself called upon to teach in the local district school, but is stated to have been also an expert carpenter and cabinet-maker. In 1861 or 1862 he entered Lenox College, in the town of Hopkinton. Later he became an instructor there. Lenox College was one of the many small denominational colleges so abundant throughout the middle west, with scanty endowment, poor equipment, and affording opportunities for only the simplest and most fundamental training. There Calvin remained until 1864 when, in company with others of the faculty and student body, he enlisted. Before he was called into serious service, the war came to an end and Calvin returned to Lenox and labored under the discouraging conditions incidental to building up a nearly wrecked institution.

In 1867 and 1868 he served as county superintendent of Delaware County, and from 1869 to 1873 was principal of one of the Dubuque schools. While at Lenox he found among other members of the faculty Thomas H. Macbride, a botanist, to whom he became warmly attached and with whom he made frequent excursions and collecting trips. In the course of this work he came in contact with Dr. C. A. White, then state geologist and later professor of geology at the State University. When Dr. White resigned to accept a call from an eastern college, Calvin in 1874 succeeded him as professor of natural history at the University and when the state survey was reorganized in 1892, became state geologist as well. It was with this organization that his name first became known to the country at large. This, it may be well to note, was the third attempt at a geological survey on the part of the state, and Calvin continued at its head until 1904, when he resigned, to be appointed again in 1906, serving until his death in 1911.

Calvin's scientific training, as is evident, was largely self-acquired. When he entered upon his work as teacher, the geology of the upper Mississippi region was known only in the most general way and it is perhaps fortunate that he began with no preconceived notions. "He found his inspiration in a deep love and enthusiastic appreciation of nature and he brought to his work a critically keen judgment and an uncompromising allegiance to simple truth which made for thoroughness and accuracy" (Shimek, *post*, p. 5). Calvin's individual research, quite aside from his teaching and executive duties, was largely paleontological and stratigraphic. It is stated that he considered his discovery and proper interpretation of an interglacial mammalian fauna in the state as his most important contribution to science. In the course of his work, he described and named some thirty species of invertebrate fossils, and in turn had eleven species and varieties named after him by others. He was one of the founders of the *American Geologist* in 1888, and its editor-in-chief until 1894; a member of the Geological Society of America (president 1908); of the Paleontological Society of America; the American Association for the Advancement of Science; and other scientific societies. In 1870 he was married to Louise Jackson by whom he had two children, a son and a daughter.

[H. Foster Bain, *Jour. of Geology*, XIX (1911), 385–91, whose statement that the family home was south of Manchester, *i.e.*, in Delaware County, is an error; B. Shimek, *Bull. Geol. Soc. of America*, vol. XXIII, 1912; full bibliography of Calvin's publications in Nickles, *Bull. 746, U. S. Geol. Survey*.]   G. P. M.

CAMBRELENG, CHURCHILL CALDOM (1786–Apr. 30, 1862), congressman, diplomat, was born in Washington, Beaufort County, N. C. Of his family and childhood little is known except that one brother became a New York attorney, another a naval officer, and Cambreleng himself a student in New Bern, N. C. He went to New York in 1802 and achieved success in commerce, at one time being associated with J. J. Astor, traveling extensively in America and abroad for the firm. At other times he was head of the firms of Cambreleng & Chrystie and Cambreleng & Pearson. He was one of the first directors for the Farmers Fire Insurance & Loan Company. He married a Miss Glover but had no children. From 1821 to 1839 he was a member of Congress, being the House administration leader for Jackson and Van Buren. His most important committee assignments were the

chairmanships of the committees on Ways and Means, on Commerce and on Foreign Affairs. He took a prominent part in the debates, his remarks being characterized by clarity and common sense. Considered an unscrupulous henchman of Jackson and Van Buren by their enemies, he was described by one of them—William Lyon Mackenzie, the Canadian rebel—as "very short made and very stout—no great orator but well acquainted with business and politics." Van Buren, on the other hand, called Cambreleng "as honest as the steelyard and as direct in the pursuit of his purpose as a shot from a culverin." Cambreleng approved Jackson's course toward the Bank of the United States and opposed the tariffs of 1824 and 1828. He favored a vigorous assertion of American claims to Oregon and a firm attitude toward France concerning the treaty of 1831, but opposed sending delegates to the Panama Congress. While traveling in Europe he was appointed minister to Russia by Van Buren and served from May 1840 to July 1841. His interest in public affairs persisted after his return. He represented Suffolk County in the constitutional convention of 1846. As chairman of the Committee on Currency and Banking he gave a masterly exposition of the nature and necessity of a sound currency. It is significant that he was frequently bracketed with such leaders as John A. Dix, Preston King, William Cullen Bryant, and Samuel J. Tilden. The "Hunkers" having secured control of the state Democratic convention in 1847, the "Barnburners" withdrew and held one of their own, presided over by Cambreleng. He took a prominent part in the convention at Utica in 1848 which nominated Van Buren for president and paved the way for the national Free-Soil convention at Buffalo. Cambreleng's published works include: his report as the chairman of the Committee on Commerce and Navigation (1830), which passed through several editions and was republished in London; *An Examination of the New Tariff Proposed by the Honorable Henry Baldwin* (1821); *A Defence of Direct Taxes and of Protective Duties for the Encouragement of Manufactures* (1822); *Eulogy Pronounced in the City of New York, July 17, 1826* (on John Adams and Jefferson); *Speech on the Proposition . . . to Amend the Constitution . . . Respecting the Election of President and Vice-President* (1826); *Speech . . . on the Bill Regulating the Deposit of Public Money* (1835). Neither the violent demagogue his enemies thought, nor the paragon his friends esteemed him, Cambreleng was an industrious, astute politician. His successful mercantile career contributed much to his success in politics. He died at his home at West Neck, Long Island, Apr. 30, 1862.

[Many Cambreleng letters are in the Van Buren Papers in the Library of Congress, a few in the libraries at Albany and N. Y., some in Wm. Lyon Mackenzie's *Lives and Opinions of Benj. Franklin Butler and Jesse Hoyt* (1845) and *The Life and Times of Martin Van Buren* (1846). Other sources are: the N. Y. and Washington newspapers of the period; "The Autobiography of Martin Van Buren," being *House Doc. No. 819*, 66 Cong., 2 Sess.; the *Documents* and *Journals* of the N.Y. Constitutional Convention of 1846; the *Annals of Cong.*; the *Reg. of Debates*; and the *Cong. Globe*. Scattered items may be found in De Alva S. Alexander, *Polit. Hist. of N. Y.* (1906); Chas. E. Fitch, *Memorial Encyc. of the State of N. Y.* (1916); Wm. T. Bonner, *N. Y.—the World Metropolis* (1924); Jas. Schouler, *Hist. of the U. S. Under the Constitution* (1880–91); and the biographies and writings of Bryant, Jackson, Polk, Tilden, and Van Buren.]   M.L.B.

CAMDEN, JOHNSON NEWLON (Mar. 6, 1828–Apr. 25, 1908), business man, senator, of Maryland descent, was the eldest of the eight children of John Scribner Camden and Nancy (Newlon) Camden. He was born at the Collins Settlement, Va. Early in 1838 he moved with his father to the neighboring Braxton County, where as a boy he obtained a thorough knowledge of woodcraft and some insight into mineral resources. His basic training for business was obtained from a brief experience as assistant to the county clerk at Weston (1842–43), two years of study at the Northwestern Academy at Clarksburg (1843–45), a year of service as deputy-clerk of the circuit court of Braxton County (1845–46), and a period of study as a cadet at the United States Military Academy at West Point (1846–48). Resigning from West Point to study law, he was admitted to the bar in 1851 and for a time held the local office of state attorney, first in Braxton County, then in Nicholas County; but, influenced by his interest in surveying and in large tracts of wild lands, he soon abandoned law for the purchase of leases for wild lands with which he combined for a time (1853–58) an assistant's position in the Exchange Bank at Weston. In 1858 he married Anna Thompson, a daughter of Judge George W. and Elizabeth (Steenrod) Thompson of Wheeling. Later he applied his business genius to the development of oil production beginning with exciting pioneer work at Burning Springs on the Little Kanawha in Wirt County in 1860 and forming a partnership with the Rathbone Brothers during the Civil War. In 1869 he sold his Little Kanawha interests and at Parkersburg entered the oil refining business which soon resulted in association with the recently organized Standard Oil Company. In the latter he became a director and was especially in charge of the prosperous Camden Consolidated Oil Company at Parkersburg and later consolidated the refin-

eries of Baltimore under a single management of which he became president. In connection with his plans for wild land development he completed a branch railroad from Clarksburg to Weston in 1879 and extended it southward to the Elk and Gauley rivers in 1889–90, merging the various branches into the West Virginia & Pittsburgh of which he became president and which in 1890 was leased to the Baltimore & Ohio Company. Meantime in 1882 he was a leader in the organization of the Ohio River Railroad which was completed from Wheeling to Parkersburg in 1884 and to Huntington in 1888.

Camden was active in movements for repeal of the state constitutional disfranchisement of Confederates. In 1868 and again in 1872 he was the Conservative-Democrat candidate for governor but was defeated. He declined to be a candidate for the nomination in 1870. In 1868, 1872, and 1876 he was a delegate to the Democratic national conventions. For the United States Senate he was strongly supported in the contest of 1874, was unanimously nominated by the Democratic caucus in 1880, and was elected by the legislature in 1881. He was the caucus nominee of 1887 for reëlection and, although defeated by the defection of twelve Democrat members of the legislature who opposed his political methods, he named his successor. With the intention of retiring from politics he declined the offer of the nomination for governor. In January 1893 he was again elected to the United States Senate to complete the unexpired term of Senator John A. Kenna (deceased) and served until Mar. 4, 1895, when he was succeeded by Senator Stephen B. Elkins.

[J. M. Callahan, *Hist. of W. Va. Old and New* (1923); Geo. W. Atkinson and Alvaro F. Gibbons, *Prominent Men of W. Va.* (1890); *Biog. Directory Am. Cong.* (1928); *Daily State Jour.* (Parkersburg, W. Va.), Apr. 27, 1908.]   J.M.C.

CAMERON, ANDREW CARR (Sept. 28, 1834–May 28, 1890), labor leader and publisher, the son of a Scotch printer, lived for the first seventeen years of his life in Berwick-on-Tweed, England. After a short but rigorous elementary education, he was placed in his father's shop, where he worked until the family emigrated to America and settled in a small village near Chicago. Within a few months the father was able to find an opening for young Cameron on a Chicago paper, at that time called the *Courant*, later merged into *Young America*, and afterward into the *Chicago Times*. With the latter reorganization, it became the official organ of Stephen A. Douglas. While working on this paper Cameron joined and became a prominent member of the Typographical Union. A printers' strike in 1864 led to the establishment of the *Workingman's Advocate,* and Cameron left the *Times* to become its editor. Two years later he took complete control. This weekly paper was the official organ of the Chicago Trades Assembly, and later of the National Labor Union. By forceful and clear editorials, Cameron extended his influence throughout the labor movement of the country, and became the greatest labor editor of his time. In editing the "paper devoted exclusively to the interests of the producing classes" his work was characterized, as an associate described it, "by all the 'vim' and independent characteristics of a Scotch Covenanter who hated tyranny and oppression from whatever source." Cameron's activities were by no means confined to his desk through this period, for during the first six years of his editorship he took part in all the leading labor deliberations, was four years president of the Chicago Trades Assembly, and was also president of the Grand Eight Hour League, and of the Illinois State Labor Association. The labor movement of the middle West during this period believed strongly in the value of independent political action and the editorial columns of the *Advocate* continually expressed this view. Cameron was one of the organizers of the National Labor Union, which had throughout its brief existence as its cardinal tenet the formation of a labor party. For six consecutive years he was chairman of the Platform Committee of the National Labor Union, and was secretary of the conference called by it which nominated Judge Davis for president of the United States. With the unemployment that came with the first attempts at deflation in 1867 and 1868, Cameron and a number of other leaders within the National Labor Union began to stress the greenback theory of "plentiful money." Independent political action, with the issues of the eight-hour day through legislative action, monetary and land reform, and coöperation were the doctrines that he continually dwelt on in the *Workingman's Advocate* and which he impressed upon the National Labor Union. As a part of his program he also emphasized the very limited possibilities of the strike. Though the *Advocate* continued publication until 1880 and was widely read, Cameron's influence began to decline from about 1870. Many workers were losing faith in the power of political action, and inclining toward a more strictly economic organization. New leaders were being heard who urged the economic value of unionism and advocated the use of the strike where necessary. Though Cameron never lost faith in his own beliefs, he was fair enough to give the new leaders a hearing and encourage-

ment through the columns of the *Advocate.* By 1875 the drift away from political action was very marked, and the National Labor Union held its last convention, with Cameron and a few more of the old leaders as the only delegates in attendance. Though he was unable to see in the tendency away from political action any reason for giving up his own beliefs, he never became bitter at the new leaders or the changed emphasis. He continued to urge political action leading to monetary reform for it would, he believed, "do more to dignify labor, secure to the laborer an equitable distribution of this world's goods than all trade unions" (*Workingman's Advocate,* Jan. 25, 1873). After sixteen years as publisher of the *Advocate,* he discontinued the paper, and became editor of the *Inland Printer,* the leading technical journal for the trade in the United States at that time. He had in no way lost his sympathy and enthusiasm for the welfare of the producing classes, but the movement had passed to other issues, issues for which Cameron had not the same zeal. After eight years he purchased the *Artist Printer,* which he edited until his death.

[See the brief biography in the *Western British American,* Mar. 19, 1888. Most of the material from the pages of the *Workingman's Advocate,* including the yearly proceedings of the National Labor Union, has been collected in John R. Commons and others, *Documentary Hist. of Am. Industrial Soc.,* vol. IX (1910), containing the significant "Address to Workingmen" prepared by Cameron for the National Labor Union. The place of Cameron in the labor movement of the period is outlined in John R. Commons and others, *Hist. of Labour in the U. S.* (1918), vol. II.]   W.E.C.

CAMERON, ARCHIBALD (*c.* 1771–Dec. 4, 1836), Presbyterian minister, was the youngest of six children born to John and Jannet (McDonald) Cameron of Ken Loch in Lochaber, Scotland. In 1773–74 the family emigrated to America and located near Redstone, on the Monongahela River in western Virginia, whence the family moved, in 1781, to Kentucky and eventually settled on a farm near Bardstown in Nelson County. The parents died soon after their arrival in Kentucky, and Angus Cameron—a strange anomaly among frontiersmen, in that he was quite at home with Greek and Latin texts—directed the early training of his younger brother, Archibald. After spending about a year at Transylvania Seminary, Lexington, Archibald finished his literary course under the guidance of James Priestley of Bardstown, and then studied theology with David Rice of Danville. Licensed to preach in 1795 and ordained the following year, he began a ministry of forty years' duration which left its imprint on Presbyterianism in Kentucky, though his labors were confined to the counties of Nelson, Shelby, and Jefferson.

Freed from "worldly cares and avocations" by an emolument, which, in 1806, amounted to $217.75 if all the subscriptions were paid, Cameron rode about the country, often swimming his horse across the Salt River, to organize new churches and to encourage the struggling congregations already established. He combated with an unbending orthodoxy the schisms which threatened to destroy the Presbyterianism his Calvinistic inheritance and training had led him to support. With New Light, Shakerism, Socinianism, and even with the "absurdities of Methodism" which he deemed "more pernicious, owing to their prevalence, than the Papist errors," he contended in church assembly and in pamphlet. He was a member of the commission appointed by the Kentucky Synod of 1804 to inquire into the Cumberland controversy. He was prominent in the state synods from the first, in 1802, until his death, and usually served on the judiciary committees so that he came to be recognized by his contemporaries as the greatest judicial theologian of Presbyterianism in Kentucky. His published works, including such titles as *The Faithful Steward* (1806), *A Defense of the Doctrines of Grace* (1816), *A Reply to Some Questions on Divine Predestination* (1822) and *An Exposure of Falsehood and Folly* (1829), were brochures, controversial in nature, opposing certain doctrines such as that of "abstracted atonement," which were fashionable in some sections of the Presbyterian church. Cameron was a tireless student, blunt and reserved in manner, and careless in dress, but possessed of a native eloquence and keen powers of satire that made him a much feared adversary. He never married.

[Manuscript copy of papers in the possession of relatives, furnished to J. H. Logan as material for a biography of Archibald Cameron, now in possession of the Presbyt. Hist. Soc. Lib., Phila.; Wm. B. Sprague, *Annals Am. Pulpit*, IV (1858), pp. 168–72; Robt. Davidson, *Hist. of the Presbyt. Ch. in the State of Ky.* (1847), pp. 120–21; the *Presbyterian*, Dec. 24, 1836.]

T. D. M.

CAMERON, JAMES DONALD (May 14, 1833–Aug. 30, 1918), railroad president, secretary of war, senator, the son of Simon Cameron [*q.v.*], and Margaret (Brua) Cameron, was born at Middletown, Pa. After graduating from Princeton in 1852, he returned to his native town to begin a business career. His father had established the Bank of Middletown, had organized and developed the Northern Central Railroad, and had interested himself in numerous other projects. Young Cameron, therefore, found ample opportunities awaiting him. He began his apprenticeship as a clerk in the bank, but was soon promoted to cashier and subsequently became president. Other family properties came under his management early because of the elder Cameron's increasing absorption in state and national politics. During the Civil War the son was active in forwarding Union troops over the "Cameron Road," and from 1863 to 1874 he was president of the company. It is said that he personally made the railroad arrangements to get Lincoln to Washington in 1861 when there were rumors of plots against the President. He seems to have had much of his father's ability, energy, and shrewdness, and to have been typical of the men of affairs who were beginning to dominate the life of the nation. But it was not as a business man that he earned a nation-wide reputation: it was as an audacious politician. Here also his father had paved the way for him, but once in the rough and tumble of politics, Don Cameron was well able to stand alone. In his father's notable struggle against Gov. Andrew G. Curtin for the senatorship in 1867, the son successfully directed the maneuvers in the legislature from start to finish. The Governor's defeat gave the Camerons undisputed domination of the politics of the state. The father also acquired great influence with President Grant and when a vacancy occurred in the War Office in 1876 he succeeded in having his son appointed as secretary of war. Don Cameron's incumbency was brief (May 22, 1876–Mar. 3, 1877), but his energetic handling of departmental business amply demonstrated his competence. He was not averse to using his office, however, to serve political ends. When Hayes's chances of winning the electoral votes of Florida and Louisiana in 1877 were doubtful, Cameron placed Federal troops at the disposal of Republican politicians in these states. For this service and for the notable assistance that he had rendered Hayes in the Republican nominating convention, the elder Cameron and other Pennsylvania Republicans demanded that the Secretary be continued in the War Department under the new administration. Hayes refused; he disapproved of the political methods of the Camerons and wanted an entirely new cabinet. Senator Cameron then decided to surrender his own place to his son as a consolation prize. The subservient Pennsylvania legislature readily acquiesced and elected Don Cameron for the remaining two years of his father's term. A more striking example of entrenched political power could hardly be found. At the same time Don also took over the active management of the state political machine which his father had built up and with the aid of lieutenants like Matthew

Quay ran it skilfully and defiantly as long as he remained in public life. It enabled him to be returned to the Senate in 1879, 1885, and 1891. Election to the chairmanship of the Republican national committee in 1879 for a time widened his influence in national politics. He promptly turned it to Grant's advantage, joining with Conkling of New York and Logan of Illinois in a strenuous campaign to have the war hero nominated for a third term. Shrewd plans were laid to control the convention of 1880, but their strategy was discovered and defeated. Although successful as a politician, Cameron never employed the arts commonly used by public men to popularize themselves with the people. He despised all such methods. He was a judicious, reticent, unemotional man. His speeches were few and brief, but direct and forceful. Like his father he worked in ante-rooms, committees, and caucuses to attain his ends. On the whole his twenty years in the Senate were undistinguished. He made politics, not statesmanship, his principal public business. At a time when the public treasury was being drained for pensions, relief measures, and the like, he was in the forefront of those serving private causes. In national legislation he generally stood with his party, but on occasion, as in the case of the "Force Bill" of 1890, showed admirable and courageous independence. And, unlike his father, he would not bend or yield to public sentiment. He was especially earnest in his support of a high tariff and other measures favorable to the rapidly expanding business interests. In 1883 he went so far as to vote against a protective tariff because its iron duty seemed too low. Yet for some unknown reason he supported free silver as "honest money, the money of the people" (*Congressional Record*, 53 Cong., 1 Sess., p. 2930), and on Oct. 30, 1893, he voted against the repeal of the Sherman Silver Purchase Law. At the end of his third full term, 1897, possibly foreseeing defeat, he retired voluntarily from the Senate and spent the rest of his life in the management of his private affairs and in the quiet enjoyment of his Lancaster farm and his houseboat on the Southern coast. Thoroughly honest in personal matters, he was held in high regard by his friends. He was married twice. His first wife, Mary McCormick, died in 1874. Four years later he married Elizabeth Sherman, niece of John and William T. Sherman.

[There is little in print about Cameron. The most extensive account is in Alexander K. McClure, *Old Time Notes of Pa.* (1905). McClure was a political opponent, but seems to write fairly. References to particular incidents in Cameron's career are to be found in Jas. F. Rhodes, *Hist. of the U. S.*, vol. VIII (1919); E. P. Oberholtzer, *Hist. of the U. S. Since the Civil War*, vol. III (1926); Jas. G. Blaine, *Twenty Years of Congress* (1884–93); G. F. Hoar, *Autobiog. of Seventy Years* (1903); Chas. R. Williams, *Life of Rutherford B. Hayes* (1914). Obituaries in the *N. Y. Times*, *N. Y. Tribune*, Phila. *Public Ledger*, and *Phila. Press*, Aug. 31, 1918, give brief but useful sketches of Cameron's life.]
A.H.M.

CAMERON, ROBERT ALEXANDER (Feb. 22, 1828–Mar. 15, 1894), Union soldier, land colonizer, was born in Brooklyn, N. Y. About the time he was fourteen years old his parents moved to Valparaiso, Ind. After finishing at the public schools he entered the Indiana Medical College, from which he graduated in 1849, later attending Rush Medical College in Chicago. In 1857 he bought the *Valparaiso Republican,* which he conducted for several years. He was a delegate to the Republican national convention, where he voted for the nomination of Lincoln, and in the fall of the year he was elected to the lower house of the legislature. On the news of the firing on Fort Sumter he began at once to organize a company of three-months' men. Two days later he telegraphed Gov. Morton that his company was ready, and on Apr. 23 he was mustered in as a captain of the 9th Indiana Volunteers. His first service was in the West Virginia campaign under McClellan. In July he reënlisted, and on the 29th was commissioned a lieutenant-colonel and transferred to the 19th Indiana. On Feb. 3, 1862, he was transferred to the 34th Indiana, of which he was made colonel on June 15. He served at Island No. 10, New Madrid, and at the capture of Memphis. For gallant conduct during the siege of Vicksburg he was recommended by Grant, with five other colonels, for promotion, and on Aug. 11, 1863, was commissioned a brigadier-general. He commanded one of the two divisions (the third) of the 13th Corps that took part in the Red River expedition in the fore part of 1864, and on the wounding of Ransom, at Sabine Cross Roads, Apr. 8, assumed command of the corps. With the defeat and return of the army to the Mississippi and the transfer of the corps to Grant in Virginia, he was placed in command of the Lafourche district of the Department of the Gulf, with headquarters at Thibodaux, La., where he remained till the close of the war. In the omnibus promotions dated Mar. 13, 1865, he was brevetted a major-general.

He resigned from the army June 22 and went to New York. Here he formed the acquaintance of Nathan C. Meeker [*q.v.*], agricultural editor of the *Tribune,* and became greatly interested in the movement for planting farm colonies in the West. On the organization, in Cooper Union, Dec. 23, 1869, of the Union Colony, he was made vice-president, and in the following year, with Meeker and A. C. Fisk, went to Colorado and selected the site now occupied by Greeley. He took a leading part in the founding of the colony, and at the first election, May 1871, was chosen one of the town trustees and subsequently was made president. Three months later, however, he resigned, to take the superintendency of the Fountain Colony, which established Colorado Springs. At the end of the year he returned to Greeley, but in the spring of 1873 took part in the founding of Fort Collins, a venture that proved personally disastrous. After an attempt to recoup his fortunes in San Francisco, he returned to Colorado and settled in Denver. For several years he was inspector of mail service in that city, a post in which he is credited with doing efficient work. In 1885 he was appointed warden of the penitentiary at Canon City, but a change in the state administration two years later caused him to lose the place before he had time to introduce the reforms he had planned. In 1888 he was engaged as immigration agent of the Fort Worth & Denver City Railway. In the outskirts of Canon City he developed a fruit farm and continued to reside there until his death.

Cameron married a daughter of J. B. Flower, one of the founders of Greeley Colony and at one time his partner. He was a large man, somewhat above six feet in height and weighing more than 200 pounds. The Denver *News*, on his death, said of him that "as a citizen" none "was more highly esteemed." Boyd, one of the Union colonists, though acknowledging that he had a certain kind of ability, speaks of him as one who "was fertile in expedients," who was "a man of policy rather than a devotee of principle" and finds fault with him for taking for himself and his partner Flower the best location in Greeley.

[F. B. Heitman, *Hist. Reg.* (1903) ; *Battles and Leaders of the Civil War,* IV (1888) ; John Formby, *The Am. Civil War* (1910) ; Jerome C. Smiley and others, *Semi-Centennial Hist. of the State of Colo.* (1913) ; Jas. F. Willard, *The Union Colony at Greeley, Colo.* (1918) ; David Boyd, *Greeley and the Union Colony of Colo.* (1890) ; obituaries in *The News* and *The Republican* of Denver, Mar. 16, 1894.] W.J.G.

CAMERON, SIMON (Mar. 8, 1799–June 26, 1889), senator, secretary of war, diplomat, was born in Lancaster County, Pa., of Scotch and German ancestry, the son of Charles and Martha (Pfoutz) Cameron. Reverses and misfortunes in his father's family cast him upon the world early and he was obliged to apprentice himself for a time in a printing business in Harrisburg. In January 1821, at the solicitation of Samuel D. Ingham, he went to Doylestown, Pa., where he edited the *Bucks County Messenger,* soon merged with the *Doylestown Democrat* as the *Bucks County Democrat.* On the decease of this paper at the close of the year 1821, he returned to

Harrisburg for a short time as partner of Charles Mowry in the management of the *Pennsylvania Intelligencer,* but during 1822 he went to Washington to study national political movements, obtained work in the printing house of Gales & Seaton who printed the congressional debates, and spent his spare time in the houses of Congress and in making useful friends,—among them Monroe and Calhoun. About 1824 he returned to Harrisburg, bought the *Republican,* and was soon exercising considerable influence in state and national politics. He was then, as later, a staunch advocate of the protective tariff. The remunerative position of state printer was given him and in 1826 he was made adjutant-general of the state. Newspaper editing did not hold him long. As soon as his position was established and his purse sufficient, he left the press and entered pursuits which promised greater financial gain. It was the era of internal improvements, and the ambitious young Cameron was quick to see money-making possibilities. He became a contractor for the construction of canals and began a network of railroads in Pennsylvania which he later united into the Northern Central Railroad. In 1832 he set up the Bank of Middletown with himself as cashier, and soon afterward entered the iron business. Subsequently he also engaged in insurance and became interested in other projects. Notwithstanding the diversity of these undertakings Cameron managed them with skill and success and amassed a fortune. At no time, however, did he lose his interest in state and national politics. It was partly through his efforts that the state legislature in 1830 was induced to head a movement for Jackson's renomination, and two years later he aided materially in having Van Buren nominated for vice-president in place of Calhoun. It was also largely through Cameron's maneuvering that James Buchanan was sent to the Senate in 1833 just at the time when he despaired of political opportunities and was seriously considering a return to the practise of law. Prior to 1838 Cameron had held no public office except the position of adjutant-general of Pennsylvania, but in that year he received an appointment as commissioner to settle certain claims of the Winnebago Indians, a place he acquired with Buchanan's assistance. Considerable scandal arose from his activities because of his adjusting the claims by the payment of notes on his own bank, an arrangement which enriched himself and earned for him the derisive sobriquet, "The Great Winnebago Chief." Following this episode, Cameron's political influence decreased for a time, but actually his career as a great politician was only beginning. In 1845 by a coalition of Whigs, Native Americans, and Protectionist Democrats he won the Senate seat vacated by Buchanan who resigned to enter Polk's cabinet. Buchanan was irritated at Cameron's defeat of the regular party candidate, George Woodward, a free-trader, and the two men parted political company. Alexander K. McClure, an old political foe, has written that from 1845 until Cameron's death nearly a half-century later, "There is not an important complete chapter of political history in the State that can be written with the omission of his defeats or triumphs, and even after his death until the present time [1905] no important chapter of political history can be fully written without recognizing his successors and assigns in politics as leading or controlling factors" (*Old Time Notes of Pennsylvania,* 1905, I, 98). Still, the victory of 1845 did not crown Cameron as the political czar of his state. He had won by fusion methods and incurred bitter Democratic opposition. In 1849 he was unable to command Democratic support and failed to effect a strong enough coalition in the legislature to win a reëlection. His first term in the Senate is of interest principally because in 1846 he made the one important speech of his career. It was in opposition to the Walker revenue tariff. Another attempt in 1855 to return to the Senate with Know-Nothing support also resulted in failure. Cameron then decided to cast his lot with the new Republican party and in 1856 actively supported Frémont for President. The following year Republican backing and three Democratic votes, obtained by bargaining, enabled him to return to the Senate. There he became an implacable foe of President Buchanan. Cameron's political somersaulting was now at an end; he remained a Republican for the rest of his life and gave much of his time and energy to the building up of a smooth-running party machine in Pennsylvania. In the management and control of it he was unequalled. His leadership was sometimes challenged; he suffered subsequent defeats; but no one ever dislodged him from control of the organization. In 1860 it helped him to make a presentable showing in the Republican national convention as a candidate for president. He could not be nominated, but his henchmen traded Pennsylvania votes for Lincoln in exchange for a cabinet post for Cameron. After much hesitation Lincoln abided by the bargain his managers had made without his consent. Cameron resigned his seat in the Senate and became secretary of war. The choice proved a most unfortunate one. Although Cameron was an able business executive, political considerations too often governed his judg-

ments and his actions in departmental administration. He dispensed civil and military offices and army contracts in a notorious fashion; corruption became rampant. Although it does not appear that he enriched himself, there were many who did profit shamefully. Complaints against his management and his favoritism poured into Washington almost daily and demands for his removal were persistent. In an effort to retrieve popular support he began to advocate the freeing and arming of slaves, policies which were rapidly gaining public favor, but which were not then acceptable to the President. So embarrassing did the Secretary's presence become that Lincoln in January 1862 appointed him minister to Russia to be rid of him. Three months later the House of Representatives censured his conduct in the handling of contracts. Cameron had no intention of remaining long in Russia, however, and was back in the United States in time to try for the Senate again in 1863. He failed of election, but in 1867, after a struggle of unexampled desperation, was successful. For ten years thereafter the Senator reigned supreme in Pennsylvania, and in 1873 returned to the Senate without a contest. He also became a power in Grant's administration, controlled the patronage of his state, and in 1876 succeeded in having his son, James Donald Cameron [*q.v.*], appointed secretary of war. When President Hayes in 1877 refused to continue the son in that office, Cameron resigned his own place in the Senate upon receiving assurances from the subservient Pennsylvania legislature that it would elect his son as his successor. With this bold stroke the Senator closed his remarkable political career. At the same time he handed over to his son the control of the state machine. No politician of his generation understood the science of politics better than Simon Cameron; none enjoyed greater power. He studied and understood individuals who could be of service to him; he knew the precise value of men and could marshal them when occasion arose. His methods were often circuitous, the means employed were often questionable, but the end in view was always clear. Cameron was of broad intellectual force, if not of fine learning; he could employ his faculties to the utmost and meet each new problem in an eminently practical way. He could be patient and conservative, or keen and aggressive, as the situation demanded. Tradition and precedent bore lightly upon him and were promptly brushed aside when new conditions and necessities arose. He lived in a time when men firmly believed that "to the victor belongs the spoils," and to this doctrine he gladly subscribed.

By patronage he built up a political despotism in Pennsylvania; with it he rewarded his friends and punished his foes. It was commonly said that he never forgot a friend or an enemy. In his senatorial career there was little that was statesmanlike or brilliant. He had no aptitude for Websterian oratory or flights of verbal fancy. He said little in public that was vital, but did much in private that was practical, far-seeing, and astute. His business in the Senate, as elsewhere, was politics, and he governed his conduct accordingly. In appearance he was tall and slim, with a "marked Scotch face," keen gray eyes, a high broad forehead crowned with a luxuriant crop of hair. His manners and speech were kindly and gentle, and his genial, democratic manner won many people to him. He prided himself on possessing the doggedness and determination of his German forebears and the aggressiveness of the "Scotch rebels." His fighting qualities were great. Time dealt lightly with him and at the end of his half-century of political activity and struggle, he was hale and hearty as ever. For twelve years after leaving the Senate he enjoyed freedom from the cares and perplexities of political life on his farm at Donegal Springs, and saw his son three times elected to the place he had surrendered to him. In his ninety-first year, rich in honors and fortune, he passed away. His wife Margaret Brua died several years before, leaving five children.

[The Coryell and Buchanan papers in the Pa. Hist. Soc. contain a number of Cameron letters relating to his earlier years. Some others written in later life are to be found in the Lib. of Cong., in the manuscript collections of his political contemporaries. The files of the War Dept. and the *Official Records* contain most of his war correspondence, and the "Report of the Committee on Contracts" (*House Report No. 2, 37 Cong., 2 Sess.*) reveals much regarding his deficiencies as secretary of war. The most useful accounts of his life are in Alexander K. McClure, *Old Time Notes of Pa.* (1905) and *Abraham Lincoln and Men of War Time* (1892). These are critical, but not unfriendly. Standard histories and the biographies of public men of Cameron's time also are helpful. Additional information is to be found in A. H. Meneely, *The War Dept., 1861* (1928) ; Ellis and Evans, *Hist. of Lancaster County, Pa.* (1883) ; *N. Y. Times*, Mar. 13, 14, 1877, June 3, 1878, June 27, 1889; *Pittsburgh Dispatch*, June 27, 1889; *Harrisburg Daily Patriot*, June 27, 1889; *Phila. Press*, Mar. 13, 14, 15, 1877, Jan. 20, June 27, 1889.]

A. H. M.

CAMERON, WILLIAM EVELYN (Nov. 29, 1842–Jan. 25, 1927), newspaper editor, governor of Virginia, son of Walker Anderson Cameron and Elizabeth Byrd Walker, was born in Petersburg, Va., of aristocratic and distinguished descent from the Scottish chieftain Ewan Lochiel. After attending local schools and a North Carolina military academy, he entered Washington University, St. Louis, but soon left college for a clerkship on a Mississippi steamboat. He was in St. Louis again, preparing for a cadetship at West Point, when the Civil War broke out, and he acted as drillmaster for the Missouri troops until captured at Fort Jackson by the Federals. Escaping the same night, he made his way home and enlisted in the 12th Virginia Regiment; fought in all the battles of Lee's army (except Sharpsburg) from Seven Pines onward; was severely wounded at second Manassas; and when he surrendered at Appomattox had risen from private to assistant adjutant-general.

Returning to Petersburg, he commenced his professional career as local editor of a daily newspaper founded by Anthony Keiley, and when Gen. Canby suppressed this for "disloyalty," obtained a similar position on the *Index*. In 1866 he was made editor of the newly-established *Norfolk Virginian*. The next year he bought the Petersburg *Index,* and waged active and effectual warfare in behalf of the conservative political policies which resulted in the election of Gilbert Carlton Walker as governor and in the state's release from carpet-bag rule. In the heat of this campaign he became involved in a duel with Judge Robert W. Hughes, and was badly wounded. In 1872 he sold the *Index,* and, with Baker P. Lee, acquired control of the *Richmond Enquirer.* He married, Oct. 1, 1868, Louisa Clara Egerton, of St. Paul.

After serving three years as mayor of Petersburg, in 1879 he allied himself with the "anti-Bourbon" forces, who, advocating a readjustment of the state debt, were read out of the Democratic party. Unshaken by this ostracism, he battled for his convictions through the columns of the *Richmond Whig;* served as a Hancock elector on his faction's presidential ticket; and in 1881, nominated for governor by the Readjuster convention, was victorious over John W. Daniel, the regular Democratic candidate. His administration, 1882–86, saw the execution of the Readjuster platform, which, although involving repudiation of the state debt and abuse of patronage, provided much progressive economic and social legislation designed to benefit the masses and to break the power of the privileged. At the end of his term of office Cameron engaged in the practise of law at Petersburg, for which profession he had qualified ten years earlier, and won recognition as a capable constitutional lawyer. During 1892–94 he was in Chicago as an official of the Columbian Exposition, served on its Jury of Awards of Liberal Arts, and was appointed historian of the enterprise. In 1901 he represented Petersburg in the Virginia Constitutional Convention, was chairman of the committee on the executive department, a member of the committees on the judiciary and on final revision, and participated in all of the proceedings of the Assembly. He moved to Norfolk in 1908 and edited the *Norfolk Virginian* until 1915, when he became editor-in-chief of the *Virginian-Pilot,* a position which he held until failing health compelled his retirement in 1919.

Impetuous, eager, courageous, and independent, his forceful personality combined with his talents to make him a leader of local political thought in his day, and although the majority of Virginians did not always agree with him,—especially in his general indorsement of Mahone policies or his treatment of the race problem— they never questioned his patriotism or his sincerity of purpose. He was equally eloquent with tongue and pen: a brilliant and uncommonly powerful editorial writer, a cultured, polished stylist, a convincing speaker, and a master of debate. Among his publications were: *History of the World's Columbian Exposition* (1893); *The Life and Character of Robert E. Lee* (1901); sketches of Tyler, Wise, and other prominent Virginians; and a number of fugitive lyrics, at least one of which, "In the Twilight," achieved a deserved and lasting popularity.

[L. G. Tyler, *Men of Mark in Va.* (1906), I, 108–11; *Who's Who in America,* 1918–19; C. C. Pearson, *The Readjuster Movement in Va.* (1917); Richmond *Times-Dispatch,* Jan. 26, 27, 1927; Norfolk *Virginian-Pilot,* Jan. 26, 27, 1927; R. L. Morton, *Hist. of Va.* (1924), vol. III.]   A.C.G.,Jr.

CAMM, JOHN (1718–1778), Anglican clergyman, president of the College of William and Mary, was the son of Thomas Camm of Hornsea, Yorkshire, England. After attending school at Beverley, in Yorkshire, he entered Trinity College, Cambridge, at the age of twenty. Soon after receiving his bachelor's degree, he emigrated to Virginia. In 1745 he was appointed minister of Newport Parish, Isle of Wight County. Four years later, the young minister was appointed professor of divinity in the College of William and Mary, to be associated with that institution for twenty-eight years. He was at the same time appointed minister of the neighboring York-Hampton parish. Camm was in sympathy a Tory, an ardent champion of the Crown and of the clergy. In December 1755, the Virginia Assembly, because of a shortage of tobacco, the common medium of exchange, enacted a law enabling the inhabitants to pay their debts in money at the rate of 16 s. 8 d. a hundred pounds, the equivalent of two pence a pound. The act, known as the Two Penny Act, did not carry the usual suspending clause for the King's pleasure. Although it was general in its application, only the clergymen protested. Their salaries had been placed by law at 1,600 pounds of tobacco. They felt that the law was not just. Commissary Dawson, John Camm, and three other professors in the College of William and Mary protested vigorously against its passage. Meanwhile, Dawson was made president of the College. Camm and his three confederates now tried in vain to have the Commissary call a convocation of the clergy to oppose the act. When he refused to grant their request, they severely criticized him and called the clergy to meet. But the clergy, finding the price of tobacco not above the normal, remained passive. Ill feeling between president and faculty, however, resulted in the resignation of one of the latter and the expulsion of three others, one of whom was Camm. In 1758, another Two Penny Act was passed, to continue in operation twelve months. The clergy now met in convocation at the college, drew up an appeal to the King to veto the act, and chose Camm to present it at Court. He was successful in having the objectionable acts of 1755 and of 1758 disallowed by the King in Council in August 1759. His attorney in Virginia, with the encouragement of his parishioners, immediately brought suit for his salary. There was great excitement in Virginia when news came of the King's action. Upon his return from England, Camm found himself the center of attack and the leader of the clergy in their fight against the Two Penny Act. He engaged in a war of pamphlets with Col. Richard Bland and Col. Landon Carter. His articles were forceful, clear, and well written. It was this quarrel which brought to public notice Patrick Henry. Camm's own case was finally appealed to the Privy Council, but was thrown out on a technicality. He did succeed, however, in securing his reinstatement, by the Privy Council, to his former position in the college. He drew another storm about himself in 1771, in advocating the establishment of a bishopric in Virginia,—a very unpopular movement, which failed. In that year he was appointed president of the College of William and Mary, rector of Bruton Parish, commissary of the Bishop of London, and member of the Governor's Council. Although his fellow Tories deserted him at the outbreak of the Revolution, Camm held his position in the college until removed in the spring of 1777. He had opposed the separation from England. Dr. Arthur Lee said that he was "the center of all the disaffection in the Colony" (*William and Mary Quarterly,* I, 69–73). On one occasion the Governor exclaimed that the Visitors of the College allowed President Camm to lead them around by the nose. In 1769, when fifty-one years old, Camm married the youthful Betsy Hansford, a descendant of one of the rebel lieutenants. There is a charming family tradition of their courtship, a story which might well rank with that of John Alden and Priscilla (see *William and Mary Quarterly*, XIX, 29; and John Fiske, *Old Virginia and Her Neighbors*, 1897, II, 127).

[See Lyon G. Tyler in *Wm. and Mary College Hist. Quart.*, I, 69–73; XIX, 28–30. Other references in that Quarterly are: III, 65; I, 237, a sprightly letter to a friend in England; the manuscript minutes of the William and Mary College faculty in volumes I, II, III, IV, V, XIII, XIV, XV; an interesting account of the part played by Camm in the Two Penny Act controversy, XX, 10 ff. Other accounts of the Two Penny Act controversy may be had in *Va. Mag. of Hist. and Biog.*, X, 350–56; Wm. Wirt Henry, *Patrick Henry, Life, Correspondence, and Speeches* (1891), I, 28–48; Chas. Campbell, *Hist. of Va.* (1860), 507–18; Bishop Wm. Meade, *Old Churches and Families of Va.* (1857), I, 216–25; H. J. Eckenrode, *Separation of Church and State in Va.* (1910); Wm. Stevens Perry, *Papers Relating to the Hist. of the Church in Va., A. D., 1650–1776* (1870).]   R. L. M—n.

CAMMERHOFF, JOHN CHRISTOPHER FREDERICK (July 28, 1721–Apr. 28, 1751), Moravian missionary, was born at Hillersleben, near Magdeburg, Germany, of religious parents who dedicated him, even before his birth, to the ministry. He was first instructed at home by private tutors, then attended the celebrated Protestant school of Kloster Bergen, and in 1738 entered the University of Jena where he came under Moravian influence in the persons of John Nitschmann and Count C. R. Zinzendorf. Upon graduation, out of deference to his parents' wishes, he accepted a position as tutor at Kloster Bergen, but he was increasingly repelled by the formality of Lutheranism and in 1743, with two fellow-teachers, Schumann and Zurmucklen, he sought admission into the Moravian Brotherhood and received an appointment in the Theological Seminary at Marienborn in Wetteravia. He found the religious views prevalent in that region entirely congenial, sharing to the full in the extreme emotionalism, the mystic emphasis upon the Passion, the delight in fantastic symbolism, and the conviction of being in a state of special grace which were characteristic of the Wetteravian group. He once more came under the direct influence of Zinzendorf, and after two years was made his amanuensis. At the early age of twenty-five, he was appointed assistant to Bishop A. G. Spangenberg [*q.v.*] in Pennsylvania. He was immediately married, on July 23, 1746, to Anna von Pahlen, a Livonian baroness; was consecrated bishop in London

two months later; and arrived in America toward the end of the year.

Spangenberg distrusted the emotional fervor of his young assistant but felt powerless to prevent his introduction of Wetteravian methods, as he soon perceived that Cammerhoff was acting under secret instructions from their mutual superiors in Germany. The influence of the younger man rapidly increased. He maintained an extensive correspondence with Zinzendorf and other officials of the Church—his letters sometimes running to more than one hundred closely written pages, preached widely among the settlers of Pennsylvania and New York, and made extensive missionary journeys among the Indians. The supposedly stolid aborigines were quick to respond to Cammerhoff's child-like enthusiasm, and he came to enjoy their confidence to a marked degree, being formally adopted into the Turtle tribe of the Oneida nation, on Apr. 15, 1748, under the name of Gallichwio, or "Good Message." His longest journey was to the Grand Council of the Iroquis Confederacy at Onondaga, N. Y., in 1750, in which accompanied by David Zeisberger, he covered 1,600 miles in three months, being exposed, in addition to the customary perils of the wilderness, to the dangers of four nights in an Indian village where all the males were crazed with drink. His health was broken by the hardships of this journey, and he died in the ensuing spring, at the age of twenty-nine. With his death the Wetteravian influence in this country came to an end.

[See *Trans. Moravian Hist. Soc.*, vols. II (1886), III (1888), V (1899); also Geo. H. Loskiel, *Hist. of the Mission of the United Brethren among the Indians of North America* (London, 1794), pt. II, ch. 9. Cammerhoff's diary of his journey to Onondaga may be found in *Moravian Jours. Relating to Central N. Y., 1745–66* (Onondaga Hist. Ass., Syracuse, N. Y., 1916). There are voluminous Cammerhoff MSS. in the Bethlehem Archives at Bethlehem, Pa., many of them unfortunately defaced by some later hand which expunged the extravagant Wetteravian phraseology.]   E. S. B.

CAMP, DAVID NELSON (Oct. 13, 1820–Oct. 19, 1916), educator, was born in Durham, Conn. His father was Elah Camp, a descendant of settlers who came from Essex County, England, in 1630; his mother, Orit (Lee) Camp, was a descendant of Theophilus Eaton, governor of the New Haven colony. Life on the farm laid hard work and many responsibilities on young Camp's shoulders. His mother, "a devout Christian woman," brought him up "in the Fear of the Lord" and taught him to read; but the Bible, Scott's *Commentaries,* psalm books, "a few religious books," some school texts, and occasional newspapers constituted the range of his early reading. Beyond the home, his education was continued in the district school, the private school of Mrs. Goodwin, Durham Academy, Hartford Grammar School, Meriden Academy, and the temporary normal school instituted by Barnard at Hartford in 1839. His own ill health, and that of his father, hindered regular preparatory schooling and frustrated his plans for college. Nevertheless, with the aid of special masters, he studied Latin, bookkeeping, surveying, higher mathematics, poetry, history, natural, moral, and intellectual philosophy, astronomy, German and French. At eighteen, he first taught at North Guilford for thirty-nine dollars a quarter, with the privilege (and necessity) of "boarding 'round." Other successful schools at Cromwell, Branford, and Meriden brought his work to the attention of Henry Barnard [q.v.]. In 1844 he was married to Sarah Adaline Howd. He began institute work in 1845, was made secretary of the State Teachers' Association in 1847, was called to a professorship in the State Normal School in 1849, and was made the associate principal in 1855. On Philbrick's resignation, in 1857, Camp became commissioner of common schools and principal of the Normal School. He resigned (1866) on account of ill health. While abroad he accepted a professorship in St. John's College, Annapolis, but resigned to become an assistant to Barnard (1867) in the United States Bureau of Education. He soon, however, retired from Washington and conducted the New Britain (Conn.) Seminary till he discontinued active school work.

Besides his teaching and administrative duties, Camp was editor of the *Connecticut Common School Journal* and the *American Year Book,* and was the author of a *History of New Britain, Farmington, and Berlin* (1889). For schools, he prepared the small *Globe Manual* (1864), *Manual of Illustrative Teaching* (1865), four different *Geographies,* with *Outline Maps,* and revised Mitchell's *Outline Maps* and the *Government Instructor.* His later life was given over to church, business, and municipal affairs. In New Britain he was councilman (1871), alderman for three years, and mayor 1887–89. He was elected to the legislature in 1889, being chairman of the Committee on Education. His educational labors and his text-books made him one of the influential educators in Connecticut in the nineteenth century.

[The most complete single source of information is Camp's *Recollections of a Long and Active Life* (1917); other sources are his widely scattered addresses, published in proceedings of various educational associations, editorials, and periodical articles, the records of his administration at Hartford, printed reports of the New Britain School Society, and the books of which he was author or editor.]   T.W.

CAMP, HIRAM (Apr. 9, 1811–July 8, 1893), clock-maker, philanthropist, was the son of Deacon Samuel Camp, a farmer of Plymouth, Conn., and of his wife Jeannette Jerome, a sister of the clock-maker, Chauncey Jerome. His grandfather, Samuel Camp, was a Revolutionary soldier who saw service at Crown Point, Ticonderoga, and on Staten Island. Hiram passed his boyhood on the farm, with slender schooling during those months when he might best be spared from farm labors. He entered the Jerome shops at Bristol in 1829 and continued in business there with his uncle for twenty-four years. During just this period metal works and machine production were being introduced into the clock industry, with their accompanying lessening of the cost of production. Chauncey Jerome and Hiram Camp were largely instrumental in effecting this change. By 1837 the Jerome works had perfected a small brass-works clock that could be sold for $6.00, the price later being reduced to seventy-five cents. A branch of the Jerome works was opened in New Haven in 1843, and when the Bristol shops burned in 1845 the whole establishment was moved to that city. Camp supervised the erection of the New Haven plant. In 1851 he went into business for himself, manufacturing clock movements, and in 1853 he organized the New Haven Clock Company (of which he was president), a joint stock company capitalized at $20,000 for the purpose of making cases. The Jerome company failed in 1855, and the New Haven Clock Company purchased its entire business. With the elimination of the Jerome competition the New Haven Clock Company soon became the world's greatest clock manufacturing organization. It reached out for world markets; it improved its clock-making machinery; it developed sound financial policies; it perfected the mass-production of cheap standardized time pieces, such as the nickel alarm clock and the pioneer "dollar watch"; it diversified production so as to cover all markets with a complete line of goods: metronomes, jewelers' regulators, electro-mechanical movements, telegraph devices, miniature clocks, and high-grade movements with periodized and ornate cases in granites and different kinds of woods. Camp continued as president of the company until 1892 and was a trustee until his death.

He found time for numerous avocations. He served his city as selectman, councilman, and chief engineer of the fire department. As a Republican he represented his district in the Connecticut legislature of 1859 and held a place on its Finance Committee. But his chief interest, aside from his regular labor, was in his church.

He memorized his daily text and he exhibited a veritable passion for evangelization; he went from house to house with his Bible in his hand, he organized Sunday-schools, he supported city and frontier missions, he built a church next door to his own home, and he subscribed liberally to charities and religious education. With the evangelist D. C. Moody [*q.v.*], he established the Mount Hermon Boys' School and the Northfield Seminary for Young Ladies. He served as trustee for these institutions and at various times donated approximately $100,000 to their support. Interest in Christian morality drew him to the Prohibition movement. He contributed to its campaign chest and he took the stump in its behalf. Finally he even accepted nomination as its candidate for governor in 1888. He was married twice: to Elvira Rockwell Skinner, and, after her death, to Lucy Davis.

[*The Daily Morning Jour. and Courier* (New Haven), July 10, 12, 1893; *New Haven Evening Reg.*, July 11, 1893; Geo. B. Chandler, "Industrial History," section on "Clocks and Watches" in *Hist. of Connecticut*, ed. by Norris G. Osborn (1925), vol. IV; Chauncey Jerome, *Hist. of the Am. Clock Business for the Past Sixty Years and Life of Chauncey Jerome* (1860); *Hist. of the City of New Haven*, ed. by Edward E. Atwater (1887), pp. 580–81; Francis Atwater, *Hist. of the Town of Plymouth, Conn.* (1895), pp. 234–35; *Industrial Advantages of New Haven* (1889), p. 134; *Commerce, Manufactures and Resources of the City of New Haven and Environs* (1882), p. 101.] E. F. H.

CAMP, JOHN LAFAYETTE (Feb. 20, 1828–July 16, 1891), Confederate officer and Texas political leader, was born on a farm near Birmingham, Ala. He was the son of John Lafayette Camp and Elizabeth (Brown) Camp. He was graduated from the University of Tennessee in 1848 and moved to Texas the next year, locating at Gilmer, in Upshur County. There he taught school and practised law, soon taking his place as the leading attorney of that section of east Texas. He was married in 1851 to Mary Ann Ward, daughter of Dr. William Ward, well-known east Texas physician. During the next ten years he established an enviable reputation as a lawyer and was a prosperous cotton planter. When the Civil War broke out he left his wife and five children to enlist in the Confederate army. He was at first captain of an Upshur County company, but was soon elected colonel of the 14th Texas Cavalry. His regiment served in the Missouri campaign, also in Louisiana and Arkansas. He distinguished himself at Murfreesboro, and participated in the battles at Richmond, Cumberland Gap, and Chickamauga. His last battle was at Altoona, Ga. He was twice wounded and twice captured and was imprisoned for many months. In 1866 he was elected by the first Texas district to serve in the national Con-

gress, but was not permitted to take his seat. He was a delegate to the Texas constitutional convention of 1866, where he advocated measures which, following the Presidential plan of reconstruction, would have restored Texas to her former place in the Union. As a delegate to the national Democratic convention in 1872 he advocated coöperation with the Liberal Republicans. In 1874 he entered the state Senate, where he was an administration leader. He advocated the more rapid settlement of the frontier portion of the state through the encouragement of railroad building by donation of state lands, and led the campaign for a new constitution. Before the legislature had decided to favor a convention, a joint committee of Senator Camp and two representatives prepared a constitution, adoption of which was proposed as amendments, and which was admitted by all to be superior to the existing constitution (S. S. McKay, *Making the Texas Constitution of 1876*, 1924, p. 57).

In 1878 Camp was appointed by Gov. Hubbard to be judge of the district court sitting at Jefferson, Marshall, Palestine, and Tyler. In 1884 he accepted an appointment from President Cleveland as registrar of the land office of Arizona, hoping the change of climate would improve his health; but, this not resulting, he resigned after two years of service. He then moved to San Antonio, where he died in 1891. Camp County, Texas, created in April 1874, was named for him.

[*Official Records* (Army); *Tex. Almanac*, 1867; J. H. Brown, *Hist. of Tex.* (2 vols., 1893); J. J. Lane, *Hist. of Education in Tex.* (1903); *Jour. of the Senate of Tex.*, 1874; Z. T. Fulmore, *Hist. and Geography of Tex. as Told in County Names* (Austin, 1915); W. C. Raines, *Yearbook of Tex.* (Austin, 1901); Dudley G. Wooten, *A Comprehensive Hist. of Tex.* (2 vols., Dallas, 1898).] S. S. M.

CAMP, JOHN LAFAYETTE (Sept. 23, 1855–Aug. 10, 1918), Texas judge and federal district attorney, was the son of John Lafayette Camp [*q.v.*], and Mary Ann (Ward) Camp. He was born at Gilmer, Upshur County, Tex., and was educated at Gilmer Academy, Texas Military Institute, and Trinity University. In 1881 he married Lamartine Felder, daughter of Dr. J. L. Felder, a well-known physician of Leesburg, Tex. He served a term in the state Senate, 1887–91 and then moved to San Antonio, where he practised law for six years. In 1897 he was appointed, by Gov. Culberson, judge of the forty-fifth district court, and he served for more than seventeen years, his work being so acceptable that he was usually reëlected without opposition. During his tenure he tried a great many notable cases and had to his credit a larger percentage of sustained decisions than any other district judge in Texas has ever had. In 1912 he was instrumental in preserving the Alamo, shrine of Texas liberty, as it stands to-day. A state law of 1905 had given the "care and custody" of the Alamo property to the Daughters of the Republic. But at the suggestion of Gov. Colquitt in 1912 the legislature appropriated $5,000 to "improve" the Alamo. When the work of dismantling began, and it became known that the governor planned to make the Alamo grounds into a state park, the Daughters of the Republic appealed to Camp. A temporary and then a permanent injunction halted the work of dismantling the building. Camp held that the act of 1912 did not repeal that of 1905, that the superintendent of public buildings and grounds was given the direction of expenditure but not the power to dismantle the property, and that the Alamo was still in charge of the Daughters of the Republic of Texas. The Governor appealed to the higher courts; but the Alamo still stands.

Camp was appointed, by President Wilson, United States district attorney for the western district of Texas, which takes in the border. The position is an important one at any time; it was particularly so during Camp's incumbency. He secured the evidence which led to the arrest of Victoriano Huerta, former president of Mexico, on June 27, 1915, at Newman, N. Mex., charged with violating the United States neutrality laws in organizing a prospective military expedition against Mexico. Huerta was released under bond, but, when additional evidence was secured by Camp, he was rearrested on July 3 and was kept under guard at Fort Bliss until his death six months later. On the retirement of Judge Maxey from the bench of the western district of Texas, Camp had the unanimous indorsement of the eighteen Texas congressmen, the two United States senators from Texas, and the attorney-general for the position of federal judge. But President Wilson had decided that no man who had reached the age of sixty should be appointed as federal judge, and Camp was a few months over that age. He accepted a second appointment as federal district attorney, and filled that office creditably during the war.

[Sketch of Camp's services in J. H. Cole, *The Federal Courts of the Southern States* (Ann Arbor, 1928); *San Antonio Light*, Aug. 11, 1818; private information.]

S.S.M.

CAMP, WALTER CHAUNCEY (Apr. 7, 1859–Mar. 14, 1925), promoter of American football, was born in New Britain, Conn., and died in his room at a New York hotel, following a football conference, his sudden death, seemingly, an anti-climax to a career devoted to the interests of health and longevity. He came of old English stock. His father, Leverett L. Camp, was a schoolmaster, and from him he probably acquired his sense of discipline; while from his mother, Ellen Cornwell, a gentle soul, he derived that patience and poise which contributed greatly to his success as a leader. He prepared for college at the Hopkins Grammar School, New Haven, and graduated from Yale in the class of 1880. For two years he attended the Yale Medical School, where he gained a knowledge of anatomy and physiology which he was later to employ in his training of youth. During his student days he engaged enthusiastically in all outdoor sports, but specialized in football which he played for six years. Upon leaving the medical school he took a subordinate position with the Manhattan Watch Company, N. Y., and in 1883 became connected with the New York office of the New Haven Clock Company, a firm with which he was associated for the remainder of his life. On June 30, 1888, he married Alice Graham Sumner.

His business connections brought him to New Haven to live in 1888, and he soon became general athletic director and head advisory football coach at Yale. While a student, as a representative of the college at a rules conference, he had suggested modifications which revolutionized the game. The "scrimmage" was substituted for the "scrum" (the ball being put into play by one side instead of being left to a free-for-all scramble), the number of players was reduced from fifteen to eleven, and the key position of quarterback was created. His influence on the game, thus early begun, now continued for nearly thirty years. He is credited with the suggestions which led to the "fourth down rule" with the accompanying "gridiron" pattern of the field, and for the permission of tackling below the waist. Team play was his great objective, and his strategic ability contributed much to the development of its technique. An even greater contribution came from his love of clean sportsmanship which directly and indirectly he instilled into players on college fields and in school yards. He created a literature of the game in books, magazines, and newspapers, some of his publications being: *Football: How to Coach a Team* (1886); *American Football* (1891); *Walter Camp's Book of College Sports* (1893); *The Substitute* (1908); *Jack Hall at Yale* (1909). In 1889 he began his custom of selecting an "All-America Team," membership on which was considered the highest football honor,—a remarkable testimonial to public confidence in Camp's knowledge of the game and his impartial sportsmanship.

In 1917, after the United States entered the World War, Camp became a national figure in a new capacity. Realizing that to endure the war strain those at home must be kept physically fit, in connection with Dr. W. G. Anderson, Director of the Yale University Gymnasium, he organized the leading citizens of New Haven into the Senior Corps for daily physical exercises. Soon he was called to Washington where by similar exercises he undertook to keep members of the cabinet and of Congress in good condition. He thus attracted the attention of the Secretary of the Navy, Josephus Daniels, who made him chairman of the Athletic Department, United States Commission on Training Camp Activities, for the physical care and development of naval officers and men. Out of these experiences came the famous "Daily Dozen" exercises. Originally the idea of Dr. Anderson who formulated three exercises for the daily use of his classes, Camp expanded them into the "Dozen," and his name and gift for publicity gave them countrywide popularity. A memorial erected at the Yale Bowl, financed by his admirers in many colleges and schools, bears testimony to the respect and affection in which he was held.

[H. W. H. Powel, *Walter Camp, the Father of Am. Football* (1926); Parke H. Davis, *Football* (1911); Wm. G. Daggett, *A Hist. of the Class of Eighty, Yale College, 1876–1910* (1910); Grantland Rice, article in *Collier's*, May 9, 1925; *Yale Alumni Weekly*, Mar. 20, 1925; *Yale Univ. Obit. Rec. of Grads.*, 1925; Spalding's *Official Foot Ball Guide for 1926*.]   N.G.O.

CAMPANIUS, JOHN (Aug. 15, 1601–Sept. 17, 1683), Lutheran clergyman, missionary among the Delaware Indians, was born in Stockholm, the son of Jonas Peter Campanius, parish clerk of St. Clara's, was educated at the Stockholm gymnasium and the University of Upsala, and was ordained on July 19, 1633. The next year he accompanied a Swedish mission to Russia and on his return became schoolmaster at Norrtälje and later chaplain and preceptor of the Stockholm Orphans' Home. When Lieutenant-Colonel John Printz was appointed governor of the colony on the Delaware, Admiral Claes Flemming, one of the King's counsellors of state, suggested that Campanius go with him as chaplain of the settlers. Printz and his company left Stockholm on Aug. 16, 1642, touched at Antigua on Dec. 20—where they remained till Jan. 3, were entertained by the English governor, and were loaded with a gift of oranges and lemons—and dropped anchor at Fort Christina (now Wilmington, Del.), Feb. 15, 1643. Campanius took his family with him. His account of the six months' voyage is incorporated in the work on New Sweden by his grandson, Thomas Campa-

nius, "Holmiensis." During his sojourn of six years in America he ministered faithfully to his scattered congregation of German and Swedish colonists, indentured servants, and transported criminals. He also attempted to Christianize the Indians. The work began awkwardly, for when the Indians first came to the services they were amazed that one man should stand alone and talk so long while the rest listened in silence, and they suspected a trap. He gained their affection, however, learned their language, and was so successful in teaching them "that those people who were wandering in darkness were able to see the light." He translated Luther's *Shorter Catechism* into the Delaware language, but his version was not printed until 1696, when Charles XI brought it out at Stockholm at his own expense and sent 500 copies to America. *Lutheri Catechismus Öfwersatt på American-Virginiske Språket* made a duodecimo volume of 160 pages, the catechism being given in both Swedish and Delaware, with a glossary filling twenty-eight pages. Campanius's labors among the Indians, which antedated by a few years those of John Eliot at Roxbury, Mass., were eminently Christian and provided a foundation for the later work of William Penn. Besides studying the Indian folkways and language, in which as a pious seventeenth century scholar he found significant affinities with Hebrew, Campanius made careful meteorological observations twice a day for several years and farmed a tract of land at the settlement of Upland. In 1646 he built a church at Tinicum (Tennakong), nine miles southwest of Philadelphia. With his family he returned to Sweden in 1648. The legend was current in the time of Acrelius that Campanius had traveled up into the interior among the Red Men and had made his way by land to Sweden. Home again, he became pastor in 1649 of the congregations at Frosthült and Hernevi, a charge that he served until his death. Johan Danielson Svedberg described him justly as a man *ob indefessum semper amorem Dei propagandi studium summopere laudandum.*

[W. J. Mann, B. M. Schmucker, W. Germann, eds., *Nachrichten von den vereinigten Deutschen Evangelische-Lutherischen Gemeinden in Nord-America*, Erster Band (Allentown, Pa., 1886); A. L. Gräbner, *Geschichte der Lutherischen Kirche in America* (St. Louis, 1892); T. E. Schmauk, *Hist. of the Luth. Ch. in Pa.* (1903); Amandus Johnson, *The Swedish Settlements on the Delaware* (1911); Thomas Campanius Holm (sic), *Description of the Province of New Sweden Now Called by the English Pennsylvania in America*, transl. from the Swedish with notes by Peter S. Du Ponceau (1834); Israel Acrelius, *Hist. of New Sweden*, transl. from the Swedish with an introduction and notes by W. M. Reynolds (1874); Otto Norberg, *Svenska Kyrkans Mission vid Delaware i Nord-Amerika* (Stockholm, 1893); J. D. Svedberg, *Dissertatio Gradualis de Svionum in America Colonia* (Upsala, 1709).] G.H.G.

CAMPAU, JOSEPH (Feb. 25, 1769–July 23, 1863), trader, belonged to a family line which has been numerous and prominent in Detroit since the time of Cadillac. His father was Jacques Campau, a native of Detroit, and his mother was Catherine Menard, a native of Montreal. He was the sixth of a family of twelve children born to his parents in the years 1762–81. In early manhood he entered upon a trading career at Detroit, in which he achieved a large measure of success. His trade was chiefly with the Indians, and in addition to his Detroit store he established outposts at numerous places—at Saginaw, St. Clair, near Mount Clemens, and elsewhere. Aside from his mercantile business, he displayed a life-long interest in real estate, and the profits he made in trade were persistently invested in Detroit property which he improved and leased but seldom willingly sold. About the year 1837 he retired from active business, and devoted the remainder of his long life to looking after his investments. The growth of Detroit made these increasingly valuable, and he is reputed to have been Michigan's first millionaire. At the time of his death he was supposed to be the largest landholder in Detroit and the wealthiest citizen of Michigan.

Business interests aside, Campau was long a man of prominence in Detroit, holding at different times many public offices. He served as trustee of the town, treasurer, overseer of the poor, assessor, and appraiser. He was appointed ensign in the local militia by Winthrop Sargent upon the American occupation of Detroit in 1796, and he subsequently achieved the title of major. Prior to the fire which destroyed Detroit in 1805 Campau owned and occupied a house on Ste. Anne St. After the fire he rebuilt on the same site (south side of Jefferson Ave. between Shelby and Griswold Sts.) ; here he lived until his death, and the house was a conspicuous feature of Jefferson Ave. for many years thereafter. On May 12, 1808, he married Adelaide Dequindre, member of one of Detroit's old French families. They lived together over half a century, and had a family of twelve children, all but two of whom lived to maturity. A sister of Campau married Thomas Williams, early Detroit merchant and magistrate. Their son, Gen. John R. Williams, was Detroit's first elective mayor and for half a century one of her leading citizens. In early life he was partner, for a time, of Campau. In 1823 Williams was defeated by Father Gabriel Richard for election as delegate to Congress. The bitterness engendered by the electoral contest (in which both contestants appealed for the ballots of the French-Catholic electors) prob-

ably materially influenced Campau in a long-continued conflict with the church authorities over the ownership of the so-called Church Farm property, a dispute which vexed the courts for a full generation after all the original contestants had passed away. In 1831 Williams was again a candidate for the delegacy and he and Campau were two of eleven associates who provided funds for establishing the *Democratic Free Press and Michigan Intelligencer,* to serve as the political organ of their party. This paper is regarded as the ancestor of the present-day *Free Press* of Detroit.

Campau was a capable business man of conservative tendencies. His character was marked by numerous eccentricities, which afforded subject matter for local gossip. Although a Catholic, he early became a Mason, and after his estrangement from the church he was fond of abusing that organization.

[Father Christian Denissen, "Detroit Genealogies" (MS. in Burton Hist. Coll.) ; *Barnabas Campau and his Descendants,* compiled by C. M. Burton (Detroit, 1916) ; C. M. Burton, *City of Detroit, Mich., 1701–1922* (1922) ; *Detroit Free Press,* July 25, 1863 ; an article by Robert B. Ross, "Detroit in 1837 : Reminiscences of Joseph and Daniel J. Campau," in the Detroit *Sunday News-Tribune,* Nov. 4, 1894.]   M. M. Q.

CAMPBELL, ALEXANDER (Sept. 12, 1788–Mar. 4, 1866), one of the founders of the Disciples of Christ, was born in County Antrim, Ireland, the son of Thomas Campbell [*q.v.*], and Jane (Corneigle) Campbell. His mother's family was of French Huguenot origin, but several of its members had settled in Ireland before his birth. His father was of a Scotch family that had long resided in Ireland. Alexander derived his features from his mother, his love of preaching and teaching from his father. He obtained his earlier education in school and at home with his father, but he was so fond of sport that he found it irksome to study. His physical frame was strengthened by farm work. As he grew older his mind became active, his memory developed remarkably, and he became fond of religious literature and philosophy. His parents scrupulously attended to his religious and moral education, and he grew up sturdy, active, and conscientious.

In order to increase his income and provide further opportunity for education to his children Thomas Campbell moved his family to the town of Rich Hill when Alexander was sixteen years old, and established an academy of which he was the principal, with Alexander as his assistant. Success followed. Alexander became thoughtful about his personal religion and joined the church. Afterward he gave much study to theology and church history in anticipation of becoming a minister. The Campbells held friendly association with John Walker, an Independent minister in the same town, who later had a part in the origin of the Plymouth Brethren. Alexander was impressed with his ideas, and contrasted his independency with the arbitrary discipline of the Presbyterian ecclesiastical system. He was influenced also by the Haldanes, prominent Independents of Scotland. Upon the departure of his father to America because of impaired health, the son carried on the school. At the father's request the whole family presently undertook to emigrate to Pennsylvania, where Thomas Campbell had located as a minister, but they were delayed by smallpox and shipwreck so that Alexander studied at the University of Glasgow for a year. The family went to America in 1809. Alexander's studies and friendships and the experiences of his father, who had had unpleasant relations with the Seceders in America, made both men inclined to independency in religion. At that time in America the spirit of religious intolerance was keen and pugnacious, and the Campbells were driven presently to a new movement. This crystallized in the organization of the Christian Association of Washington (Pennsylvania) in 1809. The organization was really a local independent church, but it was not a part of the purpose of the Campbells to establish a new denomination, though it was hoped that their principles would spread and produce other associations. To this reform of religion Alexander Campbell resolved to devote himself wholly. He was well adapted by courage, energy, conviction, fine public presence, and eloquence, to become the leader of such an independent enterprise. To prepare himself more thoroughly he set apart certain hours of the day for study, devoting himself daily to the Bible and the classical languages. He became convinced that manners and morals, especially of young people, needed reform, and he wrote articles on that subject for the press. His first sermon was preached in a grove in 1810 and made a successful impression. Within a year he had preached more than a hundred times. After the organization of a full-fledged church of Disciples at Brush Run, Pa., Alexander was licensed to preach. At that time he believed in the independence and congregational government of every local church and in the toleration of infant baptism.

Disappointed by lack of growth in the number of adherents and dreading the perpetuation of a new sect, Thomas Campbell sought affiliation of the Association with the regular Presbyterians, but they declined. After Alexander in 1811 married a Presbyterian wife, Margaret Brown, and became a father, he examined into the subject of infant baptism, a matter of perennial debate between Baptists and other denominations. He decided against it, and, believing that he had never been properly baptized, he with his wife was immersed by a Baptist minister. His father and mother followed his example. This act alienated some persons in their church. It was plain that strictness in baptism might be biblical, but that it was not likely to further the purpose of Christian union.

Alexander became pastor of the Brush Run church when his father moved to Ohio. He read much, and also engaged in farming. As a neighbor he was liked. By nature he was genial, hospitable, and exceptionally interesting as a conversationalist. The Brush Run church became a member of the Redstone Baptist Association of churches, but Campbell was not acceptable to the Baptists as a preacher, because he was not rigid enough in his Calvinism, and because he magnified the differences between them. He came to believe in baptism as necessary for the remission of sins and the appropriation of God's promise of forgiveness, while the Baptists considered the new life complete before baptism. With the hope of extending his own opinions he established Buffalo Seminary in Bethany, Virginia, for the education of young folk and especially for the training of preachers. These he boarded in his own home. This was discontinued after a few years, though the first part of his purpose was highly successful. He went about preaching where he was welcome, and debating with his opponents whenever he had the opportunity. He was a skilful debater on different subjects, and he did not hesitate to meet all comers. One of his most interesting debates was on religious skepticism with Richard Owen, the English Utopian. These debates were open to the public who attended in large numbers, and they added to the growing reputation of Campbell. He was sanguine of the success of his principles, but he made the mistake of thinking that the simple language of the Bible would explain itself and serve to unite all who honestly accepted its teachings. Denominationalism was rampant, especially in the newer sections of the country, and lines were sharply drawn.

Believing in the power of the press, Alexander Campbell started the *Christian Baptist* in 1823, and built up a successful periodical, through which he disseminated his opinions. The paper was printed at home and its success encouraged him to continue the printing business uninterruptedly for forty years. In his paper he attacked missions, Sunday-schools, and sectarian societies as then conducted, carrying the war vigorously into the enemies' camp, and censuring the clergy in particular. This attitude aroused the Redstone Association to oust the Campbellites. Forecasting this action, Campbell himself withdrew with some of his followers and organized a new church which was admitted into the Mahoning Association. After 1826 the Baptist associations adopted the practise of cutting off churches of Disciples so that they became a separate denomination. On his part Campbell opposed the Baptist method of preaching, their four circuits for one rural minister, their extreme doctrinal emphasis, and their requirement of particular religious experience.

Campbell had a mastery of the English Bible and he believed a better translation was desirable. This he undertook in 1826, and his translation was published the next spring. Years later he became an active supporter of the American Bible Union, which was organized to further Baptist opinions on the proper rendition of the Greek word to baptize. In 1828 he published a volume of one hundred and twenty-five hymns, rejecting those that did not have a biblical basis. From 1830 his interest in the second coming of Christ led him to publish the *Millennial Harbinger* instead of the *Christian Baptist*. His publishing interests in a small community were so large that the Federal government established a post office for him and made him postmaster, an office which he held for thirty years.

Campbell's interests broadened as he began to travel more. His acquaintance extended rapidly. He was a delegate to a political convention called to revise the constitution of the state of Virginia. In 1835 he was relieved of a part of his editorial work that he might have more freedom to respond to numerous calls that came to him for public addresses. He traveled frequently into Kentucky, where he had many friends, and was a welcome speaker in Lexington, the center of culture of the state. He went into the states south of Virginia where he knew many people and had some followers. He visited the North, even during the Civil War. At one time he might have been pastor of a Baptist church in one of the Northern cities, but he knew that he could not withhold his peculiar views of truth, and he did not wish to cause division.

Campbell's dislike for creeds and confessions of faith found response in a group similar to the Disciples of Christ,—which was the name preferred by Campbell for his movement—the Christians, a company recruited from three different sources. One of them was Methodist. In 1793 the Republican Methodists had seceded from the Methodist Episcopal church, because of objection to episcopacy. They were fathered by James O'Kelley, who emphasized a creedless gospel. A second source was Baptist. Abner Jones in Ver-

mont led away several churches in New Hampshire and Vermont on the same basis. A third source was Presbyterian. Barton W. Stone was its leader. These three groups combined as the Christian Connection, and were commonly known as Christians. The differences between Disciples and Christians were chiefly in the matter of emphasis. The Disciples stressed the Bible, the Christians the idea of unity. The Christians were more evangelistic, appealed to all kinds of people, and gained rapidly in numbers, which the Disciples had not done. The differences were not sufficient to keep them apart when they agreed on their special principles of fidelity to the simple Word. Local churches combined voluntarily, then the union became general in Kentucky, Tennessee, and Ohio, but the two denominations still exist independently. Campbell was enthusiastically in favor of the combination of forces. He rejoiced also over the spread of his principles to Canada and Great Britain. In 1847 he sailed abroad, preached and lectured in the leading cities, and visited Paris. Later he went to Canada.

In 1840 he started Bethany College in his own west Virginian village and became its president. Much time was required to raise an endowment and he traveled for that purpose, but he gave as much of himself as possible to teaching. He instructed classes in the Bible, in intellectual and moral philosophy, in political economy. He opposed secret societies, but he was tolerant of slavery. The relation of master and servant seemed to him to be no sin, although he thought slavery inexpedient in modern civilization. This saved his denomination from the division that certain denominations suffered. In later life his mind became impaired, but he lived to old age with the satisfaction of knowing that the opinions for which he had contended were gaining adherents steadily. Besides his pocket Testament translation he was the author of *The Christian System* (1839); *Memoirs of Elder Thomas Campbell* (1861); a revised translation of the book of Acts for the American Bible Union; and much fugitive literature.

[Robt. Richardson, *Memoirs of Alexander Campbell* (1870); B. B. Tyler, *Hist. of the Disciples of Christ* (Am. Ch. Hist. Ser., vol. XII, 1894).]   H. K. R.

CAMPBELL, ALLEN (Oct. 11, 1815–Mar. 18, 1894), civil engineer, was the fourth son of Archibald and Margaret (Adams) Campbell. His father was a native of Scotland who came to this country in 1798 and was for many years deputy secretary of the State of New York. Born in Albany, N. Y., Allan was educated at the Albany Academy. In 1832 he joined John Randall, a distinguished engineer of that time and chief engineer of the Ithaca & Oswego Railroad, one of the first railroads in the United States. He served for several years as engineer in the construction of the earliest railways in the state of Georgia and it was while there that he met and married in 1843 Julia Farlie Cooper, daughter of Thomas Cooper, the tragedian. Subsequently, while chief engineer of the extension of the Harlem Railroad, Campbell received an offer from the Government of Chile to go to that country to construct railroads. He accepted this offer and left in 1850 to start the survey and construction of the Copiapo to Caldera route. Twice he crossed the Andes to Argentina, making reconnaissance of a route to connect the oceans. While in Buenos Aires he was on intimate terms and had most friendly relations with the then president of Argentina. Upon his return to this country in 1856 he again became chief engineer of the extension of the Harlem road and subsequently president, an office which he held until superseded by Cornelius Vanderbilt, who had purchased a controlling interest in the line. Later, as president of the Consolidation Coal Company, Campbell brought that concern out of financial difficulties into dividend-paying fields, a most noteworthy accomplishment. During the Civil War he was employed on the harbor defenses of New York City.

Much interested in civic affairs, he was appointed commissioner of public works in 1876 by Mayor Wickham of New York. He resigned in 1880 to accept the comptrollership of the city, an appointment by Mayor Cooper. He was also appointed in the same year, by act of legislature, one of the assessment commissioners of the State of New York. His work in all of these offices was characterized by strict integrity, industry, and conscientious application to his duties. In 1882 he was prominently mentioned as a candidate for the governorship of New York, and in the same year was nominated as a non-partisan candidate for the mayoralty of New York City. He was, however, defeated for the latter office. His defeat was laid to organized machine politics to which he was bitterly opposed. He was an honorary member of the American Society of Civil Engineers, a member of the New York Historical Society, the St. Andrews Society, the Century Club, and for many years a vestryman of Trinity Church, succeeding John Jacob Astor as warden in that organization.

[*Proc. Am. Soc. of Civil Engineers*, vol. XX; *Engineering News*, Mar. 22, 1894; *N. Y. Times*, Mar. 20, 1894; *Sun* (N. Y.), Mar. 19, 1894.]   K. W. C—g.

CAMPBELL, ANDREW (June 14, 1821–Apr. 13, 1890), inventor, manufacturer, was born near Trenton, N. J., the son of a farmer of very

moderate means. As soon as he was physically able Andrew helped with the farm work and attended the country schools both at his birthplace and at Matawan, Monmouth County, N. J., whither his parents moved when he was eight years old. When he was thirteen, his father died, leaving a large family unprovided for, and Andrew immediately sought employment. He disliked farming and apprenticed himself to a carriage-maker, but before completing his apprenticeship he left home and went to Trenton to work for three months in a brush-maker's shop. Here he perfected his first invention, namely, a special vise for holding brushes. At the age of fifteen he left Trenton and headed westward, working his way gradually, and arriving eventually in Alton, Ill. Here he worked for a carriage-builder until he was twenty-one, during which time he devised and constructed a number of labor-saving machines as well as carriages and omnibuses. From Alton, Campbell went to St. Louis where he engaged in his two old trades, brush-making and carriage-building, and had his first experience with printing presses when engaged periodically to make repairs on the presses of the *St. Louis Republican*. During the following ten years he was variously engaged as a machine-merchant, bridge-builder, and farmer in Columbia, Mo., Paducah, Ky., and other towns of the Middle West. The announcement of a prize of $1,000, offered by George Bruce of New York City for a printing press to print 500 copies an hour, caused Campbell to turn his attention to the problem, and in 1853 he proceeded to New York with his design, only to find that the time limit for submitting plans had expired. He obtained employment almost immediately, however, with A. B. Taylor & Company, large manufacturers of printing presses, and as foreman, devised many novel improvements including paper-feed mechanisms, special presses with table distribution for illustrated magazines such as *Harper's* and *Frank Leslie's*, as well as automatic presses. At this time, too, Campbell conceived the idea of a special press for country newspapers, and, when convinced that a market was available, he left Taylor & Company in 1858, spent three years in experimental work, and with his new patented machine began business for himself. The Campbell Country Press proved very popular, and in 1866 Campbell erected a plant in Brooklyn where he not only constructed the Country Press but devised many others. Thus in 1867 the two-revolution picture press was developed, and in 1868 a large press for fine illustrations. A special press designed by Campbell in his factory permitted the printing of 120 almanacs a minute. On it 7,000,000 impressions were taken from one form without perceptible damage. Campbell also made the first press that printed, inserted, pasted, folded, and cut in one continuous operation. He retired from active business in 1880 and died of heart disease ten years later, leaving his widow whom he had married in Columbia, Mo., in 1848, and four children.

[*Am. Dict. of Printing and Bookmaking* (1894) ; *Am. Encyc. of Printing* (1871) ; *Am. Bookmaker,* May 1890 ; *N. Y. Times,* Apr. 15, 1890.]   C. W. M.

CAMPBELL, BARTLEY (Aug. 12, 1843–July 30, 1888), playwright, journalist, theatrical manager, was the son of Bartley and Mary (Eckles) Campbell, both of whom came to America from Ireland in 1840. He was born in Pittsburgh, Pa., where he was educated in private schools and for a brief period studied law. His newspaper career began on the Pittsburgh *Post,* and before he left that city he had become editor and part proprietor of the Pittsburgh *Leader.* In 1869 he founded and edited the *Southern Monthly Magazine* at New Orleans. When he began play-writing in 1871, he definitely retired from journalism, as his standards forbade him to continue as a dramatic critic while he was producing plays. After a sensational drama *Through Fire* (1871) and a social comedy *Peril; or, Love at Long Branch* (1872), he became associated with R. M. Hooley in Chicago, in the development of Hooley's Theatre, which became the chief rival to McVicker's Theatre as the home of legitimate drama. Campbell directed the plays, many of which were his own. His *Fate* (1872–73), a domestic drama, which opened the house, was played in London at the Gaiety Theatre in 1884. Among his other dramas were *Risks, or Insure Your Life* (1873), *The Virginian* (1873), and *On the Rhine* (1875), a play of the Franco-Prussian war of 1870. Campbell took his company to San Francisco in 1875, appearing at Maguire's Opera House, and anticipating in his *Bulls and Bears* (June 7, 1875), an adaptation of Gustav von Moser's *Ultimo,* Augustin Daly's version of the same play, which arrived on July 19. During this summer season Campbell met Bret Harte and Mark Twain, became a member of the Bohemian Club, and received the inspiration for his best play. In 1876 he produced *The Virginian* at St. James's Theatre in London, and while there wrote *A Heroine in Rags* (1876) and *How Women Love* (1877). The latter, a play laid in and near San Francisco, was later rewritten as *The Vigilantes; or, The Heart of the Sierras.* After a verse tragedy, *Clio* (1878), laid in Italy in the twelfth century, and revived in 1885 on a large scale at Niblo's Garden, with music by Operti, Campbell wrote his most significant play, *My Partner,* produced at

the Union Square Theatre, New York, Sept. 16, 1879. It celebrates, with sincerity and skill, the friendship which, in the frontier days in California, often sprang up between two men associated in hardships and in success. The scene in which Joe Saunders pleads for reconciliation with his murdered partner, who is apparently sitting with the divided gold beside him, is one of the most powerful in American drama. *My Partner* held the stage for many years, was performed at the Olympic Theatre, London, Apr. 10, 1884, and was played for about fifty nights at the Residenz-Theater in Berlin, beginning Sept. 15, 1884, Campbell attending the rehearsals. While *My Partner* was a great success, Campbell received a royalty of only ten dollars a performance, so he determined to produce his own plays. *The Galley Slave* (Chestnut Street Theatre, Philadelphia, Sept. 29, 1879) was a vigorous melodrama, with a European scene, which ran for eighty-three nights at the Wilhelm-Theater in Berlin in 1881. *Fairfax* (Park Theatre, Boston, Dec. 8, 1879), a romantic play of the South, has some effective character drawing. It was written for Lester Wallack, but, when a disagreement with him arose, Campbell walked out of the theatre with the play. More melodramatic was *The White Slave* (Haverley's Theatre, New York, Apr. 3, 1882) which contains the lines, "Rags are royal raiment when worn for virtue's sake," deliberately planted by Campbell for their melodramatic effect. *Siberia* (California Theatre, San Francisco, Nov. 26, 1882) portrays the terrors of exile for the Russian patriots of that day and each of its six acts possesses a telling climax. In *Separation* (Union Square Theatre, New York, Jan. 28, 1884) Campbell's theme was the puritanic prejudice against the theatre. In his last play, *Paquita,* produced at his own theatre on Fourteenth St., New York, Aug. 31, 1885, he laid the scene in the Southwest and built up a play upon a situation in which a surgeon is called upon to save the life of the lover of his wife.

Campbell was tall, with a dignified bearing and with the aspect of a scholar. He shares the honor with Augustin Daly and Bronson Howard, of establishing in America the profession of the playwright upon a firm basis. Foreign recognition came to him to an unusual degree, but his reputation has suffered from the fact that, except for one unimportant play, *Little Sunshine* (n.d., first performed in 1873), his dramas have not been published. In ten years he made and lost a large fortune, and in the effort to write, direct, and produce plays his mental powers broke down. In November 1886, he was committed to the State Hospital for the Insane at Middletown, N. Y., where he died.

[Personal information from Mr. Robt. C. Campbell, son of Bartley Campbell; G. E. M[ontgomery], *The Theatre*, I (1886), 348–49; T. Allston Brown, *A Hist. of the N. Y. Stage*, esp. II, 491–92; for the plays: A. H. Quinn, *A Hist. of the Am. Drama from the Civil War to the Present Day*, I, 118–24.]   A. H. Q.

CAMPBELL, CHARLES (May 1, 1807–July 11, 1876), historian, editor, antiquarian, was born in Petersburg, Va., the son of a local bookseller, John Wilson Campbell. When he was a mere child of six years, his father published a *History of Virginia to 1781,* which no doubt in later years had an influence in shaping the career of the son. Like many Virginians of his day, Charles Campbell went to Princeton to be educated, and, graduating from the college there in 1825, he began life as a school-teacher. In 1842 he started a classical school in Petersburg and in 1855 became the principal of Anderson Academy, a position retained until about 1870. Campbell was an industrious collector of historical manuscripts and documents and earned a reputation in scholarly circles as an antiquary. Much of his material was loaned to the well-known Bishop William Meade of Virginia, who made free use of it in his two volumes on *Old Churches and Families of Virginia* (1857). Meade published a letter from Essex to Southampton lent by Campbell with the acknowledgment that it was "furnished me by another true son of Virginia, Mr. Charles Campbell of Petersburg" (Meade, I, 130–31). As early as 1837 Campbell became a regular contributor to *The Southern Literary Messenger* (B. B. Minor, *The Southern Literary Messenger,* p. 68); and he continued this coöperation for many years both as a contributor and as one of the conductors of the Editor's Table under Minor's editorship of the periodical. In 1845, he urged, together with Minor, upon the legislature of Virginia the securing of the Colonial Records of Virginia, and in the January number of 1847 Minor announced the publication by the *Messenger* of Charles Campbell's history of Virginia. Upon this work, *An Introduction to the History of the Colony and Ancient Dominion of Virginia* (Richmond, 1847; a new and improved edition Philadelphia, 1860) rests Campbell's chief reputation as one of the best and most extensive of the writers on state history. He was the author also of a *Genealogy of the Spotswood Family* (1868), and was the editor-author of *Some Materials for a Memoir of John Daly Burk* (1868) in a manner that showed his cordial regard for past and present historians of Virginia. As an editor likewise he published the *Bland Pa-*

pers (1840–43); a reprint, with Introduction, of R. Beverley's *The History of Virginia* (1855); and the *Orderly Book of Gen. Andrew Lewis* (Richmond, 1860). He was also a contributor to the *Virginia Historical Register.*

[Beyond a brief sketch in the *South in the Building of the Nation*, XI, 169, copied from other unsatisfactory sketches, the sources of information are Campbell's own writings and those mentioned in the body of this article.]

J. C. B.

CAMPBELL, FRANCIS JOSEPH (Oct. 9, 1832–June 30, 1914), educator of the blind, was born in Winchester, Tenn., the son of Melinda and James Campbell. His father was a farmer. When about four years old Francis lost his eyesight. At the age of twelve, he was sent to the institution for the blind at Nashville. There, in spite of being told that he had no ear for music, he made himself so good a musician that he became at sixteen a music teacher. Marrying Mary F. Bond, in Massachusetts, whither he went in 1856 for collegiate study, he finally settled at Perkins Institution, Boston, where, as head of its music department for eleven years, he tested his ideas in the vocational training and placing of chosen pupils, an experience which he was to utilize in an epochal way in England. He next studied music in the conservatories of Leipzig and Berlin. By 1871, through the labors of Dr. T. R. Armitage, a blind gentleman of wealth and position in England, the way was opened for a national training school for blind youth. Armitage assured Campbell, then visiting London, that while graduates of the Paris school were succeeding in music, only about one per cent of the British blind was doing so through teaching, performing, or tuning (T. R. Armitage, *Education and Employment of the Blind*, 1886, p. 54). Thereupon, these two, having obtained the patronage of the nobility and £3,000 in money, established at Upper Norwood in 1872 the Royal Normal College and Academy of Music for the Blind. Campbell, aided by teachers from Perkins Institution and by London professors, even improved upon his Boston successes. Basing everything on a careful preparation for the vocation to be followed, with thorough mental and physical training as a groundwork, he carefully placed his graduates in positions and followed them up, eventually finding between eighty and ninety per cent of them self-sustaining. Through these achievements, unprecedented elsewhere, the college was kept in the public eye, gaining ever more assistance for its work, the greatest being the Gardner scholarship fund, which made a selection of pupils possible. Within a few years the new policy of training the blind to earn their own living and to render them independent, self-reliant citizens had become dominant. His first wife having died, Campbell married Sophia Faulkner, an American trained teacher who as lady principal of the college brought her husband seeing eyes and understanding, patience, and invaluable assistance. Small in body, he possessed tremendous energy and daring. In 1880, after climbing Mont Blanc, he became a Fellow of the Royal Geographical Society. In 1909 he was knighted by King Edward VII in recognition of his services on behalf of the blind.

[John Bernard Mannix, *Heroes of the Darkness* (1911), pp. 61–101; Wm. J. Stead in *Rev. of Revs.* (London), V, 18; *Outlook for the Blind,* July 1909, Oct. 1912, July 1913, Oct. 1914.]   E. E. A.

CAMPBELL, GEORGE WASHINGTON (Feb. 8, 1769–Feb. 17, 1848), senator, secretary of the treasury, diplomat, was born in the parish of Tongue in the shire of Sutherland, Scotland. His parents were a Scotch physician, Dr. Archibald Campbell, and Elizabeth (Mackay) Campbell, widow of Duncan Matheson. Christened George, according to tradition he himself added Washington to his name later. In 1772 his family came to Mecklenburg County, N. C., where, after his father's death, Campbell was thrown early in life upon his own resources. Working on his mother's farm and teaching school, he prepared himself for Princeton College. He entered the junior class, completed the work of two years in one, and graduated with high honors in the class of 1794. He then studied law and soon moved to Knoxville, Tenn., where he quickly took first rank among his colleagues of the bar. Public office, however, attracted him and in 1803 he entered the lower house of Congress. Here he served three successive terms, supported the Jeffersonian administration, quarreled with the vitriolic John Randolph who characterized him as "that Prince of Prigs and Puppies" (Henry Adams, *John Randolph,* p. 210), secured the chairmanship of the Committee of Ways and Means that Randolph had held, and fought a duel with B. Gardenier who had charged that the House of Representatives was controlled by French influence. Declining reëlection, he moved his residence to Nashville, served briefly as a member of Tennessee's supreme court of errors and appeals, and in 1811 as an advocate of war with Great Britain was elected to the United States Senate. In the following year he married Harriet Stoddert, daughter of Benjamin Stoddert. In 1814 he was appointed secretary of the treasury. His brief and ineffective administration of this office brought no improvement in the badly disorganized finances of the government, and in September of that year, on the plea

of impaired health but contrary to President Madison's desire, he resigned. His health improving, he returned to the Senate, served as chairman of the Committee of Finance, supported the chartering of the Second Bank of the United States, and again, in 1818, resigned, this time in order that he might accept appointment as minister to Russia. His two years at St. Petersburg were far from happy ones, however. There was no business of importance for him to conduct; within one week three of his four children died of typhus fever; and he gratefully accepted the President's permission to resign. He did not again hold public office except to serve as one of the commissioners of the United States to carry into effect the claims convention signed with France in 1831. He had long been a personal friend of Andrew Jackson, and, despite his service as one of the directors of the Nashville branch of the Bank of the United States, he continued a member of Jackson's party. Deliberate in forming his opinions and tenacious in holding to them, frankly conscious of his own abilities which he estimated highly, unwilling or unable to compete with the politicians of the new day of triumphant Jacksonian democracy, he devoted the remainder of his life to his private affairs. Before his death he was judged one of the wealthy men of his community.

[The family Bible, containing a record of Campbell's birth, and a considerable number of his papers are in the possession of his family. Occasional letters may be found in the Manuscript Division of the Lib. of Cong. Biographical sketches are in Joshua W. Caldwell, *Sketches of the Bench and Bar of Tenn.* (1898) ; and in *Proc. of the Nashville Bar, in Relation to the Death of Hon. G. W. Campbell* (1848), reprinted in *27 Tenn. Reports,* xxi.]   P. M. H.

CAMPBELL, GEORGE WASHINGTON (Jan. 12, 1817–July 15, 1898), horticulturist, was born at Cherry Valley, Cortland County, N. Y., the son of David Campbell; his ancestry was Scotch. When he was four or five years old, his father moved to Sandusky, Ohio. He went to school for a time at Westfield, N. Y., and was trained for newspaper work in which he engaged with his father at Sandusky for a time. In 1849 he moved to Delaware, Ohio, and with a partner engaged in mercantile business until 1856 when this was discontinued. Having been for many years keenly interested in fruit growing, he now turned his whole attention to horticulture. From the first in his commercial work in horticulture he specialized in grapes. It was at Delaware, and during the early period of his specialization, that the Delaware grape, so named in recognition of its place of re-discovery (not of origin), began to attract attention. Campbell propagated it extensively and became largely instrumental in the wide dissemination which it received. Early in his commercial work with grapes he erected greenhouses to provide improved facilities for rooting the cuttings. The glass for these houses he imported from Europe.

It must have been during this same period that he undertook the grape-breeding activities which later brought him into prominence. His first experiments were with seedlings and crosses of the native sorts. The results, however, were disappointing. He then turned to hybridizing the native varieties and the most healthy of the foreign sorts. His ideals were very high. They were described in a paper on the "perfect grape" which he read before the meeting of the Ohio State Horticultural Society in 1891. This was the season before his seedling grape, later to be named Campbell Early, produced its first fruit. Of all the thousands of seedling grapes he had grown and fruited, this one, he was convinced, approached most nearly the ideal for which he was striving. At the present time it is by far the most valuable of all the varieties which he originated.

For many years prior to his death, he was the leading writer and speaker in the North on grape-growing and breeding, and his work had a decided influence on the trend of viticulture. He also gained some note as a potato breeder, though none of his potato introductions are now important. In 1878 he was appointed by President Hayes as commissioner to the Universal and International Exposition at Paris. He sailed for Paris on Apr. 13 and remained in France during that season. While there he wrote a series of articles on his observations which were published in the *Ohio Farmer*. His comments on the ravages of the grape phylloxera, then devastating the vineyards of France, were particularly informing. During the last years of his life, he devoted much of his time to experimenting in plant propagation, especially with soft wood grafting and the determination of the compatibility of varieties and species.

He was married, on Aug. 29, 1846, to Elizabeth Little. They lived to celebrate their golden wedding.

[*Ann. Reports Ohio State Hort. Soc.; Trans. Mass. Hort. Soc.,* 1898; *Jour. Columbus (Ohio) Hort. Soc.,* 1898; unpublished MS. by Campbell concerning his grape-breeding; personal letters.]   H. P. G.

CAMPBELL, HENRY FRASER (Feb. 10, 1824–Dec. 15, 1891), physician, the son of James C. Campbell of Ireland and his wife, Mary R. Eve, an American, was born in Augusta, Ga. He received an academic education, supplemented by a classical course under a private tutor, and entered the Medical College (now University) of Georgia where he received his M.D. in 1842. In the same year he established himself in Augusta, where two years later on June 17, 1844, he married Sarah Bosworth, daughter of Amory Sibley. Until the outbreak of the Civil War he practised his profession in Augusta. He was commissioned surgeon in the Confederate army, 1861, and served as a member of the Army Board of Medical Examiners and as medical director of the General Military Hospital at Richmond, Va. He prepared parts of the *Confederate Manual of Military Surgery* (1863). He occupied various teaching positions at the Medical College of Georgia, as professor of comparative and microscopical anatomy (1854–57), professor of anatomy (1857–66), and from 1868 to the end of his life, professor of orthopedic surgery and gynecology. During this period he was clinical lecturer in the several hospitals of Augusta. Except for the years of the Civil War, his only lengthy absence from the city of his birth was from 1866 to 1868 when he was successively professor of anatomy and professor of surgery at the New Orleans School of Medicine. He is best known for his original studies on the nature of the autonomic nervous system. In 1850 he read an "Essay on the Influence of Dentition in Producing Disease" (*Minutes of the Medical Society of Augusta,* May 2, 1850). In 1851 he published "Law Governing the Distribution of Striped and Unstriped Muscular Fibre" (*Southern Medical and Surgical Journal,* VII, 139–42). Later came articles on excito-secretory action, on reflex vasomotor action as a basis of certain diseases, on the nervous system in febrile diseases, etc. In 1857 he was awarded the prize of one hundred dollars at the tenth annual meeting of the American Medical Association for his investigation of the excito-secretory system. His work on the sympathetic nerves in reflex phenomena was much discussed and on Mar. 2, 1857, he laid claim to priority over Claude Bernard, the famous French physiologist. Dr. Marshal Hall, F.R.S., of London, adjudicated the claim and found that "the idea and designation of excito-secretory action belonged to Dr. Campbell but his details are limited to pathology and observation. The elaborate experimental demonstration of reflex excito-secretory action is the result of the experimental labours of M. Claude Bernard."

Campbell was not only an able surgeon and physiologist but was also a pioneer in preventive medicine. His observations on the abortive treatment of gonorrhea (1845), epidemic dengue fever (1851), the nature of typhoidal fever (1853), unusual forms of dysentery (1851), registration and sanitation (1875), the railroad transmission of disease germs (1876), quarantine in relation to yellow fever germs (1879) and the non-contagiousness of that disease (1880), all reflect a clear logical mind and conceptions of the nature of communicable disease well in advance of his time. His unusual powers of observation were never better demonstrated than in his presentation of his ideas on the transmission of yellow fever before the American Public Health Association's seventh annual meeting (1880), when he vigorously defended his assertion of the portability of atmospheric germs and the non-contagiousness of the disease. From 1857 to 1861, in conjunction with his brother, Dr. Robert Campbell, he was editor of the *Southern Medical and Surgical Journal,* published at Augusta. He was president of the Georgia Medical Association (1871), correspondent of the Academy of Natural Sciences of Philadelphia (1858), corresponding member of the Imperial Academy of Medicine of St. Petersburg (1860), a founder of the American Gynecological Society (1876), and member of the Georgia Board of Health (1875). He was elected vice-president (1858) and finally president of the American Medical Association and presided at its meeting in New Orleans in 1885.

[Sketches in the *Trans. Southern Surgic. and Gynec. Ass.,* XV, 429; *Southern Practitioner,* XIV, 89; Campbell's numerous papers in his own journal, the *Southern Medic. and Surgic. Jour.,* extending over many years, and his articles read before the Am. Medic. Ass. and the Am. Pub. Health Ass., and published in their official organs; bibliography in the Index catalogue of the Surgeon-General's Lib., 1, 2 ser.]   E. E. H.

CAMPBELL, JAMES (Sept. 1, 1812–Jan. 27, 1893), postmaster-general, was born in Southwark, Pa. (now part of Philadelphia), the son of Anthony Campbell, a prosperous storekeeper, and of Catharine McGarvey, his wife, both Irish and Catholic in race and religion. His boyhood was one well-disciplined, at home, by the church, and under the schoolmasters of Southwark, John and Geraldus Stockdale, pedagogues and disciplinarians of the old school. All his early environment conspired to produce a steady-going, bookish young fellow who made a regular and industrious law student in the office of Edward D. Ingraham. In this office he applied himself, as was his habit, varying his study with such recreation as might be found in the Philadelphia Library, the Athenæum, or the debating society. He was admitted to the bar on Sept. 14, 1833. His advance was not easy; after three years of practise, he recorded in his diary, "Mind much agitated; singular that I cannot compose myself more when I am to address the

court." These were the years of the bitter anti-Catholic feeling that dominated the local partizanship of that day. Though he was not a strict religionist, Campbell was loyal to his church and became the best-known leader of the Catholic Democrats of Philadelphia. He became school commissioner in 1840 and his influential position is demonstrated by the fact that Gov. Porter appointed him to the court of common pleas in 1842 before he was thirty. He was on the bench ten years and was often called upon to bear the insults which Catholics suffered in the troublous forties. Politically he was arrayed with the Tyler forces for their brief day and then became a Buchanan man. In 1851 he was nominated for supreme court justice to strengthen the rest of the Democratic ticket among his adherents. The balance of the ticket was elected but anti-Catholic prejudice defeated Campbell. The next year Gov. Bigler appointed him attorney-general. In 1852 Campbell marshalled his forces in favor of Pierce during a campaign in which the latter was accused of anti-Catholic prejudice. As a result of this valuable service and upon the recommendations of the state chairman and of Buchanan, Pierce appointed him postmaster-general. In 1853, when Campbell undertook his new task, he was described as a fat jolly man who tended strictly to business. His ambition was to promote the efficiency of his department. He instituted new methods; he attempted to get better rates and more efficient service from the railroad and steamship companies carrying mail; he vainly strove to have the franking privilege abolished. Upon his recommendation the registry system was established. He sought more favorable postage rates with foreign nations, and his success with Bremen laid the foundation for cheaper foreign postages, although Great Britain would not yield during Campbell's term. He was an energetic and hard-working cabinet member, but he was not outstanding in the administration, and, as a Catholic, during the Know-Nothing furor of 1854–55, he probably contributed to the administration's unpopularity.

In 1857 he returned from Washington with his career behind him; Buchanan gave his confidence only to those unconnected with the Pierce administration. A few months after Campbell returned, his wife, Emilie S. Chapron whom he had married Oct. 28, 1845, died, leaving him two sons. Thenceforth, with the exception of once during the Civil War, when he was nearly elected to the United States Senate as a war Democrat, he spent his life with his law practise and as a trustee and director of various charities and institutions, among which were Girard College and Jefferson Medical College. He passed these last thirty-five years in the quiet, steady, almost monotonous mode of life devoted to duty and usefulness, which seemed best to fit his nature.

[Campbell's annual reports as postmaster-general are found in the *Senate Ex. Docs.*, 33 Cong., 34 Cong. The Pa. Hist. Soc. has a few of his letters, mostly in the Buchanan MSS., and scattering items are found in the Pierce papers in the Lib. of Cong. Campbell's son, John M. Campbell, prepared a biographical sketch which was published by the Am. Cath. Hist. Soc. in vol. V (1894) of their *Records*.]   R. F. N.

CAMPBELL, JAMES HEPBURN (Feb. 8, 1820–Apr. 12, 1895), congressman, was born in Williamsport, Pa. He was the son of Francis C. Campbell, a lawyer, and was the grandson of the Rev. John Campbell, an Episcopal clergyman. His mother was Jane Hepburn, a daughter of James Hepburn of Northumberland County, Pa., not the daughter of Judge William Hepburn, as is sometimes stated. (See John F. Meginness, *Genealogy and History of the Hepburn Family of Susquehanna Valley*, 1894.) He was admitted to the bar in 1841, having graduated from the law department of Dickinson College at Carlisle. He then located at Pottsville, Pa., where he built up a large legal practise and soon became active in politics. In 1840 he was a representative to the Young Men's Ratification Convention held at Baltimore after the nomination of William Henry Harrison. Four years later he represented his district in the national Whig convention when Henry Clay received the nomination for president. In 1845, although residing in a district largely Democratic, he was elected a Whig member of the Thirty-fourth Congress. He supported N. B. Banks for speaker, taking an active part in the protracted contest over his election. In 1856 he was defeated as a Republican by W. L. Dewart, the Democratic nominee, but two years later was returned to Congress by a vote of 7,153 as against 4,860 for this same opponent. In 1860 he was again elected. He represented his state on the Committee of Thirty-Three to which Lincoln's first inaugural address was referred, but his most important work was as chairman of the special committee on the Pacific railroad. Largely due to his energetic and adroit leadership the bill granting federal aid for the Pacific railroad by the middle route was passed in the House on May 6, 1862 (*Congressional Globe*, 37 Cong., 2 Sess., p. 1971). He was an ardent champion of protection to industry in the form of a tariff and spoke several times in favor of the Morrill Act of 1861. He supported the Legal Tender Act of 1862 and the conscription bill.

In April 1861 he left his home to aid in the defense of the national capital, and, after passing safely through the Baltimore mobs on Apr. 19, enlisted as a private in Maj. Cassius M. Clay's battalion. The following month he was elected major of the 25th Regular Pennsylvania Volunteers for three months' service. During the invasion of Pennsylvania by Gen. Lee in 1863 he aided Gen. Nagle in the recruiting of a regiment of 1,100 men and became lieutenant-colonel in command of the 39th Pennsylvania Volunteers. After he was mustered out of service, Secretary of State Seward tendered him the appointment of judge of the court for the suppression of the African slave trade, provided for by the treaty of 1862 with Great Britain. This post required residence in Capetown, Africa, and Campbell declined it. In 1864 President Lincoln appointed him United States minister to Sweden and Norway, where he resided three years. On his return he resumed his law practise in Philadelphia, later leaving the law for agricultural pursuits at his country place, Aeola, near Wayne, where he died. He was married in 1843 to Juliet H. Lewis, daughter of Chief Justice Ellis Lewis of Pennsylvania.

[*A Biog. Album of Prominent Pennsylvanians*, vol. I (1888); *Biog. Encyc. of Pa.* (1874), p. 372; *Phila. Inquirer*, Apr. 13, 1895; *Phila. Press*, Apr. 12, 1895.]   F. C. S—n.

CAMPBELL, JAMES VALENTINE (Feb. 25, 1823–Mar. 26, 1890), jurist, son of Henry Munroe Campbell, and Lois (Bushnell) Campbell, both of New England stock, was born in Buffalo, N. Y., where his father was a man of considerable prominence. In the year 1826 the family moved to Detroit, Mich. His father was affiliated with the Episcopal Church, wherefore the son was sent to the Episcopal preparatory school at Flushing, L. I. From this school he went to St. Paul's College, also located in Flushing. He graduated in 1841, and returned to Detroit, where he studied law in the office of Douglass & Walker. In 1844 he began to practise law as the partner of his two instructors. On Nov. 18, 1849, he was married to Cornelia Hotchkiss. When in the year 1858 the supreme court of Michigan was established, Campbell became one of the first three justices; and he was continuously reëlected till his death. He was, in fact, a judge and lawyer of national reputation. His opinions are recorded in seventy volumes of the *Michigan Reports*. They have left their impress not only on the jurisprudence of Michigan, but on that of the whole country. For more than half a century the state and federal judiciary and the writers of texts have cited his decisions as high authority. He was in almost all respects a non-partisan judge (see in particular his opinion in the case of *Twitchell* vs. *Blodgett*, 12 *Mich.*

127). In 1859 he was appointed professor of law in the newly-created Department of Law of the University of Michigan. Seven years later the University conferred upon him its first degree of Doctor of Laws. When he finally resigned his professorship in 1885, his loss was deeply felt by both colleagues and student body. Not only was he highly respected for his keen mind, his unflagging industry, and his sense of justice; but he also endeared himself to his friends and associates because of his sweet disposition.

In 1845 he edited Walker's *Chancery Reports,* and in 1876 he published the *Outlines of the Political History of Michigan,* a valuable contribution to American history. He also published, among others, the following addresses and papers: *The Dangers of Church Centralization* (1856); *Moravians in Michigan* (1858); *Some Remarks on the Polity of the Protestant Episcopal Church in the United States* (1865); *Our City Schools* (1869); *Does the Law Deal Unfairly with Questions of Insanity?* (1870); *Of the Taking of Private Property for Purposes of Utility* (1871); *Some Hints on Defects in the Jury System* (1876); *Law Abridgement* (1879); *Materials of Jurisprudence* (1880). On Oct. 3, 1859, at the opening of the Law Department in the University of Michigan, he delivered an address *On the Study of Law,* which was published in the same year by the University.

[*Exercises of the Supreme Court of Mich. at the Opening of the Apr. Term, 1890, in Memory of Jas. Valentine Campbell* (Lansing, 1890; also in 81 *Mich. Reports*); G. I. Reed, *Bench and Bar of Mich.* (1897), pp. 20, 236–38; R. B. Ross and G. B. Catlin, *Landmarks of Wayne County and Detroit* (1898), pp. 659–62; B. A. Hinsdale, *Hist. of the Univ. of Mich.* (1906), p. 233.]   A. H—a.

CAMPBELL, JOHN. [See LOUDOUN, JOHN CAMPBELL, FOURTH EARL OF, 1705–1782.]

CAMPBELL, JOHN (1653–Mar. 4, 1727/8), journalist, was a Scot, who emigrated to Boston before 1698 and probably before 1695. In 1702 he became postmaster at Boston under Neale's monopoly, with the "approbation" of Gov. Dudley. The General Court subsidized the post-office at first and in 1703 Campbell was freed from various civic duties during his employment. The subsidy was suspended in 1706. The archives contain a series of petitions by Campbell for its continuance as compensation for taking "due care of forwarding the public letters" and for the printing of the *Weekly Intelligencer.* The post-office was the center of information and Campbell utilized his position to write news-letters for regular patrons, which he franked through the mail (*Proceedings of the Massachusetts Historical Society,* IX, 485). From this developed his printed *Boston News-*

Letter, beginning Apr. 24, 1704. This weekly half-sheet was the first established newspaper in America, though not the first attempt. "Published by authority," the paper was careful to keep on the good side of that authority, but was not entirely immune from official censure (*Calendar of State Papers, Colonial Series, America and West Indies, 1706–08,* 231). It set the precedent of being concerned chiefly with foreign news. The paper was dull; the publisher wrote little himself and that awkwardly, and complained of meager returns, since in 1711 he could not "vend two hundred and fifty copies at one impression." He was not without business enterprise, however; for instance, during 1719 he made half the issues whole sheets in order to catch up on the foreign news, being thirteen months behind, whereby "in a little time all will become New that us'd formerly to seem Old"; and on Jan. 4, 1720, he announced that "such as have a Mind to pleasure their Friends with it per Post may have it every Monday a whole Sheet, one half with the News, the other half good Paper to write their Letter on (which will fully Obviate that insinuation of People's being prevented having it that live remote from hence) by only paying single Postage for both the News and their Letter every Post." He was no longer postmaster at this time, for he had lost the position in 1718. With the last issue of 1722 he turned the control of the *News-Letter* over to Bartholomew Green, who had printed it during most of the preceding years. During the latter part of his life Campbell was a justice of the peace and a man of considerable position. He was twice, possibly thrice, married. His last wife was Mary Pemberton (*née* Clarke) who took Herbert Lloyd as her third husband and published *Meditations on Divine Subjects* (1745).

[The local records and state archives contain various items on Campbell. Some of those on the post-office are in *Mass. Hist. Soc. Colls.,* 3 ser., VII, 60–84. Samuel Sewell gives some information in his Diary, *Mass. Hist. Soc. Colls.,* 5 ser., V–VII. Isaiah Thomas, *Hist. of Printing in America* (2d. ed., 2 vols., 1874), II, 12–28, is the chief source on Campbell's newspaper. For the controversy over earlier newspaper attempts, see *Mass. Colonial Soc. Pubs.,* X, 310.]   D. M. M.

CAMPBELL, JOHN ARCHIBALD (June 24, 1811–Mar. 12, 1889), lawyer, associate justice of the Supreme Court of the United States and assistant secretary of war for the Southern Confederacy, was born at Washington, in Wilkes County, Ga. Like so many of the inhabitants of the lower South, he was almost entirely of Scottish and Scotch-Irish blood. His paternal great-grandfather came to North Carolina from Scotland in the migration of Highlanders that followed the disaster at Culloden and the harsh enactments of the British Parliament. The grandfather whose full name he bore was an officer in the Continental Army upon the personal staff of Gen. Greene, and after the war a judge of the North Carolina court of Admiralty. His father, Duncan Green Campbell, moved to Georgia in 1808 and there married Mary Williamson, the daughter of Lieut.-Col. Micajah Williamson,— Revolutionary leader—and Sarah (Gilliam) Williamson. Sarah Williamson had been one of the most remarkable women of her period in Georgia. With great enterprise and courage she successfully managed a plantation and a large number of negro slaves, during the absence of her husband at the front, in spite of the depredations of the enemy who at times overran her property.

Campbell entered Franklin College (University of Georgia) when he was eleven years old and upon his graduation with first honor at fourteen was made a cadet at the United States Military Academy by John C. Calhoun, his father's friend, who was then secretary of war. His father died while nominee for governor of Georgia with every prospect of success, a year before John was to receive his commission. The unsatisfactory condition of his father's estate made it necessary for John to abandon a military career and come home. There he prepared for the bar under the tutelage of his uncle John W. Campbell, and Gov. Clarke, and was admitted to practise at eighteen, together with his fellow townsman Robert Toombs [q.v.], by virtue of a special act of the Georgia legislature. Within a year he moved to Alabama where he lived—first in Montgomery, then in Mobile—until his elevation to the bench. While there he married Anna Esther Goldthwaite, the sister of Henry and George Goldthwaite.

As a member of the bar of Alabama, Campbell rose rapidly. He twice declined an associate justiceship of the state supreme court, the first appointment having been tendered him when he was only twenty-four years of age. He was an indefatigable student, had an unusual memory, and his knowledge of the principles of both the civil and common law was extensive. The best known case in which he appeared during this period was that of *Gaines* vs. *Relf* (12 *Howard*, 472), where his argument in the circuit court on behalf of a pathetic woman who was to devote practically her entire life toward establishing her legitimacy, elicited high praise. The litigation was protracted for nearly half a century. Seven times, in one phase or another, was it appealed to the Supreme Court of the United States, but it was finally disposed of by the same process of reasoning pursued by Campbell in his argument in the circuit court. (For a history of this

cause celèbre see J. Carroll Payne, "A Celebrated Case, the Myra Clark Gaines Litigation," in *Report of the Fourteenth Annual Session of the Georgia Bar Association,* 1897.) Although his law practise was large, Campbell took an active interest in public affairs. He served with distinction for two terms in the Alabama legislature, and was a delegate to the Nashville Convention of June 1850, where he prepared the greater portion of the resolutions adopted. They were temperate and conciliatory, in striking contrast to the impassioned *Address* issued by the convention from the pen of Robert Barnwell Rhett (see Farrar Newberry, "The Nashville Convention and Southern Sentiment of 1850," *South Atlantic Quarterly,* XI, 259).

At forty Campbell had a national reputation as a lawyer and in March 1853, before he was forty-two, he was appointed an associate justice of the United States Supreme Court by President Pierce. His selection was made at the request of the justices of the Court and appears from articles in the press of the period to have given universal satisfaction. His judicial opinions indicate an unwillingness to further extend the liberal interpretation of the Constitution which prevailed under the chief-justiceship of Marshall, and also disclose a profound hostility toward monopolies. Having been nurtured and schooled in the Jeffersonian policies of strict construction and being familiar, as a student of history, with the tendency of courts to amplify and enlarge their jurisdictions, he was quick to sense judicial infringement upon the reserved powers of the states, and frequently found himself in disagreement with the majority of his colleagues on constitutional questions. On other points he was usually in agreement with the majority, and therefore could not be called, in the general acceptance of the term, a "dissenting judge."

Although he impressed the leading jurists of his time as possessing great ability and "supreme integrity of nature and intellect," he was in no sense a popular man and in the performance of duty often ran counter to public opinion. He was denounced in certain quarters of the South because while sitting as circuit judge in New Orleans he urged the grand jury to indict William Walker and other prominent and popular leaders of filibustering expeditions to Latin America, as violators of the neutrality laws. And he came in for his share of the torrent of abolitionist abuse heaped upon the majority of the court for their celebrated Dred Scott decision. Campbell, in an elaborate concurring opinion, supported the majority in holding that a negro was not a citizen of the United States, and that the Missouri Com-

457

promise, which undertook to prohibit slavery in
the territories north of the thirty-sixth parallel,
was without constitutional authority and void
(19 *Howard,* 493). At the time when this case
was decided he held no slaves. Upon his appointment to the Supreme Court he had emancipated
all he owned and thereafter employed as servants
only free persons of color. Although he was bitterly attacked by the extreme abolitionists, he
was generally regarded as a "moderate," and in
the crisis in the Democratic party in 1860 he was
looked upon by more than one conservative leader as an ideal compromise candidate for the
Presidency. He had no political aspirations, however, and gave no encouragement to the movement.

When, after the election of Lincoln, the lower
South was aflame with the fires of secession, he
openly and persistently opposed it. While he had
a sympathetic understanding of the Southern
point of view and believed that a failure to accord the slave states their constitutional rights
within the Union legally entitled them to withdraw, he nevertheless thought secession unnecessary, believed it would prove calamitous, and
held to the view that the differences between the
sections could be adjusted by compromise. Nor
did he cease his efforts to close the breach after
the cotton states had formed a provisional government and despatched commissioners to Washington to negotiate a treaty. He was informed
by his associate, Justice Nelson, that Secretary
of State Seward (who apparently desired to
bring about a reconciliation) was depressed by
the insistence of the Confederate commissioners
that they be officially recognized, since at the
moment President Lincoln and the rest of the
cabinet were not inclined to receive them. Campbell tendered his services as an intermediary and
was assured by Seward that, if the commissioners would not press their demand for recognition, Fort Sumter, then occupied by Federal
troops, would be evacuated in "five days." Campbell communicated this to the commissioners and
they so advised their Government. Thus was begun that strange course of conduct by Seward
concerning which much has been written. In
brief, by repeated promises to Campbell that
Sumter would be evacuated he held the commissioners dangling in Washington until an expedition was despatched to Charleston for the fort's
replenishment. It is probable that Seward believed the fortress would be given up (Nathaniel
W. Stephenson, *Lincoln and the Union,* 1921, p.
107). But whatever his motives or beliefs, he
placed Campbell in an untenable position and refused to exculpate him from the charge of treach-

ery (H. G. Connor, *post,* pp. 133 ff.). Campbell's
memoranda of the conferences with Seward,
made soon after the event, have every indication
of accuracy and show that Campbell's conduct
was above reproach (J. F. Rhodes, *post,* III, pp.
338 ff.). He forfeited for a time, however, the
confidence of the Confederates, who believed that
he had connived with the Federal Administration
in a policy of duplicity.

There can be no question of the sincerity of
Campbell's devotion to his native section, and
after he had failed in his efforts to save the
Southern people from what he believed to be inevitable catastrophe, he resigned his judicial position and joined fortunes with them. He took
no part in the struggle until October 1862, when,
the hostility toward him having abated, he was
urged by the Confederate secretary of war to become an assistant secretary with the special duty
of administering the conscription law. He accepted and, although the work was distasteful to
him, held the position until the Confederacy collapsed (see "Papers of Hon. John A. Campbell
1861–65," in *Southern Historical Society Papers,*
October 1917, pp. 3–81).

In January 1865, President Davis named him,
together with Vice-President Stephens and R.
M. T. Hunter, on the peace commission which
met with President Lincoln and Secretary Seward at Hampton Roads. Although Lincoln's
terms were unsatisfactory, Campbell believed
they could be made the basis for further negotiations; Davis thought otherwise, and the conference came to nothing.

When the Confederate capital was evacuated,
Campbell made a last attempt to lighten the burdens of his people. At some physical danger to
himself he remained in Richmond and was able
to secure an interview with President Lincoln.
It resulted in an order permitting the Virginia
legislature to convene to consider Lincoln's
terms of reconstruction (see Campbell's own account in his *Recollections of the Evacuation of
Richmond, Apr. 2nd, 1865* (1880), and *Reminiscences and Documents Relating to the Civil War
During the Year 1865* (1887)). Within a few
days Lee surrendered and Lincoln withdrew his
sanction of the meeting in a telegram to Gen.
Weitzel (Federal commander) in which he said
that Campbell had misconstrued the terms under
which the plan was to be carried out. The next
day Lincoln was assassinated. As a result of the
passion following that tragedy Campbell was arrested on the absurd charge of having misrepresented to Weitzel Lincoln's purpose in assembling the legislature—absurd, because Weitzel
had participated in both of the conferences Camp-

bell held with Lincoln and had heard everything Lincoln said. After being confined for about four months at Fort Pulaski, Campbell was released by President Johnson at the instance of his former colleagues, Justice Nelson of New York and Justice Curtis of Massachusetts.

All of Campbell's property, which consisted mainly of holdings in Mobile, had been destroyed during the war, and upon his release from prison he was faced with the necessity, at fifty-four, of beginning life anew. He went to New Orleans and soon acquired a large and lucrative law practise. He appeared in many cases of great importance in the United States Supreme Court. Among these were the famous Slaughterhouse Cases (16 *Wallace,* 36), where he again took up the cudgels against monopolies, but now, in the exigencies of the time, he was seeking the aid of the Federal power to relieve a community from the oppressive act of a state. The carpet-bag government of Louisiana had in 1869 chartered a corporation upon which it conferred for twenty-five years the exclusive right to maintain within the city and parish of New Orleans, and two adjoining parishes, all butcher-shops, slaughter-pens, stock-yards, and stables. Some thirteen hundred persons were legislated out of business. Judge Campbell attacked the statute as creating a monopoly and as being in violation of the recently adopted Fourteenth and Fifteenth Amendments to the Constitution. It was a case of first impression, as the war amendments had not before been up for judicial interpretation. Campbell's argument was elaborate and forceful, and supported by a wealth of authority, historical and judicial; but he lost his case. By a divided bench—five to four—it was held that the amendments were passed only to secure the freedom of the negro from the oppressions of those who had formerly exercised dominion over him, and would not be extended to protect rights already given to citizens by the states.

Another case in which he appeared, this time successfully, was that of *Jackson* vs. *Ludeling* (21 *Wallace,* 616), in which he prevented the consummation of what was characterized by the court as "a great wrong, perpetrated by the agency of legal forms." So too, in the case of *New York and New Hampshire* vs. *Louisiana* (108 *United States,* 76), where his argument was described by Chief Justice Waite as the greatest he had ever heard in a court of justice, he successfully defeated the collection of bonds issued by a corrupt government under "a condition bordering on anarchy," and where, as he said, "the holders knew there was no coercive power to enforce their payment."

Nearly all of Campbell's opinions as a judge, as well as his arguments at the bar, show that he had a thorough knowledge of the historical aspects of the questions involved. He had perhaps the finest private law library, in all languages, in America, and when retained in an important case he would retire to his books and lead the life of a recluse until he had completed its preparation. When he died at the age of seventy-seven he had for the second time in his life come to be recognized as one of the leading lawyers in America. He has frequently been described as austere. In fact, his large, erect frame, natural dignity, and strong, prominent features did produce a rugged aspect. But though his manners to the world were formal, to his family and intimates he was tender and considerate, and his sympathy for the unfortunate was profound. The faith of an old negro woman whose freedom he had bought and who when she was dying admonished those about her to put their "faith in God and Mr. Campbell," was no doubt shared by many beneficiaries of his charity.

[*John Archibald Campbell* (1920), by H. G. Connor, is, on the whole, excellent. It cites convincing evidence to support Campbell's memoranda and letters relating to his conferences with Seward, while the treatment of Campbell's work as a jurist leaves little to be desired. For an apparently impartial interpretation of the Sumter incident, see Jas. Ford Rhodes, *Hist. of the U. S. from the Compromise of 1850* (1893), III, 336–40; for a Northern version, see Jas. Schouler, *Hist. of the U. S. A. Under the Constitution* (1880–91), VI, 14 ff.; for a Southern view, see A. H. Stephens, *A Constitutional View of the War Between the States* (1868–70), II, 347 ff. Campbell's judicial opinions are to be found in 15–24 *Howard* (56–65 *U. S.*). An appraisal of his work as judge and advocate by leaders of the American bar may be found in 130 *U. S.*, App. VII.]   B. F.

CAMPBELL, JOHN WILSON (Feb. 23, 1782–Sept. 24, 1833), congressman, jurist, was born in Augusta County, Va., near Miller's Iron Works. His parents, William and Elizabeth (Wilson) Campbell, had come to that settlement from near Londonderry, Ireland. When he was a lad of eight or nine they moved, together with their large family, to Bourbon County, Ky. Young Campbell was not suited to the hard life on a pioneer farm, for he was not robust, and besides, he desired an education. This his parents could not afford to give him, although they had the Scotch-Presbyterian respect for learning. He grew discontented and ran away to Cincinnati, where he apprenticed himself to a carpenter. His parents prevailed on him to return home, and he was sent to a school conducted by the Rev. J. P. Campbell. His parents shortly moved to Ohio, where he was able to pay for his own schooling either by working at clearing the timberlands or by teaching school. After studying law at Morgantown, Va., with his uncle Thomas Wilson, he was admitted to the bar in 1808, and set up an office in West Union, Adams County, Ohio. Here he was shortly made prosecuting attorney and succeeded in building up a lucrative practise. In 1811 he was married to Eleanor Doak, daughter of Col. Robert Doak of Augusta County, Va. He had a short period of service in the War of 1812 (*The "Old Northwest" Genealogical Quarterly*, X, 45). In 1813 and again in 1815 he was sent by his county to the state legislature. In 1814, United States Senator Thomas Worthington resigned to become governor of Ohio, and Campbell was nominated, along with ten others, to fill the vacancy. The fact that he stood third highest in the balloting is an indication of the place he was coming to have in state politics. In 1816 he was elected to Congress by a large majority. He represented his district in five consecutive sessions (1817–27). Judging from the records, he was not an active debater. He spoke vigorously, however, against the Panama Mission, an administration measure, on Apr. 20, 1826 (*Register of Debates*, 19 Cong., 1 Sess., col. 2413 ff.). Although he was a Jackson man, he was not an intense partizan by nature, and his speeches indicate the equanimity of his disposition. In 1828 he was nominated by the state convention of the Jackson party for the governorship (*The "Old Northwest" Genealogical Quarterly*, IX, 230) but was defeated. It seems probable that he was a reluctant candidate. On the accession of Jackson to the presidency, Campbell was appointed United States district judge. In order to be near his work, he moved his residence from his farm in Brown County to Columbus, in 1831. He seems to have been well qualified both by education and disposition for his new position, but he did not live to make his mark as a judge, for he was among the victims of the cholera epidemic which decimated Ohio in 1833.

[*Biog. Sketches; with other Literary Remains of the Late John W. Campbell . . . Compiled by his Widow* (1838), containing a laudatory, but accurate sketch of his life; *Hist. Sketches of the Campbell, Pilcher and Kindred Families* (1911); obituaries in the *Cincinnati Daily Gazette*, Sept. 28, 1833, and other contemporary newspapers.] W. T. U—r.

CAMPBELL, JOSIAH A. PATTERSON (Mar. 2, 1830–Jan. 10, 1917), jurist, was of Scotch and Irish descent, the son of the Rev. Robert B. Campbell, a Presbyterian minister, and of his wife, Mary Patterson. He was born in the Waxhaw settlement, Abbeville district, S. C., and was educated at Camden Academy and Davison College, N. C. Upon leaving college he joined his father's family in Madison County, Miss., where they had settled in 1845. He

then read law, and at the age of seventeen was admitted to the bar at Kosciusko, Miss. He there practised his profession until 1865, except during the war period. At the age of twenty-one he was elected to the legislature on the Democratic ticket. As the practise of law was more congenial to him than politics, he retired from public office at the expiration of his legislative term. In 1859 he was again elected to the legislature, and became speaker of the House. When his state seceded from the Union in 1861, he was chosen one of the seven delegates from Mississippi to the Confederate constitutional convention at Montgomery and thus became a member of the Provisional Congress of the Confederacy. In March 1862 he entered the Confederate army, and was chosen captain of Company K, which became part of the 40th Regiment, and when that regiment was organized at Meridian, Miss., he was made lieutenant-colonel. He commanded his regiment in the battles of Iuka and Corinth, being wounded in the latter engagement. He rejoined his command at Grenada and went with it to Vicksburg, where he received notice from the secretary of war that he had been assigned to the military court of Gen. Polk's corps, with the rank of colonel. He served in this capacity until the end of the war. He was then elected circuit judge of his district, to fill an unexpired term, and was reëlected in 1866 for the full term. But his inability to take the test oath required by the federal government forced him to retire from the bench in 1870. He was elected professor of law at the University of Mississippi, but declined this position and opened a law office at Canton, Miss. A short time later he formed a partnership with Judge S. S. Calhoun in the same town, and this relationship lasted until Campbell received an appointment to the supreme bench of the state. Meantime, at the request of Gov. Alcorn, he served on a commission which prepared the Code of 1871. When the Democratic party resumed control of the state government in 1876, Gov. Stone appointed Campbell to the supreme bench for a term of nine years. He was then reappointed by Gov. Lowry for a second term, which gave him a tenure of eighteen years during a third of which time he was chief justice. At the request of the state legislature he also prepared the Code of 1880, which was almost wholly in force for more than a generation. Responding to a request of the legislature of Mississippi, he delivered before that body (1890) a memorial address on the "Life and Character of Jefferson Davis." In this address he said: "I have never blamed a

Northern man for supporting *his* country, . . . and before the bar of justice and fairness, I demand the same recognition for myself and countrymen in supporting *ours* . . . This is our native earth, and rights to which we are born were in jeopardy." At the time of his death, Campbell was the sole survivor of the forty-nine signers of the Confederate constitution. He was a man of imposing appearance, with a courtly bearing that befitted the high judicial position which he filled with dignity and honor. He was about six feet two in height, with erect carriage, a sonorous voice, expressive blue eyes, a high forehead, and an intellectual, bearded face. He was married, May 23, 1850, to Eugenia E., daughter of Rev. W. W. and Nancy (Dotson) Nash, of Kosciusko, Miss.

[Sketches of Campbell will be found in *Biog. and Hist. Memoirs of Miss.* (1891), I, 495–98; *Miss. Hist. Soc. Pubs.*, IV (1901), 493, footnote; Dunbar Rowland, *Mississippi* (1907), I, 349–50; *Times-Picayune* (New Orleans) and *Commercial Appeal* (Memphis), Jan. 11, 1917. His judicial decisions will be found in *Miss. Reports* from 1876 to 1894. See also his "Planters and Union Bank Bonds" in *Miss. Hist. Soc. Pubs.*, IV, 493–97 and his *Address on the Life and Character of Jefferson Davis* (pamphlet published by authority of the legislature of Miss., Jackson, Miss., (1890).]

F. L. R.

CAMPBELL, LEWIS DAVIS (Aug. 9, 1811– Nov. 26, 1882), editor, congressman, diplomat, of Highland Scotch stock, the son of Samuel and Mary (Small) Campbell, was born at Franklin, Warren County, Ohio. After serving an apprenticeship of three years (1828–31) on the *Cincinnati Gazette*, he took over the *Hamilton Intelligencer*, which heartily championed the cause of Henry Clay and the Whig party. While engaged with this weekly paper, he found time to study law and in 1835 was admitted to the bar. His practise and reputation as a lawyer grew rapidly. His marriage to Jane H. Reily, daughter of John Reily, a prominent Ohio pioneer, added to his influence. In 1848 he was elected to Congress as a Whig, and for four consecutive sessions he was reëlected. In 1858 he and C. L. Vallandigham fought for the support of the Miami Valley. Each claimed the victory, but the seat was awarded to Vallandigham by the House of Representatives. The high point of Campbell's career in Congress was his chairmanship of the Committee of Ways and Means in the Thirty-fourth Congress. In the great debates over slavery he displayed considerable force as a speaker, particularly in his opposition to the repeal of the Missouri Compromise. On the outbreak of the Civil War he served for a time as colonel of the 69th Regiment of Ohio volunteers, but ill health compelled him to leave the service. Although not in Congress,

he opposed the Congressional program of reconstruction. He was a delegate at the Philadelphia Union convention and at the Soldiers Convention at Cleveland in 1866. President Johnson appointed him minister to Mexico at a time when Secretary of State Seward was trying to compel Napoleon III to recall his troops, by diplomatic rather than military pressure. The dogged resistance of the republicans of Mexico, led by Juarez, had won the admiration of the people of the United States. Although Campbell was appointed minister in May 1866, it was not until November that he departed on his mission to the Juarez government, located somewhere in northern Mexico. To make his mission more significant diplomatically, Gen. W. T. Sherman accompanied him. They found the coast towns still in the hands of Maximilian and failed to get in touch with Juarez. Campbell for the time being set up his "Legation" at New Orleans. Gideon Welles, secretary of the navy, wrote in his diary, "The Minister, with his thumb in his mouth, stood off, went up the coast, where Sherman left him. The whole business turns out a *faux pas,* a miserable, bungling piece of business" (*Diary of Gideon Welles,* 1911, II, 649). The refusal of Maximilian to leave Mexico following the withdrawal of the French forces had by this time become the chief difficulty in the Mexican situation. Seward repeatedly ordered Campbell to depart for his post of duty with the Juarez government, but Campbell, who found his duties irksome, pleaded ill health and private business as reasons for delaying. Seward practically forced his resignation, June 15, 1867. Campbell now found himself so thoroughly out of accord with the Republican party's program, both political and economic, that he withdrew his allegiance and in 1870 ran for Congress and was elected on the Democratic ticket. In 1872 he actively supported Greeley for the presidency. He was a member and vice-president of the third Ohio constitutional convention which met in 1873. The document framed by that body did not meet with his approval and he aided the forces which accomplished its rejection. In his last years he frequently spoke and wrote in behalf of various movements for economic and political reform.

[Full sketches of Campbell were published in the *Cincinnati Commercial,* Nov. 27, 1882, and in the *Cincinnati Enquirer* of the same date. Jas. McBride, *Pioneer Biogs., Sketches of the Lives of Some of the Early Settlers of Butler County, Ohio* (1869), has a number of references to Campbell. See also *Ohio Archæol. and Hist. Quart.,* Jan., Oct. 1925. The fullest account of the Mexican episode is in Ellis P. Oberholtzer, *A Hist. of the U. S. Since the Civil War,* vol. I (1917). This author has made use of the Johnson Papers. Campbell's official correspondence as minister is to be found in

House Ex. Doc. No. 1 and No. 76, 39 Cong., 2 Sess.; House Ex. Doc. No. 30, 40 Cong., 1 Sess.; House Ex. Doc. No. 1, 40 Cong., 2 Sess., vol. I. J. M. Callahan's article "Evolution of Seward's Mexican Policy," West Va. Univ. Studies, vols. IV–VI, is useful.]

W. T. U—r.

CAMPBELL, PRINCE LUCIEN (Oct. 6, 1861–Aug. 14, 1925), college president, was of Scotch and Irish descent, the son of Thomas Franklin and Jane Eliza (Campbell) Campbell. He was born in Newmarket, Mo., but the family removed in 1869 to Monmouth, Ore., where his father became president of Christian College. There Prince Campbell graduated in 1879. He taught, reported for the *Kansas City Star,* and attended Harvard, graduating in 1886. On Sept. 12, 1887, he was married to Eugenia J. Zieber of Forest Grove, Ore. From 1886 to 1889 he was teacher of ancient languages and pedagogy in the State Normal School at Monmouth, successor to Christian College. Thereafter, to 1902, he was president of that institution. In 1902 he became president of the University of Oregon. On Aug. 20, 1908, his first wife having died in February 1891, he was married to Susan A. Church of San Francisco. The educational problems which he was called upon to meet as president of the University of Oregon were, at the outset, similar to those encountered by such institutions generally. Among these were the insignificant financial resources and limited student patronage. Campbell, during the previous four or five years, as a trusted adviser of legislative committees, had aided in establishing the public high-school system, and in the rapid multiplication of high schools he found the best assurance of student support for the university. Candidates soon began applying for admission in more generous numbers. Eventually the legislature was induced to enlarge the university's grant. But at this point the president encountered the newly adopted "Initiative and Referendum" amendment to the state constitution. This, under the existing conditions, revolutionized the history of public support for liberal higher education. No American educator had ever been called upon to present the case for higher education to the entire electorate. That is what Campbell was obliged to do, not once, but repeatedly, ultimately gaining the assured support of the people themselves. In this work, whose result was to render more secure every state-supported university in America, Campbell's inspiring personality was a major asset. Combined with rare practical judgment, organizing ability, and a positive genius for maintaining the morale of his forces, he had an abiding faith in the necessity of liberal culture for a democ-

racy and great enthusiasm in presenting the argument to the voters. He was a man of splendid physique, five feet nine in stature and weighing 180 pounds, with handsome florid countenance, glowing dark eyes, black hair and mustache. He was fond of society, a noted raconteur, a gay, charming companion, a lover of his kind.

[Jos. Schafer, *Prince Lucien Campbell* (Eugene, 1926); private MSS.; newspaper clippings; Univ. of Ore. Regents Reports, 1902–26.]
J. S.

CAMPBELL, ROBERT (March 1804–Oct. 16, 1879), fur trapper, capitalist, was born of Scotch parents in Aughlane, County Tyrone, Ireland. Nothing is known of his youth. He came to America probably in 1824, and he seems to have gone at once to St. Louis. On Oct. 30, 1825, suffering from lung trouble and advised to try the mountains for a cure, he set out with Ashley's second overland expedition. His health improved and he engaged actively in trapping, soon becoming a leader and commanding various parties organized by Ashley's successors. In close association with Fitzpatrick, Smith, Bridger, the Sublettes and other noted trappers, his operations during the first seven years covered nearly the whole of the northern region. In the battle with the Blackfeet in Pierre's Hole, July 18, 1832, made famous by Irving and others, he bore a conspicuously gallant part, incidentally saving the life of his companion, W. L. Sublette. On Dec. 20 he became a partner with Sublette in an effort to contest the hold of the American Fur Company on the upper Missouri, but at the end of the following year, after a succession of disasters, the partners decided to confine themselves to the mountain trade.

In the fall of 1835 Campbell retired from the mountains and made his home in St. Louis. The firm of Sublette & Campbell, after maintaining for seven or eight years the only serious opposition encountered during that time by the American Fur Company, was dissolved on Jan. 12, 1842. Campbell engaged in extensive real estate dealings, established a large dry-goods store, and at a later time became the proprietor of the Southern Hotel and the president of both the Bank of the State of Missouri and the Merchants' National Bank. All his affairs prospered, and he amassed great wealth. Though never a candidate for office, he took an active part in public affairs. In 1846, as a member of Gov. Edwards's staff, with the rank of colonel, he distinguished himself by his indefatigable efforts toward equipping and drilling the mounted volunteers for the Mexican War. In 1851, by appointment of President Fillmore, he was one of the commissioners in the great Indian conference held near Fort Laramie, and in 1869, by appointment of President Grant, he again served as an Indian commissioner. To the end he maintained a lively interest in the scenes wherein he had spent his young manhood, and in 1868 he paid a final visit to the region, giving a reception at Fort Laramie to his old friends and acquaintances. In his later years he suffered greatly from a bronchial affection. In the summer of 1879 he journeyed to Saratoga and the Atlantic seashore, but returned in September hopeless of relief. He died at his St. Louis home.

Campbell was married, probably in Philadelphia, to Virginia Kyle, of Raleigh, N. C., who with three children survived him. He was, for many years before his death, one of the most influential and widely known business men and capitalists of the West. He was a generous man, and his benefactions, though secret, are believed to have been many and large. Though he was somewhat distant and difficult of approach, his friendships were strong and enduring. He was greatly attached to Bridger, befriending him in various ways and undertaking the care of his children—one of whom, Virginia, lived for two years in his home. He was honest, and in an era wherein the fierce competition of rivals prompted the basest accusations against one another, his reputation seems to have escaped reproach.

[Mention of Campbell is more or less frequent in the journals and letters of the fur-trapping period and in such works as Washington Irving, *The Adventures of Capt. Bonneville* (1837), Chas. G. Coutant, *Hist. of Wyoming* (1899), E. L. Sabin, *Kit Carson Days* (1914), and J. C. Alter, *Jas. Bridger* (1925). Biographical sketches are given in H. M. Chittenden, *The Am. Fur Trade of the Far West* (1902), and J. T. Scharf, *Hist. of St. Louis City and County* (1883). There are obituaries in the *St. Louis Globe-Democrat* and the *Mo. Republican* (St. Louis), Oct. 17, 1879).]   W. J. G.

CAMPBELL, THOMAS (Feb. 1, 1763–Jan. 4, 1854), one of the founders of the Disciples of Christ, was the son of Alexander Campbell. A handsome young Irishman of Scotch descent, he was religiously minded, and, after graduating from the University of Glasgow, became a minister of the Secession Church, which was a branch of the Scottish kirk that had broken away from the parent stock of Presbyterianism. The tendency to independency was strong in the seceding body, and controversy divided it. Campbell tried to bring about a reunion, and went as a delegate to the Scotch synod in an effort to make peace. This was unsuccessful, and a later attempt to free the Irish churches from Scotch control was unavailing. The experience made Campbell an enemy of sectarianism. Ill health compelled a sea voyage in 1807, and he sailed to America, hoping to find there a task to his liking. In western Pennsylvania he discovered friends and an opportunity to preach, and he sent for his family to join him. His liking for Christian unity made him invite persons of various religious professions to join in the Lord's Supper, but his Presbyterian synod censured him, thus causing him to withdraw from the Presbyterian Church. With his son Alexander Campbell [*q.v.*] he formed the Christian Association of Washington (Pa.), out of which came later a fully organized independent church, with a declaration of principles written by Thomas Campbell. Before long it was apparent that a new denomination might grow out of the experiment. That was not the wish of the Campbells and it seemed best to join the Baptists with whom they were sympathetic on the subject of baptism. But the union did not work well, the connection was broken, and the Campbellites formed a merger with the Christians, a similar group that had been organized by Barton W. Stone. The Campbellites preferred to call themselves Disciples.

Thomas Campbell was a popular preacher, sometimes lengthy in discourse, but enlivening his subject with homely illustrations. He was never strongly rooted in one locality. In 1813 he removed from Pennsylvania to a farm in Ohio, where he started a seminary. Two years later he moved to Pittsburgh with another school as his medium of usefulness. Tiring of this after another two years, he made a home at Burlington, Vt., among the Baptists, and tried to show them how to make their emotional preaching more intellectual. Meanwhile he taught school for a living. His family was happy in these surroundings and the school was prospering when Campbell became displeased with the attitude of the community toward negroes, and he peremptorily summoned his family to return to the neighborhood of their old home in Pennsylvania. There he assisted his son Alexander in the conduct of a school near by. In his later life he itinerated as a preacher, until, becoming blind, he retired from active service. He lived to the age of ninety, dying peacefully at Bethany, W. Va.

[The chief source is *The Memoir of Elder Thos. Campbell* (1861) by his son Alexander Campbell. See also Robt. Richardson, *Memoirs of Alexander Campbell* (1868–70), *passim*.]   H. K. R.

CAMPBELL, THOMAS JOSEPH (Apr. 29, 1848–Dec. 14, 1925), Jesuit priest, was born on Manhattan Island and educated at the College of St. Francis Xavier, New York City, where he was graduated in 1866. The following year after further studies in philosophy he received the degree of M.A. In the summer of 1867 he entered the Society of Jesus at Sault-au-Recollet, Canada, and in 1870 was assigned to teach the freshman class at St. John's College, Fordham (now Fordham University). From 1873 to 1876 he studied philosophy and science at Woodstock College, Maryland. After two more years of teaching at St. Francis Xavier's, he went to Louvain, Belgium, where he devoted himself to theological branches for four years, being ordained priest in 1880.

In 1885 he was appointed president of St. John's College, Fordham, and three years later provincial of the Maryland-New York Province of the Society of Jesus. This office he held until 1893, when he became vice-rector of St. Francis Xavier's for ten months. Two years were spent in missionary preaching in the eastern states, after which he was appointed a second time president of St. John's College, Fordham. In August 1900 he joined the staff of the Apostleship of Prayer in New York, as preacher, writer, and editor. Master of a clear, attractive English style, he contributed many impressive articles to the *Messenger of the Sacred Heart* and to the *Pilgrim of Our Lady of Martyrs,* the organ of the Shrine erected at Auriesville, N. Y. His interest in the mission work of New France resulted in the publication in the pages of the *Messenger* of many biographical sketches of the missionaries. These were published later on in book-form under the title *Pioneer Priests of North America* (3 vols., 1908–11). Two further volumes were devoted to *Pioneer Laymen of North America* (1915).

Two years were spent by Father Campbell in Montreal as English preacher in the Jesuit church and as research worker in the Jesuit archives, after which in 1910 he was chosen editor of the weekly Catholic review, *America,* published by the Jesuit Fathers in New York. He conducted the review with vigor and success for four years, writing especially on historical, educational, and social subjects. During this time he translated and published *The Names of God and Meditative Summaries of the Divine Perfections* (1912), by Father Leonard Lessius, S. J. After a sojourn of two more years in Canada, he again returned to New York and among other occupations lectured on American history in the Graduate School of Fordham University. Under the title *Various Discourses* (1917) he gathered into a volume the outstanding sermons and addresses of his life. In 1921 he published *The Jesuits, 1534–1921, A History of the Society of Jesus from its Foundation to the Present Time.* It was the first attempt at a full, but popular, historical account in English, written by a member of the Society. During the latter years of his life he translated the Psalms into verse, as well as the hymns of the Roman Breviary, compiled a series of sketches of distinguished members of the Society of Jesus, and prepared a sketch of the Archdiocese of New York. The last work from his pen was a revision of his monograph on Blessed Isaac Jogues and his companion martyrs, published posthumously under the title *The Martyrs of the Mohawk* (Apostleship of Prayer, 1926). After a life of labor and merit Father Campbell retired to the Jesuit Rest House at Monroe, N. Y., where he died on Dec. 14, 1925.

[The main sources for the biography of Father Campbell are the private archives, catalogues and publications of the Md.–N.Y. Province of the Society of Jesus. A brief notice will be found in *Who's Who in America,* 1912–13. Obituaries appeared in the *N.Y. Times,* Dec. 15, 1925; *America,* Dec. 26, 1925; *Cath. Hist. Rev.,* Apr. 1926.]

J. C.

CAMPBELL, Lord WILLIAM (d. Sept. 5, 1778), colonial governor of South Carolina, was the fourth son of the fourth Duke of Argyll and the Honorable Mary Bellenden, daughter of Lord Bellenden and maid of honor to Caroline, Princess of Wales. His father had a long honorable career in public service, as an officer of the army in the Continental wars of George II and in the Rebellion of 1745, as a member of Parliament, as one of the sixteen representatives of the Scotch peerage, and as a member of the Privy Council. William Campbell entered the navy and rose rapidly to the rank of captain in 1762. Two years later he was elected to the House of Commons to represent the Shire of Argyll but resigned in 1766 when appointed governor of Nova Scotia. His governorship was marked by no notable events and was broken by three visits, one to London and two to Boston, making him absent from his station almost two years. He was evidently dissatisfied in Halifax, for he petitioned twice to be transferred, once in 1771 and again in 1773. His plea was granted in 1773 when he became governor of South Carolina, where already he had private interests, for in 1763 he had visited the colony while commanding the British ship *Nightingale,* and had (Apr. 7, 1763) married Sarah, daughter of Ralph Izard, a wealthy and influential South Carolinian. Gov. Campbell arrived at Charleston, June 17, 1775, to an ominously quiet reception, for on the preceding day the Council of Safety, appointed by the Provincial Congress, had held its first meeting. The Governor was placed in an anomalous position from the outset. His wife's relatives were all patriots. The residence he intended to occupy was unready, and he accepted perforce the hospitality of Miles Brewton, a cousin by marriage and a member of the Council of Safety. With his powers usurped by this body and in the midst of disturbed and threatening conditions, the Governor summoned an Assembly, which, uncoöperative and hostile, accomplished little. In a further effort to hold the colony loyal, he turned to the frontier, where Tory support was strongest. He carried on secret negotiations for aid not only with the frontiersmen but also with the Indians. These transactions were discovered, and only the intervention of the moderates prevented the radicals from seizing him. His term of office was destined to be short, for when word was received that the British were on their way to Charleston the patriots occupied Fort Johnson, and the Governor, dissolving his Assembly, fled to the British ship *Tamar*. The Council of Safety invited him to return, but he declined, and when the royal fleet attacked Charleston, he was in the affray as a volunteer in His Majesty's service, commanding a lower gun-deck. In the British defeat he was wounded and returned to England, dying at Southampton.

[Sir Robt. Douglas, *The Peerage of Scotland* (rev. ed., 1813); Jos. Foster, *Members of Parliament, Scotland* (2nd ed., 1882); Beamish Murdock, *Hist. of Nova Scotia* (3 vols., 1867); Edward McCrady, *Hist. of S. C. in the Revolution* (1901); *S. C. Hist. and Geneal. Mag.*, vols. I, II, VII.]   H.B-C.

CAMPBELL, WILLIAM (1745–Aug. 22, 1781), Revolutionary soldier, was born in Augusta County, Va. His branch of the famous Campbell family came from Argyll, Scotland, by way of northern Ireland and Pennsylvania. His father was Charles Campbell, his mother's surname was Buchanan. He settled in the valley of the Holston River at Aspenvale (near Abingdon), Va., and married Elizabeth, sister of Patrick Henry. He was a "typical pioneer"; very tall, of great strength and endurance, fair of complexion, grim toward his enemies, and a hater of Tories. He soon rose to prominence; as captain of militia he was active in intermittent border warfare against the Cherokees, and he held office as justice of Fincastle County. Like so many other frontiersmen, he participated in Dunmore's War against the Indians in 1774. In January 1775 he with others signed an address from the people of Fincastle County to the Continental Congress, protesting their loyalty to the Crown but declaring their willingness to fight for their "constitutional rights" (*American Archives,* 4 ser., I, 1165). Campbell led a company to join Patrick Henry's regiment at the capital, Williamsburg, and aided in the expulsion of the royal governor, Lord Dunmore. Resigning in Oc-

tober 1776, he resumed his activities on the frontier; he had a share in the irregular warfare, and was boundary commissioner between Virginia and the Cherokees; in the Virginia militia he held the rank of colonel 1777–80. He was also a justice in Washington County, and a delegate to the Virginia legislature. The great event in his life came near the close of the war. By the autumn of 1780 the prospect for independence seemed almost hopeless in the South. The Americans had lost Charleston, the battle of Camden, and their hold upon South Carolina and Georgia. Ferguson, the ablest of the Loyalist commanders, was operating in the Carolinas, encouraging the Tories and terrorizing the Whigs. To defeat him, there collected a small army of backwoodsmen, the "rear-guard of the Revolution." One of their leaders, Shelby, urged Campbell to join them. At first he declined, giving as a reason the necessity of defending Virginia against invasion by Cornwallis. Finally accepting, he marched with 400 men of Washington County to the rendezvous at Sycamore Shoals (on the upper Watauga). When the army reached Cowpens, nearly in touch with Ferguson, it numbered about 1,800 men under various commanders, Shelby, Sevier, Campbell, and others. The officers being of equal rank, Campbell was elected officer of the day to execute the decisions of the council of officers. About 900 men were picked, and the march began on a rainy night toward Ferguson's position. This was on the knob of a ridge called King's Mountain. Ferguson's ground, which he held with about 1,100 men, was supposed by him to be impregnable. During the battle (Oct. 7, 1780), Campbell is said to have been in the thick of the fight, leading his men. His part in the exploit was recognized by Cornwallis with a threat of death—in the case of capture. At the battle of Guilford, Mar. 15, 1781, Campbell brought only a few Virginians to the aid of Gen. Greene, since the Cherokees were on the frontier; with his riflemen he fought under the immediate command of Gen. Henry Lee, and he claimed later that Lee withheld his support. He received the thanks of Congress for his services, and from his state legislature a vote of thanks together with a horse and a sword. He was elected again to the legislature, was appointed brigadier-general of militia, and began the final campaign under Lafayette at Jamestown, but died shortly after at Rocky Mills, Hanover County, Va. Thirty years later Shelby and Sevier questioned Campbell's share in the victory of King's Mountain, alleging that he remained in the rear; but the charge was never proved.

[L. C. Draper, *King's Mt. and Its Heroes* (1881); Wm. H. Foote, *Sketches of Va.* (2nd ser., 1885); H. Lee, *Memoirs of the War in the Southern Dept. of the*

U. S. (1812) ; Wm. Johnson, *Sketches of the Life and Correspondence of Nathanael Greene* (1822) ; Jas. Ferguson, *Two Scottish Soldiers* (Aberdeen, 1888); *Southern Lit. Messenger*, Sept. 1845 ; *Am. Rev.*, Dec. 1848 ; *Mag. of Western Hist.*, Jan. 1887 ; *Southern Meth. Rev.*, July, Sept. 1887 ; Isaac Shelby, *Battle of King's Mt., To the Public* (1823) ; F. Moore, *Diary of the Am. Revolution* (1860).]   E. K. A.

CAMPBELL, WILLIAM BOWEN (Feb. 1, 1807–Aug. 19, 1867), congressman, governor of Tennessee, the first child of David and Catherine (Bowen) Campbell, was born on his father's farm in Sumner County, Tenn., within a few miles of Nashville. He studied law under the direction of his cousin, Gov. David Campbell of Abingdon, Va., attended the lectures of Henry St. George Tucker, and began the practise of his profession at Carthage, Tenn. Here in 1835 he married Frances Owen. In his family there was a tradition of courageous military service. Paternal and maternal ancestors had distinguished themselves in colonial wars and in the American Revolution. In 1836 Campbell volunteered for the Seminole War and fought with gallantry as a captain of a company in a regiment commanded by Col. William Trousdale. In the following year he defeated Trousdale in a campaign for the lower house of Congress, despite the fact that the latter had the support of Ex-President Jackson. Campbell now became a member of the newly formed Whig party which for almost twenty years was to be the dominant party in his state. After six years in Congress he voluntarily retired to private life. He was called from retirement by the Mexican War, when he was elected to command the 1st Regiment of Tennessee Volunteers. At Monterey, at Vera Cruz, and at Cerro Gordo, he and his men of the "Bloody First" fought with a courage and success that made him a popular hero. In 1851 he was the gubernatorial candidate of the Whigs, and again William Trousdale was his Democratic opponent. Trousdale's chief issue was condemnation of the compromise measures of 1850. Campbell championed them and denounced resistance to the laws of the United States. The Whig papers carried as their campaign slogan Campbell's cry at Monterey, "Boys, Follow Me !" and Campbell was elected. He was the last Whig governor of Tennessee. At the end of his term he voluntarily retired again to private life, made his home in Lebanon, and became president of the Bank of Middle Tennessee. The final phase of his life began with the fateful presidential campaign of 1860. He gave his support to John Bell, the Union candidate; he strenuously opposed the secession of Tennessee; and when that act had been accomplished and even John Bell had given allegiance to the Confederacy, he remained the most distinguished of those few in Middle Tennessee who still remained loyal to the Union. From the Confederate authorities he refused offers of high military command. For a brief period he accepted a brigadier-generalship in the Union army. As a "conservative unionist" he worked for the return of Tennessee to the Union. In 1865 he was elected to the lower house of Congress, and when finally seated he gave his support to the conservative policies of President Johnson, but his health had long been failing and he soon died. He was a man of courage and unquestioned integrity, who commanded the respect of those who knew him.

[Campbell's papers are in the possession of members of his family in Nashville. Some of these, relating his experiences in the Mexican War, have been edited by St. George L. Sioussat and printed in the *Tenn. Hist. Mag.*, I, 129–67. A campaign biography (anon.), *Sketch of the Life and Public Services of Gen. Wm. B. Campbell, of Tenn.*, 16 pp., was published in 1851. His genealogy, his portrait, and a sketch of his life by his son, Lemuel R. Campbell, may be found in Margaret Campbell Pilcher, *Hist. Sketches of the Campbell, Pilcher and Kindred Families* (1911). A lengthy obituary appeared in the (Nashville) *Union and Dispatch*, Aug. 29, 1867.]   P. M. H.

CAMPBELL, WILLIAM HENRY (Sept. 14, 1808–Dec. 7, 1890), clergyman, college president, was born in Baltimore, the youngest of the ten children of William and Ann (Ditchfield) Campbell. His father had emigrated to America from Ayrshire and was a thriving merchant and an elder of the Associate Reformed Church. His mother, who was of English extraction, died when William was three weeks old, and he was brought up by his sisters. He attended a small school kept by an able teacher but unfortunate man, the Rev. John Gibson, and then went to Dickinson College (1824–28) where he formed scholarly tastes and habits under the guidance of the celebrated Alexander McClelland. His course in the Princeton Theological Seminary was cut short in 1829 by the bankruptcy of his father, who had indorsed the notes of his friends. Through the offices of his brother-in-law, the Rev. Thomas M. Strong, under whom he continued his theological studies, Campbell secured a position as assistant teacher in Erasmus Hall at Flatbush, Long Island, and was licensed to preach by the Second Presbytery of New York in 1831. In the same year he married Katherine Elsie Schoonmaker, of Flatbush, who was to be his companion for almost fifty-five years. He was co-pastor with the Rev. Andrew Yates at Chittenango, N. Y., 1831–33, giving up his charge because chronic bronchitis had temporarily incapacitated him for preaching; was principal of Erasmus Hall 1833–39; pastor at East New York 1839–41, at the same time keeping a school because his parishioners could not pay him a living wage; pastor of the Third Reformed Church in Albany 1841–48; and principal of the Albany Academy 1848–51. With twenty years of varied experience as preacher and teacher behind him, he succeeded his old master, Dr. McClelland, as professor of Oriental literature in the New Brunswick Seminary and of belles-lettres in Rutgers College, 1851–63. A man of consecrated personal life, a conservative but by no means narrow-minded theologian, and a methodical, rigorous, enthusiastic teacher, he made a lasting impression on successive generations of theological students. He required all his students to study Chaldee, instructed some of them also in Syriac, and with one faithful pupil attacked Arabic. To maintain the decorum of his office, he gave up chewing and smoking, which had solaced him for years, but the reek of his friends' tobacco pipes was always grateful to his nostrils. He instigated the movement that brought about the separation of the Seminary from Rutgers College, and in 1863 was elected president of the College. Rutgers was at that time suffering severely from the depression caused by the Civil War and its supporters were beginning to lose heart, but Campbell took hold of the new work with his customary vigor and courage. Under his administration the College grew in endowments, buildings, and students. In 1864 the State of New Jersey established at Rutgers the State College for Agriculture and the Mechanic Arts, which was to exert a constantly growing influence on the College as a whole. Increasing age and failing eyesight compelled Campbell to resign in June 1881, but he retained the presidency for another year, when a successor was found. The trustees of the College then made him professor of moral philosophy, a position without teaching duties that allowed them to show their esteem for him by paying him a salary out of their own pockets. Retirement, however, did not mean inactivity; his last years were given to establishing the Suydam Street Church in New Brunswick, in which his son followed him as pastor in 1889.

[*A Memorial of the Rev. Wm. Henry Campbell, D.D., LL.D., Late President of Rutgers College* (printed for the College, 1894); *Biog. Notices Officers and Grads. Rutgers Coll. Deceased during the Academical Year Ending in June 1891* (1891); E. T. Corwin, *A Manual of the Reformed Church in America* (4th ed., 1902); *Acts and Proc. of the 85th Regular Sess. of the Gen. Synod of the Reformed Ch. in America* (1891).]

G. H. G.

CAMPBELL, WILLIAM W. (June 10, 1806–Sept. 7, 1881), jurist, historian, congressman, was born in Cherry Valley, Otsego County, N. Y., to which place his grandfather, Samuel

Campbell, had come with his parents from Londonderry, N. H., in 1742. Col. Samuel Campbell served under Gen. Nicholas Herkimer [*q.v.*] at Oriskany, and his wife, Jane, and seven-year-old son, James S., were captured at the time of the Cherry Valley massacre but later exchanged for the wife and children of Col. John Butler [*q.v.*]. James S. Campbell married Sarah Elderkin, and William W. Campbell was their son. He was graduated from Union College in 1827, and among his classmates were Preston King and Rufus W. Peckham (L. B. Proctor, *The Bench and Bar of New York*, 1870, p. 34). He took up the study of law under Chancellor Kent and began practise in New York City in 1831. His legal career was not spectacular. His service to the profession was to be in the capacity of jurist rather than of attorney. In 1841 he was appointed master in chancery, and afterward commissioner in bankruptcy, and, from 1849 until 1855, he was a justice of the superior court of New York City. His most distinguished work was done while he was justice of the state supreme court for the 6th judicial district, a post which he occupied from 1857 until 1865. During his early occupancy of the supreme court bench, he was very much under the influence of Justice Ransom Balcom, who generally wrote the opinions for the court. In 1863 Campbell became the presiding justice, and his influence among his colleagues became more apparent. He placed himself on record as opposed to the acceptance of the testimony under oath of atheists or disbelievers in a personal god, and thus helped shape the law of evidence in the state along conservative lines (*Stanbro* vs. *Hopkins,* 28 *Barbour,* 265, at p. 272). On the other hand, he took a liberal position in interpreting the married women's property acts (*White* vs. *Wagner,* 32 *Barbour,* 250).

Campbell was one of the most active members of the Native American party, and, as its nominee, he was elected to Congress, and served from 1845 until 1847. During his term of office, he addressed the House frequently on the subject of the Native American principles. Adopting as his slogan, "Americans should rule America," he made vigorous efforts to restrict the voting privileges of naturalized citizens at a time when the great Irish emigration was at its flood-tide. In his well-known speech of Jan. 27, 1846, in which he favored a compromise on the Oregon claim (*Congressional Globe,* 29 Cong., 1 Sess., p. 260; App., pp. 157–59), he attacked the proposal to give political preference to naturalized citizens. "I value too highly my American birthright to barter it for political preferment; I would not sell it for a mess of pottage," he declared. He successfully advocated restricting the right of suffrage in the Territory of Oregon to citizens of the United States, excluding those who had merely declared their intention to become citizens (*Ibid.*, p. 1204). In his public addresses he seemed unable to grasp the distinction between national and state citizenship.

Campbell made a number of historical contributions. In 1831 he published his *Annals of Tryon County; or, the Border Warfare of New-York During the Revolution,* a colorful narrative, the sources of which are chiefly regional anecdotes. Because of his researches in the field of Indian history, he staunchly favored fair treatment for the Indians (*Congressional Globe,* 29 Cong., 1 Sess., p. 409). In *The Life and Writings of De Witt Clinton* (1849), he points out the intimate personal and political association of his father and grandfather with the careers of George and De Witt Clinton. The volume comprises a brief notice of the Clintons and a selected number of Clinton's public addresses, and his Private Canal Journal for 1810. In 1813 Campbell published *An Historical Sketch of Robin Hood and Captain Kidd,* the inspiration for which was a trip a few years previously to the Yorkshire district in England. The author in his defense of the character of Kidd gave a lucid analysis of the documentary material, an analysis vindicated by modern critical scholarship.

Campbell was married twice: first on Aug. 13, 1833, to Maria Starkweather of Cooperstown, N. Y., and after her death in 1853, to Catherine, daughter of Jacob Livingston of Cherry Valley.

[*Political Reg. and Cong. Dir. 1776–1878* (1878), comp. by B. P. Poore; *Albany Jour.,* Sept. 8, 1881; C. L. Starkweather, *A Brief Geneal. Hist. of Robert Starkweather, etc.* (1904); S. T. Livermore, *A Condensed Hist. of Cooperstown* (1862); address by Campbell in *The Centennial Celebration at Cherry Valley . . . July 4th, 1840* (1840).]   R. B. M.

CANAGA, ALFRED BRUCE (Nov. 2, 1850–Dec. 24, 1906), naval engineer, the son of Elias Green Canaga and Jane (McClintock) Canaga, was born in Scio, Ohio. He was educated in the public schools of Scio (1856–68), at Scio College (1868–72), and at the United States Naval Academy (1872–74). In 1881 he was married to Ermina Carr. He was promoted through the various grades in Engineer Corps to chief engineer in 1895 and became lieutenant commander in March 1899, when the amalgamation of Line and Engineer Corps was consummated. An able, progressive, and efficient designer, he was a loyal assistant to his chief, Admiral Melville, in carrying out the latter's administrative policies.

He designed the machinery of the battleships *Alabama, Illinois, Kentucky, Maine* (second), *Missouri, Ohio,* and *Wisconsin*; of the single turret monitors *Cheyenne* (*Wyoming*), *Ozark* (*Arkansas*), *Tallahassee* (*Florida*), *Tonopah* (*Nevada*); of the armored cruisers *Maryland, West Virginia, Pennsylvania, South Dakota, Colorado, Washington.* He was on duty at the Navy Department during the war with Spain and could not be spared for service at the front. Prior to his duty as chief designer he had made a cruise in the *Chicago,* which had the most remarkable machinery of modern times, beam-engines, driving screw propellers, and cylindrical boilers of large diameter, externally fired with return tubes. Before the end of the cruise it was necessary to treat the boilers like racehorses and blanket them after a run to prevent too rapid cooling. The design of this machinery was due to the civilian engineer member of the Naval Advisory Board and was opposed by the naval engineer member, who was not supported by his naval colleagues. Owing to his imperturbable good nature, Canaga, known to all his friends as "Pop Canaga," was universally popular in the navy. He was short and stout, and died suddenly of a stroke while on duty at the Boston Navy Yard in charge of the Engineering Department.

[*Army and Navy Reg.,* Dec. 29, 1906; *Army and Navy Jour.,* Dec. 29, 1906; *Boston Transcript,* Dec. 26, 1906; *Jour. Am. Soc. Naval Engineers,* Feb. 1907.]
     W. M. M.

CANBY, EDWARD RICHARD SPRIGG (Aug. 1817–Apr. 11, 1873), Union soldier, was born in Kentucky. His father, Israel T. Canby, was later Democratic candidate for governor of Indiana, to which state the family had removed. Canby was appointed from Indiana to a cadetship at West Point in 1835, graduated there in 1839, and was commissioned second lieutenant in the 2nd Infantry. He served in the Florida War and on routine duties for some years, was promoted first lieutenant in 1846, and in 1847 was appointed an assistant adjutant-general with the rank of captain. In that capacity he accompanied Riley's brigade of Gen. Scott's army in Mexico, was present at the siege of Vera Cruz, the battles of Cerro Gordo, Contreras, and Churubusco, and the taking of the City of Mexico, and was twice brevetted for gallantry. He was employed on duties pertaining to his department, at first in San Francisco and later in Washington, until 1855, when he returned to the line by appointment as major of the 10th Infantry. He then served with his regiment at various stations on the frontier, the outbreak of the Civil War finding him in garrison at Fort Defiance, N. M. He was appointed colonel of the 19th Infantry, May 14, 1861, and assigned to the command of the Department of New Mexico. The district under his charge was an almost uninhabited region, remote from the principal theatre of the war, and the operations conducted there were little noticed at the time and are now almost forgotten. Yet they had, or might have had, a great influence upon the result of the war. When Gen. Sibley led a Confederate expedition from Texas into New Mexico, his government had larger plans than the mere occupation of that territory. California was the goal which Sibley hoped to reach. Its population was scanty, and included a considerable number of secession sympathizers. Once occupied, its reconquest by Union troops would have been a difficult matter, and meanwhile the Confederate government could have drawn from it an ample supply of the gold that it so badly needed. Canby's force was small, and was largely made up of unreliable local volunteers. He fought and lost a battle at Valverde, Jan. 21, 1862, and thereafter avoided combat, using hunger, thirst, and heat as his weapons, as he drew Sibley away from his supplies. The invasion ended in complete disaster, and Sibley's demoralized command had lost half its strength before it reached Texas again. Canby was appointed brigadier-general of volunteers, Mar. 31, 1862, and ordered east. For a year and a half he was on duty as assistant adjutant-general in Washington, except for a period of four months in 1863, following the draft riots, when he was in command of the city of New York, suppressing disorder and executing the draft. He was appointed major-general of volunteers, May 7, 1864, and assigned to the command of the Military Division of West Mississippi, embracing the Gulf States and the Southwest. As all available troops had been withdrawn to strengthen Grant's and Sherman's armies, there were no large operations in his district during 1864. He was severely wounded by guerrillas in November. Soon after his recovery he managed to assemble sufficient force for a serious campaign against Mobile. The forts covering it were successively taken, by siege or assault, and the city was entered on Apr. 12, 1865. On May 4 and May 26, Canby received the surrender of the armies of Taylor and Kirby Smith, the last two Confederate armies remaining in the field. For five years following the war he was moved from place to place in the South, being sent anywhere that the administration encountered serious difficulties. "Wherever he went," says Gen. Cullum, "order, good feeling, and tranquillity

followed his footsteps." He had been appointed a brigadier-general in the regular army, July 28, 1866, and was mustered out of the volunteer service, Sept. 1, 1866. In 1870 he was assigned to command on the Pacific coast. Always a friend to the Indian, he undertook a mission to the Modocs in northern California, endeavoring to arrange a peaceable settlement of the difficulties with the government, but was treacherously murdered by the Indian envoys during his conference with them. He was tall and soldierly in appearance, kind and courteous in manner, utterly devoid of selfish ambition. His superiors and subordinates knew him as a great commander; he was too modest and reserved to win the popular recognition that he merited.

[G. W. Cullum, *Biog. Reg.* (1891), II, 18–24; *Battles and Leaders of the Civil War* (1884), vols. II and IV; *Official Records*, IV, IX, XXVII, pt. 1, XXXIV, pts. 1, 3, 4, XXXIX, pts. 1, 2, 3, XLIX, pts. 1, 2; H. C. Wood, "The Assassination of Gen. Canby," in *Jour. of the Military Service Institution*, IX (1888), 395–98.]
T. M. S.

CANDEE, LEVERETT (June 1, 1795–Nov. 27, 1863), pioneer rubber manufacturer, was born at Oxford, Conn., the son of Job and Sarah (Benham) Candee. His father was a veteran of the Revolution, and later a captain of militia and a member of the Connecticut legislature. After a scanty education in the district school, Candee went to New Haven at the age of fifteen where he soon obtained employment with Capt. Gad Peck, then a prominent merchant in foreign trade. His next position was with Root & Atwater, dealers in dry-goods, the beginning of twenty-five years' connection with the dry-goods business. With two fellow clerks, James E. P. Dean and William Cutler, he organized the firm of Candee, Dean & Cutler which took over the business of their employers. Retiring from the firm in 1833, Candee removed to New York, where for two years he was partner in a firm of jobbers and commission merchants in dry-goods. He returned to New Haven in 1835 and entered into a partnership with Timothy Lester and Abraham Murdock in a general merchandise and commission business. Upon the dissolution of this firm Candee was interested for several years in the manufacture of book paper at Westville, Conn. This enterprise, carried on under the firm name of Candee, Page & Lester, and, after retirement of John G. Page in 1840, under the name of Candee & Lester, was unsuccessful. Its failure in 1842 wiped out the fortune accumulated by Candee over a period of twenty-five years.

Undaunted by failure, Candee turned immediately to the manufacture of elastic suspenders.

His interest aroused in rubber, he attempted in the same year (1842) to manufacture rubber shoes. Charles Goodyear, who had just discovered the process of vulcanization, offered him a license to use the process, the license to be confirmed and extended upon a grant of a patent. Backed financially by Henry and Lucius Hotchkiss of New Haven, Candee commenced the manufacture of rubber shoes at Hampden, Conn., being the "first person in the world to manufacture rubber over-shoes under the Goodyear Patent" (Edward E. Atwater, *History of the City of New Haven to the Present*, 1887, p. 591). These first over-shoes were exceedingly crude and the early years of their manufacture were largely taken up with improving the product and building a market. By the late forties the firm was solidly established, and a new impetus to its prosperity was given in 1852 by court decisions which upheld the validity of the Goodyear patents, a famous case in which Daniel Webster appeared for Goodyear. In 1852 the firm was organized as Candee & Company, with a capital of $200,000, and four partners,—the Hotchkiss brothers, Timothy Lester, and Candee himself. Candee from the start had been the actual manager and continued, with the exception of one year, as president of the concern. He retired shortly before his death in 1863. He married Jane Caroline Tomlinson and left one son.

[The best sketch is in *Representative New Eng. Manufacturers* (1879), pp. 152–58, with engraving. See also C. C. Baldwin, *The Candee Genealogy* (1882), pp. 30–31, 66.]

H. U. F.

CANDLER, ALLEN DANIEL (Nov. 4, 1834– Oct. 26, 1910), congressman, governor of Georgia, was born near Pigeon Roost gold mine, Lumpkin County, Ga. His father was Daniel Gill Candler; his mother's maiden name was Nancy Caroline Matthews. He was descended from William Candler, of English and Irish blood, who moved from North Carolina to Georgia and became a colonel in the Revolutionary War. In 1859 he was graduated from Mercer University and for two years taught school at Jonesboro, Ga. Enlisting as a private in 1861, as colonel of the 4th Georgia Reserves he surrendered in 1865 with Gen. Johnston's army. He participated in the battles of Bridgeport, Richmond (Ky.), Baker's Creek (Miss.), Missionary Ridge, Resaca, Kenesaw Mountain, where he was wounded, and Jonesboro, where the bursting of a shell caused the loss of an eye. He was also in the conflicts about Vicksburg and Atlanta. In January 1865 he married Eugenia Williams. After the war he returned to Jonesboro having, as he said, "one wife, one

baby, one dollar, and one eye." After teaching for five years (at Monroe, Jonesboro, and Griffin) he moved in 1870 to Gainesville where he became saw-miller and contractor, erecting some of the main buildings of the town, and constructing its street railway and a portion of the Gainesville, Jefferson & Southern Railroad. Of this road he was president from 1879 to 1892.

Beginning in 1872 Candler served five years as member of the House of Representatives of the state legislature and in 1879 was elected to the state Senate. In 1882, after an exciting contest, he defeated, for congressman of the ninth district, the eloquent Emory Speer who had been elected for two terms as an independent Democrat. Candler served four consecutive terms in Congress and then voluntarily retired. For one term he was chairman of the Committee on Education. In 1894 he became secretary of state for Georgia and served till 1898 when he was elected governor. In this office he continued two terms (four years). As governor he urged economy in appropriations, recommended compulsory local taxation for education, biennial instead of annual sessions of the legislature, child labor legislation, support of a home for Confederate soldiers, a bond issue for the prompter pay of teachers' salaries, exemption of college endowments from taxation, and the publication of the state's historical records. His successor, Gov. Terrell, appointed him to compile the Colonial, Revolutionary, and Confederate records of the state, and he continued at this task until his death. Thirty-six volumes edited by him have been published. While a member of Congress he made a study of his own family history and had printed for private circulation *The Candler Family from 1650 to 1890*, of which a revised edition was later published with the title *Col. William Candler of Georgia, His Ancestry and Progeny* (1902). In 1914 a newly-formed county was named in his honor.

He was short in stature, somewhat rugged in appearance, rather free and vigorous in the expression of his convictions, and effective as a "stump speaker." Early in his career he became known as the "one-eyed plow-boy of Pigeon Roost."

[*Men of Mark in Georgia* (1908), IV, 29–32; *Memoirs of Georgia* (1895), I, 1018–20; personal information derived from associates and relatives.]

E. H. J—n.

CANDLER, ASA GRIGGS (Dec. 30, 1851– Mar. 12, 1929), manufacturer, philanthropist, son of Samuel Charles and Martha (Beall) Candler, was born on a farm near Villa Rica, in Carroll County, Ga. His father was a country merchant and farmer of ability. The family consisted of eleven children, and, of the seven boys, at least four rose to prominence in public life. One of Asa's brothers (Warren A.), became a bishop in the Methodist Episcopal Church, South, another (John S.), served on the Georgia supreme court, and a third (Milton A.), held a seat in the federal congress. Candler's early years were spent on the farm. He had good educational opportunities for the times and was prepared, in several academies, for admission to the junior class in the state university, but never entered. Early in life he developed a desire to become a physician, spent some time studying medicine under private tuition, and while so engaged became a trained pharmacist. His ambition to practise medicine was never realized, but his knowledge of drugs led ultimately to his success in the business world. In 1873 he went to Atlanta and secured a position with a druggist, George J. Howard. He soon exhibited the business acumen for which he later became noted, developed a prosperous drug business, and was ready to seize his first great opportunity. In 1887 he bought the formula for Coca Cola from a business partner, improved the process, and about 1890, sold his wholesale drug business to devote his entire attention to the new venture. Under his direction, the Coca-Cola Company developed rapidly into one of the most prosperous business enterprises in the South. In 1909, the federal government, acting upon a report of the secretary of agriculture and under the provisions of the Food and Drugs Act, filed a libel praying the condemnation and forfeiture of a quantity of Coca Cola. The case was carried through the lower federal courts to the Supreme Court and remanded for trial in the federal court for the eastern district of Tennessee. Conflicting testimony was presented alleging and denying that the amount of caffeine contained in Coca Cola was deleterious to health. The company, however, without admitting the charges stated that it had made modifications in the process of manufacture. Judgment of forfeiture was then entered (1917) against the company and it was ordered to pay the costs of court (Supplement to notices of judgment under the Food and Drugs Act, No. 6117, *Service and Regulatory Announcements* published by the Bureau of Chemistry). Candler sold the business in 1919 for $25,000,000.

With rapidly increasing wealth at his disposal, Candler was among the first to see the great future in Atlanta real estate, a field of activity which he had entered in a small way almost upon his arrival in the city. He undoubtedly possessed in high degree the Midas-touch, but from the very beginning of his career he exhibited philanthropic interests. Almost single-handed he prevented a disastrous real-estate panic in Atlanta in 1907, buying great quantities of real estate to prevent a slump and in many cases turning later profits over to original holders. One of the most conspicuous of his altruistic services was in the early years of the World War. Cotton, the staple crop of the South, had declined far below the cost of production, growers were faced with ruin, and the "buy a bale" movement had proved ineffective. Candler suddenly came forward with an offer, widely circulated throughout the cotton region, to lend six cents a pound on all cotton stored in warehouses to an amount up to $30,000,000; and when this sum had been rapidly exhausted, he borrowed additional funds and continued to lend. To aid the plan he constructed a warehouse covering forty acres. In a relatively short time he had in large measure allayed the panic, and as the war went on and the demand for cotton increased the producers were enabled to market their stores at a fair price. Instances of similar character were frequent in his career. In a crisis in the affairs of the city government, he was drafted into service as mayor of Atlanta, 1917–18, aided in the reorganization of municipal administration, untangled financial difficulties, and frequently advanced from his private resources funds to accomplish needed public improvements, for which the city was not then able to pay. Throughout his life he was deeply attached to the Methodist church and a large part of his interest and of his wealth was devoted to that institution. He was instrumental in the construction of a down-town institutional church plant and of a hospital under church control. Long interested in Emory College, a small denominational institution, located near Atlanta, he made possible, by an initial gift of $1,000,000, its removal to Atlanta and its expansion into Emory University. All told, his gifts to that university amounted to $7,000,000. Always particularly concerned in medical education, he constructed on the campus of the university, adjoining its medical school, a teaching hospital at a cost of nearly $2,000,000. He was married on Jan. 15, 1878, to Lucy Elizabeth Howard, daughter of the druggist who gave him his first job in Atlanta and later became his business partner. In 1923, after the death of his first wife, he married Mrs. Mary L. Reagin.

[Wm. J. Northen, ed., *Men of Mark in Ga.*, vol. IV (1908); files of the *Atlanta Constitution, Atlanta Jour., Atlanta Georgian and American*; additional information from Bishop W. A. Candler, A. G. Candler's brother.]   T.H.J.

CANFIELD, JAMES HULME (Mar. 18, 1847–Mar. 29, 1909), educator, librarian, born in Delaware, Ohio, was the son of the Rev. Eli Hawley Canfield, of Vermont stock, and of Martha Hulme, a native of New Jersey. His boyhood and youth, except for an interval with relatives in Vermont after his mother's death, were spent in New York and Brooklyn, his father having become rector of Christ Church in the latter city. He attended the Polytechnic Institute in Brooklyn, where he knew Seth Low as a schoolmate, and he had a distinguished career at Williams College where he was graduated in 1868. Though destined by his father for the law, he took employment after graduation with an Iowa company engaged in building a branch of the Chicago, Milwaukee & St. Paul Railroad, and in two years acquired a vigorous and valuable experience of affairs. He then entered a law office in Jackson, Mich., and after admission to the bar in 1872 set up in practise at St. Joseph in that state. In 1873 he married Flavia Camp, who became the mother of Dorothy Canfield Fisher, the novelist.

In addition to his legal practise at St. Joseph, Canfield showed a sturdy interest in civic affairs and especially in educational policies. His work in this connection soon convinced him that he was better fitted for the chair than for the bar, and led to his cordial acceptance of a professorship in the University of Kansas in 1877. His chair was a wide one, extending over the fields of English language and literature, history, political science, and even other subjects; and in the fourteen years of his tenure he greatly enlarged his interests and abilities. He was soon known as a brilliant speaker and a facile writer in the interest of political reform in general and of a free-trade policy in particular. As an apostle of free trade in a protectionist stronghold he encountered several attempts to expel him from his professorship; but his suave though fearless persistence in uttering his views won him such a reputation for tact, courage, and vision, that, after serving as secretary of the National Education Association for three years from 1886, and very ably as its president in the year following, he was chosen in 1891 as chancellor of the University of Nebraska. During four years in this office he aided vigorously in the phenomenal development of the standards and the resources of the institution, and in the spread of education throughout the state. In the face of heavy odds, he had placed the institution on a firm financial and administrative basis and had won the admiration and affection of the great body of his colleagues and students when he was called, in 1895, to the presidency of Ohio State University. His four years' tenure here closed when, at the invitation of Seth Low, he accepted the position of librarian at Columbia University, where he remained until his death. Aside from the library administration, he served the University on numerous occasions as a public representative, particularly in an educational mission to France and England (1907), and was in extraordinary demand as a speaker for a great variety of occasions. He was a staunch churchman and a member of many learned societies. His presence was one of unusual vitality; thick-set and swarthy, with remarkably fine eyes, he was said to bear a striking resemblance to Stephen A. Douglas; but he had also a large fund of sympathy and humor.

His interests were scarcely those of a minute scholar, but rather of an able and amiable administrator and public servant who brought great power of thought and speech to whatever problem claimed his attention. In his well-nigh innumerable reports and addresses to civic, religious, educational, and political audiences he gave form to a mass of material the vast body of which, by his special request, was withheld from the press. Nevertheless his bibliography contains scores of articles on a wide variety of topics in learned and popular periodicals. Among his longer publications are: *Taxation, a Plain Talk for Plain People* (1883), a *History of Kansas* (1884), *Local Government in Kansas* (1889), and *The College Student and his Problems* (1902).

[Calvin Thomas, "Jas. Hulme Canfield," in the *Columbia University Quart.*, June 1909; Nicholas Murray Butler, "In Memoriam," in the *Proc. of the N. E. A.*, 1909; appreciation by Arthur E. Bostwick, *Lib. Jour.*, Apr. 1909.]   E. H. W.

CANFIELD, RICHARD A. (June 17, 1855–Dec. 11, 1914), familiarly known as "Dick" Canfield to the vast sporting public who played for high stakes in his gambling houses, art connoisseur, manufacturer, and Wall Street operator, was born in New Bedford, Mass., where his ashes now lie interred. He was the son of William and Julia (Aiken) Canfield, was of Scotch Presbyterian stock, and was married, on Aug. 31, 1882, to Genevieve Wren Martin of Pawtucket, R. I. His passion for gambling, acquired during the days of his young manhood when he clerked in summer resort hotels, led to the opening of a gambling house in Providence, R. I., which was successful for five or six years before the authorities came down on him. He served a brief sentence in Cranston jail before entering upon his spectacular career in New York in the middle eighties. After success at a house on Twenty-sixth St., he acquired the famous place at 5 East

Forty-fourth St., next door to the then new Delmonico's. This brown stone house, entered by the elect through great bronze doors put in by Canfield, extravagantly furnished, and fitted out with valuable and beautiful ancient potteries and paintings, became the center of New York gambling gentry. In the early nineties Canfield bought the old Saratoga Club which became the Monte Carlo of America. For a while he operated a house in Newport. In 1902 District Attorney William Travers Jerome with a squad of policemen literally smashed their way into the palatial home next to Delmonico's. Canfield contested the case for two years, and it was not until Jerome obtained the passage of special legislation to compel witnesses to testify, that he yielded, prompted by a desire to lessen the difficulties of his patrons, paid the ridiculous fine of $1,000, and closed his house. He devoted his time for the next five years to the Saratoga Club adding a great park that cost in the neighborhood of $25,000 a year to maintain; but public disapproval grew, and in 1907 this place, too, was closed. The business interests of the latter years of Canfield's life were glassware and bottle-manufacturing plants at Brooklyn, N. Y., and Morgantown, W. Va. For years he was active on Wall Street, working alone, and acquiring the reputation of being one of the biggest operators on the Street. He was also an art connoisseur whose collections attracted admiring attention wherever exhibited. A man of culture and refinement, he cultivated well an innate good taste. He had a collection of ancient vases, bas-reliefs, and pottery; of rare Sheraton and Hepplewhite furniture; and his collection of Whistler oils, water-colors, pastels, and drawings, was regarded as one of the largest and best in America. This Whistler collection he sold to the Knoedler Galleries in 1914 for $300,000. His estate at the time of his death was estimated at more than $1,000,000.

[See Alexander Gardiner, "A Tintype of the Flash Age," *Saturday Evening Post,* Nov. 21, Dec. 1, 8, 15, 1928, and Jan. 5, 1929. Canfield's collection of "Rare Sheraton and Hepplewhite" is the subject of an article in *House Beautiful,* June 1916. There are numerous references to him in E. R. and J. Pennell, *The Whistler Journal* (1921), with portrait, painted by Whistler, opposite p. 234. A catalogue of his Whistler collection is to be found in the N. Y. Pub. Lib.]   E.Y.

CANNON, CHARLES JAMES (Nov. 4, 1800–Nov. 9, 1860), author, was born in New York City, the son of an Irishman from whom he inherited facile sentiment, deep melancholy, a religious nature, and a love of melodramatic romance. Presumably his education was scant, since he earned his livelihood as a clerk. A portrait, frontispiece to *The Oath of Office* (1854),

reveals fine features and alert and quietly humorous eyes and mouth. Able to give to creative writing only the leisure hours of a work-a-day life, Cannon was conscious of the incompleteness of his training, and, although writing primarily for his own gratification, was sensitive to adverse critical opinion. His verse, much of which first appeared in minor periodicals of the day, was freely revised before publication in collected form. *Facts, Feelings, and Fancies,* his first book, appeared in 1835, a collection of poems and tales, the latter for the most part melodramatic and harrowing. One of them in a different vein, "Evert van Schaick," he left unfinished as too obviously an imitation of Fitz-Greene Halleck's "Fanny." *The Poet's Quest and Other Poems* followed in 1841. In addition to the title poem, the volume contains forty short poems, most of which were occasioned by the death of friends or acquaintances. Cannon is, in general, occupied with the sad retrospect of memory or the weary burden of life. In barely half a dozen poems do we find either a lighter or a more exalted strain. In 1843 a less somber collection, *The Crowning Hour and other Poems,* dealt chiefly, in the shorter poems, with religious themes. "The Crowning Hour" is a poetic version of Columbus's discovery of land; and "Love," the other long poem of the volume, details a happy poet's quest, as a concession to the critics who had complained of the "Byronic moodiness" of the previous volume. In 1855, *Ravellings from the Web of Life,* over the pseudonym of "Grandfather Greenway," was published, comprising six tales told by the members of a family group. A contemporary critic in *Brownson's Quarterly* found these tales more poetic than Cannon's poetry, saying that they displayed "nice observation, deep feeling, happy descriptive powers and now and then something of the witchery of romance." *The Oath of Office,* a tragedy of unrelieved intensity, was produced at the Bowery Theatre on Mar. 18, 1850, and was published in 1854. In characterization and power of feeling, this tragedy, the scene of which is laid in Ireland in the fifteenth century, is the best of Cannon's work. Its production, however, seems to have brought its author disappointment and bitterness, and he abandoned hope of staging his additional plays, contenting himself with their collection in two publications, *Poems, Dramatic and Miscellaneous* (1851) and *Dramas* (1857). The tragedies possess cumulative horror, rather than true dramatic quality, and have insufficient characterization or local color. Cannon was even less successful in his one comedy, "Better Late than Never" (*Dramas*), than in his tragedies. His verse, though touched with simple faith and feeling, has little originality of thought and imagery; yet it possesses an agreeable ease which enables it to rank with most transitory periodical verse. In addition to the volumes named above, Cannon's work included: *Mora Carmodi; or, Woman's Influence, A Tale* (1844); *Scenes and Characters from the Comedy of Life*, by the author of "Harry Layden" (1847); and, of uncertain date, *Father Felix, a Catholic Story*, and *Tighe Lifford*, a drama. By implication from the title of the 1847 publication, there should likewise be *Harry Layden*. Cannon is believed also to have compiled a *Practical English Spelling Book* (1852) and a series of readers.

[Prefaces and forewords to his various publications are practically the only sources of information regarding Cannon's life and work. See, however, the article reviewing *Ravellings from the Web of Life; Poems, Dramatic and Miscellaneous*; and *Dramas*, in *Brownson's Quarterly*, Oct. 1857.]   A. L. B.

CANNON, GEORGE QUAYLE (Jan. 11, 1827–Apr. 12, 1901), Apostle in the Church of Latter-day Saints, was born in Liverpool, England, the eldest child of George and Ann Quayle Cannon. His ancestors, sea-faring people, for several centuries were residents of the Isle of Man. He was thirteen years old when he and his parents were converted to Mormonism. In 1842 with other members of his family he migrated to Nauvoo, Ill. In 1847 with other Mormons he went to Salt Lake Valley. He had learned and practised the printer's trade while in Nauvoo, and his abilities in this line led to his assignment to editorial work on various periodicals. In 1855 he was sent on a mission to California, where from 1856 for two years he edited and published the *Western Standard*, a weekly. As this was during the period of the "Vigilantes," exciting experiences were common. He was called back to Utah in 1858, when there was apprehension of an attack by the United States army. There was a general migration south from Salt Lake City, and Cannon was appointed by Brigham Young to take the press and printing materials of the *Deseret News* to Fillmore, where for several months he continued the publication of the paper. In 1866 he began the publication of the *Juvenile Instructor*. During the remainder of his life he devoted much of his time and energy to this "Illustrated Monthly Magazine, Designed Expressly for the Education and Elevation of the Young." In 1867 he also took charge of the *Deseret News*, then issued semi-weekly, and immediately changed it into a daily. His connection with this paper continued for several years, and later, in 1877, he was again in charge of it for a time.

Cannon was for three years private secretary to Brigham Young. He had experience in the territorial legislature, as member of the Council, and in other political positions. In 1862, while in England, he was elected senator of the proposed State of Deseret and was called back temporarily to labor in Washington with his colleague, Senator Hooper, for the admission of the state to the Union. Their efforts proved unavailing. In August of 1872, Cannon was elected delegate to Congress. It was said at the time that Brigham Young favored his election because he was an apostle and a polygamist (Cannon's first wife was Elizabeth Hoagland; he had also four others). An attempt was made by a man (Maxwell) who had been an opposing candidate, to prevent Cannon from being sworn in as a delegate (O. F. Whitney, *History of Utah*, 1904, II, 731). Prominent members of Congress of both parties, however, supported Cannon, and he was duly sworn in. He served as a delegate for ten years, being reëlected four successive times. The operation of the Edmunds law in 1882 caused his retirement by a vote of the House 123 to 79. From 1884 onward there were many prosecutions of prominent Mormons. Some of them avoided prosecution for a time by voluntary exile. Cannon was advised by Taylor, the president of the Church, to leave the city. He was, however, arrested and brought back and placed under $45,000 bonds. At the advice again of President Taylor, he failed to appear for trial, and forfeited his bonds. Later, an act of Congress was passed to reimburse him, he having previously settled in full with his sureties (Andrew Jensen, *Latter-day Saint Biographical Encyclopedia*, 1901, I, 50). On Sept. 17, 1888, he appeared in court and surrendered. He was fined and imprisoned about five months. Several years of legal conflict of this nature were ended by a Manifesto issued by the president of the Mormon Church on Sept. 24, 1890, which advised Latter-day Saints to "refrain from contracting any marriage forbidden by the law of the land." At a general conference of the Church in the following month, Cannon was foremost in addressing the congregation in approval of the Manifesto. He was sent to California on a mission for the Church in 1849. Here he worked in the gold mines. In 1850, with several others, he was sent to the Sandwich Islands. His associates had intended to preach to the white inhabitants, but finding the opportunities limited, wished to return. Cannon insisted upon continuing their mission to the natives. He translated Mormon books into the Hawaiian language, and in three and a half years nearly four thousand persons were baptized (M. F. Cowley, *Prophets and Patriarchs*, p. 154). While he was on a church mission in the Eastern states in 1859 he was chosen to fill a vacancy in the Council of Apostles. In 1860 he was sent to England for four years to preside over the European mission, to have charge of emigration, and to edit the *Millennial Star* at Liverpool. He founded a publishing firm; helped to organize the Utah Central Railroad; served as a director of the Union Pacific; and acted as president or director of various corporations. After the death of Brigham Young no man in Utah wielded with all classes so great an influence as Cannon. He was one of the executors of the will of Brigham Young. He was first counselor consecutively to three of the immediate successors of Brigham Young in the presidency of the Mormon Church. In the autumn of 1900 he went to Hawaii as the honored guest at the Jubilee Anniversary of the opening of his mission fifty years before. The queen and her people united in demonstrations of honor and affection (Whitney, IV, 663).

[Sources in addition to the works mentioned above: E. W. Tullidge, *Hist. of Salt Lake City* (1886) and *Life of Brigham Young* (1876); personal information from sons and other relatives and acquaintances of Cannon.]   G. E. F.

CANNON, HARRIET STARR (May 7, 1823–Apr. 5, 1896), one of the founders and the first Mother Superior of the Sisterhood of St. Mary, was born in Charleston, S. C., the daughter of William and Sally (Hinman) Cannon, and a descendant of French Huguenot refugees who came to the colony of New Netherlands about 1632. Both of her parents dying of yellow fever when she was little more than a year old, she and a sister were reared by an aunt in Bridgeport, Conn. Left practically alone in the world by the death of her sister in 1855, she determined to devote herself to a life of religious service, and on Feb. 6, 1856, was received as a candidate for the Sisterhood of the Holy Communion, the first Episcopal Sisterhood in this country, formed under the auspices of Dr. William A. Muhlenberg. On Feb. 2, 1857, she was received into full membership and for the next seven years worked in the parish of the Church of the Holy Communion and in St. Luke's Hospital. Finding that this Sisterhood did not meet her ideal of the religious life, she with several others withdrew. In 1863 they accepted an invitation to take charge of the House of Mercy, a reformatory for fallen women. The following year they added to their duties the charge of the Sheltering Arms, an institution for friendless children, and in 1867 that of St. Barnabas' House for homeless women and children. In the meantime, Feb. 2, 1865, five women, including Sister Harriet, were received by Bishop Horatio Potter in St. Michael's Church

as the first members of a society "for the performance of all spiritual and corporal works of mercy that Christians can perform, and for the quest of a higher life in perfect consecration of body, soul, and spirit to our Lord," the Sisterhood of St. Mary, incorporated in May 1865. Sister Harriet was elected Mother Superior, which office she held until her death. At first the order was persecuted as "Romanist" and the sisters forced out of St. Barnabas' House and the Sheltering Arms, but under Mother Harriet's long and wise direction it grew in favor and its work expanded. It started St. Mary's School, founded St. Mary's Hospital for Children, and assisted in the work of other institutions. Southern branches were established at Memphis and Sewanee, Tenn., and Western branches at Kenosha, Wis., and Chicago, Ill. Extensive property, later known as St. Gabriel's, was purchased at Peekskill-on-the-Hudson in 1872, which became the home of the Mother Superior and the seat of training and educational and philanthropic activity. Here Mother Harriet died on Easter Sunday, 1896.

[Morgan Dix, *Harriet Starr Cannon* (1896); Geo. F. Seymour, "Mother Harriet of the Sisterhood of St. Mary," *Church Eclectic*, June 1896; Henry C. Potter, *Sisterhoods and Deaconesses* (1873).]   H. E. S.

CANNON, JAMES GRAHAM (July 26, 1858–July 5, 1916), banker, was the son of Ann Eliza (White) Cannon and George B. Cannon, a local business man of the small town of Delhi, N. Y. In 1872 his parents moved to New York City, where he graduated from Packard's Business College in 1875. He then obtained a position as a messenger in the Fifth Avenue Bank, soon transferred to the Fourth National Bank, and steadily advanced through the different grades until he became vice-president in 1890, a post which he retained for twenty years. He became president on Aug. 9, 1910, remaining in that position until the Fourth National was amalgamated in 1914 with the Mechanics & Metals National Bank.

Cannon's earliest service to the financial community, outside of the performance of his duty as a faithful and exceptionally efficient administrative officer of his own institution, was rendered in connection with the study of commercial credit. During the decade or two after he became vice-president of the Fourth National Bank credit study and analysis in American banking institutions was at a low ebb. The profession of accountancy then hardly existed in the United States, and it was not until the early nineties that credit departments began to be established even by metropolitan banks. During these formative years of the American credit system, Cannon rendered valuable service through speeches, addresses, and articles designed to enforce the necessity of sound credit analysis as a basis for careful banking.

It was not, however, in connection with credit study and analysis that he became most widely known. In the course of his work as an operating officer he had become impressed with the importance of the clearing-house system. In due time his studies of clearings were elaborated into a volume entitled *Clearing-houses, their History, Methods and Administration* (1908) which passed through various editions and became, for its time, the standard work of reference on clearing-house practise. Cannon was one of the earliest proponents of a plan to make use of the clearing-house associations of the country as institutions for the issuance of an elastic currency on a semi-emergency basis when required by the needs of trade. He advocated this view before the so-called (Pujo) Money Trust Committee of the House of Representatives in 1912–13, and both his testimony and his earlier writings furnished material for use in connection with the framing of the Federal Reserve Act.

In addition to becoming president and one of the chief factors in the National Association of Credit Men and chairman of the committee on finance and currency of the New York State Chamber of Commerce, Cannon also played an important part as a director or trustee in various commercial and financial institutions. He rendered extensive service to educational and charitable institutions and was also prominent in church work (Congregational), besides having an active share in the work of the Young Men's Christian Association. Married during his comparatively early youth to Charlotte B. Bradley, he was survived by her and by a son and two daughters. Of a somewhat stern, rather uncompromising appearance, Cannon well represented outwardly the traditional ideal of the New York banker, but associates found him an unusually kindly and well disposed chief. His career, closely bound up with a single institution, was terminated at the time when the bank was consolidated with the Mechanics & Metals, a combination brought about against Cannon's wishes and presenting a situation in which he refused to participate. His death at the comparatively early age of fifty-eight was by some regarded as having been hastened through disappointment. His writings represent the same qualities of accuracy, system, and attention to detail without great brilliancy or ingenuity, which were characteristic of their author. Both in his early work as a "credit

man," his later career as a leader in the scientific credit movement, and in his activity as an exponent of correct clearing-house practise, these were, however, precisely the traits that were of immediate practical value.

[The major facts in Cannon's life must be gathered from current newspapers and magazines or from the numerous associates with whom he worked in the various institutions and boards of directors of which he was an officer or member. See *N. Y. Times,* July 6, 1916; *Financier,* July 8, 1916; *Commercial and Financial Chronicle,* July 8, 1916; *Financial Age,* July 8, 1916; *Chamber of Commerce of the State of N. Y., Bull.,* Sept. 1916; *Who's Who in America,* 1916–17.]

H. P. W.

CANNON, JOSEPH GURNEY (May 7, 1836–Nov. 12, 1926), congressman, was born at New Garden, Guilford County, N. C. His father, Dr. Horace Franklin Cannon, who was drowned in 1851, was one of the founders of Guilford College, North Carolina; his mother, Gulielma Hollingsworth, traced her descent from George Fox. His grandfather, Samuel Cannon, of Huguenot descent, was a native of Ireland, migrating thence to New England and from there to North Carolina. While Joseph was still a child, the family removed to a new Quaker settlement at what is now Annapolis, Ind., where the boy became a clerk in a country store. He studied law under John P. Usher [*q.v.*], spent six months at the Cincinnati Law School, and in 1858 began practise at Shelbyville, Ill., removing soon after to Tuscola and later to Danville, where he made his home for the rest of his life. In January 1862 he was married to Mary P. Reed of Canfield, Ohio. From 1861 to 1868 he was state's attorney for the 27th judicial district. While holding this office he quietly disposed of a charge of theft that had been lodged, as he believed for political purposes, against Lincoln's stepmother. Defeated as a Republican candidate for Congress in 1870, he was elected to the Forty-third Congress (1873–75), and held his seat until the end of the Fifty-first Congress (1889–91). His uncouth manners and racy speech earned for him at once the popular appellation of "the Hayseed Member from Illinois," a title subsequently replaced by that of "Uncle Joe." At the beginning of his congressional term he was assigned by Speaker James G. Blaine [*q.v.*] to the Committee on Post Offices and Post Roads, and was there made chairman of a subcommittee on the revision of the postal laws. His unprogressive attitude was shown in 1875, when he opposed the resumption of specie payment, and in 1882, when he spoke and voted against an appropriation putting into effect the Civil Service Act. In 1885 he was a member of the Holman Committee which investigated conditions on the Indian reservations. From the Forty-eighth to the Fiftieth Congress, inclusive (1883–89), during the speakership of John G. Carlisle [q.v.], he and Thomas B. Reed [q.v.] were the minority members of the Committee on Rules. At the opening of the Fifty-first Congress (1889–91) he was an unsuccessful candidate for speaker, but Reed, who was elected, made him his "lieutenant in parliamentary procedure" (Busbey, *post,* p. 167), and he took an important part in the discussions which led, on Jan. 29, 1890, to Reed's action in counting a quorum. A coarse speech in the House in August 1890, which won him temporarily the name of "foul-mouthed Joe," contributed to his defeat in the Democratic wave which swept over the country in that year, but he was elected to the Fifty-third Congress (1893–95) and sat in the House until the close of the Sixty-second Congress (Mar. 3, 1913). From the Fifty-fifth to the Fifty-seventh Congress, inclusive (1897–1903), he was chairman of the Committee on Appropriations, as he had been in the Fifty-first Congress. In March 1898, at President McKinley's request, he put through a bill, without consulting his committee, appropriating $50,000,000 for national defense (*Ibid.,* pp. 186–92). An offer of appointment as a member of the peace commission after the war with Spain, however, was declined. At the opening of the Fifty-seventh Congress (1901–03) he was elected speaker, and began the arbitrary and partisan control of procedure which became known as "Cannonism." Signs of revolt appeared by 1907, when members who resented his domination were debarred from desirable committee places. At the opening of the first session of the Sixty-first Congress (March–August 1909), under the leadership of Champ Clark [q.v.], an unsuccessful attempt was made to break his power, but it was not until March 1910, at the second session, that a combination of Democrats and insurgent Republicans carried a resolution enlarging the Committee on Rules, providing for the election of the committee by the House, and excluding the speaker from membership. A motion to declare the speakership vacant, however, failed, and Cannon retained the office until the end of the Congress (Mar. 3, 1911). His overthrow did not greatly affect his personal popularity in the House. He does not seem ever to have regretted his course, and he later insisted that his policy was substantially the same as that of some of the ablest of his predecessors and the one which other speakers would be obliged to follow. For a speech in opposition to an injunction bill, in 1906, he was attacked by

Samuel Gompers [q.v.], and in 1908 was the target of President Roosevelt's sharp criticism of Congress for its refusal to remove certain limitations on the use of appropriations for the secret service. In 1904, while speaker, he was made permanent chairman of the Republican national convention at Chicago, and in the convention of 1908, at the same place, received 58 votes for president on the first ballot, all but eleven of the votes being from Illinois. He was defeated for reëlection to the Sixty-third Congress (1913–15), but regained his seat in the Sixty-fourth Congress (1915–17) when the Democrats and Progressives met with reverses, and continued a member of the House until the close of the Sixty-seventh Congress (Mar. 3, 1923), when he retired. His attitude toward President Wilson was one of distrust, and the League of Nations evoked his ridicule and scorn. The Commemoration by the House of his eightieth birthday (May 6, 1916) seems a remarkable testimonial of personal regard when one recalls his extreme reactionism, the heated attacks upon his conduct as speaker, and his failure to connect his name with any important piece of constructive legislation during his extraordinarily long period of membership in the House.

[The principal authority for Cannon's life, aside from the *Jour. of the House of Representatives* and the *Cong. Record,* is L. W. Busbey, *Uncle Joe Cannon* (1927), a book of rambling, but on the whole good-humored, reminiscence. The author, whose work was prepared for publication after his death by his wife, Katherine G. Busbey, was for twenty years Cannon's secretary. Champ Clark, *My Quarter Century of Am. Politics* (1920), gives a judicious account of the speakership controversy. A pungent view of Cannon as a politician is presented by Wm. Hard, "Uncle Joe Cannon," in *Collier's,* May 23, 30, 1908. J. Hampton Moore, *With Speaker Cannon through the Tropics* (1907), is a popular record of a voyage to the West Indies, Venezuela, and Panama, and of Cannon's observations on American policy. See also obituary in the *N. Y. Times,* Nov. 13, 1926.] W. M.

CANNON, NEWTON (May 22, 1781–Sept. 16, 1841), congressman, governor of Tennessee, was the son of Letitia (Thompson) Cannon and Minos Cannon, a Revolutionary soldier. Born in Guilford County, N. C., he came with his parents about 1790 to the frontier settlement of Cumberland. His education was limited. He learned the saddler's trade; he was a clerk, a merchant, a surveyor; and in time he became a wealthy planter in Williamson County. He was twice married: on Aug. 26, 1813 to Leah Pryor Perkins who died three years later, and on Aug. 27, 1818 to Rachel Starnes Wellborn. He was the father of eleven children. In 1811 and 1812 he was a member of the Tennessee Senate. In 1813 he served briefly in the Creek war as colonel of a regiment of mounted volunteers. Earlier in that year he had been over-whelmingly defeated by Felix Grundy for a seat in the United States Congress. In the following year, however, when Grundy resigned his seat, Cannon was chosen to fill it and this position he retained, except for one term, until 1823. Four years later he was a candidate for governor of Tennessee and announced as the major planks of his platform the development of a general system of public education, the improving of roads, the building of canals, and the promotion of river navigation. The politicians were opposed to him; he did not have the personal appeal of his chief opponent, Sam Houston; and he was defeated. In the state's constitutional convention of 1834, he served as chairman of the committee of the whole and took an active and influential part in its proceedings. In 1835 his opportunity came. A split in the hitherto solid ranks of the Democratic party in Tennessee was threatening; although Cannon had been a friend of the United States Bank and the politicians of the Jackson-Van Buren faction showed him no favors, the supporters of Hugh Lawson White for the presidency (the future Whigs) brought him out as their candidate for governor in opposition to William Carroll who announced his support of Van Buren. In an exciting campaign, in which the question of the presidency received more attention than questions of state policy, Cannon was elected and became the first Whig governor of Tennessee. Two years later he defeated Robert Armstrong for the office, but in 1839 the Democrats, determined to redeem the state for their party, induced James K. Polk to become their candidate. The two men undertook a joint canvass of the state, but Cannon was no match for Polk, whose ability as a stump speaker and powers of ridicule compelled the slower, less magnetic Cannon to refuse to continue to speak from the same platform. Though John Bell came to his support, Cannon was defeated and his public career was ended.

[Family Bible and manuscript sketch by his daughter, Mrs. Rebecca L. C. Bostick, now owned by Mrs. Harry W. Evans of Nashville; Eugene I. McCormac, *Jas. K. Polk* (1922); Jas. Phelan, *Hist. of Tennessee* (1888); letters in the Polk Papers, Lib. of Cong.; local newspapers and state documents; obituaries in *Nashville Whig*, Sept. 17, 1841 and *Niles' Reg.*, Oct. 9, 1841.]

P. M. H.

CANNON, WILLIAM (Mar. 15, 1809–Mar. 1, 1865), governor of Delaware, the son of Josiah and Nancy (Bowlin) Cannon, was born near Bridgeville, Sussex County, Del. He received only an elementary education before he entered the mercantile business in Bridgeville. He acquired considerable wealth for his day, be-ing an extensive landowner and fruit grower in Sussex County, where he married Margaret N. B. Laws. A Democrat by inheritance, he early in life became identified with politics, and was elected a member of the House of Representatives for two successive terms in 1844 and 1846, and state treasurer in 1851. Ten years later he was appointed one of the five members of Delaware's delegation to the Peace Convention, but when civil war seemed inevitable he pronounced himself decidedly in favor of the Union. It was his strongly loyal proclivities that led the Union party to nominate him, notwithstanding his previous affiliations with the Democrats, as their candidate for governor in 1862, and, although a Democratic majority was elected to the legislature, Cannon defeated his opponent in November of that year, and was inaugurated in the following January. Nathaniel B. Smithers was appointed secretary of state, and it is quite probable that the very able messages, proclamations, and other state papers issued over the Governor's name were as much the product of his subordinate as of the Governor himself. Cannon's inaugural address attracted considerable attention throughout the North as he announced that vigorous measures would be undertaken by his administration to support the federal government. His record as governor bore out his promises despite the fact that he experienced difficulties at times with the legislature. Immediately after the organization of that body it took cognizance of the charges made by Cannon's predecessor (Burton) in his last message, that the Union party had won the governorship by intimidating the Democrats with Federal troops sent into the state by the Lincoln administration for the purpose of assuring the election of a Lincoln candidate. A joint committee controlled by the Democrats held an investigation, and in a long report singled out William Cannon, Nathaniel B. Smithers, and George P. Fisher as mainly responsible for the presence of the troops at the polls. When later the legislature passed an act to prevent "illegal arrests" in the state by Federal authorities, Cannon sent a special message on Mar. 3, 1863, informing that body that it was with regret that he felt "compelled to decline co-operation with a co-ordinate branch of the Government." This message was followed on Mar. 11 by a proclamation in which the Governor stated among other things that the provisions of the above-mentioned law were "calculated to lessen the estimation in which her [Delaware's] people were held, as faithful to the government of the United States." Cannon held office just two years and two months, death overtaking him as the Civil War was nearing its close.

[J. T. Scharf, *Hist. of Del.* (1888), I, 348 ff.; Henry C. Conrad, *Hist. of the State of Del.* (1908), I, 207 ff., III, 843 ff.; Records of Executive Acts for years 1863 ff., in Governor's Office, Dover; *Jour. of the Senate of the State of Del.*, 1863–65; *Jour. of the House of Representatives of the State of Del.*, 1863–65; *Report of the Committee of the General Assembly of the State of Del. Together with the Jour. of the Committee and the Testimony Taken Before them in Regard to the Interference by the U. S. Troops with the General Election, etc., Nov. 4, 1862* (Dover, 1863).]   G. H. R.

CANONCHET (d. April 1676), Narragansett chief, known also as Nanuntenoo, was the son of Miantanomo [*q.v.*], and "was chief sachem of all the Narragansetts" (Hubbard, *post*, p. 67). During the early months of King Philip's War, the settlers prevailed upon the Narragansetts to remain loyal, and, by a treaty signed July 15, 1675, Canonchet and the other sachems agreed to deliver to the English such of the hostile Indians as should fall into their hands, and to take an active part in the conflict. Since the advantage of the war first rested largely with King Philip, the Narragansetts were reluctant to join the English, although the treaty was renewed at Boston, Oct. 18, 1675, at which time Canonchet was presented with a "silver-lac'd coat." Violation of the covenant, by the sheltering of the women and children of the Wampanoags, caused the New England Confederation to send a powerful expedition against the Narragansett fort near South Kingston, R. I. Here the "Great Swamp Fight" of Dec. 19, 1675 resulted in the destruction of nearly one thousand Narragansetts with their camp and winter food-supply. The survivors, probably led by Canonchet, on Mar. 26, 1676 lured Capt. Michael Pierce into an ambush at the Patuxet River (near Providence, R. I.) and killed him and about forty of his men. Canonchet realized that the English policy of destroying the Indians' corn was likely to starve his people, and, "foreseeing so many hundreds could not well subsist without planting," decided to raise corn in the abandoned English fields on the Connecticut River. Venturing to Seaconk (near Bristol, R. I.) with a few warriors early in April to obtain seed, he unexpectedly encountered Capt. George Denison of Stonington with over one hundred soldiers and Indian allies. Canonchet tried to escape across a stream, but, slipping on a stone, fell and wet his gun, rendering it useless. Although a man "of goodly stature, and great courage of mind, as well as strength of body," he surrendered without resistance to Robert Stanton, to whom he is reported to have said, "You much child, no understand matters of war; let your brother or your chief come, him I will an-swer." Offered his life on the condition that he make peace, the sachem proudly refused, and, when blamed for his part in the conflict, replied that "others were as forward for the war as himself, and that he desired to hear no more thereof." When informed that he was to be executed, he said that "he liked it well, that he should die before his heart was soft, or had spoken anything unworthy of himself." Capt. Denison then took Canonchet to Stonington, where he was shot and beheaded by the Pequots and Mohicans, who sent the head to the Council at Hartford "as a token of their love and fidelity." Canonchet's death was a severe blow to King Philip, since it deprived him of his ablest ally at the time of his greatest need, and, by leaving the Narragansetts without good leadership, shortened the course of the war.

[The contemporary source for Canonchet's life is Wm. Hubbard, *A Narrative of the Troubles with the Indians in New Eng.* (1677), republished, ed. by S. G. Drake, as *Hist. of the Indian Wars in New Eng.* (1865). S. G. Drake, *Book of the Indians* (1841) contains a biography.]   H. P. S.

CANONGE, LOUIS PLACIDE (June 29, 1822–Jan. 22, 1893), journalist, dramatist, was a representative Louisiana Creole, born in New Orleans of French ancestry. His father was J. F. Canonge of Santo Domingo, who had married a widow, Amelie (Mercier) Amelung of New Orleans. Intense rivalry then existed between the French and American elements of the population of Louisiana, and the parents of Canonge in order to assure to their son a position of leadership in the struggle sent him to study in France where both his parents had been educated. He attended the Collège Louis-le-Grand in Paris while the Romantic movement headed by Hugo was at its height. The exuberance of the period produced a lasting impression on the young Louisianian who returned home in 1838, his heart aglow with liberalism. The field of journalism offered the best means for the expression of his overflowing ideas. He began as a contributor to *L'Abeille*, and throughout his life he wrote for that noted French daily as well as for the numerous French journals and reviews that flourished for short intervals in Louisiana. He also took a keen interest in church publications, being editor-in-chief of *Le Propagateur Catholique*. For *La Presse*, the noted Parisian daily, he contributed a series of essays under the title of *Institutions américaines*. Politics, law, literature, and art occupied his attention in equal measure as a newspaper writer, but he showed a marked preference for theatrical criticism, being editor of *La Lorgnette*. His interest in the theatre was not limited to literary studies: tradition credits him with capacity as an an actor; and he wrote many plays: *Le maudit passeport* (1840), a vaudeville; *Gaston de St-Elme* (1840), a tragedy; *L'Ambassadeur d'Autriche* (1850); *Un grand d'Espagne*; *Le Comte de Monte-Cristo*; *Histoire sous Charles-Quint*; *France et Espagne; ou la Louisiane en 1768 et 1769* (1850); *Le Comte de Carmagnola* (1856); *Qui perd gagne,* a one-act comedy (1849) dedicated to the author of *Les Nuits*. The majority of these plays were acted in New Orleans; the last three were also published in New Orleans; and *Le Comte de Carmagnola* enjoyed a Parisian production. Canonge was also interested in the musical play, for he is reputed to have written three librettos, only one of which, *Louise de Lorraine,* is known specifically; he composed songs intensely patriotic, one of which, "La Louisiane," is preserved in the Howard Memorial Library. Canonge also served as manager of theatrical troupes, selecting one in Paris for the old Orleans Theatre immediately before the Civil War and after that struggle managing the French Opera for two seasons. In these ventures he enjoyed social and artistic, if not financial, success. Canonge took an active part in civic life. He practised law for several years. An ardent devotee of the Lost Cause he translated into French *Nojoque* (1867) written by H. R. Helper, preserving all the bitterness of the attack against the North but omitting all unpleasant allusions to his Church. He served his people as their representative at the state capital, as superintendent of education, and as professor of French at the State University. The French government decorated him twice for his labors in the field of French letters. He married Hélène Halphern who died in 1889.

Canonge's chief claim to fame resides in his journalistic work of the *feuilletoniste* type. He excelled in short articles written on the spur of the moment on all the varied topics that interested a French-speaking community fond of French literature, culture, and art. As a dramatist his work belongs solely to the French Romantic School which he imitated closely; lovers of *Les trois mousquetaires* of Dumas would find delight in his *Comte de Carmagnola,* a drama of intrigue in five acts and ten tableaux. A typical Creole he reflected the life of his times in New Orleans; a tireless energy and ready versatility characterized him as a man and as a writer.

[Three local articles of a biographical nature are extant: one in the *Daily Picayune,* Mar. 2, 1890; another, by C. P. Dimitry, in the *Times-Democrat,* Jan. 22, 1893; a recent one, by G. Wm. Nott, in the *Times-Picayune,* Feb. 6, 1927. John Kendall gives the dates of Canonge's theatrical ventures in his *Hist. of New Orleans* (1922). Alcée Fortier has contributed two short sketches as well as the plots of Canonge's most important plays in *Louisiana Studies* (1894) and in the *Lib. of Southern Lit.,* vol. II (1909). Grace King has preserved the story of the Canonge family in her *Creole Families of New Orleans* (1921). A pen picture of Canonge is to be found in *The Living Writers of the South* (1869) by J. W. Davidson.]   L. C. D.

CANONICUS (*c.* 1565–1647), Narragansett chief, ruled his powerful tribe in conjunction with his nephew Miantanomo [*q.v.*]. He was about fifty-five when the Pilgrims landed at Plymouth and he sent his well-known war challenge to them. In spite of this inauspicious beginning, he became and remained a friend to the whites. In 1633 a John Oldham was murdered by Pequots and two boys kidnapped. Canonicus and Miantanomo were found innocent, although other Narragansett sachems were implicated. The Massachusetts government then sent a punitive expedition against the Pequots, under Endicott, who behaved with great cruelty. The Pequots tried to induce Canonicus to join them in a war against the English, and Massachusetts to secure peace had to employ the good offices of the banished Roger Williams, who had obtained the grant of Rhode Island from Canonicus and always had great influence with him. In 1635 Williams was able to settle the bloody war which had been raging between the Narragansetts and the Wampanoags. The next year, Miantanomo and two sons of Canonicus went to Boston and made a new peace treaty with Massachusetts. In 1638 the tri-partite agreement between Connecticut, the Pequots, and the Narragansetts was signed, stipulating that the tribes would not war on each other without the consent of the whites.

The friendship of Canonicus was to be sorely tried. As a result of a quarrel started by the Mohegan sachem Uncas, Miantanomo received permission from the English to revenge himself, was taken prisoner by his enemy through treachery, and, when he gave himself up to the English for protection, was turned over by them to Uncas to be killed. This dastardly treatment of his nephew was naturally greatly resented by Canonicus, who treated the emissaries sent by Massachusetts, to prevent a war between the tribes, with scant courtesy. Shortly before, Canonicus and others had ceded their lands, at the instigation of some of the "Gortonites," to "the protection, care and government" of the king, and Canonicus told the Massachusetts government that the Indians were their fellow subjects and that if there were any dispute between them, it should be settled by King Charles. In spite of provocative treatment, Canonicus could well say, as he did to Williams, that he had never suffered any wrong to be done to the English and never would. Throughout his twenty-five years of relations with the whites, his record is much better than theirs, excepting that of Williams. His eldest son, Mriksah or Meika, succeeded him as sachem.

[There is a short account of Canonicus in F. W. Hodge, *Handbook of Am. Indians* (1910), and a longer one in S. G. Drake, *Book of the Indians* (1845), pp. 53–57. Otherwise his life must be patched together from scattered references in the contemporary colonial records, and the contemporary historical accounts of the colonies.]   J. T. A.

CAPEN, ELMER HEWITT (Apr. 5, 1838– Mar. 22, 1905), college president, was born in Stoughton, Norfolk County, Mass. He was educated at Pierce Academy, at the Green Mountain Institute in Woodstock, Vt., and at Tufts College, a Universalist institution, where he took his B.A. degree in 1860. While still an undergraduate he was elected to the Massachusetts legislature as a representative from his native town. He studied law, was admitted to the bar in 1864, and practised for a short time at Stoughton. Desiring, however, to enter the ministry, he studied for that purpose with the Rev. A. St. John Chambré. He preached in 1864 and was ordained the next year. His first church, where he remained until 1869, was the Independent Christian Church in Gloucester, Mass. After a year's pastorate in St. Paul, Minn., which followed the Gloucester period, he went to Providence, R. I., to the First Universalist Church, where he remained until he was asked to accept the presidency of Tufts College in 1875. He had married Letitia H. Mussey of New London, Conn. After her death he married in 1877 Mary L. Edwards, of Brookline, Mass. As president of Tufts he showed administrative ability, a capacity for work, and an ability to meet all types of conditions. He was at the head of the department of political science in which he gave four courses, and he preached regularly in the college chapel. He was also called upon frequently to speak at social, religious, educational, and political meetings. He was one of the men responsible for establishing Dean Academy, and was the first secretary of the trustees. From 1875 on he was also a trustee of the Universalist General Convention. Other important positions which he held were as chairman of the state board of education, chairman of the board of visitors of the Salem Normal School, and president of the New England Commission on Admission Examinations. He showed his interest in extra-academic matters in holding the presidency of the Citizens' Law and Order League during its entire existence and in serving in 1888 as delegate to the Republican national convention. He was a man of progressive

ideas and throughout his presidency was thoroughly in sympathy with student interests and activities. For the Universalist section of the Columbian Congress he contributed an article on the Atonement. He was the author of *Occasional Addresses* (1902), the liturgical portions of *The Gloria Patri Revised* (1903), and of *The College and the Higher Life* (1905).

[*Tufts Coll. Reg. of Officers of Instruction and Govt. and Dir. of Grads.* (1912); A. B. Start and others, *Hist. of Tufts Coll.* (1896).]   M. A. K.

CAPEN, NAHUM (Apr. 1, 1804–Jan. 8, 1886), miscellaneous writer and postmaster of Boston, the son of Andrew Capen (1757–1846) by his wife, Hannah Richards, was born at Canton, Mass. He was descended from Bernard Capen (1562–1638) who came to this country in 1630 from Dorset, England. Nahum received the ordinary Latin school education of the day and at an early age showed evidence of precocity. He read widely in the classical authors, especially Plutarch, and at nineteen he rewrote *Plutarch's Lives* for popular consumption (not published). He was also attracted to the study of the sciences, and when eighteen became enamoured of Benjamin Franklin and set out to read everything that he had written. At this time he began to study medicine under his older brother Robert, but ill health caused him to abandon this calling. In 1825 he entered the publishing house of March, Capen & Long as partner and there found ample opportunity for indulgence of his literary tastes. Soon afterward he became an aggressive protagonist of the copyright laws, making appeals to Congress and writing letters on the subject to Daniel Webster and to Henry Clay. He wrote papers on Free Trade as early as 1823, and in 1827 he published anonymously on the same subject several articles which were republished in the South. On Oct. 14, 1830 he was married to Elizabeth Ann, daughter of William and Sarah (Rand) More. During the visit of Spurzheim to the United States in 1832 Capen became the confidant and adviser of the distinguished visitor, later writing his life, and publishing his works (1833). After the death of Spurzheim, Capen organized the Boston Phrenological Society and became its secretary. The history of the early deliberations of this group was later described by Capen in a separate volume, *Reminiscences of Dr. Spurzheim and George Combe* (1881). In 1835–36 Capen spent a year abroad, where he visited hospitals, schools, asylums, and institutions for blind, deaf, dumb, and delinquent. On returning to America he did much to further the cause of popular education and was largely instrumental in securing the establishment of the State Board of Education of Massachusetts. In June 1857 he was appointed by President Buchanan postmaster of Boston, a position which he held until 1861. He is said to have been the first postmaster in the country to introduce street letter-boxes and to work out a free delivery system (*Boston Transcript*, Jan. 9, 1886). His first book, *The Republic of the United States of America, its Duties to Itself ... Embracing also a Review of the Late War between the United States and Mexico,* published anonymously in 1848, was dedicated to President James Buchanan. It is a semi-historical, semi-political work in praise of Buchanan's political activities. *The History of Democracy in the United States* was published in four parts in 1851–52, but was later withdrawn from sale, as the author contemplated a larger work, *The History of Democracy: or Political Progress, Historically Illustrated, from the Earliest to the Latest Periods,* only one volume of which was ever published (1874). This was a creditable and scholarly work of 677 pages, though marred by numerous dogmatic statements which reflect the limitations of the writer's early education.

[Edmund Burke, "Nahum Capen," *U. S. Democratic Rev.,* May 1858, pp. 397–412, portr.; *Genealogical and Personal Memoirs relating to the Families of the State of Mass.,* ed. by W. R. Cutter (1910), IV, 2157–58; J. F. Fulton, "Early Phrenological Societies and their Journals," *Boston Medic. and Surgic. Jour.,* 1927, CXCVI, 398 ff.; obituary in *Boston Transcript,* Jan. 9, 1886.]
J.F.F.

CAPEN, SAMUEL BILLINGS (Dec. 12, 1842–Jan. 29, 1914), merchant, active in church and civic affairs, the second son of Samuel Childs Capen and his wife, Anne Billings, was born in Boston, the family home since the landing of Bernard and Jane Capen, May 30, 1630. His academic training ended with his graduation from the Boston English High School in 1858. Shortly after this he went into the carpet business of Wentworth & Bright, later Torrey, Bright & Capen. Here, a partner from 1864, he remained in active business until 1909. He was married, on Dec. 8, 1869, to Helen M. Warren.

Early interested in Sunday-school work, first in the Old Colony Mission School, then in the Central Congregational Church of Jamaica Plain, to which place he had moved shortly after his marriage, he, in 1882, became president of the Congregational Sunday-school and Publishing Society, at a time when its future seemed most problematic. To this office he brought the rare combination of unselfish devotion and great business sagacity which distinguished him throughout life. Between 1882 and his resignation in

1899, under the guidance of a board of directors reorganized to include business men as well as churchmen, the capital of the society increased from $35,127 to $125,490, most of this increase coming from the profits of its own operations. In 1899 Capen became the president of the American Board of Commissioners for Foreign Missions, a position which he administered with the same competence and high endeavor which he had brought to the earlier work. To stabilize the finances of the board and to interest the business man in what he considered the all-important duty of the Christian Church, were the tasks he set himself. His eagerness to accomplish the latter purpose brought forth from him the commercial argument for missions, that "trade follows the missionary," an argument the use of which called down upon him sharp criticism.

A new field of activity was opened to him when, at a stormy time in the history of the Boston public schools, he was elected to the Boston School Committee, on which he served from 1888 to 1893, the last year as president of the committee. During his term, more businesslike methods of administration were introduced, a building programme, long delayed, was inaugurated, the curriculum was overhauled, a "parental school" for incorrigibles was established, and manual training was given a secure place in the school system. In 1900 higher education enlisted his services. He became a member of the board of trustees of Wellesley College, of which body he was a judicious and enthusiastic president from 1905 till his death.

Among Capen's other active interests may be mentioned his work for the Municipal League, local and national, for the Indian Association, for temperance reform, and for world peace. In politics he was a conservative. His address to the Boston Ministers' Meeting in 1896 did service as a campaign document (Hawkins, *post,* p. 102; *The National Crisis of 1896,* Boston, Business Men's Sound Money League). His published work, aside from fugitive contributions to religious papers, consists of various addresses, the best known of which is probably *Foreign Missions and World Peace* (Boston, 1912, World Peace Foundation, Pamphlet series, No. 7, pt. 3). In September 1913, he sailed for the Orient, as president of the American Board and representative of the World Peace Foundation. After some active weeks in India and Ceylon, he died of pneumonia in Shanghai.

[The most substantial source is Chauncy J. Hawkins, *Samuel Billings Capen: His Life and Work* (1914). Excellent sketches were published in the *Boston Transcript,* Jan. 30, 1914, the *Missionary Herald,* March 1914, and the *Congregationalist,* Feb. 5, 1914.] E.D.

CAPERS, ELLISON (Oct. 14, 1837–Apr. 22, 1908), Confederate soldier, Episcopal bishop, was born in Charleston, S. C. His mother was Susan (McGill) Capers, adopted daughter of the widow of Gen. Peter Horry. His father was William Capers [q.v.]. With the exception of two years in Oxford, Ga., Ellison spent his childhood and youth in Charleston where he attended the two private schools and the high school. He received additional training in the Conference School, Cokesbury, and in Anderson Academy. In 1854 he entered the South Carolina Military Academy and after his graduation early in 1857 remained for that year as instructor in mathematics. During 1858 he served as principal of the preparatory department at Mt. Zion College, Winnsboro, but returned to his old school in January 1859 as assistant professor of mathematics. The next month he married Charlotte Palmer of Cherry Grove Plantation.

At the outbreak of the Civil War Capers was elected major of a volunteer regiment which took part in the bombardment of Fort Sumter. This organization gave way to a permanent unit, the 24th South Carolina Infantry, of which Capers was lieutenant-colonel. After two years of fighting in the Carolinas, the most sanguinary at the battles on James Island, the regiment was ordered to go with Johnston, in May 1863, to the relief of Vicksburg. From this time until the surrender at Bentonville, Capers was in the midst of hard campaigning and much terrific fighting. He was wounded at Jackson, Miss., in May 1863, at Chickamauga in September of the same year, and at Franklin in November 1864. He was made general, succeeding Gist in command of the brigade.

A few weeks after his return to Anderson in May 1865, Capers was chosen secretary of state for South Carolina under Gov. Orr. Moved partly by the deepening experiences of war-time, he now entered the ministry, electing not the Methodist church of his father but the Episcopal church of more remote ancestors. His first charge, which he took in 1866, was Christ Church, Greenville. The following year he resigned his political position. In 1875 he went to Selma, Ala., but returned the following year to the same Greenville parish. In 1886 he was elected bishop of the Easton, Md., diocese but declined. In 1887 he was called to Trinity Church, Columbia; on July 20, 1893, he was consecrated assistant bishop of South Carolina; and in 1904 he was elected chancellor of the University of the South at Sewanee, Tenn. His death, which followed a stroke of paralysis, occurred at his home in Columbia. Devoted as a churchman in his activities and interests, Bishop Capers went beyond narrowly interpreted ecclesiastical duty. He was chaplain-general of the Confederate Veterans; he was an energetic member of the Southern Historical Association; he contributed to periodicals many reminiscent sketches and book reviews; and he edited Volume V, the South Carolina volume, of *Confederate Military History* (1899). He championed higher education as a function of both church and state and he protested in many official charges against the growth of lawlessness and crime. Most pleasant of his achievements, perhaps, was his contribution, made by personal contacts and by frequent addresses, to the return of good feeling between the once-divided sections of the Union.

[Records of the Capers family are in *S. C. Hist. and Geneal. Mag.*, Oct. 1901. A brief biographical sketch is in the volume of *Confed. Mil. Hist.* referred to above. Walter B. Capers, *"The Soldier-Bishop"* (1912), is the standard biography.]   F. P. G.

CAPERS, WILLIAM (Jan. 26, 1790–Jan. 29, 1855), Methodist bishop, was born on his father's plantation at Bull-Head Swamp in St. Thomas' Parish, about twenty miles from Charleston, S. C., the son of William and Mary (Singeltary) Capers. One of the molding forces in his life was his father, a strong character, a captain under Gen. Marion in the Revolution, and, for the most part, a convinced Methodist. The family was of Huguenot ancestry. In 1805 Capers entered the sophomore class of South Carolina College, injured his health by protracted study in an effort to make up for his desultory preparation, and on Dr. Maxcy's advice withdrew and entered the college again in 1807. But his mind was agitated by thoughts of religion; and, troubled in spirit, he left the college in 1808, intending to study law. During the summer he underwent a series of religious experiences, and before the end of November, somewhat to his own surprise and misgiving, he found himself a licensed Methodist preacher accompanying the Rev. William Gassaway on his circuit. In December 1810 he was admitted into full connection with the South Carolina Conference and was ordained deacon; two years later he was ordained elder. He married Anna White of Georgetown District, Jan. 13, 1813. She died in childbirth Dec. 30, 1815, and on Oct. 31, 1816, he married Susan McGill of Kershaw District. Besides serving various circuits Capers was at one time or another located at Wilmington, N. C.; Georgetown, Charleston, and Columbia, S. C.; Milledgeville, Oxford, and Savannah, Ga. Several of these charges he filled more than once. He became the most popular preacher of his denomination in the South and was a power in the General Conferences of the Church. He was superintendent of the missions to the Creek Indians along the Chattahoochee in Georgia and Alabama 1821–25, visited England in 1828 as an official representative of the American Methodist Church to that of Great Britain, and began in 1829 the work of which he was proudest,—his missions among the plantation negroes of the South Carolina littoral. For this work, difficult and perhaps even dangerous, he was peculiarly fitted by his sympathy and understanding, and he managed it with success. He was secretary of the Southern Missionary Department of the Church 1840–44. In the slavery controversy that finally split the Methodist Church into two general bodies in 1844, he was a dignified, good-tempered exponent of the Southern point of view. On May 14, 1846, he was consecrated a bishop of the Methodist Church South. In all he made eight episcopal visitations, his territory extending from Virginia to Texas across half a continent. He died of heart disease near Anderson Court House, S. C., while returning from a visit to Florida. With ample opportunity to make money, he died a poor man. No scholar and of no conspicuous ability as an administrator, he was nevertheless one of the leaders of the second generation of Southern Methodism by sheer strength and goodness of character.

[W. M. Wightman, *Life of Wm. Capers, Including an Autobiography* (1858); W. B. Sprague, ed., *Annals of the Am. Pulpit*, vol. VII (1861), inaccurate in some details; J. M. Buckley, *A Hist. of Methodists in the U. S.* (1896); J. D. Wade, *Augustus Baldwin Longstreet* (1924), valuable for social background.]

G. H. G.

CAPRON, HORACE (Aug. 31, 1804–Feb. 22, 1885), agriculturist, was born in Attleboro, Mass. He was fifth in descent from Banfield Capron, who came to Massachusetts from England about 1674. His father, Dr. Seth Capron, served with distinction during the Revolutionary War. His mother, Eunice (Mann) Capron, was a daughter of Dr. Bezaleel Mann of Attleboro. In 1806 his family moved to Whitesboro, Oneida County, and in 1823 to Walden, Orange County, N. Y. He received an academic education intended as preparatory for West Point. Failing to receive an appointment, he drifted into cotton manufacturing in which his father and older brother were extensively engaged. In 1829 he was called to Warren, Baltimore County, Md., as superintendent of the cotton factory of James Buchanan & Company. In 1834 the governor of Maryland commissioned him colonel of the 32nd Regiment of Maryland militia, for his services in ending the labor riots which took place in the neighborhood during the construction of the Baltimore & Ohio railroad. He married, June 5, 1834, Louisa

V. Snowden, daughter of Nicholas Snowden of Laurel. In 1836 he erected and became superintendent of a cotton factory in Laurel which later employed several hundred operatives and which under his management acquired a reputation as a model factory (*American Farmer,* 1845, pp. 36–37). Through his marriage he came into possession of a large tract of the Snowden estate and began farming on an extensive scale, applying scientific principles to his operations. He became widely known as a progressive farmer and took an active part in national, state, and local agricultural societies. In 1849 his wife died. This loss was followed by business reverses. Desiring to leave Laurel, he requested and received from President Fillmore, in the spring of 1852, an appointment as special agent over certain tribes of Indians in Texas, which appointment he held through 1853. In 1854 he married Margaret Baker of New York and moved to Illinois where he continued farming on an extensive scale, especially as a breeder of Devon cattle. In 1863 he was commissioned lieutenant-colonel of the 14th Illinois Cavalry, serving with distinction during the remainder of the war. He was commissioned brevet brigadier-general of volunteers in 1865 and brigadier-general in 1866. After the war he returned to his farm in Illinois. On Nov. 29, 1867, he was appointed United States commissioner of agriculture, to succeed Isaac Newton, deceased. He took charge, on Dec. 4, 1867, as second commissioner and served with ability and credit. He resigned on June 27, 1871, to accept an appointment by the Japanese Government as commissioner and chief adviser to the Kaitakushi Department in the development and settlement of the island of Yesso, now Hokkaido. By his introduction of American methods, implements, live stock, and produce he revolutionized the farming of that country.

In 1875 he returned to the United States and until his death resided in Washington. He was a public-spirited man of outstanding character, high ideals, great personal courage, and of courtly, distinguished bearing. His most important writings were *Reports and Official Letters to the Kaitakushi* (Tokyo, 1875); articles in various publications of the United States Department of Agriculture, including his annual reports as commissioner for 1868–71; and a series of articles entitled "On the Renovation of Worn-Out Soils" in the *American Farmer,* 1847.

[The principal sources of biographical information are Capron's unpublished memoirs in three volumes, in possession of his grandson, Horace M. Capron, Evanston, Ill. (Copies of two of the volumes, made by permission, are also in the U. S. Dept. of Ag. Lib.). See also F. A. Holden, *Genealogy of the Descendants of Banfield Capron* (1859); Merritt Starr, "Gen. Horace Capron" in *Ill. State Hist. Soc. Jour.*, XVIII, 259–349; Louisa Kirwin Capron Thiers, "An American Adviser to the Japanese Government," in *Jour. of Am. Hist.*, VII, 1415–25; C. H. Greathouse, *Hist. Sketch of the U. S. Dept. of Ag.* (1898), pp. 12–13; *Am. Influence upon the Ag. of Hokkaido, Japan* (1915, Tohoku Imperial Univ., Sapporo, Japan).] C. R. B.

CAPTAIN JACK (1837?–Oct. 3, 1873), a subchief of the Modocs, was the leader of the hostiles in the Modoc War of 1872–73. His Indian name was Kintpuash or Kientpoos, "having the water brash"; the "captain" in the name given him by the whites was due to his fondness for brass buttons and other military ornaments. He had some hereditary claims on the chieftainship, held by Sconchin, and for a number of years was regarded by a considerable following as their real chief. An attempt to compel him and his followers to return to the Klamath reservation, from which they had escaped, resulted in a fight, Nov. 29, 1872, in which both sides suffered severe losses. The Indians, in two bands, fled to the lava beds, an almost impregnable natural fortress south of Tule Lake, in California, one of the bands killing eighteen settlers on the way. Other Indians joined them, until Jack had a force of about eighty warriors. On Jan. 17, 1873, a command of about 400 men attempted to storm the Modoc stronghold, but after an all-day battle in which probably no Indian was hit, was compelled to withdraw, with a loss of nine killed and thirty wounded. Gen. E. R. S. Canby [*q.v.*], commander of the military district, in an effort to prevent further hostilities, opened negotiations with Jack, but in a conference on Apr. 11 the commissioners were treacherously attacked, and Canby and the Rev. Eleazer Thomas were killed and A. B. Meacham was desperately wounded. Col. Jefferson C. Davis assumed command, more than a thousand soldiers, volunteers and Indian scouts were assembled, and a vigorous campaign was begun. Gradually the Indians were driven from the lava beds. Dissensions arose, the force broke up into small bands, and on May 22 sixty-five of the hostiles surrendered, several of them joining the troops in pursuit of the Indians still at large. On June 1 Jack and two other warriors, with their women and children, were captured, and the war ended. Six Indians implicated in the murder of the commissioners were tried by court martial (July 5–9), for violation of the rules of war. Three Modocs largely responsible for the trouble testified for the government and received immunity. The six defendants were found guilty and sentenced to be hanged. President Grant commuted to life imprisonment the sentences of two of them (one of whom was subsequently released), but Jack, Sconchin John (a younger brother of Chief Sconchin), Black Jim, and Bos-

ton Charley were hanged at Fort Klamath Oct. 3. Jack was not distinguished in appearance, according to Bancroft; he was below medium stature, weighing about 145 pounds, with small hands and feet, thin arms, a round face, a low, square forehead, and black, sharp, watchful eyes. He was not above profiting, according to the same authority, by the prostitution of the women of his band, and at the trial he showed a disposition to be shifty and untruthful. Others have portrayed him in a better light, and a few have lauded him for his personal, no less than his military, qualities.

[Jas. Mooney, "Kintpuash," *Handbook of Am. Indians* (1907); A. S. Gatschet, "The Klamath Indians," *Contributions to North Am. Ethnology*, vol. II, pt. I (1890); H. H. Bancroft, *Hist. of Ore.*, vol. II (1888); J. P. Dunn, Jr., *Massacres of the Mountains* (1886); *Report Bd. of Indian Commissioners for 1873* (1874); Cyrus Townsend Brady, *Northwestern Fights and Fighters* (1907); Jeff C. Riddle, *The Indian Hist. of the Modoc War* (1914).] W. J. G.

CARBUTT, JOHN (Dec. 2, 1832–July 26, 1905), pioneer in photographic methods, was born in Sheffield, England, and emigrated to the United States in 1853, when he immediately became interested in photography. After a fruitful experience as official photographer of the Canadian Pacific Railway during the building of the road, he established himself in Chicago, and began experiments with gelatine as applied to the production of the photographic plate. "His contributions to this art industry began as early as 1868, when he successfully used gelatine in place of collodio-albumen in the preparation of dry plates in his photographic practise" (*Journal of the Franklin Institute*, CLX, 461). Dry plates were known and used before Carbutt made them, but the Taupenot plate,—a collodio-albumen process, which was invented in 1856—had a tendency to blister, and needed to receive its final preparation and development within a week or ten days. Carbutt, by the use of gelatine, abolished many of these defects and made a practical dry plate that need not be developed for months after it was made. Becoming interested in the gelatine intaglio printing process, known then as the Woodburytype method, Carbutt went to Philadelphia in 1871, where he established himself, working the process which he had radically modified to meet the exigencies arising from the American climatic conditions. The advent of the less complicated photo-collotype process, having immeasurably greater commercial possibilities than the other method, Carbutt abandoned this enterprise, and, in 1879, turned his attention to the manufacture of gelatine dry plates, thus placing on the market the first American product of the kind. At the same time he succeeded in standardizing the size of the photographic lantern-slide, which still remains 3¼ by 4 inches, or what was known as the quarter-plate size. His success with dry plates soon brought a train of manufacturers in his wake, but his preeminence in the production of lantern-slide plates never was menaced. Always investigating and experimenting in the photographic field, Carbutt made notable contributions to the development of chromo-photographic processes, having introduced the ortho-chromatic plate which for the first time permitted of photography with the correct color values. Through devising accurate color filters, he appreciably speeded the development of all color photography, including that of the processes of color engraving and printing. He was the first president of the Photographic Association of America. He died in Philadelphia.

[See Louis E. Levy and Samuel Sartain, a paper on Carbutt in the *Jour. of the Franklin Institute*, Dec. 1905; John Nicol, "The Late John Carbutt," *American Amateur Photographer*, Sept. 1905; *Wilson's Photographic Mag.*, Oct. 1905; *The Photographic Times*, Sept. 1905; Phila. *Public Ledger*, July 28, 1905.]   J. J.

CÁRDENAS, GARCÍA LÓPÉZ de (fl. 1540), was the discoverer of the Grand Canyon of the Colorado. The Cárdenas family, of high nobility, proceeded from the royal house of Vizcaya. The main branch of the family were lords of the Villa de Cárdenas, dukes of Maqueda, and marquises of Elche. García Lópéz de Cárdenas was an early settler in Mexico and played a prominent part in the Coronado expedition to New Mexico (1540–42). When the army left Compostela he was one of its six captains. As a reward for bravery he succeeded to Samaniego's position as *maestre de campo* of the expedition, and was chosen to accompany Corônado with the advance guard to Cíbola (Zuñi). The natives there resisted, and a battle ensued at Hawikuh in which Cárdenas and Alvarado saved Coronado's life. From Cíbola Coronado sent Pedro de Tovar to visit the Moqui pueblos of northeastern Arizona. While there Tovar heard of the Colorado River, and Cárdenas was dispatched from Cíbola with about a dozen companions "to go to see this river." Guides were obtained at the Moqui towns. Traveling thence west about twenty days, Cárdenas reached the Grand Canyon at a place where the river banks "seemed to be more than three or four leagues above the stream which flowed between them ... They spent three days on this bank looking for a passage down to the river, which looked from above as if the water was six feet across, although the Indians said it was half a league wide. It was impossible to descend, for after these three days Captain Melgosa and one Juan Galeras and another companion, who were

the three lightest and most agile men, made an attempt to go down at the least difficult place, and went down until those who were above were unable to keep sight of them. They returned about four o'clock in the afternoon, not having succeeded in reaching the bottom ... Those who staid above had estimated that some huge rocks on the sides of the cliffs seemed to be about as tall as a man, but those who went down swore that when they reached these rocks they were bigger than the great tower of Seville" (Winship, p. 489). From Zuñi, Alvarado went ahead to Ácoma, Tiguex (on the Rio Grande), and the Buffalo Plains. Cárdenas followed him to prepare winter quarters at Tiguex for the main army, which was coming behind. In the course of the winter the natives at Tiguex rose in revolt, and Cárdenas played a leading part in subduing them. In the spring of 1541 he accompanied Coronado on his journey eastward in search of Quivira (Kansas). While crossing the Buffalo Plains his horse fell and his arm was broken. Soon after the return to New Mexico, a letter arrived telling Cárdenas of the death of his brother in Spain, and summoning him thither to receive the family inheritance. Bearing dispatches, with a few companions he set out for Mexico, but finding the Sonora Indians in revolt hastened back to rejoin Coronado. Coronado himself now soon returned to Mexico and Cárdenas with him. From there Cárdenas apparently went to Spain.

[The Cárdenas family are given large space in Alberto and Arturo García Carraffa's *Dicciónario Heráldico y Genealógico de Appellidos Españoles y Americanos*, XXI, 108–69 (Madrid, 1925). The sources of information regarding Cárdenas's discovery of the Grand Canyon and his part in the Coronado expedition are the same as those cited under the article on Francisco Vásquez Coronado, *q.v.* See especially G. P. Winship, "The Coronado Expedition, 1540–1542," in the *Fourteenth Annual Report of the Bureau of Ethnology* (1896), pt. I, pp. 319–613.]   H. E. B.

CARDOZO, JACOB NEWTON (June 17, 1786–Aug. 30, 1873), editor, economist, was born in Savannah, Ga., but his father, who had been a Revolutionary soldier, moved to Charleston, S. C. in 1796. After an ordinary education, Jacob was put to mechanical and mercantile pursuits, but interested himself in authorship, and in 1817 became acting editor of the *Southern Patriot*. Six years later he bought the paper and continued as proprietor and editor until 1845. Though he made the *Southern Patriot* a free trade organ, he used it to bolster commercial restriction in one notable instance. In 1818 and 1822 Congress retaliated against prohibitions of American trade with the British West Indies. In the latter year Baltimore and Norfolk remonstrated against the measures of Congress; Charleston merchants, suffering under the stoppage of trade, became excited and meant to lead the Southern ports in a memorial. Cardozo threw the weight of his paper against the movement, believing that the commerce with the West Indies would sooner be opened by America's showing Great Britain her resentment of the Orders in Council. He persuaded an adjourned meeting to his view, and later received assurances from Washington that the failure of the threatened interference had saved the effectiveness of the government's policy. Cardozo was one of the revivers in 1823 of the old Charleston Chamber of Commerce, and in 1827 or 1828 he was asked by this body to draw up a memorial against the "Bill of Abominations." This is said to have been the first petition from the South on behalf of free trade, and was the beginning of the Nullification movement. Cardozo took no part in Nullification, but continued to preach free trade as a principle. In 1826 he published, in Charleston, *Notes on Political Economy*. He had prepared the manuscript for his private use, but published it in an effort to counteract the teachings of John McVickar's *Outlines of Political Economy* (1825). Cardozo's work is an attempted refutation of cardinal points in the system of David Ricardo, whose disciple McVickar was. It contains inklings of doctrine first clearly expressed by Daniel Raymond and later developed by the American National School, of which Henry C. Carey [*q.v.*] was the leading figure. Cardozo showed that the conditions of American economic life suggested theories opposed to those of English classical writers, finding in this country a naturalness of development rather than a long history of mistaken measures of government. He did not deny the Ricardian rent theory on the absolute grounds perceived by Carey, but quarreled with parts of the doctrine. He was alive to the principle of increasing returns in industry, and believed that at least inventiveness would counteract the tendency toward decreasing returns in agriculture. The Malthusian account of population seemed to Cardozo untenable. In 1845 he sold the *Southern Patriot* and founded the *Evening News*. Two years later he disposed of his interest in the *Evening News* but continued as commercial editor until 1861, when he left Charleston for Savannah. During the Civil War he filled editorial positions in Mobile and Atlanta. In 1863 he published *A Plan of Financial Relief Addressed to the Legislature of Georgia and Confederate States Congress*. From the close of the war until the year before his death, when his eyesight failed, he wrote for the Savannah *Morning News*. He paid a brief visit to Charleston just before his death, which occurred in Savannah.

[See Charleston *News and Courier*, Sept. 2, 3, 1873; W. L. King, *Newspaper Press of Charleston, S. C.* (1872), p. 80, and B. A. Elzas, *The Jews of S. C.* (1903), pp. 176–79. Cardozo's *Reminiscences of Charleston* (1866) contains much autobiographical matter.]

B. M—l.

CAREY, HENRY CHARLES (Dec. 15, 1793–Oct. 13, 1879), economist, publisher, was born in Philadelphia, the eldest son of Mathew Carey [*q.v.*], an Irish political refugee who, in his voluminous and spirited writings, made himself the chief advocate of protection for American manufactures. The father, after the habit of James Mill with John Stuart Mill, used to take the boy by the hand in walks through the city, impressing economic lessons upon him. The son in his ninth year attended in New York the first literary fair, and did business on his own account in a small stock of books that had been given him, attracting attention by his precociousness. Two years later he took charge for six weeks of his father's branch store in Baltimore, and on Jan. 1, 1817 he became a partner in the business and later head of the firm of Carey, Lea & Carey, which became a leading American publishing house. Lacking formal schooling, he nevertheless read widely in deciding which manuscripts and books should be issued by his firm. In this way he formed an acquaintance, though necessarily a superficial one, with many fields of learning, and this showed itself in the facility with which later he ransacked almost every department of knowledge for illustrations of his special doctrines. He became the American publisher for Thomas Carlyle, Washington Irving, and Sir Walter Scott, and, before the period of international copyright, he insisted upon making adequate payment to foreign authors. His wife, who died early, was a sister of C. R. Leslie, the painter. He was forty-two years old before he turned attention to the economic writing in which he earned his reputation. In 1835 he published his *Essay on the Rate of Wages,* and withdrew from business to devote himself exclusively to political economy. The *Essay,* which was called forth by Senior's *Lecture on Wages,* was marked by contradictory tendencies. Carey gave his assent to *laissez-faire* as a guiding principle, and accepted the efficacy of the wage-fund doctrine, but at the same time he declared that natural laws are working toward a universal harmony of interests; he denied the Ricardian principle of rent to the extent of asserting the belief that capital and invention will compensate for the infertility of poorer soils; he differed with Malthus by claiming that food increases faster than population and that distress is a consequence of human ineptitude rather than of an economic nemesis that constantly threatens mankind; he defined wealth in terms of well-being, and conceived of happiness as best promoted by attention to the nation as the unit of economic activity. In all of these latter particulars he struck the note of buoyancy and optimism which was afterward to distinguish his work from the dour forebodings of the English classical school. The following year he prepared a manuscript, "The Harmony of Nature," which, after printing, he refrained from publishing because it did not completely satisfy him. Nothing cast down, he immediately went to work on his *Principles of Political Economy*, which appeared in three volumes in 1837–38–40. This work shows his doctrinal evolution. While not denying Ricardo's implicit assumption that the best lands are those first occupied, he made the fundamental departure of declaring that land derives its value from the capital expended upon it, and thus that rent does not differ from interest. Also, he believed that progress in the "mutual fertilization" of labor and capital implies a decrease in the present labor value of all previously existing capital, necessarily involving both a relative and an absolute increase in the share of the joint product of labor and capital going to the worker, while assigning to capital a return that grows at a less rate than wages. Thus his peculiar theory of distribution, which held to a progressive diffusion of wealth among the poorest classes of society, was taking form. In another particular he foreshadowed one of his later advocacies. The panic of 1837 was confirming the administration's distrust of a paper and especially a bank-note currency, but in the midst of the banks' disgrace, Carey pointed out the virtue in a medium of exchange so readily adaptable to commercial requirements. The *Principles* enjoyed a vogue in Europe, being translated into Swedish and Italian. Carey and his friends believed that Bastiat drew from this work the inspiration for his *Harmonies Économiques* (1850), though the French economist contended that Carey's writings had not done more than confirm his own opinions. Neither his father's advocacy of protection nor the languishing prosperity which came in the wake of the tariff of 1833 shook Carey's faith in *laissez-faire*. Perhaps the ruin of a paper manufacture in New Jersey in which he had invested heavily between 1837 and 1840 helped to set his judgment against free trade, but this loss could not have had an immediate effect, for he believed that the tariff of 1842, imposing higher duties, would make matters still worse. William Elder, declaring he quoted Carey, is authority for the statement that his conversion to protectionism came like a flash in 1844. However this may be, in 1845 in his pamphlet on *Commercial Associations in France and England* and in louder tones in his *Past, Present and Future* (1848) he announced himself the foe of the free-trade system. This was in the very moment of the exaltation of free trade in the abolition of the corn laws in England, and in the reduction of duties to a revenue basis in this country in the Dallas tariff of 1847. But Carey was not deterred; rather he gathered ardor as he proceeded in his campaign for protection. He became a regular contributor to Greeley's *New York Tribune* in 1849, writing editorials as well as signed articles, and in this way continued his championing of protection until 1857, when Greeley, believing the fight was lost, supported the tariff of that year, which lowered rates on imports still further. Carey from this period forward was an intense nationalist, and opposed the cosmopolitanism of the day, particularly as impressed upon the world by England's free-trade example. In all of his writings, he was, for a number of reasons, intensely anti-British. One cannot escape the conviction that he must have been profoundly influenced by Friedrich List's *National System of Political Economy*, which appeared in 1841. In the *Past, Present and Future* he gave definitive statement to his opposition to the Ricardian theory of rent, maintaining that the order of occupation has been from poorer to better soils, and that the progress of associated labor and capital must always bring increasing rather than diminishing returns to effort. His next work, the *Harmony of Interests: Manufacturing and Commercial* (1851) further celebrated his protectionism. Particularly he developed the principle, sufficiently evident in his father's writings, that propinquity of manufactures and agriculture would render economic effort vastly more effective, lending force to that power of association which was ever his rallying cry. The centralizing tendency of England's mastership in manufactures and finance, which tended to reduce other countries to mere provinces supplying the world's workshop with raw materials, must be overcome, he declared, by the erection of protective barriers about the young industries of every nation. Ultimately, he held, a free interchange of surplus products between fully developed countries would be possible. The American tariff of 1861 commenced a reaction against unrestricted commerce in which Carey's apostleship and authority were internationally recognized. Familiarity with his works, which were translated into seven European languages and Japanese, brought him a flood of grateful correspondence from all over the world. His *Slave Trade, Domestic and Foreign* (1853) prescribed manufactures for the South; his *Letters to the President* (1858) lamented the disastrous effects of the low tariff of the year before. In 1858–59 he published the three volumes of *The Principles of Social Science,* a congeries of his doctrines, stressing the analogy between natural and social science. This marked the end of his pioneering thought. His *Unity of Law* (1872) was the only book to appear afterward, though the steady flow of pamphlets, reiterating his tenets, continued. In this same year he held his only public office, that of delegate to the state constitutional convention. He presented a striking appearance; handsome in his younger days, his face retained to the last a singular alertness and sensitiveness. The vehemence of his writings was belied by the pervasive kindliness of his personal manner. His home in Philadelphia was for years the gathering place of disciples and visitors to the city, these "Carey Vespers," as they were affectionately called, forming almost the only American counterpart to the salons of the French Physiocrats. In his robust optimism he interpreted the rapid expansion of the economic life of this country in his long span of eighty-six years. He was the leader of the only group that can be said to constitute an American school of political economy; among his followers were Stephen Colwell, Condy Raguet, E. Peshine Smith, Henry C. Baird, William Elder, Robert Ellis Thompson, Edward Atkinson, and, in a later period, Simon N. Patten. Among European disciples, Dühring, Schulze-Delitzsch, and Ferrera are the best known. Judgment of to-day, while pronouncing him uncritical in his parade of illustrations from history, and frequently fanciful in the ardor of his pursuit, cheerfully acknowledges him as not only an original thinker of power, but as the leader of the opposition to the pessimism of the classical school and also to the socialist group which took rise from the Ricardian counsel of despair.

[The main facts of Carey's life are given by Wm. Elder, *Memoir of Henry C. Carey* (1880); Henry Carey Baird, "Henry Chas. Carey," in *Am. Bookseller,* XVII, 102–06 and "Carey and Two of his Recent Critics," in *Proc. Am. Philosophical Soc.,* vol. XXIX (1891); Robt. E. Thompson, "Henry Chas. Carey," in *Penn Mo.,* X (1879), 816–34; Chas. H. Levermore, "Henry C. Carey and his Social System," in the *Political Science Quart.,* V, 553–82 which gives a condensed summary and criticism of Carey's economic writings.]   B. M.—l.

CAREY, JOSEPH MAULL (Jan. 19, 1845–Feb. 5, 1924), senator, governor of Wyoming, was born at Milton, Del., the son of Robert Hood and Susan (Davis) Carey. He attended Union College and the law school of the University of Pennsylvania, and was admitted to the bar in 1867. He practised law in Pennsylvania for two years and then was appointed by President Grant first United States attorney in the newly-created territory of Wyoming, with which he was thenceforth identified, serving on the bench of the supreme court from 1872 to 1876 and thrice as delegate of the territory in Congress. In 1890 he introduced the bill providing for the admission of Wyoming as a state, and he defended ardently and successfully the clause in the constitution which conferred the suffrage on women. He had, indeed, been a consistent supporter of equal suffrage, which had been granted by the territorial legislature by act of 1869. He was chosen first United States senator from Wyoming in 1890, serving one term. During this single term, however, he secured the passage of an act (Aug. 8, 1894) which authorized the secretary of the interior to patent lands to states containing desert areas, provided they would cause such lands to be reclaimed and irrigated. The terms of this act, commonly known as the Carey Act, were accepted by Wyoming in the following year, and large areas were patented to companies.

Although most of his constituents favored the free coinage of silver, Carey supported President Cleveland in securing the repeal of the silver-purchase act of 1878, sacrificing thereby his chances of reëlection. During President Roosevelt's administration he became a Progressive Republican, and he again paid dearly for his independence, failing to obtain the nomination of the Republicans for governor in 1910. He was then nominated by the Democrats and elected. He became a promoter, with Sir Horace Plunkett, of a development company which by extensive irrigation projects at Wheatland threw open large areas to cultivation. In this undertaking he had in mind not merely financial profit but a great Wyoming with agriculture as its corner-stone. He married in 1877 Louise David of Cheyenne. The elder of their two sons, Robert D. Carey, served also as governor of Wyoming.

[*Wyo. State Tribune and Cheyenne State Leader,* Feb. 7, 8, 1924; *Progressive Men of State of Wyo.* (1903), pp. 27–29; family records; personal information.]   G. R. H.

CAREY, MATHEW (Jan. 28, 1760–Sept. 16, 1839), publisher, economist, was born in Dublin, Ireland, the son of Christopher Carey, who was at one time in the British navy and was subsequently a contractor for the army, through which means he achieved an independence. The boy was dropped by his nurse when a year old, and was lame the rest of his life. Probably as a consequence of his deformity, he was shy and apparently backward as a schoolboy. He had only the rudiments of formal education, but read much and developed a remarkable aptitude for languages; particularly, he used Latin with familiarity in all his writings. From childhood he wanted to be a printer and bookseller; his father not approving his choice of a trade, compelled the boy to find his own master, one McDaniel, with whom he served part of an apprenticeship. A threatened encounter between fellow apprentices gave occasion for Carey's first essay, an argument against duelling, published in the *Hibernian Journal* when the author was seventeen. In 1779, incensed by the wrongs of the Irish Catholics, he published, anonymously, a pamphlet in their defense. The tract was instanced in the Lords and Commons as proof of the treasonable views of the Catholics, and a conservative group of Catholics offered £40 for the author's apprehension. Carey's family sent him to Paris, where a priest introduced him to Benjamin Franklin. He worked for some months at a little printing-office which Franklin had set up at Passy. Lafayette called on him to discover the strength of revolutionary sentiment in Ireland. Returning to Dublin in a year, Carey conducted the *Freeman's Journal,* and in 1783, when he was nearly twenty-four, his father set him up as proprietor of a new paper, the *Volunteer's Journal*, the object of which was to defend Ireland, economically and politically, against the encroachments of England. The journal's career, Carey said, "was enthusiastic and violent." Its columns were used to get up a demonstration against the Duke of Rutland, the lord-lieutenant, at Daly's Theatre, and Carey was a leader in the crowd that rushed out after the lord-lieutenant's party, groaning them through the streets and up to the gates of Dublin Castle, where a few Scotch horse dispersed the taunters. The paper was only a year old when the owner was arrested for an attack on the House of Commons and the Premier and was committed for a short time to Newgate. After his release, a new prosecution threatening, he took ship for America, Sept. 7, 1784, escaping detection by dressing as a woman. Landing at Philadelphia with twelve guineas only, and no friends, he was delighted to receive a summons from Lafayette to call on the General at his lodgings. The next day, Lafayette, with no so-

licitation on the part of the young Irish immigrant, sent him a present of $400, which he refused to receive back despite Carey's protest. The debt was repaid in 1824, however, when Lafayette returned to America in broken fortune. Carey issued the first number of his *Pennsylvania Herald,* Jan. 25, 1785; the paper, which supported the conservative party in state politics, had a good circulation, mainly owing to Carey's detailed reports of sessions of the House of Assembly, which were a novelty in American journalism. He was drawn into a bitter controversy with Col. Oswald, editor of the *Independent Gazetteer,* which resulted, January 1786, in a duel in which Oswald was not injured, but Carey was badly wounded in the thigh and did not recover from the hurt for more than a year. Following the duel, Carey characteristically published his wish for reconciliation with his antagonist, which lost him the friendship of some of his supporters. With five partners, in October 1786, Carey began the publication of the *Columbian Magazine,* but soon released himself to publish the *American Museum,* a journal made up of clippings. Despite great financial worry at this time, he married, in 1791, Bridget Flahavan, the daughter of a respectable, but poor, Philadelphian. (See Joseph Willcox, *Historical Sketches of Some of the Pioneer Catholics of Philadelphia.* No place or date.) They had nine children, of whom three died young. Relinquishing the *Museum,* which never paid, despite its excellence, Carey borrowed money and set up as a publisher and bookseller; he was frequently anxious because of his heavy speculations in this business, but at length prospered conspicuously. He volunteered, with his friend Stephen Girard and others, to serve on the committee of health during the yellow fever epidemic of 1793, and described the horrors of the pestilence in a vivid pamphlet which went through numerous editions. Early in the nineties he formed the Hibernian Society for the relief of Irish immigrants, and in 1796 joined in launching the first Sunday-school society in America. A few years later, in spite of his attempts at avoidance, he became engaged in a violent controversy with William Cobbett, who was then a bookseller in Philadelphia. In 1802 he was elected a director of the Bank of Pennsylvania. In 1810 he was one of the few Republicans in Philadelphia who worked for the renewal of the charter of the Bank of the United States. The second war with England having made a serious rift between the Federalist and Republican parties, Carey published his *Olive Branch* in 1814 to bring them together. In 1819, after much labor, he published his *Vindiciae Hibernicae,* to clear the Irish of the charge of promoting the massacre of 1641. American manufactures, which had sprung up during the war, had been seriously impaired by the flood of English goods which followed the peace and Carey took a leading part in forwarding a protective policy for this country. He was a charter member of the Philadelphia Society for the Promotion of National Industry, most of the addresses of which came from his pen. These are recognized as the classic American argument in favor of the protective system, and for them Carey will be chiefly remembered in economic authorship. He did more than any one else, if we except Hamilton, to found the American nationalist school of economic thought, his son, Henry C. Carey [*q.v.*], being his most distinguished follower. His tracts and books, running to thousands of pages, cover many subjects. He was an unceasing advocate of universal education and tirelessly insisted on the importance of internal improvements. His style was clear, vigorous, and often eloquent. He took a joy in vituperation. He was a pious Catholic, and generous in his giving to charity. His funeral was the most largely attended of any in Philadelphia to that time with the exception of that of Stephen Girard.

[Carey published *Autobiographical Sketches* (Phila., 1829; only one volume issued). The *New Eng. Mag.,* vols. V–VII, contains a very full autobiography. See also E. L. Bradsher, *Mathew Carey, Editor, Author, and Publisher* (1912); *Niles' Weekly Reg.,* Sept. 21, 1839; *Am. Bookseller,* Feb. 1, 1885; E. F. J. Maier, "Mathew Carey, Publicist and Politician," *Records of the Am. Cath. Hist. Soc.,* XXXIX, 71–154; and for samples of his work, Mathew Carey, *Miscellaneous Essays* (1830).]   B. M—l.

CARLETON, HENRY (*c.* 1785–Mar. 28, 1863), jurist, author, was born in Virginia. His name was originally Henry Carleton Cox. He attended the University of Georgia for two years and then entered Yale, where he graduated in 1806. After a residence in Mississippi, he came to New Orleans in 1814. In the campaign connected with the defense of the city against the British, he served as a lieutenant of infantry under Jackson. For a while he seems to have taught school until advised by a friend to seek a field of endeavor more congenial to his talents. Having read law in the office of Edward Livingston, the great jurist, he became a worthy and successful lawyer at a time when the bar of New Orleans was adorned by an array of eminent names. He was appointed United States district attorney in 1832, serving in this capacity until 1837. His position was a difficult one, for it was during this period that the re-

lations between this country and Mexico were of a critical nature, due to the fact that New Orleans was the center of the despatch of volunteers and munitions in aid of the struggling Texans. In view of the sympathy felt by the citizens of New Orleans for those in revolt against the rule of Santa Anna, Carleton found it practically impossible to enforce the law of Apr. 20, 1818 intended to prevent violations of neutrality. On Oct. 21, 1835 he wrote the secretary of state of the difficulties encountered by him in striving to bring within the scope of the law those going to Texas with arms in their hands (*House Executive Document, No. 74,* 25 Cong., 2 Sess.; *Statutes at Large,* III, 447–50). In December 1835 a number of business men and insurance agents requested Carleton to prevent the sailing of the *Brutus,* then fitting out as a man-of-war. Witnesses were accordingly examined by Carleton, though he failed completely to make out a case. In March 1836 he instituted proceedings against a prominent citizen, William Christy, for aiding Gen. José Antonio Mexía, who was fitting out a filibustering expedition against Mexico. But here again no evidence was forthcoming to sustain the charge. On Apr. 1, 1837 Carleton became associate justice of the supreme court of Louisiana in place of Judge George Mathews, serving with distinction in this capacity until Feb. 1, 1839, when he resigned on account of ill health. For a while he traveled in Europe, then settled in Philadelphia, where he became interested in speculations of a metaphysical and philosophical nature. The fruit of these studies appeared in his *Liberty and Necessity* (1857) and *Essay on the Will* (1863). Another volume entitled *Eight Days in England* is also ascribed to him. As a writer, however, his reputation rests on his translation in collaboration with Louis Moreau Lislet of *Las Siete Partidas,* the principal Spanish code long enforced in Louisiana. An act of the state legislature of Mar. 3, 1819 authorized this task at the expense of the state. The two volumes of the edition of 1820 contain all that portion of the work which was considered as having force in Louisiana. The translation was accepted in 1820 by the legislature on the recommendation of a committee, composed of Pierre Derbigny, Mazureau, and Livingston, appointed for the purpose of examining it. The legislature ordered the translation to be circulated "as a substantial contribution toward an understanding of the laws of Spain" (*Louisiana Historical Quarterly,* IV, 35). The translators wrote in the Introduction: "The particular care and attention the translators have bestowed, in order to render their work as perfect as possible, will, they hope, secure to them the praise of having faithfully discharged the honorable task imposed upon them by the legislature." Carleton was married on May 29, 1815, to Aglaé D'Avezac de Castera, a younger sister of Auguste D'Avezac [*q.v.*], and of Louise D'Avezac, the brilliant second wife of Edward Livingston (*Louisiana Historical Quarterly*, V, 352). A daughter, Aglaé Marie Carleton, was the mother of Carleton Hunt (1836–1921), referred to by some as the "Nestor of the Louisiana bar." After the death of his first wife Carleton married Mrs. Maria (Vanderburgh) Wiltbank, who survived him.

[A very inadequate sketch of Carleton was published by Judge Edward S. Whitaker in his *Sketches of Life and Character in La.* (1847). A brief memoir is printed in *La. Reports*, vol. CXXX (1913). See also sketch by Carleton Hunt in F. B. Dexter, *Biog. Sketches Grads. Yale Coll.*, vol. VI (1912).]   J. E. W—n.

CARLETON, HENRY GUY (June 21, 1856–Dec. 10, 1910), playwright, was born at Fort Union, N. Mex., and died in Atlantic City, N. J. His father was James Henry Carleton, a general, and his mother Sophie Garland Wolfe. He studied civil and mining engineering at Santa Clara College, San Francisco, 1865–70, and from 1873 to 1876 was a cavalry officer in the army. In 1876 he came to New Orleans to write for the *Times,* of that city, and he also opened newspaper connections in Chicago and New York. He remained enough of a soldier to become an officer of militia and to take part in the riots of 1877 incident to the final suppression of the reconstruction government in Louisiana. In 1881, he wrote a blank verse tragedy, *Memnon,* its scene laid in ancient Egypt. From the age of fifteen when he wrote a play called *The Age of Gold,* he had been intensely interested in the drama, and in 1882, encouraged by *Memnon,* he went to New York in order to be near the theatres. Play followed play rapidly, the number mounting at last to more than sixteen. Whether because he confined himself largely to themes of gloom, or for other reasons, this work was not often the means of his acquiring money. He moved to Boston, and was living there, ill and in something like poverty, when in 1892, at the suggestion of Nat Goodwin, he wrote *The Gilded Fool.* This play, a tragi-comedy of the conventional type, served Goodwin admirably for a long time. Two years later, appeared *Butterflies,* through which John Drew and Maude Adams first attained wide popularity. In spite of these and other successes and of frequent work for the magazines and newspapers, Carleton's finances were usually at low ebb. He endeavored to relieve this condition by turning to

account some of his early training as an engineer, and from 1899 to 1903 he invented and patented thirty-four electrical and chemical devices. None of these proved very remunerative. He was delightful company. When prosperous, he joined yacht clubs and gave himself to a consideration of his colonial ancestry in both Virginia and Massachusetts, but even when not prosperous he retained his inveterate humor and his disposition to tease every one with whom he had contact. Once when congratulated on his military medals, he explained that he had to thank for them the fact that he had always been a grievous stammerer. As a young man he was in charge of some troops who were surprised by hostile Indians. He was terrified, but the proper order of retreat could not be coaxed to his lips. The consequence was rout for the Indians, and medals for the routers. Such raillery characterized him even in the long period of ill health which preceded his death.

[N. C. Goodwin, *Nat Goodwin's Book* (1914); *New Internat. Year Book*, 1910; *Who's Who in America*, 1910–11.]   J. D. W.

CARLETON, WILL (Oct. 21, 1845–Dec. 18, 1912), poet, originally named William McKendree Carleton (he dropped his middle name and became Will Carleton in 1873), was born on a farm two miles east of Hudson, Mich. His father, John Hancock Carleton, a direct descendant of Edward Carleton whose name appears in the records of Rowley, Mass., in 1638, was a pioneer-farmer, industrious, religious; his mother, Celestia E. (Smith) Carleton, was a sweet-tempered woman who sang ballads while rocking her children to sleep. Will was born and grew up a delicate dreamy boy, more inclined to deliver orations to the cows than to follow the plow. He attended the country schools of the neighborhood, and graduated from Hillsdale College in 1869. Then he became editor of the *Hillsdale Standard* and the *Detroit Weekly Tribune.* In 1871, reporting a divorce case, he was inspired to write "Betsy and I are Out," which was copied throughout the country. In quick succession *Harper's Weekly* featured "Out of the Old House, Nancy," "Over the Hill to the Poor House," "Gone with a Handsomer Man." These attracted wide attention, so that *Farm Ballads,* published by Harpers in 1873, within eighteen months attained a circulation of forty thousand copies. This was followed by *Farm Legends* (1875), *Young Folks' Centennial Rhymes* (1876), *Farm Festivals* (1881). In 1878 Carleton went to Boston to live, and out of the new environment came *City Ballads* (1885), *City Legends* (1889), *City Festivals* (1892). In 1882 he was married to Adora

Niles Goodell and moved to Brooklyn, N. Y., where he resided until his death. In 1894 he founded a magazine called *Every Where*. Partly from this he gleaned in 1895–96 *Rhymes of Our Planet* and *The Old Infant and Similar Stories*. In 1902 he published the *Song of Two Centuries*. He was one of the first poets of the country to give public readings from his own writings, a venture which yielded him a large income. The secret of his poetical success lay in his ability to utter in simple language the homely sentiments of the plain people. His best-known production, "Over the Hill to the Poor House," had a pathetically human note which set in vibration a sympathetic chord in the hearts of a great multitude. Superintendents of poor houses reported to him that their inmates were decreasing in numbers because children were withdrawing their parents from these institutions, shamed into filial duty by this ballad. His imagination was not wide in its range, neither did it glow in magic words or memorable sentences; he was not an artist in poetic form, but his emotions were wholesome, and he voiced without undue sentimentality the humor and pathos in the experiences of the common people. Nature plays little part in his poems; it is the heart that predominates. He sympathized with the life of the humble and interpreted their feelings without exploiting their peculiarities.

[A. Elwood Corning has written an excellent biographical study, entitled *Will Carleton* (1917). In the *Mich. Hist. Colls.*, vol. XXXIX, appears an appreciation by Byron A. Finney, together with a full bibliography, which, however, lists two works not written by Carleton—*Geraldine: a Romance in Verse* (1881), by Alonzo Hopkins, *My Wife and I Quarrelled* (1877), by Mrs. Emerson-French. The error was first pointed out by Mr. Finney himself, who is now engaged on a definitive life of Carleton.]   C. A. D.

CARLILE, JOHN SNYDER (Dec. 16, 1817–Oct. 24, 1878), lawyer, senator, West Virginia Unionist, was born in Winchester, Va. His family was Scotch-Irish, and long settled in the Shenandoah Valley. From his widowed mother, John received the early training in books and morals which the Valley Scotch believed in. At fourteen he became a store clerk. Developing rapidly, he three years later entered business on his own account, but only to find himself soon overwhelmed with debts,—debts which he later felt in honor bound to pay. Thanks to private study, however, he was able to begin life anew in 1840 as a lawyer in the little town of Beverly. Moving soon to the larger Clarksburg, he eventually fought his way to prominence, though not to preëminence, among the lawyers of the Kanawha section. Political life, however, was his great field. A "bold and forceful speaker," of attractive personality, and blessed by the gods of western politics with early poverty, his progress was rapid. He was successively senator (1847–51), member of the constitutional convention of 1850, and congressman (1855–57),—being a member in 1856 of the House Committee of Accounts. Though he obtained in none of these positions more than local distinction and met defeat as the Know-Nothing candidate for Congress in 1857, he at all times represented faithfully the dominating pro-Union sentiments of his constituents. Accordingly they sent him to the secession convention of 1861. Here his extreme views and aggressive conduct made him the target of the *Richmond Enquirer* and put him in imminent danger of mob violence. Returning home hastily and determined to create a new state and to keep that state in the Union, he worked to secure a convention at Wheeling, notably by drafting the Address of May 22, 1861, to the people of western Virginia. When his proposal that this convention as a sovereign body create a new state was defeated as premature, he accepted the chairmanship of the convention's central committee and contributed to its campaign against ratification of the secession ordinance a widely distributed pamphlet that made no mention of a new state. A little later he embodied his ideas as to the legality of secession and the sovereignty of his people in a "Declaration of the People of Virginia," which was adopted by the second Wheeling convention, June 17, 1861. A new state government, though not a new state, having been created on the basis of Carlile's argument, he was sent by it to the United States Senate. Already the House had received him as a member, from July 4 to July 13. Now the Senate welcomed him, put him on the Committee on Public Lands and the Committee on Territories; and the chairman of the latter committee, because of Carlile's "lucid mind," soon entrusted him with entire management of a bill to create the new state of West Virginia. His great ambition now within his grasp, sense and fortune suddenly failed him. For although in the August convention of his state he had favored a West Virginia which was to be limited (for the present) to enthusiastic western counties, he now included in the bill counties of the Shenandoah Valley, which were loyal to the old state, thereby endangering the whole project. Perhaps he hoped thus to defeat the emancipation provisions of the bill, relying on aid from the border state men whom he afterward joined in opposing confiscation and military draft. Instead he was swept aside. Denounced by the home legislature, he was never again elected to office. When President Grant, mindful of Carlile's loyalty, nominated him as ambassador to Sweden, senatorial leaders refused confirmation. He died at Clarksburg.

[A brief sketch by Carlile's son in Wm. P. Willey, *An Inside View of the Formation of the State of W. Va.* (1901) ; Jas. C. McGregor, *The Disruption of Va.* (1922) ; *Bench and Bar of W. Va.* (1919), ed. by G. W. Atkinson ; *W. Va. Hist. and Govt. told by Contemporaries* (1928), ed. by I. G. Boughter and J. W. Pence.]

C. C. P.

CARLISLE, JAMES MANDEVILLE (May 22, 1814–May 19, 1877), lawyer, was the only son of Christopher Carlisle, a resident of Alexandria near Washington, D. C., and his wife, Anne Mandeville. In 1825 the family moved to Washington, D. C., where James attended the Catholic Seminary, completing his education at Partridge's military school. Of a studious disposition, he became a fine classical scholar, and showed a special aptitude for the French and Spanish languages. He studied law at Baltimore and Washington, giving lessons in modern languages in order to defray his expenses, and was admitted to the bar of the Supreme Court at Washington in 1837. Opening an office in Washington, he quickly secured a promising connection, his familiarity with French and Spanish inducing retainers in cases involving early land titles in Florida and Louisiana. In 1849 he obtained wide publicity as junior counsel to Horace Mann in the defense of Daniel Drayton and Edward Sayres who were tried for larceny in transporting and assisting slaves to escape. He was frequently consulted by the legations of the various Central and South American republics, and in 1852 was retained as standing legal adviser to the British legation. In 1862 he appeared as counsel for Costa Rica before the joint commission at Washington respecting the claims of United States citizens arising out of the occupation of Nicaragua by troops of Costa Rica. On the reorganization of the supreme court of the District of Columbia in 1863 he refused to take the new oath in that court, and thereafter confined his practise to the Supreme Court of the United States and the Court of Claims, where, however, for the next ten years he held a larger number of briefs than any other practitioner. In 1864 he was retained as counsel for Colombia before the commission of that year to consider the undecided claims against New Granada arising, *inter alia,* from the Panama Riots of 1856. In 1871 he was counsel for Spain before the mixed commission under the agreement of Feb. 12, 1871, and in the same year was retained as counsel for the British government before the mixed claims commission under Article 12 of the Treaty of Washington, acting throughout the proceedings

which lasted two years. He had for some years suffered from paralysis of the optic nerve, and after 1866 he could never read a printed book, but continued his professional work, relying largely on his phenomenal memory. He died at Washington. A remarkably sound and versatile lawyer, of quick perception, with an intuitive grasp of vital points, he was at his best in international cases involving complicated issues, where his mastery of detail, wonderful memory, and dialectical skill had full sway. Personally he was a man of much dignity and charm. He is spoken of as "an advanced boulevardier . . . immaculately attired, given to dropping in at foreign legations and chatting on familiar terms with the titled and great" (Noel and Downing, *post*).

[*Eminent and Representative Men of Va. and the District of Columbia of the 19th century* (1893) ; F. R. Noel and M. B. Downing, *Court House of the District of Columbia* (1919) ; H. W. Crew, *Centennial Hist. of Washington* (1902).]

H. W. H. K.

CARLISLE, JOHN GRIFFIN (Sept. 5, 1835–July 31, 1910), lieutenant-governor of Kentucky, congressman and senator, secretary of the treasury, was born in Campbell (now Kenton) County, of humble parentage. He was the son of L. H. and Mary A. (Reynolds) Carlisle. His early life was spent on a rocky, begrudging farm, which gave him little opportunity for an education. But having unusual ambition for a boy in his situation, he took advantage of every opportunity, and succeeded in getting all the schooling his neighborhood had to offer. Over a period of five years, beginning when he was only fifteen years old, he taught school whenever his labors on the farm permitted. He then moved to Covington where he might have greater opportunities of advancement and began the study of law under the direction of William B. Kinkhead and John W. Stephenson, who later became governor of the state. In January 1857 he married Mary Jane, daughter of John A. Goodson of Covington. He was admitted to the bar in 1858 and for a time was in partnership with Kinkhead. His first speech before a jury won him a respectful hearing and a considerable reputation. Within a short time he had developed as large a practise as could be found in Covington. He was elected in 1859 to the Kentucky legislature and was reëlected for a second term. He took a conservative course in the great sectional dispute, living too near the Ohio River to be a secessionist and yet by nature too conservative to favor coercion. He was a member of the House Committee on Federal Relations which reported the neutrality resolutions of May 16, 1861. Indeed neutrality seemed to express best Carlisle's position throughout the war, for he did not feel called upon to fight on either side. As the Federal military régime gripped Kentucky tighter, almost superseding the civil government, he joined the party of protest and helped to promote its organization at Louisville in June 1864, its position being that, "the revocation of all unconstitutional edicts and pretended laws, an immediate armistice, a national convention for the adjustment of our difficulties, are the only measures for saving our nation from unlimited calamity and ruin" (*Lexington Observer and Reporter,* July 2, 1864). Yet he refused to serve as an elector on the McClellan ticket. In August 1865 he ran for the state Senate and was defeated, as the military authorities took almost complete charge of the election throughout the state. But when the legislature met it refused to seat seven representatives and four senators, Carlisle's opponent being among the latter, and ordered new elections. Carlisle ran again and was elected, being reëlected in 1869. While in the legislature he took a decided stand in favor of granting to the Cincinnati Southern Railway a right-of-way through Kentucky and when in 1871 the Democratic convention nominated Preston H. Leslie, an opponent of the road, for the governorship, Carlisle was nominated for the lieutenant-governorship in order to please central Kentucky which favored the road. He now resigned his senatorship and was elected lieutenant-governor in August. After an intensely bitter fight, over the third attempt of the road to secure a right-of-way, the vote in the Senate stood 19 to 19. Carlisle, now presiding over that body by virtue of being lieutenant-governor, broke the tie in favor of the road. He entered upon his national career in 1877 when he took his seat in the lower house of Congress, where he soon became the recognized leader of the Democrats. He was elected speaker in 1883 and was reëlected for the next two Congresses. To-day he is generally considered to have been one of the few great speakers of the House. His knowledge of parliamentary law and of the rules of the House was unquestioned. In an age when extreme partisanship prevailed, he was scrupulously impartial. Representative Hiscock of New York, a Republican, said at the time, "He is one of the strongest of Democrats, and I am one of the strongest of Republicans; yet . . . my imagination is not strong enough to conceive of his making an unfair ruling or doing an unfair thing against the party opposed to him in this House" (A. D. White, *Autobiography,* 1905, II, 126).

As a member of the House he was the out-standing tariff reformer, and although in theory a free-trader, he stood in reality for a tariff for revenue only. As a member of the Committee on Ways and Means he played an active part in formulating the various Democratic bills, and in 1888 he with Roger Q. Mills fought the hardest for the Mills Bill. According to Champ Clark (*My Quarter Century of American Politics,* 1920, I, 236), the tariff reform movement was due more to him than to any other man. He was also greatly interested in restoring American shipping to the seas. On May 26, 1890 he resigned his seat to accept an appointment to the Senate to fill out the unexpired term of James B. Beck, who had died. On Feb. 4, 1893, he resigned from the Senate to accept under President Cleveland the post of secretary of the treasury, which position he held to the end of Cleveland's term. At a time when most politicians considered themselves financial experts, Carlisle made a close study of the money question and well realized the intricacies of it. As secretary of the treasury he showed courage and ability, but due to the extreme difficulties of the situation he added little to his reputation. He worked in harmony with the President, who said of him, "We are just right for each other. He knows all I ought to know" (R. M. McElroy, *Grover Cleveland, the Man and the Statesman,* II, 6). The new administration was immediately confronted by a panic and a fast-disappearing gold reserve. Carlisle's announcement on Apr. 15, 1893 that no more gold certificates would be issued caused a flurry which was aggravated by the further explanation that gold would be paid for treasury notes only so long as it was "lawfully available." Soon Cleveland clarified the matter by announcing that he would use every power to preserve the parity between gold and silver. Thereafter no one misunderstood the intentions of the treasury department. To maintain the gold reserve Carlisle resorted to various bond issues, authority for which he took from the old resumption act of 1875. In embracing the "sound money" position, he stirred up bitter hostility within his party. He was charged with having deserted his earlier principles, and Champ Clark later declared that Carlisle had given the best free silver arguments ever formulated and had likewise put forth the best reasons for the gold standard. In his famous silver argument, Carlisle stood against the free coinage of either metal, but favored the unlimited coinage of both. He later stated that he would rather be right than consistent.

He had bright presidential prospects in 1892, and was rejected for Cleveland only because the latter, it was thought, would receive a greater independent vote. As the campaign of 1896 approached Carlisle was considered the inevitable "sound money" candidate, but because of the failure of Cleveland to state that he would not be a candidate, Carlisle became hesitant and lost the support of many who were urging him to become an active candidate. In the campaign he came out boldly for the gold standard and supported the Palmer and Buckner "National Democratic" ticket. He made a series of speeches in Kentucky, where the hostility of the silver Democrats became so bitter against him that he was almost mobbed in his home town of Covington. Never before in Kentucky had a leader, excepting Clay and John C. Breckinridge, been more beloved, yet no one was more detested than Carlisle after 1896. The next year, feeling that the verdict of banishment from Kentucky had been pronounced, he began the practise of law in New York City. He took no further part in politics, though he opposed Imperialism and accepted a vice-presidency in the Anti-Imperialist League. He was not a great orator, but he had a gift of keen analysis and lucid statement; and no one excelled him in direct and convincing exposition of economic and financial questions.

[A short sketch of the life of Carlisle appears in *Who's Who in America*, 1910–11. Facts concerning his career in Kentucky are noted in R. H. and L. Collins, *Hist. of Ky.* (1874), vols. I, II, and in E. M. Coulter, *The Cincinnati Southern Railroad and the Struggle for Southern Commerce, 1865–72* (1922); the Louisville *Courier-Jour.*, Aug. 1, 2, 3, 1910. Short obituaries and appreciations are in *N. Y. Times*, Aug. 1, 1910; *Nation*, Aug. 4, 1910, and *Outlook*, Aug. 13, 1910.]

E. M. C—r.

CARLL, JOHN FRANKLIN (May 7, 1828–Mar. 13, 1904), civil engineer, geologist, was born in Bushwick (now Brooklyn), L. I., the son of John and Margaret (Walters) Carll. He was educated at Union Hall Academy in Flushing, L. I. At eighteen, when he had finished his schooling, he joined his father in farming and was so occupied for about three years. He then entered the publishing field in association with his brother-in-law, E. O. Crowell, and assisted in the editing and printing of the *Daily Eagle* in Newark, N. J. Four years later he disposed of his interests in that newspaper and returned to Flushing where for ten years he was engaged in the practise of civil engineering and surveying. In October 1864 he moved to Pleasantville, Pa., and became identified with work in the development of the oil fields of that state. While so occupied, he invented the static-pressure sand pump, a removable pump chamber, and adjustable sleeves for piston rods. In 1874 Prof. J. P. Lesley, chief of the Second Geological Survey of Pennsylvania, appointed Carll as one of the as-

sistant geologists, in charge of the petroleum and natural-gas surveys. The seven reports which he compiled on this work have, from their publication to the present time, been considered by oil men as standard authorities. They are models of conscientious investigation and scientific description. Carll was the first geologist to comprehend the structure of the oil regions of Pennsylvania and to furnish in his reports a reliable exposition of their essential features. These reports cover the geology of the oil regions of Warren, Venango, Clarion, and Butler counties of Pennsylvania; they also include surveys of Garland and Panama conglomerates in Warren and Crawford counties in Pennsylvania and in Chautauqua County of New York. In them Carll described oil-well rigs and tools and discussed both the pre-glacial and post-glacial drainage of Erie County, Pa. He also gave an excellent comparison of the geology of northeastern Ohio, northwestern Pennsylvania, and western New York. It is hardly too much to say that the geology of petroleum was virtually created by Carll and his service to the science in sweeping away many popular fallacies was invaluable. For eight years he exerted an influence upon the more thoughtful part of the population of the oil regions, an influence so unpretentious, steady, and consistent as almost to elude observation, but so real and fundamental as to illustrate admirably the true function of a geological survey. Carll continued with the Survey until 1885 when he resigned to enter private practise as a consulting geologist. He was married twice: in 1853 to Hannah A. Burtis of South Oyster Bay, L. I., who died in September 1859, and in 1868 to Martha Tappan of Newark, N. J., who died in 1903. At the time of his death in 1904, in Waldron, Ark., Carll was on his way south for the benefit of his health.

[The Mar. 14, 1904 issue of the *Daily Derrick* (Oil City, Pa.), now the *Oil City Derrick*; Prof. J. P. Lesley's letter of transmittal with Carll's reports to Gov. Pattison of Pa., pub. in *Geological Report on Warren County* by J. F. Carll (1883); *Who's Who in America*, 1903–05; information as to certain facts from S. E. Carll (great-nephew of J. F. Carll), 42 Idaho St., Passaic, N. J.]

K. W. C—g.

CARMACK, EDWARD WARD (Nov. 5, 1858–Nov. 9, 1908), prohibitionist, the son of F. M. and Catherine Carmack, was a native of Sumner County, Tenn. His father, a minister of the Christian or Campbellite Church, who lived near Castalian Springs, died when his son was a small boy, leaving the family entirely without means. Edward worked on farms and at a brick yard, helping to support the family. At county schools he secured some training, and friends later aided him to attend the famous Webb School at Culleoka, Tenn. He then read law at home and in a lawyer's office, and, after a short law practise in Columbia, he entered the state legislature in 1884. He next became editor of the *Columbia Herald,* and later of the *Nashville American* (1888). In April 1890 he was married to Elizabeth Cobey Dunnington of Columbia, Tenn. In 1892 he became editor of the *Memphis Commercial Appeal.* Throughout his editorial career he fought for good government and for the prohibition of the liquor traffic. He became known as an able editor who excelled in the use of ridicule and invective. In 1897 he was elected to Congress and served two terms, after which he was elected United States senator. In 1906 he contested the governorship of Tennessee with M. R. Patterson, Carmack standing for state-wide prohibition. Defeated he again became editor of the *Nashville American* and carried the prohibition fight to the Democratic state convention, in which many of his adherents were unseated. He then planned to carry the contest to the state legislature in 1908. The struggle was bitter and it was clear that a majority would support Carmack's views. Gov. Patterson strongly opposed the prohibition policy. Bitter animosities were aroused and before the legislature met Carmack was killed on the street in Nashville by Duncan B. Cooper and his son Robin, both supporters of Gov. Patterson's policies. They were sentenced to twenty years' imprisonment but Patterson immediately pardoned the older man, and his son, granted a new trial, was not further prosecuted. The legislature, however, two months later, passed over the governor's veto the state-wide prohibition law for which Carmack had struggled.

In political campaigns and in Congress Carmack was known as a popular orator and ready debater. His manner and style were those of John Randolph but Carmack possessed greater versatility. His course in public affairs always commanded enthusiastic followers and developed bitter enemies. What he decided was right he supported with all the vigor at his command and what he thought was wrong he condemned with vitriolic ridicule and wit. Few men cared to meet him in debate. He was a good writer, a brilliant speaker, a great editor of the old-fashioned type, and during his brief and restless career one of the most influential men the state of Tennessee has produced. Only four monuments have been erected on the grounds of the state capitol in Nashville: to Andrew Jackson, James K. Polk, Sam Davis, and Edward Ward Carmack.

[W. T. Hale and D. L. Merritt, *A Hist. of Tenn. and Tennesseans* (1913); J. G. Cisco, *Historic Sumner County, Tenn.* (1909); pamphlets and newspaper files in the State Library of Tennessee.]   W.L.F.

CARMICHAEL, WILLIAM (d. Feb. 9, 1795), diplomat, was born in Queen Annes County, Md. His father was also William Carmichael, who had come to the eastern shore of Maryland as a Scotch immigrant, and there married a Miss Brooke, niece of the second wife of Richard Bennett, son of a former governor of Virginia, and one of the wealthiest landed proprietors of Maryland. This fortunate inheritance enabled William Carmichael to complete his education at Edinburgh, and to tour the British Isles. He was in London, leading a gay life, in 1775, when word came of the beginning of revolution in America. He resolved to return to America and was entrusted with dispatches by Arthur Lee, then the agent in London for some of the Colonies, but on reaching Paris, he was detained there by illness until the arrival of Silas Deane. He offered his services to Deane, and served as a secretary of the Commission (Deane, Franklin and Arthur Lee), in their efforts to enlist the aid of France for the Colonies. He was individually responsible for the coming of Lafayette to America (*Stevens' Facsimiles,* vol. III, no. 248). In October 1776 he was sent to Berlin to propose treaty relations with Frederick the Great but found that old monarch too cautious to risk the enmity of England (*Ibid.,* vol. XV, no. 1453). After rendering useful service in France, Carmichael sailed from Nantes for America, February 1778, bearing important dispatches to the Continental Congress.

He served as a member of the Continental Congress in 1778–79, and then became secretary to John Jay, chosen as minister plenipotentiary to secure a treaty with Spain. The Jay commission reached Cadiz, Jan. 22, 1780, and Carmichael was sent ahead to Madrid to ascertain whether the commission would be received or not. The answer was favorable, and for more than two years they sought a treaty with Spain, but without success, as Spain refused to allow America the navigation of the Mississippi to its mouth. When Jay left for Paris in June 1782 he left Carmichael as acting chargé d'affaires, to transact routine matters while the negotiations for a treaty were transferred to Paris. Carmichael continued at Madrid or at other residences of the Court of Spain, and was formally received by the king and royal family on Aug. 23, 1783, an honor not usually accorded to any below the rank of minister (Carmichael MSS.; Library of Congress, Carmichael to Livingston, Aug. 30, 1783). His commission as chargé was dated Apr. 20, 1790. With his health much impaired, Carmichael's letters to Jefferson, Secretary of State, became infrequent, and in January 1791 he asked to be relieved and allowed to return to America. This request Jefferson refused, and, in March 1792, a new commission, in which Carmichael was joined by William Short, was appointed by President Washington to secure a treaty with Spain. On the arrival of Short, negotiations began Mar. 23, 1793, and were continued without success until June 5, 1794, when Carmichael was recalled and Short named as his successor. Before Carmichael could arrange his affairs and take formal leave of the Court, winter set in and compelled a delay until the next spring. In February 1795 he was confined to his bed by an illness felt for years past which resulted in his death, Feb. 9, 1795. He was buried in a lot adjoining the Roman Catholic Cemetery in Madrid.

His chief public service was rendered during his fourteen years in Spain, when both the reputation and credit of the nation were very bad. Under such conditions he gained the close friendship of the Spanish foreign minister, Florida Blanca, a genuine statesman, and through him secured the aid of Spain in obtaining the release of American captives in Morocco and a favorable treaty with Morocco. He was ignored by his own government, unpaid for years, and compelled to use his personal resources to keep up appearances. Every American who had occasion to visit Madrid while Carmichael was in active service testified to his good standing and influence at the Spanish Court (Jefferson MSS.; Jefferson to Madison, Jan. 30, 1787).

William Carmichael was twice married. As a youth he wed a Miss Stirling, daughter of an Episcopal rector in Queen Annes County, Md. He was a widower with no children when he went to Spain, and there married Antonia Reynon. His widow, with one daughter, Alphonsa, came to America to live near Chestertown, Md. The estate of Carmichael was so impaired by his long public service that his family was on the verge of poverty, and only some belated generosity on the part of Congress in paying the claims advanced by Mrs. Carmichael kept her from actual suffering.

[The chief source of information is The Papers of the Continental Congress, Letters of W. Carmichael in the Lib. of Cong., Manuscripts Division. See also Francis Wharton, ed., *The Revolutionary Diplomatic Correspondence* (6 vols., 1889); Jared Sparks, ed., *The Diplomatic Correspondence of the Am. Rev.* (12 vols., 1829–30); S. F. Bemis, ed., *The Am. Secretaries of State and Their Diplomacy*, vol. I (1927); Samuel G. Coe, *The Mission of Wm. Carmichael to Spain* (1928).]
S. G. C.

CARNAHAN, JAMES (Nov. 15, 1775–Mar. 3, 1859), college president, was born in Cumberland County, Pa., where his ancestors had settled early in the eighteenth century. His father, for a time an officer in the state militia during the Revolution, met an untimely death in 1788.

James, after some years of study at the academy of Canonsburg, was admitted in 1798 to the junior class of the College of New Jersey (now Princeton) whence two years later he was graduated with highest honors. For more than a score of years he divided his time between preaching and teaching. In 1801–03 he was a tutor in the College of New Jersey; in 1804 he was licensed to preach by the Presbytery of New Brunswick; in 1806–12 he served the united congregation of Utica and Whitesboro (N. Y.). Resigning on account of ill health, he spent eleven years in conducting a classical academy at Georgetown, D. C. He became well known throughout the Presbyterian communion as a man of sound judgment and unflagging diligence. In May 1823 he was elected to the presidency of the College of New Jersey. For six years he had to contend with an evil heritage, as the institution was in the midst of a period of decline. Standards were low; discipline was lax; and divided counsels rent the administration. Frequent resignations from the faculty continued to undermine the reputation of the college. In 1828 the lowest ebb was reached; the enrolment had dropped from 120 to 70. The president was keenly discouraged and thought of recommending the closing of the institution. But at this juncture a young professor, John Maclean, possessed of tremendous energy and resource, put his shoulder to the wheel. Henceforth "the administration of Dr. Carnahan . . . until his resignation in 1853 was a collegiate administration in which two colleagues labored as one man" (J. DeWitt, *post*, p. 647). Maclean advised an immediate strengthening of the faculty. The adoption of this policy inaugurated an era of prosperity. Men of the stamp of Albert Dod, Joseph Henry, and John Torrey enhanced the reputation of the college. When Carnahan retired in 1854 there were 250 students enrolled. New chairs were endowed; many scholarships were established; East and West Colleges and Clio and Whig Halls were erected. A law school flourished (for a short time), and ambitious plans for a medical school were afoot. From the time of his retirement until his death Carnahan served as a trustee of the college and as president of the board of trustees of the Theological Seminary. His wife, Mary (Van Dyke) Carnahan, died five years before him in 1854.

[See John Maclean, *Hist. of the Coll. of N. J.* (1877); V. L. Collins, *Princeton* (1914); J. DeWitt, *Princeton College* (1897); J. F. Hageman, *Hist. of Princeton* (1879); and J. W. Wilson, *An Hist. Sketch of the College of N. J.* (1859). Carnahan's writings, largely addresses and sermons, are listed in Maclean, II, 405–06. A complete collection is in the Princeton Univ. Lib.]
J. E. P.

CARNEGIE, ANDREW (Nov. 25, 1835–Aug. 11, 1919), manufacturer, publicist, and "distributor" of wealth "for the improvement of mankind,"—the word "philanthropist" he scornfully rejected—was born at Dunfermline, Scotland, the son of William Carnegie, a handloom weaver, and Margaret Morrison, the daughter of Thomas Morrison, a tanner and shoemaker. These progenitors would indicate a humble origin, but Carnegie himself regarded his family inheritance as a rich one. Though Carnegie's father lacked the imaginative resourcefulness and impatient energy that made his son so conspicuous a leader in many fields, he had the political sense, the eagerness for social progress, and the love of books that had for generations distinguished the damask trade. In Dunfermline to-day, William Carnegie is remembered, above all, as "an awfu' man to read." He was moreover an active political figure in his region, and an advanced radical,—an organizer of anti-Corn Law processions and a Chartist leader. On Carnegie's maternal side these tendencies were even more marked. His grandfather, Thomas Morrison, was one of the most irrepressible agitators of Scotland. He was the friend and correspondent of William Cobbett, and himself a contributor to Cobbett's *Register*. There was not a step intended to promote human progress or to advance liberty, enlightenment and toleration,—a reformed Commons, a democratic ballot, new factory laws, Catholic emancipation, freedom of trade, the destruction of hereditary privilege, the abolition of kings and armies—that Thomas Morrison did not advocate on the public platform,—and advocate with great native eloquence, and a wealth of argument that was the product of a lifetime spent in self-education. A collection of his newspaper letters still exists in which he vigorously assails the legislative shortcomings of Lord Dalmeny, at that time (1835) the representative of Stirling Burghs in Parliament—the same Lord Dalmeny whose son, Lord Rosebery, the Prime Minister, afterward became one of Andrew Carnegie's best friends. The elder Morrison likewise enjoys a certain fame as a pioneer in technical education; an article once widely circulated was his contribution to Cobbett's *Register* (Dec. 21, 1833) on " 'Heddekashun' and 'Handication,' " containing ideas of which his grandson afterward became an enthusiastic exponent.

The romantic strain acquired from his father found abundant nourishment in the surroundings of Carnegie's childhood. Dunfermline itself, as a great national shrine, is hardly second to Edinburgh. Here Scottish history began with King Malcolm Canmore, the successor of Macbeth on the Scottish throne, and his pious Queen Margaret. Dunfermline Abbey—the Westminster of Scotland—is the burial place of twenty Scottish royalties, including many kings and queens; and there lie the bones of King Robert the Bruce, only a few hundred yards from the humble Carnegie cottage, on the corner of Moodie St. and Priory Lane. The Abbey ruins; the nearby Stuart Palace in which Charles I was born; Loch Leven, with its memories of Mary Stuart, eight miles away; the Firth of Forth and the Pentland Hills, which Carnegie could see from the hill on which his birthplace stood—in all this historic country there was plenty to stimulate a sensitive child. Andrew's family and relatives exercised the liveliest effect upon his sentimental nature. His uncle, George Lauder, was his principal instructor. This uncle kept a grocery shop in the High St., the back room of which formed the favorite congregating place of Carnegie and his cousin, George. Here the older man, a gentle, dreamy soul, a lover of flowers, of music, of poetry, and of Scottish history, filled Andrew's mind with stories of Bruce, Wallace, Rob Roy, and other Celtic heroes. Above all, he implanted a love of Burns, teaching the boy to learn pages by heart, with the result that Carnegie, up to his last days, had the words of the national bard constantly on his lips. To "Uncle" Lauder, Burns meant more than mere romance, for to him, as always to Carnegie, the poet was one of the greatest preachers of democracy. Next to Scotland and Burns, Lauder's interest was the United States; the fervid admiration which Carnegie always evinced for American institutions was thus part of his childhood training. The influence that shaped his political opinion was another uncle, his mother's brother, "Bailie" Morrison. This reformer, like his father, Cobbett's friend, was a political firebrand; in his speeches the Royal Family and the House of Lords were always severely attacked; the Established Church, both of England and Scotland, aroused his most incendiary periods; and such time as he could spare from his trade of shoemaker, he spent in advocating the establishment of an English republic in place of the existing monarchy, and in promoting the interests of the workingmen. Once the Bailie was arrested for his part in the "labor cessation" of 1842; and the glimpse of his uncle behind prison bars, which Andrew obtained at the age of seven, likewise had its effect in arousing an antagonism to privileged institutions. "As a child," said Carnegie, "I could have slain king, duke, or lord, and considered their death a service to the state."

The poverty of the Carnegie family during Andrew's childhood was extreme. The factory system was invading the linen industry, and the day of the individual handloom weaver, who performed his daily task on the ground floor of his own cottage, assisted by wife and children, was passing. Andrew Carnegie vividly remembered the night when his father, after a day's unavailing search for a web, came home a picture of despair, and said, "Well, Andra, I canna get nae mair work." It marked the beginning of hard times in the Carnegie cottage. The mother, always the dominant partner, sought to repair the family fortunes by keeping a "sweetie shop" and binding shoes,—little Andrew sitting at her side threading the needles. The children's upbringing, however, was not neglected. Primary instruction was the natural right of every child born in the country of John Knox, and Andrew obtained this, and even a few scraps of Latin, at a Lancasterian school. But the mother's ambition for her two sons,—the second was Thomas M., eight years Andrew's junior,—was little less than a passion. She saw no future for them in Scotland. Her two sisters and one brother had already settled in the new world; and this became Margaret Carnegie's goal. The passage money proved a serious problem; friends of Margaret's childhood, however, lent her twenty pounds, the household effects were sold, and in May 1848 the four Carnegies sailed from the Broomielaw in Glasgow on the American ex-whaler *Wiscasset*. After a six weeks' voyage they reached New York, proceeded up the Hudson River and the Erie Canal to Lake Erie, and thence, by lake and canal, to Allegheny, Pa. Here they joined a little Scottish colony including the aunts and uncles already settled there; William Carnegie obtained modest employment in a cotton factory; Andrew was installed in the same building as bobbin boy at $1.20 a week; and little Tom was put to school.

The diminutive white-haired Scottish boy was quickly transformed into an American. At the age of sixteen Andrew began writing letters to friends in Scotland, comparing American life and institutions with those of Great Britain, much to the disadvantage of the latter country. At the same age, he also contributed letters to the newspapers, notably to the *New York Tribune,* on the great questions of the day, especially slavery,—a habit that became a lifelong one. His natural love of reading received a new impetus from the kindly action of Col. James Anderson, who opened his personal library of 400 volumes to working boys, delivering books to them each Saturday night. Carnegie became the most persistent borrower, and the recollection of the great benefits derived from Col. Anderson largely ex-

plains his own library gifts in after years. Indeed, a failure to emphasize Andrew Carnegie's interest in reading, as well as his absorption in politics, history, and certain phases of science and speculative thinking, would make the portrait most incomplete. The years he spent struggling up from poverty were devoted also to the development of his mind. He was a "self-made" man in a more comprehensive sense than the term usually implies, for he was self-made mentally as well as economically. His alertness and determination to succeed soon brought him opportunities. He spent a year or more as bobbin boy and engine tender, the latter the only occupation in which he was ever really unhappy, but his chance came when—he was now fourteen and small for his age—he obtained a job as messenger in the Pittsburgh telegraph office. The pay, $2.50 a week, seemed a fortune. To this experience he traced his great love of Shakespeare: he was frequently sent to deliver messages to the theatre, and usually contrived to make his appearance at night, after the curtain had gone up,—his plea to be permitted to remain being invariably granted by the manager. Most of the time Carnegie was not delivering messages he utilized by listening to the telegraph instrument as the words came over the wire. In those days telegraph operators did not take "by sound"; there was an elaborate instrument that transcribed the letters on a long tape. Andrew soon learned to distinguish the letters by sound, thus becoming one of the first two or three telegraphers in the country so gifted. His employers, discovering his skill, promoted him to an operator's key. "I have got past delivering messages," he wrote his cousin in Scotland (he was now sixteen) "and have got to operating. I am to have four dollars a week now and a good prospect of soon getting more." One of the influential Pittsburghers whom Carnegie met most frequently in the telegraph office was Thomas A. Scott, then beginning his brilliant career with the Pennsylvania Railroad. Presently the astonished Andrew found himself installed in Scott's office as private secretary and personal telegrapher. The salary was $35 a month; "I couldn't imagine," Carnegie used to say, recalling the episode, "what I could ever do with so much money!" He remained with the Pennsylvania twelve years (1853–65), advancing from position to position until he finally succeeded Scott as superintendent of the Pittsburgh Division. Probably Carnegie's greatest achievement as a railroad man was the introduction of Pullman sleeping cars; he acquired a one-eighth interest in the Woodruff Company, the original holder of the Pullman patents. This investment, which was profitable, represented the first considerable sum that Andrew Carnegie had ever earned. His most exciting experience came when he accompanied Mr. Scott to Washington on the outbreak of the Civil War. Scott was made assistant secretary of war in charge of military transportation, and Carnegie became his right-hand man. The first brigade of troops to reach Washington was transported by Carnegie, the doughty Scotsman taking his place on the engine of the first military train into the Federal capital. Soon afterward he superintended the transportation of the defeated Federal forces after the battle of Bull Run, personally loading train after train with the wounded. He organized the telegraph department that rendered such efficient service in the next four years (see Homer D. Bates, *Lincoln in the Telegraph Office*, 1907). His work in the field resulted in a slight sunstroke that made it necessary, for the rest of his life, to spend the summer in cool climates.

The American iron industry received a great impetus from the Civil War. Until that event, American iron had cut no figure in world trade. But the sudden demand for war materials, railway supplies and the like, brought fortunes to the previously struggling iron masters of Pittsburgh. In a small way Carnegie had joined one or two enterprises of the kind; in 1865, however, he resigned from the Pennsylvania Railroad, to devote all of his energies to the new field. Yet his first important venture, the Keystone Bridge Company, represented a continuation of his railroad work; his experience had taught him the inadequacy of wooden bridges for railroads and the usefulness of iron. His acquaintance with railroad men proved a great asset to his company; it was largely owing to Carnegie's infinite ability as a salesman that the success of the Keystone Bridge Company, as well as his other enterprises, was due. Carnegie was now thirty years old; whatever faults his enemies—and he had his share of them—may impute to him, on one point the judgment is unanimous: he was a man of vast personal charm. Far better read than most business men, and far better traveled, with a keen sense of humor, an unrivaled gift for anecdote, a great talent for good-natured controversy and raillery, and at times a genuine literary tang in expression, he soon became in all industrial centers a familiar dinner table companion. These personal qualities paid dividends in orders that poured into his mill. Yet at first his Keystone Bridge Company seemed merely one of several interests that engaged Carnegie's attention. It was not until 1873 that he concentrated on steel. He had made a small fortune in oil and taken several trips to Europe selling railroad securities, dealing chiefly with the London firm of Junius S. Morgan & Company. The last of these was as late as 1872, his commission on this transaction amounting to $150,000. Carnegie operations in bond selling, oil dealing, bridge building and the like were so dashing and so successful that conservative Pittsburgh business men regarded him somewhat doubtfully; what was really courage they looked upon as recklessness, and what was foresight, in their more prosaic minds was regarded as mere gambling. Carnegie's European tours, then and afterward, had results of great consequence. He came into close touch with British steel makers,—then the world's leaders; he obtained a close acquaintance with the Bessemer process, and he formed a friendship with Sir Henry Bessemer, which was maintained until the latter's death. By 1873, therefore, Carnegie was prepared to stake all his possessions, at this time considerable, on what was then a new American industry,—to begin his famous policy, as he himself described it, of "putting all his eggs in one basket, and then watching the basket." Americans did not realize it at the time, but, when Carnegie made this decision, the industrial supremacy of the United States was born. Carnegie himself was thirty-eight years old; significantly, in the same year (1873) that the J. Edgar Thomson Steel Mills were started, he made his first public gift—that of free baths for his native town of Dunfermline, Scotland. In Scottish phrase, Andrew Carnegie was "gathering gear."

Carnegie's business life for the next three decades is, in its larger outlines, the industrial history of the United States for the same period. In 1873 the relative positions of Great Britain and the United States in steel strikingly resembled their present positions in shipping,—England seemed to hold first place by a kind of natural right. Yet our conquest of the steel trade was achieved in a little more than sixteen years. By 1889 the production of America had passed that of Great Britain. In the succeeding forty years this nation increased its steel manufactures at such a rate that even the greatest industrial nations of Europe lagged far behind. More than one cause necessarily explains such a triumph. The great bodies of ore in the Lake Superior regions are an asset that no other country can duplicate. The Carnegie company ultimately purchased or leased the most valuable of these fields. Doubtless tariff favors proved helpful in the early days, though the time soon came when they were no longer needed. Carnegie always described himself as a protectionist of the John

Stuart Mill variety,—the tariff was justified in developing an "infant industry" but was a wicked device when used merely to swell the profits of an established business. Long before he retired (1901) he advocated the removal of duties on steel. Railroad rebates had little to do with the growth of Pittsburgh steel, though at times the Carnegie company received concessions; Carnegie's business life was largely one long battle against his old employer, the Pennsylvania Railroad, which, having a monopoly of Pittsburgh traffic, for years discriminated against that city in favor of Chicago, Cleveland, and other competitive points. The presence of the great Connellsville coke area (developed in the seventies and eighties by the genius of Henry Clay Frick [q.v.], who joined the Carnegie forces in 1882, becoming chairman of Carnegie Brothers, Limited, in 1889, and thus chief executive of the organization), likewise had much to do with the Carnegie triumph. Andrew Carnegie himself, in analyzing the history of his own progress, estimated one element as far more important than all the rest. The world might deprive him of his ores, his coal, his railroads, his steamship lines, his steel mills, his machinery, and, provided one thing only were left, he could guarantee to repeat his success. The one indispensable possession was his organization. The American conquest of steel was, above everything else, a personal achievement. What made Andrew Carnegie first among steel masters was the fact that he was a supreme judge of men, which is only another way of saying that he was a supreme organizer. He once suggested this as his epitaph: "Here lies the man who was able to surround himself with men far cleverer than himself." Among these forceful associates Carnegie would have placed in the first class the famous Capt. "Bill" Jones, who as a maker of steel and commander of men, as well as an inventor of new processes, has probably never had an equal; his own brother, Thomas M. Carnegie, whose early death (in 1886) at the age of forty-three has somewhat obscured his contribution, though in business ability he was entirely worthy of the name he bore; Henry Clay Frick, whose quarrel with his old associates, a sensational episode in steel history, never diminished Carnegie's admiration for his genius as an industrialist; and Charles M. Schwab. There were many more of exceptional talent.

Thus, Carnegie's steel campaign, though Napoleonic in its rapidity and the completeness of its victory, was a case of Napoleon and his marshals. He built up his organization by adhering strictly to democratic principles. His company was put together with the idea of developing talent in the rank and file. Many who ended as heads of great departments and as millionaires, started in the Carnegie works as laborers. Schwab himself began as stake driver at a dollar a day. The Carnegie company, until a few months preceding its absorption in the United States Steel, was never a corporation; not a share of its stock was publicly sold; it was a limited partnership, every dollar being held by men who were active working associates. If a member died or withdrew from the company, his stock was purchased for the treasury at book value; similarly, at any time, owners representing three-fourths of the stock could call in any shares on the same terms, thus forcing the unsuccessful partner to retire. Carnegie himself always held a majority interest; the rest was distributed among a large number of partners,—at the end, about forty. Every man acquired an interest solely on his record. If his work warranted it, he was allotted a small quota, which was increased as his value increased. He was not forced to pay for it in cash, the dividends being set aside for that purpose. The eagerness to obtain such an interest became the incentive that urged every worker to his most heroic efforts, and probably explains, more than any one circumstance, the amazing efficiency of the organization. And Andrew Carnegie, at the head, gave, for thirty years, an illustration of superb generalship. His success was the result of his optimism, enthusiasm, and courage. He was not a gambler; the speculative side of Wall Street he detested; he never bought a share of stock on margin in his life, yet he did make one gamble of titanic proportions,—and won. He wagered everything he possessed on the economic future of the United States. He was probably the most daring man in American industry; his insistence on the most up-to-date machines, his readiness to discard costly equipment as soon as something better appeared, is a tradition in the steel trade. When business was most depressed and steel was apparently facing ruin, that was always the time Carnegie took for action. It was in these periods of depression that he made immense outlays improving his plants. His competitors spent money on buildings and equipment when times were flush, but Carnegie selected hard times for two reasons: first, he could build his extensions at extremely low prices; secondly, he had unbounded faith in the United States and knew that prosperity would return. And when prosperity emerged, he proposed to be ready to supply any demand. His less far-sighted competitors, when business revived, had run-down organizations, and could not meet the requirements of the trade. They would start at once making improvements, but in good times they could do this only at high prices; Carnegie, on the other hand, was not only ready for the rush, but could sell cheaply, for his facilities had cost him so little. Thus, the era from 1893 to 1897 was one of great industrial depression and most steel factories ran to seed. This was precisely the time that Carnegie took for developing his works. When prosperity came with a flood tide, he had the whole steel industry at his mercy. The price at which he made rails, steel, and other products, meant vast profits for himself and absolute ruin for his competitors. In 1900 the profits of the Carnegie Company were $40,000,000, of which Carnegie's share was about $25,000,000.

The steel business, important as it was to Carnegie's career, seems almost to have been merely an avocation. Carnegie's early ambition inclined to journalism and authorship, and his ideas on the uses of wealth were also no improvisation of his mature years. Among his papers is a memorandum, written in 1868, before his career as a steel maker had begun: "Thirty-three," he wrote, "and an income of $50,000 per annum! . . . Beyond this never earn,—make no effort to increase fortune, but spend the surplus each year for benevolent purposes. Cast aside business for ever, except for others. Settle in Oxford and get a thorough education, making the acquaintance of literary men—this will take three years' active work—pay especial attention to speaking in public. Settle then in London and purchase a controlling interest in some newspaper or live review and give the general management of it attention, taking a part in public matters, especially those connected with education and improvement of the poorer classes. Man must have an idol—the amassing of wealth is one of the worst species of idolatry—no idol more debasing than the worship of money. Whatever I engage in I must push inordinately; therefore should I be careful to choose that life which will be the most elevating in its character. To continue much longer overwhelmed by business cares and with most of my thoughts wholly upon the way to make more money in the shortest time, must degrade me beyond hope of permanent recovery. I will resign business at thirty-five, but during the ensuing two years I wish to spend the afternoons in receiving instruction and in reading systematically."

Certain items in this program the young man did not carry out: he did not cease money making,—at least until more than thirty years afterward; he did not spend three years in Oxford;

and he did not settle permanently in London. The spirit of this memorandum, however, was precisely the spirit of Carnegie's life. He made many friends in the literary and political world. Among them were Matthew Arnold, who came to the United States in 1883 as Carnegie's guest; Sir Edwin Arnold, who gave him as a keepsake the original manuscript of "The Light of Asia"; Herbert Spencer, "the man to whom I owe most," Carnegie said; William E. Gladstone, John Morley, Lord Rosebery, Joseph Chamberlain, Sir William Vernon Harcourt, Frederic Harrison, James Bryce, William T. Stead, John Burns, and Lloyd George; while in the United States his correspondents and acquaintances included practically all the American presidents, statesmen, and writers of his time, with chief emphasis upon James G. Blaine, Theodore Roosevelt, Richard Watson Gilder, Mark Twain, Elihu Root, and Andrew D. White. The *Adventures of a Phaeton* of his friend William Black, inspired Carnegie's famous coaching trip through England and Scotland in 1881, including a triumphal entry into his birthplace, Dunfermline, where his mother, aged seventy, laid the foundation of the first Carnegie Library,—a summer experience recorded in Carnegie's book, *An American Four-in-Hand in Britain* (1883). Carnegie, though actively in business, now became a frequent contributor to serious magazines, especially the *Nineteenth Century,* under the editorship of James Knowles, and the *North American Review,* in its most influential period, under Lloyd Bryce. In 1886 he startled both America and Great Britain with his volume *Triumphant Democracy.* The book was a statistical pæan; its purpose was to exhibit the vast superiority of Republican institutions over Monarchical, and specifically of the American system over the British. The red cover displayed a representation of a royal crown, printed bottom end up, of a broken scepter and an inverted pyramid,—the latter a thrust at what Carnegie regarded as the topsy-turvy monarchical principle. The volume not only contained a glowing account of American progress, but several extremely harsh hits at the British Royal Family,— a fact that caused some scandal in England. The book first opened the eyes of Americans themselves to their rapid economic progress, and more than 40,000 copies were sold in a brief time. Carnegie's strictures on the British aristocracy implied no hostility to the British people; indeed, he loved England and Scotland with all the intensity of his nature, and one of the great purposes of his life was to do a part in making closer the bonds uniting the English-speaking nations. But he believed that the best way he could show his devotion to Britain was to assist in the reform of its political and social institutions. With this ambitious plan in mind, he purchased, in the early eighties, a string of newspapers in England, which rigorously advocated the abolition of the monarchy and the establishment of the British Republic. These manifestations never alienated Carnegie's English friendships. He was a welcome guest of Gladstone at Hawarden Castle, and to him Gladstone turned when his friend, Lord Acton, faced the possibility of losing his great library. Carnegie advanced $50,000 to prevent foreclosure, leaving the library in Acton's possession for life, and, after the great scholar's death, giving it to John Morley, who passed it on to its permanent resting place in Cambridge University. Long before this transaction John Morley had become Carnegie's closest friend. The two men corresponded for nearly forty years, from 1883 to 1919; the profound scholar and accomplished stylist discovered in the self-educated iron-master and natural philosopher the most personally congenial of his associates. In his letters Morley frequently refers to "my friends, of whom I place you and Mrs. Carnegie at the top of the list."

Carnegie caused a great stir in June 1889 when his article, "Wealth," appeared in the *North American Review.* Gladstone at once requested its republication in England, and it presently appeared in William T. Stead's *Pall Mall Gazette,* under the amended caption by which it will always be known, "The Gospel of Wealth." Gladstone was so interested that he contributed an article to the *Nineteenth Century,* and soon all the newspapers, magazines, and reviews in Europe and America were discussing Carnegie's ideas. The conception of the responsibility of rich men which Carnegie set forth was then new. The point that caught the imagination of mankind was Carnegie's central one: that the life story of a rich man should fall into two periods,—the first, that of acquiring wealth, the second, that of distributing it. The popular mind misconstrued one sentence as meaning that a "man who dies rich dies disgraced," but Carnegie never phrased the matter quite so pungently. He insisted that the first duty of every man was to provide a competence for his family. This competence, of course, should bear some relation to the manner of existence his wife and children had observed in his own lifetime. The rich man who really "died disgraced" was the one who died leaving great sums which he might himself have administered for the public good. Carnegie accepted on the whole the estab-

lished economic and political system; he was then, and so remained to his death, a disbeliever in socialism. Yet he recognized that the accumulation of enormous sums in the hands of industrial leaders was a result of capitalism that held great possibilities of evil. So far as these leaders stimulated industry and performed their part in unloosing natural and human energies for the growth of society, they were a valuable national asset, indeed, Carnegie believed, they were indispensable. But their reward, if used for their own selfish purposes, far exceeded the value of their services. Carnegie granted that the people as a whole had created the fortunes concentrated in individual hands; what the community had piled up should be returned to it. The millionaire who properly recognized his own position was merely a "trustee"; he held his surplus wealth for the benefit of his fellows. After discussing the subject in all its aspects, Carnegie concluded that the rich man should himself administer his surplus wealth in his own lifetime for the public good; the accumulator of great possessions was *prima facie* an exceptional person, and it became his duty to use the talents which had made his fortune by distributing it for "the improvement of mankind."

Carnegie was fifty-four years old when he promulgated his gospel; his fortune, in 1889, though amounting to many millions, was a small one compared with the great size it ultimately reached. In the decade from 1890 to 1900 it increased at flood tide. Yet the annual accretions did not represent his main interest. It was no secret, several years before his retirement, that he wished to sell. Certain misunderstood events, such as the Homestead strike of 1892, and personal difficulties which began to develop inside the organization, finally culminating in the break with Henry C. Frick, perhaps accentuated this desire; the main reason, however, was the same as that which had inspired the above-quoted memorandum of 1868,—a desire to use his wealth for public purposes, to cultivate his friendships, and to develop his own soul. Carnegie was a man of the deepest domestic affections. As a boy he had dreamed of becoming rich, so that his mother might dress in silks and ride in her own carriage; and the devotion he lavished on her is one of the great traditions of Pittsburgh. He remained a bachelor during his mother's lifetime; soon after her death, however, he married (1887) a lady who had been a close friend for several years,—Louise Whitfield, of New York. In his married life Carnegie was fortunate; his wife made not only an ideal companion and an accomplished hostess, but she sympathized with all his plans for distributing his wealth and assisted him in executing them. For ten years succeeding their marriage, Mr. and Mrs. Carnegie spent six months of almost every year at Cluny Castle, Kingussie, Inverness-shire, Scotland; in 1898 they acquired a large tract, eventually amounting to nearly 40,000 acres, on Dornoch Firth, Sutherlandshire, and there built Skibo Castle, which remained their favorite residence until the World War.

After one or two abortive negotiations to dispose of his business, Carnegie finally sold the Carnegie Company to the newly-formed United States Steel Corporation, in January 1901. His remark to J. P. Morgan, after signing the papers of sale, really expressed the feeling of many years. "Well, Pierpont," he said, "I am now handing the burden over to you." For his share Carnegie received $250,000,000 in five per cent fifty-year gold bonds. His first act after his retirement was to give the employees of the Carnegie Company $5,000,000 in the form of a pension and benefit fund.

Carnegie lived for nearly twenty years after abdicating his position in the industrial world, and devoted most of his time to putting into practise his own gospel of wealth. Had he merely placed his fortune at interest, subtracting the comparatively modest amount needed for personal expenses, it would have made him the first American billionaire practically in his own lifetime. But, as fortunes are estimated to-day, Carnegie died a man of moderate wealth. His benefactions amounted to $350,000,000,—for he gave away not only his annual income of something more than $12,500,000, but most of the principal as well. Of this sum, $62,000,000 was allotted to the British Empire and $288,000,000 to the United States, for Carnegie, in the main, confined his benefactions to the English-speaking nations. His largest gifts were $125,000,000 to the Carnegie Corporation of New York (this same body also became his residuary legatee), $60,000,000 to public library buildings, $20,-000,000 to colleges (usually the smaller ones), $6,000,000 to church organs, $29,000,000 to the Carnegie Foundation for the Advancement of Teaching, $22,000,000 to the Carnegie Institute of Pittsburgh, $22,000,000 to the Carnegie Institution of Washington, $10,000,000 to Hero Funds, $10,000,000 to the Endowment for International Peace, $10,000,000 to the Scottish Universities Trust, $10,000,000 to the United Kingdom Trust, and $3,750,000 to the Dunfermline Trust. These gifts fairly picture Carnegie's conception of the best ways to improve the status of the common man. They represent all his personal tastes,—

his love of books, art, music, and nature—and the reforms which he regarded as most essential to human progress,—scientific research, education both literary and technical, and, above all, the abolition of war. The expenditure the public most associates with Carnegie's name is that for public libraries. Carnegie himself frequently said that his favorite benefaction was the Hero Fund,—among other reasons, because "it came up my ain back"; but probably deep in his own mind his library gifts took precedence over all others in importance. There was only one genuine remedy, he believed, for the ills that beset the human race, and that was enlightenment. "Let there be light" was the motto that, in the early days, he insisted on placing in all his library buildings. As to the greatest endowment of all, the Carnegie Corporation, that was merely Andrew Carnegie in permanently organized form; it was established to carry on, after Carnegie's death, the work to which he had given personal attention in his own lifetime.

Many honors came to Carnegie. He received the Freedom of fifty-four cities, was granted honorary degrees from many institutions of learning, and was elected Lord Rector of the Universities of St. Andrews and Aberdeen. In 1908 King Edward, through Lord Morley, asked Carnegie if he would accept an "honor" at his hands. This clearly indicated a title. Carnegie declined: in becoming the world's second richest man, he had not surrendered his democratic principles; besides, such a distinction would mean the abandonment of his American citizenship, which he regarded as a priceless possession. All his active days Carnegie advocated world peace and arbitration; in his final years, especially as he saw the great conflagration approaching, this became his absorbing interest. Besides his peace endowments, he built the Peace Palace at The Hague, made a visit to Kaiser William II in 1907, and corresponded with that potentate on the same subject. How deeply world peace entered into Carnegie's being became painfully apparent on the outbreak of war in August 1914. Up to that time, though nearly eighty years old, he retained his activity of mind and body. He was never the same man afterward. He approved Great Britain's declaration of war, and strongly indorsed American participation in 1917. But he rapidly became a very old man, and died, at his summer home, "Shadowbrook," Mass., on Aug. 11, 1919, in his eighty-fourth year. He was survived by his wife and one daughter, Margaret Carnegie (Mrs. Roswell Miller). He was buried in Sleepy Hollow on the Hudson.

[There is as yet no adequate biography of Andrew Carnegie, though his personal papers are of great extent and value. The best account of his life is his own *Autobiography* published (and edited by John C. Van Dyke) in 1920. It is racy in style, full of character, and extremely entertaining, though most incomplete as a record of Carnegie's life,—which it was never intended to be. Wm. T. Stead's *Mr. Carnegie's Conundrum: £40,000,000: What shall I do with it?* (1900) has considerable biographical material. Bernard Alderson's *Andrew Carnegie* (1902) is a popular sketch. *The Inside Hist. of the Carnegie Steel Company* by Jas. Howard Bridge (1903) has little value as history because its all too obvious purpose is to "muckrake" the great steel magnate. Herbert Casson's *The Romance of Steel* (1907) is sprightly, informative, and accurate. *A Carnegie Anthology* (1915) privately printed, by Margaret Barclay Wilson, is a most valuable compendium of Carnegie's opinions and philosophy. There are hundreds of articles on Carnegie in the magazines and newspapers of all countries, and scores of books and biographies contain passages concerning him. Carnegie's own bibliography, consisting of books, magazine articles and speeches, is a long one. His most important books are: *Round the World* (1881); *An American Four-in-Hand in Britain* (1883); *Triumphant Democracy* (1886, revised 1893); *The Gospel of Wealth* (collected essays, 1901); *The Empire of Business* (1902); *James Watt* (1905); and *Problems of To-day* (1908). *A Book of Carnegie Libraries*, by Thos. Wesley Koch (1917) is a complete history of its subject, and *A Manual of the Public Benefactions of Andrew Carnegie* (1919), published by the Carnegie Endowment for International Peace, is a statistical study, with much historical matter, of the practical outcome of Carnegie's "Gospel."]

B. J. H.

CARNEY, THOMAS (Aug. 20, 1824–July 28, 1888), governor of Kansas, the son of James and Sarah Carney, was born on a small farm in Delaware County, Ohio. When Thomas was four years old, his father died, and the boy remained with his mother to help support the family until he was nineteen. Having secured a common-school education, he took a position with a wholesale house in Cincinnati, of which in June 1852 he became a partner. He was married in 1851 to Rebecca Ann Canaday of Kenton, Ohio. Carney, Swift & Company soon became one of the most prosperous and best-known mercantile firms in the Middle West. Several years of strenuous effort here impaired his health. Desiring to recuperate and to find a new location he purchased a farm in Illinois and engaged temporarily in the live-stock business. In 1858 or 1859 he removed to Leavenworth, Kan., where he and Thomas Stevens established a wholesale house which soon did a large business. Later he became the sole proprietor of two successful wholesale houses in St. Louis. He was elected a member of the Kansas legislature in 1861. His ability and service soon brought him into favorable notice. In September 1862 he received the Republican nomination for governor and a few weeks later was elected by a majority of 4,627 votes over W. R. Wagstaff, his opponent. He then arranged to withdraw his attention from business and to give his en-

tire time and energy to the duties of his office.

An able executive was badly needed. The state's credit was poor and its treasury empty. There were dangers incident to civil war. Guerrilla bands from Missouri threatened the state on the eastern side and hostile Indians menaced its western settlements. Under the leadership of the new governor the legislature voted a bond issue sufficient to provide for the needs of the state. Being a rich man, Carney personally endorsed the bonds and guaranteed the payment of both principal and interest when due. They were then readily sold at a satisfactory price. A military patrol was organized for the eastern counties of the state and paid from the Governor's private funds until Federal troops for guard duty were available. It was after this change was made that the Quantrill's guerrillas slipped across the border, sacked the town of Lawrence on July 21, 1863, and murdered not less than one hundred and fifty unarmed men.

During Carney's administration the state's penal, philanthropic, and higher educational institutions were established. In February 1864 he was elected United States senator for the term beginning Mar. 4, 1865. As this election was held in advance of the usual time and its legality doubtful he never claimed the seat. In the fall of 1864 he called out the entire militia of the state, 12,622 in number, to resist Gen. Price who had invaded Missouri and eastern Kansas. In January 1865 Carney retired to private life with an excellent record as a public official. His remaining years were uneventful.

[*Kansas Annual Reg.* (1864); D. W. Wilder, *Annals of Kansas* (1875–86); Wm. G. Cutler, ed., *Hist. of Kansas* (1883); Frank W. Blackmar, ed., *A Cyc. of Kansas Hist.* (1912); *Kansas Hist. Colls.*, vols. VIII (1904), XI (1910), XII (1912); *Portrait and Biog. Rec. of Leavenworth, Douglas and Franklin Counties, Kan.* (1899); *Leavenworth Evening Standard*, July 28, 1888; *Topeka Daily Capital*, July 29, 1888; the Carney family records.]

T. L. H.

CARNOCHAN, JOHN MURRAY (July 4, 1817–Oct. 28, 1887), surgeon, was born in Savannah, Ga. He was the son of John Carnochan, a wealthy Scotch merchant and planter, and of Harriet Frances Putnam, a collateral descendant of Gen. Israel Putnam [*q.v.*]. On account of delicate health he was raised in Scotland, in the Carnochan homestead (Gate House, Fleet, Kirkcudbright, Galloway) and in Edinburgh, where he graduated from the high school and University (1834) and began the study of medicine. Summoned home, he completed his medical studies in New York, registering as a pupil with Valentine Mott [*q.v.*], who was to speak of him later as "his most distinguished pupil." It was at this period that he made a remarkable minute dissection of the human foot. Having received the degree of M.D. from the College of Physicians and Surgeons, New York, in 1836, he at once returned to Europe for post-graduate study, spending six full years in the Paris hospitals, walking the hospital wards with the leading local surgeons, including such men as Lisfranc, Velpeau, and Civiale. He then removed to London where he studied surgery under Sir Astley Cooper and Sir Benjamin Brodie and was offered a partnership by the surgeon Liston. He did not return to America until 1847, when he located in New York as a general practitioner. In 1851 he received the appointment of surgeon-in-chief of the new State Emigrant Hospital at Ward's Island, then the largest in the country, while from 1851 to 1862 he was professor of surgery at the New York Medical College. Beginning in 1851 he performed and published an account of a brilliant series of operations which gave him an international reputation, and in 1858 he published his first series of *Contributions to Operative Surgery and Surgical Pathology*. Among his surgical pioneer efforts were: the cure of an apparently incurable case of elephantiasis Arabum by ligation of the femoral artery; the removal of the entire lower jaw for post-typhoid necrosis; the exsection of the entire ulna with preservation of the arm functions; and the exsection of the entire superior maxillary nerve for the radical cure of neuralgia (which he performed five times). It was said of him that he had performed every capital operation, this including five cases of successful amputation at the hip joint. He had a successful record as an ovariotomist and was a pioneer in operating for congenital dislocation of the hip, on which subject he published a large monograph, *Etiology, Pathology and Treatment of Congenital Dislocation of the Head of the Femur* (1850). Among his interesting case reports was one on survival for eleven days with a bullet in the heart, the patient having been the notorious "Bill" Poole. During 1870–71, he reappeared in public life as health officer of the port. A consultation with a colleague who had been accused of flirting with homeopathic remedies led to a breach with the medical profession, terminated by Carnochan's resignation from the New York County Medical Society. From that period his chief interest was in the New York Medico-Legal Society. Continuing to publish his *Contributions to Operative Surgery*, he issued a series in 1877–78 and was at work on another volume when stricken with apoplexy. His last monograph, *Cerebral Localization in Relation to*

Insanity, appeared in 1884. Upon his death he was highly eulogized as a surgeon and man by the Medico-Legal Society. His wife, Estelle Morris, a lineal descendant of Lewis Morris [*q.v.*], was an accomplished artist who illustrated his papers.

[S. W. Francis, "Biographical Sketches of Distinguished Living N. Y. Surgeons," *Medic. and Surgic. Reporter*, XI, 383, June 18, 1864; Clark Bell and others in *Medico-Legal Jour.*, 1887–88, V, 346.]

E. P.

CARONDELET, FRANCISCO LUIS HECTOR, Baron de (*c.* 1748–Aug. 10, 1807), governor of Louisiana and West Florida, was born at Noyelles, Flanders. He belonged to a distinguished Burgundian family, originally from Poligny and Dole, which had played an important part in the political and artistic life of Burgundy in the fifteenth and sixteenth centuries ("Mémoire sur L'Abbaye de Montbenoit et sur les Carondelet" in *Mémoires de L'Académie de Besançon*, 1865–67). He was the son of Juan Luis Nicolas de Carondelet, Baron de Carondelet y de Noyelles, Viscount hereditary of Langle, Lord of Hernue, Hayne-Saint-Pierre, la Hestre and Briâtre, and of Rosa Plunkett of Dunsany (daughter of Edward Plunkett, Baron Dunsany in the Irish peerage, and of Maria de Alen). He himself married into an influential Spanish family, for his brother-in-law, Luis de las Casas, was captain-general of Cuba and of Louisiana and the Floridas during Carondelet's administration in Louisiana. The Baron was a man of energy, moderately enlightened, conscientious, tenacious, and brave. He devoted himself to public works, built a canal that gave New Orleans an outlet to the Gulf by way of Lake Pontchartrain, reformed the police and instituted a street lighting system in the capital, strove to ameliorate the condition of the slaves, risked his career to protect the commerce of Louisiana against the unwise policy of the Spanish Court, and labored incessantly to repel the rising tide of American frontiersmen and to extend Spain's dominion over the whole of the Mississippi Valley. Despite his family connections and personal merit, his administration was most unfortunate for Spain, for the province, and for Carondelet himself. His task was one of extreme difficulty, and he was not fitted for it by either temperament or training. The pressure of the American frontiersmen and their government, the schemes of Genêt, G. R. Clark, and William Blount, the restiveness of the French Creoles, the menace of a servile insurrection, the vagaries of powerful Indian tribes and their British traders, the incompetent meddling of a distant court—in these were problems to tax a master mind; and Carondelet was a man of quite ordinary mentality. He came to his border province, from the governorship of San Salvador in Guatemala, utterly ignorant of the English language and of local conditions. He was slow to learn, loath to take the advice of his better informed subordinates, and unable to discriminate between the false and the true, the fantastic and the probable, in the many wild rumors that came to his ears from all quarters of America and Europe.

Accompanied by his wife and daughter, he arrived at New Orleans in the twenty-ninth year of his service of the king, and on Dec. 30, 1791, he took over the government and intendancy of Louisiana and West Florida. One of the first problems that received his attention was that of Indian relations. He succeeded in capturing the interloper, W. A. Bowles, in persuading Alexander McGillivray to renounce his connection with the United States, in promoting the interests of the Anglo-Spanish fur traders, Panton, Leslie & Company, among the Southern Indians, in forming a defensive alliance with the four Southern tribes (October 1793), and in instigating the Indians to attack the American frontiersmen. He revived the separatist intrigue with James Wilkinson and other American frontiersmen, built a fleet of gunboats on the Mississippi, and extended Spain's military frontier by establishing additional posts within the territory in dispute with the United States. He made land grants to the victims of Gallipolis and to the Baron de Bastrop, and otherwise sought to stimulate the growth of Louisiana. His very successes, however, only embarrassed his government, for they were a heavy tax on the disordered finances of Spain, and offended the United States at a critical moment. His domestic policy was equally unfortunate. Arbitrary arrests alienated the Creoles, and lax enforcement of the commercial restrictions led to his removal from the intendancy in October 1793. After the treaty of San Lorenzo was signed (1795), he had some influence in delaying its execution, and continued the Kentucky intrigue with unabated vigor. On Aug. 5, 1797, he closed his term of office as governor of Louisiana, having been named president of the Royal Audiencia and governor general of Quito. On June 20, 1798, he was ordered to take possession of this post, and on Feb. 20, 1799, he reported that he had done so. He was granted release from the position on May 11, 1807, but died on Aug. 10, 1807, while still discharging his duties. He was buried in the vault of St. Peter of the Cathedral Church of the city of Quito (according to documents now in the private archives of the Duke of Bailen).

[A. P. Whitaker, *Spanish-American Frontier* (1927); "Spain and the Cherokee Indians, 1783–98," *N. C. Hist. Rev.*, IV, 252; Jane M. Berry, "The Indian Policy of Spain in the Southwest, 1783–95," *Miss. Valley Hist. Rev.*, III, 462; Manuel Serrano y Sanz, *El Brigadier Jaime Wilkinson* . . . (Madrid, 1915); *España y los Indios Cherokis y Chactas* . . . (Seville, 1916); Chas. Gayarré, *Hist. of La.* (1903), vol. III; F. X. Martin, *Hist. of La.* (1882); Alcée Fortier, *Hist. of La.* (1904), vol. II; *Am. Hist. Rev.*, II, 475–505; information from José Ma. Ots, director técnico de estudios del Instituto Hispano-Cubano.]   A. P. W.

CARPENTER, CYRUS CLAY (Nov. 24, 1829–May 29, 1898), governor of Iowa, was born of pioneer stock at Harford, Susquehanna County, Pa. His parents were Asahel and Amanda M. (Thayer) Carpenter. As a boy he worked on the farm and acquired the rudiments of an education by attending the neighborhood school in the winter. In order to prepare himself to teach he enrolled in the academy at Harford. At eighteen he began teaching school, and for the next four years divided his time between teaching and attending the academy. He chose Iowa as his future home because "he liked the looks of it on the map." On his way he stopped for two years in Licking County, Ohio, where he taught school and worked on a farm in the summer. With his meager savings he again set out for the West, arriving at Fort Dodge in the summer of 1854 without funds, but endowed with robust health, a good education for that day, and ambition to become a leader. At Fort Dodge he became the first school-teacher of the community. He also engaged in the task of surveying land, and was chosen county surveyor in 1856. In the midst of these various duties he studied law and in due time was admitted to the bar. In the early spring of 1857 he joined the relief expedition from Fort Dodge to the scene of the Spirit Lake Massacre. He never forgot the hardships suffered on this journey through deep drifts of snow and the bitter cold of northwestern Iowa. Later in 1857 he was elected to a seat in the Iowa General Assembly. At the outbreak of the Civil War he enlisted as a private, but soon received a commission as captain, serving in turn on the staff of W. S. Rosecrans, Grenville M. Dodge, and John A. Logan. With the rank of lieutenant-colonel, he was commissary of subsistence in Sherman's army on the march to the sea. At the close of the war, he was mustered out with the rank of colonel by brevet. His dependability and good judgment had enabled him to perform his laborious duties in a faithful and efficient manner that won the commendation of his superior officers. In 1864 he married Susan C. Burkholder of Fort Dodge. Both were lovers of good literature and their home was "rich with the atmosphere of books."

In 1866 Carpenter was elected register of the

land office by the Republicans of Iowa. He spent two terms in this capacity, and then became the candidate of his party for governor. He was elected to this office in 1871, and reëlected in 1873. His administration was during a period of adjustment, years of industrial and social transition. State control of the railroads was a paramount issue. The Governor's attitude in this controversy was clearly indicated by his oft-quoted phrase, "the exorbitant railway rate is the skeleton in the Iowa corn crib." The so-called "Granger Law" regulating railroads in Iowa was passed during his administration. Carpenter also took a firm stand in favor of adequate support for state institutions. At the close of his second term as governor he was appointed second comptroller of the Treasury of the United States, and served in that capacity nearly two years. In 1878 he accepted a position on the newly-created railroad commission in Iowa, but soon resigned in order to run for Congress. Twice elected to the House of Representatives, he occupied a seat in that body from 1879 to 1883. Perhaps his most distinguished service in Congress was his successful support of the measure to create a Department of Agriculture (*Congressional Record,* 47 Cong., 1 Sess., XIII, pp. 3719–23). In 1884 he was again elected to the General Assembly of Iowa where his age and experience made him much respected. In his later years he served as postmaster of Fort Dodge.

[Sen. J. P. Dolliver, "Ex-Gov. Cyrus C. Carpenter," in the *Midland Mo.,* X, 75–81 ; Benj. F. Gue, *Hist. of Iowa from the Earliest Times to the Beginning of the Twentieth Century* (1903), IV, 42 ; numerous references in the *Official Records* (Army) ; Carpenter's own account of the Spirit Lake expedition and sketches of Civil War days in the *Annals of Iowa,* 3 ser., III, 481–91 ; his official utterances as governor of Iowa in *The Messages and Proclamations of the Governors of Iowa,* ed. by Benj. F. Shambaugh, IV (1903), 3–279 ; his speeches in the Forty-sixth and the Forty-seventh Congress in the *Cong. Record,* vols. IX to XIV (see Index).]   B. E. M.

CARPENTER, EDMUND JANES (Oct. 16, 1845–Feb. 21, 1924), journalist and author, found in his New England background and ancestry absorbing interests to which he gave expression in several of his printed books. On his father's side, he was descended from William Carpenter who came to Weymouth, Mass., in 1638, in the ship *Bevis.* On his mother's side he was descended from Jonathan Walcott, who was in Salem at least as early as 1662. He, himself, was born in North Attleboro, Mass., the son of George Moulton Carpenter, a minister, and, after his removal to Providence, R. I., about 1855, a presiding elder of the Methodist Episcopal Church, who, in 1843, married Sarah Lewis Walcott. They had two sons. The elder, also named George Moulton, was graduated from Brown University in 1864,

practised law, became a justice of the Supreme Court of Rhode Island, and afterward a federal judge. Edmund Janes was graduated from Brown in 1866, and received the degree of Litt.D. from that institution in 1905. After graduation, he tried his hand at several kinds of business, and finally found work to his liking, writing for the *Providence Journal.* Afterward, he worked successively on the *New Haven Palladium,* and on three Boston papers, the *Globe, Advertiser,* and *Transcript.* At the time of his death he had been writing for the last-named paper for twenty years. In 1873, he was married to Lydia Etta Snow of Providence, by whom he had six children. He died in Milton, Mass., which had been his home for many years.

Carpenter had a versatile mind and a facile pen. He was the author of short stories and occasional poems ; contributed to magazines for young people, such as *Wide Awake* and *St. Nicholas,* and also to other magazines ; made translations ; wrote book reviews, editorials, and a number of books. His earliest book, *A Woman of Shawmut* (1891), published originally in serial form in the *New England Magazine,* was a romance, gracefully told, of colonial times ; was based in part upon historical fact ; and was the first fruit of Carpenter's interest in the story of the Massachusetts Bay and Plymouth settlements. The book was dedicated to William Dean Howells, to whom, in a dedicatory letter, Carpenter made acknowledgments for suggestion as well as for encouragement. Next, he aided William Kent in preparing the latter's *Memoirs and Letters of James Kent* (1898). With the acquisition of the Hawaiian Islands, Carpenter wrote *America in Hawaii* (1899), a compact and useful historical statement of the relations between the islands and the United States which led to annexation. *The American Advance* (1903) is a similar statement of the territorial expansion of the United States. A different interest is revealed in his *Hellenic Tales* (1906), stories for boys and girls, published also the same year under the title *Long Ago in Greece.* In later works Carpenter returned to his studies of New England colonial history. His *Roger Williams* (1909), based on original sources, presented in fluent style a well tempered rather than controversial account. Following this study came *The Pilgrims and Their Monument* (1918), the latter inscribed "To the memory of my far-away kinswoman, Alice Carpenter, wife of Governor Bradford."

[*Boston Transcript,* Feb. 21, 1924 ; Arthur S. Walcott, *The Walcott Book* (1925) ; Amos B. Carpenter, *A Geneal. Hist. of the Rehoboth Branch of the Carpenter Family in America* (1898) ; *Hist. Cat. Brown Univ.* (1914).]   W. A. S.

CARPENTER, FRANCIS BICKNELL

(Aug. 6, 1830–May 23, 1900), portrait painter, was born at Homer, N. Y., the son of a farmer, Asaph A. Carpenter. As a boy he sketched pictures on smooth pieces of board and leaves torn from old account books. Later he watched an itinerant painter at work and attempted to imitate him with the crude materials that a moneyless country boy might find about the farm,—lampblack used for marking sheep, old dried lumps of Venetian red, worn carriage painters' brushes. Finally his father allowed him to spend five months at Syracuse with an artist named Sanford Thayer. With only so much training, Carpenter, now sixteen years old, set up a studio in his native village. His first big fee was ten dollars for illustrating a book on sheep husbandry by Henry Stephens Randall [q.v.], who, delighted with the pictures of the sheep, immediately ordered his own portrait. Thus encouraged, Carpenter sent examples of his work to competitions in New York, was successful, and in 1851 moved to the metropolis. The next year he married Augusta H. Prentiss, by whom he had a son and a daughter, and was made an associate of the Academy of Design. A full-length portrait of President Fillmore established his reputation, and for a number of years he enjoyed a large measure of popularity, the list of his sitters including many notable men of letters, divines, and statesmen, among them four presidents of the United States. A gentle, meditative man, with long, straight black hair and delicate features, he readily won the regard of his patrons. His exalted patriotism and generous humanitarian sympathies are expressed in a memorable historical painting of Lincoln reading the first draft of the Emancipation Proclamation to his cabinet, which now hangs in the Capitol at Washington. For painting this picture he was accorded unusual facilities. From February to July 1864, he was "turned loose"—as Lincoln put it—in the White House, setting up his huge canvas in the East Room and living on friendly terms with the President and his fractious cabinet. A second product of this association was his *Six Months at the White House* (1866), which in a subsequent edition was misnamed *The Inner Life of Abraham Lincoln* (1867). The book has an artless charm as well as the value of direct testimony. Carpenter's later career was comparatively uneventful. As a friend of Theodore Tilton, he was sucked into the vortex of the Beecher-Tilton scandal and thrown out again, disheveled and humiliated. For the last few years of his life he suffered from dropsy. He died in New York, May 23, 1900.

[*Who's Who in America*, 1899–1900; F. B. Perkins, *The Picture and the Men* (1867); *N. Y. Herald*, May 24, 1900; C. F. Marshall, *The True History of the Brooklyn Scandal* (1874); J. E. P. Doyle, *Plymouth Church and Its Pastor* (1874); J. C. Derby, *Fifty Years among Authors, Books, and Publishers* (1884).]   G. H. G.

CARPENTER, FRANK GEORGE

(May 8, 1855–June 18, 1924), journalist, traveler, author, the son of George F. and Jennette Carpenter, was born at Mansfield, Ohio. He received the degrees of A.B. and A.M. from the University of Wooster, Ohio, in 1877 and 1880. In 1879 he became legislative correspondent at Columbus of the *Cleveland Leader*. His health was so frail that when he married Joanna D. Condict, of Mansfield, in 1883, she was told by a friend that he would not live a year. In Washington, where he went as correspondent for the *Cleveland Leader*, he was at first obliged to spend much time in bed, but by dictating letters to his wife he was able to do his work. In 1888, accompanied by his wife and a new machine called a "caligraph," he started around the world, having formed his own syndicate by arranging with fifteen newspapers to publish his weekly foreign travel letters. So began the travels which extended over thirty-six years, took Carpenter to nearly every part of the world, and resulted in hundreds of syndicate articles and many books. A small son and daughter prevented Mrs. Carpenter from going on later trips as his secretary, but she was his business manager at home, collecting and filing geographical clippings, having his letters typed and sent out, and handling the finances of his syndicate. On some trips his daughter Frances traveled with him as secretary. The articles and the geographical readers and volumes of travel which grew out of them were intended, he said, "for ordinary people like myself . . . and for boys and girls." His public has always appreciated his writing. Numerous adults have found entertainment and geographical education in the Carpenter letters and there are few school children who do not know and love the Carpenter *Readers*, with their simple language, anecdotes, and interesting descriptions. Carpenter's method was to take the children on an imaginary tour and to point out in each country what would interest and instruct them. His *Readers* include: *Asia* (1897); *North America* (1898); *South America* (1899); *Europe* (1902); *Australia, Our Colonies, and Other Islands of the Sea* (1904); *Africa* (1905). The series of *Readers on Commerce and Industry* includes: *How the World is Fed* (1907); *How the World is Clothed* (1908); and *How the World is Housed* (1911). Though possessing successively several comfortable homes in

Washington, Carpenter's favorite home, after 1896, was on a mountain top in the Blue Ridge, Virginia. The mountain, entirely owned and named Joannasberg after Mrs. Carpenter, was crowned by a rambling stone house, with a smaller stone house for library and workshop. There worked, with careful consideration for rest periods, a small, wiry man, never weighing over 115 pounds, with sandy hair, homely features, and blue eyes twinkling through gold-rimmed eyeglasses. After Mrs. Carpenter's death in 1920, Carpenter lived at the Cosmos Club in Washington. In 1918 he gave up his syndicate in order to revise his *Readers,* but in 1921 he formed a new syndicate and began writing a series of *World Travels* (20 vols., published). For this purpose he started on fresh journeys. Attacks of illness failed to discourage him; his last overtook him at Nanking, China.

[*Who's Who in America,* 1922–23; *Washington Evening Star,* June 18, 1924; *Washington Post,* June 18, 1924; a series of three articles written by his daughter, Mrs. Frances Carpenter Huntington, of Washington, D. C., for the Carpenter syndicate newspapers (*Boston Globe, Dallas News, Boisé Capital News, Columbia State, Detroit News, Peoria Star, Raleigh News and Observer*), Mar. 1, 8, 15, 1925; additional information furnished by Mrs. Huntington.]   S. G. B.

CARPENTER, FRANKLIN REUBEN (Nov. 5, 1848–Apr. 1, 1910), mining engineer, was descended from a Sussex family which came to America with William Penn. He was born in Parkersburg, W. Va. His father, John Woodward Carpenter, died when Franklin was less than four years old. His mother, Sarah Rebecca (Taylor) Carpenter became a teacher at the Broaddus Seminary at Clarksburg and later was postmistress there, but she was financially unable to give her son the education he craved. At sixteen he was apprenticed to a jeweler and watchmaker but continued his studies under Dr. Late, the village physician, until he secured a teacher's certificate and was thus enabled to earn a better salary. He saved enough money to take a course in civil engineering at Rector's College in Pruntytown, W. Va. In December 1874 he was married to Annette Howe of Athens, Ohio. In 1878 he opened an engineering office in Georgetown, Colo., where he had been principal of the schools. Some of his work for the next few years included the first survey of the "loop" above Georgetown, and the location of the Loveland Pass Tunnel. In 1886 he went to the Black Hills, attracted by the tin deposits. The following year he became dean of the Territorial (Dakota) School of Mines from which position he resigned two years later. From that time on, his life was devoted to mining engineering. At Deadwood he erected the Deadwood and Dela-

ware Smelter and developed a new mode of operation in semipyritic smelting. In 1900 health conditions in his family necessitated his moving from the Black Hills. He went to Denver where he maintained a consulting mining engineering practise for the rest of his life. In 1904 he successfully turned his attention to the electrostatic concentration of the ores of the Nonesuch Copper Mine at Lake Superior. His last important work was the application of the Longmaid-Henderson process to the treatment of Sudbury copper ores, in which he showed that copper could be rendered soluble while the nickel remained insoluble, and a raw material for making nickel steel in the open-hearth furnace could be made by smelting the residual iron oxide for nickel-bearing pig iron. He contributed a score or more of valuable papers to the technical press, including "Ore-Deposits of the Black Hills of Dakota" and "Pyritic Smelting in the Black Hills" (published in the *Transactions of the American Institute of Mining and Metallurgical Engineers,* XVII, 570–98, XXX, 764–77). While in South Dakota he wrote a book on the geology of the Black Hills. He held a number of patents, largely on processes for treating metals.

[See brief notice in *Engineering News,* LXIII, 448, and the biographical sketch prepared by H. O. Hofman of Boston, in *Trans. Am. Inst. of Mining and Metallurgical Engineers,* vol. XLI.]   E. Y.

CARPENTER, GEORGE RICE (Oct. 25, 1863–Apr. 8, 1909), educator, author, was of old New England ancestry, the son of Charles Carroll Carpenter and Feronia N. (Rice) Carpenter. He was born at the Eskimo River Mission Station, on the Labrador coast, where his parents were engaged in pioneer missionary service. After preparation at Phillips Academy, Andover, he entered Harvard with the class of 1886, and on graduation gained the Rogers Fellowship, which took him abroad for two years of further study, chiefly at Paris and Berlin. On his return he became an instructor in English at Harvard (1888–90), then assistant professor at the Massachusetts Institute of Technology (till 1893), whence he was called to the chair of rhetoric at Columbia University, where he remained until death. At Columbia he showed the remarkable gifts of vision and direction which soon made him one of the natural builders of a rapidly expanding university coping with large and new problems; in various executive and advisory offices, and as leader or participant in nearly every forward movement of the institution, he exerted an influence that will long be felt in its policy. But he overspent his strength in work which, however ably done, was not of his first choice, and died on the threshold of far greater usefulness and power.

His publications were of two main kinds. He wrote and edited a large number of text-books concerned mainly with rhetoric and literary history; and if such books can scarcely win a lasting fame, the unusually high standard they set both to teachers and to publishers should not go unrecorded. More than any of his friends, he regretted that such labors, added to heavy administrative burdens, left too little time for that other work of research and criticism which was always the interest of his heart. Yet from the brilliant *Episode of the Donna Pietosa* (1888), which won him the prize of the Dante Society and a reputation among Dantists here and abroad, through a considerable body of critical writing which includes an excellent sketch of Longfellow (1901), in the Beacon Biographies, to the distinguished treatment of Whittier (1903), in the American Men of Letters Series, and of Whitman (1909), in the English Men of Letters Series, his output was varied and uniformly thoughtful. But even if he had been able to devote a lifetime to thought and writing, it would still have been the man, rather than the author or thinker, whom his friends would have desired to commemorate for his union of clarity and mysticism, of power and simplicity and very manly winsomeness.

[Articles by Wm. T. Brewster in the *Columbia Univ. Quart.*, June 1909 (with portrait), and by Jefferson B. Fletcher in the *Annual Report of the Dante Society*, Boston, 1909, pp. 7–9. A complete bibliography by H. R. Steeves is in the *Columbia Univ. Quart.*, Sept. 1909.]

E. H. W.

CARPENTER, MATTHEW HALE (Dec. 22, 1824–Feb. 24, 1881), lawyer, senator, the son of Ira and Esther Ann (Luce) Carpenter, was born in Moretown, Vt. His baptismal name was "Merritt Hammond," but not liking it, he later changed it to "Matthew Hale." His father was a man of little formal education, but of considerable influence in his community. Frail in body and precocious in mind, young Carpenter did not develop the interests usual with American youth, and he showed early two traits that ever remained with him, a cordial dislike for manual work and a great avidity for books. At fourteen he made his home with Paul Dillingham, a lawyer of Waterbury, Vt., later prominent in politics. At eighteen he entered West Point, but, chafing under military discipline, resigned and resumed his legal studies, first with Dillingham and later with Rufus Choate at Boston. Instead of remaining with either of his masters, however, he migrated to Wisconsin and settled at Beloit in June 1848. Caroline Dillingham,

youngest daughter of his benefactor, became his wife in 1855. As an ardent Democrat of the Douglas stripe he participated in the presidential campaigns of 1848, 1852, and 1856, but he did not himself accept political preferment. In the middle fifties he took up residence in Milwaukee and became for a short time the partner of E. G. Ryan, later chief justice of the Wisconsin supreme court. When the Civil War issues drew men into public controversy, Carpenter urged the election of Douglas so that secession on the part of the South would not be precipitated, something he considered inevitable if Lincoln were elected. He did not, however, believe that Republican success justified secession; that step he considered treason. Physical defects alone prevented him from taking the field. By speeches and public letters he urged vigorous prosecution of the war against the Confederates, and in 1862, in answer to the famous Ryan address—the Democratic platform of that year which arraigned Lincoln's war measures—Carpenter wrote a communication in defense of the government.

In the rôle of legal advocate Carpenter helped to shape the Reconstruction policy of the North. In the Garland case he represented an ex-Confederate, pardoned by President Johnson, who tried to establish his right to practise in United States courts; and in the case of William H. McCardle, a Mississippi editor sentenced by a military tribunal, he pleaded the cause of the United States government. This latter case involved the constitutionality of the military governments in the South as established by the Reconstruction measures of Congress. Though acting in the capacity of attorney in the interest of his clients, his arguments in both instances were in conformity with his views on Reconstruction; namely, that once rebel citizens and rebel states were restored to their position in the Union, they were entitled to full equality with other citizens and other states, but until that restoration had been effected, Congress, the omnipotent political body, had broad discretionary powers as to the method to be used in achieving that end.

Political recognition did not come to Carpenter until 1869, in which year the Republican legislature of Wisconsin sent him to the Senate. There he identified himself, for the most part, with the Radical supporters of President Grant. In one of his greatest public speeches, that at Janesville, June 26, 1873, he courageously but unwisely discussed the two most dangerous issues of the day, the "Salary Grab" and the Crédit Mobilier. He had voted for the salary increase and this mistake was not offset by his vote for its repeal the following year. Besides he had a reputation for indiscreet personal conduct and had won the enmity of the railroads by securing unfavorable decisions from the courts and by advocating federal control of interstate commerce. These obstacles proved insurmountable when he was a candidate for reëlection in 1875; even his friend, Boss E. W. Keyes, could not rally to him the united support of the party. In one of the most bitter and exciting senatorial contests in the history of the state, Carpenter was defeated by a coalition of Democrats and dissenting Republicans, most of whom were followers of the Senator's rival, the former governor, C. C. Washburn. Upon leaving the Senate, Carpenter established an office in Washington and became the attorney in two cases of nation-wide significance. He represented Secretary of War Belknap in his impeachment trial, and a little later Samuel Tilden before the electoral commission. These two unpopular causes did him no permanent harm, for when Senator Howe's third term expired in 1879, Carpenter, who had rehabilitated his political fortunes, was victor in a triangular contest between himself, the incumbent, and Boss Keyes. His second term in the Senate was cut short by his death.

[Frank A. Flower, *Life of Matthew Hale Carpenter, A View of the Honors and Achievements That in the Am. Republic are Traits of Well Directed Ambition and Persistent Industry* (Madison, 1883); Alexander MacDonald Thomson, *A Political Hist. of Wis.* (2nd ed., 1902), pp. 163–207, 308–09; John B. Cassoday, "Matthew Hale Carpenter," in *Report of the Proc. of the Meeting of the State Bar Ass. Mar. 13, 14, 1906* (Madison, 1907), pp. 155–93; "Memorial Addresses on the Life and Character of Matthew H. Carpenter" in *Cong. Record*, 47 Cong., 1 Sess.; *Proc. of the Bench and Bar of the Supreme Court of the U. S. in Memoriam, Matthew H. Carpenter* (1881); "Death of Matthew Hale Carpenter" in 52 *Wis. Reports*, 23–36.]   H.J.D.

CARPENTER, STEPHEN CULLEN (died *c.* 1820), journalist, was of Irish birth, but "led by a truant disposition into the world" (*Monthly Register, Magazine and Review of the United States*, preface to Volume II, 1806). He is reputed to have been a Parliamentary reporter for the trial of Warren Hastings (Allibone, *Dictionary of British and American Authors*, 1863). This tradition is lent color by the fact that in 1804 he reported a murder trial in Charleston (*Report of the Trial of Richard Dennis for the Murder of James Shaw on Aug. 20, 1804, by S. C. Carpenter*, 1805) and by the further fact as evidenced by his editorial writing that he had an intimate knowledge of contemporary English politics. He came to Charleston not later than 1802 (see *People's Friend* for Apr. 10, 1807). In 1803 he established there in partnership with Loring Andrews the Charleston *Courier*, which

was strongly federalist in tone. He undertook in addition to this the editing of a literary and historical review, the *Monthly Register, Magazine and Review of the United States*. In this he published his history of the American Revolution, and articles, strongly Whig in viewpoint, on the history and state of English politics. He had brought out only a few numbers of this magazine, before he removed with it to New York in 1806. There with the assistance of Elias Hicks he took over the *Daily Advertiser* which he issued from Sept. 1, 1806 to Aug. 3, 1807 as the *People's Friend*. He contributed articles and editorials intended to prove that in the United States of his day "the Forms of a free and the Ends of an Arbitrary Government are not incompatible." He was almost exclusively concerned with national politics, and grew more and more bitter in his opposition to the French, and more determined to save the country "from the colossal power and dark intrigues of Bonaparte." This national partisanship probably cost him his editorship, and in August 1807 the paper was taken over by its former proprietor, Samuel Bayard (*Daily Advertiser*, Aug. 4, 1807). Carpenter then moved to Philadelphia and published there a magazine devoted to the drama under the title, the *Mirror of Taste and Dramatic Censor*. Four volumes appeared in a year and then the magazine disappeared. In 1809 he published a prejudiced life of Jefferson which was embedded in a violently anti-French history of the United States, *Memoirs of Jefferson, Containing a Concise History of the United States, from the Acknowledgement of their Independence, with a View of the Rise and Progress of French Influence and French Principles in that Country*. In 1815 he brought out *Select American Speeches, Forensic and Parliamentary, with Prefatory Remarks; a Sequel to Dr. Chapman's Select Speeches*. He is thought to have spent his latter years in the government employ at Washington, and to have died there about 1820.

[Most of the brief notices dealing with Carpenter are inaccurate. Allibone, *Dict. of Brit. and Am. Authors*, is responsible for crediting him with the authorship of *An Overland Journey to India* under the pseudonym of "Donald Campbell." The *Dict. of Nat. Biog.* (English) attributes it to an authentic Donald Campbell. Most of the information concerning his life is to be found in scattered statements in the *People's Friend* and in the *Monthly Reg. Mag. and Rev. of the U. S.*]
M. A. M.

CARPENTER, STEPHEN HASKINS (Aug. 7, 1831–Dec. 7, 1878), educator, son of Calvin G. Carpenter, was born at Little Falls, Herkimer County, N. Y. His early education was obtained at his own home and at Munro Academy, Elbridge, N. Y. In 1848 he entered Madison University, Hamilton, N. Y., where he spent his first two college years, transferring to the University of Rochester, from which he was graduated in 1852. Coming at once to Wisconsin, he was appointed tutor in succession to Obadiah Milton Conover, holding the position for two years. During the four succeeding years he was editor and one of the publishers of the *Daily Patriot,* and later of the *Western Fireside,* whereupon he became assistant state superintendent of public instruction in Wisconsin, which position he held from 1858 to 1860. He had been married in 1856 to Frances Curtis of Madison. In 1860 he was appointed professor of ancient languages in St. Paul's College, Palmyra, Mo., holding this position until the Civil War compelled the closing of the institution. Returning to Wisconsin, he was engaged in various enterprises, serving as city clerk of Madison, 1864–68, and clerk of the board of education, 1865–72. In 1868 he was appointed professor of rhetoric and English literature in the University of Wisconsin in succession to Daniel Read who had been elected president of the University. The title of the professorship was changed in 1874 to logic and English literature. In 1875 Carpenter was elected to the presidency of the University of Kansas, but declined the appointment. His premature death occurred at Geneva, N. Y., of diphtheria which had already proved fatal to his brother and a nephew, a few days before.

The versatility of Carpenter's interests is shown in his continued participation in civil affairs, in a volume of educational addresses, a collection of "Songs for the Sabbath School," a volume of twelve lectures on Christian evidences, translations from the French, papers on logic and metaphysics in the *Transactions of the Wisconsin Academy of Sciences, Arts, and Letters,* and in his contributions in the field of Anglo-Saxon and early English languages, on which, in addition to his great power as a teacher, rest his claims to remembrance. In 1872 he published *English of the Fourteenth Century,* a critical study of the English of Chaucer. In 1875 he issued a text-book, *An Introduction to the Study of the Anglo-Saxon Language,* which was widely used. His *History of the University of Wisconsin from 1849–76,* published in 1876, tells the story of the University from its founding, in 1850, through the reörganizations of 1858 and 1866. His last publication, *Elements of English Analysis* (1877), was widely used as a grammar text.

[R. B. Anderson, "Prof. Stephen Haskins Carpenter" in *Robinson's Epitome of Lit.* (1878), p. 189; C. W. Butterfield, "Univ. of Wis., Sketches Historical and Biographical," *Wis. State Jour.,* Feb. 22, 1879; R. G.

Thwaites, *Univ. of Wis., Its Hist. and Alumni* (Madison, 1900); obituary in the *Wis. State Jour.,* Dec. 7, 1878, reprinted as a memorial in the *Trans. Wis. Acad. of Sci., Arts, and Letters,* IV, 318–20.]   V. A. C. H.

CARR, BENJAMIN (1769–May 24, 1831), musical composer, was born and brought up in England. He was taught by the most excellent church musicians, and became known as soloist in The Antient Concerts, a London enterprise. In 1793 he emigrated, settling in Philadelphia. There he established the city's first music store, known as The Musical Repository. A branch in New York, with the same name, was sold a few years later. As composer, Carr soon became well known and deservedly popular. Some of his shorter pieces are in a manuscript collection of his, now in the New York Public Library. He was successful in many fields, orchestral as well as vocal and instrumental. His music is said to have a pleasing softness of line. His "Federal Overture" was widely known, and was given on several occasions beside that of the Norfolk concert of Oct. 7, 1796, managed by Graupner. His published works include: *Masses, Vespers, and Litanies* (1805), *Lessons in Vocal Music* (1811), *A Collection of Chants* (1816), and *The Chorister* (1820). Most ambitious among his compositions was the opera *The Archers,* produced in New York on Apr. 18, 1796, repeated there twice, and given twice in Boston. The libretto, by William Dunlap, treated the episode of William Tell; but it was weakened by the anachronism of introducing Winkelried's later sacrifice, and made trivial by the introduction of comic characters, such as the amazonian Rodolpha and the adventurous Conrad. Some effective monologues and striking contrasts gave the composer scope, but the words made the lyrics tame, and gave little chance for dramatic power in the music, though Dunlap praised the score. Only two numbers are now extant, a graceful solo entitled, "Why, huntress, why?" which deplores Rodolpha's courting of danger, and a dainty rondo from the overture. The work has been called (though wrongly) the first American opera. In 1794 Carr appeared in Arne's opera *Love in a Village,* and after that became prominent as a concert soloist, chiefly in Philadelphia. As organist he was at one time the incumbent of St. Joseph's Church, where Lafayette, Rochambeau, and other French officers attended service. Carr conducted at many concerts, often in conjunction with others, as was the fashion at that time. Soon after 1800 he edited a musical journal, and published some theoretical treatises. In 1816 he organized a practise society; and when this began to languish, he infused new vigor into it by changing it, in 1820, into the Musical Fund Society, designed to aid indigent musicians. With him on the committee were Cross (his pupil), Hupfield, and Patterson. For some years the directors' meetings were held at Carr's home, 7 Powell St. The opening concert, on Apr. 24, 1821, included a glee, "Awake, Æolian Lyre," by Danby, with "orchestra accompaniments" by Carr. Another number was Beethoven's "Grand Sinfonia in C." Carr was one of the conductors of *The Creation,* given in 1822. Other society activities included an anonymous appearance of Malibran, in 1827. The society's later historian wrote, "Above all, the personality of Benjamin Carr stands out as one who, of all the early musicians of Philadelphia, wrought most vigorously to introduce the best, chiefly in the oratorio and in the church." One may praise his concert series also, as he included works of Handel, Haydn, Pleyel, Stamitz, Linley, etc. The society erected a monument to him in St. Peter's Church. His epitaph calls him "A distinguished professor of music . . . charitable without ostentation, faithful and true in his friendships."

[Oscar G. Sonneck, *Early Concert Life in America* (Leipzig, 1907), *Early Opera in America* (N. Y., 1915), and "Early Am. Opera" in *Sammelbände der Internat. Musikgesellschaft,* VI, 428–95 ; Henry Simpson, *Lives of Eminent Philadelphians* (1859), pp. 186–87 ; "Cath. Choirs and Choir Music in Phila.," in *Am. Cath. Hist. Soc. Records,* II, 115–26 ; Louis Childs Madeira, *Annals of Music in Phila.* (1896).]   A.E.

CARR, DABNEY (Apr. 27, 1773–Jan. 8, 1837), jurist, was a descendant of Thomas Carr (1678–1737) of "Bear Castle," one of the first justices of Caroline County, Va., sheriff of King William County, and representative from the latter county in the House of Burgesses. Thomas Carr's son, Dabney Carr the elder, married Martha, sister of Thomas Jefferson, and their son was Dabney Carr the younger. The latter attended Hampden Sidney College, and later studied law. In 1800 he married his first cousin, Elizabeth Carr. He was closely associated in his early legal career with James Barbour [*q.v.*], William Wirt [*q.v.*], and others of like caliber. He and Wirt corresponded frequently and intimately for fully thirty-seven years. In 1807, the two friends planned to raise a legion in Virginia, should war come with Great Britain. But they took up the pen instead, and Carr was one of the contributors to Wirt's *Old Bachelor.* So good was Carr's style that Wirt advised him to take seriously to authorship. In 1811, Carr was appointed circuit judge by the Governor and Council, but when his nomination came before the Assembly, the next year, his opponents were able to defeat the confirmation of the appointment, in spite of the fact that Carr had acquitted himself creditably in the position. A new chancery district, with the seat of justice at Winchester, was created immediately, and Carr was made its chancellor. This necessitated his moving to Winchester. In 1824 he succeeded Judge Fleming in the state supreme court of appeals. Here he served with distinction until his death. He was well-read, cultured, possessed of humor and kindness of heart. In his profession he was industrious, punctual, learned, and upright.

[*Va. Mag. of Hist. and Biog.,* II, 221–28, III, 214–17, V, 441 ; John P. Kennedy, *Memoirs of the Life of Wm. Wirt* (2 vols., 1850) ; *Richmond Whig,* Jan. 10, 1837 ; *Southern Lit. Messenger,* IV, 65–70.]   R.L.M—n.

CARR, DABNEY SMITH (Mar. 5, 1802–Mar. 24, 1854), journalist, diplomat, was born in Albemarle County, Va., son of Peter and Hester (Smith) Carr, and nephew of Dabney Carr [*q.v.*]. His grandfather, Dabney Carr the elder, was a rival of Patrick Henry in patriotic oratory and married Martha, sister of Thomas Jefferson, while his father, a lawyer of great ability, was for a time Jefferson's private secretary but retired from public life to live in lordly elegance on his estate, "Carr's Brook." Young Dabney's career began in the counting house of his uncle, Gen. Samuel Smith, head of the firm of Smith & Buchanan, famous Baltimore merchants ; but his ability as a writer and strong interest in politics led him in 1827 to found a newspaper, the *Baltimore Republican and Commercial Advertiser.* His violently partisan support of Andrew Jackson during the presidential campaign of 1828 was considered largely responsible for a sweeping victory in Maryland. For this service he was rewarded by appointment as naval officer for the port of Baltimore. To make a place for him Jackson had to remove the oldest son of Commodore Joshua Barney. This raised such a storm of criticism that for a time it was doubtful whether the Senate would consent to the President's nomination. Confirmed by a majority of one vote, Carr sold his newspaper on Apr. 16, 1829, and took up his new work. For fourteen years he held the position and became popular with local merchants through his unfailing honesty and courtesy. In 1843 President Tyler appointed him to succeed Commodore David Porter as United States minister to Turkey. There he gave six years of unostentatious but efficient service, which merited the praise of merchants, missionaries, and the Ottoman Government. Broken in health, he returned to America in 1850 and was long occupied in attempting to obtain compensation from Congress for a special mission to Syria. His wife was a daughter of Gov. W. C. Nicholas of Virginia. He died at Charlottesville, Va., and was buried at Monticello. As a political writer his style was vigorous to the point of bellicosity, though in private life he was a polished and genial gentleman.

[E. I. Carr, *The Carr Family Records* (Rockton, Ill., 1894) ; E. Woods, *Albemarle County in Va.* (Charlottesville, Va., 1901) ; J. T. Scharf, *Chronicles of Baltimore* (1874) ; *Biog. Cyc. of Md. and District of Columbia* (1882) ; *Va. Mag. of Hist. and Biog.*, II, 224 ; obituaries in *Baltimore Republican and Argus*, Mar. 28, 1854, and *Richmond* (Va.) *Enquirer*, Apr. 3, 1854.]

W.L.W.,Jr.

CARR, ELIAS (Feb. 25, 1839–July 22, 1900), governor of North Carolina, was born on the extensive and fertile "Bracebridge Farm," near Tarboro in Edgecombe County. His parents, Jonas Johnston Carr and Elizabeth Jane (Hilliard) Carr, traced their lineage back through Revolutionary fighters to Virginia emigrants who received land patents direct from the Lords Proprietors. His education was gained at the Oaks School in Orange County, the University of North Carolina, and the University of Virginia. In 1859 he married Eleanor Kearney of Warren County. Having purchased his brother's share of "Bracebridge Farm," he settled down, after the manner of his father, to its serious and intelligent cultivation. For nearly thirty years he lived the life of a country gentleman of wealth and education, entertaining his friends, raising his six children, serving his county as commissioner and his state in minor non-political ways. Then came the agrarian movement of the eighties. Disturbed by the distress of his poorer neighbors, in 1886 Carr went as state delegate to the Farmers' Convention in St. Paul and next year became president of the Farmers' Convention that met in Raleigh to foster agricultural education. When the Farmers' Alliance had been organized throughout the state, he was made its president. The year previous (1890), Alliance men had gone into the primaries of both parties and won the legislature to their program of better school facilities, especially for farmers, and regulation of railroads through a commission. Both of these movements Carr undoubtedly approved and assisted. Extreme measures such as were embodied in the St. Louis platform, however, he repudiated. Especially did he oppose the formation of a third party, fearing, it seems, that this would result in a return of negro rule, as did indeed happen a little later. In the state Democratic convention of 1892 he was nominated for governor as a compromise between the extremists of the Alliance and its opponents. This proved good party strategy, for his popularity and moderation held the party together and secured his election over a divided opposition. As governor (January 1893–January 1897) Carr suggested wholesome legislation and attended conscientiously to the state's business. "An efficient common school system," he told the legislature, "is the only hope of our people for an intelligent, thrifty laboring population upon our farms." Of roads he said, "the present system is a failure and the roads a disgrace to civilization." Unlike most of his class he was willing that taxes on realty be increased for such purposes—by constitutional amendment if necessary—though he thought, correctly enough, that intangibles should first be reached. Eschewing the exercise of political influence, he gave personal and businesslike attention to the state's institutions, especially the prison and convict farms. He supported the new railroad commission but he did not make war on railroads. Indeed his long-term lease of the state-owned North Carolina Railroad to the Southern System is now condemned by the state's historians as shortsighted policy. From the viewpoint of to-day his antagonism of the Cleveland administration seems unwise and unfortunate ; but in this he fairly represented his people. Altogether his public career exemplified the least selfish and most constructive phases of the agrarian movement. At the same time (1893–97), he was serving as first president of the North Carolina Sons of the American Revolution, of which he was a charter member. Always hospitable and jovial, he spent his remaining years pleasantly at "Bracebridge."

[There is a biographical sketch by Marshall De Lancey Haywood in the *Biog. Hist. of N. C.* (1917), VIII, 91–97 ; a eulogistic estimate in the *Raleigh Morning Post*, Aug. 30, 1900, by Capt. W. W. Carraway ; and an obituary in the Raleigh *News-Observer*, July 24, 1900. The farmers' movement is treated by J. G. de R. Hamilton, *N. C. Since 1860* (1919), and S. A. Ashe, *Hist. of N. C.* (1908).]

C.C.P.

CARR, EUGENE ASA (Mar. 20, 1830–Dec. 2, 1910), soldier, son of Clark Murwin and Delia Ann (Torrey) Carr, was born at Concord, Erie County, N. Y. Entering the United States Military Academy in 1846, he graduated in 1850, was commissioned in the Mounted Riflemen (now the 3rd Cavalry), and was sent to the Cavalry School for Practise at Carlisle, Pa., for what the present-day army would call an incubator course. For the next ten years his service was chiefly on the frontier, and included several skirmishes with Indians, in one of which (near Limpia, Tex., Oct. 10, 1854) he was severely injured by an arrow, the first of his many wounds. Upon the organization of several new regiments in 1855, he was appointed a first lieutenant in the 1st (now 4th) Cavalry, and was promoted to a captaincy in 1858. At the beginning of the Civil War he was in garrison at Fort Washita, in the Indian Territory. Sent to join Lyon's command in Missouri, he distinguished himself at the battle of Wilson's Creek, and was appointed colonel of the 3rd Illinois Cavalry a few days later. He was soon in command of a brigade and then, at the battle of Pea Ridge, of a division. Here he was three times wounded, but refused to leave the field and had his wounds bandaged as he sat on his horse. The Medal of Honor was later awarded to him for distinguished gallantry in this action. He was appointed brigadier-general of volunteers, Mar. 7, 1862. His promotion to the grade of major in the regular army followed a few months later, but this commission of course remained in abeyance so long as he held higher volunteer rank. In 1863 he commanded a division in the Vicksburg campaign, and after the surrender of the city returned to Arkansas, where he was engaged in minor operations until he joined Gen. Canby early in 1865 for the campaign which resulted in the capture of Mobile. He was mustered out of the volunteer service, Jan. 15, 1866, with the brevet rank of major-general, served for a time in North Carolina and at Washington, and then returned to the frontier. He had gained his first experience with hostile Indians before the Civil War; now began a long series of campaigns which made him, according to Gen. C. D. Rhodes, "perhaps the most famous and experienced Indian fighter of the quarter of a century following the Civil War." From 1868 until the final campaign of Pine Ridge in 1890–91, he served almost continuously in the Indian country with the 5th and 6th Cavalry, fought against Cheyenne, Sioux, and Apache, and received the thanks of the legislatures of Nebraska, Colorado, and New Mexico for bringing peace within their borders. He was promoted to lieutenant-colonel, Jan. 7, 1873, and to colonel, Apr. 29, 1879. He was appointed brigadier-general, July 19, 1892, but his active service was nearly at an end, for he was placed on the retired list, Feb. 15, 1893. Though spending the rest of his life in the East, he was a member of the Historical Society of Kansas, a state whose history he had largely helped to make. Gen. Rhodes calls him a "superb horseman" and "a born cavalry leader," and quotes Frederic Remington as saying that "Gen. Carr would rather be a colonel of cavalry than Czar of Russia." The Indians called him the War Eagle. His wife, whom he married in 1865, was Mary P. Maguire of St. Louis. He died in Washington and was buried at West Point.

[G. W. Cullum, *Biog. Reg.* (3rd ed., 1891), II, 419–21; *Bull. Ass. Grads. U. S. Mil. Acad.*, 1911, pp. 99–106; *Official Records*, ser. 1, vols. III, VIII, XIII, XXII (pts. 1, 2), XXIV (pts. 1, 2, 3), XXX (pts. 2, 3, 4), XXXIV (pts. 1, 2, 3, 4), XLI (pts. 1, 2, 3, 4), XLVIII (pt. 1), XLIX (pts. 1, 2).]   T. M. S.

CARR, JOSEPH BRADFORD (Aug. 16, 1828–Feb. 24, 1895), politician, soldier, was born in Albany, N. Y., the son of William and Ann Carr, who had come to this country from Ireland in 1824. He engaged in the tobacco business at an early age and continued in it until the outbreak of the Civil War. He was then a colonel of militia, having entered that service in 1849 and risen rapidly. On May 14, 1861, he was mustered into the service of the United States as colonel of the 2nd New York Infantry and sent to Ft. Monroe, Va. Of the experiences of the green troops there, and of the action at Big Bethel (June 10),—dignified at the time by the name of battle,—he later wrote in *Battles and Leaders of the Civil War*, II, 144–52. He soon succeeded by seniority to the command of the brigade, which belonged to the 2nd Division of the 3rd Corps, and led it in the Peninsular Campaign and at the second battle of Bull Run. On Sept. 7, 1862, he was appointed brigadier-general of volunteers, by a recess commission under which he served until Mar. 4, 1863, when the adjournment of the Senate without confirmation of his nomination terminated the appointment. He was promptly reappointed, however, Mar. 30, 1863, and in due time this nomination was confirmed. He continued to command a brigade, except for a short time when the death of Gen. Barry, killed at Chancellorsville, put him in charge of the division. The 3rd Corps (Sickles) was the one which occupied the salient in the center of the Union line and bore the brunt of the Confederate attack on the second day of the battle of Gettysburg. The division commander (Humphreys), in his report of the battle, refers to Carr's "cool courage, determination and skillful handling of troops." On Oct. 4, 1863, Carr was assigned to the command of the 3rd Division, 4th Corps. In the following spring he joined Butler's Army of the James, which was to move against Richmond from the southeast while the Army of the Potomac advanced from the north. He commanded a division of colored troops in the operations around Petersburg, and for some time was in charge of the defenses on the York and James rivers. After being mustered out of service, Aug. 24, 1865, he took up manufacturing in Troy. In 1867 he was appointed major-general of militia, and held that position for the rest of his life. For many years he was active in political life, being elected secretary of state in New York in 1879, 1881, and 1883. He was the Republican candidate for lieutenant-governor in 1885, but failed of election. He died in Troy.

[F. B. Heitman, *Hist. Reg.* (1903), I, 285; *Official Records*, ser. I, vols. XI (pt. 2), XII (pt. 2), XXI,

XXV (pts. 1, 2), XXVII (pt. 1), XXIX (pts. 1, 2), XL (pts. 1, 3), XLII (pts. 2, 3) ; C. E. Fitch, *Memorial Encyc. of Biog. of N. Y.* (1916), III, 15–18).]

T. M. S.

CARR, MATTHEW. [See CARR, THOMAS MATTHEW, 1750–1820.]

CARR, THOMAS MATTHEW (1750–Sept. 29, 1820), Austin Friar, was born probably in Galway, Ireland. He joined the Augustinians in Dublin and studied theology in Toulouse. After ordination to the priesthood he lived some years in the Dublin Friary. In 1795 he was chosen by his brethren to establish a house of the Friars in the United States. Some Friars from the Irish Province were engaged on the missions in Newfoundland, the Friars from Spain had been in Mexico since 1533 ; they had missions also in South America and the Philippines ; but there was no house of the Order in the newly-formed United States. Early in the spring of 1796 Carr came to America bearing letters from Archbishop Troy of Dublin to Bishop Carroll. The first charge assigned by the latter was at St. Mary's in Philadelphia with residence at Old St. Joseph's. Carr remained at St. Mary's directing the work of mission stations in Wilmington, New Castle, Trenton, Burlington, South Jersey, and the counties of Southeastern Pennsylvania until the rectory at St. Augustine's was completed in 1802. In the meantime Bishop Carroll had given him powers of vicar general. The work of organizing St. Augustine's was begun in June 1796, and the corner-stone of the church was laid in September of the same year. Among the contributors was George Washington, who gave fifty dollars for the new church. In 1811 Carr opened a school known as St. Augustine's Academy, for the teaching of languages and the higher branches. This school was closed in June 1815 owing probably to the pressure of work on the missions. Carr prepared the memorial address commemorating the life and work of Washington, which was delivered in St. Mary's, Philadelphia, Feb. 22, 1800. He died at St. Augustine's, Philadelphia, Sept. 29, 1820.

[F. X. McGowan, *Hist. Sketch of St. Augustine's Ch., Phila.* (1896) ; T. C. Middleton, *Hist. Sketch of Villanova College* (1893) ; *Records of the Am. Cath. Hist. Soc.*, vols. I, II, VII, X, XIII, XVI, XVII, XVIII, XIX, XXI, XXII, XXXI ; unpub. letters, registers, and records of St. Augustine's Ch., Phila.]

F. E. T.

CARRÈRE, JOHN MERVEN (Nov. 9, 1858– Mar. 1, 1911), architect, was born in Rio de Janeiro. His father, John M. Carrère, of distinguished French descent, was a coffee merchant of Baltimore. His mother, Anna Louisa Maxwell, was of a Scotch family, long resident in Baltimore, where she had been educated in a convent. John Merven Carrère, after spending his early years in Rio de Janeiro, went, at fourteen, to Switzerland to study at the Institute Breitenstein at Grenchen. His vacations were spent with his paternal grandmother at Dieppe where his architectural propensities showed themselves in the careful drawings which he made of the old house in which they lived. Entering the École des Beaux Arts at Paris, where he studied especially under Victor Robert, Charles Laisne, and Léon Ginain, the last famous for his Neo-Grèc work, he received his Diplôme in 1882. He then went to New York and in 1883 entered the office of McKim, Mead & White. Here he renewed an acquaintance, formed in Paris, with Thomas Hastings, with whom he eventually entered into partnership. Their first important commission was for Henry M. Flagler's Ponce de Leon Hotel (1887). This was followed by the Alcazar Hotel (1888) and two churches: Grace Methodist Church (1887) and the memorial Presbyterian church (1890), all of this work, in St. Augustine, Fla., in a modified Spanish Renaissance style of great brilliance. From this beginning the work of the firm known as Carrère & Hastings grew rapidly and embraced all types of buildings. The Central Congregational Church in Providence, R. I. (1891), shows the Spanish influence of their Florida work but their other buildings were more and more inspired by the French Renaissance, which was always Carrère's favorite style. This appears particularly in the Hotel Laurel-in-the-Pines, Lakewood, N. J. (1891) with many resemblances to Fontainebleau, and in the detail of their New York business buildings, especially the rich caryatid entrance of the Mail and Express Building (1891) and the charming doorway of the Life building (1893). Their other important early works were: the Benedict estate at Greenwich, Conn. (1891) ; the R. H. Townsend house, Washington, D. C. (1893) ; and the Jefferson Hotel, Richmond, Va. (1893). "Bellefontaine," for Giraud Foster at Lenox, Mass. (1897) ; the house for Mrs. Richard Gambrill at Newport, R. I. (1898) ; and "Blairsden," the Blair estate at Peapack, N. J. (1898) all show with what imaginative skill French Renaissance inspiration was applied by them to the buildings and gardens of great American country houses.

In 1901, Carrère was chief architect and chairman of the board of architects in charge of gardens, grounds, and decorations, for the Pan-American Exposition at Buffalo, and Carrère & Hastings were the architects of the memorial bridge and designed all of the gardens and

518

smaller decorative features. From this time on their work embraced a greater and greater proportion of monumental buildings. Among these were the Richmond Borough Hall, New York City (1903–07); the McKinley monument in Buffalo (1903); the St. George ferry terminal, Staten Island, N. Y. (1904); the great agricultural building at the St. Louis Exposition (1904); the approaches and architectural work, including a great triumphal arch, of the Manhattan Bridge, New York City (1905); the Traders Bank, Toronto, Canada (1905); and the Royal Bank of Canada, Montreal (1906). Their work, however, was not limited to buildings of this kind, for the same period embraced "Whitehall," the Flagler house at Palm Beach, Fla. (1901); the elaborate house of Murry Guggenheim, Elberon, N. J. (1903), awarded the A. I. A. gold medal; the First Church of Christ Scientist, New York City (1898); Carnegie Institute, Washington, D. C. (1906); Goldwin Smith Hall at Cornell University (1903); and Woolsey Hall and Memorial Hall at Yale (1906).

The greatest achievements of the firm of Carrère & Hastings were the Senate and House Office buildings (respectively 1905 and 1906) in Washington, D. C.; the New Theatre (later called the Century Theatre), New York City (1906–09); and the New York Public Library, Carrère's favorite work, won in a competition in 1897, but after long delays completed only in 1911. Carrère had always been vitally interested in city-planning matters and in the development of Washington, so that the commission for the design of the Senate Office Building, which his firm won in competition, was particularly congenial to him. This building, with its mate, the House Office Building, was designed to form an adequate frame for the open space in front of the Capitol. Although the site necessitated an irregularly shaped plan, Carrère succeeded in embodying in these buildings a feeling of great dignity and utter simplicity and, by keeping the fronts restrained in detail, and more austere than was customary in his work, in making them give an added sense of climax to the colonnades of the Capitol. In 1903 Carrère & Hastings had received the commission to reconstruct the interior of the Empire Theatre, New York City, which they had made into an auditorium of lavish yet intimate charm. This success was followed by their masterly design for the New Theatre. This attempt to give New York a quasi-municipal theatre produced a building unique in America, occupying a whole block front, which, like the Paris Opéra, was supposed to combine the gaiety of a theatre with monumentality almost official. The scheme adopted accomplished this with perfect success, and the interior of the theatre proper, with its rich proscenium arch, its coffered ceiling, and lavishly ornamented, sweeping, curved walls, is an outstanding example of its type. The New York Public Library was designed in a modernized classic style of strong French inspiration. Its plan was studied to combine simplicity and efficiency of administration with great richness and beauty of interior effect, and the exterior was devised to grow inevitably from the interior arrangement and to express frankly the functions and positions of the main interior elements. The success with which the entire building achieves these ends and the dignity of its carefully studied approach make it one of the best expressions in America of those ideals of logic in design for which the École des Beaux Arts was then particularly famous. Not only did the architects have charge of the building itself but they also designed all of its furniture and the Bryant monument (except the statue) which forms the central feature of the rear. The beauty of the detail in all of the subsidiary work is characteristic.

The last important commission which Carrère & Hastings had prior to Carrère's death was the City Hall of Portland, Me., designed by them and executed in association with Calvin Stevens of Portland. This is remarkable because of its treatment of a general composition, colonial in type, with details of French Renaissance character, and it is said that Carrère's last drawing was a study for the ship weather-vane of this building.

Carrère's interests outside of the office were extremely wide. He was an enthusiastic member of Trinity Chapel, New York. He was a tireless worker in the American Institute of Architects and its New York chapter, of which he was twice president. He was on the city plan commissions of Grand Rapids, Mich. (1909); Hartford, Conn. (1911); and Cleveland, Ohio. His interest in architectural education is shown by the fact that he helped found, and was twice president of, the Society of Beaux Arts Architects, and was a trustee of the American Academy at Rome. He was also instrumental in founding the Fine Arts Federation of New York City, and the Municipal Art Commission of New York. He succeeded D. H. Burnham [q.v.] in directing the activity of the American Institute of Architects in connection with the plan of Washington and as a result was offered but declined the post of supervising architect of the Treasury Department. Francis S. Swayles, in the

London Architectural Review (XXIX, 283), said that he was "almost the first in America to preach and practise professional ethics," and he was the author of the code of competitions which was adopted, slightly modified, by the American Institute of Architects. He published *City Improvement from the Artistic Standpoint* (1908) ; *Preliminary Report of the City Plan for Grand Rapids, Mich.* (1909), with Arnold Brunner; and *Plan of the City of Hartford* (1912). Carrère was made a Fellow of the American Institute of Architects in 1891 and elected as an Academician of the National Academy of Design in 1910. He was married on June 5, 1886, to Marian Sidonia Dell, of Houston, Tex., and San Francisco, Cal., who died Feb. 8, 1920. For many years he lived on Staten Island but during the latter part of his life in New York City itself. His country house, Red Oaks, White Plains, N. Y., designed by himself, was the home of which he was most fond. He was characterized by great generosity, and uncompromising integrity. Impulsive, on occasions fiery, he was, nevertheless, exceedingly popular with all types of people and had a great capacity for winning and holding the affection and confidence of others. Of medium height, with a very dark complexion inherited from his mother's family, and with a small beard, his appearance was almost that of a French aristocrat. Injured in an automobile accident, Feb. 12, 1911, he died at the Presbyterian Hospital, New York, on Mar. 1.

[Memorial notice by Thos. Hastings in the *N. Y. Architect*, V, 65–72; appreciations by W. R. Mead, Walter Cook, and others in *Brickbuilder*, XX, 41 ; a full and enlightening appreciation by Francis S. Swayles in the *London Architectural Rev.*, XXIX, 283–93 ; *Architectural Record*, XXVII, 1–120, fully illustrated and with a list of works; *Am. Art Annual*, IX, 308–09 ; *Am. Art News*, IX, 4 ; *Quart. Bull. of the Am. Inst. of Architects*, XI, 271, 296–99 ; London *Builder*, C, 358–60 ; *Am. Architect*, XCIX, 96, 129, 131 ; *N. Y. Tribune*, Mar. 2, 1911 ; *Who's Who in America*, 1910–11 ; information as to certain facts from Carrère's daughter, Anna M. Carrère.]   T. F. H.

CARRICK, SAMUEL (July 17, 1760–Aug. 17, 1809), Presbyterian clergyman, college president, was born in York (later Adams) County, Pa., a region from which came many of the men and women among whom he was to spend his life on the Virginia and Tennessee frontiers. At an early age he moved to the Shenandoah Valley, and here, under the instruction of William Graham who was laying the foundation for what later became Washington and Lee University, he prepared himself for the Presbyterian ministry. In 1782 he was licensed to preach, and in the following year he was installed as pastor of Rocky Spring and Wahab meeting-house in Virginia.

From the occasional references to him in the records of his church, it appears that within a few years Carrick began to go to the Tennessee frontier in something of the character of a traveling missionary. At the apex of the wedge of settlement that was being pushed rapidly down the valley of the Holston River, he gathered together such casual congregations as he could find, and with the forest as his church building, with a fallen tree or an Indian mound as his pulpit, he preached to them the gospel. By the year 1791 he had organized Lebanon Church and had made his home near the junction of the Holston and French Broad rivers. Soon he organized the first church in the near-by newly-founded Knoxville, where he continued as pastor for the remainder of his life. In September 1793, his first wife, Elizabeth Moore, whom he had married in Virginia, died, and in January of the following year he married Annis McClellen. Like many other frontier preachers, he was not only a minister of the gospel but an educator. In 1793 he opened at his home a "Seminary" where instruction was offered in Latin, Greek, English, geography, logic, natural and moral philosophy, astronomy, and rhetoric. In the following year the territorial legislature chartered Blount College, a non-denominational, co-educational college, named in honor of the governor, William Blount, and Carrick was made its president. A few years later, when this institution, that was to become in time the University of Tennessee, was transformed into East Tennessee College, he continued as its president. He was a much-needed man of culture in a pioneer community, a gentleman of commanding appearance, of great urbanity, and, as described in a brief notice of his death, "a worthy, pious man" (*Wilson's Knoxville Gazette*, Aug. 19, 1809).

[A brief sketch by R. B. McMullen is in Wm. B. Sprague, *Annals Am. Pulpit*, vol. III (1858), and a briefer one is in Wm. Henry Foote, *Sketches of Va.* (2nd ed., 1856). The little that is known about Carrick's administration as president of Blount College can be found in Moses White, *Early Hist. of the Univ. of Tenn.* (1879). See also *Knoxville Gazette*, esp. Dec. 1, 1792, Jan. 30, and Apr. 10, 1794.]   P. M. H.

CARRINGTON, HENRY BEEBEE (Mar. 2, 1824–Oct. 26, 1912), lawyer, author, the son of Miles M. and Mary (Beebee) Carrington, was born at Wallingford, Conn. His grandfather, James Carrington, was a partner of Eli Whitney from 1800 to 1825, superintendent of the manufacture of arms for the United States at Whitneyville, Conn., and inspector of work at the arsenals of Springfield and Harper's Ferry. His maternal grandfather and great-grandfather were graduates of Yale College. In his twelfth year he commenced classical studies under Rev. Epaphras Goodman and Dr. Erasmus D. Hudson. Owing to a chance address by John Brown he became an ardent abolitionist. From his early youth military affairs interested him, and, had his constitution been more rugged, he doubtless would have entered West Point. He entered Yale College in the fall of 1840, and after a temporary absence because of ill health, was graduated with the class of 1845. For a year and a half after graduation he taught in Irving Institute at Tarrytown, N. Y., where he was encouraged by Washington Irving to pursue a line of research which afterward led him to write his *Battles of the American Revolution.* Later he became a professor in the New Haven Collegiate Institute, at the same time pursuing a course of study in the Yale Law School.

In 1848 he moved to Columbus, Ohio, and entered upon the practise of the law, first with Hon. Aaron F. Perry and afterward for nine years with Hon. William Dennison, subsequently governor of Ohio. In his twelve years of law practise in Columbus he was attorney for manufacturing, banking, and railroad corporations. He was locally prominent in the organizing of the Republican party, serving with Rufus P. Spalding and other eminent leaders on the committee on resolutions in the convention of July 13, 1854, which denounced the Kansas-Nebraska policy of the national administration (Joseph Patterson Smith, *History of the Republican Party in Ohio*, 1898). He was the personal friend and supporter of Gov. Salmon P. Chase, and in 1857, at the earnest request of the latter, accepted a position on his staff to take charge of the reorganization of the militia of the state. This work was so well done that it led to Carrington's appointment as adjutant-general, a position which he held under Chase and his successor, Gov. Dennison. When President Lincoln issued his first call for troops, before the United States volunteers could be organized and mustered, nine regiments of Ohio militia were hurried across the Ohio River to save West Virginia for the Union. For this service Carrington received the thanks of the Secretary of War and of Generals Scott and Wool. Shortly afterward he was commissioned colonel of the 18th United States Infantry and placed in command of the regular army camp near Columbus, while still acting as adjutant-general of Ohio. Upon the request of Gov. Oliver P. Morton of Indiana, he was ordered to that state to organize its levies for the service. In 1862 he was promoted to the rank of brigadier-general. He was especially active in organizing and forwarding troops to the field. From In-

diana alone he superintended the recruiting of more than one hundred thousand men. Under his direction the Sons of Liberty and other disloyal orders were exposed. His course in the trial of these conspirators was bitterly denounced by the opponents of the Lincoln administration, but it was sustained by the army and by the loyal sentiment of the country. The cases were ultimately carried to the Supreme Court of the United States, where a majority of the judges held that the military court of Carrington had been illegal because held in a state that was not in rebellion (Whitelaw Reid, *Ohio in the War*, 1893). When he was mustered out of the service as brigadier-general of volunteers, Carrington rejoined his regiment in the Army of the Cumberland; was president of the commission that tried the guerrillas at Louisville in 1865, and later in the fall of the same year was ordered to the Indian service in Nebraska; built Fort Phil Kearny in the Rocky Mountain district; participated in the Red Cloud War; in 1867 established friendly relations with Spotted Tail and other Indian chiefs; was granted a year's leave of absence because of a severe wound received in the line of duty; protected the Union Pacific Railroad from Indian interruption; in 1869 was detailed as professor of military science at Wabash College (Indiana); in 1889 negotiated a treaty with the Flathead Indians of Montana and two years later moved Indians to Joco reservation, western Montana. He was a frequent contributor to periodicals and published several books, of which the following are the more important: *American Classics* (1849); *Russia Among the Nations* (1851); *Hints to Soldiers Taking the Field* (1862); *Mineral Resources of Indiana; Crisis Thoughts* (1878); *Battles of the American Revolution* (1876); *Battle Maps and Charts of the American Revolution* (1881); *The Six Nations* (1892); *Washington, the Soldier* (1898). *Ab-sa-ra-ka, Home of the Crows; or the Experience of an Officer's Wife on the Plains* (1868) was written by Carrington's first wife and in subsequent editions enlarged by Carrington himself. He was twice married: first, to Margaret Irvin Sullivant, daughter of Joseph Sullivant of Columbus, Ohio; and, second, on Apr. 3, 1871, to Fannie, widow of Col. G. W. Grummond, and daughter of Robert Courtney.

[The chief source is *Record of the Class of 1845 of Yale College, Complete to 1881*. The sketch of Carrington in this publication is autobiographical and with the exception of a few mistakes in dates, is authentic. Briefer sketches appear in *The Biog. Cyc. and Portrait Gallery, with Hist. Sketch of Ohio* (1887), IV, 1043-45, and in the *Genealogy and Family Memorial* (1874), by Jos. Sullivant.]   C. B. G—h.

CARRINGTON, PAUL (Mar. 16, 1733–June 23, 1818), jurist, was the son of George Carrington, a wealthy and influential planter of Cumberland County, Va., and of his wife, Anne Mayo—both of English descent. When he was about seventeen years old he went to that part of Lunenburg County later organized as Charlotte County, to study law with Clement Read, county clerk and a man of wealth, culture, and influence. He lived in his instructor's home, and eventually married his daughter, Margaret. His training must have been effective, for he began the practise of law when twenty-one years old, and was very successful. Fortunate family connections and his own ability brought many appointments his way. He was king's attorney of the counties of Bedford, Mecklenburg, Botetourt, and Lunenburg; was major of the Lunenburg militia; and when a portion of Lunenburg County was separated therefrom and organized as Charlotte County in 1765, was chosen as one of its representatives in the Colonial General Assembly, a position which he retained throughout the life of that body. He was also county lieutenant and presiding justice of Charlotte County. In spite of these numerous positions under the crown, he was ever loyal to the Colony. He was a member of the Mercantile Association of 1770, was chairman of the Revolutionary Committee of Charlotte County, and took an active part in each of the several Revolutionary conventions of Virginia from 1774 to 1776, inclusive, which played a large part in uniting the colonies, and in inaugurating the movement for independence. In the Virginia convention of 1776 he was a member of the committee which reported the Declaration of Rights and the Virginia Constitution of 1776. He voted for the resolutions instructing Virginia's delegates in Congress to propose independence. He was a member of the Committee of Safety (both the first and second groups) which was the revolutionary executive body in Virginia until the formation of the state government in July 1776. After representing Charlotte in the state Senate during the first two years of its existence, he began his long career on the bench as a member of the general court (created in 1779). In 1780 he was made chief justice of that body. When the new court of appeals was created in 1789, Carrington was made one of the five judges, and was continued in that position until his resignation in 1807. At that time he retired to private life after having held public office without intermission for forty-two years. The last years of his life were spent at "Mulberry Hill" on the Staunton River.

He was vigorous in body, "over six feet in height, with prominent features, bright blue eyes, and sandy hair" (Grigsby, *post*). In his sixtieth year he had married Priscilla Sims, his first wife having died in 1766. He remained active and erect until within a year of his death, which occurred at the age of eighty-five.

[See Alexander Brown, *The Cabells and Their Kin* (1895), and Hugh Blair Grigsby, *The Va. Convention of 1776* (1855). Brown had access to the manuscript material relating to the Carrington family in the possession of N. F. Cabell; Grigsby resided in the neighborhood of "Mulberry Hill," knew Carrington's children, and had access to many of the family records. Carrington's will and other documents relating to him may be found in the Charlotte County records, at Charlotte C. H., Va. Sketches of him and of his family are in Wm. Henry Foote, *Sketches of Va., Hist. and Biog.* (2nd ed., 1856), and in Bishop Wm. Meade, *Old Churches, Ministers, and Families of Va.* (1861).]

R. L. M—n.

CARROLL, CHARLES (Sept. 19, 1737–Nov. 14, 1832), Revolutionary leader, signer of the Declaration of Independence, and United States senator from Maryland, is said by his biographers to have been descended from the "old Irish princely family of the Carrolls of Ely O'Carroll, Kings County, Ireland." He was born at Annapolis, the son of Charles Carroll of Annapolis and Elizabeth (Brooke) Carroll. His early education was almost entirely in the hands of the Society of Jesus, at first in the school on Bohemia Manor in Maryland, then for six years following 1748 in the Collège de St. Omer in French Flanders. After finishing at Rheims and at the Collège de Louis le Grand in Paris, he spent the years 1753 to 1757 at Bourges and Paris, whence he went to London for the beginning of a residence of several years during which he continued the studies in civil law begun in France, though not with the intention of making professional use of his acquirements. At the age of twenty-eight, he returned to Maryland, prepared to take up the development of the ten-thousand-acre tract in Frederick County located at the mouth of the Monocacy and known as Carrollton Manor, which his father made over to him at this time. He took no part in the politics of the next few years, but lived the life of a gentleman of property, debarred from political activity by his legal disability as a Roman Catholic. On June 5, 1768, he married his cousin, Mary Darnall. In the Assembly of 1770 the question of regulating officers' fees and the stipends of the clergy of the Established Church reached such a point of bitterness between the two houses that Gov. Eden prorogued the session and issued a proclamation reaffirming the old table of fees which the lower house had been trying to reform. The bitterness aroused by this action came to a head two years later when the

Maryland Gazette, on Jan. 7, 1773, published a letter in defense of the government signed "Antilon," a pseudonym which it was generally understood concealed the identity of Daniel Dulany [*q.v.*]. This letter, in the form of a dialogue in which the arguments of "First Citizen" against the government's position were overcome by Dulany speaking as "Second Citizen," gave Carroll his opportunity. Dramatically enough he stepped into the clothes of the straw man Dulany had knocked down and under the signature of "First Citizen" reopened the argument. The controversy was carried on in the *Maryland Gazette* until July 1, 1773, and when it was over Carroll had become indeed something like the First Citizen of the province. He was active in the non-importation proceedings of 1774, and this year and the next saw him successively a member of the local Annapolis Committee of Correspondence, of the first Maryland Convention, of the provincial Committee of Correspondence, and of the Committee of Safety. In February 1776, the Continental Congress appointed a commission to visit Canada "to promote or form a union" between Canada and the colonies, naming as its members, Benjamin Franklin, Samuel Chase, and Charles Carroll. Though Carroll was not a member of Congress at this time, his standing among American Catholics and his knowledge of French fitted him peculiarly for the mission. The story of that abortive attempt, foredoomed to failure, is found in Carroll's journal of the mission. As a delegate to the Maryland Convention of 1776, he was instrumental in bringing about the passage of the resolution of separation from England that put the province into line with the other colonies on this absorbing question of the hour. Elected a delegate to the Continental Congress on July 4, Carroll went almost immediately to Philadelphia, voted for the engrossment of the Declaration of Independence on July 19 and put his name to the instrument on Aug. 2. The romantic story that he added "of Carrollton" to his name on this occasion for the first time in response to the suggestion that King George would probably hang one of the other Charles Carrolls by mistake is without foundation. He had assumed this designation first on his return to Maryland in 1765, and had used it ever since as his invariable signature to distinguish him from his father and cousins of the same name. From this time on Carroll took a prominent part in the Assembly of his state and in the Continental Congress. He was intimately concerned in the drawing up of the Maryland Constitution, and he opposed the confiscation of British property and other measures that seemed to him as tyrannical as those

from which the country was endeavoring to escape. He served in Congress from 1776 to 1778 and was appointed to the Board of War and to other important committees. In 1787 he was elected to the Constitutional Convention, but did not accept the election, though when the question of adoption was before the Maryland Senate, he allied himself with the party for adoption and remained a Federalist for the rest of his days. He represented Maryland as senator in the first federal Congress, 1789, and continued in this capacity until his resignation in 1792. His political career ended when he left the Maryland Senate in 1800 and devoted himself to the development of an estate that counted between seventy and eighty thousand acres of land in Maryland, Pennsylvania, and New York. In common with his party as a whole, he was opposed to the War of 1812, and, when the office of the *Federal Republican* of Baltimore was sacked by a mob, he contemplated moving from the state. He was a member of the Potomac Company, with its dream of a water route to Ohio and the West, and of its successor, the Chesapeake & Ohio Canal Company, organized in 1823. He was on the first board of directors of the Baltimore & Ohio Railroad and laid its corner-stone on the 4th of July 1828. His property increased with the years and when he died on Nov. 14, 1832, he was envied by many as the wealthiest citizen of the United States and revered by every one as the last surviving signer of the Declaration of Independence.

[Kate Mason Rowland, *The Life of Chas. Carroll of Carrollton, 1737–1832* (2 vols. 1898), in which are reprinted as appendices to vol. I, "Letters of the First Citizen," and the Canada "Jour. of Chas. Carroll of Carrollton," and as appendices to vol. II his will and the genealogy of the family.]   L.C.W.

CARROLL, DANIEL (July 22, 1730–May 7, 1796), was commissioner of the District of Columbia. Among the immigrant Carrolls of the sixteenth century were two descendants of a common ancestor, one of whom, Charles Carroll, established the line which was to find its greatest representative in Charles Carroll of Carrollton, and the other, Kean Carroll, was the father of Daniel Carroll of Upper Marlboro. The latter, unlike other members of the family, entered business, but, although this was considered demeaning, his character and natural presence must have inspired great respect, for about 1727 he married a provincial belle of Woodyard, Md., Eleanor Darnall (*Records of the Columbia Historical Society, Washington, D. C.,* XXI, 16–18). He had two sons who distinguished themselves; John Carroll [*q.v.*], and Daniel Carroll. In 1742 Daniel was sent for his education to Flanders where he remained for six years. After his return he married Elizabeth Carroll of Duddington, probably a first cousin of Charles Carroll of Carrollton (*American Catholic Historical Researches*, XII, 53; Peter K. Guilday, *Life and Times of John Carroll*, 1922, I, 3n.). Of his activities between the years 1753 and 1781 very little has been recorded. Upon the death of his father he probably fell heir to a large share of a considerable estate for he is spoken of much later as "a man of large fortune and influence in his state" (*Documents Illustrative of the Formation of the Union of the American States,* selected and arranged by Charles C. Tansill, 1927, p. 104). In 1781 he was elected a delegate to the Continental Congress, signing the Articles of Confederation on Mar. 1 of that year, and from that time until his death he was an active participant in the leading events. On May 26, 1787, he was appointed a delegate to the Constitutional Convention. In company with all the great propertyholders of that assembly he worked for a strongly centralized government. Opposing the payment of members of Congress by the states he declared, "The dependence of both Houses on the State Legislatures would be compleat. . . . The new government in this form is nothing more than a second edition of Congress in two volumes, instead of one, and perhaps with very few amendments" (*Ibid.,* p. 544). During the struggle for ratification he wrote a judicious and persuasive letter to the *Maryland Journal* in answer to a letter written by Samuel Chase who had advised his countrymen to delay ratification (P. L. Ford, editor, *Essays on the Constitution of the United States,* 1892, pp. 325–36). Carroll was elected senator from Maryland to the First Congress of the United States and voted for the assumption bill and the bill to locate the District of Columbia on the banks of the Potomac. His residence at what is now Forest Glen, Md., near the District, and his friendship with Washington probably induced the latter on Jan. 22, 1791, to name him one of the three commissioners to survey and limit a part of the territory of the ten-mile square. The fact that he was an uncle of Daniel Carroll of Duddington who owned considerable property in the area affected, and that he himself owned tracts near-by may have been partly responsible for the embarrassing complications which finally resulted in the resignation of L'Enfant. Carroll served as commissioner until May 1795 when his age and feeble health caused him to resign. He died at his home at Rock Creek either May 6 or 7, 1796 (see deposition of his sister published in *Records of the Columbia Historical Society, Washington, D. C.,* XXI, 17 and *Federal Gazette,* May 14, 1796).

[See Thos. F. Meehan, "Daniel Carroll," article in the *Cath. Encyc.* (1913), which, however, contains numerous errors; also, W. B. Bryan, *A Hist. of the National Capital* (1914), I, 120–22, 255. Carroll's letters to Madison on the struggle for ratification in Maryland are in the Madison Papers, Lib. of Cong.; see a summary of them in *Am. Hist. Rev.,* vol. V. There is information in "D. C. Letters and Papers, Site and Bldg. for Fed. City, Letters," vol. I, in MSS. Div., Lib. of Cong.]

C. W. G.

CARROLL, HOWARD (Sept. 17, 1854–Dec. 30, 1916), author, business man, like Benjamin Franklin preferred even in his later years to be known as a journalist. In addition to these activities he was inspector-general of all New York State troops during the Spanish-American War. This interest in military affairs he doubtless derived from his father, Brigadier-General Howard Carroll, who at the outbreak of the Civil War raised a regiment in New York City and after a short but brilliant military career was killed at Antietam. The son received his early education at Albany, the city of his birth, and in New York City, but went abroad for college training at Hanover, Göttingen, and Geneva. Upon his return to the United States in 1874 he joined the reportorial staff of the *New York Times,* a paper which he later served as correspondent first at Albany and then at Washington. In 1877 he reported the yellow fever epidemic in the South for that newspaper and gathered material for his book, *A Mississippi Incident.* While on the *New York Times* he wrote several plays, of which the most important was *The American Countess* (1884),—a comedy that had a record run of two hundred nights in New York City. In 1883 he published *Twelve Americans: Their Lives and Times,* a volume which he affectionately dedicated to George Jones of the *New York Times.* His newspaper work in Washington brought him into contact with President Arthur, who offered him the position of private secretary and also the post of minister to Belgium, both of which he declined. Always active in Republican politics, a delegate to three national conventions, he ran for office only once. A candidate in 1882 for congressman-at-large for New York State, he ran 64,000 votes ahead of his ticket but was defeated by his Democratic opponent, Gen. Henry W. Slocum. A member of numerous clubs, he was possibly proudest of the honor of being president of the New York Times Association. Twice he was on the military staff of New York governors with a rank of brigadier-general, first with Gov. Morton and then with Gov. Black. To public interests in New York City where he spent his later life he gave liberally of his time. His greatest service to the city was as president of the New York Tercentenary Commission. For his liberality in entertaining German officers during the Hudson-Fulton celebration he was decorated by the German emperor with the Order of the Red Eagle of the first class. In 1888 he married Caroline Starin, whose father John H. was a member of Congress from New York City.

[The most detailed biographical sketch may be found in the obituary in the *N. Y. Times*, Dec. 31, 1916; see also *Who's Who in America*, 1916–17.]   J.M.L.

CARROLL, JAMES (June 5, 1854–Sept. 16, 1907), bacteriologist, pathologist, investigator of yellow fever, was born in Woolwich, England, to James and Harriet Chiverton Carroll. His early education was received at Albion House Academy, Woolwich. At the age of fifteen, he emigrated to Canada and in 1874, at the age of twenty, he enlisted in the United States Army as a private of infantry. After nine years' service in the infantry, he was transferred to the Medical Department as a hospital steward. In this position he served from 1883 to 1898, during which period he studied medicine at the University of the City of New York (1886–87) and at the University of Maryland in Baltimore (1889–91), where he received his M.D. degree. The new science of bacteriology with its promise of future developments in medicine, attracted his attention and during the two winters following his graduation, he took the courses in bacteriology and pathology recently opened at Johns Hopkins University. In 1895, while still a hospital steward, he was assigned to the Army Medical Museum in Washington as assistant to the curator, Maj. Walter Reed [*q.v.*]. Upon the outbreak of the Spanish-American War in 1898, he was appointed acting assistant surgeon. His study of the fever patients in the Army camps was largely instrumental in showing that the prevailing disease was not malaria but typhoid fever. In 1899, Reed and Carroll disproved the claim of Sanarelli that the *Bacillus icteroides* was the causative agent of yellow fever. In the following year, Surgeon-General Sternberg created the so-called Yellow Fever Commission for the study of that disease in Cuba. Its members were Reed, Carroll, Jesse W. Lazear, and Aristide Agramonte. Although Reed's was the planning and organizing mind in this investigation, Carroll must be credited with much of the detailed work. It was here that his skill as a technician and his capacity for infinite pains is best shown. Reed was early convinced that the theory of mosquito transmission advanced some years before by Dr. Carlos Finlay offered the most promising line of investigation. This called for human subjects for inoculation and the Commission was naturally loath to adopt such experimentation in this highly fatal disease.

While Reed was absent in the United States, Carroll caused an infected mosquito to be applied to his arm by Lazear. Three days later, he developed a severe case of yellow fever, which nearly cost him his life. During the course of this illness, he suffered an acute dilatation of the heart, which was the beginning of the permanent lesion which caused his death seven years later. Controlled experiments upon nearly thirty subjects followed, happily without any fatal result.

Carroll's interest in yellow fever did not cease with his participation in the discovery of the method of transmission. In 1901 he returned to Cuba to make a study of the blood of patients. Perhaps his greatest individual contribution was the demonstration of the fact that the virus of yellow fever is ultra-microscopic. Either alone or in collaboration, he contributed twenty-seven articles to medical periodicals, practically all of them relating to yellow fever. His earlier contributions were written largely in collaboration with Walter Reed, with whose name that of Carroll is inseparably associated. From 1895 until Reed's death in 1902 Carroll was Reed's principal assistant. During this period he was demonstrator of bacteriology and pathology in the Medical Department of Columbian University in Washington and for a time was professor of bacteriology and pathology in the Veterinary Department of the same institution. Upon the death of Walter Reed, Carroll succeeded him in the chairs of bacteriology and pathology at Columbian University and the Army Medical School. In recognition of his contribution to the yellow fever investigation, the regulation assigning an age limit for commissions in the Army was waived and he was appointed lieutenant in the Medical Corps in October 1902. In 1907 he was given the commission of major by a special act of Congress. In the same year two universities (Maryland and Nebraska) conferred upon him the honorary degree of LL.D. Quiet, mild-mannered, soft-spoken, he was tall, with an angularity that defied all his years of army life to give him a military bearing. He had a fine high forehead, a large prominent nose and mild eyes looking out always through thick lenses. He was married in 1888 to Jennie M. G. Lucas of Cleveland, Ohio, who together with seven children survived him.

[In the *Bull. of the Johns Hopkins Hospital*, vol. XIX (1908) is contained a series of papers on Carroll by prominent men of his acquaintance. The *Mil. Surgeon*, vol. XXII (1908) contains a concise biographical sketch with portrait. The chapter on the Yellow Fever Commission in John C. Hemmeter's *Master Minds in Medicine* (1927) is largely in relation to Carroll and has a portrait and bibliography. There is also a biographical sketch by Caroline W. Latimer in Kelly and Burrage, *Am. Medic. Biogs.* (1920). Much that has been written concerning Carroll's career is colored by the feeling that the government never adequately rewarded him for his part in the yellow fever investigations.]

J.M.P.

CARROLL, JOHN (Jan. 8, 1735–Dec. 3, 1815), first Roman Catholic bishop in the United States and first archbishop of Baltimore, was the fourth of seven children born to Daniel Carroll, a merchant and landholder of Upper Marlboro, Md., and his wife, Eleanor Darnall, an heiress who traced descent to the Calverts and the English founders of the colony. Jacky Carroll, as the child was known, received his elementary training at home probably from his mother who had been schooled in France at a time when most colonial women were untutored. At the age of twelve years, he was enrolled in the short-lived local Jesuit school at Bohemia Manor. The following year along with his cousin Charles Carroll [q.v.], he was sent to St. Omer's in France, one of the best-known English refugee colleges for the Catholic gentry's sons and for British youth destined to the domestic missions of the Society of Jesus. This was quite usual for well-to-do Catholic manorial families in Maryland where the penal laws precluded the possibility of higher education for their children. Hence the Carrolls found a number of young Marylanders among their fellow students.

At the conclusion of his classical course, John entered the rigorous Jesuit novitiate at Watten (1753), not far from St. Omer's, where he passed two years in study and prayerful meditation. Here again he was associated with English and Maryland youth preparing for the Jesuit missions in the British North American plantations. Thence, he was advanced to the scholasticate at Liège where he pursued the languages and philosophical subjects for three years, before being assigned, as a teacher of boys, at St. Omer's (1758). In 1762 along with the other masters and their pupils he left for Bruges, having learned that St. Omer's was about to be seized by the French government and turned over to English seculars in preparation for the royal edict suppressing the Society of Jesus (1764).

Taking his final vows as a Jesuit, Carroll renounced all claims to a share in his late father's estate in favor of his brothers and sisters and returned to Liège, where he was ordained in 1767 or according to some authorities in 1769. At all events, he was given a leave of absence from teaching to tour Europe in 1771 as a tutor and companion of Lord Stourton's son. His manuscript journal is too fragmentary and circumspect to be interesting, although he traveled widely and met persons of rank in state and church in Germany, France, Italy, and Rome.

He had hardly returned to Liège when Pope Clement XIV, according to current expectation, suppressed the Society (Aug. 16, 1773). Like most Jesuits, Carroll was hurt and resentful but obedient. With a few Jesuits and students, he soon went to England where the penal laws were dying through non-enforcement, and as secretary of a committee drafted futile remonstrances to the Austrian government concerning property losses at Bruges. As tutor and chaplain for Lord Arundell at Wardour Castle, he lived a year in scholarly leisure, but he had no desire to continue permanently in this honorable capacity. Almost forty years old, he was anxious to visit his aged and widowed mother whom he had not seen since his departure for St. Omer's. Furthermore, he sensed the impending Revolution from the tenor of his Maryland correspondence and the tenseness of English official opinion which he gauged with unusual perspicacity. Not long after Charles Carroll had written the "Letters of the First Citizen" in answer to the loyalist arguments of the renowned Maryland lawyer, Daniel Dulany [q.v.], Father John Carroll arrived in America. Stopping with his mother at Rock Creek, Md., he lived privately, saying mass in the manorial chapel and attending to the religious needs of the surrounding country. Though an ardent patriot, he took no active part in the Revolution, save in the spring of 1776 when he was invited by Congress to accompany the American commissioners (Franklin, Chase, and Charles Carroll) to Canada. He was quite aware of the hopeless character of the mission. As an ex-Jesuit, he was not warmly welcomed by Bishop Briand of Quebec who was decidedly pro-British in tone. Carroll was, however, of service to the emissaries, and Franklin wrote (May 27, 1776) thanking him for the solicitous care which he had bestowed upon him during his illness. He was soon back in his Rock Creek retreat.

Annoyed by the chaotic condition of the Catholic Church which the Revolution had severed from any control by the vicar-apostolic of London and also annoyed by the listless character of the ex-Jesuit priests, Carroll wrote a "Plan of Reorganization" in which he pilloried the ex-Jesuits for their idleness when the possibilities of successful work were so great. The following year the arch-priest, John Lewis, called a convocation at Whitemarsh near Annapolis, which named a committee including Fathers Lewis and Carroll and three others, which petitioned Rome to recognize Lewis as superior with some essential episcopal powers (1783). Soon afterward Carroll and a few others drafted another and more respectful petition that they be allowed to select their own head. In 1784, Carroll was chosen to answer a *Letter to the Roman Catholics of the City of Worcester, England,* published in that year by his old associate, the Rev. Charles H. Wharton [*q.v.*], an ex-Jesuit who had returned to his native land as an Episcopalian minister in Burlington, N. J. Carroll's reply, *An Address to the Roman Catholics of the United States of America* (Annapolis, 1784) was highly esteemed and well received as a brilliant controversial article on a high plane.

In 1784–85 he was named prefect-apostolic by Pope Pius VI who apparently regarded Father Lewis as too old for the arduous task of organizing the infant church. Franklin in Paris heartily approved of the choice of his old friend. In the meantime there was some intriguing in French political and ecclesiastical circles to have the church in America placed under a French vicar-apostolic responsible to the papal nuncio in Paris with priests trained in a seminary in France established for that purpose. Knowledge of these schemes seems to have hurried the advancement of Carroll who was named bishop on Nov. 14, 1789, in accordance with the wishes of a convocation of clergy at Whitemarsh, and was consecrated on Aug. 15, 1790, in the Weld family chapel at Lulworth Castle by Bishop Charles Walmesley, O. S. B.

Even ere this, Carroll had been intensely active in church affairs: laying the corner-stone of St. Peter's, Barclay St., in New York City; settling difficulties in Boston; struggling against trusteeism; composing the Irish-German racial situation in Philadelphia; arranging with the bishop of Quebec about the trans-Alleghany jurisdiction; answering in a cogent document an attack on Catholicism by "Liberal" in the *Gazette of the United States* (1789) by pointing to the Revolutionary services of Catholics; carrying on an extended correspondence with English Catholic leaders in quest of financial aid; and making fatiguing visitations over great distances for the 30,000 members of his widely scattered communion. In 1789, he joined with Charles and Daniel Carroll, Thomas Fitzsimons of Philadelphia, and Dominick Lynch, a New York merchant, in drafting a felicitous *Address* to Washington on the part of the Roman Catholics, which the newly-elected President answered with equal felicity. Ten years later he was to deliver one of the finest patriotic addresses on the death of Washington (Feb. 22, 1800).

In 1791 Bishop Carroll presided over his first synod, which considered ecclesiastical regulations, administration, and education. With education he was especially concerned. In 1789 he

had established a college at Georgetown in Maryland in order that Catholic boys should no longer be compelled to go abroad for training or matriculate at the non-sectarian University of Pennsylvania which alone among American schools welcomed them. It was with relief that he saw Georgetown open in 1791 with Dr. Robert Plunkett, an English priest, as rector. Later when the Society of Jesus was revived he confided Georgetown to its care. With enthusiasm, he accepted the offer of Dr. Francis C. Nagot and his Sulpician brethren, who faced persecution in revolutionary France, to labor in America and establish a diocesan seminary (St. Mary's, Baltimore) for the training of native priests. This he urgently desired, as he dreaded and successfully combated foreign influences in the American church whether French, English, or Irish. When the Sulpicians were about to return to France after the Concordat, he begged them to remain, and, supported by Pius VII, he won the consent of their superior general in Paris. Carroll had learned to depend upon them as his most efficient aides on frontier missions or as seminary professors. In 1803, members of this community, at his desire, founded St. Mary's College for boys in Baltimore, which continued for fifty years (superseded by Loyola), and Mount St. Mary's College, Emmitsburg (1808), which has long since been assigned to secular priests. The bishop was not narrowly attracted to any particular order. He felt that there was work for all. In 1790, he welcomed the Belgian Carmelite nuns; in 1799, he gave his patronage to the Visitation Academy in Washington, the first institution of its kind in America; he received the Trappists in Baltimore and aided in the establishment of their famous monastery in Kentucky; to the Augustinians under Father Matthew Carr he assigned a parish in Philadelphia; he ardently supported the Dominicans who were engaged in the Kentucky missions; he was associated in the establishment of Mother Seton's Sisters of Charity and their College of St. Joseph at Emmitsburg (1808–09); and he sought to have a Franciscan province erected in the United States.

In 1795, the bishop commenced to collect for a cathedral, but as money came in slowly a customary lottery was tried. Not until 1806 was the corner-stone laid and not until six years after his death was the church completed. It was held by all travelers to be the finest church in the States. Growth was slow, yet, in 1808, Baltimore was made an archdiocese subdivided into the four new dioceses of Boston, New York, Philadelphia, and Bardstown, Ky. The Archbishop, however, advised concerning the affairs of all these dioceses, whose bishops he virtually nominated, and gave much thought to Louisiana, whose ecclesiastical affairs were unsettled until his administrator apostolic, Louis Dubourg [*q.v.*], was named bishop in 1815. While Archbishop Carroll had little sympathy with the anti-British group in Congress prior to 1812, he loyally supported Madison's administration during the war and ordered a *Te Deum* in his churches on the failure of the English bombardment of Baltimore, which he witnessed and vividly described in a letter to Father Plowden, an English priest. He was growing old and his work had been arduous. He was not without critics. The Irish suspected him of English sympathies; the French and Germans of being pro-Irish; the Jesuits were never altogether sure of him, yet other communities thought of him as pro-Jesuit; ardent Republicans regarded him as an aristocrat and a Federalist. Yet, he was unperturbed; he steered a straight course. He was a thorough gentleman, a good scholar, an able preacher, and a worthy bishop without any obtrusive piety in speech or correspondence. He built well and on his death left the Catholic Church in a promising condition, freed of foreign influences and well entrenched in the hearts of his people.

[Peter K. Guilday, *Life and Times of John Carroll* (1922), based on printed and archival materials and provided with a full bibliography; J. G. Shea, *Life and Times of the Most Rev. John Carroll* (1888); R. H. Clarke, *Lives of the Deceased Bishops of the Cath. Ch. in the U. S.* (1872); Daniel Brent, *Biog. Sketch of the Most Rev. John Carroll, First Archbishop of Baltimore* (1843), which appeared on Carroll's death; Thos. O'Gorman, *Hist. of the Roman Cath. Ch. in the U. S.* (1895); *Cath. Encyc.* (1913); C. H. Wharton, *Concise View of Principal Points of Controversy between Protestant and Roman Churches* (containing his 1784 address, Carroll's and his reply); Arthur O'Leary, *Review of the Important Controversy between Dr. Carroll and the Rev. Messers Wharton and Hawkins* (London, 1786).]
R. J. P.

CARROLL, JOHN LEE (Sept. 30, 1830–Feb. 27, 1911), governor of Maryland, was a great-grandson of Charles Carroll of Carrollton and his grandfather and father were also named Charles. His mother was Mary Digges Lee, grand-daughter of Thomas Sim Lee, twice governor of Maryland. John Lee Carroll was born on the Homewood estate, near Baltimore, now a part of the Johns Hopkins University campus, but was reared at the ancestral Doughoregan Manor, near Ellicott City, Md. His general education was secured from private tutors, and Roman Catholic schools of the District of Columbia and Maryland, and his legal training in the Harvard Law School and a law office in Baltimore. In 1851 he was admitted to the bar, and,

after an extensive visit to Europe, he began practise in Baltimore in 1854. Two years later he married Anita Phelps, daughter of a rich New York merchant. (She died in 1873, and in 1877 he married Mary Carter Thompson of Staunton, Va.)

He moved to New York in 1859 with the object of practising law there; but, because of his father's failing health and his own Southern sympathies in the slavery controversy, he returned to Maryland in two or three years, and took charge of Doughoregan Manor, which, a short time after their father's death, he bought from his brother Charles, and made his country home.

He was early interested in politics, and allied with the Democrats, who, in 1868, elected him state senator. In 1872 he was reëlected, and two years later, made president of the Senate. In 1875, after bitter opposition on the score of his being a Roman Catholic, he was elected governor of Maryland, a position which he filled with energy, courage, and, on the whole, interest in the common good. Especially along agricultural and commercial lines his policy was progressive. This was a time of great economic depression and resulting labor disturbances, and in July 1877, Gov. Carroll was confronted by a strike of Baltimore & Ohio Railroad employees in protest against a ten per cent reduction of wages. When substitutes were put in, the strikers became violent and began to destroy property in Cumberland. Carroll, therefore, announced that he would send state troops to the town, and when destructive rioting began in Baltimore he telegraphed President Hayes for federal troops. These came, and order was restored by July 23, after nearly a week of rioting and the loss of a number of lives; but deep bitterness survived in some labor quarters toward the Governor. After his term as state executive, Carroll refused all further political office, and spent most of his remaining years at Doughoregan, where, as "lord of the manor," he dispensed hospitality to all comers. He died at his winter home in Washington.

[The chief sources are the *Md. Senate Jour.*, 1868–74, *Md. Public Documents*, 1876–80, and the sketch, evidently based upon data furnished by Carroll himself, appearing in *The Biog. Cyc. of Representative Men of Md. and the D. C.* (1879). Heinrich Ewald Buchholz's biography of Carroll in his *Governors of Maryland* (1908) is founded almost completely upon the last-named. An obituary appears in the *Baltimore Sun* for Feb. 28, 1911.]
M. W. W.

CARROLL, SAMUEL SPRIGG (Sept. 21, 1832–Jan. 28, 1893), Union soldier, was born in Washington, D. C., a descendant of that distinguished Maryland family of whom Charles Carroll of Carrollton is the best-known member. His father, William Thomas Carroll, was for many years clerk of the Supreme Court. He was appointed a cadet at West Point in 1852 and graduated in 1856, among his classmates being Fitzhugh Lee. Commissioned in the 10th Infantry, he served on the frontier until 1860, when he returned to West Point as quartermaster of the Military Academy. He was not released for duty in the field until November 1861. Meanwhile he had been promoted to first lieutenant, Apr. 25, and to captain, Nov. 1. He was then sent to West Virginia, on Dec. 15 was appointed colonel of the 8th Ohio Infantry, and joined his regiment at Romney. He took part in the campaigns in the Shenandoah Valley and northern Virginia in the spring and summer of 1862, including the engagements at Kernstown, Port Republic, and Cedar Mountain. During part of this time he was with his regiment, but from May 24 he commanded a brigade in Shields's division, until he was wounded, Aug. 14, in a skirmish on the Rapidan. Rejoining the army in September, upon his recovery, he commanded a brigade of the 3rd Corps at Fredericksburg. He was relieved from this in April 1863, at his own request, and placed in command of a brigade of the 2nd Corps, which he led at Chancellorsville and Gettysburg. He took part in the Bristoe Station and Mine Run operations in the autumn of 1863, and in the early part of the campaign of 1864. He was wounded at the battle of the Wilderness, May 5, while commanding his brigade, but continued on duty until May 13, when he was disabled by a severe wound in the fighting around Spottsylvania, while temporarily in charge of the division. He was appointed brigadier-general of volunteers, May 12. It was December before he was again fit for duty. For a few weeks he served as a member of a court martial, and then was assigned to command in West Virginia. During the last days of the war he commanded a division in the Army of the Shenandoah. Mustered out of the volunteer service, Jan. 15, 1866, he reverted to his regular army rank of captain, but on Jan. 22, 1867, was appointed lieutenant-colonel of the 21st Infantry. His further service was short, however, for disability resulting from his wounds caused him to be placed on the retired list, June 9, 1869, the rank of major-general being given to him at the same time. He made his home in Washington, and died near that city in Montgomery County, Md. He was buried in Oak Hill Cemetery.

[G. W. Cullum, *Biog. Reg.* (3rd ed., 1891), II, 670–71; *Bull. Ass. Grads. Mil. Acad.*, 1893, pp. 102–04; *Official Records*, ser. 1, vols. XII (pts. 1, 2), XXI, XXV (pt. 1), XXVII (pt. 1), XXIX (pt. 1), XXXIII, XXXVI (pt. 1), XLVI (pts. 1, 2, 3).]   T. M S.

CARROLL, WILLIAM (Mar. 3, 1788–Mar. 22, 1844), governor of Tennessee, was born on a farm near Pittsburgh, Pa., the son of Thomas and Mary Montgomery Carroll. Thomas Carroll, a Revolutionary soldier, had moved from Maryland to Pennsylvania where he and Albert Gallatin were joint owners of a nail factory. William's early education, apparently, was meager, but he had ability, perseverance, and ambition, and such of his papers as are in existence show that he possessed an unusual clarity and vigor of thought and expression. In Pittsburgh he was a merchant, and after moving to Nashville, Tenn., about 1810, he continued for some years in the mercantile business. In Tennessee he quickly became the friend of Andrew Jackson. About 1813 he married Cecelia Bradford. During the Creek War he served with the rank of colonel, fought with great bravery against the Indians, was wounded slightly at the battle of Horse Shoe Bend, and received warm praise from Jackson. Later in 1814 when the latter was appointed major-general in the United States army, Carroll was elected to succeed him as major-general of the Tennessee militia. When the British threatened to invade Louisiana, Carroll raised a force of volunteers, transported them down the Cumberland, the Ohio, and the Mississippi, and arrived in time to give Jackson invaluable aid in repulsing the British in the battle of New Orleans.

For the next few years Carroll devoted himself to his business, but suffered severe financial losses during the depression of 1819. In 1821 he entered political life as a candidate for the office of governor. The campaign was an exciting one. His opponent, Edward Ward, was a man of wealth and superior education, and Carroll was represented as the people's candidate. He was elected by a large majority, and in 1823 and 1825 he was reëlected without opposition. The state constitution prohibited a fourth consecutive term, but in 1829, 1831, and 1833, Carroll was again elected governor without opposition. In the history of Tennessee, the twelve years of his administrations stand out as among the most notable of the period before the Civil War. Possessed of the confidence and support of the masses of the voters, he had an unusually strong influence in the legislature. He opposed successfully the popular demand for legislative interference between debtor and creditor and recommended personal economy as the remedy for the ills of the debtors. He urged a resumption of specie payments, sound banking laws, and the repeal of the act which prohibited the establishment of a branch of the United States

Bank in Tennessee. He recommended a reformation of the judicial system, the abolishment of the whipping post and the pillory, the building of a penitentiary, the development of a system of internal improvements, and the establishment of a system of public instruction for all of the children of the state. The last year of his administration saw the adoption by the state of a new and more democratic constitution, an action that was thoroughly in accord with the spirit of his administrations. Under this new constitution in 1835, he sought election to a seventh term as governor. The state was now divided into two bitter political factions, the supporters of Van Buren's candidacy for the presidency and the champions of Hugh Lawson White for that office. Carroll gave his support to the Jackson-Van Buren faction and his defeat by Newton Cannon foreshadowed the future domination of the state by the Whig party. Carroll now desired but failed to secure appointment as minister to Mexico. Yet he continued until his death an active supporter of the Democratic party in Tennessee.

[There is a brief and inadequate discussion of Carroll's career by Emma Carroll Tucker in *Am. Hist. Mag.* (Nashville), VII, 388–96. His official papers in the Tennessee archives are of slight value. A number of letters by him or about him are in the Jackson Papers, the Van Buren Papers, and the Polk Papers in the Lib. of Cong. Some have been published in J. S. Bassett (ed.), *Correspondence of Andrew Jackson* (1926). Much of the information about Carroll's public life can be secured only from newspapers and legislative journals. Information regarding his parentage has been supplied by his grand-daughter, Mrs. R. H. Vance.]

P. M. H.

CARRYL, GUY WETMORE (Mar. 4, 1873–Apr. 1, 1904), author, was born in New York City, the son of Charles Edward and Mary (Wetmore) Carryl. His father, a railroad director and member of the New York Stock Exchange, was himself the author of several volumes of fiction. The younger Carryl attended the Cutler School and Columbia College, from which he graduated in 1895. While in college he wrote plays for amateur performance and was noted for his handsome looks, good manners, literary facility, wit, and zestful enjoyment of life. A youthful epigram—"It takes two to make one seduction"—has been remembered because it scandalized his teacher, Harry Thurston Peck [*q.v.*]. He got his start in journalism as early as 1893 with a memorably vivid description in the *New York Times* of Edwin Booth's last hours. Upon his graduation he joined the staff of *Munsey's Magazine*, was promoted to managing editor, and in 1896 went to Paris as representative of Harper & Brothers. He remained in Paris until 1902, writing for *Life, Outing,*

Munsey's, and *Collier's*, and learning intimately the ways of the foreign colony in the city. On his return to the United States he made his home at Swampscott, Mass. Early in 1904 his bungalow burned. Carryl contracted rheumatic grip from exposure while fighting the fire, blood poisoning set in, and he died in the Roosevelt Hospital, New York City, in his thirty-second year. The literary career thus abruptly terminated seemed to his contemporaries to be of unusual promise. It began properly in 1898 with *Fables for the Frivolous* (*with Apologies to La Fontaine*), a volume of graceful light verse dedicated to his father. The tripping lines and genial, mildly cynical humor, aided by Peter Newell's illustrations, were well received; and its author followed it with two volumes in similar vein, *Mother Goose for Grown-Ups* (1900) and *Grimm Tales Made Gay* (1902). Time has not completely faded the humor of these verses. In 1903 Carryl turned to fiction with *The Lieutenant-Governor*, his most substantial book. It is temperately realistic and satirical, and the description and dialogue, as in his other fiction, are manipulated deftly. *Zut and Other Parisians* (1903) is a collection of short stories. Paris is also the background of *The Transgression of Andrew Vane* (1904), a story of blackmail with an incredible dénouement, well enough written to attract critical attention when it was published. After his death two more volumes appeared: *Far from the Maddening Girls* (1904), a rather slight novel, and *The Garden of Years* (1904), which contains his serious verse. The title poem is autobiographical.

[*Who's Who in America*, 1903–05; obituaries in *N. Y. Post*, Apr. 1, and *N. Y. Times*, Apr. 2, 1904; E. C. Stedman, "To the Reader" in *The Garden of Years*.]

G. H. G.

CARSON, CHRISTOPHER (Dec. 24, 1809–May 23, 1868), commonly known as Kit Carson, trapper, guide, Indian agent, soldier, was born in Madison County, Ky. His paternal grandfather, William, was an immigrant, probably from Scotland, who in 1761 received a land grant in Iredell County, N. C. His father, Lindsay (born about 1755), served in the Revolution and after the death of his first wife (1793) moved to Kentucky, where, in 1797, he married Rebecca Robinson. Of their ten children, Kit was the fifth. In the spring of 1811 the family moved to the Boone's Lick district of Missouri, a region for several years thereafter harassed by Indian forays. In September 1818, the father, while burning timber, was killed by a falling limb. Kit had no schooling and remained illiterate until the last five or six years of his life.

In 1825 his mother apprenticed him to a saddler in the near-by town of Franklin, but about the first of September, 1826, he ran away and joined a Santa Fé expedition as "cavvy boy." In the Southwest, after several shifts of occupation, he was engaged by Ewing Young as one of his party that left Taos in August 1829, crossed the Mohave Desert to California, and, after trapping the San Joaquin and other streams, returned to its starting place in April 1831.

This expedition was Carson's high school, from which he came out a certified trapper and Indian fighter. In the fall of 1831 he joined Thomas Fitzpatrick [q.v.], in a trapping venture to the North, and in the spring of 1833, after wintering at Robidou's Fort Uintah, reached the trapper's encampment at the present Pocatello, just in time to join in a fight with the Blackfeet, in which he received his only serious wound. For the next eight years, interrupted by returns to his adopted home town of Taos and by buffalo hunts to supply meat for Bent's Fort, he trapped in these regions, sometimes with Bridger's and Fitzpatrick's men but oftener with parties of his own, and many of the heroic incidents of the Carson epic date from this period. About 1836 he married, in Indian fashion, an Arapaho girl whom he called Alice, by whom he had a daughter, Adaline. In the spring of 1842, after the death of Alice, he took his five-year-old daughter to his old home in Missouri, where he placed her with relatives and provided for her education. Returning from St. Louis, he took passage on a steamboat, and on board he met Lieut. John Charles Frémont. This chance meeting opened to him a new career.

He served as guide to Frémont's first expedition (June 10–Oct. 10, 1842), and on the publication of the Pathfinder's report was brought into immediate and country-wide fame. Returning to Taos, he married, Feb. 6, 1843, Maria Josefa Jaramillo, a sister of the wife of Charles Bent. On Frémont's second expedition (1843–44) he shared the honors as guide with Thomas Fitzpatrick, while on the third, which left Bent's Fort, Aug. 26, 1845, his function at the start seems to have been undesignated. In the California conquest he bore an active and daring part until after the capture of Los Angeles, when he was appointed "lieutenant on special service" and ordered East with dispatches. Meeting Kearny's column, Oct. 6, 1846, near Socorro, N. Mex., he was compelled, against his wish, to return as guide. He fought in the battle of San Pasqual, Dec. 6, and on the third night after the disaster, with Lieut. Edward Fitzgerald Beale and a Delaware Indian, accomplished the des-

perate feat of crawling through the Californians' lines to bring succor from San Diego. He was in the battles of Jan. 8–9, 1847, for the recovery of Los Angeles, and in March, accompanied by Beale, again started East with dispatches. He reached Washington in June, to find himself a popular hero and to be appointed by President Polk (June 9) a lieutenant in the Mounted Riflemen. He was back in Los Angeles in October, and in the spring of 1848 was again sent East. A companion on the journey was Lieut. George Douglas Brewerton, who in an article in *Harper's Magazine* for August 1853 gave one of the most intimate and engaging portrayals of Carson that we have. At Santa Fé Carson learned that a majority of the Senate, eager to humiliate "the Benton-Frémont clique," had rejected his appointment (Jan. 28). From Washington he returned to Taos as a private citizen.

Various activities, including Indian fighting and an attempt to run a farm, engaged him during the next four years. In the summer of 1853 he drove a flock of 6,500 sheep to Sacramento, netting a good profit from its sale. Returning in December, he learned that he had been appointed a United States Indian agent. His charges were chiefly two tribes of Utes (after the first year or two exclusively so), and during his more than seven years in this post, with home and office in Taos, he rendered excellent service. He was still illiterate; though in the early sixties his contact with army officers was to prove a stimulus enabling him to solve the mysteries of reading and writing, he could at this time merely write (doubtless imitatively) his name and title, and had to delegate to others the preparation of his official reports. It was during this period, presumably the winter of 1857–58, that he dictated to the army surgeon, Lieut.-Col. De Witt C. Peters, and his wife a brief autobiography. The surgeon's expansion of this material, dressed in a somewhat grandiloquent style, into a book, could hardly have been satisfactory to the modest hero, who remarked, on hearing some of the pages read to him, that "Peters laid it on a leetle too thick."

At the outbreak of the Civil War he resigned his place as Indian agent and aided in organizing the 1st New Mexican Volunteer Infantry, of which he was commissioned lieutenant-colonel July 25, 1861, and colonel, Sept. 20. He took part in the battle of Valverde, Feb. 21, 1862, and in successful campaigns against the Mescalero Apaches and the Navajos, in the latter campaign finally breaking the war spirit of a tribe that for two hundred years had been a terror to the settlements. In the fall of 1864 he was sent against the Kiowas and Comanches. At Adobe Walls, in northwestern Texas, Nov. 25, 1864, with about 400 men and two pieces of artillery, he vigorously attacked a force of Indians variously estimated at from 3,000 to 5,000, but after a day's hard fighting was compelled to withdraw. This was his last battle.

In the general promotions dated Mar. 13, 1865, he was brevetted a brigadier-general of volunteers "for gallantry in the battle of Valverde and for distinguished services in New Mexico." In the summer of 1866 he took command of Fort Garland, in western Colorado, where he was visited by Gen. W. T. Sherman and Gen. James F. Rusling. A year later, owing to ill health, he resigned and on Nov. 22 was mustered out. An injury suffered on a hunting trip in the fall of 1860, when his horse fell on him, had resulted in the growth of a tumor pressing on the trachea. In the spring of 1868 he moved his family to Boggsville, a new town near the present La Junta, Colo. Though ill and in great pain, he accepted a call to Washington to take part in a conference with a deputation of Utes. On this journey he visited New York and Boston in the vain hope of getting medical relief. Returning, he reached Boggsville about the first week in April. On the 23rd his wife died. His health continued to fail, and on May 14 he was moved to Fort Lyon, where, though tenderly cared for, he died two weeks later.

Carson is said to have been about five feet eight inches tall. To Mrs. Frémont he seemed "very short and unmistakably bandy-legged, long-bodied and short-limbed." He weighed a mean of about 145 pounds. The color of his eyes, about which the testimony is amusingly discrepant, was probably gray-blue, and his hair was thin and light or sandy. He was ordinarily a man of few words, and there is agreement that his voice was "as soft and gentle as a woman's." In all things he was temperate, and though a confirmed smoker was abstemious of liquor. He has a unique place in history, and a fitting characterization is difficult. "He was not a great man," says Sabin, "nor a brilliant man," but "a great character." Certain it is that this plain, modest, and unlettered man had native qualities which to those who knew him equaled, if they did not transcend, the best they found in other men. To Brewerton he was "one of Dame Nature's gentlemen—a sort of article which she gets up occasionally, but nowhere in better style than among the backwoods of America." "With me Carson and truth are one," wrote Frémont. "His integrity is simply perfect," said Sherman to Rusling at Fort Garland, and Rusling adds:

"As simple as a child, but brave as a lion, he soon took our hearts by storm and grew upon our regard all the while we were with him." Beale, who seems unable to mention his dead comrade without a surge of emotion, apostrophizes him in 1870 as "Dear old Kit. . . . O wise of counsel, strong of frame, brave of heart and gentle of nature!" and says that Tasso "would have placed him by the side of Godfrey and made him the companion of Tancred and Rinaldo."

[De Witt C. Peters in *The Life and Adventures of Kit Carson, the Nestor of the Rocky Mts.* (1858), is the authority for much of the Carson history, and the other early biographers made copious drafts upon his material, without especial concern to look further. In *Kit Carson Days* (1914), Edwin L. Sabin made careful and effective use of all the documentary material then available and further added greatly to the knowledge of Carson, as well as of his environment, by correspondence and interviews with persons who had known him. Other material has since been found, most important of which is the MS. of the autobiography dictated to Peters and his wife. A part of this MS., with critical notes by Chas. L. Camp, was published in the *Cal. Hist. Soc. Quart.*, Oct. 1922, and all of it in a booklet, *Kit Carson's Own Story of His Life* (1926), ed. by Blanche C. Grant. An impressionistic biography, *Kit Carson, the Happy Warrior of the Old West*, by Stanley Vestal, appeared in 1928.]

W. J. G.

CARSON, JOSEPH (Apr. 19, 1808–Dec. 30, 1876), physician, the son of Joseph and Elizabeth (Lawrence) Carson, was born in Philadelphia. He was educated in private schools in that city and graduated from the collegiate department of the University of Pennsylvania in 1826. After working for a short time in a wholesale drug house he became a private pupil of Dr. Thomas T. Hewson while pursuing the medical course at the University of Pennsylvania, from which he received his M.D. in 1830. After graduation he was elected resident physician to the Philadelphia Almshouse. He then went to the East Indies as surgeon in the ship *Georgiana* and on his return to Philadelphia in 1832 began practise. Although he acquired a very large clientele, especially in obstetrics, he also carried on the study of botany throughout his life. In 1835 he became a member of the Academy of Natural Sciences of Philadelphia and for over forty years was most active in its affairs, making communications, serving on committees, and holding various offices. In 1836 he was chosen professor of materia medica in the Philadelphia College of Pharmacy and some years later he also taught in the Medical Institute of Philadelphia. From 1850 until 1876 he was professor of materia medica and pharmacy in the University of Pennsylvania. In 1849 he was elected one of the physicians to the Lying-in-Department of the Pennsylvania Hospital, having as his colleague the distinguished Hugh L. Hodge. Both of these men served the Hospital until the department was finally closed in 1854 in consequence of recurrent outbreaks of puerperal fever. For some years Carson edited the *American Journal of Pharmacy*. He brought out two editions of Pereira's *Materia Medica* with notes. In 1847 he published *Illustrations of Medical Botany*, for which he had himself drawn and colored many of the plates. Carson was very active in the decennial conventions for the revision of the Pharmacopœia. He was a fellow of the College of Physicians of Philadelphia, and a member of the American Philosophical Society, which he served as curator for seventeen years. In 1869 he published his invaluable *History of the Medical Department of the University of Pennsylvania*. He was married twice: in 1841 to Mary Goddard who died without issue in the following year; and in 1848 to Sarah Hollingsworth by whom he had four children.

[Jas. Darrach, "Memoir of Jos. Carson," in *Trans. of the Coll. of Physicians of Phila.*, XI, 45–67; John W. Harshberger, *The Botanists of Phila. and Their Work* (1899), containing a very complete bibliography of Carson's contributions to scientific literature; Thos. G. Morton, *Hist. of the Pa. Hospital* (1895).]

F.R.P.

CARTER, ELIAS (May 30, 1781–Mar. 23, 1864), architect, was born in Ward, Mass., the son of Timothy and Sarah (Walker) Carter. His father and his uncle Benjamin were partners in a building business in Worcester and the neighborhood, and although his father was killed by a fall when the boy was only three years old, and the widow, with her six children, moved to Greenwich, Mass., and remarried, it is certain that the tradition of building and designing remained strong in the family. Carter "certainly had the book which had been his father's guide, Battey Langley's *Treasury of Designs*" (Forbes, *post*, p. 59). Soon after building a church in Brimfield, Mass., in 1805, he settled in that town for a time, and while living there built a hotel and several houses, some still standing. But he was, in these early years, much on the move; his wife told a grand-daughter they had lived in forty different places. He was, at one time, probably before 1805, in the South, which may account for the Southern influence apparent in the high porticos he loved. Already, in the Wyles and Hitchcock houses in Brimfield, this element appears, with columns two stories high combined with a balcony. In Templeton, Mass., he built a church in 1811, and probably the Artemus Lee house, very likely from his own designs, though it is hard to trace the exact steps by which he developed from builder into architect. In 1815, from plans by the famous Ithiel Town, he

built the church in Thompson, Conn., and in 1818 that at Killingly, Conn. A church at Mendon, Mass. (1820), was built from designs by himself, and the pastor of the church at Milford, Mass., about the same date, speaks of him as "a skilful and faithful architect and amiable and pious man."

From 1828 till the time of his death Carter lived chiefly in Worcester, Mass. His known work there includes: the second Unitarian Church (1828); the Daniel Waldo house (1830), which excited much comment for the richness of its woodwork; the Waldo store, known as the "Granite Row"; the Insane Hospital (1832); houses for Alfred Dwight Foster (*c.* 1835), Judge Kinnicut (1835), Gov. Levi Lincoln (1836), S. M. Burnside (1836), the Burt (Smith) house, the Salisbury house, the Mason Moore and Leland houses on Main St., and the Union Church, Front St. (1836–37). Outside of Worcester he designed the Leicester Academy (1832), the Morton house in Taunton, Mass., and the Insane Asylum, Concord, N. H. (1842). His last known work is a house in Monson, Mass. (1859). He must have been a man of civic interests for he was an unsuccessful candidate for delegate to the General Court in 1834, and served on town committees in 1834 and 1837. He was married on May 25, 1807, to Eudocia Lyon who died July 23, 1869.

His importance as an architect is due to the fact that he was brought up and did his earliest work under strong "late colonial" influences, which colored his later Greek Revival work, and gave it a restraint and a harmony with its American use all too lacking in other work of the time. He was somewhat influenced by Asher Benjamin, but his work is usually more restrained, as he restricts himself, with few exceptions, to the Ionic and Doric orders. His churches were the typical white steepled churches of New England; it was the Worcester houses, in their dignity, their simple directness, and a certain monumental scale, which show best the skill and originality with which he adapted Greek detail to New England use.

[The best account of Carter is that by Harriet Merrifield Forbes, in *Old-Time New Eng.* (the Bulletin of the Soc. for the Preservation of New Eng. Antiquities), XI, 58–71. See also C. M. Hyde, *Hist. Celebration of the Town of Brimfield* (1879). A few of Carter's plans are in the possession of the Am. Antiquarian Soc. at Worcester, Mass.]

T.F.H.

CARTER, FRANKLIN (Sept. 30, 1837–Nov. 22, 1919), college president, was born in Waterbury, Conn., the son of Preserve Wood Carter, a farmer, and Ruth Wells (Holmes) Carter. At Phillips Academy, Andover, where he graduated in 1855, he was valedictorian of his class. He entered Yale with the class of 1859, but a hemorrhage at the close of his sophomore year obliged him to leave college and devote himself to restoring his shattered health. In the autumn of 1860 he joined the junior class at Williams College, taking his degree in 1862. In 1863 he married Sarah Leavenworth Kingsbury of Waterbury, with whom he spent many months traveling and studying in Europe, returning in 1865 to Williams as professor of Latin and French. Resigning in 1872, he went abroad for another year in preparation for a new position as professor of German at Yale, where he taught for the next seven years.

In 1880, upon the retirement of President Paul A. Chadbourne, Carter was called to Williams as the sixth president of that institution, being formally inaugurated on July 6, 1881. With him began the period of what Prof. Leverett Wilson Spring rightly styles "the new Williams." During the twenty years of his administration he secured funds for the college to the amount of more than a million dollars. Furthermore, eight new buildings were erected, and improvements were carried out in many of the older structures. He appointed and maintained a scholarly faculty, doubling the number of instructors and adding to the staff several remarkably brilliant men. He modernized the curriculum by announcing elective courses, first for seniors and then for juniors and sophomores also, and by dropping Greek from the list of subjects required for admission; and he adopted the honor system for examinations. While he was president, the undergraduate body increased in numbers by 68 per cent. Although he was temperamentally an aristocrat, he insisted that Williams should be democratic,—not a "refuge for rich men's sons." A thorough and cultivated scholar, Carter especially emphasized the intellectual side of college life. In 1892 Williams observed its centennial with appropriate exercises, and Carter presided over a large gathering of the alumni at Williamstown.

His health had never been rugged, and in 1901 he felt constrained to resign, being relieved from duty on Sept. 1. After that date he continued to reside in Williamstown, occasionally giving a series of "interesting and thought-provoking lectures" on "Theism," for seniors only, but going for the summer to the Adirondacks and for the winter to Florida. His wife died in 1905, leaving four children, and three years later he married Mrs. Elizabeth Sabin Leake, widow of a retired banker. He was a trustee of Phillips Academy (1891–1902) and president of Clarke School for the Deaf (1896–1919). He served as presi-

dential elector (1896), as member of the Massachusetts Board of Education (1896–1900), as president of the Massachusetts Home Missionary Society (1896–1901), and as president of the Modern Language Association (1881–86). He published *The Life of Mark Hopkins* (1892), and an edition of Goethe's *Iphigenie auf Tauris* (1879), as well as numerous articles in scholarly periodicals; but he was not a fluent or a productive writer. He died of pneumonia, Nov. 22, 1919, at Williamstown. A bronze memorial tablet was placed in the Williams College Chapel in 1924 by his daughter, Mrs. Paul C. Ransom.

Carter was tall and slender, with flowing side whiskers. Somewhat stately in his manner, he gave the impression of being reserved if not a trifle austere, but he was actually a person of warm emotions and generous purposes. Although he was quiet and unaggressive, he was a capable executive, getting the most out of his faculty by letting them put their own theories into practise. His religious views were evangelical almost to the verge of fanaticism, and his finest and most enduring influence was exerted through his chapel prayers. In judging undergraduates, he was frequently deceived, discerning piety often where it did not and could not exist. His chronic ill health, accentuated by some domestic afflictions, cast a shadow over the middle years of his life, but in his old age he mellowed, grew more genial and sociable, and was transformed into "the Sage of Williamstown."

[*Springfield Republican*, Nov. 23, 1919; *Who's Who in America*, 1918–19; *Boston Herald*, Nov. 23, 1919; *Williams College Obit. Record*, 1919, pp. 21–30; L. W. Spring, *Hist. of Williams College* (1917); personal information from the Rev. Carroll Perry of Ipswich, Mass.]   C. M. F.

CARTER, HENRY ALPHEUS PEIRCE (Aug. 7, 1837–Nov. 1, 1891), merchant, diplomat, born in Honolulu, H. I., the son of Joseph Oliver and Hannah Trufant (Lord) Carter, was descended from Thomas Carter, a graduate of Cambridge University who came from Hertfordshire, England, to Charlestown, Mass., in 1635. His father, a shipmaster and trader from Charlestown, settled in Honolulu about 1828. In 1840 he left Henry in Boston to be educated, but disastrous speculations forced him nine years later to recall to Hawaii the boy of twelve. The latter immediately went to work, by 1851 was clerk in the local post-office, and the next year was in California working in a Stockton grocery. In 1854 he was employed by the largest Honolulu mercantile firm, C. Brewer & Company, who soon recognized his remarkable business sagacity and took him into partnership when he was twenty-five. He was among the first to realize that whaling, the great business of the islands during the fifties, was on the decline, and accordingly developed a close connection with the growing sugar industry, furnishing the plantations with supplies and capital and marketing their product. In spite of financial difficulties accompanying the Civil War, he brought the company safely through and made large profits on private ventures of his own. Until his death he retained a large and profitable interest in the firm.

Carter early took a prominent place in the civic life of Honolulu, where he enjoyed a reputation as an orator, which he gained during the Civil War by speeches made whenever a Northern victory was celebrated. On Feb. 27, 1862, he married Sybil Augusta, daughter of Gerrit P. Judd, a missionary physician who was the first Hawaiian foreign minister, and thenceforth he took a great interest in governmental affairs, giving himself by extensive study an education in diplomacy. Competent associates allowed him to relieve the pressure of business activity by tours through the United States and Europe in 1866 and 1871. The sugar industry, now producing heavily, was in critical condition for lack of a profitable market. As a solution for this difficulty Carter supported a policy of tariff reciprocity with the United States, and as early as 1872 foresaw annexation as the final outcome. Having attracted official attention by his eloquent advocacy of reciprocity, he was appointed a privy counsellor in September 1874, and less than a month later was sent to Washington with Judge Elisha H. Allen to negotiate such a treaty as he had often advocated. Two years of labor resulted in the treaty of 1876, which put sugar on the free list of imports to the United States and led to a "boom" in the industry. But England, France, and Germany protested that their "most favored nation" treaties were violated by the privileges given America. Viewing the mollification of these governments as an unfinished part of his earlier negotiation, Carter willingly went to Europe as King Kalakaua's special envoy for that purpose. The British made little difficulty and the French left their decision dependent on that of Germany. At Berlin Carter found Bismarck in an aggressive mood, demanding all the privileges accorded the United States. By a skilful combination of straightforward honesty, daring, and urbanity the chancellor was made a friend, and a treaty was signed whereby the special interest of Hawaii in the large and convenient markets of the United States was recognized and less favorable terms were accepted by Germany. Returning to Honolulu in 1879, Carter plunged into business, only to be called again into government

service the following year as minister of the interior, a post which he held for almost two years. In 1882 he went to Lisbon and negotiated a treaty which greatly facilitated the immigration of Portuguese peasants to relieve the acute labor shortage which had developed with the rapid growth of sugar production. From 1883 until his death he served as Hawaiian minister to the United States, where his remarkable knowledge of diplomacy and men was constantly used to repel the attacks of American sugar producers and other interests opposed to the reciprocity treaty. In 1887 he secured an extension of the treaty for seven years, though it cost Hawaii the grant to the United States of Pearl Harbor as a naval station. On his return from a vacation in Europe he died in a New York hotel. Carter's standing as a popular and skilful diplomat was equaled by his reputation as an able and far-sighted financier, while his personal charm made famous the hospitality of his Washington home.

[Geo. F. Nellist, ed., *Story of Hawaii and Its Builders* (Honolulu, 1925); Josephine Sullivan, *Hist. of C. Brewer & Company, Ltd.* (1926); W. D. Alexander, *Hist. of the Later Years of the Hawaiian Monarchy* (Honolulu, 1896).]   W. L. W., Jr.

CARTER, HENRY ROSE (Aug. 25, 1852–Sept. 14, 1925), sanitarian and epidemiologist, was born at Clifton plantation in Caroline County, Va. The first Carters of Virginia had come from Hertfordshire, England, in 1649. They were lords of the manor of Garston in the old country and became landowners and people of consequence in the new. From the highlands of Scotland came to Virginia the family of Rose. Hill Carter of Mine Hill married Mary Rose and of the union was born the first Henry Rose Carter, who married Emma Coleman. To them was born the younger Henry Rose Carter. After a preliminary education obtained at home and in the local schools of his community, young Carter was sent to the University of Virginia, where he pursued a scientific course, with special attention to mathematics. Here he was graduated in 1873 as a civil engineer. An injury, at the time regarded a permanent disability, turned him from an engineering career and toward the study of medicine. After three years of teaching, one as assistant in applied mathematics at the University of Virginia, he entered the University of Maryland and graduated in medicine in 1879. He entered the Marine Hospital Service in May of the same year. Shortly after his assignment to Cairo, Ill., in the fall of 1879 began his contact with yellow fever, which was to occupy much of his official career. The next few years, however, were devoted to clinical medicine. His assignment to the Gulf Quarantine Station at Ship Island in 1888 brought him into contact with the problems of maritime quarantine and particularly that of yellow fever exclusion. By systematic observation he satisfied himself of the efficiency of sulphur fumigation and provisionally fixed the incubation period of yellow fever at not to exceed six days. From these observations he introduced the principle that detention of ship personnel should be for seven days following fumigation. He found maritime quarantine procedure a haphazard system without central control and subject to no uniform regulations. He was largely instrumental in causing the transfer of quarantine stations from municipal or State control to that of the Government and in causing the formulation of uniform regulations based upon rational grounds.

When in 1893, and again in 1897-98, yellow fever gained a foothold in the Southern States, Carter was the Government's representative to coöperate with the State authorities in fighting the disease. From his observations in these epidemics, he definitely fixed the incubation period of yellow fever in man at not more than six days, confirming the provisional conclusion which he had drawn from his quarantine experience. In May 1900 he published *A Note on the Interval between Infecting and Secondary Cases of Yellow Fever*, calling attention to the "extrinsic incubation" of the disease, which accounted for the discrepancy between the incubation period and the observed time elapsing between original and secondary cases. This discrepancy (ten to seventeen days) was declared necessary for "infection of the environment" or, as was later shown, for the development of the yellow fever virus in the mosquito. The publication of this article was coincident with the order for convening the so-called Army Yellow Fever Commission for research upon the disease in Cuba. In its first report, the Commission credits the observations of Carter, together with those of Carlos Finlay on yellow fever and those of Ross and the Italian workers on malaria, with having materially influenced the decision to undertake investigation of mosquito transmission. Following the proof of this mode of transmission by Reed and his colleagues, Carter took up the presentation of the epidemiology of the disease from the new viewpoint. His papers on yellow fever, though neither numerous nor long, are classical.

Following the Spanish-American War, Carter organized the quarantine service for the new government of Cuba. In 1904 he went to Panama, where, after organizing the quarantine service of the Canal Commission, he became director of hospitals, which position he held for four years. In recognition of his distinguished work in sanitation, he was commissioned assistant surgeon-general of the Public Health Service in 1915. In the field of malariology, he also was a commanding figure. In 1913 he conducted with conspicuous success the first campaign for the control of malaria attempted in the United States, and, from that time until his retirement from active duty in the Public Health Service in 1919, he was constantly engaged in directing studies and supervising control of malaria in the Southern States. The last ten years of his life were closely identified with the yellow fever campaign of the International Health Board. He served on its special councils and in 1920, while observing an epidemic in Peru was asked by the Peruvian Government to act as its sanitary adviser. Because of his three decades of acquaintance with yellow fever and his position as leading authority on the subject, he was asked by the International Health Board to prepare a *History of Yellow Fever*, which was well on toward completion when he died in Washington of angina pectoris, after a protracted illness.

Carter was of medium height with a slight figure. He was of delicate constitution all his life and suffered frequent illnesses. He was, however, not only able to continue his activities, but he spared himself no inconveniences or physical hardship in the pursuit of his work. He was sociable and companionable, with a mind of Celtic complexity in which love of nature and the arts combined with dependability and devotion to duty. His portrait shows a thoroughly human personality, a relatively large head, a full face with a drooping *fer à cheval* mustache. He was married in 1880 at Cairo, Ill., to Laura Eugenia Hook, a resident of that place.

[A sketchy autobiography taken from the files of the Public Health Service appears in the *Va. Medical Mo.*, vol. LIII, 1926. The *Am. Jour. of Tropical Medicine*, vol. V, 1925, contains a biographical sketch with portrait. Much of the material for the present article was obtained from family sources, and from manuscripts of Dr. Wade H. Frost of Baltimore, still unpublished.]

J.M.P.

CARTER, JAMES COOLIDGE (Oct. 14, 1827–Feb. 14, 1905), lawyer, was born in Lancaster, Mass., the son of Solomon and Elizabeth (White) Carter. He attended Derby Academy, Hingham, Mass., and in 1846 entered Harvard College where he won the Bowdoin Prize, was a member of the Hasty Pudding Club, and graduated in 1850, fourth in his class. Before entering the Dane Law School at Harvard, in September 1851, he spent a year in New York City as a private tutor, and law student. Having removed to New York City, he was admitted to the New York bar in 1853, and began practise as managing clerk for the firm of Davies & Scudder of which he became a member in 1854 on the retirement of Judge Davies. He was associated with this firm, with various changes in personnel, for fifty-two years. The keynote of his career was devotion to his profession. There was no divided allegiance, even on the personal side, for he never married. His cases, and defense of the common law, made up his whole life, except in a few instances which had direct relation to the law. His ability early attracted the attention of Charles O'Conor who sought him as associate in many cases. Among the most prominent of these were the Jumel Will Case, and the Tweed Ring Cases. Out of the latter litigation grew Carter's interest in municipal reform. In 1875, at the appointment of Gov. Tilden, he served as a member of a commission of twelve to devise a plan of government for the cities of New York State. A founder of the National Municipal League, he was its president for nine years. He was counsel in many important cases in New York State, including the Singer, Tilden, Hamersley and Fayerweather will cases. In the last decade of his active practise, he was engaged chiefly in arguing cases involving constitutional questions before the United States Supreme Court. Perhaps the most noted of these was the Income Tax Case, argued in 1895, in which he brilliantly but unsuccessfully supported the constitutionality of the act.

In the court room, Carter was a striking advocate. He was of medium height, strongly built, with a rugged countenance in which "sternness, sadness and benevolence struggled for ascendancy," and he had a magnificent head described as leonine. His voice was deep, rich, and powerful. He possessed a copious vocabulary and displayed fine skill in its use. He was earnest, but used few gestures, and while not wanting in a sense of humor, was more given to irony. He was combative, aggressive, and forceful. He had the unusual habit, said Joseph H. Choate, "when he embarked in a cause, of first convincing himself of its justice, before he undertook to convince court, or jury or adversary." He formed his theory of a case, and retained it to the end through each appeal. "Nothing is finally decided," he used to say, "until it is decided right." He was almost too thoroughly in earnest in contentious argument, giving sometimes the appearance of hostility toward his adversary. Being called into critical cases where a forlorn hope had to be led, he lost in the long run as many cases as he won. His power of application was phenomenal, and his aim was absolute perfection and completeness in preparation. As a young man he twice went beyond his physical strength, so that for a year

or two he had to retire from practise. Thenceforward he gave systematic attention to his health, providing for repose, sport, and exercise. His brother lawyers recognized his position of leadership by electing him president of the American Bar Association (1894–95), and president, five times, of the Association of the Bar of the City of New York, of which he was a founder. In 1890 he was a member of the New York State Commission appointed to suggest amendments to the judiciary article of the state constitution. The high point in his career as an advocate was reached when he appeared as one of counsel for the United States before the Behring Sea Fur-Seal Tribunal of Arbitration which met in Paris in February 1893. His opening argument for the United States lasted seven days.

Among lawyers, Carter's name will always be a byword because of the fight which he led against codification. When the Civil Code of substantive law drawn up by David Dudley Field had been twice adopted by a New York legislature, and twice vetoed by a governor, and when further efforts were being made to effect its passage, Carter as a member of a Committee of the Association of the Bar of the City of New York, prepared a paper entitled *The Proposed Codification of Our Common Law* (1883), which was printed and widely distributed. This began a spirited controversy with Field which lasted until the final defeat of the Code. Carter believed that Field's plan to reduce to statutory form the entire body of law governing private transactions of men was fundamentally unsound, impossible of accomplishment, and even if possible undesirable. The foundation of his argument was a series of propositions: "That human transactions, especially private transactions, can be governed only by the principles of justice; that these have an absolute existence, and cannot be made by human enactment; that they are wrapped up with the transactions which they regulate, and are discovered by subjecting those transactions to examination; that the law is consequently a science depending upon the observation of facts, and not a contrivance to be established by legislation, that being a method directly antagonistic to science." That Carter's interest was not merely controversial, but philosophical and scientific, was shown by two further studies, "The Provinces of the Written and the Unwritten Law" (*Report of Virginia State Bar Association*, 1889), and "The Ideal and the Actual in the Law" (*Report of American Bar Association*, 1890). After his retirement from active practise, he devoted a portion of his leisure to the preparation of a fuller statement of his views, which was to have been read as a series of lectures before the Harvard Law School in the spring of 1905. After his death in New York City on Feb. 14 of that year, they were published by his executors under the title *Law: Its Origin, Growth and Function* (1907).

[Geo. A. Miller, "Jas. Coolidge Carter" in W. D. Lewis, ed., *Great Am. Lawyers*, VIII (1909), pp. 1–41; Jos. H. Choate, memorial in the *Report of the Ass. of the Bar of the City of N.Y.* (1906), pp. 120–37.]
F.C.H.

CARTER, JAMES GORDON (Sept. 7, 1795– July 21, 1849), educational reformer, was the son of Capt. James Carter of Leominster, Mass., and of Betsy (Hale) Carter. As his family was poor, young Carter secured the rudiments of learning in winter schools, which relieved the tedium of long, hard summers on the New England farm. At seventeen, he resolved to make his independent way through Groton Academy and Harvard College, which he did by teaching district and singing schools and lecturing on the history of Masonry. He graduated from Harvard, with honors (1820), and entered at once upon a career, as teacher, legislator, and author of textbooks, which placed him in the forefront of the memorable common school revival of Massachusetts. He astonished and satisfied, in turn, both the committee and pupils by his instruction and discipline of a school at Cohasset, proving himself a worthy descendant of Thomas Carter who "was apt to teach." His next venture, for which many Harvard students held him in grateful remembrance, was a private school at Lancaster, for those having difficulty with college work. He taught there till 1830. He early caught the vision of education as a science. In the views of Warren Colburn [*q.v.*], on the teaching of arithmetic, he found a practical application of the Pestalozzian principle that pupils should discover truth inductively, rather than memorize the instructions of books or teachers. The adoption of this principle he constantly urged in public addresses and published articles. He himself endeavored chiefly to apply the inductive method to geography. Assuming that "we need to know most of the places which are nearest us," he prepared and published, with William H. Brooks, illustrated geographies of Essex, Middlesex, and Worcester counties (1830), leading up to a knowledge of the larger unit, the state, afforded by geographies of Massachusetts (1830) and New Hampshire (1831). Though a step in the right direction, not much more can be said for these texts.

In 1821, Carter began his efforts in behalf of public education. His papers, which appeared in the *Boston Transcript,* were collected in a pamphlet, *Letters to the Hon. William Prescott on the Free Schools of New England, with Remarks on the Principles of Instruction* (1824). They both constituted an attack on the decadent state of education and contained suggestions for improvement. More specific proposals, first appearing in the *Boston Patriot* under the name of "Franklin," were published in a pamphlet, *Essays upon Popular Education with an Outline of an Institution for the Education of Teachers* (1826). The *Essays* were widely and favorably discussed and were reviewed in the *Literary Gazette* and the *North American Review*. In a memorial to the legislature (1827) Carter sought a practical realization of the normal school idea. A favorable report on the project, and a bill to subsidize it, were vigorously presented by W. B. Calhoun [*q.v.*], but failed in the Senate by one vote. In 1830 Carter helped to found the American Institute of Instruction, of which he was an influential member and, for some time, an officer. Being elected to the legislature, he served in the House (1835–38), then in the Senate, playing an important rôle as chairman of the committee on education. Among the more notable measures reported were those securing aid to the American Institute; "an act to provide for the better instruction of youth, employed in manufacturing establishments"; one securing one-half the surplus revenue for training common-school teachers; and another for the creation of a board of education and appointment of a state secretary of public schools (1837). Many held Carter to be the best qualified person to receive the newly created secretary's post. His disappointment over not obtaining it was probably a factor in the decline of his active participation in education. He was, however, the first member appointed to the board of education. Besides being legislator and reformer, Carter was also something of a journalist, serving as editor of the *Literary Gazette,* the *United States Gazette* (1824) and *New York Review* (1826). But his permanent reputation as an educator, which would have been augmented had he given his attention to education as completely in later as in earlier life, rests on his contribution to the growth of common schools (elementary and secondary), and his influence in favor of a rational method of teaching and the establishment of normal schools. He was married in 1827 to Anne M. Packard. He died of fever while in Chicago, July 21, 1849.

[An excellent sketch appears in Henry Barnard, *Memoirs of Teachers, Educators, and Promoters and Benefactors of Education* (1859), repub. from the *Am. Jour. of Education*. Accounts also appear in David Wilder, *Hist. of Leominster* (1853), Abijah P. Marvin, *Hist. of Lancaster* (1879), and Paul Monroe, ed., *Cyc. of Education* (1925).]
T.W.

CARTER, JESSE BENEDICT (June 16, 1872–July 20, 1917), classical scholar, was born in New York City of Scotch descent, the son of a publisher, Peter Carter, and of his wife Mary Louise Benedict. Books and studies formed a natural part of the daily life of the home in which he was brought up. In 1899 he entered New York University, but after one year went to Princeton, where he was graduated at the head of his class in 1893. In college his brilliancy and mental power caused him to surpass his classmates in all studies, and he was also an assiduous reader, especially in the fields of modern letters and the fine arts. After his graduation he studied for two years at the universities of Leipzig, Berlin, and Göttingen, for the most part in the field of the classics. He was instructor in Latin at Princeton for two years, 1895–97, when he returned to Germany, where he obtained, in 1898, the degree of Ph.D. at Halle. He was assistant professor of Latin at Princeton, 1898–1902, and in 1900 was lecturer on Roman religion in the summer school of the University of Wisconsin. On Jan. 22, 1902, he married Kate Benedict Freeman of New York. In the same year he was promoted to the rank of professor, a position which he held until 1907, though from 1904 to 1907 he was on leave of absence from Princeton and served as annual professor in the American School of Classical Studies in Rome. In 1907 he was chosen director of the School, and when, in 1911, it became a part of the American Academy in Rome, he remained as director of the Classical School of the Academy. In 1913 he was chosen director of the Academy. In the same year Princeton University conferred upon him the degree of L.H.D.

As director of the American Academy in Rome Carter displayed great executive and administrative ability. The Academy had recently been enlarged in scope and now included the School of Classical Studies as well as the School of Fine Arts. It was the director's task to further and guide the intellectual and material growth of the institution. During Carter's directorship the Academy was settled in permanent and admirable buildings, and its position as an important institution became generally recognized. The Director's own importance as a scholar also received wide recognition. He was invited to deliver the Lowell Lectures in Boston, and in 1916 he delivered, by invitation of the French Minister of Public Instruction, a course of lectures at the Sorbonne and at other French universities on "The Growth of Humanism in the United States." During the World War, Carter and other officers of the Academy were actively engaged in the work of Italian war relief, and it was in recognition of his services in this work, as well as of his scholarship, that King Victor Emmanuel III conferred upon him in 1917 the rank of Commendator della Corona d'Italia. He died at Cervignano, Italy, from heart trouble aggravated by exposure to the heat, as he was on his way to the Italian front with a commission sent by the American Red Cross.

In person Carter was of medium height and rather rotund in face and figure. His exuberant vitality showed itself in mannerisms which were not always pleasing to Americans, but which added to his influence with the Italians among whom his later years were passed. He liked to be well dressed in the latest style. He was of a jovial and convivial disposition and enjoyed the good things of life whether of material or intellectual nature. His published writings treat for the most part topics in his chosen field, Roman religion. He was a regular collaborator in Roscher's *Ausführliches Lexikon der griechischen und römischen Mythologie* and in Hastings's *Encyclopædia of Religion and Ethics* and contributed to various periodicals. His separate publications were: *De Deorum Cognominibus* (1898), *The Roman Elegiac Poets* (1900), *Epitheta Deorum* (1902), *Virgil's Aeneid* (1903), *The Religion of Numa* (1906), *The Religious Life of Ancient Rome* (1911), and a translation of Huelsen's *Roman Forum* (1906). He was an able, even brilliant scholar, and in his presentation he succeeded in combining the salient features of his subject in an exceptionally vivid and striking manner.

[*Who's Who in America,* 1916–17; *Annual Rep. of the Am. Acad. in Rome,* 1916–17, pp. 31–33, 41–42; *Am. Jour. of Archæology,* XXI, 340; *N. Y. Times,* July 23, Aug. 6, 1917.]   H. N. F.

CARTER, JOHN (1737–1781), pioneer, was born in Virginia, where about 1758 he married Elizabeth Taylor. It is believed that he was a kinsman of Robert (or "King") Carter [*q.v.*], but the precise relationship has not been determined. Emigrating from Virginia about 1770, he was one of the first settlers in western North Carolina (now Tennessee) and in the Watauga community in the region of the Watauga River. By reason of his eminence he became the most prominent member of the community which included such distinguished pioneers as John Sevier and Charles and James Robertson. He formed a partnership with William Parker, in the establishment of a store, the chief enterprise of the growing colony. This store was robbed by Indians, who were forced to make reparation by granting the owners an extensive tract of land comprising the whole of Carter's Valley. In 1772 the Watauga pioneers organized the first government west of the Alleghanies and adopted a written constitution, sometimes said to be the first in America, entitled "Articles of the Watauga Association." Under this government, legislative and executive functions were vested in a board of thirteen commissioners, of which Carter was chairman. He was also chairman of the judicial body, the Watauga court.

In 1776 the inhabitants of "Washington District," which comprised what is now northeast Tennessee, petitioned the North Carolina Provincial Council to be annexed to North Carolina. The petition was granted, and the district chose Carter as one of the members of the North Carolina Provincial Congress of 1776. This congress made him a colonel of the district, in which capacity he was active throughout the Revolution in defending the frontier against the Indians. A public magazine of military stores was established at his house. In 1777, and again in 1781, he represented Washington District in the North Carolina Senate, serving on a committee for the protection of the frontier. He was a partner of Gen. John Sevier and Col. Richard Henderson in land speculations, and he served as public entry-taker, a position of great responsibility in a growing frontier settlement. At his death he was one of the largest landholders west of the Alleghany Mountains. He had one son, Landon Carter [q.v.]. Many of his descendants have filled important offices under the Tennessee or the Federal government.

[David W. Carter, *Carter of Tenn.* (Chattanooga, 1927), pp. 9–10; J. G. M. Ramsay, *Annals of Tenn.* (1853, repr. 1926); *N. C. Records*, vols. X–XII, XVII, XXIV.]   C. O. P.

CARTER, JOHN (July 21, 1745–Aug. 19, 1814), printer, editor, put behind his newspaper, the *Providence Gazette,* the resources of a strong personality, and conducted it for nearly half a century with a vigor which made it an influence in Rhode Island affairs, and an institution respected beyond state limits. He was the youngest of the five children of John and Elizabeth (Spriggs) Carter; was born in Philadelphia a few months after the death of his father, who was killed in a naval battle of the war of 1745; and learned the printing-trade of Benjamin Franklin and David Hall, whom he served as an apprentice (Isaiah Thomas, *History of Printing,* 1810, I, 430). At the age of twenty-two, he came to Providence, and became associated with Sarah Goddard in the publication of the *Providence Gazette.* The next year the business came into his possession; from that time until ill health

caused his retirement shortly before his death in 1814, he was the sole editor, and, during the same period, excepting for five or six years (Nov. 1793–May 1799), when William Wilkinson was a partner, was the sole proprietor. During the Revolutionary War, he was a member of the Committee of Correspondence. From July 1772 to June 1792 he was postmaster of Providence; a commission dated Sept. 25, 1775, was signed by Benjamin Franklin.

Carter's chief claim to remembrance rests on his work at his printing shop "at the sign of Shakespear's Head." Here, for many years, much of the local printing and publishing was done, and, for a period, all of it. Here, too, the *Gazette* was printed, with the typographical correctness which was Carter's pride, and which distinguished all of his craftsmanship (William R. Staples, *Annals of the Town of Providence,* 1843, pp. 544–45). The *Gazette* supported the Revolutionary cause; it opposed the paper-money party; it is said to have opposed the adoption of the Constitution (Edward Field, editor, *State of Rhode Island and Providence Plantations at the End of the Century,* 1902, II, 574). As the time approached of Rhode Island's final action, a paragraph in the issue of Mar. 20, 1790, was made to conclude with the words: "In short, the State is as free as an Individual in a State of Nature, and there is *no more* Reason for an Adoption of the New Constitution, than there is for such Individual to enter into a State of Government." The words in italics (so printed in the original) may hide a subtlety and imply that the writer held *some* reason to exist of a contrary tenor. In the obituary notice of Carter in the Gazette of Aug. 20, 1814, the statement is made that he "was zealous in his endeavors to induce the people of this state to adopt the Present Constitution." The opposition of the paper in 1812 to the declaration of war is unequivocal (Field, I, 297). Carter's valedictory was printed in the issue of Feb. 14, 1814. The *Providence Gazette,* he said, "since the dawn of our glorious revolution, has unceasingly disseminated the orthodox political principles of the Washington school." Miss Gertrude S. Kimball speaks of him as "the admirable and sagacious John Carter," and says that he was "possessed of that choleric and generous-hearted temperament that so frequently characterizes the Irish-American" (*Providence in Colonial Times,* 1912, pp. 318–19). He was married on May 14, 1769, to Amey Crawford, by whom he had twelve children. His name was continued in that of his great-grandson, John Carter Brown, the founder of the John Carter Brown Library at Brown University.

[A sketch of John Carter, by his great-great-grandson, John Carter Brown Woods, is printed in *R. I. Hist. Soc. Colls.*, Oct. 1918. Dates in the history of the *Providence Gazette*, and information regarding the location of files, will be found in "Bibliography of Am. Newspapers, 1690–1820, pt. 15, R. I.," by C. S. Brigham in *Proc. Am. Antiq. Soc.*, Apr. 1924. A list of Carter imprints to 1800 will be found in *R. I. Imprints, 1720–1800* (R. I. Hist. Soc., 1915).]   W. A. S.

CARTER, LANDON (Jan. 29, 1760–June 5, 1800), pioneer and public official, the only son of John [*q.v.*] and Elizabeth (Taylor) Carter, was born in Virginia and emigrated with his father to the region of the Watauga River in what is now northeast Tennessee, when he was about ten years old. He was sent to school at Liberty Hall (now Davidson College), Mecklenburg County, N. C., and was more adequately equipped for a public career than many of his Tennessee contemporaries. The last years of the Revolution found him old enough for responsible military duties. In 1780 he served as a captain in John Sevier's expedition against the Cherokees and he participated in the battle of Boyd's Creek, one of the best fought engagements of the war on the frontier. In the same year he was with Charles Robertson's command in South Carolina. In 1781–82 he fought in that state under Gen. Sevier and also under Gen. Francis Marion. On his march homeward his company was ambushed by the Indians. In 1788 the North Carolina legislature appointed him a major of horse and in 1790 Gov. Blount of the Southwest Territory made him lieutenant-colonel commandant of the militia of the Washington District. In the Indian campaign of 1792–93 he served as colonel.

In 1784 and again in 1789 Carter represented Washington County in the North Carolina House of Commons. The movement to erect what is now northeast Tennessee into the independent state of Franklin was cordially supported by Carter. He was secretary of the Jonesborough Convention of 1784 which forwarded the movement, and on the organization of Franklin he served as speaker of the first Senate and member of the first Council of State and later as secretary of state and state entry-taker. Under the government of the Southwest Territory, which was organized in 1790, he was treasurer of Washington District, one of the three districts into which the territory was divided. In 1796 he represented Washington County in the convention that adopted a constitution for the new state of Tennessee. The first legislature of the new state elected him treasurer for the two districts of Washington and Hamilton. The same legislature created Carter County which it named for him. The county seat, Elizabethton,

was named for his wife, Elizabeth Maclin, whom he married in 1784.

Carter added largely to the extensive land holdings that he inherited from his father. He received ten thousand acres from the state of North Carolina as a reimbursement for the expenses incurred by his father in connection with Col. Richard Henderson's purchase of lands from the Cherokees. Throughout his life he manifested an interest in education, serving as a trustee and incorporator of Martin Academy (later Washington College) and as trustee of Greeneville College, both located in northeast Tennessee.

[D. W. Carter, *Carter of Tenn.* (Chattanooga, 1927), pp. 10–12; S. C. Williams, *Hist. of the Lost State of Franklin* (1924), pp. 292–94; *N. C. Records*, vols. XVII–XXII, XXIV.]   C. O. P.

CARTER, ROBERT (1663–Aug. 4, 1732), colonial official, landholder, well-known as "King Carter," was the son of John and Sarah (Ludlow) Carter. He was born in Lancaster County, Va., at his father's country seat, Corotoman, situated near the Rappahannock River not far from the Chesapeake Bay. It appears that the ancestral home was in Buckinghamshire, England, and that John, the emigrant, was a distressed royalist who sought refuge in Virginia about 1649. Before his death in 1669 he had accumulated considerable wealth and had become prominent in the politics of the colony.

All that is known about Robert's education is derived from the wills of his father and elder brother. The father's will provided that a "man or youth servant" that had been brought up in a Latin school should be purchased for the son, then six years old, to teach him "his books either in English or Latin." The elder brother out of a considerable library left Robert all his law and Latin books. At the age of twenty-eight, Robert entered the colonial Assembly as a burgess from Lancaster County, in which office he served during the years 1691–92 and 1695–99. Becoming one of the most prominent members of the Assembly, he was chosen speaker in 1696 and again in 1699. In the latter year he was advanced to the Council and was also made colonial treasurer, an office that he filled for six years. That he served as treasurer while a councillor is evidence of the high esteem in which he was held, for the treasurership by right belonged to a burgess. In the council from 1699 until his death in 1732, he was for the last six years its president. After the death of Gov. Drysdale in 1726, he was for a few months acting governor of Virginia.

During the first third of the eighteenth century Carter was the most eminent resident of the

Northern Neck (the peninsula bounded by the Chesapeake Bay and the Potomac and Rappahannock rivers) and one of its chief landowners. Among the local offices that he held were those of colonel and commander-in-chief of Lancaster County, the same for Northumberland County, and naval officer for the Rappahannock River District. In 1702 he became agent for the Fairfaxes, proprietors of the Northern Neck, and he served his opulent employers in this capacity for upwards of twenty years (1702–11 and 1722–32). This was a strategic position for the acquisition of a fortune and Carter made the most of it. At his death he was one of the wealthiest of colonials, leaving more than three hundred thousand acres of land, one thousand slaves, and ten thousand pounds. Fairfax Harrison has characterized him as a "man of tremendous energy, shrewd business habits, dominant personality, and accustomed to success in whatever he undertook" (*post*, I, 197). Possibly because of the great power that he exercised, or possibly, as an enemy said, because of his excessive pride and ambition, he received the sobriquet "King Carter" or "King Robin." That so powerful a man had his enemies and doubtless his faults cannot be denied. As an antidote to the lofty eulogy composed by his parson and engraved upon his tombstone is the following verse scribbled thereon in chalk by a less friendly hand:

> "Here lies Robin, but not Robin Hood,
> Here lies Robin that never was good,
> Here lies Robin that God has forsaken,
> Here lies Robin the Devil has taken."

Carter was a friend and benefactor of William and Mary College, serving it as rector, trustee, and member of the board of visitors. Building at his own expense Christ Church, Lancaster County, still standing, he reserved, in addition to a large pew for his immediate family, one-fourth of the building for the use of his tenants and servants. The tombstones of the "King" and his wives in the churchyard were described in 1838 by Bishop Meade as probably the largest, richest, and heaviest in the United States. His first wife was Judith (Armistead) Carter (died 1699), his second, Elizabeth (Landon) Carter (died 1710), of the family of Landon, Herefordshire, England. The children of these unions married into the first families of the colony, and, as a result of a fortunate blending of superior strains, Carter had an unusual number of distinguished descendants—two presidents of the United States, six governors of Virginia, Gen. Robert E. Lee, and many others.

[The best account of the Carters is found in T. A. Glenn, *Some Colonial Mansions* (1898), pp. 217–60. A genealogy of the family was published by W. A. Standard in *The Critic* (Richmond), June 18, 24, 25, 1888. Fairfax Harrison, *Landmarks of Old Prince William* (1924), is excellent for Carter's career as a landowner and agent for the Fairfaxes. Frequent references to Carter are found in the *Jours. of the Va. House of Burgesses and Council*; Bishop Wm. Meade, *Old Churches, Ministers, and Families of Va.* (1857); *Wm. and Mary College Quart. Hist. Mag.*, and the *Va. Mag. of Hist. and Biog.* (especially vols. V–VIII).] C. O. P.

CARTER, ROBERT (Feb. 5, 1819–Feb. 15, 1879), editor, author, was born in Albany, N. Y., of Irish parentage. His formal education, which was rather fragmentary, was acquired in the common schools and in the Jesuit College of Chambly in Canada. At fifteen he was appointed an assistant to his guardian, who was state librarian, but he resigned in 1838 in order to take up journalism, some of his poems and sketches having already appeared in the Albany papers. "He had known extreme poverty, and used to tell the story of his mother and himself walking the streets of a city in central New York and spending their last half-dollar on a copy of Spenser's Faerie Queene, instead of a dinner" (T. W. Higginson, *Old Cambridge*, 1899, p. 47). In 1841, having become a Swedenborgian, he moved to Boston in order to prepare some religious pamphlets and there met James Russell Lowell, with whom he joined, in 1843, in editing the *Pioneer*, a literary monthly, which was abandoned after three issues, chiefly because of Lowell's poor health.

Carter was not the kind of man to settle down to any one occupation over a period of years. He edited several manuals of knowledge, acted as chief clerk in the Cambridge post-office during 1845, was employed as literary adviser to various publishing houses, and became private secretary to William H. Prescott, the historian. In 1846 he was married to Ann Augusta Gray, a writer of books for children, "who brought him as a dowry two eagles,—formidable pets,—whose butcher's bills made great inroads on his pay" (*Ibid.*, p. 48). An important phase of his career opened in 1848, when he identified himself with the Free-Soil party and shortly afterward was made the editor, with John G. Palfrey, of the Boston *Commonwealth*, the chief organ of the Free-Soilers. As secretary of the Free-Soil State Committee, he called a convention in Worcester, July 20, 1854, where the delegates, being too numerous for any hall in that city, held their sessions in the open air. A brief platform drafted by Carter was adopted, together with the name "Republican" suggested by him; and a committee of six, headed by John A. Andrew, was named to organize the new party in the state.

In 1855 Carter edited the Boston *Telegraph;*

in 1856 he took charge of the Boston *Atlas;* and during 1857–59 he was Washington correspondent for Greeley's *New York Tribune.* From 1859 until 1863 he assisted George Ripley and Charles A. Dana in editing the first edition of *The American Cyclopedia.* Then, after a few months in government service, he moved to Rochester, N. Y., as editor of the *Democrat,* remaining there for five years. In 1864 he was married to his second wife, Susan Nichols, an author of handbooks on art and a contributor to periodicals. Rossiter Johnson, one of his assistants on the *Democrat,* was much impressed by his marvelous memory for men and events. The old restlessness again seized him, however, and he became editor of *Appleton's Journal* (1870–73), resigning to take part in the revision of *The American Cyclopedia,* to which he contributed noteworthy articles on "Jefferson Davis" and "The Confederate States of America." In 1874 impaired health obliged him to give up writing, and he took several trips to Europe during the next three years. He died in Cambridge, Mass., Feb. 15, 1879, worn out by his ceaseless activity.

He wrote several novels, including *The Armenian's Daughter* and *The Great Tower of Tarudant* (published first in Poe's *Broadway Journal*), and a breezy book, *A Summer Cruise on the Coast of New England* (1864), which ran through several editions. One of his best-known achievements was a series of vigorous essays written for the Boston *Atlas* in reply to the attacks of Francis Bowen [q.v.], on the Hungarian revolutionists; these articles later appeared in a volume called *The Hungarian Controversy* (1852). In 1852 also, with Kossuth's sanction, Carter edited a book called *Kossuth in New England.* He was the friend of nearly all the literary men of his generation in the United States, and he left at his death some incomplete reminiscences, which, however, have never been published. He was an industrious writer, who read everything and combined an encyclopedic knowledge with a tenacious memory. It is said that, when the news of the assassination of President Lincoln reached him at Rochester, he sat down at his editor's desk and, without consulting a single reference, prepared a long article on "Notorious Regicides in History."

[See Introduction by Rossiter Johnson to Carter's *A Summer Cruise* (new ed., 1888); scattered items in Horace E. Scudder, *Jas. Russell Lowell: A Biography* (1901); obituary in *Boston Transcript,* Feb. 17, 1879.]
C. M. F.

CARTER, SAMUEL POWHATAN (Aug. 6, 1819–May 26, 1891), naval and army officer, grandson of Landon Carter [q.v.], and great-grandson of John Carter [q.v.], was the oldest of the three children of Alfred Moore Carter (1784–1850) and his second wife, Evalina B. Parry. Born at Elizabethton, Tenn., he was educated at Washington College in that state, a Presbyterian institution, and at Princeton, which he entered as a sophomore in 1837. On Feb. 14, 1840, he was appointed midshipman in the navy, making his first cruise, 1840–43, on the sloop *Dale,* of the Pacific squadron. After serving on the steamer *Michigan,* stationed on the Great Lakes, and the frigate *Potomac* of the home squadron, he late in 1845 was ordered to the Naval Academy at Annapolis where he graduated with the class of 1846. On July 11 of that year he was promoted passed midshipman. His first duty in this rank was on board the ship of the line *Ohio,* from which vessel he witnessed the fall of Vera Cruz. After periods of service at the Naval Observatory and on board the frigate *St. Lawrence* of the Mediterranean squadron, he was ordered in 1850 to the Naval Academy as assistant professor of mathematics, where he remained until 1853. He was promoted master in 1854, and lieutenant in 1855. While attached to the steam frigate *San Jacinto* of the East India squadron, he participated in the attack on the Barrier Forts, Canton River, China, in 1856. From 1857 to 1860 he was assistant to the executive officer of the Naval Academy. The outbreak of the Civil War found him serving on board the steam sloop *Seminole* of the Brazil squadron.

A letter written by Carter while on the Brazil station declaring his purpose to adhere to the Union in the event of war was widely published in his home state and led Andrew Johnson and other influential residents of east Tennessee to request his services in prosecuting the war in that quarter. Early in July 1861 he was detailed from the navy to "special duty at the War Department" and was ordered to proceed to east Tennessee for the purpose of organizing and drilling Unionist volunteers. In less than a month he had organized one full regiment and part of another,—the first Unionist troops from Tennessee. A month later he was placed in command of a Tennessee brigade and in May 1862 he was made a brigadier-general of the volunteer army. Until the close of 1862 he commanded brigades; and from that time until mustered out of service, divisions. In 1862 he commanded the first important cavalry raid made by the Unionists, in which he defeated the Confederates at Holston, Carter's Station, and Jonesville, and destroyed much valuable property. This raid brought relief to Rosecrans then hard pressed at Murfreesboro and infused new life into the Unionist cavalry. Carter received the thanks of Gen. Halleck and was recommended for promotion to the rank of major-general. At the battle of Kinston, N. C., in March 1865, he commanded the left wing of the Unionist army; and later that year, the 23rd Army Corps and the District of Goldsboro. On Mar. 13, 1865, he received the brevet of major-general of volunteers and on January 19, 1866, was honorably mustered out of service.

While serving in the army Carter in 1863 was promoted lieutenant-commander in the navy, and in 1865 commander. On his return to the navy in 1866 he was made commander of the steamer *Monocacy* of the Asiatic squadron, in which capacity he served for three years. From 1870, in which year he received his captaincy, to 1873 he was commandant of midshipmen at Annapolis. He next saw active service for two years as commander of the steamship *Alaska* on the European station. His last important duty before his retirement in 1881 was as a member of the Light-House Board, 1877–80. In 1878 he was made a commodore and in 1882 he was advanced to the grade of rear-admiral on the retired list.

Carter's career is unique. He is the only American officer who was both a rear-admiral and a major-general. He was tall, handsome and dignified, graceful in carriage, and very affable. A fellow officer described him as a "soldierly Christian" of sincere piety and undoubted courage. He married Carrie Potts, a member of the Pennsylvania family of that name. He is buried in Oak Hill Cemetery, Washington, D. C.

[Record of Officers, Bureau of Navigation, 1840–82; *Official Records* (Army), 1 ser., XX, XXX, XLVII; and *House Report No. 1858*, 48 Cong., 1 Sess.; G. C. Kniffin, "A Sailor on Horseback" in *D. C. Mil. Order of the Loyal Legion, War Papers, No. 19*; "A Sketch of the Mil. Services of Sam. P. Carter . . . 1861–65" (MS.), deposited with the Naval Hist. Foundation; sketch in the *Baltimore Weekly American*, May 20, 1882.]

C.O.P.

CARTER, THOMAS HENRY (Oct. 30, 1854–Sept. 17, 1911), senator, was born on a farm in Scioto County, Ohio. His parents, Edward C. and Margaret (Byrnes) Carter were of pure Irish blood. In 1865 they moved to central Illinois. In 1878 Thomas left his father's home and began the study of law at Burlington, Iowa. He earned his expenses by selling a book, *The Footprints of Time, a Complete Analysis of Our System of Government.* In 1882 he moved to Helena, Mont., and with Montana he was identified for the remainder of his life. He was married on Jan. 27, 1886, to Ellen L. Galen of Helena. In his early years in Montana he gave himself entirely to the practise of law, entering into part-

nership with John B. Clayberg in a firm which maintained a preeminent position for many years. In 1888 the Republican party nominated him as its candidate for territorial delegate to Congress. The territory had generally been Democratic, but this year due to a fight between Democratic leaders Carter was elected by a majority of more than 5,000 votes. The following year Montana was admitted as a state and Carter was elected its first representative in Congress. There he showed a disposition to urge free silver and was an advocate of more liberal legislation for homesteaders. In spite of his Western view-point, and of the fact that he came from a new state he gained influence rapidly. In the Democratic landslide of 1890 he was defeated for reëlection, and President Harrison gave him an appointment as commissioner of the general land office. This appointment was received with pleasure in the West where the land laws had been enforced by men with Eastern views. Carter at once satisfied the complaints of Western farmers, miners, and timbermen by a policy of liberal interpretation of the law. In 1892, four years after he had entered politics, he was selected by Harrison as chairman of the Republican national committee to manage the President's campaign for reëlection. Three years later he was elected to the United States Senate by the legislature of Montana. Upon the expiration of his term he retired to make way for a Democrat but was elected again in 1905.

Carter's chief work was as United States senator. Although a staunch Republican he strongly opposed the policy of Eastern manufacturers who desired a high tariff on finished goods and a low tariff on raw materials. Montana was a producer of wool, hides, lead, and lumber, and he advocated protection for these. His support of the Dingley Tariff and of the Payne-Aldrich Tariff was given only after protection for the raw materials of the West was included. He also forced the issue of bimetallism against the growing influence of the gold wing under Hanna, and, although he refused to bolt the St. Louis convention, after the Republican triumph in 1896 he waged a fight for international bimetallism. While McKinley was still president, Carter supported the bill for a ship subsidy and coupled it with a demand for national reclamation. He also took a leading part in many measures not of a partisan nature. He helped draft the forest reserve law of 1897 and throughout his twelve years in the Senate was an active participant in all sorts of legislation regarding the national forests. He was opposed to a policy of extensive conservation, vigorously attacking Cleveland's withdrawal of 21,000,000 acres of the public domain for forest reserve, and fighting Roosevelt's policy of conservation as primarily beneficial to the large lumber companies. In great measure he represented the older Western sentiment favorable to getting the public domain as rapidly as possible into private hands. He introduced a number of bills for the improvement of Yellowstone Park and was largely responsible for the establishment of Glacier National Park. For many years he was an advocate of postal savings banks and drafted the measure that finally became a law. He declared that this act was his greatest contribution to good government. He earnestly advocated a constitutional amendment giving Congress authority to enact a uniform marriage and divorce law. He was greatly interested in giving Alaska an adequate territorial government, and helped draft the code that went into operation in 1911. He opposed all attacks on the Civil Service Law and brought about many extensions of its regulations. Shrewd, cautious, but courageous, he was a man of great power, although his ability to obtain something for Montana and the West in all types of legislation, and the way in which he strove to reconcile opposing principles laid him open to charges of insincerity.

[There is a laudatory sketch of Carter in *Progressive Men of Mont.* (1904), and a long, eulogistic obituary in the *Helena Daily Independent*, Sept. 18, 1911. His sister, Mrs. Julia Lang, has a collection of material regarding him. His work in Congress may be followed through the *Cong. Record*, 51, 54, 56, 59, 61 Cong., vols. XXI, XXVIII, XXXIV, XL, XLVI.] P.C.P.

CARTER, WILLIAM SAMUEL (Aug. 11, 1859–Mar. 15, 1923), trade-union official, was born in Austin, Tex., the son of Samuel Miles and Margaret Frances (Oliphant) Carter. As a youth he was studious; though most of his time until his twenty-first year was spent as a cowboy, he employed his leisure in reading, and he was enabled to get some primary schooling in Williamson County and two years of instruction in the Agricultural and Mechanical College of Texas. His introduction to railroading, with which he was to be connected for many years, occurred in 1879, when he was put in charge of a wooden tramway for hauling lumber and thus became "superintendent of seven mules, a few drivers and seven miles of track." In the same year he got a job as a fireman on an old woodburning locomotive on what is now a part of the Gulf, Colorado & Santa Fé Railway. Except for an intermission of three years he worked successively as a baggageman, fireman, and engineer on various railroads until September 1894. In October he became editor of the *Brotherhood*

of Locomotive Firemen and Enginemen's Magazine, a place he retained until Jan. 1, 1904, when he became general secretary and treasurer of the Brotherhood. Five years later he became its president.

He attracted general attention in 1913 by refusing to call a strike that had been voted by his union after prolonged negotiations and by appealing to the government and public for support on the ground that the railway managers were trying to embarrass President Wilson in the furtherance of the executive's industrial policy. As a sequence of his action negotiations were reopened, and a revised wage scale was adopted. In February 1918, he was appointed director of the Division of Labor of the United States Railway Administration, an office he held until Mar. 15, 1920, continuing during the time as the nominal head of his union and afterward resuming active service. On June 30, 1922, he retired from the presidency and was made manager of the newly-created research department of the Brotherhood. He moved from Cleveland, which had been his home for many years, to Washington, where he began the organization of his department. Some months later his health failed. On Feb. 24, 1923, he was taken for treatment to the Church Home and Infirmary, at Baltimore, where three weeks later he died. His funeral, largely attended by trade-union and government officials, was held in Washington.

Carter was twice married: on Dec. 26, 1880, to Evelyn Gorsuch of Austin, who died June 22, 1892, and on Nov. 27, 1902, to Julia I. Cross of Peoria, Ill., who survived him. He was a man of high character, and, in his special field, of exceptional abilities. As the editor of the journal of his union, though without previous experience, he developed a marked capacity, bringing it to a high state of excellence, and winning for it a general recognition. As general secretary and treasurer he was an innovator of many improvements in the technique of union management, while as president, during a period in which the most important wage movements in the history of the Brotherhood took place, he showed a skill, tact, and patience in negotiations which usually brought success. His service in the government's railway administration has been highly praised by his colleagues. He had the confidence of the rank and file of his union to an extent few labor leaders have attained, and it seems not to have been disturbed by the high regard he won from the employers with whom he dealt. He was democratic and unassuming in manner, generous in disposition, and, though often in controversy, is said to have borne no resentments.

[Who's Who in America, 1922–23; Brotherhood of Locomotive Firemen and Enginemen's Mag., Apr. 1923; N. Y. Times, Mar. 16, 1923.]
W.J.G.

CARTERET, PHILIP (1639–1682), first governor of New Jersey, was the son of an attorney-general of the Island of Jersey, and fourth cousin to Sir George Carteret, prominent at the Restoration Court. After the gift of New Jersey by James, Duke of York, to Lord John Berkeley and Sir George Carteret in 1664, Philip Carteret was commissioned by them as governor. Sailing in the ship, *Philip,* with a party recruited in part in the Channel Islands, he landed in August 1665, at what is now Elizabethport. On disputed authority he is said to have given to the settlement the name of Elizabethtown in honor of the wife of Sir George. It is a tradition also that Carteret went ashore carrying a hoe to symbolize his fellowship with the planters. The youthful governor faced a task of great difficulty. Though the Dutch, already established at Bergen and elsewhere, readily accepted his authority, groups of New England settlers, who had received from Col. Nicolls at New York permission to enter the country, were not eager to submit. Accustomed to the free New England ideas of settlement and land tenure they disliked the plan of the Lords Proprietors to draw large sums from quit-rents paid in perpetuity by the colonists. On Carteret's landing he found the land already occupied by the pioneers of such a group. Though no direct collision took place between Carteret and the "Associates," out of the conflict of claims later arose the famous "Elizabethtown Controversy" which long distracted the politics of New Jersey. Carteret instituted government under the "Concessions and Agreements" of the Proprietors, and in 1668 summoned the first session of the legislature of New Jersey. But when the first payment of quit-rent came due his authority was defied. The insurgents rather illogically chose as their leader Capt. James Carteret, son of Sir George, whom they elected "President of the Country." Philip Carteret at length received aid from the Lords Proprietors and the rebellion collapsed. But directly afterward occurred the Dutch reconquest of New Netherland which included New Jersey. After the Treaty of Westminster, Philip Carteret became governor of East Jersey, for the original province had been divided between Sir George Carteret and the Quaker assigns of Berkeley. East Jersey included the northern and eastern portion looking to the Hudson. This province Philip Carteret administered with some success. But the right of East Jersey to collect customs was questioned by Sir Edmund Andros of New York, and after the death of Sir George Carteret in 1680 Andros endeavored to suppress the entire jurisdiction. After resisting successfully for some time, Philip Carteret was finally seized by a force from New York, was harshly treated and was put upon trial for usurping authority. Though declared innocent, he was compelled to desist from exercising power. Meanwhile, however, the diplomacy of William Penn and his associates had virtually forced the Duke of York to surrender his claims to New Jersey, and the authority of Philip Carteret in East Jersey was reestablished. In 1682, he gave up the office to Thomas Rudyard, and died soon after. Of his personality and appearance we have no direct account. But throughout his tempestuous career as governor, he displayed firmness, tact, and stalwart fidelity to his trust. His wife was the thrice married daughter of Richard Smith of Long Island.

[The chief source of printed information on Carteret is vol. I of the *N. J. Archives.* His relations to the land question are shown in the rare *Elizabethtown Bill in Chancery* and the still rarer *Answer to the Elizabethtown Bill in Chancery.* A brief sketch of Carteret appears in the second edition of Wm. A. Whitehead, *East Jersey under the Proprietary Govt.* (2nd ed., 1875), p. 106. See also Samuel Smith, *Hist. of the Colony of Novo-Caesaria, or N. J.* (1877); Willis F. Johnson, "The Story of the Carterets" in *Proc. N. J. Hist. Soc.,* 4 Ser., IX, 328–33; *Ibid.,* 2 Ser., I, 31.]
E.P.T.

CARTWRIGHT, PETER (Sept. 1, 1785–Sept. 25, 1872), Methodist clergyman, was born in Amherst County, Va. His father, Justinian Cartwright, a Revolutionary soldier, "was quite a poor man and not so much a bad as a good-for-nothing kind of man" (Mrs. Susannah Johnson, *Recollections of the Rev. John Johnson,* Nashville, 1869, p. 32). He married a widow Wilcox, a devout Methodist but a termagant. Among her numerous children beside Peter, one son, Edmund, became a local Methodist preacher, another, John, was hanged for murder, while a daughter, Polly, led a life of debauchery. About the year 1790 Justinian moved with his family into the wilds of Kentucky and ultimately located, in 1793, in Logan County on the extreme southern edge of the state in a section known as Rogue's Harbor from the number of escaped convicts and desperadoes who congregated there. Although the more respectable settlers eventually organized into a band called the Regulators and after several pitched battles drove out the Rogues, life in this region continued turbulent and unrestrained. Here Peter grew up, a tall and lusty youth, devoted to horse-racing, card-playing, and dancing. He was almost totally without education save for the religious instruction received from his mother which made a deep impression upon his ardently emotional nature. In his sixteenth year he fell into a conviction of sin soon followed by conversion at a camp meeting and by admission into the Methodist Church. In the service of that robust communion he was thenceforth able to express the energy which had formerly gone into more purely pagan activities. Almost immediately after his own conversion he began to convert the lads of the neighborhood with such success that in the next year (1802) he was given an exhorter's license. A little later his family moved into Lewiston County where for a time Peter attended Brown's Academy, but doctrinal disputes with the teacher and the other pupils soon interrupted his schooling and he returned to the more congenial work of exhortation. In October 1803 when a little over eighteen he became a traveling preacher. His early itineraries successively included the Red River Circuit in Kentucky, the Waynesville Circuit which covered a part of Tennessee, the Salt River and Shelbyville Circuit which extended into Indiana, and the Scioto Circuit in Ohio. Through all this wide territory, "the Kentucky Boy," as Peter was called, became a well-known and popular figure. His self-reliance, his readiness with tongue and fist, his quick sense of humor, all made him dear to the hearts of the frontier. As presiding elder he had the noted William M'Kendree [q.v.], who instructed him in English grammar and laid out for him a course of study and reading which the young disciple faithfully pursued with much profit. In 1806 Peter was ordained a deacon by Bishop Francis Asbury [q.v.], and two years later, at the age of twenty-three, he was ordained an elder. On Aug. 18, 1808, he was married to Frances Gaines, a girl of nineteen, because, as he wrote, "After mature deliberation and prayer ... I thought it was my duty to marry." He continued his work as a circuit-rider mainly in Kentucky and Tennessee until 1824 when, actuated largely by hatred of slavery, he had himself transferred to the Sangamon Circuit in Illinois, with which state he was thenceforth identified.

For almost another fifty years "the Kentucky Boy," now known as "Uncle Peter," remained a leader in the religious activities of the West. His personality was almost perfectly adapted to the demands of frontier life. Early inured to physical hardship and to poverty, delighting in herculean labors, ruggedly honest and shrewdly humorous, indifferent to refinement of thought or manners, he made his Methodism a joyous battlefield against the devil and rival sects. Baptist, Presbyterian, and Shaker he overwhelmed with torrents of abuse, ridicule, and scorn. Sin (consisting in unbelief, drinking, gambling, or the wearing of ruffles) and salvation (consisting of conversion to the Church) gave him a dual theme which he manipulated with telling force. This simple ethical code, this narrow and intense religion, above all this thunderous fighting spirit literally swept his hearers off their feet, and at his camp-meetings hundreds were felled to the ground beneath his eloquence and lay prostrate until brought to the mourners' seats, whence he led them singing and shouting into the courts of heaven. If, as not infrequently happened, intruders attempted to break up his meetings, he was quick to meet force with force and seems to have been uniformly victorious in these physical encounters. There was a point of emotional excess, however, at which Cartwright's common sense revolted. For the nervous disorders which too often accompanied his meetings,—"the jerks," "the runnings and barkings," the trances and prolonged illnesses—he assumed no responsibility, regarding them as due to the wiles of the devil, who thus sought to discredit his work. So he continued on his way, a mighty figure among the Methodists of Illinois. He was for forty-five years a presiding elder, attended forty-six meetings of the Illinois Conference, and was twelve times elected to the General Conference. He was twice a member of the Illinois legislature. The one defeat of his career came in 1846 when he ran for the United States Congress against Abraham Lincoln, attempting in vain to make the issue turn upon Lincoln's alleged "infidelism." This political campaign Cartwright forgot to mention in his noted *Autobiography,* published in 1857, a work naively self-glorifying, and unsatisfactory as a record of his life, but written with great verve, revealing the author's extraordinary ability as a raconteur. His later work, *Fifty Years as a Presiding Elder* (1871), edited by the Rev. W. S. Hooper, is considerably less interesting but contains Cartwright's celebrated letter to the devil (a polemic against Calvinism). With advancing years, although he contributed liberally to Methodist colleges and publishing houses, Cartwright found some difficulty in adapting himself to the more intellectual interests of the newer Methodism. He deplored the passing of the good old days and earnestly prayed that "camp-meetings, class-meetings, prayer-meetings, and love-feasts" might "eternally" continue. Hale and hearty he himself remained: his magnificent body, supporting a massive head, with beady black eyes and disheveled hair, hardly knew a day's ill health until extreme old age. From the time of his coming to Illinois he made his home at Pleasant Hills, where in the intervals of religious duty he farmed, and, also, reared a numerous progeny. He lived to welcome nine children, fifty grandchildren, thirty-seven great-grandchildren, and seven great-great-grandchildren.

[In addition to the works mentioned above see *Minutes of the Annual Conferences of the M. E. Ch. for the Year 1873*, pp. 115–17; Abel Stevens, *A Compendious Hist. of Am. Methodism* (1868), pp. 482–86; M. H. Chamberlin, "Rev. Peter Cartwright, D.D.," in *Trans. of the Ill. State Hist. Soc.*, 1902, pp. 47–56.] E.S.B.

CARUS, PAUL (July 18, 1852–Feb. 11, 1919), philosopher, the son of Dr. Gustav and Laura (Krueger) Carus, was born at Ilsenburg, Germany, of a family of distinguished scholars. His father, then pastor at Ilsenburg, later became First Superintendent General of the Church of Eastern and Western Prussia. Carus received a good education in mathematics and the classics at the *gymnasia* of Posen and Stettin, and afterward studied at the universities of Greifswald, Strassburg, and Tübingen where he received the degree of Ph.D. in 1876. He then became a teacher in the military academy at Dresden, but his liberal views soon brought him into opposition to the authorities, and he eventually resigned. In the early eighties he went to England and later came to America. Of stocky physique and massive head, black-bearded, intense, and voluble, with a generous spirit and extraordinarily broad interests, he was already an arresting personality. He had by now worked through a devastating period of religious skepticism into what was to remain his life-long philosophy. This consisted in a thorough-going monism of mind and matter, based on community of form and on the identity of the laws of nature and the laws of mind. Philosophy, he believed, could be reduced to a science as objective as any of the other sciences. The philosopher's brain, he wrote, "should work with the regularity of a machine." While thus opposed in principle to all subjectivism, he believed that the religious aspirations of mankind could be satisfied with a scientific conception of God as the impersonal world-order, and a historical conception of immortality as the survival of one's influence. To the working out in detail of this philosophy Carus zealously devoted the rest of his long life. His auctorial energy was stupendous, his bibliography embracing more than 1,000 titles, of which over fifty were of monographs in book form. In 1887 the Chicago zinc-manufacturer, Edward C. Hegeler, founded the *Open Court* as a journal devoted to the establishment of religion and ethics on a scientific basis. Carus contributed several articles and was then appointed editor. The magazine, first as a weekly, then as a monthly, flourished under his capable management. He threw open its columns to contributors, regardless of their previous prestige, and, with equal zest, entered into controversy with nobodies and with philosophers of established reputation. The interest of an idea, rather than its author, attracted him. His ties with Hegeler were drawn closer by his marriage on Mar. 29, 1888, to Hegeler's daughter, Mary. In 1890 Hegeler established the *Monist* as a quarterly to take care of the more technical contributions to the *Open Court*, and Carus became editor of the new magazine also. Soon the reprinting of valuable articles led to the development of the Open Court Publishing Company which, under Carus's direction, gradually enlarged its scope to include the republication at popular prices of philosophical classics, and the publication of new philosophical works and notable scientific treatises, such as those of Boole and Dedekind in mathematics, Binet and Ribot in psychology, and Mach in physics.

Carus exercised a wide popular influence on behalf of a more rational attitude toward religion and ethics than had hitherto been prevalent in America. His direct influence on American philosophy was curiously slight. In part this may be explained by the fact that philosophy, to its own loss, still tended to be the exclusive property of the universities, which looked upon any one outside their fold as an interloper and were particularly scandalized by Carus's editorial independence, but in part, also, it was due to Carus's insistent rationalism which was entirely out of harmony with the pragmatic tendencies of the time. Essentially forthright and impatient of doubt, he underrated the epistemological difficulties of his realistic position, and, in his constant endeavor toward a synthesis, sometimes strove to unify really irreconcilable doctrines. The religious tone of his writings failed to reconcile idealists to his naturalism but sufficed to alienate his fellow naturalists. Nevertheless his philosophy was well founded on his theory of forms, and it must be considered as one of the most constructive philosophical achievements in nineteenth-century America. Among his many books, probably the most important are: *Fundamental Problems* (1889); *The Soul of Man* (1891); *The Gospel of Buddha* (1894), a compilation of Buddhist scriptures, which was widely translated and was adopted in Buddhist schools in Ceylon and Japan; *De Rerum Natura*, a philosophical poem written originally in German but translated into English by Charles Alva Lane (1895) and published in its German form in the *Open Court*, September 1919; *Buddhism and Its Christian Critics* (1897); *Kant and Spencer: a Study of the Fallacies of Agnosticism* (1899); *The History of the Devil* (1900); *The Surd of Meta-*

physics (1903); *Friedrich Schiller* (1905); *Chinese Thought* (1907); *The Foundations of Mathematics* (1908); *God: an Enquiry and a Solution* (1908); *The Pleroma* (1909); *Truth on Trial* (1911), a critique of pragmatism; *Goethe, with Special Consideration of His Philosophy* (1915). Carus also translated Kant's *Prolegomena to Any Future Metaphysic* (1902) and *The Canon of Reason and Virtue . . . Being Lao-Tze's Tao Teh King* (1913). His *Philosophy as a Science* (1909) gives a synopsis of his writings to that date, and *The Point of View* (1927), edited by Catherine Cook, is a volume of well-chosen selections.

[Articles by Paul Brauns, Julius Goebel, Philip E. B. Jourdain, and Lydia G. Robinson in the *Open Court*, Sept. 1919, and by Wm. Ellery Leonard in the *Dial*, May 3, 1919; an obituary note by J. R. Kantor in the *Jour. of Philosophy, Psychology and Scientific Methods*, Apr. 10, 1919.]   E. S. B.

CARUSO, ENRICO (Feb. 25, 1873–Aug. 2, 1921), grand opera tenor, was born in Naples of peasant stock, the eighteenth son (and the first to survive infancy) of Marcellino and Anna (Baldini) Caruso. Marcellino Caruso was a rather unsuccessful mechanic, overly fond of wine, who took little interest in his son's education. Anna Caruso, however, although she died when her boy was eleven, had ambitions for the child; she labored to correct the slack Neapolitan dialect which he heard in the streets by teaching him "la lingua Toscana en bocca Romana" and she cultivated his naturally strong taste for neatness and precision in every undertaking. While he was still in the kindergarten, Errico,—the name by which he was christened and known until well into his maturity—was sent to an evening school kept by Father Giuseppe Bronzetti for training boy singers in church choirs. This school the child continued to attend for some eight years, his clear contralto voice eventually raising him to the position of chief soloist. His native talent for drawing was also carefully developed by Giuseppe Spasiano, the teacher of penmanship. When he was fourteen, Carusiello, as he was affectionately called, made his first appearance on any stage, as a comedian in a church play, "I briganti nel giardino di don Raffaele." Meanwhile, from the age of ten the boy had been put to work as a mechanic. At sixteen he had progressed to be accountant and receiving clerk in the factory of Francesco Meuricoffre where he remained for the next four years. But he took eager advantage of his scanty leisure to continue his music, earning a few much needed extra *lire* by singing at cafés, public baths, and church festivals. He also studied under Guglielmo Vergine, who recognized his talent sufficiently to make a

shrewd bargain that he should receive twenty-five per cent of Caruso's earnings for *five years of actual singing*, a contract which, since it would cover practically a lifetime, even the guileless Caruso later contested, finally compromising on terms sufficiently liberal to gratify his grasping master. Vergine, however much of a Shylock, proved to be a good teacher; under his instruction Caruso learned not to force his somewhat thin tenor voice, and at the same time was encouraged, at the age of twenty, definitely to seek an operatic career.

The next five years were devoted by Caruso to a slowly victorious struggle against obscurity, poverty, professional jealousy, and his own limitations. Always best in the *mezza voce*, and often in these early years accused of being a baritone, it was not until the end of this period that he really mastered his high notes. His acting, pronounced "awful" at first, he was never able to make more than passable. He often faced the boos and hisses with which the art-loving Italians were wont to greet a false note or absurd gesture, and through his simplicity and sincerity he was an easy victim of cabals. He made his début on Nov. 16, 1894, at the Teatro Nuovo, Naples, in the première of an unsuccessful opera, *L'Amico Francesco* by one Mario Morelli. A brief season at the Cimarosa in Caserta was followed by his appearance, owing to the illness of the regular tenor, in *Faust* at the Teatro Bellini, Naples, which led to a renewed engagement in the fall. During the next two years he did not get beyond Naples and its circle of influence (Caserta, Salerno, and several towns in Sicily), but by the autumn of 1897 he had reached northern Italy (Fiume, Milan, Genoa, Trent, Leghorn), and on Nov. 17, 1898, his gradually expanding reputation suddenly became international through his widely reported performance in the world première of *Fedora* at the Teatro Lirico, Milan. During the trying period before success, Caruso owed most to the teaching of Vincenzo Lombardi for a few months in 1896 and to the friendship of the prima donna Ada Giochetti, with whom in 1898 he formed a liaison destined to endure for eleven happy years and to give him two dearly loved sons, Rodolfo and Enrico.

Following his triumph in *Fedora*, Caruso was overwhelmed with offers. In the winter of 1898–99 he went to St. Petersburg, singing Rhadames in *Aïda* for the first time; in the spring he paid the first of many visits to Buenos Aires; in the fall he appeared at the Teatro Costanzi in Rome; in the ensuing winter he conquered the critical audience of La Scala in Milan, opening with Puccini's *La Bohême,* and taking part in the world première of *Le Maschere* and the noted revival of *Elisir d'amore.* Regarding his voice as a gift which he delighted to share with others, he went to Naples in 1901 in high hopes to please his native city, but Naples, ever critical of her own offspring, received him coldly,—so coldly that he swore never to visit the town again except "to eat a plate of spaghetti." The disappointment was soon alleviated, however, by renewed triumphs: at Monte Carlo, February 1902; London, May–July 1902; Lisbon, February–March 1903; Buenos Aires, July 1903; Rio de Janeiro, August 1903. And on Nov. 21, 1903, in *Rigoletto,* Caruso opened his first season at the Metropolitan Opera House, New York,—the goal of every opera singer's desire.

Caruso's task at the Metropolitan was not an easy one. He followed the aristocratic and intellectual Jean de Reszke, and he was neither aristocratic nor intellectual. His round, genial, plebeian face, and stocky figure inclined to strut when kingly dignity or romantic grace were called for, might easily have prejudiced the audience against him; but after a few performances the marvelous beauty of his "golden" voice, its lyric passion, its range and power, had already begun to cast a spell over the Metropolitan which was never broken. The memory of the more theatrical De Reszke paled before the far richer voice and natural even if ungainly manner of his successor. Henceforth until his death, although welcomed regularly in Europe and South America, Caruso remained especially the idol of the Metropolitan.

Extraordinarily conscientious toward both his audiences and his art, at least in all that concerned its musical side, Caruso sang on every occasion as if it were the crowning event of his career. He developed a dramatic vocal technique unequalled in variety and scope. His repertoire included no less than forty-three operas (complete list in Key, *post,* p. 396). Probably his greatest successes were in tragedy, yet he was by nature a comedian. Every week an amusing and admirably drawn cartoon from his pen appeared in *La Follia.* His fellow actors were likely to be disconcerted in some serious scene through having an egg or other awkward object surreptitiously thrust in their hands or through discovering that a needed prop had been diverted to some absurd use by the ingenious Caruso. To the end he remained the incorrigible boy, ingenuously vain, impetuously kind, quickly elated or depressed. He enjoyed the pleasures of food and drink; he smoked cigarettes incessantly and with impunity; he spent his money lavishly on mul-

titudinous garments, on collections of stamps and coins, on bronzes, enamels, pottery, tapestry, watches, and furniture, on a large estate near Florence embracing forty-seven farms. But he bestowed his wealth on others in as princely a manner as on himself. Unspoiled by success, he showed the same courtesy to kings and beggars. The tales of his generosity are legion. Besides the $70 worth of tickets to which his contract at the Metropolitan entitled him for each of his own performances, he usually gave away from $300 to $400 worth of tickets to his friends. Napoleonic in loyalty to his family and early acquaintances, he included more than a hundred in his list of pensioners; twenty-one of his relatives were at one time housed in his Florentine villa. During the World War he gave $5,000,-000 to the Italian Red Cross and raised $21,000,-000 for the Allied armies by his concerts.

On Aug. 20, 1918 he was married to Dorothy Benjamin, daughter of Park Benjamin [*q.v.*], who, convinced that the marriage would be unhappy, did his best to make it so, refusing to see his daughter afterward because she had married a "public singer." Luckily the father's prophecy of evil remained unfulfilled. The autumn of 1919 was especially joyous to Caruso for two things: his appearance as Eleazar in *La Juive* on Nov. 22,—universally considered the high point of his career; and the birth of his daughter Gloria on Dec. 18. During the ensuing year he became moody and melancholy through continued ill health but scrupulously fulfilled his contracts to sing, until, on Dec. 11, 1920, after going through a whole act of *Elisir d'amore* with a broken blood-vessel in his throat, he was obliged to close the performance. The next week he appeared thrice, as usual, but on Christmas Eve he sang for the last time. On Christmas Day he was attacked with pleurisy which developed into pneumonia; for weeks he hung between life and death, with the whole world anxiously watching the bulletins; apparently recovered, he insisted upon going in the early summer back to his beloved Italy where he suffered a relapse and died, in Naples, on Aug. 2, 1921, from an abscess of the lungs.

[*Enrico Caruso* (1922) by P. V. R. Key is a detailed biography prepared in part with Caruso's assistance. The date of birth is, however, given incorrectly; the correct date will be found in Caruso's handwriting in Emil Ledner, *Erinnerungen an Caruso* (Leipzig, 1922), facing p. 30. *Wings of Song* (1928) by Dorothy Caruso and Torrance Goddard gives an intimate and yet remarkably objective account of the singer's later life. References on Caruso's art are J. H. Wagenmann, *Enrico Caruso und das Problem der Stimmbildung* (Altenburg, 1911); Henry C. Lahee, *Grand Opera Singers of Today* (1912); Arturo Lancellotti, in *Musica D'Oggi,* V, 350–55.]   E.S.B.

CARUTHERS, WILLIAM ALEXANDER

(*c.* 1800–Aug. 29, 1846), author, was born in Virginia and died in Marietta, Ga. The only record of his youth is that he attended Washington College (now Washington and Lee University) in 1819–20 and that during that time he witnessed a much heralded ascent of the Natural Bridge, an event of some importance as the basis of an article he later wrote for the *Knickerbocker Magazine.* Sixteen years after leaving college he was still characterizing himself as a "Virginian," but it is probable that he was already a citizen of Savannah, a city which he thought of as "outstripping Philadelphia and New York, and controlled by a class of men as much like our real old-fashioned Virginia gentlemen as can well be imagined." *The Kentuckian in New York,* which he published in 1834, is a romance set forth in a series of letters between two Virginia students, one visiting in New York, the other, in Georgia and the Carolinas. In an epilogue, the Kentuckian himself is frankly apologized for as a humorous character introduced only for the sake of popularity; the writer's true interest lay elsewhere, specifically in an historical romance, *The Cavaliers of Virginia,* which he had already nearly completed. This book, published in 1837, describes with considerable accuracy the circumstances of Bacon's Rebellion. Like all its author's work, it touches at times on humor and aphorism, but remains on the whole too voluble and stilted to be of lasting interest. *The Knights of the Horseshoe, a Traditionary Tale of the Cocked Hat Gentry in the Old Dominion* (1845) deals with the rule of Gov. Spottswood. At some unknown date Caruthers became a physician. He is referred to in a Savannah newspaper of his time as being highly respected in his profession, and in 1842 he attacked a current vogue of mesmerism. He read widely and learned much, and he maintained always, even in the troubled realm of sectional disputes, an outlook which was to a degree clear and impartial. He was universally esteemed for his kindliness and his elegance of manner. His death occurred in North Georgia, where he had gone with a son, in hope of finding relief from protracted ill health.

[W. A. Caruthers, "Climbing the Natural Bridge," *Knickerbocker Mag.,* July 1838; "Sturmer, a Tale of Mesmerism," *Magnolia* (Jan. 1842); *Lecture Delivered before Ga. Hist Soc.* (1843); *Savannah Daily Georgian* and *Savannah Daily Republican,* Sept. 2, 1846; *Washington Coll. Reg. Alumni* (1858); C. Holliday, "Wm. Alexander Caruthers" in E. A. Alderman and J. C. Harris, *Lib. Southern Lit.* (1907), vol. II; J. G. Johnson, *Southern Fiction Prior to 1860* (1909).]

J. D. W.

CARVER, JOHN

(*c.* 1576–Apr. 5, 1621), one of the *Mayflower* Pilgrims, was the first governor of Plymouth. There is no Pilgrim whose services are better attested than his and no man of significance about whose life so few details are known. Born probably about 1576 in Nottinghamshire or Derbyshire, he spent his early life in business, moving to London in the last years of Elizabeth's reign, where he acquired in trade what for those days was a considerable fortune. Emigrating to Holland in 1609, independently of the Scrooby group, he joined the Pilgrims at Leyden probably in 1610–11. His high character, his stern piety, his maturity (most of the congregation being young men) gave him place at once among the leaders; his fortune, which he managed somehow to transfer from England, made him able to finance the congregation in part at least and explains perhaps the purchase of the Great House in which John Robinson, the pastor, lived and in which the congregation worshipped. As deacon, he ranked third among the officers of the church, following Robinson and William Brewster.

When the project for emigration to America was formed, Carver and Robert Cushman were sent to England in September 1617 as agents to secure permission from the Virginia Company to settle upon their territory. This mission failed, and Carver seems not to have been one of those who finally secured a grant of land on the Hudson River. He was, however, in all probability the one who persuaded a group of merchants, perhaps former friends of his, to finance the venture and the one responsible for the agreement, later called the Common Stock, under which the Pilgrims at last sailed for the New World. He was certainly the organizer of the London contingent, collecting the group which sailed direct from England, including Miles Standish and John Alden; he hired the *Mayflower;* and he sailed on her on July 15, 1620, from London, to meet the *Speedwell* with the Leyden contingent at Southampton. His wife sailed with him, and he brought also,—an attestation of his means—six servants, all "bound out" to him. One of these, John Howland, promptly proved his worth and remained for five decades among the most prominent of the Pilgrims.

On the voyage, Carver was certainly the mainstay of the group, and, when the decision was reached to settle in New England instead of on the Hudson where their charter granted them land, he was elected governor for one year of the new political society organized by the Pilgrim Compact, signed on Nov. 11, 1620. He commanded the two boat expeditions to spy out the land and was perhaps the first to step on shore at Plymouth on Dec. 11. During the winter, throughout the "sickness" in which so many died, he was active in all duties, including nursing the sick. Aside from his treaty with Massasoit in March 1621, we have no idea of his governmental activities or policies. On Mar. 23, he was reëlected governor. Weakened, however, by his own severe illness in the winter, and by excessive toil for the colony at manual labor, he died on Apr. 5, 1621, while working in the fields, overcome, they thought, by sunstroke. Of his appearance we have no inkling. His chair and sword are among the few relics of undoubted authenticity.

[The chief authority is Wm. Bradford's *Hist. of Plimouth Plantation* (ed. by Worthington C. Ford, 1912). See also E. Arber, *Pilgrim Fathers* (1897); O. S. Davis, *John Robinson* (1903); W. H. Burgess, *John Robinson* (1920); H. M. and M. Dexter, *England and Holland of the Pilgrims* (1905); R. G. Usher, *The Pilgrims and their Hist.* (1918).]
R. G. U.

CARVER, JONATHAN (Apr. 13, 1710–Jan. 31, 1780), traveler, son of David and Hannah (Dyer) Carver, was born in Weymouth, Mass. When he was eight years of age, his father moved to Canterbury, Conn., where after a prosperous career he died in 1727. Jonathan was left in care of a maternal uncle, and had as good an education as the colony afforded; it is claimed, but not proven, that he studied medicine. At Canterbury he married, Oct. 10, 1746, Abigail Robbins; thence he enlisted as sergeant and was at the siege of Fort William Henry in 1757, where he was wounded. He became lieutenant in 1759, and captain the next year in a Massachusetts regiment, having removed to Montague in that state, where in 1759 he was selectman. Gen. Gage testified to his military ability and good character. At the instance of Maj. Robert Rogers, then commandant at Mackinac, Carver set out on his travels in 1766. He went west by the route of the Great Lakes, crossed to the Mississippi by the Green Bay–Fox–Wisconsin route, ascended the great river and entered the St. Peter's (now the Minnesota). He reached Lake Superior by the Chippewa and St. Croix rivers, and finally returned in the autumn of 1767 to Mackinac, whence in the next spring he made his way back to Boston. Disappointed in the hope of publishing his volume of travels, he sailed on Feb. 22, 1769, for England, where he engaged in literary work during the rest of his life. In 1774 he married Mrs. Mary Harris in London, notwithstanding the fact that his American wife was still living. The first edition of his *Travels* appeared in 1778;

the second part was a compilation on Indian manners and customs, from other authors who were not cited, and so gave rise to the charge of plagiarism. The manuscript of Carver's *Travels* exists in the British Museum; it differs materially from the published account, which shows the hand of some literary hack in preparing it for publication. In 1779 Carver lent his name to a *New Universal Geography;* he also published a treatise on tobacco raising. Notwithstanding these publications and a payment of his accounts by the government, he died in great penury, and was buried in paupers' ground, whence his English wife had him removed by the charity of admirers. He left one daughter by his wife in England, and several children of his American marriage. The 1781 edition of his *Travels* contained a biography, portrait, and account of Carver's Indian grant, which he never claimed in his lifetime. On the strength of this grant, supposed to have been made in a cave near St. Paul, a number of speculators attempted to claim lands in Wisconsin and Minnesota.

[Carver's *Travels in Interior Parts of America* was a very popular book, and ran through many editions and translations; see John Thos. Lee, "A Bibliography of Carver's Travels" in *Proc. Wis. Hist. Soc.*, 1909, pp. 143–83; "Additional Data," by same author, *Ibid.*, 1912, pp. 87–123. E. G. Bourne, "The Travels of Jonathan Carver," in *Am. Hist. Rev.*, XI, 287–302, called attention to his plagiarism, and discredited his biography. He has been rehabilitated by Lee (as above) and by Wm. Browning, "Early Hist. of Jonathan Carver," in *Wis. Mag. of Hist.*, III, 291–305. See also M. M. Quaife, "Carver and the Carver Grant," in *Miss. Valley Hist. Rev.*, VII, 3–25; L. P. Kellogg, "Mission of Jonathan Carver," in *Wis. Mag. of Hist.*, XII, 127–45.]
L. P. K.

CARY, ALICE (Apr. 26, 1820–Feb. 12, 1871), poet, was descended from John Cary, who in 1630 taught the first Latin class in America, in Plymouth, Mass. A lineal descendant, in the sixth generation, from John, was Robert Cary, a pioneer farmer, who lived on a bit of land eight miles north of Cincinnati; a man of poetic temperament which the hardships of life had left undeveloped. His wife, Elizabeth Jessup, was a superior woman whose eagerness for culture was not quenched by the toil of bringing up a family of nine children; of these Alice was the fourth. The primitive conditions of her early life afforded few opportunities for intellectual development, yet these she improved so zealously that when she was eighteen years of age a poem from her pen appeared in a Cincinnati paper. In 1849, she, together with her sister Phœbe [*q.v.*], four years her junior, issued a volume entitled *Poems of Alice and Phœbe Cary.* The next year the two made a journey to New York and New England, which was especially significant to them because of a visit they paid to Whittier, which he commemorated in his poem "The Singer." The favorable reception given the collected poems and a disappointment in love moved Alice Cary to make her home in New York City in 1850, and later to send for Phœbe and a younger sister. Literary work was not then liberally paid, but the sisters lived economically, kept out of debt, and Alice worked so unremittingly and successfully that by 1856 she was well established and drew about her a brilliant circle of friends. To the home on Twentieth St. for the next fifteen years came on Sunday evenings a group, congenial and distinguished, of men and women of literary tastes. The social charm of the two sisters more than their reputation as poets was the chief attraction. Alice seemed to her friends greater and sweeter than any song she ever sang. Full of unselfish interest in individuals, she was an intelligent and eager champion of the great causes making for human advancement. Although of a self-effacing disposition, she reluctantly consented to become the first president of the first woman's club (now the Sorosis) in America. The breadth of her religious sympathies attached her to the Universalist Church and she accepted most of its doctrines. Despite the fact that she was an invalid during her later years, she worked unremittingly. This toil, partly necessary for maintaining the household and partly the conscientious effort to waste no moment of talent, injured to some extent the quality of her poetry. Widely read during her lifetime, her poems are too diffuse, too tinged with sadness, too didactic for the taste of to-day; but there is in them a genuine poetic feeling, a sincere love and interpretation of nature which is attractive. Her prose works, especially *Clovernook Papers* (1852), had a large sale in this country and in Great Britain; a second series was issued in 1853. In 1855 *Clovernook Children* proved popular with young people. Her other publications were *Hager, a Story of Today* (1852), *Lyra and Other Poems* (1852), *Married, not Mated* (1856), *Pictures of Country Life* (1859), *Ballads, Lyrics and Hymns* (1866), *Snow-Berries* (1867), *The Bishop's Son* (1867), *The Lover's Diary* (1868). She was at work on *The Born Thrall* at the time of her death which occurred in New York, Feb. 12, 1871.

[*Poetical Works of Alice and Phœbe Cary: with a Memorial of their Lives* by Mary Clemmer (1876); see also references under Phœbe Cary.]　　　C. A. D.

CARY, ANNIE LOUISE (Oct. 22, 1842–Apr. 3, 1921), singer, was born in Wayne, Me., a daughter of Dr. Howard Nelson Cary and of his wife, Maria Stockbridge, a descendant of Elder Brewster of *Mayflower* fame. As a young woman (1864) she began her music studies with J. Q. Wetherbee and Lyman Wheeler, in Boston. Two years later she went to Milan and prepared for an operatic career with Giovanni Corsi, and it was only fifteen months later that she made her début in Copenhagen. The Scandinavian peninsula kept the young star on the platforms of its theatres for two seasons, Miss Cary leaving only during her vacations which were devoted to study at Baden-Baden with Mme. Viardot-Garcia. A winter of study in Paris with Maurice Strakosch and Bottesini followed an appearance at Brussels, and in August 1870, Miss Cary returned to her country. After her first appearance in America as a member of Christine Nilsson's Concert Company in New York City on Sept. 19, 1870, there was in the next morning's *Sun,* the report that next to Mme. Nilsson's, Miss Cary's appearance attracted the most interest: "She has an admirable voice, full, deep, round and mellow—a voice like that of Adelaide Phillips, a great deal of that peculiarly sweet and touching quality which seems to belong more or less to all American girls who have any voice at all. She has been trained in an excellent school and is likely to prove a credit to her country." From that time until her retirement in 1882, she was one of the most celebrated of opera and concert contraltos, equally popular at the opera houses of London, St. Petersburg, and New York. Her retirement at the age of forty was simultaneous with her marriage to Charles Monson Raymond. During her short public career she attained a distinction well described by W. J. Henderson in the *New York Herald* (Apr. 10, 1921) just a week after her death: "Her repertoire included all the principal contralto parts of the day. Her voice was of rich dramatic timbre. It is pretty safe to say in the case of Miss Cary that she was the foremost contralto who trod the lyric stage within the memory of living opera-goers. No other has quite equalled her in the splendor of her tone, her command of the grand style and her heroic delivery of tragic music." Her most successful rôles were those of Siebel in *Faust,* Amneris in *Aïda,* and Martha and Pantalis in the first American performance of Boito's *Mefistofele* which antedated those of Paris and London by more than two years. After her retirement, she sang occasionally in the choir of the West Presbyterian Church in New York City. She died on Apr. 3, 1921, in her seventy-ninth year.

[H. E. Krehbiel in *Grove's Dict. of Music and Musicians* (3rd ed., 1927); Mary H. Flint in *N. Y. Times,* Apr. 10, 1921.]　　　P. V. R. K.

CARY, ARCHIBALD (1721–1787), planter, industrialist, Revolutionary statesman, son of Henry and Anne (Edwards) Cary, came from a typical great family of eighteenth-century Virginia. Before 1667, Miles Cary the immigrant, whose ancestors since 1546 had been prosperous merchants and high municipal officers in Bristol, England, was flourishing in Virginia. There the Carys maintained their mercantile position while they also became great planters, public officials, and aristocrats. Archibald's father, landholder and high sheriff, was the contracting builder of court-houses and churches. He built also the chapel and the president's house at William and Mary, and on the James River in Chesterfield County erected Ampthill House and a flour mill. Beyond the fall line in Henrico, afterward Goochland and Cumberland Counties, he acquired 12,000 acres, on part of which in 1742 he seated Archibald lately educated at William and Mary.

Here from 1747 to 1750, young Archibald served as justice of the peace, burgess, and vestryman. Then, his father having died, he removed to Ampthill, where he extended Henry Cary's manufacturing projects. He established a ropery, built a furnace and foundry, but after a decade ceased to manufacture iron. From his more successful flour mill he later supplied the War Board. Contemporaneously, he took an interest in experimental stock breeding, imported pure-bred cattle, and fostered road and bridge building. From 1756 he represented Chesterfield County in the Assembly, and in 1762 became chairman of the Public Claims Committee. Though of the committee which protested against Grenville's proposed Stamp Tax, he voted against Patrick Henry's flaming resolutions in 1765. He became, nevertheless, ardently revolutionary, signed the Associations of 1769, 1770, 1774, was on the Committee of Correspondence of 1773, sat in all the Virginian Revolutionary conventions, and as chairman of the Committee of the Whole read to the convention Virginia's Resolution of Independence.

In 1781 his mills were destroyed by a British force under Benedict Arnold. Six years afterward he died, speaker of the Virginia Senate and lord of 14,172 acres and 266 slaves, but financially in difficulties. Notably a lavish patriot, to whom the State in 1781 owed £58,000 in depreciated currency, he like other Virginians paid his British debts,—at least £10,000—in depreciated Virginian currency. When magistrate he prosecuted Virginian Baptists. Futilely he strove to forestall disestablishment and in the Convention of 1785 helped organize the incorporated

Episcopal Church. Bright-eyed, compact, and muscular, he was masterful, and was bitingly dubbed by a contemporary "Old Bruiser," but a British prisoner found him courteous, genial, and hospitable, and Washington, eleven years younger, affectionately called him "Archy." At twenty-three, he married Mary Randolph, granddaughter of the famous Turkey Island couple; through his mother, he was cousin to his fellow patriot, Benjamin Harrison; and his children's marriages additionally linked him with leading Virginian families.

[Fairfax Harrison, *The Virginia Carys* (1919); *William and Mary College Quart.*, 2 ser., V, 167–68, VI, 122–28; H. B. Grigsby, *The Virginia Convention of 1776* (1855), pp. 90–93; *Jours.* of the Va. House of Burgesses, Revolutionary Conventions, and Senate 1748–87. Cary's personal papers and correspondence were destroyed.]   K. B.

CARY, EDWARD (June 5, 1840–May 23, 1917), editor, son of Joseph and Lydia (Chase) Cary of Quaker stock, was born in Albany, N. Y. He grew up in his native city, where his elementary schooling was obtained. Having completed his junior year at Union College, Schenectady, N. Y., he returned to Albany to continue his studies at the Law School there. He soon began writing editorials for a paper called the *Statesman,* and after about a year decided on journalism as his life-work and went to Brooklyn, N. Y., to take the editorship of the daily *Union.* The editorials which he wrote for that newspaper soon began to attract the notice of other editors and publishers. Cary was at first a Republican, and a defender of the Lincoln administration, but after the Civil War he found himself less and less in sympathy with the tenets of the party in power. In 1871, George Jones, proprietor of the *New York Times,* was seeking an editorial writer. Cary at thirty-one, with eight years of newspaper writing behind him, was selected by Jones as the man to take the place. The opportunity appealed to the young man. The *Times* was in its fight with the Tweed ring and in national politics was assuming an independent attitude. Cary took the chair, which he was not to relinquish until his death after forty-six years of exacting but fruitful toil. Shortly after beginning work on the *Times,* he made a positive stand in opposition to free silver coinage. This he consistently maintained for more than a quarter of a century,—until the question was removed from the sphere of practical politics. Later he held an equally definite course on the subject of tariff reduction. In civil service reform he was one of the pioneers, not only warmly supporting the movement with his pen, but taking a personal part in the leadership, with George William Curtis, Carl Schurz, Dorman B. Eaton, and others. His advocacy in the *Times* of Grover Cleveland's candidacy was a factor of no slight importance in the national election of 1884. In both of Cleveland's terms as president the *Times* gave him able and hearty support.

By the time Cary came to the *Times* desk the old manner of editorial polemics had about run its course in New York. Editors were no longer calling one another scoundrels and liars,—in cold type. Cary was gifted in a style of writing that was suited to the new demands. Partisan pleas and vituperation were alike distasteful to him. He excelled in the calm, clear, and succinct statement of economic facts and principles, without embroidery. His audience may not have been large (in the early years), but it was influential to the degree that brains count for power in the long run. The *Times* editorials were widely quoted by other newspapers. According to estimates made by his colleagues, Cary's contributions to the editorial page averaged 6,000 words each week for the entire period of his service, reaching a total of more than 14,000,000 words,—the equivalent of two substantial volumes a year for the forty-six years. A remarkably large percentage of this output was of more than ephemeral interest; indeed much of it, in economic and political discussions, was of permanent value. In 1894 he contributed *George William Curtis* to the American Men of Letters series. Cary had been married in 1864 to Elisabeth Luther, of Albany. His daughter, Elisabeth Luther Cary, was for many years editor of the art department of the New York *Times*.

[*N. Y. Times, N. Y. Herald,* May 24, 1917; *Hist. of the Class of 1863 of Union College* (n.d.).]

W. B. S.

CARY, LOTT (1780?–Nov. 10, 1828), negro Baptist missionary, was born a slave in Charles City County, Va. In 1804 he went to Richmond, secured work in a tobacco warehouse, and for some years led a riotous life. In 1807 he was greatly impressed by a sermon based on the third chapter of John, and from this time forth his life showed the effect of a genuine conversion. Meanwhile his efforts to fit himself for service gave evidence of remarkable force of personality, and he was helped by his massive and erect figure. He learned to read, was given unusual authority in his work, and from time to time received special remuneration. About 1813, his first wife having died, he purchased his freedom and that of his two children for $850; and he received license to preach from the First Baptist Church of Richmond, which in 1815 had 1,200 negro members in its congregation. Inspired by the sermons of Luther Rice, Cary in 1815 helped to organize the Richmond African Baptist Missionary Society, which after five years had $700 in the treasury. Meanwhile he married again. He himself determined to go to Africa; and on May 1, 1819, he was received for service by the Baptist Board of Foreign Missions. Before leaving, with Collin Teague and a few other associates he organized what was to be the first Baptist church in Liberia, himself being pastor. On Jan. 23, 1821, in the brig *Nautilus,* he sailed from Norfolk in company with twenty-eight colonists and their children, the expedition being in charge of two representatives of the American Colonization Society. With this organization circumstances forced Cary to cooperate; but he never fully subscribed to its policies. Having arrived at Freetown after a voyage of forty-four days, no other provision having been made for them, the colonists were accepted by the government agent as laborers and mechanics. In December the arrival of new agents of the Colonization Society led to further negotiation for land and to the real founding of Liberia; and early in 1822 Cary and others went to Cape Montserado. Between the ravages of the fever and the hostility of the natives the outlook was far from promising; but Cary was with those colonists who determined to stay. He extended his labors, and after three years he had more than sixty members in his church. In the closing months of 1823 he was prominent in opposing the authority of Jehudi Ashmun [*q.v.*], who had brought out a company of colonists and had taken charge of the colony; but the high character of Ashmun eventually won his cooperation. In 1826 he was vice-agent of the colony. On Nov. 8, 1828, while he was assisting in the defense of the colony against the Deys, the overturning of a candle led to a powder explosion, and he was fatally injured along with several other persons. He died two days later.

[Miles Mark Fisher, "Lott Cary, the Colonizing Missionary," in *Jour. of Negro Hist.,* VII, 380 ff.; Jas. B. Taylor, *The Biography of Elder Lott Cary* (1837); sketch from "a Richmond paper" of the year 1825, with other material, in *Biog. Sketches and Interesting Anecdotes of Persons of Colour,* comp. by A. Mott (enlarged ed., 1837); Ralph R. Gurley, *Life of Jehudi Ashmun* (1835), with an appendix containing a biographical sketch of Cary.]

B. B.

CARY, PHOEBE (Sept. 4, 1824–July 31, 1871), poet, was the sixth child of Robert and Elizabeth (Jessup) Cary, and shared with her sister Alice [*q.v.*], the hardships of the farm just outside Cincinnati, and felt the same inner music and passion for self-expression. In 1849 she contributed her part to the slender volume, *Poems of Alice and Phœbe Cary*. After she had joined her sister in New York, to her fell most of the domestic duties of the home, and the increasing invalidism of Alice threw more and more responsibility upon her. In the large circle of friends who frequented the Sunday evening receptions she was considered one of the wittiest women in America. By temperament more buoyant and vigorous than her sister, she held her poetic talent in less command. The elder worked ceaselessly, the younger was more the servant of her mood. Her literary output was much less, but there is an ampler variety of feeling, more humor and spirit. Alice Cary was more generally read by contemporaries, but Phœbe Cary's verses seem to have more of that quality which keeps poetry alive, and it would not be without reason if she had in the future the greater number of admirers. Certainly her poem "One Sweetly Solemn Thought" has won for itself a permanent place in the religious poetry of the country. It was composed one Sunday morning in 1852 when the mood of the church service still possessed her. It was soon set to music and became popular and effective as an anthem. After the publication of their first volume of poems, the two sisters worked independently and published their poetry under separate covers. Although the two differed quite widely in temperament, endowments, and methods of work, they perfectly supplemented each other. Their devotion was complete and when Alice died in February 1871 her sister, weakened by constant anxiety and deprived of the one who had been the steadying and controlling influence of her life, followed in July of the same year. Phœbe had published *Poems and Parodies* (1854) and *Poems of Faith, Hope and Love* (1868), and had assisted Dr. Charles F. Deems, pastor of the Church of the Strangers in editing *Hymns for all Christians* (1869).

[*Poetical Works of Alice and Phœbe Cary: with a Memorial of their Lives* by Mary Clemmer (1876); Horace Greeley, "Alice and Phœbe Cary" in *Eminent Women of the Age* (1868) by Jas. Parton and others; R. W. Griswold, *Female Poets of America* (1859).]

C. A. D.

CASANOWICZ, IMMANUEL MOSES (July 25, 1853–Sept. 26, 1927), orientalist, archeologist, was born at Zhaludok, Province of Vilna, Russia, the son of Jekuthiel and Sara (Tanowsk) Casanowicz. His parents, though in moderate circumstances, intended that the youth should become a learned man, perhaps a rabbi. Being set apart with this purpose in view, he received such instruction as could be given in his

native town. At twenty-three years of age he was a student in the Evangelische Predigerschule at Basel, Switzerland, in which he later became a teacher. Emigrating to America about 1882, he took the position of teacher in Hebrew and church history in the German Theological School of Newark, at Bloomfield, N. J., remaining there four years (1883–86). He then studied at Johns Hopkins where he was awarded the degree of Ph.D. in 1892. In the same year he was appointed to the division of Oriental studies originated by Dr. Paul Haupt and under the immediate supervision of Dr. Cyrus Adler in the United States National Museum in Washington. Gradually rising in usefulness in this work, he was appointed assistant curator of Old World archeology in 1906 and held this position at the time of his death. He was a member of the American Oriental Society and of the Anthropological Society of Washington. He was unmarried. Short of stature, slender, and ascetic, he gave an impression of reserve force far beyond the physical. His manner declared him to be kind, considerate, and helpful, inspiring confidence and friendship. The history of religions absorbed a great part of his energies and on this subject he was an authority. His knowledge of the Semitic group of languages, as well as of several other ancient and modern tongues, rendered him one of the first students in Biblical exegesis. He arranged, in the National Museum, exhibits,— unique in America—illustrating the cult or external side of religious activities. Writing on subjects relating to religion formed the bulk of his publications. Of these his inaugural dissertation *Paronomasia in the Old Testament* (1894) attracted much attention from scholars on account of its erudition. Of his descriptive catalogues of material in the United States National Museum, *Ecclesiastical Art* (1919), *Buddhist Art* (1921), *Rosaries* (1909), and *Old World Archeology* (1924) are the most important. He left a large manuscript on the collection of objects of religious ceremonial in the United States National Museum, which may be regarded as a summation of his studies, and which is to be published.

[*Who's Who in America*, 1927–28; *Am. Anthropologist.* n.s., XXX, no. 2, 359; personal acquaintance.]

W. H.

CASE, JEROME INCREASE (Dec. 11, 1818– Dec. 22, 1891), manufacturer, was born in Williamstown, Oswego County, N. Y., where his parents, Caleb and Deborah (Jackson) Case, were among the pioneers from the eastern part of the state. As soon as he was old enough, Jerome helped in clearing and cultivating the wilderness and went to school when he could. His interest in machinery was of local comment. When he was sixteen, his father purchased a horse-treadmill threshing-machine of which Jerome was placed in charge, conducting a threshing business for five years. With his earnings he then attended an academy at Mexico, N. Y., for a year. Upon completing an elective course there, he decided to go West and start another threshing business. He purchased six horse-power threshers on credit and took them to Racine, Wis., in 1842, where he soon found buyers for five of the machines. He kept the sixth with which to earn his living and in the hope that by study and experiment he might improve it. Success crowned his efforts and in 1844, while in Rochester, Wis., he designed, built, and put into practical operation a combined thresher and separator, thus eliminating the fanning mill. He immediately rented a small shop in Racine to build the machine, and, after three hard years during which he succeeded in selling a few units, his machine was generally accepted and he had accumulated sufficient capital to erect a manufacturing plant. His business, in which he displayed much sagacity, grew rapidly. The fact that he was a practical thresher himself was of great advertising value. His plant was the largest west of Buffalo and within ten years, by 1857, was producing 1,600 machines a year. In 1863 he took in three former employees to form the J. I. Case Company, and in 1880 this company was incorporated as the J. I. Case Threshing-Machine Company. Besides his original organization Case formed the J. I. Case Plow Works, and in 1871 established the Manufacturers' National Bank of Racine and the First National Bank of Burlington, Wis. He was president of these institutions at the time of his death and was also a member of the Board of Trustees of the Northwestern Mutual Life Insurance Company of Milwaukee. As successful in banking as in manufacturing, he was later identified with national banks in Minnesota, South Dakota, and California. He was twice Republican mayor of Racine (1856, 1859), was a state senator for one term, was one of the Wisconsin State commissioners at the Centennial Exposition in 1876, and was one of the founders of the Wisconsin Academy of Science, Art, and Letters. His life-long love of fine horses was gratified in his ownership of the Glenview Stock Farm in Louisville, Ky., where many famous racers were bred, notably Jay-Eye-See. He was married in 1849 to Lydia A., daughter of De Grove Bull of Yorkville, Wis. Three daughters and a son were born

to them, all of whom as well as Case's widow survived him.

[*Milwaukee Sentinel*, Dec. 23, 1891; *Western Mo.*, vol. IV, no. 21; *National Mag.*, vol. XV, no. 5.]

C. W. M.

CASE, LEONARD (July 29, 1786–Dec. 7, 1864), Western Reserve land agent, lawyer, was born in Westmoreland County, Pa., the oldest son in a family of eight children. His father, Meshach Case, was of Dutch, and his mother, Magdalene Eckstein, of German descent. They were farmers, and Leonard passed his time as did other country boys between short terms at school and long periods of farm work. One of his early recollections was of the Whiskey Insurrection in his neighborhood. In his autobiography he makes the observation that a cause of the insurrection was the scarcity of currency, and that the presence of the Federal army soon placed in circulation a supply which relieved the situation. In the spring of 1800, tales of the country west of Pennsylvania attracted the Cases to Warren, Ohio, where they obtained a two-hundred-acre farm. In October 1801, Leonard was prostrated with fever, possibly as a result of exposure while ranging the woods for cattle. Complications left him a cripple for life, necessitating the use of a cane and a crutch. He faced the handicap with courage, purchased a Dilworth arithmetic, borrowed *Gibson on Surveying,* and set about their mastery as the first step in his new plan of life. In 1806 he secured a place as assistant to the clerk of courts at Warren and in 1807 he was appointed clerk of the supreme court. He also began the study of law and was employed for a time in the office of the Connecticut Land Company. In the latter office his association with Gen. Simon Perkins, chief agent of the company, proved to be the foundation for much of his later business success. He continued his study of law and in 1814 received his certificate of admission to the bar. In 1816, the Commercial Bank of Lake Erie was founded in Cleveland, and Case became cashier. The next year he was married to Elizabeth Gaylord. The years immediately after 1816 were precarious for the banking business in the West, and in 1819 the bank closed. Some years later, in the thirties, it was rehabilitated with Case as president, but in the meantime he had returned to his law practise and to the real estate business, with intervals in public office. From 1820 to 1824, he was auditor of Cuyahoga County; from 1821 to 1825, president of Cleveland Village. In 1824 he was elected to the state legislature where he distinguished himself for his work in behalf of the Ohio canals. From 1826 to 1830, he was prosecuting attorney of Cuyahoga County, and in 1838, after Cleveland became a city, he was elected a member of the council. When Cleveland's first railroad project, the Cleveland, Columbus & Cincinnati, was organized in 1847, Case was a director and vice-president, and for two years, until his health prevented, he took an active part in the building of the railroad. From 1827 to 1855, he was agent for the Connecticut Land Company. After closing out the land agency, Case spent the remaining years of his life caring for his own properties. His claim for remembrance by posterity rests upon his part as a builder of early Cleveland,—the advancement of its material well-being and the promotion of civic pride.

[The chief source for the life of Case is his unpublished autobiography now in possession of a relative, Mr. Eckstein Case. The latter also contributed a biographical sketch to S. P. Orth, *A Hist. of Cleveland*, I (1910), 556 ff. There is a biographical sketch in the *Western Reserve Hist. Soc. Tract 79* (1891), p. 221, by Jas. D. Cleveland, written with the use of the autobiography, aided by personal recollections.]   E. J. B.

CASE, LEONARD (June 27, 1820–Jan. 6, 1880), philanthropist, was the second son of Leonard Case [*q.v.*] and Elizabeth (Gaylord) Case. He attended the schools of Cleveland; for a time the Academy of the Rev. Colley Foster, and later that of Franklin T. Backus. Following the advice of the latter, a Yale graduate, Leonard entered Yale in 1838, and graduated with the class of 1842. The following two years he studied law in the Cincinnati Law School. After admission to the bar he opened a law office in Cleveland. His practise was never large, for he gave his attention chiefly to the real estate business which his father had developed. Meanwhile he found time to pursue mathematical, scientific, and literary studies. He and his brother, William, together with a group of friends, turned the Case office into a miniature natural-history museum. They called themselves the "Arkites" and the office, the "Ark." The "Arkites" formed a stimulating informal natural-history club. In 1845, Case went to Europe in company with Prof. St. John of Western Reserve College and Prof. Loomis, then of the University of the City of New York, formerly of Western Reserve. While in Switzerland he became seriously ill and the effects lasted the remainder of his life, necessitating constant care of his health. He was very fond of travel and though he made only one trip to Europe, he traveled extensively in the United States. He remained unmarried. His tastes were never satisfied with either his law practise or business. As soon as he came into his father's large estate he turned the active management over to another and devoted himself to his lit-

erary pursuits, to writing, to a wide correspondence, and to his growing interest in philanthropic enterprises in Cleveland. On his travels he wrote lengthy descriptive letters. He also wrote a good many poems, usually of a humorous turn, many of which were published in *Western Reserve Historical Society Tract No. 79*. His "Treasure Trove," a mixture of comedy, tragedy, and satire, about medieval knights and kings, was published in the *Atlantic Monthly*, July 1860 (reprinted in book form, 1873).

Of a kindly nature, Case was a generous giver to charities. To the Cleveland Library Association (later Case Library) he gave an endowment of $20,000. Some years later this was very largely increased by the gift of the Case building, where the library had been housed since 1866, and which was valued at the time at $300,000. When the Western Reserve Historical Society was founded in 1867, Case became one of its benefactors. His greatest work was the founding of the Case School of Applied Science, his plan for which seems to have been fully perfected by 1876. There is some evidence that his father and brother had had in mind some use of their fortune for the benefit of their fellow townsmen, but it is probable that Case's own interest in scientific matters was the main cause of this particular project. In February 1877 the trust deed was signed giving a large share of his fortune to endow a school "to teach mathematics, physics, engineering, mechanical and civil, chemistry, geology, mining, and metallurgy, natural history, languages," and such other subjects as the trustees should consider necessary. The gift consisted of real property in the business center of Cleveland and was valued at that time at about one and one-half million dollars. Case disliked publicity and the knowledge of the gift was withheld from the public until after his death. In the fall of 1881, the school opened its doors in the Case homestead on Rockwell St.

[A biography of Case, prepared by Judge Jas. D. Cleveland, is printed in the *Western Reserve Hist. Soc. Tract 79*; *Biog. Record of the Class of 1842 of Yale Coll.* (privately printed, 1878); Mr. Eckstein Case, in *Notes on the Origin and Hist. of the Ark* (Cleveland, 1902), reprints some Case letters.]   E. J. B.

CASE, WILLIAM SCOVILLE (June 27, 1863–Feb. 28, 1921), lawyer, jurist, born in Tariffville, Conn., was the son of William Cullen Case and Margaret (Turnbull) Case, and was a descendant in the eighth generation of John Case, who came to America from the southern part of England. William Cullen Case was for many years a lawyer of Connecticut, distinguished, among other things, for his oratorical ability and for his mastery of the art of cross-examination. The fragmentary early education of William Scoville Case in the local schools was supplemented by extended reading. He entered Hopkins Grammar School in New Haven in 1877, was admitted to Yale University, and graduated with his class in 1885 after four happy and well-spent years, during which he had found opportunity for the expression of his literary gift as editor of the *Yale Record*. On leaving college he studied in his father's office until his admission to the bar in 1887. On Apr. 8, 1891, he married Elizabeth Nichols of Salem, Mass., daughter of Nathan and Elizabeth Rodman Nichols. Shortly after his marriage he wrote a novel, *Forward House*, which evinced imagination and unusual powers of description. In July 1897 he became judge of the court of common pleas in Hartford County, and entered upon a judicial career that was to end only with his death twenty-four years later. Promoted to the superior court in 1901, he served there most acceptably until August 1919, when he became a justice of the supreme court of errors. Possessed of a keen, discriminating, and cultured mind, he readily mastered legal principles, and by a sort of flashing intuition rather than by studied processes— at least so it seemed—he was able to select the one that pointed out the judgment to be rendered. But this instinctive method was never permitted to dictate finality in his conclusions, until their correctness had been verified by a course of reasoning,—a test which his logical mind was abundantly able to supply. His memoranda of decisions and later his opinions in the supreme court had a felicity of style rarely equaled in law reports. He also had other means of expression, as many lifelike and clever caricatures of lawyers, witnesses, and jurors, imbedded in his evidence-books, testify; but they, unfortunately, were kept for the delectation of a few friends. A quiet dignity pervaded his court-room, and one was conscious of the firm but unobtrusive control which he exercised over its proceedings. Any deliberate violation of the proprieties met with quick rebuke, uttered occasionally in caustic and witty phrase which members of the bar delighted to recall. His varied gifts would have been certain to bring him ever greater distinction as a justice of the court of last resort, and his death before completing two years of work on that tribunal was deplored by bench and bar, and by a public he had served with conspicuous ability and fidelity.

[*Yale Univ., Quarter-Centenary of the Class of 1885* (1913); 95 *Conn. Reports*, 743; *Hartford Courant*, Mar. 1, 1921; *Who's Who in America*, 1920–21; information from Mrs. Wm. Scoville Case; personal acquaintance.]   J.P.A.

CASEY, JOSEPH (Dec. 17, 1814–Feb. 10, 1879), jurist, was the son of Joseph Casey, a native of Wicklow, Ireland, and a graduate in medicine of Edinburgh University, who in 1792 emigrated to the United States, settled in Pennsylvania, and there married Rebecca, daughter of Thomas McLaughlin of Franklin County. The younger Joseph was born at Ringgold's Manor, Washington County, Md. While he was yet a child misfortune beset his parents, the various members of the family separated, and Joseph was placed with a blacksmith's family in Newville, Pa. In 1828, having received little education, he rejoined his father at Shippensburg, Cumberland County, Pa. He there attended the common schools for about a year, but his father was in financial straits, and in 1831 Joseph was apprenticed to a hat manufacturer at Shippensburg. For the next five years he was employed in this industry, also studying at home to complete his education. In 1836, in Carlisle, Pa., he entered the law office of Charles B. Penrose, grandfather of Senator Boise Penrose, and a very astute politician. In November 1838 he was admitted to the bar at Carlisle. For four years he practised at Bloomfield, Perry County, Pa., but in 1845 moved to New Berlin, Union County, Pa., a place which offered better opportunities. There he commenced to take an active part in politics. In 1848 he was elected as Whig representative of his district in the Thirty-first Congress and served till Mar. 3, 1851, but declined a renomination. He was a moderate opponent of slavery and voted for the compromise measures of 1850 but against the fugitive-slave law. On the conclusion of his term he received the Whig nomination for judge of the district court for Mifflin and Union counties, but was defeated. In 1855, prompted by the exigencies of his growing practise, he opened an office at Harrisburg, and was appointed by Gov. Pollock commissioner to investigate and terminate the "Erie Railroad War," a somewhat difficult and delicate undertaking which he brought to a successful conclusion. In the same year he was appointed reporter of the decisions of the supreme court of Pennsylvania, a position which he occupied for six years, in the course of which he prepared and published 25–36 *Pennsylvania State Reports* (1856–61), covering the years 1855 to 1860. They are frequently cited as "Casey's Reports," and have been uniformly accepted as able and accurate. In May 1861 President Lincoln appointed him judge of the United States Court of Claims, necessitating his removal to Washington, D. C., and in 1863, when the Court was reorganized, he became its first chief justice. He went on the bench at a critical time.

Owing to the outbreak of the Civil War the business of the Court of Claims assumed an importance which hitherto it had lacked, and it fell to his lot to consider and decide many cases involving new problems of vital interest. Eminently fair to both the Federal Government and the private citizen, he enjoyed the confidence and respect of the public, and performed his judicial duties with complete success. Failing health induced his resignation, Dec. 1, 1870. During the last nine years of his life he was a professor in the National University at Washington, and took a deep interest in its success. He was married to Mary A. Krettle of Carlisle.

[*Polit. Reg. and Cong. Dir., 1776–1878* (1878), comp. by B. P. Poore; *Biog. Encyc. of Pa. of the Nineteenth Century* (1874), p. 471; *Nat. Republican*, Feb. 11, 12, 1879.]

H. W. H. K.

CASEY, SILAS (July 12, 1807–Jan. 22, 1882), Union soldier, was born at East Greenwich, R. I. He was appointed to a cadetship at West Point in 1822, graduated in 1826, and was commissioned second lieutenant in the 2nd Infantry. For the next ten years he served with his regiment at posts on the Great Lakes and on the frontier, and from 1837 to 1842 was engaged in the Florida War against the Seminole Indians. He was promoted to first lieutenant in 1836 and to captain in 1839. He was with Gen. Scott's army in its campaign against the City of Mexico, 1847, took part in the battles of Contreras, Churubusco, Molino del Rey, and Chapultepec, and was twice brevetted for gallantry in action. He was severely wounded at the storming of Chapultepec while heading a "forlorn hope" of some 265 selected officers and men (Justin H. Smith, *The War with Mexico*, 1919, II, 153–57). Between the Mexican War and the Civil War he was stationed chiefly on the Pacific coast. For a time he was a member of a board of officers to revise the manual of infantry tactics, and later he prepared the manual adopted in 1862. "Casey's Tactics" remained in use in the army for many years. In 1855, several new regiments were organized, the field officers being chosen from among the ablest officers of the old organizations. Casey was thus appointed lieutenant-colonel of the new 9th Infantry, and became its colonel in 1861. Recalled from the Pacific coast upon the outbreak of the Civil War, he was appointed brigadier-general of volunteers, Aug. 31, 1861. He served with the Army of the Potomac during its formative period and in the Peninsular campaign, where he commanded a division. For distinguished service at the battle of Fair Oaks, where his division bore the first shock of the Confederate attack, he received a brevet in the regular army and was appointed major-general of volunteers, May 31, 1862 (*Battles and Leaders of the Civil War*, 1884, II, 230–33). From August 1862 until the end of the war he commanded a division of the troops assigned to the defenses of the city of Washington. He was also, for two years, president of the board for the examination of candidates for commission as officers of colored troops. He was a member of the court martial for the trial of Fitz-John Porter. Mustered out of the volunteer service on Aug. 24, 1865, he served in command of his regiment and on special duties until retired from active service, July 8, 1868, upon his own application. He died at Brooklyn. Gen. Cullum says of him: "Casey was a reserved, unassuming gentleman, a gallant soldier, a skilled tactician, and a proficient scholar in the higher mathematics, particularly the application of calculus and quaternions."

[G. W. Cullum: *Biog. Reg.* (3rd ed., 1891); *Official Records (Army)*, 1 ser., vols. II (pts. 1, 2, 3), LI (pt. 1).]

T. M. S.

CASILEAR, JOHN WILLIAM (June 25, 1811–Aug. 17, 1893), engraver and landscape painter, was the third of the nine children of John and Rebecca (Stevens) Casilear. The Stevenses were a prominent family in New Jersey. Casilear's paternal grandfather, Francis Casilear, as a young man came from Barcelona, Spain, to New York City, where he died in 1796, and was buried in St. Paul's churchyard. John William Casilear was born in New York City. Like many artists of the Italian Renaissance period, a number of the men who became eminent as painters in the United States through the first half of the nineteenth century found a safe starting point for their more ideal flights in the practise of engraving, and especially in producing the portraits and pictorial embellishments used on both federal and state bank notes. Peter Maverick, engaged in this phase of engraving, was an early member of the National Academy of Design and it was with him that Casilear at the age of sixteen began his apprenticeship. As the only support of a widowed mother and several brothers and sisters, he worked steadily and advanced to hold an interest in the American Bank Note Company, which he did not relinquish till 1857, thus acquiring a handsome competence. Intimately associated with Asher B. Durand, Edmonds, Kensett, and Rossiter, he was in close touch with the National Academy of Design as a student and exhibitor, becoming an associate in 1835, at a time when, as he modestly said, "The Academy took in anybody." In his case, however, the producing of graceful designs for bank notes, with more than ordinary skill in the use of the graver, and the painting of landscapes, gave probably well-founded reasons for such a distinction. He knew and received advice from Thomas Cole and, in 1840, he was afforded an opportunity to go to Europe with Durand, Kensett, and Rossiter, where he visited the galleries with them and gathered a harvest of sketches and studies. Returning to New York the following year, he did not yet allow the brush entirely to displace the burin, which had so far assured his material well-being. He produced one of the finest American engravings of the period, a reproduction of Daniel Huntington's "Sibyl," which was published by the American Art Union. In sharpness and decision of line it has been considered worthy of the old master engravers. In 1851 he was elected to full membership in the National Academy of Design and after 1854 gave most of his time to landscape painting, spending his summers in the hills of Vermont, about Lake George, in the Genesee Valley, N. Y., and in the Adirondacks. During another trip to Europe in 1857, he visited Switzerland, making a number of studies and sketches of romantic landscapes, from which he afterward painted pictures. One of his earlier exhibits at the Academy, "Storm Effect"—wind and rain passing over a summer landscape—drew attention as a forceful presentation of this striking phase of natural phenomena. "Moonlight in the Glen" depicted the rushing waters of a stream between forest-clad banks, reflecting the light of a full moon rising in the clear sky above. But as a whole, Casilear's pictures, in subject and treatment, harmonized with the even tenor of his life. After he had completely relinquished his engraving interests about 1857, his studio in New York during the latter part of his career was at 51 West Tenth St., where a number of distinguished painters lived and worked. Having acquired the means that assured relief from material cares by the steady industry of his earlier years, he was now able to undertake the production of a series of pictures that reflected usually the more peaceful aspects of American landscape. He was an active member of the Artists' Fund Society which held yearly exhibitions, and at each succeeding exhibit of the National Academy of Design, his landscapes were remarked for their sunny skies, silvery clouds, quiet reaches of rivers and lakes between broad meadows and distant hills. "Lake George," "Adirondack Scenery," "Genesee Meadows," and a "Connecticut Riverside," alternated with reminiscences of European trips that would occasionally appear as "Lake Leman," "Swiss Scenery," or "The Jungfrau" by which he was represented in the Centennial Exhibition of the National Academy of Design, held at

Washington and New York in 1926. Casilear's work, like that of his companions who began their art in the precise school of engraving, was marked by careful finish, contrasting with the more self-assertive technique of the impressionists who followed. He and his associates may not have been as dexterous as their followers in the free use of the brush, and like Cole were directly or indirectly influenced by the classical landscapes of Claude Lorraine; but they were deeply in love with nature, which they approached in a reverent and poetic spirit. They produced pictures remarkable for their simple, unaffected beauty, and have a definite place in the development of American landscape art. Casilear was married in 1867 to Ellen M. Howard of Tamworth, N. H. He died of apoplexy at Saratoga, in his eighty-third year, and was buried from Dr. Houghton's church in Twenty-ninth St., New York.

[H. T. Tuckerman, *Book of the Artists* (1867), pp. 521–22; *Art Jour.* (N. Y.), II, 16–17; Mantle Fielding, *Dict. of Am. Painters, Sculptors and Engravers* (1926); various catalogues and *Academy Notes* of the National Academy of Design Exhibitions, N. Y.; information as to certain facts from Casilear's son, John W. Casilear of Brooklyn, N. Y.]   R.J.W.

CASS, GEORGE WASHINGTON (Mar. 12, 1810–Mar. 21, 1888), engineer and railroad executive, was born on a farm near Dresden, Muskingum County, Ohio. His parents were George W. and Sophia Lord Cass, both of New England stock. In 1824 he was sent to Detroit to attend the Detroit Academy, making his home with his uncle, Gen. Lewis Cass [*q.v.*], who was then governor of Michigan Territory. Appointed from Ohio to the United States Military Academy in 1827, he graduated in 1832 with special honors in mathematics. He was then appointed brevet second lieutenant in the 7th Infantry, but never joined that regiment because of assignment to duty with the Topographical Engineers in the making of a survey of Provincetown Harbor, Mass., from Sept. 12 to Dec. 5, 1832. He was next detailed for duty with the Corps of Engineers as assistant to the superintendent in charge of the construction of the Cumberland Road, east of the Ohio River, and remained on this duty until Oct. 26, 1836, when he resigned his commission as first lieutenant in the 7th Infantry; but continued in the service of the Corps of Engineers as a civil engineer until 1840. During his service (1837) he erected the first cast-iron tubular-arch bridge to be built in the United States. In 1840 he established a mercantile business in Brownsville, Pa., but soon began to turn his attention to the transportation enterprises growing out of the development of the railways. He became one of the engineers in charge of the improvement of the Monongahela River and when this work was suspended because of the inability of the State of Pennsylvania to finance it, he was instrumental in forming a private company which completed the work in 1844. He organized the first steamboat line on the Monongahela and the first fast stage lines across the mountains. In 1849 he established the Adams Express Company from Baltimore to Pittsburgh and in 1854 effected the consolidation of all the company lines between Boston and St. Louis and south to Richmond. The next year he was elected president of the consolidated company, which position he held until 1857. On July 31, 1856, he was elected president and director of the Ohio & Pennsylvania Railroad Company, which later consolidated with the Ohio & Indiana and Fort Wayne & Chicago Railroad companies under the name of the Pittsburgh, Fort Wayne & Chicago Railroad Company, of which he was elected the first president. He held this position, except for a short interval, until May 25, 1881, when, the road being leased to the Pennsylvania Railroad Company, he resigned but continued one of the directors until his death. He was also president of the Northern Pacific Railroad Company from 1872 to 1875. Besides his business activities he was interested in politics. Twice, in 1863 and again in 1868, he was the Democratic candidate for governor of Pennsylvania. In 1859 he was a member of the board of visitors to the United States Military Academy. He was an able business man although sometimes inclined to be too conservative. He possessed simple tastes and being ingenuous in all his methods scorned pretense in others. His nature was generous and he gave very largely to his church and to charities.

[G. W. Cullum, *Biog. Reg.* (1891), I, 499–501; Jas. Parton and others, *Sketches of Men of Progress* (1870–71), pp. 469–73; E. V. Smalley, *Hist. of the N. P. R. R.* (1883), pp. 190–97; Hist. of the P., F. W. & C. R. R. (MS.), p. 70; *N. Y. Tribune,* Mar. 22, 1888; *Railway Age,* Mar. 23, 1888; memorial resolutions passed by the P., F. W., & C. R. R., May 16, 1888, in their *Annual Report,* pp. 8–9.]
J.H.F.

CASS, LEWIS (Oct. 9, 1782–June 17, 1866), soldier, diplomat, statesman, was the eldest of the six children of Jonathan Cass, a skilled craftsman with an excellent record in the Revolution, and was descended through his mother, Mary Gilman, from the best New England stock. He was born at Exeter, N. H., while the peace negotiations were still pending. His childhood coincided with the "Critical Period" in American history. In 1786, serious rioting occurred in Exeter, in which the senior Cass upheld the cause of law and order, a cause his son was des-

tined to maintain throughout his life. In 1792, Lewis entered the academy at Exeter, where he won the good will of Daniel Webster, a schoolmate (McLaughlin, *post,* p. 38). Having finished his education, he taught school at Wilmington, Del., for a time in 1799, but in the same year he crossed the Alleghanies to the West and a career.

He was at Marietta, Ohio, in 1800, where he established a law practise in 1802, soon removed to Zanesville, successfully defended Judge Brown, a presiding circuit judge, in impeachment proceedings before the Ohio Senate, married Elizabeth Spencer, the daughter of a Revolutionary general, spent his honeymoon with Mr. and Mrs. Harman Blennerhassett, and was elected at the age of twenty-four to the Ohio legislature, its youngest member, but a leader. Here he opposed Aaron Burr and drew up resolutions of loyalty to Thomas Jefferson, thus early identifying himself with the cause of union, in a fashion which led Jefferson to appoint him marshal for Ohio.

Cass unquestionably felt the enthusiasm of the times for the War of 1812. As colonel of the 3rd Ohio, he went promptly to the rendezvous at Dayton, and accompanied the forces leaving for Detroit in June. His military career is inseparably connected with that of Gen. William Hull. Cass spurred his reluctant chief to action, urged him to attack Malden, himself took part in an engagement near-by, and protested against orders to abandon a strategic position. "To Col. Cass," it is related, "belongs the honor not only of being the first man to invade the enemy's territory, but also of having opened the campaign with a victory" (Young, *post,* p. 27). He was considerate of his men, shared their hardships, and won their affection. He was on a relief expedition to the River Raisin when Hull surrendered at Detroit. Cass himself was included in the capitulation. He broke his sword rather than surrender it. His indignation at Hull's conduct was vented in a letter to the Secretary of War which is one of the sources for the period (*Ibid.,* pp. 49–52). While on parole in Washington, Cass was made a colonel in the regular army and a major-general of volunteers. On his release in January 1813, he was soon brevetted and in April was given joint command with Harrison and McArthur over the Eighth Military District, including Kentucky, Ohio, Indiana, Michigan, Illinois, and Missouri. When Harrison undertook an advance on Malden, Cass arranged the troops in line, and fought with conspicuous gallantry at the battle of the Thames, Oct. 5, 1813. He led the pursuit of Proctor, and was highly praised in

Harrison's dispatches. Before the month was out he was appointed governor of the Territory of Michigan, and that winter made the tedious trip to Albany to testify at Hull's court martial.

Returning to Detroit, Cass confronted a difficult task. The *habitants* were impoverished; the Indians were menacing; but present problems did not monopolize the Governor's attention. He pioneered in developing an empire. With a view to overcoming their land titles he met the Indians at Fort Meigs, Sept. 29, 1817, where they ceded their remaining lands in Ohio, in a part of Indiana, and in a portion of Michigan. Cass signalized the year 1820 by a 5,000-mile trip, mostly by canoe, to visit tribes within his jurisdiction. The itinerary included Mackinac; Sault Ste. Marie, where he procured from the Chippewas the cession of a military post; and, on his return, Chicago.

In 1825, Cass and Gov. Clark of Missouri met the Indians at Prairie du Chien, where on Aug. 19 a treaty was sealed with numerous tribes. The liquor which customarily on such occasions was given to the Indians, Cass poured upon the ground, a courageous manifestation of his lifelong hatred of intemperance (*Ibid.*, p. 90). In this year he settled certain difficulties with the Winnebagoes in his territory, and procured, besides, a right of way for a military road from Detroit to Chicago. He had previously urged a road from Sandusky to Detroit. In helpful, firm, and constructive service, Cass labored eighteen years in his proconsulship of Michigan, to the entire satisfaction of the people whom he governed and of his superiors at Washington (*Ibid.*, p. 98).

The foundation was laid, meanwhile, for an ample personal fortune through the purchase in 1818 of 500 acres near the mouth of the Detroit River, paid for in cash in the sum of $12,000, then deemed exorbitant (Smith, *post*, p. 142), and through the acquisition as a bounty of a further 1,200 acres similarly located. Throughout his political career Cass was far removed from all pecuniary temptation.

The shake up in President Jackson's cabinet caused by the Eaton affair brought Cass into the War Department. Here he was peculiarly fitted for the problems of his office by his previous experience with the Indians. He believed their removal beyond the Mississippi a practical necessity but advanced humane ideas for organizing the new Indian territory. He acted efficiently for the suppression of the Black Hawk War, 1832, and carried his views on temperance over into army regulations. In the trouble of Georgia with the Cherokees, he sympathized with the State in its opposition to the Supreme Court. Toward similar trouble in Alabama he assumed a corresponding stand. Toward a peaceful outcome in the Nullification crisis he is believed to have exercised a powerful but anonymous influence (McLaughlin, pp. 149–50). He advocated a strong navy and coast defense. After a six years' tenure he left the cabinet because of ill health, but was promptly sent to France as minister in October 1836.

Cass brought to his mission deep anti-British prejudice, the product of his past. All his life he fought the British. When he perceived their efforts to win French acceptance of a quintuple treaty designed to legalize the right of search, acting independently he voiced a protest. (For documents in this important case, see "The Appeal of Gen. Cass to the People of France," in Smith, *post*, pp. 403–27; and "The Right of Search," in Young, pp. 136–66.) Guizot accepted Cass's advice, but Webster, the United States secretary of state, was enraged. Cass resigned. An acrimonious correspondence followed, in which Webster had the advantage of position; Cass, of argument (Young, pp. 172–207). The strong stand of Cass won the admiration of Jackson, his former chief, and undoubtedly contributed to his prestige as a national figure.

Henceforth Cass took a stand on all important issues. Revival of a national bank he did not favor. He opposed distribution to the States of funds derived from public lands. When Texas proved the campaign issue in 1844, he wrote the Hannegan Letter, May 10, strongly urging annexation. It was a bid for the Democratic nomination. When this fell instead to Polk, Cass was loyal to the party ticket. Michigan sent him to the Senate in 1845. Here he assumed a characteristically anti-British attitude toward the Oregon question: "Now the Oregon I claim is all Oregon, and no vote of mine in this Senate will surrender one *inch* of it to England" (*Ibid.*, p. 252).

Toward Mexico Cass was frankly an imperialist. On Feb. 10, 1847, he declared, "We must continue our occupation of Mexico, and push the invasion still farther" (*Ibid.*, p. 309). Opposing the Wilmot Proviso, he anticipated the Squatter Sovereignty of Douglas when he said, "Leave to the people who will be affected by this question, to adjust it upon their own responsibility and in their own manner . . ." (*Ibid.*, p. 327). This was the doctrine of the Nicholson Letter, Dec. 24, 1847, a bid for the nomination of 1848 (Smith, pp. 607–16).

Cass opposed a system of general public improvements under national auspices, but was favorable to river and harbor development, and in

No one railroad could meet the pressure alone and the roads could look for nothing but moral support from the Interstate Commerce Commission. Although the Interstate Commerce Act had been on the statute book for over a decade, all that had come from attempts to prescribe rates had been warnings from the Supreme Court that the Commission lacked the necessary power. If anything was to be done at this time, the railroads must do it themselves, but again they had just been deprived by the Supreme Court of any right to combine if such combination constituted restraint of trade. Pooling was prohibited by the Interstate Commerce Act.

Cassatt, while general manager and vice-president, had had opportunity to observe the pressure that large shippers could bring to bear upon railroads, especially in the relation of the Eastern roads to the Standard Oil Company. In the hearings conducted by the Commonwealth of Pennsylvania in 1879 Cassatt's testimony was startling in its candor and completeness and substantiated the claim of the oil men that the Pennsylvania had become the creature of the Standard Oil Company (Ida M. Tarbell, *History of the Standard Oil Company,* 1904, I, 227). It is not unreasonable to assume that this experience made a deep impression on Cassatt and turned his mind toward possible solutions of the problem. During the seventeen years that he was free from official responsibility he was by no means out of touch with railroad affairs, and his position as director gave him leisurely opportunity to mature plans which he was able to put into execution when he took the reins of management into his hands.

His plan was that of purchasing a sufficient amount of stock in competing roads to give a voice in management and was known as "community of interest." It involved an agreement with the New York Central which through the Lake Shore was to buy some of the stock of the Reading. The Pennsylvania made large investments in the Baltimore & Ohio, Chesapeake & Ohio, and Norfolk & Western. The Baltimore & Ohio in turn bought into the Reading. The strategic roads were thus so interlocked as to be able to present a united front to the industrial combinations that were depleting their revenues. The roads then announced that no further rebates would be granted. This announcement was not received kindly and the Carnegie interests especially refused to comply, first diverting traffic from the Pennsylvania and then threatening to build a road of their own to the seaboard, but the railroad combination refused to be frightened, and the worst of the discrimination in this territory was over. In 1903 the Elkins Anti-Rebate law was passed, largely at the instance of the railroad, and Cassatt was a powerful factor in the movement for its enactment. While the "community of interest" plan did not at the time appeal to the people of the country as a sound solution of the problem, and while the Northern Securities decision of 1904 and later decisions of the Supreme Court led to the dissolution of many of these corporate relationships, it must be conceded that Cassatt's plan accomplished much at the time and that it was a bold adventure and demanded ability of the highest order. That he yielded to popular opinion and sold many of his holdings did not mean that he was in agreement with the prevailing view. Up to the time of his death he held to the belief that cooperation between railroads was essential to a sound and stable rate system, but, at the time, the country, led by Roosevelt, was hostile to combination in any form, and it was not until 1920 that it came round to Cassatt's point of view. Cassatt took prompt action to eliminate the improper use of railroad passes on his lines. He believed in clothing the Commission with power to fix rates and put himself and his company behind the Roosevelt railroad program. He died a few months after the Hepburn Act had been signed which was to put real power for the first time into the hands of the Commission.

Another of Cassatt's achievements was the construction of the Pennsylvania Terminal in New York, the most gigantic project of railroad enterprise that has ever been undertaken. The disadvantageous location of the Pennsylvania Terminal on the west bank of the Hudson had been a matter of concern for thirty years before Cassatt's presidency, and many plans for crossing the river had been suggested; but all for one reason or another had been rejected. In 1901 Cassatt studied the extension of the Orleans Railway in Paris and became so impressed with the possibilities of electric traction that, upon his return, he set actively to work upon the New York tunnel and terminal project which, however, was not brought to completion until after his death. For the bold conception and for the inauguration of the work, however, the credit must be his. His statue was unveiled in the new Terminal in 1910 and on it are inscribed the words: "Whose foresight, courage, and ability achieved the extension of the Pennsylvania Railroad into New York City."

His life outside the railroad was an active one. He was a constant advocate of good roads and for nineteen years was road supervisor of

Merion Township in which he lived. He also served from time to time as director of insurance and trust companies. He was an enthusiastic horseman and was one of the two or three leading patrons of the American turf. He was associated with others in the construction of the race track at Monmouth Park and raced horses there with great success. When the sport fell into disrepute he transferred his attentions to breeding at his Chesterbrook stock farm at Berwyn, Pa., where he raised sheep, cattle, draft horses, and hackneys. He was one of the pioneers of coaching and an enthusiast over cricket, hunting, and yachting.

In 1869 Cassatt married Lois, daughter of Rev. Edward Y. Buchanan, and a niece of President James Buchanan. They had four children.

[The *Biog. Sketch of A. J. Cassatt, Dec. 28, 1906,* was issued by the authority of the Pa. R. R., at the time of Cassatt's death and reissued with addendum in 1910, at the time of the unveiling of his statue in the Pa. Station in N. Y. The *Mo. Bull. Pa. R. R. Dept. Y. M. C. A. of Phila.,* Feb. 1907, is a memorial number devoted to him. Wm. B. Wilson, *Hist. of the Pa. R. R. Dept. of Y. M. C. A. of Phila.* (1911), contains an estimate of his personality and his work. Another appraisal is to be found in an address of one of his successors to the presidency, Samuel Rea, entitled *Engineering and Transportation,* delivered before the Princeton School of Engineering in 1926, and privately printed.]   F. H. D.

CASSATT, MARY (May 22, 1845–June 14, 1926), artist, was descended from a Frenchman named Cossart, who in 1662 emigrated from France into Holland, and whose grandson emigrated to America. She was the daughter of Robert S. Cassatt, a banker, and Katharine Kelso (Johnston) Cassatt. Her eldest brother, Alexander Johnston Cassatt [*q.v.*], became president of the Pennsylvania Railroad. She was born in Allegheny City, Pa. When she was a little girl, her parents took her to Paris where they lived for five years, returning finally to Philadelphia. In 1868 she went again to Paris with her mother, who spoke and wrote French fluently. It was then that Mary Cassatt decided definitely to become an artist. She went to Italy and lived at Parma for eight months studying Correggio, then to Spain where she became filled with such admiration for Rubens that she went to Antwerp to study his work further. In 1874 she returned to Paris permanently. Her studio was in the Rue de Marignan just off the Champs-Élysées, but she spent much of her time in her Château de Beaufresne at Mesnil-Théribus dans l'Oise, seventy miles from Paris. She became a devoted disciple of Degas, with whom she enjoyed long years of friendship and mutual criticism. Degas suggested that she exhibit with his friends of the Impressionist School, and she accepted with joy. She hated conventional art and with this group, Manet, Courbet, Degas, and others, she departed from the academic tradition, working out her personal interpretation, untrammeled by precedent. She exhibited with Impressionists from 1879 to 1886. Degas's admiration for her was unbounded. Before one of her pictures he said, "I will not admit a woman can draw like that." Mellerio wrote that she "possesses an original inspiration, representative of her epoch and her race, . . . a direct and significant expression of the American character." In 1893 she gave her first independent exhibition, in the Gallery of Durand-Ruel in Paris. She was chosen among women artists to decorate the Woman's Building in the Chicago Exposition. Puvis de Chavannes and Whistler were among her close friends. She painted a number of portraits with admirable results, notably those of her mother and her devoted friend Mrs. Henry O. Havemeyer. For almost every picture and print, she chose the world-old theme of motherhood, depicting mothers and babies in intimate scenes in sunny gardens and quiet interiors, not sentimentally, but in an original and simple manner. Her pastels are not so well known, but they are in soft, light tones, and some of her best work was done in this difficult medium. Her etchings, dry-points, and color prints are of great delicacy, yet firm in line and perception. By competent critics she is esteemed the most distinguished etcher, after Whistler, that America has produced. She was, however, regarded more as a member of the French impressionist school than of any American group. She became honorary president of the "Hostel" for Girl Students, established in Paris by Mrs. John Hoff, to which she contributed money to be distributed between the two girls evincing the most talent, requiring them to study for a year the French Pastellists of the seventeenth and eighteenth centuries in the Musée St. Quentin, said to be the finest collection in France. She possessed wealth and an enviable position in the social as well as the art world. She was above the average height, dark and slender. Her voice was low, soft, and pleasantly modulated, her manner quiet, except when she was roused in some heated art discussion. During the latter years of her life, she was an invalid, becoming almost blind. She died at Mesnil-Théribus. The only portrait of her known to exist is a small sketch made many years ago by Degas, now in a private French collection. Although she did not care for medals or honors, she received many. Her work has been exhibited widely, and she is represented in the Luxembourg, and in the leading galleries and museums of America as well as in important private collections. The Memorial Exhibition held in the Pennsylvania Museum, Philadelphia, April 1927, was a valuable showing of her work in all media. It included forty oils and pastels, over a hundred prints and a series of fifteen water-colors and drawings.

[Achille Segard, *Un Peintre des Enfants et des Mères, Mary Cassatt* (Paris, 1913); Y. Rambaud, "Mary Cassatt," *L'Art dans les Deux-Mondes*, Nov. 19, 1890; Wm. Walton, "The Art of Mary Cassatt," *Scribner's Mag.*, Mar. 1896; Camille Mauclair, "Un Peintre de l'Enfance," *L'Art Décoratif*, Aug. 1902; Elisabeth L. Cary, "The Art of Mary Cassatt," *Scrip*, Oct. 1905; Christian Brinton, "Concerning Miss Cassatt and Certain Etchings," *Internat. Studio*, Feb. 1906; *Arts*, Aug. 1926; André Mellerio, "Mary Cassatt," *L'Art et les Artistes*, Nov. 1910; Frank Weitenkampf, "The Drypoints of Mary Cassatt," *Print-Collector's Quart.*, Dec. 1916; Arsène Alexandre, "Miss Mary Cassatt, Aquefortiste," *La Renaissance de l'Art Français*, Mar. 1924; *Metropolitan Museum of Art Bull.*, Jan. 1927; *Art News*, May 7, 1927; *Pa. Museum Bull.*, May 1927 (Memorial Number).]   H. W.

CASSIDY, WILLIAM (Aug. 12, 1815–Jan. 23, 1873), journalist, politician, was a son of John and Margaret Cassidy. He was named for his paternal grandfather who had migrated from Ireland late in the eighteenth century and had settled in Maiden Lane, Albany, N. Y. John Cassidy, proprietor of a meat-market, won the esteem of the Albanians and represented them as alderman. William, being a studious youth, completed his work at the Albany Academy and entered the senior year at Union College, Schenectady, where he graduated with high honors in 1833. He was trained for the law in the office of John Van Buren and Judge James McKown, and was admitted to the bar but never practised, as his tastes were markedly literary and journalistic. He devoured the contents of books amazingly fast, became conversant with Latin, French, and German, and impressed Henry James as being the best-read man of his time in French ballads. At the age of twenty-five years he was writing caustic articles for the radical *Plaindealer and Rough Hewer,* an Albany newspaper which supported the Azariah Flagg faction of the New York Democracy. His political leanings, and his satirical and witty pen, made him acceptable to the Van Buren group, who had him chosen state librarian for 1841–43, after which he became joint editor with Henry Van Dyke of the Albany daily *Atlas.* His editorials, much shorter than those of many other partisan editors, were written in a dirty corner amidst the confusion of the composing room. His drafts were never transcribed, were seldom revised, and had few erasures, though they were "a very lunacy of hieroglyphics." When the Albany *Argus* deserted Van Buren on the issue of the

annexation of Texas, Cassidy attacked its editor, Edwin Croswell [q.v.], in an editorial duel which was long remembered. Croswell finally sued Cassidy for libel, succeeded in having the office of state printer abolished, and bid in the state printing free of charge to prevent Cassidy's election as printer. After the factional fight of 1848, Cassidy turned to Pierce (1852) and through the influence of Horatio Seymour, united the *Atlas* and *Argus* (1856) to fight the Republican party. He bitterly opposed Frémont and denounced the Republican leaders as demagogues, while he urged the support of Pierce and Buchanan. Lincoln seemed to him an uncouth and dangerous man to be elected president. The *Atlas and Argus* was classed as a copperhead sheet during the Civil War, and was barred from the mails. Cassidy's bitter opposition to Lincoln did not prevent him, however, from dashing off, in the heat of the hour, one of the best eulogies on the assassinated president. He ardently supported McClellan, Johnson, and Seymour, and reluctantly aided Greeley in 1872. He served as a member of the constitutional convention of New York (1867), as secretary of the State Democratic Committee (1868–73), as president of the Argus Company (1865–73), and as a member of a commission on revision of the New York state constitution (1872).

An Irish Catholic, he was a life-long enemy of Great Britain. His paper bristles with anti-English editorials, but for consistent foreign news it fails the reader. It was simply a state partisan newspaper. The combative Cassidy was, however, courtly, dignified, and suave in manner. He became the Nestor of Democratic journalists in up-state New York, and was a lover of society, to the last. Death came to him at his birthplace, the Cassidy homestead on Maiden Lane. An estate estimated at well over $150,-000 was left to his wife, née Lucie Rochefort, and to his sons.

[The Albany *Atlas, Argus, Evening Jour.,* the *Atlas and Argus,* and the N. Y. City newspapers are the chief sources. See also Almosa J. Parker, ed., *Landmarks of Albany County* (Syracuse, 1897); Herbert D. A. Donovan, *The Barnburners* (1925); M. V. Dolan, *Centenary of the Argus* (1913); *Memoir of Wm. Cassidy* (1874).]   W. E. S.

CASSIN, JOHN (Sept. 6, 1813–Jan. 10, 1869), ornithologist, son of Thomas Cassin, a Quaker, was born on a farm in Upper Providence Township, Delaware County, Pa., about a mile from the present town of Media. He was educated at the near-by Quaker school, Westtown. Here, as in all educational institutions conducted by the Friends, natural history received especial attention, and young John Cassin was strongly influenced in this direction. Removing to Philadelphia at the age of twenty-one, he engaged in mercantile pursuits and later held a position in the United States Custom-House. Finally upon the death of Bowen, head of one of the principal engraving and lithographing establishments of the day, Cassin succeeded him in the management of the business and later produced the illustrations for many government and other scientific publications.

Soon after removing to Philadelphia, Cassin joined the Academy of Natural Sciences. The collection of birds especially attracted him and he devoted much of his spare time to its study. Dr. Thomas B. Wilson, patron and later president of the Academy, was at this time beginning to assemble the enormous collection of birds that was to make the institution famous in ornithological centers throughout the world, and upon Cassin devolved the work of arranging and identifying the 26,000 specimens which Wilson had brought together, and which formed the largest collection then in existence. Cassin's opportunities were unequaled, but unfortunately business responsibilities took so much of his time that he was forced to pursue his studies in spare hours, evenings, and holidays. He had the constant support of Dr. Wilson, who procured for the Academy's library practically every book and journal that Cassin needed in his work. Cassin published the results of his researches in many papers in the *Proceedings* of the Academy and soon established a reputation throughout the scientific world. Unlike Audubon and Alexander Wilson, he was what has been termed a "closet naturalist," his publications being mainly technical monographs or descriptions of new species dealing with taxonomy and questions of synonymy and nomenclature. Probably no ornithologist of his day had such a knowledge of the literature of the subject, and Elliott Coues has truly said of him that he was the only ornithologist the United States had produced up to that time who was as familiar with the birds of the Old World as with those of America.

Perhaps Cassin's most notable papers published by the Academy were those based upon the collections of Du Chaillu made in the then unknown regions of West Africa, which abounded in rare and curious novelties. He also contributed the ornithological portions of a number of United States Government publications: *Mammalogy and Ornithology,* being Volume VII (second edition, 1858) of the *United States Exploring Expedition*; "Narrative of the Expedition of an American Squadron to the China

Seas and Japan, Volume II," published as *Senate Executive Document No. 79* and *House Executive Document, No. 97,* 33 Cong., 2 Sess.; "United States Naval Astronomical Expedition to the Southern Hemisphere, Volume II," published as *House Executive Document No. 121,* 33 Cong., 1 Sess.; and part of the classic volume on the birds of North America, "Reports of Explorations and Surveys . . . Route for a Railroad from the Mississippi River to the Pacific Ocean, Volume IX, Part II," published as *Senate Executive Document, No. 78* and *House Executive Document, No. 91,* 33 Cong., 2 Sess. He also published a notable work, *Illustrations of the Birds of California, Texas, Oregon, British, and Russian America* (1856), covering the species discovered since the appearance of Audubon's *Birds of America* (1827–38).

[Witmer Stone, "John Cassin," in *Cassinia, a Bird Annual,* 1901, pp. 1–7; T. M. Brewer in *Proc. Boston Soc. Nat. Hist.,* Jan. 1869, reprinted in *Am. Jour. Sci.,* Mar. 1869.]   W. S.

CASTLE, VERNON BLYTHE (May 2, 1887–Feb. 15, 1918), dancer, aviator, the son of William and Jane Blythe, was born in Norwich, England. When a small boy he surprised his parents by wiring the entire house with electric bells. The family immediately planned for him a career as an electrical engineer, and he later received training as a civil engineer in London. In 1906 he came to the United States with his father and his sister, Coralie Blythe, who was to take part in a play in New York. Through association with his sister's friends Vernon was given a small unimportant part in Lew Field's *The Girl Behind the Counter,* in 1907. It was at this time that he assumed the name Castle. The short freakish dance which he did in the show was singled out by the public as unusual and eccentric. Castle soon found himself creating dances for various occasions. On May 28, 1911 he married Irene Foote, the daughter of a New Rochelle physician. His wife proved to be a competent dancing partner and appeared with him a few times in small dance acts. About a year later they went to Paris, and because of lack of funds started dancing in a Paris café. They proved a sensation to the Parisians, and when news of their success reached New York, café owners and theatrical producers besieged them with offers. They returned to America in a few months, and at times, during the next two years, were drawing as much as $6,000 a week for their performances. In 1914 they published a book of instruction in dancing, called *Modern Dancing.* Castle originated the one-step, turkey-trot, Castle-walk and many other dances, some of which have lasted and many of which have not. In February 1916 he enlisted in the Royal Flying Corps. He received the commission of lieutenant and served in the French army under Gen. Foch. He held the respect of officers for his daring and spectacular movements in the air. The Croix de Guerre was awarded him for bringing down two German planes. In 1918 he was sent to Fort Worth, Tex., to teach aviation and was as highly praised as an instructor of aviation as he had been as an instructor of dancing. He was killed in a collision with another airplane, flown by a cadet. His courage in maneuvering to save the cadet's life was highly praised by officers who witnessed the accident. He was a tall, slender, rather frail-looking man, extremely sympathetic, and above all else a lover of animals. He did well the only two things which he attempted during his short lifetime.

[*N. Y. Times, N. Y. Herald,* Feb. 16, 1918; Irene F. Castle, "My Memories of Vernon Castle," in *Everybody's Mag.,* Nov., Dec., 1918, Jan., Feb., Mar., 1919, and *My Husband* (1919).]

M.S.

CASWELL, ALEXIS (Jan. 29, 1799–Jan. 8, 1877), college president, scientist, was a twin son of Samuel and Polly (Seaver) Caswell. He came of a line of farmers which went back to Thomas Caswell, an Englishman, one of the incorporators of Taunton, Mass., in 1639. His maternal grandmother, Zibiah White, was descended from Peregrine White, born on the *Mayflower.* After three years in Taunton Academy Caswell entered Brown University, graduating in 1822 at the head of his class. For five years he taught in Columbian College, Washington, the last two years as professor of ancient languages, meanwhile studying theology with the president. He entered the ministry in 1827, and served as pastor of a Baptist church in Halifax, Nova Scotia, for nearly a year. But in 1828 he accepted the chair of mathematics and natural philosophy in Brown University, where he taught continuously for thirty-five years except for a year abroad in 1860–61. His professorships (mathematics and natural philosophy, 1828–50, mathematics and astronomy, 1850–55, natural philosophy and astronomy, 1855–63) forbade him to confine himself to one science, but his favorite field was astronomy. His lectures on this subject at the Smithsonian Institution in 1858 "were of the highest order of popular instruction," wrote Prof. Joseph Lovering of Harvard, who adds that "he was never superficial." He published admirable reviews of William Whewell's *Astronomy and General Physics* (1833) and of J. P. Nichol's *Architecture of the Heavens* (1838),

his easy, lucid style presenting scientific subjects pleasantly yet with precision (*Christian Review,* June 1836, December 1841). In 1855 he was chosen vice-president of the American Association for the Advancement of Science; in 1858, the president and vice-president being absent, he was called to the chair, and therefore gave the address as retiring president the next year, reviewing the problems of astronomy and forecasting the part American astronomers might have in solving them. His standing as a scientist is also shown by his election as associate fellow of the American Academy of Arts and Sciences in 1850, and by the government's choice of him as one of fifty incorporators of the National Academy of Sciences in 1863. His most important publication was, perhaps, the account of his own meteorological observations at Providence, R. I., from December 1831 to May 1860, in *Smithsonian Contributions to Knowledge,* vol. XII (1860).

After his retirement in 1863, he became president of the National Exchange Bank and of the American Screw Company, in Providence. In 1868 he was called to the presidency of Brown University, to meet an emergency caused by two declinations. He was sixty-nine at the time. A man of that age, called obviously to fill a gap, might only have discharged the routine duties of the office, with which Caswell was already familiar as president *pro tempore* in 1840–41, and as regent, or dean, from 1852 to 1855. But he did more, vigilantly maintaining the scholarship of the university and making some advance. Long before, in 1836, in an article in the *North American Review* he had attacked the prevailing system of higher education in America, referring to the "practise of conferring degrees on easy terms" with the result that "with us, degrees are not distinctions," adding that in England examinations "are conducted with a severity, at which, in this country, all our college fraternities [*i. e.,* the colleges] would stand aghast." In his president's report, in 1872, he spoke of "the weary task" of educating youths "who were not born to study." He retired from the presidency in 1872, but served as trustee from 1873 to 1875 and as fellow the next two years. From 1875 till his death he was president of the Rhode Island Hospital, of which he had been a trustee since its founding.

In all his work Caswell is revealed as a Yankee of the best type, cool, shrewd, kindly, able to turn his hand with confidence to varied tasks. "Dr. Caswell is universally known to be a man of imperturbable good nature," wrote President Wayland to an angry parent. "He never told your son that he was a liar, but he did tell him that he found great difficulty in believing the account which he had given." He was untroubled by the supposed conflict between science and religion; "the legitimate results of all true science, and all discovery," he wrote in 1841, "will be to fix the truths of Christianity upon a broader and deeper foundation." "Inflexible in his own peculiar theology," said Prof. Lovering, "he had no taint of illiberality in his intellect or his heart." He was married in 1830 to Esther L. Thompson, who died in 1850, and in 1855 to Elizabeth B. Edmands, who survived him.

[*New Eng. Hist. and Geneal. Reg.*, July 1877; Jos. Lovering in *Proc. Am. Acad. Arts and Sci.*, 1877, vol. XII, and J. L. Lincoln in *Providence Daily Jour.*, June 20, 1877.]   W.C.B.

CASWELL, RICHARD (Aug. 3, 1729–November 1789), Revolutionary soldier and politician, was born in Cecil County, Md. Owing to the financial misfortunes of his father, who was a merchant, he was early thrown upon his own resources and at the age of seventeen removed to Raleigh, N. C., where he became a surveyor. He was also a lawyer, and, being a versatile man, a good speaker, and highly regarded, he held political offices at an early age. He was deputy-surveyor of the colony, clerk of Orange County, and in 1754–71 a member of the North Carolina Assembly. During this long term of legislative service he was very active, particularly in reforming the courts of law. In the last two years he was speaker of the Assembly. During the insurrection of the Regulators in 1771 he served under Gov. Tryon at the battle of Alamance, commanding the right wing.

During the Revolution, Caswell was prominent in various lines. He presided over the provincial congress, and also over the convention which prepared the state constitution, being a member of the committee which framed that document. He was a delegate to the Continental Congress 1774–76. In the army he was colonel of North Carolina Partisan Rangers 1776–77, and was major-general of the state militia from 1780 to the end of the war. His military opportunity came at the battle of Moore's Creek, Feb. 27, 1776. In this action Colonels Caswell and Lillington with about 1,100 men repulsed a Loyalist army of about 1,600 led by the Scotch Highlander McDonald. The victory was complete, and decisive—for some years—of the war in North Carolina. McDonald and about 900 of his army were taken prisoners, and the captures included money, arms, and ammunition (see, for the numbers, R. D. W. Connor, *Revolutionary Leaders*, and *North Carolina Colonial Records*). Caswell had shown skill, and received the thanks of Congress.

He was governor of North Carolina, 1776–80, and helped in the organizing and equipping of troops. While governor in 1777 he received a letter from Washington, urging strong measures in dealing with deserters. His popularity suffered a temporary eclipse after the battle of Camden (Aug. 16, 1780). In this disastrous action Caswell commanded the North Carolina militia. When his men broke and fled, Caswell, having attempted vainly to rally them, shared in Gates's rapid flight northward. He was superseded for a while by Gen. Smallwood in the command of the state militia, but his influence in the state was soon recovered. He held the offices of speaker of the Senate, comptroller-general, and governor for a second time, 1785–87. While governor he was chosen delegate to the Federal Convention, but declined to serve. He showed his interest in its actions, however, by asking for information that might be of use to the Convention, and by correspondence with the delegates from his state in regard to the proceedings. When the state convention met for ratification, Caswell's influence was thrown against the new Federal Constitution. While holding his last political office as speaker of the Assembly, he was stricken with paralysis, and died a few days later at Fayetteville.

[R. D. W. Connor, *Revolutionary Leaders of N. C.* (1916); Eugene C. Brooks, "Richard Caswell," in S. A. Ashe, ed., *Biog. Hist. of N. C.*, vol. III (1905), 65; John H. Wheeler, *Hist. Sketches of N. C.* (1851).]

E.K.A.

CATESBY, MARK (*c.* 1679–Dec. 23, 1749), naturalist and traveler, was born late in 1679 or early in 1680, it is believed at Sudbury, in Suffolk, England. He developed an early interest in natural science and went to London the better to study it. He first landed in America in 1712, in Virginia, where he had relatives living. He remained there seven years, sending back to England collections of seeds and plants; then returned to England, and planned, with the assistance and encouragement of (among others) Sir Hans Sloane, Dr. William Sherard, the botanist, and Gov. Nicholson of South Carolina, an examination of the natural history of the Southern colonies and the Bahamas. He landed at Charleston, S. C., in May 1722, and spent about three years studying and collecting the fauna and flora of South Carolina, Georgia, and Florida. He also visited the Bahamas, returning to England in 1726. He then settled at Hoxton; mastered the art of etching; and wrote and illustrated his most considerable work, *The Natural History of Carolina, Florida, and the Bahama Islands*. Published in parts, in large folio, with the text in French and English, the first volume was completed in 1731, the second in 1743, and an appendix in 1748. The book was illustrated with over 200 plates, the figures etched by Catesby himself, from his own paintings, and the first colored copies tinted under his inspection. Some of the work was later reproduced on the Continent at Nürnberg. It drew considerable interest, both among the wealthy dilettanti to whom it was addressed, and also among the learned. Catesby was elected to the Royal Society in 1733, and in 1747 read a paper before that body (printed in *Philosophical Transactions* the same year) upon the migration of birds, in which he rightly refuted the belief in their hibernating under water, although so good a naturalist as Gilbert White hankered after the theory, more than a generation later. Catesby gave examples from among the South Carolina birds. He wrote, also, *Hortus Britanno-Americanus; or, a Curious Collection of Trees and Shrubs,* which illustrated work, issued posthumously in 1763–67, encouraged the introduction into Europe of North American trees and shrubs. He enjoyed many friendships, notably in the Royal Society, by "his modesty, ingenuity and upright behavior" (Pulteney, *post*). On Dec. 23, 1749, he died at his home in Old St., London, leaving a widow and two children.

[See Catesby's own preface to the *Natural Hist. of Carolina*; R. Pulteney, *Hist. and Biog. Sketches of the Progress of Botany in England* (London, 1790, II, 219–30); Britten and Boulger, *Biographical Index of British and Irish Botanists* (London, 1893, p. 32), where the reference to *Nichols' Lit. Anecdotes* should be VI, 78; Catesby's correspondence with John Bartram reprinted in W. Darlington, *Memorials of John Bartram and Humphry Marshall* (1849), pp. 319–24.] W.H.B.C.

CATHCART, JAMES LEANDER (June 1, 1767–Oct. 6, 1843), consul, was born at Mount Murragh, County of Westmeath, Ireland, the son of Malcolm Hamilton Cathcart, who had married the daughter of Edward Humphreys of Dublin. The family surname is taken from the Barony of Kethcart, County of Renfrew, now the town of Cathcart, Scotland. The founder of the family, Col. Gabriel Cathcart, accompanied the Rev. Malcolm Hamilton (later Bishop of Cashel) to Ireland in 1641. James Leander Cathcart was brought to America as a child by Capt. John Cathcart. In October 1779 he became a midshipman on the Continental frigate *Confederacy,* Capt. Seth Harding, where he served until captured by the British some months later. He was taken to New York and confined on the prison ships *Good Hope* and *Old Jersey* but escaped in March 1782 and entered the merchant service. While he was a seaman on the schooner *Maria,*

of Boston, the vessel was captured (July 25, 1785) by an Algerine xebec off Cape St. Vincent. The crew was sold into slavery in Algiers. Although a prisoner, Cathcart became clerk of the Marine (1787–88), clerk of the Bagnio Gallera (prison of the galley slaves), keeper of the prison tavern, clerk to the prime minister, and, in March 1792, chief Christian secretary to the Dey and Regency of Algiers. He seems to have had some influence with the Dey and claimed that it was only after much effort on his part that the Dey agreed to receive Joseph Donaldson, sent by the United States to negotiate for peace and the release of prisoners (1795). The treaty signed, Cathcart sailed for Philadelphia (May 8, 1796) in the barque *Independent,* which he had purchased, carrying dispatches from Joel Barlow [*q.v.*], and a letter from the Dey to President Washington. He was appointed consul at Tripoli (July 10, 1797), but remained in Philadelphia to select the presents and naval stores for the tribute to Algiers. On June 5, 1798, he married Jane Bancker Woodside of Philadelphia, by whom he had twelve children. In December 1798 he was appointed a special diplomatic agent, and accompanied William Eaton [*q.v.*] to Tunis, where they obtained alterations in the unsatisfactory treaty that had been negotiated by Joseph E. Famin in August 1797. The treaty concluded (Mar. 26, 1799), Cathcart proceeded to Tripoli and procured a settlement with the Pasha by distributing $1,500 in bribes. Later, the Pasha, observing the flourishing condition of the unprotected American commerce in the Mediterranean, made further demands, and declared war on the United States in May 1801, Cathcart retiring to Leghorn. It was upon Cathcart's suggestion that Eaton espoused the cause of Hamet Karamanli, rightful Pasha of Tripoli, then exiled in Tunis (Charles Prentiss, *Life of the Late Gen. William Eaton,* 1813, p. 225). In 1802 Cathcart was authorized to treat with the Tripolitan government, but the Pasha treated his proposals with contempt. Cathcart was then appointed consul-general at Algiers (1802), but the Dey refused to receive him and he was appointed instead consul at Tunis (1803). The Bey of Tunis, who had twice refused to receive Cathcart, whom he characterized as an *embroglione* (translated by Eaton as "troublesome litigious trifler"), rejected both consul and the terms offered and denounced Cathcart to the President, to which Jefferson made an apologetic answer. Cathcart later served as consul at Madeira (1807–15), and at Cadiz (1815–17), and after he returned to the United States became naval agent for the protection of live oak timber in Florida (1818–20). During the last twenty years of his life he was employed in the United States Treasury at Washington, D. C. He received a Revolutionary pension in 1833. Mrs. Jane B. Newkirk, Cathcart's daughter, compiled and published the journal of his Algerine captivity, *The Captives* (La Porte, Ind., 1899), and a volume of his official correspondence, *Tripoli . . . Letter-Book by James Leander Cathcart* (La Porte, 1901).

[In addition to the above: *Am. State Papers, Foreign Relations,* vols. I and II (both 1832) and *Naval Affairs,* IV (1861), 107; S. C. Blyth, *Hist. of the War between the U. S. and Tripoli, and Other Barbary Powers* (1806); *Jour. of the Captivity and Sufferings of John Foss* (1797); *Memoirs of John Quincy Adams,* vol. V (1875); G. W. Allen, *Our Navy and the Barbary Corsairs* (1905); *Daily National Intelligencer* (Washington, D. C.), Oct. 9, 1843; Revolutionary pension records in the Dept. of the Interior and records of the Dept. of State, Washington, D. C.; Cathcart MSS. in the N. Y. Pub. Lib.]   F.E.R.

CATHCART, WILLIAM (Nov. 8, 1826–July 8, 1908), Baptist minister, historian, son of James and Elizabeth (Cously) Cathcart, was born in the county of Londonderry, Ireland, where he was brought up in the strict Presbyterian faith. At about the time of his nineteenth birthday, he had a personal religious experience which he considered a conversion, and in January 1846 he was baptized by immersion. He obtained the rudiments of a classical education at a school near his home, but continued his studies at the University of Glasgow and at the Baptist school (now Rawdon College) in Horton, Yorkshire. In 1850 he married Eliza Caldwell, who was to survive him eight years. Ordained pastor of the Baptist church at Barnsley, but chafing under the restraints of a society dominated by an established church, he determined to migrate to America. Reaching New York on Nov. 18, 1853, he became, the next month, pastor at Groton, Conn. Soon after his thirtieth birthday, he was called to the Second Baptist Church of Philadelphia, beginning on Apr. 1, 1857, a pastorate of twenty-seven years. From the beginning of this ministry, its vigor was conspicuous. Cathcart participated in the broader activities of his denomination and aggressively supported the Bible Union movement in its interest in the translation rather than transliteration of the words referring to baptism. His preaching was largely a scholarly exposition of the Scriptures with an incisive application of evangelical principles, occasionally cutting across cherished views. Early in this pastorate, he assailed the prevalent Sabbatarianism of the strongly Protestant community; for this a group of fellow ministers denounced him as holding heretical views. His announcement that a recurrence of the accusation would lead to a suit for slander stifled these irrespon-

sible charges. The blend of rigor and urbanity in his temperament is revealed in the remark of an officer of his church after his retirement, "We had a master and did not know it."

Early in 1884, on account of his health he retired from the pastorate to his farm at Gwynedd, Pa., where he was able to continue historical activities which he had commenced more than a decade earlier. If his critical acumen lagged behind that of some of the more advanced historians of his day, he often delved deep for source material. He was best known as editor of the *Baptist Encyclopædia* (1883); its fulsome praise of living subjects may perhaps be ascribed to the poor taste of the period. He wrote other popular works: *The Papal System from Its Origin to the Present Time* (1872); *The Baptists and the American Revolution* (1876); *The Baptism of the Ages and of the Nations* (1878); *The Ancient British and Irish Churches Including the Life and Labors of St. Patrick* (1894).

[John B. Filson, *Hist. of the Second Baptist Ch., Phila.* (1886); Elmer W. Powell, a memorial sketch in the *Baptist Commonwealth,* July 16, 1908.]   W.H.A.

CATHERWOOD, MARY HARTWELL (Dec. 16, 1847–Dec. 26, 1902), novelist, was the daughter of Marcus and Phœbe (Thompson) Hartwell. There lay behind her a rather significant tradition of culture. Marcus Hartwell, his brother Cyrus, and his three sisters had all received from their father a small fortune and such advanced education as the Ohio of their day afforded—the girls at the Granville Female Seminary, the boys at Marietta College. Marcus, after studying medicine at Columbus, practised in the little settlement of Luray in Licking County, where Mary was born. In the latter part of the 1850's the Hartwells moved to Illinois. The young doctor had barely established a new practise at Milford when he died, his wife following him a few months later. Mary and her brother and sister were separated and cared for by maternal relatives. By the aid of school-teaching, Mary managed to work her way through the Granville Female Seminary (also called the Granville Female College). Her ambition to become a writer by this time firmly fixed, she varied her teaching at Danville, Ill., and elsewhere, by writing various stories, poems, and articles, one of them a prize story published in *Wood's Household Magazine* of Newburgh, N. Y. On Dec. 27, 1877, she was married to James Steele Catherwood. Her husband for a time conducted a confectionery store in Indianapolis, where she was a part of the little literary circle of the city. Erect and graceful, with auburn hair and bright hazel eyes, she was an attractive figure. The major part of her married life was spent at Hoopeston, Ill., where Catherwood was postmaster under Cleveland and member of a real-estate firm. Later, having separated from her husband, she spent her summers in writing, at Mackinac, her favorite resort, or in gathering material in Canada or abroad. Her last years were spent in Chicago.

Throughout her life, Mrs. Catherwood was exceptionally ambitious and prolific, carrying on several pieces of work at one time. She had, for instance, two serials, "Lilith" and "Cracque-o'-Doom," running in the 1881 numbers of *Lippincott's* and a third, "Stephen Guthrie," in the next volume. Her first novel, *A Woman in Armor,* had appeared in 1875. During the eighties she produced a number of children's books. Widespread recognition first came with her historical novel, *The Romance of Dollard* (1889), based largely on Francis Parkman. This she followed with numerous other tales dealing with the French in America: *The Story of Tonty* (1890), *The Lady of Fort St. John* (1891), *Old Kaskaskia* (1893), *The Chase of St. Castin and Other Stories of the French in the New World* (1894), *The Little Renault* (published with *The Spirit of an Illinois Town,* 1897). *The Days of Jeanne D'Arc* (1897) she regarded as in part the result of a divine hint. *The White Islander* (1893) shows the transition from French control. *The Spirit of an Illinois Town* (1897); *Spanish Peggy* (1899); *The Queen of the Swamp and Other Plain Americans* (1899); *Mackinac and Lake Stories* (1899), one of the best of her books; and an unfinished novel about Owen's colony, all treated of the Anglo-Saxon settlement of the West. Her last book, *Lazarre* (1901), dealt with the legend of the Dauphin in America. Since her death, her works have sunk into relative obscurity. It must be admitted that she fell into the pitfalls inherent in her favorite *genre* when she invented for Dollard and her other heroes loves befitting their courage, youth, and chivalry; that she was inclined to refine or sentimentalize her characters too much; and that her longer novels were marred by structural weaknesses. Nevertheless her books show careful research, a feeling for the untamed background of forest and prairie, and an intelligent sympathy with the past.

[M. L. Wilson, *Biography of Mary Hartwell Catherwood* (1904); F. L. Pattee, *Hist. of Am. Lit. since 1870* (1915); D. A. Dondore, *The Prairie and the Making of Middle America; Four Centuries of Description* (1927).]

D.A.D.

CATLIN, GEORGE (July 26, 1796–Dec. 23, 1872), artist, author, was born at Wilkesbarre, Pa., the fifth of the fourteen children of Putnam and Polly (Sutton) Catlin. When eight years old, Polly Sutton, along with her mother, had been captured by the Indians at the surrender of Forty Fort. George's early life was filled with stories, legends, and traditions of the Red Men, not only from his family but from Revolutionary soldiers, Indian fighters, trappers, hunters, and explorers, who were constant guests of the family. His scanty education was obtained at home. He loved fishing and hunting, became an accomplished sportsman, and in his early years collected Indian relics. In 1817–18 he read law in the office of Reeves & Gould in Litchfield, Conn., where he became celebrated as an amateur artist. Until 1823 he practised law at Luzerne, Pa., and in adjoining counties, but then moved to Philadelphia to devote himself to portrait painting in oil and miniature. In 1828 he visited Albany, where he painted portraits of Gov. DeWitt Clinton and many members of the legislature. While there he met and married Clara B. Gregory, who was to be an enthusiastic aid in his later western work, accompanying him on many of his trips. From 1824 to 1829 he resided mainly in Washington, D. C., painting many portraits, among others that of Dolly Madison. His painting of the Constitutional Convention at Richmond (1829–30) contains 115 figures. During all these early years he had been seeking for an idea to which he could devote the remainder of his artistic life. Upon seeing at Philadelphia a delegation of from ten to fifteen dignified-looking Indians from the wilds of the Far West, he resolved, as he wrote later, "to use my art and so much of the labors of my future life as might be required in rescuing from oblivion the looks and customs of the vanishing races of native man in America." To this one purpose he devoted enthusiastically the rest of his life and that without aid, governmental or individual. He spent his summers among the Indians; in the winters he would return to civilization, paint portraits, and save enough money to take him back to his beloved Indians in the ensuing summer. One of the most difficult things which he had to overcome was the superstition of the Indians, who believed that they would die or that the white medicine man would have power over them, if their portraits were painted. If anything did happen to the tribe, if a person died or was killed, it was supposed to be the fault of the painter, and Catlin several times escaped death only through wise counsel or by fleeing. From 1829 to 1838 he painted some 600 portraits of distinguished Indians of both sexes, in their native costume, accompanied with pictures of their villages, domestic habits, games, mysteries, and religious ceremonies. This original collection he exhibited in many cities in the United States and in Europe during a period from 1837 to 1852. In the latter year he was induced to enter into speculations which ended in financial disaster. Joseph Harrison of Philadelphia advanced him money and took the collection as security, but Catlin was never able to redeem it. Eventually the collection was given by Mrs. Harrison to the United States National Museum. There is also another collection known as the "Catlin Cartoon Collection," which consists of copies and original paintings of North and South American Indians and scenes painted between 1852 and 1870. This is the property of Catlin's heirs, and consists of 603 numbers. Catlin's writings related largely to his own experiences. They consist of: "Notes of Eight Years Travel Amongst the North American Indians," published in the New York *Daily Commercial Advertizer* from 1830 to 1839; *Letters and Notes on the Manners, Customs, and Condition of the North American Indians* (2 vols., 1841); *Catlin's North American Indian Portfolio: Hunting, Rocky Mountains and Prairies of America* (1845); *Catlin's Notes of Eight Years' Travels and Residence in Europe* (1848); *Life Among the Indians* (1867); *Last Rambles Amongst the Indians of the Rocky Mountains and the Andes* (1867). Besides the above, Catlin wrote the various catalogues of his collections and numerous articles for papers and magazines.

[Thos. Donaldson, "The Geo. Catlin Indian Gallery in the U. S. Nat. Mus.," in *Annual Report of the Board of Regents of the Smithsonian Institution*, 1885; W. Matthews, "The Catlin Collection of Indian Paintings," *Ibid.*, 1890; *U. S. Mag. and Democratic Rev.*, July 1842; *N. Y. Herald*, Dec. 24, 1872; *Nature* (London), Jan. 23, 1873; *Am. Bibliopolist*, Jan. 1873; *Pop. Sci. Mo.*, July 1891.]   R. P. T.

CATON, JOHN DEAN (Mar. 19, 1812–July 30, 1895), jurist, was born in Monroe, Orange County, N. Y. He was a son of Robert Caton, a Virginian of English descent, who, after serving through the Revolutionary War with the American forces, moved to Monroe, and married Hannah Dean. When, on the death of his father, the family moved to Oneida County, John worked as a farm hand, attending the district school in winter. In 1827 he was apprenticed to a harness maker, but was compelled to abandon this owing to impaired eyesight. He then became a common carrier between Waterville and Utica, N. Y., studying in the evenings, and in 1829 he was, for a short time, a pupil at the Utica Academy. The following summer he engaged as a farm laborer, and studied classics during the winter. In 1831 he attended the Grosvenor High School at Rome, N. Y., intermittently studying law there and at Utica and

Vernon. Two years later he went west, arriving in Chicago,—then a place of 300 inhabitants—June 19, 1833. The town had no lawyer, so he determined to locate there, and, obtaining a license to practise, opened the first law office. He instituted the first civil suit in the circuit court of the county, prosecuted the first criminal tried in a court of justice there, for which he received a fee of ten dollars—"the greatest fee he ever received," he was wont to say—and also appeared in the first jury case heard in that neighborhood. He was a member and secretary of the first political convention held in Illinois, which met at Ottawa, Mar. 4, 1834. This was followed by his election as justice of the peace. In July 1835 he married Laura Adelaide, daughter of Jacob Sherill of New Hartford, Oneida County, N. Y. In the same year he was admitted to the Illinois bar. Much of his time was taken up in traveling the circuit on horseback, which took him through practically unexplored country, involving much hardship and no little adventure. The financial panic of 1837 seriously affected him, and, his health breaking down, he retired to a farm near Plainfield, where he remained for three years, not resuming practise in Chicago till 1841. In August 1842 he was appointed associate justice of the supreme court of Illinois by Gov. Carlin, holding the office till March 1843, when he was defeated. Two months later a vacancy occurring, he was again appointed to the bench, and on the expiration of his term was unanimously nominated and elected to succeed himself. Under the new Illinois constitution of 1848, he was elected to one of the three supreme court judgeships thereby created, becoming chief justice in 1855 on the resignation of Chief Justice Treat. Reëlected in 1857, he remained chief justice till his retirement, Jan. 9, 1864. Though not a great lawyer, since he lacked the erudition which can come only through deep reading, he was an excellent judge. His opinions were always logical and expressed with great common sense and vigor. He had little respect for precedent, relying more on principles. Endowed with good business instincts, he was "one of the most practical men that ever sat upon the bench" (James B. Bradwell). Chief shareholder in the Illinois & Mississippi Telegraph Company, it is said that at one time he controlled all the telegraph lines in the state. Ultimately these were leased to the Western Union Telegraph Company, and Caton disposed of his holdings in 1867. The last thirty years of his life were spent in retirement. He had a large estate at Ottawa, where he gratified his taste for the amenities of country life. He traveled widely in the United States, Europe, and the East. He died in Chicago.

Caton contributed a number of papers on nature subjects to the Ottawa Academy of Science, and was the author of: *Matter and a Supreme Intelligence* (1864), *A Summer in Norway* (1875), *The Antelope and Deer of America* (1877), and a volume of *Miscellanies* (1880). He also contributed a series of papers to the *Chicago Legal News* in 1888–89, which were subsequently published with additional material under the title *The Early Bench and Bar of Illinois* (1893).

[A judicious study of Caton's career by M. M. Follansbee will be found in *Great Am. Lawyers,* ed. by Wm. D. Lewis (1909), VI, 307. Appreciative sketches appeared in *The Bench and Bar of Ill.,* ed. by J. M. Palmer (1899), I, 39, II, 604, and in the *Green Bag,* III, 230. See also Robt. Fergus, *Biog. Sketch of John Dean Caton* (1882); *Ill. State Bar Ass. Report,* 1896, pt. II, p. 176; 31 *Ill. R.,* p. viii; 162 *Ill. R.,* pp. 15–20.]
H. W. H. K.

CATRON, JOHN (*c.* 1786–May 30, 1865), jurist, was of German descent, at least on his father's side. His birth has been credited to both Pennsylvania and Virginia, and the date put as early as 1779 and as late as 1786. Considering all sources of information, it is believed that he was a descendant of German settlers in Pennsylvania, was born in that state about 1786, spent a part of his childhood in Virginia, and grew to manhood in Kentucky where he resided until 1812. Nothing is known of his life during this time except that his parents were poor and his educational opportunities exceedingly limited.

In 1812 he removed to Tennessee and settled near the Cumberland Mountains, and later became a prominent figure in the pioneer days of that state. He enlisted and served as a soldier under Jackson in the War of 1812. In 1815 he was admitted to the bar and, until 1818, practised on what were known as the mountain circuits, becoming, in the meantime, prosecuting attorney for one of these circuits. He was recognized as unusually proficient in land law, then the chief source of litigation. In personal appearance, he was large and well proportioned, with dark complexion, black eyes, and strong face, indicating determination and confidence in himself. He was not a pleasing or graceful speaker, having an unpleasant voice and being given to awkward and rather violent gesticulation. But his arguments were strong and convincing. As a lawyer he was studious, painstaking, and unusually successful. In 1818 he removed to Nashville where he soon enjoyed a lucrative practise, won distinction, especially as a Chancery lawyer, and acquired, for those times, a comfortable fortune. In 1824 the legislature

increased the number of the judges of the supreme court of errors and appeals (then the court of last resort) and elected Catron to the new judgeship. The bar has an apparently well-founded tradition that both the increase in the membership of the court and the election of Catron were due to the fact that land titles were unsettled to a disturbing degree on account of a division in the court as to the effect of certain statutes of limitations. Catron's views on this question were well known and insured a majority of the court for the ruling that has ever since served to quiet titles.

In 1831 the office of chief justice was created, and Catron became Tennessee's first chief justice. He held this office until a new constitution, adopted in 1834, abolished the court of which he was a member, after which he resumed his practise at Nashville. His service as a judge was of great value in developing the system of land laws which has ever since prevailed in the state. Perhaps his most noted opinion was delivered in 1829 in a case in which a lawyer was disbarred for fighting a duel and killing his man. This opinion had much to do with discrediting the then rather prevalent practise of dueling. After a most scathing arraignment of dueling and the false ideas of honor and bravery which led to it, Catron said: "We are told this is only a kind of *honorable* homicide! The law knows it as a wicked and wilful murder" (I *Yerger,* 237).

Besides being a successful lawyer, Catron was an astute politician as he showed while directing the campaign, in Tennessee, of Martin Van Buren for the presidency in 1836. He was an ardent supporter of President Jackson and had a large part in creating a sentiment in Tennessee in favor of Jackson's fight against the Bank of the United States. On Mar. 3, 1837, the day before Jackson's retirement from the presidency, Congress passed an act adding two justices to the membership of the Supreme Court. On the next day, among his last acts as president, Jackson appointed Catron. Several traditions are connected with this appointment. One is that Mrs. Catron went to the White House and personally solicited it. Another is that it was procured through the influence of Van Buren whose friendship Catron had gained. The truth probably is that, knowing his friend and supporter to be well qualified, Jackson was very glad to make the appointment when it was suggested by Mrs. Catron and possibly by Van Buren. Being self-educated, Catron was not a ripe scholar, but he had a good knowledge of the law, a keen insight into human nature, and strong common sense.

His opinions have been considered particularly strong when dealing with the common law and equity jurisprudence. In the great Dred Scott case, he was one of the justices who concurred in holding the Missouri Compromise unconstitutional. At the outbreak of the Civil War, he, as associate justice, presided over the circuit composed of Missouri, Kentucky, and Tennessee. In cooperation with the circuit judges, he was firm and determined in the effort to maintain the authority of the United States. When the Supreme Court adjourned in the spring of 1861, he hurried to Tennessee in the hope that he could aid in holding his state loyal to the Union. Tennessee had not then seceded. An election had been held and the vote had been against secession. But another election had been called. His efforts and those of many other Tennesseans, however, were unavailing and the state voted to secede.

After secession, it was Catron's purpose to remain in Tennessee, endeavor to maintain the authority of the Federal courts, and induce his friends to adhere to the cause of the Union. But this was impossible. Excitement was running too high and feeling was too bitter. Upon his return from Missouri where he had been holding court, a committee waited on him with the friendly advice that he leave the state, since otherwise he would be subjected to indignities. The state was then in control of the Confederate authorities, and, influenced, as was said, by the ill health and entreaties of his wife, he reluctantly yielded. As soon, however, as the fortunes of war made it possible to resume his judicial duties, he returned. But he was then in failing health, was near eighty years old, and soon died.

[Memorial published in 3 *Wallace* IX–XIV (1866); Joshua W. Caldwell, *Sketches of the Bench and Bar of Tenn.* (1898); Josephus C. Guild, *Old Times in Tenn.* (1878); Chas. Warren, *The Supreme Court in U. S. Hist.* (1922).]   W. L. F.

CATTELL, ALEXANDER GILMORE (Feb. 12, 1816–Apr. 8, 1894), banker, politician, was descended from Huguenot ancestors who settled in Scotland, moved to Leamington, England, and reached southern New Jersey, via Rhode Island, about 1700. He was the eldest son of Thomas W. and Keziah (Gilmore) Cattell, his father a merchant and banker of Salem, N. J., whose notes were war-time money along the lower Delaware in 1812. Owing to family reverses, Alexander left school for his father's store, but he continued his reading and wrote verses, his favorite poet being Keats. In 1840 he was elected to the legislature, in 1841–42 was clerk of the lower house, and in 1844 was the youngest member of the state constitutional convention. Moving to Philadelphia, 1846, he served on the Common Council, 1848–54, became a director of the Mechanics Bank, president of the Corn (later the Commercial) Exchange Association, 1857, and in 1858 organized the Corn Exchange Bank which he headed for thirteen years. He "did much to build up and extend the grain trade of the city" (Scharf and Westcott, *History of Philadelphia*, 1884, III, 2224). He presided at the opening of the new post-office, Feb. 23, 1863, and at the meeting to relieve Chambersburg, Aug. 3, 1864, and he headed the committee of twenty-one (July 24, 1862) to raise and equip the "Corn Exchange Regiment." He had maintained a residence in New Jersey since 1855, having interests around Merchantville, near Camden. The local Democratic victory of 1864 and the impending necessities of Republican reconstruction brought him into New Jersey politics, as a patriot with a righteous cause and money to back him.

Early in 1865 the "Union Party" (Republican) leaders of the first and second New Jersey congressional districts, "unexpectedly" urged Cattell's nomination for governor, it being understood that "a very large amount of means would be provided for the canvass" (Smith Papers, journal, pp. 159–60). But Marcus L. Ward, "the Soldier's Friend," was nominated and elected, despite knifing by the "Cattell Cabal." A little later when John Potter Stockton's election as United States senator was challenged because he had received only a plurality of the votes of the legislature, Cattell and his friends grasped the chance to seize the office. Stockton was unseated Mar. 27, 1866, and Cattell was elected in the face of an opposition which declared him mentally and morally unfit and only financially qualified (*Ibid.*, p. 124). He was seated, Dec. 3, and gave his vote for the impeachment of President Johnson. Allied with Jay Cooke and other Philadelphia interests, a sound banker, a warm friend of Grant as he had been of Lincoln, Cattell now entered his most crowded years. He did constructive work concerning tariff, taxing, national debt, and sound money; but he also became involved in the naval scandals under George M. Robeson. With his brother, Elijah G. Cattell, he "engaged in speculations in which the secretary of the navy was also involved. They gave or lent him money. They built him a house at Long Branch, purchased him horses and carriages, and managed expensive campaigns to make him a United States senator from New Jersey" (Oberholtzer, *post*, III, 182). In 1871 Cattell secured the shifting of the navy deposits in London (over a million) from Baring's to Jay Cooke's. Declining another senatorial candidacy, also a District of Columbia commissionership, he served on Grant's ineffective Civil Service Commission and, on Apr. 24, 1873, took up his headquarters at Rothschild's in London as the United States Treasury financial agent. He refunded $100,-000,000 of bonds from six per cent to five per cent, devised methods still used for quoting exchange between Great Britain and the United States, and transferred the *Alabama* claims payments to Washington. Secretary of the Treasury Bristow refused to reappoint him, because "he had positive evidence to prove that the appointment would be in the interest of dishonesty" (H. V. Boynton, "The Whiskey Ring," *North American Review,* October 1876, p. 287). Cattell served thereafter on various civic bodies, notably as president of the State Board of Assessors, but his health was none too good, partly from overstrain, partly from "a bundle of black cigars" per day (interview with nephew, E. J. Cattell). His end came while under treatment for "dementia." His wife, Eliza (Gillmore) Cattell, and an adopted daughter, had died before him.

[Cattell's letters and papers are scattered. His national career was followed with acid comment by the N. Y. *Sun,* with admiring approval by the Trenton *Daily State Gazette.* His New Jersey politics, later period, were bitterly noted by Chas. Perrin Smith in The Smith Papers (MSS.), in N. J. State Lib., Trenton. C. M. Knapp, *N. J. Politics During the Period of the Civil War and Reconstruction* (1924), and E. P. Oberholtzer, *Hist. of U. S. Since the Civil War* (1917–26) and *Jay Cooke, Financier of the Civil War* (1907) give the best view of his senatorial-financial period. For the Philadelphia navy-yard scandals see *House Misc. Docs., No. 170,* 44 Cong., 1 Sess., pt. III. Obituaries were published in Philadelphia *Evening Telegraph,* Apr. 9, 1894, and Trenton *Daily State Gazette,* Apr. 10, 1894.] 　　　　　　　　　W. L. W.

CATTELL, WILLIAM CASSADAY (Aug. 30, 1827–Feb. 11, 1898), Presbyterian clergyman, college president, was the son of Thomas W. Cattell, descended from an old family of New Jersey Quakers, and Keziah (Gilmore) Cattell. He was born at Salem, N. J., graduated from the College of New Jersey (now Princeton University) in 1848 and from the Princeton Theological Seminary in 1852, and was ordained in 1856. He began his career as an educator in 1853, as associate principal of the Edgehill Preparatory School. In 1855 he became professor of Latin in Lafayette College, Easton, Pa. On Aug. 4, 1859, he was married to Elizabeth McKeen. In 1860 he accepted the pastorate of the Pine Street Presbyterian Church at Harrisburg, Pa., where he was soon active in war work in the camps and hospitals. In 1861 he had become a trustee of Lafayette College, which, embarrassed financial-

ly and suffering from an exodus of students to join the army, was in a condition such that the trustees met to consider a suspension of operations. Instead, they elected Cattell to the presidency, which he held from 1863 to 1883. He began with thirty-nine students, a deficit, and an income insufficient to pay the $4,900 per year due the nine faculty members. A dozen years later the college, with an enrolment above 300 and proportionate increases in faculty, equipment, and endowment, was a first-class institution. Besides unusual gifts as a scholar, teacher, and administrator Cattell had a personal charm that endeared him to both faculty and students. In 1883 he was forced to resign because of ill health. While recuperating in Europe he was elected corresponding secretary of the Presbyterian Board of Ministerial Relief, in which capacity he devoted himself from 1884 to 1886 to the care of retired ministers and their dependents. From 1890 to his death he was president of the Presbyterian Historical Society. He was several times a delegate of the Presbyterian General Assembly to churches in Scotland, Bohemia, and Moravia, and he is said to have been the founder of the Sunday-school system of the Bohemian Reformed Churches. On several of these occasions he acted as a special United States commissioner of education. He was a director of the Princeton Theological Seminary, vice-president of the American Philological Society, and a councillor of the American Philosophical Society. He contributed an article on the "Tunkers" to the *Schaff-Herzog Encyclopædia,* and collected materials for a life of Lafayette and an edition of Lactantius.

[*Memoir of William C. Cattell* (1899), pp. 7–26; the *Journal* (Elmira, N. Y.), Mar. 1895; obituaries in the Phila. *Public Ledger,* Feb. 11, 1898, and in the *Presbyterian,* Feb. 16, 1898. His published addresses contain autobiographical material. See also Donald G. Mitchell, "Lafayette College," *Scribner's Mo.,* Dec. 1876; *An Hist. Sketch of the Presbyt. Board of Ministerial Relief* (1888); *Annual Report of the Presbyt. Hist. Soc.,* 1890–98.] 　　　　　　　D. L. M.

CAWEIN, MADISON JULIUS (Mar. 23, 1865–Dec. 8, 1914), poet, was born in Louisville, Ky. His father, William Cawein, descended from Jean de Herancour, a Huguenot who fled Paris at the time of the revocation of the Edict of Nantes, was born near Mannheim, Germany; his mother, born Christiana Stelsly, was of German parentage (fragment of autobiography prepared by Madison Cawein for W. W. Thum, Louisville, 1914). From his father, who gathered herbs and compounded patent medicines, Cawein learned to love the outdoors and to observe so accurately that his poems exhibit a fairly comprehensive catalogue of Kentucky flora and fauna; from his mother, who was interested in spiritualism, he probably acquired his feeling for the supernatural. His first strong impressions of wild nature were gained between the ages of nine and thirteen, the Cawein family having moved from Louisville to a house near the South Fork of Harrod's Creek and later to one near New Albany, Ind. Returning in 1879 to his native city, Cawein graduated as class poet from the Louisville Male High School in 1886. In these student days he became fond of poetry, especially that of Shelley, Tennyson, and Browning (Louisville *Courier-Journal*, Jan. 24, 1901). Working as a cashier in the Newmarket pool-room, he contrived to write verse and to have it published. His first volume, appearing when he was twenty-two, was *Blooms of the Berry* (1887). Almost accidentally it came to the notice of William Dean Howells, who praised it generously in his Editor's Study (*Harper's Monthly*, May 1888). Encouragement from such a source meant much to Cawein, and he showed his gratitude by dedicating his second book, *The Triumph of Music* (1888) to Howells. To escape from the associations of the pool-room Cawein began to dabble in real estate and in stock operations which he made lucrative and to which he devoted most of his time not given to composition. In the morning he watched stock market reports; in the afternoon he repaired to a stretch of forest a few miles south of Louisville where he could write most easily (*Louisville Herald*, Oct. 2, 1910). So tirelessly did he work that to-day his name appears on thirty-six volumes. Of the 2,700 poems included in these volumes, however, almost half are reprints or revisions. In time he came to feel that there was a disproportion between his efforts and their rewards, and at the turn of the century a note of dissatisfaction crept into his correspondence—an arraignment of his time and compatriots as being too much occupied with the materialistic. "Never in the whole history of English literature," he wrote, "was there ever less encouragement for the writing of serious poetry than there is at the present time" (Louisville *Courier-Journal*, Dec. 14, 1902). But recognition came to him, though slowly. Sir Edmund Gosse wrote the introduction for a carefully selected edition of his poems in one volume (*Kentucky Poems*, London, 1902) and in 1907 the introduction was reprinted in a five-volume edition of *The Poems of Madison Cawein* illustrated with seventeen photogravures after paintings by Eric Pape. Cawein was made an overseas member of the Authors' Club of London and a member of the National Institute of Arts and Letters.

He became the friend of many of his contemporaries who ranked high as makers of American literature. Critics were obliged to reckon with him as a sincere if over-prolific worker in a *genre* almost abandoned at that time. But increasing respect on the part of the few for his productions did not win for him a very wide public, and, having married Gertrude Foster McKelvey, on June 4, 1903, he had added reason to wish that his pen might win a large following with a consequent income sufficient to free him from business. In 1906 he met his first sharp reverse in losses incurred by the San Francisco earthquake, but it was not until some seven years later that his modest fortune began to shrink alarmingly. His health, undermined by illnesses and early carelessness, failed; his appearance, never impressive, became that of a man prematurely aged— bald, thin, stooping, with hazel eyes often clouded in sadness. Although usually modest and cheerful, he began to show, in letters from 1911 on, concern about himself and hints of concealed tragedy. He struggled against approaching poverty, opposed sickness with his pen, tried to get an appointment as United States consul in some healthful location, and attempted a scenario for a photodrama. His sudden death at the age of forty-nine rounded out the unity of ironic failure; he fell in his bath-room and struck his head against the railing of the tub, but the question whether his decease was due to the fall or to a stroke of apoplexy preceding the fall caused a long controversy with an insurance company, ultimately compromised with the question still unsettled.

Howells said of Cawein's first volume that it did not echo "any of the poets who are apt to reverberate in the pages of beginners," but this remark was more kind than just. There are unmistakable echoes of Keats and Swinburne in this sophomoric work, and Cawein never entirely threw off the spell of the Romantics and of the best known Victorians. The great bulk of his poetry—and it is unnecessary to argue that he wrote too much—displays the fields and forests, springs and flowers of Kentucky and the fairies and mythical creatures that he somewhat incongruously placed there and in whom he protested belief. The *Christian Science Monitor* declared him "the greatest nature poet his country has produced" (Jan. 24, 1920) and Joyce Kilmer adjudged him "the greatest nature poet of his time" (*Catholic World*, March 1917). Very gradually he accepted the criticism that his poetry was too unearthly, and his latter work shows that he had busied himself in understanding the problems of the modern world even to the extent of experimenting with the newer fashions in verse forms (see *The Cup of Comus*, 1915). Although nature charmed him most, he manifested an inclination toward the Arthurian romances and the Oriental. *The Giant and the Star* (1909) was written to entertain his son; *The White Snake* (1895) is a translation from the German; *The Poet and Nature and the Morning Road* (1914) reveals his horror of the war just beginning in Europe at the time of his death. His poetry is represented in some fifty anthologies of American verse.

[The chief source of information is Otto Rothert, *The Story of a Poet: Madison Cawein* (Filson Club Publications No. 30, 1921), which, not strictly a biography, is a storehouse of facts. Jessie B. Rittenhouse, *The Younger Am. Poets* (1904), ch. IX; and "Memories of Madison Cawein," *Bookman*, Nov. 1922, contain critical and personal material of interest. The best obituary was printed by the *Boston Transcript*, Dec. 19, 1914. Some information was supplied by Madison Cawein, Jr.]　　　　　　　　　　G. C. K.

CAYVAN, GEORGIA (1858–Nov. 19, 1906), actress, was born in Bath, Me. Going to Boston in childhood with her parents, she early began to appear in public, giving recitations and readings before she was fourteen. By the time she was twenty, and for some years thereafter, she was frequently engaged for entertainments by societies, clubs, and lodges in Boston and vicinity. During this period she was also taking part in amateur dramatic performances, one of her earliest recorded appearances being at Union Park Hall, Boston, May 7, 1874, when, under the auspices of the Mercantile Library Association, she played Miss Mortimer in *Naval Engagements*, and Georgiana in a condensed version of *Our American Cousin*. She studied elocution at a private school in Boston, and her first professional acting was with the Boston Ideal Opera Company as Hebe in *H. M. S. Pinafore* at the Boston Theatre, Apr. 14, 1879. On the tenth of the next month she acted Sally Scraggs in *Sketches from India* for her professional début in the drama.

Thereafter her advance was rapid. She went to New York in 1880, making her début there on May 7, at the Madison Square Theatre, as Dolly Dutton in *Hazel Kirke*, later replacing Effie Ellsler in the title character. The next year, after playing Daisy Brown in *The Professor* at the same theatre, she gained considerable added repute by her acting, in Boston and New York, of Jocasta in an English version of *Œdipus Tyrannus*, with George Riddle as *Œdipus*. She went to San Francisco to become leading lady at the California Theatre, and when she returned to New York she replaced Sara Jewett at the Union Square Theatre, playing Marcelle

in *A Parisian Romance* and Jane Learoyd in *The Long Strike*. At the Madison Square Theatre in 1885, she appeared in *Alpine Roses, Young Mrs. Winthrop,* and *May Blossom,* also playing on tour in *Divorce, Impulse,* and *La Belle Russe.* Joining the Lyceum Theatre Stock Company, then newly organized, on Nov. 1, 1888, she remained with it as leading lady until the fall of 1894, enlarging her reputation throughout the country, as well as in New York. A list of the plays in which she acted would be simply a list of the Lyceum Theatre productions, among her more important rôles being those of Helen Truman in *The Wife,* Ann Cruger in *The Charity Ball,* Minnie Gilfillan in *Sweet Lavender,* Katherine Thorpe in *Squire Kate,* and Lady Noeline in *The Amazons.* After retirement on account of ill health she returned to the stage as a star in the season of 1896–97, but with limited success. Her permanent retirement came a little later, and during her last years she was an invalid, her death occurring at Flushing, N. Y. At the height of her career she was one of the most popular American actresses of the "leading lady" type. With an attractive personality, she could always be relied upon to act a character with a certain satisfactory amount of comedy feeling and dramatic insight. She was of dark complexion, with expressive eyes that were often more eloquent even than her voice.

[Sketch by Ralph Edmunds in *Famous Am. Actors of Today* (1896), ed. by F. E. McKay and C. E. L. Wingate; J. B. Clapp and E. F. Edgett, *Players of the Present* (1899); Percy MacKaye, *Epoch, the Life of Steele MacKaye* (1927); *Brooklyn Mag.*, Feb. 1887; *Boston Herald*, Jan. 6, 1886; *N. Y. Dramatic Mirror*, July 11, 1896, Feb. 22, 1902, Dec. 1, 1906; *Toledo Globe*, Aug. 20, 1898.]　　　　E. F. E.

CAZENOVE, THÉOPHILE (Oct. 13, 1740–Mar. 6, 1811), financier and agent of the Holland Land Company, was born in Amsterdam, Holland, the fourth of nine children. His father, Théophile, belonged to a French Protestant family long resident in Switzerland; his mother, Marie, was the daughter of Paul de Raspin-Thoyras, a French Protestant historian and soldier. The younger Théophile by his marriage in 1763 to Margaretha Helena van Jever became connected with a prominent trading family of Amsterdam. For the next twenty-five years he carried on a brokerage and commercial business in Amsterdam. At the end of the period, in 1788, he was coöperating with Clavière, a Swiss banker of Paris, and Pieter Stadnitski, a wealthy financier of Amsterdam, in an unsuccessful attempt to convert the American debt to France into obligations which could be sold to private holders. By the end of 1788 he was bankrupt. Nevertheless he was now selected by Stadnitski and three other Amsterdam firms, who were speculating in American state and federal securities, to go to the United States as their purchasing agent. Arriving in America early in 1790, he established himself in Philadelphia, the seat of the federal government upon whose action largely depended the fate of the state bonds. At first he bought such securities exclusively. Then he invested for his principals in various canal and manufacturing companies, more fruitful in the development of the new country than in profits for the investors. He then persuaded his employers, who had made large profits from their bond operations, to invest in wild lands, a field in which American speculative fever was running high. Having enlarged their combination and laid the foundation for what became in 1796 the Holland Land Company, the Dutch bankers between 1792 and 1794 bought directly or through Cazenove over five million acres of land in western New York and in northern and western Pennsylvania. Cazenove's advice had determined the lands selected, but his judgment left much to be desired. The investment in New York lands, realized only forty years later, proved moderately successful; that in Pennsylvania led to heavy losses. From 1794 to 1799 Cazenove was engaged in perfecting his employers' title to the lands, in providing for their survey, and in opening some of them for sale through sub-agents. Accustomed to good living, he was something of a *grand seigneur* in Philadelphia where he kept a coach and four, a coachman, postillion, and valet. In spite of the gout, which kept him to a régime of water and vegetables, he was entertained much in the political circles of the federal capital. Hospitable and generous, he shared his own well-filled table not alone with the natives whose official positions might supply information valuable to the foreign investor but with many unfortunate French émigrés. One of them, Talleyrand, describes him as an "homme d'un esprit assez éclairé, mais lent et timide, d'un caractère fort insouciant" (*Mémoires*, 1891–92, vol. I). Timid he certainly was not in his American business dealings, but there is no doubt of his extreme carelessness. He kept almost no accounts and he carried his insouciance to the point of confusing his employers' money with his own. Early in 1799 he returned to Europe. Three years later he left the employ of the Dutch bankers and spent most of his remaining years in Paris, where renewed relations with Talleyrand, now in charge of French foreign affairs, helped him to eke out a precarious existence. He died in Paris in 1811. He had become an

American citizen in 1794, and his name is perpetuated in the village of Cazenovia in central New York. His portrait by St. Memin hangs in the Corcoran Gallery in Washington.

[R. W. Kelsey, ed., "Cazenove Journal 1794" (pub. in *Haverford Coll. Studies*, No. 13, 1922) is a diary kept by Cazenove on a trip through Pa. Two books by his descendants give some biographical data: Raoul de Cazenove, *Rapin-Thoyras, sa famille, sa vie et ses œuvres* (1866), and Q. M. A. de Cazenove, *Quatre Siècles* (1908). See also E. and E. Haag, *La France protestante* (2nd ed., Paris, 1877–88), vol. III. For Cazenove's business life and especially his relations with the bankers of the Holland Land Company see P. J. Van Winter, *Het aandeel van den Amsterdamschen handel aan den opbouw van het Amerikaansche Gemeenebest* (1927) and Paul D. Evans, "The Holland Land Company" in *Buffalo Hist. Soc. Pubs.*, vol. XXVIII (1924).]   P. D. E.

CÉLORON DE BLAINVILLE, PIERRE JOSEPH de (Dec. 29, 1693–Apr. 12, 1759), French officer and explorer, was born in Montreal. The family of Céloron de Blainville originated in Paris, whence Jean-Baptiste, the Canadian founder, emigrated to Canada in 1684. There he married, Nov. 29, 1686, Hélène Picoté de Bellestre, widow of Sieur de Brucy. Pierre Joseph was their fifth child and the oldest son. Bred like his father to the career of arms, he obtained his first commission in 1715, and was promoted to a lieutenancy in 1731. Engaged in military duties until 1734, he was in that year chosen commandant of the important post of Michilimackinac where he was so successful in his administration, that he was returned for a second term of three years (1737–40), and was again at this post in 1741–42. He was beloved by the Indians about his station, and governed them firmly, with regard to justice.

While Céloron was stationed at Mackinac, the governor of Louisiana undertook a punitive expedition against the Chickasaw tribe, which had entrapped and destroyed a contingent of French from the Illinois. The Canadian authorities agreed to cooperate and in the autumn of 1739 sent a considerable body of troops from Montreal by way of the Ohio, at the same time ordering Céloron to gather the traders and tribesmen of his post and join the expedition. He met the other contingents on the Mississippi near Memphis, where a fort was built and winter quarters prepared. It was Céloron and his detachment who saved the expedition from entire futility. In the spring of 1740 he penetrated to the Chickasaw towns, forced the Indians to make a treaty, and exacted a partial reparation. About this time he obtained a captaincy and was characterized as "intelligent, a very good officer."

In the summer of 1742 he visited Montreal with the Indians from his post; the governor told them that they could no longer keep their favorite officer. "He has been very kind to us," said the Ottawa chief regretfully. In July of that year Céloron was transferred to Detroit, where he remained somewhat over a year. In 1744 he was in command of the important fortress of Niagara, but because of some differences with the lessees was soon transferred to Fort St. Fréderic, now Crown Point. After a short term (1746–47) he was recalled, and in 1748 took command of a convoy destined to relieve Detroit, which was in danger from a revolt of the Hurons and allied tribes.

After the close of King George's War, La Gallissonnière sent Céloron on an expedition to the Ohio to expel the English traders from this region and to assert French claims. The expedition of about two hundred regulars and militia and thirty domesticated Indians left Lachine on June 15, 1749, going by way of Lake Chautauqua to the upper waters of the Allegheny River. As Céloron passed down that river and the Ohio he buried at strategic points leaden plates, with inscriptions asserting French sovereignty; some of these plates were found in the nineteenth century. He also drove off several English traders, sending by one a letter to the governor of Pennsylvania (*Pennsylvania Colonial Records*, V, 425). The ultimate object of the expedition was to break up the Miami Indian town called Pickawillany, where the English had a trading house. Céloron went up the Miami River to this place; but he was unable to induce the rebel tribesmen to return to the French alliance. He then took his way eastward by way of Detroit and the Great Lakes. The next year he was promoted to a majority and sent to command at Detroit; there he failed to reclaim the recalcitrant Miami; and after a term of three years (1750–53), he was relieved, becoming major of Montreal.

Céloron's share in the French and Indian War was not great; he was with Dieskau in 1755 on Lake George, and must have been in other battles, since his death was due to wounds. He was an able and popular officer, and left by his three wives a considerable progeny, most of whom returned to France after the British conquest of Canada. His son Paul Louis, who was born at Detroit, served as a French officer under Washington during the American Revolution.

[The best sketch of Céloron's life is in *Mich. Pioneer & Hist. Colls.*, XXXIV, 327–33; see also *Wis. Hist. Colls.*, XVII, 207, 367, XVIII, 28. The *Am. Cath. Hist. Researches*, II, 113–95 gives a sketch preliminary to the account of his voyage of 1749. His journal of that voyage has been published several times; the French original is in Margry, *Découvertes et Établissements des Français dans l'Amérique Septentrionale* (Paris, 1886), VI, 666–726; it is translated in *Wis. Hist.*

Colls., XVIII, 36–58; the chaplain's journal is in *Jesuit Relations* (Thwaites ed., 1896–1902), LXIX, 150–199; one plate is in the collections of the Am. Antiquarian Soc., and another in those of the Va. Hist. Soc.]
                                                    L. P. K.

CERRÉ, JEAN GABRIEL (Aug. 12, 1734–Apr. 4, 1805), merchant, fur-trader, son of Joseph and Marie (Picard) Cerré, was born at Montreal, Canada. Little is known of his childhood, except that he received a good education. In 1755 he was established at Kaskaskia, Ill. He pursued the vocation of merchant and trader, spending fifty years in the fur trade. In his extensive operations he went annually from Kaskaskia to Montreal. His many adventures, and the strategies used by him in dealing with Indians and protecting his goods, form an interesting story of pioneer life. The earliest hunters in the Missouri River country, excepting some occasional parties of adventurers, were men sent by Cerré from Kaskaskia. He became one of the wealthiest men in the Illinois country; a man of such eminence and influence among the people, that his assistance was enlisted by both the British and the Americans during the Revolution. Although he may have felt the traditional hatred of the French for the English, and is supposed to have served under Montcalm in defense of Quebec, he received many favors from the English commanders. Even after his espousing the American cause the British sought to break him away from his new alliance. George Rogers Clark in his "Memoir" devotes a great deal of space to his experiences with Cerré. Clark says that he had heard that Cerré was a man of great importance; that he was one of the most inveterate enemies of the American revolutionists. He also states that Cerré ultimately allied himself with the Americans, took the oath of citizenship, and was of infinite service to the United States. He gave financial aid to Clark and furnished provisions to the troops. From Clark's account of the measures taken to gain the cooperation of Cerré, there is room for suspicion that it was first gained through a species of mental coercion.

When the Virginia commandant, Col. John Todd, who had jurisdiction over the Illinois country, caused an election to be held by the people to choose magistrates, Cerré headed the list of those elected. It is doubtful if he served very long, as he appears to have turned his face westward soon thereafter and to have made St. Louis his home. If he moved in order to get out of the United States he was doomed to disappointment, as he lived to see St. Louis ceded by France. He was a soldier in the first company of St. Louis militia in 1780, and one of eight syndics in 1782. In answer to questions propounded to him by a committee of Congress in July 1786, he stated that although the people had chosen magistrates in 1779, the power of the magistrates had been annihilated and everything had fallen into a state of anarchy and confusion after the withdrawal of Todd's troops.

He was a man distinguished for his courtesy, humor, and kindness of heart. When he came to St. Louis many of his relatives in Canada joined him, and these, with his family connections, were so extensive, and his band of employees was so numerous, that he became the patriarch of a considerable portion of the inhabitants. In 1780 he founded New Madrid, Mo., when he established a trading post at that point, then called L'Anse-à-la-Graisse, and in 1781 he sent a trader to the Indians in Tennessee. He was married in 1764 to Catherine Giard and had four children, one of whom, Marie Thérèse, married Auguste Chouteau [q.v.].

[C. Tanguay, *Dictionnaire Généalogique des Familles Canadiennes*, VII (1890), 171, in which the name is spelled Séré; Kaskaskia and St. Louis Church Registers; *Report on Canadian Archives* (1882), p. 21; *Mich. Pioneer and Hist. Soc. Colls.*, XIX, 472; "Geo. Rogers Clark Papers, 1771–81," being *Colls. Ill. State Hist. Lib.*, VIII, 235, 361; W. B. Douglas, "Jean Gabriel Cerré: A Sketch" in *Mo. Hist. Soc. Colls.*, II, 58–76.]   S. D.

CESNOLA, LUIGI PALMA di (June 29, 1832–Nov. 20, 1904), soldier, archeologist, author, and museum director, was born at Rivarolo, near Turin, Italy. He was the second son of an Italian count who had served under Napoleon and whose family had come from Spain to Piedmont in 1282. His mother was Countess Eugenia Ricca di Castelvecchio. The young count was educated at the Royal Military Academy of Turin (1843–48), where he had an English tutor. His military experience began at seventeen in the Sardinian Army of Revolution. He became its youngest commissioned officer when promoted to a second-lieutenancy for bravery on the field of Novara (Mar. 23, 1849). In 1851 he graduated as full lieutenant from the Royal Military Academy of Cherasco, later becoming a staff officer in the Crimean War.

In 1860, we find him in New York for the first time, where he married (1861) Mary Isabel Reid, daughter of Capt. Samuel C. Reid, U. S. N.; taught languages; and—when the Civil War broke out—founded a military school for oticers, instructing over 700 students. Strongly in sympathy with the Northern cause, he enlisted in October 1861 as a major in the 11th New York Cavalry of which he became lieutenant-colonel. He excelled as a drill-master

and a disciplinarian. In September 1862 he became colonel of the 4th New York Volunteer Cavalry, was wounded and taken prisoner at the battle of Aldie (June 17, 1863), and was confined in Libby Prison until the spring of 1864. He fought under Sheridan throughout the Shenandoah Valley Campaign, and served till the end of the war, when Lincoln brevetted him brigadier-general of volunteers and offered him the consulship at Cyprus on condition that he would become an American citizen. This he did (1865), and on Christmas Day he landed on that island with his family.

Of his eleven years there, he has himself given us an entertaining account, in excellent English, in *Cyprus, Its Ancient Cities, Tombs, and Temples,* published in London (1877) and New York (1878). He soon made himself so respected and feared by the Turkish Government, and so trusted by the natives, that he was enabled to undertake the excavations which constitute his claim to lasting remembrance. Single-handed, save for native diggers, with no capital but his own slim purse, without training or experience, he explored sixty-five necropoli (60,-932 tombs) and at least twenty-three other sites, digging up 35,573 objects. Of these, about 5,000 were lost at sea, a selected series went to the Turkish Government, and a few were sold in Europe before he decided, in the interest of science, to keep his collection a unit. The great mass of the objects was ultimately purchased by the Metropolitan Museum of Art in New York, in three instalments, for a moderate sum, less than a quarter of what experts told Cesnola it should bring if auctioned by the piece. He finally left Cyprus in 1876 because of his wife's health, going first to London, where he brought out his book, and later to New York, where he was elected secretary of the Metropolitan Museum in 1877, and director in 1879. Both these posts he held until his death a quarter of a century later, in the face of constant fire on the authenticity of his collection, his personal honor, and his museum administration. The *Art Amateur* in August 1880 contained an attack on his collection by Gaston L. Feuardent, a well-known art dealer, and at once the press took sides with the most intolerant partisanship. In 1882 Clarence Cook, the critic, wrote for Feuardent a scathing pamphlet. Cesnola had meanwhile printed counter-attacks on Feuardent, who sued him for libel. The trial lasted from Oct. 31, 1883 to Feb. 2, 1884. The jury voted unanimously for Cesnola on the counts affecting the standing of the collection, and he had a majority of ten to two on the count which concerned his business dealings with Feuardent—this being technically a disagreement. His collection had been sustained also by the examinations of an investigating committee and by those of sculptors and stone-cutters, but the public remained skeptical and there was another attack by Dr. Max Ohnefalsch-Richter. (See *New York Herald,* May 16, 1893; *Sun,* May 23, 1893.) Later researches in Cypriote archeology have been the most satisfactory vindication of the authenticity and value of the Cesnola collection. (See John L. Myres, *Handbook of the Cesnola Collection of Antiquities from Cyprus,* 1914, for the best history and bibliography of the collection. Cesnola published *A Descriptive Atlas of the Cesnola Collection,* in three volumes, 1885–1903.) As museum director, Cesnola was accused of being hostile to the public and students, ignorant of modern art, and afraid of experts. The trustees, for the most part, credited him with laying the firm foundation on which the Museum was built by his administrative ability and tireless, devoted supervision. In the memory of his associates on the staff, he left a warm glow of affection and admiration.

Throughout his life, he gave and inspired intense loyalty and bitter enmity. Tall, martial, dark (later, iron-gray), with a ruddy color and a piercing eye, he dearly loved a fight. He retained the Italian excitability and a slight accent. When he traveled in Italy in 1900, the press featured his progress as that of a conquering hero. Among his thirteen medals and knightly orders was one struck in his honor by special order of the King of Italy (1882). Among his American decorations was the Congressional Medal of Honor.

[*Bulls. Metropolitan Mus.,* IV, 95–96, 153–54; V, 229–33, XXI, 88; *N. Y. Times, N. Y. Tribune,* Nov. 22, 1904; Henry Murray Calvert, *Reminiscences of a Boy in Blue* (1920).]   F. B. H.

CHACE, ELIZABETH BUFFUM (Dec. 9, 1806–Dec. 12, 1899), anti-slavery and woman-suffrage advocate, was born in Providence, R. I., the second daughter of Arnold Buffum [*q.v.*] and Rebecca (Gould) Buffum. She passed her childhood in Smithfield, R. I., and in Connecticut, where she attended the common schools, later studying at the Friends' School, Providence. In June 1828, at Fall River, Mass., she married Samuel Buffington Chace, a cotton manufacturer of that city, like herself an orthodox Friend. Under her father's influence she early interested herself in anti-slavery activities, and in Valley Falls, R. I., whither the Chaces removed in 1840, they conducted an Underground Railroad station. Mrs. Chace gave val-

ued counsel to officers of the New England Anti-Slavery Society, and was their agent for arranging meetings in Rhode Island, entertaining in her home Garrison, Phillips, Frederick Douglass, and other lecturers. In 1843 she resigned from the Society of Friends, alleging their indifference to the abolition cause. Thereafter she was unaffiliated with any religious sect; she retained belief in the "Inner Light," but her views became increasingly liberal. For some years she was a spiritualist, reading assiduously the *Banner of Light* and the writings of Andrew Jackson Davis, but in later life spiritualism ceased to influence her. She helped to sponsor the Woman's Rights convention held in 1850 in Worcester. With Mrs. Paulina W. Davis she organized, in 1868, the Rhode Island Woman Suffrage Association, of which she was president from 1870 till her death. For many years she was also an officer of the American Woman Suffrage Association. She worked ardently for suffrage, writing, speaking, and securing petitions for legislative action. Temperance and humanitarian activities also engaged her. In 1870 her efforts secured the passage of a state law providing for a board of women visitors to inspect Rhode Island penal and correctional institutions where women or children were confined; on this board she served for several years. At the International Congress on the Prevention and Repression of Crime, Including Penal Reformatory Treatment, in London (1872), she was a delegate and active participant. She brought about the establishment of the Rhode Island Home and School for Dependent Children (1884), and several years later reform of abuses in its management. Her wide range of interests brought her many friends, including Julia Ward Howe, Moncure D. Conway, John Weiss (Shakespearean scholar), Thomas Davidson, and Andrew Carnegie. She contributed to the *New England Magazine* and extensively to the *Providence Journal.* Her summer home at Wianno, on Cape Cod, became a literary center for reformers. After 1893 feebleness confined her to her home at Central Falls, where she died. The mother of ten children, she was the affectionate center of her home, which, amid all her activities, she never neglected. Three children only survived her; of these Lillie (Mrs. John C. Wyman) became her mother's biographer, and Arnold B. Chace chancellor of Brown University.

[Sources are Mrs. Chace's vivid *Anti-Slavery Reminiscences* (1891) and *Elizabeth Buffum Chace* (2 vols., 1914), by L. B. C. Wyman and A. C. Wyman. A shorter sketch appears in L. B. C. Wyman's *Am. Chivalry* (1913), pp. 35–50.]   R. S. B.

CHADBOURNE, PAUL ANSEL (Oct. 21, 1823–Feb. 23, 1883), college president, eldest child of Isaiah and Pandora (Dennett) Chadbourne, was born in the town of North Berwick, Me. Orphaned at the age of thirteen, he soon acquired habits of industry in working on a farm and in a carpenter's shop in his native village, meanwhile attending school. Removing to Great Falls, N. H., he became a druggist's clerk and medical student, remaining three years. Then, having prepared for college at Phillips Academy, Exeter, supporting himself by copying law papers, he entered Williams College as a sophomore, and graduated in 1848 valedictorian of his class. As an undergraduate he displayed those habits of intense application and thorough inquiry which characterized him in later years. While pursuing his theological studies at the Theological Seminary at East Windsor Hill, Conn., he was a tutor at Williams College and principal of high schools or academies in New Jersey, New Hampshire, and Connecticut. On Oct. 9, 1850, he was married to Elizabeth Sawyer Page of Exeter, N. H. In 1853 he accepted his first professorship, that of botany and chemistry at Williams College, where afterward he filled the chair of natural history. With the exception of an interval of five years, 1867 to 1872, he was closely identified with that institution till his resignation of the presidency in 1881. While discharging the duties of his professorship at Williams College, he held, for six years, subsequent to 1858, the professorship of the same branches at Bowdoin College, at the Maine Medical School, of which he was dean, and also at the Berkshire Medical Institute till its discontinuance. For twelve years he delivered courses of lectures at Mount Holyoke Seminary, and for a time taught the natural sciences at Western Reserve University.

His passion for scientific research awakened a responsive interest among his pupils, and groups of students attended him upon expeditions, the objects of which were exploration and the collection of specimens. The first was to Newfoundland in 1855, the second to Florida in 1857. In 1859 he made geological studies in Greenland, Iceland, Sweden, Norway, and Denmark, being received as a member of the Royal Society of Northern Antiquaries at Copenhagen. His last scientific expedition was to Greenland in 1861. His lectures at the Smithsonian Institution, given in 1859, were published in 1860, as *Lectures on Natural History; its Relations to Intellect, Taste, Wealth and Religion*. His Lowell Institute lectures were published under the title of *Lectures on Natural Theology* (1867)

and *Instinct, its Office in the Animal Kingdom, and its Relation to the Higher Powers in Man* (1872).

Chadbourne was by nature a practical man. His first cotton manufacturing enterprise was in 1865, and in that year and the following one came service in the Massachusetts Senate. He attended national conventions of the Republican party, once as a delegate-at-large, and was a presidential elector. While a senator he was chosen president of the then recently created Agricultural College at Amherst. During his brief incumbency he selected the site, settled the plans and contracted for the erection of three of the buildings. He also systematized the course of study, largely on the basis of President Hitchcock's classic report on the agricultural schools of Europe. He next became president of the University of Wisconsin, and from 1867 to 1870 administered its interests successfully. After leaving Wisconsin he spent nearly two years among the Rocky Mountains in the pursuit of health and the investigation of mines.

Returning to Williamstown in 1872, he followed the revered Mark Hopkins as president of Williams College, and with rare teaching and executive skill fulfilled the duties of that office for nine years, the period of his stewardship forming a significant chapter in the history of the institution. They were years of upbuilding and growth. Upon its material interests he brought to bear his unusual administrative powers. "He was the most versatile and incessantly active of Williams Presidents," but like his immediate predecessor, he was at his best in the classroom. Although he was rather short of stature and slender, his fine head, keen restless eyes, and gray, flowing beard lent impressiveness to his appearance. A strict disciplinarian, he was nevertheless affable and gracious.

In January 1882 he accepted, for the second time, the presidency of the Massachusetts Agricultural College. The institution then needed all the energy, executive ability, ripe experience and educational resources which such a man could supply. He imparted to the college an impetus which became a vigorous internal life. Even more valuable were his services in securing to it the interest and confidence of the people. In 1874 he succeeded Louis Agassiz as a member of the Massachusetts State Board of Agriculture, a position to which he had first been appointed by Gov. Andrew in 1865. He died in New York, Feb. 23, 1883, at the age of fifty-nine.

Chadbourne published some nine volumes, including *The Public Service of the State of New York* (3 vols., 1882), twelve educational addresses, and twenty-two agricultural addresses. He also contributed a series of articles to the *Congregationalist* and the *Springfield Republican,* and elsewhere articles on his scientific expeditions and was a contributor to Johnson's and other cyclopedias. His pen was seldom idle.

[S. H. Carpenter, *Hist. Sketch of the Univ. of Wis.* (1876), p. 53 ; A. B. Bassett, "Obituary Sketch of Paul A. Chadbourne," *Alumni Record, Mass. Ag. Coll.,* 1883, pp. 15–20 ; *Obit. Record of Alumni of Williams Coll., 1875–85,* pp. 312–20 ; *Mass. Ag. Coll. Gen. Cat.,* 1862–86, pp. 99–101 ; A. L. Perry, *Williamstown and Williams Coll.* (1899), *passim* ; J. M. Barker, "Memoir of Paul A. Chadbourne," *Proc. Mass. Hist. Soc.,* 2 ser., XXIII, 448–53 ; L. W. Spring, *Hist. of Williams Coll.* (1917), pp. 227–41 ; W. M. Emery, *Chadbourne-Chadbourn Genealogy* (Fall River, Mass., 1904) ; J. F. A. Pyre, *Wisconsin* (1920) ; E. H. Botsford, *Fifty Years at Williams: Bk. I, The Story of P. A. Chadbourne* (privately printed, 1928).]   F. T.

CHADWICK, FRENCH ENSOR (Feb. 29, 1844–Jan. 27, 1919), naval officer, was born in Morgantown, W. Va. (then Virginia) of good pioneer stock. He was the son of Daniel Clark and Margaret Eliza (Evans) Chadwick. His maternal grandfather was Col. John Evans, a Revolutionary soldier. He received his early schooling at the Monongalia Academy, in his native town. As a boy he read the naval classic, *History of the Navy of the United States of America* (1839) by J. Fenimore Cooper, and was fascinated by it. Entering the Naval Academy (at Newport, R. I., during the Civil War) on Sept. 28, 1861, he was graduated three years later, the fifth in a class of thirty-one members. In the summer of 1864, before his graduation, he served on the sloop of war *Marblehead,* during her pursuit of the Confederate steamers *Florida* and *Tallahassee.* Passing rapidly through the grades of ensign, master, and lieutenant, he was in 1869 promoted lieutenant commander. After serving as a junior officer on board the ships *Juniata, Sabine,* and *Tuscarora* he was in 1870–72 attached to the steamer *Guerrière,* of the European squadron. Three years of teaching at the Naval Academy as assistant professor of mathematics were followed by a tour of sea duty, 1875–78, as the executive officer of the steamer *Powhatan.*

During the two decades that preceded the Spanish-American War, Chadwick developed a great facility in investigating foreign navies and in procuring information useful in the work of constructing the new American navy. In 1879 he made an investigation in Europe, the results of which he embodied in a report on foreign systems for training seamen for the navy (*Senate Executive Document, No. 52,* 46 Cong., 2 Sess.), still a standard work on the subject. The next two years, 1880–82, were spent in "special

light-house duties," including the preparation of a valuable paper entitled "Aids to Navigation," which gave a brief history of lighthouses. In 1882 he was sent to London, where he remained almost continuously until 1889 with the American legation as naval attaché (the first American thus designated) and as the representative of the newly-organized Office of Naval Intelligence. By reason of his expert knowledge, tact, and adroitness he served his superiors so well that they were loth to displace him. Secretary of the Navy Tracy in his annual report for 1889 singled out Chadwick for especial commendation and said that his extraordinary ability and judgment had had a lasting influence upon naval development in the United States. Having been promoted commander in 1884, Chadwick, on being detached from the legation, was placed in command of the cruiser *Yorktown,* of the European station. In 1892 his services as naval attaché received recognition by his appointment as chief of the Naval Intelligence Office and a year later he was advanced to the headship of the Bureau of Equipment where he remained for the full term of four years.

A few days after his promotion to a captaincy, Nov. 7, 1897, he was made commander of the armored cruiser *New York,* the flagship of the North Atlantic squadron. When the battleship *Maine* was sunk in Havana harbor, Feb. 15, 1898, he was off the Florida coast with the squadron. His nearness to the scene of the disaster led to his selection as a member of the court of inquiry on the destruction of the *Maine,* of which Capt. W. T. Sampson [*q.v.*] was the senior member. When late in March Sampson became commander-in-chief of the squadron, Chadwick was appointed his chief of staff, retaining the command of the flagship. In this capacity he served during the eventful summer of 1898 and during the culminating action of the Spanish-American War, the battle of Santiago, July 3. When the Spanish vessels began to emerge from the harbor, the *New York* was several miles away, carrying the commander-in-chief to a conference with Gen. W. R. Shafter [*q.v.*]. She turned about and reached the scene of battle in time to join in the chase and to enable Sampson to give the final orders to his ships (*House Document, No. 3,* 55 Cong., 3 Sess., App., pp. 520–22). In recognition of his services on this day Chadwick was advanced five numbers for "eminent and conspicuous conduct in battle." Chadwick reached the climax of his naval career as president of the Naval War College, 1900–03, and as commander-in-chief of the South Atlantic squadron in 1905. On Feb. 28,

1906, he was retired as rear admiral, a rank to which he had been promoted on Oct. 11, 1903.

Admiral Chadwick belonged to a small group of learned or scientific naval officers, of which Mahan and Sampson were conspicuous members. As an author he attained considerable note, based upon the numerous articles and books which he wrote between 1892 when his first work, *Temperament, Disease and Health,* made its appearance, and 1916 when his last, *The Graves Papers and Other Documents Relating to the Naval Operations of the Yorktown Campaign,* was issued. His scholarly interest lay chiefly in the field of military and diplomatic history, in which he read widely. His most significant contributions are found in four volumes: *Causes of the Civil War* (American Nation Series, vol. XIX, 1906), *Relations of the United States and Spain: Diplomacy* (1909), and *Relations of the United States and Spain: the Spanish-American War* (2 vols., 1911). Believing that the past may serve as a guide for the present, he was inclined to draw definite conclusions, to criticize sharply historical characters, and to dwell upon the lessons of sea power. His style was clear, dignified, and vigorous.

On Chadwick's retirement to Newport in 1906 he actively interested himself in all that pertained to that city and its development, serving on its park commission and also on its representative council. He was largely instrumental in providing the city with a new charter. His wife Cornelia J. (Miller) Chadwick, formerly of Utica, N. Y., whom he married on Nov. 20, 1878, shared the intellectual interests of her husband. The admiral died in New York City, leaving no children, and was buried in Morgantown. He was somewhat above the average in height and weight, with a commanding presence. Direct and forceful in speech, he was a close observer of even the smallest details.

[Record of Officers, Bureau of Navigation, 1862–1919; *Navy Reg.,* 1862–1919; obituary in *N. Y. Times,* Jan. 28, 1919; *Report of Secretary of the Navy,* 1889–99; *Who's Who in America,* 1918–19; letters of Thos. Ray Dille, Morgantown, W. Va., to C.O.P., Nov., Dec. 1928.]   C.O.P.

CHADWICK, HENRY (Oct. 5, 1824–Apr. 20, 1908), sportsman, the son of James Chadwick, editor of the *Western Times,* published in Exeter, England, was born in Exeter but came to America when he was thirteen. The rest of his life was spent in and about Brooklyn and New York. After a good education he began contributing in 1844 to the *Long Island Star.* In 1848 he married the daughter of Alexander Botts of Richmond, Va. Turning his attention to sports, he became the first important sports writer in

America. The beginnings of his career fell at the period when, owing to the rise of cities, the vogue of field games in America, as distinct from rural pastimes, was beginning. Chadwick made it his work to promote this new outdoor life in the interest of health and good fellowship. Beginning in 1856, he reported and wrote on cricket and baseball for the *New York Times,* the *Brooklyn Eagle,* and other great dailies. For thirty-one years he was on the staff of the *New York Clipper,* a famous sporting sheet of that day. In 1886 he gave up reporting but continued to contribute to periodicals. During the Civil War he was a correspondent for the *New York Tribune.*

Heir to the best English sporting traditions, Chadwick always remained an ardent admirer and close student of cricket, but his greatest contribution to American life was in fostering interest in baseball. In the eighteen-fifties his attention was attracted to this sport, and, after playing as an amateur, he became convinced of its great possibilities and worked earnestly to develop it into a worthy national game. He had much influence in organizing professional baseball and in keeping it distinct from the amateur game. As chairman and member of the rules committee of the first National Association he dominated the development of the playing rules. The system of scoring is also practically his work. In the battle to prevent the national game from being ruined by rowdyism and gambling he did heroic service. Author of numerous athletic hand-books, he prepared, beginning in 1869, an annual baseball hand-book which developed into Spalding's *Official Baseball Guide,* a storehouse of records, edited by Chadwick from 1881 to 1908. In his later life he was widely known as "the Father of Baseball." Tall and powerful in physique and of a certain commanding presence, he was a striking exponent of the beliefs for which he stood. To a surprising degree he retained his vigor and interest to the end of his long life. Copies of Chadwick's pamphlets on various sports as well as the *Baseball Guides* are preserved in the Spalding Baseball Collection in the New York Public Library. Chadwick left his great collection of materials on the history of baseball and other sports to his friend A. G. Spalding. It constitutes the nucleus of the Spalding Collection and upon it was based in part Spalding's valuable book, *America's National Game* (1911). In the Spalding Collection are Chadwick's unpublished diaries from 1873 to 1907, relating largely to the history of sport, as well as a score of books recording baseball games from 1860 to 1907.

[*Brooklyn Eagle,* Apr. 20, 1908; *N. Y. Tribune,* Apr. 21, 1908; A. G. Spalding, *America's National Game* (1911), pp. 339–44; G. C. Richter, *Hist. and Records of Baseball* (1914), p. 278.]   E.P.T.

CHADWICK, JAMES READ (Nov. 2, 1844–Sept. 23, 1905), physician, librarian, was born in Boston, Mass., the son of Christopher Chadwick, a merchant of English extraction, who married a daughter of James Read (1789–1870). Graduated from Harvard College in 1865, and from the Harvard Medical School in 1871, in the latter year Chadwick married Katherine, daughter of Dr. George H. Lyman. After a few years of study in Berlin, Vienna, Paris, and London, he returned to Boston and began the practise of a then newly-developed department of medicine, gynecology. He assisted in the foundation of the gynecological department of the Boston City Hospital (1874) and for many years taught this specialty to the students of the Harvard Medical School. In 1876, with his father-in-law, he played an important part in the organization of the American Gynecological Society and served as its secretary for seven years; in 1897 he was president. He was largely instrumental in the publication of the early volumes of the annual *Transactions*.

Although Chadwick was greatly interested in the practise of medicine, he was at heart a book-lover. He established, with the help of a few friends, the Boston Medical Library in 1875, and served as the librarian from its inception up to the time of his death. In the early days he arranged the books in the library and did all the cataloguing. Aided by an exceptional memory, he succeeded in obtaining volumes missing from many important sets of medical journals. His "want book" was always with him in his travels in this country and abroad, and it made him a familiar figure in bookshops and libraries throughout the world. He also began an excellent collection of pamphlets, autographs, paintings, and photographs. His generosity in exchanging books and journals was one of his striking characteristics and served to make his name well-known and popular in all important medical libraries.

Chadwick was active in other fields as well. He founded the Harvard Medical Alumni Association in 1890 and for three years served as its president. Always interested in the subject of cremation, in 1892 he reorganized the decadent New England Cremation Society, assisted in the building of a model crematory and chapel near Boston, and in later years was president of the Massachusetts Cremation Society. His bibliography contains over sixty titles, dealing largely with gynecology, medical libraries, and cremation. Among his publications are a translation of Winckel's *Puerperal Fever*; a translation of two early works of J. D. Schoepff (1874–75); a study

of Schoepff's life (1905); his papers on the Boston Medical Library (1876, 1896, 1899) and the *Life of James Read* (1905).

Chadwick was artistic, even Bohemian, in temperament, generous, kind, and sympathetic, but when necessity demanded, he could be sufficiently combative to obtain a point that seemed of importance to him. He had a strong sense of the joy of living, and an equally strong sense of the joy of labor. He is perhaps best described by Oliver Wendell Holmes, as the "untiring, imperturbable, tenacious, impressible, all-subduing agitator, who neither rested nor let others rest until the success of the library project was assured." He was a good public speaker and debater and made numerous addresses throughout the country on medical libraries and on cremation.

[Obituary, with portrait and bibliography, by W. L. Burrage, in *Trans. Am. Gyn. Soc.*, XXXI, 437–45; a series of articles in the *Medic. Lib. and Hist. Jour.*, IV, 113–25; the collection of "memorials" in the Boston Medic. Lib.; John W. Farlow, *Hist. of the Boston Medic. Lib.* (Norwood, Mass., 1918).]
H.R.V.

CHADWICK, JOHN WHITE (Oct. 19, 1840–Dec. 11, 1904), Unitarian clergyman, author, came of fisher-folk, who had been settled for several generations in Marblehead, Mass., where he was born. He was the son of John White Chadwick, mentioned as a seaman or sea-captain, and Jane (Standley) Chadwick. Early apprenticed to a shoemaker, he felt a desire for more learning, entered the State Normal School at Bridgewater in 1857, and while there determined to become a minister. After studying at Phillips Exeter Academy, he entered Harvard Divinity School, from which he graduated in 1864. Immediately thereafter came an invitation to supply for three months the pulpit of the Second Unitarian Church of Brooklyn, N. Y. Chadwick accepted and made so favorable an impression that he was called to the permanent pastorate, which he held for the rest of his life. In 1865 he married Annie Horton Hathaway of Marblehead. Chadwick had a frank, open, weather-beaten countenance, and a breezy manner. Alert and eager, he had the courage of his convictions, and spoke from his pulpit against oppression, privilege, and corrupt government. But he had also a real tenderness and sympathy under his rugged exterior, and a poetic vein, in which a certain touch of mysticism was not wanting. His sermons attracted attention, and he soon became well-known as a preacher and lecturer. He called himself a Radical Unitarian, meaning thereby that he rejected the miraculous and the superhuman character of Jesus and the Bible. He welcomed the doctrine of evolution while it was still generally under suspicion in religious circles. A great lover of literature, especially of biography, with a ready pen, he became a reviewer for the *Nation* from its first volume till the last year of his life, though he wrote also for other journals. His first book to attract attention was *A Book of Poems* (1876), which ran into ten editions. It was a little book, reminiscent of earlier poets, but showed real poetic feeling. Other volumes followed in rapid succession, consisting of discussions of leading topics of religion, biographies of leaders of thought, and more poems. Of these works the most noteworthy were: *The Bible of To-Day* (1878); *The Faith of Reason* (1879); *Some Aspects of Religion* (1879); *Belief and Life* (1881); *The Man Jesus* (1883); *Origin and Destiny* (1883); *In Nazareth Town and Other Poems* (1883); *A Daring Faith* (1885); *Charles R. Darwin* (1889); *Evolution and Social Reform* (1890); *Evolution as Related to Citizenship* (1892); *The Old and New Unitarian Belief* (1894); *Theodore Parker* (1900); *Wm. E. Channing* (1903); *Later Poems* (1905).

[*Christian Reg.*, Dec. 22, 1904; *Congregationalist*, Dec. 17, 1904; *Brooklyn Eagle*, Dec. 12, 1904; *Nation*, Dec. 15, 1904; *Outlook*, Dec. 17, 1904; *Who's Who in America*, 1903–05.]   T.D.B.

CHAFFEE, ADNA ROMANZA (Apr. 14, 1842–Nov. 1, 1914), soldier, was born at Orwell, Ashtabula County, Ohio. His father, Truman Bibbins Chaffee, was descended from Thomas, who was settled at Hingham, Mass., by 1683; his mother, Grace (Hyde) Chaffee, was of Connecticut ancestry. In the summer of 1861 young Chaffee set out from home to enlist in a volunteer regiment, but encountering a recruiting party of the newly organized 6th Cavalry, of the regular army, he enlisted, July 22, 1861, in that regiment, and remained a member of it for twenty-seven years. He was with his regiment only a few weeks before being appointed a sergeant, and after serving through the Peninsular and Antietam campaigns, he was made first sergeant of his troop, Sept. 26, 1862. In the operations of the following winter and spring, reports on his conduct resulted in a note scribbled by Secretary Stanton on an envelope, still preserved in the War Department, directing his appointment as second lieutenant. This, his first commission, was dated May 12, 1863. For the remainder of the war the regiment was with the Army of the Potomac (except while serving under Sheridan in the Shenandoah Valley in the fall of 1864). In 1863 Chaffee was twice wounded, once at Fairfield, Pa., in the Gettysburg campaign, and once at Brandy Station, Va. On the first occasion he fell into the hands of the enemy, but refused to accept parole, and as his captors found themselves unable to

carry him away he did not remain a prisoner. He was promoted to first lieutenant, Feb. 22, 1865. After the war he considered giving up his military career, and finally sent in his resignation, intending to engage in business. The colonel of the regiment, absent at the time, upon his return induced Chaffee to change his mind, and telegraphed to the War Department that "he is too valuable an officer to lose and his place cannot well be filled." The resignation had taken effect on Mar. 13, 1867, but on Mar. 20 Chaffee's restoration was approved. He was promoted to captain, Oct. 12, 1867. For some twenty-five years he served with his regiment in the Southwest, except for a few periods of absence on recruiting duty or while acting as Indian agent, and was engaged summer and winter in innumerable skirmishes with Comanches, Cheyennes, Kiowas, and Apaches. One night march across the Staked Plains, in December 1874, was made in a temperature of twenty-five degrees below zero. With his promotion to major, July 7, 1888, Chaffee left his old regiment for the 9th Cavalry. He was serving as an instructor in the service school at Fort Leavenworth, when promoted to lieutenant-colonel of the 3rd Cavalry, June 1, 1897. At the outbreak of the war with Spain he was appointed brigadier-general of volunteers, May 4, 1898, and assigned to the 5th Corps, then at Tampa. He landed in Cuba, June 22, commanding the 3rd Brigade in the 2nd (Lawton's) Division. In his plan for the battle of Santiago, Gen. Shafter charged Lawton with the task of taking the fortified post of El Caney, on the right of the American line. The garrison consisted of only about 520 men, assisted by a few inhabitants of the village, but it was well entrenched, and under the command of Gen. Vara de Rey held out (July 1) for ten hours. The place was finally taken only when half its defenders, including the heroic Vara de Rey himself, were killed or wounded. The brunt of the fighting fell on Chaffee's brigade. His services were recognized by his appointment on July 8 as major-general of volunteers. After the fall of Santiago, he returned to the United States, but was sent back to Cuba in December as chief of staff of the military governor and remained there until May 1900. Meanwhile, the reduction of the volunteer army deprived him of his major-generalcy, but he was at once reappointed brigadier-general of volunteers, Apr. 13, 1899. He became a colonel in the regular army, May 8, 1899. Upon the Boxer outbreak in China, Chaffee was selected to command the American contingent of the relief expedition, and was again appointed major-general of volunteers. He commanded the American troops in the advance on Peking, the capture of the city, and the occupation of the surrounding territory. His able leadership during the fighting, and his just and considerate treatment of the inhabitants afterward, won him the admiration of the members of the invading forces and of the Chinese as well. He was made major-general in the regular army, Feb. 4, 1901. After leaving China he commanded in the Philippines until October 1902. In January 1904, he was appointed lieutenant-general, and detailed as chief of staff of the army. He retired from active service, Feb. 1, 1906, and made his home in Los Angeles, where for several years he was president of the board of public works. He died on Nov. 1, 1914, and was buried at Arlington. In appearance and in character he was a grim and determined man, but always just and humane. He possessed military abilities beyond anything demanded by the operations in which he commanded. Wholly devoid of selfish ambition, his rise was due to outstanding merit alone.

[*The Life of Lieut.-Gen. Chaffee* (1917), by his friend, Gen. W. H. Carter, is based on personal knowledge and on Chaffee's own papers. H. H. Sargent's *Campaign of Santiago de Cuba* (1914) and A. S. Daggett's *America in the China Relief Expedition* (1903) give detailed accounts of these campaigns. "The Regulars at El Caney," by A. H. Lee, British military observer, in *Scribner's Mag.*, Oct. 1898, has a very vivid description of Chaffee in action.]   T.M.S.

CHAFFEE, JEROME BONAPARTE (Apr. 17, 1825–Mar. 9, 1886), political leader, mining man and banker, second child of Warren and Elizabeth (Otto) Chaffee, was born on a farm near Lockport, Niagara County, N. Y. He received a common school education in Lockport and later in Adrian, Mich., to which place the family moved in his early youth. His subsequent career was varied, for he clerked in stores, taught school, and kept books in a bank. He married Miriam Comstock in Adrian in 1848 and had four children, all of whom died while young, save Fannie Josephine, later Mrs. U. S. Grant, Jr. In his early thirties Chaffee went to St. Joseph, becoming a banker and manager of a real-estate company. After the death of his wife, he migrated to the Pike's Peak gold region in 1860. The firm of Smith & Chaffee operated a stamp-mill in Gilpin County with profit, but the partners made more money through their investments in mines, especially in the rich Bobtail mine. After amassing a fortune in the mountains, Chaffee left them in 1865 to live in Denver. In that year he with others bought the banking house of G. T. Clark & Company and founded the First National Bank of Denver, of which he was president until 1880. While retiring from the mountains, he never gave up his interest in mining. His investments in Colorado mines were widespread, large, and usu-

ally fortunate. For a time he shared in the rich proceeds of the Little Pittsburgh in the Leadville district.

Though a successful business man, Chaffee was best known as a political leader. He was elected to the lower house of the territorial legislature in 1861 and 1863 and became its speaker in 1864. Recognized as a leader of the Republican party, he was chosen as United States senator in 1865, at a time when Colorado hoped to become a state. With John Evans, his colleague, he went to Washington and labored in vain to convert this hope into a reality. As territorial delegate from 1871 to 1875 he spent both time and money freely upon what had now become his main object in life, the admission of Colorado to statehood. Finally on Mar. 3, 1875, when President Grant signed the enabling act, his dreams came true. At the time he was given the chief credit for this accomplishment; in most ways it was the greatest moment of his life. The grateful caucus of the Republican members of the Colorado legislature nominated him by acclamation as its first choice for United States senator and he served in that capacity for the short term from 1877 to 1879. He declined to run again because of ill health. While territorial delegate and senator he was able to secure the passage of several acts benefiting his district, especially a new mining law. After years of directing the Republican party organization in Colorado, he was selected in 1884 as chairman of the national executive committee of the same party. This was his final political honor.

Chaffee was always a man of few words. He was an able organizer, open-handed in generosity to friends and party, blunt in speech, and a bitter foe to his enemies. His massive head, broad shoulders, and height made him a noticeable figure. Despite his splendid physique, his health broke in the late seventies, and he spent much of his time at his daughter Fannie's home in Westchester County, N. Y. On his last trip to Leadville in 1886, he caught a severe cold, returned to his daughter's home, and died there. His body lies beside that of his wife in Adrian.

[Sketch in the *Encyc. of Biog. of Colo.* (1901); *Denver Tribune*, Sept. 13, 1883; *Denver Tribune-Republican*, Mar. 10, 1886; Frank Hall, *Hist. of the State of Colo.* (1891); *Chaffee Geneal.* (1909), comp. by Wm. H. Chaffee.]   J.F.W.

CHAFIN, EUGENE WILDER (Nov. 1, 1852–Nov. 30, 1920), temperance leader, Prohibition candidate for president, was born at East Troy, Wis., the son of Samuel Evans and Betsey A. (Pollard) Chafin. He attended the public schools, studied law at the University of Wisconsin, from which he was graduated in 1875, and began to practise his profession in Waukesha. He took an active interest in local affairs and served as justice of the peace, police magistrate, member of the Waukesha board of education, member of the public library board, and three times as president of the Waukesha County Agricultural Society. On Nov. 24, 1881, he married Carrie A. Hunkins of Waukesha. Early in life he became interested in temperance work and joined the Good Templars at the age of fourteen. His work within the organization was soon recognized and he was elected District Chief Templar of Waukesha County. In 1885 he became Grand Counselor and in the following year Grand Chief Templar of Wisconsin. From 1893 to 1901 he was Grand Electoral Superintendent and represented his state in the International Supreme Lodge of Good Templars. He was also interested in the Epworth League, of which he was twice elected state president. In politics he was originally a Republican but in 1881 he joined the Prohibition party and ran for district attorney of Waukesha County (1881), for Congress (1882), for attorney-general (1886 and 1900), and for governor (1898). In October 1901 he moved to Chicago, where he became superintendent of the Washingtonian Home for Inebriates. His interest in politics continued unabated, and he was a candidate for Congress (1902) and for attorney-general of Illinois (1904). His law practise he gradually relinquished, and from 1904 on spent most of his time on the lecture platform, campaigning for prohibition. Within his party he had been a delegate to the Prohibition national conventions since 1884, was chairman of the Committee on the Platform in 1900, and was a member of the Prohibition National Committee from 1888 to 1896. In the Prohibition National Convention of July 1908 it seemed that William B. Palmore of Missouri had the nomination for the presidency almost within his grasp, but Chafin was put forward as a dark horse and received the nomination. He campaigned vigorously, but the result was a foregone conclusion, no Prohibition candidate having any chance of success. Four years later he was again nominated for the presidency, without opposition, but as in 1908, the Prohibition candidate received little attention, the election being for the most part a three-cornered struggle between Taft, Roosevelt, and Wilson. Nevertheless the efforts of Chafin and his colleagues did much to prepare public sentiment in the United States for Prohibition. With the adoption of the Eighteenth Amendment to the Constitution, Chafin turned his attention to world temperance and in the spring of 1919 went to Australia and New Zealand on a lecture tour in support of the Australian temperance organizations. He died in 1920 at his home in Long Beach, Cal. His writings include *The Voters' Hand-Book* (1876); *Lives of the Presidents* (1896); *Lincoln: the Man of Sorrow* (1908); and *The Master Method of the Great Reform* (1913), to which was attached a biographical sketch of the author.

[*Who's Who in America*, 1912–13; Samuel Dickie, "The Prohibitionists and Their Cause," in the *Rev. of Revs.* (N. Y.), Sept. 1908; *Los Angeles Times, Chicago Daily Tribune, Milwaukee Sentinel*, Dec. 1, 1920.]

F. E. R.

CHAILLÉ-LONG, CHARLES (July 2, 1842– Mar. 24, 1917), African explorer, was born at Princess Anne, Somerset County, Md. His ancestor, Pierre Chaillé, a French Huguenot, had settled on the Eastern Shore after the revocation of the Edict of Nantes. Pierre's grand-daughter Margaret Chaillé married Levin Long and became the mother of Littleton Long (of Chaillé). Charles Chaillé-Long was the son of the latter and of Anne Mitchell (Costen) Long. While he was a student at Washington Academy, the Civil War broke out and he left his studies and enlisted in the 1st Eastern Shore Regiment, Maryland Infantry. He was soon transferred and promoted to a captaincy in the 11th Maryland Infantry in which he served throughout the war with distinction. His war experiences and his pioneering spirit then led him to seek an appointment as an officer in the Egyptian army. He was appointed in 1869 and five years later, Feb. 19, 1874, he became chief of staff to "Chinese" Gordon who was engaged in suppressing the slave traffic in the region of the White Nile. Chaillé-Long was now charged by Khedive Ismail with a secret mission: to make a treaty with M'tesa, King of Uganda. On this journey, a vivid account of which is given in his *Naked Truths of Naked People* (1876), he conducted explorations in the upper Nile basin. Their importance in adding to the world's store of geographical knowledge was set forth in Gordon's letter published in the *New York Herald*, Jan. 23, 1880, which said, "Col. Chaillé-Long of the Egyptian staff passed down the Victoria Nile from Nyamyongo where Speke was stopped to Mooli; thus at the risk of his life settling the question, before unsolved, of the identity of the river above Urondogani with that below Mooli." On Feb. 15, 1910, the American Geographical Society conferred upon Chaillé-Long the Charles P. Daly Gold Medal which is given only to those who have made a marked contribution to geography. In 1875 he made another trip from Gondokoro which led him westsouthwest along the Congo-Nile divide region carrying him across the upper tributaries of the

Bahr-el-Ghazel system and linking his route with that of the explorer Schweinfurtter of 1870. Shortly after this last trip his health became impaired and he decided to leave Egypt. Returning to New York, he studied law at Columbia University and graduated in 1880. Two years later he went back to Alexandria to begin the practise of international law. Soon after his arrival, the Alexandria revolt of June 11 occurred. This outbreak, followed by the British bombardment of the city, caused considerable anti-foreign feeling and hundreds of lives were in jeopardy. In the absence of United States consular officials, Chaillé-Long endeavored to reëstablish the consulate and with the aid of American sailors in the harbor was able to offer protection to the refugees. For this service he was later decorated. After being relieved of his post as acting consul-general in August 1882, Chaillé-Long went to Paris where he engaged in the practise of international law. After five years he reëntered the consular service, this time as consul-general and secretary of the legation to Korea. During his two years' stay in that country he took part in a scientific expedition to Quelpart Island.

Familiar with French from his childhood, Chaillé-Long wrote a number of books in that language, including *L'Afrique Centrale* (1877); *Les Sources du Nile* (1891); *L'Égypte et ses Provinces Perdues* (1892); *La Corée ou Chosen* (1894). He also translated and edited *Les Combattants Français de la Guerre Américaine 1778–83*. Among his writings in English were *The Three Prophets; Chinese Gordon, Mohammed-Ahmed (El Maahdi), Arabi Pasha* (1884), and *My Life in Four Continents* (1912). Besides his books he made many contributions to French and American magazines and reviews, principally upon Egyptian and African subjects.

[Chaillé-Long's *Naked Truths of Naked People* (1876) and *My Life in Four Continents* (1912); articles in *Bull. Am. Geog. Soc.*, XLI, 223, XLII, 205–06; obituaries in the *N. Y. Times*, Mar. 26, 1917, and in the *Geog. Rev.*, Apr. 1917.]   G.H.B.

CHALKLEY, THOMAS (May 3, 1675–Nov. 4, 1741), Quaker minister, merchant, and mariner, son of George and Rebecca Chalkley, was born in Southwark, England. When about nine years of age he was sent for a time to a private day school, and was later apprenticed for seven years to his father, "a dealer in meal." In 1699 he decided to marry and was "inclin'd to make Choice of Martha Betterton," who like himself was an English Friends' minister. (She died in 1717, and two years later he married Martha Brown, a widow, who survived him.) Chalkley first came to America in 1698, on a preaching journey, and in 1700 brought his family over to

Maryland. The next year he removed to Philadelphia, and in 1723 to a plantation he had purchased in the near-by suburb of Frankford, later a part of the city. He was a busy, successful trader, on land and by sea, dealing principally in foodstuffs. The sea voyages apparently brought the best returns, for in times of financial stress he took to the sea to recoup his fortunes. Soon after removing to America he began, in 1701, to make trading voyages to Bermuda and Barbados. In 1716 he wrote: "My family increasing, I traded a little to sea for their support." Occasionally he made the three-cornered voyage to Barbados, thence to England, and back to Philadelphia. He accumulated a moderate fortune sufficient to enable him in 1724–25 to weather losses considerably over $10,000. During his busiest seafaring years, 1729–35, his usual voyage was from Philadelphia to Barbados and return, although he sometimes called at St. Christopher, Antigua, Anguilla, and other islands of the Windward and Leeward groups. He made, in all, at least fifteen voyages to Barbados.

His greatest enthusiasm, however, was for journeys "in the ministry." He had begun visiting meetings "under a religious concern" as early as 1695 in connection with a business trip for his father into Essex, and soon afterward had gone on a preaching tour through southwestern England into Cornwall, and a little later northward as far as Edinburgh, "where our Meeting was in the Street, we being lock'd out of our Meetinghouse by the then Power." In America his religious travels took him again and again up and down the country from New England to the Carolinas. In 1703 he "went thro' *Maryland*, and visited Friends in *Virginia* and *North Carolina*, to the river Pamphlico, where no travelling, publick [*i.e.* preaching] Friends (that ever I heard of) were before, and we had several Meetings there on each Side of the River." The next year he was in New England again, disputing with Congregational "priests" and encouraging the Quaker brethren. His religious journeys in the middle colonies near his home were too numerous to mention in particular. There are few chapters of his *Journal* that do not record preaching trips among Friends in Pennsylvania, Maryland, New Jersey, and New York. He left a valuable account of a visit made in 1706 by himself and a group of fellow Quakers to the Susquehanna Indians at Conestoga, Pa. He preached earnestly to these Indians and to the neighboring Shawnee. The Conestogas were of Iroquoian stock, and Chalkley was impressed with the fact that women spoke in their councils. He asked the interpreter the reason for the custom and the reply was:

"That some Women are wiser than some Men" (*Journal*, p. 49). He returned to England on several occasions, once remaining away from his American home for a period of three years, 1707–10. During this time he held religious meetings in Ireland, Scotland, Wales, England, and on the continent of Europe. In his continental journey, lasting for about nine weeks, in 1709, he traveled through Holland and northwestern Germany, visiting Rotterdam, Amsterdam, Hamburg, and Emden, and holding forty-five religious meetings. Next he spent a full year in England and Wales traveling, as he estimated, about 2,500 miles and attending nearly three hundred public meetings. In later life he suffered much hardship and some persecution in the course of his religious work—on one occasion (1734 or 1735) being shot and painfully wounded in Barbados for urging the islanders to treat their slaves more humanely (*Journal*, p. 273). As master of a ship he sought to engage sailors of good character, and to influence them with prayers and preaching aboard. More than once he narrowly escaped capture by privateers, or death by shipwreck. At one time, when provisions ran low and starvation seemed imminent, he offered his own body as food for the crew, but shortly afterward the capture of a dolphin ended the danger. He always ascribed his escapes to divine interposition. Even in his last years he continued his religious pilgrimages. He was in New England in 1737, rejoicing at the growth of Friends, especially on Nantucket Island. The following year he made his last journey into Virginia and North Carolina, and returned "more broken in the long and hard Travelling in this Journey, than in divers Years before" (*Journal*, p. 310). Only one more voyage awaited him. He made a religious visit in 1741 to Tortola, one of the Virgin Islands. There, after preaching zealously, he died of a fever.

Chalkley's *Journal* contains some information on the trade of the time, but deals largely with his religious activities. It displays an elevation of thought and a simple beauty of style that make it, in places, comparable to John Woolman's *Journal*. It became staple reading in Quaker families, which accounts for the reference in Whittier's *Snowbound* to "Chalkley's Journal old and quaint,—Gentlest of skippers, rare sea-saint."

[The basic source for the life of Chalkley is his *Journal*, in three parts. The original MS. of Parts I and II, covering his life to 1724, is preserved in the library of the Hist. Soc. of Pa. The *Journal* has been printed with other writings of Chalkley, under the title, *A Collection of the Works of Thos. Chalkley*. Citations above are to the first edition, printed at Phila. 1749, by Benj. Franklin and David Hall. For the various editions of the *Journal*, the *Works*, and separate epistles and exhortations, see Jos. Smith, *Descriptive Cat. of Friends' Books* (2 vols., 1867) and *Supplement* to same (1893). There are biographical sketches in the following: *Dict. of Nat. Biog.*, vol. IX (1887); *Friends Ancient and Modern* (London, 1903); *Quaker Biogs.* (First Series), vol. III (Phila., 1909); Jas. Bowden, *Hist. of the Soc. of Friends in America, 1750–54*, II (1854) 264. See also R. M. Jones, *Quakers in the Am. Colonies* (1911), *passim*. There is also valuable material on Chalkley's last days, including reprints and bibliographical notes, in Chas. F. Jenkins, *Tortola* (London, 1923).]

R. W. K.

CHALMERS, JAMES RONALD (Jan. 11, 1831–Apr. 9, 1898), lawyer, Confederate soldier, congressman, was the son of Joseph Williams and Fannie (Henderson) Chalmers. His grandfather, a Scotch planter, was a near relative of the celebrated minister, Dr. Thomas Chalmers; his father, born in Halifax County, Va., and educated at the University of Virginia, practised law in his native state, in Jackson, Tenn., and in Holly Springs, Miss. The younger Chalmers was also born in Halifax County, Va., and graduated in 1851, from South Carolina College, Columbia, S. C. After engaging in the practise of his profession for a few years at Holly Springs, he entered politics and was elected district attorney (1858). In 1861 he was chosen a delegate to the Mississippi secession convention and became chairman of the committee on military affairs. When hostilities began he entered the military service of the Confederacy, and rapidly rose from the rank of captain (March 1861) to that of colonel (April 1861), and then to that of brigadier-general (February 1862), taking part in the engagements at Santa Rosa Island, Pensacola, and in the battle of Shiloh. He was then transferred (1863) to the cavalry service, and participated in the attack on Munfordville and in the battle of Murfreesboro, gaining some distinction in the latter engagement. In April 1863 he was given command of a cavalry force in Mississippi, where he served during the remainder of the war. When he surrendered, in May 1865, he was commander of the first division of Forrest's Cavalry Army Corps. After the war he made his home at Friar's Point, Miss., and resumed the practise of law. He was married to Rebecca Arthur, by whom he had one daughter. In the upheaval by which the Democratic party regained control of the government of Mississippi in 1876, he became a member of the state Senate, and his younger brother, Judge H. H. Chalmers, was raised to the supreme bench of the state. About this time, Senator Chalmers led a force of white men that quelled an incipient negro riot at Friar's Point and drove the leader, a mulatto from Ohio who was then sheriff, out of the county. In the Congressional election, which followed, the aggressive young state senator was elected to the lower house of the Forty-fifth Congress from the celebrated "shoestring district," formed by the reapportionment act of 1876. He then moved to Vicksburg, and was elected to the Forty-sixth Congress. Two years later he received a certificate of election to the Forty-seventh Congress, but his seat was successfully contested by John R. Lynch of Natchez, Miss. (Chester H. Rowell, "Historical and Legal Digest of Contested Election Cases," *House Document, No. 510,* 56 Cong., 2 Sess., pp. 375–78). Chalmers was then appointed a special assistant to the federal district attorneys for the northern and southern districts of Mississippi. Meantime, he moved out of the "shoestring district" and made his home in Sardis, in an adjoining district, which had been represented in Congress since 1876 by Van H. Manning, a Democrat living in Holly Springs. Chalmers ran for Congress in this district (1883), on the independent ticket, with the indorsement of the Republican and Greenback conventions. He claimed a majority of the votes cast, but the Mississippi secretary of state gave a certificate of election to Manning, whose commission was duly signed by the governor. This brought on another contest before the House. After much discussion, Chalmers was finally seated, June 25, 1884 (*Ibid.,* pp. 396–98). Having been succeeded in the Forty-ninth Congress by James B. Morgan, a Democrat living in Hernando, Chalmers ran against him for the Fiftieth Congress. The election was followed by Chalmers' third contest over a seat in the House. This time he lost to his Democratic opponent (*Ibid.,* pp. 457–58). He then retired from politics and moved to Memphis, Tenn., where he engaged in the practise of law until his death, Apr. 9, 1898.

[Sketches of Chalmers in *Biog. and Hist. Memoirs of Mississippi* (1891), I, 535–56, and in Dunbar Rowland, *Mississippi* (1907), I, 390–91 ; a report of his cavalry operations, 1863, in *Southern Hist. Soc. Papers,* VIII, 222 ff.; a sketch of his father in J. D. Lynch, *The Bench and Bar of Mississippi* (1881).]   F. L. R.

CHAMBERLAIN, ALEXANDER FRANCIS (Jan. 12, 1865–Apr. 8, 1914), anthropologist, son of George and Maria (Anderton) Chamberlain, was born in Kenninghall, Norfolk, England, and was brought to America as a child, the family first settling in New York State near Rochester, but soon moving to Peterborough, Canada, where Alexander was prepared for college in the Collegiate Institute. The family then moved to Toronto that he might attend the University of Toronto, from which he graduated in 1886 with honors in languages and ethnology. While an undergraduate he had come under the influence of Sir Daniel Wilson, vice-chancellor of the University and a Canadian pioneer in anthropology, and it was doubtless due to this con-

tact that young Chamberlain turned from modern languages to anthropology. After his graduation, he made field studies among the Mississuga Indians, the results of which were presented in his thesis for the M.A. degree in 1889. This work was of such merit that he was granted a fellowship in anthropology at Clark University, where he was awarded the Ph.D. degree in 1892. This was the first such degree given for work in anthropology at an American university. Chamberlain remained at Clark until his death, beginning as lecturer in anthropology, 1893, and reaching the grade of professor in 1911. In 1898 he married Isabel Cushman. At the outset of his academic career he made field studies among the Kootenai Indians in western Canada, giving special attention to their language, but he did not carry his field-work further, devoting his time to the printed materials available. In addition to numerous special papers on anthropological subjects, he wrote two books on childhood: *The Child: A Study in the Evolution of Man* (1893); *The Child and Childhood in Folk-Thought* (1896). For many years he was editor of the *Journal of American Folk-Lore* and the *Journal of Religious Psychology,* and he contributed to each number of the *American Anthropologist,* brief comments on current articles. Mention should also be made of his work on the Indian languages of South America, and the preparation of a linguistic map for the same.

Chamberlain took a deep interest in his neighbors and the community, served as an alderman in Worcester, Mass., and as chairman of the Democratic Committee. He believed in prohibition and woman suffrage, was a follower of Henry George, and was a firm adherent of the Unitarian Church. The rights of oppressed peoples and classes was a favorite topic with him, and he was in demand as a local campaigner, and speaker in the people's forums, addressing his audiences in English, French, German, or Italian, as the occasion required. Large-limbed and awkward in appearance, with a high-pitched voice and quick jerky gestures, he was nevertheless an effective speaker. A lover of literature, especially poetry, not only did he treasure the lines of his favorite poets, but himself broke into verse at every opportunity. A volume of his poems, among which were a number of hymns, was issued in 1904.

[Albert N. Gilbertson, sketch in *Am. Anthropologist,* Apr.–June 1914, containing bibliography of Chamberlain's writings ; F. Boaz, sketch in *Jour. of Am. Folk-Lore,* July–Sept. 1914 ; *Pubs. of the Clark Univ. Lib.,* Oct. 1914 ; *Proc. Am. Antiquarian Soc.,* n.s., vol. XXIV (1914) ; *Science,* June 5, 1914 ; *Who's Who in America,* 1914–15.]   C. W.

CHAMBERLAIN, DANIEL HENRY (June 23, 1835–Apr. 13, 1907), governor of South Carolina, was the ninth child of Eli and Achsah (Forbes) Chamberlain. As a boy he worked on the farm of his birth at West Brookfield, Mass., and attended in desultory fashion the country schools. Later he had fragmentary experiences with several secondary schools, in 1849–50 at Amherst Academy, in 1854 at Phillips Academy, Andover, and for more than one session, at Worcester High School, where he graduated in 1857. The next year he taught, as he had done intermittently since 1852. In 1858 he entered Yale. His diploma, which he received four years later, indicated special distinction in oratory and English composition. At the Harvard Law School, to which he went in the same fall, he was restless, and, withdrawing in November 1863, he received his commission as lieutenant in the 5th Massachusetts, a regiment of colored troops. In December 1865, he was mustered out as captain. Visiting South Carolina in 1866 to settle the affairs of a dead classmate, he thought he saw opportunity to earn money to repay what he had borrowed for his education. Although cotton-planting on John's Island proved unprofitable, he remained in the state. In 1867 he was chosen a member for Berkeley County of the constitutional convention. Before this body opened in January 1868, he had returned North to marry, on Dec. 16, Alice Ingersoll of Bangor. In the motley convention he gained some prominence as a member of the judiciary committee and earned the favor of party leaders. In the April election of 1868 he was chosen attorney-general. Nothing of his record in this office was notable, but in the most corrupt quadrennium of South Carolina history, though an *ex-officio* member of several thieving boards, he was never charged with personal dishonesty.

After two years of law practise in Columbia, Chamberlain in 1874 won first the nomination and then the election for governor of the state. Immediately undertaking the reforms which he had promised to effect, he reduced public expenditures, revised taxation and assessment laws, eliminated abuse of the pardoning power, and curbed sharply the predatory aspirations of the state boards. His most conspicuous work was his refusal, often in the face of party insistence, to commission corrupt officials. The whites of the state gave for a time indorsement to his administration. Charleston publicly thanked him in 1875 for barring from the bench Whipper and Moses, elected by the legislature.

In the summer of 1876, looking toward renomination, he aligned himself again with the un-worthy faction of his party. He also adopted stern measures in connection with racial clashes, especially the Hamburg riot of July. His support among Democrats weakened; and though a minority of the August Democratic convention urged his claim, Wade Hampton was nominated. The contest, unprecedentedly bitter, was marked by charges and counter-charges. Both sides claimed victory. Chamberlain was inaugurated on Dec. 7, and a few days later Hampton was sworn in by a rival government. The issue was not settled until April when President Hayes, having called a conference of the competing governors, withdrew the federal troops. His government having fallen, Chamberlain engaged in law practise in New York. Honored by Cornell with appointment as non-resident professor of constitutional law in 1883, he continued an active life until 1897 when he sought retirement on the old homestead at West Brookfield. The death of a son in 1902 made that residence unhappy. Chamberlain spent a few months in South Carolina, had a year in Europe, returned for a brief stay near Charleston, lived twenty months in Egypt, and in 1906 settled at Charlottesville, Va., where he spent his remaining days.

[Biographical data are found in a prefatory note to Chamberlain's "Some Conclusions of a Free-Thinker," *North Am. Rev.*, Oct. 1907, and in the Allen, Thompson, and Reynolds references below. The standard defense of Chamberlain is Walter Allen, *Chamberlain's Administration in S. C.* (1888). Less friendly appraisals are: E. L. Godkin, "The Republican Party in S. C.," *Nation*, Apr. 19, 1877; John S. Reynolds, *Reconstruction in S. C.* (1905); Henry T. Thompson, *Ousting the Carpet-Bagger* (1926); and F. A. Porcher, "The Last Chapter in Reconstruction in S. C." in *Southern Hist. Soc. Papers*, vols. XII, XIII. The *Atlantic Monthly*, Feb. 1877, had an anonymous résumé, "Political Conditions of S. C."; the same journal for Apr. 1901 carried Chamberlain's "Reconstruction in S. C."]
             F. P. G.

CHAMBERLAIN, GEORGE EARLE (Jan. 1, 1854–July 9, 1928), lawyer, governor of Oregon, senator, was born near Natchez, Miss. His father was Charles Thomson Chamberlain, a leading physician of Natchez, whose father had been one of the foremost physicians of Newark, Del. Chamberlain's mother was Pamelia H. Archer, whose father was in turn congressman from Maryland, judge of Mississippi territory with gubernatorial powers, and at the time of his death one of the justices of the court of appeals of Maryland. Chamberlain's early education was received from private tutors and in the schools of Natchez. From sixteen to eighteen he clerked in a store, but with consciousness of his abilities and his family traditions he naturally struck out for a professional career, and, attending Washington and Lee University, he received the degrees of bachelor of arts and bachelor of law in the same year, June 1876.

On arriving in Oregon late in 1876 he first taught school in Linn County. From 1877 to 1879 he served as deputy county clerk in the same county. He then returned to Natchez and on May 21, 1879 was married to Sallie M. Welch, of New England ancestry. In 1880 Chamberlain was elected to the House of Representatives of the Oregon legislature, and, having entered upon the active practise of law, he was in 1884 elected district attorney of the 3rd judicial district. In 1891 the office of attorney-general of Oregon was created and Chamberlain was appointed by the governor to that position. At the succeeding general election he was chosen, as the Democratic candidate, running some 10,000 ahead of his party's ticket. In 1900, having taken up his residence in Portland, he was chosen district attorney of Multnomah County, his vote leading that of the party ticket by about the ratio with which he had won his previous victories. Chamberlain was twice elected governor, first in 1902 and again in 1906. As governor he moved quickly to rescue for the people valuable timbered school lands that were being rapidly filched away from them through dummy entrymen. He also used his veto freely to prevent frustration of the people's aims. The federal amendment providing for popular election of United States senators was anticipated in Oregon through the so-called "Statement No. I," submitted to candidates for election to the legislature in 1908 through which each could be pledged to vote for the man receiving the highest popular vote. This brought about the unique spectacle of a legislature strongly Republican casting its vote in 1909 for Chamberlain, a Democrat, as United States senator. In 1915, with direct election of United States senators provided by federal amendment, Chamberlain was again elected. As senator his attitude and ability had secured immediate recognition and in 1913 he had become chairman of the committee on military affairs. This position during the years immediately preceding and during American participation in the World War placed weighty responsibilities on Chamberlain's shoulders. He is credited with a large part in the formulation and the handling of the measures providing for the selective draft, food control, and the financing of the war. Dilatoriness of movement in the War Department in the early months of the war aroused him to pronounce a sharp judgment upon it in a New York City speech and to ask for an emergency organization to take over some of that department's duties.

Those nearest Chamberlain are inclined to believe that "he considered his efforts in behalf of the boys in service during the late war to have been the finest thing—the thing most fruitful of benefit to humanity—that he ever did." His action, however, was bitterly resented by President Wilson and from that time on he was out of favor with the administration. In 1920, he was defeated for reëlection. This ended his political career. He was large and impressive in appearance; an excellent speaker, whose manner inspired confidence. After his defeat his friends, both Republican and Democrat, secured his appointment as a member of the United States Shipping Board.

[*Ore. Blue Book*; *Ore. Daily Jour.*, and *Morning Oregonian*, July 10, 1928; Jos. Gaston, *Portland, Ore., Its Hist. and Builders* (1911); *Cong. Record*, 1909–20.]

F. G. Y.

CHAMBERLAIN, HENRY RICHARDSON (Aug. 25, 1859–Feb. 15, 1911), newspaper editor and foreign correspondent, was born in Peoria, Ill., where his father, Thomas Chamberlain of Boston, was spending a few months with his family. Educated in the public schools of Boston, Henry first began his newspaper work by hunting up news independently and turning it over to the *Boston Journal*. At eighteen he was a full-fledged reporter on that newspaper. Attracted by the larger salaries paid in New York City he came to the metropolis in 1888 as managing editor of the *Press*,—a position he later resigned to make a tour of Europe. Returning to New York, he became associated with the *Sun*, for which he had done considerable work as special correspondent while in Boston. This connection with the *Sun* lasted until 1891 when Chamberlain went back to Boston to become managing editor of the *Journal*. A year later he again returned to the *Sun* as its correspondent stationed in London,—possibly the highest reportorial honor in the power of any newspaper to bestow. Here he achieved his greatest distinction as a reporter of the political situation in England and also as an expert commentator upon European politics in general. In addition to his work as London correspondent for the *Sun*, he had general oversight of the European news service of that newspaper, a service that was syndicated to many papers throughout the United States. Important crises in European history Chamberlain reported in person, such as the Russian political crisis of 1906. For him the Balkans and their petty feuds had tremendous interest: he was constantly forecasting the possible results of these feuds because the quarrels of the little states were so entangled with the relations of the great European nations. Not only in London, but also in New York, newspaper men were inclined to smile over the seriousness of "H. R. C.'s war-cloud articles," even though their author was not a wailing Jeremiah. In press circles the remark was frequently made, "H. R. is always seeing things." Even his friends, believing that a general war in Europe was impossible, were often skeptical of the dispatches which Chamberlain cabled to America. He died in London in 1911, still in active service for the *Sun,* and to the very last he insisted that the great war was coming. In 1883 he married in Boston Abbie L. Sanger. Author of many short stories, he left only one book, *Six Thousand Tons of Gold* (1894). His best work as a reporter may be found in his accounts of the Macedonian disturbances, the Messina earthquake, and the Panama Canal scandal in France. He was one of the foremost representatives of the brilliant type of reporter that Charles A. Dana secured for the *Sun* when that journal was known as the newspaperman's newspaper.

[*The Story of the Sun* (1918) by Frank M. O'Brien contains a somewhat detailed sketch of Chamberlain as a newspaper man. In the *Sun,* Feb. 16, 1911, appeared an extended obituary.]   J. M. L.

CHAMBERLAIN, JACOB (Apr. 13, 1835–Mar. 2, 1908), Dutch Reformed missionary to India, was the son of Jacob Chamberlain, a farmer of Sharon, Conn., and his wife Anna Nutting. He grew up at Hudson, Ohio, where the family settled in 1838; studied at the Academy at Lodi, Mich.; graduated at Western Reserve College in 1856, and studied theology at Union Seminary and at Rutgers where he graduated in 1859. He also studied medicine at the College of Physicians and Surgeons in New York and at Western Reserve. He was ordained a missionary of the Dutch Reformed Church in May 1859, married Charlotte Close Birge of Hudson in September, sailed for India, and began his life work in the Arcot Mission in April 1860. Beginning with the Tamil language, he soon took up the Telugu in which he became proficient. His first missionary activities consisted of extensive preaching tours on which he distributed vast quantities of Bibles and tracts; but he soon added to these labors those of the medical missionary, in which he was very successful. Many thousands of natives were reached by the hospitals and dispensaries which he established. He compiled a Telugu Bible, being chairman of the revision committee from 1873 to 1896. Early in his career he began to prepare a Telugu Bible dictionary, a task that was left

uncompleted at his death. He was a pioneer champion of the union of churches on the mission field and the notable Reformed and Presbyterian unions in India have been the result of his work. The first theological seminary on the mission field, that of the Arcot mission, founded in 1887, owes its origin to him. Ill health resulting from jungle fever compelled him to spend ten years, at various periods, in the United States and other English-speaking countries where he became a most effective advocate of foreign missions.

Besides his annual reports, written in simple and beautiful English, and his numerous articles in the religious press, he wrote: *The Bible Tested in India* (1878); *In the Tiger Jungle* (1896); *The Religions of the Orient* (1896); *The Cobra's Den* (1900); *The Kingdom in India, Its Progress and its Promise* (published in 1908, with a biographical sketch of the author by Henry N. Cobb). Chamberlain combined in himself the scholar, the preacher, the physician, the inventor, and the advocate, but the missionary motive was always central. He had a sense of humor, was genial and cheerful, and was greatly beloved by his family and associates.

[Cobb's sketch (*ante*) is reprinted in the *Missionary Rev. of the World,* Aug. 1908. The same publication for May 1908 contains autobiographical material. Further material is found in *Acts and Proc. of the Gen. Synod of the Reformed Ch. in America* (1908), and in *Who's Who in America,* 1908–09.]   F. T. P.

CHAMBERLAIN, JOSHUA LAWRENCE (Sept. 8, 1828–Feb. 24, 1914), Union soldier, governor of Maine, educator, was born at Brewer, Me., the son of Joshua Chamberlain and Sarah D. Brastow. On his father's side he traced his descent from William Chamberlain, who migrated from England about 1648 and settled at Woburn, Mass.; his first maternal ancestor in this country was Jean Dupuis, a Huguenot who came to Boston from La Rochelle about 1685. His great-grandfather served in the colonial and Revolutionary wars, his grandfather was a colonel in the War of 1812, and his father acted as second in command on the American side in the so-called Aroostook War in 1839. He was educated at a military academy at Ellsworth, Me., graduated from Bowdoin College, Brunswick, in 1852, and in 1855 completed a course at the Bangor Theological Seminary. On Dec. 7, 1855, he was married to Frances Caroline, daughter of Ashur Adams of Boston and Emily (Wyllis) Adams of Hartford. In the same year he was appointed instructor in natural and revealed religion at Bowdoin; from 1856 to 1862 he was professor of rhetoric; from 1857 to 1861 instructor in modern languages; from

1861 to 1865 professor of modern languages. In 1862 he was granted leave of absence for study abroad, but, abandoning the plan in spite of the protest of the college faculty, he enlisted as lieutenant-colonel of the 20th Maine Infantry, becoming colonel in May 1863, and continuing in active service until the end of the Civil War. He took part in twenty-four engagements (among them Antietam, Fredericksburg, Chancellorsville, Gettysburg, Spottsylvania, Cold Harbor, Petersburg, and Five Forks) and was six times wounded. For his gallant defense of Little Round Top in the battle of Gettysburg he received the Congressional Medal of Honor "for daring heroism and great tenacity." On June 18, 1864, in the operations before Petersburg, where he was wounded, he was made a brigadier-general on the field by Grant, the promotion being later confirmed by the Senate. His distinguished conduct on Mar. 29, 1865, in an assault on Lee's right, caused him to be brevetted major-general of volunteers, and in the operations which ended with Lee's surrender he commanded two brigades of the 1st Division of the 5th Army Corps, and was designated to receive the surrender of the Confederate army. On June 16, 1866, he was mustered out, having declined, on account of his health, an offer of a colonelcy in the regular army and a command on the Rio Grande. In the fall of that year he was elected governor of Maine, and served in that office by reëlection for four successive annual terms. From 1871 to 1883 he was president of Bowdoin, and in addition, from 1874 to 1879, professor of mental and moral philosophy and lecturer on political science and public law, continuing to lecture on the latter subjects until 1885. During the winter of 1878-79, when the Democratic and Greenback parties, under the lead of Gov. Alonzo Garcelon, had combined to get possession of the state legislature, and the Republicans had organized a rival body, Chamberlain, acting as major-general of the state militia, kept the peace until the supreme court of the state affirmed the legality of the Republican organization. He was one of the American commissioners to the Universal Exposition at Paris in 1878, and made a valuable report on the educational exhibit. From 1884 to 1889 he was occupied with railway and industrial enterprises in Florida. In 1900 he was appointed surveyor of the port of Portland, Me., and held that office until his death. His best known and most important writings are *Maine: Her Place in History* (1877), originally prepared as an address at the Centennial Exposition at Philadelphia, Nov. 4, 1876, and *The Passing of the*

Armies (1915), a book of reminiscence dealing with the final campaigns of the Army of the Potomac. Of a number of occasional addresses or papers which were printed the best known is an address at Philadelphia on Feb. 12, 1909, before the Military Order of the Loyal Legion, Pennsylvania Commandery, on the hundredth anniversary of Lincoln's birth (published in the *Magazine of American History*, 1914, Extra No. 32). To *Universities and their Sons* (6 vols., 1898-1923), of which he was for a time editor-in-chief, he contributed a history of New York University.

[N. Cleaveland, *Hist. of Bowdoin Coll.* (1882), ed. by A. S. Packard; Louis C. Hatch, *Hist. of Bowdoin Coll.* (1927); *Gen. Cat. of Bowdoin Coll., 1794-1912* (1912); a biographical note signed G. H. P. (George Haven Putnam?) prefixed to *The Passing of the Armies* (1915); an excellent brief account of the fighting at Little Round Top in W. H. Powell, *Hist. of the Fifth Army Corps* (1896), pp. 526-31; *Official Records (Army)*; obituary in Portland *Eastern Argus*, Feb. 25, 1914.]
W. M.

CHAMBERLAIN, MELLEN (June 4, 1821-June 25, 1900), historian, was born in Pembroke, N. H., the second of the five children of Moses and Mary (Foster) Chamberlain. He attended the district schools and the Academy in Pembroke; later he assisted his father on the farm and in the business of a country store until 1836, when the family moved to Concord, N. H. He prepared for college at the Literary Institute of that place, taught in the district schools during the winters, and aided his father on the farm; he graduated from Dartmouth College in 1844 with special distinction in classical studies. During the college course he taught school three winters in Danvers, Mass., and was principal of the High School in Brattleboro, Vt., until late in 1846, when he entered the Dane (Harvard) Law School; he was soon made librarian of the school, and received his LL.B. degree in 1848. Admitted to the bar in Boston, in January 1849, he married Martha Ann Putnam on June 6 of the same year, and went to live in Chelsea, where he passed the remainder of his days. From 1849 his life was a busy one; while his chief occupation was that of a conveyancer, he soon entered public service as, successively, school committee man, selectman, alderman, and city solicitor. He was elected a representative to the General Court from the thirteenth Suffolk district in 1858 and in 1859, and was appointed a member of the special committee on the revision of the statutes. In 1863 and again in 1864 he was elected a member of the state Senate, and in the latter year was chairman of its judiciary committee. On June 29, 1866, Gov. Bullock appointed him associate justice of the newly created municipal court of

Boston; this office he held until December 1870, when Gov. Claflin appointed him chief justice of the municipal court. He remained in this position until August 1878, when he was made librarian of the Public Library of the City of Boston. His special attainments in the study of early American history proved of essential advantage to the Library in bringing that department of the institution up to the high standing already reached in other branches of knowledge. Because of failing health Chamberlain resigned in September 1890. His collection of autographs and manuscripts, begun in 1836, by will became the property of the Boston Public Library and has proved one of the richest sources of information for students of American history. From 1873 on, Chamberlain played a prominent part in the Massachusetts Historical Society and contributed valuable and interesting papers to its publications. He also wrote the chapter on "The Revolution Impending" in Justin Winsor's *Narrative and Critical History of America,* vol. VI (1888). In 1890 a selection of his writings, edited by Lindsay Swift, was published under the title of *John Adams, the Statesman of the American Revolution, with Other Essays and Addresses, Historical and Literary.* Under the auspices of a committee of publication of the Massachusetts Historical Society, there was published in 1908 *A Documentary History of Chelsea, 1624–1824,* in two volumes, from Chamberlain's incomplete manuscript and from ten folio volumes of manuscripts, plans, engravings, photographs, etc., collected and arranged by him. Uncommon literary quality, combined with judgment, sagacity, and ripe scholarship, marked the style not only of Chamberlain's writings but of his public addresses. His keen memory supplied him, when speaking, with an abundance of illustrations to strengthen and enliven his arguments. In person he was tall and erect; in bearing dignified; in nature companionable and affectionate. His strong and commanding countenance gave additional weight and meaning to his words.

["Memoir of Mellen Chamberlain," by Henry W. Haynes, in *Proc. Mass. Hist. Soc.,* 2 ser. XX, 119–46 (repr. in *Doc. Hist. of Chelsea*) ; "Tribute to Mellen Chamberlain," by Geo. B. Chase, in *Proc. Mass. Hist. Soc.,* 2 ser. XIV, 271–81.]   C. F. D. B.

CHAMBERLAIN, NATHAN HENRY (Dec. 28, 1828?–Apr. 1, 1901), Episcopalian clergyman, author, the son of Artemas White and Lydia Smith (Ellis) Chamberlain, was born in that part of Sandwich, Mass., now called Bourne, and he died about seventy-two years later in the same house. The date of his birth is uncertain. The conventional date is Dec. 25,

1830. Samuel S. Shaw, secretary of the class of 1853 (Harvard), says it is not certain whether Chamberlain was born Dec. 25, or Dec. 28, in the year 1828, '29, '30, or '31, but after careful and exhaustive study he decides on Dec. 28, 1828, as most probable. Chamberlain's early life was one continual struggle with poverty. His father was the keeper of the poor-house in Sandwich and later became a policeman in Cambridge, whither the family moved during Nathan's school-days. By mowing lawns, shoveling dirt, and snaring rabbits, the boy earned money for his needs while in Hopkins Classical School. During his college days at Harvard he taught days and studied nights in bed, being too poor to maintain a fire. He graduated from Harvard in the class of 1853 and completed his professional studies at Harvard Divinity School and at the University of Heidelberg. Ordained to the Unitarian ministry, Apr. 22, 1857, at Canton, Mass., he served Unitarian churches there and in Baltimore, Md. His convictions then led him into the Episcopal church and he was ordained priest at Middletown, Conn., in 1864. For twenty-five years he served as an Episcopalian rector in Birmingham (now Derby), Conn.; Morrisania, N. Y.; Milwaukee, Wis.; Somerville and East Boston, Mass. In 1889 he resigned from the ministry, became a teacher of elocution, and devoted much of his time to writing. He was a master in the use of the English language, lucid, direct, and graphic. His range of interests and study was broad and his themes were varied. Independent as a political thinker, in *What's the Matter? or Our Tariff and Its Taxes* (1890), he protested against protection as "anti-American, anti-republican, aristocratic and the tool of tyranny," and demanded economic as well as political freedom. Though keenly critical of Puritanism as a system of applied religion, he was liberal enough to see the elements of its power in the nation's life and paid a tribute to the same in *Samuel Sewall and the World He Lived In* (1897). A picture of life in the Pilgrim colony toned and colored by the sea is given in *The Autobiography of a New England Farm House* (1864) in which he analyzed the Tory mind and enunciated a philosophy of sorrow. During his last few years his health was seriously impaired, and he lived in retirement on Cape Cod until his death. He was married twice: first, on Feb. 19, 1855, to Hannah Simonds Tewkesbury; and, second, on Apr. 6, 1869, to Mariette Cleveland Hyde.

[*Jour. of the One Hundred Sixteenth Annual Meeting of the Convention of the Diocese of Mass.,* 1901; *Report of the Class of 1853 (Harvard), 1849–1913; Churchman,* Apr. 20, 1901.]   T. C. R.

CHAMBERLAIN, WILLIAM ISAAC (Feb. 11, 1837–June 30, 1920), agriculturist, son of Jacob and Anna (Nutting) Chamberlain, was born in Sharon, Conn. Following the tide of Connecticut movement to the Western Reserve, his parents with their two infant children moved to Ohio in 1838 and settled in Hudson. Having graduated from the public school of the town, Chamberlain entered Western Reserve College and graduated in 1859. His proficiency in the classics led to his immediate appointment as instructor of Latin and Greek in the College. On July 16, 1863, he was married to Lucy Jones Marshall. Two years later, his health and the needs of his parents made it advisable for him to give up teaching and take over the home farm. To the art of farming he applied the scholarly habits of the student, reading and testing by experiments whatever scientific facts might find practical application in the management of soils, crops, and orchards. These tests and experiments formed the basis of his frequent contributions to agricultural journals. His knowledge of Ohio agriculture led to his election as secretary of agriculture of Ohio in 1880 and to his removal to Columbus, Ohio, where he served in this capacity for six years. During this time he was instrumental in organizing throughout the state a system of farmers' institutes and of monthly crop reports, and in securing the passage of a fertilizer law and the equipment of an agricultural fair ground. In 1886 he was called to the presidency of the Iowa Agricultural College, but in 1890 he resigned to return to his experimenting, lecturing, and agricultural writing. He served as a trustee of Ohio State University and as a member of the board of control of the Ohio Agricultural Station. He was an associate editor of the *Ohio Farmer*, 1891–1908, of the *National Stockman and Farmer*, 1908–18, and published a book for practical farmers, *Tile Drainage* (1891). In 1908–09 and again in 1912 he traveled in Europe. While most of his life-work was devoted to the interests of the farmer, his love of the classics never lessened and to the end of his life, with his mind still clear and active, he read almost daily from his favorite Greek authors.

[L. S. Ivins and A. E. Winship, *Fifty Famous Farmers* (1924), pp. 309–14; *Cleveland Plain Dealer*, July 1, 1920; C. R. Aurner, *Hist. of Ed. in Iowa*, vol. IV (1916), pp. 250–57; private information.]   E. H. J.

CHAMBERLIN, THOMAS CHROWDER (Sept. 25, 1843–Nov. 15, 1928), one of the outstanding contributors to constructive thinking in the geologic sciences of the past half-century, was born in Mattoon, Ill., the son of the

Rev. John Chamberlin, a Methodist minister, and of Cecilia (Gill) Chamberlin. When he was three years old the family moved to Wisconsin where he grew to manhood. In 1866 he received the degree of A.B. at Beloit College, and for the next two years was principal of the high school at Delevan, Wis.; meanwhile, in 1867, he was married to Alma Isabel Wilson. He was a graduate student at the University of Michigan, 1868–69; professor of natural sciences at the State Normal School, Whitewater, Wis., 1870–72; professor of geology at Beloit, 1873–82. It was while he was at the latter institution that his really important work began. The fact that he resided in a region of notable glacial deposits was of great importance in the development of his career as a student of earth history. The climatic conditions in past ages, as revealed by traces of ancient glaciers, contrasted sharply with the situation obtaining to-day, and presented a series of questions for which no fully adequate answer had been obtained. His study naturally directed itself, first, to intensive examination of the material remains upon which must be based any research into the physical or climatic conditions through which these relics had been produced. Armed with the evidence secured by his investigations and stimulated by the continually increasing complexity of the problem, he extended his studies to consideration of earth climates through the known range of geological time.

In 1878 he made a special study of the glaciers of Switzerland. By 1883 he was recognized as the leading American glacialist (H. L. Fairchild, *post*, p. 611). During these years he was also the assistant state geologist of Wisconsin, 1873–76, and the chief geologist, 1877–82. Here he had the task of publishing the results of a geological survey of the whole state, made by himself and his associates, in *The Geology of Wisconsin* (4 vols., 1873–82). Volume I contained his summary of the geological history of Wisconsin, beginning with a discussion of the origin of the earth. The work attracted so much attention that a Division of Glacial Geology, of which he was appointed chief, was established in the United States Geological Survey at Washington, D. C., in 1882. He was also professor of geology in Columbian University, Washington, from 1885 to 1887. In the latter year he was called to succeed John Bascom [*q.v.*], in the presidency of the University of Wisconsin. His incumbency fell in the period when the college of liberal arts developed by his predecessor was beginning to expand into the later university. Chamberlin foresaw the future clearly and outlined the policy to be pursued. In his initial year, through the foundation of eight university fellowships, he took the first formal step toward the encouragement of graduate study; he improved the law school; and in his fifth and last year he inaugurated a university extension movement.

In 1892 Chamberlin was appointed head of the department of geology and director of the Walker Museum in the new University of Chicago. Here he remained until his death, becoming professor emeritus in 1919. In 1893 he founded the *Journal of Geology* of which he was editor-in-chief until 1922 when he became senior editor. In 1894 he accompanied the Peary Relief Expedition. In 1897 he published his first non-glacial paper, "A Group of Hypotheses Bearing on Climatic Changes," which contained the germ of his later "planetesimal hypothesis." In 1898 he outlined in "The Ulterior Basis of Time Divisions and the Classification of Geologic History" a line of approach which was to culminate in "Diastrophism as the Ultimate Basis of Correlation" (1909) and "Diastrophism and the Formative Processes" (1913, 1914, 1918). He discussed the nebular hypothesis in "An Attempt to Test the Nebular Hypothesis by the Relations of Masses and Momenta" (1900). In 1906 he published his *General Treatise on Geology,* written in collaboration with R. D. Salisbury. In 1916 his epoch-making volume, *The Origin of the Earth,* appeared, and in 1928 his last work, *The Two Solar Families.*

"Chamberlin was regarded in the profession as without question the ranking geologist of America" (C. K. Leith, in *Wisconsin Alumni Magazine,* Dec. 1928). His outstanding contributions are generally recognized as threefold: first, his detailed researches on glacial phenomena as illustrated in the relics of glaciation so widely spread through the northern United States; second, his investigations of geological climates, arising naturally out of the study of exceptional climatic conditions in the glacial period; third, the contribution to cosmic geology represented in his "planetesimal hypothesis" of the origin of the earth.

The trend of Chamberlin's researches into the geological history of the more remote ages made necessary his inquiry not only into the evolution of climates, but into questions concerning the origin of the atmosphere itself. In examination of the variation in atmospheric conditions the proportion of carbonic acid in the atmosphere appeared a critical factor. Investigation of these particular phenomena reached beyond the study of the origin of the earth climates, and involved groups of inferences relating to the development of life under varying conditions in past periods, and the possibility of linking a wide range of diverse elements in earth history through their relation to atmospheric conditions. The study of climatic changes and the origin of the atmosphere carried Chamberlin ultimately into discussion of the dynamics of the earth, with problems relating to the nature and degree of regularity of earth movements in past time. In another direction it led directly to a consideration of the origin of the earth, which could be discussed only in association with problems relating to the development of the solar system.

Always characterized by exceptional broad-mindedness, and by recognition of the need for utilization of all available materials and application of every possible hypothesis for a study of each specific case, Chamberlin illustrated to an extraordinary degree the development of these qualities in his study of problems relating to the origin of the earth. Drawing into cooperation with him a wide range of investigational efforts in the field of mathematics and astronomy, he brought practically the whole of organized study in cosmic physics to bear upon this interesting problem. In connection with these researches, special mention should be made of his long association with Forest R. Moulton, whose expression of the problem in terms of mathematics and astronomy supplemented in an extremely important manner the constructive thinking of Chamberlin.

It was clear that the widely-recognized hypotheses represented by that of La Place were not competent to account for the development of the earth and other planets, and effort was made to secure an interpretation which would fit the requirements of physics. The result was the theory that the earth and the planets owed their birth to the approach of another sun or star bringing about the partial disruption of the sun, and the expulsion of a great mass from which ultimately the earth was derived. This evolution was defined as by way of a swarm of minute, solid particles, the "planetesimals," swinging in orbits about the sun, and ultimately gathering to build the earth. Checked from every point of view, this became the "planetesimal hypothesis" of the earth's origin.

[H. L. Fairchild, "Thos. Chrowder Chamberlin—Teacher, Administrator, Geologist, Philosopher," *Science,* LXVIII, 610 ff., Dec. 21, 1928; Chas. Schuchert in *Am. Jour. Science,* ser. V, no. 98, vol. XVII, pp. 194–96, Feb. 1929; *Univ. Record* (Chicago), Jan. 1929; *Geographical Rev.,* Jan. 1929; *Sci. Mo.,* Jan. 1929; *Jour. Washington Acad. Science,* XVIII, 564, Dec. 4, 1928; *Bull. Geol. Soc. of America,* XXXVIII, 6–7, Mar. 1927; R. G. Thwaites. *The Univ. of Wisconsin* (1900), pp. 129–40; G. F. A. Pyre, *Wisconsin* (1920).]
                                                                    J.C.M.

CHAMBERS, CHARLES JULIUS. [See CHAMBERS, JAMES JULIUS, 1850–1920.]

CHAMBERS, EZEKIEL FORMAN (Feb. 28, 1788–Jan. 30, 1867), jurist, born at Chestertown, Kent County, Md., was the son of Benjamin and Elizabeth (Forman) Chambers. His father fought both in the Revolution and in the War of 1812. Ezekiel likewise distinguished himself during the War of 1812, in a militia company which was defending the Eastern Shore, Maryland, at Bel Air, against the British attack under Sir Peter Parker (*Baltimore Sun*, Feb. 2, 1867, *National Intelligencer*, Feb. 4, 1867). After a classical education in Washington College he studied law and was admitted to the bar in March 1808. After the interlude of the War of 1812 he practised until 1822 when he was elected against his will to the Maryland Senate. The famous case of *Prigg* vs. *The State of Pennsylvania,* which involved the right to recover fugitive slaves, was at this time discussed in the Senate and gave him an opportunity to pronounce his Southern state-rights views on slavery and secession. His activities in this case led the State of Maryland to appoint him commissioner to enter into negotiations with Pennsylvania regarding the return of fugitive slaves; the result of these negotiations was satisfactory to his state. Chambers served in the United States Senate from 1826 to 1834, during which time he became an ardent Whig, opposed to "Jacksonism." But he had little taste for politics and probably rejoiced when, in 1834, he was appointed chief judge of the then 2nd judicial district and judge of the court of appeals. In 1850 he was sent to the state convention which framed a new constitution. There he made himself unpopular by his unsuccessful fight against the provision that the people elect their judges. As a result, under the new constitution he was not elected to his old position. President Fillmore in 1852 offered him the appointment of secretary of the navy, which he seriously considered but declined on the ground of ill health. Instead, he turned his attention again to the bar and became celebrated as a *nisi prius* lawyer. When the menacing talk of secession grew at length into a distinct threat his sympathies were unmistakably with the movement, but like most Marylanders he advocated a calm and judicial view, advising compromise. He was in 1864 a member of the constitutional convention of Maryland where his state-rights ideas could but make his efforts ineffective, since the state was at this time controlled by the Unionists under military force. His candidacy for governor in the same year against Thomas Swann ended in fail-

ure, as it was bound to do. At the time of his death he was president of the board of trustees of his alma mater, Washington College.

[*Baltimore Sun*, Feb. 2, 1867; *Md. Hist. Mag.*, vols. XVI, XVII; *Tercentenary Hist. of Md.* (1925), IV, 852–53.]
　　　　　　　　　　　　　　　　　　C. W. G.

CHAMBERS, GEORGE (Feb. 24, 1786–Mar. 25, 1866), lawyer, was the grandson of Benjamin Chambers, a native of Antrim, Ireland, but of Scotch descent, who landed at Philadelphia in 1726 and settled near the present site of Chambersburg, Pa. Benjamin's son, also Benjamin, married Sarah, daughter of George Brown, a neighbor, and their eldest son, George, was born at Chambersburg. The family was well off, and George received a good classical education, proceeded to Princeton in October 1802, and graduated with honors in 1804. He then studied law at Chambersburg and Carlisle, and on his admission to the Cumberland County bar, Nov. 9, 1807, opened an office at Chambersburg, with every advantage which respected parentage and large local interests can confer. Devoting himself more particularly to the law of conveyancing and real property, probably because of his father's extensive land holdings, he in time acquired the reputation of being an expert in the intricate and obscure land laws of Pennsylvania. He entered public life through municipal channels, being elected a member of the Chambersburg town council in 1821, and serving as burgess from 1829 to 1833. In 1832 he was elected to Congress as Whig representative of Adams and Franklin counties, and served two terms, being reëlected in 1834. He was a delegate from Franklin County to the Pennsylvania state constitutional convention which met at Harrisburg, May 2, 1837. A bitter controversy arose in the convention anent the judiciary article, it being proposed to substitute a short tenure for judges in place of the original tenure during good behavior. This change Chambers resolutely but unsuccessfully opposed. In April 1851 he was appointed associate judge of the supreme court of Pennsylvania by Gov. Johnson, and held this office till the following December, when the new constitution came into force. Nominated by the Whig state convention of that year for continuance in office, he suffered defeat in common with the whole Whig ticket, and thereafter neither sought nor held any public position. He did not resume his law practise, but devoted much time to the promotion of education and agricultural science in his community. He was the largest landowner in Franklin County, and is said to have known every boundary line and tree throughout his extensive properties. He also engaged in literary work, publishing *A Trib-*

ute to the Principles, Virtues, Habits and Public Usefulness of the Irish and Scotch Early Settlers of Pennsylvania (1856). In addition, he prepared a biography of the Rev. John McDowell and an elaborate local history, with particular reference to the laws and usages appertaining to land. The manuscripts of these works, together with a mass of valuable private papers, were destroyed when the Confederate forces burned Chambersburg, July 30, 1864. Chambers was married to Alice A., daughter of W. Lyon, of Cumberland County. "He did not often appear in the trial of criminal cases, but led all other members of the Bar in civil suits and Orphans' Court business . . . was dignified, reserved and courteous. He had few intimates, and perhaps the general public regarded him as aristocratic, and but little disposed to concern himself about his fellow men" (John M. Cooper, *post*).

[Details of the ancestry and life of Chambers are contained in the *Kittochtinny Mag.*, I, 136, 279, 290. Further material will be found in: J. McDowell Sharpe, *Memoir of Geo. Chambers* (1873, repr. in *Hist. of Franklin County, Pa.*, 1887, p. 625) ; John M. Cooper, *Recollections of Chambersburg, Pa.* (1900), p. 104; W. D. Chambers, *Chambers Hist.* (1925), pp. 46–49).]

H. W. H. K.

CHAMBERS, JAMES JULIUS (Nov. 21, 1850–Feb. 12, 1920), journalist, born at Bellefontaine, Ohio, was the son of Joseph and Sarabella (Walker) Chambers. When he was eleven years old he decided he would work in a newspaper office and thereafter spent most of his vacations in the office of a Bellefontaine newspaper. In 1870 he was graduated from Cornell University and immediately became a reporter on the *New York Tribune* under Horace Greeley. Illness forced him to leave New York for a time, and in the summer of 1872 he explored the headwaters of the Mississippi River in a Baden-Powell canoe, going above Lake Itasca to discover Elk Lake, connected with Itasca by a stream since named Chambers Creek (see *Minnesota Historical Collections*, vol. XI, 1904). For this discovery he was made a fellow of the Royal Geographical Society. His trip furnished material for a series of letters published in the *New York Herald*, and later a book, *The Mississippi River and Its Wonderful Valley* (1910). Returning to New York and the service of the *Tribune* in August 1872, with the connivance of the city editor he arranged to be committed as insane to the Bloomingdale Asylum in order to obtain authentic information as to alleged abuses of the inmates. His friends secured his release after ten days, and his reports and stories in the *Tribune* resulted in the release of some twelve sane persons, in a general readjustment of the authorities of the institution and eventually, it is said, in the

revision of the state lunacy laws. These experiences were later published in *A Mad World and Its Inhabitants* (London, 1876 ; New York, 1877), an excellent piece of colorful and descriptive reporting. In 1873 he joined the staff of the *New York Herald*, serving as correspondent in various parts of the world, and for a time as city editor. In 1886 Bennett appointed him managing editor and in the following year called him to Paris to launch the Paris *Herald*. This done, Chambers returned to the managing desk in New York. In 1889 he was offered by Joseph Pulitzer the managing editorship of the New York *World*, which he retained until 1891. His remaining years were devoted to travel, literature, and many incidental jobs which offered themselves. He was non-resident lecturer on journalism at Cornell University in 1903–04 and at New York University in 1910. He published two hundred short stories and several volumes of fiction and had two plays produced in New York. In 1904 he began a column in the *Brooklyn Eagle,* called "Walks and Talks," which he continued until the day before he died. In 1912 he brought out a large volume called *The Book of New York,* containing his recollections of personal contacts with important personages during his newspaper career. At the time of his death he was engaged in revising a book for the press, *News Hunting on Three Continents* (1921), a good human-interest account of a reporter's life. Chambers was married twice: first, to Ida L. Burgess, and second, to Margaret Belvin.

[In addition to the autobiographical works cited above, see *Biog. Hist. of Cornell* (1916) ; *Who's Who in America*, 1918–19; obituaries in the *Brooklyn Eagle* and *N. Y. Times, Tribune, Herald, World,* and *Evening Post* for Feb. 13, 1920. Chambers wrote as Julius Chambers but stated in a letter to the Lib. of Cong. that his full name was James Julius; the "Charles Julius" given in some reference works is an error.] M. S.

CHAMBERS, JOHN (Oct. 6, 1780–Sept. 21, 1852), congressman, governor of the territory of Iowa, was born at Bromley Bridge, Somerset County, N. J. His parents were Rowland Chambers, a veteran of the American Revolution, and Phœbe (Mullican) Chambers of Long Island. When John was fourteen years of age the family removed to Washington, then the county seat of Mason County, Ky. Shortly after the family settled in their new home John found employment in a store. During the following March he was sent by his brother to Transylvania Seminary at Lexington, Ky., where he remained until the summer vacation, a period of four months which constituted the sum total of his higher education. Upon his return to Washington he again worked in a store until he was appointed deputy clerk of the district court. During the time unoccupied in performing the duties of his new office he studied law, and applied himself so diligently that in November 1800, one month after reaching the age of twenty, he was given a license to practise. On June 16, 1803, he married Margaret Taylor of Hagerstown, Md., who died on Mar. 4, 1807. On Oct. 29, 1807, he married Hannah Taylor, a sister of his first wife. Two ivory miniatures made about this time show him as a sturdy young man with short brown hair, and his second wife as a young woman of unusual beauty. Twelve children were born of their union. During the War of 1812 he served with distinction on the staff of Gen. William Henry Harrison. As a civil officer he held many positions. In 1812 he was chosen to represent his county in the state legislature of Kentucky, and in 1815 was reëlected. In 1828 he was chosen to fill a vacancy in the House of Representatives at Washington, D. C. In 1830 and 1832 he was again elected to the state legislature. In 1835 he was returned to Congress and was reëlected in 1837. On Mar. 25, 1841, he was commissioned governor of the territory of Iowa by President Harrison. He arrived at Burlington, Ia., on May 12 where he succeeded Robert Lucas in the dual capacity of governor and superintendent of Indian affairs in the territory. Despite the fact that the Democratic party predominated at that time in Iowa and Chambers was a Whig, he succeeded in administering the affairs of the territory in a way that won both local approbation and the commendation of the administration at Washington. He gave much attention to the management of Indian affairs; and as the commissioner of the United States government concluded a treaty with the Sauks and Foxes in 1842 whereby these Indians agreed to give up the remainder of their land in Iowa and to remove to Kansas. In 1844 he was reappointed to the office of governor of Iowa territory by President Tyler, but in 1845 he was removed from office by President Polk. White-haired, somewhat stooped, and with impaired health, he retired to his farm "Grouseland," a few miles west of Burlington. Shortly afterward he returned to Kentucky. In 1849 he made a journey to Minnesota to serve as a commissioner with Gov. Alexander Ramsey to treat with the Sioux. Three years later during a visit to his daughter at Paris, Ky., he was taken ill and, after a few weeks, died on Sept. 21, 1852.

[The chief source of information about Chambers is his *Autobiography* (1908), ed. by John Carl Parish (repr. from the *Iowa Jour. of Hist. and Politics*, Apr. 1908). An excellent sketch written, but not signed, by his oldest son, Jos. Sprigg Chambers, appears in the *Annals of Iowa*, ser. 1, IX, 553–61. *John Chambers* (1909), written by John Carl Parish, is a critical study.]

B. E. M.

CHAMBERS, JULIUS. [See CHAMBERS, JAMES JULIUS, 1850–1920.]

CHAMBERS, TALBOT WILSON (Feb. 25, 1819–Feb. 3, 1896), Dutch Reformed clergyman, theologian, was born at Carlisle, Pa., the son of William C. Chambers, a physician, and of Mary Ege. He was of Irish stock on his father's side and of German on his mother's. At the age of eleven he entered Dickinson College but transferred at the end of two years to Rutgers so as to study under Dr. Alexander McClelland, formerly of Dickinson, whose vigorous intellect and vivid personality exercised a decisive influence over his pupil. Upon graduating from Rutgers in 1834, he continued to study under McClelland at the New Brunswick Theological Seminary until ill health—he was frail from childhood and subject to pulmonary trouble—compelled him to leave. The year 1836–37 he spent at the Princeton Seminary. This time his course was interrupted by the financial difficulties of his parents, and in order to support himself and a younger brother he tutored in private families in Mississippi from 1837 to 1839. On Oct. 21, 1838, he was licensed to preach by the Presbytery of Clinton, Miss., but, finding himself almost immediately involved in a theological controversy in which his family was on one side and he on the other, he withdrew from the Presbyterian Church and united with the Dutch Reformed, which he had come to know during the years in New Brunswick. From 1840 to 1849 he was pastor of the Second Reformed Church of Raritan, at Somerville, N. J. On May 21, 1841, he married Louise Mercer Frelinghuysen, a daughter of Gen. John Frelinghuysen, by whom he had eleven children. During the Somerville years he dabbled surreptitiously in Whig politics, writing political editorials for a local newspaper. In December 1849 he became one of the ministers of the Collegiate Reformed Church in New York City, which he served till the end of his life. The sudden death of his wife in 1892 visibly weakened his hold on mortality, and he succumbed to pneumonia on Feb. 3, 1896.

His ministry of over half a century was active and influential. Although diligent in discharging his pastoral duties, he was chiefly interested in scholarship. He was a good linguist, with a mastery of Hebrew that made him for ten years a member of the Old Testament Company of the American Committee on the Revision of the English Bible, and with a knowledge of numerous other languages that helped him materially as chairman of the committee on versions of the American Bible Society. He was well versed in theology and in church history, and for short periods taught at Union, Lane, Alleghany, Hartford, and New Brunswick Theological Seminaries. In 1863 he was president of the General Synod of the Reformed Church. Together with Philip Schaff and James McCosh he helped to organize the Alliance of Reformed Churches Holding the Presbyterian System; in 1884 he became chairman of the Western Section and in 1892 president of the Alliance. Although his books are few and unimportant, he was a prolific writer of articles on theological and ecclesiastical topics. In his theology he was a thorough-going conservative, believing unreservedly in the integrity and sufficiency of the Bible as the revelation of God's will, and holding to the doctrines of his church as they were formulated in the early years of the Reformation. Thus cherishing the faith of his fathers, he would have seen no reproach in the fact that he displayed no originality of thought. His conservatism also manifested itself in more personal forms. He was the last minister of the Collegiate Church to maintain the use of the *exordium remotum* in the Sunday morning service, and the last to wear a dress-coat on the street in the daytime. As a divine of a now vanishing type, able, learned, devout, kind, and generous, he deserved the affection and veneration in which he was held.

[E. T. Corwin, *Manual of the Reformed Ch. in America* (4th ed., 1902); *Acts and Proc. of the 90th Regular Session of the General Synod of the Reformed Ch. in America,* June 1896, pp. 496–99; E. B. Coe, *Discourse Commemorative of the Rev. Talbot Wilson Chambers* (1896); J. P. Searle, "The Rev. Talbot Wilson Chambers," in *Presbyt. and Reformed Rev.,* VII, 577–94; bibliographies in Coe and Corwin.]   G. H. G.

CHAMPLAIN, SAMUEL de (*c.* 1567–Dec. 25, 1635), explorer and founder of Canada, was the son of a naval captain, Antoine Champlain, and his wife Marguérite, née Le Roy. He was born at Brouage in Saintonge (now Charente Inférieure), at present a neglected hamlet ten miles from Rochefort on the Bay of Biscay but in the latter half of the sixteenth century an important port, frequented by many vessels from overseas. All we know of Champlain's early life is that he eagerly listened to tales of the New World, and had a vivid curiosity to see the transAtlantic lands, of which he heard so much. He also had a good, practical education, was well versed in navigation, and was posted on the discoveries being made by Spanish and English vessels on the high seas. He was early drawn into the vortex of the religious wars of France,—for Brouage was the prize contended for by both Huguenot and Catholic leaguers, at one time sustaining a siege of several months, and being fortified after capture by Condé, the great Huguenot

leader. By 1589 Champlain was serving in the army of Henry of Navarre, and later joined the naval arm of Navarre's forces. Finally when peace came and the treaty of Vervins was signed in 1598, Champlain's coveted opportunity came. An uncle was chosen to pilot home a Spanish contingent in the ship *St. Julien,* and took his nephew with him. In Spain the vessel was impressed to accompany the annual Spanish flotilla to New Spain, and Champlain was selected as its commander. The Spanish as a rule excluded foreigners from their overseas possessions; this was, therefore, an unusual opportunity for a Frenchman, and one of which Champlain took full advantage. The fleet left San Lucar in January 1599, and the *St. Julien* was absent from Spain for two years and eight months; its commander visited the West Indies, Mexico, Cartagena, and the Isthmus of Panama. At the latter place he remarked on the utility of a possible canal. He made careful observations and drawings of the plants, animals, and products of New Spain, and upon his return to France drew up an elaborate report for the King. (The manuscript of this report with the original illustrations is now in the John Carter Brown Library, Providence, R. I.)

Henry IV was pleased with Champlain's observations, and gave him a pension and a patent of nobility, so that he was thereafter the Sieur de Champlain. The King also persuaded his young subject to join a French expedition setting forth to explore in the region discovered by French navigators two generations earlier. Although several of his projects had come to naught, the King, interested not only in exploration but in colonization, was eager to have Champlain attempt another. The voyage of 1603 was a preparatory one. Champlain accompanied a furtrading expedition, which under the patronage of Aymer de Chastes, governor of Dieppe, was sailing to the Gulf of St. Lawrence under command of François Gravé, Sieur du Pont (usually called Pontgravé). After reaching Tadoussac, at the mouth of the Saguenay, where Pontgravé had already established a post, and where many natives came from the interior bringing rich furs to trade, Champlain in a pinnace ascended the St. Lawrence River, noting its natural features and its availability for a colony. He was stopped by the Lachine Rapids, but not before he had heard from Indian comrades of the great bodies of water lying at the source of the river, a report which stimulated his desire to explore interior North America. Upon his return to France in the autumn he published his first book entitled *Des Sauvages,* descriptive both of his voyage and of the inhabitants of the St. Lawrence Valley.

Chastes, the patron of the North American enterprise, had died during the summer of 1603, but the King found for the enterprise another patron in Sieur de Monts, a Huguenot noble of Champlain's own province of Saintonge. Monts was determined to found a colony in a more genial climate than that of the St. Lawrence, and, despite Champlain's protests, he directed the expedition of 1604 to a more southerly region. The first colony was founded on Douchet Island in the mouth of the St. Croix River, New Brunswick, and, that proving unhealthful, the entire enterprise was transferred in 1605 to Port Royal near the modern Annapolis Royal, Nova Scotia. Champlain was the steadying influence in the little group of exiles which maintained a precarious hold on this shore until 1607; he founded the Order of Good Company, and by his example and good cheer kept the colony alive. During these years, also, he made three exploring expeditions along the coast of New England. In the first he discovered and named Mount Desert Island, and ascended the Penobscot to the site of Bangor. In 1605 he went farther along the coast, discovered the Kennebec, Androscoggin, and Saco Rivers, sighted the White Mountains from Casco Bay, passed Cape Ann and entered Plymouth Harbor —which he named for St. Louis—and finally turned back from Nauset Harbor on Cape Cod. His third survey followed the track of the second, going as far as Stage Harbor off Vineyard Sound, where a hostile attack by the natives forced the French navigators to return to Nova Scotia.

In 1608 Champlain attained the wish of his heart when he persuaded the King to permit him to found a colony on the St. Lawrence. He and Pontgravé sailed in the ship Le Don de Dieu, and on July 3 Champlain laid the foundation of what proved to be the first permanent French colony in America, at Quebec. In what he called the "habitation," with twenty-eight companions, he spent the ensuing winter. In the spring he was visited by a group of Huron Indians on their way to attack their enemies the Iroquois, in central New York. Champlain consented to accompany them and on the way entered the beautiful lake that still bears his name. There, on July 30, 1609, occurred the first clash with the Iroquois, in which the French firearms put them to flight.

The assassination of Henry IV in 1610 recalled Champlain to France, where he was obliged to make new arrangements to sustain his colony and his own personal fortune. In behalf of the latter, he entered late in 1610 into a marriage contract with Hélène Boullé, twelve-year-old daughter of one of the royal secretaries. Because of the youth of the bride it was stipulated that she should remain some time with her parents. She finally came to Quebec with her husband, and passed there four years, 1616–20, after which she separated from Champlain, and ultimately entered a French convent. They never had children. Hélène Champlain's name is retained by St. Helen Island, south of Montreal, which her husband named in her honor. For the colony Champlain arranged a new charter, taken out in 1611, and found for Canada a royal patron in the person of the Prince de Condé. He then determined to undertake explorations westward and to find if possible a route to the western sea. One of his subordinates, whom he had left among the Indians, came to France with the story of a journey to the northern ocean, and in 1613 Champlain set forth to ascertain the truth of this report. He advanced up the Ottawa River, noting its rapids and portages, as far as Morrison Island, where was the Indian village his man had previously visited. There he learned to his sorrow that he had been deceived, and that his informant had never been beyond this point. He learned here, however, more of the inland lakes and planned to explore them at his first opportunity.

This came in 1615 when he accompanied a band of Huron Indians to their home on Georgian Bay. As he had been preceded to Huronia by several traders and a Recollect missionary all of the Great Lakes had been seen by white men before him; he was, however, the first to describe, map, and name Lake Huron, and may well be called its discoverer. He reached it by the Ottawa River, Lake Nipissing, and its outlet into Georgian Bay, and called it La Mer Douce, the Fresh Sea. Coasting southward along the bay to the Huron habitat he encountered Ottawa Indians, whom, because of the crests they wore, he spoke of as the "Nation of the Staring Hairs." Arrived at Huronia he was welcomed with acclaim, and soon set out with his Indian allies on another excursion against the Iroquois. Leaving the Huron villages, Sept. 1, the war party passed southeastward to Lake Ontario, which Champlain named "Great Lake of the Entouhonorons," and recognized as the source of the St. Lawrence.

The party then crossed the eastern end of the lake and went inland along the Oneida River until on Oct. 10 they came in sight of an Iroquois fort, located probably on Nichols Pond, Madison County, N. Y. A siege began, in which after desperate fighting—Champlain being severely wounded by poisoned arrows—the French and Hurons were repulsed. They rapidly retreated by the way they had come, and although

Champlain had planned to go to Quebec via the St. Lawrence, his wounded condition made it necessary for him to accompany the Hurons home. There he recovered during the winter, and explored for some distance beyond Huronia to the west. After returning to France in 1616 he embodied his knowledge of the Great Lakes in a map, which was published with the edition of his *Voyages* in 1632.

This voyage of 1615–16 marks the extent of Champlain's personal explorations. Thenceforward he devoted himself to the upbuilding of the colony of New France, and to its economic and agricultural development. From 1620 to 1624 he remained in Canada, and in 1625 succeeded in interesting Cardinal Richelieu in France's overseas domain so that two years later this minister formed the Company of One Hundred Associates to provide and equip colonists for New France. Meanwhile Champlain succeeded in making a treaty of alliance with the formidable Iroquois, and all promised well for the colony's progress. Suddenly, while France and England were engaged in a petty war, a fleet of British freebooters descended upon the St. Lawrence and captured Quebec. Champlain and all his officials were transported. During his exile of four years (1629–33) in Europe, he brought out the final edition of his *Voyages*.

In 1632 France and England signed the treaty of St. Germain by which Canada was restored to the French Crown. Early in the succeeding year Champlain returned as governor of his colony, never more to leave it during life. His arrival was hailed with acclaim both by colonists and tribesmen. With the latter he rebuilt his alliances and arranged in 1634 to send his envoy Jean Nicolet to explore the West. Nicolet's return the next year, with the news of the discovery of Lake Michigan and Green Bay, cheered the veteran governor. By this expedition New France was extended westward many leagues. This was the last important act of Champlain's administration. His death on Christmas Day was deplored by the entire colony, for he had no enemies. He was buried in a new chapel of the parish church of Quebec.

As none of the so-called portraits of Champlain are authentic, we have no knowledge of his physical appearance. His characteristics appear in his writings: he was simple, sincere, and steadfast, without ostentation or pride; he preferred life in the open to that of courts, yet he was no mean courtier and was respected by king and nobles alike. His appreciation of the natives of America was deep and sincere, and by his sympathy for them he had much influence over the savages. His vision and foresight for the colony's needs earned for him the title of Father of New France.

[Champlain's writings were voluminous and appeared at frequent intervals during his lifetime. After *Des Sauvages* describing his voyage of 1603, appeared *Les Voyages du Sieur de Champlain* (Paris, 1613), in which was included his map of 1612. *Voyages et Descouvertes faites en la Nouvelle France* (Paris, 1619), carried his account to 1618. While in exile from his colony (1629–33) he prepared a third volume entitled: *Les Voyages de la Nouvelle France Occidentale dicte Canada . . . depuis l'an 1603 jusques en l'an 1629* (Paris, 1632), including a map of the St. Lawrence and its sources. He also wrote a treatise on navigation entitled *Traitté de la Marine et du Devoir d'un bon Marinier de la Navigation.* His *Brief Discours* of his West Indies voyage was not published until the 19th century. *Œuvres de Champlain*, edited by Abbé C. H. Laverdière (6 vols., Quebec, 1870) is the standard edition. *The Works of Samuel de Champlain* published by the Champlain Society (Toronto, 1922–27) contains the French text and English translation. His biographers are C. W. Colby, *The Founder of New France* (Toronto, 1915); Edwin A. Dix, *Champlain* (N. Y., 1903); Ralph Flenley, *Samuel de Champlain* (Toronto, 1924); Gabriel Gravier, *Vie de Samuel Champlain* (Paris, 1900).]   L. P. K.

CHAMPLIN, JOHN DENISON (Jan. 29, 1834–Jan. 8, 1915), editor, author, traced his ancestry to Geoffrey Champlin who settled at Newport, R. I., in 1638. He was the son of John Denison and Sylvia (Bostwick) Champlin. The name Denison, borne by his father and himself, was derived from William Denison, of Bishop Stortford, Hertfordshire, England.

He received his early education at the Hopkins Grammar School, New Haven, Conn., whence he entered Yale College in 1852, graduating in 1856. With a strong leaning toward law, he began its study in the office of Gideon H. Hollister at Litchfield, Conn., where in 1859 he was admitted to the bar. After practising for a time in Milwaukee, he became a member of the law firm of Hollister, Cross, & Champlin in New York City, whither Hollister had removed. Champlin's literary interests were, however, already gaining the ascendency, and he collaborated in the writing of a tragedy, *Thomas à Becket* (1866), produced by Edwin Booth in New Orleans in 1861. After a period of free-lancing, in 1864 he became associate editor of the Bridgeport *Evening Standard*. Finding himself hampered in his work by his associates, he decided to remove to Litchfield, and start a paper of his own. So in 1865 he established the *Litchfield Sèntinel*, a weekly newspaper devoted to Democratic interests. After four years, he sold this paper in order to remove to New York and engage in other literary enterprises. From the Journal of J. F. Loubart, he wrote a *Narrative of the Mission to Russia, in 1866, of the Honorable Gustavus Vasa Fox,* which occupied him during the years 1872–73. Toward the end of the latter year, he became one of the revisers of the *American Cyclopædia,* becoming associate editor in 1875, especially in charge of the maps and engravings. Between the years 1878 and 1881 he originated and edited a series of Young Folk's Cyclopædias covering common things, persons and places, astronomy and history. Going to Europe in 1884, he accompanied Andrew Carnegie on a coaching trip along the south coast of England, and this he described in his *Chronicle of the Coach* (1886). In conjunction with Arthur E. Bostwick, he published the *Young Folk's Cyclopædia of Games and Sports* in 1890. As an editor of books he was first engaged by Charles Scribner's Sons, producing for that firm the *Cyclopædia of Painters and Paintings* (1886–87) and the *Cyclopædia of Music and Musicians* (1888–90). He then joined the editorial staff of the *Standard Dictionary* (1892–94). In 1901 he added to the Young Folk's Cyclopædia series a volume on *Literature and Art,* and in 1905 one on *Natural History.* In 1910 he edited the *Orations, Addresses, and Speeches of Chauncey M. Depew.* His "One Hundred Allied Families of the Seventeenth Century in England and New England," and "Anne Hutchinson : Her Life, Her Ancestry and Her Descendants," both written in 1912, remained unpublished. He was married, on Oct. 8, 1873, to Franka Eliza, daughter of Capt. George M. Colvocoresses [*q.v.*], of the United States Navy.

[*Records of the Colony of R. I. and Providence Plantations,* I, 91; "John Denison Champlin," by his son John D. Champlin, Jr. in *N. Y. Geneal. and Biog. Record,* Oct. 1915; *Records of the Class of 1856 of Yale College* (1878, 1892); *Obit. Record of Grads. of Yale Univ.* (1915); *Who's Who in America,* 1914–15.]

F. H. V.

CHAMPLIN, JOHN WAYNE (Feb. 7, 1831–July 24, 1901), jurist, was a descendant in the direct line of Geoffrey Champlin, who, coming from England to Rhode Island, settled at Newport. John's father, Jeffrey Champlin, married Ellis Champlin, a member of a collateral branch of the family, and resided at Kingston, Ulster County, N. Y., where John was born. Shortly afterward the family moved to a farm at Harpersfield, Delaware County, where John spent his early youth, attending the village school in winter and working on the farm in the summer. In 1844 he went to Stamford Grammar School, proceeding later to Rhinebeck and Harpersfield Academies, and then taking a course of civil engineering at Delaware Literary Institute, Franklin, N. Y. In 1852 he began to practise as a civil engineer in Delaware County but two years later, seeking a wider field, joined his brother Stephen G. Champlin in Grand Rapids, Mich., and took up the study of law in the latter's office. On his admission to the Michigan bar in June 1855 he commenced practise in Grand Rapids, with which city he continued associated for the remainder of his life. Evincing at the outset a deep interest in municipal problems he was retained in 1856 to draft the charter of the City of Grand Rapids which was passed by the legislature in the following year. Champlin was also appointed city solicitor in 1857, continuing as such for three years, in the course of which he became recognized as the leading authority in the state on the subject of municipal law and practise. He retired in 1861 and became judge of the recorder's court of Grand Rapids, retaining that position for two years. In 1863 he was an unsuccessful candidate for the position of circuit judge, but in 1864 was elected prosecuting attorney for Kent County and as such displayed great efficiency and impartiality. In 1867 he was elected mayor of Grand Rapids on the Democratic ticket. During his tenure of office he incurred great unpopularity by opposing the issue of bonds of the city for the purpose of bonusing railways, and failed of reëlection, but was subsequently vindicated by the supreme court of Michigan which pronounced the city's action unconstitutional. In 1883 he was nominated by the Fusion party for the office of justice of the supreme court, was elected by a large vote, and took his seat on the bench, Jan. 1, 1884. Becoming chief justice in 1890, he retired, Dec. 31, 1891, and resumed practise in Grand Rapids. In 1892 he was appointed professor in the law department of the University of Michigan where he lectured on corporations and torts, but resigned in 1896. He died at Grand Rapids, July 24, 1901. He was married to Ellen, daughter of John B. More of Roxbury, N. Y.

In legal circles he was esteemed as a competent, conscientious, careful judge, though not distinguished by any deep learning except in relation to municipal law, in which he was an expert. His opinions were marked by extreme clarity of thought, and both at the bar and as a judge he was the essence of courtesy, exhibiting marvelous patience on the bench in listening to arguments of counsel. Politically, he was a Democrat, but never extreme in his convictions, and he supported the Lincoln administration in its war measures. In his later years he abstained from active participation in public affairs.

[*Mag. of Western Hist.,* IV, 692; *City of Grand Rapids and Kent County, Mich. up to Date* (1900), p. 25; *Green Bag,* II, 394; 91 *Mich.,* 47; *Grand Rapids Herald,* July 25, 1901.]

H. W. H. K.

CHAMPLIN, STEPHEN (Nov. 17, 1789–Feb. 20, 1870), naval officer, was born at South Kingston, R. I. His father, Stephen, had served in the Revolution, probably at sea, and his mother Elizabeth Perry was an aunt of Commodores O. H. and M. C. Perry [qq.v.]. About 1795 the family moved to a farm near Lebanon, Conn., where Stephen worked and went to school till he was sixteen, when he ran away to sea. By 1812 he had risen to captain and made numerous voyages, one with his cousin Oliver Perry, a midshipman on leave. When war was declared he became a sailing master in the navy, May 22, 1812, serving in Perry's gunboats at Newport and then accompanying him to the Great Lakes in February 1813. As second in command of the *Asp* on Lake Ontario he engaged in the expeditions against York and Fort George. In command of the small, fast schooner *Scorpion* (2 guns) at the battle of Lake Erie, he was in the van throughout the action and in the thick of the fighting, firing the first shot and also the last. His narrative of the battle, in strong support of Perry, figures in the literature of the Perry-Elliott controversy. The *Scorpion* was later engaged in transporting Harrison's army to Malden and accompanying it up the Thames; and during the winter Champlin had charge of the prizes *Detroit* and *Queen Charlotte* at Put-in-Bay. In command of the *Tigress* he took part in the unsuccessful attack on Mackinac, Aug. 4, 1814, and was afterward left to blockade the post. On the night of Sept. 3 an overwhelming enemy force in batteaux and canoes surprised and captured his schooner in the St. Mary's River. Though perhaps negligent in permitting the surprise, Champlin and his men defended their vessel vigorously, all the officers being wounded, and Champlin receiving a canister shot through the thigh, shattering the bone. After detention for thirty-eight days, with great suffering, he was paroled to Erie, and thence went to Connecticut, arriving in March 1815. During 1816–18 he commanded the *Porcupine* on the upper lakes, surveying the Canadian boundary. Thereafter, owing to recurrent trouble from his wound, he saw little active service, living in Connecticut until 1834 and then in Buffalo. For a month in 1828 he was attached to the steam battery *Fulton* in New York; in 1838 during the "Patriot War" he commanded two steamers, operating to prevent movement of armed men into Canada; and in 1845–48 he commanded the lake station ship *Michigan*. He remained on the active list until 1855, being promoted lieutenant, Dec. 9, 1814, captain, 1850, and commodore, retired, 1867. At his death he was the last

officer survivor of the battle of Lake Erie. He was a stout, thickset man, thoroughly upright in character, strictly abstemious, simple and rather rough in manner and dress. Generally esteemed, he was spoken of for mayor of Buffalo, but declined the nomination because of his naval position. He was married to Minerva L. Pomeroy of Buffalo on Jan. 5, 1817, and was survived by three sons and two daughters.

[Geo. Clinton, in *Buffalo Hist. Soc. Pubs.*, VIII, 381 ff., an excellent sketch based on Champlin's private papers; the "Dobbins Papers" in the same volume; Usher Parsons, "Brief Sketches of the Officers Who Were in the Battle of Lake Erie," in *New Eng. Hist. and Geneal. Reg.*, Jan. 1863; J. B. Lossing, *Pictorial Field-Book of the War of 1812* (see index).]   A. W.

CHAMPNEY, BENJAMIN (Nov. 17, 1817–Dec. 11, 1907), painter, born at New Ipswich, N. H., was one of the seven children of Ebenezer and Rebecca (Brooks) Champney. The father, a lawyer, died young, leaving his widow poor. Benjamin at the age of ten was sent to an aunt at Lebanon, N. H., where he attended the district school twelve weeks each winter and worked in a cotton-mill forty weeks. After four years he returned to his mother and entered Appleton Academy, intending to take advantage of a West Point cadetship promised him by Franklin Pierce, then a representative. "Like many other congressmen he made too many promises," Champney afterward wrote of Pierce. Disappointed, the boy obtained a clerkship with Henry L. Daggett, a Boston shoe-dealer. From the shop's back window he looked into a lithographer's studio where he saw artists and engravers at work. For years he had drawn pictures and he was now emboldened to think of this as a means of livelihood. He went one day into the lithographic place, but, receiving only discouragement, resumed selling shoes. A little later, however, Robert Cooke, head draftsman at the lithographer's, took a room at Champney's boarding-house and the two became friends. Cooke directed Champney's drawing and aided him in securing admittance as an apprentice in Moore's lithographic establishment. Here Champney did commercial work, having among his associates William Rimmer [q.v.]. Then, together with Cooke, he opened a studio for portraiture. The two had success, and saved money for study abroad, sailing May 1, 1841. At Paris they studied with Boudin, and copied at the Louvre. Champney became friendly with J. F. Kensett and the veteran John Vanderlyn, the latter employing him as assistant in painting "The Landing of Columbus," for the Capitol at Washington. Kensett and Champney made trips to Fontainebleau, where they painted from nature, then an unusual practise. Champney exhibited in the Salon and sent to Boston copies from old masters which were sold. In 1846 he returned to America in the *Anglo-Saxon*, wrecked off Nova Scotia. After a brief stay, he sailed back to Europe with W. Allan Gay to paint a panorama of the Rhine. Though interrupted by the political upheaval of 1848 they finished the gigantic piece which was exhibited in 1849 at the Horticultural Building, Boston. It was financially unsuccessful and in 1853 was destroyed in the Crystal Palace fire in New York. Turning his attention to landscape, Champney in 1850 discovered North Conway, N. H., as painting ground. He was joined by Kensett, Alfred Ordway, and others. "By 1853," he wrote, "the meadows and banks of the Saco were dotted all about with white umbrellas." In 1853 he married Mary C. Brooks and bought at North Conway a house which was their summer home. Their winters were spent at Woburn. In 1855 Champney was one of the founders of the Boston Art Club, of which he became president in 1856 and in whose exhibitions he was frequently represented. His later life was quiet and uneventful. As a painter he followed the formula of the so-called Hudson River school which lost its vogue in the late nineteenth century. He was a catholic critic of other artists' work,— an admirer of the Barbizon painters long before their merits were generally appreciated and of Claude Monet before the impressionists' theory of values was popularly understood. He is well represented at the Boston Art Club and the Woburn Public Library.

[Champney's autobiographical *Sixty Years' Memories of Art and Artists* (1900), and the *Boston Post*, Dec. 12, 1907.]   F. W. C.

CHAMPNEY, JAMES WELLS (July 16, 1843–May 1, 1903), painter, illustrator, a son of James H. and Sarah (Wells) Champney, was born at Boston where when he was sixteen years old he was apprenticed to a wood engraver. He enlisted in the 45th Massachusetts Volunteers and saw service at Gettysburg. After the war he taught drawing at Dr. Dio Lewis's school in Lexington, Mass., and then, in 1866, went to Paris, where he studied with Edouard Frère, a genre painter. He had also a year at Antwerp under Van Lerius. He exhibited in the 1869 Salon, signing his pictures "Champ" to distinguish himself from the other American Champneys. Back in Boston in 1870, he returned to France in 1871 in time to witness the excitement of the Commune. He then made a sketching tour of Germany which included studies of the Passion Play at Ober-Ammergau,—

a topic on which he afterward lectured. In 1873 he accompanied Edward King to make drawings for a series of *Scribner's Monthly* articles on the "Great South." They traveled about 20,000 miles and Champney did more than 500 sketches. During the same year he married Elizabeth Williams. As illustrator and war correspondent he visited the camp of Don Carlos, then campaigning for the Spanish crown. In 1877 he accepted the professorship of art at Smith College, a position which he held seven years. For *Scribner's* he made a sketching tour of South America in 1878, illustrating articles by Herbert Smith. He directed the art classes of the Hartford Society of Decorative Art, and maintained a winter studio at New York. In 1885 he began to make pastel portraits, having among his sitters Hon. John Bigelow, Henry M. Stanley, William Winter, and many theatrical people. He was represented at the Chicago Exposition, 1893, by his portraits of the Rev. Robert Collyer, Miss Suzanna Sheldon, and his wife. He painted many "translations" into pastel of famous masterpieces in the European galleries. In 1898 he did important decorations for the Hotel Manhattan, New York. As a painter he was one of the first Americans to understand and apply the theory of "values" which the French impressionists, Manet, Monet, and others, had developed. Among pastellists he was ranked in his own day with Whistler and Robert Blum.

[S. G. W. Benjamin, *Our Am. Artists* (1881), pp. 32–35; G. C. de Soisson, "J. Wells Champney, an Am. Pastellist," in the *Artist*, XXIX, 159–61.]   F. W. C.

CHANCHE, JOHN MARY JOSEPH (Oct. 4, 1795–July 22, 1852), first Roman Catholic bishop of Natchez, Miss., was the son of John Chanche, a merchant and, it was said, a man of considerable wealth, who, fleeing from the negro disturbances in San Domingo, came to Baltimore with his wife Catherine Provost. There John Mary Joseph was born. He entered St. Mary's College at the age of eleven and presently joined the Sulpician community which conducted it, receiving Holy Orders at Baltimore, June 5, 1819. Following some years of teaching he was made vice-president and, in 1834, president of his alma mater. After twice refusing nomination as bishop-coadjutor of eastern sees, he accepted (Dec. 15, 1840) appointment to the newly-erected diocese of Natchez. Soon after his consecration at Baltimore by Archbishop Eccleston, Mar. 14, 1841, he set out for the South. Though the church in Mississippi was then over a century old and had received the support of the Spanish government probably until 1791, its state was such that Bishop Chanche virtually had to found it anew. The land and buildings in Natchez with which Spain had provided the mission had been lost when the American government took possession of the region, probably because title to them had been vested in the Spanish government. No claim was entered until Bishop Chanche came in May 1841. The search for evidence of ecclesiastical right to these properties led the bishop to Cuba in 1844 and to other parts of Spanish America. He presented the evidence which he discovered to Congress and petitioned that the church be indemnified in money or in lands of equal extent or value with those originally granted. His petition was never returned. Bishop Chanche was, however, too practical a man to wait the issue of this claim. He drew immediately on funds which the Association for the Propagation of the Faith had prior to his coming annually deposited with the bishop of New Orleans for the support of the Natchez mission. He solicited contributions from European missionary societies. He pressed the congregation which had led a precarious existence at Natchez during the American period. His determination to succeed was plainly stated in his first address to it the day after his arrival. "If I meet encouragement I will stay with you; if not I seek a home elsewhere. I am not bound to Natchez, but to the state of Mississippi." His success may be concretely measured by the progress of his cathedral, in its day a large church, and noted for its Gothic architectural beauty. The corner-stone of the edifice was laid on Feb. 28, 1842, and it was dedicated on Christmas Day. At this time however Bishop Chanche had but two priests and a hundred communicants. The Catholic population was thinly distributed over about fifty thousand square miles of territory. When he died he had eleven priests, and he had laid the foundations of an educational system that would indirectly develop vocations. In 1848 he had introduced Sisters of Charity from Emmitsburg, Md., and they promptly opened a school and presently an orphan asylum in Natchez. In the state at large there were on his death eleven churches and seventeen attendant missions, and missionary activity among the negroes also was well under way. Returning to Natchez from the First Plenary Council of Baltimore, of which he had been an earnest promoter, Bishop Chanche fell ill of cholera morbus, and died at Frederick City, Md., July 22, 1852. His was a tall and commanding figure, graceful and dignified of carriage, and an attractive and winning personality, urbane and cultivated of manner.

[See John G. Shea, *Hist. of the Cath. Ch. in the U. S.* (1892), IV, 275–79; Richard Henry Clarke, *Lives of the Deceased Bishops of the Cath. Ch. in the U. S.* (1872), II, 166–90; Francis Janssens, *Sketch of the Cath. Ch. in the City of Natchez . . .* (1886); *Metropolitan Cath. Almanac and Laity's Directory . . . 1853* (1852). The *Am. Cath. Hist. Researches* (1884) printed Bishop Chanche's memorial to Congress (IV, 146–47) and other items relating to the Natchez mission prior to his coming (IV, 147–51; XIX, 64; XX, 48). Scattered data of value may be found in the *Catholic Almanac* for 1853, and the *Annalen der Verbreitung des Glaubens* (Einsiedeln-Mainz, 1832).] F.J.T.

CHANDLER, CHARLES FREDERICK (Dec. 6, 1836–Aug. 25, 1925), industrial chemist, was born in Lancaster, Mass., in the house of his grandfather, and his boyhood was spent with his parents, Charles and Sarah (Whitney) Chandler, at New Bedford, Mass., where his father owned and conducted a dry-goods store. A few lectures by Louis Agassiz that he heard as a boy aroused his scientific curiosity, and at the age of sixteen he was a student of chemistry at the Lawrence Scientific School of Harvard University. As a youth he had been diligent in making chemical experiments and in collecting minerals, and when in 1855, acting on the advice of Charles A. Joy, professor of chemistry at Union College, he sailed for Europe to study under Woehler at Göttingen, he took his collection with him, having learned that it would be likely to interest Woehler. This Yankee shrewdness, together with Chandler's earnestness and personal attractiveness, soon won for him the favor of being made Woehler's private assistant for the semester. He then went to Berlin to study analytical chemistry under Heinrich Rose, whose private assistant he became, while also studying mineralogy under Gustav Rose. Later he returned to Göttingen where he obtained his doctorate. Coming home, he first sought consulting practise in New Bedford among the whale-oil merchants, but could not make a living at it. He offered an article to the *Scientific American* on the preparation and use for lamps of mineral oil obtained from shale in Scotland, but it was rejected on the ground that the use of mineral oil in lamps was too fantastic a notion for publication. He then heard that Prof. Joy needed an assistant at Union College, and he made the journey thither to apply for the post in person, only to learn that, while Prof. Joy did need an assistant the trustees had decided to secure a janitor instead. So Chandler accepted the position of janitor at a wage of $400 a year, swept and cleaned the laboratory before and after hours, and meanwhile acted as Prof. Joy's assistant during the day. As a side issue, the janitor taught mineralogy. Soon fortune rewarded him. Prof. Joy was called to Columbia College, and the twenty-year-old janitor became full professor of chemistry.

Chandler had a tiger's appetite for work. He taught chemistry (including assaying), geology, and mineralogy; he made an outstanding collection of minerals; and for eight years he did important consulting work in regard to water supplies and other subjects at Schenectady. In 1864 he was invited by Prof. Egleston, theretofore a mining engineer, to join him in establishing a school of mines at Columbia. Professors were to get their living from tuition fees, and $3,000 had been raised to equip the laboratories. This, in 1864, was the beginning of the Columbia School of Mines, of which Chandler was dean for many years. On Prof. Joy's death he took over his work for the College, remaining at the head of the department of chemistry at Columbia after it became a university, until his retirement in 1910.

Few teachers have exercised so great an influence on so many students. They were like sons to him, he was jealous for their welfare, was always available for advice and help, and constantly took the position that to study chemistry was easy and intensely interesting rather than hard or dull. He worked day and night with extraordinary intensity, and yet never seemed hurried. And he regarded physical science as the grandest sport of his day. At the time of his retirement grateful alumni established in his honor the Chandler Lectureship and the Chandler medal for research in chemistry.

Chandler's work at Columbia, however, was only a small part of his total achievement. The New York College of Pharmacy, then a struggling little school, had no one to teach chemistry, and no money to pay for it. Chandler gave the lectures and laboratory instruction at nights, free, until the school grew and could pay. Later he became president of the College of Pharmacy which was eventually taken over by Columbia. In 1866 he had an income of $1,500 a year and he needed more. Without giving up any of his teaching, paid or unpaid, he engaged with Booth & Edgar, sugar refiners, to do their chemical work and conduct research as to improvement in their methods. This he did from 6 to 8 a. m. daily in a laboratory in the refinery at King and West Sts., some four or five miles distant from Columbia. Thus he doubled his income to $3,000 a year. In 1872 the College of Physicians and Surgeons invited him to become adjunct professor of chemistry. Soon he was made full professor of chemistry and also professor of medical jurisprudence.

He became a leading authority on water supplies, sanitation, oil refining, and assaying. The system of assay weights now in general use, whereby the amount of metal in a ton of ore is easily and quickly computed in grams or ounces, was worked out by him in 1866. He served the United States government on many commissions, but his outstanding public service was to New York City as president of its Board of Health. In 1866 members of the Board had asked him to make scientific studies of their sanitary problems. They had no appropriation for the purpose, but that did not deter the young professor, who was then but twenty-nine years of age, working from six to eight every morning in the laboratory of a sugar refinery, struggling all day to build up the School of Mines, and lecturing and teaching several nights a week without pay at the College of Pharmacy. In time a modest honorarium was appropriated by the city for his services, and in 1873 he was appointed to the presidency of the Board by Mayor Havemeyer, the appointment being renewed for a term of six years more by Mayor Ely in 1877. Chandler immediately addressed himself to the food and water supplies of the city, the adulteration of liquors, poisonous cosmetics, and gas nuisances. The water was good, foods were fair, adulteration of liquors less than anticipated, but poisonous cosmetics, kerosene accidents, and gas nuisances were common. Milk he found generally adulterated with one-third water after some of the cream had been removed. He established flash-point tests for kerosene and reduced lamp explosions in such a marked degree that he was invited to appear before the House of Lords to enlighten the British government on the subject. His war against milk adulteration and his subsequent control of the supply was probably the hardest battle of his life, but he succeeded and became a pioneer in municipal milk control. He fought the gas companies and made them put a stop to their nuisances. Another battle against offenses was with slaughterhouses and rendering establishments, and still other difficult undertakings were the control of contagious diseases and the establishment of compulsory vaccination. He reduced the child death rate so as to save 5,000 young lives annually. Plumbing was crude and very defective. He designed the flush closet now in general use and made no attempt to patent the idea, giving it to the plumbing trade in the hope of more healthful homes. He was, as Elihu Root said, "one of the most effective crusaders of his time in behalf of the public good." Eminent as a sanitarian, he was equally eminent as an industrial chemist. He established the 66° Baumé test for sulphuric acid when standards were in a state of conspicuous confusion, and in the early development of the petroleum industry he was the foremost consultant in America. In 1920 the Perkin Medal of the Society of Chemical Industries was conferred on him because he had made "such valuable contributions to applied chemistry" as to place the entire world in his debt.

Chandler was married twice. His only child, the first wife of the present Viscount Exmouth, died before him.

[*Columbia Alumni News,* June 15, 1926, being the Chandler Memorial Number; *Industrial and Engineering Chem.,* Oct. 1925; *N. Y. Times,* Aug. 26, 1925.]

E.H.

CHANDLER, ELIZABETH MARGARET (Dec. 24, 1807–Nov. 2, 1834), author, born at Centre, Del., was the youngest of the three children of Thomas Chandler, descended from English Quaker settlers along the Delaware River, and his wife, Margaret Evans of Burlington, N. J. Her mother died while Elizabeth was a baby, and Thomas Chandler removed to Philadelphia, where he placed his daughter in the care of her grandmother Evans. Elizabeth attended schools managed by the Society of Friends and was strictly trained in religion by her grandmother. When she was nine her father died, and this loss, combined with her religious education, made her unchildishly reflective. At thirteen she left school, but she had acquired the habits of reading and writing, which were her favorite occupations throughout her short life. Friends published some of her essays and poems, anonymously, for she was timid and feared publicity. At sixteen she was writing much for the press and her articles were copied by various newspapers. She had never cared for the amusements of her day and seldom went out except to meetings of the Friends. She had become much interested in philanthropy, especially in the anti-slavery cause, and most of her writing was now concerning the wrongs of slavery. Her best known poem, "The Slave Ship," published in the *Casket,* received a prize and was copied by Benjamin Lundy, editor of the *Genius of Universal Emancipation,* who asked its author to become a regular contributor. Many of her poems on slavery appeared in the *Genius,* among them "The Wife's Lament," "The Recaptured Slave," and "The Slave's Appeal." In 1829 she took charge of the "female department" of the *Genius,* where she soon published an "Appeal to the Ladies of the United States" concerning slavery, which is said to have caused some women to emancipate their slaves. In 1830 she went with her brother and aunt to make a new home in the Territory of Michigan. There on a farm, which they christened "Hazelbank," in Lenawee County, she continued by mail her editorial work for the *Genius.* Her work was interrupted by an illness, called

"remittent fever," which after some months ended in her death. A portrait of her shows a full oval face, with large dark eyes under heavy arching brows, dark hair piled high on her head, a bow mouth, and an expression of happy alertness not suggestive of her serious nature. Two volumes of her writings were published after her death: *Essays, Philanthropic and Moral* (1836) and *Poetical Works of Elizabeth Margaret Chandler; with a Memoir of Her Life and Character* (1836), by Benjamin Lundy. Her work is inspired by a burning moral purpose, but viewed as literature, her best poetry is not her slavery verse but that expressing her love of beauty and tenderness for associations, as in "The Brandywine," "Schuylkill," "The Sunset Hour," and "Summer Morning."

[Benj. Lundy, *ante*; Rufus W. Griswold, *The Female Poets of America* (1859); *Phila. Am. Sentinel,* Nov. 28, 1834.]

S.G.B.

CHANDLER, JOHN (Feb. 1, 1762–Sept. 25, 1841), soldier, senator, a descendant of William Chandler, who settled in Roxbury in 1637, and the son of Capt. Joseph and Lydia (Eastman) Chandler, was born in Epping, N. H. In 1777, a year after the death of his father, who was a veteran of the Seven Years' War and a soldier of the Revolution, Chandler enlisted in the patriot army for three months, participating in the battle of Saratoga. In January 1779 he joined the crew of the privateer *Arnold,* which was later captured by the British ship-of-war *Enterprise.* Chandler escaped from the prison ship on which he was confined and made his way home to New Hampshire. In 1780 he served a further term of six months in the army. Influenced by a fellow townsman and faithful friend who afterward was a great help to him in business, politics, and military affairs, he took part in the "Epping exodus" and purchased land in the plantation of Wales in the District of Maine (incorporated as the town of Monmouth in 1792). He settled there late in February 1784 with his wife, Mary Whittier (also spelled Whitcher) whom he had married on Aug. 28, 1783. In a community of poor men, he was perhaps the poorest, but by constant industry—shoeing horses, keeping tavern and store, building and operating sawmills, farming —he soon acquired a competence, shrewd practises, according to his neighbors, aiding his natural diligence and frugality. His scanty education had been added to after he reached manhood by studies under the local schoolmaster. He therefore filled acceptably various local offices, including those of postmaster and town clerk. During 1803, 1804, and 1819 he was a Massachusetts state senator, and in 1805 and 1806 a member of the national House of Representatives. As sheriff of Kennebec County, 1808–12 (John Chandler, *post*, p. 2), he performed with credit the difficult task of bringing harmony and order out of the animosities resulting from land controversies. Having all this time been a zealous member of the Massachusetts militia, in which he had risen to be major-general of the 17th Division, he resigned on Nov. 18, 1812, to accept a commission as brigadier-general in the United States Army. During the War of 1812 he served for the most part in New York and Upper Canada, being injured and captured in the battle of Stony Creek, June 6, 1813. His conduct during the battle was the cause of some controversy, from which he emerged with credit, although it cannot be said that his attainments as a military officer were exceptional. He was exchanged on Apr. 19, 1814, but his injuries, from which he suffered the remainder of his life, did not permit him to engage in service again until August, when he took charge of the United States forces in Maine. Later he had charge of the defenses of Portsmouth, N. H., performing his duties tactfully with due regard to militia politics. After the treaty of peace he retired from the army and returned to Monmouth to devote himself to business and politics. Influenced to favor the separation of Maine from Massachusetts by political considerations and by the dilatory conduct of Massachusetts while the coast of Maine was being ravaged in the war, he was a member of the convention which met at Portland, Oct. 11, 1819, to form the constitution of Maine. The first state legislature elected him and his political friend, John Holmes, to the United States Senate. In 1823 he was reëlected. As a Jacksonian he opposed internal improvements and the United States Bank. He took a prominent part, however, in the debate which resulted in the construction of the military road from the Penobscot River to Houlton, Me. He was also a member of the board of directors of the United States Branch Bank at Portland in 1829 and 1830. By appointment of President Jackson he served eight years as collector of customs for the district of Portland and Falmouth, declining reappointment at the age of seventy-five.

[The most important account of Chandler's life is his manuscript autobiography owned by the Me. Hist. Soc. Extracts from this have been printed with many changes in punctuation and grammar in the *Me. Hist. Soc. Colls.*, IX, 167–206. The references to Chandler in H. H. Cochrane's *Hist. of Monmouth and Wales* (1894), vol. I, *passim*, successfully counterbalance the fulsome eulogy of W. H. Smith in the *Granite Mo.*, VII, 5–12. Geo. Chandler's *Chandler Family* (1883), gives the Chandler ancestry in detail and contains a short sketch of John Chandler on pages 401–04.]　　　R. E. M.

CHANDLER, JOSEPH RIPLEY (Aug. 25, 1792–July 10, 1880), journalist, congressman, the son of Joseph and Saba (Ripley) Chandler of Kingston, Mass., was educated in the common schools of Kingston and at the University of Pennsylvania. He taught in the common schools for a time and in 1815 opened a seminary for young ladies in Philadelphia. This he conducted for a number of years. In 1822 he became editorial writer on the *Gazette of the United States,* the celebrated Federalist organ started in 1780 by John Fenno. In 1826, together with two others, Chandler purchased the paper (later merged with the *North American*), editing it until 1847 when he resigned because of ill health. From October 1843 to December 1849, he edited *Graham's American Monthly Magazine of Literature, Art and Fashion.* When Girard College was established, he became president of the first board of directors in 1848. The same year he published his *Grammar of the English Language* for use in the public schools. A Freemason from his early manhood, he had become Grand Master of Pennsylvania when in 1849 he was converted to Catholicism. The same year he was elected as a Clay Whig to Congress where he served three terms. In 1855 he delivered in the House a brilliant speech on "The Temporal Power of the Pope" (*Congressional Globe,* 33 Cong., 2 Sess., App.), which was an attack on the movement to deny full rights of citizenship to Roman Catholics. Abhorring religious intolerance, he delivered an equally commendable oration in 1855 at the celebration of the landing of "the Pilgrims of Maryland." Both speeches were published in book form. In 1858 he was appointed by President Buchanan minister to the Two Sicilies, where he remained for three years. On his return, he became deeply interested in a variety of philanthropic enterprises, especially in the reform of county prison conditions, personally visiting many prisons every year. In 1872, the Philadelphia Society for Alleviating the Miseries of Public Prisons sent him as representative to the international Congress in London. He visited many European penal establishments and upon his return wrote a most comprehensive report of the Congress, with discriminating criticism and explanatory remarks—all in the space of one hundred pages. In 1847 he published an essay entitled *Outline of Penology,* written for the Social Science Association of Philadelphia, and in 1875 he brought out a book of fiction called *The Beverly Family or Home Influence of Religion,* which was of no literary value but perhaps aided in spreading his philosophy of religious tolerance.

[Phila. *Press, Phila. Inquirer, North American,* all of July 12, 1880; Grand Lodge of Pa., *Abstract of Proceedings for 1880;* Biog. Dir. of the Am. Congress (1928).]   M.S.

CHANDLER, PELEG WHITMAN (Apr. 12, 1816–May 28, 1889), lawyer, was descended from Edmond Chaundeler who settled at Duxbury, Mass., in 1633. His grandfather, Peleg Chandler, became one of the pioneers of New Gloucester, Me.; his father, also Peleg, married Esther, daughter of Col. Isaac Parsons. The third Peleg was born at New Gloucester, received his early education at Bangor Theological College, and graduated from Bowdoin in 1834. He then studied law in his father's office at Bangor for a short time, later entering the Dane Law School at Harvard and reading with a relative, Prof. Theophilus Parsons. At the same time he reported legal cases for the Boston *Daily Advertiser.* On Nov. 30, 1837, he was married to Martha Ann Bush, daughter of Prof. Parker Cleaveland of Brunswick, Me. In the same year he was admitted to the Suffolk County bar and commenced practise in Boston, continuing to maintain his association with the press. In 1838 he established a monthly law journal, the *Law Reporter,* remaining its editor for a number of years. He also commenced work on a series of twelve volumes of *American Criminal Trials,* the first of which was published in 1841, followed by a second in 1844, but the subsequent growth of his law practise prevented the completion of his design. In addition to his legal and literary work he threw himself with ardor into the civic life of Boston, being elected a member of the common council in 1843, and president of that body in 1844 and 1845. He had been elected a member of the Massachusetts House of Representatives in 1844 and served one term. In 1846 he became city solicitor. He held the position of United States commissioner in bankruptcy for a time, during which he published *Bankruptcy Laws of the United States, and the Outline of the System with Rules and Forms in Massachusetts* (1842). He was also engaged in collecting and revising the civic ordinances, and these, in their revised form, were published in 1850, together with a digest of the law pertaining to them, under the title *Revised Ordinances, Boston.* He resigned the city solicitorship in November 1853, but always remained closely associated with the legal interests of Boston, advising on legislative projects and preparing the revised charter. He took a prominent part in the "Back Bay Improvement" scheme and devoted a large amount of his time and ability to the advancement of projects for the beautifying and adornment of the city. In 1854 he became a member of the executive council of

the commonwealth and in 1862–63 was again a member of the state House of Representatives. Endowed with a strong constitution, capable of intense application, and always at work, in spite of his other varied interests he enjoyed one of the largest practises in the state. An expert in municipal and commercial law, he confined himself to civil cases. He was an excellent speaker with a fund of anecdote and humor. His arguments were distinguished by their appeal to common sense and his presentation of facts was invariably simple, concise, and devoid of ornament. Judge Rockwood Hoar, a competent authority, said that in his prime Chandler was the best jury lawyer in Massachusetts with the possible exception of Choate. Unfortunately, at the very height of his career Chandler became almost entirely deaf and was compelled to retire from jury work, gradually withdrawing from active business and during his last years being more or less of an invalid. He was the author of *Observations on the Authority of the Gospels, By a Layman* (2nd ed., 1867); *Memoir of Gov. Andrew, with Personal Reminiscences* (1880), a work of considerable biographical value; and a number of legal, political, and historical articles.

[Mary C. Lowell, *Chandler-Parsons & Allied Families* (1911), p. 44; T. H. Haskell, *New Gloucester Centennial* (1875); *Am. Law Rev.,* XXII, 280–84, XXIII, 824–27; N. Cleaveland, *Hist. of Bowdoin Coll.* (1882), p. 453; Conrad Reno, ed., *The Judiciary and the Bar of New Eng.* (1900), I, 592; *Green Bag,* I, 270.]   H.W.H.K.

CHANDLER, SETH CARLO (Sept. 17, 1846–Dec. 31, 1913), astronomer, was born in Boston, a son of Seth Carlo and Mary (Cheever) Chandler. He was educated in the Boston public schools (finishing with the English High School), and at Harvard College. During his senior year in college he did some computing for Prof. Benjamin Pierce. After graduation in 1861 he became a private assistant of the astronomer Benjamin A. Gould. This was the beginning of a lasting friendship. From 1864 to 1870 he held a position in the United States Coast Survey. In the latter year he married Caroline Herman of Boston, and soon accepted a position as actuary with the Continental Life Insurance Company of New York, but in 1877 returned to Boston to a similar position which he held for several years. In 1881 he moved to Cambridge, where he became associated with the Harvard College Observatory, and resumed his astronomical work. He was at this time interested in the computation of cometary orbits. Together with John Ritchie, Jr., he devised a telegraphic code for the distribution of astronomical news. He also constructed the almucantar—an instrument for finding time by equal-altitude observations—which constituted his chief contribution to instrumental astronomy. Leaving the Observatory in 1885, he continued privately his work in astronomy, becoming especially interested in variable stars, on which subject he was soon a leading authority. He was the discoverer of several variable stars, and the author of many papers on the classification and general laws of stellar variation. He compiled three catalogues of variable stars, and shortly before his death was engaged in the discussion of a standard system of magnitudes. His greatest work was the demonstration of the variation of latitude, a subject on which he worked many years. His first paper on this subject appeared in 1891. He succeeded Dr. Gould in the editorship of the *Astronomical Journal,* which became an absorbing interest to him. He received the degree of LL.D. from De Pauw University in 1891, the Gold Medal of the National Academy of Sciences in 1895, and the Gold Medal of the Royal Astronomical Society in 1896. The University of Glasgow desired to confer upon him the doctor's degree in 1901, but he was unable to go abroad. With a brilliant creative mind and great nervous energy, he worked at high speed. In his later years his health was broken, chiefly by his excessive zeal. He was unpretentious and social, kind and constant in friendship. He died in Wellesley, Mass., whither he had moved in 1904.

[*Science,* XXXIX, 348–50; *Nature,* XCII, 611–12; *Astronomical Jour.,* XXVIII, 101–02; *Pubs. Astronomical Soc. of the Pacific,* XXVI, 39–41; *Popular Astronomy,* XXII, 271–75; *British Astronomical Ass. Jour.,* XXIV, 221.]   R. S. D.

CHANDLER, THOMAS BRADBURY (Apr. 26, 1726–June 17, 1790), Anglican clergyman, Loyalist, was the eldest of the ten children of Capt. William and Jemima (Bradbury) Chandler. He was born in Woodstock, Conn., where, on his father's farm, he spent his early years. Entering Yale College he came under the strong Episcopalian influence that had clung to the institution since 1722 when its first president, Timothy Cutler [*q.v.*], had publicly announced his doubt of the validity of Presbyterian ordination and had joined himself to the Church of England. After his graduation in 1745 Chandler taught school at Woodstock for two years, at the same time reading theology under the guidance of the Rev. Samuel Johnson [*q.v.*], first president of King's College. In 1747 St. John's Church at Elizabethtown, N. J., being deprived by death of the ministry of the Rev. Edward Vaughan, called Chandler to its service. He accepted the invitation, and being yet too young for ordination undertook the duties of lay reader and catechist. Four years later he went to London to receive orders, returned to Elizabethtown, and long served St. John's Church and adjacent missionary stations with ability and devotion. In 1750 he married Jane M. Emott of Elizabethtown, by whom he had one son and five daughters. In 1753 he received the degree of M.A. from the University of Oxford and was admitted to the degree of D.D. in 1766 and 1767 at Oxford and Columbia respectively. His refusal to allow George Whitefield to speak in his church in 1763 caused resentment and division within his flock, but in spite of many defections he would not compromise.

The clergy of New York, New Jersey, and Pennsylvania delegated him as a leading advocate of American episcopacy to prepare a plea for the sending of bishops to America, and in 1767 he published *An Appeal to the Public in Behalf of the Church of England in America,* which provoked wide controversy. He also wrote *An Address from the Clergy of New York and New Jersey to the Episcopalians in Virginia* (1771). Although he had advised the repeal of the Stamp Act, he was as ardent a Loyalist as churchman, and the events of the next few years moved him to vigorous protest against the drift toward revolution. In 1775 appeared his pamphlet *What Think Ye of Congress Now?* which was a spirited attack upon the authority and actions of the Continental Congress. The occurrences of April 1775 were too much for his Loyalist fervor and he departed for England the following month. During the next ten years he labored for the family he had left behind him, for his destitute brethren, and for an American episcopate. Returning in 1785 he rejoined his family in St. John's rectory, but failing health would not permit him to undertake any but the lightest parochial duties, nor to accept elevation to the episcopate of Nova Scotia, an honor tendered him in 1786. He died at Elizabethtown, June 17, 1790, and was buried in the church whose minister he had been for forty-three years.

[F. B. Dexter, *Biog. Sketches Grads. Yale Coll.,* vol. II (1896); A. H. Hoyt, *Sketch of the Life of the Rev. Thos. Bradbury Chandler, D.D.* (1873), a reprint from the *New Eng. Hist. and Geneal. Reg.,* XXVII, 227–36; J. C. Rudd, *Hist. Notices of St. John's Ch.* (1825); J. D. McVickar, *The Early Life and Professional Years of Hobart* (1838); S. A. Clark, *Hist. of St. John's Ch.* (1857); W. S. Perry, *Hist. of the Am. Episc. Ch.* (2 vols., 1885); Arthur Lyon Cross, *The Anglican Episcopate and the Am. Colonies* (1902).]   H. J. T.

CHANDLER, WILLIAM EATON (Dec. 28, 1835–Nov. 30, 1917), secretary of the navy, senator, was during his entire life identified with Concord, N. H., where he was born, and where he died. His parents, Nathan S. and Mary Ann (Tucker) Chandler, gave him an education at the local schools and academies, and sent him to the

Harvard Law School, where he received his degree in 1854. After a few years as court reporter, he turned politician and journalist; and with the Concord *Monitor and Statesman* (which he controlled for many years) for an ally, he justified the nickname of the "stormy petrel" of New Hampshire politics. Slight, lithe, bearded, and agreeable, he had great talents as a manager and controversialist, which brought him to power in the rough and tumble of the Civil War. Elected to the legislature in 1863, he was reëlected in the two succeeding years, in both of which he was also speaker of the New Hampshire Assembly. It was no disadvantage that his father-in-law, Joseph A. Gilmore, was at the same time, 1863–65, governor of the state. Chandler established his character as a war Republican, advocating a confiscation of the property of rebels, and the right of soldiers in the field to vote. He gave vigorous support to the Lincoln administration, and was appointed, first, to prosecute frauds in the Philadelphia navy-yard, and then, at the beginning of Lincoln's second administration, to be solicitor and judge-advocate general of the navy department. President Johnson transferred him to the treasury, where he was assistant secretary, 1865–67; after which he returned to the practise of law and politics in his native state. As national committeeman from New Hampshire he assisted in directing party strategy in the four presidential campaigns, 1868, 1872, 1876, and 1880. In the first two of these he was secretary of the Republican National Committee.

Immediately after the election of 1876, although he had ceased to be secretary, he appeared at the headquarters of the national committee in New York City, and took a large share in the maneuvers that secured the outcome of the election. He refused to concede the election of Tilden, inspired the fights before the returning boards of Florida, Louisiana, and South Carolina, and was counsel for the Florida electors before the electoral commission. The installation of Hayes as president was commonly regarded as a triumph of his tactics. He was not, however, appointed to important office in the government, and was soon disgusted with the friendliness shown by Hayes to the South, and with the somewhat non-partisan course of the administration. The Hayes circular directing office-holders to refrain from the official management of political campaigns seemed to him hypocrisy. After the refusal of the Senate to confirm the Hayes appointees to the New York Custom-House, Chandler came out with a public manifesto (*New York Times*, Dec. 27, 1877) addressed to the Republicans of New Hampshire. In this he charged that Hayes was guilty of a corrupt bargain with the Democrats, whereby he received the presidency in return for a pledge to relax Northern control over the South.

In 1880 Chandler led the Blaine faction of the national Republican committee against Cameron, who was manager for Gen. Grant. When Garfield eventually secured the nomination from the Republican convention, Chandler gave him his support, and was rewarded in the spring of 1881 by a nomination to be solicitor-general, which, however, the Senate refused to confirm. In the next winter he was appointed secretary of the navy by President Arthur after the retirement of William H. Hunt. The appointment was interpreted as a civil gesture toward the friends of James G. Blaine; and it gave to Chandler a chance to preside over the navy in a momentous period of its history. He reminded Congress in his first annual report, as Arthur had done in the annual message of the preceding year, that the navy of the United States, as a fighting force, was extinct. Its leading warship was the *Tennessee,* a wooden ship of 4,840 tons displacement. Only the United States, among major nations, had refrained from profiting by the new methods of naval architecture. In Chandler's first year of office, on Aug. 5, 1882, Congress authorized the preparation of plans for two steel cruisers; and on Mar. 3, 1883, it made appropriations for constructing these, and for adding two more steel vessels to the new navy. Under Chandler's direction the plans were drawn and the keels were laid for the *Chicago, Boston, Atlanta,* and a despatch boat, the *Dolphin.* The contracts were let to John Roach who had been building steel ships on the Delaware for several years. It was determined to proceed no more rapidly than American building resources would justify, but to manufacture the new ships and their armament in the United States rather than attempt to buy them abroad. Several years elapsed before the American shipyards and gun foundries were ready for contracts for armored cruisers or battleships. Naval architecture was not beyond the point at which it was possible to argue that the ships should possess complete sailing equipment as well as steam; and at which it was possible to mount the boilers over brick furnaces (as was done in the *Chicago*). As might have been expected, none of these four vessels was a triumph. The *Dolphin* was a scandal. Chandler was publicly charged with favoritism; but he had established the new program of steel construction before he handed over his office to William C. Whitney in 1885.

After 1885, Chandler continued active with his newspaper, fought vigorously against the great railroad combinations of his state, and secured in

1887 election to the United States Senate for the last two years of the term of Austin F. Pike. In 1889 he was elected for a full term, after a bitter fight with Jacob H. Gallinger in the New Hampshire legislature. He was again reëlected in 1895, but was defeated in 1901 by Judge Henry E. Burnham, whereupon President McKinley made him chairman of the Spanish Treaty Claims Commission. Chandler's style of speech and writing may be judged from his *New Hampshire A Slave State* (1891), popularly known as the "Book of Bargains." He was married twice: in 1859 to Ann Caroline Gilmore (d. 1871), and in 1874 to Lucy Lambert Hale, daughter of a former senator, John P. Hale.

[There is a good obituary in the *New Eng. Hist. and Geneal. Reg.*, LXXII, 54, and several less important sketches are to be found in the *Granite Mo.*, vols. VI, X, XII, and XXXIV ; the *Daily Patriot* (Concord, N. H.), Nov. 30, 1917, and the *Manchester Union*, Dec. 1, 1917.]
F. L. P—n.

CHANDLER, ZACHARIAH (Dec. 10, 1813– Nov. 1, 1879), senator, Republican boss, was born at Bedford, N. H. His father, Samuel Chandler, was a descendant of William Chandler, who emigrated from England and settled at Roxbury, Mass., about 1637 (George Chandler, *The Chandler Family*, 1872, p. 818). His mother, Margaret Orr, was the oldest daughter of Col. John Orr. He received a common school education, and in 1833 removed to Detroit, where he opened a general store, and eventually through trade, banking, and land speculation became one of the richest men in Michigan. On Dec. 10, 1844, he was married to Letitia Grace Douglass of New York. He made campaign speeches for Taylor in 1848, served for a year (1851–52) as mayor of Detroit, and in 1852 offered himself as a Whig candidate for governor and was defeated. He was one of the signers of the call for the meeting at Jackson, Mich., July 6, 1854, which launched the Republican party, and "the leading spirit" of the Buffalo convention called to aid free state migration to Kansas (George F. Hoar, *Autobiography*, 1903, II, 75). In 1856 he was a delegate to the Republican national convention at Pittsburgh, and was made a member of the national committee of the party. In January 1857, he was elected to the United States Senate in succession to Lewis Cass [*q.v.*], and held his seat until Mar. 3, 1875. In the Senate he allied himself with the radical anti-slavery element of the Republicans, although hostile to Charles Sumner, and was later recognized as one of the most outspoken enemies of secession. From March 1861 to 1875 he was chairman of the Committee on Commerce, to whose jurisdiction

the appropriations for rivers and harbors, later known as the "pork barrel," were assigned. At the outbreak of the Civil War he exerted himself to raise and equip the first regiment of Michigan volunteers. He was a member of the Joint Committee on the Conduct of the War ; initiated acts for the collection and administration of abandoned property in the South (Mar. 3, 1863) and for the further regulation of intercourse with the insurrectionary states (July 2, 1864) ; bitterly denounced the incompetence of McClellan in a speech at Jackson, Mich. (July 6, 1862) which he regarded as one of his most important public services ; supported the proposal of a national bank ; voted for greenbacks as an emergency measure while strongly resisting inflation of the currency ; and approved of the Reconstruction acts although criticizing them as in some respects too lax. His aggressive Republicanism was matched by his clamorous jingoism in regard to Great Britain ; on Jan. 15, 1866, he offered a resolution, which was tabled, for non-intercourse with Great Britain for its refusal to entertain the *Alabama* claims, and in 1867, when the question of recognizing Abyssinia as a belligerent in its war with Great Britain was under consideration, he submitted (Nov. 29) a resolution "recognizing to Abyssinia the same rights which the British had recognized to the Confederacy" (*Congressional Globe*, 40 Cong., 1 Sess., p. 810). He was one of the promoters and most influential members of the Republican Congressional Committee, serving as its chairman in the campaigns of 1868 and 1876. From the beginning of his senatorial career he used his Federal patronage to strengthen his political power, and by methods openly partisan and despotic if not actually corrupt obtained control of the Republican machine in Michigan, and was for years the undisputed boss of his party in the state. The Democratic landslide of 1874, however, broke his power, and he was defeated for reëlection to the Senate. In October 1875, he became secretary of the interior, retaining the office until the close of Grant's second administration. His reorganization of the department was attended by wholesale dismissals for alleged dishonesty or incompetence. He was again elected to the Senate in February 1879, to fill a vacancy caused by the resignation of Isaac P. Christiancy [*q.v.*].

[Aside from the *Biog. Cong. Dir.* (1913), the *Journals of the Senate*, the *Cong. Globe*, and *Cong. Record*, the chief source is the anonymous *Zachariah Chandler : an Outline Sketch of His Life and Public Services* (1880), which is supplemented in a number of details by Wilmer C. Harris, *Public Life of Zachariah Chandler, 1851–75* (1917), a doctoral dissertation of the University of Chicago.]
W. M.